GO!
Premium Media Site

Improve your grade with hands-on tools and resources!

- Master *Key Terms* to expand your vocabulary.
- Assess your knowledge with fun *Crossword Puzzles* and *Flipboards*, which let you flip through the definitions of the key terms and match them with the correct term.
- Prepare for exams by taking practice quizzes in the *Online Chapter Review*.
- Download *Student Data Files* for the application projects in each chapter.
- Answer matching and multiple choice questions to test what you learned in each chapter.

And for even more tools, you can access the following Premium Resources using your Access Code. Register now to get the most out of *GO!*.

- *Student Training Videos* for each Objective have been created by the author - a real instructor teaching the same types of courses that you take.*
- *GO! to Work* videos are short interviews with workers showing how they use Office in their job.*
- *GO! for Job Success* videos related to the projects in the chapter cover such important topics as Dressing for Success, Time Management, and Making Ethical Choices.*

*Access code required for these premium resources

Your Access Code is:

Note: If there is no silver foil covering the access code, it may already have been redeemed, and therefore may no longer be valid. In that case, you can purchase online access using a major credit card or PayPal account. To do so, go to **www.pearsonhighered.com/go**, select your book cover, click on "Buy Access" and follow the on-screen instructions.

To Register:

- To start you will need a valid email address and this access code.
- Go to **www.pearsonhighered.com/go** and scroll to find your text book.
- Once you've selected your text, on the Home Page for the book, click the link to access the Student Premium Content.
- Click the Register button and follow the on-screen instructions.
- After you register, you can sign in any time via the log-in area on the same screen.

System Requirements

Windows 7 Ultimate Edition; IE 8
Windows Vista Ultimate Edition SP1; IE 8
Windows XP Professional SP3; IE 7
Windows XP Professional SP3; Firefox 3.6.4
Mac OS 10.5.7; Firefox 3.6.4
Mac OS 10.6; Safari 5

Technical Support

http://247pearsoned.custhelp.com

Photo credits: Goodluz/wrangler/Elena Elisseeva/Shutterstock

GO!

with Microsoft®

Office 2013

Volume 2

GO!

with Microsoft®

Office 2013

Volume 2

Shelley Gaskin, Carol Martin, Debra Geoghan, Nancy Graviett, and Suzanne Marks

PEARSON

Boston   Columbus   Indianapolis   New York   San Francisco   Upper Saddle River
Amsterdam   Cape Town   Dubai   London   Madrid   Milan   Munich   Paris   Montréal   Toronto
Delhi   Mexico City   São Paulo   Sydney   Hong Kong   Seoul   Singapore   Taipei   Tokyo

Editor in Chief: Michael Payne
Executive Acquisitions Editor: Jenifer Niles
Editorial Project Manager: Carly Prakapas
Product Development Manager: Laura Burgess
Development Editor: Shannon LeMay-Finn, Ginny Monroe,
   Toni Ackley, and Cheryl Slavik
Editorial Assistant: Andra Skaalrud
Director of Marketing: Maggie Leen
Marketing Manager: Brad Forrester
Marketing Coordinator: Susan Osterlitz
Marketing Assistant: Darshika Vyas
Managing Editor: Camille Trentacoste

Senior Production Project Manager: Rhonda Aversa
Operations Specialist: Maura Zaldivar-Garcia
Senior Art Director: Jonathan Boylan
Cover Photo: © photobar/Fotolia
Associate Director of Design: Blair Brown
Director of Media Development: Taylor Ragan
Media Project Manager, Production: Renata Butera
Full-Service Project Management: PreMediaGlobal
Composition: PreMediaGlobal
Printer/Binder: Webcrafters, Inc.
Cover Printer: Lehigh-Phoenix Color/Hagerstown
Text Font: MinionPro

ISBN 10: 0-13-341179-6
ISBN 13: 978-0-13-341179-9

Brief Contents

PowerPoint

Table of Contents

Word

Chapter 4   Using Styles and Creating Multilevel Lists and Charts............................ 49

Chapter 5   Using Advanced Table Features **97**

Chapter 6   Building Documents from Reusable Content and Using Markup Tools 147

Excel

Chapter 4 Use Financial and Lookup Functions, Define Names, Validate Data, and Audit Worksheets

Access

PowerPoint

Chapter 4 Creating Templates and Reviewing, Publishing, Comparing, Combining, and Protecting Presentations

About the Authors

Shelley Gaskin, Series Editor, is a professor in the Business and Computer Technology Division at Pasadena City College in Pasadena, California. She holds a bachelor's degree in Business Administration from Robert Morris College (Pennsylvania), a master's degree in Business from Northern Illinois University, and a doctorate in Adult and Community Education from Ball State University (Indiana). Before joining Pasadena City College, she spent 12 years in the computer industry, where she was a systems analyst, sales representative, and director of Customer Education with Unisys Corporation. She also worked for Ernst & Young on the development of large systems applications for their clients. She has written and developed training materials for custom systems applications in both the public and private sector, and has also written and edited numerous computer application textbooks.

This book is dedicated to my students, who inspire me every day.

Carol L. Martin is recently retired from the faculty at Harrisburg (Pennsylvania) Area Community College. She holds a bachelor's degree in Secondary Education—Mathematics from Millersville (Pennsylvania) University and a master's degree in Training and Development from Pennsylvania State University. For over 40 years, she has instructed public school students and educators in the use of various computer applications. She has written and edited a variety of textbooks dealing with Microsoft Office applications and has co-authored several training manuals for use in Pennsylvania Department of Education in-service courses.

This book is dedicated to my husband Ron—a constant source of encouragement and technical support; and to my delightful grandsons, Tony and Josh, who keep me young at heart.

Debra Geoghan is a professor in the Science, Technology, Engineering, and Mathematics (STEM) Department at Bucks County Community College in Pennsylvania where she is coordinator of the Computer Science area. Deb teaches computer classes ranging from basic computer literacy to cybercrime, computer forensics, and networking. She holds a B.S. in Secondary Science Education from Temple University and an M.A. in Computer Science Education from Arcadia University, and has earned certifications from Microsoft, CompTIA, and Apple. Deb has taught at the college level since 1996 and also spent 11 years in the high school classroom.

Throughout her teaching career Deb has worked with educators to integrate technology across the curriculum. At Bucks she serves on many technology committees, presents technology workshops for faculty, and runs a summer workshop for local K-12 teachers interested in using technology in their classrooms. Deb is an avid user of technology, which has earned her the nickname "gadget lady."

This book is dedicated to my husband Joe, and my sons Joe and Mike, whose love and support have made this project possible.

Nancy Graviett is a professor in the Business and Computer Science department at St. Charles Community College in Cottleville, Missouri, where she is the program coordinator for the Business Administrative Systems program and teaches within the program. Nancy is also very active with distance learning and teaches in face-to-face, hybrid, and online formats. She holds a master's degree from University of Missouri. Nancy holds Microsoft® Certified Application Specialist certification in multiple applications and provides training both on and off campus. In her free time, Nancy enjoys quilting and spending time with family and friends.

I dedicate this book to my husband, David, my children (Matthew and Andrea), and my parents, whose love and support I cherish more than they could ever know.

Suzanne Marks is a faculty member in Business Technology Systems at Bellevue Community College, Bellevue, Washington. She holds a bachelor's degree in Business Education from Washington State University, and was project manager for the first IT Skills Standards in the United States.

This book is dedicated to my sister, Janet Curtis, for her unfailing support.

GO! with Office 2013

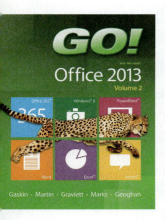

GO! with Office 2013 is the right solution for you and your students in today's fast-moving, mobile environment. The GO! Series content focuses on the real-world job skills students need to succeed in the workforce. They learn Office by working step-by-step through practical job-related projects that put the core functionality of Office in context. And as has always been true of the GO! Series, students learn the important concepts when they need them, and they never get lost in instruction, because the GO! Series uses Microsoft procedural syntax. Students learn how and learn why—at the teachable moment.

After completing the instructional projects, students are ready to apply the skills in a wide variety of progressively challenging projects that require them to solve problems, think critically, and create projects on their own. And, for those who want to go beyond the classroom and become certified, GO! provides clear MOS preparation guidelines so students know what is needed to ace the Core exam!

What's New

New Design reflects the look of Windows 8 and Office 2013 and enhances readability.

Enhanced Chapter Opener now includes a deeper introduction to the A and B instructional projects and more highly defined chapter Objectives and Learning Outcomes.

New Application Introductions provide a brief overview of the application and put the chapters in context for students.

Coverage of New Features of Office 2013 ensures that students are learning the skills they need to work in today's job market.

New Application Capstone Projects ensure that students are ready to move on to the next set of chapters. Each Application Capstone Project can be found on the Instructor Resource Center and is also a Grader project in MyITLab.

More Grader Projects based on the E, F, and G mastering-level projects, both homework and assessment versions! These projects are written by our GO! authors, who are all instructors in colleges like yours!

New Training and Assessment Simulations are now written by the authors to match the book one-to-one!

New MOS Map on the Instructor Resource Site and in the Annotated Instructor's Edition indicates clearly where each required MOS Objective is covered.

Three Types of Videos help students understand and succeed in the real world:

- *Student Training Videos* are broken down by Objective and created by the author—a real instructor teaching the same types of courses that you do. Real personal instruction.
- *GO! to Work* videos are short interviews with workers showing how they use Office in their jobs.
- *GO! for Job Success* videos relate to the projects in the chapter and cover important career topics such as *Dressing for Success*, *Time Management*, and *Making Ethical Choices*. **Available for Chapters 1–3 only**.

New GO! Learn It Online Section at the end of the chapter indicates where various student learning activities can be found, including multiple choice and matching activities.

New Styles for In-Text Boxed Content: Another Way, Notes, More Knowledge, Alerts, and **new *By Touch* instructions** are included in line with the instruction and not in the margins so that the student is more likely to read this information.

Clearly Indicated Build from Scratch Projects: GO! has always had many projects that begin "from scratch," and now we have an icon to really call them out!

New Visual Summary focuses on the four key concepts to remember from each chapter.

New Review and Assessment Guide summarizes the end-of-chapter assessments for a quick overview of the different types and levels of assignments and assessments for each chapter.

New Skills and Procedures Summary Chart (online at the Instructor Resource Center) summarizes all of the shortcuts and commands covered in the chapter.

New End-of-Chapter Key Term Glossary with Definitions for each chapter, plus a comprehensive end-of-book glossary.

New Flipboards and Crossword Puzzles enable students to review the concepts and key terms learned in each chapter by completing online challenges.

A Microsoft® Office textbook designed for student success!

Project-Based – Students learn by creating projects that they will use in the real world.

Microsoft Procedural Syntax – Steps are written to put students in the right place at the right time.

■ **Teachable Moment –** Expository text is woven into the steps—at the moment students need to know it—not chunked together in a block of text that will go unread.

■ **Sequential Pagination –** Students have actual page numbers instead of confusing letters and abbreviations.

New Feature

Student Outcomes and Learning Objectives – Objectives are clustered around projects that result in student outcomes.

New Design – Provides a more visually appealing and concise display of important content.

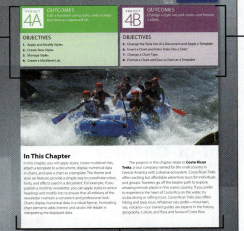

New Application Introductions – Provide an overview of the application to prepare students for the upcoming chapters.

Simulation Training and Assessment – Give your students the most realistic Office 2013 experience with open, realistic, high-fidelity simulations.

Scenario – Each chapter opens with a job-related scenario that sets the stage for the projects the student will create.

Project Activities – A project summary stated clearly and quickly.

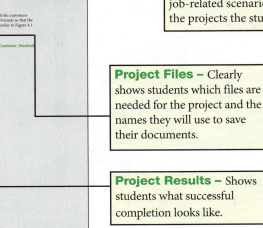

Project Files – Clearly shows students which files are needed for the project and the names they will use to save their documents.

New Build from Scratch Icons – Enable you to easily see all the projects that the student builds from scratch.

Project Results – Shows students what successful completion looks like.

In-Text Features
Another Way, Notes, More Knowledge, Alerts, and By Touch Instructions

Microsoft Procedural Syntax – Steps are written to put the student at the right place at the right time.

Color Coding – Each chapter has two instructional projects, which is less overwhelming for students than one large chapter project. The two projects are differentiated by different colored numbering and headings.

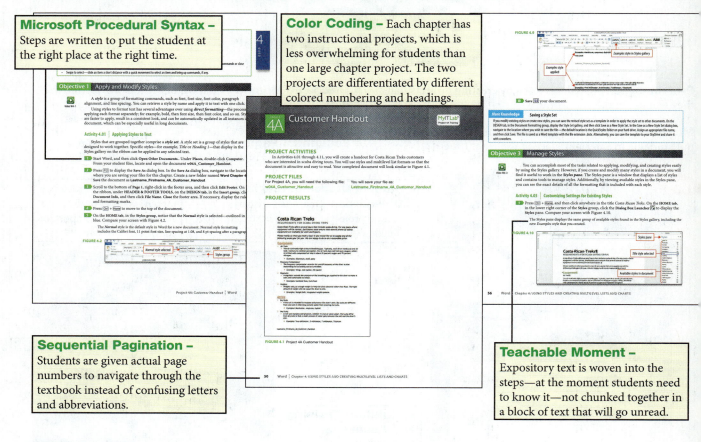

Sequential Pagination – Students are given actual page numbers to navigate through the textbook instead of confusing letters and abbreviations.

Teachable Moment – Expository text is woven into the steps—at the moment students need to know it—not chunked together in a block of text that will go unread.

End-of-Chapter
Content-Based Assessments – Assessments with defined solutions.

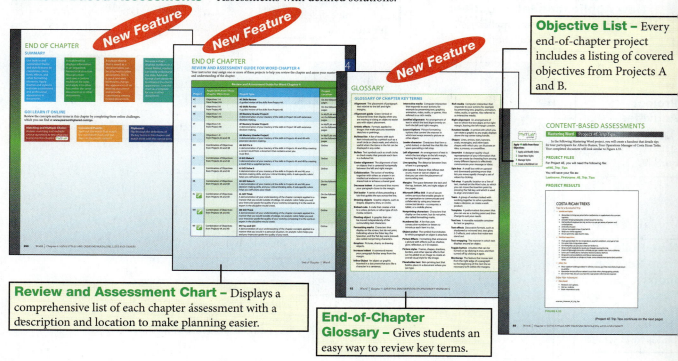

Objective List – Every end-of-chapter project includes a listing of covered objectives from Projects A and B.

Review and Assessment Chart – Displays a comprehensive list of each chapter assessment with a description and location to make planning easier.

End-of-Chapter Glossary – Gives students an easy way to review key terms.

End-of-Chapter

Content-Based Assessments – Assessments with defined solutions. (continued)

Grader Projects – Each chapter has six MyITLab Grader projects—three homework and three assessment—clearly indicated by the MyITLab logo.

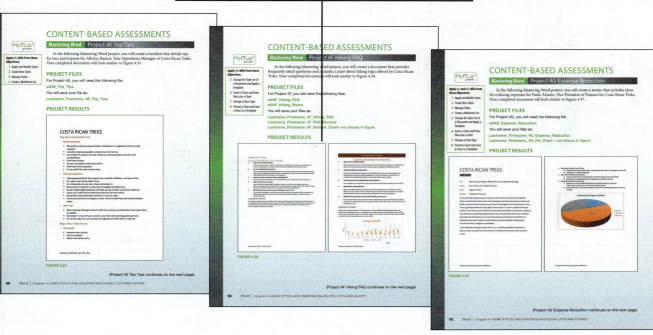

Task-Specific Rubric – A matrix specific to the GO! Solve It projects that states the criteria and standards for grading these defined-solution projects.

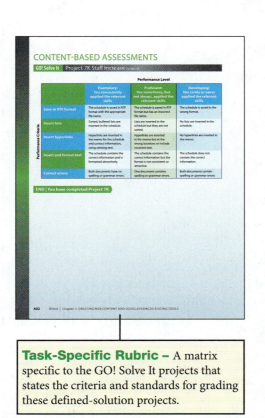

End-of-Chapter

Outcomes-Based Assessments – Assessments with open-ended solutions.

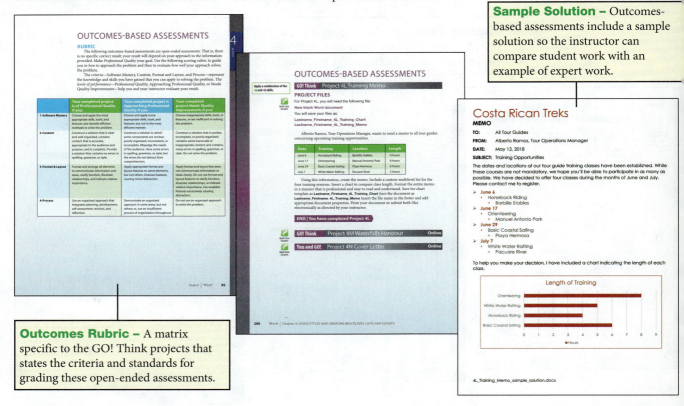

Sample Solution – Outcomes-based assessments include a sample solution so the instructor can compare student work with an example of expert work.

Outcomes Rubric – A matrix specific to the GO! Think projects that states the criteria and standards for grading these open-ended assessments.

Student Materials

Student Data Files – All student data files are available to all on the companion website: www.pearsonhighered.com/go.

Three Types of Videos help students understand and succeed in the real world:

- *Student Training Videos* are by Objective and created by the author—a real instructor teaching the same types of courses that you teach.
- *GO! to Work* videos are short interviews with workers showing how they use Office in their job.

Flipboards and Crossword Puzzles provide a variety of review options for content in each chapter.

Available on the companion website using the access code included with your book.
pearsonhighered.com/go.

All instructor and student materials available at pearsonhighered. com/go

Instructor Materials

Student Assignment Tracker (previously called Assignment Sheets) – Lists all the assignments for the chapter. Just add the course information, due dates, and points. Providing these to students ensures they will know what is due and when.

Scripted Lectures – A script to guide your classroom lecture of each instructional project.

Annotated Solution Files – Coupled with the scorecards, these create a grading and scoring system that makes grading easy and efficient.

PowerPoint Lectures – PowerPoint presentations for each chapter.

Audio PowerPoints – Audio versions of the PowerPoint presentations for each chapter.

Scoring Rubrics – Can be used either by students to check their work or by you as a quick check-off for the items that need to be corrected.

Syllabus Templates – For 8-week, 12-week, and 16-week courses.

MOS Map – Provided at the Instructor Resource Center site and in the Annotated Instructor's Edition, showing where each required MOS Objective is covered either in the book or via additional instructional material provided.

Test Bank – Includes a variety of test questions for each chapter.

Companion Website – Online content such as the Online Chapter Review, Glossary, and Student Data Files are all at www.pearsonhighered.com/go.

Reviewers

GO! Focus Group Participants

Kenneth Mayer	Heald College
Carolyn Borne	Louisiana State University
Toribio Matamoros	Miami Dade College
Lynn Keane	University of South Carolina
Terri Hayes	Broward College
Michelle Carter	Paradise Valley Community College

GO! Reviewers

Abul Sheikh	Abraham Baldwin Agricultural College
John Percy	Atlantic Cape Community College
Janette Hicks	Binghamton University
Shannon Ogden	Black River Technical College
Karen May	Blinn College
Susan Fry	Boise State University
Chigurupati Rani	Borough of Manhattan Community College / CUNY
Ellen Glazer	Broward College
Kate LeGrand	Broward College
Mike Puopolo	Bunker Hill Community College
Nicole Lytle-Kosola	California State University, San Bernardino
Nisheeth Agrawal	Calhoun Community College
Pedro Diaz-Gomez	Cameron
Linda Friedel	Central Arizona College
Gregg Smith	Central Community College
Norm Cregger	Central Michigan University
Lisa LaCaria	Central Piedmont Community College
Steve Siedschlag	Chaffey College
Terri Helfand	Chaffey College
Susan Mills	Chambersburg
Mandy Reininger	Chemeketa Community College
Connie Crossley	Cincinnati State Technical and Community College
Marjorie Deutsch	City University of New York - Queensborough Community College
Mary Ann Zlotow	College of DuPage
Christine Bohnsak	College of Lake County
Gertrude Brier	College of Staten Island
Sharon Brown	College of The Albemarle
Terry Rigsby	Columbia College
Vicki Brooks	Columbia College
Donald Hames	Delgado Community College
Kristen King	Eastern Kentucky University
Kathie Richer	Edmonds Community College
Gary Smith	Elmhurst College
Wendi Kappersw	Embry-Riddle Aeronautical University
Nancy Woolridge	Fullerton College
Abigail Miller	Gateway Community & Technical College
Deep Ramanayake	Gateway Community & Technical College
Gwen White	Gateway Community & Technical College
Debbie Glinert	Gloria K School
Dana Smith	Golf Academy of America
Mary Locke	Greenville Technical College
Diane Marie Roselli	Harrisburg Area Community College
Linda Arnold	Harrisburg Area Community College - Lebanon
Daniel Schoedel	Harrisburg Area Community College - York Campus
Ken Mayer	Heald College
Xiaodong Qiao	Heald College
Donna Lamprecht	Hopkinsville Community College
Kristen Lancaster	Hopkinsville Community College
Johnny Hurley	Iowa Lakes Community College
Linda Halverson	Iowa Lakes Community College
Sarah Kilgo	Isothermal Community College
Chris DeGeare	Jefferson College
David McNair	Jefferson College
Diane Santurri	Johnson & Wales University
Roland Sparks	Johnson & Wales University
Ram Raghuraman	Joliet Junior College
Eduardo Suniga	Lansing Community College
Kenneth A. Hyatt	Lone Star College - Kingwood
Glenn Gray	Lone Star College - North Harris
Gene Carbonaro	Long Beach City College
Betty Pearman	Los Medanos College
Diane Kosharek	Madison College
Peter Meggison	Massasoit Community College
George Gabb	Miami Dade College
Lennie Alice Cooper	Miami Dade College
Richard Mabjish	Miami Dade College
Victor Giol	Miami Dade College
John Meir	Midlands Technical College
Greg Pauley	Moberly Area Community College
Catherine Glod	Mohawk Valley Community College
Robert Huyck	Mohawk Valley Community College
Kevin Engellant	Montana Western
Philip Lee	Nashville State Community College
Ruth Neal	Navarro College
Sharron Jordan	Navarro College
Richard Dale	New Mexico State University
Lori Townsend	Niagara County Community College
Judson Curry	North Park University
Mary Zegarski	Northampton Community College
Neal Stenlund	Northern Virginia Community College
Michael Goeken	Northwest Vista College
Mary Beth Tarver	Northwestern State University
Amy Rutledge	Oakland University
Marcia Braddock	Okefenokee Technical College
Richard Stocke	Oklahoma State University - OKC
Jane Stam	Onondaga Community College
Mike Michaelson	Palomar College
Kungwen (Dave) Chu	Purdue University Calumet
Wendy Ford	City University of New York - Queensborough Community College
Lewis Hall	Riverside City College
Karen Acree	San Juan College
Tim Ellis	Schoolcraft College
Dan Combellick	Scottsdale Community College
Pat Serrano	Scottsdale Community College
Rose Hendrickson	Sheridan College
Kit Carson	South Georgia College
Rebecca Futch	South Georgia State College
Brad Hagy	Southern Illinois University Carbondale
Mimi Spain	Southern Maine Community College
David Parker	Southern Oregon University
Madeline Baugher	Southwestern Oklahoma State University
Brian Holbert	St. Johns River State College
Bunny Howard	St. Johns River State College
Stephanie Cook	State College of Florida
Sharon Wavle	Tompkins Cortland Community College
George Fiori	Tri-County Technical College
Steve St. John	Tulsa Community College
Karen Thessing	University of Central Arkansas
Richard McMahon	University of Houston-Downtown
Shohreh Hashemi	University of Houston-Downtown
Donna Petty	Wallace Community College
Julia Bell	Walters State Community College
Ruby Kowaney	West Los Angeles College
Casey Thompson	Wiregrass Georgia Technical College
DeAnnia Clements	Wiregrass Georgia Technical College

Introduction to Microsoft Office 2013 Features

PROJECT 1A

OUTCOMES
Create, save, and print a Microsoft Office 2013 document.

OBJECTIVES

1. Use File Explorer to Download, Extract, and Locate Files and Folders
2. Use Start Search to Locate and Start a Microsoft Office 2013 Desktop App
3. Enter, Edit, and Check the Spelling of Text in an Office 2013 Program
4. Perform Commands from a Dialog Box
5. Create a Folder and Name and Save a File
6. Insert a Footer, Add Document Properties, Print a File, and Close a Desktop App

PROJECT 1B

OUTCOMES
Use the ribbon and dialog boxes to perform commands in Microsoft Office 2013.

OBJECTIVES

7. Open an Existing File and Save It with a New Name
8. Sign In to Office and Explore Options for a Microsoft Office Desktop App
9. Perform Commands from the Ribbon and Quick Access Toolbar
10. Apply Formatting in Office Programs
11. Compress Files and Use the Microsoft Office 2013 Help System
12. Install Apps for Office and Create a Microsoft Account

etse1112/Fotolia

In This Chapter

In this chapter, you will use File Explorer to navigate the Windows folder structure, create a folder, and save files in Microsoft Office 2013 programs. You will also practice using features in Microsoft Office 2013 that work similarly across Word, Excel, Access, and PowerPoint. These features include managing files, performing commands, adding document properties, signing in to Office, applying formatting, and using Help. You will also practice compressing files and installing Apps for Office from the Office Store. In this chapter, you will also learn how to set up a free Microsoft account so that you can use SkyDrive.

The projects in this chapter relate to **Skyline Metro Grill**, which is a chain of 25 casual, full-service restaurants based in Boston. The Skyline Metro Grill owners are planning an aggressive expansion program. To expand by 15 additional restaurants in Chicago, San Francisco, and Los Angeles by 2018, the company must attract new investors, develop new menus, develop new marketing strategies, and recruit new employees, all while adhering to the company's quality guidelines and maintaining its reputation for excellent service. To succeed, the company plans to build on its past success and maintain its quality elements.

Note Form

PROJECT
1A

PROJECT ACTIVITIES

In Activities 1.01 through 1.09, you will create a note form using Microsoft Word, save it in a folder that you create by using File Explorer, and then print the note form or submit it electronically as directed by your instructor. Your completed note form will look similar to Figure 1.1.

PROJECT FILES

For Project 1A, you will need the following file: You will save your file as:

New blank Word document   **Lastname_Firstname_1A_Note_Form**

PROJECT RESULTS

Build from
Scratch

> ### Skyline Metro Grill, Chef's Notes
> ### Executive Chef, Sarah Jackson
>
> Lastname_Firstname_1A_Note_Form

FIGURE 1.1 Project 1A Note Form

Objective 1   Use File Explorer to Download, Extract, and Locate Files and Folders

Video OF1-1

A *file* is a collection of information stored on a computer under a single name, for example, a Word document or a PowerPoint presentation. A file is stored in a *folder*—a container in which you store files—or a *subfolder*, which is a folder within a folder. The Windows operating system stores and organizes your files and folders, which is a primary task of an operating system.

You *navigate*—explore within the organizing structure of Windows—to create, save, and find your files and folders by using the *File Explorer* program. File Explorer displays the files and folders on your computer and is at work anytime you are viewing the contents of files and folders in a *window*. A window is a rectangular area on a computer screen in which programs and content appear; a window can be moved, resized, minimized, or closed.

Activity 1.01 | Using File Explorer to Download, Extract, and Locate Files and Folders

1 Sign in to Windows 8 with your Microsoft account—or the account provided by your instructor—to display the Windows 8 **Start screen**, and then click the **Desktop** tile. Insert a **USB flash drive** in your computer; **Close** ☒ any messages or windows that display.

The *desktop* is the screen in Windows that simulates your work area. A *USB flash drive* is a small data storage device that plugs into a computer USB port.

2 On the taskbar, click **Internet Explorer** 🌐. Click in the **address bar** to select the existing text, type **www.pearsonhighered.com/go** and press Enter. Locate and click the name of this textbook, and then click the **STUDENT DATA FILES tab**.

The *taskbar* is the area along the lower edge of the desktop that displays buttons representing programs—also referred to as desktop apps. In the desktop version of Internet Explorer 10, the *address bar* is the area at the top of the Internet Explorer window that displays, and where you can type, a *URL—Uniform Resource Locator*—which is an address that uniquely identifies a location on the Internet.

3 ▶ On the list of files, move your mouse pointer over—*point* to—**Office Features Chapter 1** and then *click*—press the left button on your mouse pointing device one time.

4 ▶ In the **Windows Internet Explorer** dialog box, click **Save As**.

A *dialog box* is a small window that contains options for completing a task.

5 ▶ In the **Save As** dialog box, on the left, locate the **navigation pane**, and point to the vertical **scroll bar**.

The Save As dialog box is an example of a *common dialog box*; that is, this dialog box looks the same in Excel and in PowerPoint and in most other Windows-based desktop applications—also referred to as programs.

Use the *navigation pane* on the left side of the Save As dialog box to navigate to, open, and display favorites, libraries, folders, saved searches, and an expandable list of drives. A *pane* is a separate area of a window.

A *scroll bar* displays when a window, or a pane within a window, has information that is not in view. You can click the up or down scroll arrows—or the left and right scroll arrows in a horizontal scroll bar—to scroll the contents up and down or left and right in small increments.

You can also drag the *scroll box*—the box within the scroll bar—to scroll the window or pane in either direction.

This is a *compressed folder*—also called a *zipped folder*—which is a folder containing one or more files that have been reduced in size. A compressed folder takes up less storage space and can be transferred to other computers faster.

> **NOTE**   **Comparing Your Screen with the Figures in This Textbook**
>
> Your screen will match the figures shown in this textbook if you set your screen resolution to 1280 × 768. At other resolutions, your screen will closely resemble, but not match, the figures shown. To view your screen's resolution, on the desktop, right-click in a blank area, and then click Screen resolution.

---

6 ▶ In the **navigation pane**, if necessary, on the scroll bar click ☑ to scroll down. If necessary, to the left of **Computer**, click ▷ to expand the list. Then click the name of your **USB flash drive**.

7 ▶ With *Office_Features* displayed in the **File name** box, in the lower right corner click **Save**.

At the bottom of your screen, the *Notification bar* displays information about pending downloads, security issues, add-ons, and other issues related to the operation of your computer.

8 ▶ In the **Notification bar**, when the download is complete, click **Open folder** to display the folder window for your **USB flash drive**.

A *folder window* displays the contents of the current location—folder, library, or drive—and contains helpful parts so that you can navigate within the file organizing structure of Windows.

9 ▶ With the compressed **Office_Features** folder selected, on the ribbon, click the **Extract tab** to display the **Compressed Folder Tools**, and then click **Extract all**.

The *ribbon* is a user interface in both Office 2013 and Windows 8 that groups the commands for performing related tasks on tabs across the upper portion of a window.

In the dialog box, you can *extract*—decompress or pull out—files from a compressed folder.

You can navigate to some other location by clicking the Browse button and navigating within your storage locations.

10 In the **Extract Compressed (Zipped) Folders** dialog box, click to the right of the selected text, and then press Backspace until only the drive letter of your USB and the colon following it display—for example G:—and then click **Extract**. Notice that a progress bar indicates the progress of the extract process, and that when the extract is complete, the **Office_Features** folder displays on the file list of your **USB flash drive**.

In a dialog box or taskbar button, a *progress bar* indicates visually the progress of a task such as a download or file transfer.

The *address bar* in File Explorer displays your current location in the folder structure as a series of links separated by arrows, which is referred to as the *path*—a sequence of folders that leads to a specific file or folder.

By pressing Backspace in the Extract dialog box, you avoid creating an unneeded folder level.

11 Because you no longer need the compressed (zipped) version of the folder, be sure it is selected, click the **Home tab**, and then click **Delete**. In the upper right corner of the **USB drive** folder window, click **Close** ☒. **Close** ☒ the **Internet Explorer** window and in the Internet Explorer message, click **Close all tabs**.

Your desktop redisplays.

Objective 2 | Use Start Search to Locate and Start a Microsoft Office 2013 Desktop App

Video OF1-2

The term *desktop app* commonly refers to a computer program that is installed on your computer and requires a computer operating system such as Microsoft Windows or Apple OS to run. The programs in Microsoft Office 2013 are considered to be desktop apps. Apps that run from the *device software* on a smartphone or a tablet computer—for example, iOS, Android, or Windows Phone—or apps that run from *browser software* such as Internet Explorer, Safari, Firefox, or Chrome on a desktop PC or laptop PC are referred to simply as *apps*.

Activity 1.02 | Using Start Search to Locate and Start a Microsoft Office 2013 Desktop App

The easiest and fastest way to search for an app is to use the *Start search* feature—simply display the Windows 8 Start screen and start typing. By default, Windows 8 searches for apps; you can change it to search for files or settings.

1 With your desktop displayed, press ⊞ to display the Windows 8 **Start screen**, and then type **word 2013** With *word 2013* bordered in white in the search results, press Enter to return to the desktop and open Word. If you want to do so, in the upper right corner, sign in with your Microsoft account, and then compare your screen with Figure 1.2.

Documents that you have recently opened, if any, display on the left. On the right, you can select either a blank document or a *template*—a preformatted document that you can use as a starting point and then change to suit your needs.

 BY TOUCH Swipe from the right edge of the screen to display the charms, and then tap Search. Tap in the Apps box, and then use the onscreen keyboard that displays to type *word 2013*. Tap the selected Word 2013 app name to open Word.

FIGURE 1.2

Recently opened documents, if any, display here

Start a blank document here

User signed in; this is optional

Templates to start different types of documents

2 Click **Blank document**. Compare your screen with Figure 1.3, and then take a moment to study the description of these screen elements in the table in Figure 1.4.

NOTE   **Displaying the Full Ribbon**

If your full ribbon does not display, click any tab, and then at the right end of the ribbon, click ⊞ to pin the ribbon to keep it open while you work.

FIGURE 1.3

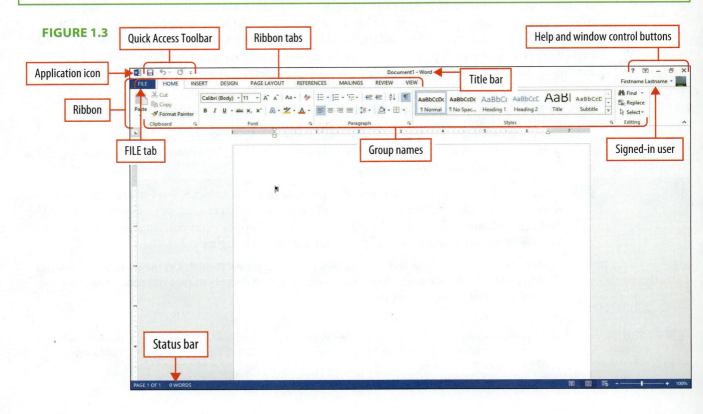

Quick Access Toolbar

Ribbon tabs

Help and window control buttons

Application icon

Ribbon

FILE tab

Title bar

Group names

Signed-in user

Status bar

FIGURE 1.4

MICROSOFT OFFICE SCREEN ELEMENTS	
SCREEN ELEMENT	**DESCRIPTION**
FILE tab	Displays Microsoft Office Backstage view, which is a centralized space for all of your file management tasks such as opening, saving, printing, publishing, or sharing a file—all the things you can do *with* a file.
Group names	Indicate the names of the groups of related commands on the displayed tab.
Help and window control buttons	Display Word Help and Full Screen Mode and enable you to Minimize, Restore Down, or Close the window.
Application icon	When clicked, displays a menu of window control commands including Restore, Minimize, and Close.
Quick Access Toolbar	Displays buttons to perform frequently used commands and use resources with a single click. The default commands include Save, Undo, and Redo. You can add and delete buttons to customize the Quick Access Toolbar for your convenience.
Ribbon	Displays a group of task-oriented tabs that contain the commands, styles, and resources you need to work in an Office 2013 desktop app. The look of your ribbon depends on your screen resolution. A high resolution will display more individual items and button names on the ribbon.
Ribbon tabs	Display the names of the task-oriented tabs relevant to the open program.
Status bar	Displays file information on the left; on the right displays buttons for Read Mode, Print Layout, and Web Layout views; on the far right displays Zoom controls.
Title bar	Displays the name of the file and the name of the program. The Help and window control buttons are grouped on the right side of the title bar.
Signed-in user	Name of the Windows 8 signed-in user.

Objective 3 | Enter, Edit, and Check the Spelling of Text in an Office 2013 Program

Video OF1-3

All of the programs in Office 2013 require some typed text. Your keyboard is still the primary method of entering information into your computer. Techniques to enter text and to *edit*—make changes to—text are similar among all of the Office 2013 programs.

Activity 1.03 | Entering and Editing Text in an Office 2013 Program

1 On the ribbon, on the HOME tab, in the Paragraph group, if necessary, click Show/Hide ¶ so that it is active—shaded. If necessary, on the VIEW tab, in the Show group, select the Ruler check box so that rulers display below the ribbon and on the left side of your window.

The *insertion point*—a blinking vertical line that indicates where text or graphics will be inserted—displays. In Office 2013 programs, the mouse *pointer*—any symbol that displays on your screen in response to moving your mouse device—displays in different shapes depending on the task you are performing and the area of the screen to which you are pointing.

When you press Enter, Spacebar, or Tab on your keyboard, characters display to represent these keystrokes. These screen characters do not print and are referred to as *formatting marks* or *nonprinting characters*.

2 ▸ Type **Skyline Grille Info** and notice how the insertion point moves to the right as you type. Point slightly to the right of the letter *e* in *Grille* and click to place the insertion point there. Compare your screen with Figure 1.5.

A *paragraph symbol* (¶) indicates the end of a paragraph and displays each time you press Enter. This is a type of formatting mark and does not print.

FIGURE 1.5

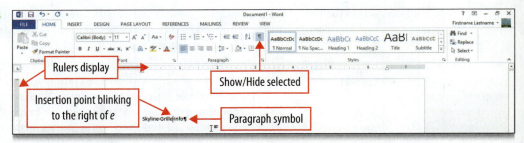

3 ▸ On your keyboard, locate and then press the Backspace key to delete the letter *e*.

Pressing Backspace removes a character to the left of the insertion point.

4 ▸ Press → one time to place the insertion point to the left of the *I* in *Info*. Type **Chef's** and then press Spacebar one time.

By *default*, when you type text in an Office program, existing text moves to the right to make space for new typing. Default refers to the current selection or setting that is automatically used by a program unless you specify otherwise.

5 ▸ Press Del four times to delete *Info* and then type **Notes**

Pressing Del removes a character to the right of the insertion point.

6 ▸ With your insertion point blinking after the word *Notes*, on your keyboard, hold down the Ctrl key. While holding down Ctrl, press ← three times to move the insertion point to the beginning of the word *Grill*.

This is a *keyboard shortcut*—a key or combination of keys that performs a task that would otherwise require a mouse. This keyboard shortcut moves the insertion point to the beginning of the previous word.

A keyboard shortcut is commonly indicated as Ctrl + ← (or some other combination of keys) to indicate that you hold down the first key while pressing the second key. A keyboard shortcut can also include three keys, in which case you hold down the first two and then press the third. For example, Ctrl + Shift + ← selects one word to the left.

7 ▸ With the insertion point blinking at the beginning of the word *Grill*, type **Metro** and press Spacebar.

8 ▸ Press Ctrl + End to place the insertion point after the letter *s* in *Notes*, and then press Enter one time. With the insertion point blinking, type the following and include the spelling error: **Exective Chef, Madison Dunham**

9 With your mouse, point slightly to the left of the *M* in *Madison*, hold down the left mouse button, and then ***drag***—hold down the left mouse button while moving your mouse—to the right to select the text *Madison Dunham* but not the paragraph mark following it, and then release the mouse button. Compare your screen with Figure 1.6.

The ***mini toolbar*** displays commands that are commonly used with the selected object, which places common commands close to your pointer. When you move the pointer away from the mini toolbar, it fades from view.

Selecting refers to highlighting, by dragging or clicking with your mouse, areas of text or data or graphics so that the selection can be edited, formatted, copied, or moved. The action of dragging includes releasing the left mouse button at the end of the area you want to select.

The Office programs recognize a selected area as one unit to which you can make changes. Selecting text may require some practice. If you are not satisfied with your result, click anywhere outside of the selection, and then begin again.

 BY TOUCH   Tap once on *Madison* to display the gripper—small circle that acts as a handle—directly below the word. This establishes the start gripper. If necessary, with your finger, drag the gripper to the beginning of the word. Then drag the gripper to the end of Dunham to select the text and display the end gripper.

FIGURE 1.6

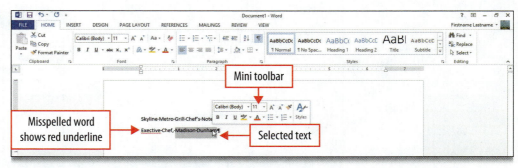

10 With the text *Madison Dunham* selected, type **Sarah Jackson**

In any Windows-based program, such as the Microsoft Office 2013 programs, selected text is deleted and then replaced when you begin to type new text. You will save time by developing good techniques for selecting and then editing or replacing selected text, which is easier than pressing the Del key numerous times to delete text.

Activity 1.04 | Checking Spelling

Office 2013 has a dictionary of words against which all entered text is checked. In Word and PowerPoint, words that are not in the dictionary display a wavy red line, indicating a possible misspelled word or a proper name or an unusual word—none of which are in the Office 2013 dictionary.

In Excel and Access, you can initiate a check of the spelling, but red underlines do not display.

1 Notice that the misspelled word *Exective* displays with a wavy red underline.

2 Point to *Exective* and then ***right-click***—click your right mouse button one time.

A ***shortcut menu*** displays, which displays commands and options relevant to the selected text or object. These are ***context-sensitive commands*** because they relate to the item you right-clicked. These types of menus are also referred to as ***context menus***. Here, the shortcut menu displays commands related to the misspelled word.

 BY TOUCH   Tap and hold a moment to select the misspelled word, then release your finger to display the shortcut menu.

3 Press [Esc] to cancel the shortcut menu, and then in the lower left corner of your screen, on the **status bar**, click the **Proofing** icon ⌷x, which displays an *X* because some errors are detected. Compare your screen with Figure 1.7.

> The Spelling pane displays on the right. Here you have many more options for checking spelling than you have on the shortcut menu. The suggested correct word, *Executive*, is highlighted.

> You can click the speaker icon to hear the pronunciation of the selected word. You can also see some synonyms for *Executive*. Finally, if you have not already installed a dictionary, you can click *Get a Dictionary*—if you are signed in to Office with a Microsoft account—to find and install one from the online Office store; or if you have a dictionary app installed, it will display here and you can search it for more information.

> In the Spelling pane, you can ignore the word one time or in all occurrences, change the word to the suggested word, select a different suggestion, or add a word to the dictionary against which Word checks.

FIGURE 1.7

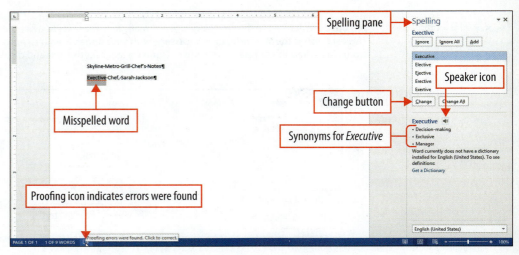

 **ANOTHER WAY**   Press [F7] to display the Spelling pane; or, on the Review tab, in the Proofing group, click Spelling & Grammar.

4 In the **Spelling** pane, click **Change** to change the spelling to *Executive*. In the message box that displays, click **OK**.

Objective 4   Perform Commands from a Dialog Box

Video OF1-4

In a dialog box, you make decisions about an individual object or topic. In some dialog boxes, you can make multiple decisions in one place.

Activity 1.05 | Performing Commands from a Dialog Box

1 On the ribbon, click the **DESIGN tab**, and then in the **Page Background group**, click **Page Color**.

2 At the bottom of the menu, notice the command **Fill Effects** followed by an **ellipsis** (...). Compare your screen with Figure 1.8.

> An *ellipsis* is a set of three dots indicating incompleteness. An ellipsis following a command name indicates that a dialog box will display when you click the command.

FIGURE 1.8

DESIGN tab active

Page Color button

Fill Effects followed by ellipsis

3 ▶ Click **Fill Effects** to display the **Fill Effects** dialog box. Compare your screen with Figure 1.9.

Fill is the inside color of a page or object. The Gradient tab is active. In a *gradient fill*, one color fades into another. Here, the dialog box displays a set of tabs across the top from which you can display different sets of options. Some dialog boxes display the option group names on the left.

FIGURE 1.9

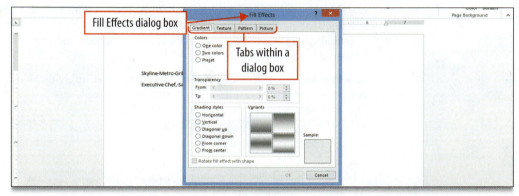

Fill Effects dialog box

Tabs within a dialog box

4 ▶ Under **Colors**, click the **One color** option button.

The dialog box displays settings related to the One color option. An *option button* is a round button that enables you to make one choice among two or more options.

5 ▶ Click the **Color 1 arrow**—the arrow under the text *Color 1*—and then in the third column, point to the second color to display the ScreenTip *Gray-25%, Background 2, Darker 10%*.

A *ScreenTip* displays useful information about mouse actions, such as pointing to screen elements or dragging.

6 ▶ Click **Gray-25%, Background 2, Darker 10%**, and then notice that the fill color displays in the **Color 1** box. In the **Dark Light** bar, click the **Light arrow** as many times as necessary until the scroll box is all the way to right. Under **Shading styles**, click the **Diagonal down** option button. Under **Variants**, click the upper right variant. Compare your screen with Figure 1.10.

FIGURE 1.10

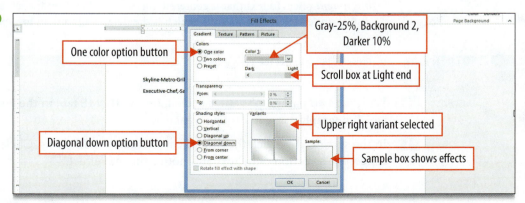

One color option button

Gray-25%, Background 2, Darker 10%

Scroll box at Light end

Upper right variant selected

Diagonal down option button

Sample box shows effects

7 At the bottom of the dialog box, click **OK**, and notice the subtle page color.

In Word, the gray shading page color will not print—even on a color printer—unless you set specific options to do so. However a subtle background page color is effective if people will be reading the document on a screen. Microsoft's research indicates that two-thirds of people who open Word documents never edit them; they only read them.

Activity 1.06 | Using Undo

1 Point to the *S* in *Skyline*, and then drag down and to the right to select both paragraphs of text and include the paragraph marks. On the mini toolbar, click **Styles,** and then *point to* but do not click **Title**. Compare your screen with Figure 1.11.

A *style* is a group of *formatting* commands, such as font, font size, font color, paragraph alignment, and line spacing that can be applied to a paragraph with one command. Formatting is the process of establishing the overall appearance of text, graphics, and pages in an Office file—for example, in a Word document.

Live Preview is a technology that shows the result of applying an editing or formatting change as you point to possible results—before you actually apply it.

FIGURE 1.11

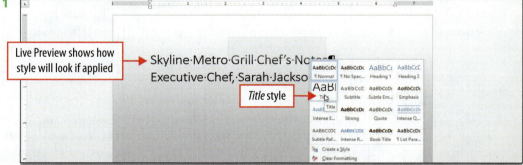

2 In the **Styles** gallery, click **Title**.

A *gallery* is an Office feature that displays a list of potential results.

3 On the ribbon, on the **HOME tab**, in the **Paragraph group**, click **Center** to center the two paragraphs.

Alignment refers to the placement of paragraph text relative to the left and right margins. *Center alignment* refers to text that is centered horizontally between the left and right margins. You can also align text at the left margin, which is the default alignment for text in Word, or at the right.

4 With the two paragraphs still selected, on the **HOME tab**, in the **Font Group**, click **Text Effects and Typography** to display a gallery.

5 In the second row, click the first effect—**Gradient Fill – Gray**. Click anywhere to *deselect*—cancel the selection—the text and notice the text effect.

6 ▶ Because this effect might be difficult to read, in the upper left corner of your screen, on the **Quick Access Toolbar**, click **Undo** ↺.

The **Undo** command reverses your last action.

↻ **ANOTHER WAY**   Press [Ctrl] + [Z] as the keyboard shortcut for the Undo command.

7 ▶ Display the **Text Effects and Typography** gallery again, and then in the second row, click the second effect—**Gradient Fill – Blue, Accent 1, Reflection**. Click anywhere to deselect the text and notice the text effect. Compare your screen with Figure 1.12.

As you progress in your study of Microsoft Office, you will practice using many dialog boxes and applying interesting effects such as this to your Word documents, Excel worksheets, Access database objects, and PowerPoint slides.

FIGURE 1.12

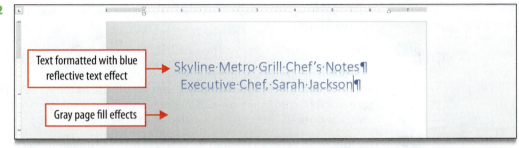

Text formatted with blue reflective text effect →

Skyline·Metro·Grill·Chef's·Notes¶
Executive·Chef,·Sarah·Jackson¶

Gray page fill effects →

Objective 5   Create a Folder and Name and Save a File

Video OF1-5

A *location* is any disk drive, folder, or other place in which you can store files and folders. Where you store your files depends on how and where you use your data. For example, for your college classes, you might decide to store on a removable USB flash drive so that you can carry your files to different locations and access your files on different computers.

If you do most of your work on a single computer, for example your home desktop system or your laptop computer that you take with you to school or work, then you can store your files in one of the Libraries—Documents, Music, Pictures, or Videos—that the Windows 8 operating system creates on your hard drive.

The best place to store files if you want them to be available anytime, anywhere, from almost any device is on your *SkyDrive*, which is Microsoft's free *cloud storage* for anyone with a free Microsoft account. Cloud storage refers to online storage of data so that you can access your data from different places and devices. *Cloud computing* refers to applications and services that are accessed over the Internet, rather than to applications that are installed on your local computer.

Because many people now have multiple computing devices—desktop, laptop, tablet, smartphone—it is common to store data *in the cloud* so that it is always available. *Synchronization*, also called *syncing*—pronounced SINK-ing—is the process of updating computer files that are in two or more locations according to specific rules. So if you create and save a Word document on your SkyDrive using your laptop, you can open and edit that document on your tablet. And then when you close the document again, the file is properly updated to reflect your changes.

You need not be connected to the Internet to access documents stored on SkyDrive because an up-to-date version of your content is synched to your local system and available on SkyDrive. You must, however, be connected to the Internet for the syncing to occur. Saving to SkyDrive will keep the local copy on your computer and the copy in the cloud synchronized for as long as you need it. If you open and edit on a different computer, log into the SkyDrive website, and then edit using Office 2013, Office 2010, or the **Office Web Apps**, you can save any changes back to SkyDrive. Office Web Apps are the free online companions to Microsoft Word, Excel, PowerPoint, Access, and OneNote. These changes will be synchronized back to any of your computers that run the SkyDrive for Windows application, which you get for free simply by logging in with your Microsoft account at skydrive.com.

The Windows operating system helps you to create and maintain a logical folder structure, so always take the time to name your files and folders consistently.

Activity 1.07 | Creating a Folder and Naming and Saving a File

A Word document is an example of a file. In this activity, you will create a folder on your USB flash drive in which to store your files. If you prefer to store on your SkyDrive or in the Documents library on your hard drive, you can use similar steps.

1 If necessary, insert your **USB flash drive** into your computer.

As the first step in saving a file, determine where you want to save the file, and if necessary, insert a storage device.

2 At the top of your screen, in the title bar, notice that *Document1 – Word* displays.

The Blank option on the opening screen of an Office 2013 program displays a new unsaved file with a default name—*Document1, Presentation1*, and so on. As you create your file, your work is temporarily stored in the computer's memory until you initiate a Save command, at which time you must choose a file name and a location in which to save your file.

3 In the upper left corner of your screen, click the **FILE tab** to display **Backstage** view. Compare your screen with Figure 1.13.

Backstage view is a centralized space that groups commands related to *file* management; that is why the tab is labeled *FILE*. File management commands include opening, saving, printing, publishing, or sharing a file. The **Backstage tabs**—*Info, New, Open, Save, Save As, Print, Share, Export*, and *Close*—display along the left side. The tabs group file-related tasks together.

Here, the **Info tab** displays information—*info*—about the current file, and file management commands display under Info. For example, if you click the Protect Document button, a list of options that you can set for this file that relate to who can open or edit the document displays.

On the right, you can also examine the **document properties**. Document properties, also known as **metadata**, are details about a file that describe or identify it, such as the title, author name, subject, and keywords that identify the document's topic or contents. To close Backstage view and return to the document, you can click ⬅ in the upper left corner or press [Esc].

FIGURE 1.13

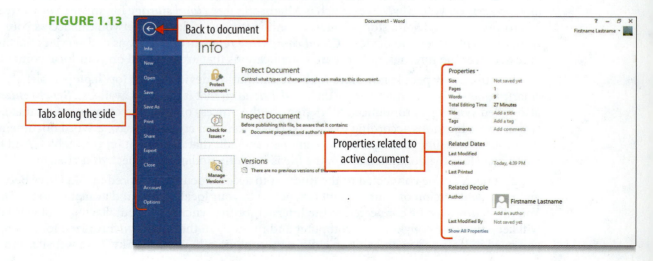

4 On the left, click **Save As**, and notice that the default location for storing Office files is your **SkyDrive**—if you are signed in. Compare your screen with Figure 1.14.

> When you are saving something for the first time, for example a new Word document, the Save and Save As commands are identical. That is, the Save As commands will display if you click Save or if you click Save As.

FIGURE 1.14

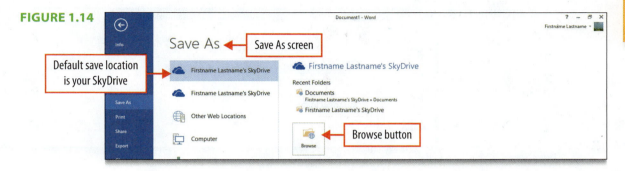

N O T E   **Saving after Your File Is Named**

After you name and save a file, the Save command on the Quick Access Toolbar saves any changes you make to the file without displaying Backstage view. The Save As command enables you to name and save a *new* file based on the current one—in a location that you choose. After you name and save the new document, the original document closes, and the new document—based on the original one—displays.

---

5 To store your Word file on your **USB flash drive**—instead of your SkyDrive—click the **Browse** button to display the **Save As** dialog box. On the left, in the navigation pane, scroll down, and then under **Computer**, click the name of your **USB flash drive**. Compare your screen with Figure 1.15.

> In the Save As dialog box, you must indicate the name you want for the file and the location where you want to save the file. When working with your own data, it is good practice to pause at this point and determine the logical name and location for your file.

> In the Save As dialog box, a *toolbar* displays. This is a row, column, or block of buttons or icons, that usually displays across the top of a window and that contains commands for tasks you perform with a single click.

FIGURE 1.15

6 > On the toolbar, click **New folder**.

In the file list, Word creates a new folder, and the text *New folder* is selected.

7 > Type **Office Features Chapter 1** and press [Enter]. Compare your screen with Figure 1.16.

In Windows-based programs, the [Enter] key confirms an action.

FIGURE 1.16

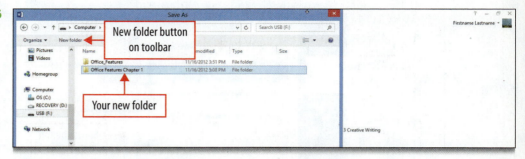

8 > In the **file list**, double-click the name of your new folder to open it and display its name in the **address bar**.

9 > In the lower portion of the dialog box, click in the **File name** box to select the existing text. Notice that Office inserts the text at the beginning of the document as a suggested file name.

10 > On your keyboard, locate the hyphen [-] key. Notice that the [Shift] of this key produces the underscore character. With the text still selected and using your own name, type **Lastname_Firstname_1A_Note_Form** and then compare your screen with Figure 1.17.

You can use spaces in file names, however, some people prefer not to use spaces. Some programs, especially when transferring files over the Internet, may insert the extra characters *%20* in place of a space. This can happen in ***SharePoint***, so using underscores instead of spaces can be a good habit to adopt. SharePoint is Microsoft's collaboration software with which people in an organization can set up team sites to share information, manage documents, and publish reports for others to see. In general, however, unless you encounter a problem, it is OK to use spaces. In this textbook, underscores are used instead of spaces in file names.

FIGURE 1.17

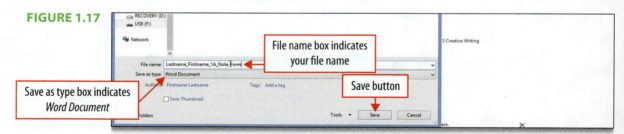

11 > In the lower right corner, click **Save** or press [Enter]. Compare your screen with Figure 1.18.

The Word window redisplays and your new file name displays in the title bar, indicating that the file has been saved to a location that you have specified.

FIGURE 1.18

12 In the first paragraph, click to place the insertion point after the word *Grill* and type **,** (a comma). In the upper left corner of your screen, on the **Quick Access Toolbar**, click **Save** 🖫.

> After a document is named and saved in a location, you can save any changes you have made since the last Save operation by using the Save command on the Quick Access Toolbar. When working on a document, it is good practice to save your changes from time to time.

Objective 6   Insert a Footer, Add Document Properties, Print a File, and Close a Desktop App

Video OF1-6

For most of your files, especially in a workplace setting, it is useful to add identifying information to help in finding files later. You might also want to print your file on paper or create an electronic printout. The process of printing a file is similar in all of the Office applications.

Activity 1.08 | Inserting a Footer, Inserting Document Info, and Adding Document Properties

> **N O T E**   **Are You Printing or Submitting Your Files Electronically?**
>
> In this activity, you can either produce a paper printout or create an electronic file to submit to your instructor if required.

1 On the ribbon, click the **INSERT tab**, and then in the **Header & Footer group**, click **Footer**.

2 At the bottom of the list, click **Edit Footer**. On the ribbon, notice that the **HEADER & FOOTER TOOLS** display.

> The *Header & Footer Tools Design* tab displays on the ribbon. The ribbon adapts to your work and will display additional tabs like this one—referred to as ***contextual tabs***—when you need them.

> A ***footer*** is a reserved area for text or graphics that displays at the bottom of each page in a document. Likewise, a ***header*** is a reserved area for text or graphics that displays at the top of each page in a document. When the footer (or header) area is active, the document area is dimmed, indicating it is unavailable.

3 On the ribbon, under **HEADER & FOOTER TOOLS**, on the **DESIGN tab**, in the **Insert group**, click **Document Info**, and then click **File Name** to insert the name of your file in the footer, which is a common business practice. Compare your screen with Figure 1.19.

> Ribbon commands that display ▼ will, when clicked, display a list of options for the command.

FIGURE 1.19

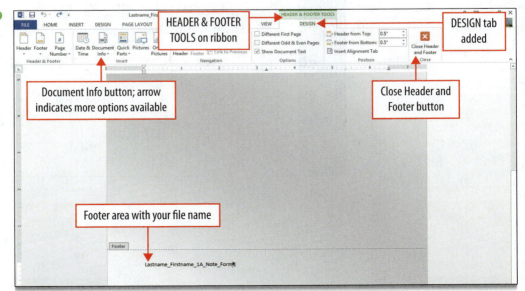

4 At the right end of the ribbon, click **Close Header and Footer**.

↻ **ANOTHER WAY**   Double-click anywhere in the dimmed document to close the footer.

5 Click the **FILE tab** to display **Backstage** view. On the right, at the bottom of the **Properties** list, click **Show All Properties**.

↻ **ANOTHER WAY**   Click the arrow to the right of Properties, and then click Show Document Panel to show and edit properties at the top of your document window.

6 On the list of **Properties**, click to the right of **Tags** to display an empty box, and then type **chef, notes, form**

> *Tags*, also referred to as *keywords*, are custom file properties in the form of words that you associate with a document to give an indication of the document's content. Adding tags to your documents makes it easier to search for and locate files in File Explorer and in systems such as Microsoft SharePoint document libraries.

↻ **BY TOUCH**   Tap to the right of Tags to display the Tags box and the onscreen keyboard.

7 Click to the right of **Subject** to display an empty box, and then type your course name and section #; for example *CIS 10, #5543*.

8 Under **Related People**, be sure that your name displays as the author. If necessary, right-click the author name, click Edit Property, type your name, click outside of the Edit person dialog box, and then click OK. Compare your screen with Figure 1.20.

FIGURE 1.20

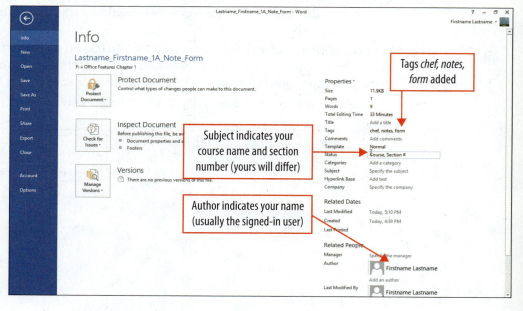

Activity 1.09 | Printing a File and Closing a Desktop App

1 On the left, click **Print**, and then compare your screen with Figure 1.21.

> Here you can select any printer connected to your system and adjust the settings related to how you want to print. On the right, the ***Print Preview*** displays, which is a view of a document as it will appear on paper when you print it.

> At the bottom of the Print Preview area, in the center, the number of pages and page navigation arrows with which you can move among the pages in Print Preview display. On the right, the Zoom slider enables you to shrink or enlarge the Print Preview. ***Zoom*** is the action of increasing or decreasing the viewing area of the screen.

 **ANOTHER WAY**   From the document screen, press Ctrl + P or Ctrl + F2 to display Print in Backstage view.

FIGURE 1.21

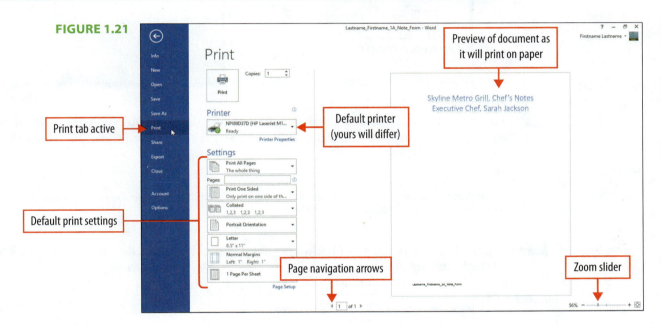

2 To submit your file electronically, skip this step and continue to Step 3. To print your document on paper using the default printer on your system, in the upper left portion of the screen, click the **Print** button.

> The document will print on your default printer; if you do not have a color printer, the blue text will print in shades of gray. The gray page color you applied to the document does not display in Print Preview nor does it print unless you specifically adjust some of Word's options. Backstage view closes and your file redisplays in the Word window.

3 To create an electronic file, on the left click **Export**. On the right, click the **Create PDF/XPS** button to display the **Publish as PDF or XPS** dialog box.

> ***PDF*** stands for ***Portable Document Format***, which is a technology that creates an image that preserves the look of your file. This is a popular format for sending documents electronically, because the document will display on most computers.

> ***XPS*** stands for ***XML Paper Specification***—a Microsoft file format that also creates an image of your document and that opens in the XPS viewer.

4 On the left in the **navigation pane**, if necessary expand ▷ Computer, and then navigate to your **Office Features Chapter 1** folder on your **USB flash drive**. Compare your screen with Figure 1.22.

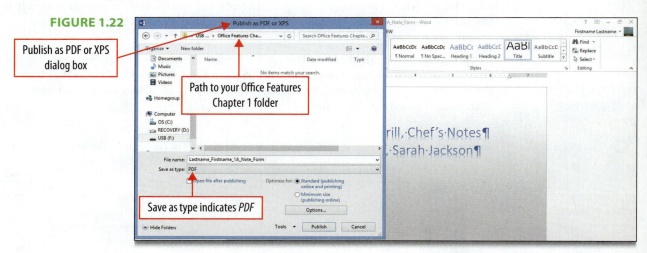

Publish as PDF or XPS dialog box

Path to your Office Features Chapter 1 folder

Save as type indicates *PDF*

5 In the lower right corner of the dialog box, click **Publish**; if your Adobe Acrobat or Adobe Reader program displays your PDF, in the upper right corner, click Close . Notice that your document redisplays in Word.

 ANOTHER WAY   In Backstage view, click Save As, navigate to the location of your Chapter folder, click the Save as type arrow, on the list click PDF, and then click Save.

6 Click the **FILE tab** to redisplay **Backstage** view. On the left, click **Close**, if necessary click Save, and then compare your screen with Figure 1.23.

FIGURE 1.23

Word window with all documents closed

Close button

7 In the upper right corner of the Word window, click **Close** [x]. If directed by your instructor to do so, submit your paper or electronic file.

END | You have completed Project 1A

PROJECT ACTIVITIES

In Activities 1.10 through 1.21, you will open, edit, and then compress a Word file. You will also use the Office Help system and install an app for Office. Your completed document will look similar to Figure 1.24.

PROJECT FILES

For Project 1B, you will need the following file:

of01B_Rehearsal_Dinner

You will save your file as:

Lastname_Firstname_1B_Rehearsal_Dinner

PROJECT RESULTS

Skyline Metro Grill

TO: Sarah Jackson, Executive Chef

FROM: Laura Mabry Hernandez, General Manager

DATE: February 17, 2016

SUBJECT: Wedding Rehearsal Dinners

In the spring and summer months, wedding rehearsal dinners provide a new marketing opportunity for Skyline Metro Grill at all of our locations. A rehearsal dinner is an informal meal following a wedding rehearsal at which the bride and groom typically thank those who have helped them make their wedding a special event.

Our smaller private dining rooms with sweeping city views are an ideal location for a rehearsal dinner. At each of our locations, I have directed the Sales and Marketing Coordinator to partner with local wedding planners to promote Skyline Metro Grill as a relaxed yet sophisticated venue for rehearsal dinners. The typical rehearsal dinner includes the wedding party, the immediate family of the bride and groom, and out-of-town guests.

Please develop six menus—in varying price ranges—to present to local wedding planners so that they can easily promote Skyline Metro Grill to couples who are planning a rehearsal dinner. In addition to a traditional dinner, we should also include options for a buffet-style dinner and a family-style dinner.

This marketing effort will require extensive communication with our Sales and Marketing Coordinators and with local wedding planners. Let's meet to discuss the details and the marketing challenges, and to create a promotional piece that begins something like this:

Skyline Metro Grill for Your Rehearsal Dinner

Lastname_Firstname_1B_Rehearsal_Dinner

FIGURE 1.24 Project 1B Memo

Video OF1-7

In any Office program, you can display the *Open dialog box*, from which you can navigate to and then open an existing file that was created in that same program.

The Open dialog box, along with the Save and Save As dialog boxes, is a common dialog box. These dialog boxes, which are provided by the Windows programming interface, display in all Office programs in the same manner. So the Open, Save, and Save As dialog boxes will all look and perform the same regardless of the Office program in which you are working.

Activity 1.10 | Opening an Existing File and Saving It with a New Name

In this activity, you will display the Open dialog box, open an existing Word document, and then save it in your storage location with a new name.

1 Sign in to your computer, and then on the Windows 8 Start screen, type **word 2013** Press Enter to open Word on your desktop. If you want to do so, on the taskbar, right-click the **Word icon**, and then click **Pin this program to taskbar** to keep the Word program available from your desktop.

2 On Word's opening screen, on the left, click **Open Other Documents**. Under **Open**, click **Computer**, and then on the right click **Browse**.

3 In the **Open** dialog box, on the left in the **navigation pane**, scroll down, if necessary expand ▷ Computer, and then click the name of your **USB flash drive**. In the **file list**, double-click the **Office_Features** folder that you downloaded.

4 Double-click **of01B_Rehearsal_Dinner**. If **PROTECTED VIEW** displays at the top of your screen, in the center click **Enable Editing**.

In Office 2013, a file will open in *Protected View* if the file appears to be from a potentially risky location, such as the Internet. Protected View is a security feature in Office 2013 that protects your computer from malicious files by opening them in a restricted environment until you enable them. *Trusted Documents* is another security feature that remembers which files you have already enabled.

You might encounter these security features if you open a file from an email or download files from the Internet; for example, from your college's learning management system or from the Pearson website. So long as you trust the source of the file, click Enable Editing or Enable Content—depending on the type of file you receive—and then go ahead and work with the file.

5 With the document displayed in the Word window, be sure that **Show/Hide** is active; if necessary, on the HOME tab, in the Paragraph group, click Show/Hide to activate it. Compare your screen with Figure 1.25.

FIGURE 1.25

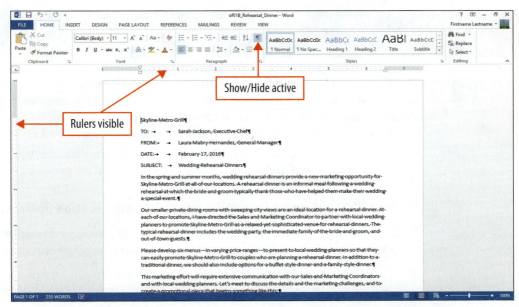

6 Click the **FILE tab** to display **Backstage** view, and then on the left, click **Save As**. On the right, click the folder under **Current Folder** to open the **Save As** dialog box. Notice that the current folder is the **Office_Features** folder you downloaded.

ANOTHER WAY   Press F12 to display the Save As dialog box.

7 In the upper left corner of the **Save As** dialog box, click the **Up** button ⬆ to move up one level in the File Explorer hierarchy. In the **file list**, double-click your **Office Features Chapter 1** folder to open it.

8 Click in the **File name** box to select the existing text, and then, using your own name, type **Lastname_Firstname_1B_Rehearsal_Dinner** Compare your screen with Figure 1.26.

FIGURE 1.26

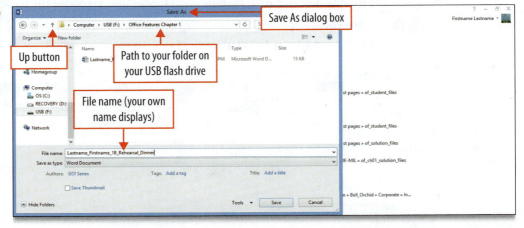

9 Click **Save** or press Enter; notice that your new file name displays in the title bar.

The original document closes, and your new document, based on the original, displays with the name in the title bar.

More Knowledge   **Read-Only**

Some files might display **Read-Only** in the title bar, which is a property assigned to a file that prevents the file from being modified or deleted; it indicates that you cannot save any changes to the displayed document unless you first save it with a new name.

Video OF1-8

If you sign in to Windows 8 with a Microsoft account, you may notice that you are also signed in to Office. This enables you to save files to and retrieve files from your SkyDrive and to **collaborate** with others on Office files when you want to do so. To collaborate means to work with others as a team in an intellectual endeavor to complete a shared task or to achieve a shared goal.

Within each Office application, an **Options dialog box** enables you to select program settings and other options and preferences. For example, you can set preferences for viewing and editing files.

Activity 1.11 | Signing In to Office and Viewing Application Options

1 In the upper right corner of your screen, if you are signed in with a Microsoft account, click the arrow to the right of your name, and then compare your screen with Figure 1.27.

Here you can change your photo, go to About me to edit your profile, examine your Account settings, or switch accounts to sign in with a different Microsoft account.

FIGURE 1.27

2 Click the **FILE tab** to display **Backstage** view. On the left, click the last tab—**Options**.

3 In the **Word Options** dialog box, on the left, click **Display**, and then on the right, locate the information under **Always show these formatting marks on the screen**.

4 Under **Always show these formatting marks on the screen**, be sure the last check box, **Show all formatting marks**, is selected—select it if necessary. Compare your screen with Figure 1.28.

FIGURE 1.28

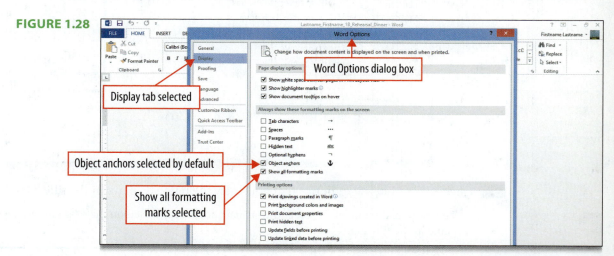

5 In the lower right corner of the dialog box, click **OK**.

Objective 9 | Perform Commands from the Ribbon and Quick Access Toolbar

Video OF1-9

The ribbon that displays across the top of the program window groups commands in a manner that you would most logically use them. The ribbon in each Office program is slightly different, but all contain the same three elements: *tabs*, *groups*, and *commands*.

Tabs display across the top of the ribbon, and each tab relates to a type of activity; for example, laying out a page. Groups are sets of related commands for specific tasks. Commands—instructions to computer programs—are arranged in groups and might display as a button, a menu, or a box in which you type information.

You can also minimize the ribbon so only the tab names display, which is useful when working on a smaller screen such as a tablet computer where you want to maximize your screen viewing area.

Activity 1.12 | Performing Commands from and Customizing the Ribbon and the Quick Access Toolbar

1 Take a moment to examine the document on your screen. If necessary, on the ribbon, click the VIEW tab, and then in the Show group, click to place a check mark in the Ruler check box. Compare your screen with Figure 1.29.

This document is a memo from the General Manager to the Executive Chef regarding a new restaurant promotion for wedding rehearsal dinners.

When working in Word, display the rulers so that you can see how margin settings affect your document and how text and objects align. Additionally, if you set a tab stop or an indent, its location is visible on the ruler.

FIGURE 1.29

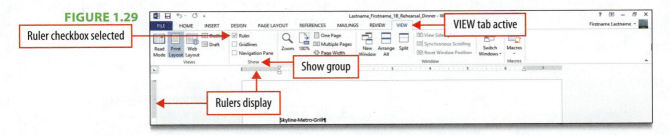

Ruler checkbox selected

VIEW tab active

Show group

Rulers display

2 In the upper left corner of your screen, above the ribbon, locate the **Quick Access Toolbar**.

Recall that the Quick Access Toolbar contains commands that you use frequently. By default, only the commands Save, Undo, and Redo display, but you can add and delete commands to suit your needs. Possibly the computer at which you are working already has additional commands added to the Quick Access Toolbar.

3 At the end of the **Quick Access Toolbar**, click the **Customize Quick Access Toolbar** button ⎸▾⎹, and then compare your screen with Figure 1.30.

A list of commands that Office users commonly add to their Quick Access Toolbar displays, including New, Open, Email, Quick Print, and Print Preview and Print. Commands already on the Quick Access Toolbar display a check mark. Commands that you add to the Quick Access Toolbar are always just one click away.

Here you can also display the More Commands dialog box, from which you can select any command from any tab on the ribbon to add to the Quick Access Toolbar.

 BY TOUCH   Tap once on Quick Access Toolbar commands.

FIGURE 1.30

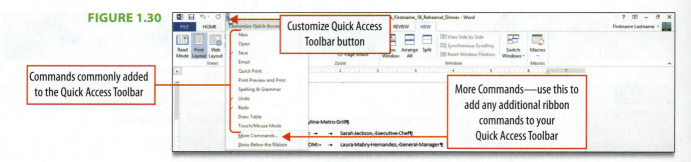

4 On the list, click **Print Preview and Print**, and then notice that the icon is added to the **Quick Access Toolbar**. Compare your screen with Figure 1.31.

The icon that represents the Print Preview command displays on the Quick Access Toolbar. Because this is a command that you will use frequently while building Office documents, you might decide to have this command remain on your Quick Access Toolbar.

ANOTHER WAY   Right-click any command on the ribbon, and then on the shortcut menu, click Add to Quick Access Toolbar.

FIGURE 1.31

5 In the first line of the document, if necessary, click to the left of the *S* in *Skyline* to position the insertion point there, and then press Enter one time to insert a blank paragraph. Press ↑ one time to position the insertion point in the new blank paragraph. Compare your screen with Figure 1.32.

FIGURE 1.32

6 On the ribbon, click the **INSERT tab**. In the **Illustrations group**, *point* to the **Online Pictures** button to display its ScreenTip.

Many buttons on the ribbon have this type of *enhanced ScreenTip*, which displays useful descriptive information about the command.

7 Click **Online Pictures**, and then compare your screen with Figure 1.33.

In the Insert Pictures dialog box you can search for online pictures using Microsoft's Clip Art collection. *Clip art* refers to royalty-free photos and illustrations you can download from Microsoft's Office.com site.

Here you can also search for images using the Bing search engine, and if you are signed in with your Microsoft account, you can also find images on your SkyDrive or on your computer by clicking Browse. At the bottom, you can click the Flickr logo and download pictures from your Flickr account if you have one.

FIGURE 1.33

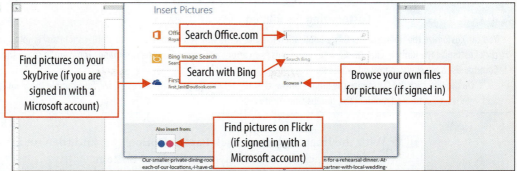

Search Office.com

Find pictures on your SkyDrive (if you are signed in with a Microsoft account)

Search with Bing

Browse your own files for pictures (if signed in)

Find pictures on Flickr (if signed in with a Microsoft account)

---

8 Click **Office.com Clip Art** and in the box that displays to the right, type **salad in a bowl** and press Enter. As shown in Figure 1.34, point to the illustration of the salad bowl to display its keywords.

You can use various keywords to find clip art that is appropriate for your documents.

FIGURE 1.34

ScreenTip displays keywords for this clip

Insert button

---

9 Click the illustration of the salad to select it, and then in the lower right corner, click **Insert**. In the upper right corner of the picture, point to the **Layout Options** button ▣ to display its ScreenTip, and then compare your screen with Figure 1.35. If you cannot find the image, select a similar image, and then drag one of the corner sizing handles to match the approximate size shown in the figure.

Inserted pictures anchor—attach to—the paragraph at the insertion point location—as indicated by the anchor symbol. *Layout Options* enable you to choose how the *object*—in this instance an inserted picture—interacts with the surrounding text. An object is a picture or other graphic such as a chart or table that you can select and then move and resize.

When a picture is selected, the PICTURE TOOLS become available on the ribbon. Additionally, *sizing handles*—small squares that indicate an object is selected—surround the selected picture.

FIGURE 1.35

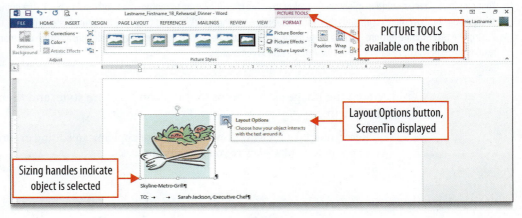

PICTURE TOOLS available on the ribbon

Layout Options button, ScreenTip displayed

Sizing handles indicate object is selected

10 ▶ With the image selected, click **Layout Options**, and then under **With Text Wrapping**, in the second row, click the first layout—**Top and Bottom**.

11 ▶ Point to the image to display the pointer, hold down the left mouse button to display a green line at the left margin, and then drag the image to the right and slightly upward until a green line displays in the center of the image and at the top of the image, as shown in Figure 1.36, and then release the left mouse button. If you are not satisfied with your result, on the Quick Access Toolbar, click Undo and begin again.

Alignment Guides are green lines that display to help you align objects with margins or at the center of a page.

FIGURE 1.36

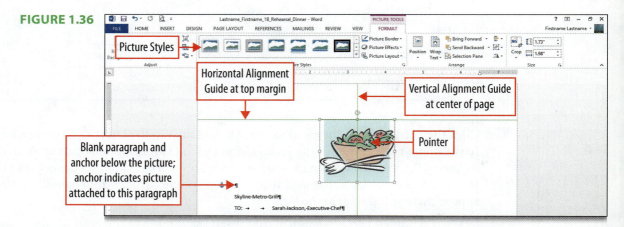

12 ▶ On the ribbon, in the **Picture Styles group**, point to the first style to display the ScreenTip *Simple Frame, White*, and notice that the image displays with a white frame.

N O T E | **The Size of Groups on the Ribbon Varies with Screen Resolution**

Your monitor's screen resolution might be set higher than the resolution used to capture the figures in this book. At a higher resolution, the ribbon expands some groups to show more commands than are available with a single click, such as those in the Picture Styles group. Or, the group expands to add descriptive text to some buttons, such as those in the Adjust group. Regardless of your screen resolution, all Office commands are available to you. In higher resolutions, you will have a more robust view of the ribbon commands.

13 ▶ Watch the image as you point to the second picture style, and then to the third, and then to the fourth.

Recall that Live Preview shows the result of applying an editing or formatting change as you point to possible results—*before* you actually apply it.

14 In the **Picture Styles group**, click the second style—**Beveled Matte, White**—and then click anywhere outside of the image to deselect it. Notice that the *PICTURE TOOLS* no longer display on the ribbon. Compare your screen with Figure 1.37.

Contextual tabs on the ribbon display only when you need them.

FIGURE 1.37

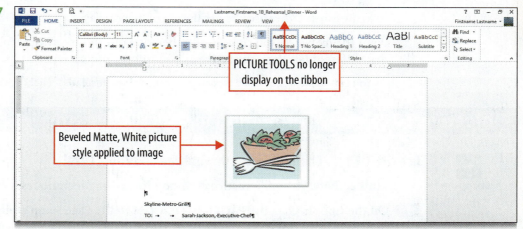

PICTURE TOOLS no longer display on the ribbon

Beveled Matte, White picture style applied to image

15 On the **Quick Access Toolbar**, click **Save** 💾 to save the changes you have made.

Activity 1.13 | Minimizing and Using the Keyboard to Control the Ribbon

Instead of a mouse, some individuals prefer to navigate the ribbon by using keys on the keyboard.

1 On your keyboard, press Alt, and then on the ribbon, notice that small labels display. Press N to activate the commands on the **INSERT tab**, and then compare your screen with Figure 1.38.

Each label represents a *KeyTip*—an indication of the key that you can press to activate the command. For example, on the INSERT tab, you can press F to open the Online Pictures dialog box.

FIGURE 1.38

KeyTips indicate that keyboard control of the ribbon is active

2 Press Esc to redisplay the KeyTips for the tabs. Then, press Alt or Esc again to turn off keyboard control of the ribbon.

3 Point to any tab on the ribbon and right-click to display a shortcut menu.

Here you can choose to display the Quick Access Toolbar below the ribbon or collapse the ribbon to maximize screen space. You can also customize the ribbon by adding, removing, renaming, or reordering tabs, groups, and commands, although this is not recommended until you become an expert Office user.

4 ▶ Click **Collapse the Ribbon**. Notice that only the ribbon tabs display. Click the **HOME tab** to display the commands. Click anywhere in the document, and notice that the ribbon goes back to the collapsed display.

5 ▶ Right-click any ribbon tab, and then click **Collapse the Ribbon** again to remove the check mark from this command.

Many expert Office users prefer the full ribbon display.

6 ▶ Point to any tab on the ribbon, and then on your mouse device, roll the mouse wheel. Notice that different tabs become active as you roll the mouse wheel.

You can make a tab active by using this technique instead of clicking the tab.

Objective 10   Apply Formatting in Office Programs

Video OF1-10

Activity 1.14 | Changing Page Orientation and Zoom Level

In this activity, you will practice common formatting techniques used in Office applications.

1 ▶ On the ribbon, click the **PAGE LAYOUT tab**. In the **Page Setup group**, click **Orientation**, and notice that two orientations display—*Portrait* and *Landscape*. Click **Landscape**.

In ***portrait orientation***, the paper is taller than it is wide. In ***landscape orientation***, the paper is wider than it is tall.

2 ▶ In the lower right corner of the screen, locate the **Zoom slider**.

Recall that to zoom means to increase or decrease the viewing area. You can zoom in to look closely at a section of a document, and then zoom out to see an entire page on the screen. You can also zoom to view multiple pages on the screen.

3 ▶ Drag the **Zoom slider** to the left until you have zoomed to approximately *60%*. Compare your screen with Figure 1.39.

FIGURE 1.39

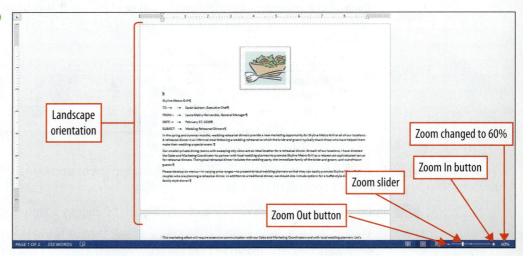

| BY TOUCH | Drag the Zoom slider with your finger. |

4 ▶ Use the technique you just practiced to change the **Orientation** back to **Portrait**.

The default orientation in Word is Portrait, which is commonly used for business documents such as letters and memos.

5 ▸ In the lower right corner, click the **Zoom In** button ⊞ as many times as necessary to return to the **100%** zoom setting.

Use the zoom feature to adjust the view of your document for editing and for your viewing comfort.

 **ANOTHER WAY** You can also control Zoom from the ribbon. On the VIEW tab, in the Zoom group, you can control the Zoom level and also zoom to view multiple pages.

6 ▸ On the **Quick Access Toolbar**, click **Save** 🖫 .

More Knowledge | **Zooming to Page Width**

Some Office users prefer Page Width, which zooms the document so that the width of the page matches the width of the window. Find this command on the VIEW tab, in the Zoom group.

Activity 1.15 | **Formatting Text by Using Fonts, Alignment, Font Colors, and Font Styles**

1 ▸ If necessary, on the right side of your screen, drag the vertical scroll box to the top of the scroll bar. To the left of *Skyline Metro Grill*, point in the margin area to display the 🔏 pointer and click one time to select the entire paragraph. Compare your screen with Figure 1.40.

Use this technique to select complete paragraphs from the margin area—drag downward to select multiple-line paragraphs—which is faster and more efficient than dragging through text.

FIGURE 1.40

2 ▸ On the ribbon, click the **HOME tab**, and then in the **Paragraph group**, click **Center** ≣ to center the paragraph.

3 ▸ On the **HOME tab**, in the **Font group**, click the **Font button arrow** Calibri (Body) ▾ . On the alphabetical list of font names, scroll down and then locate and *point to* **Cambria**.

A *font* is a set of characters with the same design and shape. The default font in a Word document is Calibri, which is a *sans serif* font—a font design with no lines or extensions on the ends of characters.

The Cambria font is a *serif font*—a font design that includes small line extensions on the ends of the letters to guide the eye in reading from left to right.

The list of fonts displays as a gallery showing potential results. For example, in the Font gallery, you can point to see the actual design and format of each font as it would look if applied to text.

4 ▸ Point to several other fonts and observe the effect on the selected text. Then, scroll back to the top of the **Font** gallery. Under **Theme Fonts**, click **Calibri Light**.

A *theme* is a predesigned combination of colors, fonts, line, and fill effects that look good together and is applied to an entire document by a single selection. A theme combines two sets of fonts—one for text and one for headings. In the default Office theme, Calibri Light is the suggested font for headings.

5 With the paragraph *Skyline Metro Grill* still selected, on the **HOME tab**, in the **Font group**, click the **Font Size button arrow** 11 ▾, point to **36**, and then notice how Live Preview displays the text in the font size to which you are pointing. Compare your screen with Figure 1.41.

FIGURE 1.41

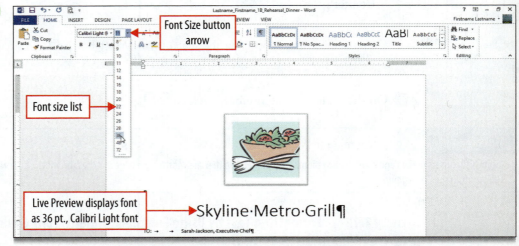

6 On the list of font sizes, click **20**.

Fonts are measured in ***points***, with one point equal to 1/72 of an inch. A higher point size indicates a larger font size. Headings and titles are often formatted by using a larger font size. The word *point* is abbreviated as ***pt***.

7 With *Skyline Metro Grill* still selected, on the **HOME tab**, in the **Font group**, click the **Font Color button arrow** A ▾. Under **Theme Colors**, in the last column, click the last color—**Green, Accent 6, Darker 50%**. Click anywhere to deselect the text.

8 To the left of *TO:*, point in the left margin area to display the pointer, hold down the left mouse button, and then drag down to select the four memo headings. Compare your screen with Figure 1.42.

Use this technique to select complete paragraphs from the margin area—drag downward to select multiple paragraphs—which is faster and more efficient than dragging through text.

🔄 **BY TOUCH**   Tap once on TO: to display the gripper, then with your finger, drag to the right and down to select the four paragraphs.

FIGURE 1.42

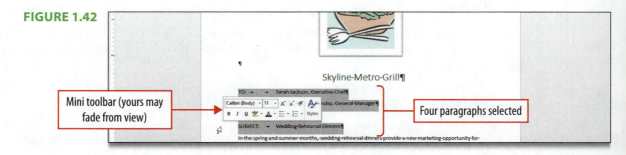

9 With the four paragraphs selected, on the mini toolbar, click the **Font Color** button [A ▾], and notice that the text color of the four paragraphs changes.

The font color button retains its most recently used color—Green, Accent 6, Darker 50%. As you progress in your study of Microsoft Office, you will use other buttons that behave in this manner; that is, they retain their most recently used format. This is commonly referred to as *MRU*—most recently used.

Recall that the mini toolbar places commands that are commonly used for the selected text or object close by so that you reduce the distance that you must move your mouse to access a command. If you are using a touchscreen device, most commands that you need are close and easy to touch.

10 On the right, drag the vertical scroll box down slightly to position more of the text on the screen. Click anywhere in the paragraph that begins *In the spring*, and then *triple-click*—click the left mouse button three times—to select the entire paragraph. If the entire paragraph is not selected, click in the paragraph and begin again.

11 With the entire paragraph selected, on the mini toolbar, click the **Font Color button arrow** [A ▾], and then under **Theme Colors**, in the sixth column, click the last color— **Orange, Accent 2, Darker 50%**.

12 In the memo headings, select the guide word *TO:* and then on the mini toolbar, click **Bold** [B] and **Italic** [I].

Font styles include bold, italic, and underline. Font styles emphasize text and are a visual cue to draw the reader's eye to important text.

13 On the mini toolbar, click **Italic** [I] again to turn off the Italic formatting.

A *toggle button* is a button that can be turned on by clicking it once, and then turned off by clicking it again.

Activity 1.16 | Using Format Painter

Use the Format Painter to copy the formatting of specific text or of a paragraph and then apply it in other locations in your document.

1 With *TO:* still selected, on the mini toolbar, click **Format Painter** [🖌]. Then, move your mouse under the word *Sarah*, and notice the [▲I] mouse pointer. Compare your screen with Figure 1.43.

The pointer takes the shape of a paintbrush, and contains the formatting information from the paragraph where the insertion point is positioned. Information about the Format Painter and how to turn it off displays in the status bar.

FIGURE 1.43

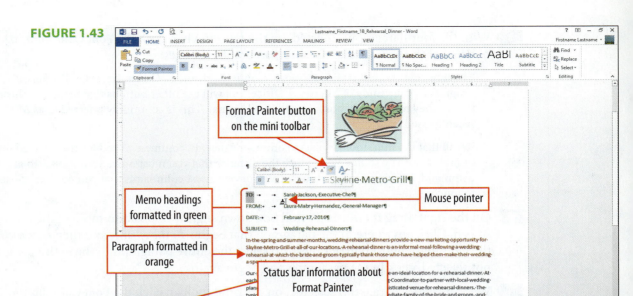

Format Painter button on the mini toolbar

Mouse pointer

Memo headings formatted in green

Paragraph formatted in orange

Status bar information about Format Painter

---

2 With the ▲I pointer, drag to select the guide word *FROM:* and notice that Bold formatting is applied. Then, point to the selected text *FROM:* and on the mini toolbar, *double-click* **Format Painter** .

3 Select the guide word *DATE:* to copy the Bold formatting, and notice that the pointer retains the ▲I shape.

> When you *double-click* the Format Painter button, the Format Painter feature remains active until you either click the Format Painter button again, or press Esc to cancel it—as indicated on the status bar.

4 With Format Painter still active, select the guide word *SUBJECT:*, and then on the ribbon, on the **HOME tab**, in the **Clipboard group**, notice that **Format Painter** is selected, indicating that it is active. Compare your screen with Figure 1.44.

FIGURE 1.44

Format Painter button on ribbon active

Memo headings formatted with Bold; *SUBJECT:* still selected

5 On the ribbon, click **Format Painter** to turn the command off.

 **ANOTHER WAY** Press Esc to turn off Format Painter.

---

6 In the paragraph that begins *In the spring*, triple-click again to select the entire paragraph. On the mini toolbar, click **Bold** $\boxed{\text{B}}$ and **Italic** $\boxed{\text{I}}$. Click anywhere to deselect.

7 On the **Quick Access Toolbar**, click **Save** $\boxed{\text{H}}$ to save the changes you have made to your document.

Activity 1.17 | Using Keyboard Shortcuts and Using the Clipboard to Copy, Cut, and Paste

The ***Clipboard*** is a temporary storage area that holds text or graphics that you select and then cut or copy. When you ***copy*** text or graphics, a copy is placed on the Clipboard and the original text or graphic remains in place. When you ***cut*** text or graphics, a copy is placed on the Clipboard, and the original text or graphic is removed—cut—from the document.

After copying or cutting, the contents of the Clipboard are available for you to ***paste***—insert—in a new location in the current document, or into another Office file.

1 Hold down $\boxed{\text{Ctrl}}$ and press $\boxed{\text{Home}}$ to move to the beginning of your document, and then take a moment to study the table in Figure 1.45, which describes similar keyboard shortcuts with which you can navigate quickly in a document.

FIGURE 1.45

KEYBOARD SHORTCUTS TO NAVIGATE IN A DOCUMENT	
TO MOVE	**PRESS**
To the beginning of a document	$\boxed{\text{Ctrl}}$ + $\boxed{\text{Home}}$
To the end of a document	$\boxed{\text{Ctrl}}$ + $\boxed{\text{End}}$
To the beginning of a line	$\boxed{\text{Home}}$
To the end of a line	$\boxed{\text{End}}$
To the beginning of the previous word	$\boxed{\text{Ctrl}}$ + $\boxed{\leftarrow}$
To the beginning of the next word	$\boxed{\text{Ctrl}}$ + $\boxed{\rightarrow}$
To the beginning of the current word (if insertion point is in the middle of a word)	$\boxed{\text{Ctrl}}$ + $\boxed{\leftarrow}$
To the beginning of the previous paragraph	$\boxed{\text{Ctrl}}$ + $\boxed{\uparrow}$
To the beginning of the next paragraph	$\boxed{\text{Ctrl}}$ + $\boxed{\downarrow}$
To the beginning of the current paragraph (if insertion point is in the middle of a paragraph)	$\boxed{\text{Ctrl}}$ + $\boxed{\uparrow}$
Up one screen	$\boxed{\text{PgUp}}$
Down one screen	$\boxed{\text{PgDn}}$

2 To the left of *Skyline Metro Grill*, point in the left margin area to display the $\boxed{\text{A}}$ pointer, and then click one time to select the entire paragraph. On the **HOME tab**, in the **Clipboard group**, click **Copy** $\boxed{\text{🖹}}$.

Because anything that you select and then copy—or cut—is placed on the Clipboard, the Copy command and the Cut command display in the Clipboard group of commands on the ribbon. There is no visible indication that your copied selection has been placed on the Clipboard.

🔄 **ANOTHER WAY** Right-click the selection, and then click Copy on the shortcut menu; or, use the keyboard shortcut $\boxed{\text{Ctrl}}$ + $\boxed{\text{C}}$.

3 ▶ On the **HOME tab**, in the **Clipboard group**, to the right of the group name *Clipboard*, click the **Dialog Box Launcher** button 🔽, and then compare your screen with Figure 1.46.

The Clipboard pane displays with your copied text. In any ribbon group, the *Dialog Box Launcher* displays either a dialog box or a pane related to the group of commands. It is not necessary to display the Clipboard in this manner, although sometimes it is useful to do so.

FIGURE 1.46

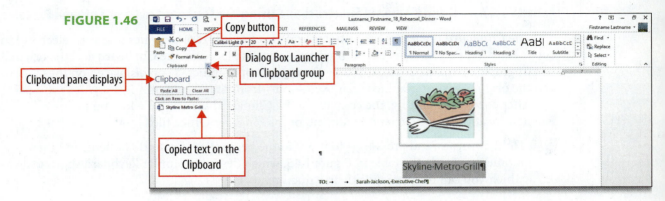

4 ▶ In the upper right corner of the **Clipboard** pane, click **Close** ✖.

5 ▶ Press Ctrl + End to move to the end of your document. Press Enter one time to create a new blank paragraph. On the **HOME tab**, in the **Clipboard group**, point to **Paste**, and then click the *upper* portion of this split button.

The Paste command pastes the most recently copied item on the Clipboard at the insertion point location. If you click the lower portion of the Paste button, a gallery of Paste Options displays. A *split button* is divided into two parts; clicking the main part of the button performs a command, and clicking the arrow displays a list or gallery with choices.

🔄 **ANOTHER WAY**   Right-click, on the shortcut menu under Paste Options, click the desired option button; or, press Ctrl + V.

6 ▶ Below the pasted text, click **Paste Options** 📋 as shown in Figure 1.47.

Here you can view and apply various formatting options for pasting your copied or cut text. Typically you will click Paste on the ribbon and paste the item in its original format. If you want some other format for the pasted item, you can choose another format from the *Paste Options gallery*.

The Paste Options gallery provides a Live Preview of the various options for changing the format of the pasted item with a single click. The Paste Options gallery is available in three places: on the ribbon by clicking the lower portion of the Paste button—the Paste button arrow; from the Paste Options button that displays below the pasted item following the paste operation; or on the shortcut menu if you right-click the pasted item.

FIGURE 1.47

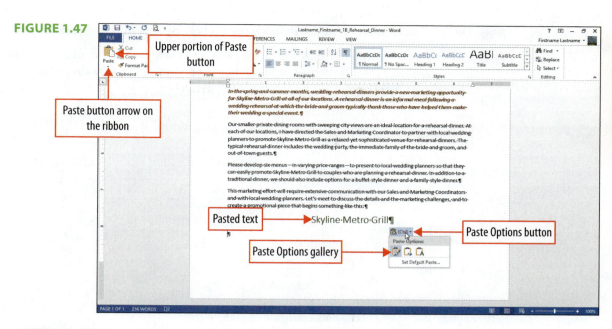

Upper portion of Paste button

Paste button arrow on the ribbon

Pasted text

Paste Options gallery

Paste Options button

---

7 In the **Paste Options** gallery, *point* to each option to see the Live Preview of the format that would be applied if you clicked the button.

The contents of the Paste Options gallery are contextual; that is, they change based on what you copied and where you are pasting.

8 Press Esc to close the gallery; the button will remain displayed until you take some other screen action.

9 Press Ctrl + Home to move to the top of the document, and then click the **salad image** one time to select it. While pointing to the selected image, right-click, and then on the shortcut menu, click **Cut**.

Recall that the Cut command cuts—removes—the selection from the document and places it on the Clipboard.

 ANOTHER WAY   On the HOME tab, in the Clipboard group, click the Cut button; or, use the keyboard shortcut Ctrl + X.

10 Press Del one time to remove the blank paragraph from the top of the document, and then press Ctrl + End to move to the end of the document.

11 With the insertion point blinking in the blank paragraph at the end of the document, right-click, and notice that the **Paste Options** gallery displays on the shortcut menu. Compare your screen with Figure 1.48.

FIGURE 1.48

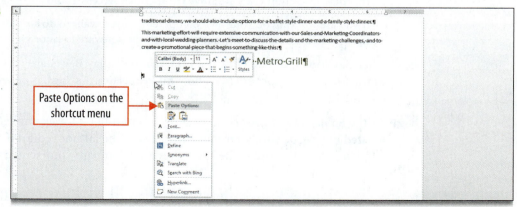

Paste Options on the shortcut menu

12 On the shortcut menu, under **Paste Options**, click the first button—**Keep Source Formatting**.

13 Point to the picture to display the pointer, and then drag to the right until the center green **Alignment Guide** displays and the blank paragraph is above the picture, as shown in Figure 1.49. Release the left mouse button.

⟳ BY TOUCH   Drag the picture with your finger to display the Alignment Guide.

FIGURE 1.49

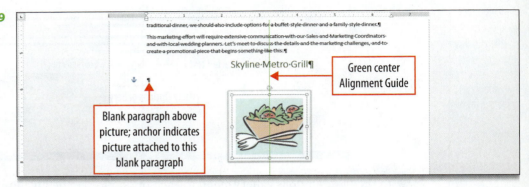

14 Above the picture, click to position the insertion point at the end of the word *Grill*, press Spacebar one time, type **for Your Rehearsal Dinner** and then **Save** 🖫 your document. Compare your screen with Figure 1.50.

FIGURE 1.50

15 On the **INSERT tab**, in the **Header & Footer group**, click **Footer**. At the bottom of the list, click **Edit Footer**, and then with the **HEADER & FOOTER Design tab** active, in the **Insert group**, click **Document Info**. Click **File Name** to add the file name to the footer.

16 On the right end of the ribbon, click **Close Header and Footer**.

17 On the **Quick Access Toolbar**, point to the **Print Preview and Print icon** 🔍 you placed there, right-click, and then click **Remove from Quick Access Toolbar**.

If you are working on your own computer and you want to do so, you can leave the icon on the toolbar; in a lab setting, you should return the software to its original settings.

18 Click **Save** 🖫 and then click the **FILE tab** to display **Backstage** view. With the **Info tab** active, in the lower right corner click **Show All Properties**. As **Tags**, type **weddings, rehearsal dinners, marketing**

19 As the **Subject**, type your course name and number—for example *CIS 10, #5543*. Under **Related People**, be sure your name displays as the author (edit it if necessary), and then on the left, click **Print** to display the Print Preview. Compare your screen with Figure 1.51.

FIGURE 1.51

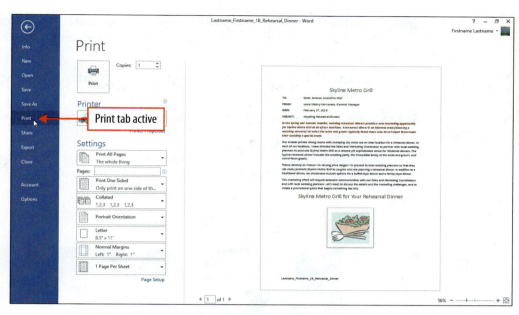

20 On the left side of **Backstage** view, click **Save**. As directed by your instructor, print or submit your file electronically as described in Project 1A, and then in the upper right corner of the Word window, click **Close** [×].

21 If a message indicates *Would you like to keep the last item you copied?* click **No**.

This message displays if you have copied some type of image to the Clipboard. If you click Yes, the items on the Clipboard will remain for you to use in another program or document.

Objective 11 | Compress Files and Use the Microsoft Office 2013 Help System

Video OF1-11

A ***compressed file*** is a file that has been reduced in size. Compressed files take up less storage space and can be transferred to other computers faster than uncompressed files. You can also combine a group of files into one compressed folder, which makes it easier to share a group of files.

Within each Office program, the Help feature provides information about all of the program's features and displays step-by-step instructions for performing many tasks.

Activity 1.18 | Compressing Files

In this activity, you will combine the two files you created in this chapter into one compressed file.

1 On the Windows taskbar, click **File Explorer** [icon]. On the left, in the **navigation pane**, navigate to your **USB flash drive**, and then open your **Office Features Chapter 1** folder. Compare your screen with Figure 1.52.

FIGURE 1.52

2 In the **file list**, click your **Lastname_Firstname_1A_Note_Form** Word file one time to select it. Then, hold down `Ctrl`, and click your **Lastname_Firstname_1B_Rehearsal_Dinner** file to select the files in the list.

> In any Windows-based program, holding down `Ctrl` while selecting enables you to select multiple items.

3 On the **File Explorer** ribbon, click **Share**, and then in the **Send group**, click **Zip**. Compare your screen with Figure 1.53.

> Windows creates a compressed folder containing a *copy* of each of the selected files. The folder name is selected—highlighted in blue—so that you can rename it.

↻ BY TOUCH   Tap the ribbon commands.

FIGURE 1.53

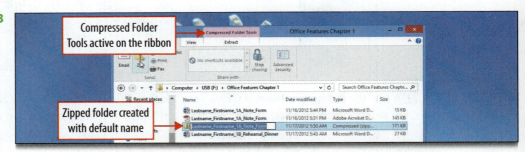

↻ ANOTHER WAY   Point to the selected files in the File List, right-click, point to Send to, and then click Compressed (zipped) folder.

4 Using your own name, type **Lastname_Firstname_Office_Features_Chapter_1** and press `Enter`.

> The compressed folder is ready to attach to an email or share in some other format.

5 In the upper right corner of the folder window, click **Close** ⊠.

Activity 1.19 │ Using the Microsoft Office 2013 Help System in Excel

In this activity, you will use the Microsoft Help feature to find information about formatting numbers in Excel.

1 Press ⊞ to display the Windows 8 **Start screen**, and then type **excel 2013** Press `Enter` to open the Excel desktop app.

2 On Excel's opening screen, click **Blank workbook**, and then in the upper right corner, click **Microsoft Excel Help** ❓.

↻ ANOTHER WAY   Press `F1` to display Help in any Office program.

3 In the **Excel Help** window, click in the **Search online help** box, type **formatting numbers** and then press `Enter`.

4 On the list of results, click **Format numbers as currency**. Compare your screen with Figure 1.54.

FIGURE 1.54

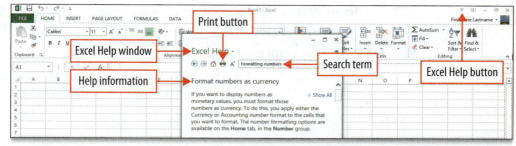

> **5** If you want to do so, at the top of the **Excel Help** window, click Print 🖶 to print a copy of this information for your reference.

> **6** In the upper right corner of the Help window, click **Close** ☒.

> **7** Leave Excel open for the next activity.

Objective 12 | Install Apps for Office and Create a Microsoft Account

ALERT!   **Working with Web-Based Applications and Services**

Computer programs and services on the web receive continuous updates and improvements. Thus, the steps to complete the following web-based activities may differ from the ones shown. You can often look at the screens and the information presented to determine how to complete the activity.

Video OF1-12

Apps for Office 2013 and SharePoint 2013 are a collection of downloadable apps that enable you to create and view information within your familiar Office programs. Some of these apps are developed by Microsoft, but many more are developed by specialists in different fields. As new apps are developed, they will be available from the online Office Store.

An *app for Office* is a webpage that works within one of the Office applications, such as Excel, that you download from the Office Store. Office apps combine cloud services and web technologies within the user interface of Office and SharePoint. For example, in Excel, you can use an app to look up and gather search results for a new apartment by placing the information in an Excel worksheet, and then use maps to determine the distance of each apartment to work and to family members.

Activity 1.20 | Installing Apps for Office

ALERT!   **You Must Be Signed In to Office with a Microsoft Account to Complete This Activity**

To download an Office app, you must be signed in to Office with a free Microsoft account. If you do not have a Microsoft account, refer to the next activity to create one by using Microsoft's outlook.com email service, which includes free SkyDrive cloud storage.

> **1** On the Excel ribbon, click the **INSERT tab**. In the **Apps group**, click the **Apps for Office** arrow, and then click **See All**.

> **2** Click **FEATURED APPS**, and then on the right, click in the **Search for apps on the Office Store** box, type **Bing Maps** and press Enter.

> **3** Click the **Bing logo**, and then click the **Add** button, and then if necessary, click Continue.

> **4** **Close** ☒ Internet Explorer, and then **Close** ☒ the **Apps for Office** box.

5 ▶ On the **INSERT tab**, in the **Apps group**, click **Apps for Office**, click **See All**, click **MY APPS**, click the **Bing Maps** app, and then in the lower right corner, click **Insert**.

6 ▶ On the Welcome message, click **Insert Sample Data**.

Here, the Bing map displays information related to the sample data. Each state in the sample data displays a small pie chart that represents the two sets of data. Compare your screen with Figure 1.55.

This is just one example of many apps downloadable from the Office store.

FIGURE 1.55

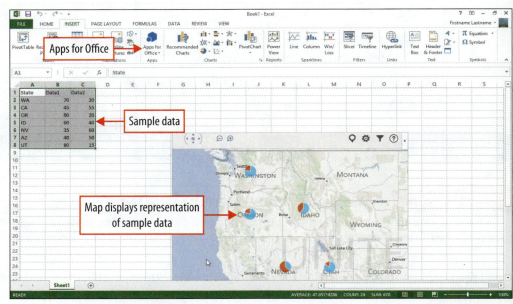

7 ▶ **Close** ☒ Excel without saving.

Activity 1.21 | Creating a Microsoft Account

In Windows 8, you can create a Microsoft account, and then use that account to sign in to *any* Windows 8 PC. Signing in with a Microsoft account is recommended because you can:

- Download Windows 8 apps from the Windows Store.
- Get your online content—email, social network updates, updated news—automatically displayed in an app on the Windows 8 Start screen when you sign in.
- Synch settings online to make every Windows 8 computer you use look and feel the same.
- Sign in to Office so that you can store documents on your SkyDrive and download Office apps.

1 ▶ Open Internet Explorer 🌐, and then go to **www.outlook.com**

2 Locate and click **Sign up now** to display a screen similar to Figure 1.56. Complete the form to create your account.

FIGURE 1.56

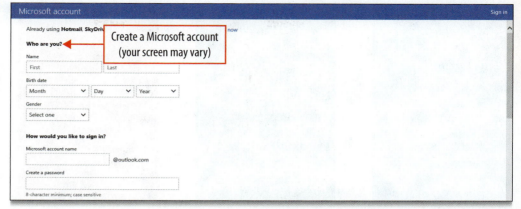

3 Close ⊠ Internet Explorer.

END | You have completed Project 1B

END OF CHAPTER

SUMMARY

Many Office features and commands, such as the Open and Save As dialog boxes, performing commands from the ribbon and from dialog boxes, and using the Clipboard are the same in all Office desktop apps.

A desktop app is installed on your computer and requires a computer operating system such as Microsoft Windows or Apple OS to run. The programs in Microsoft Office 2013 are considered to be desktop apps.

Apps that run on a smartphone or tablet computer—for example, iOS, Android, or Windows Phone—or apps that run from browser software such as Internet Explorer or Chrome on a PC, are referred to as apps.

Within each Office app, you can install additional Apps for Office from the Office Store. You must have a Microsoft account, which includes free SkyDrive storage, to download Windows 8 or Office apps.

GO! LEARN IT ONLINE

Review the concepts and key terms in this chapter by completing these online challenges, which you can find at **www.pearsonhighered.com/go**.

Matching and Multiple Choice: Answer matching and multiple choice questions to test what you learned in this chapter. **MyITLab®**

Crossword Puzzle: Spell out the words that match the numbered clues, and put them in the puzzle squares.

Flipboard: Flip through the definitions of the key terms in this chapter and match them with the correct term.

GLOSSARY

GLOSSARY OF CHAPTER KEY TERMS

Address bar (Internet Explorer) The area at the top of the Internet Explorer window that displays, and where you can type, a URL—Uniform Resource Locator—which is an address that uniquely identifies a location on the Internet.

Address bar (Windows) The bar at the top of a folder window with which you can navigate to a different folder or library, or go back to a previous one.

Alignment The placement of text or objects relative to the left and right margins.

Alignment guides Green lines that display when you move an object to assist in alignment.

App The term that commonly refers to computer programs that run from the device software on a smartphone or a tablet computer—for example, iOS, Android, or Windows Phone—or computer programs that run from the browser software on a desktop PC or laptop PC—for example Internet Explorer, Safari, Firefox, or Chrome.

App for Office A webpage that works within one of the Office applications, such as Excel, and that you download from the Office Store.

Apps for Office 2013 and SharePoint 2013 A collection of downloadable apps that enable you to create and view information within your familiar Office programs.

Backstage tabs The area along the left side of Backstage view with tabs to display screens with related groups of commands.

Backstage view A centralized space for file management tasks; for example, opening, saving, printing, publishing, or sharing a file. A navigation pane displays along the left side with tabs that group file-related tasks together.

Center alignment The alignment of text or objects that is centered horizontally between the left and right margins.

Click The action of pressing and releasing the left button on a mouse pointing device one time.

Clip art Downloadable predefined graphics available online from Office.com and other sites.

Clipboard A temporary storage area that holds text or graphics that you select and then cut or copy.

Cloud computing Refers to applications and services that are accessed over the Internet, rather than to applications that are installed on your local computer.

Cloud storage Online storage of data so that you can access your data from different places and devices.

Collaborate To work with others as a team in an intellectual endeavor to complete a shared task or to achieve a shared goal.

Commands An instruction to a computer program that causes an action to be carried out.

Common dialog boxes The set of dialog boxes that includes Open, Save, and Save As, which are provided by the Windows programming interface, and which display and operate in all of the Office programs in the same manner.

Compressed file A file that has been reduced in size and thus takes up less storage space and can be transferred to other computers quickly.

Compressed folder A folder that has been reduced in size and thus takes up less storage space and can be transferred to other computers quickly; also called a *zipped* folder.

Context menus Menus that display commands and options relevant to the selected text or object; also called *shortcut menus*.

Context-sensitive commands Commands that display on a shortcut menu that relate to the object or text that you right-clicked.

Contextual tabs Tabs that are added to the ribbon automatically when a specific object, such as a picture, is selected, and that contain commands relevant to the selected object.

Copy A command that duplicates a selection and places it on the Clipboard.

Cut A command that removes a selection and places it on the Clipboard.

Default The term that refers to the current selection or setting that is automatically used by a computer program unless you specify otherwise.

Deselect The action of canceling the selection of an object or block of text by clicking outside of the selection.

Desktop In Windows, the screen that simulates your work area.

Desktop app The term that commonly refers to a computer program that is installed on your computer and requires a computer operating system like Microsoft Windows or Apple OS to run.

Dialog box A small window that contains options for completing a task.

Dialog Box Launcher A small icon that displays to the right of some group names on the ribbon, and which opens a related dialog box or pane providing additional options and commands related to that group.

Document properties Details about a file that describe or identify it, including the title, author name, subject, and keywords that identify the document's topic or contents; also known as *metadata*.

Drag The action of holding down the left mouse button while moving your mouse.

Edit The process of making changes to text or graphics in an Office file.

Ellipsis A set of three dots indicating incompleteness; an ellipsis following a command name indicates that a dialog box will display if you click the command.

Enhanced ScreenTip A ScreenTip that displays more descriptive text than a normal ScreenTip.

Extract To decompress, or pull out, files from a compressed form.

File A collection of information stored on a computer under a single name, for example, a Word document or a PowerPoint presentation.

File Explorer The program that displays the files and folders on your computer, and which is at work anytime you are viewing the contents of files and folders in a window.

Fill The inside color of an object.

Folder A container in which you store files.

Folder window In Windows, a window that displays the contents of the current folder, library, or device, and contains helpful parts so that you can navigate the Windows file structure.

Font A set of characters with the same design and shape.

Font styles Formatting emphasis such as bold, italic, and underline.

Footer A reserved area for text or graphics that displays at the bottom of each page in a document.

Formatting The process of establishing the overall appearance of text, graphics, and pages in an Office file—for example, in a Word document.

Formatting marks Characters that display on the screen, but do not print, indicating where the Enter key, the Spacebar, and the Tab key were pressed; also called *nonprinting characters*.

Gallery An Office feature that displays a list of potential results instead of just the command name.

Gradient fill A fill effect in which one color fades into another.

Groups On the Office ribbon, the sets of related commands that you might need for a specific type of task.

Header A reserved area for text or graphics that displays at the top of each page in a document.

Info tab The tab in Backstage view that displays information about the current file.

Insertion point A blinking vertical line that indicates where text or graphics will be inserted.

Keyboard shortcut A combination of two or more keyboard keys, used to perform a task that would otherwise require a mouse.

KeyTip The letter that displays on a command in the ribbon and that indicates the key you can press to activate the command when keyboard control of the ribbon is activated.

Keywords Custom file properties in the form of words that you associate with a document to give an indication of the document's content; used to help find and organize files. Also called *tags*.

Landscape orientation A page orientation in which the paper is wider than it is tall.

Layout Options A button that displays when an object is selected and that has commands to choose how the object interacts with surrounding text.

Live Preview A technology that shows the result of applying an editing or formatting change as you point to possible results—*before* you actually apply it.

Location Any disk drive, folder, or other place in which you can store files and folders.

Metadata Details about a file that describe or identify it, including the title, author name, subject, and keywords that identify the document's topic or contents; also known as *document properties*.

Mini toolbar A small toolbar containing frequently used formatting commands that displays as a result of selecting text or objects.

MRU Acronym for *most recently used*, which refers to the state of some commands that retain the characteristic most recently applied; for example, the Font Color button retains the most recently used color until a new color is chosen.

Navigate The process of exploring within the organizing structure of Windows.

Navigation pane In a folder window, the area on the left in which you can navigate to, open, and display favorites, libraries, folders, saved searches, and an expandable list of drives.

Nonprinting characters Characters that display on the screen, but do not print, indicating where the Enter key, the Spacebar, and the Tab key were pressed; also called *formatting marks*.

Notification bar An area at the bottom of an Internet Explorer window that displays information about pending downloads, security issues, add-ons, and other issues related to the operation of your computer.

Object A text box, picture, table, or shape that you can select and then move and resize.

Office Web Apps The free online companions to Microsoft Word, Excel, PowerPoint, Access, and OneNote.

Open dialog box A dialog box from which you can navigate to, and then open on your screen, an existing file that was created in that same program.

Option button In a dialog box, a round button that enables you to make one choice among two or more options.

Options dialog box A dialog box within each Office application where you can select program settings and other options and preferences.

Pane A separate area of a window.

Paragraph symbol The symbol ¶ that represents the end of a paragraph.

Paste The action of placing text or objects that have been copied or cut from one location to another location.

Paste Options gallery A gallery of buttons that provides a Live Preview of all the Paste options available in the current context.

Path A sequence of folders that leads to a specific file or folder.

PDF The acronym for Portable Document Format, which is a file format that creates an image that preserves the look of your file; this is a popular format for sending documents electronically because the document will display on most computers.

Point The action of moving your mouse pointer over something on your screen.

Pointer Any symbol that displays on your screen in response to moving your mouse.

Points A measurement of the size of a font; there are 72 points in an inch.

Portable Document Format A file format that creates an image that preserves the look of your file, but that cannot be easily changed; a popular format for sending documents electronically, because the document will display on most computers.

Portrait orientation A page orientation in which the paper is taller than it is wide.

Print Preview A view of a document as it will appear when you print it.

Progress bar In a dialog box or taskbar button, a bar that indicates visually the progress of a task such as a download or file transfer.

Protected View A security feature in Office 2013 that protects your computer from malicious files by opening them in a restricted environment until you enable them; you might encounter this feature if you open a file from an email or download files from the Internet.

pt The abbreviation for *point*; for example, when referring to a font size.

Quick Access Toolbar In an Office program window, the small row of buttons in the upper left corner of the screen from which you can perform frequently used commands.

Read-Only A property assigned to a file that prevents the file from being modified or deleted; it indicates that you cannot save any changes to the displayed document unless you first save it with a new name.

Ribbon A user interface in both Office 2013 and File Explorer that groups the commands for performing related tasks on tabs across the upper portion of the program window.

Right-click The action of clicking the right mouse button one time.

Sans serif font A font design with no lines or extensions on the ends of characters.

ScreenTip A small box that that displays useful information when you perform various mouse actions such as pointing to screen elements or dragging.

Scroll bar A vertical or horizontal bar in a window or a pane to assist in bringing an area into view, and which contains a scroll box and scroll arrows.

Scroll box The box in the vertical and horizontal scroll bars that can be dragged to reposition the contents of a window or pane on the screen.

Selecting Highlighting, by dragging with your mouse, areas of text or data or graphics, so that the selection can be edited, formatted, copied, or moved.

Serif font A font design that includes small line extensions on the ends of the letters to guide the eye in reading from left to right.

SharePoint Collaboration software with which people in an organization can set up team sites to share information, manage documents, and publish reports for others to see.

Shortcut menu A menu that displays commands and options relevant to the selected text or object; also called a *context menu*.

Sizing handles Small squares that indicate a picture or object is selected.

SkyDrive Microsoft's free cloud storage for anyone with a free Microsoft account.

Split button A button divided into two parts and in which clicking the main part of the button performs a command and clicking the arrow opens a menu with choices.

Start search The search feature in Windows 8 in which, from the Start screen, you can begin to type and by default, Windows 8 searches for apps; you can adjust the search to search for files or settings.

Status bar The area along the lower edge of an Office program window that displays file information on the left and buttons to control how the window looks on the right.

Style A group of formatting commands, such as font, font size, font color, paragraph alignment, and line spacing that can be applied to a paragraph with one command.

Subfolder A folder within a folder.

Synchronization The process of updating computer files that are in two or more locations according to specific rules— also called *syncing*.

Syncing The process of updating computer files that are in two or more locations according to specific rules— also called *synchronization*.

Tabs (ribbon) On the Office ribbon, the name of each activity area.

Tags Custom file properties in the form of words that you associate with a document to give an indication of the document's content; used to help find and organize files. Also called *keywords*.

Taskbar The area along the lower edge of the desktop that displays buttons representing programs.

Template A preformatted document that you can use as a starting point and then change to suit your needs.

Theme A predesigned combination of colors, fonts, and effects that look good together and is applied to an entire document by a single selection.

Title bar The bar at the top edge of the program window that indicates the name of the current file and the program name.

Toggle button A button that can be turned on by clicking it once, and then turned off by clicking it again.

Toolbar In a folder window, a row of buttons with which you can perform common tasks, such as changing the view of your files and folders or burning files to a CD.

Triple-click The action of clicking the left mouse button three times in rapid succession.

Trusted Documents A security feature in Office that remembers which files you have already enabled; you might encounter this feature if you open a file from an email or download files from the Internet.

Uniform Resource Locator An address that uniquely identifies a location on the Internet.

URL The acronym for Uniform Resource Locator, which is an address that uniquely identifies a location on the Internet.

USB flash drive A small data storage device that plugs into a computer USB port.

Window A rectangular area on a computer screen in which programs and content appear, and which can be moved, resized, minimized, or closed.

XML Paper Specification A Microsoft file format that creates an image of your document and that opens in the XPS viewer.

XPS The acronym for XML Paper Specification—a Microsoft file format that creates an image of your document and that opens in the XPS viewer.

Zipped folder A folder that has been reduced in size and thus takes up less storage space and can be transferred to other computers quickly; also called a *compressed* folder.

Zoom The action of increasing or decreasing the size of the viewing area on the screen.

Using Styles and Creating Multilevel Lists and Charts

GO! to Work
Video W4

PROJECT 4A

OUTCOMES
Edit a handout using styles and arrange text into an organized list.

OBJECTIVES

1. Apply and Modify Styles
2. Create New Styles
3. Manage Styles
4. Create a Multilevel List

PROJECT 4B

OUTCOMES
Change a style set and create and format a chart.

OBJECTIVES

5. Change the Style Set of a Document and Apply a Template
6. Insert a Chart and Enter Data into a Chart
7. Change a Chart Type
8. Format a Chart and Save a Chart as a Template

evron.info/Fotolia

In This Chapter

In this chapter, you will apply styles, create multilevel lists, attach a template to a document, display numerical data in charts, and save a chart as a template. The theme and style set features provide a simple way to coordinate colors, fonts, and effects used in a document. For example, if you publish a monthly newsletter, you can apply styles to article headings and modify lists to ensure that all editions of the newsletter maintain a consistent and professional look. Charts display numerical data in a visual format. Formatting chart elements adds interest and assists the reader in interpreting the displayed data.

The projects in this chapter relate to **Costa Rican Treks**, a tour company named for the small country in Central America with a diverse ecosystem. Costa Rican Treks offers exciting but affordable adventure tours for individuals and groups. Travelers go off the beaten path to explore amazing remote places in this scenic country. If you prefer to experience the heart of Costa Rica on the water, try scuba diving or rafting tours. Costa Rican Treks also offers hiking and Jeep tours. Whatever you prefer—mountain, sea, volcano—our trained guides are experts in the history, geography, culture, and flora and fauna of Costa Rica.

Customer Handout

PROJECT ACTIVITIES

In Activities 4.01 through 4.11, you will create a handout for Costa Rican Treks customers who are interested in scuba diving tours. You will use styles and multilevel list formats so that the document is attractive and easy to read. Your completed document will look similar to Figure 4.1.

PROJECT FILES

For Project 4A, you will need the following file:

w04A_Customer_Handout

You will save your file as:

Lastname_Firstname_4A_Customer_Handout

PROJECT RESULTS

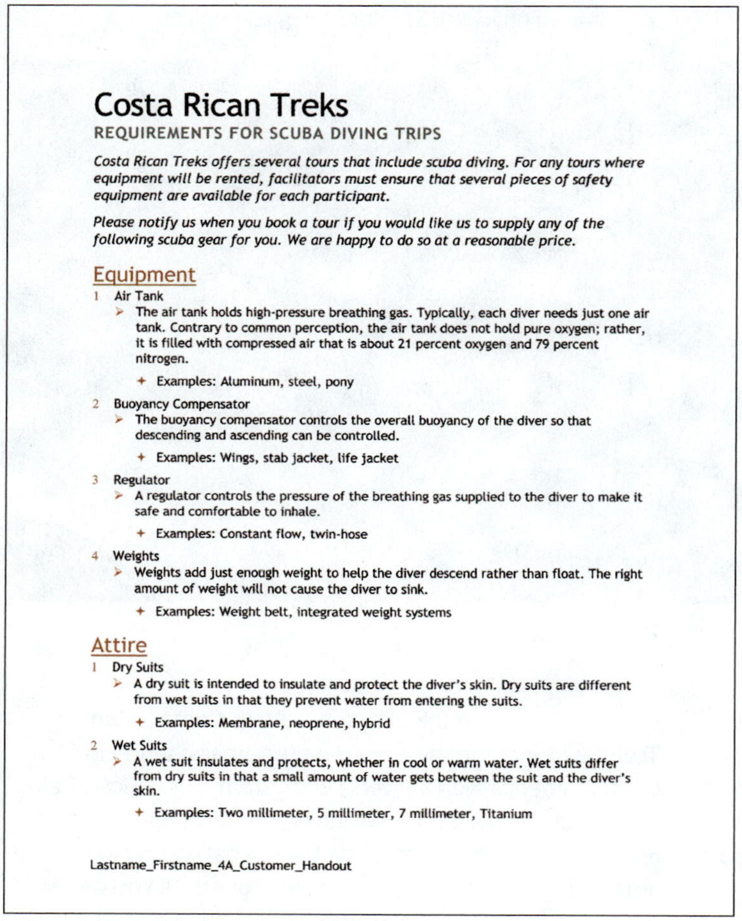

Costa Rican Treks

REQUIREMENTS FOR SCUBA DIVING TRIPS

Costa Rican Treks offers several tours that include scuba diving. For any tours where equipment will be rented, facilitators must ensure that several pieces of safety equipment are available for each participant.

Please notify us when you book a tour if you would like us to supply any of the following scuba gear for you. We are happy to do so at a reasonable price.

Equipment
1. Air Tank
   - The air tank holds high-pressure breathing gas. Typically, each diver needs just one air tank. Contrary to common perception, the air tank does not hold pure oxygen; rather, it is filled with compressed air that is about 21 percent oxygen and 79 percent nitrogen.
     - Examples: Aluminum, steel, pony
2. Buoyancy Compensator
   - The buoyancy compensator controls the overall buoyancy of the diver so that descending and ascending can be controlled.
     - Examples: Wings, stab jacket, life jacket
3. Regulator
   - A regulator controls the pressure of the breathing gas supplied to the diver to make it safe and comfortable to inhale.
     - Examples: Constant flow, twin-hose
4. Weights
   - Weights add just enough weight to help the diver descend rather than float. The right amount of weight will not cause the diver to sink.
     - Examples: Weight belt, integrated weight systems

Attire
1. Dry Suits
   - A dry suit is intended to insulate and protect the diver's skin. Dry suits are different from wet suits in that they prevent water from entering the suits.
     - Examples: Membrane, neoprene, hybrid
2. Wet Suits
   - A wet suit insulates and protects, whether in cool or warm water. Wet suits differ from dry suits in that a small amount of water gets between the suit and the diver's skin.
     - Examples: Two millimeter, 5 millimeter, 7 millimeter, Titanium

Lastname_Firstname_4A_Customer_Handout

FIGURE 4.1 Project 4A Customer Handout

Objective 1   Apply and Modify Styles

Video W4-1

A **style** is a group of formatting commands, such as font, font size, font color, paragraph alignment, and line spacing. You can retrieve a style by name and apply it to text with one click.

Using styles to format text has several advantages over using **direct formatting**—the process of applying each format separately; for example, bold, then font size, then font color, and so on. Styles are faster to apply, result in a consistent look, and can be automatically updated in all instances in a document, which can be especially useful in long documents.

Activity 4.01   Applying Styles to Text

Styles that are grouped together comprise a **style set**. A style set is a group of styles that are designed to work together. Specific styles—for example, *Title* or *Heading 1*—that display in the Styles gallery on the ribbon can be applied to any selected text.

1   Start Word, and then click **Open Other Documents..** Under **Places**, double-click **Computer**. From your student files, locate and open the document **w04A_Customer_Handout**.

2   Press F12 to display the **Save As** dialog box. In the **Save As** dialog box, navigate to the location where you are saving your files for this chapter. Create a new folder named **Word Chapter 4 Save** the document as **Lastname_Firstname_4A_Customer_Handout**

3   Scroll to the bottom of **Page 1**, right-click in the footer area, and then click **Edit Footer**. On the ribbon, under **HEADER & FOOTER TOOLS**, on the **DESIGN tab**, in the **Insert group**, click **Document Info**, and then click **File Name. Close** the footer area. If necessary, display the rulers and formatting marks.

4   Press Ctrl + Home to move to the top of the document.

5   On the **HOME tab**, in the **Styles group**, notice that the **Normal** style is selected—outlined in blue. Compare your screen with Figure 4.2.

The **Normal** style is the default style in Word for a new document. Normal style formatting includes the Calibri font, 11 point font size, line spacing at 1.08, and 8 pt spacing after a paragraph.

FIGURE 4.2

6 Including the paragraph mark, select the first paragraph, which forms the title of the document. On the **HOME tab**, in the **Styles group**, click **More** ⊡ to display the **Styles gallery.** Point to the style named **Title**, and then compare your screen with Figure 4.3.

Live Preview displays how the text will look with the Title style applied.

FIGURE 4.3

7 Click **Title**, and then click anywhere in the document to deselect the title.

The Title style includes the 28 point Calibri Light font, single line spacing, and 0 pt spacing after the paragraph.

8 Select the second paragraph, which begins *Requirements for*, and is the subtitle of the document. In the **Styles group**, click **More** ⊡, and then in the gallery, click **Subtitle**.

The Subtitle style includes a Text 1 font color and expands the text by 0.75 pt.

9 Select the third and fourth paragraphs, beginning with *Costa Rican Treks offers* and ending with the text *at a reasonable price*. In the **Styles group**, click **More** ⊡, and then in the gallery, click **Emphasis**. Click anywhere to deselect the text, and then compare your screen with Figure 4.4.

FIGURE 4.4

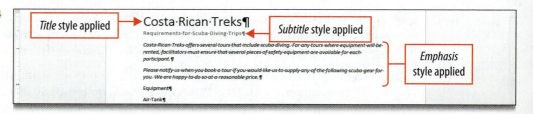

10 **Save** 🖫 your document.

Activity 4.02 | Modifying Existing Style Attributes

You are not limited to the exact formatting of a style—you can change it to suit your needs. For example, you might like the effect of a style with the exception of the font size. If you plan to use a customized style repeatedly in a document, it's a good idea to modify the style to look exactly the way you want it, and then save it as a *new* style.

1 Select the heading *Equipment*. Using the technique you practiced, apply the **Heading 1** style.

The Heading 1 style includes the 16 point Calibri Light font, an Accent 1 font color, 12 pt spacing before the paragraph, and 0 pt spacing after the paragraph.

A small black square displays to the left of the paragraph indicating that the Heading 1 style also includes the ***Keep with next*** and ***Keep lines together*** formatting—Word commands that keep a heading with its first paragraph of text on the next page, or prevent a single line from displaying by itself at the bottom of a page or at the top of a page.

2 With the paragraph selected, on the mini toolbar, change the **Font Size** to **18**, and then click **Styles**. In the **Styles** gallery, right-click **Heading 1**, and then compare your screen with Figure 4.5.

 **ANOTHER WAY**   On the HOME tab, display the Styles gallery, and then right-click the Heading 1 style.

FIGURE 4.5

3 From the shortcut menu, click **Update Heading 1 to Match Selection**, and then click anywhere to deselect the text.

> By updating the heading style, you ensure that the next time you apply the Heading 1 style in *this* document, it will retain these new formats. In this manner, you can customize a style. The changes to the Heading 1 style are stored *only* in this document and will not affect the Heading 1 style in any other documents.

4 Scroll down to view the lower portion of **Page 1**, and then select the heading *Attire*. On the **HOME tab**, in the **Styles** group, click **Heading 1**, and notice that the *modified* **Heading 1** style is applied to the paragraph. Click anywhere in the document to deselect the text. **Save** 🖫 your document.

Activity 4.03 │ Changing the Document Theme

Recall that a theme is a predefined combination of colors, fonts, and effects; the *Office* theme is the default setting. Styles use the font scheme, color scheme, and effects associated with the current theme. If you change the theme, the styles adopt the fonts, colors, and effects of the new theme.

1 Press Ctrl + Home. Click the **DESIGN tab**, and then in the **Document Formatting group**, click **Themes**. In the gallery, point to the various themes and notice the changes in your document.

> Live Preview enables you to see the effects that a theme has on text with styles applied.

2 Click **Facet**, and then compare your screen with Figure 4.6.

> The Facet theme's fonts, colors, and effects display in the document. All the styles will now use the Facet theme.

FIGURE 4.6

3 Select the subtitle, which begins *Requirements for*. On the mini toolbar, change the **Font Size** to **14** and click **Bold** [B].

In this handout, this emphasis on the subtitle is useful. Because there are no other subtitles and you will not be applying this style again in this document, it is not necessary to modify the actual style.

4 With the subtitle still selected, click the **HOME tab**. In the **Font group**, click **Change Case** [Aa ▾], and then from the list, click **UPPERCASE**.

The ***Change Case*** feature allows you to quickly change the capitalization of characters. In the selection, all characters now display in uppercase letters.

5 Select the third and fourth paragraphs, beginning with *Costa Rican Treks offers* and ending with the text *at a reasonable price*. On the mini toolbar, change the **Font Size** to **12**, and then click **Styles**. In the **Styles** gallery, right-click **Emphasis**, and then click **Update Emphasis to Match Selection**. Click anywhere to deselect the text. **Save** [💾] your document.

Objective 2   Create New Styles

Video W4-2

You can create a new style based on formats that you specify. For example, if you frequently use a 12 point Verdana font with bold emphasis and double spacing, you can create a style to apply those settings to a paragraph with a single click, instead of using multiple steps each time you want that specific formatting. Any new styles that you create are stored with the document and are available any time that the document is open.

Activity 4.04   Creating Custom Styles and Assigning Shortcut Keys

You can assign a shortcut key to a style, which allows you to apply the style using the keyboard instead of clicking the style in the Styles gallery.

1 Select the paragraph that begins *Examples: Aluminum*, and then on the mini toolbar, change the **Font Size** to **12**, click **Bold** [B], and then click **Italic** [I].

2 With the paragraph still selected, on the **HOME tab**, in the **Styles group**, click **More** [▾]. In the lower portion of the gallery, click **Create a Style**.

 **ANOTHER WAY**   On the mini toolbar, click Styles, and then click Create a Style.

3 In the **Create New Style from Formatting** dialog box, in the **Name** box, type **Examples** Compare your screen with Figure 4.7.

> Select a name for your new style that will remind you of the type of text to which the style applies. A preview of the style displays in the Paragraph style preview box.

FIGURE 4.7

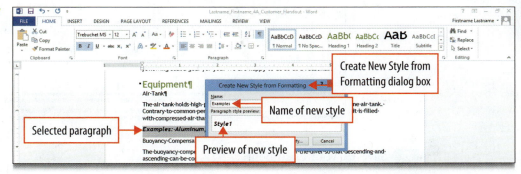

4 At the bottom of the dialog box, click **Modify**.

5 In the **Create New Style from Formatting** dialog box, at the bottom left, click **Format**, and then click **Shortcut key**.

6 In the **Customize Keyboard** dialog box, with the insertion point in the **Press new shortcut key** box, press Ctrl + Alt + E. Compare your screen with Figure 4.8.

> The Command box indicates that the shortcut key will be assigned to the Examples style. The text *Alt+Ctr+E* indicates the keys that have been pressed. A message indicates that the shortcut key is currently unassigned.

FIGURE 4.8

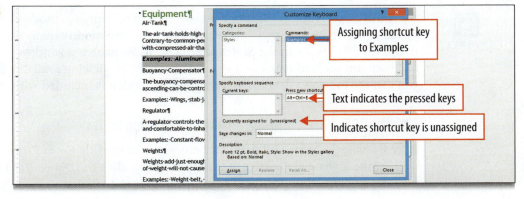

7 In the **Customize Keyboard** dialog box, click **Close**, and then in the **Create New Style from Formatting** dialog box, click **OK**.

> The *Examples* style is added to the available styles for this document and displays in the Styles gallery. The shortcut key Ctrl + Alt + E is assigned to the *Examples* style.

8 Scroll down as necessary and select the paragraph that begins *Examples: Wings*. Press Ctrl + Alt + E to apply the new style *Examples*.

9 Using the technique you just practiced, select the four remaining paragraphs that begin *Examples:*, and then apply the **Examples** style. Click anywhere to deselect the text, and then compare your screen with Figure 4.9.

FIGURE 4.9

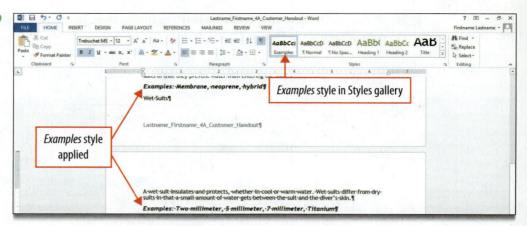

Examples style in Styles gallery

Examples style applied

10 ▶ **Save** 🖫 your document.

Objective 3 | Manage Styles

Video W4-3

You can accomplish most of the tasks related to applying, modifying, and creating styles easily by using the Styles gallery. However, if you create and modify many styles in a document, you will find it useful to work in the ***Styles pane***. The Styles pane is a window that displays a list of styles and contains tools to manage styles. Additionally, by viewing available styles in the Styles pane, you can see the exact details of all the formatting that is included with each style.

Activity 4.05 | Customizing Settings for Existing Styles

1 ▶ Press Ctrl + Home, and then click anywhere in the title *Costa Rican Treks*. On the **HOME tab**, in the lower right corner of the **Styles** group, click the **Dialog Box Launcher** 🔲 to display the **Styles** pane. Compare your screen with Figure 4.10.

The Styles pane displays the same group of available styles found in the Styles gallery, including the new *Examples* style that you created.

FIGURE 4.10

Styles pane

Title style selected

Available styles in document

2 In the **Styles** pane, point to **Title** to display a ScreenTip with the details of the formats associated with the style. In the **ScreenTip**, under **Style**, notice that *Style Linked* is indicated.

3 Move your mouse pointer into the document to close the ScreenTip. In the **Styles** pane, examine the symbols to the right of each style, as shown in Figure 4.11.

A *character style*, indicated by the symbol **a**, contains formatting characteristics that you apply to text—for example, font name, font size, font color, bold emphasis, and so on.

A *paragraph style*, indicated by the symbol ¶, includes everything that a character style contains, plus all aspects of a paragraph's appearance—for example, text alignment, tab stops, line spacing, and borders.

A *linked style*, indicated by the symbol ¶**a**, behaves as either a character style or a paragraph style, depending on what you select.

List styles, which apply formats to a list, and *table styles*, which apply a consistent look to the borders, shading, and so on of a table, are also available but do not display here.

FIGURE 4.11

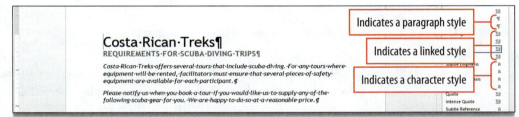

4 In the **Styles** pane, point to **Heading 1**, and then click the arrow to display a list of commands. Compare your screen with Figure 4.12.

ANOTHER WAY   In the Styles gallery, right-click Heading 1.

FIGURE 4.12

5 From the displayed list, click **Modify**. In the **Modify Style** dialog box, under **Formatting**, click **Underline** [U]. Click the **Font Color arrow**, and then in the eighth column, click the fifth color—**Orange, Accent 4, Darker 25%**. Compare your screen to Figure 4.13.

The Modify command allows you to make changes to the selected style In this case, the font color is changed and underline formatting is added to the style.

FIGURE 4.13

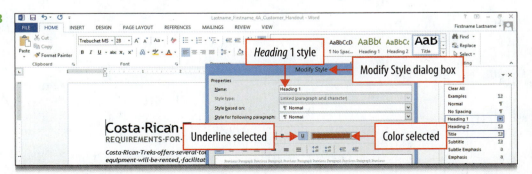

6 Click **OK** to close the **Modify Styles** dialog box. Scroll as necessary, and then notice that both headings—*Equipment* and *Attire*—are underlined and display as an orange font color. **Save** 🖫 your document.

Activity 4.06 | Viewing Style Formats

You can examine existing styles in several ways—for example, when you want to review the formatting characteristics of selected text.

1 Scroll to view the upper portion of **Page 1**, and then select the heading *Equipment*. Notice that in the **Styles** pane *Heading 1* is selected.

🔄 **BY TOUCH** Tap the document and then slide up to view the upper portion of Page 1. Tap and drag the heading *Equipment*.

2 At the bottom right of the **Styles** pane, click **Options**. In the **Style Pane Options** dialog box, in the **Select styles to show** box, click the **arrow** to display specific selection styles.

The selected option—in this case, the default option *Recommended*—determines the styles that display in the Styles pane. The Recommended option causes the most commonly used styles to display.

3 At the bottom of the **Style Pane Options** dialog box, click **Cancel** to close the dialog box.

4 Near the bottom of the **Styles** pane, select the **Show Preview** check box.

The *Show Preview* feature causes a visual representation of each style to display in the Styles window.

5 Clear the **Show Preview** check box, and then at the bottom of the **Styles** pane, click **Style Inspector** 🔠. In the **Style Inspector** pane, notice the name of the style applied to the selected text displays.

The *Style Inspector* pane displays the name of the style with formats applied and contains paragraph-level and text-level formatting options that allow you to modify the style or reset to default formats.

6 At the bottom of the **Style Inspector** pane, click **Reveal Formatting** 🔡 to display the **Reveal Formatting** pane. If necessary, drag the **Styles** pane to the left until it is docked. Compare your screen with Figure 4.14. Note: Your view may differ.

The *Reveal Formatting* pane displays the formatted selection—in this case, *Equipment*—and displays a complete description of the formats applied to the selection.

FIGURE 4.14

7. **Close** ✖ the **Style Inspector** pane, the **Reveal Formatting** pane, and the **Styles** pane. **Save** 🖫 your document.

Activity 4.07 | Clearing Existing Formats

There may be instances where you wish to remove all formatting from existing text—for example, when you create a multilevel list.

1. Scroll to view the upper portion of **Page 1**, and then select the paragraph that begins *Examples: Aluminum*. On the **HOME tab**, in the **Font group**, click **Clear Formatting** 🖌. Compare your screen with Figure 4.15.

The Clear Formatting command removes all formatting of the applied style from the selected text. Text returns to the *Normal* style formatting for the current theme.

FIGURE 4.15

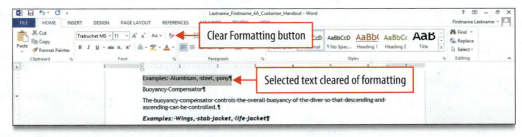

🔄 **ANOTHER WAY**   Select the desired text, and then at the top of the Styles pane, click the Clear All command.

2. With the text still selected, in the **Styles group**, right-click **Examples**, and then click **Update Examples to Match Selection**.

All instances of text formatted with the Examples style now display with the Normal style formatting.

3. **Save** 🖫 your document.

Activity 4.08 | Removing a Style

If a style that you created is no longer needed, you can remove it from the Styles gallery.

1. In the **Styles group**, right-click **Examples**, and then click **Remove from Style Gallery**.

The Examples style is removed from the Styles gallery. The style is no longer needed because all the paragraphs that are examples of scuba gear will be included in a multilevel list. Although the Examples style is removed from the Styles gallery, it is not deleted from the document.

2. **Save** 🖫 your document.

Objective 4 | Create a Multilevel List

Video W4-4

When a document includes a list of items, you can format the items as a bulleted list, as a numbered list, or as a *multilevel list*. Use a multilevel list when you want to add a visual hierarchical structure to the items in the list.

Activity 4.09 | Creating a Multilevel List with Bullets and Modifying List Indentation

1 On **Page 1**, scroll to position the heading *Equipment* near the top of your screen. Beginning with the paragraph *Air Tank*, select the 12 paragraphs between the headings *Equipment* and *Attire*.

2 On the **HOME tab**, in the **Paragraph group**, click **Multilevel List** to display the gallery. Under **List Library**, locate the ❖, ➤, • (bullet) style, which is the multilevel bullet list style. Compare your screen with Figure 4.16.

Word provides several built-in styles for multilevel lists. You can customize any style.

FIGURE 4.16

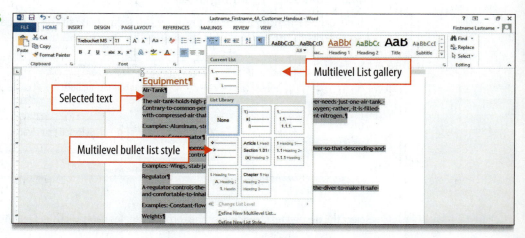

3 Click the **multilevel bullet list** style. Compare your screen with Figure 4.17.

All the items in the list display at the top level; the items are not visually indented to show different levels.

FIGURE 4.17

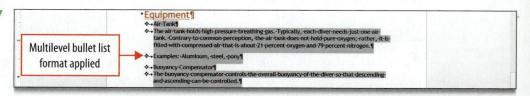

4 ▸ Click anywhere in the second list item, which begins *The air tank*. In the **Paragraph group**, click **Increase Indent** ⬚, and then compare your screen with Figure 4.18.

The list item displays at the second level which uses the ➤ symbol. The Increase Indent command demotes an item to a lower level; the Decrease Indent command promotes an item to a higher level. To change the list level using the Increase Indent command or Decrease Indent command, it is not necessary to select the entire paragraph.

FIGURE 4.18

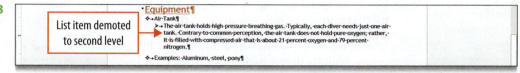

🔄 **ANOTHER WAY**   Select the item, and press ⎇Tab to demote the item or press ⇧Shift + ⎇Tab to promote it.

---

5 ▸ Click in the third item in the list, which begins *Examples: Aluminum*. In the **Paragraph group**, click **Increase Indent** ⬚ two times, and then compare your screen with Figure 4.19.

The list item displays at the third level, which uses the ■ symbol.

FIGURE 4.19

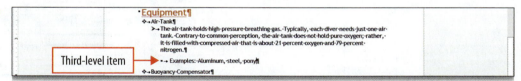

6 ▸ Using the technique you just practiced, continue setting levels for the remainder of the multilevel list as follows: Apply the second-level indent for the descriptive paragraphs that begin *The buoyancy*, *A regulator*, and *Weights add*. Apply the third-level indent for the paragraphs that begin *Examples*.

7 ▸ Compare your screen with Figure 4.20. If necessary, adjust your list by clicking **Increase Indent or Decrease Indent** so that your list matches the one shown in Figure 4.20.

FIGURE 4.20

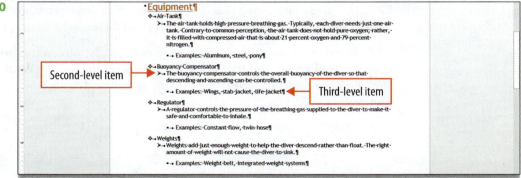

8 ▸ **Save** 💾 your document.

Activity 4.10 | Modifying the Numbering and Formatting in a Multilevel List Style

1 Select the entire multilevel list. Click **Multilevel List** ⊞. At the bottom of the gallery, click **Define New List Style**.

In the Define New List Style dialog box, you can select formatting options for each level in your list. By default, the dialog box displays formatting options starting with the *1st level*.

2 Under **Properties**, in the **Name** box, type **Equipment List** Under **Formatting**, in the small toolbar above the preview area, to the right of *Bullet:* ❖, click the **Numbering Style arrow**.

3 In the list, scroll to the top of the list, and then click the **1, 2, 3** style. Click the **Font Color arrow**, which currently displays black, and then in the eighth column, click the fifth color—**Orange, Accent 4, Darker 25%**. Compare your screen with Figure 4.21.

The numbering style and font color change will be applied only to first-level items. The style changes are visible in the preview area.

FIGURE 4.21

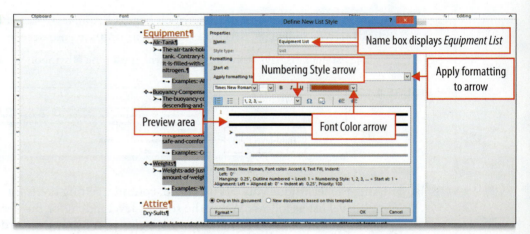

4 Under **Formatting**, click the **Apply formatting to arrow**, and then click **2nd level**. Click the **Font Color arrow**, and then in the eighth column, click the first color—**Orange, Accent 4**—to change the bullet color for the second-level items.

5 Click the **Apply formatting to arrow**, and then click **3rd level**. Click the **Font Color arrow**, and then in the eighth column, click the fifth color—**Orange, Accent 4, Darker 25%**.

6 Click **Insert Symbol** Ω. In the **Symbol** dialog box, be sure **Wingdings** displays. If necessary, click the **Font arrow**, and then click **Wingdings**. At the bottom of the **Symbol** dialog box, in the **Character code** box, select the existing text, type **170** and then compare your screen with Figure 4.22.

The ✦ symbol, represented by the character code 170 is selected.

FIGURE 4.22

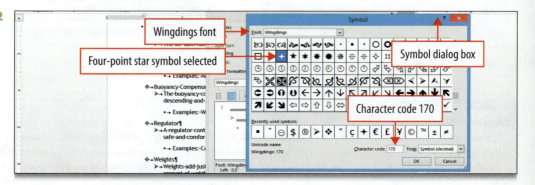

7 ▶ Click **OK** to apply the selected symbol and close the **Symbol** dialog box.

Third-level items will display with the ◆ symbol and orange font color.

8 ▶ In the **Define New List Style** dialog box, notice the preview of your changes, and then click **OK** to close the dialog box. Click anywhere to deselect the text, and then compare your screen with Figure 4.23.

FIGURE 4.23

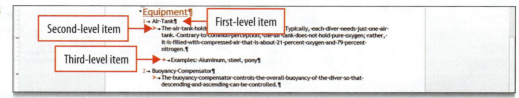

9 ▶ Select the entire list. With all 12 paragraphs selected, click the **PAGE LAYOUT tab**, and then in the **Paragraph group**, click the **Spacing After spin box down arrow** to **6 pt. Save** 🔲 your changes.

Activity 4.11 │ Applying the Current List Style and Changing the List Levels

After you define a new list style, you can apply the style to other similar items in your document.

1 ▶ Scroll to display the heading *Attire* and all remaining paragraphs in the document. Beginning with the paragraph *Dry Suits*, select the remaining paragraphs of the document.

2 ▶ Click the **HOME tab**, and then in the **Paragraph group**, click **Multilevel List** 📑. In the gallery, under **Current List**, click the displayed style. Compare your screen with Figure 4.24.

The current list style formats each paragraph as first-level items.

FIGURE 4.24

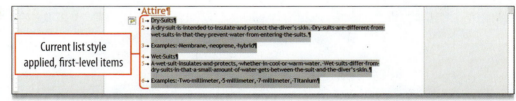

3 ▶ Under the *Attire* heading, select the two descriptive paragraphs that begin *A dry suit* and *A wet suit*. Click **Multilevel List** 📑, and then click **Change List Level**. Compare your screen with Figure 4.25.

All available list levels display for the selected paragraphs. You can increase or decrease the list level for selected items in a list by assigning the desired level.

FIGURE 4.25

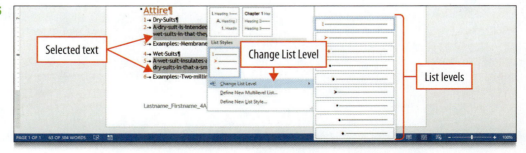

4 From the levels list, select the second list level that displays the symbol ➤—**Level 2**.

5 Select the two paragraphs that begin *Examples*, and then using the technique you just practiced, assign the third list level that displays the symbol ◆—**Level 3**.

6 Select the entire list. With all six paragraphs selected, click the **PAGE LAYOUT tab**, and then in the **Paragraph group**, click the **Spacing After spin box down arrow** to **6 pt**. Deselect the text, and then compare your screen with Figure 4.26.

FIGURE 4.26

7 Click the **FILE tab** to display **Backstage** view. On the right, at the bottom of the **Properties** list, click **Show All Properties**. In the **Tags** box, type **scuba diving, trip handout** and then in the **Subject** box, type your course name and section number. If necessary, edit the author name to display your name.

8 In **Backstage** view, click **Print** to display the **Print Preview**. Examine the **Print Preview**, make any necessary adjustments, and then **Save** your document.

9 Print your document or submit it electronically as directed by your instructor. **Close** ☒ Word.

END | You have completed Project 4A

Planning Memo with a Chart

PROJECT ACTIVITIES

In Activities 4.12 through 4.23, you will edit a memo to all the company tour guides regarding the planning session. The Tour Operations Manager of Costa Rican Treks is preparing for a planning session in which he and other key decision makers will discuss the types of tours the company will offer in the coming year. They want to use information gathered from customer research to provide an appropriate mix of tour types that will appeal to a wide audience. You will add a chart to illustrate plans for tour types in the coming year. Your completed documents will look similar to Figure 4.27.

PROJECT FILES

For Project 4B, you will need the following files:

w04B_Planning_Memo
w04B_Custom_Styles

You will save your files as:

Lastname_Firstname_4B_Planning_Memo
Lastname_Firstname_4B_Planning_Revised
Lastname_Firstname_4B_Chart_Template—not shown in figure

PROJECT RESULTS

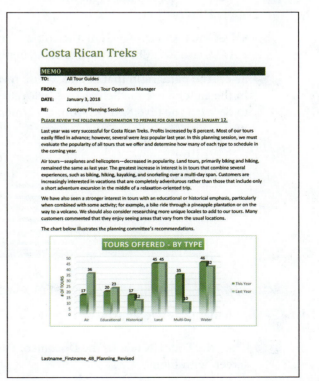

FIGURE 4.27 Project 4B Planning Memo

Video W4-5

Recall that a style set is a group of styles that is designed to work together. A style set is useful when you want to change the look of all the styles in a document in one step rather than modifying individual styles. You can modify the document using a built-in style set or by attaching a template.

Activity 4.12 | Formatting a Memo

A **memo**, also referred to as a **memorandum**, is a written message to someone working in the same organization. Among organizations, memo formats vary, and there are many acceptable memo formats. Always consult trusted references or the preferences set by your organization when deciding on the proper formats for your professional memos.

1 **Start** Word. From your student files, locate and open the file **w04B_Planning_Memo**.

2 Save the document in your **Word Chapter 4** folder as **Lastname_Firstname_4B_Planning_Memo**. Scroll to the bottom of the page, right-click in the footer area, and then click **Edit Footer**. On the ribbon, under **HEADER & FOOTER TOOLS**, on the **DESIGN tab**, in the **Insert group**, click **Document Info**, and then click **File Name**. **Close** the footer area. If necessary, display the rulers and formatting marks.

3 Select the first paragraph of the document—*Costa Rican Treks*. On the **HOME tab**, in the **Styles group**, click **More** ⏷, and then in the gallery, click **Title**.

4 Select the second paragraph, the heading *MEMO*, click **More** ⏷, and then in the gallery, apply **Heading 1**.

5 Select the text *TO:*—include the colon—hold down Ctrl, and then select the text *FROM:*, *DATE:*, and *RE:*. On the mini toolbar, apply **Bold** B to these four memo headings.

6 Select the paragraph that begins *Please review*. In the **Styles** group, click **More** ⏷. In the gallery, use the ScreenTips to locate and then click **Intense Reference**. Click anywhere to deselect the text. **Save** 🖫 your document. Compare your screen with Figure 4.28.

FIGURE 4.28

Title style applied

Heading 1 style applied

Memo headings in bold

Intense Reference style applied

Activity 4.13 | Changing the Style Set of a Document

By changing a style set, you can apply a group of styles to a document in one step.

1 Click the **DESIGN tab**. In the **Document Formatting group**, click **More** ⏷. Compare your screen with Figure 4.29.

All available style sets display in the Style Set gallery; there are seventeen built-in style sets. The default style set is Word 2013. The style set currently applied to a document displays under This Document.

FIGURE 4.29

2 In the gallery, under **Built-In**, in the second row, click the first style—**Minimalist**. Compare your screen with Figure 4.30, and then **Save** 🖫 your document.

Minimalist is the name of a particular style set. Applying the *Minimalist* style set, which includes a default font size of 10.5, causes styles—such as Title, Heading 1, and Intense Reference—to display a different format.

FIGURE 4.30

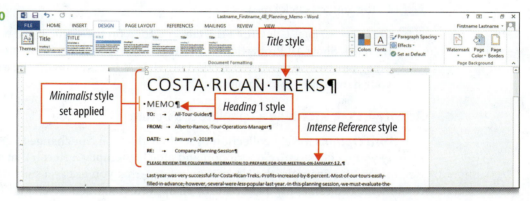

Activity 4.14 | Changing the Paragraph Spacing of a Document

Each style set reflects the font scheme and color scheme of the current theme, including the paragraph spacing formats. Built-in paragraph spacing formats allow you to change the paragraph spacing and line spacing for an entire document in one step.

1 On the **DESIGN tab**, in the **Document Formatting group**, click **Paragraph Spacing**. Compare your screen with Figure 4.31, and then take a moment to study the table shown in Figure 4.32.

Word provides six built-in styles for paragraph spacing. The *Minimalist* style set uses custom paragraph spacing that includes line spacing of 1.3, 0 pt spacing before, and 8 pt spacing after a paragraph.

FIGURE 4.31

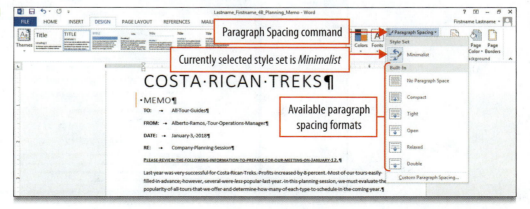

FIGURE 4.32

PARAGRAPH SPACING FORMATS			
OPTION	**SPACING BEFORE**	**SPACING AFTER**	**LINE SPACING**
No paragraph spacing	0 pt	0 pt	1
Compact	0 pt	4 pt	1
Tight	0 pt	6 pt	1.15
Open	0 pt	10 pt	1.15
Relaxed	0 pt	6 pt	1.5
Double	0 pt	8 pt	2

2 In the gallery, point to **Double**. Notice that the ScreenTip describes the paragraph spacing format and that Live Preview displays how the document would look with this paragraph spacing format applied.

3 In the gallery, click **Open**.

4 Press Ctrl + Home. Click the **FILE tab**, and then on the right, at the bottom of the **Properties** list, click **Show All Properties**. In the **Tags** box, type **memo, draft** and then in the **Subject** box, type your course name and section number. If necessary, edit the author name to display your name. **Save** your document.

Activity 4.15 | Attaching a Template to a Document

Word Options form a collection of settings that you can change to customize Word. In this activity you will customize the ribbon and attach a template. Recall that a template is an existing document—for example, the Normal template—that you use as a starting point for a new document. You can apply a template to an existing document to change the appearance of the document.

1 Press F12 to display the **Save As** dialog box. Navigate to your **Word Chapter 4** folder, and then **Save** the document as **Lastname_Firstname_4B_Planning_Revised** Right-click in the footer area, and then click **Edit Footer**. In the footer, right-click the existing file name, and then click **Update Field**. **Close** the footer area.

2 Press Ctrl + Home. Click the **FILE tab**, and then on the left, click **Options** to display the **Word Options** dialog box. Compare your screen with Figure 4.33, and then take a few moments to study the table in Figure 4.34.

In an organizational environment such as a college or business, you may not have access or permission to change some or all of the settings.

FIGURE 4.33

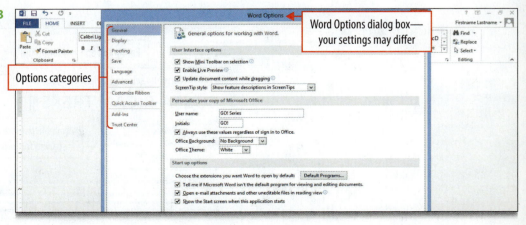

FIGURE 4.34

WORD OPTIONS	
CATEGORY	**OPTIONS TO:**
General	Set up Word for your personal way of working—for example, changing the Office Background—and personalize Word with your name and initials.
Display	Control the way content displays pages on the screen and when it prints.
Proofing	Control how Word corrects and formats your text—for example, how AutoCorrect and spell checker perform.
Save	Specify where you want to save your Word documents by default and set the AutoRecover time for saving information.
Language	Set the default language and add additional languages for editing documents.
Advanced	Control advanced features, including editing and printing options.
Customize Ribbon	Add commands to existing tabs, create new tabs, and set up your own keyboard shortcuts.
Quick Access Toolbar	Customize the Quick Access Toolbar by adding commands.
Add-Ins	View and manage add-in programs that come with the Word software or ones that you add to Word.
Trust Center	Control privacy and security when working with files from other sources or when you share files with others.

3 ▶ In the **Word Options** dialog box, on the left, click **Customize Ribbon**.

The Word Options dialog box displays a list of popular commands on the left and main tabs display on the right. Under Main Tabs, the checkmarks to the left of the tab names indicate tabs that are currently available on the ribbon.

4 ▶ In the **Word Options** dialog box, in the **Main Tabs** list, select the **Developer** check box. Compare your screen with Figure 4.35.

The Developer tab extends the capabilities of Word—including commands for using existing templates.

FIGURE 4.35

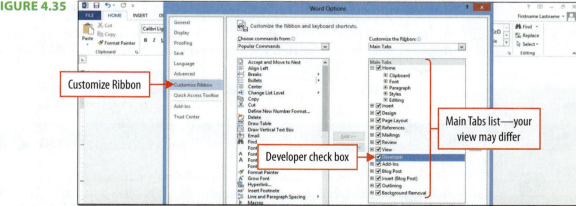

5 ▶ Click **OK** to close the **Word Options** dialog box.

The DEVELOPER tab displays on the ribbon to the right of the VIEW tab.

6 ▶ Click the **DEVELOPER tab**, and then in the **Templates group**, click **Document Template**.

7 ▶ In the **Templates and Add-ins** dialog box, to the right of the **Document template** box, click **Attach** to display the **Attach Template** dialog box.

8 In the **Attach Template** dialog box, navigate to the location of your student files, click **w04B_Custom_Styles**, and then click **Open**.

The file w04B_Custom_Styles is a Word template that contains styles created by the marketing director to be used in all Costa Rican Treks documents.

9 In the **Templates and Add-ins** dialog box, to the left of **Automatically update document styles**, select the check box, and then compare your screen with Figure 4.36.

FIGURE 4.36

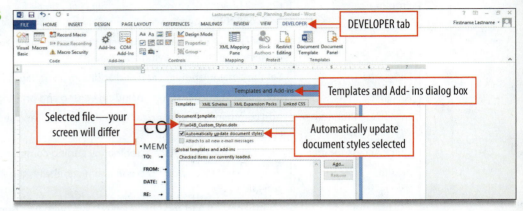

10 In the **Templates and Add-ins** dialog box, click **OK**. Compare your screen with Figure 4.37.

All styles contained in the w04B_Custom_Styles template are applied to your Lastname_Firstname_4B_Planning_Revised document.

FIGURE 4.37

11 Right-click the **DEVELOPER tab**, and then from the shortcut menu, click **Customize the Ribbon**. Under **Main Tabs**, clear the **Developer** check box, and then click **OK**. **Save** 🖫 your document.

The DEVELOPER tab no longer displays on the ribbon.

Objective 6 | Insert a Chart and Enter Data into a Chart

Video W4-6

A *chart* is a visual representation of *numerical data*—numbers that represent facts. Word provides the same chart tools that are available in Excel. A chart that you create in Word is stored in an Excel worksheet, and the worksheet is saved with the Word document. Excel, which is part of Microsoft Office 2013, is a spreadsheet application that makes calculations on numbers. An Excel worksheet is a set of cells, identified by row and column headings, that is part of a worksheet. Charts make numbers easier for the reader to understand.

Activity 4.16 | Selecting a Chart Type

1 Press **Ctrl** + **End**. Press **Enter**, and then type **The chart below illustrates the planning committee's recommendations.** Press **Enter**.

2 Click the **INSERT tab**, and then in the **Illustrations group**, click **Chart** to display the **Insert Chart** dialog box. Take a moment to examine the chart types described in the table shown in Figure 4.38.

> Ten chart types display on the left side of the Insert Chart dialog box. The most commonly used chart types are column, bar, pie, line, and area.

FIGURE 4.38

COMMONLY USED CHART TYPES AVAILABLE IN WORD	
CHART TYPE	**PURPOSE OF CHART**
Column, Bar	Show comparison among related data
Pie	Show proportion of parts to a whole
Line, Area	Show trends over time

3 On the left side of the **Insert Chart** dialog box, click **Bar**. In the right pane, at the top, click the fourth style—**3-D Clustered Bar**. Compare your screen with Figure 4.39.

> A bar chart is a good choice because this data will *compare* the number of tours offered in two different years.

FIGURE 4.39

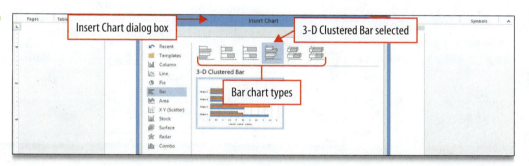

4 Click **OK** to insert the chart in your document and open the related Chart in Microsoft Word worksheet, which is an Excel worksheet. Compare your screen with Figure 4.40.

> The chart displays on Page 2 of your Word document. Sample data displays in the worksheet.

> The process of inserting a chart in your document in this manner is referred to as *embedding*—the object, in this case a chart, becomes part of the Word document. When you edit the data in the worksheet, the chart in your Word document updates automatically.

FIGURE 4.40

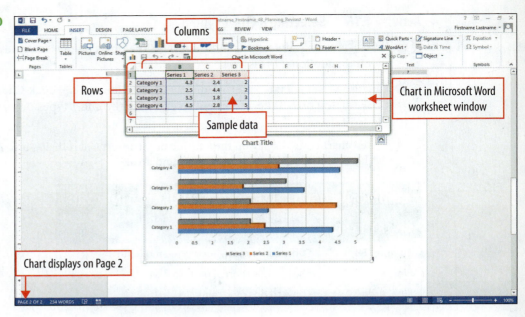

Columns

Rows

Chart in Microsoft Word worksheet window

Sample data

Chart displays on Page 2

Activity 4.17 | Entering Chart Data

You can replace the sample data in the worksheet with specific tour data for your chart.

1 In the **Chart in Microsoft Word** worksheet, point to the small box where **column B** and **row 1** intersect—referred to as cell **B1**—and click. Compare your screen with Figure 4.41.

A *cell* is the location where a row and column intersect. The cells are named by their column and row headings. For example, cell B1, containing the text *Series 1*, is in column B and row 1.

FIGURE 4.41

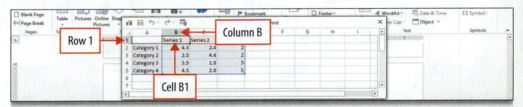

Row 1

Column B

Cell B1

2 With cell **B1** selected, type **This Year** and then press Tab. With cell **C1** selected, type **Last Year** and then click cell **A2**—which displays the text *Category 1*.

3 With cell **A2** selected, type **Air** and then press Tab to move to cell **B2**. Type **17** and then press Tab. In cell **C2** type **36** and then press Tab two times to move to **row 3**.

As you enter data in the worksheet, the chart is automatically updated in the Word document. When entering a large amount of data in a cell, it may not fully display. If necessary, the data worksheet or chart can be modified to display the data completely.

4 Without changing any values in **column D**, type the following data—after typing *42* in C7, press Tab to select cell D7.

	THIS YEAR	LAST YEAR	SERIES 3
Air	17	36	2
Educational	13	9	2
Historical	17	12	3
Land	45	45	5
Multi-Day	35	10	
Water	46	42	

5 Compare your screen with Figure 4.42. If necessary, position the ⬉ pointer at the top of the worksheet window, and then drag up to fully display your data.

The red lines and shading for cells B1 through D1 indicate data headings. The purple lines and shading for cells A2 through A7 indicate category headings. The blue line—the *data range border*—surrounds the cells containing numerical data that display in the chart. The group of cells with red, purple, and blue shading is referred to as the *chart data range*—the range of data that will be used to create the chart.

FIGURE 4.42

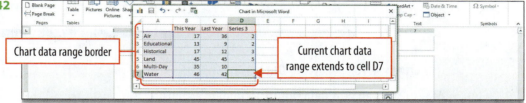

6 In the **Chart in Microsoft Word** worksheet, point to the lower right corner of the blue border to display the ⬉ pointer, and then drag to the left to select only cells **A1** through **C7**. Compare your screen with Figure 4.43.

FIGURE 4.43

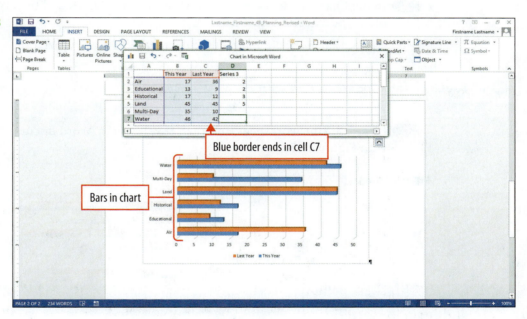

7 In the upper right corner of the worksheet window, click **Close** ✕ . Click the chart border to select the chart. If necessary, point to the top border of the chart until the ⬉ pointer displays, and then drag the chart upward so that it displays near the top of **Page 2** of your document. **Save** 🖫 your Word document, and then compare your screen with Figure 4.44.

The *chart area* refers to the entire chart and all its elements. The categories—the tour type names—display along the left side of the chart on the *vertical axis*, which is also referred to as the *Y-axis*. The scale—based on the numerical data—displays along the lower edge of the chart on the *horizontal axis*, which is also referred to as the *X-axis*.

Data markers, the bars in your chart, are the shapes representing each of the cells that contain data, referred to as the *data points*. A *data series* consists of related data points represented by a unique color. For example, this chart has two data series—*This Year* and *Last Year*. The *legend* identifies the colors assigned to each data series or category.

With the chart selected, the CHART TOOLS display on the ribbon and include two additional tabs—DESIGN and FORMAT—to provide commands with which you can modify and format chart elements.

FIGURE 4.44

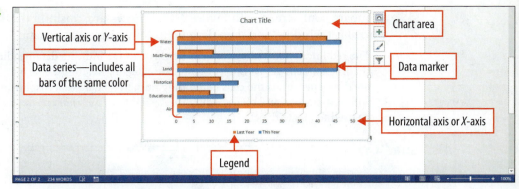

Activity 4.18 | Editing Data

You can edit data points to update a chart.

1 ▶ Be sure your chart is selected; if necessary, click the chart border to select it. On the ribbon, under **CHART TOOLS**, click the **DESIGN tab**, and then in the **Data group**, click **Edit Data** to redisplay the embedded Chart in Microsoft Word worksheet.

2 ▶ In the **Chart in Microsoft Word** worksheet, click cell **B3**, and then type **20** Click cell **C3**, and then type **23** Press Enter.

Word automatically updates the chart to reflect these data point changes.

⟳ BY TOUCH   Double-tap a cell, and then type the number.

3 ▶ **Close** ☒ the worksheet, and then **Save** 🖫 your Word document. Compare your screen with Figure 4.45.

FIGURE 4.45

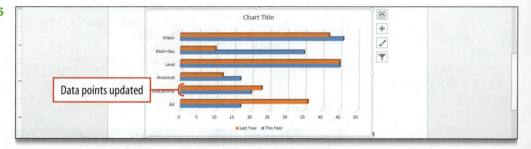

Objective 7 | Change a Chart Type

Video W4-7

A chart commonly shows one of three types of relationships—a comparison among data, the proportion of parts to a whole, or trends over time. You may decide to alter the chart type—for example, change a bar chart to a column chart—so that the chart displays more attractively in the document. You can modify, add, or delete chart elements such as the chart title, data labels, and text boxes.

Activity 4.19 | Changing the Chart Type

The data in the tour types chart compares tour numbers for two years and is appropriately represented by a bar chart. A column chart is also appropriate to compare data.

1 > With the chart selected, on the ribbon, under **CHART TOOLS**, on the **DESIGN tab**, in the **Type group**, click **Change Chart Type**.

2 > In the **Change Chart Type** dialog box, on the left, click **Column**, and then in the right pane, at the top, click the fourth chart type—**3-D Clustered Column**. Click **OK**, and then compare your screen with Figure 4.46.

> The category names display in alphabetical order on the horizontal axis; the number scale displays on the vertical axis.

FIGURE 4.46

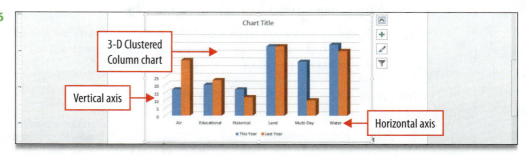

3 > **Save**  your document.

Activity 4.20 | Adding Chart Elements

Add chart elements to help the reader understand the data in your chart. For example, you can add a title to the chart and to individual axes, or add *data labels*, which display the value represented by each data marker.

1 > Four buttons—*Layout Options*, *Chart Elements*, *Chart Styles*, and *Chart Filters*—display to the right of the selected chart. Take a moment to read the descriptions of each button in the table in Figure 4.47.

FIGURE 4.47

AVAILABLE CHART BUTTONS		
CHART BUTTON	**ICON**	**PURPOSE**
Layout Options		To set how a chart interacts with the text around it
Chart Elements		To add, remove, or change chart elements—such as a chart title, legend, gridlines, and data labels
Chart Styles		To apply a style and color scheme to a chart
Chart Filters		To define what data points and names display on a chart

2 > To the right of the chart, click **Chart Elements** +. In the list, point to **Gridlines**, and then with the **Gridlines** check box selected, click the **arrow.** Notice that *Primary Major Horizontal* is selected.

> Gridlines assist the reader in identifying specific values. The major gridlines in this chart extend horizontally from the vertical axis to the right of the last data marker. Use the Gridlines command to display or hide vertical or horizontal gridlines—either major or minor—based on the complexity of the chart.

ANOTHER WAY   Under CHART TOOLS, on the DESIGN tab, in the Chart Layouts group, click Add Chart Element, and then point to Gridlines.

3 In the **Chart Elements** list, point to **Axes**, and then click the **arrow**. Notice that both *Primary Horizontal* and *Primary Vertical* are selected.

4 Press Esc to close the **Chart Elements** list. Above the chart, click in the text box that displays *Chart Title*, delete the existing text, and then type **Tours Offered – By Type**

5 If necessary, click in an empty corner of the chart to display the buttons at the right. Click **Chart Elements** ➕, and then select the **Axis Titles** check box. Click the **arrow**, and then clear the **Primary Horizontal** check box to remove the primary horizontal title text box from the chart. Compare your screen with Figure 4.48.

By default, when you select Axis Titles, both the primary horizontal axis title and primary vertical axis title text boxes display in the chart. In this case, because the chart title identifies the categories, the primary horizontal axis title is not needed.

FIGURE 4.48

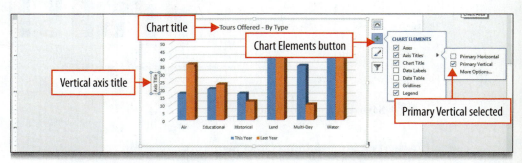

6 To the left of the vertical axis, select the text **Axis Title**, and then type **# of Tours** Notice that the text displays vertically in the text box.

7 Click in an empty corner of the chart to deselect the text box. Click **Chart Elements** ➕, and then select the **Data Labels** check box. **Save** 💾 your document.

The data point values display above each data marker column in the chart. In addition to the scale on the vertical axis, data labels are helpful for the reader to understand the values represented in the columns.

Objective 8   Format a Chart and Save a Chart as a Template

Video W4-8

You can format a chart to change the appearance of chart elements. After formatting a chart, you can save the chart as a template. If a document contains several charts, using a chart template provides consistency in style and formatting.

Activity 4.21 │ Changing the Chart Style and Formatting Chart Elements

A *chart style* refers to the overall visual look of a chart in terms of its graphic effects, colors, and backgrounds. For example, you can have flat or beveled columns, colors that are solid or transparent, and backgrounds that are dark or light. Individual chart elements can also be formatted to enhance the appearance of the chart.

1 To the right of the chart, click **Chart Styles** 🖌️. With **STYLE** selected, scroll down and click the eighth style—**Style 8**. At the top of the **Chart Styles** list, click **COLOR**. Under **Monochromatic**, in the sixth row, click the green color scheme—**Color 10**. Compare your screen with Figure 4.49.

FIGURE 4.49

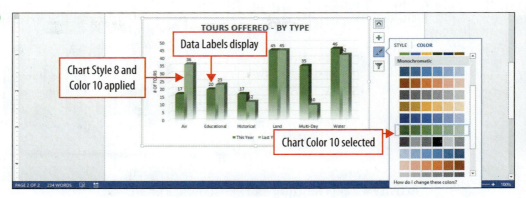

ANOTHER WAY   Under CHART TOOLS, on the DESIGN tab, in the Chart Styles group, click the More button to display the Chart Styles gallery and click the Change Colors button to display the Color Gallery.

2 ▶ Click in the document to close the Chart Styles list. Select the chart title. On the ribbon, under **CHART TOOLS**, click the **FORMAT tab**, and then in the **Shape Styles group**, click **More** ⬇. In the gallery, in the fifth row, click the last style—**Moderate Effect – Green, Accent 6**. Click in an empty corner of the chart to deselect the chart title, and then compare your screen with Figure 4.50.

FIGURE 4.50

3 ▶ To the left of the vertical axis, select the text *# of Tours*. On the mini toolbar, click the **Font Color arrow** ⬛ ▾, and then in the last column, click the last color—**Green, Accent 6, Darker 50%**.

4 ▶ Above the **Air** columns, click **17** to select the data labels for each data marker in the *This Year* data series.

5 ▶ On the **FORMAT tab**, in the **WordArt Styles group**, click **More** ⬇. In the gallery, click the first style—**Fill – Black, Text 1, Shadow**.

   All the data labels in the *This Year* data series display with the WordArt style applied.

6 ▶ Using the technique you just practiced, apply the **Fill – Black, Text 1, Shadow** WordArt style to the data labels in the *Last Year* data series.

7 ▶ Click the border of the chart. On the **FORMAT tab**, in the **Shape Styles group**, click **Shape Outline** ✎, and then in the last column, click the first color—**Green, Accent 6**. Deselect the chart, and then compare your screen with Figure 4.51.

   A border surrounds the entire chart.

FIGURE 4.51

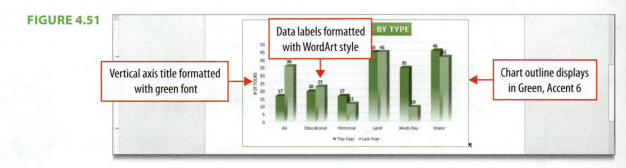

Data labels formatted with WordArt style

Vertical axis title formatted with green font

Chart outline displays in Green, Accent 6

Activity 4.22 | Resizing and Positioning a Chart

You can resize and position both the chart and individual chart elements. You can also position the chart on the page relative to the left and right margins.

1 Click in the chart. To the right of the chart, click **Chart Elements** ⊞, and then point to **Legend**. With *Legend* selected, click the **arrow,** and then click **Right**.

The legend displays on the right side of the chart.

2 To the right of the chart, click **Layout Options** 🖾.

When you insert a chart, the default text wrapping setting is In Line with Text.

3 Near the bottom of the gallery, click **See more** to display the **Layout** dialog box.

The Layout dialog box allows you to change the position, text wrapping, and size of a chart.

4 In the **Layout** dialog box, click the **Size tab**, and then under **Height**, click the **Absolute down spin arrow** to **2.7**. Click **OK** to close the dialog box.

When you change the position, text wrapping, or size of a chart, the chart may display differently in the document. In this case, the chart displays at the bottom of Page 1.

5 With the chart selected, press Ctrl + E to center the chart horizontally on the page. Compare your screen with Figure 4.52.

FIGURE 4.52

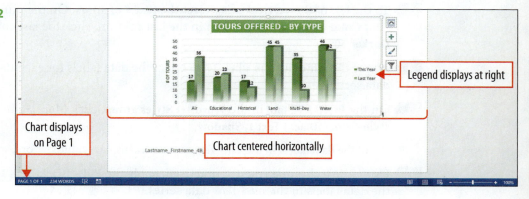

Legend displays at right

Chart displays on Page 1

Chart centered horizontally

🔁 **ANOTHER WAY**   On the FORMAT tab, in the Arrange group, you can modify the text wrapping and alignment of the chart; and in the Size group, you can change the size.

6 Save 🖫 your document.

Activity 4.23 | Saving a Chart as a Template

After formatting the chart and chart elements, you can save the chart as a template. If a document contains several charts, using a chart template provides consistency in style and formatting.

1 ▶ Right-click the border of the chart, and then from the shortcut menu, click **Save as Template**.

2 ▶ In the **Save Chart Template** dialog box, navigate to your **Word Chapter 4** folder, and then save the chart as **Lastname_Firstname_4B_Chart_Template**

The chart template is saved with the file extension .crtx.

3 ▶ Press Ctrl + Home. Click the **FILE tab** to display **Backstage** view. On the right, at the bottom of the **Properties** list, click **Show All Properties**, if necessary. In the **Tags** box, delete any text, and then type **planning memo, tours data**

4 ▶ In **Backstage** view, click **Print**. Examine the **Print Preview**, and make any necessary adjustments. **Save** your document.

5 ▶ Print your two documents or submit all three files electronically as directed by your instructor. **Close** ☒ Word.

More Knowledge | **Saving a Chart Template to Your SkyDrive**

If you save the template to your SkyDrive and share it with coworkers, all charts created within the department or organization can have a consistent appearance.

END | You have completed Project 4B

END OF CHAPTER

SUMMARY

Use built-in and customized theme and style features to coordinate colors, fonts, effects, and other formatting elements. Apply themes and styles to maintain a consistent and professional appearance in documents.

A multilevel list displays information in an organized, hierarchical structure. You can create and save a custom multilevel list style, and apply it to other lists within the same document or in other documents.

A custom theme that is saved as a Word template can be attached to other documents. This is a quick and easy method to change the appearance of an existing document and provide consistency among related documents.

Because a chart displays numbers in a visual format, readers can easily understand the data. Add and format chart elements to enhance the chart's appearance. Save the chart as a template for use in other documents.

GO! LEARN IT ONLINE

Review the concepts and key terms in this chapter by completing these online challenges, which you can find at **www.pearsonhighered.com/go**.

Matching and Multiple Choice:
Answer matching and multiple choice questions to test what you learned in this chapter. **MyITLab®**

Crossword Puzzle:
Spell out the words that match the numbered clues, and put them in the puzzle squares.

Flipboard:
Flip through the definitions of the key terms in this chapter and match them with the correct term.

END OF CHAPTER

REVIEW AND ASSESSMENT GUIDE FOR WORD CHAPTER 4

Your instructor may assign one or more of these projects to help you review the chapter and assess your mastery and understanding of the chapter.

Review and Assessment Guide for Word Chapter 4			
Project	**Apply Skills from These Chapter Objectives**	**Project Type**	**Project Location**
4C	Objectives 1-4 from Project 4A	**4C Skills Review** A guided review of the skills from Project 4A.	On the following pages
4D	Objectives 5-8 from Project 4B	**4D Skills Review** A guided review of the skills from Project 4B.	On the following pages
4E	Objectives 1-4 from Project 4A	**4E Mastery (Grader Project)** A demonstration of your mastery of the skills in Project 4A with extensive decision making.	In MyITLab and on the following pages
4F	Objectives 5-8 from Project 4B	**4F Mastery (Grader Project)** A demonstration of your mastery of the skills in Project 4B with extensive decision making.	In MyITLab and on the following pages
4G	Objectives 1-8 from Projects 4A and 4B	**4G Mastery (Grader Project)** A demonstration of your mastery of the skills in Projects 4A and 4B with extensive decision making.	In MyITLab and on the following pages
4H	Combination of Objectives from Projects 4A and 4B	**4H GO! Fix It** A demonstration of your mastery of the skills in Projects 4A and 4B by creating a correct result from a document that contains errors you must find.	Online
4I	Combination of Objectives from Projects 4A and 4B	**4I GO! Make It** A demonstration of your mastery of the skills in Projects 4A and 4B by creating a result from a supplied picture.	Online
4J	Combination of Objectives from Projects 4A and 4B	**4J GO! Solve It** A demonstration of your mastery of the skills in Projects 4A and 4B, your decision-making skills, and your critical thinking skills. A task-specific rubric helps you self-assess your result.	Online
4K	Combination of Objectives from Projects 4A and 4B	**4K GO! Solve It** A demonstration of your mastery of the skills in Projects 4A and 4B, your decision-making skills, and your critical thinking skills. A task-specific rubric helps you self-assess your result.	On the following pages
4L	Combination of Objectives from Projects 4A and 4B	**4L GO! Think** A demonstration of your understanding of the chapter concepts applied in a manner that you would outside of college. An analytic rubric helps you and your instructor grade the quality of your work by comparing it to the work an expert in the discipline would create.	On the following pages
4M	Combination of Objectives from Projects 4A and 4B	**4M GO! Think** A demonstration of your understanding of the chapter concepts applied in a manner that you would outside of college. An analytic rubric helps you and your instructor grade the quality of your work by comparing it to the work an expert in the discipline would create.	Online
4N	Combination of Objectives from Projects 4A and 4B	**4N You and GO!** A demonstration of your understanding of the chapter concepts applied in a manner that you would in a personal situation. An analytic rubric helps you and your instructor grade the quality of your work.	Online

GLOSSARY

GLOSSARY OF CHAPTER KEY TERMS

Area chart A chart type that shows trends over time.

Bar chart A chart type that shows a comparison among related data.

Cell The intersection of a column and row.

Change Case A formatting command that allows you to quickly change the capitalization of selected text.

Character style A style, indicated by the symbol **a**, that contains formatting characteristics that you apply to text, such as font name, font size, font color, bold emphasis, and so on.

Chart A visual representation of numerical data.

Chart area The entire chart and all its elements.

Chart data range The group of cells with red, purple, and blue shading that is used to create a chart.

Chart Elements A Word feature that displays commands to add, remove, or change chart elements, such as the legend, gridlines, and data labels.

Chart Filters A Word feature that displays commands to define what data points and names display on a chart.

Chart style The overall visual look of a chart in terms of its graphic effects, colors, and backgrounds.

Chart Styles A Word feature that displays commands to apply a style and color scheme to a chart.

Column chart A chart type that shows a comparison among related data.

Contiguous Items that are adjacent to one another.

Data labels The part of a chart that displays the value represented by each data marker.

Data markers The shapes in a chart representing each of the cells that contain data.

Data points The cells that contain numerical data used in a chart.

Data range border The blue line that surrounds the cells containing numerical data that display in in the chart.

Data series In a chart, related data points represented by a unique color.

Direct formatting The process of applying each format separately, for example bold, then font size, then font color, and so on.

Embedding The process of inserting an object, such as a chart, into a Word document so that it becomes part of the document.

Horizontal axis (*X*-axis) The axis that displays along the lower edge of a chart.

Keep lines together A formatting feature that prevents a single line from displaying by itself at the bottom of a page or at the top of a page.

Keep with next A formatting feature that keeps a heading with its first paragraph of text on the same page.

Layout Options A Word feature that displays commands to control the manner in which text wraps around a chart or other object.

Legend The part of a chart that identifies the colors assigned to each data series or category.

Line chart A chart type that shows trends over time.

Linked style A style, indicated by the symbol ¶**a**, that behaves as either a character style or a paragraph style, depending on what you select.

List style A style that applies a format to a list.

Memorandum (Memo) A written message sent to someone working in the same organization.

Multilevel list A list in which the items display in a visual hierarchical structure.

Noncontiguous Items that are not adjacent to one another.

Normal The default style in Word for new documents and which includes default styles and customizations that determine the basic look of a document; for example, it includes the Calibri font, 11 point font size, line spacing at 1.08, and 8 pt spacing after a paragraph.

Numerical data Numbers that represent facts.

Paragraph style A style, indicated by ¶, that includes everything that a character style contains, plus all aspects of a paragraph's appearance; for example text alignment, tab stops, line spacing, and borders.

Pie chart A chart type that shows the proportion of parts to a whole.

Reveal Formatting A pane that displays the formatted selection and includes a complete description of formats applied.

Show Preview A formatting feature that displays a visual representation of each style in the Styles window.

Style A group of formatting commands, such as font, font size, font color, paragraph alignment, and line spacing, which can be applied to selected text with one command.

Style Inspector A pane that displays the name of the selected style with formats applied and contains paragraph- and text-level formatting options.

Style set A group of styles that are designed to work together.

Styles pane A window that displays a list of styles and contains tools to manage styles.

Table style A style that applies a consistent look to borders, shading, and so on of a table.

Vertical axis (*Y*-axis) The axis that displays along the left side of a chart.

Word Options A collection of settings that you can change to customize Word.

CHAPTER REVIEW

Apply 4A skills from these Objectives:

1 Apply and Modify Styles
2 Create New Styles
3 Manage Styles
4 Create a Multilevel List

Skills Review Project 4C Training Classes

In the following Skills Review, you will add styles and a multilevel list format to a document that describes training classes for Costa Rican Treks tour guides. Your completed document will look similar to Figure 4.53.

PROJECT FILES

For Project 4C, you will need the following file:

w04C_Training_Classes

You will save your file as:

Lastname_Firstname_4C_Training_Classes

PROJECT RESULTS

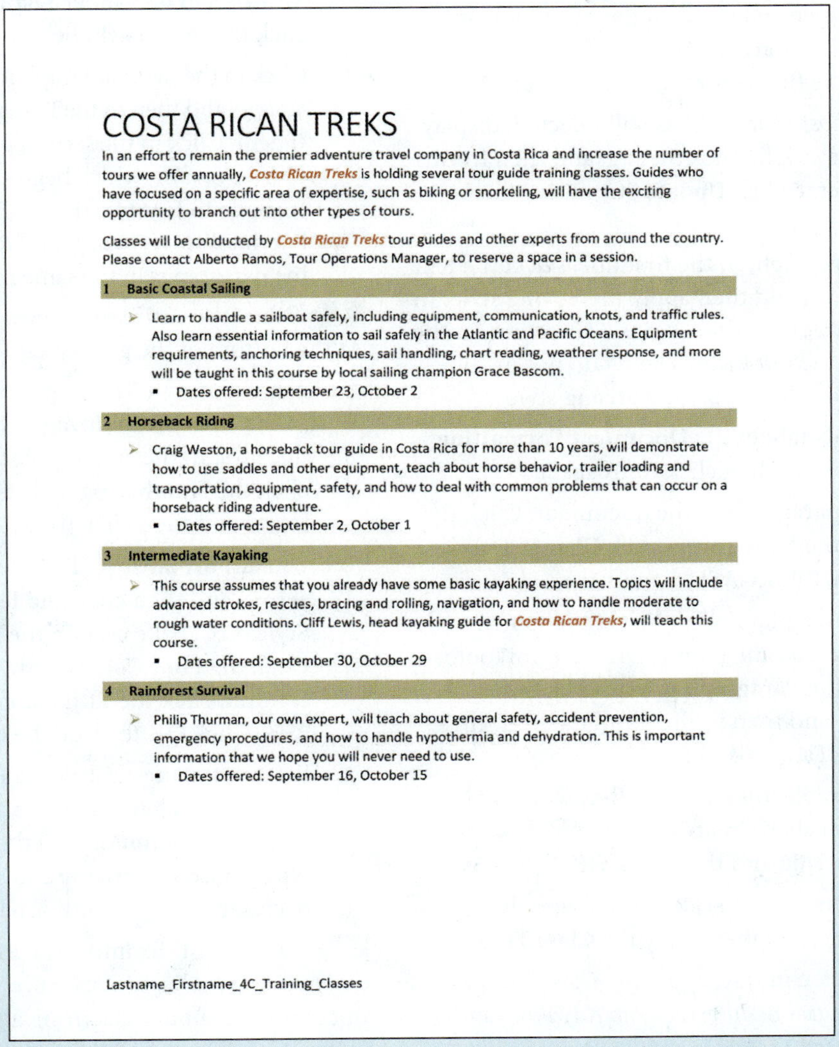

COSTA RICAN TREKS

In an effort to remain the premier adventure travel company in Costa Rica and increase the number of tours we offer annually, ***Costa Rican Treks*** is holding several tour guide training classes. Guides who have focused on a specific area of expertise, such as biking or snorkeling, will have the exciting opportunity to branch out into other types of tours.

Classes will be conducted by ***Costa Rican Treks*** tour guides and other experts from around the country. Please contact Alberto Ramos, Tour Operations Manager, to reserve a space in a session.

1 Basic Coastal Sailing

- Learn to handle a sailboat safely, including equipment, communication, knots, and traffic rules. Also learn essential information to sail safely in the Atlantic and Pacific Oceans. Equipment requirements, anchoring techniques, sail handling, chart reading, weather response, and more will be taught in this course by local sailing champion Grace Bascom.
  - Dates offered: September 23, October 2

2 Horseback Riding

- Craig Weston, a horseback tour guide in Costa Rica for more than 10 years, will demonstrate how to use saddles and other equipment, teach about horse behavior, trailer loading and transportation, equipment, safety, and how to deal with common problems that can occur on a horseback riding adventure.
  - Dates offered: September 2, October 1

3 Intermediate Kayaking

- This course assumes that you already have some basic kayaking experience. Topics will include advanced strokes, rescues, bracing and rolling, navigation, and how to handle moderate to rough water conditions. Cliff Lewis, head kayaking guide for ***Costa Rican Treks***, will teach this course.
  - Dates offered: September 30, October 29

4 Rainforest Survival

- Philip Thurman, our own expert, will teach about general safety, accident prevention, emergency procedures, and how to handle hypothermia and dehydration. This is important information that we hope you will never need to use.
  - Dates offered: September 16, October 15

Lastname_Firstname_4C_Training_Classes

FIGURE 4.53

(Project 4C Training Classes continues on the next page)

CHAPTER REVIEW

1 Start Word. From your student files, open the file **w04C_Training_Classes**. **Save** the document in your **Word Chapter 4** folder as **Lastname_Firstname_4C_ Training_Classes** Scroll to the bottom of the page, right-click in the footer area, and then click **Edit Footer**. On the ribbon, in the **Insert group**, click **Document Info**, and then click **File Name**. **Close** the footer area.

   a. Select the first paragraph. On the **HOME tab**, in the **Styles group**, click **More**, and then in the gallery, click **Title**.

   b. In the second paragraph, in the second line, select the text *Costa Rican Treks*. Display the **Styles** gallery, and then click **Strong**.

   c. Right-click the selected text. On the mini toolbar, click the **Font Color arrow**, and then in the sixth column, click the first color—**Orange, Accent 2**.

   d. With the text *Costa Rican Treks* still selected, display the **Styles** gallery, right-click **Strong**, and then from the shortcut menu, click **Update Strong to Match Selection**.

   e. In the third paragraph, in the first line, select the text *Costa Rican Treks*, and then apply the **Strong** style. In the eleventh paragraph that begins *This course*, in the third line, select *Costa Rican Treks*—do not include the comma—and then apply the **Strong** style.

2 On the **DESIGN tab**, in the **Document Formatting group**, click **Themes**, and then click **Retrospect**.

   a. Select the first paragraph of the document. Click the **HOME tab**. In the **Font group**, click **Change Case**, and then click **UPPERCASE**.

   b. Including the paragraph mark, select the fourth paragraph *Basic Coastal Sailing*. On the mini toolbar, apply **Bold**. In the **Paragraph group**, click the **Shading arrow**, and then in the ninth column, click the first color—**Tan, Accent 5**.

   c. With the paragraph still selected, display the **Styles** gallery, and then click **Create a Style**. In the **Name** box, type **Class Title** and then click **OK**.

   d. Scroll down as necessary, select the paragraph *Horseback Riding*, and then apply the **Class Title** style.

   e. Using the same technique, apply the **Class Title** style to the paragraphs *Intermediate Kayaking* and *Rainforest Survival*.

3 Press Ctrl + Home. In the **Styles group**, click the **Dialog Box Launcher**.

   a. In the **Styles** pane, point to **Strong**, click the **arrow**, and then click **Modify**.

   b. In the **Modify Style** dialog box, under **Formatting**, click **Italic**. Click **OK** to close the dialog box and update all instances of the *Strong* style. **Close** the **Styles** pane.

4 Click to position the insertion point to the left of the paragraph *Basic Coastal Sailing*, and then from this point, select all remaining text in the document.

   a. On the **HOME tab**, in the **Paragraph group**, click **Multilevel List**. Under **List Library**, locate and then click the ❖, ➤, • (bullet) style.

   b. Click in the first paragraph following *Basic Coastal Sailing*, and then in the **Paragraph group**, click **Increase Indent**. Click in the second paragraph following *Basic Coastal Sailing*, which begins *Dates*, and then click **Increase Indent** two times. Under *Horseback Riding*, *Intermediate Kayaking*, and *Rainforest Survival*, format the paragraphs in the same manner.

5 Select the entire multilevel list. Click **Multilevel List**. At the bottom of the gallery, click **Define New List Style**.

   a. Name the style **Training Class** Under **Formatting**, in the **Apply formatting to** box, be sure *1st level* displays. In the small toolbar above the preview area, click the **Numbering Style arrow**, in the list, scroll to locate and then click the **1, 2, 3** style.

   b. Under **Formatting**, click the **Apply formatting to arrow**, and then click **2nd level**. In the **Numbering Style** box, make certain the **Bullet:** ➤ style displays. Click the **Font Color arrow**, and then in the ninth column, click the fifth color—**Tan, Accent 5, Darker 25%**. Click **OK** to close the dialog box.

   c. Press Ctrl + Home. Click the **FILE tab**, and then click **Show All Properties**. In the **Tags** box, type **training classes, description** and then in the **Subject** box, type your course name and section number. If necessary, edit the author name to display your name.

6 Click **Print**. Examine the **Print Preview**, and make any necessary adjustments. **Save** your changes. Print your document or submit electronically as directed by your instructor. **Close** Word.

END | You have completed Project 4C

CHAPTER REVIEW

Skills Review | Project 4D Strategy Session

Apply 4B skills from these Objectives:

5 Change the Style Set of a Document and Apply a Template

6 Insert a Chart and Enter Data into a Chart

7 Change a Chart Type

8 Format a Chart and Save a Chart as a Template

In the following Skills Review, you will create a memo for Maria Tornio, President of Costa Rican Treks, which details the company's financial performance and provides strategies for the upcoming year. Your completed documents will look similar to Figure 4.54.

PROJECT FILES

For Project 4D, you will need the following files:

w04D_Strategy_Session
w04D_Memo_Styles

You will save your files as:

Lastname_Firstname_4D_Strategy_Session
Lastname_Firstname_4D_Revised_Strategy
Lastname_Firstname_4D_Tour_Chart – not shown in figure

PROJECT RESULTS

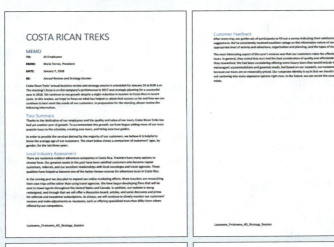

FIGURE 4.54

(Project 4D Strategy Session continues on the next page)

CHAPTER REVIEW

1 Start Word. From your student files, locate and then open the file **w04D_Strategy_Session**. **Save** the document in your **Word Chapter 4** folder as **Lastname_Firstname_4D_Strategy_Session** Scroll to the bottom of **Page 1**, right-click in the footer area, and then click **Edit Footer**. On the ribbon, in the **Insert group**, click **Document Info**, and then click **File Name**. **Close** the footer area.

a. Select the first paragraph—*Costa Rican Treks*. On the **HOME tab**, in the **Styles** group, click the **More** button, and then click **Title**. Select the second paragraph—*MEMO*, display the **Styles** gallery, and then click **Heading 1**.

b. Select the memo heading TO:—include the colon—hold down Ctrl and then select the memo headings FROM:, DATE:, and RE:. On the mini toolbar, click **Bold**.

c. Select the paragraph *Tour Summary*, press and hold Ctrl, and then select the paragraphs *Local Industry Assessment* and *Customer Feedback*. Apply the **Heading 2** style.

d. Click the **DESIGN tab**, and then in the **Document Formatting group**, click the **More** button. In the gallery, under **Built-In**, in the first row, click the first style set—**Basic (Elegant)**. In the **Document Formatting group**, click **Paragraph Spacing**, and then click **Open**.

e. Press Ctrl + Home. Click the **FILE tab**, and then click **Show All Properties**. In the **Tags** box, type **strategy memo, draft** and then in the **Subject** box, type your course name and section number. If necessary, edit the author name to display your name.

f. In **Backstage** view, click **Save**.

2 Click the **FILE tab**, and then click **Save As**. Navigate to your **Word Chapter 4** folder, and then save the document as **Lastname_Firstname_4D_Revised_Strategy** Right-click in the footer area, and then click **Edit Footer**. In the footer area, right-click the existing file name, and then click **Update Field**. **Close** the footer area.

a. Click the **FILE tab**, and then click **Options**. In the **Word Options** dialog box, click **Customize Ribbon**. In the **Main Tabs** list, select the **Developer** check box, and then click **OK**.

b. On the **DEVELOPER tab**, in the **Templates group**, click **Document Template**. In the **Templates and Add-ins** dialog box, click **Attach**. In the **Attach Template** dialog box, navigate to your student files, click **w04D_Memo_Styles**, and then click **Open**. Select the **Automatically update document styles** check box, and then click **OK**.

c. Click the **FILE tab**, and then click **Options**. In the **Word Options** dialog box, click **Customize Ribbon**. In the **Main Tabs** list, click to deselect the **Developer** check box, and then click **OK**.

d. On **Page 1**, below *Tour Summary*, locate the paragraph that begins *In order to provide*. Position the insertion point at the end of the paragraph, and then press Enter.

3 Click the **INSERT tab**, and then in the **Illustrations group**, click **Chart**.

a. On the left side of the **Insert Chart** dialog box, be sure **Column** is selected. At the top of the right pane, click the first chart type—**Clustered Column**—and then click **OK**.

b. In the **Chart in Microsoft Word** worksheet, click cell **B1**, type **Male** and then press Tab. With cell **C1** selected, type **Female** and then click cell **A2**.

c. With cell **A2** selected, type **2015** and then press Tab. In cell **B2**, type **36**, press Tab, and then in cell **C2**, type **32**. Press Tab two times to move to **row 3**.

d. Using the technique you just practiced, and without changing the values in **column D**, enter the following data:

	Male	Female	Series 3
2015	36	32	2
2016	**47**	**39**	**2**
2017	**52**	**43**	**3**

e. Point to the lower right corner of the blue border to display the ⤡ pointer, and then drag to the left and up to select only cells **A1** through **C4**.

f. **Close** the **Chart** in Microsoft Word worksheet, and then **Save** your document. Scroll as necessary to display the entire chart.

(Project 4D Strategy Session continues on the next page)

CHAPTER REVIEW

4 If necessary, click in an empty area of the chart to select it. Under **CHART TOOLS**, on the **DESIGN tab**, in the **Data group**, click **Edit Data** to redisplay the worksheet.

a. In the worksheet, click cell **C4**, type **45** press Enter, and then **Close** the worksheet.

b. With the chart selected, under **CHART TOOLS**, on the **DESIGN tab**, in the **Type group**, click **Change Chart Type**.

c. In the **Change Chart Type** dialog box, on the left, click **Bar**, and then on the right, at the top, click the first chart type—**Clustered Bar**. Click **OK**.

5 Select the text *Chart Title*, and then type **3-Year Tour Summary**

a. Click in an empty area of the chart, and then to the right of the chart, click **Chart Elements**. Select the **Axis Titles** check box, click the arrow, and then clear the **Primary Vertical** check box. Below the horizontal axis, select the text *Axis Title*, and then type **Average Age of Participants**

b. Click in an empty area of the chart, and then to the right of the chart, click **Chart Elements**. Select the **Data Labels** check box.

c. Click **Chart Styles**. Scroll down, and then click the fifth style—**Style 5**. At the top of the list, click **COLOR**, and then under **Colorful**, in the fourth row, click the color scheme **Color 4** to display the chart with blue and green data markers.

d. Select the chart title. Click the **FORMAT tab**, and then in the **WordArt Styles group**, click **More**. In the gallery, in the second row, click the second style—**Gradient Fill – Blue, Accent 1, Reflection**. Click in an empty corner area of the chart. On the **FORMAT tab**, in the **Shape Styles group**, click **Shape Outline**, and then in the last column, click the first color—**Green, Accent 6**.

e. Click **Chart Elements**, point to **Legend**, click the arrow, and then click **Right**. Click in an empty corner of the chart so that the entire chart is selected.

f. Click **Layout Options**, and then click **See more**. In the **Layout** dialog box, Click the **Size tab** and under **Height**, change the **Absolute down spin arrow** to **3.3"** Click **OK** to close the dialog box. Press Ctrl + E.

6 Right-click in an empty area of the chart, and then from the shortcut menu, click **Save as Template**. Save the chart in your **Word Chapter 4** folder as **Lastname_Firstname_4D_Tour_Chart**

a. Click the **FILE tab**, and then click **Show All Properties**. In the **Tags** box, delete the existing text, and then type **strategy session, memo**

7 In **Backstage** view, click **Save**. Print your two documents or submit your three files electronically as directed by your instructor. **Close** Word.

END You have completed Project 4D

CONTENT-BASED ASSESSMENTS

MyITLab® grader

Apply 4A skills from these Objectives:

1 Apply and Modify Styles
2 Create New Styles
3 Manage Styles
4 Create a Multilevel List

Mastering Word Project 4E Trip Tips

In the following Mastering Word project, you will create a handout that details tips for tour participants for Alberto Ramos, Tour Operations Manager of Costa Rican Treks. Your completed document will look similar to Figure 4.55.

PROJECT FILES

For Project 4E, you will need the following file:

w04E_Trip_Tips

You will save your file as:

Lastname_Firstname_4E_Trip_Tips

PROJECT RESULTS

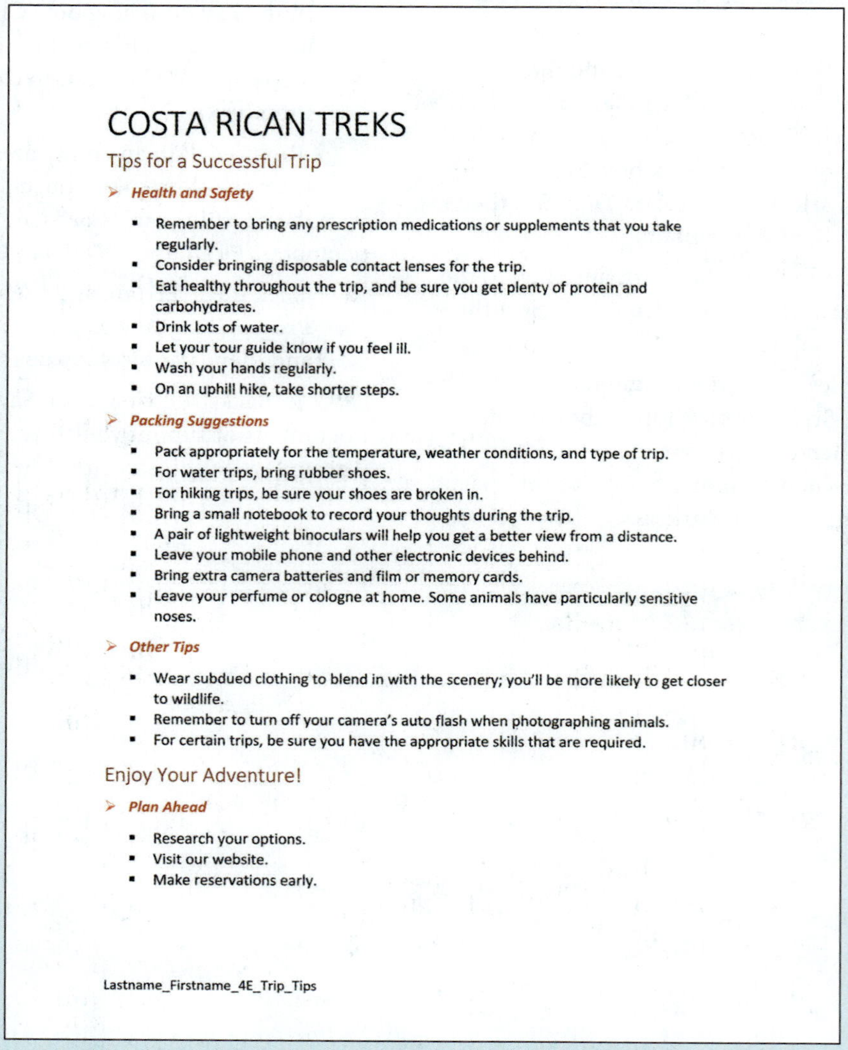

COSTA RICAN TREKS

Tips for a Successful Trip

➢ ***Health and Safety***

- Remember to bring any prescription medications or supplements that you take regularly.
- Consider bringing disposable contact lenses for the trip.
- Eat healthy throughout the trip, and be sure you get plenty of protein and carbohydrates.
- Drink lots of water.
- Let your tour guide know if you feel ill.
- Wash your hands regularly.
- On an uphill hike, take shorter steps.

➢ ***Packing Suggestions***

- Pack appropriately for the temperature, weather conditions, and type of trip.
- For water trips, bring rubber shoes.
- For hiking trips, be sure your shoes are broken in.
- Bring a small notebook to record your thoughts during the trip.
- A pair of lightweight binoculars will help you get a better view from a distance.
- Leave your mobile phone and other electronic devices behind.
- Bring extra camera batteries and film or memory cards.
- Leave your perfume or cologne at home. Some animals have particularly sensitive noses.

➢ ***Other Tips***

- Wear subdued clothing to blend in with the scenery; you'll be more likely to get closer to wildlife.
- Remember to turn off your camera's auto flash when photographing animals.
- For certain trips, be sure you have the appropriate skills that are required.

Enjoy Your Adventure!

➢ ***Plan Ahead***

- Research your options.
- Visit our website.
- Make reservations early.

Lastname_Firstname_4E_Trip_Tips

FIGURE 4.55

(Project 4E Trip Tips continues on the next page)

CONTENT-BASED ASSESSMENTS

1 Start Word. From your student files, open the document **w04E_Trip_Tips**. Save the file in your **Word Chapter 4** folder as **Lastname_Firstname_4E_Trip_Tips** Insert the file name in the footer.

2 Select the first paragraph—*Costa Rican Treks*. Apply the **Title** style, and then **Change Case** to UPPERCASE. Select the second paragraph that begins *Tips for*, apply the **Heading 2** style. Change the **Font Size** to **16**, change the **Font Color** to **Green, Accent 6, Darker 50%**—in the last column, the last color, and then change the **Spacing After** to **6 pt**. Display the **Styles** gallery, right-click **Heading 2**, and then click **Update Heading 2 to Match Selection**.

3 Near the bottom of **Page 1**, select the paragraph *Enjoy Your Adventure!* Apply the **Heading 2** style. Change the document **Theme** to **Celestial**.

4 Near the top of **Page 1**, select the third paragraph, *Health and Safety*. Apply **Italic** emphasis, and then change the **Font Color** to **Red, Accent 6, Darker 25%**—in the last column, the fifth color. With the text selected, display the **Styles** gallery. Click **Create a Style**, and then name the new style **Tip Heading** Apply the **Tip Heading** style to the paragraphs *Packing Suggestions*, *Other Tips*, and *Plan Ahead*. **Modify** the **Tip Heading** style by applying **Bold** emphasis.

5 Select the block of text beginning with *Health and Safety* and ending with *that are required* near the bottom of **Page 1**. Apply a **Multilevel List** with the ❖, ➤, • style. Select the paragraphs below each *Tip Heading* paragraph, and then **Increase Indent** one time.

6 Select the entire list, and then display the **Define New List Style** dialog box. Name the style **Tips List** Change the **1st level** to **Bullet: ➤** and set the color to **Red, Accent 6**—in the last column, the first color. Set the **2nd level** to **Bullet: ■**. Be sure the bullet ■ displays in black. Click **OK**.

7 At the bottom of **Page 1**, beginning with *Plan Ahead*, select the last four paragraphs. Apply the **Tips List** multilevel list style. Select the last three paragraphs, and then **Increase Indent** one time.

8 Click the **FILE tab**, and then click **Show All Properties**. In the **Tags** box, type **trip tips list** and then in the **Subject** box, type your course name and section number. If necessary, edit the author name to display your name.

9 Check your document in **Print Preview**, and then make any necessary corrections. **Save** the document, and then print the document or submit electronically as directed by your instructor. **Close** Word.

END | You have completed Project 4E

CONTENT-BASED ASSESSMENTS

Apply 4B skills from these Objectives:

5 Change the Style Set of a Document and Apply a Template

6 Insert a Chart and Enter Data into a Chart

7 Change a Chart Type

8 Format a Chart and Save a Chart as a Template

In the following Mastering Word project, you will create a document that provides frequently asked questions and includes a chart about hiking trips offered by Costa Rican Treks. Your completed documents will look similar to Figure 4.56.

PROJECT FILES

For Project 4F, you will need the following files:

w04F_Hiking_FAQ
w04F_Hiking_Styles

You will save your files as:

Lastname_Firstname_4F_Hiking_FAQ
Lastname_Firstname_4F_FAQ_Revised
Lastname_Firstname_4F_Rainfall_Chart– not shown in figure

PROJECT RESULTS

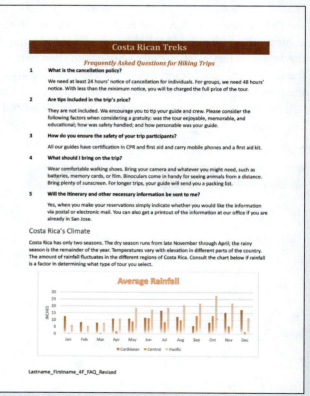

FIGURE 4.56

(Project 4F Hiking FAQ continues on the next page)

CONTENT-BASED ASSESSMENTS

1 ▸ Start Word. From your student files, open the file **w04F_Hiking_FAQ**, and then **Save** the document in your **Word Chapter 4** folder as **Lastname_Firstname_4F_Hiking_FAQ** Insert the file name in the footer.

2 ▸ Format the first paragraph *Costa Rican Treks* with the **Heading 1** style, and then change the **Font Size** to **18**. Select the second paragraph, and then apply the **Heading 2** style. Select the paragraph *Costa Rica's Climate*, and then apply the **Subtitle** style. Change the **Style Set** to **Basic (Stylish)**. Change the **Paragraph Spacing** style to **Compact**. Select all the numbered paragraphs, and then apply **Bold**. For each single paragraph following a numbered paragraph, click **Increase Indent** one time.

3 ▸ **Show All Properties**, add the tags **FAQ, hiking** Insert your course name and section number, and display your name as the author. **Save** your document.

4 ▸ Click the **FILE tab**, and then click **Save As**. **Save** the document to your **Word Chapter 4** folder as **Lastname_Firstname_4F_FAQ_Revised** In the footer, **Update Field**.

5 ▸ Display the **Word Options** dialog box, and then click **Customize Ribbon**. Display the **DEVELOPER tab**. Display the **Templates and Add-ins** dialog box, and then click **Attach**. From your student files, **Open** the file **w04F_Hiking_Styles**, and then **Automatically update document styles**. Hide the **DEVELOPER tab**.

6 ▸ Move the insertion point to the end of the document, and then press Enter. **Insert** a **Clustered Column** chart, and then beginning in cell **B1**, type the following data, pressing Tab to move from one cell to the next.

	Caribbean	Central	Pacific
Jan	12.5	0.4	6.3
Feb	8.3	0.2	5.7
Mar	8	0.5	8
Apr	10.9	1.7	11
May	11	8.9	18.9
Jun	11.7	11.3	17.5
Jul	16.8	8.5	18.9
Aug	12.3	9.8	20.9
Sep	5.7	13	22
Oct	8.2	13	27.7
Nov	15.4	5.6	22.3
Dec	17.5	1.6	11.6

7 ▸ With the chart range **A1** through **D13** selected, **Close** the worksheet. Select the text *Chart Title*, and then type **Average Rainfall** Display a **Primary Vertical Axis Title** with the title **Inches**

8 ▸ Change the **Chart Style** to **Style 9**, and then change the chart **Color** scheme to **Color 6**—under **Monochromatic**, in the second row, the orange color scheme. Format the chart title with the **WordArt** style **Fill – Orange, Accent 2, Outline – Accent 2**.

9 ▸ Display the **Layout** dialog box, and then change the **Absolute Height** of the chart **2.4"**. **Center** the chart horizontally on the page. **Save** the chart as a **chart template** in your **Word Chapter 4** folder as **Lastname_Firstname_4F_Rainfall_Chart**

10 ▸ **Show All Properties**, and then change the tags to **FAQ, final Save** your document. Print both documents or submit all three files electronically as directed by your instructor. **Close** Word.

END | You have completed Project 4F

CONTENT-BASED ASSESSMENTS

Mastering Word   Project 4G Expense Reduction

Apply 4A and 4B skills from these Objectives:

1 Apply and Modify Styles
2 Create New Styles
3 Manage Styles
4 Create a Multilevel List
5 Change the Style Set of a Document and Apply a Template
6 Insert a Chart and Enter Data into a Chart
7 Change a Chart Type
8 Format a Chart and Save a Chart as a Template

In the following Mastering Word project, you will create a memo that includes ideas for reducing expenses for Paulo Alvarez, Vice President of Finance for Costa Rican Treks. Your completed document will look similar to Figure 4.57.

PROJECT FILES

For Project 4G, you will need the following file:

w04G_Expense_Reduction

You will save your files as:

Lastname_Firstname_4G_Expense_Reduction
Lastname_Firstname_4G_Pie_Chart – not shown in figure

PROJECT RESULTS

FIGURE 4.57

(Project 4G Expense Reduction continues on the next page)

CONTENT-BASED ASSESSMENTS

1 Start Word. From your student files, open the file **w04G_Expense_Reduction**, and then save the document in your **Word Chapter 4** folder as **Lastname_Firstname_4G_Expense_Reduction** Insert the file name in the footer.

2 Apply the **Title** style to the first paragraph. Apply the **Strong** style to the second paragraph *Memo*, With *Memo* selected, change the **Font Size** to **26**, and then change the text to **UPPERCASE**. Select the text *TO:*—include the colon—and then apply **Bold** and change the **Font Color** to **Orange, Accent 2, Darker 25%**. Save the selection as a new style with the name **Memo Heading** Apply the **Memo Heading** style to the memo headings *FROM:*, *DATE:*, and *SUBJECT:*.

3 Change the **Style Set** to **Basic (Elegant)**, and then change the **Paragraph Spacing** style to **Relaxed**. On **Page 1**, beginning with the heading *TO:*, change the **Font Size** of all the remaining text in the document to **12**. Select the text on **Page 2**, and then apply a **Multilevel List** with the format **1., a., i**. For the paragraphs beginning *Mobile phone*, *Reduction*, *Focus*, *Research*, *Evaluate*, and *Utilize*, **Increase Indent** one time.

4 Select the entire list, and then display the **Define New List Style** dialog box. Name the style **Reduction List** Change the **2nd level** letter style to **A, B, C**.

5 Position the insertion point at the end of the document. Insert a **3-D Pie** chart. Type the following chart data:

	Projected Savings in Dollars
Employee	15,000
Operations	43,000
Marketing	26,000

6 Select the chart data range **A1** through **B4**, and then **Close** the worksheet. Apply the **Style 5** chart style. Display **Data Labels** in the **Center** position. Format the chart **Shape Outline** as **Orange, Accent 2, Darker 25%**. Display the **Legend** to the **Right** of the chart. **Center** the chart horizontally on the page.

7 **Save** the chart as a **Chart Template** in your **Word Chapter 4** folder as **Lastname_Firstname_4G_Pie_Chart**

8 **Show All Properties**. Add the tags **expenses, reduction** Add your course name and section number, and make sure your name displays as the author. Check your document in **Print Preview**, and then make any necessary corrections. **Save** your document. Print your document or submit both files as directed by your instructor. **Close** Word.

END | You have completed Project 4G

CONTENT-BASED ASSESSMENTS

GO! Fix It	Project 4H New Tours	Online
GO! Make It	Project 4I Newsletter	Online
GO! Solve It	Project 4J Fall Newsletter	Online
GO! Solve It	Project 4K Custom Adventure	

Apply a combination of the 4A and 4B skills.

PROJECT FILES

For Project 4K, you will need the following file:

w04K_Custom_Adventure

You will save your file as:

Lastname_Firstname_4K_Custom_Adventure

Open the file **w04K_Custom_Adventures** and save it in your **Word Chapter 4** folder as **Lastname_Firstname_4K_Custom_Adventure** Change the theme, and apply existing styles to the first two and last two paragraphs of the document. Create a new style for *Choose a Region*, and apply the style to *Choose Your Favorite Activities* and *Develop Your Skills*. Define a new multilevel list style and apply the style to all lists in the document. Adjust paragraph and text formats to display the information appropriately in a one-page document. Include the file name in the footer, add appropriate document properties, and print your document or submit electronically as directed by your instructor.

Performance Level

Performance Criteria		Exemplary: You consistently applied the relevant skills	Proficient: You sometimes, but not always, applied the relevant skills	Developing: You rarely or never applied the relevant skills
	Change theme and apply existing styles	All existing styles are applied correctly using an appropriate theme.	Existing styles are applied correctly but an appropriate theme is not used.	One or more styles are not applied correctly.
	Create a new style	A new style is created and applied correctly.	A new style is created but not applied correctly.	A new style is not created.
	Create a multilevel list	A multilevel list style is created and applied correctly.	A multilevel list style is applied correctly but the default style is used.	A multilevel list style is not applied correctly.
	Format attractively and appropriately	Document formatting is attractive and appropriate.	The document is adequately formatted but is unattractive or difficult to read.	The document is formatted inadequately.

END | You have completed Project 4K

OUTCOMES-BASED ASSESSMENTS

RUBRIC

The following outcomes-based assessments are *open-ended assessments*. That is, there is no specific correct result; your result will depend on your approach to the information provided. Make *Professional Quality* your goal. Use the following scoring rubric to guide you in *how* to approach the problem and then to evaluate *how well* your approach solves the problem.

The *criteria*—Software Mastery, Content, Format and Layout, and Process—represent the knowledge and skills you have gained that you can apply to solving the problem. The *levels of performance*—Professional Quality, Approaching Professional Quality, or Needs Quality Improvements—help you and your instructor evaluate your result.

	Your completed project is of Professional Quality if you:	Your completed project is Approaching Professional Quality if you:	Your completed project Needs Quality Improvements if you:
1-Software Mastery	Choose and apply the most appropriate skills, tools, and features and identify efficient methods to solve the problem.	Choose and apply some appropriate skills, tools, and features, but not in the most efficient manner.	Choose inappropriate skills, tools, or features, or are inefficient in solving the problem.
2-Content	Construct a solution that is clear and well organized, contains content that is accurate, appropriate to the audience and purpose, and is complete. Provide a solution that contains no errors in spelling, grammar, or style.	Construct a solution in which some components are unclear, poorly organized, inconsistent, or incomplete. Misjudge the needs of the audience. Have some errors in spelling, grammar, or style, but the errors do not detract from comprehension.	Construct a solution that is unclear, incomplete, or poorly organized; contains some inaccurate or inappropriate content; and contains many errors in spelling, grammar, or style. Do not solve the problem.
3-Format & Layout	Format and arrange all elements to communicate information and ideas, clarify function, illustrate relationships, and indicate relative importance.	Apply appropriate format and layout features to some elements, but not others. Overuse features, causing minor distraction.	Apply format and layout that does not communicate information or ideas clearly. Do not use format and layout features to clarify function, illustrate relationships, or indicate relative importance. Use available features excessively, causing distraction.
4-Process	Use an organized approach that integrates planning, development, self-assessment, revision, and reflection.	Demonstrate an organized approach in some areas, but not others; or, use an insufficient process of organization throughout.	Do not use an organized approach to solve the problem.

OUTCOMES-BASED ASSESSMENTS

Apply a combination of the **4A** and **4B** skills.

Build from Scratch

GO! Think   Project 4L Training Memo

PROJECT FILES

For Project 4L, you will need the following file:

New blank Word document

You will save your files as:

Lastname_Firstname_4L_Training_Chart
Lastname_Firstname_4L_Training_Memo

Alberto Ramos, Tour Operations Manager, wants to send a memo to all tour guides concerning upcoming training opportunities.

Date	Training	Location	Length
June 6	Horseback Riding	Barbille Stables	4 hours
June 17	Orienteering	Manuel Antonio Park	8 hours
June 29	Basic Coastal Sailing	Playa Hermosa	6 hours
July 7	White Water Rafting	Pacuare River	5 hours

Using this information, create the memo. Include a custom multilevel list for the four training sessions. Insert a chart to compare class length. Format the entire memo in a manner that is professional and easy to read and understand. Save the chart template as **Lastname_Firstname_4L_Training_Chart** Save the document as **Lastname_Firstname_4L_Training_Memo** Insert the file name in the footer and add appropriate document properties. Print your document or submit both files electronically as directed by your instructor.

END | You have completed Project 4L

Build from Scratch

GO! Think   Project 4M Waterfalls Handout   Online

Build from Scratch

You and GO!   Project 4N Cover Letter   Online

Using Advanced Table Features

GO! to Work
Video W5

PROJECT 5A	**OUTCOMES** Use advanced table features such as custom table styles, sort, and properties.

OBJECTIVES

1. Create and Apply a Custom Table Style
2. Format Cells
3. Use Advanced Table Features
4. Modify Table Properties

PROJECT 5B	**OUTCOMES** Create a custom table that includes a nested table and an Excel spreadsheet.

OBJECTIVES

5. Draw a Freeform Table
6. Use Nested Tables
7. Insert an Excel Spreadsheet

JackF/Fotolia

In This Chapter

A table provides a convenient way to organize text. In addition to using the Table command, there are other methods for inserting a table in a document. For example, you can draw a table, convert existing text into a table format, or insert Excel spreadsheets. You can insert formulas in a table to perform calculations on numerical data. Formatting a table makes data easier to read and provides a professional appearance. You can create and apply custom table styles, merge and split cells, and change the way text displays within the cells. The Organizer allows you to copy custom styles from one document to another.

The projects in this chapter relate to **Chesterfield Creations**, a manufacturer of high-quality leather and fabric accessories for men and women. Products include wallets, belts, handbags, key chains, backpacks, business cases, laptop sleeves, and travel bags. The Toronto-based company distributes its products to department stores and specialty shops throughout the United States and Canada. Chesterfield Creations also has a website from which over 60 percent of its products are sold. The company pays shipping costs for both delivery and returns, and bases its operating philosophy on exceptional customer service.

Product Summary

MyITLab®
Project 5A Training

PROJECT ACTIVITIES

In Activities 5.01 through 5.12, you will create, modify, and format tables containing new product information to produce a document that will be distributed to the Chesterfield Creations sales team. Chesterfield Creations is introducing new products for the spring season. Charles Ferguson, Marketing Vice President, has asked you to create a document that summarizes the new product lines. Your completed document will look similar to Figure 5.1.

PROJECT FILES

For Project 5A, you will need the following files:

w05A_Product_Summary
w05A_Custom_Styles

You will save your file as:

Lastname_Firstname_5A_Product_Summary

PROJECT RESULTS

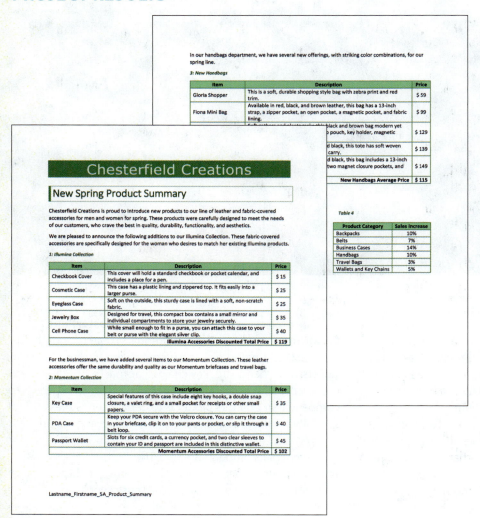

FIGURE 5.1 Project 5A Product Summary

Video W5-1

N O T E   **If You Are Using a Touchscreen**

- Tap an item to click it.
- Press and hold for a few seconds to right-click; release when the information or command displays.
- Touch the screen with two or more fingers and then pinch together to zoom in or stretch your fingers apart to zoom out.
- Slide your finger on the screen to scroll—slide left to scroll right and slide right to scroll left.
- Slide to rearrange—similar to dragging with a mouse.
- Swipe from edge: from right to display charms; from left to expose open apps, snap apps, or close apps; from top or bottom to show commands or close an app.
- Swipe to select—slide an item a short distance with a quick movement to select an item and bring up commands, if any.

Objective 1   Create and Apply a Custom Table Style

Recall that a *style* is a group of formatting commands—such as font, font size, and font color—that can be applied with a single command. Styles in an existing document can be copied to another document. You can create a *table style* and apply it repeatedly to give your tables a consistent format. A table style can include formatting for the entire table and specific table elements, such as rows and columns. You can use the *Split Table* feature to divide an existing table into two tables in which the selected row—where the insertion point is located—becomes the first row of the second table.

Activity 5.01   Using the Organizer to Manage Styles

You can copy styles using the *Organizer*—a dialog box where you can modify a document by using styles stored in another document or template.

1 Start Word. From your student files, locate and open the file **w05A_Product_Summary**. If necessary, display the rulers and formatting marks. If any words are flagged as spelling or grammar errors, right-click, and then click **Ignore All**.

2 Press F12 to display the **Save As** dialog box. Navigate to the location where you are saving your files for this chapter. Create a new folder named **Word Chapter 5** and then **Save** the document as **Lastname_Firstname_5A_Product_Summary** Right-click in the footer area, and then click **Edit Footer**. Under **HEADER & FOOTER TOOLS**, on the **DESIGN tab**, in the **Insert group**, click **Document Info**, and then click **File Name**. **Close** the footer area.

3 Press Ctrl + Home. Click the **FILE tab** to display **Backstage** view, and then click **Options**. In the **Word Options** dialog box, click **Add-Ins**.

4 At the bottom of the **Word Options** dialog box, click the **Manage box arrow**, and then click **Templates**. Compare your screen with Figure 5.2.

FIGURE 5.2

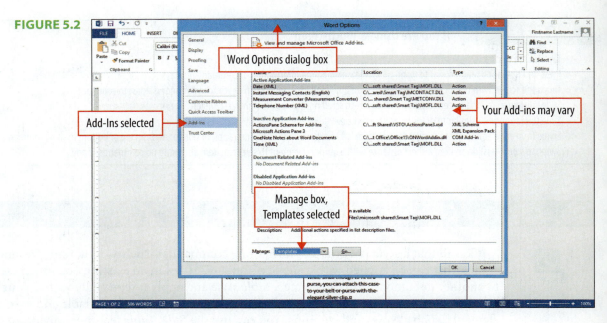

5 ▶ To the right of the **Manage** box, click **Go**.

6 ▶ In the **Templates and Add-ins** dialog box, at the bottom left, click **Organizer**.

7 ▶ On the left side of the **Organizer** dialog box, be sure that *Lastname_Firstname_5A_Product_Summary (Document)* displays in the **Styles available in** box. On the right side of the dialog box, click **Close File**. Notice the button changes to an **Open File** button.

8 ▶ Click **Open File**, navigate to your student files, select the file **w05A_Custom_Styles**, and then click **Open**. Compare your screen with Figure 5.3.

The styles stored in the *w05A_Custom_Styles (Template)* display on the right side of the dialog box.

FIGURE 5.3

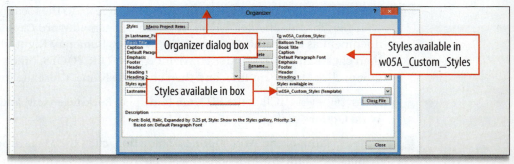

9 ▶ In the top right box, scroll down, and then click **Heading 2**. Press and hold Ctrl, scroll down, and then click **Title**.

You can select one or more styles that you want to copy to another document. In this case, two styles are selected.

10 ▶ In the center of the **Organizer** dialog box, click **Copy**. If a message box displays asking if you want to overwrite the existing style entry **Heading 2**, click **Yes to All**. Click **Close** to close the dialog box. Compare your screen with Figure 5.4.

The Heading 2 and Title styles are copied to your *Lastname_Firstname_5A_Product_Summary* document.

FIGURE 5.4

Heading 2 and Title styles

Activity 5.02 | Creating a Table Style and Splitting a Table

When you create a table style, you can apply formats, such as borders, to the entire table and add special formats to individual parts of the table, such as bold emphasis and shading to specific cells. Creating a table style saves time when formatting multiple tables and provides a uniform appearance.

1 Select the first paragraph of the document—the company name *Chesterfield Creations*. On the **HOME tab**, in the **Styles group**, click **Title**.

2 Select the second paragraph that begins *New Spring*, and then in the **Styles group**, click **Heading 2**. Click anywhere in the third paragraph, and then compare your screen with Figure 5.5.

FIGURE 5.5

Title and Heading 2 styles applied

3 On the **HOME tab**, in the **Styles group**, click the **Dialog Box Launcher** to display the **Styles** pane.

4 At the bottom of the **Styles** pane, click the **New Style** button. In the **Create New Style from Formatting** dialog box, under **Properties**, in the **Name** box, type **Chesterfield Creations** Click the **Style type arrow**, and then click **Table**.

A sample table displays in the preview area. You can create a new style to apply a set of formats to a table by using the Create New Style from Formatting dialog box.

5 Under **Formatting**, click the **Border button arrow**, and then click **All Borders**. Click the **Line Weight arrow** , and then click **1 pt**. Click the **Border Color arrow** , and then under **Theme Colors**, in the last column, click the fifth color— **Green, Accent 6, Darker 25%**. Compare your screen with Figure 5.6.

Notice that under *Formatting*, in the *Apply formatting to* box, the formatting will be applied to the whole table. By default, notice at the bottom of the dialog box that this style is available only in this document.

FIGURE 5.6

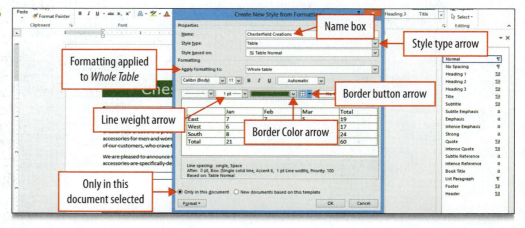

Formatting applied to *Whole Table*

Name box

Style type arrow

Border button arrow

Line weight arrow

Border Color arrow

Only in this document selected

6 Click **OK** to close the dialog box, and then **Close** ☒ the **Styles** pane.

7 In the seventh row of the first table, click to position the insertion point in the first cell that contains the text *Item*. Under **TABLE TOOLS**, on the **LAYOUT tab**, in the **Merge group**, click **Split Table**.

> The original table is divided into two separate tables and a new, blank paragraph is inserted above the second table.

8 If necessary, position the insertion point in the blank paragraph above the second table, and then press ⎆Enter. Type **For the businessman, we have added several items to our Momentum Collection. These leather accessories offer the same durability and quality as our Momentum briefcases and travel bags.**

 BY TOUCH Tap in the blank paragraph, and then on the taskbar, tap the Touch Keyboard button. Tap the appropriate keys to type the text, and then on the Touch Keyboard, tap the X button.

9 Save 🖫 your changes.

More Knowledge **Creating a Custom Table Style from the Table Styles Gallery**

If the insertion point is in an existing table, you can create a custom table style from the Table Styles gallery. Under TABLE TOOLS, on the DESIGN tab, in the Table Styles group, click More, and then click New Table Style to display the Create New Style from Formatting dialog box.

Activity 5.03 | Applying and Modifying a Table Style

You can apply a table style to an existing table. Additionally, you can modify an existing style or make formatting changes after a style has been applied to a table.

1 Display the first table in the document, and then click in the top left cell that contains the text *Item*.

> You can apply a table style when the insertion point is positioned anywhere within a table.

2 Under **TABLE TOOLS**, on the **DESIGN tab**, in the **Table Styles group**, click **More** ⊽.

3 In the **Table Styles** gallery, under **Custom**, point to the style. Notice that the ScreenTip—*Chesterfield Creations*—displays.

4 Click the **Chesterfield Creations** style to apply the table style to the table. Compare your screen with Figure 5.7.

FIGURE 5.7

Table style applied to table

5 ▶ Scroll as necessary, and then click to position the insertion point anywhere in the second table of the document—the table is split, displaying across two pages. Under **TABLE TOOLS**, on the **DESIGN tab**, in the **Table Styles group**, click **More** ⌄, and then under **Custom**, click **Chesterfield Creations**.

In the Table Styles group, at the extreme left, the *Chesterfield Creations* table style displays.

6 ▶ In the **Table Styles** gallery, right-click the **Chesterfield Creations** style. A shortcut menu displays several options for working with styles as described in the table in Figure 5.8.

FIGURE 5.8

TABLE STYLE OPTIONS	
STYLE OPTION	**DESCRIPTION**
Apply (and Clear Formatting)	Table style applied; text formatting reverts to Normal style
Apply and Maintain Formatting	Table style applied, including text formatting
New Table Style	Option to create a new, custom table style
Modify Table Style	Option to edit the table style
Delete Table Style	Removes the style from the Table Styles gallery
Set as Default	Style is used as the default for all tables created in the document
Add Gallery to Quick Access Toolbar	Table Styles gallery is added to the Quick Access Toolbar

7 ▶ From the shortcut menu, click **Modify Table Style**. In the **Modify Style** dialog box, under **Formatting**, click the **Apply formatting to arrow**, and then click **Header row**.

You can apply formatting to specific table elements. In the *Chesterfield Creations* style, you want to change formats that only apply to the *header row*—the first row of a table containing column titles.

8 ▶ Click **Bold** B , and then click the **Fill Color arrow** No Color ⌄ . Under **Theme Colors**, in the last column, click the fourth color—**Green, Accent 6, Lighter 40%**. Compare your screen with Figure 5.9.

FIGURE 5.9

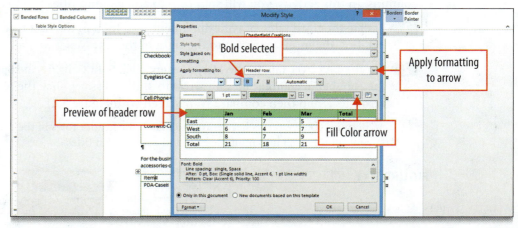

9 ▶ Click **OK** to close the dialog box, and then press Ctrl + Home. On the **VIEW tab**, in the **Zoom group**, click **Multiple Pages**. Compare your screen with Figure 5.10.

The additional formatting has been applied to the header rows in the first and second tables.

FIGURE 5.10

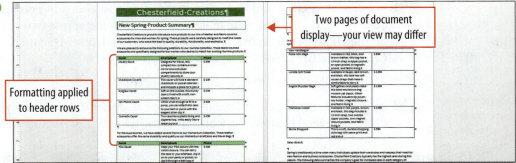

On the **VIEW tab**, in the **Zoom group**, click **100%**, and then **Save** 🖫 your changes.

More Knowledge | **Repeating Header Rows**

When a table is large enough to cause part of the table to display on a second page, the header row of the table can be repeated on the second page. With the insertion point in the header row, on the LAYOUT tab, in the Table group, click Properties. In the Table Properties dialog box, click the Row tab, and then under Options, click *Repeat as header row at the top of each page*.

Objective 2   Format Cells

Video W5-2

Special formatting features that are unavailable for use with paragraph text are available in tables. For example, you can combine or divide cells and adjust the positioning of text.

Activity 5.04 | Merging and Splitting Cells

You can *merge* or *split* cells to change the structure of a table. Merging is the process of combining two or more adjacent cells into one cell so that the text spans across multiple columns or rows. Splitting divides selected cells into multiple cells with a specified number of rows and columns. In this activity, you will split cells to add column titles to a header row.

1. Locate the third table of your document, and then in the first row, in the first cell, click to position the insertion point to the right of the text *New Handbags*.

2. On the **LAYOUT tab**, in the **Merge group**, click **Split Cells**. In the **Split Cells** dialog box, click the **Number of columns up spin arrow** to **3**. If necessary, click the **Number of rows down spin arrow** to **1**, and then compare your screen with Figure 5.11.

   Because you want this header row to match the header rows in the other two product tables, you will split the cell into multiple cells and add column titles.

FIGURE 5.11

3. Click **OK** to close the dialog box. Notice that the selected cell has been split into three cells.

   When splitting a cell that contains text, the text is automatically moved to the top left cell created by the division. When you change the structure of a table, some formatting features may be removed.

4 In the first cell of the header row, select the existing text *New Handbags*, and then type **Item** Press `Tab` to move to the second cell of the header row, and then type **Description** Press `Tab`, and then in the last cell of the header row type **Price** Under **TABLE TOOLS**, on the **DESIGN tab**, in the **Table Styles group**, click **More** ⏷. In the **Table Styles** gallery, under **Custom**, click **Chesterfield Creations**. **Save** 🖫 your changes, and then compare your screen with Figure 5.12.

FIGURE 5.12

More Knowledge | **Splitting Multiple Cells**

You can modify the number of rows or columns for any group of adjacent cells in a table. Select the cells you want to modify, and then on the LAYOUT tab, in the Merge group, click Split Cells. In the Split Cells dialog box, change the number of columns or rows to the desired values.

Activity 5.05 | Positioning Text within Cells

You can align text horizontally—left, center, or right—and vertically—top, center, or bottom—within cells. The default setting is to align text at the top left of a cell. Changing cell alignments creates a table with a professional appearance.

1 Locate the first table in your document, and then select the **header row**. On the **LAYOUT tab**, in the **Alignment group**, click **Align Center** 🔲.

All text in the header row is centered horizontally and vertically within the cell.

2 Below the header row, select all the cells in the first and second columns, and then in the **Alignment group**, click **Align Center Left** 🔲.

The selected text is left aligned and centered vertically within the cells.

3 Below the header row, select all the cells in the third column, and then in the **Alignment group**, click **Align Center** 🔲. Deselect the text, and then compare your screen with Figure 5.13.

FIGURE 5.13

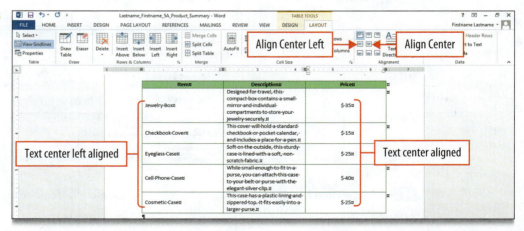

4 Using the technique you just practiced, format the **header row** in the second and third tables to match the formatting of the header row in the first table—**Align Center** 🔲. In the second and third tables, **Align Center Left** 🔲 the first and second columns below the header row, and then **Align Center** 🔲 the text in the third column below the header row. Deselect the text, and then **Save** 🖫 your changes.

Video W5-3

Word tables have some capabilities similar to those in an Excel spreadsheet—for example, sorting data and performing simple calculations. Additionally, you can convert existing text to a table format and resize tables in several ways.

Activity 5.06 | Sorting Tables by Category

In this activity, you will sort the data in the three product tables by price and item to make it easier for the sales team to reference specific items.

1 Scroll as necessary to display the entire contents of the first table in the document, and then position the insertion point anywhere in the table.

Recall that data in a table can be sorted in ascending—from the smallest to the largest number or from A to Z order—or descending order—from the largest to the smallest number or from Z to A order. Regardless of the columns that are selected in the sort, all cells in each row are moved to keep the data intact.

2 On the **LAYOUT tab**, in the **Data group**, click **Sort**.

The Sort dialog box allows you to sort text alphabetically, by number, or by date. The Sort feature can be applied to entire tables, selected data within tables, paragraphs, or body text that is separated by characters, such as tabs or commas. You can sort information using a maximum of three columns.

3 In the **Sort** dialog box, under **Sort by**, click the **Sort by arrow**, and then click **Price**. Compare your screen with Figure 5.14.

You are sorting the data in the table by the product's price. When a table has a header row, Word displays each column's header text in the Sort by list. By default, the Header row option is selected at the bottom left of the Sort dialog box. If a table does not have a header row, select the No header row option button. Without a header row, the sort options for a table will display as *Column 1*, *Column 2*, and so on.

Because the Price column contains numbers, the Type box displays *Number*. When working in tables, the Using box displays the default *Paragraphs*.

FIGURE 5.14

Sort by set to *Price*
Type set to *Number*
Using set to *Paragraphs*
Header row selected

4 Under **Then by**, click the **Then by arrow**, and then click **Item**. Notice that the **Type** box displays *Text*.

It is important to designate the columns in the order that you want them sorted. Word will first sort the data by price in ascending order. If two or more items have the same price, Word will arrange those items in alphabetical order.

5 Click **OK** to close the dialog box and notice that the two items with the same price of **$ 25** are listed in alphabetical order. Deselect the table, and then compare your screen with Figure 5.15.

FIGURE 5.15

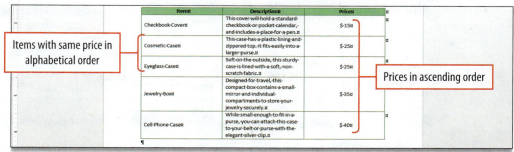

Items with same price in alphabetical order

Prices in ascending order

6 ▸ Click to position the insertion point anywhere in the second table of the document. On the **LAYOUT tab**, click **Sort**.

> The Sort by box displays *Price*, and the Then by box displays *Item*. In the Sort dialog box, Word retains the last sort options used in a document.

7 ▸ Click **OK**, and notice that the table is sorted similarly to the first table.

8 ▸ Click to position the insertion point anywhere in the third table of the document. On the **LAYOUT tab**, click **Sort**, and then click **OK**. Notice that the table is sorted in the same manner as the previous tables.

9 ▸ Deselect the table, and then **Save** 🖫 your changes.

Activity 5.07 | Converting Text to a Table and Modifying Fonts within a Table

To improve the appearance of a document, you can convert existing text, such as a list of information, to a table. In this activity, you will convert text to a table so that you can apply the same table style used for the other tables of the document.

1 ▸ Scroll as necessary, and then immediately below the third table, select the paragraph *Sales Goals*. On the mini toolbar, change the **Font Size** to **14**, apply **Bold** [B], and then change the **Font Color** [A ▾] to **Green, Accent 6, Darker 25%**—in the last column, the fifth color. Press [Ctrl] + [E] to center the paragraph.

2 ▸ Beginning with the paragraph that begins *Product Category*, drag down to select all the remaining text in the document. Be sure to include the text on *Page 3*—you should have seven paragraphs selected.

3 ▸ On the **INSERT tab**, in the **Tables group**, click **Table**, and then click **Convert Text to Table** to display the **Convert Text to Table** dialog box. Compare your screen with Figure 5.16.

> Word uses characters such as tabs, commas, or hyphens to determine the number of columns. The selected text consists of seven paragraphs—or rows—with each paragraph containing a single tab. By default, Word uses the tab formatting mark to separate each paragraph into two parts—forming the two columns of the table. Under the Separate text at section of the dialog box, you can define the character Word uses to separate the text into columns. You can also change the number of columns or rows, based on the text you are converting.

FIGURE 5.16

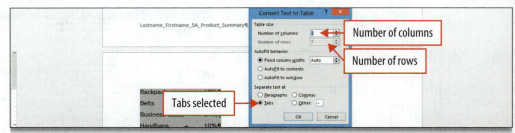

4 Click **OK** to close the dialog box.

Word creates a table that contains two columns and seven rows. The table is split, displaying across two pages.

5 With the table selected, on the **HOME tab**, in the **Font group**, click the **Font arrow** Calibri (Body), and then click **Calibri (Body)**.

6 Save 💾 your changes.

More Knowledge | **Converting a Table to Text**

To convert an existing table to text, on the LAYOUT tab, in the Data group, click Convert to Text, and then in the Convert Table to Text dialog box, select the type of text separator you want to use.

Activity 5.08 | Defining the Dimensions of a Table and Setting AutoFit Options

Word provides several methods for resizing a table. The ***AutoFit*** feature automatically adjusts column widths or the width of the entire table. ***AutoFit Contents*** resizes the column widths to accommodate the maximum field size. You can change a row height or column width by dragging a border, or designating specific width and height settings. To improve the overall appearance of the document, you will modify column widths.

1 In the first table in the document, point to the top border of the first column—*Item*—and when the ⬇ pointer displays, click to select the entire column. On the **LAYOUT tab**, in the **Cell Size group**, click the **Width down spin arrow** to **1.5"**. Select the second column in the table—*Description*—and then in the **Cell Size group**, click the **Width up spin arrow** to **4.5"**. Select the last column in the table—*Price*—and then in the **Cell Size group**, click the **Width down spin arrow** to **0.5"**. Deselect the column, and then compare your screen with Figure 5.17.

FIGURE 5.17

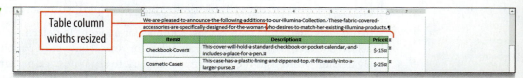

2 In the second and third tables of the document, using the technique you just practiced, change the **Width** of the first column to **1.5"**, the **Width** of the second column to **4.5"**, and the **Width** of the third column to **0.5"**.

All product tables have the same structure—the first, second, and third column widths in all tables are identical.

3 Below the second table, click to position the insertion point to the left of the paragraph that begins *In our handbags department*, and then press Ctrl + Enter to insert a page break.

4 ▸ Click to position your insertion point anywhere in the last table of the document. On the **LAYOUT tab**, in the **Cell Size group**, click **AutoFit**, and then click **AutoFit Contents**. Compare your screen with Figure 5.18.

AutoFit Contents resizes a table by changing the column widths to fit the existing data. In this table, the widths of both columns were decreased.

FIGURE 5.18

5 ▸ Click to position the insertion point anywhere in the table, and then under **TABLE TOOLS**, on the **DESIGN tab**, in the **Table Styles group**, click **More** ▾. In the **Table Styles** gallery, under **Custom**, click **Chesterfield Creations**.

6 ▸ Select the **header row**, and then on the **LAYOUT tab**, in the **Alignment group**, click **Align Center** ▤. Select the remaining cells in the second column, and then click **Align Center** ▤. **Save** 🖫 your changes.

More **Knowledge** | **Using the Sizing Handle**

At the lower right of a table, drag the sizing handle to change the entire table to the desired size.

Activity 5.09 | Using Formulas in Tables and Creating Custom Field Formats

To perform simple calculations, you can insert a ***formula*** in a table. A formula is a mathematical expression that contains ***functions***, operators, constants, and properties, and returns a value to a cell. A function is a predefined formula that performs calculations by using specific values in a particular order. Word includes a limited number of built-in functions—for example, SUM and AVERAGE.

1 ▸ Click anywhere in the first table of the document, and then point to the bottom left corner of the table to display the **One-Click Row/Column Insertion** button ⊕. Compare your screen with Figure 5.19.

The One-Click Row/Column Insertion button provides a quick method to insert a row or column in a table.

FIGURE 5.19

2 ▸ Click the **One-Click Row/Column Insertion** button ⊕ to insert a new row at the bottom of the table.

 **ANOTHER WAY** | On the LAYOUT tab, in the Rows & Columns group, click Insert Below.

3 In the new row, select the first two cells, and then on the **LAYOUT tab**, in the **Merge group**, click **Merge Cells**. In the merged cell, type **Illumina Accessories Total Price** Select the text, and then on the mini toolbar, apply **Bold** B . On the **LAYOUT tab**, in the **Alignment group**, click **Align Center Right** . Press Tab to move to the last cell in the table. Compare your screen with Figure 5.20.

FIGURE 5.20

4 On the **LAYOUT tab**, in the **Data group**, click **Formula**. In the **Formula** dialog box, under **Number format**, click the **Number format arrow**, and then click **#,##0**. Click to position the insertion point to the left of the Number format text, and then type **$** Compare your screen with Figure 5.21.

The Formula dialog box contains the default formula =SUM(ABOVE). All formulas begin with an equal sign = . This formula includes the SUM function and calculates the total of the numbers in all of the cells above the current cell—up to the first empty cell or a cell that contains text—and places the result in the current cell. You can specify a special number format—in this case a whole number preceded by a dollar sign.

FIGURE 5.21

5 Click **OK** to close the dialog box. Notice that *$ 140*—the sum of the prices for the Illumina accessories—displays in the active cell.

A formula is a type of *field*—a placeholder for data. The displayed number is a formula field representing the value calculated by the formula.

6 Select the inserted text, and then on the mini toolbar, apply **Bold** B .

7 Position the insertion point anywhere in the second table. Point to the lower left border of the table, and then click the **One-Click Row/Column Insertion** button . In the new row, select the first two cells, right-click and then from the shortcut menu, click **Merge Cells**. In the merged cell, type **Momentum Accessories Total Price** and then apply **Bold** B and **Align Center Right** . Press Tab .

8 On the **LAYOUT tab**, in the **Data group**, click **Formula**. In the **Formula** dialog box, under **Number format**, click the **Number format arrow**, and then click **#,##0**. Click to position the insertion point to the left of the Number format text, and then type **$** Click **OK**. Compare your screen with Figure 5.22.

The sum of the prices for the Momentum accessories—*$ 120*—displays in the active cell.

FIGURE 5.22

9 ▶ Select the inserted text, and then on the mini toolbar, apply **Bold** [B].

10 ▶ In the third table of the document, use the technique you practiced to insert a new row at the bottom of the table. In the new row, select the first two cells, and then using any technique you practiced, **Merge Cells**. In the merged cell, type **New Handbags Average Price** and then apply **Bold** [B] and **Align Center Right** [≣].

11 ▶ Press [Tab] to position the insertion point in the last cell of the table, and then click **Formula**. In the **Formula** dialog box, in the **Formula** box, delete the existing text, and then type = Under **Paste function**, click the **Paste function arrow**, and then click **AVERAGE**. In the **Formula** box, notice that =*AVERAGE* displays followed by *()*. With the insertion point between the left and right parentheses, type **ABOVE**

> You can use the Paste function box to specify a built-in function—such as AVERAGE, PRODUCT, MIN, the minimum value in a list, or MAX, the maximum value in a list. By typing *ABOVE*, the calculation includes all of the values listed above the current cell in the table. You are using the AVERAGE function to calculate the average price of the new handbags.

12 ▶ In the **Formula** dialog box, under **Number format**, click the **Number format arrow**, and then click **#,##0**. Click to position the insertion point to the left of the Number format text, and then type **$** Compare your screen with Figure 5.23.

FIGURE 5.23

13 ▶ Click **OK** to close the **Formula** dialog box. Select the inserted text, and then apply **Bold** [B]. **Save** [💾] your changes.

> The average price of the five handbags—*$ 117*—displays in the active cell.

More Knowledge | **Inserting Rows and Columns in a Table**

To insert a new row in an existing table, point to the left of the border between two existing rows, and then click the One-Click Row/Column Insertion button. To insert a new column, point above the border between two existing columns, and then click the One-Click Row/Column Insertion button. To insert a column at the extreme right of the table, point to the top right corner of the table, and then click the One-Click Row/Column Insertion button.

Activity 5.10 | Updating Formula Fields in Tables

You can edit an existing formula in a table. Additionally, if a value is changed in a table, it is necessary to manually update the field containing the formula.

1 ▶ In the first table, in the last row, click to position the insertion point to the left of *Total*, type **Discounted** and then press [Spacebar]. Press [Tab], right-click the selection, and then from the shortcut menu, click **Edit Field**. In the **Field** dialog box, under **Field properties**, click **Formula**.

2 ▶ In the **Formula** dialog box, in the **Formula** box, be sure the insertion point displays to the right of the formula =*SUM(ABOVE)*, and then type ***.85** Compare your screen with Figure 5.24.

> Formulas are not restricted to the built-in functions. You can also create your own. Customers purchasing the entire accessories collection receive a 15 percent discount. The modified formula reflects this discounted price. The total price is multiplied by 85 percent (.85), representing 100 percent minus the 15 percent discount.

FIGURE 5.24

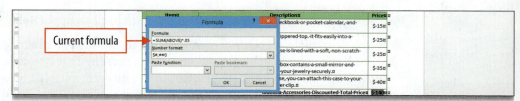

Current formula

3 Click **OK**, and notice that a new, lower value—*$ 119*—displays in the active cell.

4 In the second table, in the last row, click to position the insertion point to the left of *Total*, type **Discounted** and then press Spacebar. Press Tab, right-click the selection, and then from the shortcut menu, click **Edit Field**. In the **Field** dialog box, under **Field properties**, click **Formula**.

5 In the **Formula** dialog box, in the **Formula** box, click to position the insertion point to the right of the displayed formula *=SUM(ABOVE)*, if necessary, and then type ***.85** Click **OK**.

The discounted total for the Momentum accessories—*$ 102*—displays in the active cell.

6 In the third table, in the last column, below the header row, click in the third cell—the price of the Angela Shoulder Bag. Select only the number *139*, and then type **129**

Unlike Excel, when you change a value that is used in a formula, the resulting calculation is not automatically updated.

7 In the bottom right cell of the table, select the text. Right-click the selection, and then from the shortcut menu, click **Update Field**.

The value *$ 115* displays in the active cell and represents a formula field. If a number used in the calculation is changed, you must use the Update Field command to recalculate the value.

8 **Save** 🖫 your changes.

> **N O T E** **Summing Rows**
>
> The default formula is =SUM(ABOVE), assuming the cell above the selected cell contains a number. If there is a number in the cell to the left of the selected cell and no number in the cell above, the default is =SUM(LEFT). If you want to sum the entire range, be sure to avoid leaving a cell empty within a range. If there is no value, then enter a 0.

Activity 5.11 | Adding Captions, Excluding Labels from Captions, and Setting Caption Positions

Captions are titles that can be added to Word objects; Word numbers them sequentially as they are added to the document. You can add a caption to each table in a document to make it easier to refer to specific tables in the body text.

1 Click to position the insertion point anywhere in the first table. On the **REFERENCES tab**, in the **Captions group**, click **Insert Caption**.

Because the object selected is a table, in the Caption box, the default caption *Table 1* displays. Word automatically numbers objects sequentially. If the selected object is not a table, you can change the object type by clicking the Label arrow in the Caption dialog box.

2 In the **Caption** dialog box, select the **Exclude label from caption** check box.

The label *Table* is removed, and only the number *1* displays in the Caption box.

3 In the **Caption** box, to the right of *1,* type **:** and press Spacebar, and then type **Illumina Collection** If necessary, under **Options**, click the **Position arrow**, and then click **Above selected item**. Compare your screen with Figure 5.25.

You can adjust the position of a caption to display above or below the document element. In this case, the caption is set to display above the table.

FIGURE 5.25

4 ▶ Click **OK** to close the **Caption** dialog box. Notice that the caption displays above the table.

5 ▶ Using the technique you just practiced, add captions to the second and third tables. For the second table caption, insert the caption **2: Momentum Collection** above the table, and then for the third table, insert the caption **3: New Handbags** above the table.

6 ▶ **Save** 🖫 your changes.

Objective 4 Modify Table Properties

Video W5-4

Tables, like all other Word objects, have properties that can be altered. For example, you can change how text wraps around tables and define cell spacing. Modifying table properties can improve the overall appearance of your document.

Activity 5.12 │ Wrapping Text around Tables and Changing Caption Formats

If you have a long document with several tables and body text, you can apply text wrapping to have the text flow around the table. This can create a shorter document and improve the overall appearance of the document.

1 ▶ In the last table of the document, click anywhere in the table, and then point to the upper left corner of the table to display the **table move handle** ⊞. Drag the table until the top border is aligned with the top of the paragraph that begins *Spring is*, and the right border is at approximately **6.5 inches on the horizontal ruler**. Deselect the table, and then compare your screen with Figure 5.26. If your table position does not match the figure, click **Undo** ↻ and begin again.

FIGURE 5.26

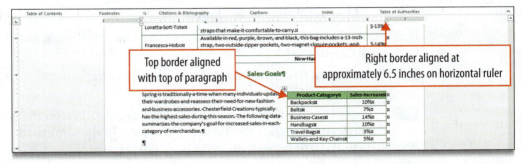

2 ▶ Click to position the insertion point anywhere in the table. On the **LAYOUT tab**, in the **Table group**, click **Properties**. In the **Table Properties** dialog box, on the **Table tab**, under **Text wrapping**, be sure **Around** is selected, and then click **Positioning**. In the **Table Positioning** dialog box, under **Distance from surrounding text**, click the **Left up spin arrow** to **0.5"**. Compare your screen with Figure 5.27.

You can define how close existing text displays in relation to the top, bottom, left, or right of a table. By changing the Left box value to 0.5", the text will display one-half inch from the left border of the table.

FIGURE 5.27

3 ▸ Click **OK** two times to close the dialog boxes.

4 ▸ With the insertion point in the table, on the **REFERENCES tab**, in the **Captions group**, click **Insert Caption**. In the **Caption** dialog box, clear the **Exclude label from caption** check box. With *Table 4* displayed in the **Caption** box and *Above selected item* displayed in the **Position** box, click **OK** to close the dialog box and insert the caption at the left margin.

5 ▸ Select the caption. On the mini toolbar, change the **Font Size** to **10**, apply **Bold** B, and then change the **Font Color** A⌄ to **Green, Accent 6, Darker 50%**—in the last column, the last color. At the left end of the horizontal ruler, if necessary, click the **Tab Alignment** button to display the **Left tab** button L. To set a left tab stop, on the horizontal ruler, click at **4.0 inches on the horizontal ruler**. Click to the left of the caption, and then press Tab. Compare your screen with Figure 5.28.

> You can format a caption, just as you would format body text. In this case, you format the caption to display above the table and coordinate with the color scheme of the table.

FIGURE 5.28

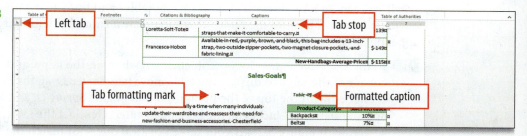

6 ▸ In the last sentence of the document, select the text *The following data*, and then type **Table 4**

> Adding a caption to a table enables you to refer to the table in the body text.

7 ▸ Select the caption *Table 4*. On the mini toolbar, click **Styles**, and then in the **Styles** gallery, click **Create a Style**.

8 ▸ In the **Create New Style from Formatting** dialog box, in the **Name** box, type **Table Caption** and then click **OK**.

9 ▸ Press Ctrl + Home. Select the first table caption, and then on the mini toolbar, click **Styles**. In the **Styles** gallery, click the **Table Caption** style. In the same manner, apply the **Table Caption** style to the remaining two captions in the document.

10 ▸ Press Ctrl + Home. Click the **FILE tab** to display **Backstage** view. On the right, at the bottom of the **Properties** list, click **Show All Properties**. In the **Tags** box, type **product summary, tables** In the **Subject** box, type your course name and section number. If necessary, edit the author name to display your name.

11 ▸ **Save** 💾 your document. Print your document or submit electronically as directed by your instructor. **Close** ✕ Word.

END | You have completed Project 5A

PROJECT 5B

Expense Form

MyITLab®
Project 5B Training

5 WORD

PROJECT ACTIVITIES

In Activities 5.13 through 5.22, you will create an expense form by drawing a table, use nested tables to display expense codes, and insert an Excel spreadsheet. Rachel Anders, Chief Financial Officer for Chesterfield Creations, has asked you to design an expense reimbursement form to be used by the company's sales representatives. Your completed document will look similar to Figure 5.29.

PROJECT FILES

For Project 5B, you will need the following files:

New blank Word document
w05B_Logo

You will save your file as:

Lastname_Firstname_5B_Expense_Form

PROJECT RESULTS

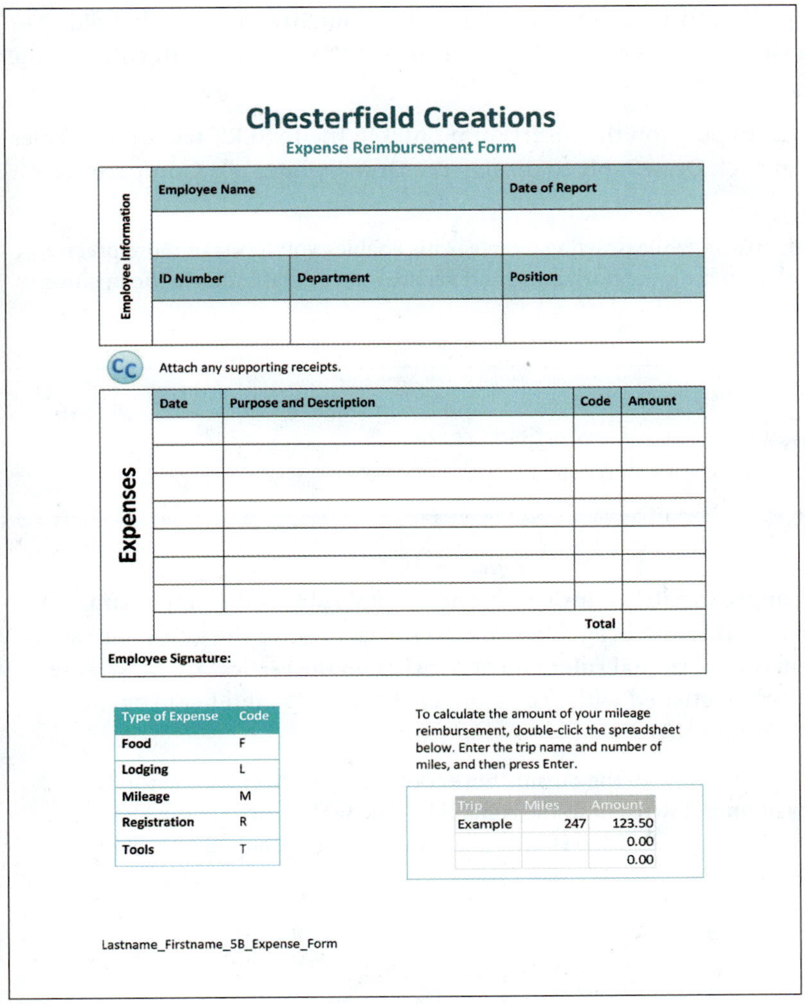

Chesterfield Creations

Expense Reimbursement Form

Employee Information	Employee Name		Date of Report
	ID Number	Department	Position

Attach any supporting receipts.

Expenses	Date	Purpose and Description	Code	Amount
			Total	

Employee Signature:

Type of Expense	Code
Food	F
Lodging	L
Mileage	M
Registration	R
Tools	T

To calculate the amount of your mileage reimbursement, double-click the spreadsheet below. Enter the trip name and number of miles, and then press Enter.

Trip	Miles	Amount
Example	247	123.50
		0.00
		0.00

Lastname_Firstname_5B_Expense_Form

FIGURE 5.29 Project 5B Expense Form

Video W5-5

When a table is inserted into a Word document, the result is a table structure that consists of rows and columns of a uniform size. Sometimes you must modify the table structure to create rows and columns of varying sizes, such as on a purchase order or employee expense form. Word provides tools that work like an electronic pencil and eraser to draw the table objects. After the table is drawn, you can use the features on the DESIGN and LAYOUT tabs to refine the table format.

Activity 5.13 | Drawing a Freeform Table

1 Start Word, and then open a new blank document. **Save** the document in your **Word Chapter 5** folder as **Lastname_Firstname_5B_Expense_Form** Insert the file name in the footer. If necessary, change the zoom level to 100%. Display the rulers and formatting marks.

2 On the **DESIGN tab**, in the **Document Formatting group**, click **Colors**, and then click **Green**.

3 On the **HOME tab**, in the **Styles group**, click the second style—**No Spacing**. Type **Chesterfield Creations** Press Enter, type **Expense Reimbursement Form** and then press Enter.

4 Select the first paragraph. On the mini toolbar, change the **Font Size** to **26**, apply **Bold** B and then change the **Font Color** A to **Aqua, Accent 5, Darker 50%**—in the ninth column, the last color. Press Ctrl + E.

5 Select the second paragraph. On the mini toolbar, change the **Font Size** to **14**, apply **Bold** B, and then change the **Font Color** A to **Aqua, Accent 5, Darker 25%**—in the ninth column, the fifth color. Press Ctrl + E.

6 In the third paragraph, click to position the insertion point. On the **INSERT tab**, in the **Tables group**, click **Table**, and then click **Draw Table** to display the **Draw** pointer. Compare your screen with Figure 5.30.

> It is a good idea to view the rulers while drawing a table. This enables you to make more precise measurements. Lines display on both the horizontal and vertical rulers that indicate the position of the Draw pointer.

FIGURE 5.30

7 Position the pointer at approximately **0 inch on the horizontal ruler** and at approximately **0.75 inch on the vertical ruler**. Click and drag down and to the right until the guides are at approximately **6.5 inches on the horizontal ruler** and at **6 inches on the vertical ruler**. Release the mouse button. If you are dissatisfied with the result, click **Undo** and begin again. Compare your screen with Figure 5.31.

> When drawing a table, always begin with the outside border of the table. Begin at the top left corner and drag the Draw pointer down and to the right. After the table is drawn, the Draw pointer continues to display, the LAYOUT tab is active, and in the Draw group, the Draw Table button is turned on.

FIGURE 5.31

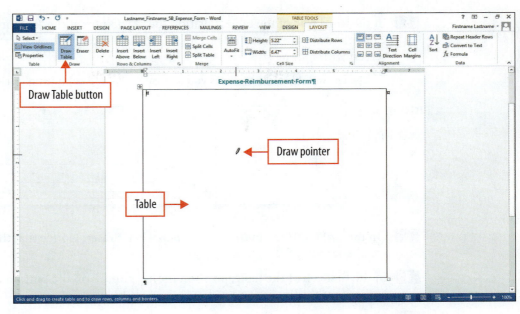

Draw Table button

Draw pointer

Table

Expense·Reimbursement·Form¶

Click and drag to create table and to draw rows, columns and borders.

8 Save 🔲 your changes.

Wrapping Text When Drawing a Table

To cause existing text to flow around the table you are drawing, click the Draw Table command, and then press and hold Ctrl as you draw the table.

Activity 5.14 │ Adding and Removing Columns and Rows

You can draw horizontal and vertical lines inside the table to create cells of various sizes. Your table requires a section for entering employee information and another section for listing expenses incurred. Each section requires cells that vary in size.

1 On the **LAYOUT tab**, in the **Draw group**, click **Draw Table**. Position the tip of the ✏ pointer on the top border of the table at **0.5 inch on the horizontal ruler**. Drag down, and then, when you see the dotted vertical line extending to the bottom table border, release the mouse button.

By drawing a vertical dividing line, you have created an inside border forming two columns in the table.

2 Position the ✏ pointer on the left border of the table at **1.25 inches on the vertical ruler**. Drag to the right, and when you see the line extending to the right table border, release the mouse button to create the first row of the table. Compare your screen with Figure 5.32.

By drawing a horizontal line, you have created an inside border forming two rows in the table.

FIGURE 5.32

Expense·Reimbursement·Form¶

Inside column border

Inside row border

3 Draw three more horizontal lines—one beginning at **1.5 inches on the vertical ruler**, one beginning at **1.75 inches on the vertical ruler**, and one beginning at **2 inches on the vertical ruler**.

4 In the first row of the table, position the ✏ pointer at the top border at **4.25 inches on the horizontal ruler**. Drag down four rows to draw a vertical line.

5 In the third row of the table, position the ✎ pointer at the top border of the second cell at **2 inches on the horizontal ruler**. Drag down two rows to draw a vertical line. Compare your screen with Figure 5.33.

The Draw Table feature allows you to create rows and columns of various sizes.

FIGURE 5.33

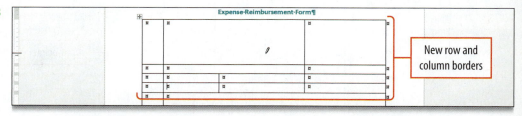

6 On the **LAYOUT tab**, in the **Draw group**, click **Eraser**. Notice that the pointer displays as a small eraser ⌦.

7 In the first cell of the table, position the ⌦ pointer on the bottom cell border, and click. Notice that the line is removed.

8 In the newly merged cell, position the ⌦ pointer on the bottom cell border, and then click to remove the line. Position the ⌦ pointer on the bottom cell border, click to remove the line, and then compare your screen with Figure 5.34.

FIGURE 5.34

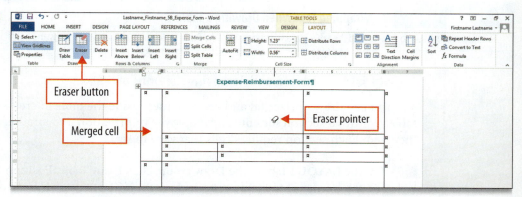

9 On the **LAYOUT tab**, in the **Draw group**, click **Draw Table**. In the last row of the table, in the first cell, position the ✎ pointer at the left border of the cell at **2.5 inches on the vertical ruler**. Drag across to draw a horizontal line extending to the right border of the table.

10 On the **LAYOUT tab**, in the **Draw group**, click **Draw Table** to turn off the feature. Click in the last table cell. On the **LAYOUT tab**, in the **Merge group**, click **Split Cells**. In the **Split Cells** dialog box, click the **Number of columns down spin arrow** to **1**, and then click the **Number of rows up spin arrow** to **9**. Click **OK**. Click in the paragraph immediately above the table, and then compare your screen with Figure 5.35.

You can use the Draw Table feature to create new rows, but sometimes it is faster to use Split Cells.

FIGURE 5.35

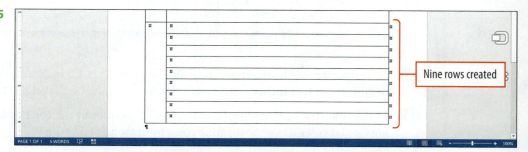

11 Click anywhere in the table. On the **LAYOUT tab**, in the **Draw group**, click **Draw Table**. In the sixth row of the table—the top row of the rows you just inserted—position the ✐ pointer at the top border of the row at **1.25 inches on the horizontal ruler**. Drag down to draw a vertical line extending to the bottom border of the table.

12 In the same row, draw two more vertical lines—one beginning at **5 inches on the horizontal ruler** and one beginning at **5.5 inches on the horizontal ruler**. On the **LAYOUT tab**, in the **Draw group**, click **Draw Table** to turn it off. **Save** 💾 your changes, and then compare your screen with Figure 5.36.

FIGURE 5.36

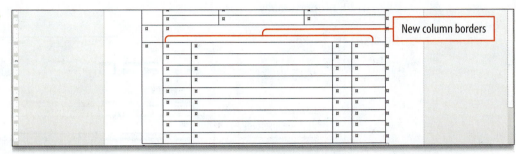

New column borders

Activity 5.15 | Inserting Text and Graphics

You can insert text and objects, such as pictures and WordArt, into table cells.

1 In the first row of the table, position the insertion point in the second cell, and then type **Employee Name** Press [Tab], and type **Date of Report**

2 Press [Tab] five times to move to the second cell in the third row of the table, and type **ID Number** Press [Tab], type **Department** press [Tab], and then type **Position**

3 In the sixth row, position the insertion point in the second cell, and then type **Date** Press [Tab], and then type **Purpose and Description** Press [Tab], type **Code** press [Tab], and then type **Amount**

4 Select the first six rows of the table, and then on the **LAYOUT tab**, in the **Alignment group**, click **Align Center Left** ▤.

5 In the first row, select the text *Employee Name*, and on the mini toolbar, apply **Bold** B . Using the same technique, apply **Bold** B to all the remaining text in the table, being careful not to apply Bold to empty cells. Compare your screen with Figure 5.37.

FIGURE 5.37

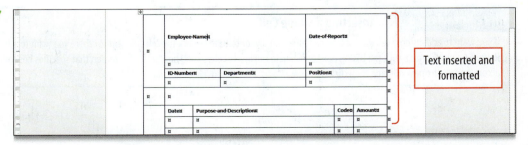

Text inserted and formatted

6 In the first column, position your insertion point in the second cell. On the **INSERT tab**, in the **Illustrations group**, click **Pictures**. Navigate to the location where your student data files are stored, select the file **w05B_Logo**, and then click **Insert**. Notice that the picture—the company logo—is inserted in the cell.

The size of the graphic causes the column width and row height to increase.

7 With the graphic selected, on the **FORMAT tab**, in the **Size group**, click the **Shape Width down spin arrow** ⌷ Width: 6.49" to **0.4"**. Compare your screen with Figure 5.38.

Using this method to reduce the size of the image automatically reduces the row height and column width proportionally.

FIGURE 5.38

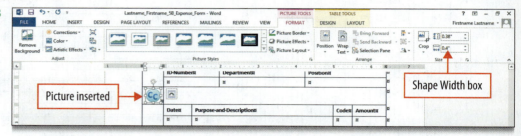

8 In the fifth row, to the right of the graphic, click in the second cell, and then type **Attach any supporting receipts.**

9 In the last row of the table, select the second, third, and fourth cells. On the **LAYOUT tab**, in the **Merge group**, click **Merge Cells**. In the **Alignment group**, click **Align Center Right** ▤.

10 Click in the merged cell, and type **Total** Select the text. On the mini toolbar, apply **Bold** B, click **Insert**, and then click **Insert Below**.

The mini toolbar contains buttons to insert or delete rows and columns—in this case, to insert a row.

11 In the last row of the table, with all the cells selected, on the **LAYOUT tab**, in the **Merge group**, click **Merge Cells**. In the **Alignment group**, click **Align Center Left** ▤. If necessary, in the **Cell Size group**, change the **Height** to **0.4"**.

12 With the insertion point in the last row of the table, type **Employee Signature:** Select the text, and on the mini toolbar, apply **Bold** B. Deselect the text, **Save** 🖫 your changes, and then compare your screen with Figure 5.39.

FIGURE 5.39

***More* Knowledge**   **Inserting a Single Cell**

If you want to add a single cell to a table—not an entire row or column—click the cell adjacent to where you want to add the cell. On the LAYOUT tab, in the Rows & Columns group, click the Dialog Box Launcher. In the Insert Cells dialog box, select the option that specifies how adjacent cells should be moved to accommodate the new cell, and then click OK.

Activity 5.16 | Changing Text Direction

Word tables include a feature that enables you to change the text direction. This is effective for column titles that do not fit at the top of narrow columns or for row headings that cover multiple rows.

1 Click to position the insertion point in the first cell of the table. On the **LAYOUT tab**, in the **Alignment group**, click **Text Direction** two times. Notice that the insertion point displays horizontally in the cell.

> Use the Text Direction button to change the positioning of text within a cell. The appearance of the Text Direction button changes to indicate the direction of the text within the currently selected cell.

2 Type **Employee Information** On the **LAYOUT tab**, in the **Alignment group**, click **Align Center** 🔲. Select the text, and then on the mini toolbar, apply **Bold** B. Deselect the text, and then compare your screen with Figure 5.40.

FIGURE 5.40

3 In the first column, click to position the insertion point in the third cell. On the **LAYOUT tab**, in the **Alignment group**, click **Text Direction** two times. Notice that the insertion point displays horizontally in the cell.

4 Type **Expenses** On the **LAYOUT tab**, in the **Alignment group**, click **Align Center** 🔲. Select the text, and then on the mini toolbar, change the **Font Size** to **20** and apply **Bold** B. **Save** 💾 your changes.

Activity 5.17 | Distributing Rows and Columns

When you draw a freeform table, you may have rows that you want to be exactly the same height or columns that you want to be the same width. The **Distribute Columns** command adjusts the width of the selected columns so that they are equal. Similarly, the **Distribute Rows** command causes the height of the selected rows to be equal.

1 In the first four rows of the table, select all of the cells to the right of the first column. On the **LAYOUT tab**, in the **Cell Size group**, click **Distribute Rows** 🔳. Deselect the cells, and then compare your screen with Figure 5.41.

> The four rows are equal in height.

FIGURE 5.41

2 **Save** 💾 your changes.

Activity 5.18 | Formatting a Table

Table cells can be formatted to enhance the appearance of a table. You will add shading to cells and modify the borders of the table.

1 In the first row, select the second and third cells. Under **TABLE TOOLS**, on the **DESIGN tab**, in the **Table Styles group**, click the **Shading button arrow**, and then under **Theme Colors**, in the ninth column, click the third color—**Aqua, Accent 5, Lighter 60%**.

2 In the third row, select the second, third, and fourth cells, and then in the **Table Styles group**, click the **Shading** button—not the **Shading button arrow**. In the sixth row, select cells two through five, and in the **Table Styles group**, click **Shading**. Deselect the cells, and then compare your screen with Figure 5.42.

The Shading button retains the color that was last selected. By clicking the Shading button, the current color is applied to the selected cells.

FIGURE 5.42

Shading applied to cells

3 If necessary, on the **LAYOUT tab**, in the **Table group**, click **View Gridlines** to turn on the feature. In the first column, position the insertion point in the second cell that contains the graphic. Be careful not to select the graphic. Under **TABLE TOOLS**, on the **DESIGN tab**, in the **Borders group**, click the **Borders button arrow**, and then click **Left Border**. Click the **Borders button arrow**, and then click **Right Border**. Notice that the left and right borders of the cell no longer display; instead they are replaced by the dashed lines as shown in Figure 5.43.

Gridlines—the dashed lines—are nonprinting cell borders that can be used as a guide for viewing table cells. They are useful when positioning content in a table when you are not using a table border. Removing borders can improve the appearance of certain content—for example, the graphic in this table.

FIGURE 5.43

Gridlines

4 Press ⌧Tab. In the **Borders group**, click **Borders**—not the **Borders button arrow**.

The Border button retains the last setting—in this case, Right Border. A gridline displays at the right of the cell.

5 On the **LAYOUT tab**, in the **Table group**, click **View Gridlines** to turn it off. **Save** 🖫 your changes.

Hiding the gridlines allows you to see how a table will display in print.

Objective 6   Use Nested Tables

Video W5-6

A *nested table* is a table within a table. You can insert a table in any cell of an existing table. Using nested tables can enhance the readability of the displayed data. You can also improve the appearance of data within tables by changing *cell margins* and *cell spacing*. Cell margins are the amount of space between a cell's content and the left, right, top, and bottom borders of the cell. Cell spacing is the distance between the individual cells of a table.

Activity 5.19 | Changing Cell Margins and Cell Spacing and Using the Border Painter

To create a nested table, you must first have an existing table.

1 Press Ctrl + End to move to the end of the document. Press Enter.

2 On the **INSERT tab**, in the **Tables group**, click **Table**, and then under **Insert Table**, in the **Table** grid, in the second row, click the second square to insert a 2 × 2 table.

> A table with two rows and two columns displays at the insertion point location, and the insertion point displays in the upper left cell.

3 On the **LAYOUT tab**, in the **Alignment group**, click **Cell Margins**.

> The Table Options dialog box allows you to set the cell margins and cell spacing for a table.

4 In the **Table Options** dialog box, under **Default cell margins**, click the **Top up spin arrow** to **0.1"**. Using the same technique, change the **Bottom**, **Left**, and **Right** cell margins to **0.1"**.

> Contents of each cell within the table will be displayed 0.1" from each cell border.

5 Under **Default cell spacing**, click to select the **Allow spacing between cells** check box, and then click the **Allow spacing between cells up spin arrow** to **0.05"**. Compare your screen with Figure 5.44.

> All cells in the table will be separated by 0.05" of space.

FIGURE 5.44

6 Click **OK**. In the table, select the two cells in the first column, and then on the **LAYOUT tab**, in the **Merge group**, click **Merge Cells**. Compare your screen with Figure 5.45.

FIGURE 5.45

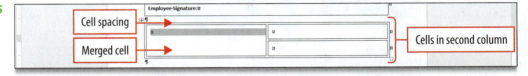

7 Point slightly outside of the upper left corner of the table to display the **table move handle** ⊞. With the ⊹ pointer displayed, click the **table move handle** ⊞ to select the entire table.

8 On the **LAYOUT tab**, in the **Table group**, click **View Gridlines** to turn on the feature. Under **TABLE TOOLS**, on the **DESIGN tab**, in the **Borders group**, click the **Borders button arrow**, and then click **No Border**.

9 In the second column, position the insertion point in the second cell. Under **TABLE TOOLS**, on the **DESIGN tab**, in the **Borders group**, click **Pen Color**, and then under **Theme Colors**, in the ninth column, click the first color—**Aqua, Accent 5**.

> By default, in the Borders group, when you change the Border Style, Pen Color, or Line Weight, the *Border Painter* feature becomes active. The Border Painter applies selected formatting to specific borders of a table. When the Border Painter is turned on, the pointer takes the shape of a small brush.

10 In the second column, above the second cell, click the border. Notice that the border color changes to the selected color.

11 In a similar manner, use the **Border Painter** to change the color of the left, right, and bottom borders of the cell. Compare your screen with Figure 5.46.

FIGURE 5.46

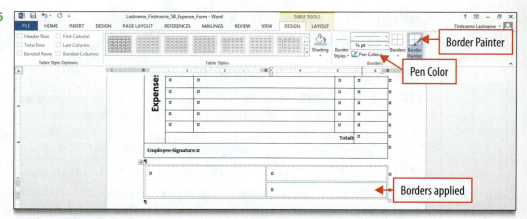

12 In the **Borders group**, click the **Pen Color arrow**, and then click **Automatic**. Click the **Border Painter** to turn off the feature. **Save** 🖫 your changes.

Activity 5.20 | Inserting a Nested Table and Setting a Table Title by Adding Alternative Text

In this activity, you will create a nested table to display the codes that are used on the expense form.

1 Click to position the insertion point in the first cell of the second table. On the **INSERT tab**, in the **Tables group**, click **Table**, and then in the **Table** grid, in the sixth row, click the second cell.

A table containing two columns and six rows is created—or nested—within the first cell of the table.

2 In the first cell of the nested table, type **Type of Expense** Press ⇥, and then type **Code**

3 In the same manner, enter the following data in the remaining cells of the table:

TYPE OF EXPENSE	CODE
Food	F
Lodging	L
Mileage	M
Registration	R
Tools	T

4 If necessary, click to position the insertion point in the nested table. On the **LAYOUT tab**, in the **Cell Size group**, click **AutoFit**, and then click **AutoFit Contents** to resize the nested table to fit the existing text.

5 Under **TABLE TOOLS**, on the **DESIGN tab**, in the **Table Styles group**, click **More** ⤓. In the **Table Styles** gallery, scroll down, and then under **List Tables**, in the third row, click the sixth style—**List Table 3 – Accent 5**. Compare your screen with Figure 5.47.

FIGURE 5.47

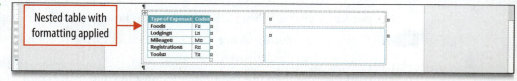

Nested table with formatting applied

6 With the insertion point in the table, on the **LAYOUT tab**, in the **Table group**, click **Properties**.

7 ▷ In the **Table Properties** dialog box, click the **Alt Text tab**.

Alternative text can be added to the properties of an object—for example, a table, chart, or picture. This is useful for a person with vision or cognitive impairments who may not be able to view or understand the object as it displays in the document. The title of the object—in this case, the table—can be read to the person with the disability. If applicable, the description can also be read to provide more information.

8 ▷ In the **Title** box, type **Expense Codes** In the **Description** box, type **The table contains the codes to be used when completing the expense form.**

9 ▷ Click **OK** to close the dialog box, and then **Save** 🖫 your changes.

Objective 7 | Insert an Excel Spreadsheet

Video W5-7

You can insert an Excel spreadsheet in a document to provide a table that performs calculations.

Activity 5.21 | Inserting an Excel Spreadsheet

In this activity, you will insert an Excel spreadsheet to assist employees with calculating mileage reimbursements.

1 ▷ On the right side of the status bar, on the **Zoom Slider**, click **Zoom In** ⊞ two times to change the zoom level to 120%.

Each click of the Zoom In button causes the zoom level to increase in 10 percent increments.

🔁 **BY TOUCH**   On the status bar, tap the Zoom In button to increase the zoom level in 10 percent increments.

2 ▷ In the original table that contains the nested table, in the second column, position the insertion point in the top cell. Type **To calculate the amount of your mileage reimbursement, double-click the spreadsheet below. Enter the trip name and number of miles, and then press Enter.**

3 ▷ Click to position the insertion point in the remaining empty cell. On the **INSERT tab**, in the **Tables group**, click **Table**, and then click **Excel Spreadsheet**.

An Excel spreadsheet and part of the table display on **Page 2** of the document.

4 ▷ In cell **A1**, type **Trip** and then press Tab. In cell **B1**, type **Miles** and then press Tab. In cell **C1**, type **Amount** Compare your screen with Figure 5.48.

FIGURE 5.48

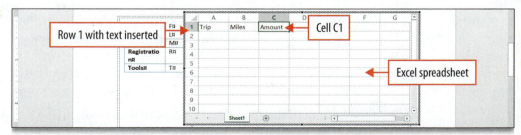

5 ▷ Click in cell **A2**, type **Example** and then press Tab. In cell **B2**, type **247** and then press Tab. In cell **C2**, type **=B2*0.5**

The formula is based on a mileage reimbursement rate of 50 cents per mile.

6 Press `Ctrl` + `Enter`, and notice that the value *123.50* displays in cell **C2**.

> Calculations can be performed in the spreadsheet with the full capability of Excel. In Excel, all formulas are preceded by the = symbol. In this case, the formula prompts the program to multiply the number in cell B2 by 0.50, the company's mileage reimbursement rate. The calculated value displays in cell C2.

7 With cell **C2** selected, on the **HOME tab**, in the **Number group**, click **Increase Decimal** .

8 With cell **C2** selected, in the lower right corner of the cell, point to the **fill handle**—the small square—until the ➕ pointer displays, as shown in Figure 5.49.

FIGURE 5.49

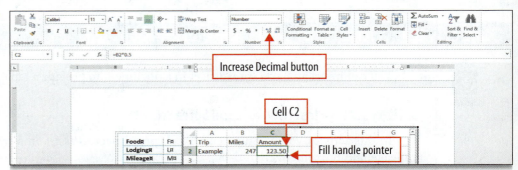

9 With the ➕ pointer displayed, drag down to cell **C8**. Notice that the number *0.00* displays in cells **C3** through **C8**.

> Dragging the fill handle copies the formula in C2 to the cells below. Excel changes the cell references in the formula to match the row number—for example, in cell C3 the formula is copied as =B3*0.5. Because you haven't entered any data in rows 3 through 8, the Amount column displays a value of 0 for those rows. You have copied the formula so that the person using the form can calculate the reimbursement amount for several trips without having to delete any data in the spreadsheet.

10 Select cells **A1** through **C1**. On the **HOME tab**, in the **Styles group**, click **Cell Styles**. In the **Cell Styles** gallery, under **Themed Cell Styles**, in the fourth row, click the third style—**Accent 3**.

11 On the right edge of the spreadsheet, point to the middle sizing handle until the ↔ pointer displays. Compare your screen with Figure 5.50.

FIGURE 5.50

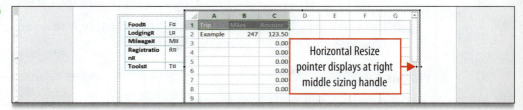

12 Drag to the left until only **columns A, B,** and **C** display. If necessary, on the right side of the spreadsheet, drag the middle sizing handle to fully display **columns A, B,** and **C**.

13 At the bottom of the spreadsheet, point to the middle sizing handle until the ↕ pointer displays. Drag upward until only **rows 1** through **4** display. If necessary, at the bottom of the spreadsheet, drag the middle sizing handle up or down to fully display **rows 1** through **4**. Compare your screen with Figure 5.51.

FIGURE 5.51

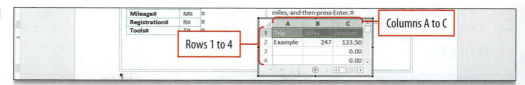

14 ▶ To close the Excel spreadsheet, click in a blank area of the document. Click in a blank area of the cell containing the Excel table, and then on the **LAYOUT tab**, in the **Alignment group**, click **Align Center** ▦.

15 ▶ In the **Table group**, click **View Gridlines** to turn off the feature. **Save** 🖫 your changes.

Activity 5.22 | Modifying the Dimensions of a Table

1 ▶ On the status bar, click **Zoom Out** ▬ two times to restore the document view to 100%.

2 ▶ At the bottom of the page, position the insertion point in the table containing the expense codes. At the lower right corner of the table, point to the corner sizing handle. With the 🡖 pointer displayed, drag down until the bottom border of the table is aligned with the 8.5-inch mark on the vertical ruler. Compare your screen with Figure 5.52.

Use the corner sizing handle to quickly change the dimensions of a table.

FIGURE 5.52

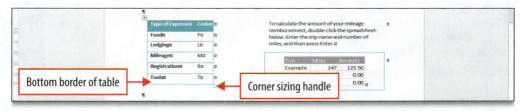

3 ▶ Press [Ctrl] + [Home]. Click the **FILE tab** to display **Backstage** view. In the **Tags** box, type **expense form, nested table** In the **Subject** box, type your course name and section number. If necessary, edit the author name to display your name.

4 ▶ **Save** 🖫 your changes. Print your document, or submit electronically, as directed by your instructor. **Close** ✕ Word.

END | You have completed Project 5B

END OF CHAPTER

SUMMARY

Creating and applying a table style standardizes the appearance of multiple tables in a document. The style can include formatting for the entire table and for specific elements—such as rows and columns.

Word has advanced tools that enable you to present table data efficiently and attractively—such as changing alignment within cells, merging and splitting cells, sorting data, and changing text direction.

The Draw Table and Table Eraser features function as an electronic pencil and eraser. By drawing and erasing borders, you can create a table with rows and columns of varying sizes—for example, in a form.

Insert a nested table or modify the cell margins and cell spacing to improve readability of data within a table. To perform simple or complex calculations within a document, insert an Excel spreadsheet.

GO! LEARN IT ONLINE

Review the concepts and key terms in this chapter by completing these online challenges, which you can find at **www.pearsonhighered.com/go**.

Matching and Multiple Choice:
Answer matching and multiple choice questions to test what you learned in this chapter. MyITLab®

Crossword Puzzle:
Spell out the words that match the numbered clues, and put them in the puzzle squares.

Flipboard:
Flip through the definitions of the key terms in this chapter and match them with the correct term.

END OF CHAPTER

REVIEW AND ASSESSMENT GUIDE FOR WORD CHAPTER 5

Your instructor may assign one or more of these projects to help you review the chapter and assess your mastery and understanding of the chapter.

		Review and Assessment Guide for Word Chapter 5		
Project	**Apply Skills from These Chapter Objectives**	**Project Type**		**Project Location**
5C	Objectives 1–4 from Project 5A	**5C Skills Review** A guided review of the skills from Project 5A.		On the following pages
5D	Objectives 5–7 from Project 5B	**5D Skills Review** A guided review of the skills from Project 5B.		On the following pages
5E	Objectives 1–4 from Project 5A	**5E Mastery (Grader Project)** A demonstration of your mastery of the skills in Project 5A with extensive decision making.		In MyITLab and on the following pages
5F	Objectives 5–7 from Project 5B	**5F Mastery (Grader Project)** A demonstration of your mastery of the skills in Project 5B with extensive decision making.		In MyITLab and on the following pages
5G	Objectives 1–7 from Projects 5A and 5B	**5G Mastery (Grader Project)** A demonstration of your mastery of the skills in Projects 5A and 5B with extensive decision making.		In MyITLab and on the following pages
5H	Combination of Objectives from Projects 5A and 5B	**5H GO! Fix It** A demonstration of your mastery of the skills in Projects 5A and 5B by creating a correct result from a document that contains errors you must find.		Online
5I	Combination of Objectives from Projects 5A and 5B	**5I GO! Make It** A demonstration of your mastery of the skills in Projects 5A and 5B by creating a result from a supplied picture.		Online
5J	Combination of Objectives from Projects 5A and 5B	**5J GO! Solve It** A demonstration of your mastery of the skills in Projects 5A and 5B, your decision-making skills, and your critical thinking skills. A task-specific rubric helps you self-assess your result.		Online
5K	Combination of Objectives from Projects 5A and 5B	**5K GO! Solve It** A demonstration of your mastery of the skills in Projects 5A and 5B, your decision-making skills, and your critical thinking skills. A task-specific rubric helps you self-assess your result.		On the following pages
5L	Combination of Objectives from Projects 5A and 5B	**5L GO! Think** A demonstration of your understanding of the chapter concepts applied in a manner that you would outside of college. An analytic rubric helps you and your instructor grade the quality of your work by comparing it to the work an expert in the discipline would create.		On the following pages
5M	Combination of Objectives from Projects 5A and 5B	**5M GO! Think** A demonstration of your understanding of the chapter concepts applied in a manner that you would outside of college. An analytic rubric helps you and your instructor grade the quality of your work by comparing it to the work an expert in the discipline would create.		Online
5N	Combination of Objectives from Projects 5A and 5B	**5N You and GO!** A demonstration of your understanding of the chapter concepts applied in a manner that you would in a personal situation. An analytic rubric helps you and your instructor grade the quality of your work.		Online

GLOSSARY

GLOSSARY OF CHAPTER KEY TERMS

AutoFit A table feature that automatically adjusts column widths or the width of the entire table.

AutoFit Contents A table feature that resizes the column widths to accommodate the maximum field size.

Border Painter: A table feature that applies selected formatting to specific borders of a table.

Caption A title that is added to a Word object and numbered sequentially.

Cell margins The amount of space between a cell's content and the left, right, top, and bottom borders of the cell.

Cell spacing The distance between the individual cells in a table.

Distribute Columns A command that adjusts the width of the selected columns so that they are equal.

Distribute Rows A command that causes the height of the selected rows to be equal.

Field A placeholder for data.

Formula A mathematical expression that contains functions, operators, constants, and properties, and returns a value to a cell.

Function A predefined formula that performs calculations by using specific values in a particular order.

Gridlines Nonprinting lines that indicate cell borders.

Header row The first row of a table containing column titles.

Merge A table feature that combines two or more adjacent cells into one cell so that the text spans across multiple columns or rows.

Nested table A table inserted in a cell of an existing table.

Organizer A dialog box where you can modify a document by using styles stored in another document or template.

Split A table feature that divides selected cells into multiple cells with a specified number of rows and columns.

Split Table A table feature that divides an existing table into two tables in which the selected row—where the insertion point is located—becomes the first row of the second table.

Style A group of formatting commands—such as font, font size, and font color—that can be applied with a single command.

Table style A style that includes formatting for the entire table and specific table elements, such as rows and columns.

CHAPTER REVIEW

Skills Review   Project 5C Sales Conference

In the following Skills Review, you will format tables and insert formulas to create a memo regarding a conference for Sales Managers at Chesterfield Creations. Your completed document will look similar to Figure 5.53.

PROJECT FILES

For Project 5C, you will need the following files:

w05C_Sales_Conference
w05C_Sales_Styles

You will save your file as:

Lastname_Firstname_5C_Sales_Conference

PROJECT RESULTS

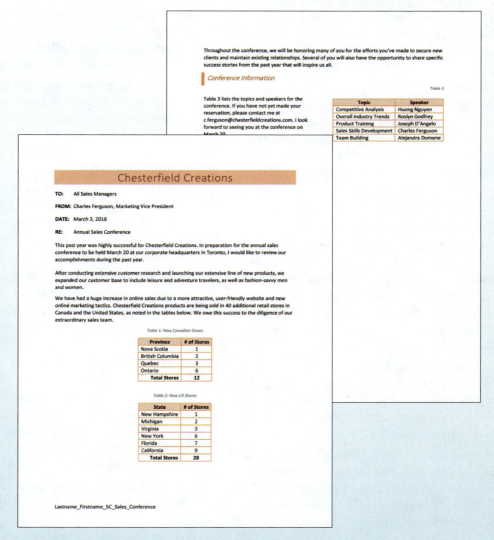

FIGURE 5.53

(Project 5C Sales Conference continues on the next page)

CHAPTER REVIEW

1 Start Word. Navigate to your student files and open the file **w05C_Sales_Conference**. **Save** the document in your **Word Chapter 5** folder as **Lastname_Firstname_5C_ Sales_Conference** Insert the file name in the footer. Display the rulers and formatting marks. If any words are flagged as spelling errors, click **Ignore All**.

a. Click the **FILE tab**, and then click **Options**. In the **Word Options** dialog box, click **Add-Ins**.

b. At the bottom of the **Word Options** dialog box, click the **Manage box arrow**, click **Templates**, and then click **Go**.

c. In the **Templates and Add-ins** dialog box, click **Organizer**.

d. On the left side of the **Organizer** dialog box, be sure that the *Lastname_Firstname_5C_Sales_Conference* file displays. On the right side of the **Organizer**, click **Close File**. Click **Open File**, navigate to your student files, select the file **w05C_Sales_Styles**, and then click **Open**.

e. On the right side of the **Organizer**, scroll as necessary, select **Heading 2**, press and hold Ctrl, and then select **Title**. In the middle of the **Organizer** dialog box, click **Copy**. **Close** the **Organizer**. **Save** your changes.

2 Select the first paragraph, and then apply the **Title** style. For each of the next four paragraphs, select the heading—including the colon—and apply **Bold**.

a. On the **HOME tab**, in the **Styles group**, click the **Dialog Box Launcher** to display the **Styles** pane. At the bottom of the **Styles** pane, click the **New Style** button. In the **Create New Style from Formatting** dialog box, under **Properties**, in the **Name** box, type **Sales Conference** Click the **Style type arrow**, and then click **Table**.

b. Under **Formatting**, click the **Border button arrow**, and then click **All Borders**. Click the **Line Weight arrow**, and then click **1 pt**. Click the **Border Color arrow**, and then in the sixth column, click the first color—**Orange, Accent 2**.

c. Under **Formatting**, click the **Apply formatting to arrow**, and then click **Header row**. Click the **Fill Color arrow**, and then in the sixth column, click the third color—**Orange, Accent 2, Lighter 60%**. Click **OK**. **Close** the **Styles** pane.

d. In the sixth row of the table, click in the first cell that contains the text *State*. On the **LAYOUT tab**, in the **Merge group**, click **Split Table**.

3 In the first table in the document, click in the first cell. Under **TABLE TOOLS**, on the **DESIGN tab**, in the **Table Styles group**, click the **Sales Conference** table style. In a similar manner, click in the first cell in the second table of the document, and then apply the **Sales Conference** table style.

a. Under **TABLE TOOLS**, on the **DESIGN tab**, in the **Table Styles group**, right-click the **Sales Conference** table style, and then click **Modify Table Style**. Click the **Apply formatting to arrow**, and then click **Header row**. Apply **Bold**, and then click **OK**.

b. In the first table, position the insertion point to the right of *Province*. On the **LAYOUT tab**, in the **Merge group**, click **Split Cells**, and then click **OK**. In the first row, click in the second cell, and type **# of Stores**

c. Select the **header row**, and then on the **LAYOUT tab**, in the **Alignment group**, click **Align Center**. In the first column, select all cells below the header row, and then click **Align Center Left**. In the second column, select all cells below the header row, and then click **Align Center**.

d. In the second table, position the insertion point to the right of *State*. On the **LAYOUT tab**, in the **Merge group**, click **Split Cells**, and then click **OK**. In the first row, click in the second cell, and type **# of Stores**

e. Select the **header row**, and then on the **LAYOUT tab**, in the **Alignment group**, click **Align Center**. In the first column, select all cells below the header row, and then click **Align Center Left**. In the second column, select all cells below the header row, and then click **Align Center**.

4 Click anywhere in the first table, and then on the **LAYOUT tab**, in the **Data group**, click **Sort**. Click the **Sort by arrow**, click **# of Stores**, and then click **OK**. Click anywhere in the second table, and then in the **Data group**, click **Sort**. In the **Sort** dialog box, click the **Sort by arrow**, click **# of Stores**, and then click **OK**.

5 Near the bottom of **Page 1**, select the paragraph *Conference Information,* and then apply the **Heading 2** style.

(Project 5C Sales Conference continues on the next page)

a. Locate the paragraph that begins *Topic*, and then drag to select all the remaining text in the document—a total of six paragraphs.

b. On the **INSERT tab**, in the **Tables group**, click **Table**, and then click **Convert Text to Table**. Click **OK** to close the dialog box.

6 Click to position your insertion point anywhere in the table you inserted. Under **TABLE TOOLS**, on the **DESIGN tab**, in the **Table Styles group**, click the **Sales Conference** table style.

a. On the **LAYOUT tab**, in the **Cell Size group**, click **AutoFit**, and then click **AutoFit Contents**.

b. Select the **header row**, and then in the **Alignment group**, click **Align Center**. Select the remaining cells in the table, and then click **Align Center Left**.

7 In the first table, click to position the insertion point in the first cell of the last row. On the **LAYOUT tab**, in the **Cell Size group**, click **AutoFit**, and then click **AutoFit Contents**. Point to the bottom left corner of the table, and then click the **One-Click Row/Column Insertion** button.

a. In the new last row of the table, click in the first cell, and then type **Total Stores** Select the text, and apply **Bold**. In the **Alignment group**, click **Align Center Right**. Press [Tab], and then in the **Data group**, click **Formula**.

b. In the **Formula** dialog box, with *=SUM(ABOVE)* displayed, click the **Number format arrow**, and then click **0**. Click **OK**. Select the inserted text, and apply **Bold**.

8 In the second table, click to position the insertion point in the first cell of the last row. On the **LAYOUT tab**, in the **Cell Size group**, click **AutoFit**, and then click **AutoFit Contents**. Point to the bottom left corner of the table, and then click the **One-Click Row/Column Insertion** button.

a. In the new last row, click in the first cell, and then type **Total Stores** Select the text, and apply **Bold**. In the **Alignment group**, click **Align Center Right**. Press [Tab], and then in the **Data group**, click **Formula**.

b. In the **Formula** dialog box, with *=SUM(ABOVE)* displayed, click the **Number format arrow**, and then click **0**. Click **OK**. Select the inserted text, and apply **Bold**.

c. In the first table, in the second column, click in the fifth cell. Select *5*, and then type **6** In the last cell of the table, select *11*, right-click the selection, and then click **Update Field**.

d. In the second table, in the second column, click in the sixth cell. Select *8*, and then type **7** In the last cell of the table, select *29*, right-click the selection, and then click **Update Field**.

9 Click to position the insertion point anywhere in the first table. On the **REFERENCES tab**, in the **Captions group**, click **Insert Caption**. In the **Caption** dialog box, with the insertion point to the right of *Table 1,* type **:** Press [Spacebar], and then type **New Canadian Stores** If necessary, under **Options**, click the **Position arrow**, and then click **Above selected item**. Click **OK**.

a. Click to position the insertion point anywhere in the second table. In the **Captions group**, click **Insert Caption**. In the **Caption** dialog box, with the insertion point to the right of *Table 2,* type **:** Press [Spacebar], and then type **New US Stores** If necessary, under **Options**, click the **Position arrow**, and then click **Above selected item**. Click **OK**.

b. Click to position the insertion point anywhere in the last table. On the **LAYOUT tab**, in the **Table group**, click the **Properties** button. In the **Table Properties** dialog box, if necessary, under **Text wrapping**, click **Around**, and then click **Positioning**.

c. In the **Table Positioning** dialog box, under **Distance from surrounding text**, click the **Left up spin arrow** to **0.5"**. Click **OK** two times to close the dialog boxes. Display the **Table Move Handle**, and drag the table up and to the right until the top border is even with the first line of the last paragraph and the right border is aligned with the right margin.

d. Click anywhere in the table. On the **REFERENCES tab**, in the **Captions group**, click **Insert Caption**. In the **Caption** dialog box, with *Table 3* displayed, click **OK**. Select the caption, and then on the **HOME tab**, in the **Paragraph group**, click **Align Right**. In the last paragraph of the document, select the text *Listed below are*, and then type **Table 3 lists**

(Project 5C Sales Conference continues on the next page)

CHAPTER REVIEW

10 Click to position the insertion point anywhere in the first table. On the **LAYOUT tab**, in the **Table group**, click **Properties**. In the **Table Properties** dialog box, under **Alignment**, click **Center**, and then click **OK**. Click to position the insertion point anywhere in the second table. In the **Table group**, click **Properties**. In the **Table Properties** dialog box, under **Alignment**, click **Center**, and then click **OK**. Select the captions for *Table 1* and *Table 2*, and then press Ctrl + E.

11 Press Ctrl + Home. Click the **FILE tab**, and then click **Show All Properties**. In the **Tags** box, type **sales conference** In the **Subject** box, type your course name and section number. If necessary, edit the author name to display your name. **Save** your document.

12 Print your document or submit electronically as directed by your instructor. **Close** Word.

END | You have completed Project 5C

CHAPTER REVIEW

Apply 5B skills from these Objectives:

5 Draw a Freeform Table

6 Use Nested Tables

7 Insert an Excel Spreadsheet

Skills Review | Project 5D Registration Form

In the following Skills Review, you will create a registration form for the Employee Charity Bowling Tournament sponsored by Chesterfield Creations. Your completed document will look similar to Figure 5.54.

PROJECT FILES

For Project 5D, you will need the following file:

w05D_Registration_Form

You will save your file as:

Lastname_Firstname_5D_Registration_Form

PROJECT RESULTS

Chesterfield Creations

Annual Employee Charity Bowling Tournament

The administrative team of Chesterfield Creations hosts a bowling tournament each year for its employees. Proceeds from the tournament are given to the Greater Toronto Food Bank. This year the tournament will be held at the Regency Bowling Lanes in Toronto on May 14 and 15. Various prizes are awarded to individuals and teams of four. In addition to the three games of bowling each day, continental breakfast and lunch are available for an additional fee. Consider joining us this year for fun and fellowship with your coworkers.

Registration Form

Employee Information	Name:	Department:
	Phone:	Email:
	Home Address:	

Use the Excel spreadsheet below to calculate the total amount due.

Day	Item	Charge	Your Cost
	Entry Fee	$150	
Friday	Breakfast	$10	
Friday	Lunch	$20	
Saturday	Breakfast	$10	
Saturday	Lunch	$20	
	Total	$210	0

Amount Enclosed: $

Please send your check and a copy of the completed registration form to Rachel Anders, Chief Financial Officer, at our Toronto address. Make checks payable to Chesterfield Creations Bowling Tournament.

Lastname_Firstname_5D_Registration_Form

FIGURE 5.54

(Project 5D Registration Form continues on the next page)

CHAPTER REVIEW

1 Start Word. Navigate to your student files and open the file **w05D_Registration_Form**. **Save** the document in your **Word Chapter 5** folder as **Lastname_Firstname_5D_Registration_Form** Insert the file name in the footer. Display the rulers and formatting marks.

a. Select the first two paragraphs. Change the **Font Size** to **18**, apply **Bold**, and then change the **Font Color** to **Orange, Accent 2, Darker 25%**. Press Ctrl + E. Select the fourth paragraph—*Registration Form*. Change the **Font Size** to **16**, apply **Bold**, and then change the **Font Color** to **Orange, Accent 2, Darker 50%**. Press Ctrl + E.

2 Click to position the insertion point in the fifth paragraph, which is blank. On the **INSERT tab**, in the **Tables group**, click **Table**, and then click **Draw Table**.

a. Position the ✐ pointer at the left margin and at approximately **2.75 inches on the vertical ruler**. Drag down and to the right until the guides are at approximately **6.5 inches on the horizontal ruler** and at **8 inches on the vertical ruler**. Release the mouse button. If necessary, under **TABLE TOOLS**, on the **DESIGN tab**, in the **Borders group**, change the **Line Weight** to **½ pt** and the **Pen Color** to **Automatic**.

b. With the insertion point in the table, on the **HOME tab**, in the **Styles group**, click the **No Spacing** style, and then change the **Font Size** to **12**.

c. On the **LAYOUT tab**, in the **Draw group**, click **Draw Table**. Position the ✐ pointer on the left border of the table at approximately **0.75 inch on the vertical ruler**, and drag to the right table border. In a similar manner, draw horizontal lines at **1.25 inches**, **2 inches**, and **4.5 inches on the vertical ruler**.

d. Position the ✐ pointer on the top border of the table at **0.5 inch on the horizontal ruler**, and drag down three rows. Position the ✐ pointer on the top border at approximately **3.25 inches on the horizontal ruler**, and drag down to the bottom of the table. Click **Draw Table** to turn off the feature.

e. On the **LAYOUT tab**, in the **Draw group**, click **Eraser**. In the first cell of the table, position the ✐ pointer on the bottom cell border and click. In the newly merged cell, position the ✐ pointer on the bottom cell border and click. In the fourth row, in the first cell, position the ✐ pointer on the right cell border and click. Click **Eraser** to turn it off.

3 Starting in the second column, select the first three rows of the table. On the **LAYOUT tab**, in the **Cell Size group**, click **Distribute Rows**. Click in the fourth row. Under **TABLE TOOLS**, on the **DESIGN tab**, in the **Borders group**, click the **Borders button arrow**, and then click **Left Border**. Click the **Borders button arrow**, and then click **Right Border**. Select the last row, click the **Borders button arrow**, and then click **No Border**. If necessary, on the **LAYOUT tab**, in the **Table group**, click the **View Gridlines** button to display the gridlines.

a. In the first row of the table, in the second cell, type **Name:** Press Tab, and then type **Department:** In the second row, in the cell below *Name*, type **Phone:** Press Tab, and then type **Email:** In the third row, in the cell below *Phone*, type **Home Address:** Select the text in the three rows, and then on the **LAYOUT tab**, in the **Alignment group**, click **Align Center Left**.

b. In the third row of the table, select the second and third cells, and then on the **LAYOUT tab**, in the **Merge group**, click **Merge Cells**. Position the insertion point in the first cell of the table, and then on the **LAYOUT tab**, in the **Alignment group**, click **Text Direction** two times. Type **Employee Information** In the **Alignment group**, click **Align Center**, and then apply **Bold**.

c. In the last row of the table, click in the first cell, and then in the **Alignment group**, click **Align Center Right**. Type **Amount Enclosed:** Press Tab, and then type **$** In the **Alignment group**, click **Align Center Left**. In the last row, select both cells, and then apply **Bold**.

4 Click to position the insertion point in the fourth row of the table. On the **LAYOUT tab**, in the **Alignment group**, click **Align Center**.

a. With the insertion point in the fourth row, on the **INSERT tab**, in the **Tables group**, click the **Table** button, and then under **Insert Table**, in the **Table** grid, in the second row, click the second square to insert a 2 × 2 table.

b. On the **LAYOUT tab**, in the **Alignment group**, click **Cell Margins**. In the **Table Options** dialog box, under **Default cell margins**, change the **Top** and **Bottom** margins to **0.01"**, and then change the **Left** and **Right** margins to **0.4"**.

(Project 5D Registration Form continues on the next page)

c. Under **Default cell spacing**, select the **Allow spacing between cells** check box, and then change the cell spacing to **0.1"**. Click **OK**.

d. In the nested table, select the two cells in the first column, and then on the **LAYOUT tab**, in the **Merge group**, click **Merge Cells**. Select the nested table. Under **TABLE TOOLS**, on the **DESIGN tab**, in the **Borders group**, click the **Borders button arrow**, and then click **No Border**.

5 Click to position the insertion point in the first cell of the nested table. On the **LAYOUT tab**, in the **Alignment group**, click **Align Center**. On the **INSERT tab**, in the **Illustrations group**, click **Online Pictures**. In the **Insert Pictures** dialog box, in the **Office.com Clip Art** box, type **bowling** and then press Enter. Click the image shown in Figure 5.54, or select a similar graphic, and then click **Insert**.

a. Click in the top right cell of the nested table, and then type **Use the Excel spreadsheet below to calculate the total amount due.** Click to position the insertion point in the bottom right cell of the nested table. On the **INSERT tab**, in the **Tables group**, click **Table**, and then click **Excel Spreadsheet**.

b. Click to position the insertion point in cell **A1**, if necessary, and then type **Day** Press Tab, and then in cell **B1**, type **Item** Press Tab, and then in cell **C1**, type **Charge** Press Tab, and then in cell **D1**, type **Your Cost** Type the following text in the appropriate cells under the headings you typed:

	A	B	C
1	Day	Item	Charge
2		**Entry Fee**	**$150**
3	**Friday**	**Breakfast**	**$10**
4	**Friday**	**Lunch**	**$20**
5	**Saturday**	**Breakfast**	**$10**
6	**Saturday**	**Lunch**	**$20**
7		**Total**	

c. Click in cell **C7**, type **=SUM(C2:C6)** and then press Tab. In cell **D7**, type **=SUM(D2:D6)** and then press Enter. Select cells **A1** through **D7**. On the **HOME tab**, in the **Styles group**, click the **Cell Styles** button. In the **Cell Styles** gallery, under **Themed Cell Styles**, click **40% –Accent 4**.

d. On the right edge of the spreadsheet, point to the middle sizing handle, and drag to the left until only **columns A** through **D** display. At the bottom of the spreadsheet, point to the middle sizing handle, and drag upward until only **rows 1** through **7** display. To close the Excel spreadsheet, click in a blank area of the document. On the **LAYOUT tab**, in the **Table group**, click **View Gridlines** to turn it off.

6 Press Ctrl + Home. Click the **FILE tab**, and then click **Show All Properties**. In the **Tags** box, type **registration, bowling tournament** In the **Subject** box, type your course name and section number. If necessary, change the author name to display your name. **Save** your document. Print your document or submit electronically as directed by your instructor. **Close** Word.

END | You have completed Project 5D

CONTENT-BASED ASSESSMENTS

Mastering Word Project 5E Travel Bags

In the following Mastering Word project, you will create a memo to all Chesterfield Creations Sales Managers announcing the Flair Collection of travel bags. Your completed document will look similar to Figure 5.55.

Apply 5A skills from these Objectives:

1 Create and Apply a Custom Table Style

2 Format Cells

3 Use Advanced Table Features

4 Modify Table Properties

PROJECT FILES

For Project 5E, you will need the following file:

w05E_Travel_Bags

You will save your file as:

Lastname_Firstname_5E_Travel_Bags

PROJECT RESULTS

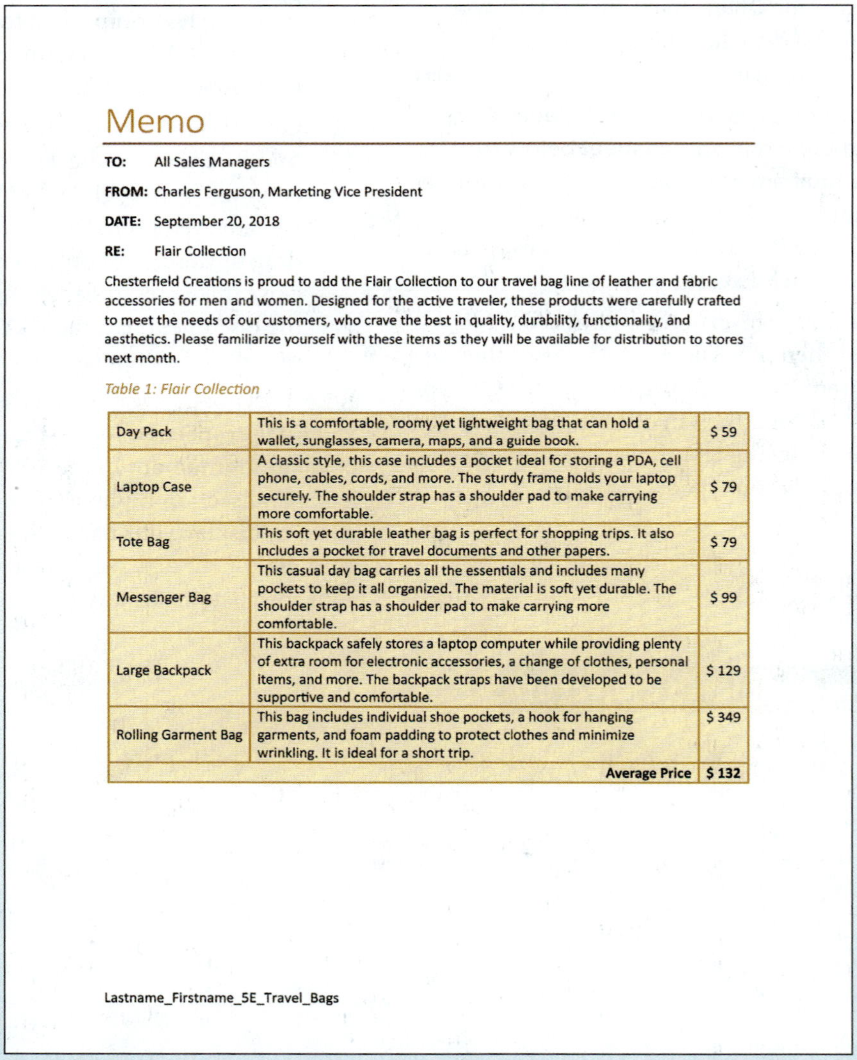

Memo

TO:	All Sales Managers
FROM:	Charles Ferguson, Marketing Vice President
DATE:	September 20, 2018
RE:	Flair Collection

Chesterfield Creations is proud to add the Flair Collection to our travel bag line of leather and fabric accessories for men and women. Designed for the active traveler, these products were carefully crafted to meet the needs of our customers, who crave the best in quality, durability, functionality, and aesthetics. Please familiarize yourself with these items as they will be available for distribution to stores next month.

Table 1: Flair Collection

Day Pack	This is a comfortable, roomy yet lightweight bag that can hold a wallet, sunglasses, camera, maps, and a guide book.	$ 59
Laptop Case	A classic style, this case includes a pocket ideal for storing a PDA, cell phone, cables, cords, and more. The sturdy frame holds your laptop securely. The shoulder strap has a shoulder pad to make carrying more comfortable.	$ 79
Tote Bag	This soft yet durable leather bag is perfect for shopping trips. It also includes a pocket for travel documents and other papers.	$ 79
Messenger Bag	This casual day bag carries all the essentials and includes many pockets to keep it all organized. The material is soft yet durable. The shoulder strap has a shoulder pad to make carrying more comfortable.	$ 99
Large Backpack	This backpack safely stores a laptop computer while providing plenty of extra room for electronic accessories, a change of clothes, personal items, and more. The backpack straps have been developed to be supportive and comfortable.	$ 129
Rolling Garment Bag	This bag includes individual shoe pockets, a hook for hanging garments, and foam padding to protect clothes and minimize wrinkling. It is ideal for a short trip.	$ 349
	Average Price	**$ 132**

Lastname_Firstname_5E_Travel_Bags

FIGURE 5.55

(Project 5E Travel Bags continues on the next page)

CONTENT-BASED ASSESSMENTS

Mastering Word | Project 5E Travel Bags (continued)

1 ▸ Start Word. Navigate to your student files, and open the file **w05E_Travel_Bags**. **Save** the document in your **Word Chapter 5** folder as **Lastname_Firstname_5E_Travel_Bags** Insert the file name in the footer, and display the rulers and formatting marks.

2 ▸ Select the first paragraph and apply the **Title** style. For each of the next four paragraphs, select the heading—including the colon—and apply the **Strong** style.

3 ▸ Display the **Styles** pane, and then click the **New Style** button. In the **Create New Style from Formatting** dialog box, for the **Name**, type **Flair Collection** Change the **Style type** to **Table**. Apply the border style to **All Borders**. Change the **Line Weight** to **1 ½ pt**. Change the **Border Color** to **Gold, Accent 4, Darker 25%**. Change the **Fill Color** to **Gold, Accent 4, Lighter 80%**, and then click **OK**. **Close** the **Styles** pane.

4 ▸ Locate the paragraph that begins *Rolling Garment Bag*, drag to select the remaining six paragraphs of the document, and then **Convert Text to Table**. With the insertion point anywhere in the table, **Sort** the table by **Column 3** in **Ascending** order. Apply the **Flair Collection** table style. Select the first two columns of the table, and change the alignment to **Align Center Left**. Select the third column, and change the alignment to **Align Center**. Resize the table to **AutoFit Contents**. In the second column, select all six cells, and then change the **Width** to **4.5"**.

5 ▸ At the bottom of the table, insert a new row. In the last row, select the first and second cells, and then **Merge Cells**. Change the alignment to **Align Center Right**, type **Average Price** and then apply **Bold**. In the last cell of the table, click **Formula**, change the **Formula** to **=AVERAGE(ABOVE)** Change the **Number format** to **#,##0**, and then to the left of the number format, type **$** Click **OK**. Select the displayed value, and apply **Bold**.

6 ▸ Display the **Table Properties** dialog box, and then change the table alignment to **Center**.

7 ▸ Display the **Caption** dialog box, and then modify the text as necessary to display above the table as *Table 1: Flair Collection*. Select the caption, change the **Font Size** to **12**, and then change the **Font Color** to **Gold, Accent 4, Darker 25%**.

8 ▸ Press Ctrl + Home. Click the **FILE tab**, and then click **Show All Properties**. In the **Tags** box, type **travel bags, Flair** In the **Subject** box, type your course name and section number. If necessary, change the author name to display your name. **Save** your document.

9 ▸ Print your document or submit electronically as directed by your instructor. **Close** Word.

END | You have completed Project 5E

CONTENT-BASED ASSESSMENTS

Mastering Word | Project 5F Buyer Program

Apply 5B skills from these Objectives:

5 Draw a Freeform Table

6 Use Nested Tables

7 Insert an Excel Spreadsheet

In the following Mastering Word project, you will create a flyer explaining the Frequent Buyer Program to Chesterfield Creations customers. Your completed document will look similar to Figure 5.56.

PROJECT FILES

For Project 5F, you will need the following file:

w05F_Buyer_Program

You will save your file as:

Lastname_Firstname_5F_Buyer_Program

PROJECT RESULTS

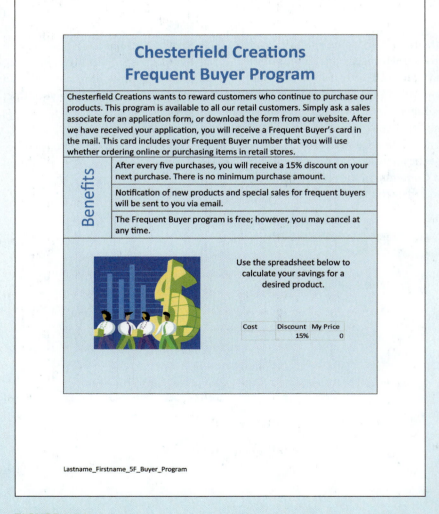

FIGURE 5.56

(Project 5F Buyer Program continues on the next page)

CONTENT-BASED ASSESSMENTS

1 Start Word. Navigate to your student files, and open the file **w05F_Buyer_Program**. **Save** the document in your **Word Chapter 5** folder as **Lastname_Firstname_5F_Buyer_Program** Insert the file name in the footer, and display rulers and formatting marks.

2 Select the first cell of the table, and change the **Width** to 1". Select the second cell, and change the **Width** to 5.5".

3 On the **LAYOUT tab**, in the **Rows & Columns group**, click **Insert Above**. Click anywhere in the second row, and then click **Insert Below**. In the last row, change the **Height** to 4.8". In the first row, change the **Height** to 1.2".

4 In the **Draw group**, click **Draw Table**. Begin at the left border of the table and at **5.5 inches on the vertical ruler**, and draw a horizontal line extending to the right border of the table. Begin at the right border of the first column and at **4.5 inches on the vertical ruler**, and draw a horizontal line extending to the right table border. In a similar manner, draw a horizontal line positioned at **5 inches on the vertical ruler**. In the first row, use the **Eraser** to remove the border between the two cells. In a similar manner, use the **Eraser** to remove the inside border in the second and sixth rows. Turn off the **Eraser**.

5 In the first row of the table, type **Chesterfield Creations** Press Enter, and then type **Frequent Buyer Program** Select the text, change the **Font Size** to **28 pt**, apply **Bold**, and then change the **Font Color** to **Blue, Accent 1, Darker 25%**. Click **Align Center**.

6 In the third row, select the first cell, change the **Height** to 0.75", click **Align Center**, and then click **Text Direction** two times. Type **Benefits** Select the text, change the **Font Size** to **28 pt**, and then change the **Font Color** to **Blue, Accent 1, Darker 25%**.

7 In the second row, select the last sentence that begins *The Frequent*, and drag to move the text to the second cell in the fifth row. In a similar manner, move the sentence that begins *Notification* to the fourth row, and then move the two sentences beginning with *After every five* and ending with *amount* to the third row. Select all three cells to the right of *Benefits*, click **Align Center Left**, and then click **Distribute Rows**. Remove any unnecessary spaces that display at the end of the paragraphs in **rows 2** through **5**.

8 Select the entire main table, and then change the **Shading** to **Blue, Accent 1, Lighter 80%**.

9 In the last row of the table, insert a nested table that contains two rows and two columns. Select the entire nested table, and apply **No Border**. If necessary, turn on **View Gridlines**. Change all **Default cell margins** to 0.1", change **Default cell spacing** to 0.3", and then click **Align Center**. Select the first column, and then **Merge Cells**. In the nested table, click in the first cell. Insert an online picture from **Office.com Clip Art**—search for **teamwork dollars** and then select the image shown in Figure 5.56 or a similar graphic. Click the **Shape Height up spin arrow** to 2".

10 In the nested table, in the first cell of the second column, type **Use the spreadsheet below to calculate your savings for a desired product.** In the second cell of the second column, insert an **Excel Spreadsheet**. In cell **A1**, type **Cost** In cell **B1**, type **Discount** and then in cell **C1**, type **My Price** In cell **B2**, type **15%** and then in cell **C2**, type **=A2*.85** Press Enter. Resize the spreadsheet to display only **columns A** through **C** and **rows 1** and **2**, and then click in a blank area of the document.

11 Press Ctrl + Home. Click the **FILE tab**, and then click **Show All Properties**. In the **Tags** box, type **frequent buyer program** In the **Subject** box, type your course name and section number. If necessary, change the author name to display your name. **Save** your document. Print your document or submit electronically as directed by your instructor. **Close** Word.

END | You have completed Project 5F

CONTENT-BASED ASSESSMENTS

MyITLab® grader

Apply 5A and 5B skills from these Objectives:

1. Create and Apply a Custom Table Style
2. Format Cells
3. Use Advanced Table Features
4. Modify Table Properties
5. Draw a Freeform Table
6. Use Nested Tables
7. Insert an Excel Spreadsheet

Mastering Word Project 5G Holiday Special

In the following Mastering Word project, you will create a flyer that provides descriptions of new products available for holiday shopping at Chesterfield Creations. Your completed document will look similar to Figure 5.57.

PROJECT FILES

For Project 5G, you will need the following file:

w05G_Holiday_Special

You will save your file as:

Lastname_Firstname_5G_Holiday_Special

PROJECT RESULTS

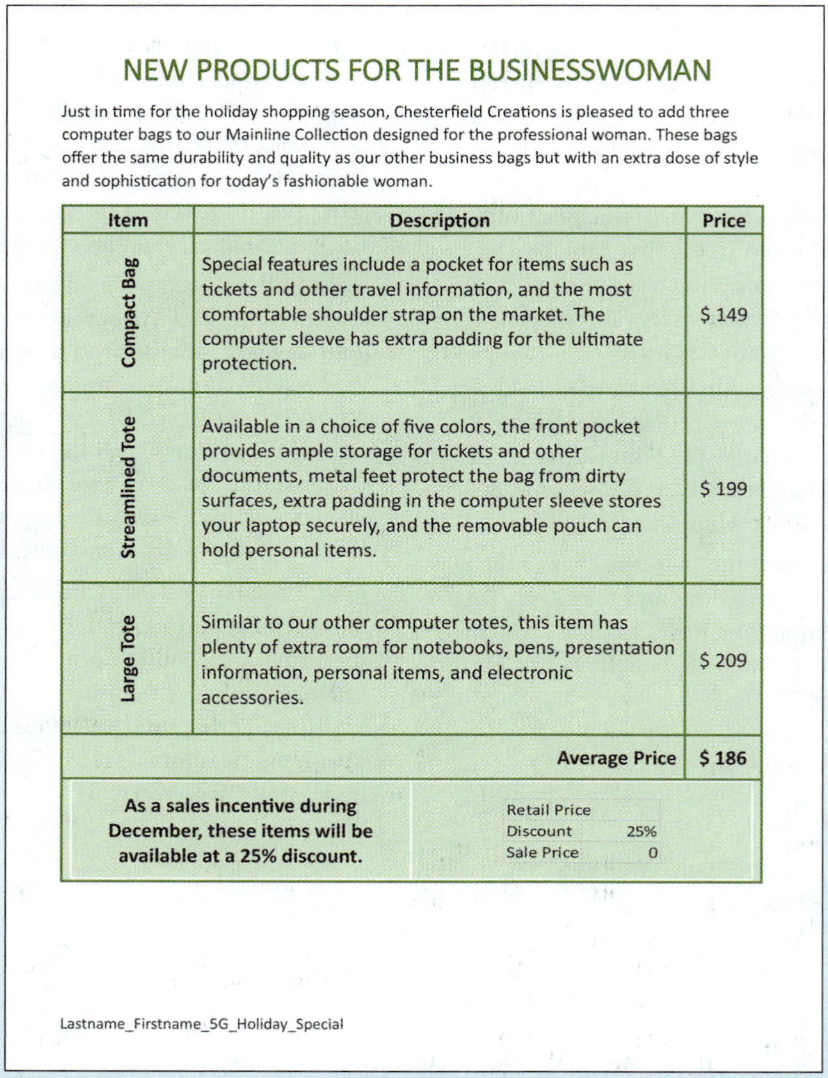

NEW PRODUCTS FOR THE BUSINESSWOMAN

Just in time for the holiday shopping season, Chesterfield Creations is pleased to add three computer bags to our Mainline Collection designed for the professional woman. These bags offer the same durability and quality as our other business bags but with an extra dose of style and sophistication for today's fashionable woman.

Item	Description	Price
Compact Bag	Special features include a pocket for items such as tickets and other travel information, and the most comfortable shoulder strap on the market. The computer sleeve has extra padding for the ultimate protection.	$ 149
Streamlined Tote	Available in a choice of five colors, the front pocket provides ample storage for tickets and other documents, metal feet protect the bag from dirty surfaces, extra padding in the computer sleeve stores your laptop securely, and the removable pouch can hold personal items.	$ 199
Large Tote	Similar to our other computer totes, this item has plenty of extra room for notebooks, pens, presentation information, personal items, and electronic accessories.	$ 209
	Average Price	**$ 186**

As a sales incentive during December, these items will be available at a 25% discount.	Retail Price Discount 25% Sale Price 0

Lastname_Firstname_5G_Holiday_Special

FIGURE 5.57

(Project 5G Holiday Special continues on the next page)

CONTENT-BASED ASSESSMENTS

1 Start Word, and then open the file **w05G_Holiday_Special**. **Save** the document in your **Word Chapter 5** folder as **Lastname_Firstname_5G_Holiday_Special** Insert the file name in the footer, and display rulers and formatting marks.

2 Select the first paragraph, and then apply the **Heading 1** style. Select the second paragraph, and then change the **Font Size** to **12**. Select the remaining three paragraphs of the document, change the **Font Size** to **14**, and then with the text still selected, **Convert Text to Table**.

3 Display the **Styles** pane, and then click the **New Style** button. In the **Create New Style from Formatting** dialog box, create a new style named **Holiday** Set the **Style type** to **Table**. Apply the style to **All Borders**. Set the **Line Weight** to **1 ½ pt**, and then set the **Border Color** to **Green, Accent 6, Darker 25%**. Change the **Fill Color** to **Green, Accent 6, Lighter 80%**. Apply the **Holiday** style to the entire table.

4 Select the first column, and then change the column **Width** to **1.2"**. Change the second column **Width** to **4.5"**, and the third column **Width** to **0.7"**. Position the insertion point anywhere in the first row, and then click **Insert Above**. In the first cell of the table, type **Item** and then press Tab. Type **Description** Press Tab and then type **Price** Select the **header row**, apply **Bold**, and then click **Align Center**. Change the **Height** of **rows 2, 3,** and **4** to **1.5", 1.8",** and **1.4"**, respectively.

5 In the first column, select all the cells below the header row. Apply **Bold**, click **Align Center**, and then click **Text Direction** two times. In the second column, select all the cells below the header row, and then click **Align Center Left**. In the last column, select all the cells below the header row, and click **Align Center**.

6 Point to the bottom left corner of the table, and then click the **One-Click Row/Column Insertion** button. In the last row, change the **Height** to **0.4"**. Select the first and second cells, and then **Merge Cells**. Click **Text Direction**, and then click **Align Center Right**. Type **Average Price** and then apply **Bold**. In the last cell of the table, insert the **Formula: =AVERAGE(ABOVE)** Change the **Number format** to **#,##0**, and to the left of the number format, type **$** and then click **OK**. Select the displayed text, and then apply **Bold**.

7 Point to the bottom left corner of the table, and then click the **One-Click Row/Column Insertion** button. Select both cells in the last row, and then **Merge Cells**. Insert a nested table containing one row and two columns. Select both cells, and then apply **No Border**. Change all **Cell Margins** to **0.1"**, set **Allow spacing between cells** to **0.02"**. Click **Align Center**.

8 In the first cell of the nested table, type **As a sales incentive during December, these items will be available at a 25% discount.** In the second cell of the nested table, insert an **Excel Spreadsheet**. In cell **A1**, type **Retail Price** and then in cell **A2**, type **Discount** In cell **A3**, type **Sale Price** In cell **B2**, type **25%** and then in cell **B3**, type **=B1*.75** Press Enter. Resize the spreadsheet to display only **columns A** and **B** and **rows 1** through **3**, and then click in a blank area of the document.

9 Press Ctrl + Home. Click the **FILE tab**, and then click **Show All Properties**. In the **Tags** box, type **holiday special, Mainline** In the **Subject** box, type your course name and section number. If necessary, edit the author name to display your name. **Save** your document. Print the document or submit electronically as directed by your instructor. **Close** Word.

END | You have completed Project 5G

CONTENT-BASED ASSESSMENTS

Apply a combination of the **5A** and **5B** skills.

GO! Fix It	Project 5H Safety Program	Online

GO! Make It	Project 5I Product Flyer	Online

GO! Solve It	Project 5J Planning Committee	Online

GO! Solve It	Project 5K Wallet Collection	

PROJECT FILES

For Project 5K, you will need the following file:

w05K_Wallet_Collection

You will save your file as:

Lastname_Firstname_5K_Wallet_Collection

Open the file **w05K_Wallet_Collection** and save it to your **Word Chapter 5** folder as **Lastname_Firstname_5K_Wallet_Collection** Using the information for the specific wallets, convert the text to a table. Insert a header row, add appropriate column headings, and then sort the table by price and item name. Create a formula to display the average price of the items. Create and apply a table style. Adjust paragraph, text, table, and cell formats to display attractively in a one-page document. Insert the file name in the footer and add appropriate document properties. Print your document or submit electronically as directed by your instructor.

Performance Level

		Exemplary: You consistently applied the relevant skills	Proficient: You sometimes, but not always, applied the relevant skills	Developing: You rarely or never applied the relevant skills
Performance Criteria	**Convert text to table**	All appropriate text is displayed in a table.	At least one item of text is not displayed in a table.	No text is displayed in a table.
	Sort the table	The data in the table is sorted by both price and item name.	The data in the table is sorted only by price or item name.	The data in the table is not sorted.
	Create a formula	The average price is calculated using a formula and displays in a new row.	The average price displays in a new row, but a formula is not used.	The average price does not display in a new row.
	Create and apply a table style	A new table style is created and applied to the table.	A table style is applied to the table, but it is a built-in style—not new.	No table style is applied to the table.
	Format the document	All items in the document are formatted appropriately.	At least one item in the document is not formatted appropriately.	No items in the document are formatted.

END | You have completed Project 5K

OUTCOMES-BASED ASSESSMENTS

RUBRIC

The following outcomes-based assessments are open-ended assessments. That is, there is no specific correct result; your result will depend on your approach to the information provided. Make *Professional Quality* your goal. Use the following scoring rubric to guide you in *how* to approach the problem and then to evaluate *how well* your approach solves the problem.

The *criteria*—Software Mastery, Content, Format and Layout, and Process—represent the knowledge and skills you have gained that you can apply to solving the problem. The *levels of performance*—Professional Quality, Approaching Professional Quality, or Needs Quality Improvements—help you and your instructor evaluate your result.

	Your completed project is of Professional Quality if you:	Your completed project is Approaching Professional Quality if you:	Your completed project Needs Quality Improvements if you:
1-Software Mastery	Choose and apply the most appropriate skills, tools, and features and identify efficient methods to solve the problem.	Choose and apply some appropriate skills, tools, and features, but not in the most efficient manner.	Choose inappropriate skills, tools, or features, or are inefficient in solving the problem.
2-Content	Construct a solution that is clear and well organized, contains content that is accurate, appropriate to the audience and purpose, and is complete. Provide a solution that contains no errors in spelling, grammar, or style.	Construct a solution in which some components are unclear, poorly organized, inconsistent, or incomplete. Misjudge the needs of the audience. Have some errors in spelling, grammar, or style, but the errors do not detract from comprehension.	Construct a solution that is unclear, incomplete, or poorly organized; contains some inaccurate or inappropriate content; and contains many errors in spelling, grammar, or style. Do not solve the problem.
3-Format & Layout	Format and arrange all elements to communicate information and ideas, clarify function, illustrate relationships, and indicate relative importance.	Apply appropriate format and layout features to some elements, but not others. Overuse features, causing minor distraction.	Apply format and layout that does not communicate information or ideas clearly. Do not use format and layout features to clarify function, illustrate relationships, or indicate relative importance. Use available features excessively, causing distraction.
4-Process	Use an organized approach that integrates planning, development, self-assessment, revision, and reflection.	Demonstrate an organized approach in some areas, but not others; or, use an insufficient process of organization throughout.	Do not use an organized approach to solve the problem.

OUTCOMES-BASED ASSESSMENTS

Apply a combination of the **5A** and **5B** skills.

Build from
Scratch

GO! Think Project 5L Company Picnic

PROJECT FILES

For Project 5L, you will need the following file:

New blank Word document

You will save your file as:

Lastname_Firstname_5L_Company_Picnic

Every year, Chesterfield Creations holds a picnic for employees and their families. This year the picnic will be held on June 16 from 10 a.m. to 4 p.m. at High Park in Toronto. Lunch and snacks are provided. There will be music and an assortment of games for young and old. In addition, other park activities are available for a fee—such as pony rides and miniature golf.

Using this information, create a flyer to distribute to employees as an email attachment. Create a document that explains the picnic and lists the schedule of events in a table format. Insert a second table that lists fees for specific activities. Use a formula to provide the total cost for these events. Create a table style and apply it to both tables. Format the flyer, including table and cell properties, so that it is attractive and easy to read. Save the file as **Lastname_Firstname_5L_Company_Picnic** Insert the file name in the footer and add appropriate document properties. Print the document or submit as directed by your instructor.

END | You have completed Project 5L

Build from
Scratch

GO! Think Project 5M Employee Newsletter   Online

Build from
Scratch

You and GO! Project 5N Personal Budget   Online

Building Documents from Reusable Content and Using Markup Tools

GO! to Work
Video W6

6
WORD 2013

PROJECT 6A

OUTCOMES
Create reusable content and construct a document with building blocks and theme templates.

OBJECTIVES

1. Create Custom Building Blocks
2. Create and Save a Theme Template
3. Create a Document by Using Building Blocks

PROJECT 6B

OUTCOMES
Collaborate with others to edit, review, and finalize a document.

OBJECTIVES

4. Use Comments in a Document
5. Track Changes in a Document
6. View Side by Side, Compare, and Combine Documents

Blend Images/Fotolia

In This Chapter

In this chapter you will work with building blocks—objects that can be reused in multiple documents. You will customize predefined building blocks and create your own reusable content. You will create a theme—by defining the colors, fonts, and effects—to give documents a customized appearance. You will build a new document from the custom building blocks and theme. Word includes features to review revisions and comments made in a document. This makes it easy to work with a team to collaborate on documents. You will insert comments, track changes, review changes made by others, and then accept or reject those changes.

The projects in this chapter relate to **Mountain View Public Library**, which serves the Claremont, Tennessee community at three locations—the Main library, the East Branch, and the West Branch. The library's extensive collection includes books, audio books, music CDs, video DVDs, magazines, and newspapers—for all ages. The Mountain View Public Library also provides sophisticated online and technology services, youth programs, and frequent appearances by both local and nationally known authors. The citizens of Claremont support the Mountain View Public Library with local taxes, donations, and special events fees.

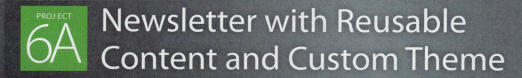

PROJECT 6A

Newsletter with Reusable Content and Custom Theme

PROJECT ACTIVITIES

In Activities 6.01 through 6.09, you will assist Benedetta Herman, Director of Operations at Mountain View Public Library, in designing a custom look for documents that the library produces by creating a custom theme and building blocks for content that can be reused. Your completed documents will look similar to Figure 6.1.

PROJECT FILES

Build from Scratch

For Project 6A, you will need the following files:

Three new blank Word documents
w06A_February_Articles
w06A_Classes

You will save your files as:

Lastname_Firstname_6A_Building_Blocks
Lastname_Firstname_6A_February_Newsletter
Lastname_Firstname_6A_Library_Theme—not shown in figure

PROJECT RESULTS

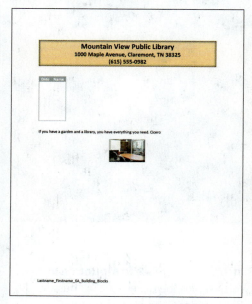

FIGURE 6.1 Project 6A February Newsletter

- Tap an item to click it.
- Press and hold for a few seconds to right-click; release when the information or command displays.
- Touch the screen with two or more fingers and then pinch together to zoom in or stretch your fingers apart to zoom out.
- Slide your finger on the screen to scroll—slide left to scroll right and slide right to scroll left.
- Slide to rearrange—similar to dragging with a mouse.
- Swipe from edge: from right to display charms; from left to expose open apps, snap apps, or close apps; from top or bottom to show commands or close an app.
- Swipe to select—slide an item a short distance with a quick movement to select an item and bring up commands, if any.

Objective 1   Create Custom Building Blocks

Video W6-1

Building blocks are reusable pieces of content or other document parts—for example, headers, footers, page number formats—that are stored in galleries. The Headers gallery, the Footers gallery, the Page Numbers gallery, and the Bibliographies gallery, some of which you have already used, are all examples of building block galleries. You can also create your own building blocks for content that you use frequently.

| ALERT! | Completing This Project in One Working Session |

If you are working in a school lab, plan to complete Project 6A in one working session. Building blocks are stored on the computer at which you are working. Thus, in a school lab, if you close Word before completing the project, the building blocks might be deleted and will not be available for your use—you will have to re-create them. On your own computer, you can close Word, and the building blocks will remain until you purposely delete them.

Activity 6.01 | Inserting a Text Box and Creating a Custom Building Block

Recall that a ***text box*** is a movable, resizable container for text or graphics. In this activity, you will create a distinctive text box that the library can use for any documents requiring the library's contact information.

1 Start Word, and then click **Blank document**. Press F12. In the **Save As** dialog box, navigate to the location where you are saving your files for this chapter, and then create a folder named **Word Chapter 6** Save the document as **Lastname_Firstname_6A_Building_Blocks** At the bottom of the document, right-click in the footer area, and then click **Edit Footer**. On the ribbon, in the **Insert group**, click **Document Info**, and then click **File Name**. **Close** the footer area. If necessary, display the rulers and formatting marks.

2 Press Enter two times, and then position the insertion point in the first blank paragraph.

3 On the **INSERT tab**, in the **Text group**, click **Text Box**. Notice that predesigned, built-in building blocks display in the **Text Box** gallery. Click the first text box—**Simple Text Box**.

A text box containing placeholder text displays at the top of your document. Text boxes can be formatted like other graphic elements in Word and saved as building blocks.

4 On the **FORMAT tab**, in the **Shape Styles group**, click **More** ⏷. In the **Shape Styles** gallery, in the fourth row, click the fifth style—**Subtle Effect – Gold, Accent 4**.

5 On the **FORMAT tab**, if the **Size group** is visible, change the **Shape Width** [Width: 6.49"] to **6.5"**; otherwise, to the right of the **Arrange group**, click **Size**, and then change the **Shape Width** [Width: 6.49"] to **6.5"**. Compare your screen with Figure 6.2.

Depending on the resolution setting of your monitor, either the Size group or the Size button will display.

FIGURE 6.2

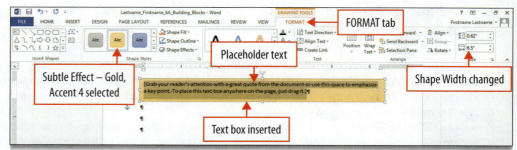

Subtle Effect – Gold, Accent 4 selected

Placeholder text

FORMAT tab

Shape Width changed

Text box inserted

▶ **6** On the **FORMAT tab**, in the **Shape Styles group**, click **Shape Effects**. Point to **Shadow**, and then under **Inner**, in the second row, click the second style—**Inside Center**.

▶ **7** In the text box, type the following text to replace the placeholder text: **Mountain View Public Library** Press Enter, and then type **1000 Maple Avenue, Claremont, TN 38325** Press Enter, and then type **(615) 555-0982**

▶ **8** Select all three paragraphs. On the mini toolbar, click **Styles**, and then in the **Styles** gallery, click **No Spacing**. With the three paragraphs selected, press Ctrl + E to center the paragraphs. Select the first paragraph, change the **Font Size** to 20, and then apply **Bold** B . Select the second and third paragraphs, change the **Font Size** to 16, and then apply **Bold** B . Notice that the height of the text box automatically adjusts to accommodate the text.

▶ **9** Click in the first paragraph to deselect the text. Click the outer edge of the text box so that none of the text is selected, but that the text box itself is selected and displays sizing handles. Compare your screen with Figure 6.3.

FIGURE 6.3

Sizing handles indicate text box is selected

Mountain·View·Public·Library¶
1000·Maple·Avenue,·Claremont,·TN·38325¶
(615)·555-0982¶

Text entered and formatted

▶ **10** On the **INSERT tab**, in the **Text group**, click **Text Box**, and then click **Save Selection to Text Box Gallery**. In the **Create New Building Block** dialog box, in the **Name** box, type **Library Information** Notice that the **Gallery** box displays *Text Boxes*.

By selecting the Text Boxes gallery, this building block will display in the gallery of other text box building blocks.

▶ **11** In the **Description** box, type **Use as the library contact information in newsletters, flyers, public meeting agendas, and other publications** Compare your screen with Figure 6.4.

FIGURE 6.4

Create New Building Block dialog box

Building block stored in Text Boxes gallery

Building block name

Description of building block

▶ **12** Click **OK** to close the dialog box and save the building block. **Save** 💾 your document.

Activity 6.02 | Using the Building Blocks Organizer to View, Edit, and Move Building Blocks

The **Building Blocks Organizer** enables you to view—in a single location—all of the available building blocks from all the different galleries.

1 On the **INSERT tab**, in the **Text group**, click **Quick Parts**.

> **Quick Parts** refers to all of the reusable pieces of content that are available to insert into a document, including building blocks, document properties, and fields.

2 From the list, click **Building Blocks Organizer**. In the **Building Blocks Organizer** dialog box, in the upper left corner, click **Name** to sort the building blocks alphabetically by name.

> Here you can view all of the building blocks available in Word. In this dialog box, you can also delete a building block, edit its properties—for example, change the name, description, or gallery location—or select and insert it into a document.

3 By using the scroll bar in the center of the **Building Blocks Organizer** dialog box, scroll down until you see your building block that begins *Library*, and then click to select it. Compare your screen with Figure 6.5.

> You can see that Word provides numerous building blocks. In the preview area on the right, notice that under the preview of the building block, the name and description that you entered displays.

FIGURE 6.5

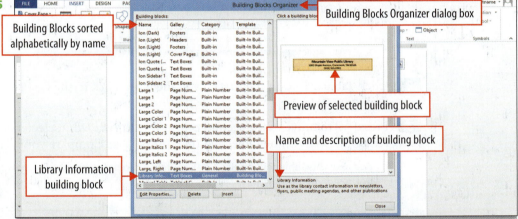

4 In the **Building Blocks Organizer** dialog box, click **Edit Properties**. In the **Modify Building Block** dialog box, click the **Save in box arrow**. In the displayed list, notice that *Building Blocks* is selected.

> By default, the text box building block you created is saved in a folder that contains all predefined building blocks. You can move a building block to a document template by selecting the name of the file from the list. In this case, only the Normal template displays in the list.

5 Be sure *Building Blocks* is selected in the list, and then in the **Modify Building Block** dialog box, click in the **Description** box.

6 In the **Description** box, select the text *public*, and then press [Delete].

> You can edit building block properties in the Modify Building Block dialog box. In this case, you are changing the description of the text box building block.

7 ▶ In the **Modify Building Block** dialog box, click **OK**. In the **Microsoft Word** message box, when asked if you want to redefine the building block entry, click **Yes**. In the lower right corner of the **Building Blocks Organizer** dialog box, click **Close**.

Activity 6.03 | Saving a Custom Building Block as a Quick Table

Quick Tables are tables that are stored as building blocks. Word includes many predesigned Quick Tables, and you can also create your own tables and save them as Quick Tables in the Quick Tables gallery. In this activity you will modify an existing Quick Table and then save it as a new building block. Benedetta Herman will use this table to announce staff birthdays in the quarterly newsletter and in the monthly staff bulletin.

1 ▶ Below the text box, position the insertion point in the second blank paragraph. On the **INSERT tab**, in the **Tables group**, click **Table**, and then at the bottom of the list, point to **Quick Tables**. In the **Quick Tables** gallery, scroll down to locate **Tabular List**, as shown in Figure 6.6.

FIGURE 6.6

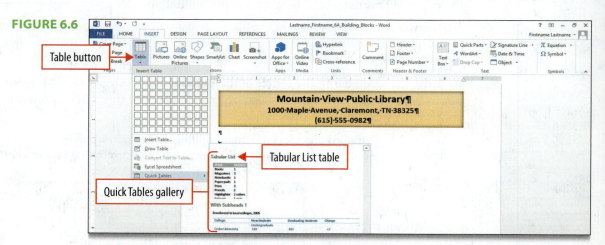

2 ▶ Click **Tabular List**. In the first row of the table, click in the first cell, select the text *ITEM*, and then type **Date**

3 ▶ Press <kbd>Tab</kbd> to move to the second cell, and with *NEEDED* selected, type **Name** Select all the remaining cells of the table, and then press <kbd>Delete</kbd>. Compare your screen with Figure 6.7.

Because this table will be used as a building block to enter birthday information, the sample text is not needed.

FIGURE 6.7

A L E R T !   **Viewing Gridline**

If the table borders do not display, under TABLE TOOLS, click the LAYOUT tab, and then in the Table group, click View Gridlines.

4 ▶ Click in the table, point slightly outside of the upper left corner of the table, and then click the **table move handle** to select the entire table.

5 With the table selected, on the **INSERT tab**, in the **Tables group**, click **Table**. In the displayed list, point to **Quick Tables**, and then at the bottom of the list, click **Save Selection to Quick Tables Gallery**.

6 In the **Create New Building Block** dialog box, in the **Name** box, type **Birthday Table** In the **Description** box, type **Use for staff birthdays in newsletters and bulletins** Compare your screen with Figure 6.8.

FIGURE 6.8

7 Click **OK** to save the table in the **Quick Tables** gallery. **Save** 💾 your document.

Activity 6.04 | Saving a Picture and an AutoText Entry as Quick Parts

In this activity, you will modify an image and save it as a building block so that Benedetta Herman can use it in any document that includes information about library classes.

1 Click in the second blank paragraph below the table. On the same line, point to display the pointer at approximately **3.25 inches on the horizontal ruler** as shown in Figure 6.9.

> The *click and type pointer* is the text select—I-beam—pointer with various attached shapes that indicate which formatting—left-aligned, centered, or right-aligned—will be applied when you double-click in a blank area of the document. In this case, if you double-click, the paragraph will be formatted with center alignment.

FIGURE 6.9

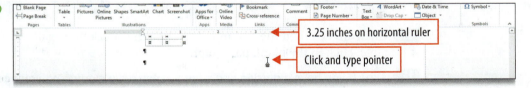

2 At the **3.25 inches mark on the horizontal ruler**, double-click to change the blank paragraph formatting to center alignment. On the **INSERT tab**, in the **Illustrations group**, click **Pictures**.

3 In the **Insert Picture** dialog box, navigate to your student files, select the file **w06A_Classes**, and then click **Insert**.

4 With the picture selected, on the **FORMAT tab**, in the **Picture Styles group**, click **Picture Effects**. Point to **Bevel**, and then under **Bevel**, in the first row, click the fourth bevel—**Cool Slant**.

5 On the **FORMAT tab**, in the **Size group**, change the **Shape Width** to **1.3"**.

🔄 **BY TOUCH**   Tap the picture, and then press and drag the picture's resize handle.

6 With the picture selected, on the **INSERT tab**, in the **Text group**, click **Quick Parts**. From the list, click **Save Selection to Quick Part Gallery**.

> By choosing the Save Selection to Quick Part Gallery command, building blocks that you create are saved in the Quick Parts gallery and assigned to the General category. However, you can save the building block in any of the other relevant galleries or create your own custom gallery. You can also create your own category if you want to do so.

7 In the **Create New Building Block** dialog box, in the **Name** box, type **Classes Picture** and then in the **Description** box, type **Use this picture in documents containing information about the library classes** Compare your screen with Figure 6.10.

You can create and then select any content and save it as a building block in this manner.

FIGURE 6.10

8 Click **OK** to close the dialog box and save the **Classes Picture** building block.

Your new building block is saved; you can insert it in a document by selecting it from the Quick Parts gallery.

9 On the **INSERT tab**, in the **Text group**, click **Quick Parts**, and then point to **Classes Picture**. Compare your screen with Figure 6.11.

Your picture displays under General in the Quick Parts gallery.

FIGURE 6.11

10 Click anywhere in the document to close the **Quick Parts** gallery. Immediately below the table, click in the blank paragraph, and then press Enter.

11 Type **If you have a garden and a library, you have everything you need. Cicero**

12 Select the text you just typed. Be careful not to select the paragraph mark. On the **INSERT tab**, in the **Text group**, click **Quick Parts**. From the list, click **AutoText**, and then click **Save Selection to AutoText Gallery**.

13 In the **Create New Building Block** dialog box, in the **Name** box, type **Library Quote** and then in the **Description** box, type **Quote for newsletter** Click the **Save in box arrow**, and then click **Building Blocks**. Compare your screen with Figure 6.12.

FIGURE 6.12

14 ▶ Click **OK** to close the dialog box, and then press Ctrl + Home. Click the **FILE tab**, click the **Info tab**, and then click **Show All Properties**. In the **Tags** box, type **library newsletter, building blocks** In the **Subject** box, type your course name and section number. If necessary, edit the author name to display your name.

15 ▶ From **Backstage** view, click **Save**. Press Ctrl + W to close the document and leave Word open for the next activity.

> The purpose of this document is to submit a copy of your building blocks to your instructor. After the building blocks are stored in a gallery, they are saved on your system and no document is required unless you want to distribute your building blocks to someone else who would like to use the building blocks on his or her computer.

 **ANOTHER WAY**   Click the FILE tab, and then click Close to close a document and leave Word open.

A L E R T !   **What Happens If I Accidentally Close Word?**

If you accidentally close Word, in the dialog box regarding changes to building blocks, click Save to accept the changes.

Objective 2 | Create and Save a Theme Template

Video W6-2

Recall that a ***theme*** is a predefined combination of colors, fonts, and line and fill effects that look good together and is applied to an entire document by a single selection. Word comes with a group of predefined themes—the default theme is named *Office*. You can also create your own theme by selecting any combination of colors, fonts, and effects, which, when saved, creates a ***theme template***. A theme template, which stores a set of colors, fonts, and effects—lines and fill effects—can be shared with other Office programs, such as Excel and PowerPoint.

Activity 6.05 | Creating Custom Theme Colors and Theme Fonts

In this activity, you will create a custom theme.

1 ▶ Press Ctrl + N to display a new blank document.

2 ▶ On the **DESIGN tab**, in the **Document Formatting group**, click **Themes**. In the **Themes** gallery, click **Organic**.

3 ▶ On the **DESIGN tab**, in the **Document Formatting group**, click **Colors** ▦. In the **Theme Colors** gallery, take a moment to examine the various color schemes, scrolling as necessary, and then at the bottom of the list, click **Customize Colors**.

4 ▶ In the **Create New Theme Colors** dialog box, click the **Text/Background – Dark 1 arrow**, and then under **Theme Colors**, in the seventh column, click the fifth color—**Blue-Gray, Accent 3, Darker 25%**. Using the same technique, change **Accent 1** to **Red, Accent 4**—in the eighth column, the first color, and then change **Accent 4** to **Blue-Gray, Accent 3, Lighter 40%**—in the seventh column, the fourth color. In the **Name** box, delete the existing text, and then type **Newsletter Colors** Compare your screen with Figure 6.13.

> A set of theme colors contains four text and background colors, six accent colors, and two hyperlink colors. You can select a new color for any category and save the combination of colors with a new name. In this case, you are changing the colors for the Text/Background – Dark 1, Accent 1, and Accent 4 categories, and saving the color combination with the name Newsletter Colors. The Sample box displays the modified theme color scheme.

FIGURE 6.13

Create New Theme Colors dialog box

Text Background – Dark 1

Accent 1

Accent 4

Name

5 Click **Save** to close the **Create New Theme Colors** dialog box. In the **Document Formatting group**, click **Fonts** A , and then at the bottom of the list, click **Customize Fonts**.

Theme fonts contain a heading font—the upper font—and a body text font—the lower font. You can use an existing set of built-in fonts for your new theme, or define new sets of fonts.

6 In the **Create New Theme Fonts** dialog box, click the **Heading font arrow**, scroll as necessary to locate and then click **Arial**. Click the **Body font arrow**, scroll as necessary, and then click **Calibri**. In the **Name** box, delete the existing text, and then type **Newsletter Fonts**

The custom Theme Fonts—Newsletter Fonts—includes the Arial heading font and the Calibri body text font.

7 Click **Save** to close the **Create New Theme Fonts** dialog box. In the **Document Formatting group**, click **Effects** .

Theme effects are sets of lines and fill effects. Here you can see the lines and fill effects for each predefined theme. You cannot create your own set of theme effects, but you can choose any set of effects to combine with other theme colors and theme fonts.

8 In the **Theme Effects** gallery, click **Office**.

9 Leave Word open—you will save your custom theme in the next activity.

Activity 6.06 | Creating a Custom Theme Template

To use your custom theme in other Microsoft Office files, you can save it as a theme template.

1 In the **Document Formatting group**, click **Themes**, and then at the bottom of the **Themes** gallery, click **Save Current Theme** to display the **Save Current Theme** dialog box. Compare your screen with Figure 6.14.

By default, saving a new theme displays the Templates folder, which includes the Document Themes folder, containing separate folders for Theme Colors, Theme Effects, and Theme Fonts. The Save as type box specifies the file type *Office Theme*.

If you save your theme in the Templates folder, it is available to the Office programs on the computer at which you are working. In a college or organization, you may not have permission to update this folder, but on your own computer, you can save your themes here if you want to do so.

FIGURE 6.14

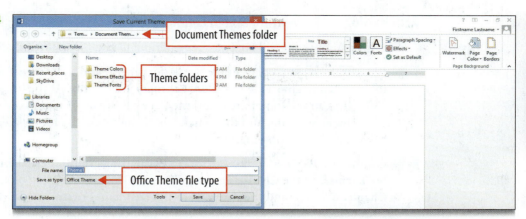

2 In the **Save Current Theme** dialog box, navigate to your **Word Chapter 6** folder. In the **File name** box, type **Lastname_Firstname_6A_Library_Theme** and then click **Save**.

For the purpose of this instruction, you are saving the theme to your Word Chapter 6 folder.

3 In the **Document Formatting group**, click **Themes**, and then click **Browse for Themes**. In the **Choose Theme or Themed Document** dialog box, navigate to your **Word Chapter 6** folder, right-click your file **Lastname_Firstname_6A_Library_Theme**, and then click **Properties**. Compare your screen with Figure 6.15.

The Properties dialog box for the Theme displays. A Microsoft Office theme is saved with the file extension .thmx. By default, a theme template is set to open with PowerPoint; however, the theme can also be applied in Word or Excel.

FIGURE 6.15

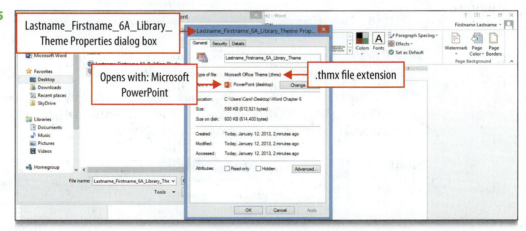

4 Click **OK** to close the **Properties** dialog box, and then **Close** ⊠ the **Choose Theme or Themed Document** dialog box. Click the **FILE tab**, and then **Close** the blank document without saving changes. Keep Word open for the next activity.

Objective 3   Create a Document by Using Building Blocks

Video W6-3

One of the benefits of creating building blocks and theme templates is that they can be used repeatedly to create individual documents. The building blocks ensure consistency in format and structure, and the theme template provides consistency in colors, fonts, and effects.

Activity 6.07 | Formatting Text in Columns

In this activity, you will apply a theme template and format text in columns.

1 Press **Ctrl** + **N** to display a new blank document, and then Save it in your **Word Chapter 6** folder as **Lastname_Firstname_6A_February_Newsletter** At the bottom of the document, right-click in the footer area, and then click **Edit Footer**. On the ribbon, in the **Insert group**, click **Document Info**, and then click **File Name**. **Close** the footer area. If necessary, display the rulers and formatting marks.

2 On the **DESIGN tab**, in the **Document Formatting group**, click **Themes**, and then click **Browse for Themes**. In the **Choose Theme or Themed Document** dialog box, navigate to your **Word Chapter 6** folder, and then click your file **Lastname_Firstname_6A_Library_Theme**. Compare your screen with Figure 6.16.

FIGURE 6.16

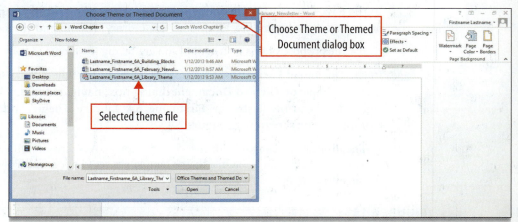

3 Click **Open** to apply the theme, and notice that the colors on the buttons in the Document Formatting group change to reflect the new theme.

4 On the **DESIGN tab**, in the **Page Background group**, click **Page Color**, and then click **Fill Effects**. In the **Fill Effects** dialog box, click the **Texture tab**, and then in the fourth row, click the fourth texture–**Stationery**. Compare your screen with Figure 6.17.

FIGURE 6.17

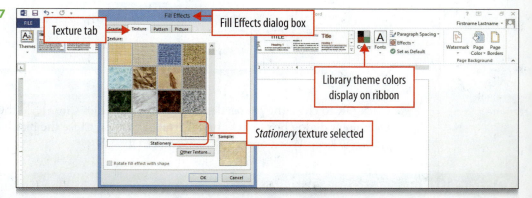

5 Click **OK** to apply the textured background.

6 Press **Enter** two times. Type **Staff Newsletter** press **Tab** two times, type **February** and then press **Enter**. Select the paragraph you just typed, on the mini toolbar, click **Styles**, and then click **Title**. Press **Ctrl** + **E** to center the paragraph.

7 Above the title, select the two blank paragraphs, and then on the **HOME tab**, in the **Styles group**, click **No Spacing**. Below the title, position the insertion point in the blank paragraph. On the **HOME tab**, in the **Styles group**, click **Normal**. Select the paragraph mark, and then compare your screen with Figure 6.18.

FIGURE 6.18

Text entered and formatted → Staff·Newsletter · · February¶

Paragraph mark selected

8 With the paragraph mark selected, on the **PAGE LAYOUT tab**, in the **Page Setup group**, click **Columns**, and then click **Two**. Click to the left of the paragraph mark, and then compare your screen with Figure 6.19.

A continuous section break is inserted at the end of the previous paragraph. The remainder of the document will be formatted in two columns.

FIGURE 6.19

Two-column format

Staff·Newsletter · · February¶ ← Section break

9 On the **INSERT tab**, in the **Text group**, click the **Object arrow**, and then click **Text from File**. In the **Insert File** dialog box, navigate to your student files, click **w06A_February_Articles**, and then click **Insert**.

Word inserts the text in the first column.

10 On the **PAGE LAYOUT tab**, in the **Page Setup group**, click the **Columns arrow**, and then click **More Columns** to display the **Columns** dialog box.

You can modify column formats in the Columns dialog box. For example, you can change the number of columns, the width of the columns, the spacing after columns, and insert a line to separate the columns.

11 In the **Columns** dialog box, select the **Line between** check box, and then click **OK**. Compare your screen with Figure 6.20.

A line displays between the two columns.

FIGURE 6.20

Text inserted →

New·Classes·at·the·Library¶

We·still·need·leaders·for·the·following·sessions.·Please·contact·Abigail·Gardner·if·you·can·help.¶

Story·and·Craft:·The·topic·is·kites.·A·class·for·children·ages·5–12.¶
When:·February·27·at·4·p.m.¶
Where:·West·Branch¶

Line inserted between columns

12 Select the paragraph *New Classes at the Library*. Press and hold Ctrl, and then select the paragraphs *Valentine's Day Fundraiser* and *Card Shower*. On the mini toolbar, click **Styles**, and then click **Heading 1**.

13 In the *New Classes* section, select the headings *Story and Craft:*, *E-mail Basics:*, and *Adult Literacy Volunteers:*—be sure to include each colon. Display the **Styles** gallery, and then click **Intense Emphasis**.

14 At the top of the second column, click in the blank paragraph.

15 ▸ Type **February Birthdays** and then press Enter. Select the text you just typed, display the **Styles** gallery, and then click **Heading 1**. Compare your screen with Figure 6.21, and then **Save** 🖫 your document.

FIGURE 6.21

Activity 6.08 | Inserting Quick Parts and Customizing Building Blocks, and Manually Hyphenating a Document

In this activity, you will complete the newsletter by using the building blocks that you created.

1 ▸ Press Ctrl + Home. On the **INSERT tab**, in the **Text group**, click **Text Box**. Scroll to the bottom of the **Text Box** gallery, and then under **General**, click the **Library Information** building block.

The theme colors of your custom theme are applied to the building block and the text in the columns is redistributed.

2 ▸ Near the beginning of the first column, locate the paragraph that begins *We still need leaders*, and then click to position the insertion point at the end of the paragraph. Press Enter, and then press Ctrl + E. On the **INSERT tab**, in the **Text group**, click **Quick Parts**. Under **General**, click the **Classes Picture** building block.

3 ▸ Click to select the picture. On the **FORMAT tab**, in the **Size group**, change the **Shape Height** Height: 0.19" to **1.7"**. Deselect the picture, and then compare your screen with Figure 6.22.

FIGURE 6.22

4 ▸ At the bottom of the first column, position the insertion point to the left of the heading *Valentine's Day Fundraiser*. On the **PAGE LAYOUT tab**, in the **Page Setup group**, click **Breaks**, and then under **Page Breaks**, click **Column**.

You can insert a manual column break to define the point where text should flow to the next column. In this case, the heading is moved to the beginning of the second column.

5 ▸ With the insertion point to the left of *Valentine's*, on the **PAGE LAYOUT tab**, in the **Paragraph group**, change the **Spacing Before** to **18 pt**.

6 ▸ In the second column, click in the blank paragraph below *February Birthdays*. On the **INSERT tab**, in the **Tables group**, click **Table**, point to **Quick Tables**, scroll toward the bottom of the list, and then under **General**, click **Birthday Table**.

7 ▸ In the second row of the table, position the insertion point in the first cell, and then type **11** Press Tab, and then type **Eleanor Willis** Press Tab. Use the same technique to type the following text in the table.

17	Lydia Barton
18	Anthony Sanchez
20	Trent Zimmer
27	Susan Matthews

8 ▸ Select the last three empty rows of the table. On the mini toolbar, click **Delete**, and then click **Delete Rows**. Click the **table move handle** 🖈, and then on the mini toolbar, change the **Font Size** to **14**.

9 ▸ At the bottom of the second column, select the blank paragraph mark. With the paragraph mark selected, on the **PAGE LAYOUT tab**, in the **Page Setup group**, click **Columns**, and then click **One**.

> The existing text remains formatted in two columns; however, the bottom of the document returns to one column—full page width.

10 ▸ With the paragraph mark selected, on the **INSERT tab**, in the **Text group**, click **Quick Parts**, click **AutoText**, and then click **Library Quote**. Select the inserted text. On the mini toolbar, click **Styles**, click **Intense Reference**, and then change the **Font Size** to **14**. Press Ctrl + E, and then deselect the text. Compare your screen with Figure 6.23.

> The Library Quote AutoText is inserted and centered between the left and right margins.

FIGURE 6.23

11 ▸ **Save** 💾 your document.

12 ▸ Press Ctrl + Home. On the **PAGE LAYOUT tab**, in the **Page Setup group**, click **Hyphenation**, and then click **Manual** to display the **Manual Hyphenation: English (United States)** dialog box.

> *Hyphenation* is a tool in Word that controls how words are split between two lines. By selecting Manual, you can control which words are hyphenated.

13 ▸ In the **Manual Hyphenation: English (United States)** dialog box, in the **Hyphenate at** box, with *at-tach-ments* displayed, click **No** to reject hyphenating the word. In the **Hyphenate at** box, with *ses-sion* displayed, click **Yes** to accept the hyphenated word. Using the same technique, click **Yes** to accept all remaining hyphenated words.

14 ▸ When a message displays indicating that the hyphenation is complete, click **OK**. **Save** 💾 your document.

Activity 6.09 | Deleting Custom Building Blocks, Theme Colors, and Theme Fonts

You can delete user-created building blocks, theme colors, and theme fonts if they are no longer needed. If you are sharing a computer with others, you must restore Word to its default settings. In this activity, you will delete the building blocks, theme colors, and theme fonts that you created.

1 ▸ On the **INSERT tab**, in the **Text group**, click **Quick Parts**. Right-click the **Classes Picture** building block, and then click **Organize and Delete**. Compare your screen with Figure 6.24.

> The Classes Picture building block is selected in the Building Blocks Organizer dialog box. A preview of the building block displays on the right. The name and description of the building block displays below the preview.

FIGURE 6.24

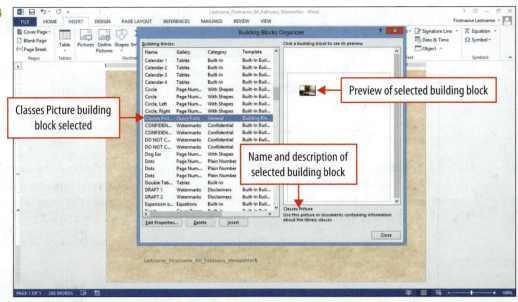

2 ▶ Click **Delete**. When a message displays to confirm the deletion, click **Yes**.

3 ▶ In the **Building Blocks Organizer** dialog box, in the upper left corner, click **Name** to sort the building blocks alphabetically by name.

4 ▶ By using the scroll bar in the center of the **Building Blocks Organizer** dialog box, scroll down until you see your building block that begins *Birthday*, and then click to select it. Click **Delete**, and then click **Yes** to confirm the deletion.

5 ▶ Using the same technique, scroll to locate your building block *Library Information*, and then delete it. Delete the **Library Quote** building block. **Close** the **Building Blocks Organizer** dialog box.

6 ▶ On the **DESIGN tab**, in the **Document Formatting group**, click **Colors** ▨. At the top of the **Theme Colors** gallery, right-click **Newsletter Colors**, and then click **Delete**. When a message displays to confirm the deletion, click **Yes**. Using the same technique, display the **Theme Fonts** gallery, and then delete the **Newsletter Fonts**.

Because the theme—including the custom theme colors and theme fonts—has been saved, you no longer need the Newsletter Colors and Newsletter Fonts to display in the respective lists.

7 ▶ Click the **FILE tab**, click the **Info tab**, and then click **Show All Properties**. In the **Tags** box, type **library newsletter, February** In the **Subject** box, type your course name and section number. If necessary, edit the author name to display your name.

8 ▶ Save 🖫 your document. Print your two Word documents—you cannot print the theme file— or submit all three files electronically as directed by your instructor. **Close** ❌ Word. When a message displays regarding changes to building blocks, click **Save** to accept the changes.

END | You have completed Project 6A

Events Schedule with Tracked Changes

PROJECT ACTIVITIES

In Activities 6.10 through 6.19, you will assist Abigail Gardner, Director of Programs and Youth Services, in using the markup tools in Word to add comments and make changes to a schedule of events. You will accept or reject each change, and then compare and combine your document with another draft version to create a final document. Your completed documents will look similar to Figure 6.25.

PROJECT FILES

For Project 6B, you will need the following files:

w06B_Events_Schedule
w06B_Schedule_Revisions

You will save your files as:

Lastname_Firstname_6B_Events_Schedule
Lastname_Firstname_6B_Schedule_Revisions
Lastname_Firstname_6B_Schedule_Combined

PROJECT RESULTS

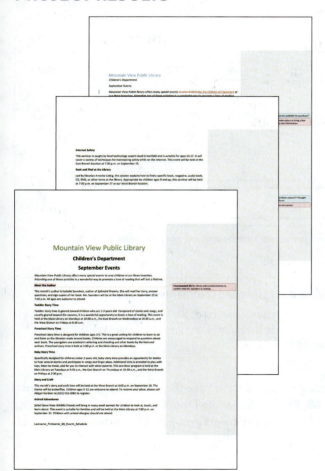

FIGURE 6.25 Project 6B Events Schedule

Video W6-4

Building a final document often involves more than one person. One person usually drafts the original and becomes the document *author*—or *owner*—and then others add their portions of text and comment on, or propose changes to, the text of others. A *reviewer* is someone who reviews and marks changes on a document.

A *comment* is a note that an author or reviewer adds to a document. Comments are a good way to communicate when more than one person is involved with the writing, reviewing, and editing process. Comments are like sticky notes attached to the document—they can be viewed and read by others but are not part of the document text.

Activity 6.10 | Inserting Comments

For the library's monthly schedule of events, Abigail Gardner has created a draft document; edits and comments have been added by others. In this activity, you will insert a comment to suggest confirming a scheduled guest.

1 Start Word. From your student files, locate and open the file **w06B_Events_Schedule**. If necessary, display the rulers and formatting marks. Compare your screen with Figure 6.26.

The document displays in *Simple Markup* view, in which *revisions*—changes made to a document—are indicated by vertical red lines in the left margin, and comments that have been made are indicated by icons in the right margin.

FIGURE 6.26

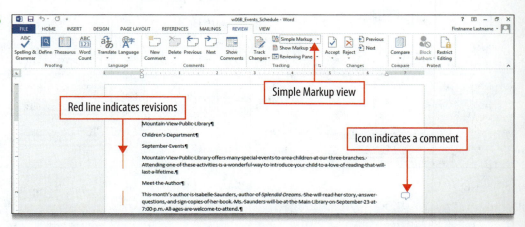

Red line indicates revisions

Simple Markup view

Icon indicates a comment

ALERT! **Displaying a Document in Simple Markup View and Displaying Comments as Icons**

If you are sharing a computer, tracking changes features may have been used previously, causing your document to display in a different view. To display the document in Simple Markup view, on the REVIEW tab, in the Tracking group, click the Display for Review arrow, and then click Simple Markup. If the comments do not display as icons, in the Comments group, click Show Comments to turn off the command.

---

2 Click the **FILE tab**, display the **Save As** dialog box, and then **Save** the document in your **Word Chapter 6** folder as **Lastname_Firstname_6B_Events_Schedule** Double-click in the footer area, and then delete the existing text. On the ribbon, in the **Insert group**, click **Document Info**, and then click **File Name**. **Close** the footer area.

3 Press Ctrl + Home. On the **REVIEW tab**, in the **Comments group**, click **Show Comments**. Compare your screen with Figure 6.27.

The comments display in *balloons* in the nonprinting *markup area*. A balloon is the outline shape in which a comment or formatting change displays. The markup area is the space to the right or left of the document where comments and also formatting changes—for example, applying italic—display. Each comment includes the name of the reviewer who made the comment. Each reviewer's comments are identified by a distinct color. An image will also display if the reviewer is signed in with a Microsoft personal account or an Active Directory at work and has a picture associated with the profile.

FIGURE 6.27

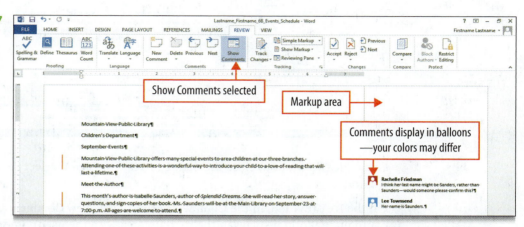

4 On the **REVIEW tab**, in the **Tracking group**, click the **Dialog Box Launcher**. In the **Track Changes Options** dialog box, click **Change User Name**.

5 In the **Word Options** dialog box, under **Personalize your copy of Microsoft Office**, on a piece of paper, make a note of the user name and initials—if you are using your own computer, your own name and initials may display.

The user name identifies the person who makes comments and changes in a document.

ALERT! **Changing the User Name and Initials**

In a school lab or organization, you may not be able to change the user name and initials, so make a note of the name and initials currently displayed so that you can identify your revisions in this document.

---

6 If you are able to do so, in the **User name** box, delete any existing text, and then type your own first and last names. In the **Initials** box, delete any existing text, and then type your initials. Below the **Initials** box, select the **Always use these values regardless of sign in to Office** check box. Compare your screen with Figure 6.28. If you are unable to make this change, move to Step 7.

FIGURE 6.28

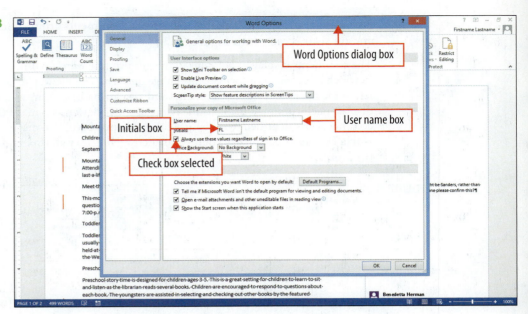

7 ▶ Click **OK** two times to close the dialog boxes. On **Page 1**, select the fifth paragraph *Meet the Author*.

8 ▶ On the **REVIEW tab**, in the **Comments group**, click **New Comment**, and notice that the comment balloon displays in the markup area with the user name. Type **Check with Barry Smith to confirm that Ms. Saunders is coming.** Click anywhere outside of the comment, and then compare your screen with Figure 6.29.

You can insert a comment at a specific location in a document or to selected text, such as an entire paragraph. Your name—or the name configured for the computer at which you are working—displays at the beginning of the comment.

FIGURE 6.29

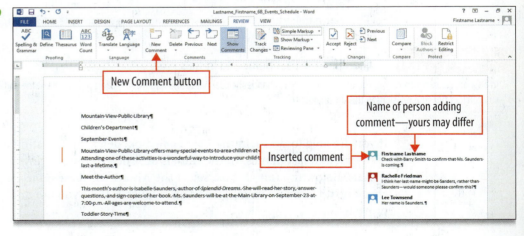

ANOTHER WAY On the INSERT tab, in the Comments group, click New Comment.

9 ▶ Near the bottom of **Page 1**, locate the comment by Rachelle Friedman that begins *Should we mention*. Point to the balloon containing the comment and notice that shaded text displays in the document indicating where the comment was inserted.

10 ▶ In the top right corner of the balloon, click **Reply** 🖵. Compare your screen with Figure 6.30.

Your name is inserted in the balloon. It is indented, indicating that this is a *reply* to Rachelle Friedman's comment. The insertion point displays below your name.

FIGURE 6.30

11 With the insertion point in the balloon, type **The program is scheduled for approximately one hour.** Click anywhere outside the comment, and then compare your screen with Figure 6.31.

FIGURE 6.31

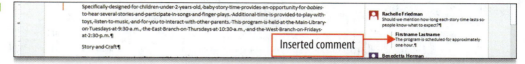

12 **Save** 🖫 your document.

Activity 6.11 | Editing and Deleting Comments

Typically, comments are temporary. One person inserts a comment, another person answers the question or clarifies the text based on the comment—and then the comments are removed before the document is final. In this activity, you will replace text in your comment and delete comments.

1 Locate the comment you inserted referencing *Barry Smith*—the first comment in the document. Select the text *Barry Smith*, and then type **Caroline Marina** If necessary, press Spacebar.

In this manner, you can edit your comments.

2 Immediately below your comment, locate the comment created by Rachelle Friedman, which begins *I think her last name*, and the following comment created by *Lee Townsend*. Compare your screen with Figure 6.32.

Because the question asked by Rachelle Friedman has been answered by Lee Townsend, both comments can be deleted.

FIGURE 6.32

3 Click anywhere in the comment by *Rachelle Friedman*, and then in the **Comments group**, click **Delete**.

4 Point to the comment by *Lee Townsend*, right-click, and then from the shortcut menu, click **Delete Comment**.

Use either technique to delete a comment.

5 In the **Comments group**, click **Next**. In the markup area, notice that the balloon containing a comment by *Benedetta Herman* is selected. Compare your screen with Figure 6.33.

In the Comments group, you can use the Next and Previous buttons in this manner to navigate through the comments in a document.

FIGURE 6.33

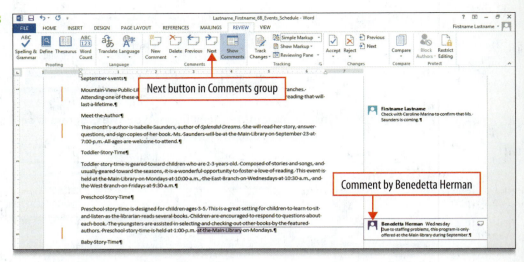

Next button in Comments group

Comment by Benedetta Herman

6 ▶ With the comment that begins *Due to staffing problems* selected, right-click, and then click **Delete Comment**.

7 ▶ In the **Comments group**, click **Next** three times to select the comment by Benedetta Herman that begins *Do we have*, and then use any technique you have practiced to delete the comment.

8 ▶ Scroll as necessary, and delete the two comments by Rachelle Friedman that begin *No, the room* and *We considered*. **Save** 🖫 your document.

Four comments remain in the document.

More Knowledge | **Printing Comments**

To print the comments in a document, click the FILE tab, and then click Print. Under Settings, click the Print All Pages arrow, and then under Document Info, click List of Markup.

Objective 5 | Track Changes in a Document

Video W6-5

When you turn on the *Track Changes* feature, it makes a record of—*tracks*—the changes made to a document. As you revise the document with your changes, Word uses markup to visually indicate insertions, deletions, comments, formatting changes, and content that has moved.

Each reviewer's revisions and comments display in a different color. This is useful if, for example, you want to quickly scan only for edits made by your supervisor or only for edits made by a coworker. After the document has been reviewed by the appropriate individuals, you can locate the changes and accept or reject the revisions on a case-by-case basis or globally in the entire document.

Activity 6.12 | Viewing All Changes in a Document

After one or more reviewers have made revisions and inserted comments, you can view the revisions in various ways. You can display the document in its original or final form, showing or hiding revisions and comments. Additionally, you can choose to view the revisions and comments by only some reviewers or view only a particular type of revision—for example, only formatting changes.

1 Press Ctrl + Home. On the **REVIEW tab**, in the **Tracking group**, locate the **Display for Review** box that displays the text *Simple Markup*. Click the **Display for Review arrow** to display a list. Compare your screen with Figure 6.34.

> Recall that *Simple Markup* view is a view for tracking changes; revisions are indicated by a vertical red bar in the left margin and comments are indicated by an icon in the right margin.
>
> *All Markup* view displays the document with all revisions and comments visible.
>
> *No Markup* view displays the document in its final form—with all proposed changes included and comments hidden.
>
> *Original* view displays the original, unchanged document with all revisions and comments hidden.

FIGURE 6.34

2 On the list, click **No Markup**. Notice that all comments and indicated changes are hidden. The document displays with all proposed changes included.

> When you are editing a document in which you are proposing changes, this view is useful because the revisions of others or the markup of your own revisions is not distracting.

3 In the **Tracking group**, click the **Display for Review arrow**, and then from the list, click **All Markup**. Compare your screen with Figure 6.35.

> At the stage where you, the document owner, must decide which revisions to accept or reject, you will find this view to be the most useful. The document displays with revisions—changes are shown as *markup*. Markup refers to the formatting Word uses to denote the revisions visually. For example, when a reviewer changes text, the original text displays with strikethrough formatting by default. When a reviewer inserts new text, the new text is underlined. A *vertical change bar* displays in the left margin next to each line of text that contains a revision. In All Markup view, the vertical change bar displays in gray; in Simple Markup view, it displays in red.
>
> In All Markup view, shaded text indicates where a comment has been inserted.

FIGURE 6.35

ANOTHER WAY Click any vertical change bar to toggle between Simple Markup view and All Markup view.

BY TOUCH Tap any vertical change bar to toggle between Simple Markup view and All Markup view.

4 In the **Tracking group**, click **Show Markup**, and then point to **Balloons**.

> The default setting *Show Only Comments and Formatting in Balloons* is selected. In this default setting, insertions and deletions *do not* display in balloons. Rather, insertions and deletions display directly in the text with insertions underlined and deletions struck out with a line. Comments and formatting *do* display in balloons.

5 Display the **Show Markup** list, if necessary, and then point to **Specific People** to see the name of each individual who proposed changes to this document. Compare your screen with Figure 6.36.

Here you can turn off the display of revisions by one or more reviewers. For example, you might want to view only the revisions proposed by a supervisor—before you consider the revisions proposed by others—by clearing the check box for all reviewers except the supervisor.

In the Show Markup list, you can also determine which changes display by deselecting one or more of the options. *Ink* refers to marks made directly on a document by using a stylus on a Tablet PC.

FIGURE 6.36

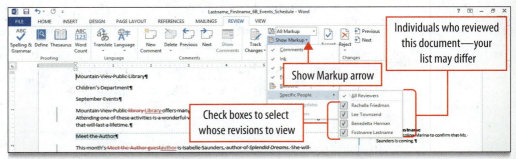

6 Click anywhere in the document to close the **Show Markup** list and leave all revision types by all reviewers displayed.

7 In the fifth paragraph, point to the shaded text *Meet the Author*, where you inserted a comment. Notice that the comment displays as a ScreenTip—indicating the date and time that the comment was created.

8 Near the bottom of **Page 1**, locate the comment by Rachelle Friedman that begins *Should we mention*, and then point to the image. Compare your screen with Figure 6.37.

A *Person Card* related to the reviewer displays. The Person Card allows you to communicate with a reviewer—using email, instant messaging, phone, or video—directly from the comment. Users must be signed in with a Microsoft account or an Active Directory account at work. In this instruction, because no reviewers are signed in, the commands are inactive.

FIGURE 6.37

 BY TOUCH   In a comment, tap the image to display the Person Card.

9 Save 🖫 your changes.

Activity 6.13 | Setting Tracking and Markup Options

In this activity, you will change the way the markup area displays in the document.

1 Press [Ctrl] + [Home] to move to the top of the document. In the **Tracking group**, click the **Dialog Box Launcher**.

2 In the **Track Changes Options** dialog box, click **Advanced Options** to display the **Advanced Track Changes Options** dialog box. Take a moment to study Figure 6.38 and the table shown in Figure 6.39.

Here you can change how markup, moved text, table revisions, and balloons display.

FIGURE 6.38

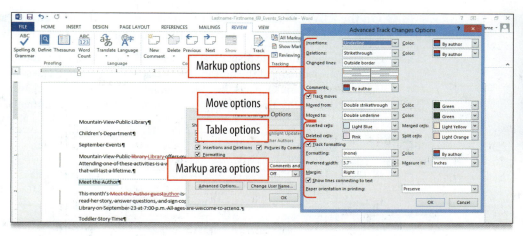

FIGURE 6.39

SETTINGS IN THE ADVANCED TRACK CHANGES OPTIONS DIALOG BOX	
OPTION	**SETTINGS YOU CAN ADJUST**
Markup	Specify the format and color of inserted text, deleted text, and changed lines. By default, inserted text is underlined, deleted text displays with strikethrough formatting, and the vertical change bar indicating changed lines displays on the outside border—left margin. Click an arrow to select a different format, and click the Color arrow to select a different color.
	By author, the default, indicates that Word will assign a different color to each person who inserts comments or tracks changes.
Move	Specify the format of moved text. The default is green with double strikethrough in the moved content and a double underline below the content in its new location. To turn off this feature, clear the Track moves check box.
Table	Specify the color that will display in a table if cells are inserted, deleted, merged, or split.
Markup area	Specify the location and width of the markup area. By default the location is at the right margin and the preferred width for balloons is set to 3.7″. You can also control the display of connecting lines to text.

3 In the **Advanced Track Changes Options** dialog box, locate and verify that the **Track formatting** check box is selected. Below the check box, click the **Preferred width spin box down arrow** to **3″**.

This action will cause the markup area to display with a width of 3″.

4 Click **OK** two times, and then **Save** 🖫 your document.

Use the Advanced Track Changes Options dialog box in this manner to set Track Changes to display the way that works best for you.

Activity 6.14 | Using the Reviewing Pane

The ***Reviewing Pane***, which displays in a separate scrollable window, shows all of the changes and comments that currently display in your document. In this activity you will use the Reviewing Pane to view a summary of all changes and comments in the document.

1 On the **REVIEW tab**, in the **Tracking group**, click the **Reviewing Pane arrow**. From the list, click **Reviewing Pane Vertical**, and then compare your screen with Figure 6.40.

The Reviewing Pane displays at the left of the document. Optionally, you can display the Reviewing Pane horizontally at the bottom of the document window. The summary section at the top of the Reviewing Pane displays the exact number of visible tracked changes and comments that remain in your document. Recall that this document contains four comments.

FIGURE 6.40

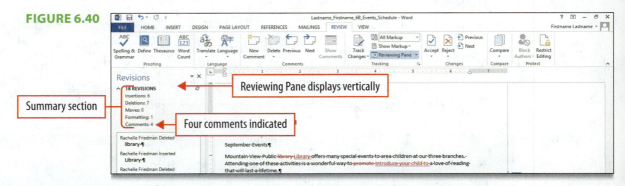

2 Take a moment to read the entries in the **Reviewing Pane**.

In the Reviewing Pane, you can view each type of revision, view the name of the reviewer associated with each item, and read long comments that do not fit within a comment balloon. The Reviewing Pane is also useful for ensuring that all tracked changes have been *removed* from your document when it is ready for final distribution.

3 At the top of the **Reviewing Pane**, click **Close** ☒.

ALERT! **Completing the Remainder of This Project in One Working Session**

Plan to complete the remaining activities of this project in one working session. For purposes of instruction, some revisions in documents must be made within a restricted time frame. If you must take a break, save the document, and then close Word. When you return to complete the project, reopen your file Lastname_Firstname_6B_Events_Schedule. If you are sharing a computer, be sure the user name and initials are the same as in the previous activities.

Activity 6.15 │ Tracking Changes and Locking Tracking to Restrict Editing

The Track Changes feature is turned off by default; you must turn on the feature each time you want to begin tracking changes in a document.

1 Press Ctrl + Home, if necessary, to move to the top of the document. In the **Tracking group**, click the upper portion of the **Track Changes** button to enable tracking. Notice that the button displays in blue to indicate that the feature is turned on.

2 In the **Tracking group**, click the **Track Changes arrow**, and then click **Lock Tracking**.

The *Lock Tracking* feature prevents reviewers from turning off Track Changes and making changes that are not visible in markup.

3 In the **Lock Tracking** dialog box, in the **Enter password (optional)** box, type **1721** In the **Reenter to confirm** box, type **1721** Compare your screen with Figure 6.41.

The Track Changes feature will remain turned on, regardless of who edits the document—the author or reviewers. The password only applies to tracking changes; it does not protect the document.

FIGURE 6.41

4 ▶ Click **OK** to close the **Lock Tracking** dialog box. Notice that the **Track Changes** button no longer displays in blue.

5 ▶ Select the first paragraph—*Mountain View Public Library*. Be sure to include the paragraph mark. On the mini toolbar, change the **Font Size** to **28**, change the **Font Color** [A ▾] to **Green, Accent 6, Darker 25%**—in the last column, the fifth color. With the paragraph selected, press [Ctrl] + [E]. Click anywhere to deselect the text, and then compare your screen with Figure 6.42.

As you make each change, the markup displays in the markup area, and the vertical change bar displays to the left of the paragraph. The types of changes—formatted text and center alignment—are indicated in balloons, and lines point to the location of the revisions.

FIGURE 6.42

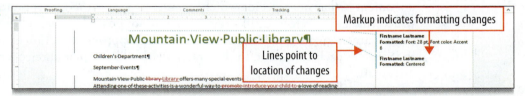

6 ▶ Select the second and third paragraphs, change the **Font Size** to **20**, apply **Bold** [B], and then press [Ctrl] + [E].

7 ▶ Select the paragraph heading *Meet the Author*, hold down [Ctrl], and then by using the **vertical scrollbar down arrow** [⌄], move through the document and select the remaining paragraph headings—*Toddler Story Time*, *Preschool Story Time*, *Baby Story Time*, *Story and Craft*, *Animal Adventures*, *Internet Safety*, and *Seek and Find at the Library*. Apply **Bold** [B] to the selected headings.

8 ▶ Scrolling as necessary, locate the paragraph below *Baby Story Time* that begins *Specifically designed*. In the third line, click to position the insertion point to the left of *program*, type **one-hour** and then press [Spacebar].

The inserted text is underlined and displays with your designated color.

9 ▶ Point to the inserted text, and then compare your screen with Figure 6.43.

A ScreenTip displays, showing the revision that was made, which reviewer made the change, and the date and time of the change.

FIGURE 6.43

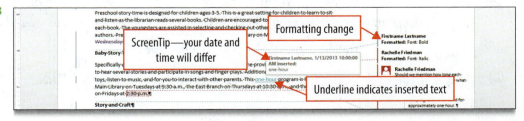

10 At the top of **Page 2**, locate the paragraph that begins *Safari Steve*, and then click to position the insertion point at the end of the paragraph. Press [Spacebar], and then type **Children with animal allergies should not attend.** Notice that the inserted text is underlined and displays with the same color as your previous insertion.

11 In the markup area, read the comment that begins *We should mention*. Use any technique you practiced to delete the comment. **Save** 🖫 your document.

Having responded to this suggestion by inserting appropriate text, you can delete the comment. When developing important documents, having others review the document can improve its content and appearance.

More Knowledge   **Sharing a Document Using SkyDrive**

Use the Share command to allow reviewers to insert comments or edit a document that has been saved to the SkyDrive. To share a saved document, open the document. Click the FILE tab, click Share, and then click Invite People. Under Invite People, enter the names or email addresses of the individuals you want to review the document. Click Can Edit to allow your coworkers to change the file, and then click Share.

Activity 6.16 | Accepting or Rejecting Changes in a Document

After all reviewers have made their proposed revisions and added their comments, the document owner must decide which changes to accept and incorporate into the document and which changes to reject. Unlike revisions, it is not possible to accept or reject comments; instead, the document owner reads the comments, takes appropriate action or makes a decision, and then deletes each comment. In this activity you will accept and reject changes to create a final document.

1 Press [Ctrl] + [Home].

When reviewing comments and changes in a document, it is good practice to start at the beginning of the document to be sure you do not miss any comments or revisions.

2 On the **REVIEW tab**, in the **Tracking group**, click the **Track Changes arrow**, and then click **Lock Tracking**. In the **Unlock Tracking** dialog box, in the **Password** box, type **1721** and then click **OK**.

Because you are finalizing the changes in a document, it is necessary to unlock tracking. After entering the password, you have unlocked tracking. In the Tracking group, the Track Changes button displays in blue, which indicates that the feature is turned on.

3 On the **REVIEW tab**, in the **Changes group**, click **Next**—be careful to select **Next** in the **Changes group**, *not* the **Comments group**. Notice that the first paragraph is selected.

In the Changes group, the Next button and the Previous button enable you to navigate from one revision or comment to the next or previous one, respectively.

4 In the **Changes group**, click the upper portion of the **Accept** button.

The text formatting is accepted for the first paragraph, the related balloon no longer displays in the markup area, and the next change—center alignment for the first three paragraphs—is selected. When reviewing a document, changes can be accepted or rejected individually, or all at one time.

5 In the **Changes group**, click **Accept** to accept the alignment change.

The centering change is applied to all three paragraphs.

 **ANOTHER WAY**   Right-click the selection, and then click Accept.

---

6 In the **Changes group**, click **Accept** to accept the text formatting for the second and third paragraphs.

7 In the next paragraph, point to the strikethrough text *library* and notice that the ScreenTip indicates that Rachelle Friedman deleted *library*. Then, point to the underline directly below *Library* to display a ScreenTip. Compare your screen with Figure 6.44.

When a reviewer replaces text—for example, when Rachelle replaced *library* with *Library*—the inserted text displays with an underline and in the color designated for the reviewer. The original text displays with strikethrough formatting.

FIGURE 6.44

8 In the **Changes group**, click **Accept** two times to accept the deletion of *library* and the insertion of *Library*.

The next change, the deletion of *promote* is selected.

9 In the **Changes group**, click **Reject**, and then point to the selected text *introduce your child to*, to display a ScreenTip. Compare your screen with Figure 6.45.

The original text *promote* is reinserted in the sentence. As the document owner, you decide which proposed revisions to accept; you are not required to accept every change in a document.

FIGURE 6.45

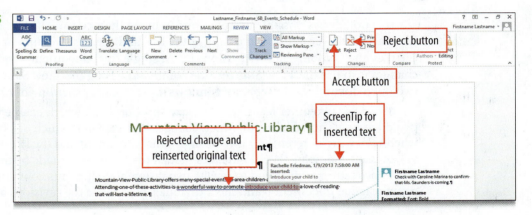

10 Click **Reject** again to reject the insertion of *introduce your child to* and to select the next change.

11 On the **REVIEW tab**, in the **Comments group**, click **Next** two times to select the comment by Rachelle Friedman—be careful to select **Next** in the **Comments group,** *not* in the **Changes group**. Read the comment, and then delete the comment.

Because you replied to Rachelle Friedman's comment, your comment is also deleted. Recall that you cannot accept or reject comments. Rather, you can take appropriate action, and then delete the comment when it is no longer relevant. Because you entered text indicating the program length, you can delete the comment.

12 In the **Changes group**, click the **Accept arrow**. From the list, click **Accept All Changes and Stop Tracking**.

All remaining changes in the document are accepted and Track Changes is turned off.

13 In the **Tracking group**, click the **Dialog Box Launcher** ⬚, and then click **Advanced Options**. In the **Advanced Track Changes Options** dialog box, below the **Track formatting** check box, click the **Preferred width spin box up arrow** to **3.7"**. Click **OK** two times to close the dialog boxes.

This action restores the system to the default settings. One comment remains, and the markup area is still visible.

14 Press ⌨Ctrl + ⌨Home, verify that the remaining comment displays, and then compare your screen with Figure 6.46.

FIGURE 6.46

15 Click the **FILE tab**, click the **Info tab**, and then click **Show All Properties**. In the **Tags** box, type **events schedule, reviewed** In the **Subject** box, type your course name and section number. If necessary, edit the author name to display your name.

16 **Save** 💾 your document; leave it open for the next activity.

Objective 6 | View Side by Side, Compare, and Combine Documents

Video W6-6

It is not always possible for reviewers to make their comments and edits on a single Word file. Each reviewer might edit a copy of the file, and then the document owner must gather all of the files and combine all the revisions into a single final document. One method to examine the changes is to use the *View Side by Side* command. Using the View Side by Side command displays two open documents, in separate windows, next to each other on your screen.

Word has two other features, *Compare* and *Combine*, which enable you to view revisions in two documents and determine which changes to accept and which ones to reject. Compare is useful when reviewing differences between an original document and the latest version of the document. When using Compare, Word indicates that all revisions were made by the same individual. The Combine feature enables you to review two different documents containing revisions—both based on an original document—and the individuals who made the revisions are identified.

Activity 6.17 | Using View Side by Side

Abigail Garner has received another copy of the original file, which contains revisions and comments from two additional reviewers—Angie Harper and Natalia Ricci. In this activity, you will use View Side by Side to compare the new document with the version you finalized in the previous activity.

1 With your file **Lastname_Firstname_6B_Events_Schedule** open and the insertion point at the top of the document, navigate to your student files, and then open the file **w06B_Schedule_Revisions**.

2 On the **VIEW tab**, in the **Window group**, click **View Side by Side** to display both documents.

This view enables you to see whether there have been any major changes to the original document that should be discussed by the reviewers before making revisions. Both documents contain the same basic text.

3 In the **w06B_Schedule_Revisions** document, if necessary, drag the horizontal scroll bar to the right so that you can see the markup area. Notice that both documents scroll. Compare your screen with Figure 6.47. Depending on your screen resolution, your view may differ.

Edits and comments made by Angie Harper and Natalia Ricci display in the w06B_Schedule_Revisions file. When View Side by Side is active, *synchronous scrolling*—both documents scroll simultaneously—is turned on by default.

FIGURE 6.47

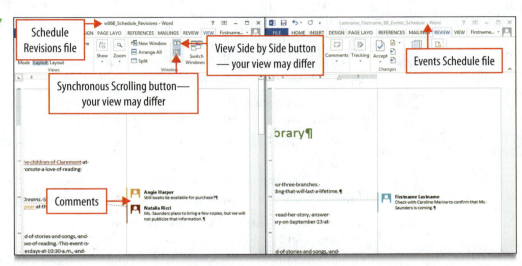

4 In the **w06B_Schedule_Revisions** document, in the **Window group**, click **View Side by Side** to restore program windows to their original size.

5 In the **w06B_Schedule_Revisions** document, select the first paragraph, and then on the mini toolbar, click **Styles**. In the **Styles** gallery, click **Heading 1**.

For purposes of instruction, you are making a formatting change to the same paragraph that you modified in your Lastname_Firstname_6B_Events_Schedule document. A reviewer usually makes revisions in only one version of a document.

6 Display the **Save As** dialog box, and then **Save** the file in your **Word Chapter 6 folder** as **Lastname_Firstname_6B_Schedule_Revisions**

7 Close the **Lastname_Firstname_6B_Schedule_Revisions** document. Notice your **Lastname_Firstname_6B_Events_Schedule** document displays.

8 Press Ctrl + W to close your **Lastname_Firstname_6B_Events_Schedule**, without closing Word.

Activity 6.18 | Combining Documents and Resolving Multi-Document Style Conflicts

In this activity, you will combine the document containing revisions and comments by Angie Harper and Natalia Ricci with your finalized version of the events schedule. Then, you will accept or reject the additional revisions to create a final document ready for distribution to the public.

1 On the **REVIEW tab**, in the **Compare group**, click **Compare**. From the list, click **Combine** to display the **Combine Documents** dialog box.

When using the Combine feature, it is not necessary to have an open document.

2 In the **Combine Documents** dialog box, click the **Original document arrow**, and then click **Browse**. In the **Open** dialog box, navigate to your **Word Chapter 6** folder, select the file **Lastname_Firstname_6B_Schedule_Revisions**, and then click **Open**.

Recall that this file includes revisions and comments from two additional reviewers. *Original document* usually refers to a document without revisions or, in this case, the document that you have not yet reviewed. The file also includes the formatting change you made to the first paragraph.

ANOTHER WAY — To the right of the Original document box, click Browse.

3 Under **Original document**, in the **Label unmarked changes with** box, if your name does not display, delete the existing text, and then type your first and last names.

4 Click the **Revised document arrow**, and then click **Browse**. Navigate to your **Word Chapter 6** folder, select **Lastname_Firstname_6B_Events_Schedule**, and then click **Open**.

Revised document refers to the latest version of the document—in this case, the document where you accepted and rejected changes.

5 Under **Revised document**, in the **Label unmarked changes with** box, if your name does not display, delete the existing text, and then type your first and last names.

6 In the **Combine Documents** dialog box, click **More**, and then under **Show changes in**, be sure the **New document** option is selected. Compare your screen with Figure 6.48.

The More button expands the dialog box to display additional settings. By selecting the New document option, all changes in both files display in a new document.

FIGURE 6.48

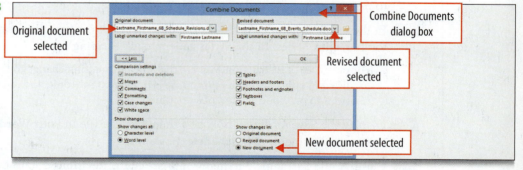

7 In the **Combine Documents** dialog box, click **Less**, and then click **OK**. In the message box indicating that Word can only store one style of formatting changes in the final merged document, under **Keep formatting changes from**, select **The other document (Lastname_ Firstname_6B_Events_Schedule)** option button. Note: If the message box does not display, proceed to Step 8, the second sentence—compare your screen with Figure 6.49.

> When combining two documents, style conflicts can exist when formatting changes are made to the same text in different versions of the document in the same time frame. In this case, the conflict exists because both files contain a formatting change applied to the first paragraph. The message box allows you to select the document that contains the formatting change you want to display in the combined document.

8 In the message box, click **Continue with Merge**. Compare your screen with Figure 6.49.

> The tri-pane Review Panel displays with the combined document in the left pane, the original document in the top right pane, and the revised document in the bottom right pane. The Reviewing Pane displays to the left of your screen, indicating all accepted changes in your Lastname_Firstname_6B_Events_Schedule file with your user name.

FIGURE 6.49

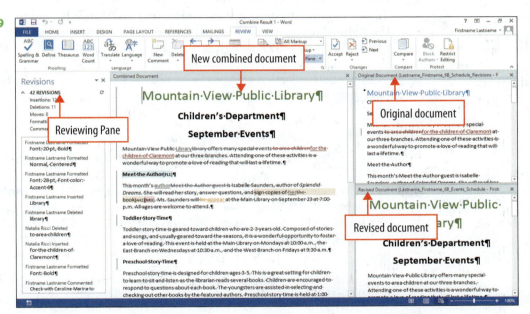

A L E R T !   **Should Both Documents Display?**

If only the combined document displays, in the Compare group, click Compare, click Show Source Documents, and then click Show Both. If the Reviewing Pane does not display, in the Tracking group, click the Reviewing Pane arrow, and then click Reviewing Pane Vertical.

---

9 If necessary, click to position the insertion point at the beginning of the **Combined Document**. **Save** the document in your **Word Chapter 6** folder as **Lastname_Firstname_6B_Schedule_Combined**

10 At the top of the **Reviewing Pane**, locate the summary and notice that there are six comments in the combined document. Take a moment to read each comment.

11 On the **REVIEW tab**, in the **Comments group**, click the **Delete arrow**, and then click **Delete All Comments in Document**. If necessary, press Ctrl + Home.

All comments have been reviewed and are no longer needed.

12 In the **Changes group**, click **Next**, and then click **Accept** to accept the first change. Continue to click **Accept** until the revision *to area children* is selected. Compare your screen with Figure 6.50.

FIGURE 6.50

13 On the **REVIEW tab**, in the **Changes group**, with the revision *to area children* selected, click **Reject** two times.

14 In the **Changes group**, click the **Accept arrow**, and then click **Accept All Changes and Stop Tracking**. In the **Reviewing Pane**, notice that no further revisions or comments remain. On the right of your screen, **Close** ☒ the two panes—the original and revised documents. **Close** ☒ the **Reviewing Pane**, and then **Save** 🖫 your changes.

Because all remaining revisions in the document are accepted, there is no longer a need to view the original or revised documents.

Activity 6.19 | Restoring Default Settings

In this activity, you will change the user name settings and finalize the document.

1 In the **Tracking group**, click the **Dialog Box Launcher**, and then in the **Track Changes Options** dialog box, click **Change User Name**. If you made changes to the user name, delete your name and initials and type the name and initials that displayed originally. Clear the **Always use these values regardless of sign in to Office** check box. Click **OK** two times to close the dialog boxes.

When sharing a computer with others, if you have made any changes, it is good practice to restore the settings when you are finished.

2 Press Ctrl + Home. On the **DESIGN tab**, in the **Page Background group**, click **Page Color**, and then click **Fill Effects**. In the **Fill Effects** dialog box, click the **Texture tab**, and then in the fourth row, click the first texture—**Newsprint**. Click **OK**.

The page background is added to improve the final appearance of the document. Because you have been assigned the task of preparing the final document for distribution, it is appropriate to make this formatting change.

NOTE   **Printing Page Backgrounds**

Page backgrounds do not display in Print Preview and do not print by default.

---

3 At the bottom of **Page 1**, right-click in the footer area, and then click **Edit Footer**. Right-click the file name, and then click **Update Field**. **Close** the footer area.

4 Click the **FILE tab**, click the **Info tab**, and then click **Show All Properties**. In the **Tags** box, type **events schedule, reviewed, combined** In the **Subject** box, type your course name and section number. If necessary, edit the author name to display your name.

5 From **Backstage** view, click **Print** to display the **Print Preview**. Examine the **Print Preview**, check for any spelling or grammatical errors, and then **Save** 🖫 your document. Print all three documents or submit electronically as directed by your instructor. **Close** ☒ Word.

More Knowledge | **Printing Page Backgrounds**

To print the background color or fill effect of a document, display the Word Options dialog box, select Display, and under Printing Options, select the Print background colors and images check box. Click OK.

END | You have completed Project 6B

END OF CHAPTER

SUMMARY

Inserting building blocks—such as text boxes, pictures, Quick Tables, and AutoText—can save time and provide consistency in your documents. Use built-in document elements or create your own building blocks.

A theme template, defined by colors, fonts, and effects, enhances the appearance of a document. Attach a theme template to multiple documents to create documents that have a coordinated appearance.

The Track Changes feature enables a group of individuals to work together on a document. Reviewers can insert comments; reply to comments made by others; insert, edit, delete, and move text; and format documents.

The author of the document can accept or reject revisions. The author can compare two different versions of a document that has been revised using the Track Changes feature or combine them in a new document.

GO! LEARN IT ONLINE

Review the concepts and key terms in this chapter by completing these online challenges, which you can find at **www.pearsonhighered.com/go**.

Matching and Multiple Choice: Answer matching and multiple choice questions to test what you learned in this chapter. **MyITLab®**

Crossword Puzzle: Spell out the words that match the numbered clues and put them in the puzzle squares.

Flipboard: Flip through the definitions of the key terms in this chapter and match them with the correct term.

END OF CHAPTER

REVIEW AND ASSESSMENT GUIDE FOR WORD CHAPTER 6

Your instructor may assign one or more of these projects to help you review the chapter and assess your mastery and understanding of the chapter.

	Review and Assessment Guide for Word Chapter 6		
Project	**Apply Skills from These Chapter Objectives**	**Project Type**	**Project Location**
6C	Objectives 1–3 from Project 6A	**6C Skills Review** A guided review of the skills from Project 6A.	On the following pages
6D	Objectives 4–6 from Project 6B	**6D Skills Review** A guided review of the skills from Project 6B.	On the following pages
6E	Objectives 1–3 from Project 6A	**6E Mastery (Grader Project)** A demonstration of your mastery of the skills in Project 6A with extensive decision making.	In MyITLab and on the following pages
6F	Objectives 4–6 from Project 6B	**6F Mastery (Grader Project)** A demonstration of your mastery of the skills in Project 6B with extensive decision making.	In MyITLab and on the following pages
6G	Objectives 1–6 from Projects 6A and 6B	**6G Mastery (Grader Project)** A demonstration of your mastery of the skills in Projects 6A and 6B with extensive decision making.	In MyITLab and on the following pages
6H	Combination of Objectives from Projects 6A and 6B	**6H GO! Fix It** A demonstration of your mastery of the skills in Projects 6A and 6B by creating a correct result from a document that contains errors you must find.	Online
6I	Combination of Objectives from Projects 6A and 6B	**6I GO! Make It** A demonstration of your mastery of the skills in Projects 6A and 6B by creating a result from a supplied picture.	Online
6J	Combination of Objectives from Projects 6A and 6B	**6J GO! Solve It** A demonstration of your mastery of the skills in Projects 6A and 6B, your decision-making skills, and your critical thinking skills. A task-specific rubric helps you self-assess your result.	Online
6K	Combination of Objectives from Projects 6A and 6B	**6K GO! Solve It** A demonstration of your mastery of the skills in Projects 6A and 6B, your decision-making skills, and your critical thinking skills. A task-specific rubric helps you self-assess your result.	On the following pages
6L	Combination of Objectives from Projects 6A and 6B	**6L GO! Think** A demonstration of your understanding of the chapter concepts applied in a manner that you would outside of college. An analytic rubric helps you and your instructor grade the quality of your work by comparing it to the work an expert in the discipline would create.	On the following pages
6M	Combination of Objectives from Projects 6A and 6B	**6M GO! Think** A demonstration of your understanding of the chapter concepts applied in a manner that you would outside of college. An analytic rubric helps you and your instructor grade the quality of your work by comparing it to the work an expert in the discipline would create.	Online
6N	Combination of Objectives from Projects 6A and 6B	**6N You and GO!** A demonstration of your understanding of the chapter concepts applied in a manner that you would in a personal situation. An analytic rubric helps you and your instructor grade the quality of your work.	Online

GLOSSARY

GLOSSARY OF CHAPTER KEY TERMS

All Markup A Track Changes view that displays the document with all revisions and comments visible.

Author The owner, or creator, of the original document.

Balloon The outline shape in which a comment or formatting change displays.

Building blocks Reusable pieces of content or other document parts—for example, headers, footers, and page number formats—that are stored in galleries.

Building Blocks Organizer A feature that enables you to view—in a single location—all of the available building blocks from all the different galleries.

Click and type pointer The text select—I-beam—pointer with various attached shapes that indicate which formatting—left-aligned, centered, or right-aligned—will be applied when you double-click in a blank area of a document.

Combine A Track Changes feature that allows you to review two different documents containing revisions, both based on an original document.

Comment A note that an author or reviewer adds to a document.

Compare A Track Changes feature that enables you to review differences between an original document and the latest version of the document.

Hyphenation A tool in Word that controls how words are split between two lines.

Ink Revision marks made directly on a document by using a stylus on a Tablet PC.

Lock Tracking A feature that prevents reviewers from turning off Track Changes and making changes that are not visible in markup.

Markup The formatting Word uses to denote a document's revisions visually.

Markup area The space to the right or left of a document where comments and formatting changes display in balloons.

No Markup A Track Changes view that displays the document in its final form—with all proposed changes included and comments hidden.

Original A Track Changes view that displays the original, unchanged document with all revisions and comments hidden.

Person Card A feature that allows you to communicate with a reviewer—using email, instant messaging, phone, or video—directly from a comment.

Quick Parts All of the reusable pieces of content that are available to insert into a document, including building blocks, document properties, and fields.

Quick Tables Tables that are stored as building blocks.

Reviewer An individual who reviews and marks changes on a document.

Reviewing Pane A separate scrollable window that shows all of the changes and comments that currently display in a document.

Revisions Changes made to a document.

Simple Markup The default Track Changes view that indicates revisions by vertical red lines in the left margin and indicates comments by icons in the right margin.

Synchronous scrolling The setting that causes two documents to scroll simultaneously.

Text box A movable, resizable container for text or graphics.

Theme A predesigned set of colors, fonts, and line and fill effects that look good together and is applied to an entire document by a single selection.

Theme template A stored, user-defined set of colors, fonts, and effects that can be shared with other Office programs.

Track Changes A feature that makes a record of the changes made to a document.

Vertical change bar A line that displays in the left margin next to each line of text that contains a revision.

View Side by Side A view that displays two open documents in separate windows, next to each other on the screen.

CHAPTER REVIEW

Skills Review   Project 6C Literacy Program

Apply **6A** skills from these Objectives:

1 Create Custom Building Blocks

2 Create and Save a Theme Template

3 Create a Document by Using Building Blocks

Build from Scratch

In the following Skills Review, you will create and save building blocks and create a theme to be used in a flyer seeking volunteers for Mountain View Public Library's Adult Literacy Program. Your completed documents will look similar to Figure 6.51.

PROJECT FILES

For Project 6C, you will need the following files:

Two new blank Word documents
w06C_Literacy_Information
w06C_Literacy_Image

You will save your files as:

Lastname_Firstname_6C_Literacy_Blocks
Lastname_Firstname_6C_Literacy_Program
Lastname_Firstname_6C_Literacy_Theme—not shown in the figure

PROJECT RESULTS

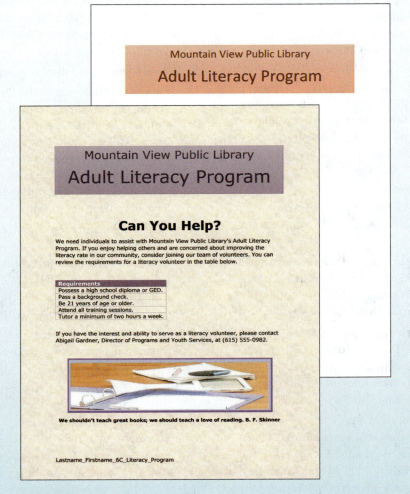

FIGURE 6.51

(Project 6C Literacy Program continues on the next page)

CHAPTER REVIEW

1 Start Word to display a new blank document. If necessary, display the rulers and formatting marks. Click the **FILE tab**, display the **Save As** dialog box, navigate to your **Word Chapter 6** folder, and then **Save** the document as **Lastname_Firstname_6C_Literacy_Blocks** Insert the file name in the footer.

a. Press Enter three times, and then position the insertion point in the first blank paragraph. On the **INSERT tab**, in the **Text group**, click **Text Box**, and then locate and click **Simple Text Box**. On the **FORMAT tab**, in the **Shape Styles group**, click **More**. In the fourth row, click the third style—**Subtle Effect – Orange, Accent 2**. In the **Size group**, change the **Shape Width** to 6.5".

b. Replace the placeholder text by typing **Mountain View Public Library** Press Enter, and then type **Adult Literacy Program** Select both lines of text, change the **Font Color** to **Orange, Accent 2, Darker 50%**, and then apply **Center**. Select the first line of text, and then change the **Font Size** to **24**. Select the second line of text, and then change the **Font Size** to **36**.

c. Click the outside edge of the text box to select it. On the **INSERT tab**, in the **Text group**, click **Text Box**, and then click **Save Selection to Text Box Gallery**. In the **Name** box, type **Literacy Heading** In the **Description** box, type **Use as the heading for all literacy documents** Click **OK**.

2 Position the insertion point in the second blank paragraph. On the **INSERT tab**, in the **Tables group**, click **Table**, point to **Quick Tables**, scroll down, and then click **Tabular List**.

a. Select the text *ITEM*, and then type **Requirements** Press Tab. Right-click, on the mini toolbar, click **Delete**, and then click **Delete Columns**. Select the text in all the remaining cells of the table, and then press Delete.

b. Position the insertion point in the first cell of the table. Under **TABLE TOOLS**, on the **DESIGN tab**, in the **Table Styles group**, click **More**. In the **Table Styles** gallery, under **List Tables**, in the fourth row, click the third style—**List Table 4 – Accent 2**.

c. Point slightly outside of the upper left corner of the table, and then click the **table move handle** ⊞ to select the entire table. On the **INSERT tab**, in the **Tables group**, click **Table**. Point to **Quick Tables**, and then at the bottom of the gallery, click **Save Selection**

to **Quick Tables Gallery**. In the **Name** box, type **Job Information** In the **Description** box, type **Use for listing job requirements** Click **OK**.

d. Press Ctrl + End. Type **We shouldn't teach great books; we should teach a love of reading. B. F. Skinner** and then select the text you just typed. On the **INSERT tab**, in the **Text group**, click **Quick Parts**, click **AutoText**, and then click **Save Selection to AutoText Gallery**. In the **Create New Building Block** dialog box, in the **Name** box, type **Literacy Quote** and then in the **Description** box, type **Quote for program** Click the **Save in arrow**, and then click **Building Blocks**. Click **OK**.

e. Click the **FILE tab**, and then click **Show All Properties**. In the **Tags** box, type **literacy, building blocks** In the **Subject** box, type your course name and section number. If necessary, edit the author name to display your name. **Save** your changes. Click the **FILE tab**, and then **Close** the document but leave Word open.

3 Press Ctrl + N to display a new blank document.

a. On the **DESIGN tab**, in the **Document Formatting group**, click **Colors**, and then click **Customize Colors**. Click the **Accent 2 arrow**, and then under **Theme Colors**, in the last column, click the first color—**Purple, Followed Hyperlink**. Click the **Accent 3 arrow**, and then in the last column, click the fifth color—**Purple, Followed Hyperlink, Darker 25%**. **Save** the theme colors with the name **Literacy Colors**

b. Click **Fonts**, and then click **Customize Fonts**. Click the **Body font arrow**, scroll down, and then click **Verdana**. **Save** the theme fonts with the name **Literacy Fonts**

c. Click **Themes**, and then click **Save Current Theme**. Navigate to your **Word Chapter 6** folder, and **Save** the theme as **Lastname_Firstname_6C_Literacy_Theme**

d. On the **DESIGN tab**, in the **Document Formatting group**, click **Colors**, right-click **Literacy Colors**, and then click **Delete**. When a message displays to confirm the deletion, click **Yes**. Using the same technique, click **Fonts**, and then **Delete** the **Literacy Fonts**.

e. Click the **FILE tab**, and then **Close** the document without saving changes, but leave Word open.

(Project 6C Literacy Program continues on the next page)

4 Press Ctrl + N. **Save** the document in your **Word Chapter 6** folder as **Lastname_Firstname_6C_Literacy_Program** Insert the file name in the footer, and display rulers and formatting marks, if necessary.

a. On the **DESIGN tab**, in the **Document Formatting group**, click **Themes**, and then click **Browse for Themes**. Navigate to your **Word Chapter 6** folder, select your **Lastname_Firstname_6C_Literacy_Theme**, and then click **Open**. In the **Page Background group**, click **Page Color**, and then click **Fill Effects**. In the **Fill Effects** dialog box, click the **Texture tab**, and then in the fourth row, click the third texture—**Parchment**. Click **OK**.

b. Press Enter two times, and then position the insertion point in the first blank paragraph. On the **INSERT tab**, in the **Text group**, click **Text Box**. Scroll to the bottom of the gallery, and then under **General**, click your **Literacy Heading** building block. Press Ctrl + End.

c. On the **INSERT tab**, in the **Text group**, click the **Object arrow**, and then click **Text from File**. Navigate to your student files, click **w06C_Literacy_Information**, and then click **Insert**. At the end of the paragraph that ends *in the table below*, position the insertion point after the period, and then press Enter two times.

5 On the **INSERT tab**, in the **Tables group**, click **Table**, point to **Quick Tables**, scroll toward the bottom of the gallery, and then under **General**, click **Job Information**.

a. Position the insertion point in the second row of the table. Type the following text in the table, pressing Tab after each line:

Possess a high school diploma or GED.

Pass a background check.

Be 21 years of age or older.

Attend all training sessions.

Tutor a minimum of two hours a week.

b. Select the last three empty rows of the table. On the mini toolbar, click **Delete**, and then click **Delete Rows**.

6 Press Ctrl + End, press Enter, and then press Ctrl + E. On the **INSERT tab**, in the **Illustrations group**, click **Pictures**. In the **Insert Picture** dialog box, navigate to your student data files, select the file **w06C_Literacy_Image**, and then click **Insert**. On the **FORMAT tab**, change the **Shape Height** to 1.6".

a. Position the insertion point to the right of the picture, and then press Enter. On the **INSERT tab**, in the **Text group**, click **Quick Parts**, click **AutoText**, and then click **Literacy Quote**. Select the inserted text, change the **Font Size** to **10**, and then apply **Bold**. If necessary, at the end of the document, delete the blank paragraph.

b. Press Ctrl + Home. Click the **FILE tab**, and then click **Show All Properties**. In the **Tags** box, type **literacy program, volunteers** In the **Subject** box, type your course name and section number. If necessary, edit the author name to display your name.

c. On the **INSERT tab**, in the **Text group**, click **Quick Parts**, and then click **Building Blocks Organizer**. In the **Building Blocks Organizer** dialog box, in the upper left corner, click **Name** to sort the building blocks alphabetically by name. Locate your building block **Job Information**, click to select it, click **Delete**, and then click **Yes** to confirm the deletion. Using the same technique, scroll to locate and then delete your building blocks **Literacy Heading** and **Literacy Quote**. **Close** the dialog box, and then **Save** the document.

7 Print your two documents—you cannot print your theme—or submit all three files electronically as directed by your instructor. **Close** Word. When a message displays regarding changes to building blocks, click **Save** to accept the changes.

END | You have completed Project 6C

CHAPTER REVIEW

Skills Review Project 6D User Guide

In the following Skills Review, you will edit a user guide for Mountain View Public Library by creating and deleting comments, inserting text, applying formatting, and accepting changes made by others. Your completed documents will look similar to Figure 6.52.

PROJECT FILES

For Project 6D, you will need the following files:

w06D_User_Guide
w06D_Reviewed_Guide

You will save your files as:

Lastname_Firstname_6D_User_Guide
Lastname_Firstname_6D_Combined_Guide

PROJECT RESULTS

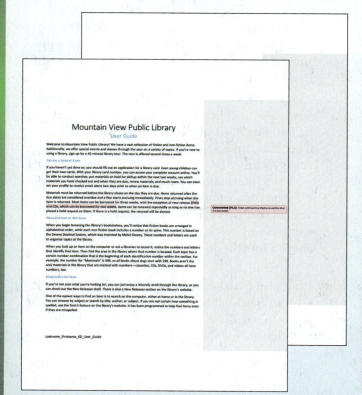

FIGURE 6.52

(Project 6D User Guide continues on the next page)

CHAPTER REVIEW

Skills Review Project 6D User Guide (continued)

1 ▶ Start Word. Navigate to your student files and open the file **w06D_User_Guide**. **Save** the document in your **Word Chapter 6** folder as **Lastname_Firstname_6D_User_ Guide** In the footer, delete any existing text, and then insert the file name.

a. On the **REVIEW tab**, in the **Tracking group**, click the **Dialog Box Launcher**. In the **Track Changes Options** dialog box, click **Change User Name**. Under **Personalize your copy of Microsoft Office**, on a piece of paper, make a note of the user name and initials. In the **User name** box, type your own first and last names, and then in the **Initials** box, type your initials, if necessary. Immediately below the **Initials** box, be sure the check box is selected. Click **OK** two times.

b. On the **REVIEW tab**, in the **Tracking group**, click the **Display for Review arrow**, and then click **All Markup**, if necessary. In the paragraph beginning *Materials must be*, select the text *DVDs and CDs, which can be borrowed for two weeks.* On the **REVIEW tab**, in the **Comments group**, click **New Comment**. In the comment, type **Check with Angie Harper to confirm that it is two weeks.**

c. Press Ctrl + Home. Click to position the insertion point in the text for the *Benedetta Herman* comment that begins *I thought*, and then in the **Comments group**, click **Delete**. Using the same technique, delete the *Caroline Marina* comment that begins *We offer*.

d. Locate your comment, and then replace *Angie Harper* with **Caroline Marina**

2 ▶ To enable tracking, in the **Tracking group**, click **Track Changes** so that it displays in blue. Select the first paragraph—the title—and then apply **Center**. Select the second paragraph, change the **Font Size** to **18**, change the **Font Color** to **Blue, Accent 1**—in the fifth column, the first color—and then apply **Center**.

a. In the paragraph that begins *When you begin browsing*, in the third line, replace the text *Melville* with **Melvil** and then delete the related *Benedetta Herman* comment. On **Page 2**, in the paragraph that begins *The branches of*, in the second line, delete the sentence *We have many comfortable desks and chairs.*

b. Press Ctrl + End. Press Enter, and then type **To find out more information about any library services, please contact us at (615) 555-0982.** Select the text you just

typed, change the **Font Size** to **12**, and apply **Italic**. Delete the *Benedetta Herman* comment that begins *Please add*.

c. Press Ctrl + Home. On the **REVIEW tab**, in the **Changes group**, click the **Accept arrow**, and then click **Accept All Changes and Stop Tracking**.

d. In the **Tracking group**, click the **Dialog Box Launcher**. In the **Track Changes Options** dialog box, click **Change User Name**. If you made changes to the user name, delete your name and initials and type those that displayed originally. Click **OK** two times.

e. Click the **FILE tab**, and then click **Show All Properties**. In the **Tags** box, type **user guide, edited** In the **Subject** box, type your course name and section number. If necessary, edit the author name to display your name. **Save** your document. Click the **FILE tab**, and then **Close** the document but leave Word open.

3 ▶ On the **REVIEW tab**, in the **Compare group**, click **Compare**, and then click **Combine**. In the **Combine Documents** dialog box, click the **Original document arrow**, and then click **Browse**. Navigate to your student files, select the file **w06D_Reviewed_Guide**, and then click **Open**.

a. Click the **Revised document arrow**, and then click **Browse**. Navigate to your **Word Chapter 6** folder, select the file **Lastname_Firstname_6D_User_Guide**, and then click **Open**.

b. In the **Combine Documents** dialog box, click **More**, and then under **Show changes in**, select the **New document** option, if necessary. Click **Less**, and then click **OK**. If necessary, on the right of your screen, **Close** the **Original Document Pane** and the **Revised Document Pane**, and then on the left, **Close** the **Reviewing Pane**, if necessary.

c. If necessary, position the insertion point at the beginning of the **Combined Document**. Click **Save**, and then **Save** the document in your **Word Chapter 6** folder as **Lastname_Firstname_6D_Combined_Guide**

4 ▶ On the **REVIEW tab**, in the **Changes group**, click the **Accept arrow**, and then click **Accept All Changes and Stop Tracking**.

a. On **Page 2**, locate the *Angie Harper* comment. Select the two sentences that begins *Be aware*, and ends *wireless device*. delete the two sentences.

b. On the **REVIEW tab**, in the **Comments group**, click the **Delete arrow**, and then click **Delete All Comments in Document**.

(Project 6D User Guide continues on the next page)

CHAPTER REVIEW

5 Right-click in the footer area, and then click **Edit Footer**. Right-click the existing text, and then from the shortcut menu, click **Update Field**. **Close** the footer area.

a. On the **DESIGN tab**, in the **Page Background group**, click **Page Color**, and then click **Fill Effects**. In the **Fill Effects** dialog box, click the **Texture tab**, scroll as necessary, and then in the next to last row, click the first texture—**Blue tissue paper**. Click **OK**.

b. Press [Ctrl] + [Home]. Click the **FILE tab**, and then click **Show All Properties**. In the **Tags** box, type **user guide, reviewed, combined** In the **Subject** box, type your course name and section number. If necessary, edit the author name to display your name.

c. **Save** your document.

6 Print both documents or submit them electronically as directed by your instructor. **Close** Word.

> **END | You have completed Project 6D**

CONTENT-BASED ASSESSMENTS

Mastering Word   Project 6E Seminar Agenda

In the following Mastering Word project, you will create and save building blocks and create a theme for an agenda for Mountain View Public Library's seminar on Public Libraries and the Internet. Your completed documents will look similar to Figure 6.53.

Apply 6A skills from these Objectives:

1 Create Custom Building Blocks

2 Create and Save a Theme Template

3 Create a Document by Using Building Blocks

Build from Scratch

PROJECT FILES

For Project 6E, you will need the following files:

New blank Word document
w06E_Seminar_Agenda

You will save your files as:

Lastname_Firstname_6E_Seminar_Blocks
Lastname_Firstname_6E_Seminar_Agenda
Lastname_Firstname_6E_Seminar_Theme—not shown in the figure

PROJECT RESULTS

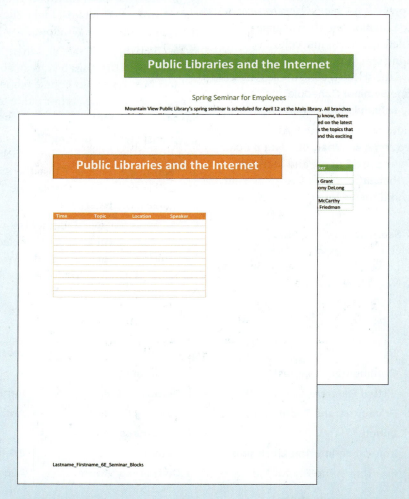

FIGURE 6.53

(Project 6E Seminar Agenda continues on the next page)

CONTENT-BASED ASSESSMENTS

1 Start Word. Display a blank document. Be sure rulers and formatting marks display. **Save** the document in your **Word Chapter 6** folder as **Lastname_Firstname_6E_Seminar_Blocks** Insert the file name in the footer.

2 Press Enter three times. In the first blank paragraph, **Insert** a **Simple Text Box**, change the **Shape Height** to **0.7"**, and then change the **Shape Width** to **6.5"**. Apply the shape style **Colored Fill – Orange, Accent 2**. In the text box, type **Public Libraries and the Internet** Select the text you typed, change the **Font Size** to **28** and then apply **Bold** and **Center**. Select and then **Save** the text box in the **Text Box** gallery with the name **Internet Seminar** and the **Description Use in all Internet Seminar documents**

3 In the third blank paragraph, display the **Quick Tables** gallery, and then insert a **Double Table**. Above the table, delete the text *The Greek Alphabet*. Replace the text *Letter name* with **Time** and then press Tab. Change *Uppercase* to **Topic** Change *Lowercase* to **Location** and then change *Letter name* to **Speaker** Delete the remaining columns, and then delete the remaining text. Apply the table style **List Table 4 – Accent 2**. **Save** the selected table in the **Quick Tables** gallery with the name **Seminar Schedule** and the **Description Use to display schedules for seminars**

4 Click the **FILE tab**, and then click **Show All Properties**. In the **Tags** box, type **seminar, building blocks** In the **Subject** box, type your course name and section number. If necessary, edit the author name to display your name. **Save** your changes, and then **Close** the document but leave Word open.

5 Open the file **w06E_Seminar_Agenda**, **Save** it in your **Word Chapter 6** folder as **Lastname_Firstname_6E_Seminar_Agenda** and then insert the file name in the footer. Display the **Create New Theme Colors** dialog box. Change **Accent 1** to **Green, Accent 6, Darker**

25%, and then change **Accent 2** to **Green, Accent 6**. **Save** the Theme Colors as **Internet Colors Save** the current theme in your **Word Chapter 6** folder as **Lastname_Firstname_6E_Seminar_Theme**

6 In the first blank paragraph, display the **Text Box** gallery, and then insert your **Internet Seminar** text box.

7 Select the text *Spring Seminar for Employees*, apply the **Heading 1** style, and then apply **Center**. On the **PAGE LAYOUT tab**, in the **Paragraph group**, change the **Spacing After** to **6 pt**. Select the text *AGENDA*, apply the **Heading 2** style, apply **Center**, and then change the **Spacing After** to **12 pt**. Position the insertion point in the blank paragraph following *AGENDA*, display the **Quick Tables** gallery, and then insert your **Seminar Schedule**. In the table, enter the text shown in Table 1 below. Delete empty rows as necessary.

8 Select the table, right-click, point to **AutoFit**, and then click **AutoFit to Contents**. Right-click, point to **AutoFit**, and then click **AutoFit to Window**. Press Ctrl + Home.

9 Click the **FILE tab**, and then click **Show All Properties**. In the **Tags** box, type **seminar, agenda** In the **Subject** box, type your course name and section number. If necessary, edit the author name to display your name. **Save** the document.

10 Display the **Building Blocks Organizer** dialog box, and then delete your building blocks **Internet Seminar** and **Seminar Schedule**. **Close** the **Building Blocks Organizer** dialog box. Display the **Theme Colors** list, and then delete the **Internet Colors**.

11 Print your two documents—you cannot print your theme—or submit all three files electronically as directed by your instructor. **Close** Word. When a message displays regarding changes to building blocks, click **Save** to accept the changes.

TABLE 1

Time	Topic	Location	Speaker
8 a.m. – 9 a.m.	Continental Breakfast	Community Room	
9 a.m. – 10 a.m.	Virtual Reference Desks	Computer Lab A	Irene Grant
10 a.m. – Noon	Privacy versus Technology	Serenity Room	Anthony DeLong
Noon – 1 p.m.	Lunch	Community Room	
1 p.m. – 3 p.m.	Innovative Internet Librarians	Computer Lab A	Josh McCarthy
3 p.m. – 5 p.m.	Fair Use in the Digital Age	Community Room	Alice Friedman

END | You have completed Project 6E

(Return to Step 8)

CONTENT-BASED ASSESSMENTS

Mastering Word Project 6F Library Classes

In the following Mastering Word project, you will edit a user guide for Mountain View Public Library by creating and deleting comments, inserting text, applying formatting, and accepting changes made by others. Your completed documents will look similar to Figure 6.54.

Apply 6B skills from these Objectives:

4 Use Comments in a Document

5 Track Changes in a Document

6 View Side by Side, Compare, and Combine Documents

PROJECT FILES

For Project 6F, you will need the following files:

w06F_Library_Classes
w06F_Classes_Reviewed

You will save your files as:

Lastname_Firstname_6F_Library_Classes
Lastname_Firstname_6F_Classes_Combined

PROJECT RESULTS

FIGURE 6.54

(Project 6F Library Classes continues on the next page)

CONTENT-BASED ASSESSMENTS

1 Start Word, and then open the file **w06F_Library_ Classes**. **Save** the document in your **Word Chapter 6** folder as **Lastname_Firstname_6F_Library_Classes** In the footer, delete the existing text, and then insert the file name. On the **REVIEW tab**, in the **Tracking group**, display the **Track Changes Options** dialog box, and then click **Change User Name**. Note the existing user name and initials. Under **Personalize your copy of Microsoft Office**, type your name in the **User name** box, and then type your initials in the **Initials** box, if necessary. Immediately below Initials, be sure the check box is selected. In the **Tracking group**, change **Display for Review** to **All Markup**, if necessary.

2 In the fourth paragraph, select the text *This month's book selection*. Insert a new comment, and then type **Should we purchase additional copies for the library?** Delete the *Abigail Gardner* comment and the *Caroline Marina* comment.

3 Turn on **Track Changes**. Select the first two paragraphs, and then apply the **Book Title** style. Change the **Font Size** to **28**, change the **Font Color** to **Orange, Accent 2, Darker 25%**, and then apply **Center**. On **Page 2**, locate the paragraph that begins *Microsoft Word*. Delete the text *101*, and then press Ctrl + End. Press Enter, and then type **To register for a class or to obtain more information, contact Abigail Gardner at (615) 555-0982.** Select the sentence you just typed, and then apply **Italic** and **Center**.

4 Press Ctrl + Home, and then **Accept All Changes and Stop Tracking**. Display the **Track Changes Options** dialog box, and then click **Change User Name**. If necessary, delete your name in the **User Name** box, delete your

initials in the **Initials** box, and then restore the original text and settings. Click the **FILE tab**, and then click **Show All Properties**. In the **Tags** box, type **library classes, edited** In the **Subject** box, type your course name and section number. If necessary, edit the author name to display your name. **Save** your document, click the **FILE tab**, and then **Close** the document but leave Word open.

5 Display the **Combine Documents** dialog box. For the **Original document**, in your student data files, select the file **w06F_Classes_Reviewed**. For the **Revised document**, in your **Word Chapter 6** folder, select the file **Lastname_Firstname_6F_Library_Classes**. Click **More**, and then select the **New document** option. Click **Less**, and then click **OK**.

6 **Save** the document in your **Word Chapter 6** folder as **Lastname_Firstname_6F_Classes_Combined** If necessary, **Close** the two document panes on the right side of your screen, and then **Close** the **Reviewing Pane**. **Accept All Changes and Stop Tracking**. Delete the comment that contains your name. Change the **Page Color** to the **Newsprint** fill effect—on the **Texture tab**, in the fourth row, the first texture.

7 Double-click in the footer area, right-click the file name field, and then click **Update Field**. **Close** the footer area. Press Ctrl + Home. Click the **FILE tab**, and then click **Show All Properties**. In the **Tags** box, type **library classes, reviewed, combined** In the **Subject** box, type your course name and section number. If necessary, edit the author name to display your name. **Save** your document.

8 Print both documents or submit electronically as directed by your instructor. **Close** Word.

END | You have completed Project 6F

CONTENT-BASED ASSESSMENTS

Mastering Word | Project 6G Website Flyer

In the following Mastering Word project, you will create a document to announce the launch of Mountain View Public Library's new website by creating and inserting building blocks, creating a custom theme, inserting text, applying formatting, and accepting changes made by others. Your completed documents will look similar to Figure 6.55.

Apply 6A and 6B skills from these Objectives:

1 Create Custom Building Blocks

2 Create and Save a Theme Template

3 Create a Document by Using Building Blocks

4 Use Comments in a Document

5 Track Changes in a Document

6 View Side by Side, Compare, and Combine Documents

Build from Scratch

PROJECT FILES

For Project 6G, you will need the following files:

New blank Word document
w06G_Website_Flyer

You will save your files as:

Lastname_Firstname_6G_Website_Blocks
Lastname_Firstname_6G_Website_Flyer
Lastname_Firstname_6G_Website_Theme—not shown in the figure

PROJECT RESULTS

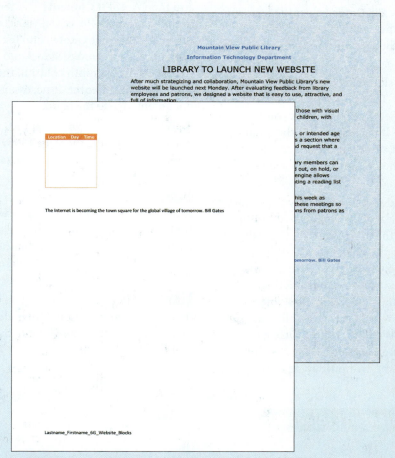

FIGURE 6.55

(Project 6G Website Flyer continues on the next page)

CONTENT-BASED ASSESSMENTS

1 Start Word, and then display a new document. **Save** the document in your **Word Chapter 6** folder as **Lastname_Firstname_6G_Website_Blocks** Insert the file name in the footer. Be sure rulers and formatting marks display.

2 Display the **Quick Tables** gallery, and insert a **Tabular List**. In the first cell, replace the text *ITEM* with **Location** In the second cell, replace the text *NEEDED* with **Day** Right-click to display the mini toolbar, click **Insert**, and then click **Insert Right** to create a third column. In the first cell of the third column, type **Time** Delete all remaining text in the table, and then apply the **List Table 3 – Accent 2** table style. **Save** the table in the **Quick Tables** gallery with the name **Training Schedule** and the **Description Use to display schedules for training**

3 Press Ctrl + End. Press Enter two times, and then type **The Internet is becoming the town square for the global village of tomorrow. Bill Gates** Select the text, and then **Save** the selection in the **AutoText** gallery with the name **Internet Quote** and the **Description Use in website documents**

4 Press Ctrl + Home. Click the **FILE tab**, and then click **Show All Properties**. In the **Tags** box, type **IT Department, building blocks** In the **Subject** box, type your course name and section number. If necessary, edit the author name to display your name. **Save** your changes. Click the **FILE tab**, and then **Close** the document but leave Word open.

5 Display a new blank document. Display the **Create New Theme Colors** dialog box, change **Accent 2** to **Blue, Accent 5, Darker 25%**—in the ninth column, the fifth color; and then **Save** the theme colors with the name **Website Colors** Display the **Create New Theme Fonts** dialog box, change **Body font** to **Verdana**, and then save the theme fonts with the name **Website Fonts Save** the current theme in your **Word Chapter 6** folder as **Lastname_Firstname_6G_Website_Theme** Delete the **Website Colors** and **Website Fonts**. Click the **FILE tab**, and then **Close** the document, without saving changes, but leave Word open.

6 Open the file **w06G_Website_Flyer**, and then **Save** it in your **Word Chapter 6** folder as **Lastname_Firstname_6G_Website_Flyer** In the footer, delete the existing text, and then insert the file name. Apply your custom theme—**Lastname_Firstname_6G_Website_Theme**.

7 Select the first two paragraphs of the document. Change the **Font Color** to **Blue, Accent 5**, and then apply **Bold** and **Center**. Press Ctrl + End, and then insert the **Training Schedule** Quick Table. Beginning in the first cell of the second row, type the following text in the table.

East Branch	Tuesday	2 p.m.
Main Library	Monday	9 a.m.
West Branch	Friday	3 p.m.

8 Delete all empty rows in the table. Select the table, and then **AutoFit Contents**. **Center** the table horizontally in the document. Press Ctrl + End, and then press Enter. Insert the **Internet Quote** AutoText. Select the inserted text, change the **Font Size** to **9** and the **Font Color** to **Blue, Accent 5**—in the ninth column, the first color; and then apply **Bold** and **Center**. If necessary, at the end of the document, delete the blank paragraph.

9 Press Ctrl + Home. **Accept All Changes** in the document. Change the **Page Color** to the **Blue tissue paper** fill effect—on the **Texture tab**, in the next to last row, the first texture.

10 Click the **FILE tab**, and then click **Show All Properties**. In the **Tags** box, type **website flyer, reviewed** In the **Subject** box, type your course name and section number. If necessary, edit the author name to display your name. **Save** your document. Delete the **Training Schedule** and **Internet Quote** building blocks.

11 Print both documents—you cannot print the theme—or submit all three files electronically as directed by your instructor. **Close** Word, and **Save** changes to building blocks.

END | You have completed Project 6G

CONTENT-BASED ASSESSMENTS

Apply a combination of the 6A and 6B skills.

GO! Fix It	Project 6H Internship Memo	Online

GO! Make It	Project 6I Request Form	Online

GO! Solve It	Project 6J Employee Newsletter	Online

Build from Scratch

GO! Solve It	Project 6K Library Rules

Build from Scratch

PROJECT FILES

For Project 6K, you will need the following files:

New blank Word document
w06K_Library_Rules

You will save your files as:

Lastname_Firstname_6K_Rules_Blocks
Lastname_Firstname_6K_Library_Rules

Display a new blank document and save it in your **Word Chapter 6** folder as **Lastname_Firstname_6K_Rules_Blocks** Insert a graphic related to a library and save it as a building block. Save a text box as a building block that includes the text **Library Rules** Insert the file name in the footer and add appropriate document properties.

From your student files, open the document **w06K_Library_Rules**. Accept all changes. Save the file to your **Word Chapter 6** folder as **Lastname_Firstname_6K_Library_Rules** Modify the theme colors and format the text to improve readability. Insert the building blocks you created. Adjust the building blocks and text to create an attractive, one-page document. Insert the file name in the footer and add appropriate document properties. Print both documents or submit electronically as directed by your instructor.

Performance Element

Performance Criteria		Exemplary: You consistently applied the relevant skills	Proficient: You sometimes, but not always, applied the relevant skills	Developing: You rarely or never applied the relevant skills
	Create a graphic building block	An appropriate graphic is saved as a building block.	A graphic is saved as a building block but is not related to the topic.	No graphic is saved as a building block.
	Create a text box building block	A text box containing the correct information is saved as a building block.	A text box is saved as a building block but contains incorrect information.	No text box is saved as a building block.
	Accept changes	All changes are accepted.	Some changes are accepted but others are not.	No changes are accepted.
	Modify theme colors and format text	The theme colors are modified and the text is formatted attractively.	The theme colors are not modified or the text is not formatted attractively.	The theme colors are not modified and the text is not formatted.
	Insert building blocks	Both building blocks are inserted and positioned appropriately.	One building block is not inserted or is positioned inappropriately.	Both building blocks are not inserted or are positioned inappropriately.

END | You have completed Project 6K

OUTCOMES-BASED ASSESSMENTS

RUBRIC

The following outcomes-based assessments are *open-ended assessments*. That is, there is no specific correct result; your result will depend on your approach to the information provided. Make *Professional Quality* your goal. Use the following scoring rubric to guide you in *how* to approach the problem and then to evaluate *how well* your approach solves the problem.

The *criteria*—Software Mastery, Content, Format and Layout, and Process—represent the knowledge and skills you have gained that you can apply to solving the problem. The *levels of performance*—Professional Quality, Approaching Professional Quality, or Needs Quality Improvements—help you and your instructor evaluate your result.

	Your completed project is of Professional Quality if you:	**Your completed project is Approaching Professional Quality if you:**	**Your completed project Needs Quality Improvements if you:**
1-Software Mastery	Choose and apply the most appropriate skills, tools, and features and identify efficient methods to solve the problem.	Choose and apply some appropriate skills, tools, and features, but not in the most efficient manner.	Choose inappropriate skills, tools, or features, or are inefficient in solving the problem.
2-Content	Construct a solution that is clear and well organized, contains content that is accurate, appropriate to the audience and purpose, and is complete. Provide a solution that contains no errors in spelling, grammar, or style.	Construct a solution in which some components are unclear, poorly organized, inconsistent, or incomplete. Misjudge the needs of the audience. Have some errors in spelling, grammar, or style, but the errors do not detract from comprehension.	Construct a solution that is unclear, incomplete, or poorly organized; contains some inaccurate or inappropriate content; and contains many errors in spelling, grammar, or style. Do not solve the problem.
3-Format & Layout	Format and arrange all elements to communicate information and ideas, clarify function, illustrate relationships, and indicate relative importance.	Apply appropriate format and layout features to some elements, but not others. Overuse features, causing minor distraction.	Apply format and layout that does not communicate information or ideas clearly. Do not use format and layout features to clarify function, illustrate relationships, or indicate relative importance. Use available features excessively, causing distraction.
4-Process	Use an organized approach that integrates planning, development, self-assessment, revision, and reflection.	Demonstrate an organized approach in some areas, but not others; or, use an insufficient process of organization throughout.	Do not use an organized approach to solve the problem.

OUTCOMES-BASED ASSESSMENTS

Build from
Scratch

GO! Think   Project 6L Fundraising Flyer

PROJECT FILES

For Project 6L, you will need the following file:

New blank Word document

You will save your files as:

Lastname_Firstname_6L_Fundraising_Blocks
Lastname_Firstname_6L_Fundraising_Flyer

The Mountain View Public Library is conducting a fundraising campaign with a goal of $200,000 needed to upgrade the computer lab at the Main library and fund library programs. Donations can be sent to 1000 Maple Avenue, Claremont, TN 38325. Benedetta Herman, Director of Operations, is chairing the fundraising committee and can be reached at (615) 555-0982. Donor levels include:

Type of Recognition	Amount of Gift
Bronze Book Club	$ 100 or more
Silver Book Club	$ 500 or more
Gold Book Club	$ 1,000 or more

Create a document that includes a text box containing the name and address of the library, an appropriate clip art image, and an appropriate quotation. Save all three objects as building blocks. Save the document as **Lastname_Firstname_6L_Fundraising_Blocks** Create a flyer explaining the campaign and how donors will be acknowledged. Customize the theme, add appropriate text, and insert your building blocks. Include a Quick Table to display the recognition types. Format the flyer in a professional manner. Save the file as **Lastname_Firstname_6L_Fundraising_Flyer** For both documents, insert the file name in the footer and add document properties. Submit both documents as directed by your instructor.

END | You have completed Project 6L

OUTCOMES-BASED ASSESSMENTS

Build from
Scratch

| **GO! Think** | Project 6M Reading Certificate | Online |

Build from
Scratch

| **You and GO!** | Project 6N Personal Calendar | Online |

Use Financial and Lookup Functions, Define Names, Validate Data, and Audit Worksheets

GO! to Work
Video E4

EXCEL 2013

4

Yuri Arcurs/Fotolia

In This Chapter

In this chapter, you will use Financial functions and What-If Analysis tools to make your worksheets more valuable for analyzing data and making financial decisions. In addition, you will define names and use them in a formula. You will use the Lookup functions to locate information that is needed in a form and create a validation list to ensure that only accurate data is entered. In this chapter, you will also use Excel's auditing features to help you understand the construction of formulas in a worksheet, and locate and correct any errors. For example, by tracing relationships you will be able to test your formulas for accuracy.

The projects in this chapter relate to **Jesse Jewelers**, a Toronto-based retailer of jewelry and accessories for men and women. Jesse sells unique and beautiful items at a great price. Products include necklaces, bracelets, key chains, business cases, jewelry boxes, handmade bags, and personalized items. Founded in 2005 by two college friends, this growing company has several retail locations and an online store. It distributes its products to department and specialty stores throughout the United States and Canada. Jesse Jewelers provides exceptional customer service from a well-trained staff of product experts.

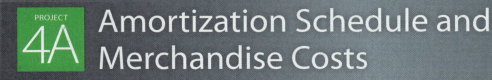

Amortization Schedule and Merchandise Costs

PROJECT 4A

MyITLab®
Project 4A Training

PROJECT ACTIVITIES

In Activities 4.01 through 4.09, you will create a worksheet for Alaina Dubois, International Sales Director for Jesse Jewelers, that details the loan information to purchase furniture and fixtures for a new store in Houston. You will also define names for ranges of cells in a workbook containing quarterly and annual merchandise costs for the new store. Your completed worksheets will look similar to Figure 4.1.

PROJECT FILES

For Project 4A, you will need the following files:

e04A_Merchandise_Costs
e04A_Store_Loan

You will save your workbooks as:

Lastname_Firstname_4A_Merchandise_Costs
Lastname_Firstname_4A_Store_Loan

PROJECT RESULTS

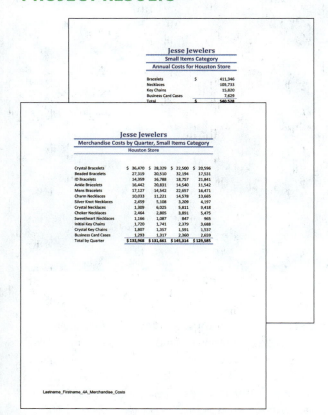

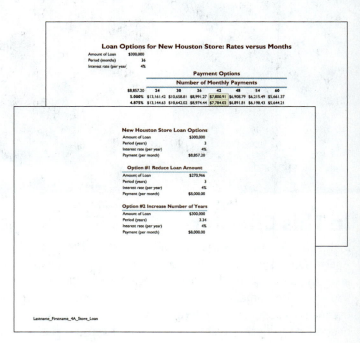

FIGURE 4.1 Project 4A Amortization Schedule and Merchandise Costs

- Tap an item to click it.
- Press and hold for a few seconds to right-click; release when the information or commands display.
- Touch the screen with two or more fingers and then pinch together to zoom in or stretch your fingers apart to zoom out.
- Slide your finger on the screen to scroll—slide left to scroll right and slide right to scroll left.
- Slide to rearrange—similar to dragging with a mouse.
- Swipe from edge: from right to display charms; from left to expose open apps, snap apps, or close apps; from top or bottom to show commands or close an app.
- Swipe to select—slide an item a short distance with a quick movement—to select an item and bring up commands, if any.

Objective 1   Use Financial Functions

Video E4-1

Financial functions are prebuilt formulas that make common business calculations such as calculating a loan payment on a vehicle or calculating how much to save each month to buy something. Financial functions commonly involve a period of time such as months or years.

When you borrow money from a bank or other lender, the amount charged to you for your use of the borrowed money is called *interest*. Loans are typically made for a period of years, and the interest that must be paid is a percentage of the loan amount that is still owed. In Excel, this interest percentage is called the *rate*.

The initial amount of the loan is called the *Present value (Pv)*, which is the total amount that a series of future payments is worth now, and is also known as the *principal*. When you borrow money, the loan amount is the present value to the lender. The number of time periods—number of payments—is abbreviated *Nper*. The value at the end of the time periods is the *Future value (Fv)*—the cash balance you want to attain after the last payment is made. The future value is usually zero for loans, because you will have paid off the full amount at the end of the term.

Activity 4.01 | Inserting the PMT Financial Function

In this activity, you will calculate the monthly payments that Jesse Jewelers must make to finance the purchase of the furniture and fixtures for a new store in Houston, the total cost of which is $300,000. You will calculate the monthly payments, including interest, for a three-year loan at an annual interest rate of 4.0%. To stay within Alaina's budget, the monthly payment must be approximately $8,000.

1 ▶ Start Excel. From your student files, open **e04A_Store_Loan**. Display the **Save As** dialog box, navigate to the location where you will store your workbooks for this chapter, and then create a new folder named **Excel Chapter 4** Open the folder, and then **Save** the workbook as **Lastname_Firstname_4A_Store_Loan**

2 ▶ In the range **A2:B5**, enter the following row titles and data. Recall that you can format the numbers as you type by typing them with their symbols as shown. Compare your screen with Figure 4.2.

Amount of Loan	$300,000
Period (years)	3
Interest Rate (per year)	4%
Payment (per month)	

FIGURE 4.2

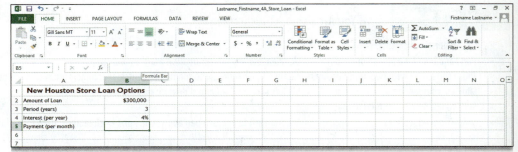

3 ▶ Click cell **B5**. On the **FORMULAS tab**, in the **Function Library group**, click **Financial**. In the list, scroll down as necessary, and then click **PMT**.

The Function Arguments dialog box displays. Recall that *arguments* are the values that an Excel function uses to perform calculations or operations.

4 ▶ If necessary, drag the Function Arguments dialog box to the right side of your screen so you can view columns A:B.

The **PMT function** calculates the payment for a loan based on constant payments and at a constant interest rate.

5 ▶ With your insertion point positioned in the **Rate** box, type **b4/12** and then compare your screen with Figure 4.3.

Excel will divide the annual interest rate of 4%, which is 0.04 in decimal notation, located in cell B4 by 12 (months), which will result in a *monthly* interest rate.

When borrowing money, the interest rate and number of periods are quoted in years. The payments on a loan, however, are usually made monthly. Therefore, the number of periods, which is stated in years, and the *annual* interest rate, must be changed to a monthly equivalent in order to calculate the monthly payment amount. You can see that calculations like these can be made as part of the argument in a function.

FIGURE 4.3

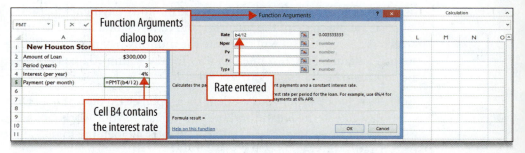

6 ▶ Press Tab to move the insertion point to the **Nper** box. In the lower portion of the dialog box, notice Excel points out that *Nper is the total number of payments for the loan* (number of periods).

7 ▶ Type **b3*12** to have Excel convert the number of years in the loan in cell **B3** (3 years) to the total number of months.

Recall that the PMT function calculates a *monthly* payment. Therefore, all values in the function must be expressed in months. To complete the PMT function, you must determine the total number of loan payment periods (months), which is 3 years × 12 months, or 36 months.

8 ▶ Press Tab to move to the **Pv** box, and then type **b2** to indicate the cell that contains the amount of the loan.

Pv represents the present value—the amount of the loan before any payments are made. In this instance, the Pv is $300,000.

9 In cell **B5** and on the **Formula Bar**, notice that the arguments that comprise the PMT function are separated by commas. Notice also, in the **Function Arguments** dialog box, that the value of each argument displays to the right of the argument box. Compare your screen with Figure 4.4.

NOTE **Optional Arguments**

The PMT function has two arguments not indicated by bold; these are optional. The Future value (Fv) argument assumes that the unpaid portion of the loan should be zero at the end of the last period. The **Type argument** indicates when the loan payment is due. If not specified, the Type argument assumes that the payment will be made at the end of each period. These default values are typical of most loans and may be left blank.

FIGURE 4.4

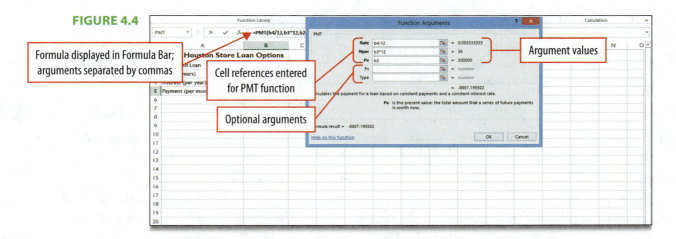

Formula displayed in Formula Bar; arguments separated by commas

Cell references entered for PMT function

Optional arguments

Argument values

10 In the lower right corner of the **Function Arguments** dialog box, click **OK**.

The monthly payment amount—($8,857.20)—displays in cell B5. The amount displays in red and in parentheses to show that it is a negative number, a number that will be paid out. This monthly payment of $8,857.20 is over the $8,000 per month that Alaina has budgeted for her payments.

11 Click in the **Formula Bar**, and then using the arrow keys on the keyboard, position the insertion point between the equal sign and PMT. Type **–** (minus sign) to insert a minus sign into the formula, and then press Enter.

By placing a minus sign in the formula, the monthly payment amount, $8,857.20, displays in cell B5 as a *positive* number, which is more familiar and simpler to work with.

12 Save 💾 your workbook.

Objective 2 Use Goal Seek

Video E4-2

What-If Analysis is a process of changing the values in cells to determine how those changes affect the outcome of formulas on the worksheet; for example, you might vary the interest rate to determine the amount of loan payments.

Goal Seek is part of a suite of data tools used for a What-If Analysis. It is a method to find a specific value for a cell by adjusting the value of one other cell. With Goal Seek, you can work backward from the desired outcome to find the number necessary to achieve your goal. If you have a result in mind, you can try different numbers in one of the cells used as an argument in the function until you get close to the result you want.

Activity 4.02 | Using Goal Seek to Produce a Desired Result

Alaina knows that her budget cannot exceed $8,000 per month for the new store loan. The amount of $300,000 is necessary to purchase the furniture and fixtures to open the new store. Now she has two options: borrow less money and reduce the amount or quality of the furniture and fixtures in the store or extend the time to repay the loan. To find out how much she can borrow for three years to stay within the budget or how much to increase the repayment period, you will use the Goal Seek tool.

1 Click cell **B5**. On the **DATA tab**, in the **Data Tools group**, click **What-If Analysis**, and then in the list, click **Goal Seek**. In the **Goal Seek** dialog box, in the **Set cell** box, confirm that *B5* displays.

The cell address in this box is the cell that will display the desired result.

2 Press Tab. In the **To value** box, type the payment goal of **8000** and press Tab. In the **By changing cell** box, type **b2** which is the amount of the loan, and then compare your dialog box with Figure 4.5.

FIGURE 4.5

3 Click **OK**, and then in the **Goal Seek Status** dialog box, click **OK**.

Excel's calculations indicate that to achieve a monthly payment of $8,000.00 using a three-year loan, Alaina can borrow only *$270,966*—not *$300,000*.

4 Click cell **A7**. Type **Option #1 Reduce Loan Amount** and then on the **Formula Bar**, click **Enter** ✓ to keep the cell active. **Merge and Center**  this heading across the range **A7:B7**, on the **HOME tab**, display the **Cell Styles** gallery, and then under **Titles and Headings**, click the **Heading 2** cell style.

5 Select the range **A2:B5**, right-click, and then click **Copy**. Point to cell **A8**, right-click, point to **Paste Special**, and then under **Paste Values**, click the **second** button—**Values & Number Formatting (A)** 📋. Press Esc to cancel the moving border.

🔄 **ANOTHER WAY**   Click cell A8, right-click, and then click Paste Special. In the Paste Special dialog box, under Paste, click the Values and number formats option button, and then click OK.

---

6 Save 💾 your workbook, and then compare your worksheet with Figure 4.6.

Recall that by using the Paste Special command, you can copy the *value* in a cell, rather than the formula, and the cell formats are retained—cell B5 contains the PMT function formula, and here you need only the value that *results* from that formula.

FIGURE 4.6

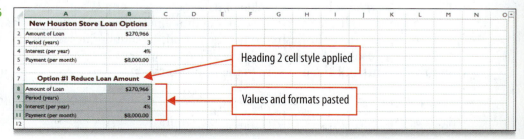

Activity 4.03 | Using Goal Seek to Find an Increased Period

For Alaina's purchase of furniture and fixtures for the new store in Houston, an alternative to borrowing less money—which would mean buying fewer items or items of lesser quality—would be to increase the number of years of payments.

1 ▸ In cell **B2**, replace the existing value by typing **300000** and then press Enter to restore the original loan amount. Click cell **B5**. On the **DATA tab**, in the **Data Tools group**, click **What-If Analysis**, and then click **Goal Seek**.

2 ▸ In the **Set cell** box, confirm that *B5* displays. Press Tab. In the **To value** box, type **8000** and then press Tab. In the **By changing cell** box, type **b3** which is the number of years for the loan. Compare your screen with Figure 4.7.

FIGURE 4.7

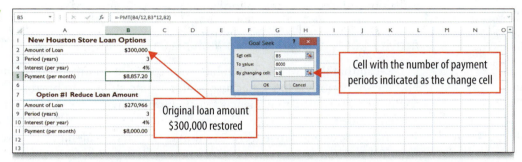

3 ▸ Click **OK** two times.

Excel's calculations indicate that by making payments for 3.3 years—*3.343845511*—the monthly payment is the desired amount of $8,000.00.

4 ▸ Click cell **A13**. Type **Option #2 Increase Number of Years** and then press Enter. Right-click over cell **A7**, on the mini toolbar, click **Format Painter** , and then click cell **A13** to copy the format.

5 ▸ Select the range **A2:B5**, right-click, and then click **Copy**. Point to cell **A14**, right-click, point to **Paste Special**, and then under **Paste Values**, click the **second** button—**Values & Number Formatting (A)** . Press Esc to cancel the moving border.

6 ▸ Click cell **B15**, right-click to display the mini toolbar, and then click **Decrease Decimal** until the number of decimal places displayed is two. Click cell **B3**. Type **3** and then press Enter to restore the original value. **Save** your workbook, and then compare your screen with Figure 4.8.

FIGURE 4.8

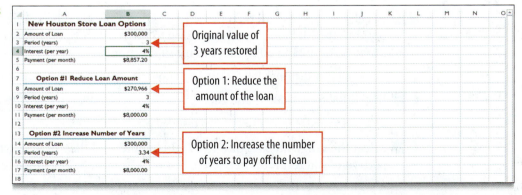

Video E4-3

A **data table** is a range of cells that shows how changing certain values in your formulas affects the results of those formulas. Data tables make it easy to calculate multiple versions in one operation, and then to view and compare the results of all the different variations.

For example, banks may offer loans at different rates for different periods of time, which require different payments. By using a data table, you can calculate the possible values for each argument.

A **one-variable data table** changes the value in only one cell. For example, use a one-variable data table if you want to see how different interest rates affect a monthly payment. A **two-variable data table** changes the values in two cells—for example, if you want to see how different interest rates and different payment periods will affect a monthly payment.

Activity 4.04 | Designing a Two-Variable Data Table

Recall that the PMT function has three required arguments: Present value (Pv), Rate, and Number of periods (Nper). Because Alaina would still like to borrow $300,000 and purchase the fixtures and furniture that she has selected for the new store in Houston, in this data table, the present value will *not* change. The two values that will change are the Rate and Number of periods. Possible periods will range from 24 months (2 years) to 60 months (5 years) and the rate will vary from 5% to 3%.

1 At the lower edge of the worksheet, click the **New sheet** button ⊕. Double-click the **Sheet1 tab**, type **Payment Table** and then press Enter.

2 In cell **A1**, type **Loan Options for New Houston Store: Rates versus Months** and then press Enter. **Merge and Center** 🖃▾ this title across the range **A1:J1**, and then apply the **Title** cell style.

3 In the range **A2:B4**, enter the following row titles and data:

Amount of Loan	$300,000
Period (months)	36
Interest rate (per year)	4%

4 Point to the border between **columns A** and **B** and double-click to AutoFit **column A**. In cell **C5**, type **Payment Options** and press Enter, and then **Merge and Center** 🖃▾ this title across the range **C5:I5**. From the **Cell Styles** gallery, under **Titles and Headings**, click the **Heading 1** cell style.

5 In cell **C6**, type **Number of Monthly Payments** and press Enter, and then use the **Format Painter** 🖌 to apply the format of cell **C5** to cell **C6**.

6 In cell **C7**, type **24** and then press Tab. Type **30** and then press Tab. Select the range **C7:D7**, point to the fill handle, and then drag to the right through cell **I7** to fill in a pattern of months from 24 to 60 in increments of six months.

Recall that the Auto Fill feature will duplicate a pattern of values that you set in the beginning cells.

7 In cell **B8**, type **5.000%** and then press Enter. In cell **B9**, type **4.875%** and then press Enter.

Excel rounds both values to two decimal places.

8 Select the range **B8:B9**. Point to the fill handle, and then drag down through cell **B24** to fill a pattern of interest rates in decrements of .125 from 5.00% down to 3.00%.

9 Right-click anywhere over the selected range, and then on the mini toolbar, click **Increase Decimal** ⬚. **Save** 💾 your workbook. Compare your screen with Figure 4.9.

Row 7 represents the number of monthly payments, and column B represents a range of possible annual interest rates. These two arguments will be used to calculate varying payment arrangements for a loan of $300,000.

FIGURE 4.9

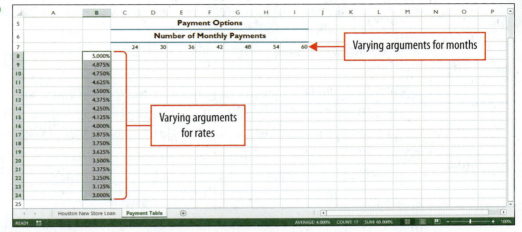

10 In cell **A8**, type **Rates** and then press ⏎. Select the range **A8:A24**. On the **HOME tab**, in the **Alignment group**, click **Merge and Center** ⬚, click **Align Right** ☰, and then click **Middle Align** ☰. Display the **Cell Styles** gallery, and then under **Data and Model**, click the **Explanatory Text** style. Compare your screen with Figure 4.10.

FIGURE 4.10

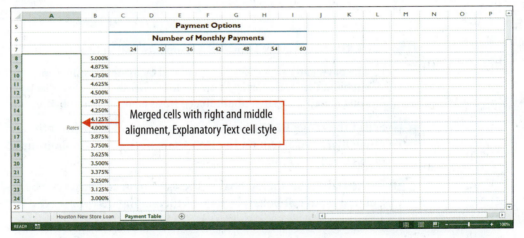

Activity 4.05 | Using a Data Table to Calculate Options

Recall that a data table is a range of cells that shows how changing certain values in your formulas affects the results of those formulas.

In this activity, you will create a table of payments for every combination of payment periods, which are represented by the column titles under *Number of Monthly Payments*, and interest rates, which are represented by the row titles to the right of *Rates*. From the resulting table, Alaina can find a combination of payment periods and interest rates that will enable her to go forward with her plan to borrow $300,000 to purchase the necessary furniture and fixtures for the new store in Houston.

1 Press Ctrl + Home to view the top of your worksheet. Then, in cell **B7**, type **=** Notice that in the upper left corner of your screen, in the **Name Box**, *PMT* displays indicating the most recently used function. Click in the **Name Box** to open the **Function Arguments** dialog box and select the **PMT** function.

When creating a data table, you enter the PMT function in the upper left corner of your range of data, so that when the data table is completed, the months in row 7 and the rates in column B will be substituted into each cell's formula and will fill the table with the range of months and interest rate options.

2 In the **Rate** box, type **b4/12** to divide the interest rate per year shown in cell **B4** by 12 and convert it to a monthly interest rate.

3 Press Tab to move the insertion point to the **Nper** box. Type **b3** which is the cell that contains the number of months, and then press Tab.

The periods in cell B3 are already stated in months and do not need to be changed.

4 In the **Pv** box, type **-b2** to enter the amount of the loan as a negative number. Compare your dialog box with Figure 4.11.

FIGURE 4.11

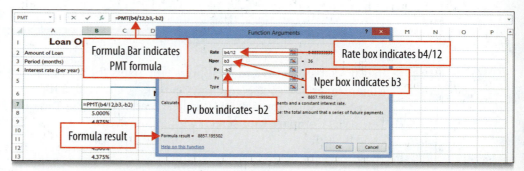

5 Click **OK** to close the **Function Arguments** dialog box and display the result in cell **B7**.

The payment—*$8,857.20*—is calculated by using the values in cells B2, B3, and B4. This is the same payment that you calculated on the first worksheet. Now it displays as a positive number because you entered the loan amount in cell B2 as a negative number.

6 Select the range **B7:I24**, which encompasses all of the months and all of the rates. With the range **B7:I24** selected, on the **DATA tab**, in the **Data Tools group**, click **What-If Analysis**, and then click **Data Table**.

7 In the **Data Table** dialog box, in the **Row input cell** box, type **b3** and then press Tab. In the **Column input cell** box, type **b4** and then compare your screen with Figure 4.12.

The row of months will be substituted for the value in cell B3, and the column of interest rates will be substituted for the value in cell B4.

FIGURE 4.12

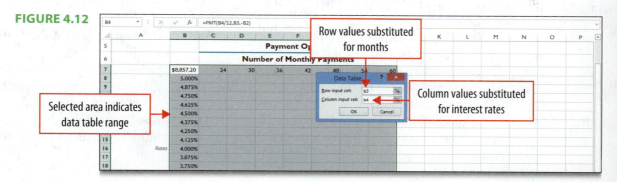

8 ▸ Click **OK**. Click cell **F8**, and then examine the formula in the **Formula Bar**. Compare your screen with Figure 4.13.

The table is filled with payment options that use the month and interest rate corresponding to the position in the table. So, if Alaina chooses a combination of 42 months at an interest rate of 5.0%, the monthly payment will be $7,800.91, which is slightly under the monthly payment she wanted. The data table is one of a group of Excel's What-If Analysis tools.

FIGURE 4.13

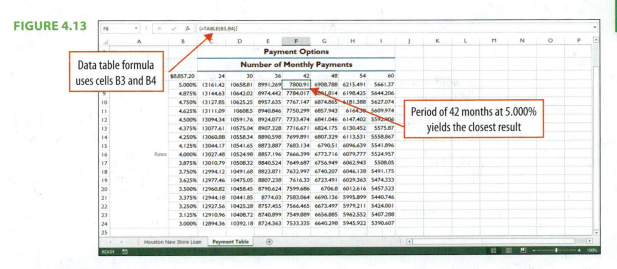

9 ▸ Point to cell **B7**, right-click, and then on the mini toolbar, click **Format Painter**. With the pointer, select the range **C8:I24** to apply the same format. AutoFit columns **C:I** to display all values.

10 ▸ Select the range **F8:F19**. From the **HOME tab**, display the **Cell Styles** gallery, and then under **Data and Model**, click the **Note** cell style to highlight the desired payment options.

11 ▸ Select the range **B8:B24**, hold down Ctrl, and then select the range **C7:I7**. Right-click over the selection, and then on the mini toolbar, click **Bold** B and then click **Center**. Click anywhere to deselect the range, and then compare your worksheet with Figure 4.14.

BY TOUCH　　Swipe to select the range B8:B24, hold it, and then select the range C7:I7.

By using a data table of payment options, you can see that Alaina must get a loan for a 42-month period (3.5 years) for any of the interest rates between 5.000% and 3.000% in order to purchase the furniture and fixtures she wants and still keep the monthly payment under $8,000.

FIGURE 4.14

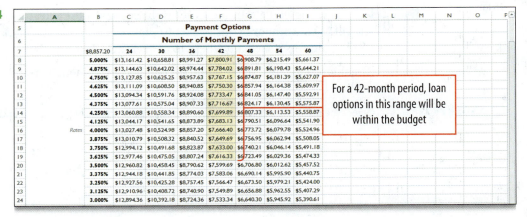

12 ▸ Right-click the **Payment Table sheet tab** and click **Select All Sheets**. With the two sheets grouped, insert a footer in the **left section** that includes the **file name**. Click outside the footer area. On the status bar, click **Normal** ⊞. Press Ctrl + Home to move to the top of the worksheet. Click the **PAGE LAYOUT tab**, in the **Page Setup group**, set the **Orientation** to **Landscape**. Click **Margins**, and then click **Custom Margins**. In the **Page Setup** dialog box, under **Center on page**, select **Horizontally**, and then click **OK**.

13 ▸ Click the **FILE tab** to display **Backstage** view. On the right, at the bottom of the **Properties** list, click **Show All Properties**. On the list of **Properties**, in the **Tags** box, type **amortization schedule, payment table** In the **Subject** box, type your course name and section #. Under **Related People**, be sure that your name displays as the author. If necessary, right-click the author name, click Edit Property, type your name, click outside of the Edit person dialog box, and then click OK.

14 ▸ Click **Print**, examine the **Print Preview**, make any necessary adjustments, and then **Save** 🖫 and Close your workbook.

15 ▸ Hold this workbook until the end of this project, and then print or submit the two worksheets in this workbook electronically as directed by your instructor. If required, print or create an electronic version of your worksheets with formulas displayed using the instructions in Project 1A.

Objective 4   Use Defined Names in a Formula

Video E4-4

A **name**, also referred to as a **defined name**, is a word or string of characters in Excel that represents a cell, a range of cells, a formula, or a constant value. A defined name that is distinctive and easy to remember typically defines the *purpose* of the selected cells. When creating a formula, the defined name may be used instead of the cell reference.

All names have a **scope**, which is the location within which the name is recognized without qualification. The scope of a name is usually either to a specific worksheet or to an entire workbook.

Activity 4.06 | Defining a Name

In this activity, you will use three ways to define a name for a cell or group of cells. After defining a name, you can use the name in a formula to refer to the cell or cells. Names make it easier for you and others to understand the meaning of formulas in a worksheet.

1 ▸ From your student files, open the file **e04A_Merchandise_Costs**, and then **Save** the file in your **Excel Chapter 4** folder as **Lastname_Firstname_4A_Merchandise_Costs**

2 ▸ Select the range **B6:E17**. In the lower right corner of the selection, click **Quick Analysis** 🖽. Click **TOTALS**, compare your screen to Figure 4.15, and then click the first **Sum** button to total the columns. Click anywhere to cancel the selection.

Use this technique to sum a group of columns or rows simultaneously.

🔁 **ANOTHER WAY**   Select the range B6:E18, which includes the adjacent empty cells in row 18, and then click AutoSum.

FIGURE 4.15

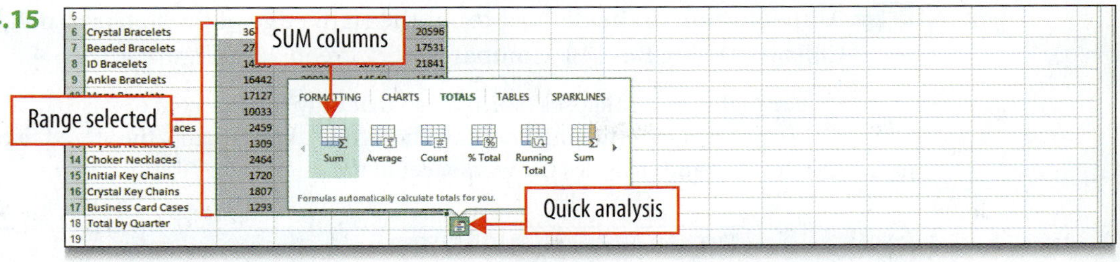

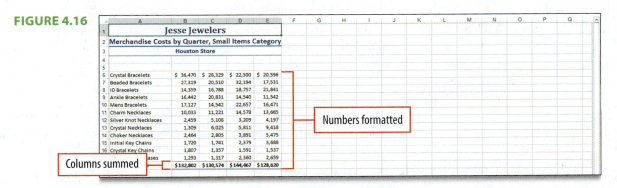

3 ▸ Select the range **B6:E6**, hold down Ctrl, and select the range **B18:E18**. From the **Cell Styles** gallery, under **Number Format**, click the **Currency [0]** cell style. Select the range **B7:E17**, display the **Cell Styles** gallery, and then, under **Number Format**, click **Comma [0]**.

You can use these number formats in the Cell Styles gallery in a manner similar to the Accounting Number Format button and the Comma Style button on the ribbon. The advantage to using these styles from the Cell Styles gallery is that you can select the option that formats automatically with zero [0] decimal places.

4 ▸ Select the range **B18:E18**, and then from the **Cell Styles** gallery, under **Titles and Headings**, click the **Total** cell style. Press Ctrl + Home to move to the top of the worksheet, and then compare your screen with Figure 4.16.

FIGURE 4.16

5 ▸ Select the range **B6:E9**. On the **FORMULAS tab**, in the **Defined Names group**, click **Define Name**. Compare your screen with Figure 4.17.

The New Name dialog box displays. In the Name box, Excel suggests *Crystal_Bracelets* as the name for this range of cells, which is the text in the first cell adjacent to the selected range. Excel will attempt to suggest a logical name for the selected cells. Notice that Excel replaces the blank space with an underscore, as defined names cannot contain spaces.

FIGURE 4.17

6 ▸ With *Crystal_Bracelets* selected, type **Bracelet_Costs** as the name.

Naming cells has no effect on the displayed or underlying values; it simply creates an easy-to-remember name that you can use when creating formulas that refer to this range of cells.

7 At the bottom of the dialog box, at the right edge of the **Refers to** box, point to and click **Collapse Dialog Box** ⬛. Compare your screen with Figure 4.18.

> The dialog box collapses (shrinks) so that only the *Refers to* box is visible, and the selected range is surrounded by a moving border. When you define a name, the stored definition is an absolute cell reference and includes the worksheet name.

FIGURE 4.18

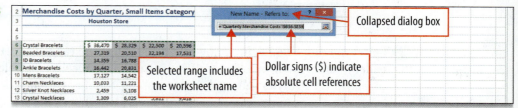

8 If necessary, drag the collapsed dialog box by its title bar to the right of your screen so that it is not blocking the selection. Then, change the range selection by selecting the range **B6:E10**.

> A moving border surrounds the new range. The range, formatted with absolute cell references, displays in the *Refers to* box of the collapsed dialog box. In this manner, it is easy to change the range of cells referred to by the name.

9 Click **Expand Dialog Box** ⬛ to redisplay the entire **New Name** dialog box, and then click **OK**.

10 Select the range **B11:E14**. In the upper left corner of the Excel window, to the left of the **Formula Bar**, click in the **Name Box**, and notice that the cell reference *B11* moves to the left edge of the box and is highlighted in blue. Type **Necklace_Costs** as shown in Figure 4.19.

FIGURE 4.19

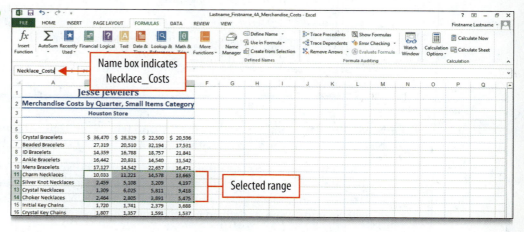

11 Press Enter, and then take a moment to study the rules for defining names, as described in the table in Figure 4.20.

FIGURE 4.20

RULES FOR DEFINING NAMES
The first character of the defined name must be a letter, an underscore (_), or a backslash (\).
After the first character, the remaining characters in the defined name can be letters, numbers, periods, and underscore characters.
Spaces are not valid in a defined name; use a period or the underscore character as a word separator, for example, 1st.Quarter or 1st_Qtr.
The single letter C or R in either uppercase or lowercase cannot be defined as a name, because these letters are used by Excel for selecting a row or column when you enter them in a Name or a Go To text box.
A defined name can be no longer than 255 characters; short, meaningful names are the most useful.
Defined names cannot be the same as a cell reference, for example M$10.
Defined names can contain uppercase and lowercase letters; however, Excel does not distinguish between them. So, for example, if you create the name Sales and then create another name SALES in the same workbook, Excel considers the names to be the same and prompts you for a unique name.

12 ▶ Click any cell to cancel the selection. Then, click the **Name Box arrow** and compare your screen with Figure 4.21. If necessary, resize the Name Box by dragging the three vertical dots to the right, to display the full names.

Your two defined names display in alphabetical order.

FIGURE 4.21

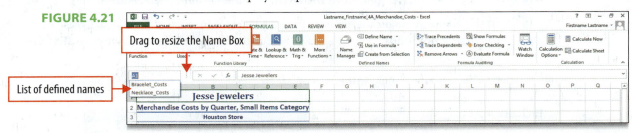

13 ▶ From the list, click **Bracelet_Costs** and notice that Excel selects the range of values that comprise the cost of various Bracelet styles.

14 ▶ Click the **Name Box arrow** again, and then click **Necklace_Costs** to select the range of values that comprise the Necklace costs.

15 ▶ Select the range **B15:E16**. On the **FORMULAS tab**, in the **Defined Names group**, click **Name Manager,** and notice that the two names that you have defined display in a list.

16 ▶ In the upper left corner of the **Name Manager** dialog box, click **New**. With *Initial_Key_Chains* selected, type **Key_Chain_Costs** and then click **OK**. Compare your screen with Figure 4.22. **Close** the **Name Manager** dialog box and **Save** your workbook.

This is another method to define a name—by creating a new name in the Name Manager dialog box. The Name Manager dialog box displays the three range names that you have created, in alphabetical order.

FIGURE 4.22

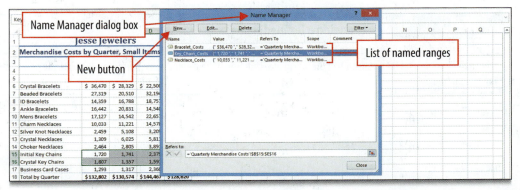

Activity 4.07 | Inserting New Data into a Named Range

You can insert new data into the range of cells that a name represents. In this activity, you will modify the range named *Necklace_Costs* to include new data.

1 On the left side of your window, click the **row 15** heading to select the entire row. Right-click over the selected row, and then click **Insert** to insert a new blank row above.

> A new row 15 is inserted, and the remaining rows move down one row. Recall that when new rows are inserted in this manner, Excel adjusts formulas accordingly.

2 Click the **Name Box arrow**, and then click **Key_Chain_Costs**. Notice that Excel highlights the correct range of cells, adjusting for the newly inserted row.

> If you insert rows, the defined name adjusts to the new cell addresses to represent the cells that were originally defined. Likewise, if you move the cells, the defined name goes with them to the new location.

3 In cell **A15**, type **Sweetheart Necklaces** and then press Tab. In cell **B15**, type **1166** and press Tab. In cell **C15**, type **1087** and press Tab. In cell **D15**, type **847** and press Tab. In cell **E15**, type **965** and press Enter.

> The cells in the newly inserted row adopt the Currency [0] format from the cells above.

4 On the **FORMULAS tab**, from the **Defined Names group**, click **Name Manager**.

5 In the **Name Manager** dialog box, in the **Name** column, click **Necklace_Costs**. At the bottom of the dialog box, click in the **Refers to** box and edit the reference, changing $E$14 to $E$15 as shown in Figure 4.23.

> This action will include the Sweetheart Necklace values in the named range.

FIGURE 4.23

6 In the **Name Manager** dialog box, click **Close**, and click **Yes** to save the changes you made to the name reference. In the upper left corner of the window, click the **Name Box arrow** and then click the range name **Necklace_Costs**. Notice that the selected range now includes the new row 15. **Save** your workbook.

NOTE   Changing a Defined Name

If you create a defined name and then decide to change it, you can use the Name Manger to edit the name. Display the Name Manager dialog box, select the defined name, and then at the top of the dialog box, click Edit. If the defined name is used in a formula, the new name is automatically changed in any affected formulas.

Activity 4.08 | Creating a Defined Name by Using Row and Column Titles

You can use the Create from Selection command to use existing row or column titles as the name for a range of cells.

1 Select the range **A18:E18**. On the **FORMULAS tab**, in the **Defined Names group**, click **Create from Selection**. Compare your screen with Figure 4.24.

> The Create Names from Selection dialog box displays. A check mark displays in the *Left column* check box, which indicates that Excel will use the value of the cell in the leftmost column of the selection as the range name, unless you specify otherwise.

FIGURE 4.24

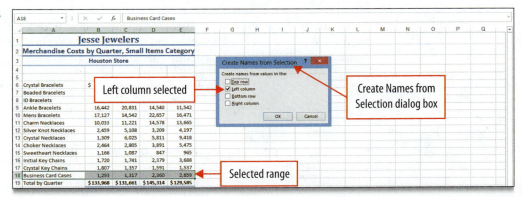

2 In the **Create Names from Selection** dialog box, click **OK**, and then click anywhere to cancel the selection.

3 Click the **Name Box arrow**, and then click the name **Business_Card_Cases**, and notice that in the new range name, Excel inserts the underscore necessary to fill a blank space in the range name. Also notice that the actual range consists of only the numeric values, as shown in Figure 4.25. **Save** your workbook.

> This method is convenient for naming a range of cells without having to actually type a name—Excel uses the text of the first cell to the left of the selected range as the range name and then formats the name properly.

FIGURE 4.25

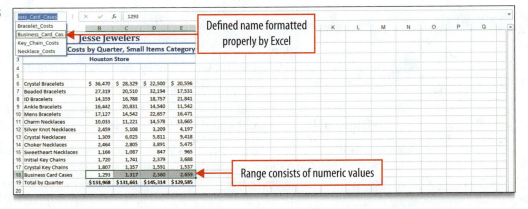

Activity 4.09 | Using Defined Names in a Formula

The advantage to naming a range of cells is that you can use the name in a formula in other parts of your workbook. The defined name provides a logical reference to data. For example, referring to data as Bracelet_Costs is easier to understand than referring to data as B6:E10.

When you use a defined name in a formula, the result is the same as if you typed the cell references.

1 Display the **Annual Merchandise Costs** worksheet.

2 In cell **B5**, type **=sum(B** and then scroll to the bottom of the AutoComplete list; compare your screen with Figure 4.26.

The Formula AutoComplete list displays containing all of Excel's built-in functions that begin with the letter B and any defined names in this workbook that begin with the letter B. To the left of your defined name *Bracelet_Costs*, a defined name icon displays.

FIGURE 4.26

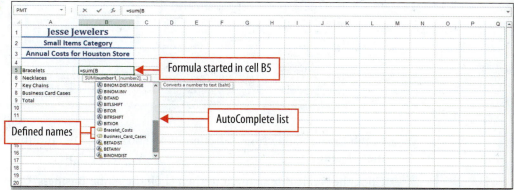

3 Double-click **Bracelet_Costs** and then press Enter.

Your result is *411346*. Recall that SUM is a function—a formula already built by Excel—that adds all the cells in a selected range. Therefore, Excel sums all the cells in the range you defined as Bracelet_Costs on the first worksheet in the workbook, and then places the result in cell B5 of this worksheet.

> 🔄 **ANOTHER WAY**   You can simply type the defined name in the formula.

4 In cell **B6**, type **=sum(N** and then on the **Formula AutoComplete** list, double-click **Necklace_ Costs** to insert the formula. Press Enter to display the result *105,733*.

5 In cell **B7**, type **=sum(** and then on the **FORMULAS tab**, in the **Defined Names group**, click **Use in Formula**. In the list, click **Key_Chain_Costs**, and then press Enter to display the total *15,820*.

6 In cell **B8**, use any of the techniques you just practiced to sum the cells containing the costs for **Business Card Cases** and to display a result of *7,629*. In cell **B9**, in the **Function Library group**, click **AutoSum** Σ AutoSum ▾ to sum **column B** and display a result of *540,528*.

7 Select the nonadjacent cells **B5** and **B9**, and then on the **HOME tab**, display the **Cell Styles** gallery. Under **Number Format**, click the **Currency [0]** cell style. Select the range **B6:B8**, display the **Cell Styles** gallery, and then under **Number Format**, click **Comma [0]**.

8 ▸ Click cell **B9** and under **Titles and Headings**, click the **Total** cell style. Click cell **B5** and then compare your screen with Figure 4.27.

FIGURE 4.27

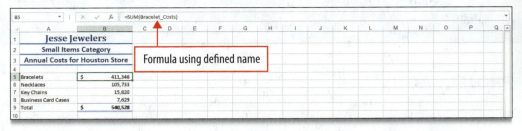

9 ▸ Select both worksheets so that *[Group]* displays in the title bar. With the two worksheets grouped, insert a footer in the **left section** that includes the file name. Return to **Normal** view and make cell **A1** active. **Center** the worksheets **Horizontally** on the page.

10 ▸ Click the **FILE tab** to display **Backstage** view. On the right, at the bottom of the **Properties** list, click **Show All Properties**. Under **Related People**, be sure that your name displays as the author. If necessary, right-click the author name, click Edit Property, and then type your name. In the **Subject** box, type your course name and section #, and in the **Tags** box, type **small items category, merchandise costs** Display the grouped worksheets in **Print Preview**, **Close** the **Print Preview**, and then make any necessary corrections or adjustments. Right-click any of the grouped sheet tabs, and then click **Ungroup Sheets**.

11 ▸ Save 🖫 your workbook. Print or submit the two worksheets in this workbook electronically as directed by your instructor. If required, print or create an electronic version of your worksheets with formulas displayed using the instructions in Project 1A. **Close** Excel.

END | You have completed Project 4A

Lookup Form and Revenue Report

PROJECT ACTIVITIES

In Activities 4.10 through 4.18, you will assist Mike Connor, the Vice President of Marketing at Jesse Jewelers, by adding lookup functions to a phone order form so that an order taker can complete the form quickly. You will use the Formula Auditing features to review a revenue worksheet and to resolve the errors and you will use the Watch Window to monitor changes in sales worksheets. Your completed workbooks will look similar to Figure 4.28.

PROJECT FILES

For Project 4B, you will need the following files:

e04B_First_Quarter_Sales
e04B_Miami_Revenue
e04B_Phone_Form

You will save your workbooks as:

Lastname_Firstname_4B_First_Quarter_Sales
Lastname_Firstname_4B_Miami_Revenue
Lastname_Firstname_4B_Phone_Form

PROJECT RESULTS

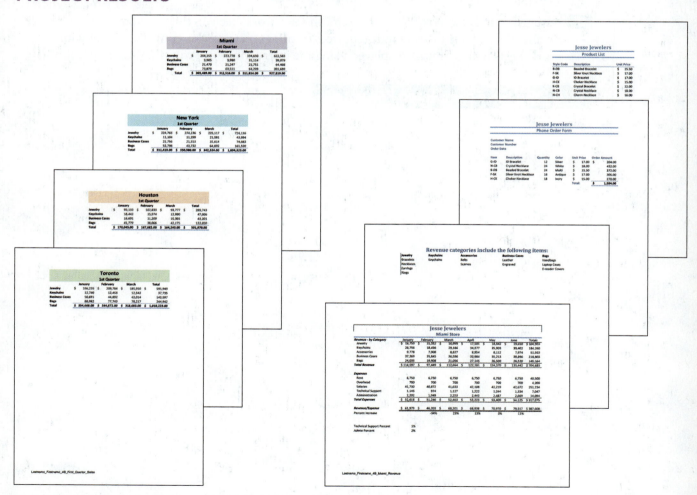

FIGURE 4.28 Project 4B Lookup Form and Revenue Report

Video E4-5

Lookup functions look up a value in a defined range of cells located in another part of the workbook to find a corresponding value. For example, you can define a two-column range of cells containing names and phone numbers. Then, when you type a name in the cell referred to by the lookup formula, Excel fills in the phone number by looking it up in the defined range. In the lookup formula, the defined range is referred to as the **table array**.

The **VLOOKUP** function looks up values in a table array arranged as vertical columns. The function searches the first column of the table array for a corresponding value, and then returns a value from any cell on the same row. The **HLOOKUP** function looks up values in a table array arranged in horizontal rows. The function searches the top row of the table array for a corresponding value, and then returns a value from any cell in the same column. The **LOOKUP** function looks up values in either a one-row or a one-column range.

There is one requirement for the lookup functions to work properly. The data in the table array, which can be numbers or text, must be sorted in ascending order. For the VLOOKUP function, the values must be sorted on the first column in ascending order. For the HLOOKUP function, the values must be sorted on the first row in ascending order.

Activity 4.10 │ Defining a Range of Cells for a Lookup Function

The first step in using a lookup function is to define the range of cells that will serve as the table array. In the Jesse Jewelers Phone Order form, after an Item Number is entered on the form, Mr. Connor wants the description of the item to display automatically in the Description column. To accomplish this, you will define a table array that includes the item number in one column and a description of the item in the second column.

1 Start Excel. From your student files, open the file **e04B_Phone_Form**, and then **Save** the file in your **Excel Chapter 4** folder as **Lastname_Firstname_4B_Phone_Form**

2 With cell **A1** active, display the **Cell Styles** gallery, and then, under **Titles and Headings**, click **Title**. Right-click cell **A1**, and on the mini toolbar, click the **Format Painter** , and then click cell **A2**. Compare your screen with Figure 4.29.

When store managers call Jesse Jewelers headquarters to place an order, the order taker uses this type of worksheet to record the information.

FIGURE 4.29

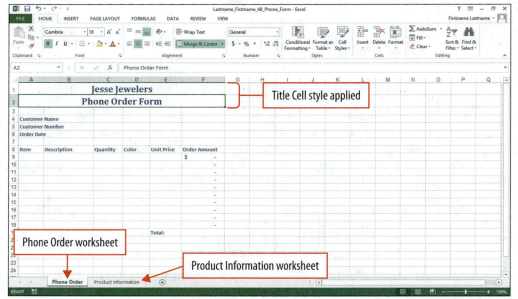

3 Click the **Product Information sheet tab** to display the second worksheet.

The Product Information worksheet contains the Style Code, Description, and Unit Price of specific bracelets and necklaces.

4 On the **Product Information** worksheet, select the range **A4:C11**. On the **DATA tab**, in the **Sort & Filter group**, click **Sort**. If necessary, drag the Sort dialog box to the right side of your screen so you can view columns A:C.

To use this list to look up information with the Excel VLOOKUP function, you must sort the list in ascending order by Style Code, which is the column that will be used to look up the matching information.

5 In the **Sort** dialog box, under **Column**, click the **Sort by arrow**. Notice that the selected range is now **A5:C11** and that the column titles in the range **A4:C4** display in the **Sort by** list. Compare your screen with Figure 4.30.

When the selected range includes a header row that should remain in place while the remaining rows are sorted, Excel usually recognizes those column headings, selects the *My data has headers* check box, and then displays the column headings in the Sort by list.

FIGURE 4.30

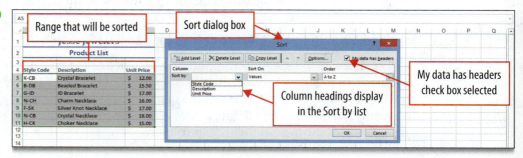

6 On the **Sort by** list, click **Style Code**, which is the first column heading and the column heading that Excel selects by default.

7 Under **Sort On**, verify that *Values* displays, and under **Order**, verify that *A to Z* displays.

Values indicates that the sort will be based on the values in the cells of the first column, rather than cell color or some other cell characteristic. *A to Z* indicates that the cell will be sorted in ascending order.

8 Click **OK** to sort the data by *Style Code* in ascending order.

Excel sorts the data alphabetically by Style Code; *B-DB* is first in the list and *N-CH* is last.

9 Save 🖫 your workbook.

Activity 4.11 | Inserting the VLOOKUP Function

Recall that the VLOOKUP function looks up values in a range of cells arranged as vertical columns. The arguments for this function include *lookup_value*—the value to search in the first column of the table array, *table_array*—the range that contains the data, and *col_index_num*—the column number (1, 2, 3, 4, and so on) in the table array that contains the result you want to retrieve from the table, which in this instance is the Description.

1 Display the **Phone Order** worksheet. In cell **A9**, type **G-ID** and press Tab.

2 With cell **B9** as the active cell, on the **FORMULAS tab**, in the **Function Library group**, click **Lookup & Reference**, and then click **VLOOKUP**.

The Function Arguments dialog box for VLOOKUP displays.

3 With the insertion point in the **Lookup_value** box, click cell **A9** to look up the description of Item G-ID.

4 Click in the **Table_array** box, and then at the bottom of the workbook, click the **Product Information sheet tab**. On the **Product Information** worksheet, select the range **A4:C11**, and then press ⌐F4⌐.

> This range (table array) includes the value that will be looked up—*G-ID* and the corresponding value to be displayed—*ID Bracelet*. By pressing ⌐F4⌐, the absolute cell reference is applied to the table array so that the formula can be copied to the remainder of the column in the Phone Order sheet.

BY TOUCH Tap in the Table_array box, and then at the bottom of the workbook, tap the Product Information sheet tab. On the Product Information sheet, select the range A4:C11, and then edit the reference to $A$4:$C$11 to make it absolute.

5 Click in the **Col_index_num** box and type **2** Compare your screen with Figure 4.31.

> The description for the selected item—the value to be looked up—is located in column 2 of the table array.

FIGURE 4.31

6 Click **OK**.

> The description for Item G-ID displays in cell B9.

7 With cell **B9** as the active cell and containing the VLOOKUP formula, point to the fill handle in the lower right corner of the cell, and then drag to fill the VLOOKUP formula down through cell **B18**. Compare your screen with Figure 4.32.

> The #*N/A* error notation displays in the cells where you copied the formula. Excel displays this error when a function or formula exists in a cell but has no value available with which to perform a calculation; values have not yet been entered in column A in those rows.

FIGURE 4.32

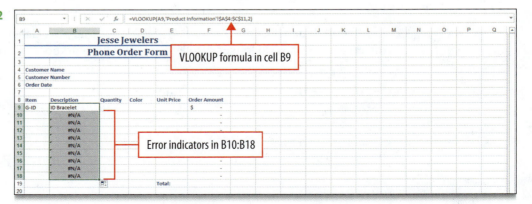

8 Click cell **C9**, type **12** as the quantity ordered and press Tab. In cell **D9**, type **Silver** and press Tab.

9 With cell **E9** as the active cell, on the **FORMULAS tab**, in the **Function Library group**, click **Lookup & Reference**, and then click **VLOOKUP**.

10 With the insertion point in the **Lookup_value** box, click cell **A9** to look up information for Item G-ID. Click in the **Table_array** box, display the **Product Information** sheet, and then select the range **A4:C11**. Press F4 to make the values in the range absolute.

11 In the **Col_index_num** box, type **3** to look up the price in the third column of the range, and then click **OK**.

The Unit Price for the ID Bracelet—*$17.00*—displays in cell E9.

12 Click cell **F9**, and notice that a formula to calculate the total for the item, Quantity times Unit Price, has already been entered in the worksheet.

This formula has also been copied to the range F10:F18.

13 Click cell **E9**, and then copy the VLOOKUP formula down through cell **E18**. Compare your screen with Figure 4.33.

The *#N/A* error notation displays in the cells where you copied the formula, and also in cells F10:F18, because the formulas there have no values yet with which to perform a calculation—values have not yet been entered in column A in those rows.

FIGURE 4.33

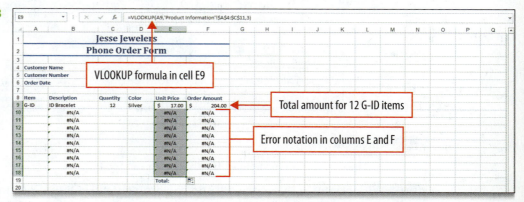

14 Click cell **A10**, type **N-CB** and press Tab two times.

Excel looks up the product description and the product price in the vertical table array on the Product Information sheet, and then displays the results in cells B10 and E10.

15 In cell **C10**, type **24** and press Tab. Notice that Excel calculates the total for this item in cell **F10**—*432.00*.

16 In cell **D10**, type **White** and then press Enter. Notice that after data is entered in the row, the error notations no longer display. **Save** 🖫 your workbook. Compare your screen with Figure 4.34.

FIGURE 4.34

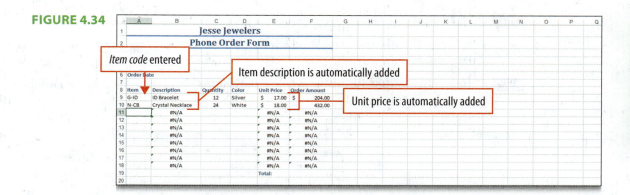

Objective 6 Validate Data

Video E4-6

Another technique to improve accuracy when completing a worksheet is **data validation**—a technique in which you control the type of data or the values that are entered into a cell. This technique improves accuracy because it limits and controls the type of data an individual, such as an order taker, can enter into the form.

One way to control the type of data entered is to create a **validation list**—a list of values that are acceptable for a group of cells. Only values in the list are valid; any value *not* in the list is considered invalid. For example, in the Phone Order sheet, it would be useful if in the Item column, only valid Style Codes could be entered.

Activity 4.12 | Creating a Validation List

A list of valid values must either be on the same worksheet as the destination cell, or if the list is in another worksheet, the cell range must be named. In this activity, you will create a defined name for the Style Codes, and then create a validation list for column A of the Phone Order worksheet.

1 Display the **Product Information** worksheet. Select the range **A4:A11**. On the **FORMULAS tab**, in the **Defined Names group**, click **Create from Selection**.

> Recall that by using the Create from Selection command, you can automatically generate a name from the selected cells that uses the text in the top row or the leftmost column of a selection.

2 In the **Create Names from Selection** dialog box, be sure the **Top row** check box is selected, and then click **OK** to use *Style Code* as the range name.

3 In the **Defined Names group**, click **Name Manager**, and then notice that the new defined name is listed with the name *Style_Code*.

> *Style_Code* displays as the defined name for the selected cells. Recall that Excel replaces spaces with an underscore when it creates a range name.

4 **Close** the **Name Manager** dialog box. Display the **Phone Order** sheet, and then select the range **A9:A18**.

> Before you set the validation requirement, you must first select the cells that you want to restrict to only valid entries from the list.

5 On the **DATA tab**, in the **Data Tools group**, click **Data Validation**. In the **Data Validation** dialog box, be sure the **Settings tab** is selected.

6 Under **Validation criteria**, click the **Allow arrow**, and then click **List**.

A Source box displays as the third box in the Data Validation dialog box. Here you select or type the source data.

7 Click to position the insertion point in the **Source** box, type **=Style_Code** and then compare your screen with Figure 4.35.

FIGURE 4.35

8 Click **OK**. Click cell **A11**, and notice that a list arrow displays at the right edge of the cell.

9 In cell **A11**, click the **list arrow** to display the list, and then compare your screen with Figure 4.36.

FIGURE 4.36

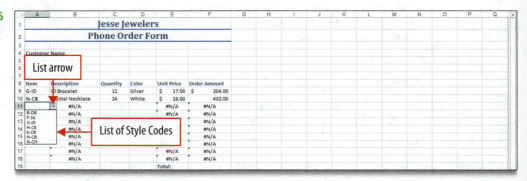

10 From the list, click **B-DB**.

The Style Code is selected from the list and the Item, Description, and Unit Price cells are filled in for row 11.

11 Press Tab two times, type **24** and press Tab, type **Multi** and then press Enter to return to the beginning of the next row. Compare your screen with Figure 4.37.

You can see that when taking orders by phone, it will speed the process if all of the necessary information can be filled in automatically. Furthermore, accuracy will be improved if item codes are restricted to only valid data.

FIGURE 4.37

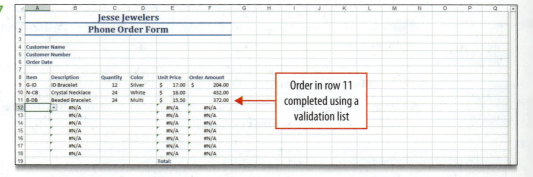

12 ▶ With cell **A12** active, click the **list arrow**, and then click **F-SK**. As the **Quantity**, type **18** and as the **Color**, type **Antique** and then press Enter.

13 ▶ In cell **A13**, type **G-W** and press Tab.

An error message displays indicating that you entered a value that is not valid; that is, it is not on the validation list you created. If the order taker mistakenly types an invalid value into the cell, this message will display.

Restricting the values that an order taker can enter will greatly improve the accuracy of orders. Also, encouraging order takers to select from the list, rather than typing, will reduce the time it takes to fill in the order form.

14 ▶ In the error message, click **Cancel**. Click the **list arrow** again, click **H-CK,** and press Tab two times. As the **Quantity**, type **18** and as the **Color**, type **Ivory** and then press Enter.

15 ▶ Select the unused rows **14:18**, right-click over the selection, and then click **Delete**.

16 ▶ In cell **F14**, sum the **Order Amount** column, and apply the **Total** cell style.

17 ▶ Select both worksheets so that *[Group]* displays in the title bar. With the two worksheets grouped, insert a footer in the **left section** that includes the file name. **Center** the worksheets **Horizontally** on the page. Return to **Normal** view and make cell **A1** active.

18 ▶ Click the **FILE tab** to display **Backstage** view. On the right, at the bottom of the **Properties** list, click **Show All Properties**. On the list of **Properties**, in the **Tags** box, type **phone order form** In the **Subject** box, type your course name and section #. Under **Related People**, be sure that your name displays as the author. If necessary, right-click the author name, click Edit Property, type your name, click outside of the Edit person dialog box, and then click OK. Display the grouped worksheets in **Print Preview**, **Close** the **Print Preview**, and then make any necessary corrections or adjustments.

19 ▶ Ungroup the worksheets and then **Save** 🖫 your workbook. Hold this workbook until the end of this project, and then print or submit the two worksheets in this workbook electronically as directed by your instructor. If required, print or create an electronic version of your worksheets with formulas displayed using the instructions in Project 1A. **Close** this workbook.

More Knowledge	**Creating Validation Messages**

In the Data Validation dialog box, you can use the Input Message tab to create a ScreenTip that will display when the cell is selected. The message can be an instruction that tells the user what to do. You can also use the Error Alert tab to create a warning message that displays if invalid data is entered in the cell.

Objective 7 | Audit Worksheet Formulas

Video E4-7

Auditing is the process of examining a worksheet for errors in *formulas*. Formulas are equations that perform calculations on values in your worksheet. A formula consists of a sequence of values, cell references, names, functions, or operators in a cell, which together produce a new value. Recall that a formula always begins with an equal sign.

Excel includes a group of *Formula Auditing* features, which consists of tools and commands accessible from the FORMULAS tab that help you to check your worksheet for errors. In complex worksheets, use these Formula Auditing features to show relationships between cells and formulas, to ensure that formulas are logical and correct, and to resolve error messages. Although sometimes it is appropriate to hide the error message, at other times error notations can indicate a problem that should be corrected.

Activity 4.13 | Tracing Precedents

Precedent cells are cells that are referred to by a formula in another cell. The ***Trace Precedents command*** displays arrows that indicate what cells affect the values of the cell that is selected. By using the Trace Precedents command, you can see the relationships between formulas and cells. As an auditing tool, the process of tracing a formula is a way to ensure that you constructed the formula correctly.

1 From your student files, open the file **e04B_Miami_Revenue,** and then **Save** the file in your **Excel Chapter 4** folder as **Lastname_Firstname_4B_Miami_Revenue** Compare your screen with Figure 4.38.

The worksheet details the revenue and expenses related to the Miami store over a six-month period. Several error notations are present (#VALUE!, #REF!, #DIV/0!), green triangles display in the top left corners of several cells indicating a potential error, and two columns are too narrow to fit the data which Excel indicates by displaying pound signs—####.

FIGURE 4.38

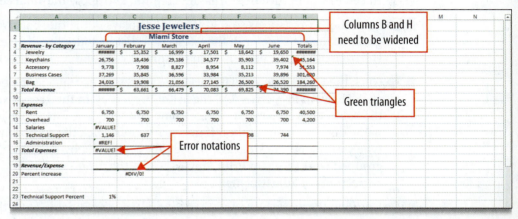

2 Click the **FILE tab,** and then on the left, click **Options**. In the **Excel Options** dialog box, click **Formulas.** Under **Error checking rules,** point to the small information icon after the first Error checking rule to display the ScreenTip. Compare your screen with Figure 4.39.

Here you can control which error checking rules you want to activate, and you can get information about each of the rules by clicking the small blue information icon at the end of each rule. By default, all but the next to last rule are selected, and it is recommended that you maintain these default settings. This textbook assumes the default settings.

FIGURE 4.39

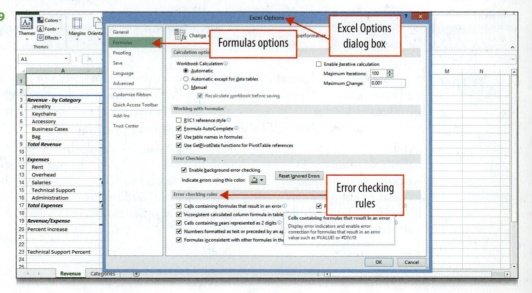

3 In the lower right corner of the dialog box, click **Cancel** to close the dialog box.

4 Take a moment to study the table in Figure 4.40, which details some common error values that might display on your worksheet.

An **error value** is the result of a formula that Excel cannot evaluate correctly.

MICROSOFT EXCEL ERROR VALUES		
ERROR VALUE	**MEANING**	**POSSIBLE CAUSE**
#####	Cannot see data.	The column is not wide enough to display the entire value.
#DIV/0!	Cannot divide by zero.	The divisor in a formula refers to a blank cell or a cell that contains zero.
#NAME?	Does not recognize a name you used in a formula.	A function or a named range may be misspelled or does not exist.
#VALUE!	Cannot use a text field in a formula.	A formula refers to a cell that contains a text value rather than a numeric value or a formula.
#REF!	Cannot locate the reference.	A cell that is referenced in a formula may have been deleted or moved.
#N/A	No value is available.	No information is available for the calculation you want to perform.
#NUM!	Invalid argument in a worksheet function.	An unacceptable argument may have been used in a function. Or, a formula result could be too large or too small.
#NULL!	No common cells.	A space was entered between two ranges in a formula to indicate an intersection, but the ranges have no common cells.

5 On your worksheet, in the **column heading area**, select **column B**, hold down Ctrl, and then select **column H**. Point to the right edge of either of the selected column headings to display the ⊞ pointer, and then double-click to apply AutoFit.

AutoFit widens the columns to accommodate the longest values in each column; the ##### errors no longer display.

⟳ BY TOUCH Tap the column B heading and hold it, then tap column H. With both columns selected double-tap the border to the right edge of either of the selected column headings to apply AutoFit.

6 Click cell **C9**, and then notice the **green triangle** in the top left corner of the cell.

A green triangle in the upper left corner of a cell indicates that the formula in the cell is suspect for some reason. Typically, this is because the formula does not match the formula in the cells next to it, or because it does not include all of the adjacent cells.

7 In cell **C9**, to the left of the cell, point to **Error Checking** ◆ ▾ , and then read the **ScreenTip** that displays. Compare your screen with Figure 4.41.

The ScreenTip indicates that adjacent cells containing numbers are not included in the formula. It is possible that the formula purposely consists of a group of cells that excludes some of the cells adjacent to it. However, because that is not as common as including *all* of the cells that are adjacent to one another, Excel flags this as a potential error.

FIGURE 4.41

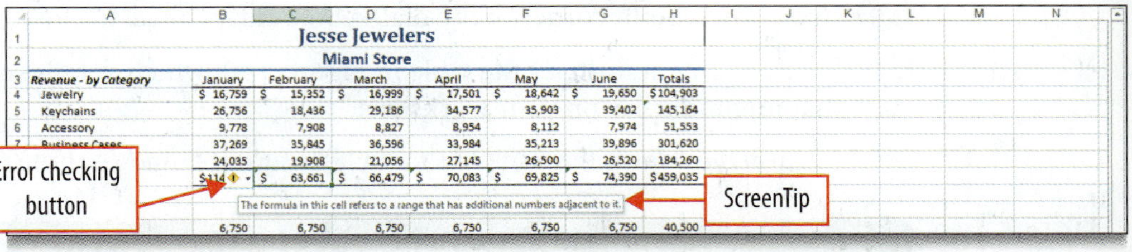

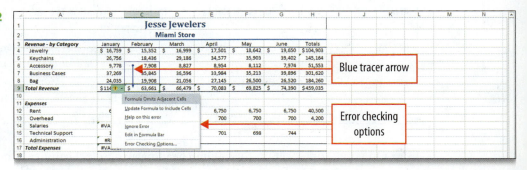

On the **FORMULAS tab**, in the **Formula Auditing group**, click **Trace Precedents**. Notice that the range **C6:C8** is bordered in blue and a blue arrow points to cell **C9**.

> Recall that precedent cells are cells that are referred to by a formula in another cell. Here, the precedent cells are bordered in blue. A blue arrow, called a *tracer arrow*, displays from C6:C8, pointing to the selected cell C9. A tracer arrow shows the relationship between the active cell and its related cells. Tracer arrows are blue when pointing from a cell that provides data to another cell.

> Because this total should include *all* of the revenue categories for February, this is an error in the formula—the formula should include the range C4:C8. By tracing the precedents, you can see that two cells were mistakenly left out of the formula.

To the left of cell **C9**, click **Error Checking** ◈ ▾ to display a list of error checking options. Compare your screen with Figure 4.42.

FIGURE 4.42

In the list, notice that Excel indicates the potential error highlighted in blue—*Formula Omits Adjacent Cells*. Notice also that you can update the formula, seek help with the error, ignore the error, edit the formula in the **Formula Bar**, or display the **Error Checking Options** in the **Excel Options** dialog box. Click **Update Formula to Include Cells**, and then look at the formula in the **Formula Bar**.

> As shown in the Formula Bar, the formula is updated to include the range C4:C8; the green triangle no longer displays in the cell.

Click cell **D9**, which also displays a green triangle, and then point to **Error Checking** ◈ ▾ to display the **ScreenTip**.

> The same error exists in cell D9—not all adjacent cells in the column were included in the formula. This error also exists in the range E9:G9. You can click in each cell and use the Error Checking button's options list to correct each formula, or, you can use the fill handle to copy the corrected formula in cell C9 to the remaining cells.

Click cell **C9,** drag the fill handle to copy the corrected formula to the range **D9:G9** and then notice that all the green triangles are removed from the range.

Click cell **H5**, point to **Error Checking** ◈ ▾, and read the **ScreenTip**.

> The formula in this cell is not the same as the formula in the other cells in this area of the worksheet.

14 On the **FORMULAS tab**, in the **Formula Auditing group**, click **Trace Precedents**. Compare your screen with Figure 4.43.

> A blue border surrounds the range B8:G8, and a blue tracer arrow displays from the cell B8 to cell H5. This indicates that the formula in cell H5 is summing the values in row 8 rather than the values in row 5.

FIGURE 4.43

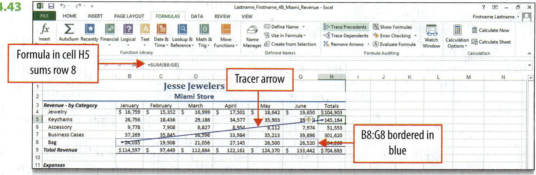

15 To the left of cell **H5**, click **Error Checking** ◈ ▾ to display the list of error checking options, notice the explanation *Inconsistent Formula*, examine the formula in the **Formula Bar**, and then click **Copy Formula from Above**. If necessary, AutoFit column H to display the values correctly.

16 Look at the **Formula Bar** to verify that the formula is summing the numbers in **row 5**—the range **B5:G5**. With cell **H5** still selected, from the **HOME tab**, display the **Cell Styles** gallery, and then, under **Number Format**, click the **Comma [0]** number format.

> The blue tracer arrow no longer displays, the formula sums row 5, and the proper number format is applied.

17 Click cell **H4**. On the **FORMULAS tab**, in the **Formula Auditing group**, click **Trace Precedents**. Notice the tracer arrow indicates that the appropriate cells are included in the formula, as shown in Figure 4.44.

FIGURE 4.44

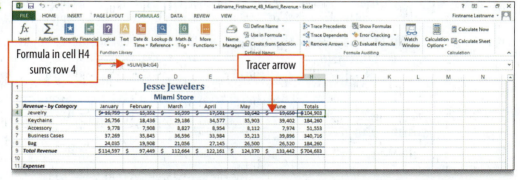

18 Click cell **H5**, click **Trace Precedents**, notice the **tracer arrow**, and then click cell **H6**. Click **Trace Precedents**, notice the tracer arrow, and verify that the correct cells are included in the formula.

19 Click cell **H7**, click **Trace Precedents**, and then click cell **H8**. Click **Trace Precedents**. Compare your screen with Figure 4.45.

Cells H7 and H8 display blue tracer arrows that are inconsistent with the other formulas in this column. However, green triangle indicators do not display in either of these cells. When auditing a worksheet, you cannot rely on the error notations and triangle indicators alone. To ensure the accuracy of a worksheet, you should use the tracer arrows to verify that all of the formulas are logical and correct.

FIGURE 4.45

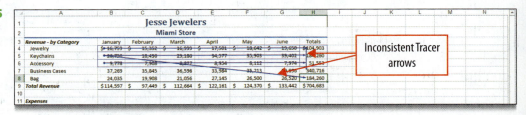

20 In the **Formula Auditing group**, click **Remove Arrows**. Click cell **H6** and then use the fill handle to copy the correct formula down to cells **H7:H8**.

21 Save 💾 your workbook.

Activity 4.14 | Tracing Dependents

Dependent cells are cells that contain formulas that refer to other cells—they depend on the values of other cells to display a result. The ***Trace Dependents command*** displays arrows that indicate what cells are affected by the value of the currently selected cell.

1 Click cell **B14**, which displays the error *#VALUE!*. To the left of the cell, point to **Error Checking** ⬧ and read the ScreenTip.

This formula contains a reference to a cell that is the wrong data type—a cell that does not contain a number.

2 In the **Formula Auditing group**, click **Trace Precedents**.

A blue tracer arrow indicates that cell B3 is included in the formula. Because cell B3 contains text—*January*—and not a number, no mathematical calculation is possible. The salaries should be calculated as 5% of *Total Revenue*, plus the constant amount of $36,000.

3 In the **Formula Auditing group**, click **Trace Dependents**. Compare your screen with Figure 4.46.

A red tracer arrow displays showing that the formula in cell B17 depends on the result of the formula in cell B14. Tracer arrows are red if a cell contains an error value, such as #VALUE!.

FIGURE 4.46

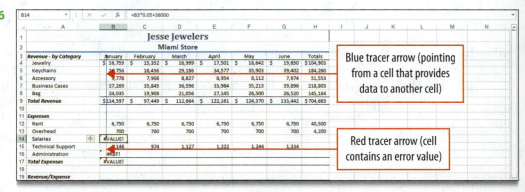

4 ▶ Click **Error Checking** ⬦ ▾ and then click **Show Calculation Steps**.

The Evaluate Formula dialog box opens and indicates the formula as =*"January"**0.05+36000. January is not a number, nor is it a range name that refers to a group of numbers; so, it cannot be used in a mathematical formula. At the bottom of the dialog box, Excel indicates that the next evaluation will result in an error.

5 ▶ At the bottom of the dialog box, click **Evaluate**.

The formula in the Evaluation box indicates *#Value!+36000*. You can use this box to evaluate each step of the formula. With complex formulas, this can be helpful in examining each piece of a formula to see where the error has occurred.

6 ▶ **Close** the **Evaluate Formula** dialog box. With cell **B14** still the active cell, click in the **Formula Bar** and edit the formula to change cell **B3** to **B9**, and then press Enter. If necessary, AutoFit column B.

The error is removed and the result—41,730—displays in cell B14.

7 ▶ Click cell **B14**. Drag the fill handle to copy the corrected formula in cell **B14** across the row to cells **C14:G14**.

8 ▶ Click cell **B9**. In the **Formula Auditing group**, click **Trace Dependents**. Compare your screen with Figure 4.47.

Each cell where an arrowhead displays indicates a dependent relationship.

FIGURE 4.47

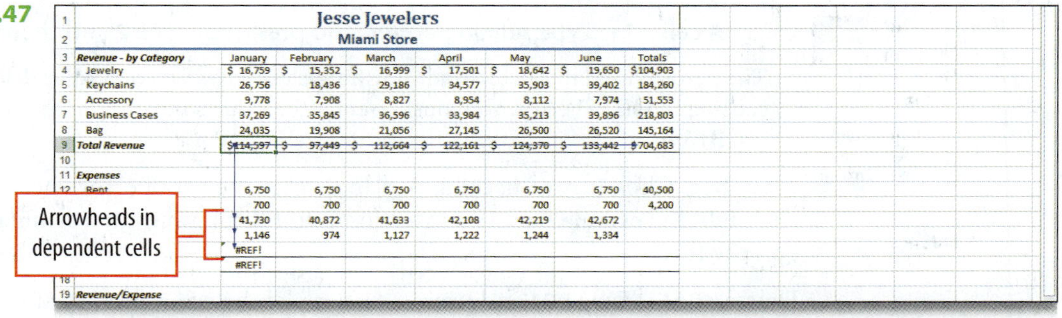

9 ▶ In the **Formula Auditing group**, click **Remove Arrows**. **Save** 🖫 your workbook.

Activity 4.15 | Tracing Formula Errors

Another tool you can use to help locate and resolve an error is the ***Trace Error command***. Use this command to trace a selected error value such as #VALUE!, #REF!, #NAME?, or #DIV/0!.

1 ▶ Click cell **B16**, point to **Error Checking** ⬦ ▾ and read the **ScreenTip**.

The error message indicates that a cell that was referenced in the formula has been moved or deleted, or the function is causing an invalid reference error. In other words, Excel does not know where to look to get the value that should be used in the formula.

2 ▶ In the **Formula Auditing group**, click the **Error Checking arrow** to display a list, and then compare your screen with Figure 4.48.

FIGURE 4.48

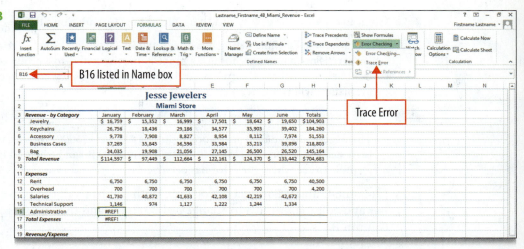

3 In the list, click **Trace Error**.

A precedent arrow is drawn from cell B9 to B16.

4 In the **Formula Auditing group**, click the **Error Checking arrow** again, and then click **Trace Error** again.

An arrow is drawn between cells B9 and B4 and the range B4:B8 is bordered in blue. The blue border indicates that this range is used in the formula in cell B9, which sums the values.

5 Click in cell **A24**. Type **Admin Percent** and press Tab, type **2** and then press Enter.

The percent used to calculate administrative expenses was moved or deleted from the worksheet causing the #REF! error. You must re-enter the value so that it can be referenced in the formula in cell B16.

6 Click **B16**. Click **Error Checking** ◆ ▾ to display the list of error checking options, and then click **Edit in Formula Bar**. The insertion point displays in the **Formula Bar** so that you can edit the formula.

7 Delete **#REF!**. Type **b24** and press F4 to make the cell reference absolute, and then press Enter.

The error notation in cell B16 is replaced with 2,292. The corrected formula needs to be copied across row 16, and it needs to use an absolute reference. That way, the 2% Admin Percent will be applied for each month.

8 Click cell **B16** and then drag the fill handle to copy the formula to the right into cells **C16:G16**.

9 **Save** 🖫 your workbook, press Ctrl + Home, and then compare your screen with Figure 4.49.

FIGURE 4.49

	A	B	C	D	E	F	G	H	I	J	K	L	M	N
1			Jesse Jewelers											
2			Miami Store											
3	Revenue - by Category	January	February	March	April	May	June	Totals						
4	Jewelry	$ 16,759	$ 15,352	$ 16,999	$ 17,501	$ 18,642	$ 19,650	$104,903						
5	Keychains	26,756	18,436	29,186	34,577	35,903	39,402	184,260						
6	Accessory	9,778	7,908	8,827	8,954	8,112	7,974	51,553						
7	Business Cases	37,269	35,845	36,596	33,984	35,213	39,896	218,803						
8	Bag	24,035	19,908	21,056	27,145	26,500	26,520	145,164						
9	Total Revenue	$114,597	$ 97,449	$ 112,664	$ 122,161	$ 124,370	$ 133,442	$704,683						
10														
11	Expenses													
12	Rent	6,750	6,750	6,750	6,750	6,750	6,750	40,500						
13	Overhead	700	700	700	700	700	700	4,200						
14	Salaries	41,730	40,872	41,633	42,108	42,219	42,672							
15	Technical Support	1,146	974	1,127	1,222	1,244	1,334							
16	Administration	2,292	1,949	2,253	2,443	2,487	2,669							
17	Total Expenses	$ 52,618												
18														
19	Revenue/Expense													
20	Percent increase		#DIV/0!											
21														
22														
23	Technical Support Percent	1%												
24	Admin Percent	2%												
25														

Activity 4.16 | Using Error Checking

The **Error Checking command** checks for common errors that occur in formulas. The behavior is similar to checking for spelling; that is, the command uses a set of rules to check for errors in formulas. The command opens the Error Checking dialog box, which provides an explanation about the error and enables you to move from one error to the next. Therefore, you can review all of the errors on a worksheet.

1 Be sure that cell **A1** is the active cell. In the **Formula Auditing group**, click the **Error Checking arrow**, and then click **Error Checking**.

The Error Checking dialog box displays, and indicates the first error—in cell C20. Here the error notation *#DIV/0!* displays. The Error Checking dialog provides an explanation of this error—a formula or function is trying to divide by zero or by an empty cell.

2 In the **Error Checking** dialog box, click **Show Calculation Steps**.

The Evaluate Formula dialog box displays, and in the Evaluation box, *0/0* displays.

3 In the **Evaluate Formula** dialog box, click **Evaluate**.

The Evaluation box displays the error *#DIV/0!* And the Evaluate button changes to Restart.

4 Click **Restart**.

The formula *(C19-B19)/C19* displays; the first reference to C19 is underlined. The underline indicates that this is the part of the formula that is being evaluated. Each time you click the Evaluate button, it moves to the next cell reference or value in the formula.

5 In the **Evaluate Formula** dialog box, click **Step In**. Compare your screen with Figure 4.50.

A second box displays, which normally displays the value in the referenced cell. In this instance, the cell that is referenced is empty, as indicated in the message in the lower part of the dialog box. In a complex formula, this dialog box can help you examine and understand each part of the formula and identify exactly where the error is located.

FIGURE 4.50

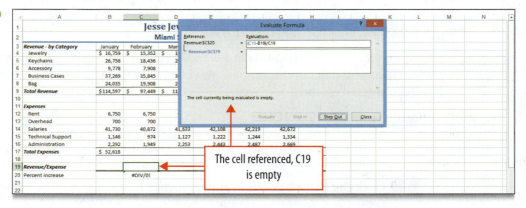

6 Click **Step Out**.

The cell evaluation box closes and the underline moves to the next cell in the formula—B19—which you can visually verify is empty by looking at the worksheet. To remove this error, you must complete the remainder of the worksheet.

7 Close the **Evaluate Formula** dialog box. In the **Error Checking** dialog box, click **Next**.

A message box displays stating that the error checking is complete for the entire sheet.

8 Click **OK**.

Both the message box and the Error Checking dialog box close.

9 Click cell **H13** and then use the fill handle to copy this formula down to cells **H14:H16**. Click cell **B17** and use the fill handle to copy this formula to the right into cells **C17:H17**. AutoFit any columns, if necessary, to display all of the data.

The formulas in the rows and columns are completed.

10 Click cell **B19** and type **=b9-b17** Press [Enter], and then copy the formula to the right into cells **C19:H19**.

The revenue/expense for each month is calculated. Notice that the *#DIV/0!* error in cell C20 is removed, but the formatting of the cell needs to be changed from dollars to percent.

11 Click cell **C20**, and on the **HOME tab**, in the **Number group**, click **Percent Style** [%]. Copy the formula to the right into cells **D20:G20**.

This formula calculates the percent change in revenue versus expenses, month to month.

12 Press [Ctrl] + [Home], **Save** [💾] your workbook. Compare your screen with Figure 4.51.

FIGURE 4.51

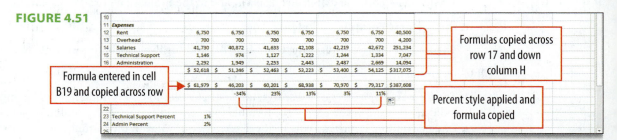

More Knowledge

One common error in Excel worksheets is a *circular reference*, in which a formula directly or indirectly refers to itself. The result is an *iterative calculation*, where Excel recalculates the formula over and over. To prevent this, Excel flags the formula as an error and does not perform the calculation. If you need to, you can enable iterative calculations and specify the maximum number of iterations Excel performs in the Excel Options dialog box.

Activity 4.17 | Circling Invalid Data

If you use validation lists in a worksheet, you can apply data validation and instruct Excel to circle invalid data. In this manner you can verify that valid values—values from the list—have been entered on the worksheet.

1 Click the **Categories sheet tab**.

This worksheet lists the merchandise types included in each category; only merchandise types from these categories are valid.

2 Click the **Name Box arrow**, and then click **Items**, which is the only range name that displays in the list box. Compare your screen with Figure 4.52.

The named range in row 2 is highlighted.

FIGURE 4.52

b

d

f

h

j

n

p

r

3 ▶ Display the **Revenue** worksheet. On the **DATA tab**, in the **Data Tools group**, click the **Data Validation arrow**, and then click **Circle Invalid Data**. Compare your screen with Figure 4.53.

Red circles display around Accessory and Bag.

FIGURE 4.53

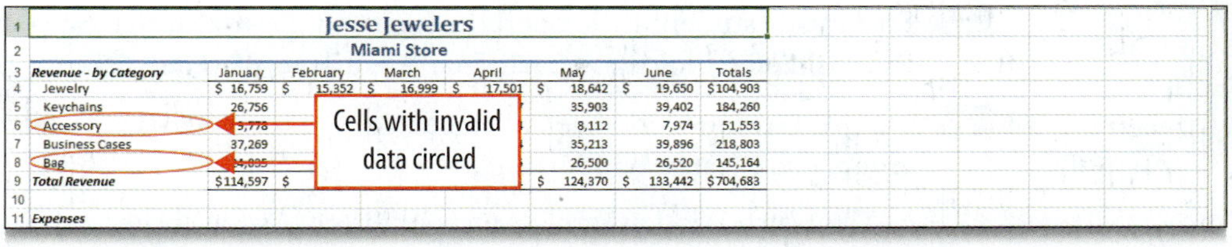

1				Jesse Jewelers					
2				Miami Store					
3	*Revenue - by Category*	January	February	March	April	May	June	Totals	
4	Jewelry	$ 16,759	$ 15,352	$ 16,999	$ 17,501	$ 18,642	$ 19,650	$104,903	
5	Keychains	26,756				35,903	39,402	184,260	
6	Accessory	5,778	Cells with invalid			8,112	7,974	51,553	
7	Business Cases	37,269	data circled			35,213	39,896	218,803	
8	Bag	14,095				26,500	26,520	145,164	
9	*Total Revenue*	$114,597	$			$ 124,370	$ 133,442	$704,683	
10									
11	Expenses								

4 ▶ Click cell **A6** and click the arrow that displays at the right side of the cell.

The validation list displays.

5 ▶ In the list, click **Accessories**.

The item is corrected but the red circle is not removed.

6 ▶ Click cell **A8**, click the arrow, and then click **Bags**.

7 ▶ In the **Data Tools group**, click the **Data Validation arrow**, and then click **Clear Validation Circles** to remove the circles.

8 ▶ In the **Data Tools group**, click the **Data Validation arrow**, and then click **Circle Invalid Data**.

No circles are applied, which confirms that the data is now valid against the validation list.

9 ▶ **Save** 🖫 your workbook.

10 ▶ Select both worksheets so that *[Group]* displays in the title bar. With the two worksheets grouped, insert a footer in the **left section** that includes the file name. **Center** the worksheets **Horizontally** on the page and set the **Orientation** to **Landscape**. On the status bar, click **Normal** ⊞. Press Ctrl + Home.

11 ▶ Click the **FILE tab** to display **Backstage** view. On the right, at the bottom of the **Properties** list, click **Show All Properties**. On the list of **Properties**, in the **Tags** box, type **Miami revenue** In the **Subject** box, type your course name and section #. Under **Related People**, be sure that your name displays as the author. If necessary, right-click the author name, click Edit Property, type your name, click outside of the Edit person dialog box, and then click OK. Display the grouped worksheets in **Print Preview**, **Close** the print preview, and then make any necessary corrections or adjustments.

12 ▶ Ungroup the worksheets, **Save** 🖫 and **Close** your workbook.

13 ▶ Hold this workbook until the end of this project, and then print or submit the two worksheets in this workbook electronically as directed by your instructor. If required, print or create an electronic version of your worksheets with formulas displayed using the instructions in Project 1A.

Objective 8   Use the Watch Window to Monitor Cell Values

Video E4-8

You can monitor cells in one part of a workbook while working on another part of the workbook using the *Watch Window*—a window that displays the results of specified cells. You can monitor cells on other worksheets and see the results as soon as formulas are calculated or changes are made that affect the outcome of the watched cells. This feature is also useful on large worksheets for which the total rows and columns are not visible on the screen with the details.

Activity 4.18 | Using the Watch Window to Monitor Changes

Mike Connor's assistant is preparing the 1st Quarter sales worksheets using the Watch Window for sales totals for the four largest retail stores.

1 From your student files, open the file **e04B_First_Quarter_Sales** and then **Save** the file in your **Excel Chapter 4** folder as **Lastname_Firstname_4B_First_Quarter_Sales**

2 On the **Toronto** worksheet, click cell **E8**. On the **FORMULAS tab**, in the **Formula Auditing group**, click **Watch Window**.

The Watch Window displays on your screen. As you create totals for the columns and rows on each worksheet in this activity, you will be able to use the Watch Window to view the results for all the worksheets at once.

3 In the upper left corner of the **Watch Window**, click **Add Watch**. Drag the window below your data, and then compare your screen with Figure 4.54.

The Add Watch dialog box displays the address for the selected cell—Toronto!$E$8

FIGURE 4.54

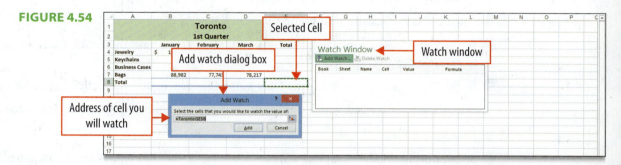

4 In the **Add Watch** dialog box, click **Add**.

Because there is no value or formula in the cell at this time, the Name, Value, and Formula columns are empty.

5 Display the **Houston** worksheet and then click cell **E8**. In the **Watch Window**, click **Add Watch**, and then in the **Add Watch** dialog box, click **Add**. Compare your screen with Figure 4.55.

A second cell is added to the Watch Window.

FIGURE 4.55

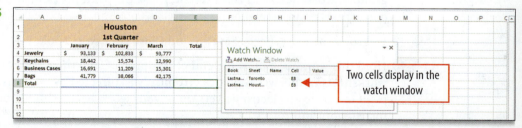

6 Following the same procedure, add cell **E8** from the **New York** sheet and from the **Miami** sheet to the **Watch Window**. Adjust the size of the **Watch Window** columns as necessary to view all four sheets. Compare your screen with Figure 4.56, and verify cell **E8** is listed for each of the four worksheets.

FIGURE 4.56

Four worksheet names

E8 from each worksheet

7 With the **Miami** worksheet active, hold down Shift, and then click the **Toronto sheet tab**.

The four store worksheets are selected and *[Group]* displays in the title bar.

8 In the **Miami** worksheet, select the range **B4:E8**.

This includes the data and the empty row and column immediately adjacent to the data. Because the sheets are grouped, this action is taking place on all four worksheets.

9 On the **FORMULAS tab**, in the **Function Library group**, click **AutoSum**. Compare your screen with Figure 4.57.

The totals for the rows and columns in this worksheet, as well as in the other three worksheets, are calculated. The results display immediately in the Watch Window, indicating that calculations took place on all four sheets simultaneously.

FIGURE 4.57

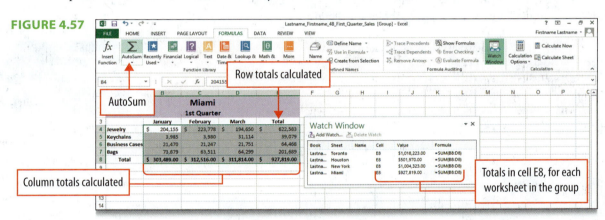

AutoSum

Row totals calculated

Column totals calculated

Totals in cell E8, for each worksheet in the group

10 Close the **Watch Window**.

11 With the four worksheets grouped, insert a footer in the **left section** that includes the file name. **Center** the sheets **Horizontally**. On the status bar, click **Normal**. Press Ctrl + Home to move to the top of the worksheet.

12 Click the **FILE tab** to display **Backstage** view. On the right, at the bottom of the **Properties** list, click **Show All Properties**. On the list of **Properties**, in the **Tags** box, type **first quarter sales** In the **Subject** box, type your course name and section #. Under **Related People**, be sure that your name displays as the author. If necessary, right-click the author name, click Edit Property, type your name, click outside of the Edit person dialog box, and then click OK. Display the grouped worksheets in **Print Preview**, and then view your worksheets. **Close** the print preview, and then make any necessary corrections or adjustments.

13 Right-click any sheet tab and click **Ungroup Sheets**. **Save** and **Close** your workbook and **Exit** Excel. Print or submit the four worksheets in this workbook electronically as directed by your instructor. If required, print your worksheets with formulas displayed using the instructions in Project 1A.

END | You have completed Project 4B

END OF CHAPTER

SUMMARY

The PMT function is used to calculate the payment for a loan. The PMT function has three required arguments: Rate (interest), Nper (number of payments), and Pv (present value), and two optional arguments.

Two of Excel's What-If Analysis tools are Goal Seek—used to find a specific value for a cell by adjusting the value of another cell; and Data Tables—which display the results of different inputs into a formula.

A defined name can represent a cell, range of cells, formula, or constant value and can be used in a formula. A Lookup function looks up data located in another part of a workbook to find a corresponding value.

Data validation is used to control the type of data or the values that are entered into a cell. Formula auditing improves the accuracy of data entry and checks a worksheet for various types of errors.

GO! LEARN IT ONLINE

Review the concepts and key terms in this chapter by completing these online challenges, which you can find at **www.pearsonhighered.com/go**.

Matching and Multiple Choice:
Answer matching and multiple choice questions to test what you learned in this chapter. MyITLab®

Crossword Puzzle:
Spell out the words that match the numbered clues, and put them in the puzzle squares.

Flipboard:
Flip through the definitions of the key terms in this chapter and match them with the correct term.

END OF CHAPTER

REVIEW AND ASSESSMENT GUIDE FOR EXCEL CHAPTER 4

Your instructor may assign one or more of these projects to help you review the chapter and assess your mastery and understanding of the chapter.

	Review and Assessment Guide for Excel Chapter 4		
Project	**Apply Skills from These Chapter Objectives**	**Project Type**	**Project Location**
4C	Objectives 1–4 from Project 4A	**4C Skills Review** A guided review of the skills from Project 4A.	On the following pages
4D	Objectives 5–8 from Project 4B	**4D Skills Review** A guided review of the skills from Project 4B.	On the following pages
4E	Objectives 1–4 from Project 4A	**4E Mastery (Grader Project)** A demonstration of your mastery of the skills in Project 4A with extensive decision making.	In MyITLab and on the following pages
4F	Objectives 5–8 from Project 4B	**4F Mastery (Grader Project)** A demonstration of your mastery of the skills in Project 4B with extensive decision making.	In MyITLab and on the following pages
4G	Combination of Objectives from Projects 4A and 4B	**4G Mastery (Grader Project)** A demonstration of your mastery of the skills in Projects 4A and 4B with extensive decision making.	In MyITLab and on the following pages
4H	Combination of Objectives from Projects 4A and 4B	**4H GO! Fix It** A demonstration of your mastery of the skills in Projects 4A and 4B by creating a correct result from a document that contains errors you must find.	Online
4I	Combination of Objectives from Projects 4A and 4B	**4I GO! Make It** A demonstration of your mastery of the skills in Projects 4A and 4B by creating a result from a supplied picture.	Online
4J	Combination of Objectives from Projects 4A and 4B	**4J GO! Solve It** A demonstration of your mastery of the skills in Projects 4A and 4B, your decision making skills, and your critical thinking skills. A task-specific rubric helps you self-assess your result.	Online
4K	Combination of Objectives from Projects 4A and 4B	**4K GO! Solve It** A demonstration of your mastery of the skills in Projects 4A and 4B, your decision making skills, and your critical thinking skills. A task-specific rubric helps you self-assess your result.	On the following pages
4L	Combination of Objectives from Projects 4A and 4B	**4L GO! Think** A demonstration of your understanding of the Chapter concepts applied in a manner that you would outside of college. An analytic rubric helps you and your instructor grade the quality of your work by comparing it to the work an expert in the discipline would create.	On the following pages
4M	Combination of Objectives from Projects 4A and 4B	**4M GO! Think** A demonstration of your understanding of the Chapter concepts applied in a manner that you would outside of college. An analytic rubric helps you and your instructor grade the quality of your work by comparing it to the work an expert in the discipline would create.	Online
4N	Combination of Objectives from Projects 4A and 4B	**4N You and GO!** A demonstration of your understanding of the Chapter concepts applied in a manner that you would in a personal situation. An analytic rubric helps you and your instructor grade the quality of your work.	Online

GLOSSARY

Arguments The values that an Excel function uses to perform calculations or operations.

Auditing The process of examining a worksheet for errors in formulas.

Circular reference An Excel error that occurs when a formula directly or indirectly refers to itself.

Data table A range of cells that shows how changing certain values in your formulas affect the results of those formulas and that makes it easy to calculate multiple versions in one operation.

Data validation A technique by which you can control the type of data or the values that are entered into a cell by limiting the acceptable values to a defined list.

Defined name A word or string of characters in Excel that represents a cell, a range of cells, a formula, or a constant value; also referred to as simply a *name*.

Dependent cells Cells that contain formulas that refer to other cells.

Error Checking command A command that checks for common errors that occur in formulas.

Error value The result of a formula that Excel cannot evaluate correctly.

Financial functions Pre-built formulas that perform common business calculations such as calculating a loan payment on a vehicle or calculating how much to save each month to buy something; financial functions commonly involve a period of time such as months or years.

Formula An equation that performs mathematical calculations on values in a worksheet.

Formula Auditing Tools and commands accessible from the FORMULAS tab that help you check your worksheet for errors.

Future value (Fv) The value at the end of the time periods in an Excel function; the cash balance you want to attain after the last payment is made—usually zero for loans.

Goal Seek One of Excel's What-If Analysis tools that provides a method to find a specific value for a cell by adjusting the value of one other cell—find the right input when you know the result you want.

HLOOKUP An Excel function that looks up values that are displayed horizontally in a row.

Interest The amount charged for the use of borrowed money.

Iterative calculation When Excel recalculates a formula over and over because of a circular reference.

LOOKUP An Excel function that looks up values in either a one-row or one-column range.

Lookup functions A group of Excel functions that look up a value in a defined range of cells located in another part of the workbook to find a corresponding value.

Name A word or string of characters in Excel that represents a cell, a range of cells, a formula, or a constant value; also referred to as *a defined name*.

Nper The abbreviation for *number of time periods* in various Excel functions.

One-variable data table A data table that changes the value in only one cell.

PMT function An Excel function that calculates the payment for a loan based on constant payments and a constant interest rate.

Precedent cells Cells that are referred to by a formula in another cell.

Present value (Pv) The total amount that a series of future payments is worth now; also known as the *principal*.

Principal The total amount that a series of future payments is worth now; also known as the *Present value (Pv)*.

Rate In the Excel PMT function, the term used to indicate the interest rate for a loan.

Scope The location within which a defined name is recognized without qualification—usually either to a specific worksheet or to the entire workbook.

Table array A defined range of cells, arranged in a column or a row, used in a VLOOKUP or HLOOKUP function.

Trace Dependents command A command that displays arrows that indicate what cells are affected by the value of the currently selected cell.

Trace Error command A tool that helps locate and resolve an error by tracing the selected error value.

Trace Precedents command A command that displays arrows to indicate what cells affect the value of the cell that is selected.

Tracer arrow An indicator that shows the relationship between the active cell and its related cell.

Two-variable data table A data table that changes the values in two cells.

Type argument An optional argument in the PMT function that assumes that the payment will be made at the end of each time period.

Validation list A list of values that are acceptable for a group of cells; only values in the list are valid and any value *not* in the list is considered invalid.

VLOOOKUP An Excel function that looks up values that are displayed vertically in a column.

Watch Window A window that displays the results of specified cells.

What-If Analysis The process of changing the values in cells to see how those changes affect the outcome of formulas in a worksheet.

CHAPTER REVIEW

Apply 4A skills from these Objectives:

1 Use Financial Functions
2 Use Goal Seek
3 Create a Data Table
4 Use Defined Names in a Formula

Skills Review | Project 4C Auto Loan

In the following Skills Review, you will create a worksheet for Patricia Murphy, U.S. Sales Director, which details loan information for purchasing seven automobiles for Jesse Jewelers sales representatives. The monthly payment for the seven automobiles cannot exceed $3,500. You will also help Ms. Murphy calculate quarterly Store Supply costs using Defined Names. Your completed two worksheets will look similar to Figure 4.58.

PROJECT FILES

For Project 4C, you will need the following files:

e04C_Auto_Loan
e04C_Store_Supplies

You will save your workbooks as:

Lastname_Firstname_4C_Auto_Loan
Lastname_Firstname_4C_Store_Supplies

PROJECT RESULTS

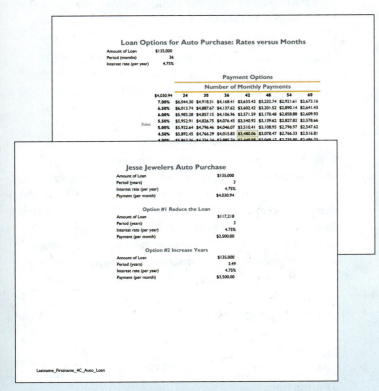

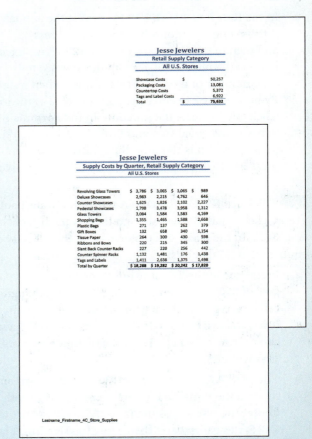

FIGURE 4.58

(Project 4C Auto Loan continues on the next page)

CHAPTER REVIEW

1 Start Excel. From your student files, open the file e04C_Auto_Loan, and then **Save** the file in your **Excel Chapter 4** folder as **Lastname_Firstname_4C_Auto_Loan**

a. In the range **A2:B5**, enter the following row titles and data.

Amount of Loan	$135,000
Period (years)	3
Interest Rate (per year)	4.75%
Payment (per month)	

b. Click cell **B5**. On the **FORMULAS tab**, in the **Function Library group**, click **Financial**, and then scroll down and click **PMT**. Drag the **Function Arguments** dialog box to the right side of your screen so you can view **columns A:B**.

c. In the **Rate** box, type **b4/12** to convert the annual interest rate to a monthly interest rate. Press Tab, and then in the **Nper** box, type **b3*12** to have Excel convert the number of years in the loan (3) to the total number of months. Press Tab, and then in the **Pv** box, type **b2** to enter the present value of the loan. Click **OK** to create the function. In the **Formula Bar**, between the equal sign and PMT, type **–** (minus sign) to insert a minus sign into the formula, and then press Enter to display the loan payment as a positive number.

2 Click cell **B5**. On the **DATA tab**, in the **Data Tools group**, click **What-If Analysis**, and then in the list, click **Goal Seek**. In the **Goal Seek** dialog box, in the **Set cell** box, confirm that B5 displays.

a. Press Tab. In the **To value** box, type the payment goal of **3500** and then press Tab. In the **By changing cell** box, type **b2** which is the amount of the loan. Click **OK** two times. For three years at 4.75%, Lauren can borrow only $117,218 if she maintains a monthly payment of $3,500.

b. Click cell **A7**. Type **Option #1 Reduce the Loan** and then on the **Formula Bar**, press **Enter**. **Merge and Center** the title across the range **A7:B7**, display the **Cell Styles** gallery, and then apply the **Heading 2** cell style.

c. Select the range **A2:B5**, right-click, and then click **Copy**. Point to cell **A8**, right-click, point to **Paste**

Special, and then under **Paste Values**, click the second button—**Values & Number Formatting (A)**. Press Esc to cancel the moving border.

d. In cell **B2**, type **135000** and then press Enter to restore the original loan amount. Click cell **B5**. On the **DATA tab**, in the **Data Tools group**, click **What-If Analysis**, and then click **Goal Seek**.

e. In the **Set cell** box, confirm that B5 displays. Press Tab. In the **To value** box, type **3500** and then press Tab. In the **By changing cell** box, type **b3** which is the number of years for the loan. Click **OK** two times.

f. Click **A13**. Type **Option #2 Increase Years** and then press Enter. Use the **Format Painter** to copy the format from cell **A7** to cell **A13**. Select the range **A2:B5**, right-click, and then click **Copy**. Point to cell **A14**, right-click, point to **Paste Special**, and then under **Paste Values**, click the second button—**Values & Number Formatting (A)**. Press Esc to cancel the moving border.

g. Point to cell **B15**, right-click to display the mini toolbar, and then click **Decrease Decimal** until the number of decimal places is two. Click cell **B3**. Type **3** and then press Enter to restore the original value. Press Ctrl + Home to move to the top of the worksheet. **Save** your workbook.

3 To determine how variable interest rates and a varying number of payments affect the payment amount, Lauren will set up a two-variable data table. Click the **New sheet** button to create a new worksheet. Double-click the **Sheet1 tab**, rename it **Payment Table** and then press Enter. In cell **A1**, type **Loan Options for Auto Purchase: Rates versus Months** and then press Enter. **Merge and Center** this title across the range **A1:I1**, and then apply the **Title** cell style.

a. In the range **A2:B4**, enter the following row titles and data.

Amount of Loan	$135,000
Period (months)	36
Interest Rate (per year)	4.75%

b. Change the width of **column A** to 20. Click cell **C8**. Type **24** and then press Tab. Type **30** and then press Tab. Select the range **C8:D8**. Drag the fill handle to

(Project 4C Auto Loan continues on the next page)

CHAPTER REVIEW

the right through cell **I8** to fill a pattern of months from 24 to 60 in increments of six months.

c. In cell **B9**, type **7.0%** and press Enter. Type **6.5%** and press Enter. Select the range **B9:B10**, and then drag the fill handle down through cell **B16** to fill a pattern of interest rates in increments of .5% from 7.00% down to 3.50%. If necessary, adjust to display two decimal places.

d. Click cell **C6**. Type **Payment Options** and then press Enter. **Merge and Center** this title across the range **C6:I6**. Apply the **Heading 1** cell style. Click cell **C7**. Type **Number of Monthly Payments** and then use the **Format Painter** to apply the format of cell **C6** to cell **C7**.

e. Click cell **A9**, type **Rates** and then press Enter. Select the range **A9:A16**. On the **HOME tab**, in the **Alignment group**, click **Merge and Center**, click **Align Right**, and then click **Middle Align**. Apply the **Explanatory Text** cell style.

f. Click cell **B8**. On the **FORMULAS tab**, in the **Function Library group**, click **Financial**, and then click **PMT**. In the **Rate** box, type **b4/12** to divide the interest rate per year by 12 to convert it to a monthly interest rate. Press Tab, and then in the **Nper** box, type **b3** and press Tab. In the **Pv** box, type **-b2** and then click **OK**.

g. Select the range **B8:I16**. On the **DATA tab**, in the **Data Tools group**, click **What-If Analysis**, and then in the list, click **Data Table**. In the **Data Table** dialog box, in the **Row input cell** box, type **b3** and then press Tab. In the **Column input cell** box, type **b4** In the **Data Table** dialog box, click **OK** to create the data table. Click in any cell outside of the table to deselect.

h. Use the **Format Painter** to copy the format from cell **B8** to the range **C9:I16**.

i. Select the range **F14:F16** and apply the **Note** cell style to highlight the desired payment option. Select the nonadjacent ranges **C8:I8** and **B9:B16**, apply **Bold** and **Center**. On the **PAGE LAYOUT tab**, set the **Orientation** for this worksheet to **Landscape**.

j. Group both worksheets. Click the **INSERT tab**, insert a footer, and then in the left section, click **File Name**. Click in a cell just above the footer to exit the **Footer area** and view your file name. From the **PAGE LAYOUT tab**, display the **Page Setup** dialog

box, and on the **Margins tab**, select the **Horizontally** check box. Click **OK**, and then on the status bar, click **Normal**. AutoFit **columns C:I**. Press Ctrl + Home to move to the top of the worksheet.

k. Click the **FILE tab** to display **Backstage** view. On the right, at the bottom of the **Properties** list, click **Show All Properties**. On the list of **Properties**, in the **Tags** box, type **amortization schedule, payment table** In the **Subject** box, type your course name and section #. Under **Related People**, be sure that your name displays as the author. If necessary, right-click the author name, click Edit Property, type your name, click outside of the Edit person dialog box, and then click OK. Return to **Normal** view and make cell **A1** active. Display each worksheet in **Print Preview**, and then make any necessary corrections or adjustments. **Close** the **Print Preview**.

l. Ungroup the worksheets, **Save** and **Close** your workbook but leave Excel open. Print or submit the two worksheets in this workbook electronically as directed by your instructor. If required, print or create an electronic version of your worksheets with formulas displayed using the instructions in Project 1A.

4 Open the file **e04C_Store_Supplies**, and then **Save** the file in your **Excel Chapter 4** folder as **Lastname_Firstname_4C_Store_Supplies**

a. Select the range **B6:E18**, which includes the empty cells in **row 18**, and then click **AutoSum**. Click anywhere to cancel the selection. Select the range **B6:E6**, hold down Ctrl and select the range **B18:E18**, and then from the **Cell Styles** gallery, under **Number Format**, apply the **Currency [0]** cell style. Select the range **B7:E17**, display the **Cell Styles** gallery, and then under **Number Format**, click **Comma [0]**. Select the range **B18:E18**, and then apply the **Total** cell style.

b. Select the range **B6:E9**. On the **FORMULAS tab**, in the **Defined Names group**, click **Define Name**. With *Revolving_Glass_Towers* selected, type **Showcase_Costs** as the name. At the bottom of the dialog box, at the right edge of the **Refers to** box, point to and click **Collapse Dialog Box**. Change the range by selecting the range **B6:E10**.

c. Click **Expand Dialog Box** to redisplay the **New Name** dialog box, and then click **OK**. Select the

(Project 4C Auto Loan continues on the next page)

CHAPTER REVIEW

range **B11:E14**. In the upper left corner of the Excel window, to the left of the **Formula Bar**, click in the **Name Box**. Type **Wrapping_Costs** and press Enter.

d. Select the range **B15:E16**. On the **FORMULAS tab**, in the **Defined Names group**, click **Name Manager**. In the upper left corner of the **Name Manager** dialog box, click **New**. With *Slant_Back_Counter_Racks* selected, type **Countertop_Costs** and then click **OK**. **Close** the **Name Manager** dialog box and **Save** your workbook.

e. On the left side of your window, in the **row heading area**, point to the **row 15** heading and right-click to select the entire row and display a shortcut menu. Click **Insert** to insert a new blank row above. Click cell **A15**, type **Ribbons and Bows** and then press Tab. In cell **B15**, type **220** and press Tab. In cell **C15**, type **215** and press Tab. In cell **D15**, type **345** and press Tab. In cell **E15**, type **300** and press Enter.

f. On the **FORMULAS tab**, from the **Defined Names group**, display the **Name Manager** dialog box. In the **Name Manager** dialog box, in the **Name** column, click **Wrapping_Costs**. At the bottom of the dialog box, click in the **Refers to** box and edit the reference, changing $E$14 to $E$15 to include the new row in the range. **Close** the **Name Manager** dialog box, and click **Yes** to save the changes you made to the name reference.

g. On the **FORMULAS tab**, from the **Defined Names group**, display the **Name Manager** dialog box. Click **Wrapping_Costs**, and then click **Edit**. In the **Edit Name** dialog box, with *Wrapping_Costs* selected, type **Packaging_Costs** Click **OK**, and then **Close** the **Name Manager** dialog box. In the upper left corner of the window, click the **Name Box arrow** and notice the modified range name, Packaging_Costs. Click any cell to close the list, and then **Save** your workbook.

h. Select the range **A18:E18**. On the **FORMULAS tab**, in the **Defined Names group**, click **Create from Selection**. In the **Create Names from Selection** dialog box, click **OK**, and then click anywhere to cancel the selection. Click the **Name Box arrow**, and then click the name **Tags_and_Labels**. Notice that in the new range name, Excel inserted the underscore necessary to fill a blank space in the range name.

5 Display the **Annual Supply Costs** worksheet.

a. In cell **B5**, type **=sum(S** Continue typing **Showcase_Costs** and then press Enter. Your result is 50257. In cell **B6**, type **=sum(P** and then on the **Formula AutoComplete list**, double-click **Packaging_Costs** to insert the formula. Press Enter to display the result 13081.

b. In cell **B7**, type **=sum(** and then on the **FORMULAS tab**, in the **Defined Names group**, click **Use in Formula**. In the list, click **Countertop_Costs** and then press Enter to display the total 5372.

c. In cell **B8**, use any of the techniques you just practiced to sum the cells containing the costs for **Tags and Labels Costs** and to display a result of 6922. Click cell **B9**, hold down Alt and press = to insert the SUM function, and then press Enter to display a total of *75632*.

d. Select the nonadjacent cells **B5** and **B9**, and then from the **HOME tab**, display the **Cell Styles** gallery. Under **Number Format**, click the **Currency [0]** cell style. To the range **B6:B8**, apply the **Comma [0]** cell style. Click cell **B9** and apply the **Total** cell style.

e. Select both worksheets so that [*Group*] displays in the title bar. With the two worksheets grouped, insert a footer in the left section that includes the file name. **Center** the worksheets **Horizontally** on the page.

f. Click the **FILE tab** to display **Backstage** view. On the right, at the bottom of the **Properties** list, click **Show All Properties**. On the list of **Properties**, in the **Tags** box, type **retail supply category, supply costs** In the **Subject** box, type your course name and section #. Under **Related People**, be sure that your name displays as the author. If necessary, right-click the author name, click Edit Property, type your name, click outside of the Edit person dialog box, and then click OK. Return to **Normal** view and make cell **A1** active, display the grouped worksheets in **Print Preview**, **Close** the **Print Preview**, and then make any necessary corrections or adjustments. Right-click any of the grouped sheet tabs, and then click **Ungroup Sheets**.

g. **Save** your workbook. Print or submit the two worksheets in both workbooks electronically as directed by your instructor. If required, print or create an electronic version of your worksheets with formulas displayed using the instructions in Project 1A. **Close** Excel.

END | You have completed Project 4C

CHAPTER REVIEW

EXCEL

4

Apply 4B skills from these Objectives:

5 Use Lookup Functions

6 Validate Data

7 Audit Worksheet Formulas

8 Use the Watch Window to Monitor Cell Values

Skills Review — Project 4D Quarterly Cost Report and Lookup Form

In the following Skills Review, you will assist Mike Connor, the Vice President of Marketing at Jesse Jewelers by adding lookup functions to a Packing Slip form so that an order taker can complete the form quickly. You will use the Formula Auditing tools to review a revenue worksheet for the Houston store and you will use the Watch Window to edit the store's utility cost worksheets. Your completed workbooks will look similar to Figure 4.59.

PROJECT FILES

For Project 4D, you will need the following files:

e04D_Houston Revenue
e04D_Packing_Slip
e04D_Utilities

You will save your workbooks as:

Lastname_Firstname_4D_Houston Revenue
Lastname_Firstname_4D_Packing_Slip
Lastname_Firstname_4D_Utilities

PROJECT RESULTS

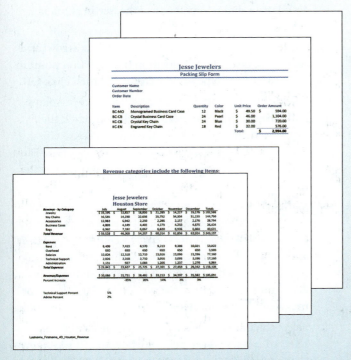

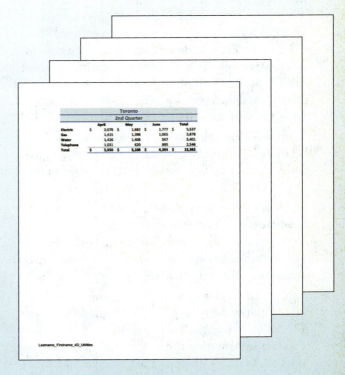

FIGURE 4.59

(Project 4D Quarterly Cost Report and Lookup Form continues on the next page)

CHAPTER REVIEW

1 From your student files, open the file **e04D_Packing_Slip**, and then **Save** the file in your **Excel Chapter 4** folder as **Lastname_Firstname_4D_Packing_Slip**

a. Display the **Product Information** worksheet. Select the range **A4:C11**. On the **DATA tab**, in the **Sort & Filter group**, click **Sort**. If necessary, drag the Sort dialog box to the right side of your screen so you can view columns A:C.

b. In the **Sort** dialog box, under **Column**, click the **Sort by arrow**. Notice that the selected range is now **A5:C11** and that the column titles in the range **A4:C4** display in the **Sort by** list. In the **Sort by** list, click **Style Code**. Under **Sort On**, verify that Values displays, and under **Order**, verify that A to Z displays. Click **OK** to sort the data by Style Code in ascending order. **Save** your workbook.

c. Display the **Packing Slip** worksheet. In cell **A9**, type **BC-MO** and press Tab. With cell **B9** as the active cell, on the **FORMULAS tab**, in the **Function Library group**, click **Lookup & Reference**, and then click **VLOOKUP**.

d. With the insertion point in the **Lookup_value** box, click cell **A9** to look up the description of Item BC-MO. Click in the **Table_array** box, and then at the bottom of the workbook, click the **Product Information sheet tab**. On the **Product Information** sheet, select the range **A4:C11**, and then press F4 . Click in the **Col_index_num** box, type **2** and then click **OK**.

e. With cell **B9** as the active cell and containing the VLOOKUP formula, point to the fill handle in the lower right corner of the cell, and then drag to fill the VLOOKUP formula down through cell **B18**.

f. Click cell **C9**, type **12** as the quantity ordered, and then press Tab. In cell **D9**, type **Black** and press Tab. With cell **E9** as the active cell, on the **FORMULAS tab**, in the **Function Library group**, click **Lookup & Reference**, and then click **VLOOKUP**.

g. With the insertion point in the **Lookup_value** box, click cell **A9** to look up information for Item BC-MO. Click in the **Table_array** box, display the **Product Information** sheet, and then select the range **A4:C11**. Press F4 to make the values in the range absolute.

h. In the **Col_index_num** box, type **3** to look up the price in the third column of the range, and then

click **OK**. The Unit Price for the Monogrammed Business Card Case displays in cell **E9**. Click cell **F9**, and notice that a formula to calculate the total for the item, Quantity times Unit Price, has already been entered in the worksheet.

i. Click cell **E9**, and then copy the VLOOKUP formula down through cell **E18**.

j. Click cell **A10**, type **BC-CB** and press Tab two times. In cell **C10**, type **24** and press Tab. Notice that Excel calculates the total for this item in cell **F10**—1,104.00. In cell **D10**, type **Pearl** and then press Enter. **Save** your workbook.

2 Display the **Product Information** sheet. Select the range **A4:A11**. On the **FORMULAS** tab, in the **Defined Names** group, click **Create from Selection**.

a. In the **Create Names from Selection** dialog box, be sure only the **Top row** check box is selected, and then click **OK**.

b. Display the **Packing Slip** worksheet, and then select the range **A9:A18**. On the **DATA tab**, in the **Data Tools group**, click **Data Validation**. In the **Data Validation** dialog box, be sure the **Settings tab** is selected.

c. Under **Validation criteria**, click the **Allow arrow**, and then click **List**. Click to position the insertion point in the **Source** box, type **=Style_Code** and then click **OK**.

d. Click cell **A11**, and notice that a list arrow displays at the right edge of the cell. In cell **A11**, click the list arrow to display the list. In the list, click **KC-CB**. Press Tab two times, type **24** and press Tab, type **Blue** and then press Enter to return to the beginning of the next row.

e. With cell **A12** active, click the **list arrow**, and then click **KC-EN**. As the **Quantity**, type **18** and as the **Color**, type **Red** and press Enter. In cell **A13**, type **B-W** and press Tab. An error message displays indicating that you entered a value that is not valid; that is, it is not on the validation list you created. In the error message, click **Cancel** and then **Save** your workbook.

f. Select the unused **rows 13:18**, right-click over the selected rows, and then click **Delete**. In cell **F13**, **Sum** the order amounts and then apply the **Total** cell style.

3 Select both worksheets so that [Group] displays in the title bar. With the two worksheets grouped, insert

(Project 4D Quarterly Cost Report and Lookup Form continues on the next page)

CHAPTER REVIEW

a footer in the left section that includes the file name. **Center** the worksheets **Horizontally** on the page.

a. Click the **FILE tab** to display **Backstage** view. On the right, at the bottom of the **Properties** list, click **Show All Properties**. On the list of **Properties**, in the **Tags** box, type **luggage, bag, order form** In the **Subject** box, type your course name and section #. Under **Related People**, be sure that your name displays as the author. If necessary, right-click the author name, click Edit Property, type your name, click outside of the Edit person dialog box, and then click OK.

b. Return to **Normal** view and make cell **A1** active, display the grouped worksheets in **Print Preview**, **Close** the **Print Preview**, and then make any necessary corrections or adjustments. Ungroup the worksheets, **Save** and **Close** your workbook.

c. Print or submit the two worksheets in this workbook electronically as directed by your instructor. If required, print or create an electronic version of your worksheets with formulas displayed using the instructions in Activity 1.16 in Project 1A.

4 From your student files, open the file **e04D_ Houston Revenue**. In your **Excel Chapter 4** folder, **Save** the file as **Lastname_Firstname_4D_Houston Revenue**

a. In the **column heading area**, select **column B**, hold down Ctrl, and then select **column H**. Point to the *right* edge of either of the selected column headings to display the pointer, and then double-click to AutoFit the columns.

b. Click cell **C9**. On the **FORMULAS tab**, in the **Formula Auditing group**, click **Trace Precedents**. To the left of the cell, click **Error Checking**, and then click **Update Formula to Include Cells**. Drag the fill handle to copy the corrected formula in cell **C9** to the range **D9:G9**.

c. Click cell **H5**, and then point to the **Error Checking** button to read the ScreenTip. On the **FORMULAS tab**, in the **Formula Auditing group**, click **Trace Precedents**. To the left of cell **H5**, click **Error Checking** to display the list of error checking options, click **Copy Formula from Above**, and then look at the **Formula Bar** to verify that the formula is summing the numbers in **row 5**. With cell **H5** still selected, from the **HOME tab**, display the **Cell Styles** gallery, and then click the **Comma [0]** number format.

d. Click cell **H6**, on the **FORMULAS tab**, click **Trace Precedents**, and then verify that the row is correctly summed. Click cell **H7**, click **Trace Precedents**. Notice that the formula is not correct. Click cell **H8**, click **Trace Precedents**; notice that the formula is not correct. In the **Formula Auditing group**, click **Remove Arrows**. Click cell **H6**, and then use the fill handle to copy the correct formula down to cells **H7:H8**.

5 Click cell **B14**, which displays the error *#VALUE!*. To the left of the cell, point to **Error Checking** and read the ScreenTip. In the **Formula Auditing group**, click **Trace Precedents**.

a. Click **Error Checking**, and then, click **Show Calculation Steps**. Notice that the formula is multiplying by a text value.

b. **Close** the **Evaluate Formula** dialog box. With cell **B14** still the active cell, click in the **Formula Bar**, and then edit the formula to change the reference to cell **B3** to **B9** and press Enter. Click cell **B14**, and then drag the fill handle to copy the corrected formula across the row to cells **C14:G14**.

6 Click cell **B16**, point to **Error Checking**, and read the ScreenTip. In the **Formula Auditing group**, click the **Error Checking arrow** to display a list. Click **Trace Error**. In the **Formula Auditing group**, click the **Error Checking arrow**, and then click **Trace Error** again to view the precedent cells. Click in cell **A24**. Type **Admin Percent** and press Tab, and then type **2** to fill in the missing data.

a. Click **B16**. Remove the arrows. Click **Error Checking** to display the list of error checking options, and then click **Edit in Formula Bar**. Delete *#REF!*. Type **b24** and press F4 to make the cell reference absolute. Press Enter. Click cell **B16**, and then use the fill handle to copy the formula to the right into cells **C16:G16**.

7 Click cell **A1**. In the Formula Auditing group, click the **Error Checking arrow**, and then click **Error Checking**—cell **C20** is selected. In the **Error Checking** dialog box, click **Show Calculation Steps**; notice that the divisor is an empty cell. In the **Evaluate Formula** dialog box, click **Evaluate**. Click **Restart**.

a. In the **Evaluate Formula** dialog box, click **Step In** to examine the formula. Click **Step Out**. Close the **Evaluate Formula** dialog box.

(Project 4D Quarterly Cost Report and Lookup Form continues on the next page)

CHAPTER REVIEW

b. In the **Error Checking** dialog box, click **Next**. Click **OK**. Click cell **H13**, and then use the fill handle to copy this formula down to cells **H14:H16**. Click cell **B17** and drag the fill handle to copy this formula to the right into cells **C17:H17**.

c. Click cell **B19** and type **=b9-b17** Press Enter, and then copy the formula to the right into cells **C19:H19**. Click cell **C20**, and then on the **HOME tab**, in the **Number group**, click **Percent Style**. Copy the formula to the right into cells **D20:G20**.

8 Display the **Categories** worksheet. To the left of the **Formula Bar**, click the **Name Box** arrow, and then click **Items**—the only range name in the worksheet. Examine the selected range.

a. Redisplay the **Revenue** worksheet. On the **DATA tab**, in the **Data Tools group**, click the **Data Validation arrow**, and then click **Circle Invalid Data**.

b. Click cell **A8**, and then click the arrow at the right side of the cell. From the list, click **Bags**. In the **Data Tools group**, click the **Data Validation arrow**, and then click **Clear Validation Circles**.

c. Select both worksheets so that *[Group]* displays in the title bar. With the two worksheets grouped, insert a footer in the **left section** that includes the file name. **Center** the worksheets **Horizontally**. Set the **Orientation** to **Landscape**. On the status bar, click **Normal**. Press Ctrl + Home.

d. Click the **FILE tab** to display **Backstage** view. On the right, at the bottom of the **Properties** list, click **Show All Properties**. On the list of **Properties**, in the **Tags** box, type **Houston revenue** In the **Subject** box, type your course name and section #. Under **Related People**, be sure that your name displays as the author. If necessary, right-click the author name, click Edit Property, type your name, click outside of the Edit person dialog box, and then click OK.

e. Display the grouped worksheets in **Print Preview**, close the print preview, and then make any necessary corrections or adjustments. Ungroup the worksheets, **Save** and **Close** your workbook. Print or submit the two worksheets in this workbook electronically as directed by your instructor. If required, print or create an electronic version of your worksheets with formulas displayed using the instructions in Project 1A.

9 From your student files, open the file **e04D_Utilities**, and then **Save** the file in your **Excel Chapter 4** folder as **Lastname_Firstname_4D_Utilities** Display the **Toronto** worksheet, and then click cell **E8**. On the **FORMULAS tab**, in the **Formula Auditing group**, click **Watch Window**. In the upper left corner of the **Watch Window**, click **Add Watch**. In the **Add Watch** dialog box, click **Add**.

a. Display the **Houston** worksheet, and using the same technique, add cell **E8** from the **Houston** worksheet. Repeat this for the **New York** worksheet and for the **Miami** worksheet. Adjust the size of the **Watch Window** and columns as necessary to view all four sheets, and verify that cell **E8** is listed for each of the four worksheets.

b. With the **Miami** worksheet active, hold down Shift and click the **Toronto sheet tab** to select all four worksheets. In the **Miami** worksheet, select the range **B4:E8**. On the **FORMULAS tab**, in the **Function Library group**, click **AutoSum**. **Close** the **Watch Window**. Select the range **E5:E7**, and then apply **Comma Style** with zero decimal places.

c. With the four worksheets grouped, insert a footer in the **left section** that includes the file name. **Center** the sheets **Horizontally**. On the status bar, click **Normal**. Press Ctrl + Home to move to the top of the worksheet.

d. Click the **FILE tab** to display **Backstage** view. On the right, at the bottom of the **Properties** list, click **Show All Properties**. On the list of **Properties**, in the **Tags** box, type **Utilities** In the **Subject** box, type your course name and section #. Under **Related People**, be sure that your name displays as the author. If necessary, right-click the author name, click Edit Property, type your name, click outside of the Edit person dialog box, and then click OK.

e. Display the grouped worksheets in **Print Preview**. Redisplay the worksheets. Make any necessary corrections or adjustments. Right-click any of the grouped sheet tabs, and then click **Ungroup Sheets**. **Save** your workbook. Print or submit the four worksheets in this workbook electronically as directed by your instructor. If required, print or create an electronic version of your worksheets with formulas displayed using the instructions in Project 1A. **Close** Excel.

END | You have completed Project 4D

CONTENT-BASED ASSESSMENTS

Mastering Excel | Project 4E Condo Loan and Quarterly Cost Report

Apply 4A skills from these Objectives:

1 Use Financial Functions
2 Use Goal Seek
3 Create a Data Table
4 Use Defined Names in a Formula

In the following Mastering Excel project, you will create a worksheet for Jacques Celestine, President of Jesse Jewelers, which analyzes loan options for a condo in Toronto that the company is considering purchasing. Jacques wants to provide a lodging facility for company visitors, but would like to keep the monthly loan payment below $6,250. You will also define names for ranges of cells in a workbook containing quarterly Advertising costs. The worksheets of your workbooks will look similar to Figure 4.60.

PROJECT FILES

For Project 4E, you will need the following files:

e04E_Advertising_Costs
e04E_Condo_Loan

You will save your workbooks as:

Lastname_Firstname_4E_Advertising_Costs
Lastname_Firstname_4E_Condo_Loan

PROJECT RESULTS

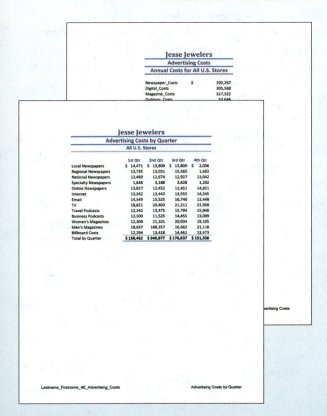

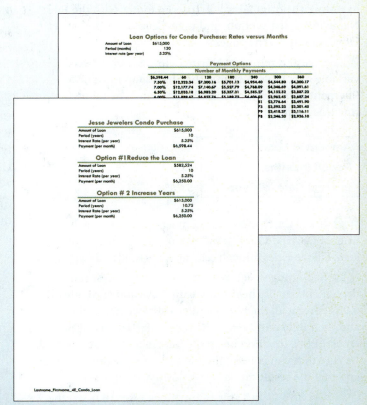

FIGURE 4.60

(Project 4E Condo Loan and Quarterly Cost Report continues on the next page)

CONTENT-BASED ASSESSMENTS

1 Start Excel. From your student files, locate and **open** **e04E_Condo_Loan**. **Save** the file in your **Excel Chapter 4** folder as **Lastname_Firstname_4E_Condo_Loan** In cell **B5**, insert the **PMT** function using the data from the range **B2:B5**—be sure to divide the interest rate by 12, multiply the years by 12, and display the payment as a positive number. The result, $6,598.44, is larger than the payment of $6,250.

2 Use **Goal Seek** to change the amount of the loan so that the payment is under $6,250. Then, in **A7**, type **Option #1 Reduce the Loan** and then **Copy** the format from cell **A1** to cell **A7**. **Copy** the range **A2:B5**, and then **Paste** the **Values & Number Formatting (A)** to cell **A8**. In cell **B2**, type **615000** to restore the original loan amount.

3 Use **Goal Seek** to change the period of the loan so that the payment does not exceed $6,250. In **A13**, type **Option #2 Increase Years** Format the cell the same as cell **A7**. **Copy** the range **A2:B5**, and then **Paste** the **Values & Number Formatting (A)** to cell **A14**. Display the value in **B15** with two decimal places, and then in cell **B3**, type **10** to restore the original value. Insert a footer with the **File Name** in the left section, and then **Center** the worksheet **Horizontally** on the page.

4 **Save** and return to **Normal** view. Set up a two-variable data table. Rename the **Sheet2 tab** to **Condo Payment Table** In the range **A2:B4**, enter the following row titles and data.

Amount of Loan	$615,000
Period (months)	120
Interest Rate (per year)	5.25%

5 In cell **C8**, type **60**—the number of months in a five-year loan. In **D8**, type **120**—the number of months in a 10-year loan. Fill the series through cell **H8**; apply **Bold** and **Center**.

6 Beginning in cell **B9**, enter varying interest rates in decrements of .5% beginning with **7.5%** and ending with **4.0%** Format all the interest rates with two decimal places, and then **Bold** and **Center** the range **B8:B16**. In cell **B8**, enter a **PMT** function using the information in cells **B2:B4**. Be sure that you convert the interest rate to a monthly rate and that the result displays as a positive number.

7 Create a **Data Table** in the range **B8:H16** using the information in cells **B2:B4** in which the **Row input cell**

is the **Period** and the **Column input cell** is the **Interest rate**. **Copy** the format from **B8** to the results in the data table. Format cell **D16** with the **Note** cell style as payment option that is close to but less than $6,250 per month. Change the **Orientation** to **Landscape**. Insert a footer with the **File Name** in the left section, and **Center** the worksheet **Horizontally** on the page. Return to **Normal** view and move to cell **A1**.

8 Click the **FILE tab** to display **Backstage** view. On the right, at the bottom of the **Properties** list, click **Show All Properties**. On the list of **Properties**, in the **Tags** box, type **condo, payment table** In the **Subject** box, type your course name and section #. Under **Related People**, be sure that your name displays as the author. If necessary, right-click the author name, click Edit Property, type your name, click outside of the Edit person dialog box, and then click OK.

Print Preview, make any necessary corrections or adjustments, ungroup the worksheets, and **Save** and **Close** your workbook. Print or submit electronically as directed.

9 From your student files, open **e04E_Advertising_Costs**. **Save** it in your **Excel Chapter 4** folder as **Lastname_Firstname_4E_Advertising_Costs** Display the **Advertising Costs by Quarter** worksheet, and then apply appropriate **Currency [0]**, **Comma [0]**, and **Total** cell styles.

10 Name the following ranges: **B6:E10 Newspaper_Costs**; **B10:E14 Digital_Costs**; **B15:E16 Magazine_Costs**; **B17:E17 Billboard_Costs** Insert a new **row 15**. In cell **A15**, type **Business Podcasts** In cell **B15**, type **12500** In cell **C15**, type **11525** In cell **D15**, type **14455** In cell **E15**, type **13009**.

11 Display **Name Manager**, click **Digital_Costs**, and then change cell **E14** to **E15**. Select the **Billboard_Costs**, and **Edit** the name to **Outdoor_Costs**. Display the **Annual Advertising Costs** sheet. In cell **B5**, type **=sum(N** and sum Newspaper costs using its defined name in the formula. Do this for the other named ranges. Sum all the costs. Apply **Currency [0]**, **Comma [0]**, and **Total** cell styles to the appropriate cells. Group the worksheets, insert a footer that includes the file name. **Center** the worksheets **Horizontally** on the page. Document properties should include the tags **advertising costs** Ungroup the worksheets, **Save** your file and then print or submit your worksheet electronically as directed by your instructor. **Close** Excel.

END | You have completed Project 4E

CONTENT-BASED ASSESSMENTS

MyITLab® grader

Mastering Excel Project 4F Lookup Form and Sales Revenue

Apply 4B skills from these Objectives:

5 Use Lookup Functions

6 Validate Data

7 Audit Worksheet Formulas

8 Use the Watch Window to Monitor

In the following Mastering Excel project, you will assist Mike Connor, the Vice President of Marketing at Jesse Jewelers, by adding lookup functions to an Advertising Order form so that an order taker can complete the form quickly. You will also use the Formula Auditing features and visual inspection to find and correct several types of errors. Your completed workbooks will look similar to Figure 4.61.

PROJECT FILES

For Project 4F, you will need the following files:

e04F_Advertising_Form
e04F_New_York_Revenue

You will save your workbooks as:

Lastname_Firstname_4F_Advertising_Form
Lastname_Firstname_4F_New_York_Revenue

PROJECT RESULTS

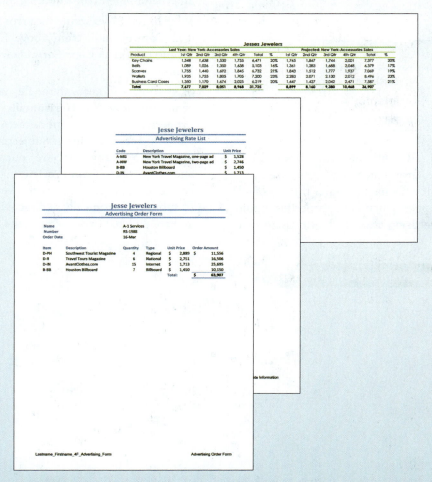

FIGURE 4.61

(Project 4F Lookup Form and Sales Revenue continues on the next page)

CONTENT-BASED ASSESSMENTS

1 Open **e04F_Advertising_Form**. **Save** the file in your **Excel Chapter 4** folder as **Lastname_Firstname_4F_Advertising_Form** Display the **Advertising Rate Information** sheet, select the range **A4:C11**, and **Sort** by **Code**. Name the range **A4:A11** using **Create from Selection**. Display the **Advertising Order Form** sheet; in the range **A9:A18** create a **data validation list** using the **defined name** *Code*.

2 Click cell **A9**, click the **list arrow**, click **D-PH**. With cell **B9** as the active cell, insert a **VLOOKUP** function that will look up the **Description** from the **Advertising Rate Information** sheet using the **Item** number.

3 With cell **B9** as the active cell, fill the VLOOKUP formula through cell **B18**. In cell **C9**, type **4** and in cell **D9**, type **Regional** With cell **E9** as the active cell, insert a **VLOOKUP** function to look up Unit Price. **Copy** the VLOOKUP formula through cell **E18**. Add the following orders:

Item	Quantity	Type
D-R	6	National
D-IN	15	Internet
B-BB	7	Billboard

4 Delete unused rows, sum the **Order Amount**, and apply **Total** cell style. Group the worksheets, insert a footer that includes the file name. **Center** the worksheets **Horizontally** on the page. Document properties should include the tags **advertising costs** and **form** Ungroup the worksheets, **Save** and **Close** your workbook but leave Excel open.

5 Open the file **e04F_New_York_Revenue**, and then **Save** the file in your **Excel Chapter 4** folder as **Lastname_Firstname_4F_New_York_Revenue**

6 Click cell **I5**, which displays a green triangle indicating a potential error, and then on the **FORMULAS tab**, click **Trace Precedents**. Click **Error Checking**, and then click **Edit in Formula Bar**. Change *$B$14* to *$B$15* so that the formula is using the Growth Assumption for *Belts*, not for Key Chains.

7 On the **FORMULAS tab**, in the **Formula Auditing group**, click **Error Checking** to begin checking for errors from this point in the worksheet. In cell **M6**, the flagged error, notice the formula is trying to divide by cell **L10**, which is empty. Click **Edit in Formula Bar**, change **10** to **9** and then in the **Error Checking** dialog box, click **Resume**.

8 In cell **F7**, examine the error information, and then click **Copy Formula from Above**. Examine the error in cell **J8**, and then click **Copy Formula from Left**. Use **Format Painter** to copy the format in cell **M5** to cell **M6**.

9 Insert a footer with the file name in the **left section**, center the worksheet **Horizontally**. Display the **Document Properties**, add your name as the **Author**, type your course name and section # in the **Subject** box, and as the **Tags**, type **New York revenue** Save your workbook. Display and examine the **Print Preview**, make any necessary corrections, ungroup the worksheets, **Save**, and then print or submit electronically as directed by your instructor. If you are directed to do so, print the formulas. **Close** Excel.

END | You have completed Project 4F

CONTENT-BASED ASSESSMENTS

Mastering Excel | Project 4G Warehouse Loan and Staff Lookup Form

Apply 4A and 4B skills from these Objectives:

1 Use Financial Functions
2 Use Goal Seek
3 Create a Data Table
4 Use Defined Names in a Formula
5 Use Lookup Functions
6 Validate Data
7 Audit Worksheet Formulas
8 Use the Watch Window to Monitor Cell Values

In the following Mastering Excel project, you will create a worksheet for Jacques Celestine, President of Jesse Jewelers, which analyzes loan options for a warehouse that the company is considering purchasing. Jacques wants to establish an additional storage facility in the United States, but would like to keep the monthly loan payment below $10,000. You will also assist Mike Connor, the Vice President of Marketing at Jesse Jewelers by adding lookup functions to a Staff Planning Form so that a manager can complete the form quickly. You will also use Formula Auditing to check a workbook for errors. Your completed workbooks will look similar to Figure 4.62.

PROJECT FILES

For Project 4G, you will need the following files:

e04G_Online_Bracelet_Revenue
e04G_Staff_Form
e04G_Warehouse_Loan

You will save your workbooks as:

Lastname_Firstname_4G_Online_Bracelet_Revenue
Lastname_Firstname_4G_Staff_Form
Lastname_Firstname_4G_Warehouse_Loan

PROJECT RESULTS

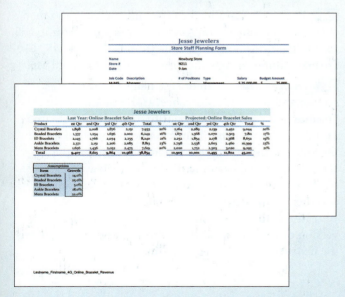

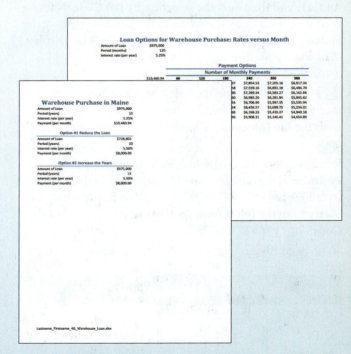

FIGURE 4.62

(Project 4G Warehouse Loan and Staff Lookup Form continues on the next page)

CONTENT-BASED ASSESSMENTS

1 In your student files, locate and **open** the file **e04G_Warehouse_Loan**, and **Save** it in your **Excel Chapter 4** folder as **Lastname_Firstname_4G_Warehouse_Loan** Display the **Warehouse Payment Table** sheet. In cell **B9**, enter rates in decrements of .5% beginning with **7.5%** and ending with **4%** in cell **B16**. Format rates with two decimal places.

2 In cell **B8**, enter a **PMT** function using the information in cells **B2:B4**. Create a **Data Table** in the range **B8:H16** using the information in cells **B2:B4** in which the **Row input cell** is the **Period** and the **Column input cell** is the **Interest rate**. Apply the format from **B8** to the results in the data table. Select the payment option closest to $10,000 per month and format the option with the **Note** cell style.

3 Insert a footer that includes the file name, and document properties that include your firstname and lastname as the **Author**, your course name and section # as the **Subject**, and the tags **warehouse loan** Change the **Orientation** to **Landscape**, **center Horizontally**, and return to **Normal** view. **Print Preview**, **Save**, and then print or submit electronically as directed. **Close** this workbook.

4 Open the file **e04G_Staff_Form**, and **Save** it in your **Excel Chapter 4** folder as **Lastname_Firstname_4G_Staff_Form** On the **Job Information** sheet, select the range **A4:C11**, and then **Sort** the selection by **Job Code**. Name the range **A4:A11** by the name in the top row. Display the **Staffing Plan** sheet, and select the range **A9:A18**. Display the **Data Validation** dialog box, and validate from a **List** using the **Source =Job_Code**

5 Click cell **A9**, and then click **M-MG**. Click cell **B9**, and insert a **VLOOKUP** function that looks up the **Description** from the **Job Information** worksheet using the **Job Code**.

6 With cell **B9** as the active cell, fill the VLOOKUP formula through cell **B18**. In cell **C9**, type **1** as the **# of Positions** and in cell **D9**, type **Management** as the **Type**. In cell **E9**, insert the **VLOOKUP** function that looks up the **Salary** from the **Job Information** worksheet using the **Job Code** Copy the VLOOKUP formula down into cell **E18**.

7 Beginning in cell **A10**, add these staff positions:

8 Delete any unused rows between the last item and the Total row. Sum the **Budget Amount** column and apply the **Total** cell style. Group the worksheets, insert a footer in the left section with the file name, **center** the worksheets **Horizontally**, and change the **Orientation** to **Landscape**. Update the document properties with your name and course name and section #, and add the **Tags planning, staff Print Preview**, ungroup the worksheets, **Save**, and then submit it as directed. **Close** this workbook.

9 From your student files, open **e04G_Online_Bracelet_Revenue**, and then **Save** the file in your **Excel Chapter 4** folder as **Lastname_Firstname_4G_Online_Bracelet_Revenue**

10 Click cell **I5**, and then on the **FORMULAS tab**, click **Trace Precedents**. Click **Error Checking**, and then click **Edit in Formula Bar**. Change *$B$14* to **$B$15** so that the formula is using the Growth Assumption for *Beaded Bracelets*, not for *Crystal Bracelets*.

11 On the **FORMULAS tab**, in the **Formula Auditing group**, click **Error Checking**. In cell **M6**, notice the formula is trying to divide by cell **L10**, which is empty. Click **Edit in Formula Bar**, change **10** to **9** and then in the **Error Checking** dialog box, click **Resume**.

12 In cell **F7**, examine the error information, and then click **Copy Formula from Above**. Examine the error in cell **J8**, and then click **Copy Formula from Left**. Click **OK**. Use **Format Painter** to copy the format in cell **M5** to cell **M6**.

13 Insert a footer with the file name in the **left section** and **center** the worksheet **Horizontally**. To the **Document Properties**, add your firstname and lastname as the **Author**, add your course name and section # as the **Subject**, and add **online bracelet revenue** as the **Tags**. Display and examine the **Print Preview**, make any necessary corrections, ungroup the worksheets, **Save**, and then print or submit electronically as directed by your instructor. If required, print or create an electronic version of your worksheets with formulas displayed using the instructions in Project 1A. **Close** Excel.

Item	# of Positions	Type
C-CASH	3	Cashier
C-CSA	1	Customer Service
M-AMG	3	Management

END | You have completed Project 4G

CONTENT-BASED ASSESSMENTS

Apply a combination of the 4A and 4B skills.

| GO! Fix It | Project 4H Bag Costs by Quarter | Online |

| GO! Make It | Project 4I Arizona Store Loan | Online |

| GO! Solve It | Project 4J Store Furnishings | Online |

| GO! Solve It | Project 4K Order Form |

PROJECT FILES

For Project 4K, you will need the following file:

e04K_Order_Form

You will save your workbook as:

Lastname_Firstname_4K_Order_Form

Open the file **e04K_Order_Form** and save it as **Lastname_Firstname_4K_Order_Form** Prepare the Product Information worksheet for a VLOOKUP function by sorting the items by Style Code, and then create a named range for the Style Code information. On the Order Form worksheet, using the named range, set data validation for the Item column. Insert the VLOOKUP function in column B and column E, referencing the appropriate data in the Product Information worksheet. Then enter the data below.

Item	Description	Quantity	Color
C-S		12	White
C-T		15	Natural
M-MC		25	Assorted
M-CF		50	Green

Delete the unused row. Construct formulas to total the order, and then apply appropriate financial formatting. On both sheets, include your file name in the footer, add appropriate properties, and then submit them as directed.

CONTENT-BASED ASSESSMENTS

GO! Solve It | Project 4K Order Form (continued)

Performance Level

		Exemplary	Proficient	Developing
Performance Criteria	**Use Lookup Functions**	The VLOOKUP function correctly looks up data on the Validation List.	The VLOOKUP function looks up some but not all data on the Validation List.	The VLOOKUP function does not look up any of the correct information.
	Validate Data	The Validation List is sorted correctly and used on the order form.	The Validation List was sorted, but not used on the order form.	The Validation List is not sorted and not used on the order form.
	Calculate and Format the Order Amount	The Order Amount and financial information is properly calculated and formatted.	Some, but not all, of the Order Amount and financial information is properly calculated and formatted.	Incorrect formulas and/or incorrect financial formatting were applied in most of the cells.

END | You have completed Project 4K

OUTCOMES-BASED ASSESSMENTS

RUBRIC

The following outcomes-based assessments are open-ended assessments. That is, there is no specific correct result; your result will depend on your approach to the information provided. Make Professional Quality your goal. Use the following scoring rubric to guide you in how to approach the problem and then to evaluate how well your approach solves the problem.

The criteria—Software Mastery, Content, Format and Layout, and Process—represent the knowledge and skills you have gained that you can apply to solving the problem. The levels of performance—Professional Quality, Approaching Professional Quality, or Needs Quality Improvements—help you and your instructor evaluate your result.

	Your completed project is of Professional Quality if you:	Your completed project is Approaching Professional Quality if you:	Your completed project Needs Quality Improvements if you:
1-Software Mastery	Choose and apply the most appropriate skills, tools, and features and identify efficient methods to solve the problem.	Choose and apply some appropriate skills, tools, and features, but not in the most efficient manner.	Choose inappropriate skills, tools, or features, or are inefficient in solving the problem.
2-Content	Construct a solution that is clear and well organized, contains content that is accurate, appropriate to the audience and purpose, and is complete. Provide a solution that contains no errors in spelling, grammar, or style.	Construct a solution in which some components are unclear, poorly organized, inconsistent, or incomplete. Misjudge the needs of the audience. Have some errors in spelling, grammar, or style, but the errors do not detract from comprehension.	Construct a solution that is unclear, incomplete, or poorly organized; contains some inaccurate or inappropriate content; and contains many errors in spelling, grammar, or style. Do not solve the problem.
3-Format & Layout	Format and arrange all elements to communicate information and ideas, clarify function, illustrate relationships, and indicate relative importance.	Apply appropriate format and layout features to some elements, but not others. Overuse features, causing minor distraction.	Apply format and layout that does not communicate information or ideas clearly. Do not use format and layout features to clarify function, illustrate relationships, or indicate relative importance. Use available features excessively, causing distraction.
4-Process	Use an organized approach that integrates planning, development, self-assessment, revision, and reflection.	Demonstrate an organized approach in some areas, but not others; or, use an insufficient process of organization throughout.	Do not use an organized approach to solve the problem.

OUTCOMES-BASED ASSESSMENTS

Apply a combination of the **4A** and **4B** skills.

GO! Think Project 4L Key Chains

PROJECT FILES

For Project 4L, you will need the following file:

e04L_Key_Chains

You will save your workbook as:

Lastname_Firstname_4L_Key_Chains

From your student files, open the file **e04L_Key_Chains**, and then save it in your chapter folder as **Lastname_Firstname_4L_Key_Chains** So that order takers do not have to type the Style Code, Description, and Unit Price in the Order Form worksheet, use the information on the Product Information sheet to create a validation list for the Item and then insert a VLOOKUP function in the Description and Unit Price columns. Then create an order for two of the Plush Animal Key Chains (K-S) and two of the Classic Key Chains (M-TF). Delete unused rows, create appropriate totals, apply financial formatting, and then save and submit it as directed.

Build from
Scratch

END | You have completed Project 4L

Build from
Scratch

GO! Think Project 4M Delivery Van Purchase **Online**

Build from
Scratch

You and GO! Project 4N Vehicle Loan **Online**

Managing Large Workbooks and Using Advanced Sorting and Filtering

GO! to Work
Video E5

PROJECT 5A	**OUTCOMES**	Manage large workbooks, create attractive workbooks, and save workbooks to share with others.

OBJECTIVES

1. Navigate and Manage Large Worksheets
2. Enhance Worksheets with Themes and Styles
3. Format a Worksheet to Share with Others
4. Save Excel Data in Other File Formats

PROJECT 5B	**OUTCOMES**	Analyze information in a database format using advanced sort, filter, subtotaling, and outlining.

OBJECTIVES

5. Use Advanced Sort Techniques
6. Use Custom and Advanced Filters
7. Subtotal, Outline, and Group a List of Data

Stephen Coburn/Fotolia

In This Chapter

In this chapter, you will navigate within a large worksheet, insert a hyperlink in a worksheet, and save a worksheet as a webpage or other file formats that you can share with others. You will practice applying and modifying themes, styles, lines, and borders to enhance the format of your worksheets. You will use Excel's advanced table features and database capabilities to organize data in a useful manner. You will use advanced sorting, sorting on multiple columns, and custom filtering to compare subsets of data. You will also limit data to display records that meet one or more specific conditions, add subtotals, and outline data.

The projects in this chapter relate to **Laurel College**. The college offers this diverse geographic area in Pennsylvania a wide range of academic and career programs, including associate degrees, certificate programs, and noncredit continuing education courses. Over 2,100 faculty and staff make student success a top priority. The college makes positive contributions to the community through cultural and athletic programs and partnerships with businesses and nonprofit organizations. The college also provides industry-specific training programs for local businesses through its Economic Development Center.

Large Worksheet for a Class Schedule

PROJECT ACTIVITIES

In Activities 5.01 through 5.13, you will assist Michael Schaeffler, Vice President, Instruction, in formatting and navigating a large worksheet that lists the class schedule for the Business Office Systems and Computer Information Systems departments at Laurel College. You will also save Excel data in other file formats. The worksheets in your completed workbooks will look similar to Figure 5.1.

PROJECT FILES

For Project 5A, you will need the following files:

e05A_Class_Schedule
e05A_Faculty_Contacts
e05A_Fall_Classes
e05A_Teaching_Requests

You will save your workbooks as:

Lastname_Firstname_5A_Class_Schedule
Lastname_Firstname_5A_Faculty_Contacts
Lastname_Firstname_5A_Fall_PDF
Lastname_Firstname_5A_Fall_XPS
Lastname_Firstname_5A_Schedule_CVS
Lastname_Firstname_5A_Schedule_Webpage

PROJECT RESULTS

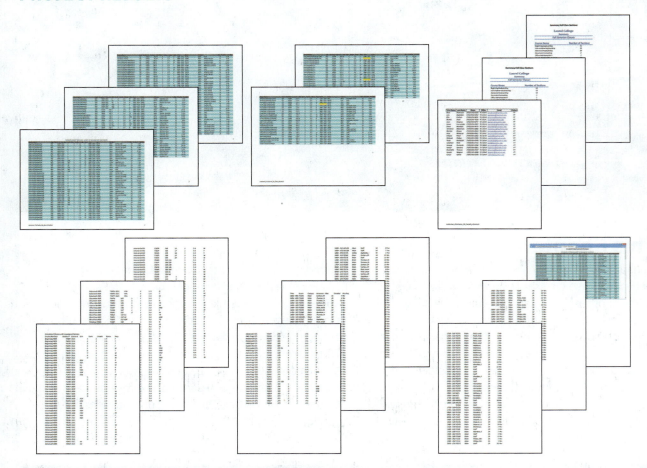

FIGURE 5.1 Project 5A Large Worksheet for a Class Schedule

Objective 1   Navigate and Manage Large Worksheets

Video E5-1

Because you cannot view all the columns and rows of a large worksheet on your screen at one time, Excel provides features that help you control the screen display and navigate the worksheet so you can locate information quickly. For example, you can hide columns or use the *Freeze Panes* command, which sets the column and row titles so that they remain on the screen while you scroll. The locked rows and columns become separate *panes*—portions of a worksheet window bounded by and separated from other portions by vertical or horizontal lines.

You can also use the *Find* command to find and select specific text, formatting, or a type of information within the workbook quickly.

Activity 5.01   Using the Go To Special Command

Use the *Go To Special* command to move to cells that have special characteristics, for example, to cells that are blank or to cells that contain constants, as opposed to formulas.

1 Start Excel. From your student files, open **e05A_Class_Schedule**. In your storage location, create a new folder named **Excel Chapter 5** and then press F12 and **Save** the file as **Lastname_Firstname_5A_Class_Schedule**

This worksheet lists the computer courses that are available for the upcoming semester in three college departments.

2 On the **HOME tab,** in the **Editing group**, click **Find & Select**, and then click **Go To Special**. Compare your screen with Figure 5.2.

In the Go To Special dialog box, you can click an option button to move to cells that contain the special options listed.

FIGURE 5.2

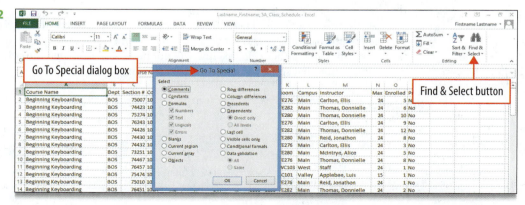

3 In the first column, click **Blanks**, and then click **OK**.

All blank cells in the active area of the worksheet are located and selected, and the first blank cell—J124—is active. The active area is the area of the worksheet that contains data or has contained data—it does not include any empty cells that have not been used in this worksheet. Cell J124 is missing the time for a Linux/UNIX class held on Tuesday.

4 Point to cell **J124** and right-click. On the mini toolbar, click the **Fill Color arrow** and then under **Standard Colors**, click the fourth color—**Yellow**—to highlight the blank cells.

This missing information must be researched before a time can be entered, and the yellow fill color will help locate this cell later, when the correct time for the class is determined.

5 Scroll down and locate the other two cells identified as blank—**J148** and **J160**— **Save** your workbook and compare your screen with Figure 5.3.

When you initiated the Go To Special command for Blank cells, Excel located and selected *all* blank cells in the active area. As a result, the formatting you applied to the first blank cell, yellow fill, was applied to all the selected cells.

FIGURE 5.3

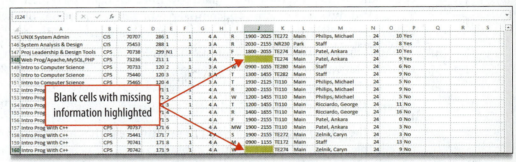

Blank cells with missing information highlighted

Activity 5.02 | Hiding Columns

In a large worksheet, you can hide columns that are not necessary for the immediate task, and then unhide them later. You can also hide columns or rows to control the data that will print or to remove confidential information from view—hidden data does not print. For example, to create a summary report, you can hide the columns between the row titles and the totals column, and the hidden columns would not display on the printed worksheet, resulting in a summary report.

1 Press Ctrl + Home. From the column heading area, select **columns E:H**.

2 Right-click over the selected columns, and then click **Hide**. Compare your screen with Figure 5.4.

Columns E, F, G, and H are hidden from view—the column headings skip from D to I. A dark line between columns D and I indicates that columns from this location are hidden from view. After you click in another cell, this line will not be visible; however, the column letters provide a visual indication that some columns are hidden from view.

FIGURE 5.4

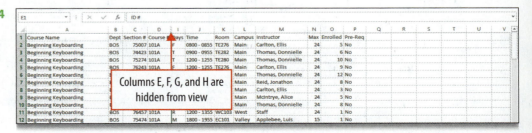

Columns E, F, G, and H are hidden from view

ANOTHER WAY On the HOME tab, in the Cells group, click the Format button. Under Visibility, point to Hide & Unhide, and then click Hide Columns.

BY TOUCH Drag to select the columns, tap and hold over the selected columns, and then click Hide.

3 Notice that the line between the **column D heading** and the **column I heading** is slightly wider, indicating hidden columns. Press Ctrl + Home, and then **Save** 💾 your workbook.

Activity 5.03 | Using the Go To Command

Use the *Go To* command to move to a specific cell or range of cells in a large worksheet.

1 On the **HOME tab**, in the **Editing group**, click **Find & Select**, and then click **Go To**. In the **Go To** dialog box, with the insertion point blinking in the **Reference** box, type **m172** and then click **OK**.

2 With cell **M172** active, on the **FORMULAS tab**, in the **Functions Library group**, click **More Functions**, point to **Statistical**, scroll down the list, and then click **COUNTIF**. As the **Range**, type **m2:m170** and as the **Criteria**, type **Staff** Click **OK**. Compare your screen with Figure 5.5.

Your result is 47, indicating that 47 courses still indicate *Staff* and need an instructor assigned.

FIGURE 5.5

3 In cell **J172**, type **Unassigned classes** and press Enter.

4 Press Ctrl + Home, and then **Save** 💾 your workbook.

Activity 5.04 | Arranging Multiple Workbooks and Splitting Worksheets

If you need to refer to information in one workbook while you have another workbook open, you can arrange the window to display sheets from more than one workbook—instead of jumping back and forth between the two workbooks from the taskbar. This is accomplished by using the *Arrange All* command, which tiles all open Excel windows on the screen. Additionally, you can view separate parts of the *same* worksheet on your screen by using the *Split* command, which splits the window into multiple resizable panes to view distant parts of your worksheet at once.

1 Press Ctrl + F12 to display the **Open** dialog box, and then from your student files, open the file **e05A_Teaching_Requests**.

The e05A_Teaching_Requests file opens, and your Lastname_Firstname_5A_Class_Schedule file is no longer visible on your screen. This worksheet contains a list of instructors who submitted requests for classes they would like to teach. You do not need to save this file; it is for reference only.

2 On the **VIEW tab**, in the **Window group**, click **Switch Windows**, and, click your **Lastname_Firstname_5A_Class_Schedule** file to make it the active worksheet.

3 On the **VIEW tab**, in the **Window group**, click **Arrange All**. Click **Horizontal** and then compare your screen with Figure 5.6.

Here, in the Arrange Windows dialog box, you can control how two or more worksheets from multiple open workbooks are arranged on the screen.

FIGURE 5.6

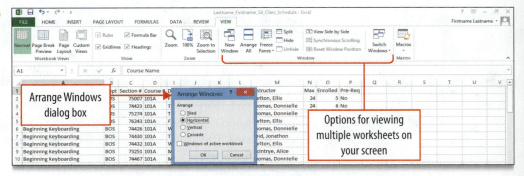

Arrange Windows dialog box

Options for viewing multiple worksheets on your screen

---

4 Click **OK**. Compare your screen with Figure 5.7.

The screen is split horizontally, and the e05A_Teaching_Requests worksheet displays below your Lastname_Firstname_5A_Class_Schedule worksheet. The active window title bar displays the file name in a darker shade of gray, and the row and column headings are shaded to indicate active cells. When multiple worksheets are open on the screen, only one is active at a time. To activate a worksheet, click anywhere on the worksheet or click the worksheet's title bar.

FIGURE 5.7

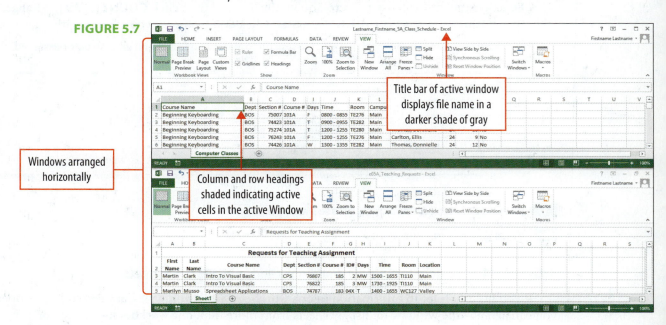

Title bar of active window displays file name in a darker shade of gray

Windows arranged horizontally

Column and row headings shaded indicating active cells in the active Window

---

5 Press **Ctrl** + **End** to move to cell **P172**, which is now the end of the active area of the worksheet.

6 Click cell **A172**. On the **VIEW tab**, in the **Window group**, click **Split** to split this upper window horizontally at row 172. Compare your screen with Figure 5.8.

A light gray horizontal bar displays at the top of row 172, and two sets of vertical scroll bars display in the Lastname_Firstname_5A_Class_Schedule worksheet—one in each of the two worksheet panes displayed in this window. You can drag the horizontal bar up slightly to make the lower pane easier to see.

FIGURE 5.8

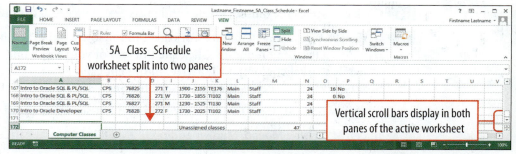

5A_Class_Schedule worksheet split into two panes

Vertical scroll bars display in both panes of the active worksheet

7 Above the **split bar,** click in any cell in **column C.** Press Ctrl + F to display the **Find tab** of the **Find and Replace** dialog box.

Column C lists the Section # for each class. This is a unique number that identifies each class.

↻ **BY TOUCH**   On the HOME tab, in the Editing group, tap Find.

8 Drag the title bar of the dialog box into the upper right area of your screen. Then, in the lower half of your screen, look at the first request in the **e05A_Teaching_Requests** worksheet, which is from *Martin Clark* to teach *Intro to Visual Basic Section # 76807.* In the **Find what** box, type **76807** so that you can locate the course in the **Lastname_Firstname_5A_Class_Schedule** worksheet.

9 Click **Find Next,** be sure that you can see the **Name Box,** and then compare your screen with Figure 5.9.

Section # 76807 is located and selected in cell C163 of the Class Schedule worksheet.

FIGURE 5.9

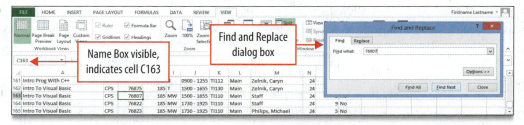

Name Box visible, indicates cell C163

Find and Replace dialog box

10 In your **Lastname_Firstname_5A_Class_Schedule** worksheet, click in cell **M163,** type **Clark, Martin** to delete *Staff* and assign the class to Mr. Clark. Press Enter.

The class is assigned to Mr. Clark, and the number of unassigned classes, which you can view below the split bar, goes down by one, to 46. Use the Split command when you need to see two distant parts of the same worksheet simultaneously.

11 In the **e05A_Teaching_Requests** worksheet, look at **row 4** and notice that the next request, also from Mr. Clark, is to teach *Section # 76822.*

This class is listed in the next row of your Lastname_Firstname_5A_Class_Schedule worksheet—row 164.

12 In cell **M164,** type **Clark, Martin** and press Enter. Notice below the split bar that the number of unassigned classes in cell **M172** goes down to *45.*

13 In the **Find and Replace** dialog box, in the **Find what** box, type **74787** which is the next requested Section #, and then click **Find Next.**

Section # 74787 in cell C66 is selected. Marilyn Musso has requested to teach this class.

14 Click cell **M66**, type **Musso, Marilyn** and press Enter; notice that the unassigned number is now *44*.

15 In the **e05A_teaching_Requests** worksheet in the lower pane, scroll down to view the remaining teaching requests. Click the title bar of your **Lastname_Firstname_5A_Class_Schedule** worksheet to make it active. In the **Find and Replace** dialog box, in the **Find what** box, type **75451** which is the next requested Section #, and then click **Find Next**.

Section # 75451 in cell C78 is selected. Marilyn Musso has requested to teach this class also.

16 In cell **M78**, type **Musso, Marilyn** and press Enter; *43* classes remain unassigned.

17 Continue to use the **Find and Replace** dialog box to locate the remaining two **Section #s** listed in the **e05A_Teaching_Requests** worksheet, and enter the appropriate instructor name for each class in **column M** of your **Lastname_Firstname_5A_Class_Schedule** worksheet.

18 In the **Find and Replace** dialog box, click **Close**. In cell **M172**, notice that *41* classes remain unassigned.

19 Click any cell in the **e05A_Teaching_Requests** worksheet to make it the active sheet. Compare your screen with Figure 5.10.

FIGURE 5.10

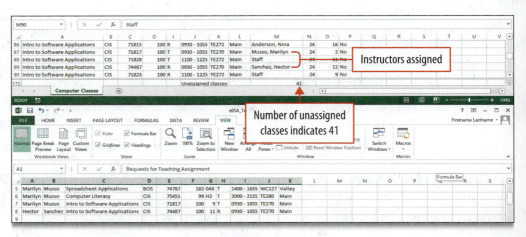

20 Click **Close** ⊠ to close the **e05A_Teaching_Requests** workbook. Then, on the title bar of your **Lastname_Firstname_5A_Class_Schedule** workbook, click **Maximize** 🗖 to restore the size of the worksheet to its full size.

21 On the **VIEW tab**, in the **Window group**, click **Split** to remove the split.

22 Press Ctrl + Home. From the **column heading area**, select **columns D:I**—recall that columns E:H are still hidden. Right-click over the selected area, and then click **Unhide**.

To redisplay hidden columns, first select the columns on either side of the hidden columns—columns D and I in this instance.

23 Press Ctrl + Home, and then **Save** 💾 your workbook.

Objective 2   Enhance Worksheets with Themes and Styles

Video E5-2

Worksheets used to be uninteresting grids of columns and rows viewed primarily on paper by accountants and managers. Now individuals may commonly use worksheets to communicate information both within an organization and to the public. A worksheet might be seen by individuals in an email, in a PowerPoint presentation, or in public blogs and publications. Accordingly, you will want to use some creative elements when preparing your worksheets.

A *theme* is a predesigned set of colors, fonts, lines, and fill effects that look good together and that can be applied to your entire Office 2013 file or to specific items. A theme combines two sets of fonts—one for text and one for headings. In the default Office theme, Calibri Light is the font for headings and Calibri is the font for body text.

In Excel, the applied theme has a set of complimentary *cell styles*—a defined set of formatting characteristics, such as fonts, font sizes, number formats, cell borders, and cell shading. The applied theme also has a set of complimentary table styles for data that you format as a table.

You can create your own themes, cells styles, and table styles.

Activity 5.05 | Changing and Customizing a Workbook Theme

1 Point to the **row 1 heading** to display the ➡ pointer, right-click, and then click **Insert** to insert a new blank row. In cell **A1**, type **Schedule of Classes with Unassigned Sections** and press Enter. On the **HOME tab**, **Merge & Center** this title across the range **A1:P1**, and then apply the **Title** cell style.

2 On the **PAGE LAYOUT tab**, in the **Themes group**, click **Themes**. Compare your screen with Figure 5.11.

The gallery of predesigned themes that come with Microsoft Office displays. Office—the default theme—is selected.

FIGURE 5.11

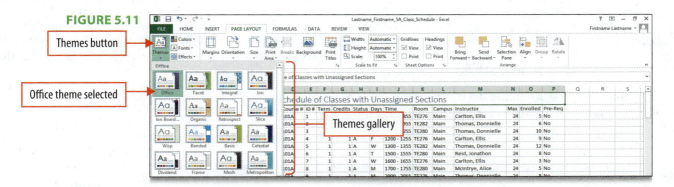

3 Point to several of the themes and notice how Live Preview displays the colors and fonts associated with each theme. Then, click the **Ion** theme.

4 In the **Themes group**, point to **Fonts** and read the **ScreenTip**.

The font associated with the Ion theme for both headings and body text is Century Gothic, but you can customize a theme by mixing the Colors, Fonts, and Effects from any of the supplied themes.

5 Click **Fonts**. If necessary, scroll to the top and click **Office**. **Save** 🖫 your workbook.

Activity 5.06 | Creating and Applying a Custom Table Style

Excel comes with many predefined table styles, but if none of these meets your needs, you can create and apply a custom table style of your own design. Custom table styles that you create are stored only in the current workbook, so they are not available in other workbooks.

1 On the **HOME tab**, in the **Styles group**, click **Format as Table**. At the bottom, click **New Table Style**.

2 In the **New Table Style** dialog box, in the **Name** box, replace the existing text by typing **Class Schedule**

3 In the list under **Table Element**, click **First Row Stripe**, and then compare your screen with Figure 5.12.

Here you can select one or more elements of the table, and then customize the format for each element.

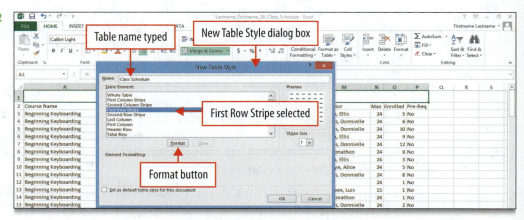

4 Below the list of table elements, click **Format**. In the **Format Cells** dialog box, click the **Fill tab**. In the fourth column of colors, click the second color, and notice that the **Sample** area previews the color you selected.

5 In the lower right corner, click **OK**. In the list of table elements, click **Second Row Stripe**, click **Format**, and then in the fourth column of colors, click the third color. Click **OK**. Notice the **Preview** shows the two colors.

6 In the list of table elements, click **Header Row**, click **Format**, and then in the third column of colors, click the second color.

7 Click **OK**, notice the **Preview**, and then compare your screen with Figure 5.13.

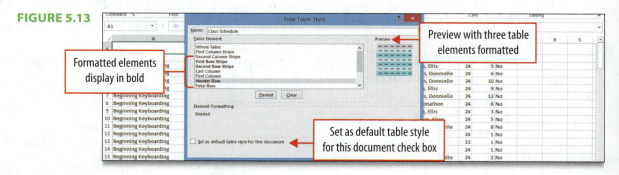

8 In the lower left corner of the dialog box, click to select the check box **Set as default table style for this document**. Click **OK**.

You must select this check box to make your table style available in the gallery of table styles.

9 Select the range **A2:P171**—do *not* include row 1 in your selection—and then in the **Styles group**, click **Format as Table**. At the top of the gallery, under **Custom**, point to your custom table style to display the **ScreenTip** *Class Schedule*. Compare your screen with Figure 5.14.

FIGURE 5.14

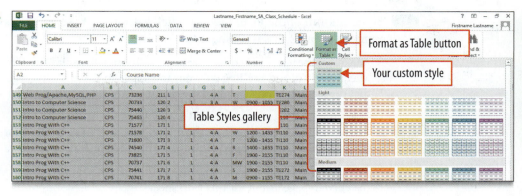

10 Click your **Class Schedule** table style, and then in the **Format As Table** dialog box, click **OK**. Then, because you do not need to filter the table, in the **Tools group**, click **Convert to Range**, and then click **Yes**.

> If you do not want to work with your data in a table by filtering and sorting, you can convert the table to a normal range to keep the table style formatting that you applied.

11 Press Ctrl + Home to deselect and move to cell **A1**, and then **Save** 🖫 your workbook.

Objective 3 | Format a Worksheet to Share with Others

Video E5-3

You can share a worksheet with others by printing and distributing paper copies, sending it electronically as an Excel file or some other file format, or posting it to the web or to a shared workspace. Regardless of how you distribute the information, a large worksheet will be easier for others to view if you insert appropriate page breaks and repeat column or row titles at the top of each page.

You can also add a *hyperlink* to a worksheet, which, when clicked, takes you to another location in the worksheet, to another file, or to a webpage on the Internet or on your organization's intranet.

Activity 5.07 | Previewing and Modifying Page Breaks

Before you print or electronically distribute a large worksheet, preview it to see where the pages will break across the columns and rows. You can move the page breaks to a column or row that groups the data logically, and you can change the orientation between portrait and landscape if you want to display more rows on the page (portrait) or more columns on the page (landscape). You can also apply *scaling* to the data to force the worksheet into a selected number of pages. Scaling reduces the horizontal and vertical size of the printed data by a percentage or by the number of pages that you specify.

1 From the column heading area, select **columns A:P**, in the **Cells group**, click **Format**, and then click **AutoFit Column Width**.

 **ANOTHER WAY** After selecting the columns, in the column heading area, point to any of the column borders and double-click.

2 Click cell **A1**, and then press Ctrl + F2 to view the **Print Preview**. Notice that as currently formatted, the worksheet will print on eight pages.

3 At the bottom of the **Print Preview**, click **Next Page** ▶ seven times to view the eight pages required to print this worksheet.

As you view each page, notice that pages 5 through 8 display the Time, Room, Campus, Instructor, Max, Enrolled, and Pre-Req columns that relate to the first four pages of the printout. You can see that the printed worksheet will be easier to read if all the information related to a class is on the same page.

4 Return to the worksheet. Click the **VIEW tab**, and then in the **Workbook Views group**, click **Page Break Preview**. Compare your screen with Figure 5.15.

The Page Break Preview window displays blue dashed lines to show where the page breaks are in the current page layout for this worksheet.

FIGURE 5.15

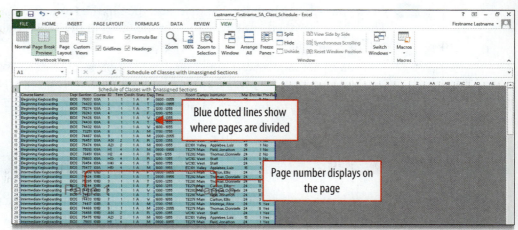

> **N O T E** | **Welcome to Page Break Preview**
>
> The Welcome to Page Break Preview dialog box may display with a message informing you that page breaks can be adjusted by clicking and dragging the breaks with your mouse. If this box displays, click OK to close it.

5 Scroll down to view the other pages and see where the page breaks are indicated. Then, in the **Workbook Views group**, click **Normal** to redisplay the worksheet in Normal view.

Dashed lines display at the page break locations on the worksheet.

6 On the **PAGE LAYOUT tab**, in the **Page Setup group**, set the **Orientation** to **Landscape**. Then, in the **Scale to Fit group**, click the **Width arrow**, and then click **1 page**.

In the Scale to Fit group, there are two ways to override the default printout size. In the Scale box, you can specify a scaling factor from between 10% and 400%. Or, you can use the Width and Height arrows to fit the printout to a specified number of pages. To return to a full-size printout after scaling, in the Scale box, type 100 as the percentage.

🔁 **ANOTHER WAY** | On the PAGE LAYOUT tab, in the Page Setup group, click the Dialog Box Launcher to display the Page Setup dialog box.

7 From the **INSERT tab**, insert a footer that includes the file name in the **left section** and the **Page Number** in the **right section**.

It is good practice to insert any headers or footers *before* making the final page break decisions on your worksheet.

8 Click any cell above the footer to exit the footer area. Press `Ctrl` + `F2` to display the **Print Preview**, and at the bottom, notice that the worksheet is now a total of four pages.

> By applying the scaling, each complete row of data will fit on one page.

9 Return to the worksheet, click the **VIEW tab**, and in the **Workbook Views group**, click **Page Break Preview**. Scroll to view the page break between **Page 2** and **Page 3**.

10 If necessary, scroll left to view column A. Point to the horizontal page break line between **Page 2** and **Page 3**. When the vertical resize pointer ↕ displays, drag the line up between **row 77** and **row 78**; this will break the pages between the BOS courses and the CIS courses. Compare your screen with Figure 5.16.

FIGURE 5.16

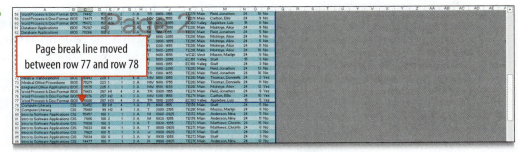

Page break line moved between row 77 and row 78

11 Scroll down to view the page break line between **Page 4** and **Page 5**. Drag the line up to break the page between **row 147** and **row 148**, which is the end of the CIS section.

12 Display the **Print Preview**. At the bottom of the window, click **Next Page** ▶ four times to scroll through the five pages that will print.

> With the new page breaks that you have inserted, the pages will break when a new Department begins.

A L E R T ! | **Page Breaks Differ**

The default printer and screen resolution on your computer may cause the page breaks to differ from those in this text.

---

13 Return ⊖ to the worksheet. On the **VIEW tab**, in the **Workbook Views group**, click **Normal** to redisplay the worksheet in Normal view. Press `Ctrl` + `Home`, and then click **Save** 💾.

Activity 5.08 | Repeating Column or Row Titles

When your worksheet layout spans multiple pages, you will typically want to repeat the column titles on each page. If your worksheet is wider than one page, you will also want to repeat the row titles on each page.

1 Display the **Print Preview** scroll through the pages, and notice that the column titles display only on the first page. Return ⊖ to the worksheet.

> Repeating the column titles on each page will make it easier to understand and read the information on the pages.

2 On the **PAGE LAYOUT tab**, in the **Page Setup group**, click **Print Titles** to display the **Sheet tab** of the **Page Setup** dialog box.

> Here you can select rows to repeat at the top of each page and columns to repeat at the left of each page.

3 Under **Print titles**, click in the **Rows to repeat at top** box, and then from the **row heading area**, select **row 2**. Compare your screen with Figure 5.17.

> A moving border surrounds row 2, and the mouse pointer displays as a black select row arrow. The absolute reference $2:$2 displays in the Rows to repeat at top box.

FIGURE 5.17

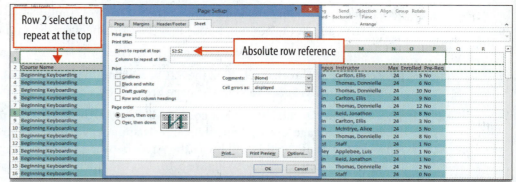

Absolute row reference

4 Click **OK**. Display the **Print Preview**, scroll through the pages and notice that the column titles display at the top of each page. Verify that the page breaks are still located between each department. Display **Page 2**, and then compare your screen with Figure 5.18. **Save** your worksheet.

FIGURE 5.18

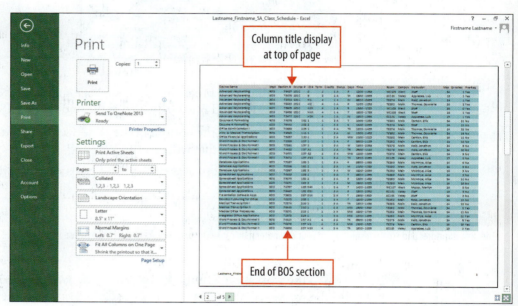

Column title display at top of page

End of BOS section

> **N O T E** **To Print a Multi-Sheet Workbook**
>
> To print all the pages in a multi-page workbook, either group the sheets, or under Settings, select Print Entire Workbook.

Activity 5.09 | Inserting a Hyperlink in a Worksheet

When a hyperlink is colored and underlined text that you can click to go to a file, a location in a file, a webpage on the Internet, or a webpage on your organization's intranet. Hyperlinks can be attached to text or to graphics. In this activity, you will add a hyperlink that will open a file containing the contact information for instructors.

1 Click cell **M2**. On the **INSERT tab**, in the **Links group**, click **Hyperlink** to display the **Insert Hyperlink** dialog box.

2 Under **Link to**, if necessary, click **Existing File or Web Page**. Click the **Look in arrow**, navigate to your student files, and then select the file **e05A_Faculty_Contacts**, which contains faculty contact information.

3 In the upper right corner of the **Insert Hyperlink** dialog box, click **ScreenTip**.

4 In the **Set Hyperlink ScreenTip** dialog box, in the **ScreenTip text** box, type **Click here for contact information** Compare your dialog box with Figure 5.19.

> When you point to the hyperlink on the worksheet, this is the text of the ScreenTip that will display.

FIGURE 5.19

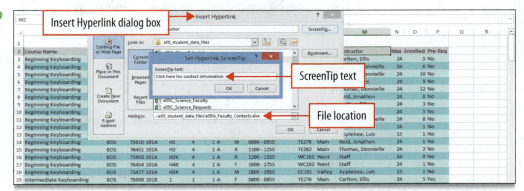

5 Click **OK** in the **Set Hyperlink ScreenTip** dialog box, and then click **OK** in the **Insert Hyperlink** dialog box.

> In the Ion theme, the color for a hyperlink is light blue.

6 Point to the **Instructor hyperlink** and read the **ScreenTip** that displays. Compare your screen with Figure 5.20.

> When you point to the hyperlink, the Link Select pointer 🖑 displays and the ScreenTip text displays.

FIGURE 5.20

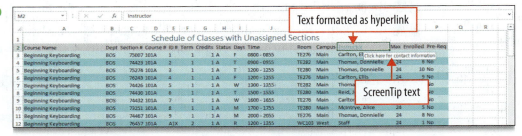

7 Click the **Instructor hyperlink**.

> The e05A_Faculty_Contacts file opens in a new window and displays the contact information.

8 Click **Close** ⊠ to close the **e05A_Faculty_Contacts** file and redisplay your **Lastname_Firstname_5A_Class_Schedule** worksheet.

9 On the **PAGE LAYOUT** tab, in the **Themes group**, click the **Colors arrow**. At the bottom of the page, click **Customize Colors**. At the bottom of the dialog box, locate the colors for **Hyperlink** and **Followed Hyperlink**. Compare your screen with Figure 5.21.

> Each color scheme uses a set of colors for a hyperlink and for a hyperlink that has been clicked (followed) one time. Now that you have followed your inserted hyperlink one time, the text displays in the Followed Hyperlink color. Here you can also change the colors for any of the colors associated with a theme.

FIGURE 5.21

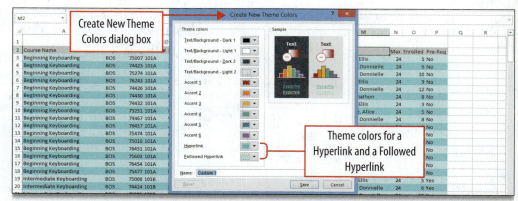

> **10** In the lower corner of the dialog box, click **Cancel**, and then **Save** 🖫 your workbook.

Activity 5.10 │ Modifying a Hyperlink

If the file to which the hyperlink refers is moved or renamed, or a webpage to which a hyperlink refers gets a new address, the hyperlink must be modified to reflect the change.

> **1** In cell **M2**, click the **Instructor hyperlink** to open the **e05A_Faculty_Contacts** workbook.

> **2** Save this file in your **Excel Chapter 5** folder as **Lastname_Firstname_5A_Faculty_Contacts**

> **3** Insert a footer in the **left section** with the file name, return to **Normal** view, click **Save** 🖫, and then click **Close** ⊠ to close your **Lastname_Firstname_5A_Faculty_Contacts** file and redisplay your **Lastname_Firstname_5A_Class_Schedule** file.

> **4** Right-click cell **M2**—the Instructor hyperlink—and then click **Edit Hyperlink**.

> **5** In the **Edit Hyperlink** dialog box, click the **Look in arrow**, navigate to your **Excel Chapter 5** folder, and then select your **Lastname_Firstname_5A_Faculty_Contacts** file, as shown in Figure 5.22.

FIGURE 5.22

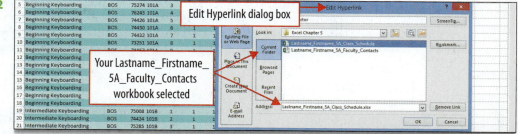

> **6** Click **OK**. In cell **M2**, click the hyperlinked text—**Instructor**.
>
> Verify that your Lastname_Firstname_5A_Faculty_Contacts file opens, and your hyperlink is now up to date.

> **7** Click **Close** ⊠ to close **Lastname_Firstname_5A_Faculty_Contacts**.

> **8** Click the **FILE tab** to display **Backstage** view. On the right, at the bottom of the **Properties** list, click **Show All Properties**. On the list of **Properties**, in the **Tags** box, type **class schedule** In the **Subject** box, type your course name and section #. Under **Related People**, be sure that your name displays as the author. If necessary, right-click the author name, click Edit Property, type your name, click outside of the Edit person dialog box, and then click OK.

> **9** Click **Save**, leave the **Lastname_Firstname_5A_Class_Schedule** workbook open.

Video E5-4

By default, Excel 2013 files are saved in the Excel Workbook file format with the *.xlsx file name extension*, which is a set of characters that helps your Windows operating system understand what kind of information is in a file and what program should open it.

Using the Save As command, you can choose to save an Excel file in another file format from the Save as type list. Some frequently used file formats are: Excel 97-2003 Workbook, Excel Template, Single File Web Page, Web Page, Excel Macro-Enabled Workbook, Text (Tab Delimited), and CSV (Comma Delimited).

For the purpose of posting Excel data to a website or transferring data to other applications, you can save your Excel file in a variety of other file formats. For example, saving an Excel worksheet as a *tab delimited text file* separates the cells of each row with tab characters. Saving an Excel worksheet as a *CSV (comma separated values) file* separates the cells of each row with commas. This type of file is also referred to as a *comma delimited file*. Text formats are commonly used to import data into a database program.

You can also save an Excel file in an electronic format that is easy to read for the viewer of the workbook. Such files are not easily modified and are considered to be an electronic printed version of the worksheet.

You can also add a hyperlink to a worksheet, which, when clicked, takes you to another location in the worksheet, to another file, or to a webpage on the Internet or on your organization's intranet.

Activity 5.11 Viewing and Saving a Workbook as a Web Page

Before you save a worksheet as a webpage, it is a good idea to view it as a webpage to see how it will display. When saving a multiple-page workbook as a webpage, all of the worksheets are available and can be accessed. You can also save a single worksheet as a webpage. Excel changes the contents of the worksheet into *HTML (Hypertext Markup Language)*, which is a language web browsers can interpret, when you save a worksheet as a webpage. In this activity, you will save and publish a worksheet as a webpage.

1 ▶ Be sure your **Lastname_Firstname_5A_Class_Schedule** workbook is open and displayed on your screen. Press F12 to display the **Save As** dialog box, navigate to your **Excel Chapter 5** folder, in the lower portion of the dialog box, click the **Save as type arrow**, and then click **Web Page**.

Your Excel files no longer display in the dialog box, because only files with the type Web Page are visible. The file type changes to Web Page and additional web-based options display below.

2 ▶ In the lower portion of the dialog box, click **Change Title**.

The text that you type here will become the title when the file displays as a webpage.

3 ▶ In the **Enter Text** dialog box, in the **Page title** box, using your own name, type **Computer Courses Lastname Firstname** Compare your screen with Figure 5.23.

FIGURE 5.23

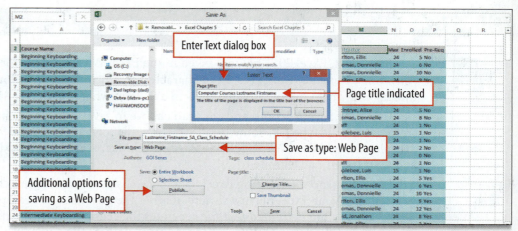

4 > In the **Enter Text** dialog box, click **OK**, and notice that in the **Page title** box, your typed text displays.

5 > In the **Save As** dialog box, click **Publish**.

6 > In the **Publish as Web Page** dialog box, click the **Choose arrow**, notice the objects that can be published as a webpage, and then click **Items on Computer Classes**—recall that the worksheet name is *Computer Classes*. In the lower left corner, click to select (place a check mark in) the **Open published web page in browser** check box. Compare your screen with Figure 5.24.

Under Item to publish, you can choose which elements to include. You can select the entire workbook, a specific worksheet in the workbook, a range of cells, or previously published items that you are modifying. The *Open published web page in browser* selection ensures that the Internet browser software, for example Internet Explorer, will automatically start and display the page.

FIGURE 5.24

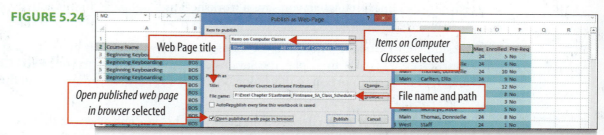

7 > Click **Browse** to display the **Publish As** dialog box.

8 > If necessary, navigate to your **Excel Chapter 5** folder. In the **File name** box, type **Lastname_Firstname_5A_Schedule_Webpage** Compare your screen with Figure 5.25.

FIGURE 5.25

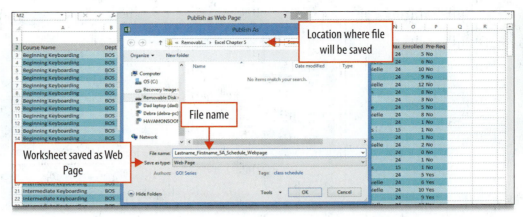

9 ▶ Click **OK**, and then on the **Publish as Web Page** dialog box, click **Publish**. Compare your screen with Figure 5.26.

> The webpage is saved in your selected folder, and the Class Schedule file opens in your default Internet browser. The browser title bar displays the text you typed in the Enter Text dialog box.

FIGURE 5.26

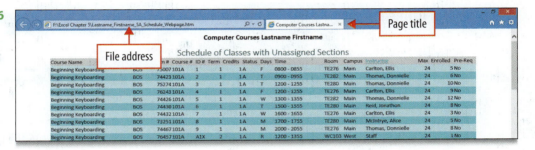

10 ▶ If you are instructed to print your webpage on paper, consult the instructions to print from your specific browser software.

> Your printed results will vary depending on which browser software you are using. Do not be concerned about the printout; webpages are intended for viewing, not printing.

11 ▶ On the browser title bar, click **Close** ✖.

Activity 5.12 | Saving Excel Data in CSV File Format

You can save an Excel worksheet as a CSV file, which saves the contents of the cells by placing commas between them and an end-of-paragraph mark at the end of each row.

1 ▶ With your **Lastname_Firstname_5A_Class_Schedule** workbook open, display the **Save As** dialog box, click the **Save as type arrow**, and then click **CSV (Comma delimited)**. Be sure you save the file in your **Excel Chapter 5** folder. In the **File name** box, using your own name, type **Lastname_Firstname_5A_Schedule_CSV** Compare your screen with Figure 5.27.

> Your Excel files no longer display, because only CSV files are displayed.

FIGURE 5.27

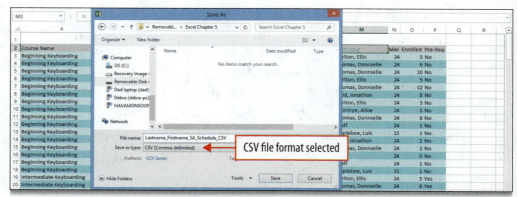

CSV file format selected

> **2** Click **Save**. Compare your screen with Figure 5.28.

> A dialog box displays to inform you that some features of the file may not be compatible with the CSV format. Features such as merged cells and formatting are lost. You can save the file and leave out incompatible features by clicking Yes, preserve the file in an Excel format by clicking No, or see what might be lost by clicking Help.

FIGURE 5.28

Three options displayed

> **3** Click **Yes** to keep the CSV format.

> The file is saved in the new format. The new file name displays in the title bar. If file extensions—the three letters that identify the type of files—are displayed on your computer, you will also see .csv after the file name.

> **4** **Close** ✖ your **Lastname_Firstname_5A_Schedule_CSV** file. Click **Save** to save changes, and then click **Yes** to acknowledge the warning message.

Activity 5.13 | Saving Excel Data as a PDF or XPS File

You can create portable documents to share across applications and platforms with accurate visual representations. To publish a document and ensure that the appearance of the document is the same no matter what computer it is displayed on, save the document in *PDF (Portable Document Format)* or *XPS (XML Paper Specification)* format. PDF is a widely used format developed by Adobe Systems. XPS is a format developed by Microsoft. Both formats let you create a representation of *electronic paper* that displays your data on the screen as it would look when printed. Use one of these formats if you want someone to be able to view a document but not change it. In this activity, you will create PDF and XPS portable documents.

> **1** In Excel, from your student files, open the file **e05A_Fall_Classes**. Display the footer area, click in the **left section**, and then type **Lastname_Firstname_5A_Fall_PDF** Click in a cell just above the footer to exit the Footer. In the lower right corner of your screen, on the status bar, click **Normal** ⊞ to return to **Normal** view.

> **2** Press [F12] to display the **Save As** dialog box and navigate to your **Excel Chapter 5** folder. Click the **Save as type arrow**, and then click **PDF**.

 **ANOTHER WAY**   From Backstage view, click Export, and then click Create PDF/XPS document to open the Publish as PDF or XPS dialog box.

3 In the lower right section of the dialog box, if necessary, select the **Open file after publishing** check box. As the file name, type **Lastname_Firstname_5A_Fall_PDF** and then click **Save**.

The file is saved in PDF format, and then opens as a PDF document using the default PDF program on your computer.

4 **Close** ✖ the **Lastname_Firstname_5A_Fall_PDF** document.

5 With the **e05A_Fall_Classes** file open, edit the footer in the left section and type **Lastname_Firstname_5A_Fall_XPS** Click in a cell just above the footer to exit the Footer. In the lower right corner of your screen, on the status bar, click **Normal** ▦ to return to **Normal** view.

6 Press F12 to display the **Save As** dialog box, navigate to your **Excel Chapter 5** folder, and then in the **File name** box, type **Lastname_Firstname_5A_Fall_XPS**

7 At the bottom of the **Save As** dialog box, click the **Save as type arrow**, and then click **XPS Document**. In the lower right section of the **Save As** dialog box, if necessary, select the **Open file after publishing** check box, and then compare your screen with Figure 5.29.

FIGURE 5.29

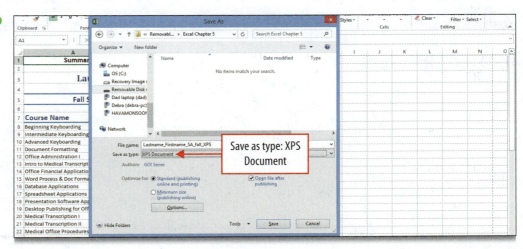

8 Click **Save**.

The file is saved in XPS format, and then opens as an XPS document in the XPS Viewer window.

ALERT! **XPS Viewer**

If the Open with dialog box opens, choose XPS viewer and then click OK to open the file.

---

9 **Close** ✖ the **XPS Viewer** window. **Close** the **e05A_Fall_Classes** file. **Don't Save** when the message displays—you do not need to save this file.

10 Submit your six files from this project as directed by your instructor, and then **Close** Excel.

More Knowledge **Converting a Tab Delimited Text File to a Word Table**

By choosing Text File as the file type, you can save an Excel worksheet as a text file, which saves the contents of the cells by placing a tab character, rather than commas, between the cells and an end-of-paragraph mark at the end of each row. This type of file can be readily exchanged with various database programs, in which it is referred to as a tab delimited text file. A text file can be converted from tab delimited text to a Word table. Word has a *Convert Text to Table* command that can easily convert a tabbed file into a table. A table displays in a row and column format, like an Excel spreadsheet.

END | You have completed Project 5A

Sorted, Filtered, and Outlined Database

MyITLab®
Project 5B Training

PROJECT ACTIVITIES

In Activities 5.14 through 5.21 you will use advanced table features to provide Dr. Kesia Toomer, the Dean of the Computer and Business Systems Division, information about the Fall course sections and assigned faculty in the Division. Your completed worksheets will look similar to Figure 5.30.

PROJECT FILES

For Project 5B, you will need the following files:

e05B_Fall_Advising
e05B_Fall_Faculty
e05B_Fall_Sections

You will save your workbooks as:

Lastname_Firstname_5B_Fall_Advising
Lastname_Firstname_5B_Fall_Faculty
Lastname_Firstname_5B_Fall_Sections

PROJECT RESULTS

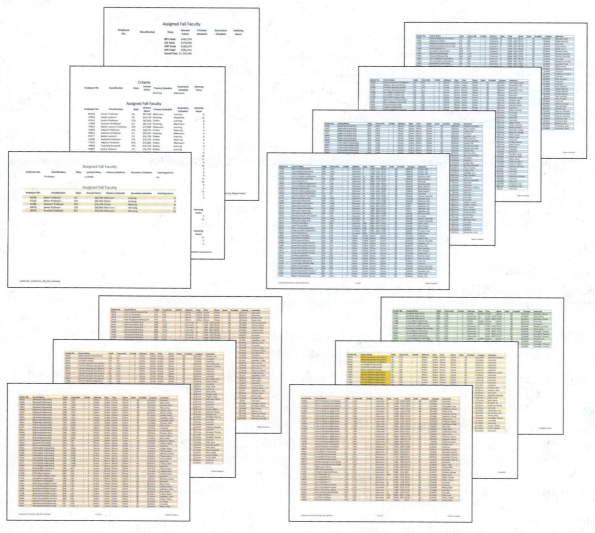

FIGURE 5.30 Project 5B Advising

Video E5-5

Sort means to organize data in a particular order; for example, alphabetizing a list of names. An *ascending* sort refers to text that is sorted alphabetically from A to Z, numbers sorted from lowest to highest, or dates and times sorted from earliest to latest. A *descending* sort refers to text that is sorted alphabetically from Z to A, numbers sorted from highest to lowest, or dates and times sorted from latest to earliest.

Sorting helps you to visualize your data. By sorting in various ways, you can find the data that you want, and then use your data to make good decisions. You can sort data in one column or in multiple columns. Most sort operations are column sorts, but you can also sort by rows.

Activity 5.14 | Sorting on Multiple Columns

To sort data based on several criteria at once, use the *Sort dialog box*, which enables you to sort by more than one column or row. For example, Dean Toomer wants to know, by department, how each course is delivered—either online or in a campus classroom. She also wants to examine the data to determine if there are any conflicts in room assignments. In this activity, you will convert the data into an Excel table, and then use the Sort dialog box to arrange the data to see the information the Dean needs.

1 ▶ Start Excel. From your student files, open **e05B_Fall_Sections**, and then **Save** the file in your **Excel Chapter 5** folder as **Lastname_Firstname_5B_Fall_Sections**

2 ▶ Be sure that the first worksheet, **Room Conflicts**, is the active sheet. In the **Name Box**, type **a1:m170** and press Enter to select this range. On the **INSERT tab**, in the **Tables group**, click **Table**. In the **Create Table** dialog box, be sure that the **My table has headers** check box is selected, and then click **OK**.

ANOTHER WAY   With cell A1 active, on the INSERT tab, in the Tables group, click Table, and Excel will select all the contiguous data as the range.

3 ▶ On the **DESIGN tab**, in the **Table Styles group**, click **More** ⏷, and then under **Light**, click **Table Style Light 16**. Click any cell to deselect the table, and then compare your screen with Figure 5.31.

A table of data like this one forms a *database*—an organized collection of facts related to a specific topic. In this table, the topic relates to the Fall course sections for this division of the college.

Each table row forms a *record*—all of the categories of data pertaining to one person, place, thing, event, or idea. In this table, each course section is a record. Each table column forms a *field*—a single piece of information that is stored in every record, such as a name or course number.

When information is arranged as records in rows and fields in columns, then you can *query*—ask a question of—the data. A query restricts records through the use of criteria conditions that will display records that will answer a question about the data.

FIGURE 5.31

4 ▸ On the **DATA tab**, in the **Sort & Filter group**, click **Sort**.

In the Sort dialog box, you can sort on up to 64 columns (levels) of data.

> **NOTE** **Defining Data as a Table Prior to Sort Operations Is Optional**
>
> Defining your range of data as an Excel table is not required to perform sort operations. Doing so, however, is convenient if you plan to perform sorts on all of the data, because any sort commands will be performed on the entire table. Defining the data as a table also freezes the column titles automatically, so they will not move out of view as you scroll down a worksheet that contains many rows. If you want to sort only part of a list of data, do not convert the data to a table. Instead, select the range, and then click the Sort button.

5 ▸ In the **Sort** dialog box, under **Column**, click the **Sort by arrow**. Notice that the list displays in the order of the field names—the column titles. In the list, click **Dept**.

6 ▸ Under **Sort On**, click the **arrow**, and then click **Values**. Under **Order**, click the **arrow**, and then click **A to Z**. Compare your screen with Figure 5.32.

The default Sort On option *Values* indicates that the sort will be based on the values in the cells of the Sort by column—the Dept. column. The default sort Order *A to Z* indicates that the values in the column will be sorted in ascending alphabetical order.

FIGURE 5.32

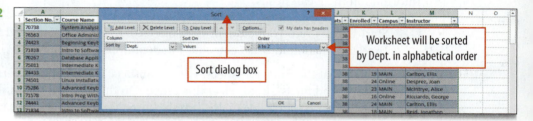

7 ▸ In the upper left corner of the **Sort** dialog box, click **Add Level**. In the second level row, click the **Then by arrow**, and then click **Course No**. Be sure that **Sort On** indicates *Values* and **Order** indicates *Smallest to Largest*.

When you initiate the sort operation, these numeric values will be sorted from the smallest number to the largest.

8 ▸ Click **Add Level** again. In the new row, under **Column**, click the **Then by arrow**, and then click **Section No**. Sort on the default options **Values**, from **Smallest to Largest**. Compare your screen with Figure 5.33.

FIGURE 5.33

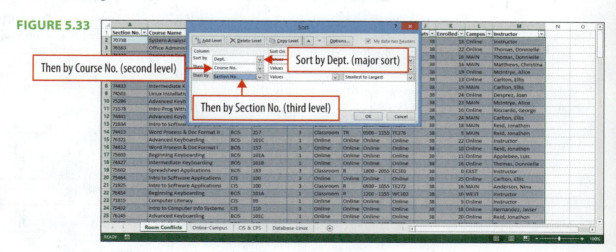

9 Click **OK**. Scroll down until **row 139** is at the top of the worksheet, take a moment to examine the arrangement of the data, and then compare your screen with Figure 5.34.

The first sort level, sometimes referred to as the *major sort*, is by the Dept. field in alphabetic order, so after the BOS department, the CIS department sections are listed, then the CNT department sections, then the CPS department sections, and so on.

The second sort level is by the Course No. field in ascending order, so within each department, the courses are sorted in ascending order by course number.

The third sort level is by the Section No. field in ascending order, so within each Course No. the section numbers display in ascending order.

FIGURE 5.34

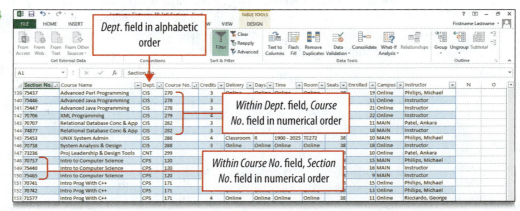

10 From the row heading area, select **rows 148:150**, and then notice that all three sections of the course *CPS 120 Intro to Computer Science* are offered in a campus classroom.

By studying the information in this arrangement, Dean Toomer can consider adding an additional section of this course in an online delivery.

11 Click any cell to deselect. On the **DATA tab**, in the **Sort & Filter group**, click **Sort** to redisplay the **Sort** dialog box.

12 Under **Column**, in the first row, click the **Sort by arrow**, and then click **Days**, change the second sort level to **Time**, and change the third sort level to **Room**. For each sort level, sort on **Values** in **A to Z** order. Compare your screen with Figure 5.35.

FIGURE 5.35

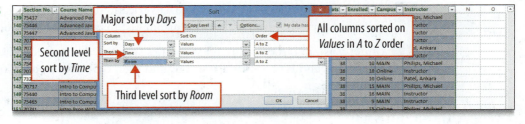

🔄 **ANOTHER WAY**   Click any row in the dialog box, click Delete Level, and then add new levels.

13 Click **OK**, and then scroll to view the top of the worksheet.

Because the days are sorted alphabetically, F (for Friday) is listed first, and then the times for the Friday classes are sorted in ascending order. Within the Friday group, the classes are further sorted from the earliest to the latest. Within each time period, the data is further sorted by room.

14 ▶ Examine the sorted data. Notice that the first three classes listed are on *Friday*, at *12:00*, in room *TE276*, with *Ellis Carlton* as the instructor.

These are all keyboarding classes, and the instructor teaches the three levels of keyboarding at the same time, so this is not a room conflict.

15 ▶ Scroll down to row 24. Notice in **rows 24:25** that two *Intro to Visual Basic* classes are scheduled on *MW* from 8:00 to 9:25 in room *TE110* with two different instructors listed. Press [Ctrl] + [Home] to move to the top of the worksheet.

This is a conflict of room assignment that will need to be resolved. Sorting data can help you identify such problems.

16 ▶ On the **PAGE LAYOUT tab**, in the **Page Setup group**, click **Print Titles**. On the **Sheet tab** of the **Page Setup** dialog box, click in the **Rows to repeat at top** box, point to the **row 1** heading to display the pointer, and click to select **row 1** so that the column titles will print on each sheet. In the dialog box, click **OK**.

17 ▶ Save 🖫 your workbook.

Activity 5.15 | Sorting by Using a Custom List

You can use a ***custom list*** to sort in an order that you define. Excel includes a day-of-the-week and month-of-the-year custom list, so that you can sort chronologically by the days of the week or by the months of the year from January to December.

Optionally, you can create your own custom list by typing the values you want to sort by, in the order you want to sort them, from top to bottom; for example, *Fast, Medium, Slow*. A custom list that you define must be based on a value—text, number, date, or time.

In this activity, you will provide Dean Toomer with a list showing all the Fall sections sorted first by Delivery, with all online courses listed first. Within each delivery type—Online and Classroom—the data will be further sorted by Dept. and then by Course Name.

1 ▶ In the **sheet tab area**, click **Online-Campus** to display the *second* worksheet in the workbook.

2 ▶ In the **Name Box**, type **a1:m170** and press [Enter] to select the range. Click **Quick Analysis** 📧, click **TABLES**, and then click **Table**. On the **DESIGN tab**, in the **Table Styles group**, click **More**, and then click **Table Style Light 17**. On the **DATA tab**, in the **Sort & Filter group**, click **Sort** to display the **Sort** dialog box.

3 ▶ Set the first (major) level to sort by **Delivery** and to sort on **Values**. Then, click the **Order arrow** for this sort level, and click **Custom List** to display the **Custom Lists** dialog box.

4 ▶ Under **Custom Lists**, be sure **NEW LIST** is selected. Then, under **List entries**, click in the empty box and type **Online** Press [Enter], and then type **Classroom** Compare your screen with Figure 5.36.

FIGURE 5.36

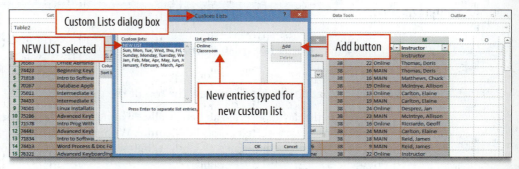

5 In the **Custom Lists** dialog box, click **Add**. On the left, under **Custom lists**, verify **Online, Classroom** is selected, and then click **OK** to redisplay the **Sort** dialog box.

6 In the **Sort** dialog box, click **Add Level**, and then as the second level sort, click the **Sort by arrow**, and then click **Dept**. Click **Add Level** again, and as the third level sort, select **Course Name**. Compare your screen with Figure 5.37.

FIGURE 5.37

7 Click **OK** and then click any cell to deselect the table. Scroll down the worksheet, and notice that all of the online courses are listed first, and then scroll down to display **row 76**. Notice the **Classroom** sections begin in **row 92**. Compare your screen with Figure 5.38.

> Within each grouping, Online and Classroom, the sections are further sorted alphabetically by *Dept.* and then by *Course Name*.

FIGURE 5.38

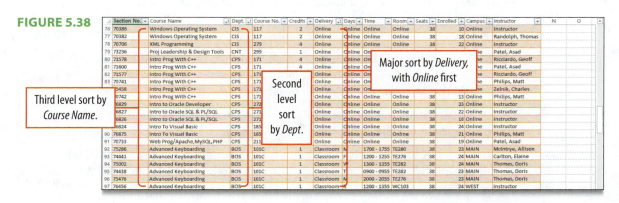

8 Press Ctrl + Home to move to cell **A1**. On the **PAGE LAYOUT tab**, in the **Page Setup group**, click **Print Titles**. On the **Sheet tab** of the **Page Setup** dialog box, click in the **Rows to repeat at top** box, point to the **row 1** heading to display the pointer, and click to select **row 1**, and then click **OK**. **Save** your workbook.

More Knowledge   **A Custom List Remains Available for All Workbooks in Excel**

When you create a custom list, the list remains available for all workbooks that you use in Excel. To delete a custom list, display Excel Options, on the left click Advanced, under General, click the Edit Custom Lists button, select the custom list, and then click the Delete button to permanently delete the custom list. Click OK to confirm the deletion. Click OK two more times to close both dialog boxes.

Video E5-6

Filtering displays only the rows that meet the *criteria*—conditions that you specify to limit which records are included in the results—and hides the rows that do not meet your criteria.

When you format a range of data as a table, or select a range and click the Filter command, Excel displays filter arrows in the column headings, from which you can display the *AutoFilter menu* for a column—a drop-down menu from which you can filter a column by a list of values, by a format, or by criteria.

Use a *custom filter* to apply complex criteria to a single column. Use an *advanced filter* to specify three or more criteria for a particular column, to apply complex criteria to two or more columns, or to specify computed criteria. You can also use an advanced filter for extracting—copying the selected rows to another part of the worksheet, instead of displaying the filtered list.

Activity 5.16 | Filtering by Format and Value Using AutoFilter

There are three types of filters that you can create with AutoFilter. You can filter by one or more values, for example *CIS* for the CIS department. You can filter by a format, such as cell color. Or, you can filter by criteria; for example, course sections that are greater than two credits, which would display courses that have three or more credits. Each of these filter types is mutually exclusive for the column; that is, you can use only one at a time.

1 Click the **CIS & CPS sheet tab** to display the *third* worksheet in the workbook.

2 Be sure that cell **A1** is the active cell, and then on the **INSERT tab**, in the **Tables group**, click **Table**. In the **Create Table** dialog box, be sure that the data indicates the range *$A$1:$M$170* and the *My table has headers* checkbox is selected.

> The Table command causes Excel to suggest a table range based on the contiguous cells surrounding the active cell.

3 Click **OK** to accept the selection as the table range. On the **DESIGN tab**, in the **Table Styles group**, click **More** ⊽, and then click **Table Style Light 19**. Click cell **A1** to deselect the table.

4 Click the **DATA tab**. In the **Sort & Filter group**, notice that **Filter** is active—it displays green. In **row 1**, notice the **filter arrows** ⊡ in each column title.

> When you format a range of data as an Excel table, filter arrows are automatically added in the header row of the table. A filter arrow, when clicked, displays the AutoFilter menu. On the ribbon, the active Filter button indicates that the data is formatted to use filters.

5 In **column B**, notice that some courses are formatted with a yellow fill color, which indicates courses that have been designated as introductory courses recommended for high school seniors who want to take a college class.

6 In cell **B1**, click the **Course Name filter arrow** ⊡. On the **AutoFilter** menu, below **Filter by Color**, click the **yellow block**.

> Only courses with a yellow fill color in column B display; the status bar indicates that 79 of the 169 records display.

7 Point to the filter arrow in cell **B1**, and notice the **ScreenTip** *Course Name: Equals a Yellow cell color*. Notice also that a small funnel displays to the right of the arrow. Compare your screen with Figure 5.39.

> The funnel indicates that a filter is applied, and the ScreenTip indicates how the records are filtered.

FIGURE 5.39

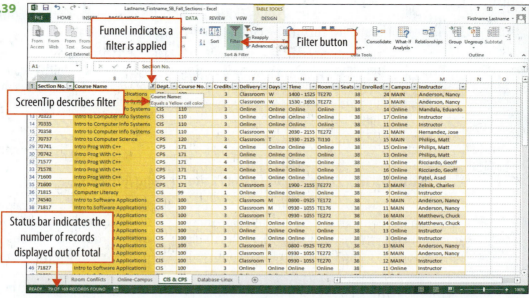

8 In cell **B1**, click the **Course Name filter arrow** ⏷, and then click **Clear Filter from "Course Name"**. Then, in cell **B1**, point to the **Course Name filter arrow**, and notice that *(Showing All)* displays.

> The funnel no longer displays. The status bar no longer indicates that a filter is active. A filter arrow without a funnel means that filtering is enabled but not applied; if you point to the arrow, the ScreenTip will display (Showing All).

9 Click cell **I5**, which contains the value *TE280*. Right-click over the selected cell, point to **Filter**, and then click **Filter by Selected Cell's Value**. Notice that only the courses that meet in Room TE280 display; all the other records are hidden.

> Excel filters the records by the selected value—TE280—and indicates in the status bar that 10 of the 169 records are displayed. This is a quick way to filter a set of records.

10 On the **DATA tab**, in the **Sort & Filter group**, click **Clear** 🗙 to clear all of the filters.

> Use this command to clear all filters from a group of records. This command also clears any sorts that were applied.

11 In cell **C1**, click the **Dept. filter arrow** ⏷. Click the **(Select All)** check box to clear all the check boxes, and then select the **CIS** and **CPS** check boxes. Click **OK**.

> The records are filtered so that only course sections in the CIS and CPS departments display. The status bar indicates that 93 of 169 records are found; that is, 93 course sections are either in the CIS or CPS departments.

12 In cell **E1**, click the **Credits filter arrow** ⏷, click the **(Select All)** check box to clear all the check boxes, and then select the **3** check box. Click **OK**.

> The status bar indicates that 61 of 169 records are found. That is, of the sections in either the CIS or CPS departments, 61 are three-credit courses. You can see that filtering actions are *additive*—each additional filter that you apply is based on the current filter, which further reduces the number of records displayed.

13 In cell **F1**, click the **Delivery filter arrow** ▾, and then using the technique you just practiced, filter the list further by **Online**.

The status bar indicates 30 of 169 records found. That is, 30 course sections are either in the CIS or CPS departments and three-credit courses are offered online. The filter drop-down lists make it easy to apply filters that provide quick views of your data. For best results, be sure the data in the filtered column has the same data type; for example, in a column, be sure all the values are numbers or text.

14 Save 🖫 your workbook.

Activity 5.17 | Filtering by Custom Criteria Using AutoFilter

By using a custom filter, you can apply complex criteria to a single column. For example, you can use comparison criteria to compare two values by using the *comparison operators* such as Equals (=), Greater Than (>), or Less Than (<) singly or in combinations. When you compare two values by using these operators, your result is a logical value that is either true or false.

1 Click **Database-Linux sheet tab** to display the *fourth* worksheet in the workbook.

2 Be sure that cell **A1** is the active cell, and then on the **INSERT tab**, in the **Tables group**, click **Table**. In the **Create Table** dialog box, be sure that the data indicates the range *$A$1:$M$170* and the *My table has headers checkbox* is selected. Click **OK**, and then apply **Table Style Light 21**. Click any cell to deselect.

3 In cell **K1**, click the **Enrolled filter arrow** ▾, point to **Number Filters**, and then click **Less Than Or Equal To**. On the **Custom AutoFilter** dialog box in the first box, be sure that *is less than or equal to* displays, and then in the second box type **12** Compare your screen with Figure 5.40.

In the Custom AutoFilter dialog box, you can create a *compound filter*—a filter that uses more than one condition—and one that uses comparison operators.

FIGURE 5.40

🔄 **ANOTHER WAY**   Click Custom Filter, click the first arrow in the first row, and then click is less than or equal to.

4 Click **OK** to display 49 records.

This filter answers the question, *Which course sections have 12 or fewer students enrolled?*

5 On the **DATA tab**, in the **Sort & Filter group**, click **Clear** 🐾 to clear all filters.

6 In cell **B1**, click the **Course Name filter arrow** ▾, point to **Text Filters**, and then click **Contains**.

7 In the **Custom AutoFilter** dialog box, under **Course Name**, in the first box, be sure that *contains* displays. In the box to the right, type **database**

8 Between the two rows of boxes, select **Or**. For the second filter, in the first box, click the arrow, scroll down as necessary, and then click **contains**. In the second box, type **linux** and then compare your screen with Figure 5.41.

> For the *Or comparison operator*, only one of the two comparison criteria that you specify must be true. By applying this filter, only courses that contain the words *database* or *linux* will display.

> For the *And comparison operator*, each and every one of the comparison criteria that you specify must be true.

FIGURE 5.41

9 Click **OK** to display 14 records. **Save** 💾 your workbook.

> This filter answers the question, Which course sections relate to either databases or the Linux operating system?

Activity 5.18 | Inserting the Sheet Name and Page Numbers in a Footer

You have practiced inserting the file name into the footer of a worksheet. In this activity, you will add the sheet name to the footer.

1 Point to the **Database-Linux sheet tab**, right-click, and then click **Select All Sheets**. With the sheets grouped, insert a footer in the left section that includes the file name.

2 In the footer area, click in the **center section** of the footer, and then on the **DESIGN tab**, in the **Header & Footer Elements group**, click **Page Number**. Press Spacebar one time, type **of** and press Spacebar again, and then click **Number of Pages**.

3 In the footer area, click in the **right section** of the footer, and then on the **DESIGN tab**, in the **Header & Footer Elements group**, click **Sheet Name**. Click a cell outside of the footer and compare your screen with Figure 5.42.

FIGURE 5.42

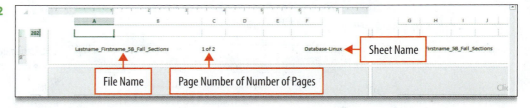

4 On the **PAGE LAYOUT tab**, set the **Orientation** to **Landscape**, and set the **Width** to **1 page**. On the status bar, click **Normal** ▦. Press Ctrl + Home to move to cell **A1**.

5 Click the **FILE tab**, and then in the lower right portion of the screen, click **Show all properties**. In the **Tags** box, type **sort, filter, sections** and in the **Subject** box type your course name and section #. In the **Author** box, replace the existing text with your first and last name. Display **Print Preview**.

> Ten pages display in Print Preview. The four worksheets in the workbook result in 10 pages—the first worksheet has four pages (blue), the second worksheet has four pages (pink), the third worksheet has one page (gold), and the fourth worksheet has one page (green).

6 ▸ Redisplay the workbook, and then make any necessary corrections or adjustments. Right-click any of the grouped sheet tabs, and then click **Ungroup Sheets**.

7 ▸ **Save** 🖫 your workbook. Hold this workbook until the end of this project, and then print or submit the four worksheets—10 total pages—in this workbook electronically as directed by your instructor. There are no formulas in these worksheets. **Close** this workbook, but leave Excel open.

Activity 5.19 | Filtering by Using Advanced Criteria

Use an advanced filter when the data you want to filter requires complex criteria; for example, to specify three or more criteria for a particular column, to apply complex criteria to two or more columns, or to specify computed criteria. When you use the Advanced Filter command, the Advanced dialog box displays, rather than the AutoFilter menu, and you type the criteria on the worksheet above the range you want to filter.

In this activity, you will create an advanced filter to determine which faculty members whose classification includes Professor and that have an annual salary of $70,000 or more, have 8 or more hours of assigned advising hours.

1 ▸ From your student files, open **e05B_Fall_Advising** and then **Save** the file in your **Excel Chapter 5** folder as **Lastname_Firstname_5B_Fall_Advising**

2 ▸ Select the range **A6:G7**, right-click, and then click **Copy**.

> The first step in filtering by using advanced criteria is to create a ***criteria range***—an area on your worksheet where you define the criteria for the filter. The criteria range indicates how the displayed records are filtered.

> Typically, the criteria range is placed *above* the data. The criteria range must have a row for the column headings and at least one row for the criteria—you will need additional rows if you have multiple criteria for a column. You can also add a title row. Separate the criteria range from the data by a blank row.

3 ▸ Point to cell **A1**, right-click, under **Paste Options**, click the first button, **Paste (P)** 📋, and then press Esc to cancel the moving border. Click cell **A1**, type **Criteria** and then press Enter.

4 ▸ Select **rows 1:2**, on the **HOME tab**, in the **Cells group**, click **Format**, and then click **AutoFit Row Height**. Compare your screen with Figure 5.43.

> By copying the title and field names, you also copy the formatting that has been applied.

FIGURE 5.43

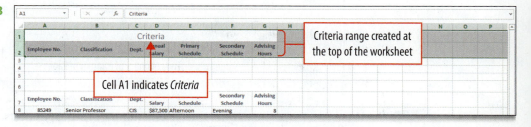

5 ▸ Select the range **A2:G3**—the column names and the blank row in the Criteria range. Click in the **Name Box**, type **Criteria** and then press Enter. Compare your screen with Figure 5.44.

> By naming the range Criteria, which is a predefined name recognized by Excel, the reference to this range will automatically display as the Criteria range in the Advanced Filter dialog box. This defined criteria range includes the field names and one empty row, where the limiting criteria will be placed. It does not include the title Criteria.

FIGURE 5.44

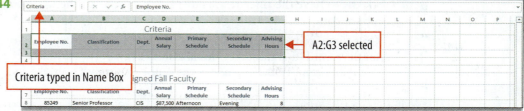

A2:G3 selected

Criteria typed in Name Box

6 Select the range **A7:G34**, on the **INSERT tab**, in the **Tables group**, click **Table**. In the **Create Table** dialog box, be sure that *My table has headers checkbox* is selected. Click **OK**, and then apply **Table Style Light 5**. Click anywhere in the table to deselect.

7 On the **FORMULAS tab**, in the **Defined Names** group, click **Name Manager**, and then compare your screen with Figure 5.45.

By defining the range as a table, Excel automatically assigns a name to the range. It is not required to format the range as a table. You can select the range and name it Table or Database; however, doing so enables you to use the Table Tools, such as formatting and inserting a Total row into the filtered data.

The defined table range will automatically display as the List range in the Advanced Filter dialog box.

FIGURE 5.45

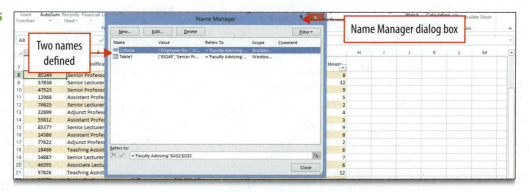

Two names defined

Name Manager dialog box

8 **Close** the **Name Manager** dialog box.

9 Scroll to view the top of the worksheet, click cell **D3**, type **>=70000** and then press Enter.

This action creates a criteria using a comparison operator to look for salary values that are greater than or equal to $70,000. Do not include a comma when you type this value, because the comma is a cell format, not part of the value.

10 Click cell **A7**. On the **DATA tab**, in the **Sort & Filter group**, click **Advanced**.

11 In the **Advanced Filter** dialog box, locate the **List range**, and verify the range indicates **$A$7:$G$34**, which is your Excel table. Be sure the **Criteria range** is identified as cells **$A$2:$G$3**. Compare your screen with Figure 5.46.

Here you define the database area—the List range—and the Criteria range where the results will display. Both ranges use an absolute reference. Under Action, you can choose to display the results in the table—in-place—or copy the results to another location.

FIGURE 5.46

Filter the list, in-place option button selected

List range defined as the Excel table you inserted

Criteria range defined

12 ▶ Click **OK** to have the filter results display in-place—in the table. Press Ctrl + Home and compare your screen with Figure 5.47.

Only the records for faculty members whose salary is $70,000 or more display. The row numbers for the records that meet the criteria display in blue. The Advanced command disables the AutoFilter command and removes the AutoFilter arrows from the column headings.

FIGURE 5.47

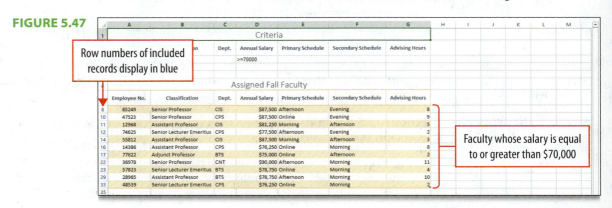

Row numbers of included records display in blue

Faculty whose salary is equal to or greater than $70,000

13 ▶ Click cell **B3**, type ***Professor** and then press Enter.

The asterisk (*) is a wildcard. Use a **_wildcard_** to search a field when you are uncertain of the exact value or you want to widen the search to include more records. The use of a wildcard enables you to include faculty whose classification ends with the word *Professor*. It directs Excel to find Professor and anything before it. The criterion in the Salary field still applies.

The use of two or more criteria on the same row is known as **_compound criteria_**—all conditions must be met for the records to be included in the results.

14 ▶ Click cell **A7**. On the **DATA tab**, in the **Sort & Filter group**, click **Advanced**. Verify that the database range is correctly identified in the **List range** box and that the **Criteria range** still indicates *$A$2:$G$3*. Click **OK**. Compare your screen with Figure 5.48.

Only the eight faculty members with a classification containing *Professor* and a salary of $70,000 or more display.

FIGURE 5.48

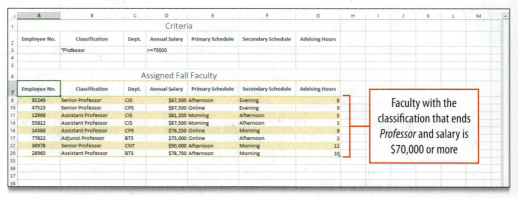

Faculty with the classification that ends *Professor* and salary is $70,000 or more

15 ▶ Using the techniques you just practiced, filter the data further by adding an additional criteria—faculty who are assigned 8 hours or more of advising. Compare your result with Figure 5.49.

Five faculty members meet all three of the criteria in the Criteria range.

FIGURE 5.49

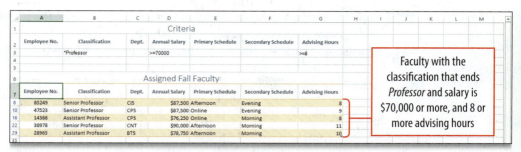

Faculty with the classification that ends *Professor* and salary is $70,000 or more, and 8 or more advising hours

16 ▶ Insert a footer in the **left section** that includes the file name, click outside the footer area, and then on the **PAGE LAYOUT tab**, set the **Orientation** to **Landscape**. On the status bar, click **Normal** ⊞. Press Ctrl + Home to move to cell **A1**.

17 ▶ Click the **FILE tab**, and then in the lower right portion of the screen, click **Show all properties**. In the **Tags** box, type **advanced filter, advising** and in the **Subject** box type your course name and section #. In the **Author** box, replace the existing text with your first and last name.

18 ▶ Display the **Print Preview**. Near the bottom of the window, click **Page Setup** to display the **Page Setup** dialog box. Click the **Margins tab**, center the worksheet horizontally, and then click **OK**. Redisplay the worksheet and make any necessary corrections or adjustments.

19 ▶ **Save** 🖫 your workbook. Hold this workbook until the end of this project, and then print or submit electronically as directed; there are no formulas in this worksheet. **Close** this workbook, but leave Excel open.

More Knowledge **Using Wildcards**

A wildcard can help you locate information when you are uncertain how the information might be displayed in your records. The placement of the asterisk in relationship to the known value determines the result. If it is placed first, the variable will be in the beginning of the string of characters. For example, in a list of names if you used *son as the criteria, it will look for any name that ends in son. The results might display Peterson, Michelson, and Samuelson. If the asterisk is at the end of the known value in the criteria, then the variable will be at the end. You can also include the asterisk wildcard at the beginning and at the end of a known value. You can also use an asterisk wildcard in the middle, so searching for m*t will result in both mat and moist.

A question mark (?) can also be used as part of your search criteria. Each question mark used in the criteria represents a single position or character that is unknown in a group of specified values. Searching for m?n would find, for example, min, men, and man; whereas searching for m??d would find, for example, mind, mend, mold.

Activity 5.20 | Extracting Filtered Rows

You can copy the results of a filter to another area of your worksheet instead of displaying a filtered list as you did in the previous activity. The location to which you copy the records is the ***Extract area***, and is commonly placed below the table of data. Using this technique you can *extract*—pull out—multiple sets of data for comparison purposes.

In this activity, you will extract data to compare how many faculty have a Morning-Evening schedule and how many have a Morning-Afternoon schedule.

1 ▶ From your student files, open **e05B_Fall_Faculty**. Display the **Save As** dialog box, navigate to your **Excel Chapter 5** folder, and then save the workbook as **Lastname_Firstname_5B_Fall_Faculty**

2 ▶ Verify that the first worksheet, **Schedule Comparison**, is the active sheet. **Copy** the range **A6:G7**, **Paste** it in cell **A1**, and then change the title in cell **A1** to **Criteria**

3 ▶ Select the range **A2:G3**, and then in the **Name Box**, type **Criteria** and then press Enter to name this range.

4 ▶ **Copy** the range **A1:G2**, scroll down to view **row 36**, point to cell **A36**, right-click, and then under **Paste Options**, click the first **Paste (P)** 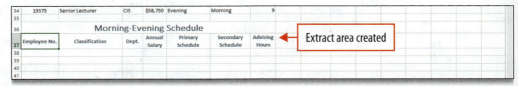 button. Click cell **A36**, change the title to **Morning-Evening Schedule** and then press Enter. Compare your screen with Figure 5.50.

FIGURE 5.50

5 ▶ Select the range **A37:G37** and then in the **Name Box**, name this range **Extract**

This action defines the Extract area so that the range will display automatically in the Copy to box of the Advanced Filter dialog box. Excel recognizes *Extract* as the location in which to place the results of an advanced filter.

6 ▶ Select the range **A7:G34** and then in the **Name Box**, name this range **Database**

Excel recognizes the name Criteria as a criteria range, the name Database as the range to be filtered, and the name Extract for the area where you want to paste the result.

7 ▶ At the top of your worksheet, in cell **E3**, type **Morning** In cell **F3**, type **Evening** and then press Enter.

When applied, the filter will display only those records where the Primary Schedule is Morning and the Secondary Schedule is Evening.

8 ▶ On the **DATA tab**, in the **Sort & Filter group**, click **Advanced**.

9 ▶ Under **Action**, click **Copy to another location**. Verify that in the **Copy to** box, the absolute reference to the Extract area—*$A$37:$G$37*—displays. Compare your screen with Figure 5.51.

FIGURE 5.51

10 ▶ Click **OK**, and then scroll to view the lower portion of your worksheet. Compare your screen with Figure 5.52.

Two records meet the criteria and are copied to the Extract area on your worksheet. When you use an Extract area in this manner, instead of reformatting the table to display the qualifying records, Excel places a copy of the qualifying records in the Extract area.

FIGURE 5.52

11 ▶ **Copy** the range **A36:G37**, and then **Paste** it in cell **A41**. In cell **A41**, change the word *Evening* to **Afternoon**

12 At the top of your worksheet, in cell **F3**, change the criteria to **Afternoon** Display the **Advanced Filter** dialog box, and then click **Copy to another location**.

13 In the **Copy to** box, click the **Collapse Dialog** button 📱, scroll down as necessary, and then select the range **A42:G42**. Click the **Expand Dialog** button 📱, and then click **OK**. Scroll to view the lower portion of the worksheet, and then compare your screen with Figure 5.53.

Three records meet the criteria and are copied to the Extract area on your worksheet.

FIGURE 5.53

Three records display in the Morning-Afternoon Extract area

14 Save 💾 and then leave this workbook open for the next activity.

Objective 7 | Subtotal, Outline, and Group a List of Data

Video E5-7

You can group and summarize a *list*—a series of rows that contains related data—by adding subtotals. The first step in adding subtotals is to sort the data by the field for which you want to create a subtotal.

Activity 5.21 | Subtotaling, Outlining, and Grouping a List of Data

In this activity, you will assist Dean Toomer in summarizing the faculty salaries by department.

1 In your **Lastname_Firstname_5B_Fall_Faculty** workbook, click the **Salaries by Department sheet tab**.

2 Select the range **A2:G29**. On the **DATA tab**, in the **Sort & Filter group**, click **Sort**. In the **Sort** dialog box, click the **Sort by arrow**, and then click **Dept.** Click **Add Level**, click the **Then by arrow**, and then click **Annual Salary**. Compare your **Sort** dialog box with Figure 5.54.

FIGURE 5.54

Sort by *Dept.* and then *Annual Salary*

Sort dialog box

3 Click **OK**. With the range still selected, on the **DATA tab**, in the **Outline group**, click **Subtotal**.

The *Subtotal command* totals several rows of related data together by automatically inserting subtotals and totals for the selected cells.

4 In the **Subtotal** dialog box, in the **At each change in** box, click the arrow to display the list, and then click **Dept**. In the **Use function** box, display the list and, if necessary, click **Sum**. In the **Add subtotal to** list, select the **Annual Salary** check box, and then scroll the list and *deselect* any other check boxes that are selected. Compare your screen with Figure 5.55.

These actions direct Excel to create a group for each change in value in the Dept. field. Excel will then use the Sum function to add a subtotal in the Annual Salary field. The check boxes at the bottom of the dialog box indicate how the subtotals will display.

FIGURE 5.55

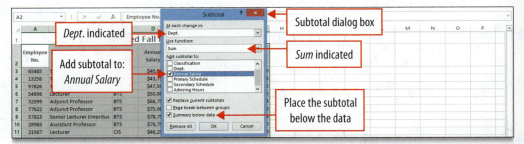

5 Click **OK**, press Ctrl + Home, scroll to view the lower portion of the data, **AutoFit column C**, and then compare your screen with Figure 5.56.

At the end of each Dept. group, inserted rows containing the subtotals for the salaries within each department display.

FIGURE 5.56

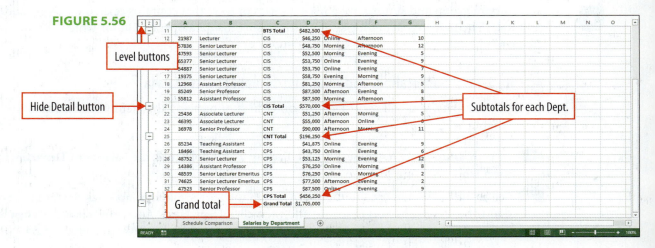

6 Along the left edge of your workbook, locate the outline.

When you add subtotals, Excel defines groups based on the rows used to calculate a subtotal. The groupings form an outline of your worksheet based on the criteria you indicated in the Subtotal dialog box, and the outline displays along the left side of your worksheet.

The outline bar along the left side of the worksheet enables you to show and hide levels of detail with a single mouse click. For example, you can show details with the totals, which is the default view. Or, you can show only the summary totals or only the grand total.

There are three types of controls in the outline. Hide Detail (–) collapses a group of cells, Show Detail (+) expands a collapsed group of cells, and the level buttons (1, 2, 3) can hide all levels of detail below the number clicked.

7 To the left of **row 25**, click **Hide Detail** (–) to collapse the detail for the **CNT** department.

Detail data refers to the subtotaled rows that are totaled and summarized. Detail data is typically adjacent to and either above or to the left of the summary data.

8 Select **rows 13:17**, and then on the **DATA tab**, in the **Outline group**, click **Group**. Compare your screen with Figure 5.57.

A fourth group is created and a bar spans the group.

FIGURE 5.57

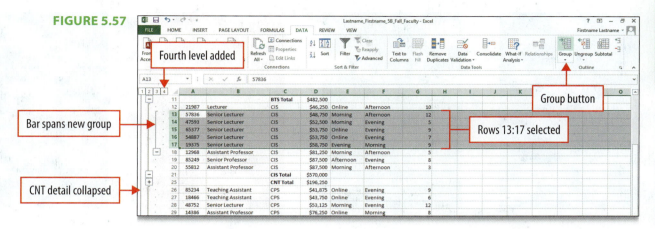

9 To the left of **row 18**, click **Hide Detail** (−) for the new group, and notice that the group is collapsed and a break in the row numbers indicates that some rows are hidden from view.

Hiding the detail data in this manner does not change the subtotal for the CIS group—it remains $570,000.

10 At the top of the outline area, click the **Level 2** button to hide all Level 3 and 4 details and display only the Level 2 summary information and the Level 1 Grand Total. Press Ctrl + Home and compare your screen with Figure 5.58.

FIGURE 5.58

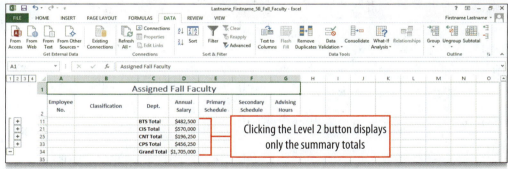

11 Group the two worksheets. Insert a footer that includes the file name in the **left section**, and in the **right section**, insert the **Sheet Name**. Click any cell to exit the footer area, and then on the status bar, click **Normal**. Press Ctrl + Home to move to cell **A1**. On the **PAGE LAYOUT tab**, set the **Width** to **1 page** and set the **Height** to **1 page.**

12 Click the **FILE tab** to display **Backstage** view. On the right, at the bottom of the **Properties** list, click **Show All Properties**. On the list of **Properties**, in the **Tags** box, type **faculty, schedule, salaries** In the **Subject** box, type your course name and section #. Under **Related People**, be sure that your name displays as the author. If necessary, right-click the author name, click Edit Property, type your name, click outside of the Edit person dialog box, and then click OK.

13 Display the **Print Preview**, redisplay the workbook, and then make any necessary corrections or adjustments. Ungroup the worksheets, and then **Save** your workbook. Along with your other two workbooks from this project, print or submit electronically as directed. **Close** Excel.

END | You have completed Project 5B

END OF CHAPTER

SUMMARY

You can navigate a large worksheet using the Freeze Panes, Go To, and Find commands. Control the screen display by hiding rows and columns and work with multiple workbooks using the Arrange All command.

A theme is a set of formatting characteristics, such as fonts, number formats, borders, and shading. Insert page breaks, repeat column or row titles, and use Landscape orientation for worksheets with many columns.

By default, Excel files are saved in the Excel Workbook file format with the .xlsx file name extension. Excel data can also be saved in other file formats such as HTML, CSV, PDF, and XPS.

Sorting organizes data in a particular order. Filtering displays only the rows that meet specific criteria. Sorting and filtering along with subtotaling, outlining, and grouping are used for data analysis.

GO! LEARN IT ONLINE

Review the concepts and key terms in this chapter by completing these online challenges, which you can find at **www.pearsonhighered.com/go**.

Matching and Multiple Choice:
Answer matching and multiple choice questions to test what you learned in this chapter. MyITLab®

Crossword Puzzle:
Spell out the words that match the numbered clues and put them in the puzzle squares.

Flipboard:
Flip through the definitions of the key terms in this chapter and match them with the correct term.

END OF CHAPTER

REVIEW AND ASSESSMENT GUIDE FOR EXCEL CHAPTER 5

Your instructor may assign one or more of these projects to help you review the chapter and assess your mastery and understanding of the chapter.

	Review and Assessment Guide for Excel Chapter 5		
Project	**Apply Skills from These Chapter Objectives**	**Project Type**	**Project Location**
5C	Objectives 1–4 from Project 5A	**5C Skills Review** A guided review of the skills from Project 5A.	On the following pages
5D	Objectives 5–7 from Project 5B	**5D Skills Review** A guided review of the skills from Project 5B.	On the following pages
5E	Objectives 1–4 from Project 5A	**5E Mastery (Grader Project)** A demonstration of your mastery of the skills in Project 5A with extensive decision making.	In MyITLab and on the following pages
5F	Objectives 5–7 from Project 5B	**5F Mastery (Grader Project)** A demonstration of your mastery of the skills in Project 5B with extensive decision making.	In MyITLab and on the following pages
5G	Combination of Objectives from Projects 5A and 5B	**5G Mastery (Grader Project)** A demonstration of your mastery of the skills in Projects 5A and 5B with extensive decision making.	In MyITLab and on the following pages
5H	Combination of Objectives from Projects 5A and 5B	**5H GO! Fix It** A demonstration of your mastery of the skills in Projects 5A and 5B by creating a correct result from a document that contains errors you must find.	Online
5I	Combination of Objectives from Projects 5A and 5B	**5I GO! Make It** A demonstration of your mastery of the skills in Projects 5A and 5B by creating a result from a supplied picture.	Online
5J	Combination of Objectives from Projects 5A and 5B	**5J GO! Solve It** A demonstration of your mastery of the skills in Projects 5A and 5B, your decision-making skills, and your critical thinking skills. A task-specific rubric helps you self-assess your result.	Online
5K	Combination of Objectives from Projects 5A and 5B	**5K GO! Solve It** A demonstration of your mastery of the skills in Projects 5A and 5B, your decision-making skills, and your critical thinking skills. A task-specific rubric helps you self-assess your result.	On the following pages
5L	Combination of Objectives from Projects 5A and 5B	**5L GO! Think** A demonstration of your understanding of the chapter concepts applied in a manner that you would outside of college. An analytic rubric helps you and your instructor grade the quality of your work by comparing it to the work an expert in the discipline would create.	On the following pages
5M	Combination of Objectives from Projects 5A and 5B	**5M GO! Think** A demonstration of your understanding of the chapter concepts applied in a manner that you would outside of college. An analytic rubric helps you and your instructor grade the quality of your work by comparing it to the work an expert in the discipline would create.	Online
5N	Combination of Objectives from Projects 5A and 5B	**5N You and GO!** A demonstration of your understanding of the chapter concepts applied in a manner that you would in a personal situation. An analytic rubric helps you and your instructor grade the quality of your work.	Online

GLOSSARY

GLOSSARY OF CHAPTER KEY TERMS

Additive The term that describes the behavior of a filter when each additional filter that you apply is based on the current filter, and that further reduces the number of records displayed.

Advanced Filter A filter that can specify three or more criteria for a particular column, apply complex criteria to two or more columns, or specify computed criteria.

And comparison operator The comparison operator that requires each and every one of the comparison criteria to be true.

Arrange All The command that tiles all open program windows on the screen.

Ascending The term that refers to the arrangement of text that is sorted alphabetically from A to Z, numbers sorted from lowest to highest, or dates and times sorted from earliest to latest.

AutoFilter menu A drop-down menu from which you can filter a column by a list of values, by a format, or by criteria.

Cell style A defined set of formatting characteristics, such as font, font size, font color, cell borders, and cell shading.

Comma delimited file A file type that saves the contents of the cells by placing commas between them and an end-of-paragraph mark at the end of each row; also referred to as a CSV (comma separated values) file.

Comparison operators Symbols that evaluate each value to determine if it is the same (=), greater than (>), less than (<), or in between a range of values as specified by the criteria.

Compound criteria The use of two or more criteria on the same row—all conditions must be met for the records to be included in the results.

Compound filter A filter that uses more than one condition—and one that uses comparison operators.

Criteria Conditions that you specify in a logical function or filter.

Criteria range An area on your worksheet where you define the criteria for the filter, and that indicates how the displayed records are filtered.

CSV (comma separated values) file A file type in which the cells in each

row are separated by commas and an end-of-paragraph mark at the end of each row; also referred to as a comma delimited file.

Custom Filter A filter with which you can apply complex criteria to a single column.

Custom list A sort order that you can define.

Database An organized collection of facts related to a specific topic.

Descending The term that refers to the arrangement of text that is sorted alphabetically from Z to A, numbers sorted from highest to lowest, or dates and times sorted from latest to earliest.

Detail data The subtotaled rows that are totaled and summarized; typically adjacent to and either above or to the left of the summary data.

Extract The process of pulling out multiple sets of data for comparison purposes.

Extract area The location to which you copy records when extracting filtered rows.

Field A specific type of data such as name, employee number, or social security number that is stored in columns.

Filtering A process in which only the rows that meet the criteria display; rows that do not meet the criteria are hidden.

Find A command that finds and selects specific text or formatting.

Freeze Panes A command that enables you to select one or more rows or columns and freeze (lock) them into place so that they remain on the screen while you scroll; the locked rows and columns become separate panes.

Go To A command that moves to a specific cell or range of cells that you specify.

Go To Special A command that moves to cells that have special characteristics, for example, to cells that are blank or to cells that contain constants, as opposed to formulas.

HTML (Hypertext Markup Language) A language web browsers can interpret.

Hyperlink Text or graphics that, when clicked, take you to another location

in the worksheet, to another file, or to a webpage on the Internet or on your organization's intranet.

List A series of rows that contains related data that you can group by adding subtotals.

Major sort A term sometimes used to refer to the first sort level in the Sort dialog box.

Or comparison operator The comparison operator that requires only one of the two comparison criteria that you specify to be true.

Pane A portion of a worksheet window bounded by and separated from other portions by vertical and horizontal bars.

PDF (Portable Document Format) A file format developed by Adobe Systems that creates a representation of electronic paper that displays your data on the screen as it would look when printed, but that cannot be easily changed.

Query A process of restricting records through the use of criteria conditions that will display records that will answer a question about the data.

Record All the categories of data pertaining to one person, place, thing, event, or idea.

Scaling The group of commands by which you can reduce the horizontal and vertical size of the printed data by a percentage or by the number of pages that you specify.

Sort The process of arranging data in a specific order.

Sort dialog box A dialog box in which you can sort data based on several criteria at once, and that enables a sort by more than one column or row.

Split The command that enables you to view separate parts of the same worksheet on your screen; splits the window into multiple resizable panes to view distant parts of the worksheet at one time.

Subtotal command The command that totals several rows of related data together by automatically inserting subtotals and totals for the selected cells.

Tab delimited text file A file type in which cells are separated by tabs; this type of file can be readily exchanged with various database programs.

Theme A predesigned set of colors, fonts, lines, and fill effects that look good together and that can be applied to your entire document or to specific items.

Wildcard A character, for example the asterisk or question mark, used to search a field when you are uncertain of the exact value or when you want to widen the search to include more records.

.xlsx file name extension The default file format used by Excel 2013 to save an Excel workbook.

XPS (XML Paper Specification) A file type, developed by Microsoft, which creates a representation of electronic paper that displays your data on the screen as it would look when printed.

CHAPTER REVIEW

Apply 5A skills from these Objectives:

1 Navigate and Manage Large Worksheets

2 Enhance Worksheets with Themes and Styles

3 Format a Worksheet to Share with Others

4 Save Excel Data in Other File Formats

In the following Skills Review, you will assist Susanne Black, Program Chair for Science, in formatting and navigating a large worksheet that lists the class schedule for the Science departments at Laurel College. You will also save Excel data in other file formats. Your completed workbooks will look similar to Figure 5.59.

PROJECT FILES

For Project 5C, you will need the following files:

e05C_Science_Faculty

e05C_Science_Requests

e05C_Science_Schedule

You will save your workbooks as:

Lastname_Firstname_5C_Science_CSV

Lastname_Firstname_5C_Science_Faculty

Lastname_Firstname_5C_Science_Schedule

Lastname_Firstname_5C_Science_Webpage

PROJECT RESULTS

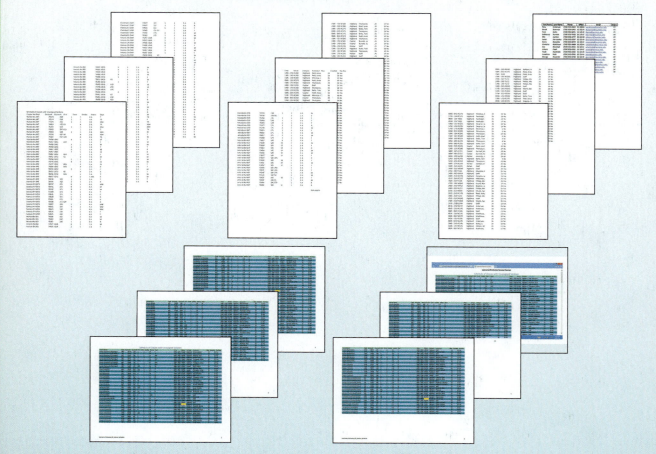

FIGURE 5.59

(Project 5C Science Schedule continues on the next page)

CHAPTER REVIEW

1 Start Excel. From your student files, open the file **e05C_Science_Schedule**. Display the **Save As** dialog box, navigate to your **Excel Chapter 5** folder, and then **Save** the workbook as **Lastname_Firstname_5C_Science_Schedule**

a. On the **HOME tab**, in the **Editing group**, click **Find & Select**, and then click **Go To Special**. In the first column, click **Blanks**, and then click **OK** to select all blank cells in the worksheet's active area. Point to the selected cell **K31** and right-click. On the mini toolbar, click the **Fill Color button arrow**, and then under **Standard Colors**, click the fourth color—**Yellow**—to fill all the selected blank cells. These cells still require Room assignments.

b. Press Ctrl + Home. From the column heading area, select **columns E:H**. Right-click over the selected area, and then click **Hide**.

c. On the **HOME tab**, in the **Editing group**, click **Find & Select**, and then click **Go To**. In the **Go To** dialog box, in the **Reference** box, type **m172** and then click **OK**. With cell **M172** active, on the **FORMULAS tab**, in the **Function Library** group, click **More Functions**, point to **Statistical**, and then click **COUNTIF**. As the **Range**, type **m2:m170** and as the **Criteria**, type **Staff** Click **OK**. Your result is *27*, indicating that 27 courses still indicate *Staff* and need an instructor assigned. In cell **I172**, type **Still need instructor assigned** and press Enter. Press Ctrl + Home and click **Save**.

2 From your student files, open **e05C_Science_Requests**. On the **VIEW tab**, in the **Window group**, click **Switch Windows**, and then at the bottom of the list, click your **Lastname_Firstname_5C_Science_Schedule** file to make it the active worksheet. On the **VIEW tab**, in the **Window group**, click **Arrange All**. Click **Horizontal**, and then click **OK**. If necessary, click the title bar of your Lastname_Firstname_5C_Science_Schedule worksheet to make it the active worksheet. Press Ctrl + End to move to cell **P172**.

a. Click cell **A172**. In the **Window group**, click **Split**. Above the split bar, click any cell in **column C**. Press Ctrl + F to display the **Find and Replace** dialog box. Locate the first request in the **e05C_Science_Requests** worksheet, which is from *Eric Marshall* to teach *Survey of Astronomy Section # 76822*. In the

Find what box, type **76822** so that you can locate the course in the worksheet.

b. Click **Find Next**. Drag the title bar of the dialog box into the upper right area of your screen so that you can see the **Name Box**, which indicates *C38*. In your **Lastname_Firstname_5C_Science_Schedule** worksheet, click in cell **M38**, type **Marshall, Eric** to delete *Staff* and assign the class to Mr. Marshall. Press Enter.

c. Continue to use the **Find and Replace** dialog box to locate the remaining three **Section #s** listed in the **e05C_Science_Requests** worksheet, and enter the appropriate instructor name for each class in **column M** of your **Lastname_Firstname_5C_Science_Schedule** worksheet. **Close** the **Find and Replace** dialog box. In cell **M172**, notice that *23* classes remain unassigned.

d. Click any cell in the **e05C_Science_Requests** worksheet, and then on this worksheet's title bar, click **Close**. Then, on the title bar of your **Lastname_Firstname_5C_Science_Schedule** worksheet, click **Maximize** to restore the size of the worksheet to its full size. On the **VIEW tab**, in the **Window group**, click **Split** to remove the split.

e. From the **column heading area**, select **columns D:I**. Right-click over the selected area, and then click **Unhide**. Press Ctrl + Home, and then **Save** your workbook.

3 Point to the **row 1 heading**, right-click, and then click **Insert**. In cell A1, type **Schedule of Classes with Unassigned Sections Merge & Center** this title across the range A1:P1, and then apply the **Title** cell style.

a. On the **PAGE LAYOUT tab**, in the **Themes group**, click **Themes**, and then, click the **Slice** theme. In the **Themes group**, click **Fonts**. Scroll to the top and then click the **Office** fonts.

b. On the **HOME tab**, in the **Styles group**, click **Format as Table**. At the bottom, click **New Table Style**. In the **New Table Style** dialog box, in the **Name** box, replace the existing text by typing **Science Schedule** In the list under **Table Element**, click **First Row Stripe**, and then click **Format**. In the **Format Cells** dialog box, click the **Fill tab**. In the fifth column of colors, click the second color. In the lower right corner, click **OK**.

(Project 5C Science Schedule continues on the next page)

CHAPTER REVIEW

c. In the list of table elements, click **Second Row Stripe**, click **Format**, and then in the third column of colors, click the sixth color. Click **OK**. In the list of table elements, click **Header Row**, click **Format**, and then in the seventh column, click the fourth color. Click **OK**, in the lower left corner of the dialog box, click to select the check box **Set as default table style for this document**, and then click **OK**.

d. Select the range **A2:P171**, and then in the **Styles group**, click **Format as Table**. At the top of the gallery, under **Custom**, locate and then click your custom **Science Schedule** table style. In the **Format As Table** dialog box, click **OK**. Then, because you do not need to filter the table, in the **Tools group**, click **Convert to Range**, and then click **Yes**. Press Ctrl + Home to deselect and move to cell **A1**. Click **Save**.

4 Select **columns A:P**, in the **Cells group**, click **Format**, and then click **AutoFit Column Width**. On the **PAGE LAYOUT tab**, in the **Page Setup group**, set the **Orientation** to **Landscape**. Then, in the **Scale to Fit group**, click the **Width arrow**, and then click **1 page.**

a. From the **INSERT tab**, insert a footer in the **left section** that includes the file name. Click in the right section, and then in the **Header & Footer Elements group**, click **Page Number**. Click in a cell just above the footer to exit the footer area.

b. On the **VIEW tab**, in the **Workbook Views group**, click **Page Break Preview**, and close the dialog box if necessary. Point to the horizontal page break line between **Page 1** and **Page 2**, and then drag the line up between **row 42** and **row 43**. Position the break between **Page 2** and **Page 3** between **row 74** and **row 75**. Position the break between **Page 3** and **Page 4** between **row 116** and **row 117**. Position the break between **Page 4** and **Page 5** between **row 152** and **row 153**.

c. On the **VIEW tab**, in the **Workbook Views group**, click **Normal** to redisplay the worksheet in **Normal** view, and then press Ctrl + Home.

d. Display the **Print Preview**, scroll through the pages, and notice that the column titles display only on the first page. Redisplay the worksheet. Click the **PAGE LAYOUT tab**, in the **Page Setup group**, click **Print Titles** to display the **Sheet tab** of the **Page Setup** dialog box.

e. Under **Print titles**, click in the **Rows to repeat at top** box, and then in the worksheet, select **row 2**. Click **OK**. Click **Save**.

5 From **Backstage** view, display the **Open** dialog box, and then from your student files, open the file **e05C_Science_Faculty**. Display the **Save As** dialog box, navigate to your **Excel Chapter 5** folder, and then **Save** the file as **Lastname_Firstname_5C_Science_Faculty** Insert a footer in the **left section** with the file name, click outside the footer area, press Ctrl + Home and return to **Normal** view. Click **Save**, and then **Close** this workbook to redisplay your **Lastname_Firstname_5C_Science_Schedule** workbook.

a. Click cell **M2**. On the **INSERT tab**, in the **Links group**, click **Hyperlink**. Under **Link to**, click **Existing File or Web Page**. Click the **Look in arrow**, navigate to your **Excel Chapter 5** folder, and then select your **Lastname_Firstname_5C_Science_Faculty** workbook. Click **OK**.

b. Point to cell **M2** to display the 🖑 pointer, and then click to confirm that the link opens the workbook containing the contact information. **Close** the workbook with the faculty contacts.

c. Point to cell **M2**, right-click, and then click **Edit Hyperlink**. In the upper right corner of the **Insert Hyperlink** dialog box, click **ScreenTip**. In the **ScreenTip text** box, type **Click here for contact information** Click **OK** two times. Point to cell **M2** and confirm that your **ScreenTip** displays.

d. Display the **document properties** and under **Related People**, be sure that your name displays as the author. If necessary, right-click the author name, click Edit Property, and then type your name. In the **Subject** box, type your course name and section number, and in the **Tags** box, type **science schedule** Click **Save**. Leave the workbook open.

6 Press F12 to display the **Save As** dialog box and navigate to your **Chapter 5** folder. In the lower portion, click the **Save as type arrow**, and then click **Web Page**.

a. Click **Change Title**. In the **Enter Text** dialog box, in the **Page title** box, using your own name, type **Lastname Firstname Science Courses** Click **OK**, and notice that in the **Page title** box, your typed text displays. In the **Save As** dialog box, click **Publish**.

(Project 5C Science Schedule continues on the next page)

CHAPTER REVIEW

b. In the **Publish as Web Page** dialog box, click the **Choose arrow**, and then click **Items on Science Classes**—recall that the worksheet name is *Science Classes*. In the lower left corner, if necessary, click to select (place a check mark in) the **Open published web page in browser** check box.

c. Click **Browse** to display the **Publish As** dialog box. If necessary, navigate to your **Excel Chapter 5** folder. In the **File name** box, type **Lastname_Firstname_5C_Science_Webpage** Click **OK**, and then in the **Publish as Web Page** dialog box, click **Publish**.

d. If you are instructed to print your webpage on paper, consult the instructions to print from your specific browser software. On the browser title bar, click **Close**. Leave your **Lastname_Firstname_5C_Science_Schedule** workbook open for the next step.

e. Display the **Save As** dialog box, be sure you are saving in your **Excel Chapter 5** folder, set the **Save as type** to **CSV (Comma delimited)**, and as the **File name**, type **Lastname_Firstname_5C_Science_CSV** Click **Save**, and then click **Yes**.

f. **Close** your **Lastname_Firstname_5C_Science_CSV** file, click **Save**, and then click **Yes**. **Close** Excel. As directed by your instructor, submit the four files that comprise the results of this project.

END | You have completed Project 5C

CHAPTER REVIEW

Apply 5B skills from these Objectives:

5 Use Advanced Sort Techniques

6 Use Custom and Advanced Filters

7 Subtotal, Outline, and Group a List of Data

Skills Review Project 5D Spring Sections

In the following Skills Review, you will use advanced table features to provide Dr. Marshall Eaton, the Dean of the Arts Division, information about the Spring course sections and assigned faculty in the Division. Your completed worksheets will look similar to Figure 5.60.

PROJECT FILES

For Project 5D, you will need the following files:

e05D_Spring_Faculty

e05D_Spring_Sections

You will save your workbooks as:

Lastname_Firstname_5D_Spring_Faculty

Lastname_Firstname_5D_Spring_Sections

PROJECT RESULTS

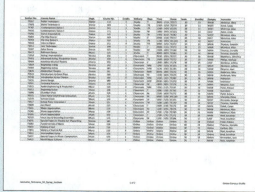

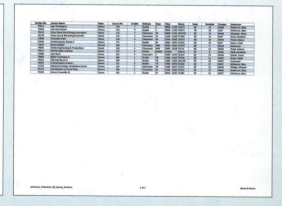

FIGURE 5.60

(Project 5D Spring Sections continues on the next page)

CHAPTER REVIEW

1 Start Excel. From your student files, open the file **e05D_Spring_Sections**, and then **Save** the file in your **Excel Chapter 5** folder as **Lastname_Firstname_5D_Spring_Sections** Be sure the first worksheet, **Online-Campus-Studio** displays.

a. On the **DATA tab**, in the **Sort & Filter group**, click **Sort**. In the **Sort** dialog box, under **Column**, click the **Sort by arrow**, and then click **Delivery**. Under **Sort On**, click the **arrow**, and then click **Values**. Under **Order**, click the **Order arrow** for this sort level, and then click **Custom List**. In the dialog box, under **Custom lists**, be sure **NEW LIST** is selected. Then, under **List entries**, click in the empty box and type **Studio** Press Enter, type **Classroom** Press Enter, and then type **Online**

b. In the **Custom Lists** dialog box, click **Add**, and then click **OK**. If necessary, in the Sort dialog box, click the Order arrow, and then click your Studio, Classroom, Online custom list so that it displays in the Order box. Click **Add Level**, and then as the second level sort, click **Dept**. Click **Add Level** again, and as the third level sort, click **Course Name**. Click **OK**.

2 Click the **Music & Dance sheet tab** to display the *second* worksheet. In cell **C1**, click the **Dept. filter arrow**. Click the **(Select All)** check box to clear all the check boxes, and then select the **Drama** and the **Music** check boxes. Click **OK**.

a. In cell **E1**, click the **Credits filter arrow**, and then filter the list further by selecting **3**. In cell **F1**, click the **Delivery filter arrow**, and filter the list further by **Online**. The status bar information reveals that *4* of the *39* course sections that are either in the Music or Drama departments are three-credit courses offered online.

b. On the **DATA tab**, in the **Sort & Filter group**, **Clear** all filters. In cell **K1**, click the **Enrolled filter arrow**, point to **Number Filters**, and then click **Less Than Or Equal To**. In the first box, be sure that *is less than or equal to* displays, and then in the second box type **15** Click **OK** to display *16* records.

c. Right-click over either of the two sheet tabs, and then click **Select All Sheets**. With the sheets grouped, insert a footer in the **left section** that includes the file name. Click in the **center section**

of the footer, and then on the **DESIGN tab**, in the **Header & Footer Elements group**, click **Page Number**. Press Spacebar one time, type **of** and press Spacebar again, and then click **Number of Pages**. Click in the **right section** of the footer, and then on the **DESIGN tab**, in the **Header & Footer Elements group**, click **Sheet Name**.

d. Click a cell outside of the footer, and then on the **PAGE LAYOUT tab**, set the **Orientation** to **Landscape**, and set the **Width** to **1 page**. Click **Normal**, and then move to cell **A1**.

e. Display the **document properties** and under **Related People**, be sure that your name displays as the author. If necessary, right-click the author name, click Edit Property, and then type your name. In the **Subject** box, type your course name and section #, and in the **Tags** box, type **sort, filter, sections** Display **Print Preview**. Make any necessary corrections or adjustments.

f. Ungroup the worksheets and **Save** your workbook. Hold this workbook until the end of this project, and then print or submit the two worksheets in this workbook electronically as directed by your instructor. **Close** this workbook, but leave Excel open.

3 From your student files, open **e05D_Spring_Faculty**. Display the **Save As** dialog box, navigate to your **Excel Chapter 5** folder, and then **Save** the workbook as **Lastname_Firstname_5D_Spring_Faculty** Be sure the **Schedule Comparison** worksheet is active. **Copy** the range **A6:G7**, **Paste** it in cell **A1**, and then change the title in cell **A1** to **Criteria**

a. Select the range **A2:G3**, and then in the **Name Box**, name this range **Criteria** Copy the range **A1:G2**, scroll down to view **row 34**, point to cell **A34**, right-click, and then click **Paste**. Click cell **A34**, and then change the title to **Morning-Evening Schedule** and then press Enter. Select the range **A35:G35** and then in the **Name Box**, name this range **Extract** Select the range **A7:G32** and then in the **Name Box**, name this range **Database**

b. At the top of your worksheet, in cell **E3**, type **Morning** and in cell **F3**, type **Evening** On the **DATA tab**, in the **Sort & Filter group**, click **Advanced**. Under **Action**, click **Copy to another location**. Verify that in the **Copy to** box—*$A$35:$G$35*—displays.

(Project 5D Spring Sections continues on the next page)

CHAPTER REVIEW

Click **OK**, and then scroll to view the lower portion of your worksheet. Two records meet the criteria.

c. Copy the range **A34:G35**, and then **Paste** it in cell **A39**. In cell **A39**, change the word *Evening* to **Afternoon** In cell **F3**, change the criteria to **Afternoon** Display the **Advanced Filter** dialog box, and then click **Copy to another location**.

d. In the **Copy to** box, click the **Collapse Dialog** button, and then select the range **A40:G40**. Click the **Expand Dialog** button and then click **OK**. *Three* records meet the criteria and are copied to the Extract area on your worksheet. **Save** the workbook.

4 Display the **Salaries by Department** worksheet. Select the range **A2:G30**. On the **DATA tab**, in the **Sort & Filter group**, click **Sort**. In the **Sort** dialog box, sort by the **Dept.** column, and then by the **Annual Salary** column. Click **OK**.

a. With the range still selected, on the **DATA tab**, in the **Outline group**, click **Subtotal**. In the **Subtotal** dialog box, in the **At each change in** box, display the list, and then click **Dept**. In the **Use function** box, display the list and click **Sum**. In the **Add subtotal to** list, select the **Annual Salary** check box, and then deselect any other check boxes. Click **OK**.

b. Click any cell to deselect, and then along the left edge of your workbook, locate the outline. To the left of **row 29**, click the **Hide Detail** button to collapse the detail for the **Music** department.

c. Select **rows 17:19**, and then on the **DATA tab**, in the **Outline group**, click **Group**. To the left of **row 20**, click the **Hide Detail** button. At the top of the outline area, click the **Level 2** button to hide all Level 3 and 4 details, and display only the Level 2 summary information, and the Level 1 Grand Total.

d. Group the two worksheets. Insert a footer in the **left section** that includes the file name, and in the **right section**, insert the **Sheet Name**. Click any cell to exit the footer area. On the **PAGE LAYOUT Tab**, set the **Width** to **1 page** and set the **Height** to **1 page**—this will scale each worksheet to fit on a single page. Click **Normal** and then move to cell **A1**.

e. Display the **document properties** and under **Related People**, be sure that your name displays as the author. If necessary, right-click the author name, click Edit Property, and then type your name. In the **Subject** box, type your course name and section #, and in the **Tags** box, type **faculty, schedule, salaries** Display the **Print Preview**. Make any necessary corrections or adjustments.

f. Ungroup the worksheets and **Save** your workbook, and then close it. Along with your other workbook from this project, print or submit electronically as directed. If required, print or create an electronic version of your worksheets with formulas displayed, using the instructions in Project 1A. **Close** Excel.

> **END | You have completed Project 5D**

CONTENT-BASED ASSESSMENTS

Mastering Excel   Project 5E Sports Schedule

In the following Mastering Excel project, you will assist Damian Howard, Athletic Director at Laurel College, in formatting and navigating a large worksheet that lists the sports events schedule for spring sports. You will also save Excel data in other file formats. Your completed workbooks will look similar to Figure 5.61.

Apply 5A skills from these Objectives:

1 Navigate and Manage Large Worksheets

2 Enhance Worksheets with Themes and Styles

3 Format a Worksheet to Share with Others

4 Save Excel Data in Other File Formats

PROJECT FILES

For Project 5E, you will need the following files:

e05E_Sports_Coaches

e05E_Referee_Requests

e05E_Sports_Schedule

You will save your workbooks as:

Lastname_Firstname_5E_Sports_Coaches

Lastname_Firstname_5E_Sports_PDF

Lastname_Firstname_5E_Sports_Schedule

Lastname_Firstname_5E_Sports_Webpage

PROJECT RESULTS

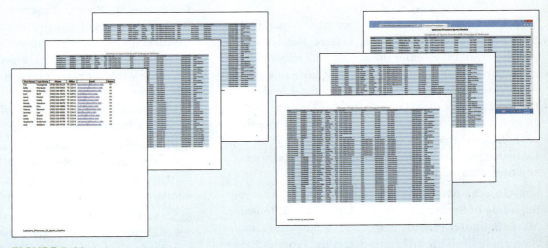

FIGURE 5.61

(Project 5E Sports Schedule continues on the next page)

CONTENT-BASED ASSESSMENTS

1 Start Excel. Open the file **e05E_Sports_Schedule** and **Save** it in your **Excel Chapter 5** folder as **Lastname_Firstname_5E_Sports_Schedule** Go to cell **M82**, and then insert the **COUNTIF** function. Set the **Range** as **m2:m80** and the **Criteria** as **Staff** resulting in *23* sporting events that still require a Referee assignment. In cell **K82**, type **Events with Unassigned Referees** and press Ctrl + Home. Open the file **e05E_Referee_Requests**. Switch windows, and then click your **Lastname_Firstname_5E_Sports_Schedule** workbook. **Arrange All** so the files are **Horizontal** with your **Lastname_Firstname_5E_Sports_Schedule** as the active worksheet in the top window.

2 Go to cell **A82**, **Split** the window horizontally, and then click in any cell above the split in **column C**. Display the **Find and Replace** dialog box. Locate the first request in the **e05E_Referee_Requests** worksheet. Use **Find** to locate **76243** and then type **Danny Litowitz** in the appropriate cell to assign him as the *Referee*.

3 Use the **Find** command to locate the remaining three **Event #s** listed in the **e05E_Referee_Requests** worksheet, and then enter the appropriate referee for each sports event in **column M** of your **Lastname_Firstname_5E_Sports_Schedule** worksheet. **Close** the **Find and Replace** dialog box. In cell **M82**, notice that *19* sports events still need a referee assigned. **Close** the **e05E_Referee_Requests** workbook. **Maximize** your **Lastname_Firstname_5E_Sports_Schedule** worksheet, and then remove the **Split**.

4 Insert a new blank row at row 1. In cell **A1**, type **Schedule of Sports Events with Unassigned Referees Merge & Center** the title across the range **A1:M1**, and then apply the **Title** cell style. Select the range **A2:M81** and **Format as Table**, and then create a **New Table Style** named **Sports Schedule** Format the **First Row Stripe** from the **Fill tab** and in the fifth column of colors, click the second color. For the **Second Row Stripe**, in the fifth column of colors, click the third color. For the **Header Row**, in the fourth column of colors click the

fourth color. Select the check box **Set as default table style for this document**. Apply the **Custom** table style, *Sports Schedule* to the table. Convert the table to a Range. Press Ctrl + Home to deselect the table and move to cell **A1**.

5 AutoFit columns A:M. Set the **Orientation** to **Landscape**, set the **Width** to **1 page**, and **Center** the worksheets **Horizontally**. Insert a footer in the **left section** that includes the file name, and in the **right section**, insert a page number. Apply **Page Break Preview**, and then drag the line to break **Page 1** after **row 49**— to end the page with *TENNIS* and begin **Page 2** with *TRACK*. Return to **Normal** view. Set **Print Titles** to repeat **row 2** at the top of each page. Display **Print Preview** and examine the pages. Redisplay the workbook, make any necessary adjustments, and then **Save**. Leave this workbook open.

6 Open the file **e05E_Sports_Coaches** and **Save** it in your **Excel Chapter 5** folder as **Lastname_Firstname_5E_Sports_Coaches** Insert a footer in the **left section** with the file name, and then return to **Normal** view. **Save** and then **Close** this workbook to redisplay your **Lastname_Firstname_5E_Sports_Schedule** workbook. In cell **J2**, **Insert** a **Hyperlink** to link to your **Lastname_Firstname_5E_Sports_Coaches** workbook and display the **ScreenTip Click here for contact information**

7 Display the **document properties** and be sure that your name displays as the author. In the **Subject** box, type your course name and section #, and in the **Tags** box, type **sports schedule**

8 Save your **Lastname_Firstname_5E_Sports_Schedule** workbook as a **Web Page** with the name **Lastname_Firstname_5E_Sports_Webpage** Change the **Page title** to **Lastname Firstname Sports Schedule** and then **Publish**. If you are instructed to print your webpage on paper, consult the instructions to print from your specific browser software. **Close** your browser. Leave your **Lastname_Firstname_5E_Sports_Schedule** workbook open.

(Project 5E Sports Schedule continues on the next page)

CONTENT-BASED ASSESSMENTS

9 ▶ Display the **Save As** dialog box and save your **Lastname_Firstname_5E_Sports_Schedule** workbook as a **PDF**, with the name **Lastname_Firstname_5E_Sports_PDF Close** all files. As directed by your instructor, print or submit electronically the four files that comprise the results of this project—two Excel files, a PDF file, and an HTML file.

END | You have completed Project 5E

CONTENT-BASED ASSESSMENTS

Mastering Excel   Project 5F Vocational Programs

In the following Mastering Excel project, you will edit a worksheet for Michael Schaeffler, Vice President of Instruction, with data that has been sorted, filtered, and grouped that analyzes vocational programs at Laurel College. The worksheets of your workbook will look similar to Figure 5.62.

Apply 5B skills from these Objectives:

5 Use Advanced Sort Techniques

6 Use Custom and Advanced Filters

7 Subtotal, Outline, and Group a List of Data

PROJECT FILES

For Project 5F, you will need the following file:

e05F_Vocational_Programs

You will save your workbook as:

Lastname_Firstname_5F_Vocational_Programs

PROJECT RESULTS

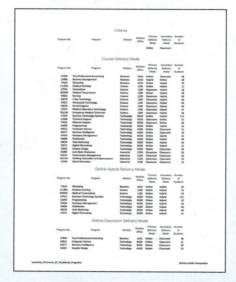

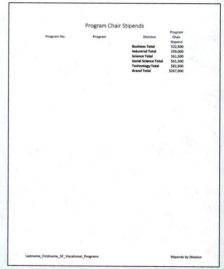

FIGURE 5.62

(Project 5F Vocational Programs continues on the next page)

CONTENT-BASED ASSESSMENTS

1 Start Excel. **Open** the file **e05F_Vocational_Programs**. **Save** the file in your **Excel Chapter 5** folder as **Lastname_Firstname_5F_Vocational_Programs** Display the *first* worksheet, **Main-East-West**. Select the range **A1:J40**, insert a table. Apply **Table Style Light 16**. Click anywhere to deselect, on the **DATA tab**, from the **Sort & Filter group**, display the **Sort** dialog box.

For the first sort level, sort by **Campus**, sort on **Values**, and then under **Order**, create a **Custom List: Main, East, West** Add a second level, sort by **Division** in alphabetical order on **Values**. Add a third level, sort by **Program Name** in alphabetical order on **Values**.

2 Convert the data to a range. Display the *second* worksheet, **Delivery Mode Comparison**. **Copy** the range **A6:G7**. **Paste** it in cell **A1**, and then change the title in cell **A1** to **Criteria** In the **Name Box**, name the range **A2:G3 Criteria**

Copy the range **A1:G2**, and **Paste** it into cell **A36**. Change the title in cell **A36** to **Online-Hybrid Delivery Mode** Select the range **A37:G37** and then in the **Name Box**, name this range **Extract** Select the range **A7:G34** and then in the **Name Box**, name this range **Database**

3 At the top of your worksheet, in cell **E3**, type **Online** and in cell **F3**, type **Hybrid** On the **DATA tab**, in the **Sort & Filter group**, click **Advanced**. Under **Action**, click **Copy to another location**. Verify that in the **Copy to** box, the absolute reference to the Extract area—**$A$37:$G$37**—displays. **Copy** the range **A36:G37**, and then **Paste** it in cell **A48**. In cell **A48** change the

word *Hybrid* to **Classroom** In cell **F3**, change the criteria to **Classroom**

Display the **Advanced Filter** dialog box, and then click **Copy to another location**. In the **Copy to** box, change the range to **A49:G49**.

4 Display the *third* worksheet—**Stipends by Division**. Select the range **A2:D41**. Display the **Sort** dialog box, **Sort** first by the **Division**, then by the **Program Chair Stipend**. **Subtotal** at each change in **Division**, select the **Sum** function, add the subtotal to the **Program Chair Stipend**. **Group** the data so each **Division** is collapsed and a break in the row numbers indicates that some rows are hidden from view. **AutoFit columns C:D** to display the **Grand Total**.

5 Select all three worksheets. Insert a footer in the **left section** that includes the file name, and in the **right section**, insert the **Sheet Name**. Return to **Normal** view, and move to cell **A1**. Set the **Width** to **1 page** and set the **Height** to **1 page**, and **Center** the worksheets **Horizontally**.

6 Display the **document properties** and be sure that your name displays as the author. In the **Subject** box, type your course name and section number, and in the **Tags** box, type **vocational programs** Examine the **Print Preview**, make any necessary corrections or adjustments, and then **Save** your workbook. Print or submit your workbook electronically as directed. If required, print or create an electronic version of your worksheets with formulas displayed, using the instructions in Project 1A. **Close** all files and **Close** Excel.

END | You have completed Project 5F

CONTENT-BASED ASSESSMENTS

Mastering Excel   Project 5G Sports Programs

Apply **5A** and **5B** skills from these Objectives:

1 Navigate and Manage Large Worksheets

2 Enhance Worksheets with Themes and Styles

3 Format a Worksheet to Share with Others

4 Save Excel Data in Other File Formats

5 Use Advanced Sort Techniques

6 Use Custom and Advanced Filters

7 Subtotal, Outline, and Group a List of Data

In the following Mastering Excel project, you will create a worksheet for Sandy Chase, Assistant Director of Athletics, with data that has been sorted, filtered, and grouped and that analyzes sports programs. Assistant Director Chase will use this information to make decisions for these sports programs for the upcoming academic year. The worksheets of your workbook will look similar to Figure 5.63.

PROJECT FILES

For Project 5G, you will need the following files:

e05G_Coach_Information
e05G_Sports_Programs

You will save your workbooks as:

Lastname_Firstname_5G_Coach_Information
Lastname_Firstname_5G_Sports_Programs

PROJECT RESULTS

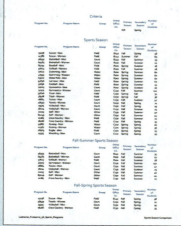

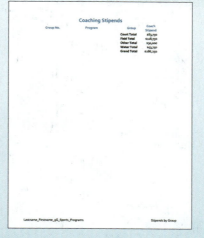

FIGURE 5.63

(Project 5G Sports Programs continues on the next page)

CONTENT-BASED ASSESSMENTS

Mastering Excel Project 5G Sports Programs (continued)

1 Start Excel. From your student files, locate and open **e05G_Sports_Programs**. **Save** the file in your **Excel Chapter 5** folder as **Lastname_Firstname_5G_Sports_ Programs** Display the **Valley-Park-West** worksheet. Select the range **A1:J40**, insert a table, and then apply **Table Style Light 17**. In the **Sort** dialog box, **Sort** by **Campus**, sort on **Values**, and then click **Custom List**. With **NEW LIST** selected, under **List entries**, create entries for **Valley** and **Park** and **West**

As the second level, sort the **Sport Group** column alphabetically on **Values**. As the third level, sort the **Program Name** column alphabetically on **Values**. Convert the table to a range.

2 Display the **Sports Season Comparison** worksheet. Copy the range **A6:G7**, **Paste** it in cell **A1**, and then change the title in cell **A1** to **Criteria** Select the range **A2:G3**, and then in the **Name Box**, name this range **Criteria**

Copy the range **A1:G2**, and then **Paste** the copied range in cell **A36**. Change the title in cell **A36** to **Fall-Summer Sports Season** Name the range **A37:G37 Extract** and then name the range **A7:G34 Database**

3 At the top of your worksheet, in cell **E3**, type **Fall** and in cell **F3**, type **Summer** On the **DATA tab**, in the **Sort & Filter group**, click **Advanced**. Under **Action**, click **Copy to another location**. Verify that in the **Copy to** box, the absolute reference to the Extract area—**$A$37:$G$37**—displays.

4 Scroll to view the lower portion of your worksheet. Copy the range **A36:G37**, and then **Paste** it in cell **A48**. In cell **A48**, change the word *Summer* to **Spring** In cell **F3**, change the criteria to **Spring**

Display the **Advanced Filter** dialog box, and then click **Copy to another location**. In the **Copy to** box, change the range **A49:G49**.

5 Display the **Stipends by Group** worksheet. Select the range **A2:D41**. **Sort** by **Group**, then by the **Coach**

Stipend. **Subtotal** at each change in **Group**, select the **Sum** function, select the **Add subtotal to** the **Coach Stipend**. Display the **Level 2** summary information, and the **Level 1** Grand Total. **AutoFit** columns as necessary.

6 Select all three worksheets. Insert a footer in the **left section** that includes the file name, and in the **right section**, insert the **Sheet Name**.

Return to **Normal** view, and then move to cell **A1**. Change the theme to **Slice**, and then change the **Fonts** to **Corbel**. Set the **Width** to **1 page** and set the **Height** to **1 page**, and **Center** the worksheets **Horizontally**. Display the **document properties** and be sure that your name displays as the author. In the **Subject** box, type your course name and section #, and in the **Tags** box, type **sports programs, campus, sports season, stipends** Display the worksheet in **Print Preview**, make any necessary corrections or adjustments.

7 Open the file **e05G_Coach_Information** and **Save** it in your **Excel Chapter 5** folder as **Lastname_Firstname_5G_Coach_Information** Insert a footer in the **left section** with the file name, and then return to **Normal** view. **Save** and then **Close** this workbook to redisplay your **Lastname_Firstname_5G_Sports_Programs** workbook.

8 On the **Valley-Park-West** worksheet, in cell **J1**, **Insert** a **Hyperlink** to link to your **Lastname_Firstname_5G_Coach_Information** workbook and the **ScreenTip text** box displays, type **Click here for contact information** Change the **Hyperlink Font Color** in cell **J1** to **Orange, Accent 5, Darker 25%**.

9 Save your **Lastname_Firstname_5G_Sports_Programs** workbook as an **XPS Document** with the **File name Lastname_Firstname_5G_Sports_XPS** As directed by your instructor, print or submit electronically the three files that comprise the results of this project—two Excel files and one XPS file. **Close** all files and **Close** Excel.

END | You have completed Project 5G

CONTENT-BASED ASSESSMENTS

GO! Fix It	Project 5H Programs	Online

GO! Make It	Project 5I Arts Faculty	Online

GO! Solve It	Project 5J Organizations	Online

GO! Solve It	Project 5K Dept Tutors	

Apply a combination of the **5A** and **5B** skills.

PROJECT FILES

For Project 5K, you will need the following file:

e05K_Dept_Tutors

You will save your workbook as:

Lastname_Firstname_5K_Dept_Tutors

Open the file e05K_Dept_Tutors and save it in your Excel Chapter 5 folder as **Lastname_Firstname_5K_Dept_Tutors**

The Director of the Tutoring Center wants to know which tutors who are classified as grad student tutors are available in the afternoons from the CNT and CPS departments. By using the table feature and filtering, filter the data to present the information requested. Include the file name in the footer, add appropriate properties, and then save your workbook. Submit as directed.

Performance Level

Performance Criteria		Exemplary	Proficient	Developing
	Convert Data to a Table	The data is properly converted to a table.	Only part of the data is in the form of a table.	The data is not properly converted to a table.
	Filter on Multiple Columns	The Filter Function is properly applied using supplied criteria.	The Filter Function is properly applied to some but not all supplied criteria.	The Filter Function is not properly applied and did not meet the supplied criteria.

END | You have completed Project 5K

OUTCOMES-BASED ASSESSMENTS

RUBRIC

The following outcomes-based assessments are *open-ended assessments*. That is, there is no specific correct result; your result will depend on your approach to the information provided. Make *Professional Quality* your goal. Use the following scoring rubric to guide you in *how* to approach the problem and then to evaluate *how well* your approach solves the problem.

The *criteria*—Software Mastery, Content, Format and Layout, and Process—represent the knowledge and skills you have gained that you can apply to solving the problem. The *levels of performance*—Professional Quality, Approaching Professional Quality, or Needs Quality Improvements—help you and your instructor evaluate your result.

	Your completed project is of Professional Quality if you:	Your completed project is Approaching Professional Quality if you:	Your completed project Needs Quality Improvements if you:
1-Software Mastery	Choose and apply the most appropriate skills, tools, and features and identify efficient methods to solve the problem.	Choose and apply some appropriate skills, tools, and features, but not in the most efficient manner.	Choose inappropriate skills, tools, or features, or are inefficient in solving the problem.
2-Content	Construct a solution that is clear and well organized, contains content that is accurate, appropriate to the audience and purpose, and is complete. Provide a solution that contains no errors in spelling, grammar, or style.	Construct a solution in which some components are unclear, poorly organized, inconsistent, or incomplete. Misjudge the needs of the audience. Have some errors in spelling, grammar, or style, but the errors do not detract from comprehension.	Construct a solution that is unclear, incomplete, or poorly organized; contains some inaccurate or inappropriate content; and contains many errors in spelling, grammar, or style. Do not solve the problem.
3-Format & Layout	Format and arrange all elements to communicate information and ideas, clarify function, illustrate relationships, and indicate relative importance.	Apply appropriate format and layout features to some elements, but not others. Overuse features, causing minor distraction.	Apply format and layout that does not communicate information or ideas clearly. Do not use format and layout features to clarify function, illustrate relationships, or indicate relative importance. Use available features excessively, causing distraction.
4-Process	Use an organized approach that integrates planning, development, self-assessment, revision, and reflection.	Demonstrate an organized approach in some areas, but not others; or, use an insufficient process of organization throughout.	Do not use an organized approach to solve the problem.

OUTCOMES-BASED ASSESSMENTS

Apply a combination of the 5A and 5B skills.

GO! Think   Project 5L Summer Sections

PROJECT FILES

For Project 5L, you will need the following file:

e05L_Summer_Sections

You will save your workbook as:

Lastname_Firstname_5L_Summer_Sections

From your student files, open the file e05L_Summer_Sections, and then save it in your Excel Chapter 5 folder as **Lastname_Firstname_5L_Summer_Sections** Select the entire range and insert a table with headers. Create a custom table style, name it **Summer Sections** and then apply it to the table. Create a custom sort, and then custom sort the Campus information in Online, Valley, Park, West order. Include the file name in the footer, add appropriate properties, include **summer sections** as Tags, set orientation to landscape and width to 1 page, save the file as a PDF, and then submit as directed.

END | You have completed Project 5L

Build from Scratch

GO! Think   Project 5M Social Science   Online

Build from Scratch

You and GO!   Project 5N Personal Expenses   Online

Creating Charts, Diagrams, and Templates

GO! to Work
Video E6

6 EXCEL 2013

auremar/Fotolia

In This Chapter

In this chapter, you will create charts and diagrams to communicate data visually. Charts make a set of numbers easier to understand by displaying data in a graphical format. Excel's SmartArt illustrations make diagrams, like an organizational chart or process cycle, easy to comprehend.

In this chapter, you will also work with templates. Templates have built-in formulas for performing calculations and are used for standardization and protection of data. You will use predefined templates that can be used for financial reports such as an expense report or purchase order, and you will create a template for an order form.

The Dallas – Ft. Worth Job Fair is a nonprofit organization that brings together employers and job seekers in the Dallas – Ft. Worth metropolitan area. Each year the organization holds a number of targeted job fairs and the annual Dallas – Ft. Worth fair draws over 900 employers in more than 75 industries and registers more than 30,000 candidates. Candidate registration is free; employers pay a nominal fee to display and present at the fairs. Candidate resumes and employer postings are managed by a state-of-the-art database system, allowing participants quick and accurate access to job data and candidate qualifications.

Attendance Charts and Diagrams

PROJECT ACTIVITIES

In Activities 6.01 through 6.17, you will create and format column and line charts for the Dallas – Ft. Worth Job Fair that display attendance patterns at the fairs over a five-year period. You will also create a process diagram and an organization chart. Your completed worksheets will look similar to Figure 6.1.

PROJECT FILES

For Project 6A, you will need the following file:

e06A_Attendance

You will save your workbook as:

Lastname_Firstname_6A_Attendance

PROJECT RESULTS

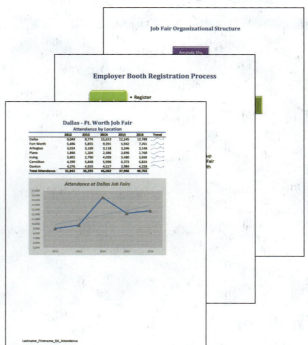

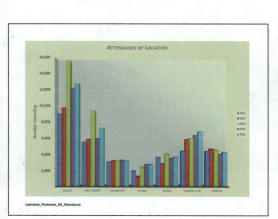

FIGURE 6.1 Project 6A Attendance Charts and Diagrams

Objective 1 | Create and Format Sparklines and a Column Chart

Video E6-1

Recall that *sparklines* are tiny charts that fit within a cell and give a visual trend summary alongside your data. Also recall that a *column chart*, which presents data graphically in vertical columns, is useful to make comparisons among related data.

Activity 6.01 | Creating and Formatting Sparklines

To create sparklines, first select the data you want to plot—represent graphically—and then select the range of cells alongside each row of data where you want to display the sparklines.

1 Start Excel. From your student files, open the file **e06A_Attendance**. Press F12 to display the **Save As** dialog box, navigate to the location where you will store your workbooks for this chapter, and then create a new folder named **Excel Chapter 6** Open your folder, and then **Save** the workbook as **Lastname_Firstname_6A_Attendance**

This data shows the number of applicants who have attended job fairs held over a five-year period at various locations in the greater Dallas - Ft. Worth area.

2 Select the range **B4:F10**. Click **Quick Analysis** 📊, and then click **SPARKLINES**. Compare your screen with Figure 6.2.

 **ANOTHER WAY** On the INSERT tab, in the Sparklines group, click Line.

FIGURE 6.2

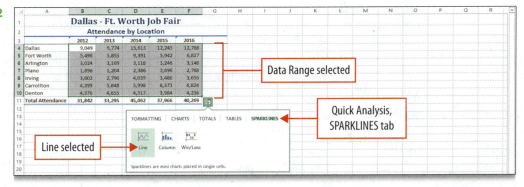

3 On the **SPARKLINES** tab, click **Line**. Compare your screen with Figure 6.3.

Sparklines display alongside each row of data and provide a quick visual trend summary for each city's job fair attendance. The sparklines provide a quick indication that for each location, attendance has had an overall upward trend over the five-year period.

FIGURE 6.3

4 On the **DESIGN tab**, in the **Show group**, select the **High Point** check box and the **Last Point** check box.

By adding the High Point and Last Point markers, you further emphasize the visual story that sparklines depict.

5 On the **DESIGN tab**, in the **Style group**, click **More** , and then in the third row, click the first style—**Sparkline Style Accent 1, (no dark or light)**.

6 In cell **G3**, type **Trend** and press Enter. Press Ctrl + Home, **Save** 🖫 your workbook, and then compare your screen with Figure 6.4.

Use styles in this manner to further enhance your sparklines.

FIGURE 6.4

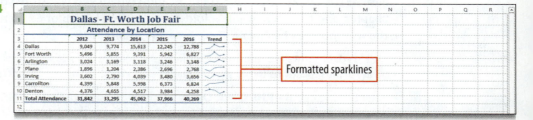

Activity 6.02 | Creating a Column Chart

A chart is a graphic representation of data. When you create a chart, first decide whether you are going to plot the values representing totals or the values representing details—you cannot plot both in the same chart. Excel's **Recommended Charts** feature can help you make this decision by previewing suggested charts based upon patterns in your data. In this activity, you will select the details—the number of attendees at each location each year. To help the reader understand the chart, you will also select the **labels** for the data—the column and row headings that describe the values. Here, the labels are the location names and the years.

1 Take a moment to study the data elements shown in Figure 6.5.

FIGURE 6.5

2 > Select the range **A3:F10**. On the **INSERT tab**, in the **Charts group**, click **Recommended Charts**. Compare your screen with Figure 6.6.

> Excel recommends several charts based upon your data. The Clustered Column chart is displayed in the preview window.

FIGURE 6.6

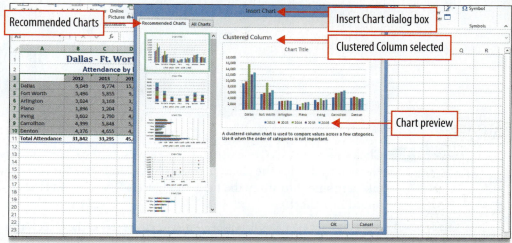

🔄 **ANOTHER WAY**   Click Quick Analysis , click CHARTS, and then click More Charts to open the Insert Chart dialog box.

3 > In the **Insert Chart** dialog box, with the **Clustered Column** chart selected, click **OK**.

4 > On the **DESIGN tab**, in the **Location group**, click **Move Chart**.

> The Move Chart dialog box displays. You can accept the default to display the chart as an object within the worksheet, which is an ***embedded chart***. Or, you can place the chart on a separate sheet, called a ***chart sheet***, in which the chart fills the entire page. A chart sheet is useful when you want to view a chart separately from the worksheet data.

5 > In the Move Chart dialog box, click **New sheet**. In the **New sheet** box, type **Attendance Chart** and then click **OK**.

6 > On the **DESIGN tab**, in the **Type group**, click **Change Chart Type**. In the **Change Chart Type** dialog box, on the **All Charts** tab, if necessary, click **Column** on the left, and then click the fourth chart icon—**3-D Clustered column**. Click **OK**.

> In this manner you can change the chart type.

7 > In the upper right corner of the chart, click **Chart Styles** 🖌. Click **Style 3**. Compare your screen with Figure 6.7.

🔄 **ANOTHER WAY**   On the DESIGN tab, in the Chart Styles group, click More ⬇, and then click Style 3.

FIGURE 6.7

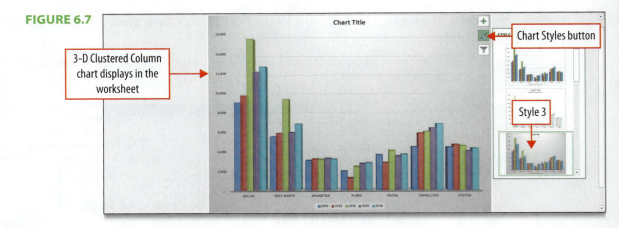

8 Click **Chart Styles** ✎ to close the chart styles. In the **Chart Layouts group**, click **Add Chart Element** to display the **Chart Elements** list. Compare your screen with Figure 6.8, and then take a moment to study the table in Figure 6.9, which lists the elements that are typically found in a chart.

The Chart Elements list displays. *Chart elements* are the objects that make up a chart. From the Chart Elements list, you can select a chart element to format it.

FIGURE 6.8

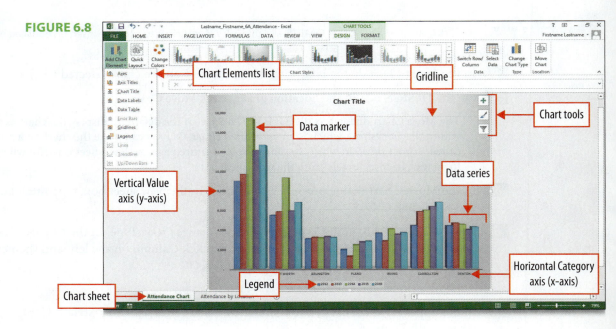

FIGURE 6.9

6

EXCEL

MICROSOFT EXCEL CHART ELEMENTS	
OBJECT	**DESCRIPTION**
Axis	A line that serves as a frame of reference for measurement and that borders the chart plot area.
Category labels	The labels that display along the bottom of the chart to identify the category of data.
Chart area	The entire chart and all its elements.
Data labels	Labels that display the value, percentage, and/or category of each particular data point and can contain one or more of the choices listed—Series name, Category name, Value, or Percentage.
Data marker	A column, bar, area, dot, pie slice, or other symbol in a chart that represents a single data point.
Data points	The numeric values of the selected worksheet.
Data series	A group of related data points that are plotted in a chart.
Gridlines	Lines in the plot area that aid the eye in determining the plotted values.
Horizontal Category axis (x-axis)	The axis that displays along the bottom of the chart to identify the category of data. Excel uses the row titles as the category names.
Legend	A key that identifies patterns or colors that are assigned to the categories in the chart.
Major unit value	The value that determines the spacing between tick marks and between the gridlines in the plot area.
Plot area	The area bounded by the axes, including all the data series.
Tick mark labels	Identifying information for a tick mark generated from the cells on the worksheet used to create the chart.
Tick marks	The short lines that display on an axis at regular intervals.
Vertical Value axis (y-axis)	The axis that displays along the left side of the chart to identify the numerical scale on which the charted data is based.
Walls and floor	The areas surrounding a 3-D chart that give dimension and boundaries to the chart. Two walls and one floor display within the plot area.

9 If necessary, click the **Add Chart Elements arrow**. In the **Chart Elements** list, point to **Legend**, and then click **Right**.

The legend is easier to see on the right side of the chart.

BY TOUCH   In the upper right corner of the chart, tap the Chart Elements button, tap Legend, and then tap Right.

10 In the **Chart Area**, click the **Chart Title** to select it. In the **Formula Bar**, type **Attendance** as the chart title, and then press Enter to display the text in the chart.

11 Click the tallest column displayed for the Dallas category. Compare your screen with Figure 6.10.

All the columns representing the Series *2014* are selected—selection handles display at the corners of each column in the series—and a ScreenTip displays the value for the column you are pointing to. Recall that a data series is a group of related data—in this case, the attendees to all the job fairs that were held in 2014. Also notice that the Formula Bar displays the address for the selected data series.

FIGURE 6.10

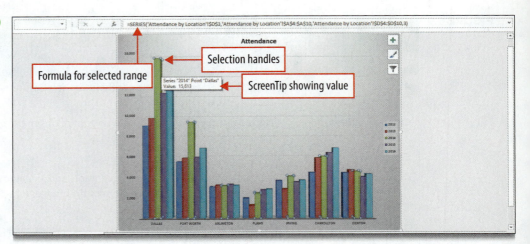

12 ▶ Locate the **Plano** category, and then click the shortest column in that group.

> The selected series changes to those columns that represent the attendees at the job fairs in 2013. The Formula Bar and Chart Elements box change and a new ScreenTip displays.

13 ▶ Click outside the chart area to deselect the series.

More Knowledge | **Sizing Handles and Selection Handles**

Sizing handles and selection handles look the same, and the terms are often used interchangeably. If a two-headed resize arrow—⬍, ↔, ⬀, ⤢—displays when you point to boxes surrounding an object, it is a sizing handle; otherwise, it is a selection handle. Some objects in a chart cannot be resized, such as the category axis or the value axis, but they can be selected and then reformatted.

Activity 6.03 | Changing the Display of Chart Data

As you create a chart, you make choices about the data to include, the chart type, chart titles, and location. You can change the chart type, change the way the data displays, add or change titles, select different colors, and modify the background, scale, and chart location.

In the column chart you created, the attendance numbers are displayed along the value axis—the vertical axis—and the locations for each job fair are displayed along the category axis—the horizontal axis. The cells you select for a chart include the row and column labels from your worksheet. In a column or line chart, Excel selects whichever has more items—either the rows or the columns—and uses those labels to plot the data series, in this case, the locations.

After plotting the data series, Excel uses the remaining labels—in this example, the years identified in the row headings—to create the data series labels on the legend. The legend is the key that defines the colors used in the chart; here it identifies the data series for the years. A different color is used for each year in the data series. The chart, as currently displayed, compares the change in attendance year to year grouped by category location. You can change the chart to display the years on the category axis and the locations as the data series identified in the legend.

1 ▶ In the **Dallas** category, click the fourth column.

> All columns with the same color are selected. The ScreenTip displays *Series "2015" Point "Dallas" Value: 12,245.*

2 ▶ Point to each of the other purple columns that are selected and notice that the ScreenTip that displays identifies each purple column as being in the *Series "2015."*

3 ▶ On the **DESIGN tab**, in **the Data group**, click **Switch Row/Column**, and then compare your screen with Figure 6.11.

> The chart changes to display the locations as the data series. The locations are the row headings in the worksheet and are now identified in the legend. The years display as the category labels.

FIGURE 6.11

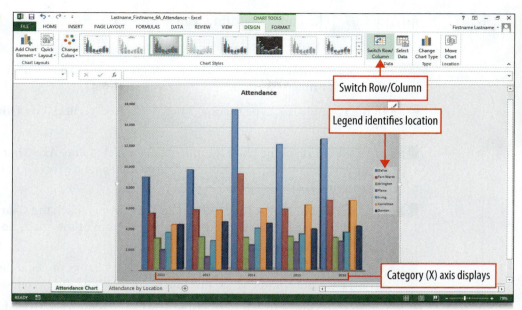

4 ▶ Click one of the purple columns. Point to each purple column and read the ScreenTip.

> The ScreenTips for the purple columns now identify this as the Plano series.

5 ▶ On the **DESIGN tab**, in the **Data group**, click **Switch Row/Column** again, and then **Save** 🖫 your workbook.

> The chart changes back to the more useful arrangement with the years identified in the legend and the locations displayed as the category labels.

More Knowledge | **Changing the Data in a Chart**

After you have created a chart, you can adjust the range of data that is displayed in the chart or add an additional data series. To do so, on the DESIGN tab, in the Data group, click Select Data. Edit the source address displayed in the Chart data range box, or drag the data in the worksheet to adjust the range as needed.

Activity 6.04 | Editing and Formatting the Chart Title

The data displayed in the chart focuses on the attendance by location. It is good practice to create a chart title to reflect your charted data.

1 ▶ Click the **Chart Title**—*Attendance*—to select it, and then click to position the mouse pointer to the right of *Attendance*.

> To edit a title, click once to select the chart object, and then click a second time to position the insertion point in the title and change to editing mode.

2 ▶ Press Spacebar one time, and then type **by Location**

3 ▶ Point to the **Chart Title**—*Attendance by Location*—right-click the border of the chart title, and then click **Font** to display the **Font** dialog box.

4 ▶ Set the **Font style** to **Bold Italic** and change the **Font Size** to **20**. Click the **Font color arrow**, and then under **Theme Colors**, in the first column, click the last color—**White, Background 1, Darker 50%.** Apply the **Small Caps** effect. Click **OK**, and then **Save** 🖫 your workbook.

> Use the Font dialog box in this manner to apply multiple formats to a chart title.

Activity 6.05 | Adding, Formatting, and Aligning Axis Titles

You can add a title to display with both the value axis and the category axis.

1 On the **DESIGN tab**, in the **Chart Layouts group**, click **Add Chart Element**, click **Axis Titles**, and then click **Primary Vertical**.

2 In the **Formula Bar**, type **Number Attending** as the **Vertical Axis Title**, and then press ⏎ to display the title text in the chart.

3 On the left side of the chart, point to the **Vertical (Value) Axis Title** you just added, select the text, and then on the mini toolbar, change the **Font Size** to **14** and the **Font Color** to **White, Background 1, Darker 50%**.

4 On the **FORMAT tab**, in the **Current Selection group**, click the **Chart Elements arrow**, click **Horizontal (Category) Axis**, and then at the bottom of the chart, notice that the **Category axis** is selected.

5 Point to the selected axis, right-click, click **Font**, and in the **Font dialog box**, click the **Font style arrow**, click **Bold**, and change the **Font Color** to **White, Background 1, Darker 50%**. Click **OK**.

6 On the left side of the chart, point to any value in the **Vertical (Value) Axis**, and then right-click to select the axis. Click the **HOME tab**, and then in the **Font group**, change the **Font Size** to **12**.

7 **Save** 🖫 your workbook, and then compare your screen with Figure 6.12.

FIGURE 6.12

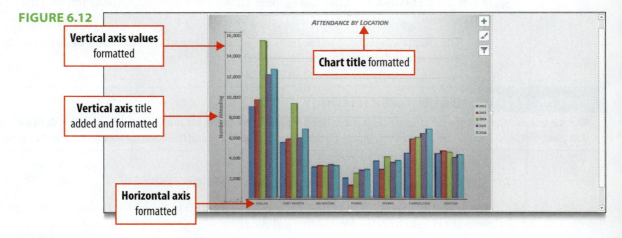

Vertical axis values formatted

Chart title formatted

Vertical axis title added and formatted

Horizontal axis formatted

Activity 6.06 | Editing Source Data

One of the characteristics of an Excel chart is that it reflects changes made to the underlying data.

1 In the **Fort Worth** column cluster, point to the last column—**2016**. Notice that the *Value* for this column is *6,827*.

2 Display the **Attendance by Location** worksheet, and then in cell **F5**, type **7261** and press ⏎.

3 Redisplay the **Attendance Chart** worksheet, **Save** 🖫 your workbook, and then point to the **Fort Worth** column for 2016. Compare your screen with Figure 6.13.

FIGURE 6.13

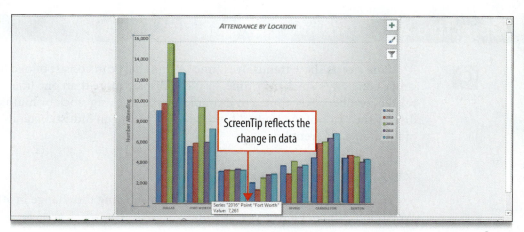

ScreenTip reflects the change in data

Activity 6.07 | Formatting the Chart Floor and Chart Walls

If your chart style includes shaded walls and a floor, you can format these elements.

1 On the **FORMAT tab**, in the **Current Selection group**, click the **Chart Elements arrow**, and then click **Back Wall**. Then in the same group, click **Format Selection**.

2 In the **Format Wall** pane, if necessary, click ▷ to expand **FILL**, click **Solid fill**, and then click the **Fill Color arrow**. Under **Theme Colors**, in the fourth column, click the fourth color—**Dark Blue, Text 2, Lighter 40%**—and then drag the slider to set the **Transparency** to **75%**.

3 Click the arrow to the right of **WALL OPTIONS** to display the **Chart Elements** list. Select **Side Wall**, and then apply the same fill, but with a **Transparency** of **60%**.

4 From the **Chart Elements** list, select the **Floor**, and then apply a **Solid fill** using the last Theme color in the first column—**White, Background 1, Darker 50%** with **0% Transparency**.

5 From the **Chart Elements** list, select the **Chart Area**, and then apply a **Solid fill** using **Olive Green, Accent 3, Lighter 60%**—in the seventh column, the third color. **Close** ✖ the **Format Chart Area** pane, click **Save** 🖫, and then compare your screen with Figure 6.14.

FIGURE 6.14

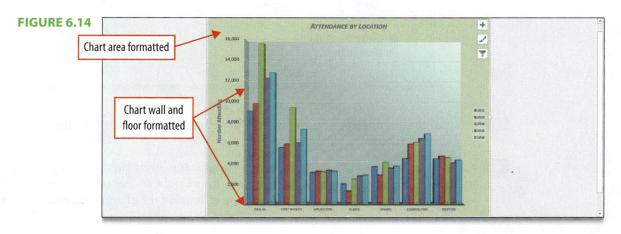

Chart area formatted

Chart wall and floor formatted

Video E6-2

Line charts show trends over time. A line chart can consist of one line, such as the price of a single company's stock over time, or it can display more than one line to show a comparison of related numbers over time. For example, charts tracking stock or mutual fund performance often display the price of the mutual fund on one line and an industry standard for that particular type of fund on a different line.

Activity 6.08 | Creating a Line Chart

In this activity, you will create a line chart showing the change in attendance at the Dallas – Ft. Worth Job Fair over a five-year period.

1 Display the **Attendance by Location** worksheet.

2 Select the range **A3:F4**, and then, on the **INSERT tab**, in the **Charts group**, click **Insert Line Chart** . In the second row, click the first chart type—**Line with Markers**. Compare your screen with Figure 6.15.

> Cell A3 must be included in the selection, despite being empty, because the same number of cells must be in each selected row. Excel identifies the first row as a category because of the empty first cell.

FIGURE 6.15

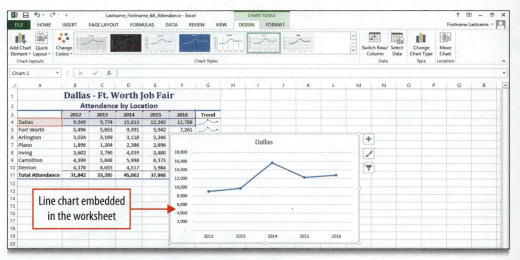

Line chart embedded in the worksheet

3 Point to the chart border to display the pointer, and then drag the upper left corner of the chart inside the upper left corner of cell **A13**.

4 Scroll down as necessary to view **row 30**. Point to the lower right corner of the chart to display the pointer, and then drag the lower right corner of the chart inside the lower right corner of cell **G29**. Click anywhere outside the chart to deselect. **Save** your workbook. Compare your screen with Figure 6.16.

> When you use the corner sizing handles to resize an object, the proportional dimensions—the relative height and width—are retained.

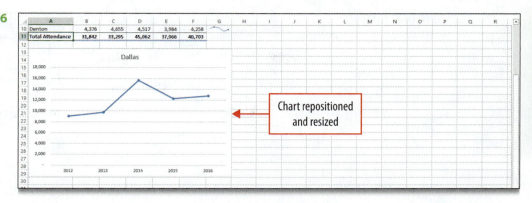

FIGURE 6.16

Activity 6.09 | Changing a Chart Title

When you select the chart type, the resulting chart might contain elements that you want to delete or change. For example, the chart title can be more specific.

1 Click the **Chart Title**—*Dallas*. In the **Formula Bar**, type **Attendance at Dallas Job Fairs** as the chart title, and then press Enter to display the title text in the chart.

2 Point to the **Chart Title**, right-click, and then click **Font**. Change the **Font Size** to **16** and the **Font Style** to **Bold Italic**. Click **OK**. Click outside of the chart to deselect it, **Save** 🖫 your workbook, and then compare your chart with Figure 6.17.

The size of the title increases, and the plot area decreases slightly.

FIGURE 6.17

Activity 6.10 | Changing the Values on the Value Axis

You can change the values on the value axis to increase or decrease the variation among the numbers displayed. The *scale* is the range of numbers in the data series; the scale controls the minimum, maximum, and incremental values on the value axis. In the line chart, the attendance figures for Dallas are all higher than 7,000, but the scale begins at zero, so the line occupies only the upper area of the chart. Adjust the scale as necessary to make your charts meaningful to the reader.

1 On the left side of the line chart, point to any number, and then when the ScreenTip displays *Vertical (Value) Axis*, right-click, and then click **Format Axis**.

2 In the **Format Axis** pane, if necessary, click ▷ to expand **AXIS OPTIONS**. Under **Bounds**, in the **Minimum** box, type **5000** Under **Units**, change the **Major unit** to **1000** and then press Enter. Compare your screen with Figure 6.18.

Here you can change the beginning and ending numbers displayed on the chart and also change the unit by which the major gridlines display. Excel formats the values with one decimal.

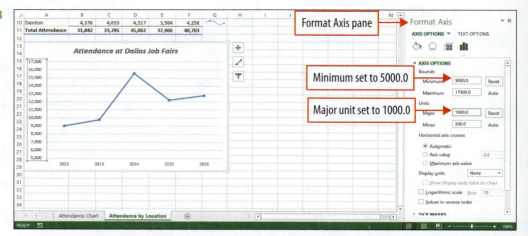

FIGURE 6.18

3 In the upper right corner of the **Format Axis** pane, click **Close** ☒. Click **Save** 🖫, and then compare your screen with Figure 6.19.

> The Value Axis begins at 5000 with major gridlines at intervals of 1000. This will emphasize the change in attendance over the five years by starting the chart at a higher number and decreasing the interval for gridlines.

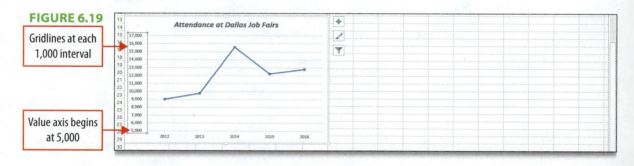

FIGURE 6.19

Gridlines at each 1,000 interval

Value axis begins at 5,000

Activity 6.11 | Formatting the Plot Area and the Data Series

1 Right-click anywhere within the lined **Plot Area**, and then click **Format Plot Area**.

> The Format Plot Area pane displays. Here you can change the border of the plot area or the background color.

2 In the **Format Plot Area** pane, if necessary, click ▷ to expand **FILL**. Click **Solid fill**. Click the **Fill Color arrow**, and then under **Theme Colors**, in the first column, click the fourth color— **White, Background 1, Darker 25%**.

3 Point to the blue chart line, right-click, and then click **Format Data Series**.

> In the Format Data Series pane, you can change the data markers—the indicators for a data point value, which on the line chart is represented by a diamond shape. You can also change the line connecting the data markers.

4 In the **Format Data Series** pane, click **Fill & Line** 🖎. Under **LINE**, click **Solid line**. Use the spin box arrows to set the **Width** to **4 pt**.

5 Under the **Fill & Line** icon, click **MARKER**. Click ▷ to expand **MARKER OPTIONS**. Click **Built-in**, click the **Type arrow**, and then click the **triangle**—the third symbol in the list. Set the **Size** of the **Marker Type** to **12**

6 Under **FILL**, click **Solid fill**, and then click the **Fill Color arrow**. Under **Theme Colors**, in the first column, click the last color—**White, Background 1, Darker 50%**.

7 ▸ Under **Border**, click **No line**, and **Close** ☒ the **Format Data Series** pane.

8 ▸ On the **FORMAT tab**, in the **Current Selection** group, click the **Chart Elements arrow**, and then click **Chart Area**. In the same group, click **Format Selection** to display the **Format Chart Area** pane, and then apply a **Solid fill** using **White, Background 1, Darker 15%**—in the first column, the third color. **Close** ☒ the **Format Data Series** pane.

9 ▸ Click in any cell outside of the chart, **Save** 🖫 your workbook, and then compare your screen with Figure 6.20.

FIGURE 6.20

Activity 6.12 | Inserting a Trendline

A *trendline* is a graphic representation of trends in a data series, such as a line sloping upward to represent increased sales over a period of months. A trendline is always associated with a data series, but it does not represent the data of that data series. Rather, a trendline depicts trends in the existing data.

1 ▸ Click slightly inside the chart border to select the entire chart. Next to the chart, click **Chart Elements** ➕, click **Trendline**, and then click **Linear**. **Save** 🖫 your workbook, and then compare your screen with Figure 6.21.

A linear trendline displays in the chart. The chart shows a significant increase in attendance for 2014, a drop in attendance in 2015, but the trendline indicates an overall increasing trend in attendance over the past five years.

FIGURE 6.21

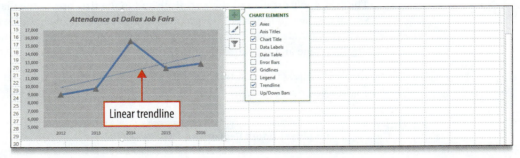

Objective 3 | Create and Modify a SmartArt Graphic

Video E6-3

A *SmartArt graphic* is a visual representation of your information and ideas. You can create SmartArt graphics by choosing from among many different layouts to communicate complex messages and relationships easily and effectively.

Unlike charts, a SmartArt graphic does not depend on any underlying data in a worksheet; rather, it is a graphical tool that depicts ideas or associations. In the following activities, you will create a process diagram to illustrate how to register for an employer booth at the job fair.

Activity 6.13 | Creating a Process SmartArt Graphic

In this activity, you will use a Process SmartArt graphic, which shows steps in a process or timeline.

1 Click **New sheet** ⊕. Double-click the **Sheet1 tab**, and rename the sheet tab **Process Chart** In cell **A1** type **Employer Booth Registration Process** and then press Enter.

2 Merge and center the text you just typed across **A1:H1**, apply the **Title** cell style, and then change the **Font Size** to **22**.

3 On the **INSERT tab**, in the **Illustrations group**, click **SmartArt** ⊞.

4 On the left, notice the types of SmartArt graphics that are available, and then take a moment to examine the table in Figure 6.22.

FIGURE 6.22

SMARTART	
USE THIS SMARTART TYPE:	**TO DO THIS:**
List	Show non-sequential information
Process	Show steps in a process or timeline
Cycle	Show a continual process
Hierarchy	Create an organization chart or show a decision tree
Relationship	Illustrate connections
Matrix	Show how parts relate to a whole
Pyramid	Use a series of pictures to show relationships
Picture	Display pictures in a diagram

5 On the left, click **Process**, and then in the first row, click the third option—**Step Down Process**. Click **OK**.

6 With your insertion point blinking in the first bullet of the **Text Pane**, type **Apply**

The text *Apply* displays in the Text Pane and in the first box in the diagram. Use the *Text Pane*, which displays to the left of the graphic, to input and organize the text in your graphic. The Text Pane is populated with placeholder text that you replace with your information. If you prefer, close the Text Pane and type directly into the graphic.

7 In the **Text Pane**, click the next bullet, which is indented, and then type **Register for Booth** Compare your screen with Figure 6.23.

FIGURE 6.23

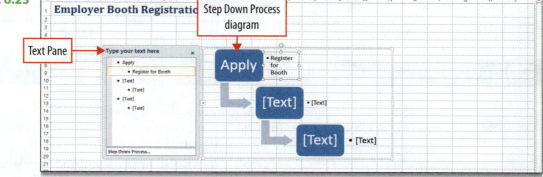

8 In the **Text Pane**, click the next bullet, and then type **Prepare** Under *Prepare* click the indented bullet and type **Booth Number Assigned**

9 Click the next bullet and type **Attend** Click the next bullet, and then type **Set up Job Fair Booth** Compare your diagram with Figure 6.24.

The Text Pane entries display on the left in the Text Pane, and the process diagram with entries displays on the right in the process diagram.

FIGURE 6.24

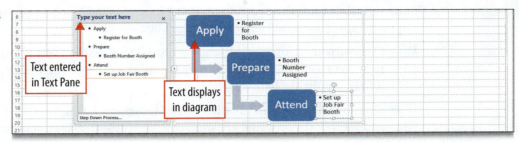

10 Close ✕ the **Text Pane**, and then Save 🖫 your workbook.

Activity 6.14 | Modifying the Diagram Style

Excel offers preformatted SmartArt styles that can be applied to a diagram.

1 With the SmartArt still selected, on the **DESIGN tab**, in the **SmartArt Styles group**, click **More** ⤓. Under **3-D**, click the first style—**Polished**.

2 In the **SmartArt Styles group**, click **Change Colors**, and then under **Colorful**, click the third option—**Colorful Range – Accent Colors 3 to 4**.

3 By using the pointer, drag the upper left corner of the graphic border inside the upper left corner of cell **A4**. Point to the lower right corner of the graphic's border to display the �pointer, and then drag to resize the graphic and position the lower right corner inside the lower right corner of cell **H22**. Save 🖫 your workbook, and then compare your screen with Figure 6.25.

FIGURE 6.25

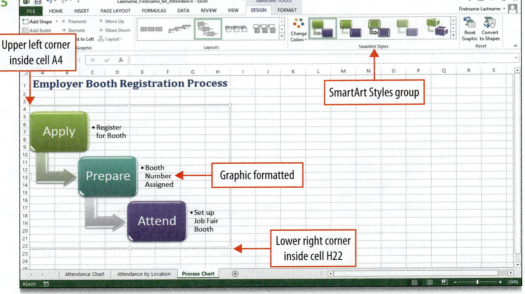

Video E6-4

An *organization chart* depicts reporting relationships within an organization.

Activity 6.15 | Creating and Modifying a SmartArt Organization Chart

In this activity, you will create an organizational chart that shows the reporting relationship among the Job Fair Director, Employer Relations Manager, Job Applicant Program Manager, Tech Support Supervisor, and Help Desk Technician.

1 Click **New sheet** ⊕. Double-click the **Sheet2 tab** and rename it **Organization Chart** In cell **A1**, type **Job Fair Organizational Structure** and then merge and center this title across the range **A1:H1**. Apply the **Title** cell style.

2 On the **INSERT tab**, in the **Illustrations group**, click **SmartArt** 📊. On the left, click **Hierarchy**, and then in the first row, click the first graphic—**Organization Chart**. Click **OK**. If the Text Pane displays, close it.

> **NOTE**   **Displaying the Text Pane**
>
> Typing in the Text Pane is optional. If you have closed the Text Pane and want to reopen it, select the graphic, click the DESIGN tab, and then in the Create Graphic group, click Text Pane. Alternatively, click the arrow on left border of SmartArt graphic to display the Text Pane.

3 In the graphic, with the first [**Text**] box selected, type **Amanda Shy, Job Fair Director**

4 In the box below the *Job Fair Director*, click on the *edge* of the box to display a solid line border—if a dashed border displays, click the edge of the box again. With the box bordered with a solid line, press Delete. Compare your screen with Figure 6.26.

Three shapes comprise the second level of the organization chart.

FIGURE 6.26

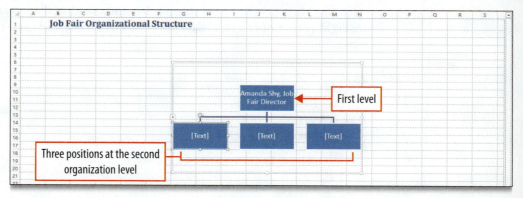

5 In leftmost shape on the second level of the organization chart, type **Linda Wong, Employer Relations Manager**

6 Click in the middle shape, and type **Miriam Ruiz, Job Applicant Program Manager** In the rightmost shape, type **Michael Gold, Tech Support Supervisor**

7 With *Michael Gold* shape selected, on the **DESIGN tab**, in the **Create Graphic group**, click the **Add Shape arrow**, and then click **Add Shape Below**.

A new shape displays below the Tech Support Supervisor shape.

ANOTHER WAY   Right-click the shape, click Add Shape, and then click Add Shape Below.

8 ▸ Type **Ivan Soklov, Help Desk Technician**

9 ▸ In the **SmartArt Styles group**, click **More** ⎤, and then under **3-D**, click the first style—
Polished. Click **Change Colors**, and then under **Colorful**, click the fifth color arrangement—
Colorful Range – Accent Colors 5 to 6. Click **Save** 🖫 and then compare your screen with
Figure 6.27.

FIGURE 6.27

Activity 6.16 | Adding Effects to a SmartArt Graphic

In this activity, you will change the formatting and layout of the graphic.

1 ▸ With the *Ivan Soklov* shape selected, on the **FORMAT tab**, in the **Shape Styles group**, click the
Shape Fill arrow, and then under **Theme Colors**, in the seventh column, click the fifth color—
Olive **Green, Accent 3, Darker 25%**.

2 ▸ Click the edge of the *Ivan Soklov* shape so that it is surrounded by a solid line and sizing
handles and the polished shape displays. Hold down Ctrl, and click each of the other shapes
until all five are selected.

3 ▸ With all five shapes selected, on the **FORMAT tab** in the **Shape Styles group**, click the **Shape
Effects arrow**, point to **Bevel**, and then under **Bevel**, in the third row, click the second bevel
shape—**Riblet**.

4 ▸ By using the 🔾 pointer, drag the upper left corner of the graphic inside the upper left corner
of cell **A4**. By using the 🔾 pointer, drag the lower right corner of the chart inside the lower
right corner of cell **H20**.

5 ▸ In the shape for *Amanda Shy*, click to position the insertion point after the comma, hold
down Shift, and then press Enter to insert a line break. Press Delete to delete the extra space. Use
the same technique in the remaining shapes to move the job title to the second line.

6 ▸ Click cell **A1**, and then **Save** 🖫 your workbook. Compare your screen with Figure 6.28.

FIGURE 6.28

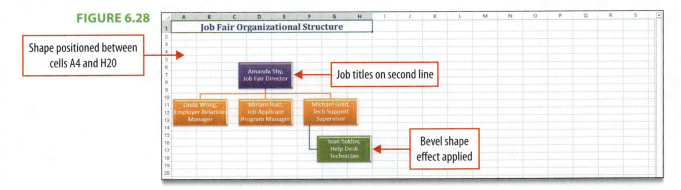

Activity 6.17 | Preparing Worksheets Containing Charts and Diagrams for Printing

1 ▸ Display the **Attendance Chart** worksheet. On the **INSERT tab**, in the **Text group**, click **Header & Footer**, and then in the **Page Setup** dialog box, click **Custom Footer**.

2 ▸ With the insertion point in the **left section**, in the small toolbar in the center of the dialog box, click **Insert File Name** 📄, and then click **OK** two times.

3 ▸ Click the **Attendance by Location sheet tab**, hold down Ctrl, and then click the **Process Chart sheet tab** and the **Organization Chart sheet tab** to select the remaining three worksheets and group them.

4 ▸ With the three sheets grouped, insert a footer in the **left section** that includes the file name. Click outside the footer area, and then on the **PAGE LAYOUT tab**, click **Margins**, click **Custom Margins**, and then center the sheets horizontally. Click **OK**. Press Ctrl + Home and return to **Normal** ▦ view.

5 ▸ Click the **FILE tab** to display **Backstage** view. On the right, at the bottom of the **Properties** list, click **Show All Properties**. On the list of **Properties**, in the **Tags** box, type **attendance statistics, organization charts** In the **Subject** box, type your course name and section #. Under **Related People**, be sure that your name displays as the author. If necessary, right-click the author name, click **Edit Property**, type your name, click outside of the Edit person dialog box, and then click OK.

6 ▸ Click **Print** and examine the **Print Preview**, make any necessary adjustments, and then **Save** 💾 your workbook. Right-click any of the grouped sheet tabs, and then click **Ungroup Sheets**.

7 ▸ Print or submit your workbook electronically as directed by your instructor. **Close** Excel.

> ### END | You have completed Project 6A

PROJECT
6B

Order Form Template

PROJECT ACTIVITIES

In Activities 6.18 through 6.25, you will create, format, and edit a booth registration order form template for use by Job Fair staff to ensure that totals for items ordered are calculated accurately. You will also protect the template. Your completed worksheets will look similar to Figure 6.29.

PROJECT FILES

For Project 6B, you will need the following files:

e06B_Logo
New blank Excel workbook

You will save your workbooks as:

Lastname_Firstname_6B_Booth_Order
Lastname_Firstname_6B_Order_Template
Lastname_Firstname_6B_Topaz_Order

PROJECT RESULTS

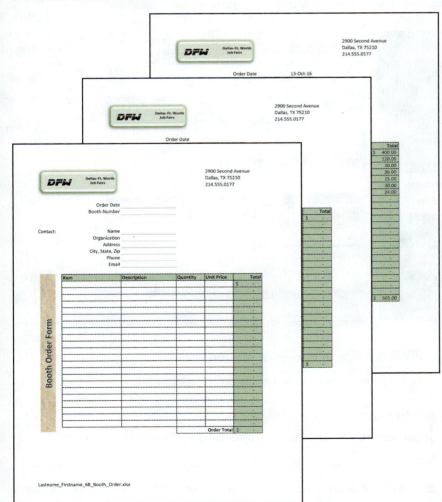

FIGURE 6.29 Project 6B Order Form Template

Video E6-5

A *template* is a workbook that you create and use as the basis for other similar workbooks. Excel also has predesigned templates that include, among others, financial forms to record expenses, time worked, balance sheet items, and other common financial reports.

Standardization and protection are the two main reasons for creating templates for commonly used forms in an organization. *Standardization* means that all forms created within the organization will have a uniform appearance; the data will always be organized in the same manner. *Protection* means that individuals entering data cannot change areas of the worksheet that are protected, and therefore cannot alter important formulas and formats built in to the template.

Activity 6.18 | Entering Template Text

To create a template, start with a blank worksheet; enter the text, formatting, and formulas needed for the specific worksheet purpose, and then save the file as a template. Saving a workbook as a template adds the extension *.xltx* to the file name. In this activity, you will start a workbook for the purpose of creating a purchase order template.

1 Start Excel. Scroll through the various templates and compare your screen with Figure 6.30.

From the *Search online templates box*, you can find and download many different predesigned templates from Microsoft's Office.com site. Microsoft updates this list frequently.

FIGURE 6.30

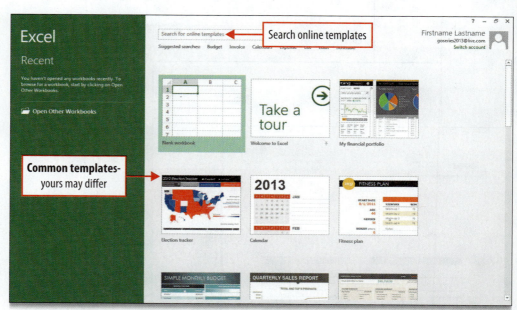

2 Click **Blank workbook**. In cell **A1**, type **Dallas - Ft. Worth Job Fair**

A blank workbook is created from the built-in Normal template in Excel.

More Knowledge | **Setting the Default Font for New Worksheets**

To change the default body font used in the Excel Normal template, from Backstage view display Excel Option dialog box. On the General tab, under When creating new workbooks, change the default font.

---

3 Click in cell **E1**, type **2900 Second Avenue** and then press Enter. In cell **E2**, type **Dallas, TX 75210** and press Enter. In cell **E3**, type **214.555.0177** and press Enter. Click cell **B6**, type **Order Date** and press Enter. In cell **B7**, type **Booth Number** and press Enter.

4 Click cell **B10**. Type **Name** and press Enter. In cell **B11**, type **Organization** and press Enter. In cell **B12**, type **Address** and press Enter. In cell **B13**, type **City, State, Zip** and press Enter. In cell **B14**, type **Phone** and press Enter. In cell **B15**, type **Email** and press Enter. Click cell **A10**. Type **Contact:** and press Enter.

> These labels will comprise the form headings.

5 Click cell **B17**. Type **Item** and press Tab to move to cell **C17**. Continuing across **row 17**, in cell **C17**, type **Description** and press Tab, in cell **D17**, type **Quantity** and press Tab, in cell **E17**, type **Unit Price** and press Tab, and in cell **F17**, type **Total** and press Enter. Select the range **B17:F17**, and then in the **Font** group, click **Bold** **B**.

> The column headings are added to the order form.

6 Save the file in your **Excel Chapter 6** folder as **Lastname_Firstname_6B_Booth_Order** Compare your screen with Figure 6.31, and then make any necessary corrections.

> Until the format and design of the order form is complete, you will save your work as a normal workbook.

FIGURE 6.31

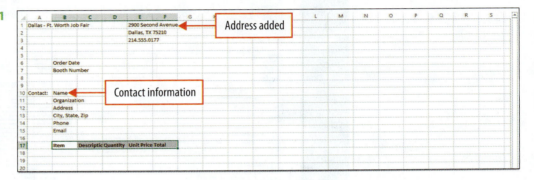

Activity 6.19 | Formatting a Template

One of the goals in designing a template is to make it easy for others to complete. It should be obvious to the person completing the form what information is necessary and where to place the information.

1 Select **column B**. On the **HOME tab**, in the **Cells group**, click **Format**, and then click **Column Width**. In the **Column Width** dialog box, type **21.5** and then click **OK**. In the same manner, widen **column C** to **20.0** Select **columns D:F** and widen to **10.0**

2 Select the range **B6:B15**, and on the **HOME tab**, in the **Alignment group**, click **Align Right**.

3 Click cell **F17**, and then in the **Alignment group**, click **Align Right**.

4 Select the range **C6:C7**. In the **Alignment group**, click the **Dialog Box Launcher**. In the **Format Cells** dialog box, click the **Border tab**. Under **Line**, in the **Style** list, click the second line in the first column—**the dotted line**.

5 Click the **Color arrow**, and then under **Theme Colors**, in the sixth column, click the third color—**Orange, Accent 2, Lighter 60%**. Under **Border**, click **Middle Border**, and **Bottom Border**. Click **OK**.

6 With the range **C6:C7** still selected, in the **Alignment group**, click **Align Right**. Then, with the range still selected, right-click, and on the mini toolbar, click the **Format Painter**, and then select the range **C10:C15** to copy the format.

> Inserting borders on cells in a template creates lines as a place to record information when the form is filled out. This provides a good visual cue to the person filling out the form as to where information should be placed.

7 Select the range **B17:F40**. Right-click the selected area and click **Format Cells**. In the **Format Cells** dialog box, if necessary, click the **Border tab**. Under **Presets**, click **Outline** ⊞ and **Inside** ⊞, and then click **OK**.

This action applies a grid of columns and rows, which is helpful to those individuals completing the form.

8 Select the range **B17:F17**, hold down Ctrl and select the nonadjacent range **F18:F40**. In the **Font group**, click the **Fill Color arrow** 🎨 ▾, and then under **Theme Colors**, in the last column, click the third color—**Green, Accent 6, Lighter 60%**. Press Ctrl + Home.

The fill color is applied to the column headings and to the Total column that will contain the formulas for the template.

9 Press Ctrl + F2 to view the **Print Preview**, and then compare your screen with Figure 6.32.

FIGURE 6.32

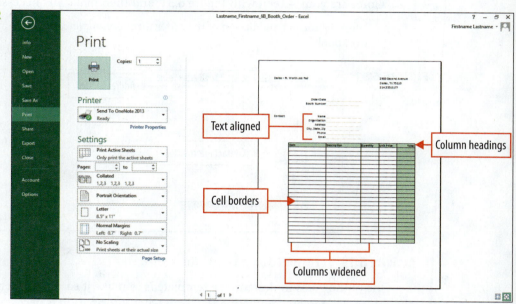

10 Click **Save** to save and return to your workbook.

A dotted line on the worksheet indicates where the first page would end if the worksheet were printed as it is currently set up. As you develop your template, use the Print Preview to check your progress.

Activity 6.20 | Entering Template Formulas

After the text is entered and formatted in your template, add formulas to the cells where you want the result of the calculations to display. In this activity, you will create a formula in the Total column to determine the dollar value for the quantity of each item ordered, and then create another formula to sum the Total column.

1 In cell **F18**, type **=d18*e18** and click **Enter** ✓.

A value of 0 displays in cell F18. However, when the person entering information into the worksheet types the Quantity in cell D18 and the Unit Price in cell E18, the formula will multiply the two values to calculate a total for the item.

2 Use the fill handle to copy the formula in cell **F18** down through cell **F39**.

3 Click cell **F40**. On the **HOME tab**, in the **Editing group**, click **AutoSum** Σ AutoSum ▾. Be sure the range displays as *F18:F39*, and then press Enter.

4 Select the range **E18:E39**. On the **HOME tab**, in the **Number group**, click **Comma Style** .

The Comma Style is applied. When values are typed into the form, they will display with two decimals and commas in the appropriate locations.

5 Click cell **F18**, hold down Ctrl, and then click cell **F40**. In the **Number group**, click **Accounting Number Format** $. Select the range **F19:F39**, and then click **Comma Style** .

Formats are applied to the Total column, and the zero in each cell displays as a hyphen.

6 Select the range **D40:E40**. In the **Alignment group**, click **Merge and Center**. Type **Order Total** and click **Enter** . In the **Alignment group**, click **Align Right** . In the **Font** group, click **Bold B**.

A label is added and formatted to identify the total for the entire order.

7 Select the range **B40:C40**, right-click, and then click **Format Cells**. In the **Format Cells** dialog box, if necessary, click the **Border tab**, and then in the **Border preview** area, click **Left Border**, **Middle Border** , and **Bottom Border** to *remove* these borders from the preview—be sure the right and top lines remain in the preview area. Compare your dialog box with Figure 6.33.

FIGURE 6.33

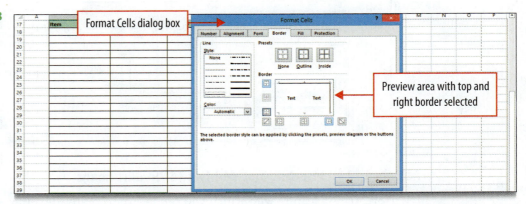

8 Click **OK**. Press Ctrl + F2 to view the **Print Preview**. Compare your screen with Figure 6.34.

FIGURE 6.34

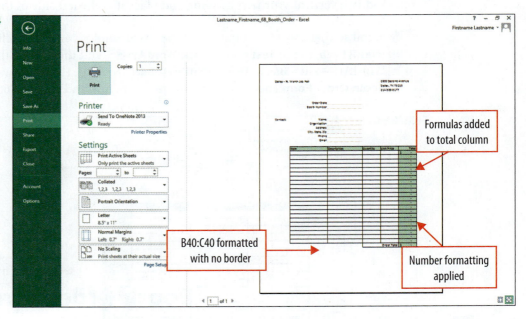

9 In the **Backstage** view, click **Save** to save and return to your workbook.

Activity 6.21 | Inserting and Modifying an Image

In the following activity, you will add a logo image to the form.

1 Click cell **A1** and press Delete to remove the company name. On the **INSERT tab**, in the **Illustrations group**, click **Pictures**.

2 In the **Insert Picture** dialog box, navigate to your student files, and then insert the file **e06B_Logo**.

The Dallas – Ft. Worth Job Fair logo displays in the upper left corner of the worksheet. The Picture Tools contextual tab displays when the object is selected.

3 With the image selected, on the **FORMAT tab**, in the **Picture Styles group**, click **More** , and then, in the third row, click the last style—**Bevel Rectangle**.

4 In the **Picture Styles group**, click the **Picture Effects arrow**, point to **Glow**, and then under **Glow Variations**, in second row, click the last effect—**Green, 8 pt. glow, Accent color 6**. Point to the image to display the pointer, and then drag the image down and to the right slightly, as shown in Figure 6.35. **Save** your workbook.

FIGURE 6.35

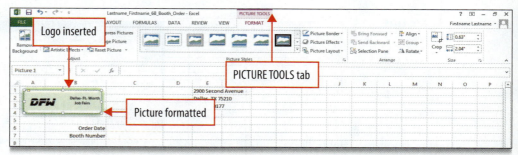

Activity 6.22 | Inserting and Modifying a WordArt Image

WordArt is a feature with which you can insert decorative text in your document, for example to create a stylized image for a heading or logo. Because WordArt is a graphical object, it can be moved and resized. In addition, you can change its shape and color. In this activity, you will create and modify a vertical WordArt heading and place it at the left side of the order form grid.

1 Scroll so that **row 16** is at the top of the Excel window, and then, click cell **A17**. On the **INSERT tab**, in the **Text group**, click **WordArt** , and then in the third row, click the first WordArt—**Fill – Black, Text 1, Outline – Background 1, Hard Shadow – Background 1**. Type **Booth Order Form** and then compare your screen with Figure 6.36.

FIGURE 6.36

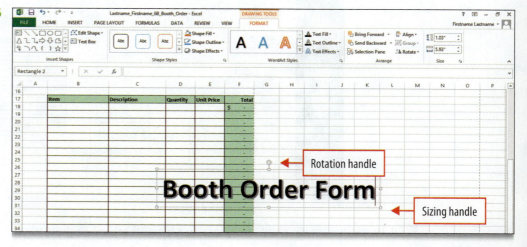

2 Select the text you just typed, and then from the mini toolbar, change the **Font Size** to **20**.

The WordArt image floats on your screen. Sizing handles display around the outside of the WordArt, and a *rotation handle* displays on the top side of the image. Use the rotation handle to rotate an image to any angle.

3 Point to the **rotation handle** until the 🔄 pointer displays, drag to the left until the WordArt is vertical, as shown in Figure 6.37, and then release the mouse button.

You can use the rotation handle to revolve the image 360 degrees.

FIGURE 6.37

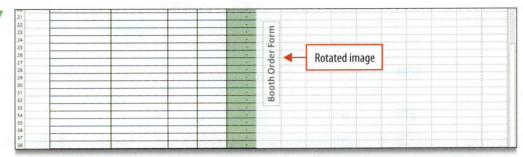

4 Point to the edge of the **WordArt** image to display the ✥ pointer. Drag the WordArt image to **column A** and align the top of the image with the top of cell **A17**—centered in the column.

5 At the lower edge of the WordArt image, point to the center resize handle and drag down so the end of the image aligns at the lower edge of cell **A39**.

6 With the WordArt image still selected, on the **FORMAT tab**, in the **Shape Styles group**, click the **Shape Fill arrow**, point to **Texture**, and then in the fourth row, click the last texture—**Stationery**. Compare your screen with Figure 6.38.

The WordArt text box fills with Stationery texture and color.

FIGURE 6.38

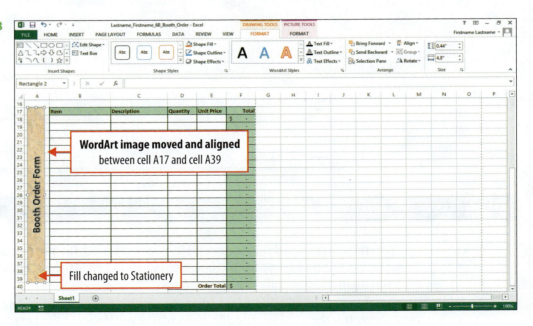

7 In the **left section**, insert a footer that includes the file name. Click any cell outside the footer to deselect. On the status bar, click **Normal** 🔳. Press Ctrl + Home to move to the top of the worksheet. **Save** 💾 your workbook.

Activity 6.23 | Saving a File as a Template

After you complete the formatting and design of a worksheet that you would like to use over and over again, save it as a template file. When saved as a template file, the *.xltx* file extension is added to the file name instead of *.xlsx*.

If a template is saved in the Templates folder on the hard drive of your computer, or the network location where the Excel software resides, the template will be available to other people who have access to the same system from the New tab in Backstage view.

Regardless of where the template file is saved, when the template is opened, a new *copy* of the workbook opens, preserving the original template for future use.

Instead of the Custom Office Templates folder, which might be restricted in a college lab, you will save the template in your **Excel Chapter 6** folder.

1 Press F12 to display the **Save As** dialog box, and then click the **Save as type arrow**. On the list, click **Excel Template**.

2 Navigate to your **Excel Chapter 6** folder.

3 In the **File name** box, change the **File name** to **Lastname_Firstname_6B_Order_Template** and then click **Save**.

A copy of the template is saved with your other files.

4 **Close** the file and **Close** Excel.

5 From the **Windows Taskbar**, click **File Explorer**. Navigate to your **Excel Chapter 6** folder, and then notice that the *Lastname_Firstname_6B_Order_Template* **Type** is listed as *Microsoft Excel Template*. Compare your screen with Figure 6.39. **Close** [**x**] the **File Explorer** window.

FIGURE 6.39

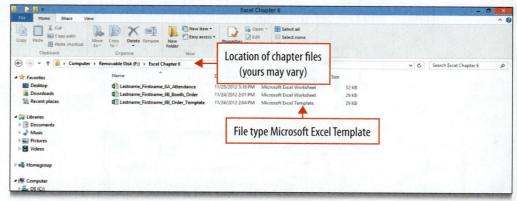

Objective 6 | Protect a Worksheet

Video E6-6

When the template design is complete, you can enable the protection of the worksheet. Protection prevents anyone from changing the worksheet—they cannot insert, modify, delete, or format data in a locked cell.

For purposes of creating a form that you want someone to complete, you can protect the worksheet, and then unlock specific areas where you do want the person completing the form to enter data.

By default, all cells in Excel are *locked*—data cannot be typed into them. However, the locked feature is disabled until you protect the worksheet. After protection is enabled, the locked cells cannot be changed. Of course, you will want to designate some cells to be *unlocked*, so that individuals completing your form can type in their data into those cells.

The basic process is to determine the cells that you will allow people to change or unlock, and then protect the entire worksheet. Then, only the cells that you designated as unlocked will be available to any person using the worksheet. You may add an optional ***password*** to prevent someone from disabling the worksheet protection. The password can be any combination of numbers, letters, or symbols up to 15 characters long. The password should be shared only with people who have permission to change the template.

Activity 6.24 | Protecting a Worksheet

1 Start Excel. From your **Excel Chapter 6** folder, open your template file **Lastname_Firstname_6B_Order_Template**. Select the range **C6:C7**, hold down Ctrl, select the nonadjacent ranges **C10:C15** and **B18:E39**.

The selected cells are the ones that you want individuals placing booth orders to be able to fill in—they should *not* be locked when protection is applied.

> **A L E R T !** **Opening a Template**
>
> If you double-click the template from File Explorer, you will create a new document based on the template, but you will not open the template itself.

2 With the three ranges selected, on the **HOME tab**, in the **Cells group**, click **Format**, and then click **Format Cells**. In the **Format Cells** dialog box, click the **Protection tab**.

3 Click to *clear* the check mark from the **Locked** check box, and then compare your screen with Figure 6.40.

Recall that all cells are locked by default, but the locking feature is enabled only when protection is applied. Therefore, you must *unlock* the cells you want to have available for use in this manner *before* you protect the worksheet.

FIGURE 6.40

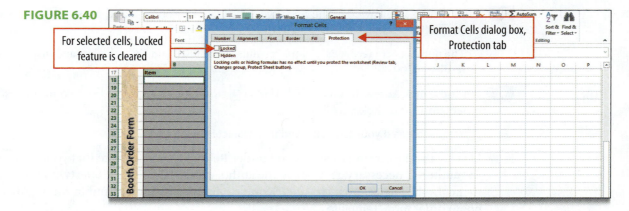

For selected cells, Locked feature is cleared

Format Cells dialog box, Protection tab

4 Click **OK** to close the **Format Cells** dialog box.

5 In the **Cells group**, click **Format**, and then under **Protection**, click **Protect Sheet**.

The Protect Sheet dialog box displays. Under *Allow all users of this worksheet to*, the *Select locked cells* and *Select unlocked cells* check boxes are selected by default. The *Select locked cells* option allows the user to click the locked cells and *view* the formulas, but because the cells are locked, they cannot *change* the content or format of the locked cells. If you deselect this option, the user cannot view or even click in a locked cell.

For the remaining check boxes, you can see that, because they are not selected, users are restricted from performing all other actions on the worksheet.

6 Leave the first two check boxes selected. At the top of the dialog box, be sure the **Protect worksheet and contents of locked cells** check box is selected. In the **Password to unprotect sheet** box type **goseries** Compare your screen with Figure 6.41.

> The password does not display—rather bullets display as placeholders for each letter or character that is typed. Passwords are case sensitive; therefore, *GOSeries* is different from *goseries*.

FIGURE 6.41

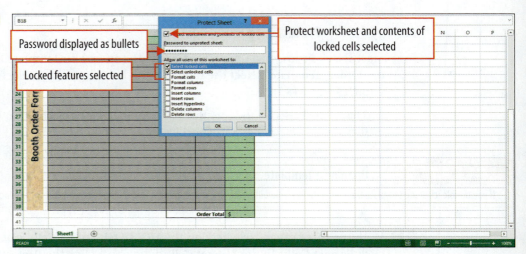

Password displayed as bullets

Locked features selected

Protect worksheet and contents of locked cells selected

7 Click **OK**. In the **Confirm Password** dialog box, type **goseries** to confirm the password, and then click **OK** to close both dialog boxes.

8 Click in any cell in the **Total** column, type **123** and observe what happens.

> The number is not entered; instead a message informs you that the cell you are trying to change is protected and therefore, read-only.

9 Click **OK** to acknowledge the message. Click cell **D18**, type **2** and press Tab, type **150** and press Enter.

> The numbers are recorded and the formulas in cell F18 and F40 calculate and display the results—$300.00.

10 On the **Quick Access Toolbar**, click **Undo** 🔄 two times to remove the two numbers that you typed, and then click **Save** 💾.

> You have tested your template, and it is protected and saved.

11 Display the **document properties** and under **Related People**, be sure that your name displays as the author. If necessary, right-click the author name, click Edit Property, and then type your name. In the **Subject** box, type your course name and section #, and in the **Tags** box, type **booth order form, template**

12 Display the **Print Preview**, redisplay the workbook, and then make any necessary corrections or adjustments.

13 **Save** 💾 your workbook, and then print or submit electronically as directed by your instructor. If required, print or create an electronic version of your worksheet with formulas displayed. **Close** the workbook, but leave Excel open.

More Knowledge   **Modifying a Template**

If you need to make changes to a template after it is protected, you must first remove the protection.

Video E6-7

After the template is protected, it is ready for use. If the template is stored in the Templates folder, anyone using the system or network on which it is stored can open it from the New tab in Backstage view. When opened from this location, Excel opens a new copy of the template as a workbook. Then the user can enter information in the unlocked cells and save it as a new file. Templates can be provided to coworkers by storing them on a company intranet, or they can be made available to customers through a website.

Activity 6.25 | Creating a Worksheet Based on a Template

1 From **Backstage** view, open your **Lastname_Firstname_6B_Order_Template** file.

2 Press F12 to display the **Save As** dialog box, and then set the **Save as type box** to **Excel Workbook**—the first choice at the top of the list. Navigate to your **Excel Chapter 6** folder, and then in the File name box, type **Lastname_Firstname_6B_Topaz_Order** Compare your screen with Figure 6.42.

FIGURE 6.42

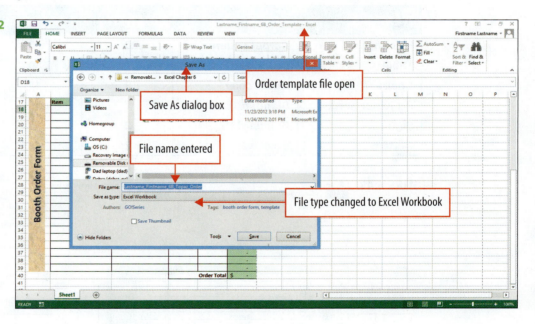

> **NOTE** Creating a Workbook from a Template in the My Templates Folder in Backstage View
>
> When you are able to open a template from the Templates folder in Backstage view, a new copy of the template opens as a workbook, not as a template, and displays a 1 at the end of the file name in the title bar. The 1 indicates a new workbook. If you are able to work from the Templates folder, the Save operation will automatically set the file type to Excel Workbook.

3 Click **Save**. Click cell **C6**, type **October 13, 2016** and press Enter, and notice that Excel applies the default date format. As the booth number, type **A-3421** and then press Tab to move to cell **C10**.

4 Starting in cell **C10**, enter the company information as follows:

Name	**Peter Marsden**
Company	**Topaz Business, Inc.**
Address	**6553 Riverside Drive**
City, State, Postal code	**Ft. Worth, TX 76111**
Phone	**214.555.0230**
Email	**pmarsden@topaz.net**

5 In cell **B18**, type **Booth space** and press Tab, type **10 feet by 10 feet** and press Tab, type **1** and press Tab, type **400.00** and then press Tab.

6 Complete the order by entering the following items, pressing Tab to move from cell to cell. When you are finished, scroll to display **row 16** at the top of your screen, and then compare your screen with Figure 6.43.

ITEM	DESCRIPTION	QUANTITY	UNIT PRICE
Flooring	**Carpet squares**	**20**	**6**
Table	**6 feet, skirted**	**1**	**30**
Chairs	**Guest chair**	**3**	**12**
Projector screen	**Standard**	**1**	**25**
Sign	**Standard**	**2**	**15**
Curtain	**Back wall**	**2**	**12**

FIGURE 6.43

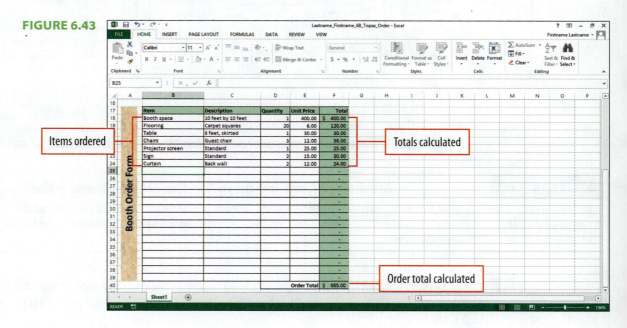

7 Display the **document properties**. Be sure your name displays in the **Author** box and your course name and section # displays in the **Subject** box. Change the **Tags** box to **Topaz booth order**

8 Display the **Print Preview**, be sure the file name displays in the **left section** of the footer. Redisplay the workbook. Make any necessary corrections or adjustments.

9 **Save** 🖫 your workbook, and then print or submit electronically as directed by your instructor. If required, print or create an electronic version of your worksheet with formulas displayed. **Close** Excel.

END | You have completed Project 6B

END OF CHAPTER

SUMMARY

Excel's Recommended Charts feature displays suggested charts based upon your data and helps you to decide the best chart type to use. You can easily modify, create, and format various chart elements.

Excel includes many different chart types, including column and line charts. A column chart shows a comparison among related numbers and a line chart displays a trend over time.

A SmartArt graphic is a visual representation of your information and ideas. SmartArt diagrams are not linked to the underlying worksheet data but float on top of the worksheet like other images.

Templates have built-in formulas and are used for standardization and protection of data. You created a template using text, formatting, formulas, locked and unlocked cells, and password protection.

GO! LEARN IT ONLINE

Review the concepts and key terms in this chapter by completing these online challenges, which you can find at **www.pearsonhighered.com/go.**

Matching and Multiple Choice:
Answer matching and multiple choice questions to test what you learned in this chapter. MyITLab®

Crossword Puzzle:
Spell out the words that match the numbered clues, and put them in the puzzle squares.

Flipboard:
Flip through the definitions of the key terms in this chapter and match them with the correct term.

END OF CHAPTER

REVIEW AND ASSESSMENT GUIDE FOR EXCEL CHAPTER 6

Your instructor may assign one or more of these projects to help you review the chapter and assess your mastery and understanding of the chapter.

		Review and Assessment Guide for Excel Chapter 6	
Project	**Apply Skills from These Chapter Objectives**	**Project Type**	**Project Location**
6C	Objectives 1–4 from Project 6A	**6C Skills Review** A guided review of the skills from Project 6A.	On the following pages
6D	Objectives 5–7 from Project 6B	**6D Skills Review** A guided review of the skills from Project 6B.	On the following pages
6E	Objectives 1–4 from Project 6A	**6E Mastery (Grader Project)** A demonstration of your mastery of the skills in Project 6A with extensive decision making.	In MyITLab and on the following pages
6F	Objectives 5–7 from Project 6B	**6F Mastery (Grader Project)** A demonstration of your mastery of the skills in Project 6B with extensive decision making.	In MyITLab and on the following pages
6G	Combination of Objectives from Projects 6A and 6B	**6G Mastery (Grader Project)** A demonstration of your mastery of the skills in Projects 6A and 6B with extensive decision making.	In MyITLab and on the following pages
6H	Combination of Objectives from Projects 6A and 6B	**6H GO! Fix It** A demonstration of your mastery of the skills in Projects 6A and 6B by creating a correct result from a document that contains errors you must find.	Online
6I	Combination of Objectives from Projects 6A and 6B	**6I GO! Make It** A demonstration of your mastery of the skills in Projects 6A and 6B by creating a result from a supplied picture.	Online
6J	Combination of Objectives from Projects 6A and 6B	**6J GO! Solve It** A demonstration of your mastery of the skills in Projects 6A and 6B, your decision-making skills, and your critical thinking skills. A task-specific rubric helps you self-assess your result.	Online
6K	Combination of Objectives from Projects 6A and 6B	**6K GO! Solve It** A demonstration of your mastery of the skills in Projects 6A and 6B, your decision-making skills, and your critical thinking skills. A task-specific rubric helps you self-assess your result.	On the following pages
6L	Combination of Objectives from Projects 6A and 6B	**6L GO! Think** A demonstration of your understanding of the chapter concepts applied in a manner that you would outside of college. An analytic rubric helps you and your instructor grade the quality of your work by comparing it to the work an expert in the discipline would create.	On the following pages
6M	Combination of Objectives from Projects 6A and 6B	**6M GO! Think** A demonstration of your understanding of the chapter concepts applied in a manner that you would outside of college. An analytic rubric helps you and your instructor grade the quality of your work by comparing it to the work an expert in the discipline would create.	Online
6N	Combination of Objectives from Projects 6A and 6B	**6N You and GO!** A demonstration of your understanding of the chapter concepts applied in a manner that you would in a personal situation. An analytic rubric helps you and your instructor grade the quality of your work.	Online

GLOSSARY

GLOSSARY OF CHAPTER KEY TERMS

Axis A line that serves as a frame of reference for measurement and that borders the chart plot area.

Category labels The labels that display along the bottom of a chart to identify the categories of data.

Chart area The entire chart and all of its elements.

Chart elements Objects that make up a chart.

Chart sheet A workbook sheet that contains only a chart.

Column chart A chart in which the data is arranged in columns and that is useful for showing data changes over a period of time or for illustrating comparisons among items.

Cycle A category of SmartArt graphics that illustrates a continual process.

Data labels Labels that display the value, percentage, and/or category of each particular data point and can contain one or more of the choices listed—Series name, Category name, Value, or Percentage.

Data marker A column, bar, area, dot, pie slice, or other symbol in a chart that represents a single data point; related data points form a data series.

Data point A value that originates in a worksheet cell and that is represented in a chart by a data marker.

Data series Related data points represented by data markers; each data series has a unique color or pattern represented in the chart legend.

Embedded chart A chart that is inserted into the same worksheet that contains the data used to create the chart.

Gridlines Lines in the plot area that aid the eye in determining the plotted values.

Hierarchy A category of SmartArt graphics used to create an organization chart or show a decision tree.

Horizontal Category axis (x-axis) The area along the bottom of a chart that identifies the categories of data; also referred to as the x-axis.

Labels Column and row headings that describe the values and help the reader understand the chart.

Legend A chart element that identifies the patterns or colors that are assigned to the categories in the chart.

Line charts A chart type that is useful to display trends over time; time displays along the bottom axis and the data point values are connected with a line.

List A category of SmartArt graphics used to show non-sequential information.

Locked [cells] In a protected worksheet, data cannot be inserted, modified, deleted, or formatted in these cells.

Major unit value A number that determines the spacing between tick marks and between the gridlines in the plot area.

Matrix A category of SmartArt graphics used to show how parts relate to a whole.

Organization chart A type of graphic that is useful to depict reporting relationships within an organization.

Password An optional element of a template added to prevent someone from disabling a worksheet's protection.

Picture A category of SmartArt graphics that is used to display pictures in a diagram.

Plot area The area bounded by the axes of a chart, including all the data series.

Process A category of SmartArt graphics that is used to show steps in a process or timeline.

Protection This prevents anyone from altering the formulas or changing other template components.

Pyramid A category of SmartArt graphics that uses a series of pictures to show relationships.

Recommended Charts An Excel feature that helps you choose a chart type by previewing suggested charts based upon patterns in your data.

Relationship A category of SmartArt graphics that is used to illustrate connections.

Rotation handle A circle that displays on the top side of a selected object used to rotate the object up to 360 degrees.

Scale The range of numbers in the data series that controls the minimum, maximum, and incremental values on the value axis.

SmartArt graphic A visual representation of information and ideas.

Sparklines Tiny charts that fit within a cell and give a visual trend summary alongside data.

Standardization All forms created within the organization will have a uniform appearance; the data will always be organized in the same manner.

Template A special workbook which may include formatting, formulas, and other elements, that is used as a pattern for creating other workbooks.

Text Pane The pane that displays to the left of the graphic, is populated with placeholder text, and is used to build a graphic by entering and editing text.

Tick mark labels Identifying information for a tick mark generated from the cells on the worksheet used to create the chart.

Tick marks The short lines that display on an axis at regular intervals.

Trendline A graphic representation of trends in a data series, such as a line sloping upward to represent increased sales over a period of months.

Unlocked [cells] Cells in a protected worksheet that may be filled in.

Vertical Value axis (y-axis) A numerical scale on the left side of a chart that shows the range of numbers for the data points; also referred to as the y-axis.

Walls and floor The areas surrounding a 3-D chart that give dimension and boundaries to the chart.

WordArt A feature with which you can insert decorative text in your document.

CHAPTER REVIEW

Apply 6A skills from these Objectives:

1 Create and Format Sparklines and a Column Chart

2 Create and Format a Line Chart

3 Create and Modify a SmartArt Graphic

4 Create and Modify an Organization Chart

Skills Review Project 6C Employer Attendance

In the following Skills Review, you will assist Linda Wong, Employer Relations Manager, in displaying the employer participation for the Dallas – Ft. Worth Job Fair in charts and diagrams. Your completed workbook will look similar to Figure 6.44.

PROJECT FILES

For Project 6C, you will need the following file:

e06C_Employer_Participation

You will save your workbook as:

Lastname_Firstname_6C_Employer_Participation

PROJECT RESULTS

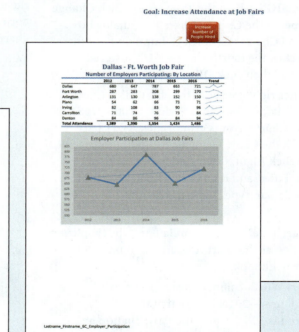

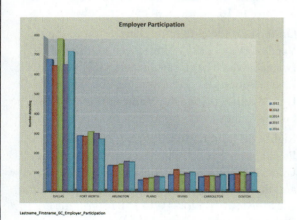

FIGURE 6.44

(Project 6C Employer Attendance continues on the next page)

CHAPTER REVIEW

1 Start Excel. From your student files, open **e06C_Employer_Participation**. **Save** the file in your **Excel Chapter 6** folder as **Lastname_Firstname_6C_Employer_Participation**

a. Select the range **B4:F10**. Click **Quick Analysis**, click **SPARKLINES**, and then click **Line**. On the **DESIGN tab**, in the **Show group**, select the **High Point** check box and the **Last Point** check box. On the **DESIGN tab**, in the **Style group**, click **More**, and then in the third row, click the first style—**Sparkline Style Accent 1, (no dark or light)**. In cell **G3**, type **Trend**

b. Select the range **A3:F10**. On the **INSERT tab**, in the **Charts group**, click **Recommended Charts**. With the **Clustered Column** chart selected, click **OK**. On the **DESIGN tab**, in the **Location group**, click **Move Chart**. Click **New sheet**, name the new sheet **Participation Chart** and then click **OK**.

c. On the **DESIGN tab**, in the **Type group**, click **Change Chart Type**. In the **Change Chart Type** dialog box, click the **All Charts** tab. Click **Column** on the left, and then click the fourth chart—**3-D Clustered Column,** and then click **OK**.

d. In the upper right corner of the chart, click **Chart Styles**. Scroll down and click **Style 3**. On the **DESIGN tab**, in the **Chart Layouts group**, click **Add Chart Element**. In the **Chart Elements** list, point to **Legend**, and then click **Right**. Click **Add Chart Element**, click **Axis Titles**, and then click **Primary Vertical**. In the **Formula Bar**, type **Number Attending** and then press Enter.

e. Click **Chart Title**, in the **Formula Bar**, type **Employer Participation** as the chart title, and then press Enter. **Save** your workbook.

f. In the **Fort Worth** column cluster, point to the last column—**2016**. Notice that the Value for this column is 306. Display the **Participation by Location** worksheet, and then in cell **F5**, type **270** and press Enter. Display the **Participation Chart** worksheet and verify the value for the column has changed.

g. On the **FORMAT tab**, in the **Current Selection group**, click the **Chart Elements arrow**, and then click **Back Wall**. Then in the same group, click **Format Selection**. In the **Format Wall** pane, click **Fill**, click **Solid fill**, and then click the **Fill Color arrow**. Under

Theme Colors, in the fourth column, click the fourth color—**Dark Blue, Text 2, Lighter 40%**—and then set the **Transparency** to **75%**.

h. In the **Format** pane, click the arrow to the right of **WALL OPTIONS** to display the **Chart Elements** list. Select **Side Wall**, and then apply the same fill, but with a **Transparency** of **60%**. To the **Floor**, apply a **Solid fill** using the last color in the first column—**White, Background 1, Darker 50%** with **0% Transparency**. To the **Chart Area**, apply a **Solid fill** using **Tan, Background 2, Darker 10%**—in the third column, the second color. **Close** the **Format** pane.

2 Display the **Participation by Location** worksheet. Select the range **A3:F4**, and then on the **INSERT tab**, in the **Charts group**, click **Insert Line Chart**. In the second row, click the first chart type—**Line with Markers**. Drag the upper left corner of the chart inside the upper left corner of cell **A13**. Drag the lower right corner of the chart inside the lower right corner of cell **G29**.

a. In the embedded chart, click the **Chart Title** Dallas, in the **Formula bar** type **Employer Participation at Dallas Job Fairs**. Point to the **Chart Title**, right-click, click **Font**, and then change the font size to **16**.

b. On the left side of the line chart, point to the **Vertical (Value) axis**, right-click, and then click **Format Axis**. If necessary, expand AXIS OPTIONS. Under **Bounds**, in the **Minimum** box, type **500** Under **Units**, change the **Major unit** to **25 Close** the **Format** pane.

c. Right-click anywhere within the **Plot Area**, click **Format Plot Area**, and if necessary, expand FILL. Under **Fill**, click **Solid fill**, click the **Fill Color arrow**, and then under **Theme Colors**, in the first column, click the fourth color—**White, Background 1, Darker 25%**.

d. Point to the chart line, right-click, and then click **Format Data Series**. Under SERIES OPTIONS, click **Fill & Line**. Under **Line**, click **Solid line**. Use the spin box arrows to set the **Width** to **4 pt**. Under the **Fill & Line** icon, click **MARKER**. Expand **MARKER OPTIONS**. Click **Built-in**, click the **Type arrow**, and then click the **triangle**—the third symbol in the list. Set the **Size** of the **Marker Type** to **14**

(Project 6C Employer Attendance continues on the next page)

e. Under **FILL**, click **Solid fill**, and then click the **Fill Color arrow**. Under **Theme Colors**, in the first column, click the sixth color—**White, Background 1, Darker 50%**.

f. Under **BORDER**, click **No line**. Using any of the techniques you have practiced to select a chart element, select the **Chart Area** and apply a **Solid fill** using **White, Background 1, Darker 15%**—in the first column, the third color. **Close** the **Format pane**. Click in any cell outside of the chart.

g. Click slightly inside the chart border to select the entire chart. On the **DESIGN tab**, in the **Charts Layouts group**, click **Add Chart Element**, point to **Trendline**, and then click **Linear**. **Save** your workbook.

3 ▶ Click **New sheet**, and then rename the sheet **Process Chart** In cell **A1**, type **Goal: Increase Attendance at Job Fairs** and then press Enter. Merge and center the text across the range **A1:H1** and apply the **Title** cell style. On the **INSERT tab**, in the **Illustrations group**, click **SmartArt**. On the left, click **Cycle**, and then in the first row, click the third option—**Block Cycle**. Click **OK**.

a. On the **DESIGN tab**, in the **Create Graphic group**, if necessary, click **Text Pane**. As the first bullet, type **Increase Number of People Hired** Click the next bullet, and then type **Attract More Attendees** As the third bullet, type **Attract More Employers** As the fourth bullet, type **Reduce Costs** As the last bullet, type **Increase Profits Close** the **Text Pane**.

b. Click the edge of the graphic to select it. On the **DESIGN tab**, in the **SmartArt Styles group**, click **More**. Under 3-D, click the first style—**Polished**. Click **Change Colors**, and then under **Colorful**, click the first option—**Colorful – Accent Colors**. Drag the upper left corner of the graphic into the left corner of cell **A3**. Drag the lower right corner inside the lower right corner of cell **H20**. Click cell **A1**, and then click **Save**.

4 ▶ Click **New sheet**, and rename the sheet tab **Organization Chart** In cell **A1**, type **Job Fair Employer Services Structure** and then merge and center this title across the range **A1:H1**. Apply the **Title** cell style. On the **INSERT tab**, in the **Illustrations group**, click **SmartArt**. On the left, click **Hierarchy**, and then in the first row,

click the third graphic—**Name and Title Organization Chart**. Click **OK**.

a. If the **Text Pane** displays, close it. In the graphic, click in the first [**Text**] box, and then type **Holly Lance** Click the edge of the small white box below Holly Lance to select it and type **Employer Manager** In the [**Text**] box below Employer Manager, click on the edge of the box to display a solid line border—if a dashed border displays, click the edge of the box again. With the box bordered with a solid line, press Delete.

b. On the second level, click in the leftmost shape, and then using the technique you just practiced, type **Jack Nix** and **Operations Manager** In the next shape, type **MJ Marks** and **Marketing Specialist** In the rightmost shape, type **Mary Treo** and **Finance Analyst** Hold down Ctrl, and then click the edge of each of the smaller title boxes to select all four. Then, on the **HOME tab**, in the **Font group**, change the font size to **8**, and click **Center**.

c. Drag the upper left corner of the graphic into cell **A3** and the lower right corner into cell **H20**. On the **DESIGN tab**, in the **SmartArt Styles group**, apply **Intense Effect style**. Change the colors to **Colorful – Accent Colors**.

d. Display the **Participation Chart** sheet. On the **INSERT tab**, click **Header & Footer**, and then click **Custom Footer**. With the insertion point in the **left section**, from the small toolbar in the dialog box, click **Insert File Name**. Click **OK** two times.

e. Display the **Participation by Location** sheet. Hold down Ctrl and select the remaining two worksheets to group the three sheets. Insert a footer with the file name in the **left section**. Click outside the footer area to deselect. On the **PAGE LAYOUT tab**, click **Margins**, click **Custom Margins**, and then center the sheets horizontally. Click **OK**. Return to **Normal** view and press Ctrl + Home to move to cell **A1**.

f. Right-click any of the grouped sheet tabs and click **Ungroup Sheets**. Click the **FILE tab** to display **Backstage** view. On the right, at the bottom of the **Properties** list, click **Show All Properties**. On the list of **Properties**, in the **Tags** box, type **employer**

(Project 6C Employer Attendance continues on the next page)

CHAPTER REVIEW

participation, organization chart In the **Subject** box, type your course name and section #. Under **Related People**, be sure that your name displays as the author. If necessary, right-click the author name, click Edit Property, type your name, click outside of the Edit person dialog box, and then click OK.

g. Click **Save**. Display and examine the **Print Preview**, make any necessary corrections, **Save**, and then print or submit electronically as directed by your instructor. If you are directed to do so, print the formulas on the Participation by Location worksheet. **Close** Excel.

END | You have completed Project 6C

CHAPTER REVIEW

Skills Review Project 6D Purchase Order

Apply 6B skills from these Objectives:

5 Create an Excel Template
6 Protect a Worksheet
7 Create a Worksheet Based on a Template

Build from Scratch

In the following Skills Review, you will assist Job Fair Director, Amanda Shay, in creating a template for a Purchase Order, and then a Purchase Order for items with a logo and name imprint of the Dallas – Ft. Worth Job Fair. Your completed worksheets will look similar to Figure 6.45.

PROJECT FILES

For Project 6D, you will need the following files:

E06D_Logo
New blank Excel workbook

You will save your workbooks as:

Lastname_Firstname_6D_Hancock_PO
Lastname_Firstname_6D_PO_Template
Lastname_Firstname_6D_Purchase_Order

PROJECT RESULTS

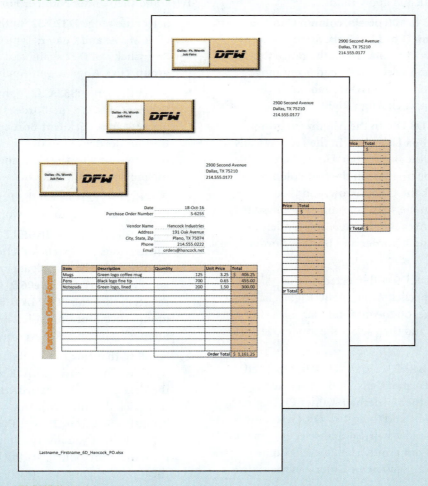

FIGURE 6.45

(Project 6D Purchase Order continues on the next page)

CHAPTER REVIEW

1 Start Excel and display a new blank workbook. **Save** the file in your **Excel Chapter 6** folder as **Lastname_Firstname_6D_Purchase_Order** Beginning in cell **E1**, type **2900 Second Avenue** and press Enter. In cell **E2**, type **Dallas, TX 75210** and in cell **E3**, type **214.555.0177** and press Enter.

a. Click cell **C8**, type **Date** and press Enter. In cell **C9**, type **Purchase Order Number** Click cell **C11**. Type **Vendor Name** and press Enter. In cell **C12**, type **Address** In cell **C13**, type **City, State, Zip** In cell **C14**, type **Phone** In cell **C15**, type **Email**

b. Click cell **B18**. Type **Item** and press Tab to move to cell **C18**. Continuing across **row 18**, in cell **C18**, type **Description** and press Tab, in cell **D18**, type **Quantity** and press Tab, in cell **E18**, type **Unit Price** and press Tab, and in cell **F18**, type **Total** and press Enter. Select the range **B18:F18** and apply **Bold**.

c. Widen **column B** to **100 pixels**, **column C** to **165 pixels** and **column D** to **145 pixels**. Select **columns E:F** and widen to **75 pixels**. Select the range **C8:C9**, hold down Ctrl and select the nonadjacent range **C11:C15**, and then on the **HOME tab**, in the **Alignment group**, click **Align Right**.

d. Select the range **D8:D9**. In the **Alignment group**, click the **Dialog Box Launcher**. In the **Format Cells** dialog box, click the **Border tab**. Under **Line**, in the **Style** list, click the first line in the first column—a dotted line. Click the **Color arrow**, and then under **Theme Colors**, in the sixth column, click the sixth color—**Orange, Accent 2, Darker 50%**. Under **Border**, click **Middle Border** and **Bottom Border**. Click **OK**.

e. With the range **D8:D9** still selected, in the **Alignment group**, click **Align Right**. Right-click over the selected range, on the mini toolbar, click the **Format Painter**, and then select the range **D11:D15** to copy the format.

f. Select the range **B18:F32**. Right-click the selected range and click **Format Cells**. In the **Format Cells** dialog box, click the **Border tab**. Under **Presets**, click **Outline** and **Inside**, and then click **OK**. Select the range **B18:F18**, hold down Ctrl and select the range **F19:F32**. In the **Font group**, click the **Fill Color arrow**, and then under **Theme Colors**, in the sixth column, click the third color—**Orange, Accent 2, Lighter 60%**.

g. Press Ctrl + Home. Press Ctrl + F2 to examine the **Print Preview**. Click **Save** to save and return to your workbook.

2 To construct a formula to multiply the Quantity times the Unit Price, in cell **F19**, type **=d19*e19** and click **Enter**. Use the fill handle to copy the formula in cell **F19** down through cell **F31**. Click cell **F32**. On the **HOME tab**, in the **Editing group**, click **AutoSum**. Be sure the range displays as **F19:F31**, and then press Enter. Select the range **E19:E31**. In the **Number group**, click **Comma Style**. Click cell **F19**, hold down Ctrl, and then click cell **F32**. In the **Number group**, click **Accounting Number Format**. Select the range **F20:F31**, and then click **Comma Style**. Select the range **D19:D31**, and then in the **Styles group**, click **Cell Styles**, and then under **Number Format**, click **Comma [0]**.

a. Select the range **D32:E32**. In the **Alignment group**, click **Merge and Center**. Type **Order Total** and press Enter. Click cell **D32** again, and then in the **Alignment group**, click **Align Right**. Apply **Bold**.

b. Select the range **B32:C32**, right-click, and then click **Format Cells**. On the **Border tab**, in the **Border** preview area, click **Left Border**, **Middle Border**, and **Bottom Border** to remove these borders from the preview—be sure the right and top lines remain in the preview area. Click **OK**.

c. Press Ctrl + F2 to view the **Print Preview**. Click **Save** to save and return to your workbook.

d. Click cell **A1**. On the **INSERT tab**, in the **Illustrations group**, click **Pictures**. In the **Insert Picture** dialog box, navigate to your student files, and then insert the file **e06D_Logo**. With the image selected, click the **FORMAT tab**, in the **Picture Styles group**, click **More**, and then locate and click the **Simple Frame, Black**. **Save** your workbook.

e. Scroll so that **row 16** is at the top of the Excel window. Then, click cell **A18**. On the **INSERT tab**, in the **Text group**, click **WordArt**, and then in the first row, click the third WordArt—**Fill – Orange, Accent 2, Outline – Accent 2**. Type **Purchase Order Form** Select the text you just typed, right-click, and then from the mini toolbar, set the **Font Size** to **20**. Drag the rotation handle to the left until the WordArt is

(Project 6D Purchase Order continues on the next page)

CHAPTER REVIEW

vertical. Then, drag the WordArt image to **column A** and align the top of the image with the top of cell **A18**—centered in the column. At the lower edge of the WordArt image, point to the center resize handle and drag down so the end of the image aligns at the lower edge of cell **A32**.

f. With the WordArt still selected, on the **FORMAT tab**, in the **Shape Styles group**, click the **Shape Fill arrow**, click **Texture**, and then in the fourth row, click the second texture—**Recycled Paper**. Click to deselect the WordArt, and then press Ctrl + Home. Insert a footer in the **left section** that includes the file name. Click any cell outside the footer to deselect. On the status bar, click **Normal**. Press Ctrl + Home to move to the top of the worksheet. From **Backstage** view, display the **document properties**, type your firstname and lastname as the **Author**, your course name and section # as the **Subject**, and **purchase order** as the **Tags**, and then **Save** your workbook.

g. Press F12 to display the **Save As** dialog box, and then click the **Save as type arrow**. On the list, click **Excel Template**. Navigate to your **Excel Chapter 6** folder. In the **File name** box, change the **File name** to **Lastname_Firstname_6D_PO_Template** and then click **Save**.

3 Select the range **D8:D9**, hold down Ctrl, select the range **D11:D15** and the range **B19:E31**. With the three ranges selected, on the **HOME tab**, in the **Cells group**, click **Format**, and then click **Format Cells**. In the **Format Cells** dialog box, click the **Protection tab**. Click to clear the check mark from the **Locked** check box. Click **OK**.

a. In the **Cells group**, click **Format**, and then under **Protection**, click **Protect Sheet**. Under **Allow all users of this worksheet to:** leave the first two check boxes selected. At the top of the dialog box, be sure the **Protect worksheet and contents of locked cells** check box is selected. In the **Password to unprotect sheet** box, type **goseries** Click **OK**. In the displayed **Confirm Password** dialog box, type **goseries** to confirm the password, and then click **OK** to close both dialog boxes. Click **Save**.

b. Display the **document properties**. The **Author** and **Subject** boxes contain your previous information. As the **Tags**, type **purchase order form, template**

c. Check the **Print Preview**, and then **Save** your template.

4 To create a purchase order from your template, display the **Save As** dialog box, and then set the **Save as type** box to **Excel Workbook**—the first choice at the top of the list. Navigate to your **Excel Chapter 6** folder, and then in the **File name** box, type **Lastname_Firstname_6D_Hancock_PO** Click **Save**.

a. Click cell **D8**, type **October 18, 2016** and press Enter—Excel applies the default date format. As the Purchase Order Number, type **S-6255** and then press Enter two times to move to cell **D11**. Beginning in cell **D11**, enter the vendor information as follows:

Vendor Name:	**Hancock Industries**
Address	**191 Oak Avenue**
City, State, ZIP	**Plano, TX 75074**
Phone	**214.555.0222**
Email	**orders@hancock.net**

b. Click cell **B19**, and then complete the order by entering the items as shown in the following table, pressing Tab to move from cell to cell.

Item	Description	Quantity	Unit Price
Mugs	Green logo coffee mug	125	3.25
Pens	Black logo fine tip	700	0.65
Notepads	Green logo, lined	200	1.50

c. Display the **document properties**. Be sure your name displays in the **Author** box and your course name and section # displays in the **Subject** box. Change the **Tags** to **Hancock, promotional items** Check the **Print Preview** to be sure the file name updated and displays in the **left section** of the footer.

d. **Save** your workbook. As directed by your instructor, print or submit electronically the three workbooks you created in this project. If required to do so, print or create an electronic version of your worksheets that contain formulas. **Close** Excel.

END | You have completed Project 6D

CONTENT-BASED ASSESSMENTS

Mastering Excel Project 6E Hires

Apply 6A skills from these Objectives:

1. Create and Format Sparklines and a Column Chart
2. Create and Format a Line Chart
3. Create and Modify a SmartArt Graphic
4. Create and Modify an Organization Chart

In the following project, you will assist Linda Wong, Employer Relations Manager, in tracking the number of people who get hired by an employer at each fair. You will create and modify a chart to display the number of people hired at the fairs in the past five years, create a diagram of the communities served, and create an organizational chart for staff at the Job Fair. Your completed worksheets will look similar to Figure 6.46.

PROJECT FILES

For Project 6E, you will need the following file:

e06E_Hires

You will save your workbook as:

Lastname_Firstname_6E_Hires

PROJECT RESULTS

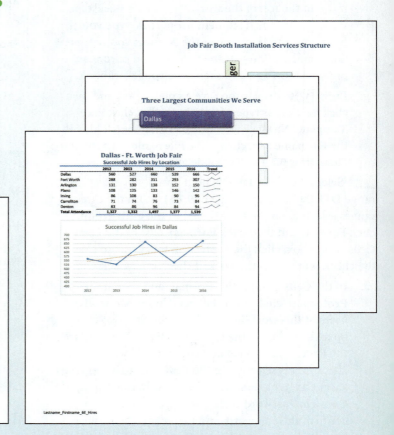

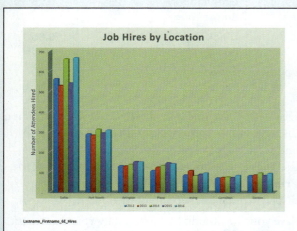

FIGURE 6.46

(Project 6E Hires continues on the next page)

CONTENT-BASED ASSESSMENTS

Mastering Excel | Project 6E Hires (continued)

1 Start Excel. From your student files, open **e06E_Hires** and **Save** the file in your **Excel Chapter 6** folder as **Lastname_Firstname_6E_Hires** Using the data in the range **A4:F10**, insert **Sparklines** using the **Line** format. Place the sparklines in the range adjacent to the **2016** column, show the **High Point** and **Last Point**, and then apply Sparkline **Style Accent 4, Darker 25%**. Type **Trend** in the cell above the sparklines.

2 Using the data for the years and for each location (not the totals), create a **3-D Clustered Column** chart on a separate chart sheet named **Hires by Location Chart** Apply **Style 11**, and change the **Chart Title** to **Job Hires by Location** Set the title's font size to **28**. Format the **Chart Area** with a solid fill using **Olive Green, Accent 3, Lighter 80%**. Format the **Plot Area** with a solid fill two shades darker—**Olive Green, Accent 3, Lighter 40%**. Format the floor and the side wall with a solid fill color using **Aqua, Accent 5, Darker 50%** and **60%** transparency. Add a title to the vertical axis with the text **Number of Attendees Hired** and change the font size to **16**.

3 On the **Job Hires by Location** worksheet, using the data for Dallas, insert a **Line with Markers** line chart. Position the chart between cells **A13** and **G26**. Change the chart title to **Successful Job Hires in Dallas** and set the title's font size to **16**. Format the **Vertical (Value) Axis** so that the **Minimum** value is **400** and the **Major unit** is **25** Add a **Linear Trendline**. Format the **Line Color** of the trendline with **Orange, Accent 6** and set the **Line Style** to a width of **2 pt**.

4 Insert a new sheet and name it **List Chart** In cell **A1**, type **Three Largest Communities We Serve** Merge and center this title across the range **A1:G1** and apply the **Title** cell style. Insert a **SmartArt** graphic using the **Vertical Box List**. In the three boxes, type, in order, **Dallas** and

Fort Worth and **Carrollton** Position the graphic between cells **A3** and **G16**. Apply the **Inset** style and change the colors to **Colorful Range – Accent Colors 4 to 5**. Click cell **A1**.

5 Insert a new sheet and name it **Organization Chart** In cell **A1**, type **Job Fair Booth Installation Services Structure** Merge and center this title across the range **A1:H1** and apply the **Title** cell style. Insert a **SmartArt** graphic using **Horizontal Multi-Level Hierarchy**. In the vertical box, type **Booth Manager** and in the three remaining boxes, type **Safety Inspectors** and **Electricians** and **Carpenters** Position the graphic between cells **A4** and **H16**. Apply the **Subtle Effect** style and change the colors to **Colorful Range – Accent Colors 4 to 5**. Click cell **A1** to deselect.

6 Display the **Hires by Location Chart** sheet. On the **INSERT tab**, click **Header & Footer**, click **Custom Footer** and then insert the File name in the **left section**.

7 Display the **Job Hires by Location** sheet. Hold down Ctrl and select the remaining two worksheets to group the three sheets. Insert a footer with the file name in the **left section**. Return to **Normal** view and move to cell **A1**. On the **PAGE LAYOUT tab**, click **Margins**, click **Custom Margins**, and then center the sheets horizontally.

8 Ungroup the worksheets. Display the **document properties**, type your firstname and lastname as the author, type your course name and section # in the **Subject** box, and as the **Tags**, type **hires by location** and **Save**. Display and examine the **Print Preview**, make any necessary corrections, **Save**, and then print or submit electronically as directed by your instructor. If you are directed to do so, print the formulas on the Job Hires by Location worksheet. **Close** Excel.

END | You have completed Project 6E

CONTENT-BASED ASSESSMENTS

Mastering Excel Project 6F Event Budget

In the following Mastering Excel project, you will create a budget template for the Dallas location of the Dallas - Ft. Worth Job Fair. You will also create a worksheet based on the budget template for review by Milton Hyken, Dallas Job Fair Director. Your completed worksheets will look similar to Figure 6.47.

Apply 6B skills from these Objectives:

5 Create an Excel Template

6 Protect a Worksheet

7 Create a Worksheet Based on a Template

Build from Scratch

PROJECT FILES

For Project 6F, you will need the following files:

New blank Excel workbook
e06F_Logo

You will save your workbooks as:

Lastname_Firstname_6F_Budget_Template
Lastname_Firstname_6F_Dallas_Budget

PROJECT RESULTS

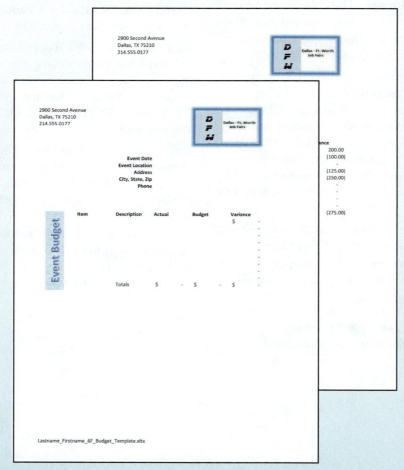

FIGURE 6.47

(Project 6F Event Budget continues on the next page)

CONTENT-BASED ASSESSMENTS

1 Start Excel and display a new blank workbook. In cell **A1**, type **2900 Second Avenue** In cell **A2**, type **Dallas, TX 75210** In cell **A3**, type **214.555.0177**

In cell **C8**, type **Event Date** In cell **C9**, type **Event Location** In cell **C10**, type **Address** In cell **C11**, type **City, State, Zip** In cell **C12**, type **Phone**

In cell **B16**, type **Item** and press Tab . In cell **C16**, type **Description** In cell **D16**, type **Actual** In cell **E16**, type **Budget** In cell **F16**, type **Variance** Click cell **C26** and type **Totals**

2 To the ranges **C8:C12** and **B16:F16**, apply **Bold**. To the range **C8:C12**, apply **Align Right**. To the range **D8:D12**, apply **Align Left**. Widen columns **A:F** to **95 pixels**.

To construct a formula to compute the Variance (Variance = Actual – Budget) for each budget item, in cell **F17**, type **=d17-e17** and copy the formula through cell **F25**. In the range **D26:F26**, insert appropriate formulas to sum these columns. To the range **D18:F25**, apply **Comma Style**. To the ranges **D17:F17** and **D26:F26**, apply **Accounting Number Format**.

3 In cell **E1**, insert the picture **e06F_Logo**. Click cell **A16**, insert a **WordArt** using **Fill – Blue, Accent 1, Outline – Background 1, Hard Shadow – Accent 1**—in the third row, the third WordArt. As the text, type **Event Budget** and set the **Font Size** to **24**. Rotate the WordArt vertically, and align it between cells **A16** and **A26**. In the **Shape Styles group**, click the **Shape Fill arrow**, click **Texture**, and then click **Blue tissue paper**.

4 Select the ranges **D8:D12** and **B17:E25**. Remove the **Locked** formatting from the selected cells, and then protect the worksheet. Be sure the check box at the top and the first two check boxes in the list are selected, and as the password type **goseries**

Insert a footer in the **left section** with the file name. Add your name, course information, and the **Tags budget template** to the **document properties**, and

then check the **Print Preview**. **Save** your workbook as an **Excel Template** in your **Excel Chapter 6** folder as **Lastname_Firstname_6F_Budget_Template**

5 To create a new budget report using the template as your model, display the **Save As** dialog box again, and then **Save** the template as an **Excel Workbook** in your **Excel Chapter 6** folder as **Lastname_Firstname_6F_Dallas_Budget** Enter the following data:

Event Date	**October 22, 2016**
Event Location	**Dallas**
Address	**288 Alba Drive**
City, State, ZIP	**Dallas, TX 75210**
Phone	**214.555.6575**

Complete the order by entering the items as shown in the following table.

Item	Description	Actual	Budget
Venue	**Hall rental fee**	**7200**	**7000**
Personnel	**Site staff**	**500**	**600**
Equipment	**Computers**	**400**	**400**
Publicity	**Signage**	**725**	**850**
Speakers	**Speaking fees**	**1750**	**2000**

6 Change the **Tags** to **Dallas event budget** Examine the **Print Preview**. **Save** your workbook. As directed by your instructor, print or submit electronically the two workbooks you created in this project. If required to do so, print or create an electronic version of your worksheets that contain formulas. **Close** Excel.

END | You have completed Project 6F

CONTENT-BASED ASSESSMENTS

Mastering Excel Project 6G Internships and Travel Template

In the following project, you will assist Ann Takei, Internship Coordinator, in tracking the number of internships by industry at each job fair and in creating a template to use for travel expenses. Your completed worksheets will look similar to Figure 6.48.

Apply 6A and 6B skills from these Objectives:

1 Create and Format Sparklines and a Column Chart
2 Create and Format a Line Chart
3 Create and Modify a SmartArt Graphic
4 Create and Modify an Organization Chart
5 Create an Excel Template
6 Protect a Worksheet
7 Create a Worksheet Based on a Template

PROJECT FILES

For Project 6G, you will need the following files:

e06G_Internships
e06G_Travel_Expense

You will save your workbooks as:

Lastname_Firstname_6G_Internships
Lastname_Firstname_6G_Jackson_Report
Lastname_Firstname_6G_Travel_Template

PROJECT RESULTS

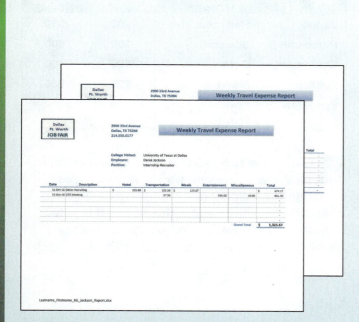

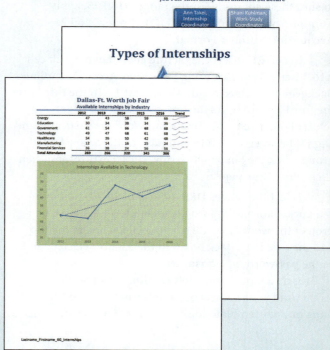

FIGURE 6.48

(Project 6G Internships and Travel Template continues on the next page)

CONTENT-BASED ASSESSMENTS

1 Start Excel. From your student files, locate and open **e06G_Internships**. **Save** the file in your **Excel Chapter 6** folder as **Lastname_Firstname_6G_Internships** Using the range **A4:F10**, insert **Sparklines** in the **Line** format in the range adjacent to the last year of data. Show the **High Point** and **Last Point** and apply Sparkline **Style Accent 4, (no dark or light)**. In cell **G3**, type **Trend** and apply the format from cell **F3**.

2 Select the ranges representing the years (including the blank cell **A3**) and the data for **Technology** internships. Insert a line chart using the **Line with Markers** chart style. Reposition the chart between cells **A13** and **G29**. Change the **Chart Title** to **Internships Available in Technology** Edit the **Vertical (Value) Axis** to set the **Minimum** to **35** and the **Major unit** to **5**

3 Format the **Plot Area** with a solid fill using **Olive Green, Accent 3, Lighter 60%**. Format the **Chart Area** with a solid fill using **Olive Green, Accent 3, Lighter 40%**. Insert a **Linear Trendline** and change the width of the line to **2.5 pt**.

4 Insert a new sheet and name it **List Chart** In cell **A1**, type **Types of Internships** Merge and center the text across the range **A1:H1**, apply the **Title** cell style, and then set the **Font Size** to **36**. Insert a **SmartArt** graphic using the **Pyramid List**. Position the graphic between cells **A3** and **H19**. In the top text box, type **Paid** In the second text box, type **Work-Study** and in the last box, type **Unpaid** Apply the **Inset** style and change the colors to **Colored Fill – Accent 1**.

5 Insert a new sheet and name it **Organization Chart** In cell **A1**, type **Job Fair Internship Coordination Structure** and then merge and center this title across the range **A1:I1**. Apply the **Title** cell style. Insert a **SmartArt** graphic using the **Hierarchy List**. Position the graphic between cells **A3** and **I17**. On the left, create a list with the following names and titles: **Ann Takei, Internship Coordinator** and **Dennis Maslin, Specialist** and **Cory**

Finley, Specialist On the right, create a list with the following names and titles: **Shani Kuhlman, Work-Study Coordinator** and **Anand Singh, Specialist** and **Vanessa Lopez, Specialist** Apply the **Inset** style and **Gradient Range – Accent 1**.

6 Group the three sheets, insert a footer with the file name in the **left section**, and then center the sheets horizontally. Display the **document properties**. Add your name, your course name and section #, and the **Tags internship organization** Examine the **Print Preview**, ungroup the worksheets, **Save** and **Close** this workbook, but leave Excel open.

7 From your student files, open the file **e06G_Travel_Expense**. Display the **Save As** dialog box, and then **Save** the workbook as an **Excel Template** in your **Excel Chapter 6** folder with the name **Lastname_Firstname_6G_Travel_Template** In the range **H15:H21**, create formulas to sum the data in each row—do not include the Date or Description columns. In cell **H22**, create a formula to create a grand total of expenses. Apply appropriate financial formatting to all the cells that will contain expenses, including the **Total** cell style in cell **H22**—refer to Figure 6.48.

8 Select the nonadjacent ranges **D8:D10** and **A15:G21**. Remove the **Locked** formatting from the selected cells and protect the worksheet. Be sure the top check box and the first two check boxes in the list are selected. As the password, type **goseries** Add your name, course information, and the **Tags travel template** to the document properties. Insert a footer with the file name in the **left section**. Click **Save**.

9 To use the template for an employee's report, **Save** it as an **Excel Workbook** in your **Excel Chapter 6** folder with the file name **Lastname_Firstname_6G_Jackson_Report** As the College Visited, type **University of Texas at Dallas** As the Employee, type **Derek Jackson** and as the Position, type **Internship Recruiter** Use the data in Table 1 to complete the report:

TABLE 1

Date	Description	Hotel	Transport	Meals	Entertainment	Misc.
11-Oct-16	Dallas Recruiting	325	225.50	123.67		
12-Oct-16	UTD Meeting		37.50		595	19

(Project 6G Internships and Travel Template continues on the next page)

CONTENT-BASED ASSESSMENTS

10 Change the **Tags** to **UTD meeting** Examine the **Print Preview**; notice the file name is updated and displays in the **left section** of the footer. **Save** your workbook.

11 As directed by your instructor, print or submit electronically the two workbooks you created in this project. If required to do so, print or create an electronic version of your worksheets that contain formulas. **Close** Excel.

END | You have completed Project 6G

CONTENT-BASED ASSESSMENTS

Apply a combination of the 6A and 6B skills.

GO! Fix It	Project 6H Operations Chart	Online
GO! Make It	Project 6I Advertisers	Online
GO! Solve It	Project 6J Sponsors	Online
GO! Solve It	Project 6K Time Card	

PROJECT FILES

For Project 6K, you will need the following file:

e06K_Time_Card

You will save your workbook as:

Lastname_Firstname_6K_Time_Template

Open the file **e06K_Time_Card** and save it as a template in your **Excel Chapter 6** file with the name **Lastname_Firstname_6K_Time_Template** Insert formulas to calculate daily pay (Regular Hours X Rate Per Hour) using an absolute cell reference, to total the hours for the week, and a formula to calculate the total pay. Apply appropriate number and financial formatting. Reposition the WordArt above the Time Card chart. Unlock the cells in which an individual would enter variable data, and then protect the sheet with the password **goseries** Insert the file name in the footer, add appropriate information to the document properties including the **Tags time card, payroll** and submit as directed by your instructor.

(Project 6K Time Card continues on the next page)

CONTENT-BASED ASSESSMENTS

Performance Level

	Exemplary	Proficient	Developing
Place WordArt Object and Apply Financial Formatting	Appropriate formulas, cell formatting, and WordArt placement are applied.	Appropriate formulas, cell formatting, and WordArt placement are partially applied.	Appropriate formulas, cell formatting, and WordArt placement are not applied.
Lock Formulas	Formula cells are locked and variable data cells are unlocked.	Only one of the formula cells or variable data cells has the locked or unlocked feature applied appropriately.	Formula cells are unlocked and variable data cells are locked.
Protect Worksheet	The worksheet is protected with the password goseries.	The worksheet is protected but not with the password goseries.	The worksheet is not protected with the password goseries.

Performance Criteria (vertical label)

END | You have completed Project 6K

OUTCOMES-BASED ASSESSMENTS

RUBRIC

The following outcomes-based assessments are open-ended assessments. That is, there is no specific correct result; your result will depend on your approach to the information provided. Make Professional Quality your goal. Use the following scoring rubric to guide you in how to approach the problem and then to evaluate how well your approach solves the problem.

The *criteria*—Software Mastery, Content, Format and Layout, and Process—represent the knowledge and skills you have gained that you can apply to solving the problem. The *levels of performance*—Professional Quality, Approaching Professional Quality, or Needs Quality Improvements—help you and your instructor evaluate your result.

	Your completed project is of Professional Quality if you:	Your completed project is Approaching Professional Quality if you:	Your completed project Needs Quality Improvements if you:
1-Software Mastery	Choose and apply the most appropriate skills, tools, and features and identify efficient methods to solve the problem.	Choose and apply some appropriate skills, tools, and features, but not in the most efficient manner.	Choose inappropriate skills, tools, or features, or are inefficient in solving the problem.
2-Content	Construct a solution that is clear and well organized, contains content that is accurate, appropriate to the audience and purpose, and is complete. Provide a solution that contains no errors in spelling, grammar, or style.	Construct a solution in which some components are unclear, poorly organized, inconsistent, or incomplete. Misjudge the needs of the audience. Have some errors in spelling, grammar, or style, but the errors do not detract from comprehension.	Construct a solution that is unclear, incomplete, or poorly organized; contains some inaccurate or inappropriate content; and contains many errors in spelling, grammar, or style. Do not solve the problem.
3-Format & Layout	Format and arrange all elements to communicate information and ideas, clarify function, illustrate relationships, and indicate relative importance.	Apply appropriate format and layout features to some elements, but not others. Overuse features, causing minor distraction.	Apply format and layout that does not communicate information or ideas clearly. Do not use format and layout features to clarify function, illustrate relationships, or indicate relative importance. Use available features excessively, causing distraction.
4-Process	Use an organized approach that integrates planning, development, self-assessment, revision, and reflection.	Demonstrate an organized approach in some areas, but not others; or, use an insufficient process of organization throughout.	Do not use an organized approach to solve the problem.

OUTCOMES-BASED ASSESSMENTS

GO! Think — Project 6L Tech Industry

PROJECT FILES

For Project 6L, you will need the following file:

e06L_Tech_Industry

You will save your workbook as:

Lastname_Firstname_6L_Tech_Industry

From your student files, open the file **e06L_Tech_Industry**, and then save it in your **Excel Chapter 6** folder as **Lastname_Firstname_6L_Tech_Industry** Format the data attractively, add appropriate formulas, add sparklines, and insert a line chart in the sheet that tracks the data for the Irving location. Create a 3-D chart on a separate page based on the data in the worksheet, and format it attractively. Change the Fort Worth 2016 data point from 84 to 96. Insert the file name in the footer on each page, format each sheet for printing, add appropriate information to the document properties including the **Tags technology employers** and submit as directed by your instructor.

END | You have completed Project 6L

Build from
Scratch

GO! Think — Project 6M Location List — Online

You and GO! — Project 6N Job Finding — Online

Enhancing Tables

GO! to Work
Video A4

PROJECT 4A	OUTCOMES Maneuver and manage data.

OBJECTIVES

1. Manage Existing Tables
2. Modify Existing Tables
3. Change Data Types
4. Attach Files to Records

PROJECT 4B	OUTCOMES Format tables and validate data entry.

OBJECTIVES

5. Create a Table in Design View
6. Create a Lookup Field
7. Set Field Properties
8. Create Data Validation Rules and Validation Text

In This Chapter

In this chapter, you will enhance tables and improve data accuracy and data entry. You will begin by identifying secure locations where databases will be stored and by backing up existing databases to protect the data. You will edit existing tables for more effective design and copy data and table design across tables. You will create a new table in Design view and determine the best data type for each field based on its characteristics. You will use the field properties to enhance the table and to improve data accuracy and data entry, including looking up data in another table and attaching an existing document to a record.

Golden Grove, California, is a growing city located between Los Angeles and San Diego. Just 10 years ago the population was under 100,000; today it has grown to almost 300,000. Its growth in population is based on its growth as a community. Community leaders have always focused on quality of life and economic development in decisions on housing, open space, education, and infrastructure, making the city a model for other communities its size around the United States. The city provides many recreational and cultural opportunities with a large park system and library system, thriving arts, and a friendly business atmosphere.

City Directory

PROJECT ACTIVITIES

Dario Soto, the new city manager of Golden Grove, has a database of city directory information. This database has three tables that have duplicate information in them. In Activities 4.01 through 4.12, you will redesign the tables, edit and proofread data, change data types, and attach files to records. Your completed tables will look similar to those in Figure 4.1.

PROJECT FILES

For Project 4A, you will need the following files:

a04A_GG_Directory
a04A_GG_Employees
a04A_PZ_Schedule
a04A_Bldg_Permit_App

You will save your databases as:

Lastname_Firstname_4A_GG_Directory
Lastname_Firstname_a04A_GG_
    Directory_2015-08-22 (date will vary)
Lastname_Firstname_4A_GG_Employees

PROJECT RESULTS

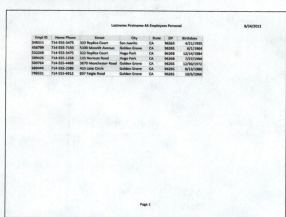

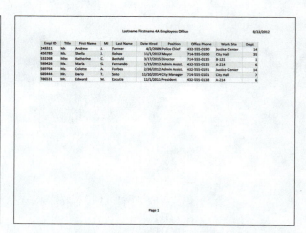

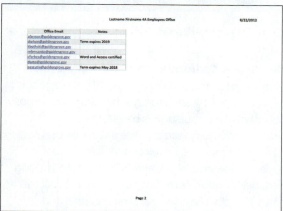

FIGURE 4.1 Project 4A City Directory

Video A4-1

A database is most effective when the data is maintained accurately and efficiently. It is important to back up your database often to be sure you can always obtain a clean copy if the data is corrupted or lost. Maintaining the accuracy of the field design and data is also critical to have a useful database; regular reviews and updates of design and data are necessary. It is also helpful to avoid rekeying data that already exists in a database; using copy/paste or appending records reduces the chances for additional errors as long as the source data is accurate.

Activity 4.01 | Backing Up a Database

Before modifying the structure of an existing database, it is important to ***back up*** the database so that a copy of the original database will be available if you need it. It is also important to back up databases regularly to avoid losing data.

1 **Start** Access. Navigate to the location where the student data files for this textbook are saved. Locate and open the **a04A_GG_Directory** file and enable the content.

2 Display **Backstage** view, click **Save As**, and then, under **Save Database As**, double-click **Back Up Database**. In the **Save As** dialog box, navigate to the drive on which you will be saving your folders and projects for this chapter. Create a new folder named **Access Chapter 4** and then compare your screen with Figure 4.2.

> Access appends the date to the file name as a suggested name for the backed-up database. Having the date as part of the file name assists you in determining the copy that is the most current.

FIGURE 4.2

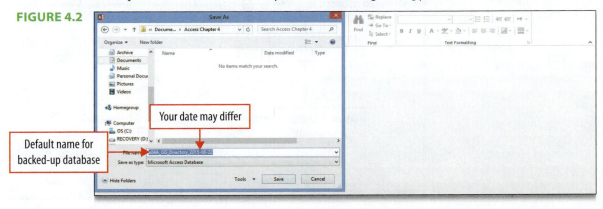

3 In the **File name** box, before the file name, type **Lastname_Firstname_** In the **Save As** dialog box, click **Save**. In the title bar, notice that the original database file—not the backed-up file—is open.

4 On the taskbar, click **File Explorer** 📁, and then navigate to the location of your **Access Chapter 4** folder. Open the folder to verify that the backed-up database exists, but do not open the file. **Close** the Access Chapter 4 window.

5 **Save As** an **Access Database** in your **Access Chapter 4** folder, and then name the database **Lastname_Firstname_4A_GG_Directory**

> This is another method of making a copy of a database. The original file exists with the original name—the date is not appended to the database name, and the newly saved file is open.

***More* Knowledge** | **Recover Data from a Backup**

If your database file is damaged, restore a backup to replace the damaged file.

- Open File Explorer, and Browse to the location where the good copy (backup) is stored.
- Copy the backup file to the location where the damaged file is located, replacing the existing file if necessary.

Activity 4.02 | Adding File Locations to Trusted Locations

In this activity, you will add the location of your database files for this chapter and the location of the student data files to the **Trust Center**—a security feature that checks documents for macros and digital signatures. When you open any database from a location displayed in the Trust Center, no security warning will display. You should not designate the My Documents folder as a trusted location because others may try to gain access to this known folder.

1 Display **Backstage** view, and click the **Enable Content** button. Click **Advanced Options** to display the **Microsoft Office Security Options** dialog box. In the lower left corner, click **Open the Trust Center**.

2 In the **Trust Center** window, in the left pane, click **Trusted Locations**. Compare your screen with Figure 4.3.

The right pane displays the locations that are trusted sources. A **trusted source** is a person or organization that you know will not send you databases with malicious code. Under Path and User Locations, there is already an entry. A **path** is the location of a folder or file on your computer or storage device.

FIGURE 4.3

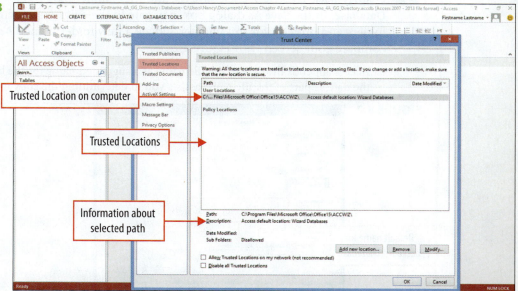

3 In the **Trusted Locations** pane, at the lower right, click **Add new location**. In the **Microsoft Office Trusted Location** dialog box, click **Browse**. In the **Browse** dialog box, navigate to where you saved your *Access Chapter 4* folder, double-click **Access Chapter 4**, and then click **OK**. Compare your screen with Figure 4.4.

The Microsoft Office Trusted Location dialog box displays the path to a trusted source of databases. Notice that you can trust any subfolders in the *Access Chapter 4* folder by checking the *Subfolders of this location are also trusted* option.

FIGURE 4.4

4 In the **Microsoft Office Trusted Location** dialog box, under **Description**, using your own first and last name, type **Databases created by Firstname Lastname** and then click **OK**.

> The Trusted Locations pane displays the path of the *Access Chapter 4* folder. You will no longer receive a security warning when you open databases from this location.

5 Using the technique you just practiced, add the location of your student data files to the Trust Center. For the description, type **Student data files created for GO! Series**

> Only locations that you know are secure should be added to the Trust Center. If other people have access to the databases and can change the information in the database, the location is not secure.

6 At the lower right corner of the **Trust Center** dialog box, click **OK**. In the displayed **Microsoft Office Security Options** dialog box, click **OK**.

> The message bar no longer displays—you opened the database from a trusted location.

7 Display **Backstage** view, and then click **Close**. Open **Lastname_Firstname_4A_GG_Directory**.

> The database opens, and the message bar with the Security Alert does not display. Using the Trust Center button is an efficient way to open databases that are saved in a safe location.

More Knowledge | **Remove a Trusted Location**

Display Backstage view, and then click the Options button. In the Access Options dialog box, in the left pane, click Trust Center. In the right pane, click the Trust Center Settings button, and then click Trusted Locations. Under Path, click the trusted location that you want to remove, and then click the Remove button. Click OK to close the dialog box.

Activity 4.03 | Duplicating a Table and Modifying the Structure

In this activity, you will duplicate the *4A Departments* table, modify the structure by deleting fields and data that are duplicated in other tables, and then designate a primary key field.

1 In the **Navigation Pane**, double-click **4A Departments** to open the table. **Close** `«` the **Navigation Pane**. Click the **FILE tab**, and then, from **Backstage** view, click **Save As**. Under **Database File Types**, double-click **Save Object As**. Compare your screen to Figure 4.5.

> The Save As command displays the Save As dialog box where you can name and save a new object based on the currently displayed object. After you name and save the new table, the original table closes, and the new table—based on the original one—displays.

FIGURE 4.5

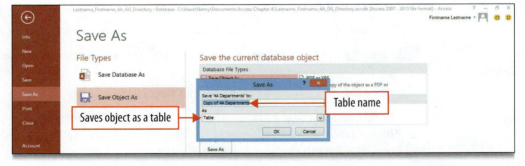

2 In the displayed **Save As** dialog box, under **Save '4A Departments' to:**, type **Lastname Firstname 4A Departments Revised** and then click **OK**.

> The *4A Departments Revised* table is open; it is an exact duplicate of the *4A Departments* table. Working with a duplicate table ensures that the original table will be available if needed.

3 Point to the **Dept Head** field name until the ↓ pointer displays. Drag to the right to the **Admin Asst** field name to select both fields. On the **HOME tab**, in the **Records group**, click the **Delete** button. In the displayed message box, click **Yes** to permanently delete the fields and the data.

> The names of the employees are deleted from this table to avoid having employee data in more than one table. Recall that a table should store data about one subject—this table now stores only departmental data. In addition to removing duplicate data, the fields that you deleted were also poorly designed. They combined both the first and last names in the same field, limiting the use of the data to entire names only.

4 Switch to **Design** view. To the left of **Department**, click the row selector box. On the **TABLE TOOLS DESIGN tab**, in the **Tools group**, click the **Insert Rows** button to insert a blank row (field) above the *Department* field.

5 Under **Field Name**, click in the blank field name box, type **Dept ID** and then press Tab. In the **Data Type** box, type **a** and then press Tab. Alternatively, click the Data Type arrow, and then select the AutoNumber data type. On the **TABLE TOOLS DESIGN tab**, in the **Tools group**, click the **Primary Key** button, and then compare your screen with Figure 4.6.

> Recall that a primary key field is used to ensure that each record is unique. Because each department has a unique name, you might question why the *Department* field is not designated as the primary key field. Primary key fields should be data that does not change often. When organizations or companies are reorganized, department names are often changed.

FIGURE 4.6

Field added to the table

Primary key field

6 Switch to **Datasheet** view, and in the displayed message box, click **Yes** to save the table.

> Because the *Dept ID* field has a data type of AutoNumber, each record is sequentially numbered. The data in this field cannot be changed because it is generated by Access.

7 In the datasheet, next to **Department**, click the **Sort and Filter arrow** ▾, and then click **Sort A to Z**.

> Sorting the records by the department name makes it easier to locate a department.

8 Save ⊟ the table. **Close** ✕ the table. **Open** » the **Navigation Pane**.

Activity 4.04 | Copying and Appending Records to a Table

In this activity, you will copy the *4A City Council Members* table to use as the basis for a single employees table. You will then copy the data in the *4A Police Dept Employees* table and *append*—add on—the data to the new employees table.

1 In the **Navigation Pane**, click **4A City Council Members**. On the **HOME tab**, in the **Clipboard group**, click the **Copy** button. In the **Clipboard group**, click the **Paste** button.

> *Copy* sends a duplicate version of the selected table to the Clipboard, leaving the original table intact. The *Clipboard* is a temporary storage area in Office that can store up to 24 items. *Paste* moves the copy of the selected table from the Clipboard into a new location. Because two tables cannot have the same name in a database, you must rename the pasted version.

2 In the displayed **Paste Table As** dialog box, under **Table Name**, type **Lastname Firstname 4A Employees** and then compare your screen with Figure 4.7.

Under Paste Options, you can copy the structure only, including all the items that are displayed in Design view—field names, data types, descriptions, and field properties. To make an exact duplicate of the table, click Structure and Data. To copy the data from the table into another existing table, click Append Data to Existing Table.

FIGURE 4.7

Copies fields, data types, field descriptions, and field properties only

Table name

Adds the data in the table to an existing table

Copies structure from above and the data

🔄 **ANOTHER WAY**

There are two other methods to copy and paste selected tables:

- In the Navigation Pane, right-click the table, and from the displayed list, click Copy. To paste the table, right-click the Navigation Pane, and click Paste from the options listed.
- In the Navigation Pane, click the table, hold down [Ctrl], and then press [C]. To paste the table, point to the Navigation Pane, hold down [Ctrl], and then press [V].

3 Under **Paste Options**, be sure that the **Structure and Data** option button is selected, and then click **OK**. Notice that the copied table displays in the **Navigation Pane**. Resize the **Navigation Pane** so that all table names display entirely.

An exact duplicate of the *4A City Council Members* table is created. The *4A Employees* table will be used to build a table of all employees.

More Knowledge **Table Description**

To provide more information about a table, you can add a Table Description:

- In the Navigation Pane, right-click the table name, and then click Table Properties.
- In the Properties dialog box, click in the Description box, and then type information about the table. For example, in the 4A Employees table, you could type *Table copied from the 4A City Council Members table*.

4 Open the **4A Employees** table, and notice the duplicate records that were copied from the *4A City Council Members* table.

5 **Copy** the **4A Police Dept Employees** table, and then click the **Paste** button. In the **Paste Table As** dialog box, under **Table Name**, type **Lastname Firstname 4A Employees** Under **Paste Options**, click the **Append Data to Existing Table** option button, and then click **OK**. With the **4A Employees table** active, in the **Records group**, click the **Refresh All** button, and then compare your screen with Figure 4.8.

The table to which you are appending the records must exist before using the Append option. Clicking the Refresh All button causes Access to refresh or update the view of the table, displaying the newly appended records. The *4A Employees* table then displays the two records for the Police department employees—last names of *Farmer* and *Forbes*—and the records are arranged in ascending order by the first field. The records still exist in the *4A Police Dept Employees* table. If separate tables existed for the employees for each department, you would repeat these steps until every employee's record is appended to the *4A Employees* table.

FIGURE 4.8

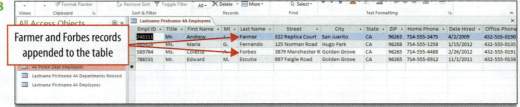

---

6 ▸ **Close** the table.

More **Knowledge**   **Appending Records**

Access appends all records from the ***source table***—the table from which you are copying records—into the ***destination table***—the table to which the records are appended—as long as the field names and data types are the same in both tables. Exceptions include:

- If the source table does not have all of the fields that the destination table has, Access will still append the records, leaving the data in the missing fields blank in the destination table.
- If the source table has a field name that does not exist in the destination table or the data type is incompatible, the append procedure will fail.

Before performing an append procedure, carefully analyze the structure of both the source table and the destination table.

Activity 4.05 | Splitting a Table into Two Tables

The *4A Employees* table stores personal data and office data about the employees. Although the table contains data about one subject—employees—you will split the table into two separate tables to keep the personal information separate from the office information.

1 ▸ Double-click the **4A Employees** table to open it in **Datasheet** view. **Close** « the **Navigation Pane**. Click the **FILE tab**, and then from **Backstage** view, click **Save As**. Under **Database File Types**, double-click **Save Object As**.

2 ▸ In the **Save As** dialog box, in the **Save to** box, type **Lastname Firstname 4A Employees Office** Notice the *As* box displays Table, and then click **OK**. Using the techniques you just practiced, create a copy of the open table named **Lastname Firstname 4A Employees Personal**

These two new tables will be used to split the *4A Employees* table into two separate tables, one storing personal data and the other storing office data.

3 ▸ In the **4A Employees Personal** table, scroll to the right, if needed, to display the **Date Hired**, **Office Phone**, **Position**, **Office Email**, and **Notes** fields. Select all five fields. On the **HOME tab**, in the **Records group**, click the **Delete** button. In the displayed message box, click **Yes** to permanently delete the fields and data.

Because these fields contain office data, they are deleted from the *4A Employees Personal* table. These fields will be stored in the *4A Employees Office* table.

4 ▸ Select the **Title, First Name, MI**, and **Last Name** fields, and then delete the fields. **Save** 🖫 and **Close** ✕ the table.

The fields you deleted are stored in the *4A Employees Office* table. You have deleted redundant data from the *4A Employees Personal* table.

5 Open the **Navigation Pane**. Open the **4A Employees Office** table. **Close** the **Navigation Pane**. Point to the **Street** field name until the pointer displays. Drag to the right to the **Home Phone** field name, and then compare your screen with Figure 4.9.

> Five fields are selected and will be deleted from this table. This is duplicate data that exists in the *4A Employees Personal* table. The *Empl ID* field will be the common field between the two tables.

FIGURE 4.9

Common field—4A Employees Office table and 4A Employees Personal table

Duplicate data—also stored in 4A Employees Personal table

6 Delete the selected fields and data from the table.

> The *4A Employees Office* table now stores only office data about the employees and can be linked to the *4A Employees Personal* table through the common field, *Empl ID*.

7 Click the **Position** field name. On the **TABLE TOOLS FIELDS tab**, in the **Add & Delete group**, click the **Number** button.

> A blank field is inserted between the *Position* field and the *Office Email* field, and it holds numeric data. Because this field will be used to link to the *4A Departments Revised* Dept ID field, which has a data type of AutoNumber, this field must use a data type of Number, even though it will not be used in a calculation.

8 The default name *Field1* is currently selected; type **Dept** to replace it and name the new field. Press Enter.

9 Open the **Navigation Pane**. Open the **4A Departments Revised** table.

> The *4A Departments Revised* table opens in Datasheet view, and the records are sorted in ascending order by the *Department* field.

10 Locate the **Dept ID** for the City Police department. On the **tab row**, click the **4A Employees Office tab** to make the table active. In the record for Andrew Farmer, enter the City Police Dept ID, **14** in the **Dept** field. Press ↓ two times. In the third record, for Colette Forbes, type **14**

11 Using the techniques you just practiced, find the **Dept ID** for the City Council department, and then enter that number in the **Dept** field for the second and fourth records in the **4A Employees Office** table. Compare your screen with Figure 4.10.

> The *Dept* field is a common field with the *Dept ID* field in the *4A Departments Revised* table and will be used to link or join the two tables.

FIGURE 4.10

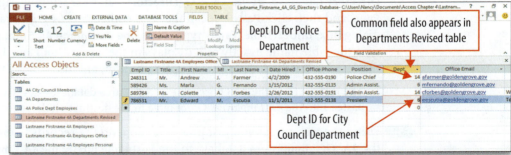

Dept ID for Police Department

Common field also appears in Departments Revised table

Dept ID for City Council Department

12 On the **tab row**, right-click any table tab, and then click **Close All**.

Activity 4.06 | Appending Records from Another Database

Additional employee records are stored in another database. In this activity, you will open a second database to copy and paste records from tables in the second database to tables in the *4A_GG_Directory* database.

🔄 BY TOUCH   Tap the Start screen icon.

1 ▶ Point to the lower left corner of your screen to display the **Start** screen icon ▦, and then click one time to display the Start screen. Right-click **Access 2013**, and then, from the taskbar, click **Open new window** to open a second instance of Access.

2 ▶ On the left side of the Access startup window, at the bottom, click **Open Other Files**. Under **Places**, click **Computer**, and then on the right, click **Browse**. In the **Open** dialog box, navigate to the location where the student data files for this textbook are saved. Locate and open the **a04A_GG_Employees** file. Display **Backstage** view, click **Save As**, and save the database as **Lastname_Firstname_4A_GG_Employees** in your **Access Chapter 4** folder.

🔄 BY TOUCH   On the taskbar, use the Swipe to Select technique—swipe upward with a short quick movement—to display the Jump List. On the list, tap Open new window.

3 ▶ In the **4A_GG_Employees** database window, in the **Navigation Pane**, right-click **4A Office**, and then click **Copy**. Click the **Access icon** in the taskbar to see two instances of Access open. Compare your screen with Figure 4.11.

Each time you start Access, you open an ***instance*** of it. Two instances of Access are open, and each instance displays in the taskbar.

FIGURE 4.11

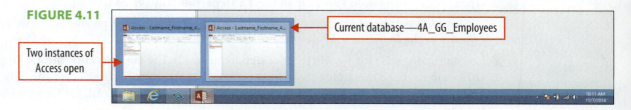

Two instances of Access open

Current database—4A_GG_Employees

You cannot open multiple databases in one instance of Access. If you open a second database in the same instance, Access closes the first database. You can, however, open multiple instances of Access that display different databases. The number of times you can start Access at the same time is limited by the amount of your computer's available RAM.

4 ▶ Point to each thumbnail to display the ScreenTip, and then click the button for the **4A_GG_Directory** database. In the **4A_GG_Directory** database window, right-click the **Navigation Pane**, and then click **Paste**—recall that you copied the *4A Office* table. In the **Paste Table As** dialog box, under **Table Name**, type **Lastname Firstname 4A Employees Office** being careful to type the table name exactly as it displays in the **Navigation Pane**. Under **Paste Options**, click the **Append Data to Existing Table** option button, and then click **OK**.

The records from the *4A Office* table in the source database—*4A_GG_Employees*—are copied and pasted into the *4A Employees Office* table in the destination database—*4A_GG_Directory*.

5 ▶ Using the techniques you just practiced, append the records from the **4A Personal** table in the **4A_GG_Employees** database to the **Lastname Firstname 4A Employees Personal** table in the **4A_GG_Directory** database.

6 ▶ Make the **4A_GG_Employees** database active, and then on the title bar for the **4A_GG_Employees** database window, click the **Close** button. If a message displays, click **Yes**.

7 If the **4A_GG_Directory** database is not current, on the taskbar, click the **Microsoft Access** button. Open the **4A Employees Personal** table, and then open the **4A Employees Office** table. **Close** « the **Navigation Pane**.

8 If necessary, on the tab row, click the 4A Employees Office tab to make the table active, and then compare your screen with Figure 4.12.

In addition to appending records, you can copy a single record or data in a field from a table in the source database file to a table in the destination database file. Now that you have finished restructuring the database, you can see that it is wise to plan your database before creating the tables and entering data.

FIGURE 4.12

Three appended records

9 On the **tab row**, right-click any table tab, and then click **Close All**.

Objective 2 | Modify Existing Tables

Video A4-2

Data in a database is usually **dynamic**—changing. Records can be created, deleted, and edited in a table. It is important that the data is always up-to-date and accurate in order for the database to provide useful information.

Activity 4.07 | Finding and Deleting Records

1 **Open** » the **Navigation Pane**. Open the **4A Departments Revised** table. **Close** « the **Navigation Pane**. In the datasheet, next to Dept ID, click the **Sort and Filter arrow** ▾, and then click **Sort Smallest to Largest**.

Sorting the records by the department ID returns the data to its primary key order.

2 In the table, in the **Department** field, click in the record containing the City Treasurer— Record 8. On the **HOME tab**, in the **Find group**, click the **Find** button. Alternatively, hold down Ctrl, and then press F.

The Find and Replace dialog box displays with the Find tab active.

3 In the **Find and Replace** dialog box, in the **Find What** box, type **Assessor**

The Look In box displays *Current field*, which refers to the Department field because you clicked in that field before you clicked the Find button.

4 In the **Find and Replace** dialog box, click the **Look in box arrow**. Notice that Access can search for the data in the entire Contacts table instead of only the Department field. Leaving the entry as **Current field**, click the **Look in box arrow** one time to close the list, and then click the **Find Next** button. Compare your screen with Figure 4.13.

If Access did not locate Record 5, ensure that you typed *Assessor* correctly in the Find What box. If you misspelled *Assessor* in the table, type the misspelled version in the Find What box. This is an example of how important accuracy is when entering data in your tables.

FIGURE 4.13

5 ▶ In the **Find and Replace** dialog box, click **Cancel** to close the dialog box.

> The table displays with *Assessor* selected in Record 5. Even though you can locate this record easily in the table because there are a limited number of records, keep in mind that most database tables contain many more records. Using the Find button is an efficient way to locate a record in the table.

6 ▶ Point to the **Record Selector** box for the *Assessor* record until the ➡ pointer displays. Click one time to ensure that the entire record is selected, and then compare your screen with Figure 4.14.

FIGURE 4.14

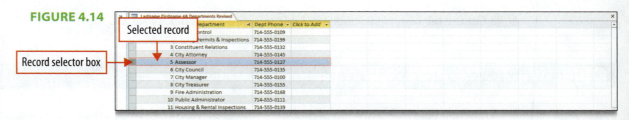

7 ▶ On the **HOME tab**, in the **Records group,** click the **Delete** button to delete the active record, and then compare your screen with Figure 4.15.

> Notice that Access displays a message stating that you are about to delete one record and will be unable to undo the Delete operation.

ANOTHER WAY There are two other methods to delete selected records in a table:
- On the selected record, right-click and then click Delete Record.
- From the keyboard, press Delete.

FIGURE 4.15

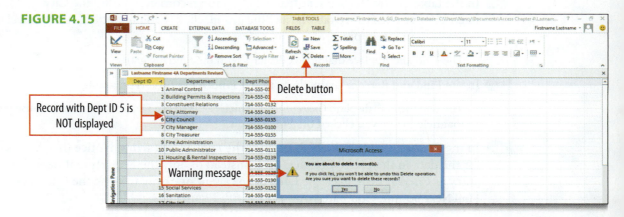

8 ▶ In the message box, click **Yes** to confirm the deletion.

> The record holding information for *Assessor* no longer displays in the table; it has been permanently deleted from the table, and will no longer display in any other objects that were created using the Contacts table. The record number of Dept ID 6—City Council—is now record 5 and is the current record.

More Knowledge **Why the Dept ID Field Data Did Not Renumber Sequentially**

You added the Dept ID field with an AutoNumber data type. Because of this, when data is entered into the table, Dept ID is automatically numbered sequentially, and those numbers are not changed as records are added, deleted, or modified.

4 ACCESS

Activity 4.08 | Finding and Modifying Records

When data needs to be changed or updated, you must locate and modify the record with the data. Recall that you can move among records in a table using the navigation buttons at the bottom of the window and that you can use Find to locate specific data. Other navigation methods include using keys on the keyboard and using the Search box in the navigation area.

1. Take a moment to review the table in Figure 4.16, which lists the key combinations you can use to navigate within an Access table.

FIGURE 4.16

KEY COMBINATIONS FOR NAVIGATING A TABLE	
KEYSTROKE	**MOVEMENT**
↑	Moves the selection up one record at a time.
↓	Moves the selection down one record at a time.
PageUp	Moves the selection up one screen at a time.
PageDown	Moves the selection down one screen at a time.
Ctrl + Home	Moves the selection to the first field in the table or the beginning of the selected field.
Ctrl + End	Moves the selection to the last field in the table or the end of the selected field.
Tab	Moves the selection to the next field in the table.
Shift + Tab	Moves the selection to the previous field in the table.
Enter	Moves the selection to the next field in the table.

2. On the keyboard, press ↓ to move the selection down one record. Record 6—*City Manager*—is now the current record.
3. On the keyboard, hold down Ctrl, and then press Home to move to the first field of the first record in the table—Dept ID *1*.
4. In the navigation area, click the **Next record** button six times to navigate to Record 7—Dept ID 8.
5. On the keyboard, hold down Ctrl, and then press End to move to the last field in the last record in the table—Dept Phone *714-555-0151*.
6. On the keyboard, hold down Shift, and then press Tab to move to the previous field in the same record in the table—*City Planner* in the Department field.
7. In the navigation area, click in the **Search** box. In the **Search** box, type **b**

   Record 2 is selected, and the letter *B* in *Building Permits & Inspections* is highlighted. Search found the first occurrence of the letter *b*. It is not necessary to type capital letters in the Search box; Access will locate the words regardless of capitalization.

8 In the **Search** box, type **sani**

Record 15 is selected, and the letters *Sani* in *Sanitation* are highlighted. Search found the first occurrence of the letters *sani*. This is the record that needs to be modified. It is not necessary to type an entire word in the Search box to locate a record containing that word.

9 In the field box, double-click the word *Sanitation* to select it. Type **Trash Pickup** to replace the current entry. The **Small Pencil** icon in the **Record Selector** box means that the record is being edited and has not yet been saved. Press ⬇ to move to the next record and save the change.

If you must edit part of a name, drag through letters or words to select them. You can then type the new letters or words over the selection to replace the text without having to press ⌦Delete or ⌫Backspace.

10 Save 💾 and **Close** ✕ the table. **Open** » the **Navigation Pane**.

Activity 4.09 | Adding and Moving Fields in Design View and Datasheet View

In this activity, you will add and move fields in Design view and in Datasheet view.

1 Right-click the **4A Employees Personal** table to display a shortcut menu, and click **Design View** to open the table in **Design** view. Alternatively, double-click the table name in the Navigation Pane to open the table in Datasheet view, and then click the View button to switch to Design view. **Close** « the **Navigation Pane**.

2 In the **Field Name** column, click the **Field Name** box below the **Home Phone** field name.

A new row is inserted below the *Home Phone* field. Recall that a row in Design view is a field.

3 In the empty **Field Name** box, type **Birthdate** and then press ⇥Tab to move to the **Data Type** column. Click the **Data Type arrow** to display the list of data types, and then click **Date/Time** to set the data type for this field. Compare your screen with Figure 4.17.

A new field to display the employee's date of birth has been created in the *Lastname Firstname 4A Employees Personal* table. An advantage of adding a field in Design view is that you name the field and set the data type when you insert the field.

FIGURE 4.17

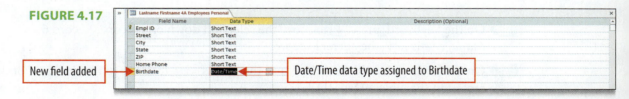

4 In the **Field Name** column, locate **Home Phone**, and then click the **Row Selector** box to select the field. Point to the **Row Selector** box to display the ➡ pointer. Drag the field up until you see a dark horizontal line following *Empl ID*, and then release the mouse button.

5 Switch the **Lastname Firstname 4A Employees Personal** table to **Datasheet** view. In the displayed message box, click **Yes** to save the design changes.

The *Home Phone* field displays to the left of the *Street* field.

6 In the first record—248311—click in the **Birthdate** field. Using the techniques you have practiced, enter the birthdate for each record shown in the following list, pressing ↓ after each entry to move to the next record. Compare your screen with Figure 4.18.

Empl ID	Birthdate
248311	4/21/1955
456789	6/1/1964
532268	12/14/1984
589426	7/27/1990
589764	12/30/1972
689444	8/13/1980
786531	10/6/1966

FIGURE 4.18

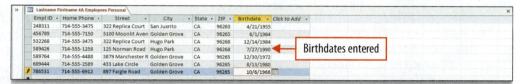

7 Adjust all column widths, ensuring that all of the field names and all of the field data display. View the table in **Print Preview**. On the **PRINT PREVIEW tab**, in the **Page Layout group**, click the **Landscape** button. If you are instructed to submit this result, create a paper or electronic printout. On the **PRINT PREVIEW tab**, in the **Close Preview group**, click the **Close Print Preview** button.

8 Close the **4A Employees Personal** table. Open » the **Navigation Pane**. Open the **4A Employees Office** table in **Datasheet** view. Close « the **Navigation Pane**.

9 Select the **Office Phone** column. On the **TABLE TOOLS FIELDS tab**, in the **Add & Delete group**, click **Short Text**. Alternatively, right-click the selected field and, from the shortcut menu, click Insert Column. A new column is inserted to the right of *Office Phone*.

10 If necessary, double-click Field1—the name of your field may differ if you have been experimenting with adding fields—to select the field name. Type **Work Site** and press Enter to save the field name.

11 In the first record—248311—click in the **Work Site** field. Using the techniques you have practiced, enter the work site for each record shown in the following list, pressing ↓ after each entry to move to the next record.

Empl ID	Work Site
248311	Justice Center
456789	City Hall
532268	B-121
589426	A-214
589764	Justice Center
689444	City Hall
786531	A-214

12 Point to **Position** until the pointer displays, and then click one time to select the column. Drag the field left until you see a dark vertical line between *Date Hired* and *Office Phone*, and then release the mouse button. Compare your screen with Figure 4.19.

The *Position* field is moved after the *Date Hired* field and before the *Office Phone* field. If you move a field to the wrong position, select the field again, and then drag it to the correct position. Alternatively, on the Quick Access Toolbar, click the Undo button to place the field back in its previous position.

FIGURE 4.19

Position field moved between Date Hired and Office Phone fields

---

More Knowledge **Hide/Unhide Fields in a Table**

If you do not want a field to display in Datasheet view or on a printed copy of the table, you can hide the field.

- Right-click the field name at the top of the column.
- From the shortcut menu, click **Hide Fields**.
- To display the field again, right-click any column heading. From the shortcut menu, click Unhide Fields. In the dialog box, click the fields to unhide, and then click OK.

Activity 4.10 | Checking Spelling

In this exercise, you will use the Spell Check feature to find spelling errors in your data. It is important to realize that this will not find all data entry mistakes, so you will need to use additional proofreading methods to ensure the accuracy of the data.

1 In the first record—248311—click in the **Empl ID** field. On the **HOME tab**, in the **Records group**, click the **Spelling** button. Alternatively, press F7. Compare your screen with Figure 4.20.

The Spelling dialog box displays, and *Bothski* is highlighted because it is not in the Office dictionary. Many proper names will be *flagged*—highlighted—by the spelling checker. Take a moment to review the options in the Spelling dialog box; these are described in the table in Figure 4.21.

FIGURE 4.20

Word not in dictionary

Suggested alternatives

FIGURE 4.21

SPELLING DIALOG BOX BUTTONS	
BUTTON	**ACTION**
Ignore 'Last Name' Field	Ignores any words in the selected field.
Ignore	Ignores this one occurrence of the word but continues to flag other instances of the word.
Ignore All	Discontinues flagging any instance of the word anywhere in the table.
Change	Changes the identified word to the word highlighted under Suggestions.
Change All	Changes every instance of the word in the table to the word highlighted under Suggestions.
Add	Adds the highlighted word to a custom dictionary, which can be edited. This option does not change the built-in Office dictionary.
AutoCorrect	Adds the flagged word to the AutoCorrect list, which will subsequently correct the word automatically if misspelled in the future.
Options	Displays the Access Options dialog box.
Undo Last	Undoes the last change.

2 In the **Spelling** dialog box, click the **Ignore 'Last Name' Field** button.

Present, which displays in the Position field, is flagged by the spelling checker. In the Spelling dialog box under Suggestions, *President* is highlighted.

3 In the **Spelling** dialog box, click the **Change** button to change the word from *Present* to *President*.

When the spelling checker has completed checking the table and has found no other words missing from its dictionary, a message displays stating *The spelling check is complete*.

4 In the message box, click **OK**.

Objective 3 Change Data Types

Video A4-3

Before creating a table, it is important to decide on the data types for the fields in the table. Setting a specific data type helps to ensure that the proper data will be entered into a field; for example, it is not possible to enter text into a field with a Currency data type. It is also important to choose a number data type when it is appropriate to avoid problems with calculations and sorting.

Activity 4.11 | Changing Data Types

Once data is entered into a field, caution must be exercised when changing the data type—existing data may not be completely visible or may be deleted. You can change the data type in either Datasheet view or Design view.

1 With the **4A Employees Office** table open, switch to **Design** view. Change the **Data Type** for the **Date Hired** field to **Date/Time**. Press F6 to move to the **Field Properties** pane at the bottom of the screen. Click in the **Format** property and select **Short Date**.

The data type of Date/Time is more appropriate for this field because it will display dates and restrict other entries. This will also allow the field to be accurately used in calculations, comparisons, and sorts.

2 Change the data type for the **Notes** field to **Long Text**, and then compare your screen with Figure 4.22.

> The data type of Long Text is more appropriate for this field because it may require more than 255 characters and spaces to effectively describe notes associated with an employee.

FIGURE 4.22

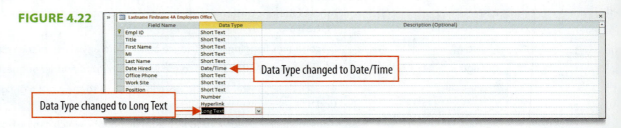

3 Switch to **Datasheet** view, saving changes to the table. Adjust all column widths, ensuring that all of the field names and all of the field data display. View the table in **Print Preview**, and then change the orientation to **Landscape**. If you are instructed to submit this result, create a paper or electronic printout. **Close Print Preview**.

4 Close ☒ the **4A Employees Office** table, saving changes.

Objective 4 | Attach Files to Records

Video A4-4

The attachment data type can be used to add one or more files to the records in a database. For example, if you have a database for an antique collection, you can attach a picture of each antique and a Word document that contains a description of the item. Access stores the attached files in their native formats—if you attach a Word document, it is saved as a Word document. By default, fields contain only one piece of data; however, you can attach more than one file by using the attachment data type. As you attach files to a record, Access creates one or more *system tables* to keep track of the multiple entries in the field. You cannot view or work with these system tables.

Activity 4.12 | Attaching a Word Document to a Record

In this activity, you will attach documents to records in the *4A Departments Revised* table.

1 **Open** ☒ the **Navigation Pane**. Open the **4A Departments Revised** table, and then switch to **Design** view. **Close** ☒ the **Navigation Pane**. Click in the empty **Field Name** box under **Dept Phone**, type **Information** and then press Tab to move to the **Data Type** box. Click the **Data Type arrow**, click **Attachment**, and then press Enter. Under **Field Properties**, on the **General tab**, notice that only two field properties—**Caption** and **Required**—are displayed for an **Attachment** field.

2 Switch to **Datasheet** view, saving changes to the table. In the **Attachment** field, notice that the field name of *Information* does not display; instead, a paper clip symbol displays. In the first record, *(0)* displays after the paper clip symbol, indicating that there are no attachments for this record.

> Because multiple files can be attached to a record, the name of the field displays the paper clip symbol.

3 In record 12, double-click in the **Attachment** field. In the displayed **Attachments** dialog box, click **Add**. Navigate to the location where the student data files for this textbook are saved. In the **Choose File** dialog box, double-click **a04A_PZ_Schedule**, and then compare your screen with Figure 4.23.

> The Word document will be added to the Attachments dialog box. You can attach multiple files to the same record.

FIGURE 4.23

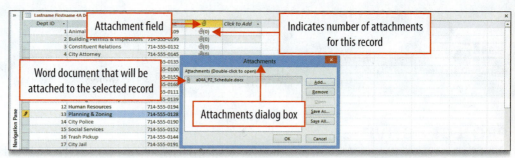

> **4** In the **Attachments** dialog box, click **OK**. Notice that the **Attachment** field now indicates there is **1** attachment for record 12. Double-click in the **Attachment** field. In the **Attachments** dialog box, click **a04A_PZ_Schedule.docx**, and then click **Open**.

> Word opens, and the document displays. You can make changes to the document, and then save it in the database.

> **5** **Close** Word. In the **Attachments** dialog box, click **OK**. Press ⬇ to save the record.

> **6** In the second record, double-click in the **Attachment** field. In the displayed **Attachments** dialog box, click **Add**. Navigate to the location where the student data files for this textbook are saved. In the **Choose File** dialog box, double-click **a04A_Bldg_Permit_App**. In the **Attachments** dialog box, click **OK**.

> The PDF document is added to the Attachments dialog box.

NOTE | **Saving Changes to an Attached File**

When you open an attached file in the program that was used to create it, Access places a temporary copy of the file in a temporary folder on the hard drive of your computer. If you change the file and save changes, Access saves the changes in the temporary copy. Closing the program used to view the attachment returns you to Access. When you click OK to close the Attachments dialog box, Access prompts you to save the attached file again. Click Yes to save the changes to the attached file in the database, or click No to keep the original, unedited version in the database.

To find the location of your temporary folder, start Internet Explorer. On the Tools menu, click Internet options. On the General tab, in the Browsing History section, click Settings. In the Website Data Settings dialog box, the temporary folder path displays in the Current location section.

> **7** Adjust all column widths, ensuring that all of the field names and all of the field data display. View the table in **Print Preview**. If you are instructed to submit this result, create a paper or electronic printout.

> **8** **Close** the table, saving changes. **Open** » the **Navigation Pane**. **Close** the database, and **Exit** Access.

> **9** As directed by your instructor, submit your database and the paper or electronic printout of the three tables that are the result of this project. Specifically, in this project, using your own name you created the following database and printouts or electronic printouts:

1. Lastname_Firstname_4A_GG_Directory	Database file
2. Lastname Firstname 4A Employees Personal	Table (printed or electronic printout)
3. Lastname Firstname 4A Employees Office	Table (printed or electronic printout)
4. Lastname Firstname 4A Departments Revised	Table (printed or electronic printout)

END | You have completed Project 4A

PROJECT ACTIVITIES

Matthew Shoaf, director of the information technology department, has created a table to keep track of tasks that he has assigned to the employees in his department. In Activities 4.13 through 4.23, you will create a table in Design view that stores records about assigned tasks, modify its properties, and customize its fields. You will add features to the database table that will help to reduce data entry errors and that will make data entry easier. Your completed tables will look similar to the tables shown in Figure 4.24.

PROJECT FILES

For Project 4B, you will need the following file:

a04B_IT_Workload

You will save your database as:

Lastname_Firstname_4B_IT_Workload

PROJECT RESULTS

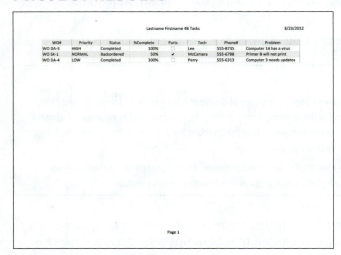
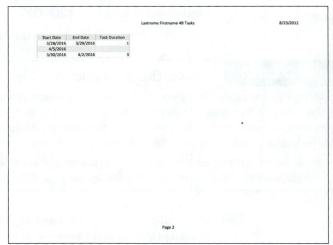

FIGURE 4.24 Project 4B IT Tasks

Video A4-5

In this activity, you will create a second table in a database using Design view.

Activity 4.13 | Creating a Table in Design View

In this activity, you will create a table to keep track of the tasks that the IT department will be completing. Creating a table in Design view gives you the most control over the characteristics of the table and the fields. Most database designers use Design view to create tables, setting the data types and formats before entering any records. Design view is a good way to create a table when you know exactly how you want to set up your fields.

1 **Start** Access. On the left side of the Access startup window, click **Open Other Files**. Under **Open Places**, click **Computer**, and then on the right, click **Browse**. In the **Open** dialog box, navigate to the student data files for this textbook. Locate and open **a04B_IT_Workload** file. **Save** the database in the **Microsoft Access Database** format in your **Access Chapter 4** folder as **Lastname_Firstname_4B_IT_Workload**

2 If you did not add the **Access Chapter 4** folder to the Trust Center, enable the content. In the **Navigation Pane**, under **Tables**, rename **4B Employees** by adding **Lastname Firstname** to the beginning of the table name. **Close** « the **Navigation Pane**.

3 On the Ribbon, click the **CREATE tab**. In the **Tables group**, click the **Table Design** button to open an empty table in Design view, and then compare your screen with Figure 4.25.

FIGURE 4.25

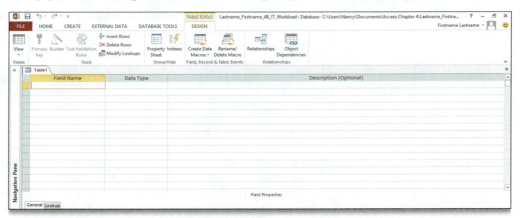

4 In the first **Field Name box**, type **WO#** press Tab, and then on the **DESIGN tab**, in the **Tools group**, click the **Primary Key** button.

5 Click the **Data Type arrow** to display a list of data types, as shown in Figure 4.26. Take a moment to study the table in Figure 4.27 that describes all 12 possible data types.

In Design view, all the data types are displayed. In Datasheet view, the list depends on the data entered in the field and does not display Lookup Wizard.

FIGURE 4.26

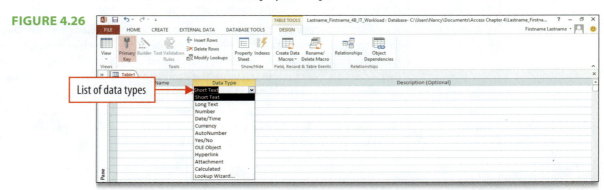

List of data types

FIGURE 4.27

DATA TYPES		
DATA TYPE	**DESCRIPTION**	**EXAMPLE**
Short Text	Text or combinations of text and numbers; also, numbers that are not used in calculations. Limited to 255 characters or length set on field, whichever is less. Access does not reserve space for unused portions of the text field. This is the default data type.	An inventory item, such as towels, or a phone number or postal code that is not used in calculations and that may contain characters other than numbers
Long Text	Lengthy text or combinations of text and numbers that can hold up to 65,535 characters depending on the size of the database.	A description of a product
Number	Numeric data used in mathematical calculations with varying field sizes.	A quantity, such as 500
Date/Time	Date and time values for the years 100 through 9999.	An order date, such as 11/10/2012 3:30 p.m.
Currency	Monetary values and numeric data that can be used in mathematical calculations involving data with one to four decimal places. Accurate to 15 digits on the left side of the decimal separator and to 4 digits on the right side. Use this data type to store financial data and when you do not want Access to round values.	An item price, such as $8.50
AutoNumber	Available in Design view. A unique sequential or random number assigned by Access as each record is entered that cannot be updated.	An inventory item number, such as 1, 2, 3, or a randomly assigned employee number, such as 3852788
Yes/No	Contains only one of two values—Yes/No, True/False, or On/Off. Access assigns 1 for all Yes values and 0 for all No values.	Whether an item was ordered—Yes or No
OLE Object	An object created by programs other than Access that is linked to or embedded in the table. *OLE* is an abbreviation for *object linking and embedding*, a technology for transferring and sharing information among programs. Stores up to two gigabytes of data (the size limit for all Access databases). Must have an OLE server registered on the server that runs the database. Should usually use Attachment data type instead.	A graphics file, such as a picture of a product, a sound file, a Word document, or an Excel spreadsheet stored as a bitmap image
Hyperlink	Web or email addresses.	An email address, such as dwalker@ityourway.com, or a Web page, such as http://www.ityourway.com
Attachment	Any supported type of file—images, spreadsheet files, documents, or charts. Similar to email attachments.	Same as OLE Object
Calculated	Available in Design view. Opens the Expression Builder to create an expression based on existing fields or numbers. Field must be designated as a Calculated field when it is inserted into the table; the expression can be edited in the Field Properties.	Adding two existing fields such as [field1]+[field2], or performing a calculation with a field and a number such as [field3]*.5
Lookup Wizard	Available in Design view. Not really a data type, but will display in the list of data types. Links to fields in other tables to display a list of data instead of having to manually type the data.	Link to another field in the same or another table

6 From the displayed list, click **Short Text**, and then press [Tab] to move to the **Description** box. In the **Description** box, type **Identification number assigned to task reported on work order form**

> Field names should be short; use the description box to display more information about the contents of the field.

7 Press [F6] to move to the **Field Properties** pane at the bottom of the screen. In the **Field Size** box, type **8** to replace the 255. Compare your screen with Figure 4.28.

> Pressing [F6] while in the Data Type column moves the insertion point to the first field property box in the Field Properties pane. Alternatively, click in the Field Size property box.

> Recall that a field with a data type of Short Text can store up to 255 characters. You can change the field size to limit the number of characters that can be entered into the field to ensure accuracy. For example, if you use the two-letter state abbreviations for a state field, limit the size of the field to two characters. When entering a state in the field, you will be unable to type more than two characters.

FIGURE 4.28

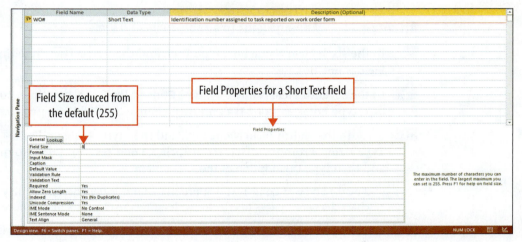

Field Size reduced from the default (255)

Field Properties for a Short Text field

8 Click in the second **Field Name** box, type **Priority** and then press [Tab] two times to move to the **Description** box. Type **Indicate the priority level of this task** Press [F6] to move to the **Field Properties** pane at the bottom of the screen. Click in the **Format** box and type **>**

> Because Short Text is the default data type, you do not have to select it if it is the correct data type for the field. Additionally, if the field name is descriptive enough, the Description box is optional.

> A greater than symbol (>) in the Format property box in a Text field converts all entries in the field to uppercase. Using a less than symbol (<) would force all entries to be lowercase.

More Knowledge   **About the Caption Property**

The Caption property is used to give a name to fields used on forms and reports. Many database administrators create field names in tables that are short and abbreviated. In a form or report based on the table, a more descriptive name is desired. The value in the Caption property is used in label controls on forms and reports instead of the field name. If the Caption property is blank, the field name is used in the label control. A caption can contain up to 2,048 characters.

---

9 In the third **Field Name** box, type **Status** and then press [Tab] three times to move to the next **Field Name** box.

10 In the fourth **Field Name** box, type **%Complete** Press Tab and then click the **Data Type arrow**. From the displayed list, click **Number**. Press Tab to move to the **Description** box, and then type **Percentage of the task that has been completed** Press F6 to move to the **Field Properties** pane. Click the **Field Size** property arrow and select **Single**. Click the **Format** property arrow and select **Percent**. Set the **Decimal Places** property to 0.

> The data type of Number is appropriate for this field because it will display only the amount of a task that has been completed. Defining the number as a percent with zero decimal places further restricts the entries. This allows the field to be used accurately in calculations, comparisons, and sorts.

11 In the fifth **Field Name** box, type **Parts** Press Tab and then click the **Data Type arrow**. From the displayed list, click **Yes/No**. Press Tab to move to the **Description** box. Type **Click the field to indicate parts have been ordered to complete the task**

> The data type of Yes/No is appropriate for this field because there are only two choices, parts are on order (yes) or parts are not on order (no). In Datasheet view, click the check box to indicate yes with a checkmark.

Activity 4.14 | Adding Fields to a Table in Design View

1 In the sixth **Field Name** box, type **Tech** and then press Tab three times to move to the next **Field Name** box.

2 In the seventh **Field Name** box, type **Phone#** Press Tab two times to move to the **Description** box, type **Enter as ###-####** and then change the **Field Size** property to **8**

3 Click in the eighth **Field Name** box, and then type **Problem** Press Tab and then click the **Data Type arrow**. From the displayed list, click **Long Text**. Press Tab to move to the **Description** box, and then type **Description of the IT problem**

> The data type of Long Text is appropriate for this field because it may require more than 255 characters and spaces to effectively describe the IT problem that needs attention.

4 Click in the ninth **Field Name** box, and then type **Start Date** Press Tab and then click the **Data Type arrow**. From the displayed list, click **Date/Time**.

> The data type of Date/Time is appropriate for this field because it will only display date information. Because Date/Time is a type of number, this field can be used in calculations.

5 Click in the tenth **Field Name** box and then type **End Date** Press Tab and then click the **Data Type arrow**. From the displayed list, click **Date/Time**.

6 Click in the eleventh **Field Name** box and then type **Task Duration** Press Tab and then click the **Data Type arrow**. From the displayed list, click **Calculated**. Press Tab, and the **Expression Builder** dialog box appears. In the **Expression Builder** dialog box, type **[End Date]-[Start Date]** and then compare your screen to Figure 4.29.

> The data type of Calculated is appropriate for this field because the entry is calculated with an expression—subtracting *Start Date* from *End Date*. The *Task Duration* field will remain blank if the task has not yet been completed; nothing can be entered in the field.
>
> The *Expression Builder* is a feature used to create formulas (expressions) in calculated fields, query criteria, form and report properties, and table validation rules. An expression can be entered using field names or numbers where the only spaces included are those that separate words in field names. Any time a field name is used in the expression, it should be enclosed in square brackets. An existing field cannot be changed to a Calculated data type; it must be assigned when the field is added to the table. The expression can be edited in the Field Properties.

FIGURE 4.29

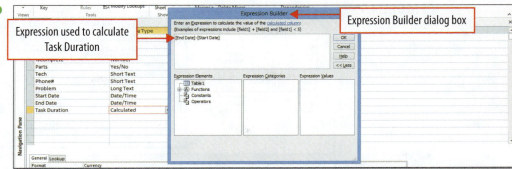

Expression used to calculate Task Duration

Expression Builder dialog box

7 ▸ Click **OK**. In the **Description** box, type **Number of days necessary to complete the task** Press F6 to move to the **Field Properties** pane at the bottom of the screen. Click in the **Result Type** property arrow, and then select **Single**.

8 ▸ On the **Quick Access** toolbar, click **Save** 🖫. In the **Save As** dialog box, type **Lastname Firstname 4B Tasks** and then click **OK**. Switch to **Datasheet** view to view the table you have just created; there are no records in the table yet.

Objective 6 | Create a Lookup Field

Video A4-6

Creating a ***lookup field*** can restrict the data entered in a field because the person entering data selects that data from a list retrieved from another table, query, or list of entered values. The choices can be displayed in a ***list box***—a box containing a list of choices—or a ***combo box***—a box that is a combination of a list box and a text box. You can create a lookup field by using the Lookup Wizard or manually by setting the field's lookup field properties. Whenever possible, use the Lookup Wizard because it simplifies the process, ensures consistent data entry, automatically populates the associated field properties, and creates the needed table relationships.

Activity 4.15 | Creating a Lookup Field Based on a List of Values

In this activity, you will create a lookup field for the Status field.

1 ▸ With the **4B Tasks** table open, switch to **Design** view. In the **Status** field, click in the **Data Type** box, and then click the **arrow**. From the displayed list of data types, click **Lookup Wizard**.

2 ▸ In the first **Lookup Wizard** dialog box, click the **I will type in the values that I want** option button, and then click **Next**. Compare your screen with Figure 4.30.

The first step of the Lookup Wizard enables you to choose whether you want Access to locate the information from another table or query or whether you would like to type the information to create a list.

The second step enables you to select the number of columns you want to include in the lookup field. The values are typed in the grid, and you can adjust the column width of the displayed list.

FIGURE 4.30

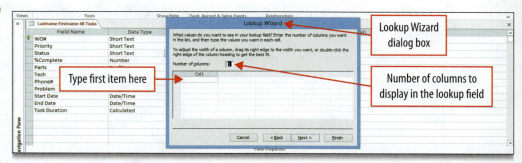

3 Be sure the number of columns is **1**. Under **Col1**, click in the first row, type **Not Started** and then press `Tab` or `↓` to save the first item.

> If you mistakenly press `Enter`, the next dialog box of the wizard displays. If that happens, click the Back button.

4 Type the following data, and then compare your screen with Figure 4.31.

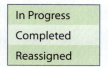

In Progress

Completed

Reassigned

FIGURE 4.31

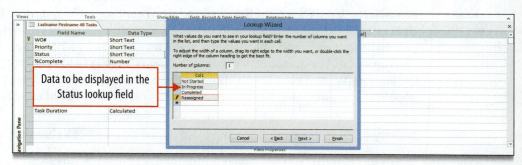

5 Double-click the right edge of Col1 to adjust the column width so all entries display, if necessary, and then click **Next**. In the final dialog box, click **Finish**. With the **Status** field selected, under **Field Properties**, click the **Lookup tab**.

> The Lookup Wizard populates the Lookup property boxes. The *Row Source Type* property indicates that the data is retrieved from a Value List, a list that you created. The *Row Source* property displays the data you entered in the list. The *Limit to List* property displays No, so you can type alternative data in the field if necessary.

6 **Save** the changes, and switch to **Datasheet** view. Click the **Status** field in the first record, and then click the **arrow** to view the lookup list. Press `Esc` to return to a blank field.

Activity 4.16 | Creating a Lookup Field Based on Data in Another Table

In this activity, you will create a lookup field for the Tech field.

1 In the **4B Tasks** table, switch to **Design** view. In the **Tech** field, click in the **Data Type** box, and then click the **Data Type arrow**. From the displayed list of data types, click **Lookup Wizard**.

2 In the first **Lookup Wizard** dialog box, be sure that the **I want the lookup field to get the values from another table or query** option button is selected.

3 ▸ Click **Next**. The **4B Employees** table is selected.

4 ▸ Click **Next** to display the third **Lookup Wizard** dialog box. Under **Available Fields**, click **Last Name**, and then click the **Add Field** (>) button to move the field to the **Selected Fields** box. Move the **First Name** and **Job Title** fields from the **Available Fields** box to the **Selected Fields** box. Compare your screen with Figure 4.32.

> Because there might be several people with the same last name, the First Name field and the Job Title field are included.

FIGURE 4.32

5 ▸ Click **Next** to display the fourth **Lookup Wizard** dialog box. In the **1** box, click the **arrow**, and then click **Last Name**. In the **2** box, click the **arrow**, and then click **First Name**. In the **3** box, click the **arrow**, and then click **Job Title**. Leave all three sort orders as **Ascending**.

> The list will first display last names in ascending order. If there are duplicate last names, then the duplicate last names will then be sorted by the first name in ascending order. If there are duplicate last names and first names, then those names will be sorted in ascending order by the job title.

6 ▸ Click **Next** to display the fifth **Lookup Wizard** dialog box. This screen enables you to change the width of the lookup field and to display the primary key field. Be sure the **Hide key column (recommended)** check box is selected, and then click **Next** to display the sixth and final **Lookup Wizard** dialog box.

> The actual data that is stored in the lookup field is the data in the primary key field.

7 ▸ Under **What label would you like for your lookup field?**, leave the default of **Tech** and be sure that **Allow Multiple Values** is *not* selected.

> Because you have already named the field, the default name is appropriate. If you were creating a new field that had not yet been named, a label should be entered on this screen. If you want to allow the selection of more than one last name when the lookup field displays and then store the multiple values, select the Allow Multiple Values check box, which changes the lookup field to a multivalued field. A *multivalued field* holds multiple values, such as a list of people to whom you have assigned the same task.

8 ▸ Click **Finish**. A message displays stating that the table must be saved before Access can create the needed relationship between the *4B Tasks* table and the *4B Employees* table. Click **Yes**.

9 ▸ With the **Tech** field selected, under **Field Properties**, click the Lookup tab, if necessary.

> The Lookup Wizard populates the Lookup properties boxes. The *Row Source Type* property indicates that the data is retrieved from a table or query. The *Row Source* property displays the SQL statement that is used to retrieve the data from the fields in the *4B Employees* table. The *Limit to List* property displays Yes, which means you must select the data from the list and cannot type data in the field.

10 ▸ Click the **General tab** to display the list of general field properties.

Video A4-7

A *field property* is an attribute or characteristic of a field that controls the display and input of data. You previously used field properties to change the size of a field and to specify a specific format for data types. When you click in any of the property boxes, a description of the property displays to the right. Available field properties depend upon the data type of each field.

Activity 4.17 | Creating an Input Mask Using the Input Mask Wizard

An *input mask* is a field property that determines the data that can be entered, how the data displays, and how the data is stored. For example, an input mask can require individuals to enter telephone numbers in a specific format like (636) 555-1212. If you enter the telephone number without supplying an area code, you will be unable to save the record until the area code is entered. Input masks provide *data validation*—rules that help prevent individuals from entering invalid data—and help ensure that individuals enter data in a consistent manner. By default, you can apply input masks to fields with a data type of Short Text, Number, Currency, and Date/Time. The Input Mask Wizard can be used to apply input masks to fields with a data type of Short Text or Date/Time only.

1 ▶ Under **Field Name**, click **Phone#**. Under **Field Properties**, click in the **Input Mask** box. At the right side of the Field Properties, notice the description given for this property. In the **Input Mask** box, click the **Build** ⸱⸱⸱ button. Compare your screen with Figure 4.33.

The Build button displays after you click in a field property box so you can further define the property. The Input Mask Wizard starts, which enables you to create an input mask using one of several standard masks that Access has designed, such as Phone Number, Social Security Number, Zip Code, and so on. Clicking in the Try It box enables you to enter data to test the input mask.

FIGURE 4.33

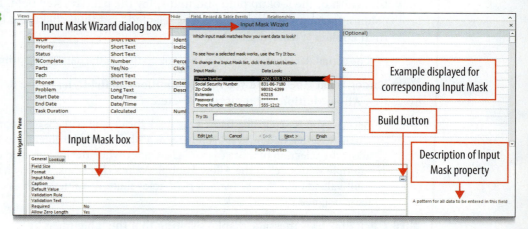

2 ▶ In the displayed **Input Mask Wizard** dialog box, with **Phone Number** selected, click **Next**, and then compare your screen with Figure 4.34. In the **Input Mask Wizard** dialog box, notice the entry in the **Input Mask** box.

A *0* indicates a required digit; a *9* indicates an optional digit or space. The area code is enclosed in parentheses, and a hyphen (-) separates the three-digit prefix from the four-digit number. The exclamation point (!) causes the input mask to fill in from left to right. The Placeholder character indicates that the field will display an underscore character (_) for each digit before data is entered in Datasheet view.

FIGURE 4.34

3 In the **Input Mask Wizard** dialog box, click **Back**, and then click **Edit List**.

The Customize Input Mask Wizard dialog box displays, which enables you to edit the default input mask or add an input mask.

4 In the **Customize Input Mask Wizard** dialog box, in the navigation area, click the **New (blank) record** button. In the **Description** box, type **Local Phone Number** Click in the **Input Mask** box, and type **!000-0000** Click in the **Placeholder** box, and type **#** Click in the **Sample Data** box, and type **555-2090** Compare your screen with Figure 4.35.

Because tasks are assigned to local personnel, the area code is unnecessary. Instead of displaying an underscore as the placeholder in the field, the number sign (#) displays.

FIGURE 4.35

5 In the **Customize Input Mask Wizard** dialog box, click **Close**.

The newly created input mask for Local Phone Number displays below the input mask for Password.

6 Under **Input Mask**, click **Local Phone Number**, and then click **Next**. Click the **Placeholder character arrow** to display other symbols that can be used as placeholders. Be sure that # is displayed as the placeholder character, and then click **Next**.

After creating an input mask to be used with the Input Mask Wizard, you can change the placeholder character for individual fields.

7 The next wizard screen enables you to decide how you want to store the data. Be sure that the **Without the symbols in the mask, like this** option button is selected, as shown in Figure 4.36.

Saving the data without the symbols makes the database size smaller.

FIGURE 4.36

8 Click **Next**. In the final wizard screen, click **Finish**. Notice that the entry in the **Input Mask** box displays as **!000\-0000;;#**. Save 🖫 the table.

Recall that the exclamation point (!) fills the input mask from left to right, and the 0s indicate required digits. The two semicolons (;) are used by Access to separate the input mask into three sections. This input mask has data in the first section—the 0s—and in the third section—the placeholder of #.

The second and third sections of an input mask are optional. The second section, which is not used in this input mask, determines whether the literal characters—in this case, the hyphen (-)—are stored with the data. A *0* in the second section will store the literal characters; a *1* or leaving it blank stores only the characters entered in the field. The third section of the input mask indicates the placeholder character—in this case, the # sign. If you want to leave the fill-in spaces blank instead of using a placeholder, type " "—there is a space between the quotation marks—in the third section.

9 Take a moment to study the table shown in Figure 4.37, which describes the characters that can be used to create a custom input mask.

FIGURE 4.37

MOST COMMON INPUT MASK CHARACTERS	
CHARACTER	**DESCRIPTION**
0	Required digit (0 through 9).
9	Optional digit or space.
#	Optional digit, space, plus sign, or minus sign; blank positions are converted to spaces.
L	Required letter (A through Z).
?	Optional letter.
A	Required digit or letter.
a	Optional digit or letter.
&	Any character or space; required.
C	Any character or space; optional.
<	All characters that follow are converted to lowercase.
>	All characters that follow are converted to uppercase.
!	Characters typed into the mask are filled from left to right. The exclamation point can be included anywhere in the input mask.
\	Character that follows is displayed as text. This is the same as enclosing a character in quotation marks.
Password	Creates a password entry box that displays asterisks (*) as you type. Access stores the characters.
" "	Used to enclose displayed text.
.	Decimal separator.
,	Thousands separator.
: ; - /	Date and time separators; character used depends on your regional settings.

Activity 4.18 | Creating an Input Mask Using the Input Mask Properties Box

In addition to using the wizard, input masks can be created directly in the Input Mask Properties box. In this activity, you will use the Input Mask Properties box to create a mask that will ensure the Work Order # is entered according to departmental policy. An example of a work order number used by the Information Technology department is WO CM-46341. WO is an abbreviation for Work Order. CM represents the initials of the person entering the work order data. A hyphen separates the initials from a number assigned to the work order.

1 With the **4B Tasks** table displayed in **Design** view, click in the **WO#** field. Under **Field Properties**, click in the **Input Mask** box, type **WO** press the Spacebar, type **>LL-99** and then compare your screen with Figure 4.38.

> The letters *WO* and a space will display at the beginning of every Work Order # (WO#). The greater than (>) sign converts any text following it to uppercase. Each *L* indicates that a letter (not a number) is required. A hyphen (-) follows the two letters, and the two 9s indicate optional numbers.

> Take a moment to study the examples of input masks shown in Figure 4.39.

FIGURE 4.38

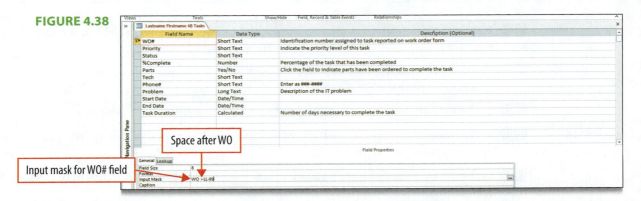

Space after WO

Input mask for WO# field

FIGURE 4.39

EXAMPLES OF INPUT MASKS		
INPUT MASK	**SAMPLE DATA**	**DESCRIPTION**
(000) 000-0000	(712) 555-5011	Must enter an area code because of the 0s enclosed in parentheses.
(999) 000-0000!	(702) 555-6331 ( ) 555-6331	Area code is optional because of the 9s enclosed in parentheses. Exclamation point causes mask to fill in from left to right.
(000) AAA-AAAA	(712) 555-TELE	Enables you to substitute the last seven digits of a U.S.–style phone number with letters. Area code is required.
#999	-20 2009	Can accept any positive or negative number of no more than four characters and no thousands separator or decimal places.
>L????L?000L0	GREENGR339M3 MAY R 452B7	Allows a combination of required (L) and optional (?) letters and required numbers (0). The greater than (>) sign changes letters to uppercase.
00000-9999	23703-5100	Requires the five-digit postal code (0) and optional plus-four section (9).
>L<???????????????	Elizabeth Rose	Enables up to 15 letters in which the first letter is required and is capitalized; all other letters are lowercase.
ISBN 0-&&&&&&&&&&-0	ISBN 0-13-232762-7	Allows a book number with text of ISBN, required first and last digits, and any combination of characters between those digits.
>LL00000-0000	AG23703-0323	Accepts a combination of two required letters, both uppercase, followed by five required numbers, a hyphen, and then four required numbers. Could be used with part or inventory numbers.

2 Click in the **Start Date** field to make the field active. Under **Field Properties**, click in the **Format** box, and then click the **arrow**. From the displayed list, click **Short Date**. Also set the format of **End Date** to **Short Date**.

| *More* **Knowledge** | **The Differences Between Input Masks and Display Formats** |

You can define input masks to control how data is entered into a field and then apply a separate display format to the same data. For example, you can require individuals to enter dates in a format such as 30 Dec. 2015 by using an input mask of DD MMM. YYYY. By using the Format property, you can specify a format of Short Date, which will display the data as 12/30/2015, regardless of how the data was entered.

---

3 Switch to **Datasheet** view, click **Yes** to save the table. In the **WO#** field in the first record, type **da3** and then press Tab or Enter to go to the next field.

The input mask adds the WO and a space. The da is automatically capitalized, and the hyphen is inserted before the 3.

4 In the **Priority** field, type **High** and then press Tab or Enter to go to the next field.

5 In the **Status** field, type **C** to display the **Completed** item in the lookup list, and then press Tab or Enter to move to the next field.

6 In the **%Complete** field, type **100** and then press Tab or Enter three times to bypass the **Parts** and **Tech** fields.

Leaving the Yes/No field blank assigns a No value in the Parts field, so parts are not on order for this task.

7 In the **Phone#** field, type **5558735** and then press Tab or Enter to move to the next field.

8 In the **Problem** field, type **Computer 14 has a computer virus** and then press Tab or Enter to move to the next field.

9 In the **Start Date** field, type **3/28/2016** and then press Tab or Enter to move to the next field.

10 In the **End Date** field, type **3/29/16** and then press Tab or Enter to move to the **Task Duration** field. Notice the calculated field now displays a 1. Compare your screen with Figure 4.40.

FIGURE 4.40

Task Duration is calculated

11 Switch to **Design** view. The data entry is automatically saved when the record is complete.

Activity 4.19 | Specifying a Required Field

Recall that if a table has a field designated as the primary key field, an entry for the field is *required*; it cannot be left empty. You can set this requirement on other fields in either Design view or Datasheet view. In this activity, you will require an entry in the Status field. Use the Required field property to ensure that a field contains data and is not left blank.

1 Click in the **Status** field, and then under **Field Properties**, click in the **Required** box. Click the **Required arrow**, and then compare your screen with Figure 4.41.

Only Yes and No options display in the list.

FIGURE 4.41

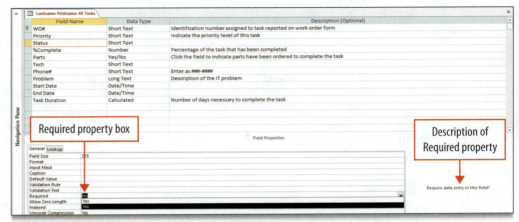

Required property box

Description of Required property

> **2** Click **Yes** to require an individual to enter the status for each record. **Save** 💾 the changes to the table.
>
> A message displays stating that data integrity rules have been changed and that existing data may not be valid for the new rules. This message displays when you change field properties where data exists in the field. Clicking Yes requires Access to examine the field in every record to see if the existing data meets the new data validation rule. For each record Access finds where data does not meet the new validation rule, a new message displays that prompts you to keep testing with the new setting. You also can revert to the prior validation setting and continue testing or cancel testing of the data.

> **3** If the message is displayed, click **No**. Switch to **Datasheet** view. Click in the **Status** field. On the **TABLE TOOLS FIELDS tab**, in the **Field Validation group**, notice that the **Required** check box is selected.

> **4** In the table, click in the **Tech** field. On the **TABLE TOOLS FIELDS tab**, in the **Field Validation group**, click the **Required** check box. Compare your screen with Figure 4.42.
>
> A message displays stating that the existing data violates the Required property for the Tech field because the field is currently blank.

FIGURE 4.42

Warning message

> **5** In the message box, click **Cancel**. Click the **arrow** at the right of the **Tech** field, and then select **Ron Lee**.

More Knowledge | **Allowing Blank Data in a Required Text or Memo Field**

By default, all fields except the primary key field can be empty—null. If the Required property for a field is set to Yes, a value must be entered into the field. If data is required, Access will not save the record until a value is entered; however, you may not have the data to enter into a text or memo field where the Required property is set to Yes. To allow for this situation, you can set the Allow Zero Length property for the field to Yes. A *zero-length string* is created by typing two quotation marks with no space between them (""), which indicates that no value exists for a required text or memo field.

Activity 4.20 | Setting Default Values for Fields

You can use the Default Value field property to display a value in a field for new records. As you enter data, you can change the *default value* in the field to another value within the parameters of any validation rules. Setting a default value for fields that contain the same data for multiple records increases the efficiency of data entry. For example, if all of the employees in the organization live in California, set the default value of the state field to CA. If most of the employees in your organization live in the city of Golden Grove, set the default value of the city field to Golden Grove. If an employee lives in another city, type the new value over the displayed default value.

1 Switch to **Design** view. Under **Field Name**, click the **Priority** field. Under **Field Properties**, click in the **Default Value** box, and then type **Low** Switch to **Datasheet** view, and then **Save** 🖫 changes to the table. Notice that the **Priority** field displays *LOW* in the **New Record** row.

> Setting a default value does not change the data in saved records; the default value will display in new records and will be saved only if nothing else is typed in the field.

2 Switch back to **Design** view. Using the technique you just practiced, for the **Status** field, set the **Default Value** property to **Not Started** If necessary, for the %Complete field, set the Default Value property to **0**

3 For the **Start Date** field, set the **Default Value** to **3/30/16** Switch to **Datasheet** view, saving changes to the table. Compare your screen with Figure 4.43.

> The Status field shows a default value of *Not "Started"*. *Not* is an Access logical operator; therefore, Access excluded the word *Not* from the text expression.

FIGURE 4.43

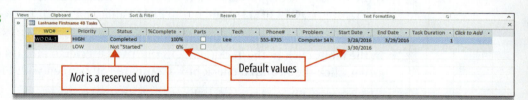

4 Switch to **Design** view. Click in the **Status** field. Under **Field Properties**, in the **Default Value** box, select the text, and then type **"Not Started"** Click in the **Start Date** field, and notice that in the **Default Value** box, Access displays the date as **#3/30/2016#**. Switch to **Datasheet** view, saving changes to the table, and then view the default value in the **Status** field.

> Inserting quotation marks around *Not Started* informs Access that both words are part of the text expression.

More Knowledge | **Using the Current Date as a Default Value**

To use the current date as the default value for a Date/Time field, in the Default Value box, type date()

Activity 4.21 | Indexing Fields in a Table

An *index* is a special list created in Access to speed up searches and sorting—such as the index at the back of a book. The index is visible only to Access and not to you, but it helps Access find items much faster. You should index fields that you search frequently, fields that you sort, or fields used to join tables in relationships. Indexes, however, can slow down the creation and deletion of records because the data must be added to or deleted from the index.

1 ▷ Switch to **Design** view. Under **Field Name**, click **WO#**. Under **Field Properties**, locate the **Indexed** property box, and notice the entry of **Yes (No Duplicates)**.

By default, primary key fields are indexed. Because WO# is the primary key field, the field is automatically indexed, and no duplicate values are permitted in this field.

2 ▷ Under **Field Name**, click **Tech**. Under **Field Properties**, click in the **Indexed** property box, and then click the displayed **arrow**. Compare your screen with Figure 4.44.

Three options display for the Indexed property—No, Yes (Duplicates OK), and Yes (No Duplicates).

FIGURE 4.44

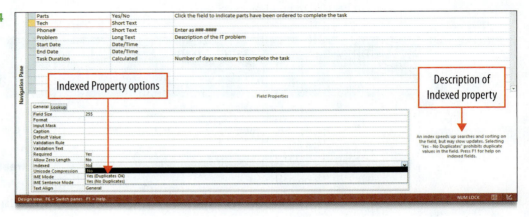

3 ▷ Click **Yes (Duplicates OK)**.

By adding an index to the field and allowing duplicates, you create faster searches and sorts on this field, while allowing duplicate data. Because a person may be assigned more than one task, allowing duplicate data is appropriate.

4 ▷ Save 🔲 the table design.

5 ▷ On the **TABLE TOOLS DESIGN tab**, in the **Show/Hide group**, click the **Indexes** button.

An Indexes dialog box displays the indexes in the current table. Opening the Indexes dialog box is an efficient way to determine the fields that have been indexed in a table.

6 ▷ In the **Indexes: 4B Tasks** dialog box, click **Close** ☒ .

Objective 8   Create Validation Rules and Validation Text

Video A4-8

You have practiced different techniques to help ensure that data entered into a field is valid. Data types restrict the type of data that can be entered into a field. Field sizes control the number of characters that can be entered into a field. Field properties further control how data is entered into a field, including the use of input masks to require individuals to enter data in a specific way.

Another way to ensure the accuracy of data is by using the Validation Rule property. A *validation rule* is an expression that precisely defines the range of data that will be accepted in a field. An *expression* is a combination of functions, field values, constants, and operators that brings about a result. *Validation text* is the error message that displays when an individual enters a value prohibited by the validation rule.

Activity 4.22 | Creating Data Validation Rules and Validation Text

In this activity, you will create data validation rules and validation text for the %Complete field, the Start Date field, and the Priority field.

1 Under **Field Name**, click **%Complete**. Under **Field Properties**, click in the **Validation Rule** box, and then click the **Build** button `...`.

The Expression Builder dialog box displays. Recall that the Expression Builder is a feature used to create formulas (expressions) in query criteria, form and report properties, and table validation rules. Take a moment to study the table shown in Figure 4.45, which describes the operators that can be used in building expressions.

FIGURE 4.45

OPERATORS USED IN EXPRESSIONS		
OPERATOR	**FUNCTION**	**EXAMPLE**
Not	Tests for values NOT meeting a condition.	**Not** >10 (the same as <=10)
In	Tests for values equal to existing members in a list.	**In** ("High","Normal","Low")
Between…And	Tests for a range of values, including the values on each end.	**Between** 0 **And** 100 (the same as >=0 **And** <=100)
Like	Matches pattern strings in Text and Memo fields.	**Like** "Car*"
Is Not Null	Requires individuals to enter values in the field. If used in place of the Required field, you can create Validation Text that better describes what should be entered in the field.	**Is Not Null** (the same as setting Required property to Yes)
And	Specifies that all of the entered data must fall within the specified limits.	>=#01/01/2016# **And** <=#03/01/2016# (Date must be between 01/01/2016 and 03/01/2016) Can use And to combine validation rules. For example, **Not** "USA" **And Like** "U*"
Or	Specifies that one of many entries can be accepted.	"High" **Or** "Normal" **Or** "Low"
<	Less than.	<100
<=	Less than or equal to.	<=100
>	Greater than.	>0
>=	Greater than or equal to.	>=0
=	Equal to.	=Date()
<>	Not equal to.	<>#12/24/53#

2 In the upper box of the **Expression Builder** dialog box, type **>=0 and <=1** Alternatively, type the expression in the Validation Rule property box. In the **Expression Builder** dialog box, click **OK**.

The %Complete field has a data type of Number and is formatted as a percent. Recall that the Format property changes the way the stored data displays. To convert the display of a number to a percent, Access multiplies the value by 100 and appends the percent sign (%). Therefore, 100% is stored as 1—Access multiples 1 by 100, resulting in 100. A job that is halfway completed—50%—has the value stored as .5 because .5 times 100 equals 50.

ANOTHER WAY When using the Expression Builder to create an expression, you can either type the entire expression or, on the small toolbar in the dialog box, click an existing button, such as the > button, to insert operators into the expression.

3 Click in the **Validation Text** box, and then type **Enter a value between 0 and 100** so that the percentages are reflected accurately. Compare your screen with Figure 4.46.

FIGURE 4.46

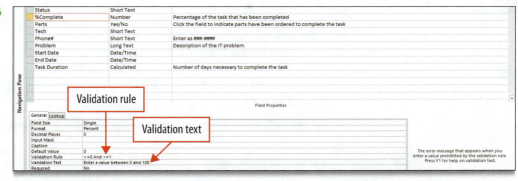

4 Under **Field Name**, click **Start Date** to make the field active. Under **Field Properties**, click in the **Validation Rule** box, and then type **>=3/15/2016** Click in the **Validation Text** box, and then type **You cannot enter a date prior to 3/15/2016** Compare your screen with Figure 4.47.

In expressions, Access inserts a number or pound sign (#) before and after a date. This validation rule ensures that the person entering data cannot enter a date prior to 3/15/2016.

FIGURE 4.47

5 Under **Field Name**, click **Priority**. Under **Field Properties**, click in the **Validation Rule** box, and then type **in ("High","Normal","Low")** Click in the **Validation Text** box, and then type **You must enter High, Normal, or Low** Compare your screen with Figure 4.48.

The operators are not case sensitive; Access will capitalize the operators when you click in another property box. With the *In* operator, the members of the list must be enclosed in parentheses, and each member must be enclosed in quotation marks and separated from each other by commas. Another way to specify the same validation rule is: "High" Or "Normal" Or "Low".

FIGURE 4.48

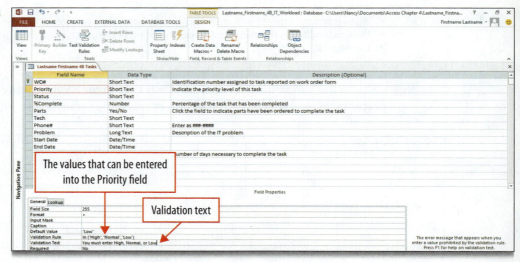

The values that can be entered into the Priority field

Validation text

6 Save the changes to the table. Switch to **Datasheet** view.

A message displays stating that data integrity rules have changed. Even though you have clicked No in previous message boxes, click Yes. In a large database, you should click Yes to have Access check the data in all of the records before moving on.

Activity 4.23 | Testing Table Design and Field Properties

In this activity, you will add records to the *4B Tasks* table to test the design and field properties.

1 With the **4B Tasks** table open in **Datasheet** view, in the second record in the **WO#** field, type **sk1** and then press Tab or Enter to go to the next field.

2 In the **Priority** field, type **Medium** to replace the default entry *Low*, and then press Tab or Enter to go to the next field. The message *You must enter High, Normal, or Low* appears on your screen because the validation rule limits the entry in this field. Compare your screen with Figure 4.49.

FIGURE 4.49

Validation rule prohibits entry of *Medium*

Warning message— Validation text

3 Click **OK** and type **Normal** in the **Priority** field to replace *Medium*. Press Tab or Enter to go to the next field.

4 In the **Status** field, **Not Started** automatically appears because it is the default entry. Type **Backordered** and then press Tab or Enter to move to the next field.

Recall that the Limit to List property setting is set to No for the lookup field, enabling you to type data other than that displayed in the list box. If the purpose of the lookup field is to restrict individuals to entering only certain data, then the Limit to List property setting should be set to Yes.

5 In the **%Complete** field, with the **0%** selected, type **50** and then press [Tab] or [Enter] to move to the next field.

6 In the **Parts** field, click in the **check box** to add a checkmark and indicate parts are on order to complete the task. Press [Tab] or [Enter] to move to the next field.

7 In the **Tech** field, select **William McCamara**. Press [Tab] or [Enter] to move to the next field.

> **↻ ANOTHER WAY**   You can locate an entry in a long list faster if you type the first letter of the data for which you are searching. For example, if you are searching for a last name that begins with the letter *m*, when the list displays, type m or M The selection will move down to the first entry that begins with the letter.

8 In the **Phone#** field, type **aaa** and notice that Access will not allow a letter entry because the input mask you just created requires numbers in this field. Type **5556798** and then press [Tab] or [Enter] to move to the next field.

9 In the **Problem** field, type **Printer B will not print** Press [Tab] or [Enter] to move to the next field

10 In the **Start Date** field, type **4/5/2016** Press [Tab] or [Enter] three times to move past **Task Duration** and move to the next record.

Notice the calendar icon that appears to the right of the date fields. Clicking the icon enables you to choose a date from a calendar.

End Date is not a required field, so it accepts a blank entry. Because End Date is blank, there is nothing to calculate in the Task Duration field.

11 In the third record, in the **WO#** field, type **da4** and then press [Tab] or [Enter] two times to move to the **Status** field.

12 In the **Status** field, select **Completed**. Press [Tab] or [Enter] to move to the next field.

13 In the **%Complete** field, with the *0%* selected, type **110** and then press [Tab] or [Enter] to move to the next field.

A message *Enter a value between 0 and 100* appears on your screen because the validation rule limits the entry in this field.

14 Click **OK** to close the dialog box. Select the *110%* and type **100** Press [Tab] or [Enter] two times. In the **Tech** field, type **Rukstad** Press [Tab] or [Enter] to move to the next field. Compare your screen with Figure 4.50.

A message *The text you entered isn't an item in the list* appears on your screen. Recall that the Limit to List property setting is set to Yes for the lookup field, which restricts you from entering anything that is not on the list.

FIGURE 4.50

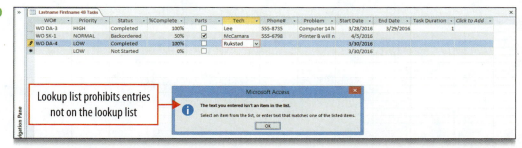

15 Click **OK** and select **Angelina Perry** from the lookup list. Press [Tab] or [Enter] to move to the next field.

16 In the **Phone#** field, type **5556313** Press `Tab` or `Enter` to move to the next field. In the **Description** field, type **Computer 3 needs updates** Press `Tab` or `Enter` to move to the next field

17 In the **Start Date** field, notice the default date of 3/30/2016, and press `Tab` or `Enter` to move to the next field. In the **End Date** field, type **4/2/2016** Press `Tab` or `Enter` to move to the next field.

18 Adjust all column widths, ensuring that all of the field names and all of the field data display. View the table in **Print Preview**, and then change the orientation to **Landscape**. If you are instructed to submit this result, create a paper or electronic printout. **Close Print Preview**.

19 **Close** `×` the table, saving changes. **Close** the database, and **Exit** Access.

20 As directed by your instructor, submit your database and the paper or electronic printout of the table that is the result of this project. Specifically, in this project, using your own name you created the following database and printout or electronic printout:

1. Lastname_Firstname_4B_IT_Workload	Database file
2. Lastname Firstname 4B Tasks	Table (printed or electronic printout)

END | You have completed Project 4B

END OF CHAPTER

SUMMARY

Backup files are copies of a database created to protect the data. Adding trustworthy storage locations to the Trust Center as secure locations allows the user full use of the content in the database.

Using existing tables as the basis to create new ones eliminates the chances of mistakes in table design, and they can be continually modified and updated to keep the data useful over time.

Creating a table in Design view allows control over the fields in the table, the choice of the data type based on the content, and the ability to set field properties to minimize errors in data entry.

Reducing errors starts with a lookup or calculated data type to minimize manual entry, formatting properties and input masks to ensure accurate presentation, and validation rules to restrict data entry.

GO! LEARN IT ONLINE

Review the concepts and key terms in this chapter by completing these online challenges, which you can find at **www.pearsonhighered.com/go**.

Matching and Multiple Choice:
Answer matching and multiple choice questions to test what you learned in this chapter. MyITLab®

Crossword Puzzle:
Spell out the words that match the numbered clues, and put them in the puzzle squares.

Flipboard:
Flip through the definitions of the key terms in this chapter and match them with the correct term.

END OF CHAPTER

REVIEW AND ASSESSMENT GUIDE FOR ACCESS CHAPTER 4

Your instructor may assign one or more of these projects to help you review the chapter and assess your mastery and understanding of the chapter.

Project	Apply Skills from These Chapter Objectives	Project Type	Project Location
		Review and Assessment Guide for Access Chapter 4	
4C	Objectives 1–4 from Project 4A	**4C Skills Review** A guided review of the skills from Project 4A.	On the following pages
4D	Objectives 5–8 from Project 4B	**4D Skills Review** A guided review of the skills from Project 4B.	On the following pages
4E	Objectives 1–4 from Project 4A	**4E Mastery (Grader Project)** A demonstration of your mastery of the skills in Project 4A with extensive decision making.	In MyITLab and on the following pages
4F	Objectives 5–8 from Project 4B	**4F Mastery (Grader Project)** A demonstration of your mastery of the skills in Project 4B with extensive decision making.	In MyITLab and on the following pages
4G	Objectives 1–7 from Projects 4A and 4B	**4G Mastery (Grader Project)** A demonstration of your mastery of the skills in Projects 4A and 4B with extensive decision making.	In MyITLab and on the following pages
4H	Combination of Objectives from Projects 4A and 4B	**4H GO! Fix It** A demonstration of your mastery of the skills in Projects 4A and 4B by creating a correct result from a document that contains errors you must find.	Online
4I	Combination of Objectives from Projects 4A and 4B	**4I GO! Make It** A demonstration of your mastery of the skills in Projects 4A and 4B by creating a result from a supplied picture.	Online
4J	Combination of Objectives from Projects 4A and 4B	**4J GO! Solve It** A demonstration of your mastery of the skills in Projects 4A and 4B, your decision making skills, and your critical thinking skills. A task-specific rubric helps you self-assess your result.	Online
4K	Combination of Objectives from Projects 4A and 4B	**4K GO! Solve It** A demonstration of your mastery of the skills in Projects 4A and 4B, your decision making skills, and your critical thinking skills. A task-specific rubric helps you self-assess your result.	On the following pages
4L	Combination of Objectives from Projects 4A and 4B	**4L GO! Think** A demonstration of your understanding of the chapter concepts applied in a manner that you would use outside of college. An analytic rubric helps you and your instructor grade the quality of your work by comparing it to the work an expert in the discipline would create.	On the following pages
4M	Combination of Objectives from Projects 4A and 4B	**4M GO! Think** A demonstration of your understanding of the chapter concepts applied in a manner that you would use outside of college. An analytic rubric helps you and your instructor grade the quality of your work by comparing it to the work an expert in the discipline would create.	Online
4N	Combination of Objectives from Projects 4A and 4B	**4N You and GO!** A demonstration of your understanding of the chapter concepts applied in a manner that you would use in a personal situation. An analytic rubric helps you and your instructor grade the quality of your work.	Online

GLOSSARY

GLOSSARY OF CHAPTER KEY TERMS

Append A feature that allows you to add data to an existing table.

Back up A feature that creates a copy of the original database to protect against lost data.

Clipboard A temporary storage area in Windows that can hold up to 24 items.

Combo box A box that is a combination of a list box and a text box in a lookup field.

Copy A command that duplicates a selection and places it on the Clipboard.

Data validation Rules that help prevent invalid data entries and ensure data is entered consistently.

Default value A value displayed for new records.

Destination table The table to which records are appended.

Dynamic An attribute applied to data in a database that changes.

Expression A combination of functions, field values, constants, and operators that produces a result.

Expression Builder A feature used to create formulas (expressions) in calculated fields, query criteria, form and report properties, and table validation rules.

Field property An attribute or a characteristic of a field that controls the display and input of data.

Flagged A highlighted word that Spell Check does not recognize from the Office dictionary.

Index A special list created in Access to speed up searches and sorting.

Input mask A field property that determines the how the data displays and is stored.

Instance Each simultaneously running Access session.

List box A box containing a list of choices for a lookup field.

Lookup field A way to restrict data entered in a field.

Multivalued field A field that holds multiple values.

Paste An option that moves the copy of the selected table from the Clipboard into a new location.

Path The location of a folder or file on your computer or storage device.

Required A field property that ensures a field cannot be left empty.

Source table The table from which you are copying records.

System tables Tables used to keep track of multiple entries in an attachment field that you cannot view or work with.

Trust Center A security feature that checks documents for macros and digital signatures.

Trusted source A person or organization that you know will not send you databases with malicious content.

Validation rule An expression that precisely defines the range of data that will be accepted in a field.

Validation text The error message that displays when an individual enters a value prohibited by the validation rule.

Zero-length string An entry created by typing two quotation marks with no spaces between them ("") to indicate that no value exists for a required text or memo field.

CHAPTER REVIEW

Apply 4A skills from these Objectives:

1 Manage Existing Tables
2 Modify Existing Tables
3 Change Data Types
4 Attach Files to Records

Skills Review   Project 4C Commerce

Dario Soto, the city manager of Golden Grove, has a database of the city's industry information. This database has five tables. The Industries table contains summary information from the other four tables. Each update to an individual industry table would require updates to the summary table. In the following Skills Review, you will redesign the tables, taking advantage of table relationships to avoid entering and storing redundant data. Your completed tables and relationships will look similar to those in Figure 4.51.

PROJECT FILES

For Project 4C, you will need the following files:

a04C_Commerce
a04C_GCH_Contacts

You will save your databases as:

Lastname_Firstname_4C_Commerce
a04C_Commerce_2016-10-30 (date will vary)

PROJECT RESULTS

FIGURE 4.51

(Project 4C Commerce continues on the next page)

CHAPTER REVIEW

1 ▶ **Start** Access. Locate and open the **a04C_Commerce** database.

a. On the **FILE tab**, click **Save As**, and then, under **Save Database As**, double-click **Back Up Database**. In the **Save As** dialog box, navigate to the drive on which you will be storing your folders and projects for this chapter, and then click **Save** to accept the default name.

b. **Save** the database in the **Microsoft Access Database** format in your **Access Chapter 4** folder as **Lastname_Firstname_4C_Commerce**.

2 ▶ In the **Navigation Pane**, double-click **4C Industries**. Take a moment to review the contents of the table. Close the **Navigation Pane**.

a. Click the **FILE tab**, and click **Save As**. Under **File Types**, double-click **Save Object As**.

b. In the displayed **Save As** dialog box, under **Save '4C Industries' to**, type **Lastname Firstname 4C Industries Revised** and then click **OK**.

3 ▶ Point to the **Business #5** field name until the pointer displays. Drag to the left to the **Business #1** field name to select the five fields. On the **Home tab**, in the **Records group**, click the **Delete** button. In the displayed message box, click **Yes** to permanently delete the fields and the data.

4 ▶ Switch to **Design** view. To the left of **Industry Code**, click the **row selector** box, and then in the **Tools group**, click the **Primary Key** button. **Close** the table, saving any changes. Open the **Navigation Pane**.

5 ▶ In the **Navigation Pane**, click **4C Agriculture**.

a. On the **Home tab**, in the **Clipboard group**, click the **Copy** button.

b. On the **Home tab**, in the **Clipboard group**, click the **Paste** button.

c. In the **Paste Table As** dialog box, under **Table Name**, type **Lastname Firstname 4C Business Contacts** Under **Paste Options**, verify that the **Structure and Data** option button is selected, and then click **OK**.

6 ▶ In the **Navigation Pane**, click **4C Manufacturing**.

a. On the **Home tab**, in the **Clipboard group**, click the **Copy** button, and then click the **Paste** button.

b. In the **Paste Table As** dialog box, under **Table Name**, type **Lastname Firstname 4C Business Contacts** Under **Paste Options**, click the **Append Data to Existing Table** option button, and then click **OK**.

c. Using the same procedure, append the **4C Medical Centers** table and the **4C E-Commerce** table to the **Lastname Firstname 4C Business Contacts** table.

7 ▶ Save the **4C Business Contacts** table as **Lastname Firstname 4C Business Stats** One table will contain only contact information, and the other table will contain only statistical information.

8 ▶ In the **4C Business Stats** table, select the **Business Name** field, and then press `Delete`. Click **Yes** to delete the field and data. If necessary, scroll to the right to display the **Address, City, State, ZIP, Contact,** and **Phone#** fields. Select all six fields, and then press `Delete`. Click **Yes** to delete the fields and data.

a. Switch to **Design** view, and click in the **Business ID** field. On the **TABLE TOOLS DESIGN tab**, in the **Tools group**, click the **Primary Key** button. Change the data type of the **First Year** field to **Number**. **Save** the changes, and then switch to **Datasheet** view.

b. Click in the **Employees** field in the first record. On the **HOME tab**, in the **Find group**, click the **Find** button. In the **Find What** box, type **12** In the Look In box, select Current field, if necessary. Click **Find Next** to select the next occurrence in the **current field**. Click **Cancel** in the **Find and Replace** dialog box.

c. Click the **Record Selector** box to select the record containing *12*. On the **HOME tab**, in the **Records group**, click the **Delete** button. In the displayed message box, click **Yes** to permanently delete the record.

d. Adjust all column widths to view the field names and data. View the table in **Print Preview**. If you are instructed to submit the results, create a paper or electronic printout. **Close Print Preview**.

9 ▶ Open the **4C Business Contacts** table. Close the **Navigation Pane**. Select the **Employees, Gross Sales,** and **First Year** fields. On the **Home tab**, in the **Records group**, click the **Delete** button. In the displayed message box, click **Yes** to permanently delete the fields and data.

(Project 4C Commerce continues on the next page)

CHAPTER REVIEW

10 Click the **Business Name** field name. On the **FIELDS tab**, in the **Add & Delete group**, click the **Short Text** button. Type **Industry Code** to replace **Field1,** and then press Enter. **Save** your work.

a. In the first record, click in the **Industry Code** field. Open the **Navigation Pane**, and open the **4C Industries Revised** table. Under **Industry Category**, locate the record for the **Agriculture**, and notice the **Industry Code** of AGR. On the **tab row**, click the **4C Business Contacts tab** to make the table active. In the **Business ID** of **189018**, in the **Industry Code** field, type **AGR** Locate the **Business ID** of **675234**, and then in the **Industry Code** field, type **AGR** Locate the **Business ID** of **234155**, type **AGR**

b. Using the techniques you just practiced, locate the **Industry Codes** for the **Manufacturing, Medical Center**, and **E-Commerce** Industry Categories. In Business IDs **258679, 399740, 479728, 927685**, and **966657**, type **MAN** In Business IDs **252479, 295738, 362149**, and **420879**, type **MED** and then in Business IDs **129741, 329718**, and **420943**, type **INT**

11 In the **Search** box in the navigation area at the bottom of the window, type **adv** Click at the end of **AdventuCom**. Press the Spacebar and type **Resources** Move to the next record to save the changes.

12 Switch the **4C Business Contacts** table to **Design** view. With the insertion point in the **Business ID** field, on the **TABLE TOOLS DESIGN tab**, in the **Tools group**, click the **Primary Key** button. **Save** the changes.

13 To the left of **Contact**, click the **row selector** box. Drag the field up until you see a dark horizontal line between *Industry Code* and *Address*, and then release the mouse button. **Save** the changes.

14 Click in the blank field name box under **Phone#**, type **Contact List** and then press Tab to move to the **Data Type** box. Click the **Data Type arrow**, and click **Attachment**.

15 Switch to **Datasheet** view, saving changes to the table.

a. In the fourth record (Greater Community Hospital), double-click in the **Attachment** field. In the displayed **Attachments** dialog box, click **Add**.

b. Navigate to the location where the student data files for this textbook are stored. In the **Choose File** dialog box, double-click **a04C_GCH_Contacts**. In the **Attachments** dialog box, click **OK**.

16 On the **HOME tab**, in the **Records group**, click the **Spelling** button. Ignore the entries until it selects *Makets*, and **Change** the spelling to *Markets*. Ignore the other names it selects as the process continues.

17 Adjust all column widths to view the field names and data. View the table in **Print Preview**, and then change the orientation to **Landscape**. If you are instructed to submit the results, create a paper or electronic printout.

18 On the **tab row**, right-click any table tab, and then click **Close All**, saving changes if necessary. **Close** the database, and **Exit** Access.

19 As directed by your instructor, submit your database and the paper or electronic printout of the two tables that are the result of this project. Specifically, in this project, using your own name you created the following database and printouts or electronic printouts:

1. Lastname_Firstname_4C_Commerce	Database file
2. Lastname Firstname 4C Business Stats	Table (printed or electronic printout)
3. Lastname Firstname 4C Business Contacts	Table (printed or electronic printout)

END | You have completed Project 4C

CHAPTER REVIEW

Skills Review | Project 4D City Airport

Dario Soto, city manager of Golden Grove, California, has created a table to keep track of airport personnel. In the following Skills Review, you will add a table that stores records about the employees, modify the properties, and customize the fields in the table. You will add features to the database table that will help to reduce data entry errors and that will make data entry easier. Your completed table will look similar to the table shown in Figure 4.52.

PROJECT FILES

For Project 4D, you will need the following files:

a04D_City_Airport
Two new blank Word documents

You will save your files as:

Lastname_Firstname_4D_City_Airport
Lastname_Firstname_4D_Indexes
Lastname_Firstname_4D_Validation

PROJECT RESULTS

FIGURE 4.52

(Project 4D City Airport continues on the next page)

CHAPTER REVIEW

1 **Start** Access. Locate and open the **a04D_City_Airport** database. **Save** the database in the **Microsoft Access Database** format in your **Access Chapter 4** folder as **Lastname_Firstname_4D_City_Airport**

2 Close the **Navigation Pane**. On the **CREATE tab**, in the **Tables group**, click the **Table Design** button to open an empty table in **Design** view.

a. In the first **Field Name** box, type **Empl ID** and press Tab. On the **Table Tools DESIGN tab**, in the **Tools group**, click the **Primary Key** button. Press F6 to move to the **Field Properties** pane at the bottom of the screen. In the **Field Size** box, type **6** to replace the 255.

b. In the second **Field Name** box, type **Vacation** In the **Data Type** box, click the **arrow**, and then click **Number**. Press Tab to move to the **Description** box. Type **Indicate how many weeks of vacation the employee receives per year** Press Tab or Enter to move to the next field.

c. In the third **Field Name** box, type **Coverage** In the **Data Type** box, click the **arrow**, and from the displayed list of data types, click **Lookup Wizard**. In the first **Lookup Wizard** dialog box, click **I will type in the values that I want** option button, and then click **Next**. Verify the number of columns is **1**. Click in the first row under **Col1**, type **Emp** and then press Tab or ↓ to save the first item. In the next three rows type the following data: **Emp + C** and **Fam** and **None** and then click **Next**. In the final dialog box, click **Finish**.

d. Click in the **Description** box, and type **Indicate the type of insurance coverage the employee has selected**

e. Click in the fourth **Field Name** box, and type **LT Care** Click the **Data Type arrow**, and then click **Number**. Press Tab to move to the **Description** box. Type **Indicate the benefit period option selected by the employee**

f. Press F6 to move to the **Field Properties** pane at the bottom of the screen, and then click in the **Validation Rule** box. Click the **Build** button. In the upper box of the **Expression Builder** dialog box, type **>=0 and <=2** and then click **OK**. Click in the **Validation Text** box, and then type **Enter a value between 0 and 2** Hold down Alt, and then press PrintScrn.

g. Start **Word 2013**. In a new, blank document, type your first and last names, press Enter, and then type **4D Validation** Press Enter, and then press Ctrl + V. **Save** the document in your **Access Chapter 4** folder as **Lastname_Firstname_4D_Validation** If you are instructed to submit this result, create a paper or electronic printout. **Exit** Word.

h. Click in the fifth **Field Name** box, and type **401K** Click the **Data Type arrow**, and then click **Yes/No**. Press Tab to move to the **Description** box. Type **Indicate whether or not the employee participates in the 401K plan**

i. Save the table as **Lastname Firstname 4D Employee Benefits** Switch to **Datasheet** view and enter the records in the table below.

If you are instructed to submit this result, create a paper or electronic printout of the **4D Employee Benefits** table. If you are to submit your work electronically, follow your instructor's directions. Close the table.

3 In the **Navigation Pane**, under **Tables**, rename the **4D Employees** table by adding your **Lastname Firstname** to the beginning of the table name. Double-click **4D Employees** to open the table. Close the **Navigation Pane**.

a. Switch to **Design** view. Make **Empl ID** the **Primary Key** field. Change the data type for the **Date Hired** field to **Date/Time**. Change the data type for the **Annual Salary** field to **Currency**. Change the data

Empl ID	Vacation	Coverage	LT Care	401K
589734	3	Emp	0	Yes
986458	2	None	1	No
564897	2	Emp + C	2	Yes
233311	4	Fam	1	Yes
722859	2	Fam	2	Yes

(Project 4D City Airport continues on the next page)

type for the **Office E-mail** field to **Hyperlink**. **Save** your work. You will see a message box warning that some data may be lost. Click **Yes** to continue.

b. In the **Dept** field, click in the **Data Type** box, click the **arrow**, and then click **Lookup Wizard**. In the first **Lookup Wizard** dialog box, verify that **I want the lookup field to get the values from another table or query** option button is selected. Click **Next**. Select the **4D Departments** table. Click **Next** to display the third **Lookup Wizard** dialog box. Under **Available Fields**, with **Department** selected, click the **Add Field** button to move the field to the **Selected Fields** box.

c. Click **Next** to display the fourth **Lookup Wizard** dialog box. In the **1** box, click the **arrow**, and then click **Department**. Leave the sort order as **Ascending**. Click **Next** to display the fifth **Lookup Wizard** dialog box. Click **Next** to display the sixth and final **Lookup Wizard** dialog box. Under **What label would you like for your lookup field?**, leave the default of **Dept** and be sure that **Allow Multiple Values** is *not* selected. Click **Finish**. Click **Yes** to save the table.

d. Under **Field Name**, click **Office Phone**. Under **Field Properties**, click in the **Input Mask** box and then click the **Build** button.

e. In the displayed **Input Mask Wizard** dialog box, with **Phone Number** selected, click **Edit List**. In the **Customize Input Mask Wizard** dialog box, click the **New (blank) record** button. In the **Description** box, type **Phone Number with Extension** In the **Input Mask** box, type **!(999) 000-0000 \X999** Click in the **Placeholder** box, and then change _ to # Click in the **Sample Data** box, and type **714 5551234236** In the **Customize Input Mask Wizard** dialog box, click **Close**.

f. Under **Input Mask**, scroll down, click **Phone Number with Extension**, and then click **Next**. Verify that # is displayed as the placeholder character, and then click **Next**. The next wizard screen enables you to decide how you want to store the data. Verify that the **Without the symbols in the mask, like this** option button is selected, and then click **Next**. In the final wizard screen, click **Finish**.

g. Click in the **Date Hired** field. Under **Field Properties**, click in the **Format** box, and then click the **Format arrow**. From the displayed list, click **Medium Date**. Click in the **Required** box. Click the **Required arrow**,

and then click **Yes**. Click in the **Monthly Earn** field. Under **Field Properties**, click in the **Expression** box, and edit the expression to read **[Annual Salary]/12** Click the **Format arrow**, and then select **Currency** from the displayed list.

h. Under **Field Name**, click **State**. Under **Field Properties**, click in the **Format** box, and then type **>** Click in the **Default Value** box, and then type **CA** Using the same technique, set the **Default Value** of the **City** field to **Golden Grove**

i. Under **Field Name**, click **Last Name**. Under **Field Properties**, click in the **Indexed** property box, and then click the displayed **arrow**. Click **Yes (Duplicates OK)**. **Save** your work. In the message box, click **Yes** to test the existing data with the new rules. On the **TABLE TOOLS DESIGN tab**, in the **Show/Hide group**, click the **Indexes** button. Hold down [Alt], and then press [PrintScrn].

j. Start **Microsoft Word**. In a new, blank document, type your first and last names, press [Enter], and then type **4D Indexes** Press [Enter], and then press [Ctrl] + [V]. **Save** the document in your **Access Chapter 4** folder as **Lastname_Firstname_4D_Indexes** If you are instructed to submit this result, create a paper or electronic printout. **Exit** Word. **Close** the **Indexes** dialog box.

4 ▶ Switch to **Datasheet** view, saving changes to the table if necessary.

a. Click the **New (blank) record** button. Type the following data:

Empl ID	543655
Title	Mr.
First Name	Mark
Last Name	Roberts
Street	1320 Woodbriar Court
City	Golden Grove
State	CA
ZIP	96265
Dept	Operations
Date Hired	3/9/2012
Salary	92000
Office Phone	714 555 0167 101
Office E-Mail	mroberts@goldengrove.gov

(Project 4D City Airport continues on the next page)

CHAPTER REVIEW

b. If you are instructed to submit this result, create a paper or electronic printout of the **4D Employees** table in **Landscape** orientation. This table will print on two pages. **Close 4D Employees**. If you are to submit your work electronically, follow your instructor's directions.

5 Open the **Navigation Pane**. **Close** the database, and **Exit** Access.

6 As directed by your instructor, submit your database and the paper or electronic printout of the four objects—two tables and two Word documents—that are the result of this project. Specifically, in this project, using your own name you created the following database and printouts or electronic printouts:

1. Lastname_Firstname_4D_City_Airport	Database file
2. Lastname_Firstname_4D_Validation	Word document (printed or electronic printout)
3. Lastname Firstname 4D Employee Benefits	Table (printed or electronic printout)
4. Lastname_Firstname_4D_Indexes	Word document (printed or electronic printout)
5. Lastname Firstname 4D Employees	Table (printed or electronic printout)

END | You have completed Project 4D

CONTENT-BASED ASSESSMENTS

Mastering Access Project 4E Cultural Events

In the following Mastering Access project, you will manage and modify tables in a database that contains cultural information about the city of Golden Grove. The database will be used by the arts council. Your completed tables and report will look similar to those in Figure 4.53.

Apply 4A skills from these Objectives:

1 Manage Existing Tables

2 Modify Existing Tables

3 Change Data Types

4 Attach Files to Records

PROJECT FILES

For Project 4E, you will need the following files:

a04E_Cultural_Events

a04E_Concert_Flyer

a04E_Quilts_Flyer

You will save your database as:

Lastname_Firstname_4E_Cultural_Events

PROJECT RESULTS

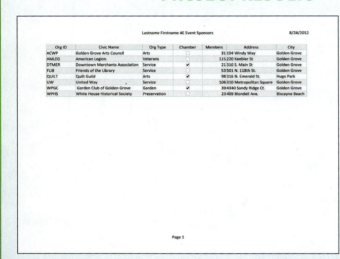

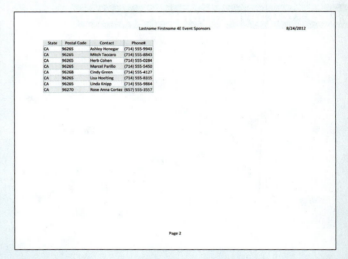

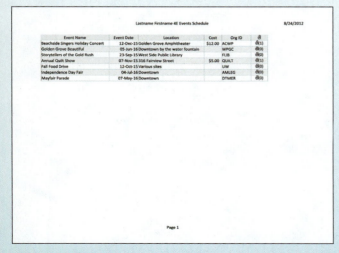

FIGURE 4.53

(Project 4E Cultural Events continues on the next page)

CONTENT-BASED ASSESSMENTS

Mastering Access   Project 4E Cultural Events (continued)

1 ▶ **Start** Access. Locate and open the **a04E_Cultural_Events** file. **Save** the database in the **Microsoft Access Database** format in your **Access Chapter 4** folder as **Lastname_Firstname_4E_Cultural_Events**

2 ▶ Open the **4E Cultural Events** table. From **Backstage** view, click **Save As**. Under **File Types**, double-click **Save Object As**. In the **Save As** dialog box, type **Lastname Firstname 4E Events Schedule** Click **OK**.

3 ▶ Make a second copy of the table. Name the table **Lastname Firstname 4E Event Sponsors**

4 ▶ Open the **4E Event Sponsors** table in **Datasheet** view. Select the first four columns, the **Event Name** field through the **Cost** field. Press [Delete], and then click **Yes** to delete the fields and data. Switch to **Design** view, and then make the **Org ID** field the **Primary Key** field.

5 ▶ Insert a row above the **Members** field, and add a field named **Chamber** with a data type of **Yes/No**. Switch to **Datasheet** view, saving the changes.

6 ▶ In **Datasheet** view, click the **Chamber** field to place a checkmark for the **Downtown Merchants Association**, **Quilt Guild**, and **Garden Club of Golden Grove**. If you are instructed to submit this result, create a paper or electronic printout of the **4E Event Sponsors** table in **Landscape** orientation. It will print on two pages. **Close Print Preview** and the table.

7 ▶ Open the **4E Events Schedule** table in **Datasheet** view. Close the **Navigation Pane**. Select and delete the following fields: **Civic Name**, **Org Type**, **Members**, **Address**, **City**, **State**, **Postal Code**, **Contact**, and **Phone#**.

8 ▶ Using **Find**, find **1876** in the **Event Name** field; in the **Match** field, select Any Part of Field, if necessary. Select and delete the record.

9 ▶ In the navigation area at the bottom of the window, search for *k* in the records. When it stops at *Make Golden Grove Beautiful*, delete the word **Make** and the space following the word from the **Event Name**.

10 ▶ Switch to **Design** view. Select the **Event Date** field, and drag it up until it is between **Event Name** and **Location**. Add a **Flyer** field at the bottom of the field list using an **Attachment** data type.

11 ▶ Switch to **Datasheet** view, saving the changes to the table design. Attach the **a04E_Concert_Flyer** to the *Beachside Singers Holiday Concert* record, and add the **a04E_Quilts_Flyer** to the *Annual Quilt Show* record.

12 ▶ On the **HOME tab**, in the **Records group**, click **Spelling**. Make any spelling corrections necessary in the table. If you are instructed to submit this result, create a paper or electronic printout of the **4E Events Schedule** table in **Landscape** orientation. Close the table.

13 ▶ **Close** the database, and **Exit** Access.

14 ▶ As directed by your instructor, submit your database and the paper or electronic printout of the two tables that are the result of this project. Specifically, in this project, using your own name you created the following database and printouts or electronic printouts:

1. Lastname_Firstname_4E_Cultural_Events	Database file
2. Lastname Firstname 4E Event Sponsors	Table (printed or electronic printout)
3. Lastname Firstname 4E Events Schedule	Table (printed or electronic printout)

END | You have completed Project 4E ▶

CONTENT-BASED ASSESSMENTS

Mastering Access | Project 4F Library System

Dario Soto, city manager, has asked Ron Singer, database manager for the city, to improve the library database. In the following Mastering Access project, you will create a table that stores records about the library programs in Design view, and then modify the properties and customize the fields in the table. You will add features to the database table that will help to reduce data entry errors and that will make data entry easier. Your completed table will look similar to the table shown in Figure 4.54.

Apply 4B skills from these Objectives:

5 Create a Table in Design View

6 Create a Lookup Field

7 Set Field Properties

8 Create Data Validation Rules and Validation Text

PROJECT FILES

For Project 4F, you will need the following file:

a04F_Library_System

You will save your database as:

Lastname_Firstname_4F_Library_System

PROJECT RESULTS

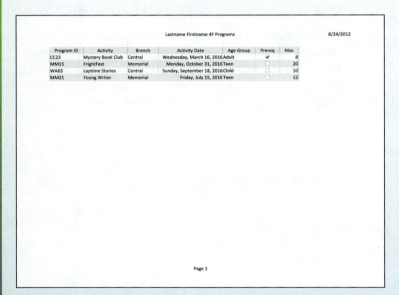

FIGURE 4.54

(Project 4F Library System continues on the next page)

CONTENT-BASED ASSESSMENTS

1 **Start** Access. Locate and open the **a04F_Library_System** file. **Save** the database in the **Microsoft Access Database** format in your **Access Chapter 4** folder as **Lastname_Firstname_4F_Library_System** Rename the table by adding your **Lastname Firstname** to the beginning of the table name. Close the **Navigation Pane**.

2 Create a table in **Design** view. In the first **Field Name** box, type **Program ID** and set the field as the **Primary Key**. Change the **Field size** to **5**

3 In the second **Field Name** box, type **Activity** In the **Field Properties**, click the **Indexed down arrow**, and then select **Yes (Duplicates OK)**. Make it a **Required** field.

4 In the third **Field Name** box, type **Branch** and select **Lookup Wizard** as the data type. Verify that **I want the lookup field to get the values from another table or query** is selected. Click **Next**. There is only one other table in this database from which to choose—*4F Branches*—and it is selected. Click **Next**. Add **Branch** to the Selected Fields. Click **Next**. In the **1** box, click the **arrow**, and then click **Branch**. Leave the sort order as **Ascending**. Click **Next** two times. Under **What label would you like for your lookup field?**, accept the default of **Branch**, and then verify that **Allow Multiple Values** is *not* selected. Click **Finish**. In the message box, click **Yes**.

5 **Save** the table as **Lastname Firstname 4F Programs**

6 In the fourth **Field Name** box, type **Activity Date** and then select the **Date/Time** data type. Click in the **Format** box, and select **Long Date**.

7 In the fifth **Field Name** box, type **Age Group** Set the **Default Value** to **Teen** In the **Validation Rule** box, type **"Child" OR "Teen" OR "Adult"** For the **Validation Text**, type **Entry must be Child, Teen, or Adult**

8 In the sixth **Field Name** box, type **Prereq** Select the **Yes/No** data type. In the **Description** box, type **Click to indicate a prerequisite is required before enrolling in this activity**

9 In the seventh **Field Name** box, type **Max** and select **Number** data type. Change the **Field Size** to **Integer**. In the **Validation Rule** box, type **<=20** In the **Validation Text** box, type **Participation is limited to 20**

10 Switch to **Datasheet** view, saving the changes to the design. Populate the table with the data shown at the bottom of the page.

11 Adjust the column widths so all data is visible. If you are instructed to submit this result, create a paper or electronic printout of the **4F Programs** table in **Landscape** orientation. **Close** the table, saving the changes. Open the **Navigation Pane**.

12 Open the **4F Branches** table in **Design** view. In the **Postal Code** field, under **Input Mask**, click the **Build** button. If prompted, **Save** the table. From the **Input Mask Wizard**, under **Input Mask**, select **Zip Code**, and then click **Next**. Accept the default "_" as the placeholder character. Click **Next**. Store the data without the symbols in the mask, click **Next**, and then click **Finish**.

13 Switch to **Datasheet** view, saving the changes to the table design. Update the data for each branch.

Central	96265-0001
Memorial	96270-0030
West Side	96268-0010

14 Adjust column widths as needed to display all of the data and field names. **Save** the changes. If you are instructed to submit this result, create a paper or electronic printout of the **4F Branches** table. **Close** the table.

15 **Close** the database, and **Exit** Access.

Program ID	Activity	Branch	Activity Date	Age Group	Prereq	Max
CC23	Mystery Book Club	Central	3/16/16	Adult	Yes	8
MM15	FrightFest	Memorial	10/31/16	Teen	No	20
WA63	Laptime Stories	Central	9/8/16	Child	No	10
MM21	Young Writer	Memorial	7/15/16	Teen	No	12

(Project 4F Library System continues on the next page)

CONTENT-BASED ASSESSMENTS

16 As directed by your instructor, submit your database and the paper or electronic printout of the two tables that are the result of this project.

Specifically, in this project, using your own name you created the following database and printouts or electronic printouts:

1. Lastname_Firstname_4F_Library_System	Database file
2. Lastname Firstname 4F Programs	Table (printed or electronic printout)
3. Lastname Firstname 4F Branches	Table (printed or electronic printout)

END | You have completed Project 4F

CONTENT-BASED ASSESSMENTS

MyITLab®
grader

Mastering Access Project 4G Parks and Recreation

Yvonne Guillen is the chair of the Parks & Recreation Commission for Golden Grove, California. The database she is using has separate tables that should be combined. In the following Mastering Access project, you will combine these tables into a facilities table. You will modify the existing tables, set field properties to ensure more accurate data entry, and add driving directions to the facilities as an attached document. You will also create a table to organize youth sports programs that use the facilities. Your completed work will look similar to Figure 4.55.

Apply 4A and 4B skills from these Objectives:

1 Manage Existing Tables
2 Modify Existing Tables
3 Change Data Types
4 Attach Files to Records
5 Create a Table in Design View
6 Create a Lookup Field
7 Set Field Properties
8 Create Data Validation Rules and Validation Text

PROJECT FILES

For Project 4G, you will need the following files:

a04G_Parks_and_Recreation
a04G_Biscayne_Park
a04G_Hugo_West
One blank Word document

You will save your files as:

Lastname_Firstname_4G_Parks_and_Recreation
Lastname_Firstname_4G_Phone_Properties

PROJECT RESULTS

FIGURE 4.55

(Project 4G Parks and Recreation continues on the next page)

1 **Start** Access. Locate and open the **a04G_Parks_ and_Recreation** file. **Save** the database in the **Microsoft Access Database** format in your **Access Chapter 4** folder as **Lastname_Firstname_4G_Parks_and_Recreation** Rename all tables by adding your **Lastname Firstname** to the beginning of each table name.

2 Select the **4G Community Centers** table. **Copy** and **Paste** the table. Name the table **Lastname Firstname 4G Facilities** In the **Paste Table As** dialog box, verify the **Structure and Data** option is selected. Click **OK**.

3 Select the **4G Parks** table. **Copy** and **Paste** the table. In the **Table Name** box, type **Lastname Firstname 4G Facilities** Under **Paste Options**, select **Append Data to Existing Table**, and then click **OK** to create one table that contains all of the facility information for the Parks & Recreation Department.

4 Open the **4G Facilities** table in **Design** view. Change the data type for the **Entry Fee** field to **Currency**. In the **Contact** field, change the field size to **20**

5 Add a new **Monthly Pass** field between the **Entry Fee** and **Contact** fields, and use a data type of **Calculated**. In the **Expression Builder** dialog box, type **[Entry Fee]*15** Change the **Result Type** to **Currency**.

6 Below the **Phone#** field add a new **Directions** field to the table and assign a data type of **Attachment**. In the description box, type **Directions to facility**

7 Select the **Phone#** field. In the **Input Mask** box, type **!000-0000** Change the field size to **8** Set the **Field Property** of **Required** to **Yes**. Using the Clipboard and Word, submit a printed copy of the **Phone#** Field Properties if you are requested to do so. **Save** the document as **Lastname_ Firstname_4G_Phone_Properties** Switch to **Datasheet** view. Save your changes. You will see a message box warning that some data may be lost. Click **Yes** to continue. You will also see a message explaining that data integrity rules have changed, click **No** to testing the data with the new rules.

8 In the **Biscayne Park** record, in the **Attachment** field, double-click, and then from the student data files, attach **a04G_Biscayne_Park**. Click **OK**.

9 Using the same technique, for the **Hugo West Center**, add the directions that are in the **a04G_Hugo_West** file.

10 Create a table in **Design** view. In the first **Field Name** box, type **Sport ID** Select an **AutoNumber** data type. Set this as the primary key.

11 In the second **Field Name** box, type **Sport** In the third **Field Name** box, type **Season** and select a **Lookup Wizard** data type. Type the following four items into the lookup list: **Winter Spring Summer** and **Fall** Save the table as **Lastname Firstname 4G Youth Sports**

12 Switch to **Datasheet** view, and populate the table with the following data.

Sport ID	Sport	Season
1	t-ball	Spring
2	baseball	Summer
3	fast pitch softball	Fall
4	basketball	Winter
5	volleyball	Fall

13 Adjust the column widths as needed to display all of the data and field names.

14 If you are instructed to submit this result, create a paper or electronic printout of the **4G Facilities** table and **4G Youth Sports** table. Be sure that all field names and data display.

15 **Close** the tables, saving changes if necessary. **Close** the database, and **Exit** Access.

16 As directed by your instructor, submit your database and the paper or electronic printout of the three objects—two tables and one Word document—that are the result of this project. Specifically, in this project, using your own name you created the following database and printouts or electronic printouts:

1. Lastname_Firstname_4G_Parks_and_Recreation	Database file
2. Lastname_Firstname_4G_Phone_Properties	Word (printed or electronic printout)
3. Lastname Firstname 4G Facilities	Table (printed or electronic printout)
4. Lastname Firstname 4G Youth Sports	Table (printed or electronic printout)

END | You have completed Project 4G

CONTENT-BASED ASSESSMENTS

GO! Fix It   Project 4H Permit Applications   Online

GO! Make It   Project 4I Medical Centers   Online

GO! Solve It   Project 4J Fire Department   Online

GO! Solve It   Project 4K City Zoo

> **Apply a combination of the 4A and 4B skills.**

PROJECT FILES

For Project 4K, you will need the following files:

a04K_City_Zoo
a04K_Dragonfly

You will save your database as:

Lastname_Firstname_4K_City_Zoo

From the student files that accompany this textbook, open the a04K_City_Zoo database file, and then save the database in your Access Chapter 4 folder as **Lastname_Firstname_4K_City_Zoo**

Mandi Cartwright, public relations director of Golden Grove, California, and City Manager Dario Soto are meeting with the mayor, Sheila Kehoe, to discuss the funding for the city zoo. The Corporate and Foundation Council provides citizens and corporations with a partnering opportunity to support the city zoo. Mandi has outlined a database to organize the sponsorships.

In this project, you will open the a04K_City_Zoo database and examine the tables. Rename the tables by adding your **Lastname Firstname** to the beginning of each table name. Modify the 4K Sponsored Events table to eliminate redundancy between it and the 4K Sponsors table. Also, change data types to match the data, including a lookup field for the Sponsor field, and apply an applicable input mask to the Event Date. In the 4K Sponsors table, create data validation for sponsor type; it must be Individual, Family, or Corporate. In the 4K Sponsors table, use the 4K Sponsor Levels table as a lookup field. To the 4K Sponsor Levels table, add an attachment field named Logo. Add the a04K_Dragonfly file from the student data files to the appropriate record. If you are instructed to submit this result, create a paper or electronic printout of the tables and the Object Definition report.

(Project 4K City Zoo continues on the next page)

CONTENT-BASED ASSESSMENTS

Performance Level

Performance Element	Exemplary: You consistently applied the relevant skills	Proficient: You sometimes, but not always, applied the relevant skills	Developing: You rarely or never applied the relevant skills
Modify the 4K Sponsored Events table to eliminate redundancy	Table was modified with correct fields in easy-to-follow format.	Table was modified with no more than two missing elements.	Table was modified with more than two missing elements.
Change data types and field properties in the 4K Sponsored Events and 4K Sponsors tables	Data types and field properties were assigned effectively for the data that each field will hold.	Data types and field properties were assigned with no more than two missing or incorrect elements.	Data types and field properties were assigned with more than two missing or incorrect elements.
Add field to 4K Sponsor Levels and populate field	Field was added with correct data type and correct data was added to the table.	Field was added with no more than two missing or incorrect elements.	Field was added with more than two missing or incorrect elements.

END | You have completed Project 4K

OUTCOMES-BASED ASSESSMENTS

RUBRIC

The following outcomes-based assessments are open-ended assessments. That is, there is no specific correct result; your result will depend on your approach to the information provided. Make Professional Quality your goal. Use the following scoring rubric to guide you in how to approach the problem and then to evaluate how well your approach solves the problem.

The *criteria*—Software Mastery, Content, Format and Layout, and Process—represent the knowledge and skills you have gained that you can apply to solving the problem. The *levels of performance*—Professional Quality, Approaching Professional Quality, or Needs Quality Improvements—help you and your instructor evaluate your result.

	Your completed project is of Professional Quality if you:	Your completed project is Approaching Professional Quality if you:	Your completed project Needs Quality Improvements if you:
1-Software Mastery	Choose and apply the most appropriate skills, tools, and features and identify efficient methods to solve the problem.	Choose and apply some appropriate skills, tools, and features, but not in the most efficient manner.	Choose inappropriate skills, tools, or features, or are inefficient in solving the problem.
2-Content	Construct a solution that is clear and well organized, contains content that is accurate, appropriate to the audience and purpose, and is complete. Provide a solution that contains no errors in spelling, grammar, or style.	Construct a solution in which some components are unclear, poorly organized, inconsistent, or incomplete. Misjudge the needs of the audience. Have some errors in spelling, grammar, or style, but the errors do not detract from comprehension.	Construct a solution that is unclear, incomplete, or poorly organized; contains some inaccurate or inappropriate content; and contains many errors in spelling, grammar, or style. Do not solve the problem.
3-Format & Layout	Format and arrange all elements to communicate information and ideas, clarify function, illustrate relationships, and indicate relative importance.	Apply appropriate format and layout features to some elements, but not others. Overuse features, causing minor distraction.	Apply format and layout that does not communicate information or ideas clearly. Do not use format and layout features to clarify function, illustrate relationships, or indicate relative importance. Use available features excessively, causing distraction.
4-Process	Use an organized approach that integrates planning, development, self-assessment, revision, and reflection.	Demonstrate an organized approach in some areas, but not others; or, use an insufficient process of organization throughout.	Do not use an organized approach to solve the problem.

OUTCOMES-BASED ASSESSMENTS

Apply a combination of the 4A and 4B skills.

PROJECT FILES

For Project 4L, you will need the following files:

a04L_Streets_Department
a04L_Work_Order

You will save your database as:

Lastname_Firstname_4L_Streets_Department

In this project, you will examine the database that has been created to help the Deputy City Manager of Infrastructure Services organize and track the constituent work requests for the city street repairs. Save the database as **Lastname_Firstname_4L_Streets_Department** Rename all of the tables by adding your **Lastname_Firstname** to the beginning of each table name. Modify the design of the 4L Work Requests table. Set the Work Order # field as the primary key field, and then create an input mask to match the data for that field in the first record. For the Type field, create a lookup table using the 4L Repair Types table. In the Repair Team field, create a Lookup Wizard data type using the 4L Repair Teams table. In the Priority field, create a validation rule requiring an entry of 1, 2, or 3. Explain this rule with appropriate validation text. Add a long text field called Description between Type and Repair Team. Open a04L_Work_Order, and then use the data to add information to the first record in the table. Use today's date as the start date. Add an attachment field to the table, and then add a04L_Work_Order as the attachment. If you are instructed to submit this result, create a paper or electronic printout of the 4L Work Requests table.

END | You have completed Project 4L

GO! Think | Project 4M Police Department | Online

You and GO! | Project 4N Club Directory | Online

Enhancing Queries

GO! to Work
Video A5

PROJECT **5A**	**OUTCOMES** Create special-purpose queries.

OBJECTIVES
1. Create Calculated Fields in a Query
2. Use Aggregate Functions in a Query
3. Create a Crosstab Query
4. Find Duplicate and Unmatched Records
5. Create a Parameter Query

PROJECT **5B**	**OUTCOMES** Create action queries and modify join types.

OBJECTIVES
6. Create a Make Table Query
7. Create an Append Query
8. Create a Delete Query
9. Create an Update Query
10. Modify the Join Type

Carlos Caetano/Fotolia

In This Chapter

Queries can do more than extract data from tables and other queries. You can create queries to perform special functions, such as calculate and summarize numeric data. Queries can also be used to find duplicate and unmatched records in tables, which is useful for maintaining data integrity. You can create a parameter query, where an individual is prompted for the criteria each time the query is run, for more flexibility in the data extracted. Queries can create additional tables in the database, append records to an existing table, delete records from a table, and modify data in the tables based on specific criteria.

S-Boards, Inc., a snowboard and surf shop, combines the expertise and favorite sports of two friends after they graduated from college. Gina Pollard and Steven Michaels grew up in the sun of Southern California, but they also spent time in the mountain snow. The store carries top brands of men's and women's apparel, goggles and sunglasses, boards and gear. The surfboard selection includes both classic boards and the latest high-tech boards. Snowboarding gear can be purchased in packages or customized for the most experienced boarders. Pollard and Michaels are proud to serve Southern California's board enthusiasts.

PROJECT
5A Store Inventory

PROJECT ACTIVITIES

In Activities 5.01 through 5.10, you will help Miles Gorden, purchasing manager of S-Boards, Inc. Surf and Snowboard Shop, create special-purpose queries to calculate data, summarize and group data, display data in a spreadsheet-like format, and find duplicate and unmatched records. You will also create a query that prompts individuals to enter the criteria. Your completed queries will look similar to Figure 5.1.

PROJECT FILES

For Project 5A, you will need the following file:

a05A_Store_Inventory

You will save your database as:

Lastname_Firstname_5A_Store_Inventory

PROJECT RESULTS

FIGURE 5.1 Project 5A Store Inventory

Objective 1 Create Calculated Fields in a Query

Video A5-1

Queries can be used to create a ***calculated field***—a field that obtains its data by performing a calculation or computation, using a formula. For example, to determine the profit that will be made from the sale of an item, subtract the cost of the item from the sale price of the item. Another example is to create a calculated field that computes the gross pay for an employee. There are two steps needed to produce a calculated field in a query. First, in the design grid of the query, in a blank column, type the name of the field that will store the results of the calculated field—the name must be followed by a colon (:). Second, type the ***expression***—the formula—that will perform the calculation. *Each field name* used in the expression must be enclosed within *its own pair* of square brackets, [ ]. If you are using a number in the expression—for example, a decimal—type only the decimal; do not enclose it in brackets.

Activity 5.01 | Creating a Calculated Field Based on Two Existing Fields

In this activity, you will create a calculated field to determine the profit for each item in the inventory database.

1. **Start** Access. Navigate to the location where the student data files for this textbook are saved. Locate and open the **a05A_Store_Inventory** file. Display **Backstage** view. Click **Save As**, and then, under *File Types*, double-click **Save Database As**. In the **Save As** dialog box, navigate to the drive on which you will be saving your folders and projects for this chapter. Create a new folder named **Access Chapter 5** and then save the file as **Lastname_Firstname_5A_Store_Inventory** in the folder.

2. If necessary, enable the content or add the Access Chapter 5 folder to the Trust Center. In the **Navigation Pane**, rename each table by adding your **Lastname Firstname** to the beginning of each table name. Resize the **Navigation Pane** so all table names are visible.

3. In the **Navigation Pane**, double-click **5A Inventory**. If the Field List pane opens, close it. Take a moment to study the fields in the table.

   Snowboarding items have a catalog number beginning with 8; surfing items have a catalog number beginning with 9. The Category field is a Lookup column. If you click in the Category field, and then click the arrow, a list of category numbers and their descriptions display. The Supplier field identifies the supplier numbers. Cost is the price the company pays to a supplier for each item. Selling Price is what the company will charge its customers for each item. On Hand refers to the current inventory for each item.

4. Switch to **Design** view, and then take a moment to study the data structure. Notice the Category field has a data type of Number; this reflects the autonumber field (ID field) in the Category table used in the Lookup field. When you are finished, **Close** [×] the table, and then **Close** [«] the **Navigation Pane**.

5. On the Ribbon, click the **CREATE tab**. In the **Queries group**, click the **Query Design** button. In the **Show Table** dialog box, double-click **5A Inventory** to add the table to the Query design workspace, and then click **Close**. Resize the list so the table name and all fields are visible.

   If you add the wrong table to the workspace or have two copies of the same table, right-click the extra table, and click Remove Table.

BY TOUCH To resize the file list, touch the file list with two or more fingers and then stretch your fingers apart to zoom out.

6 From the **5A Inventory** field list, add the following fields, in the order specified, to the design grid: **Catalog#**, **Item**, **Cost**, and **Selling Price**.

Recall that you can double-click a field name to add it to the design grid, or you can drag the field name to the field box on the design grid. You can also click in the field box, click the arrow, and click the field name from the displayed list.

7 On the **QUERY TOOLS DESIGN tab**, in the **Results group**, click the **Run** button to display the four fields used in the query, and then compare your screen with Figure 5.2.

FIGURE 5.2

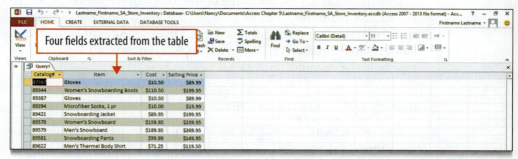

Four fields extracted from the table

8 Switch to **Design** view. In the **Field row**, right-click in the first empty column—the fifth column—to display a shortcut menu, and then click **Zoom**. *Arithmetic operators* are mathematical symbols used to build expressions in calculated fields. Take a moment to study the arithmetic operators as described in Figure 5.3.

FIGURE 5.3

ARITHMETIC OPERATORS			
OPERATOR	**DESCRIPTION**	**EXAMPLE**	**RESULT**
+	Addition	Cost:[Price]+[Tax]	Adds the value in the Price field to the value in the Tax field and displays the result in the Cost field.
−	Subtraction	Cost:[Price]-[Markdown]	Subtracts the value in the Markdown field from the value in the Price field and displays the result in the Cost field.
*	Multiplication	Tax:[Price]*.05	Multiplies the value in the Price field by .05 (5%) and displays the result in the Tax field. (Note: This is an asterisk, not an x.)
/	Division	Average:[Total]/3	Divides the value in the Total field by 3 and displays the result in the Average field.
^	Exponentiation	Required:2^[Bits]	Raises 2 to the power of the value in the Bits field and stores the result in the Required field.
\	Integer division	Average:[Children]\[Families]	Divides the value in the Children field by the value in the Families field and displays the integer portion—the digits to the left of the decimal point—in the Average field.

9 In the **Zoom** dialog box, type **Per Item Profit:[Selling Price]-[Cost]** and then compare your screen with Figure 5.4.

The first element of the calculated field—Per Item Profit—is the new field name that will display the calculated value. The field name must be unique for the table being used in the query. Following the new field name is a colon (:). A colon in a calculated field separates the new field name from the expression. Selling Price is enclosed in square brackets because it is an existing field name in the 5A Inventory table and contains data that will be used in the calculation. Following [Selling Price] is a hyphen (-), which, in math calculations, signifies subtraction. Finally, Cost, an existing field in the 5A Inventory table, is enclosed in square brackets. This field also contains data that will be used in the calculation.

FIGURE 5.4

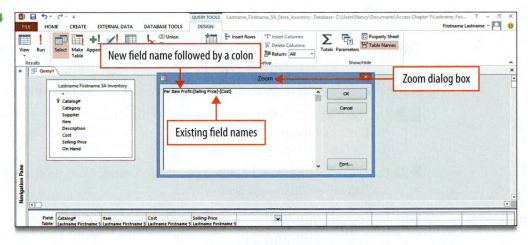

> **NOTE**   **Using Square Brackets Around Field Names in Expressions**
>
> Square brackets are not required around a field name in an expression if the field name is only one word. For example, if the field name is Cost, it is not necessary to type brackets around it—Access will automatically insert the square brackets. If a field name has a space in it, however, you must type the square brackets around the field name. Otherwise, Access will display a message stating that the expression you entered contains invalid syntax.

10 In the **Zoom** dialog box, click **OK**, and then **Run** the query. Adjust the column width of the *Per Item Profit* field to display the entire field name, and then compare your screen with Figure 5.5.

A fifth column—the calculated field—with a field name of Per Item Profit displays. For each record, the value in the Per Item Profit field is calculated by subtracting the value in the Cost field from the value in the Selling Price field.

FIGURE 5.5

Catalog#	Item	Cost	Selling Price	Per Item Profit
87127	Gloves	$10.50	$89.99	$79.49
89344	Women's Snowboarding Boots	$110.50	$199.95	$89.45
89387	Gloves	$10.50	$89.99	$79.49
89394	Microfiber Socks, 1 pr	$10.00	$19.99	$9.99
89421	Snowboarding Jacket	$89.95	$199.95	$110.00
89578	Women's Snowboard	$159.95	$239.95	$80.00
89579	Men's Snowboard	$189.95	$269.95	$80.00
89581	Snowboarding Pants	$99.99	$149.95	$49.96
89622	Men's Thermal Body Shirt	$71.25	$119.50	$48.25
89647	Goggles	$15.00	$71.95	$56.95
89683	Hood	$12.99	$39.95	$26.96
96145	Surfboard Fin	$58.35	$63.95	$5.60
96244	Hybrid Surfboard	$514.25	$729.95	$215.70
96276	Sunscreen	$7.25	$10.95	$3.70
96412	Booties	$22.45	$49.95	$27.50
96450	Short Surfboard	$489.99	$641.95	$151.96
96466	Shortboard Travel Bag	$45.00	$100.00	$55.00
96475	Superlite Traction Pad	$15.00	$32.00	$17.00

Calculated field

Selling Price minus *Cost*

11 On the **tab row**, right-click the **Query1 tab**, and then click **Save** 💾. In the **Save As** dialog box, under **Query Name**, type **Lastname Firstname 5A Per Item Profit** and then click **OK**. View the query in **Print Preview**, ensuring that the query prints on one page; if you are instructed to submit this result, create a paper or electronic printout. **Close** Print Preview. **Close** ☒ the query.

Activity 5.02 | Creating a Calculated Field Based on One Existing Field and a Number

In this activity, you will calculate the sale prices of each surfboarding item for the annual sale. During this event, all surfboarding supplies are discounted by 15 percent.

1 On the Ribbon, click the **CREATE tab**. In the **Queries group**, click the **Query Design** button. Add the **5A Inventory** table to the Query design workspace, and then **Close** the **Show Table** dialog box. Resize the field list.

2 From the **5A Inventory** field list, add the following fields, in the order specified, to the design grid: **Catalog#**, **Item**, and **Selling Price**.

3 In the **Field row**, right-click in the field cell in the first empty column—the fourth column—to display a shortcut menu, and then click **Zoom**. In the **Zoom** dialog box, type **Discount:[Selling Price]*.15** and then compare your screen with Figure 5.6.

The value in the Discount field is calculated by multiplying the value in the Selling Price field by .15—15%. Recall that only field names are enclosed in square brackets.

FIGURE 5.6

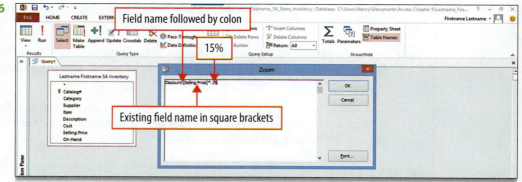

4 In the **Zoom** dialog box, click **OK**, and then **Run** the query.

The Discount field displays the results of the calculation. The data is not formatted with a dollar sign, and the first record displays a discount of 13.4985. When using a number in an expression, the values in the calculated field may not be formatted the same as in the existing field.

5 Switch to **Design** view. On the **QUERY TOOLS DESIGN tab**, in the **Show/Hide group**, click the **Table Names** button.

In the design grid, the Table row no longer displays. If all of the fields in the design grid are from one table, you can hide the Table row. The Table Names button is a toggle button; if you click it again, the Table row displays in the design grid.

6 ▶ Click in the **Field row**, in the **Discount** field box. On the **QUERY TOOLS DESIGN tab**, in the **Show/Hide group**, click the **Property Sheet** button. Alternatively, right-click in the field box and click Properties, or hold down [Alt] and press [Enter].

> The Property Sheet for the selected field—Discount—displays on the right side of the screen. In the Property Sheet, under the title of Property Sheet, is the subtitle—Selection type: Field Properties.

ALERT!   **Does the Property Sheet Display a Subtitle of Selection Type: Query Properties?**

To display the Property Sheet for a field, you must first click in the field; otherwise, the Property Sheet for the query might display. If this occurs, in the Field row, click the Discount field box to change the Property Sheet to this field.

7 ▶ In the **Property Sheet**, on the **General tab**, click in the **Format** box, and then click the displayed **arrow**. Compare your screen with Figure 5.7.

FIGURE 5.7

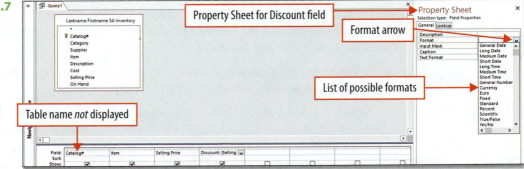

8 ▶ From the list of formats, click **Currency**. On the **Property Sheet** title bar, click the **Close** button. **Run** the query to display the results.

> The values in the Discount field now display with a dollar sign, and the first record's discount—$13.50—displays with two decimal places.

9 ▶ Switch to **Design** view. In the **Field row**, right-click in the first empty column, and then click **Zoom**. In the **Zoom** dialog box, type **Sale Price:[Selling Price]-[Discount]** and then click **OK**. **Run** the query to display the results.

> The Sale Price for Catalog #87387, Gloves, is $76.49. The value in the Sale Price field is calculated by subtracting the value in the Discount field from the value in the Selling Price field. The field names are not case sensitive—you can type a field name in lower case, such as [selling price]. Because you used only existing fields in the expression that were formatted as currency, the values in the Sale Price field are formatted as currency.

10 ▶ Switch to **Design** view. In the design grid, click in the **Criteria row** under **Catalog#**, type **9*** and then press [Enter].

> Recall that the asterisk (*) is a wildcard. With the criteria, Access will extract those records where the catalog number begins with 9 followed by one or more characters. Also, recall that Access formats the criteria. For example, you typed 9*, and Access formatted the criteria as Like "9*".

11 ▶ **Run** the query. Notice that only the records with a **Catalog#** beginning with a **9** display—surfboarding items.

12 ▶ **Save** 🖫 the query as **Lastname Firstname 5A Surfboarding Sale** View the query in **Print Preview**, ensuring that the query prints on one page. If you are instructed to submit this result, create a paper or electronic printout. **Close** Print Preview. **Close** ☒ the query.

Video A5-2

In Access queries, you can use *aggregate functions* to perform a calculation on a column of data and return a single value. Examples are the Sum function, which adds a column of numbers, and the Average function, which adds a column of numbers and divides by the number of records with values, ignoring null values. Access provides two ways to use aggregate functions in a query—you can add a total row in Datasheet view or create a totals query in Design view.

Activity 5.03 | Adding a Total Row to a Query

In this activity, you will create and run a query. In Datasheet view, you will add a Total row to insert an aggregate function in one or more columns without having to change the design of the query.

1 Create a new query in **Query Design**. Add the **5A Inventory** table to the Query design workspace, and then **Close** the **Show Table** dialog box. Resize the field list. From the **5A Inventory** field list, add the following fields, in the order specified, to the design grid: **Catalog#**, **Item**, **Cost**, and **On Hand**.

2 In the **Field row**, right-click in the first empty column, and then click **Zoom**. In the **Zoom** dialog box, type **Inventory Cost:[Cost]*[On Hand]**

The value in the Inventory Cost field is calculated by multiplying the value in the Cost field by the value in the On Hand field. This field will display the cost of all of the inventory items, not just the cost per item.

3 In the **Zoom** dialog box, click **OK**, and then **Run** the query to display the results in **Datasheet** view. Adjust the column width of the **Inventory Cost** field to display the entire field name, and then compare your screen with Figure 5.8.

If the *Inventory Cost* for Catalog #87387, Gloves, is not $525.00, switch to Design view and edit the expression you entered for the calculated field.

FIGURE 5.8

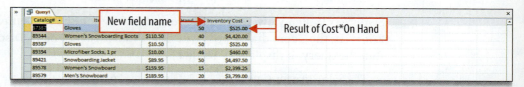

4 On the **HOME tab**, in the **Records group**, click the **Totals** button. If necessary, scroll down until the newly created Total row displays. In the **Total row** under **Inventory Cost**, click in the empty box to display an arrow at the left edge. Click the **arrow**, and then compare your screen with Figure 5.9. Take a moment to study the aggregate functions that can be used with both the **Total row** and the design grid, as described in the table in Figure 5.10.

The Total row displays after the New record row. The first field in a Total row contains the word Total. The Total row is not a record. The list of aggregate functions displayed will vary depending on the data type for each field or column; for example, number types display a full list of functions, whereas a text field will display only the Count function.

FIGURE 5.9

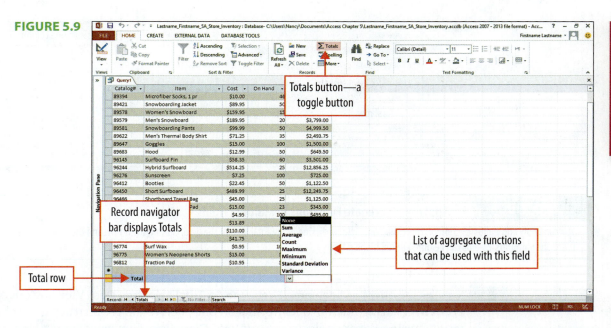

FIGURE 5.10

AGGREGATE FUNCTIONS		
FUNCTION	**DESCRIPTION**	**CAN BE USED WITH DATA TYPE(S)**
Sum	Adds the values in a column.	Currency, Decimal, Number
Average	Calculates the average value for a column, ignoring null values.	Currency, Date/Time, Decimal, Number
Count	Counts the number of items in a column, ignoring null values.	All data types, except complex repeating scalar data, such as a column of multivalued lists
Maximum	Displays the item with the highest value. Can be used with text data only in Design view. With text data, the highest value is *Z*. Case and null values are ignored.	Currency, Date/Time, Decimal, Number, Text
Minimum	Displays the item with the lowest value. Can be used with text data only in Design view. For text data, the lowest value is *A*. Case and null values are ignored.	Currency, Date/Time, Decimal, Number, Text
Standard Deviation	Measures how widely values are dispersed from the mean value.	Currency, Decimal, Number
Variance	Measures the statistical variance of all values in the column. If the table has less than two rows, a null value is displayed.	Currency, Decimal, Number

5 From the displayed list, click **Sum**, and then compare your screen with Figure 5.11.

A sum of $67,186.25 displays, which is the total of all the data in the Total Cost On Hand field.

FIGURE 5.11

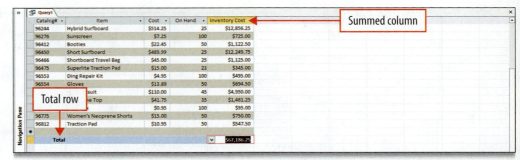

Applying Aggregate Functions to Multiple Fields

You can apply aggregate functions to more than one field by clicking in the Total row for the field, clicking the arrow, and then clicking the function. The functions for multiple fields can be different functions.

6 ▶ **Save** 🖫 the query as **Lastname Firstname 5A Total Inventory Cost** View the query in **Print Preview**, ensuring that the query prints on one page; if you are instructed to submit this result, create a paper or electronic printout. **Close** Print Preview. **Close** ☒ the query.

More **Knowledge**   **Removing the Aggregate Function and Removing the Total Row**

To remove an aggregate function from a column, on the Total row under the field, click the arrow and then click None. To remove the Total row, on the HOME tab, in the Records group, click the Totals button. You cannot cut or delete a Total row; you can only turn it on or off. You can copy a Total row and paste it into another file—for example, an Excel worksheet or a Word document.

Activity 5.04 | Creating a Totals Query

In this activity, you will create a *totals query*—a query that calculates subtotals across groups of records. For example, to subtotal the number of inventory items by suppliers, use a totals query to group the records by the supplier and then apply an aggregate function to the On Hand field. In the previous activity, you created a Total row, which applied an aggregate function to one column—field—of data. A totals query is used when you need to apply an aggregate function to some or all of the records in a query. A totals query can then be used as a source for another database object, such as a report.

1 ▶ Create a new query in **Query Design**. Add the **5A Suppliers** table and the **5A Inventory** table to the Query design workspace, and then **Close** the **Show Table** dialog box. Resize both field lists. Notice that there is a one-to-many relationship between the tables—*one* supplier can supply *many* items. From the **5A Inventory** field list, add **On Hand** to the first field box in the design grid.

2 ▶ On the **QUERY TOOLS DESIGN tab**, in the **Show/Hide group**, click the **Totals** button.

Like the Totals button on the HOME tab, this button is a toggle button. In the design grid, a Total row displays under the Table row, and Group By displays in the box.

3 ▶ In the design grid, click in the **Total row** under **On Hand** to display the arrow. Click the **arrow**, and then compare your screen with Figure 5.12.

A list of aggregate functions displays. This list displays more functions than the list in Datasheet view, and the function names are abbreviated.

FIGURE 5.12

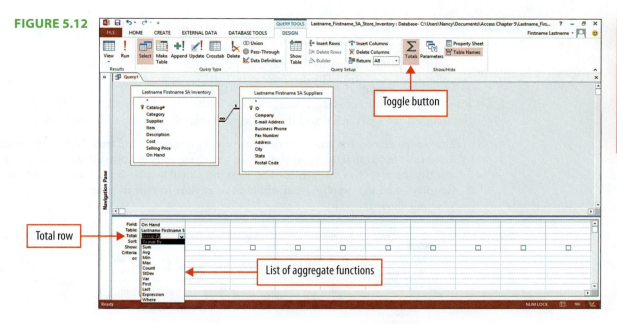

Total row

4 ▶ From the displayed list, click **Sum**. **Run** the query, and then adjust the width of the column to display the entire field name. Compare your screen with Figure 5.13.

When you run a totals query, the result—*1244*—of the aggregate function is displayed; the records are not displayed. The name of the function and the field used are displayed in the column heading.

FIGURE 5.13

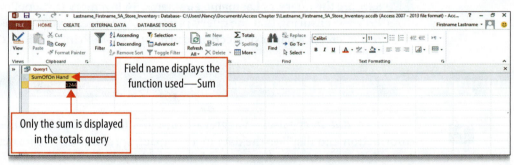

More Knowledge   Changing the Name of the Totals Query Result

To change the name from the combination aggregate function and field name to something more concise and descriptive, in Design view, in the Field row, click in the On Hand field box. On the DESIGN tab, in the Show/Hide group, click the Property Sheet button. In the Property Sheet, on the General tab, click in the Caption box, and type the new name for the result.

5 ▶ Switch to **Design** view. In the **5A Inventory** field list, double-click **Item** to insert the field in the second column in the design grid. In the design grid, click in the **Total row** under **Item**, click the displayed **arrow**, and then click **Count**. **Run** the query. Adjust the width of the second column to display the entire field name.

The number of records—25—displays. You can include multiple fields in a totals query, but each field in the query must have an aggregate function applied to it. If you include a field but do not apply an aggregate function, the query results will display every record and will not display a single value for the field or fields. The exception to this is when you group records by a category, such as supplier name.

6 Switch to **Design** view. From the **5A Suppliers** field list, drag **Company** to the design grid until the field is on top of **On Hand** and then release the mouse button.

> Company is inserted as the first field, and the On Hand field moves to the right. In the Total row under Company, Group By displays.

7 **Run** the query. If necessary, adjust column widths to display all of the field names and all of the data under each field, and then compare your screen with Figure 5.14.

> The results display the total number of inventory items on hand from each supplier and the number of individual items purchased from each supplier. By using this type of query, you can identify the suppliers that provide the most individual items—Bob's Sporting Shop and Wetsuit Country—and the supplier from whom the company has the most on-hand inventory items—Bob's Sporting Shop.

FIGURE 5.14

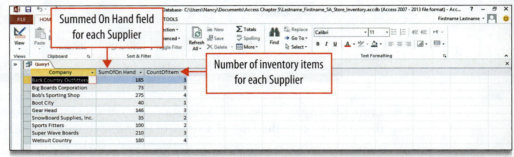

8 **Save** 🖫 the query as **Lastname Firstname 5A Inventory By Supplier** View the query in **Print Preview**, ensuring that the query prints on one page. If you are instructed to submit this result, create a paper or electronic printout. **Close** Print Preview. **Close** ☒ the query.

Objective 3   Create a Crosstab Query

Video A5-3

A **crosstab query** uses an aggregate function for data that is grouped by two types of information and displays the data in a compact, spreadsheet-like format. A crosstab query always has at least one row heading, one column heading, and one summary field. Use a crosstab query to summarize a large amount of data in a small space that is easy to read.

Activity 5.05   Creating a Select Query as the Source for a Crosstab Query

In this activity, you will create a select query displaying suppliers, the category of the inventory item, the inventory item, and the number on hand. Recall that a select query is the most common type of query, and it extracts data from one or more tables or queries, displaying the results in a datasheet. After creating the select query, you will use it to create a crosstab query to display the data in a format that is easier to analyze. Because most crosstab queries extract data from more than one table or query, it is best to create a select query containing all of the fields necessary for the crosstab query.

1 Create a new query in **Query Design**. Add the following tables to the Query design workspace: **5A Category**, **5A Inventory**, and **5A Suppliers**. In the **Show Table** dialog box, click **Close**. Resize the field lists.

2 In the **5A Suppliers** field list, double-click **Company** to add it to the first field box in the design grid. In the **5A Category** field list, double-click **CatName** to add it to the second field box in the design grid. In the **5A Inventory** field list, double-click **On Hand** to add it to the third field box in the design grid. In the design grid, click in the **Sort** box under **Company**. Click the **arrow**, and then click **Ascending**. Sort the **CatName** field in **Ascending** order.

3 On the **DESIGN tab**, in the **Show/Hide group**, click the **Totals** button. Click in the **Total row** under **On Hand**, click the **arrow**, and then click **Sum**. Compare your screen with Figure 5.15.

FIGURE 5.15

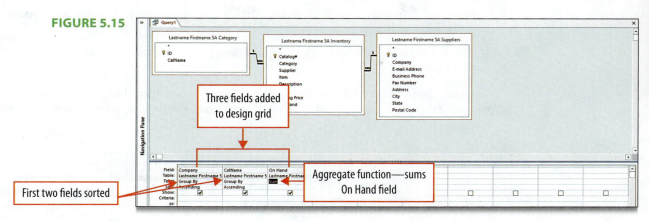

Three fields added to design grid

First two fields sorted

Aggregate function—sums On Hand field

> **N O T E** | **Selecting Multiple Fields for Row Headings**
>
> You can select up to three fields for row headings in a crosstab query. An example would be sorting first by state, then by city, and then by postal code. State would be the first row heading, city would be the second row heading, and postal code would be the third row heading. Regardless of the number of fields used for row headings, at least two fields must remain available to complete the crosstab query.

4 **Run** the query. In the datasheet, adjust all column widths to display the entire field name and the data for each record, and then compare your screen with Figure 5.16.

The select query groups the totals vertically by company and then by category.

FIGURE 5.16

Grouped first by company

Grouped second by category

SumOfOn Hand items by the company within the category

5 Switch to **Design** view. On the **DESIGN tab**, in the **Show/Hide group**, click the **Totals** button to remove the **Total row** from the design grid.

This select query will be used to create the crosstab query. When you create a crosstab query, you will be prompted to use an aggregate function on a field, so it should not be summed prior to creating the query.

6 Save 🖫 the query as **Lastname Firstname 5A On Hand Per Company and Category** and then Close ✕ the query.

Activity 5.06 | Creating a Crosstab Query

In this activity, you will create a crosstab query using the 5A Cost Per Company and Category query as the source for the crosstab query.

1 On the Ribbon, click the **CREATE tab**. In the **Queries group**, click the **Query Wizard** button. In the **New Query** dialog box, click **Crosstab Query Wizard**, and then click **OK**.

In the first Crosstab Query Wizard dialog box, you select the table or query to be used as the source for the crosstab query.

2 In the middle of the dialog box, under **View**, click the **Queries** option button. In the list of queries, click **Query: 5A On Hand Per Company and Category**, and then click **Next**.

In the second Crosstab Query Wizard dialog box, you select the fields with data that you want to use as the row headings.

3 Under **Available Fields**, double-click **Company**, and then compare your screen with Figure 5.17.

Company displays under Selected Fields. At the bottom of the dialog box, in the Sample area, a preview of the row headings displays. Each company name will be listed on a separate row in the first column.

FIGURE 5.17

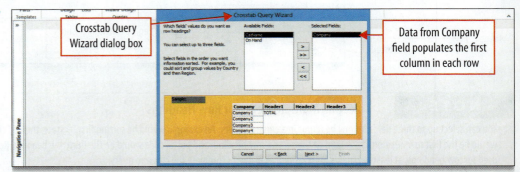

4 In the **Crosstab Query Wizard** dialog box, click **Next**.

In the third dialog box, you select the fields with data that you want to use as column headings.

5 In the displayed list of fields, **CatName** is selected; notice in the sample area that the category names display in separate columns. Click **Next**. Under **Functions**, click **Sum**, and then compare your screen with Figure 5.18.

This dialog box enables you to apply an aggregate function to one or more fields. The function will add the number on hand for every item sold by each company for each category. Every row can also be summed.

FIGURE 5.18

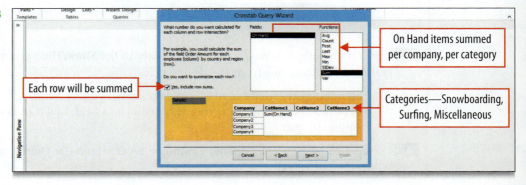

6 On the left side of the **Crosstab Query Wizard** dialog box, above the **Sample** area, clear the **Yes, include row sums** check box, and then click **Next**.

If the check box is selected, a column will be inserted between the first and second column that sums all of the numeric data per row.

7 ▶ Under **What do you want to name your query?**, select the existing text, type **Lastname Firstname 5A Crosstab Query** and then click **Finish**. Adjust all of the column widths to display the entire field name and the data in each field, and then compare your screen with Figure 5.19. Then take a moment to compare this screen with Figure 5.16, the select query you created with the same extracted data.

The same data is extracted using the select query as shown in Figure 5.16; however, the crosstab query displays the data differently. A crosstab query reduces the number of records displayed as shown by the entry for Bob's Sporting Shop. In the select query, there are two records displayed, one for the Miscellaneous category and one for the Surfing category. The crosstab query combines the data into one record.

FIGURE 5.19

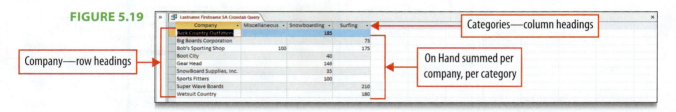

Categories—column headings

Company—row headings

On Hand summed per company, per category

NOTE | **Including Row Sums**

If you include row sums in a crosstab query, the sum will display in a column following the column for the row headings. In this activity, the row sums column would display following the Company column. For Bob's Sporting Shop, the row sum would be 275—100 plus 175.

---

8 ▶ View the query in **Print Preview**, ensuring that the query prints on one page. If you are instructed to submit this result, create a paper or electronic printout. **Close** Print Preview. **Close** ⟨×⟩ the query, saving changes—you adjusted the column widths.

Objective 4 | Find Duplicate and Unmatched Records

Video A5-4

Even when a table contains a primary key, it is still possible to have duplicate records in a table. For example, the same inventory item can be entered with different catalog numbers. You can use the **Find Duplicates Query** Wizard to locate duplicate records in a table. As databases grow, you may have records in one table that have no matching records in a related table; these are **unmatched records**. For example, there may be a record for a supplier in the Suppliers table, but no inventory items are ordered from that supplier. You can use the **Find Unmatched Query** Wizard to locate unmatched records.

Activity 5.07 | Finding Duplicate Records

In this activity, you will find duplicate records in the *5A Inventory* table by using the Find Duplicates Query Wizard.

1 ▶ On the **CREATE tab**, in the **Queries group**, click the **Query Wizard** button. In the **New Query** dialog box, click **Find Duplicates Query Wizard**, and then click **OK**.

2 ▶ In the first **Find Duplicates Query Wizard** dialog box, in the list of tables, click **Table: 5A Inventory**, and then click **Next**.

The second dialog box displays, enabling you to select the field or fields that may contain duplicate data. If you select all of the fields, then every field must contain the same data, which cannot be the case for a primary key field.

3 Under **Available fields**, double-click **Item** to move it under **Duplicate-value fields**, and then click **Next**.

> The third dialog box displays, enabling you to select one or more fields that will help you distinguish duplicate from nonduplicate records.

4 Under **Available fields**, add the following fields, in the order specified, to the **Additional query fields** box: **Catalog#**, **Category**, **Supplier**, **Cost**, and **Selling Price**. Compare your screen with Figure 5.20.

FIGURE 5.20

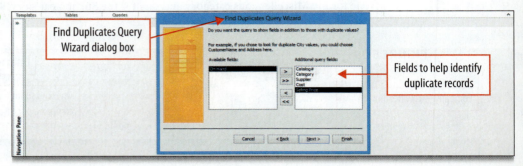

5 Click **Next**. Click **Finish** to accept the suggested query name—*Find duplicates for Lastname Firstname 5A Inventory*—and then compare your screen with Figure 5.21.

> Three records display with a duplicate value in the *Item* field. Using the displayed fields, you can determine that the second and third records are duplicates; the *Catalog#* was entered incorrectly for one of the records. By examining the *5A Inventory* table, you can determine that Category 1 is Snowboarding and Category 2 is Surfing. You must exercise care when using the Find Duplicates Query Wizard. If you do not include additional fields to help determine whether the records are duplicates or not, you might mistakenly determine that they are duplicates.

FIGURE 5.21

6 Adjust all column widths, as needed. View the query in **Print Preview**, ensuring that the query prints on one page. If you are instructed to submit this result, create a paper or electronic printout. **Close** ☒ the query, saving changes.

> Normally, you would delete the duplicate record, but your instructor needs to verify that you have found the duplicate record by using a query.

More Knowledge | **Removing Duplicate Records**

If you choose to delete duplicate records, you must first deal with existing table relationships. If the record you want to delete exists in the table on the *many* side of the relationship, you can delete the record without taking additional steps. If the record exists in the table on the *one* side of the relationship, you must first delete the relationship, and then delete the record. You should then re-create the relationship between the tables. You can either manually delete the duplicate records or create a delete query to remove the duplicate records.

Activity 5.08 | Finding Unmatched Records

In this activity, you will find unmatched records in related tables—*5A Suppliers* and *5A Inventory*—by using the Find Unmatched Query Wizard.

1 On the **CREATE tab**, in the **Queries group**, click the **Query Wizard** button. In the **New Query** dialog box, click **Find Unmatched Query Wizard**, and then click **OK**.

2 In the first **Find Unmatched Query Wizard** dialog box, in the list of tables, click **Table: 5A Suppliers**, and then click **Next**.

The second dialog box displays, enabling you to select the related table or query that you would like Access to compare to the first table to find unmatched records.

3 In the list of tables, click **Table: 5A Inventory**, and then click **Next**.

The third dialog box displays, enabling you to select the matching fields in each table.

4 Under **Fields in '5A Suppliers'**, if necessary, click ID. Under **Fields in '5A Inventory'**, if necessary, click **Supplier**. Between the two fields columns, click the button that displays <=>. Click **Next**.

At the bottom of the dialog box, Access displays the matching fields of ID and Supplier.

5 Under **Available fields**, double-click **ID**, and then double-click **Company** to move the field names under **Selected fields**. Notice that these fields will display in the query results, and then compare your screen with Figure 5.22.

FIGURE 5.22

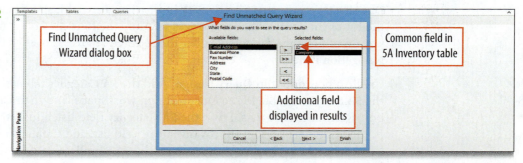

6 Click **Next.**In the last dialog box, under **What would you like to name your query?**, type **Lastname Firstname 5A Find Unmatched Query** and then click **Finish**. Compare your screen with Figure 5.23.

The query results display one company—*Cold Sports Club*—that has no inventory items in the *5A Inventory* table. Normally, you would either delete the Cold Sports Club record from the *5A Suppliers* table or add inventory items in the related *5A Inventory* for the Cold Sports Club, but your instructor needs to verify that you have located an unmatched record by using a query.

FIGURE 5.23

7 Adjust all column widths. View the query in **Print Preview**, ensuring that the query prints on one page. If you are instructed to submit this result, create a paper or electronic printout. **Close** Print Preview. **Close** ⊠ the query, saving changes.

More Knowledge | **Finding Unmatched Records in a Table with Multivalued Fields**

You cannot use the Find Unmatched Query Wizard with a table that has **multivalued fields**—fields that appear to hold multiple values. If your table contains multivalued fields, you must first create a query, extracting all of the fields except the multivalued fields, and then create the query to find unmatched records.

Video A5-5

A *parameter query* prompts you for criteria before running the query. For example, if you had a database of snowboarding events, you might need to find all of the snowboarding events in a particular state. You can create a select query for a state, but when you need to find information about snowboarding events in another state, you must open the original select query in Design view, change the criteria, and then run the query again. With a parameter query, you can create one query—Access will prompt you to enter the state and then display the results based upon the criteria you enter in the dialog box.

Activity 5.09 | Creating a Parameter Query Using One Criterion

In this activity, you will create a parameter query to display a specific category of inventory items. You can enter a parameter anywhere you use text, number, or date criteria.

1 **Open** » the **Navigation Pane**. Under **Tables**, double-click **5A Inventory** to open the table in **Datasheet** view. In any record, click in the **Category** field, and then click the **arrow** to display the list of categories. Take a moment to study the four categories used in this table. Be sure you do not change the category for the selected record. **Close** ☒ the table, and **Close** « the **Navigation Pane**.

2 Create a new query in **Query Design**. Add the **5A Category** table, the **5A Inventory** table, and the **5A Suppliers** table to the Query design workspace, and then **Close** the **Show Table** dialog box. Resize the field lists. From the **5A Category** field list, add **CatName** to the first column in the design grid. From the **5A Inventory** field list, add **Catalog#** and **Item** to the second and third columns in the design grid. From the **5A Suppliers** field list, add **Company** to the fourth column in the design grid.

3 In the **Criteria row** under **CatName**, type **[Enter a Category]** and then compare your screen with Figure 5.24.

> The brackets indicate a *parameter*—a value that can be changed—rather than specific criteria. When you run the query, a dialog box will display, prompting you to *Enter a Category*. The category you type will be set as the criteria for the query. Because you are prompted for the criteria, you can reuse this query without resetting the criteria in Design view.

FIGURE 5.24

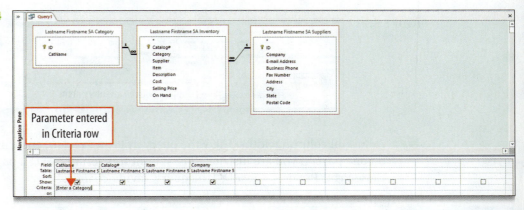

4 **Run** the query. In the **Enter Parameter Value** dialog box, type **Surfing** and then compare your screen with Figure 5.25.

FIGURE 5.25

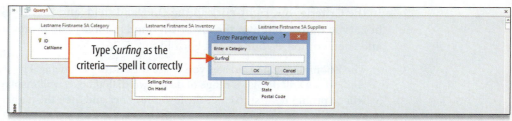

ALERT!   **Does Your Screen Differ?**

If the Enter Parameter Value dialog box does not display, you may have typed the parameter incorrectly in the design grid. Common errors include using parentheses or curly braces instead of square brackets around the parameter text, causing Access to interpret the text as specific criteria. If you use parentheses, when you run the query, there are no records displayed. If you use curly braces, the query will not run. To correct, display the query in Design view, and then correct the parameter entered in the criteria row.

---

5   In the **Enter Parameter Value** dialog box, click **OK**.

> Thirteen records display where the CatName field is Surfing.

6   Adjust column widths, if necessary, and **Save** 🖫 the query as **Lastname Firstname 5A Category Parameter Query Close** ☒ the query, and then **Open** 》 the **Navigation Pane**.

7   In the **Navigation Pane**, under **Queries**, double-click **5A Category Parameter Query**. In the **Enter Parameter Value** dialog box, type **Snowboarding** and then click **OK**.

> Eleven items categorized as Snowboarding display. Recall that when you open a query, Access runs the query so that the most up-to-date data is extracted from the underlying table or query. When you have entered a parameter as the criteria, you will be prompted to enter the criteria every time you open the query.

8   Switch to **Design** view. Notice that the parameter—[**Enter a Category**]—is stored with the query. Access does not store the criteria entered in the **Enter Parameter Value** dialog box.

9   **Run** the query, and in the **Enter Parameter Value** dialog box, type **Miscellaneous** being careful to spell it correctly. Click **OK** to display one record. Adjust all column widths.

10   View the query in **Print Preview**, ensuring that the query prints on one page. If you are instructed to submit this result, create a paper or electronic printout. **Close** Print Preview. **Close** ☒ the query, saving changes, and then **Close** 《 the **Navigation Pane**.

More Knowledge   **Parameter Query Prompts**

When you enter the parameter in the criteria row, make sure that the prompt—the text enclosed in the square brackets—is not the same as the field name. For example, if the field name is Category, do not enter [Category] as the parameter. Because Access uses field names in square brackets for calculations, no prompt will display. If you want to use the field name by itself as a prompt, type a question mark at the end of the prompt; for example, [Category?]. You cannot use a period, exclamation mark (!), square brackets ([ ]), or the ampersand (&) as part of the prompt.

Activity 5.10 | Creating a Parameter Query Using Multiple Criteria

In this activity, you will create a parameter query to display the inventory items that fall within a certain range in the On Hand field.

1   Create a new query in **Query Design**. Add the **5A Suppliers** table and the **5A Inventory** table to the Query design workspace, and then **Close** the **Show Table** dialog box. Resize the field lists. From the **5A Inventory** field list, add **Item** and **On Hand** to the first and second columns in the design grid. From the **5A Suppliers** field list box, add **Company** to the third column in the design grid.

2 In the **Criteria row**, right-click in the **On Hand** field, and then click **Zoom**. In the **Zoom** dialog box, type **Between [Enter the lower On Hand number] and [Enter the higher On Hand number]** and then compare your screen with Figure 5.26.

The Zoom dialog box enables you to see the entire parameter. The parameter includes *Between* and *And*, which will display a range of data. Two dialog boxes will display when you run the query. You will be prompted first to enter the lower number and then the higher number.

FIGURE 5.26

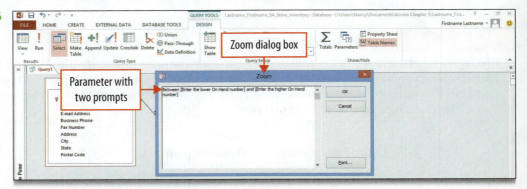

3 After verifying that you have entered the correct parameter, in the **Zoom** dialog box, click **OK**, and then **Run** the query. In the first **Enter Parameter Value** dialog box, type **10** and then click **OK**. In the second **Enter Parameter Value** dialog box, type **25** and then click **OK**. Compare your screen with Figure 5.27.

Six records have On Hand items in the range of 10 to 25. These might be inventory items that need to be ordered soon.

FIGURE 5.27

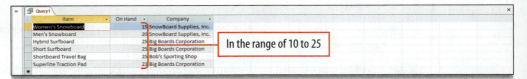

More Knowledge   **Creating a Parameter Query Using Multiple Criteria**

When you create a query using more than one field with parameters, the individual sees the prompts in the order that the fields are arranged from left to right in the design grid. When you create a query using more than one parameter in a single field, the individual sees the prompts in the order displayed, from left to right, in the Criteria box.

If you want the prompts to display in a different order, on the DESIGN tab, in the Show/Hide group, click the Parameters button. In the Parameter column, type the prompt for each parameter exactly as it was typed in the design grid. Enter the parameters in the order you want the dialog boxes to display when the query is run. In the Data Type column, next to each entered parameter, specify the data type by clicking the arrow and displaying the list of data types. Click OK, and then run the query.

---

4 Adjust all column widths, and **Save** 🖫 the query as **Lastname Firstname 5A On Hand Parameter Query**

5 View the query in **Print Preview**, ensuring that the query prints on one page. If you are instructed to submit this result, create a paper or electronic printout. **Close** Print Preview. **Close** ✕ the query.

6 **Open** » the **Navigation Pane**. **Close** the database, and **Exit** ✕ Access.

7 As directed by your instructor, submit your database and the paper or electronic printouts of the nine queries that are the result of this project. Specifically, in this project, using your own name you created the following database and printouts or electronic printouts:

1. Lastname_Firstname_5A_Store_Inventory	Database file
2. Lastname Firstname 5A Per Item Profit	Query (printed or electronic printout)
3. Lastname Firstname 5A Surfboarding Sale	Query (printed or electronic printout)
4. Lastname Firstname 5A Total Inventory Cost	Query (printed or electronic printout)
5. Lastname Firstname 5A Inventory by Supplier	Query (printed or electronic printout)
6. Lastname Firstname 5A Crosstab Query	Query (printed or electronic printout)
7. Find duplicates for Lastname Firstname 5A Inventory	Query (printed or electronic printout)
8. Lastname Firstname 5A Find Unmatched Query	Query (printed or electronic printout)
9. Lastname Firstname 5A Category Parameter Query	Query (printed or electronic printout)
10. Lastname Firstname 5A On Hand Parameter Query	Query (printed or electronic printout)

END | You have completed Project 5A

PROJECT ACTIVITIES

In Activities 5.11 through 5.19, you will help Miko Adai, sales associate for S-Boards, Inc. Surf and Snowboard Shop, keep the tables in the database up-to-date and ensure that the queries display pertinent information. You will create action queries that will create a new table, update records in a table, append records to a table, and delete records from a table. You will also modify the join type of relationships to display different subsets of the data when the query is run. Your completed queries will look similar to Figure 5.28.

PROJECT FILES

For Project 5B, you will need the following files:

a05B_Customer_Orders
a05B_Potential_Customers

You will save your databases as:

Lastname_Firstname_5B_Customer_Orders
Lastname_Firstname_5B_Potential_Customers

PROJECT RESULTS

FIGURE 5.28 Project 5B Customer Orders

Objective 6　Create a Make Table Query

Video A5-6

An **action query** enables you to create a new table or change data in an existing table. A **make table query** is an action query that creates a new table by extracting data from one or more tables. Creating a new table from existing tables is useful when you need to copy or back up data. For example, you may wish to create a table that displays the orders for the past month. You can extract that data and store it in another table, using the new table as a source for reports or queries. Extracting data and storing it in a new table reduces the time to retrieve **static data**—data that does not change—and creates a convenient backup of the data.

Activity 5.11　Creating a Select Query

In this activity, you will create a select query to extract the fields you wish to store in the new table.

1 **Start** Access. Navigate to the location where the student data files for this textbook are saved. Locate and open the **a05B_Customer_Orders** file. **Save** the database in your **Access Chapter 5** folder as **Lastname_Firstname_5B_Customer_Orders**

2 If you did not add the **Access Chapter 5** folder to the Trust Center, enable the content. In the **Navigation Pane**, under **Tables**, rename the four tables by adding **Lastname Firstname** to the beginning of each table name. Resize the **Navigation Pane** so all table names are visible. Take a moment to open each table and observe the data in each. In the **5B Orders** table, make a note of the data type for the **Order#** field and the pattern of data entered in the field. When you are finished, close all of the tables, and **Close** 《 the **Navigation Pane**.

In the *5B Orders* table, the first record contains an Order# of 7-11-17-0002. The first section of the order number is the month of the order, the second section is the day of the month, and the third section is the year. The fourth section is a sequential number. Records with orders for July, August, and September are contained in this table.

> **ALERT!**　**Action Queries and Trusted Databases**
>
> To run an action query, the database must reside in a trusted location, or you must enable the content. If you try running an action query and nothing happens, check the status bar for the following message: *This action or event has been blocked by Disabled Mode*. Either add the storage location to Trusted Locations or enable the content. Then, run the query again.

3 Create a new query in **Query Design**. From the **Show Table** dialog box, add the following tables to the Query design workspace: **5B Customers**, **5B Orders**, and **5B Shippers**. **Close** the **Show Table** dialog box, and then resize the field lists. Notice the relationships between the tables.

The *5B Customers* table has a one-to-many relationship with the *5B Orders* table—*one* customer can have *many* orders. The *5B Shippers* table has a one-to-many relationship with the *5B Orders* table—*one* shipper can ship *more* than one order.

4 From the **5B Orders** field list, add **Order#** to the first column of the design grid. From the **5B Customers** field list, add **Last Name** and **First Name** to the second and third columns of the design grid. From the **5B Shippers** field list, add **Shipping Company** to the fourth column of the design grid.

5 In the design grid, click in the **Criteria row** under **Order#**, type **9*** and then compare your screen with Figure 5.29.

Recall that the asterisk is a wildcard that stands for one or more characters—Access will extract the records where the Order# starts with a 9, and it does not matter what the following characters are. The first section of the Order# contains the month the order was placed without any regard for the year; all September orders will display whether they were placed in 2016, 2017, or any other year. You do not need criteria in a select query to convert it to a make table query.

FIGURE 5.29

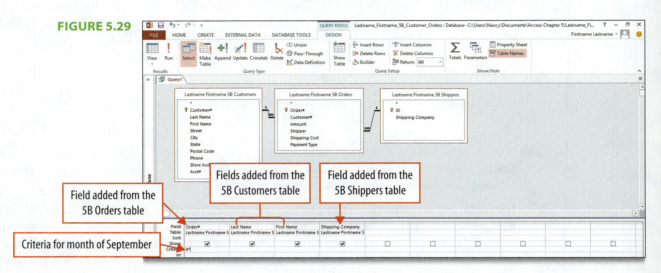

Field added from the 5B Orders table

Fields added from the 5B Customers table

Field added from the 5B Shippers table

Criteria for month of September

> **NOTE** **Using Expressions and Aggregate Functions in a Make Table Query**
>
> In addition to using criteria in a select query upon which a make table query is based, you can use expressions to create a calculated field; for example, *Gross Pay:[Hourly Wage]*[Hours Worked]*. You can also use aggregate functions; for example, you may want to sum the *Hours Worked* field.

6 **Run** the query, and notice that four orders were placed in September.

The select query displays the records that will be stored in the new table.

Activity 5.12 | Converting a Select Query to a Make Table Query

In this activity, you will convert the select query you just created to a make table query.

1 Switch to **Design** view. On the **QUERY TOOLS DESIGN tab**, in the **Query Type group**, click the **Make Table** button. Notice the exclamation point (!) in several of the buttons in the Query Type group—these are action queries. In the **Make Table** dialog box, in the **Table Name** box, type **Lastname Firstname 5B September Orders** and then compare your screen with Figure 5.30.

The table name should be a unique table name for the database in which the table will be saved. If it is not, you will be prompted to delete the first table before the new table can be created. You can save a make table query in the current database or in another existing database.

FIGURE 5.30

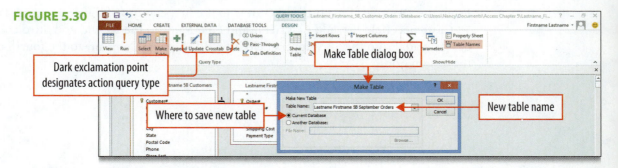

Dark exclamation point designates action query type

Make Table dialog box

Where to save new table

New table name

2 In the **Make Table** dialog box, be sure that **Current Database** is selected, and then click **OK**. **Run** the query.

A message displays indicating that *You are about to paste 4 row(s) into a new table* and that you cannot use the Undo command.

3 In the displayed message box, click **Yes**. **Close** ☒ the query, click **Yes** in the message box prompting you to save changes, and then name the query **Lastname Firstname 5B Make Table Query**

4 Open ⟫ the **Navigation Pane**. Notice that under **Tables**, the new table you created—**5B September Orders**—is displayed. Under **Queries**, the **5B Make Table Query** is displayed.

5 In the **Navigation Pane**, click the title—**All Access Objects**. Under **Navigate To Category**, click **Tables and Related Views**, widen the **Navigation Pane**, and then compare your screen with Figure 5.31.

The Navigation Pane is grouped by tables and related objects. Because the 5B Make Table Query extracted records from three tables—*5B Customers*, *5B Orders*, and *5B Shippers*—it is displayed under all three tables. Changing the grouping in the Navigation Pane to Tables and Related Views enables you to easily determine which objects are dependent upon other objects in the database.

FIGURE 5.31

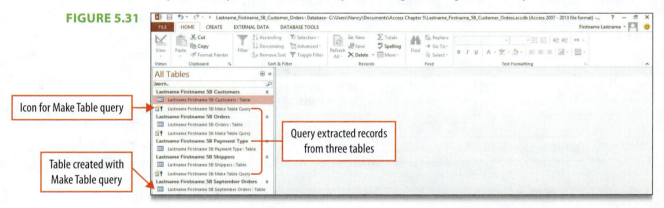

6 In the **Navigation Pane**, double-click **5B September Orders** to open the table in **Datasheet** view.

If you click the category title instead of the table, the category will close—if that happens, double-click the category title to redisplay the table, and then double-click the table.

7 Switch to **Design** view. Notice that the **Order#** field does not have an input mask associated with it and that there is no **Primary Key** field for this table.

When using a make table query to create a new table, the data in the new table does not inherit the field properties or the Primary Key field setting from the original table.

8 Switch to **Datasheet** view, and then adjust all column widths. **Close** ☒ the table, saving changes.

N O T E   **Updating a Table Created with a Make Table Query**

The data stored in a table created with a make table query is not automatically updated when records in the original tables are modified. To keep the new table up-to-date, you must run the make table query periodically to be sure the information is current.

Objective 7   Create an Append Query

Video A5-7

An ***append query*** is an action query that adds new records to an existing table by adding data from another Access database or from a table in the same database. An append query can be limited by criteria. Use an append query when the data already exists and you do not want to manually enter it into an existing table. Like the make table query, you first create a select query and then convert it to an append query.

Activity 5.13 | Creating an Append Query for a Table in the Current Database

In this activity, you will create a select query to extract the records for customers who have placed orders in August and then append the records to the *5B September Orders* table.

1 **Close** `«` the **Navigation Pane**. Create a new query in **Query Design**. From the **Show Table** dialog box, add the following tables to the Query design workspace: **5B Customers**, **5B Orders**, and **5B Shippers**. **Close** the **Show Table** dialog box, and then resize the field lists.

2 From the **5B Customers** field list, add **First Name** and **Last Name**, in the order specified, to the first and second columns of the design grid. From the **5B Orders** field list, add **Order#** and **Shipping Cost**, in the order specified, to the third and fourth columns of the design grid. From the **5B Shippers** field list, add **Shipping Company** to the fifth column of the design grid.

3 In the design grid, click in the **Criteria row** under **Order#**, type **8*** and then press ↓. Compare your screen with Figure 5.32.

FIGURE 5.32

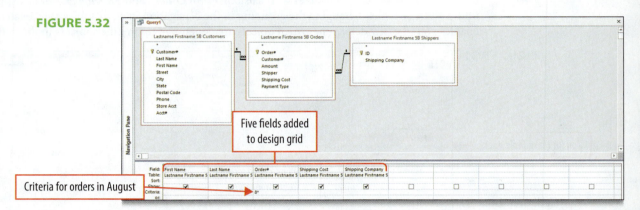

Five fields added to design grid

Criteria for orders in August

4 **Run** the query, and notice that four customers placed orders in August.

5 Switch to **Design** view. On the **QUERY TOOLS DESIGN tab**, in the **Query Type group**, click the **Append** button. In the **Append** dialog box, click the **Table Name arrow**, and from the displayed list, click **5B September Orders**, and then click **OK**. Compare your screen with Figure 5.33.

In the design grid, Access inserts an *Append To* row above the Criteria row. Access compares the fields in the query with the fields in the ***destination table***—the table to which you are appending the fields—and attempts to match fields. If a match is found, Access adds the name of the destination field to the Append To row in the query. If no match is found, Access leaves the destination field blank. You can click the box in the Append To row and select a destination field.

FIGURE 5.33

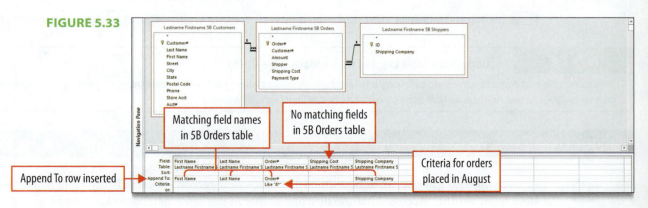

Matching field names in 5B Orders table

No matching fields in 5B Orders table

Criteria for orders placed in August

Append To row inserted

6 **Run** the query. In the displayed message box, click **Yes** to append the four rows to the *5B September Orders* table.

7 ▶ **Close** × the query, and then save it as **Lastname Firstname 5B Append August Orders**

8 ▶ **Open** » the **Navigation Pane**. Notice that **5B Append August Orders** displays under the three tables from which data was extracted.

9 ▶ In the **Navigation Pane**, click the title—**All Tables**. Under **Navigate To Category**, click **Object Type** to group the **Navigation Pane** objects by type. Under **Queries**, notice the icon that displays for **5B Append August Orders**. Recall that this icon indicates the query is an action query.

10 ▶ Under **Tables**, double-click **5B September Orders** to open the table in **Datasheet** view, and then compare your screen with Figure 5.34.

> Four orders for August are appended to the *5B September Orders* table. Because there is no match in the *5B September Orders* table for the Shipping Cost field in the 5B Append August Orders query, the field is ignored when the records are appended.

FIGURE 5.34

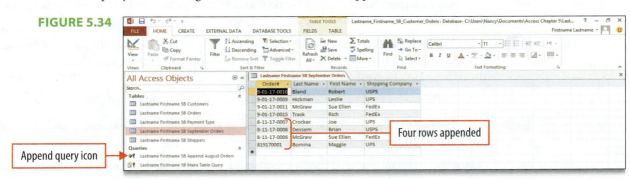

11 ▶ **Close** × the table. In the **Navigation Pane**, under **Tables**, right-click **5B September Orders**, and then click **Rename**. **Rename** the table as **Lastname Firstname 5B August & September Orders**

12 ▶ With **5B August & September Orders** selected, display **Backstage** view and view the table in **Print Preview**. If you are instructed to submit this result, create a paper or electronic printout of the table, and then **Close** the **Print Preview** window.

Activity 5.14 | Creating an Append Query for a Table in Another Database

Miko Adai recently discovered that the marketing manager has been keeping a database of persons who have requested information about the S-Boards, Inc. Surf and Snowboard Shop. These names need to be added to the *5B Customers* table so those potential clients can receive catalogs when they are distributed. In this activity, you will create an append query to add the records from the marketing manager's table to the *5B Customers* table.

1 ▶ On the Access window title bar, click the **Minimize** ▭ button. Display the **Start screen**, and then open **Access**. Navigate to the location where the student data files for this textbook are saved. Locate and open the **a05B_Potential_Customers** file. **Save** the database in your **Access Chapter 5** folder as **Lastname_Firstname_5B_Potential_Customers**

> **⟳ BY TOUCH**   To display the Start screen, always swipe in from the right and tap Start. To scroll, slide your finger to the left to scroll to the right.

2 If you did not add the **Access Chapter 5** folder to the Trust Center, enable the content. In the **Navigation Pane**, under **Tables**, rename the table by adding **Lastname Firstname** to the beginning of **5B Potential Customers**. Take a moment to open the table, noticing the fields and field names. When you are finished, **Close** ⊠ the table, and **Close** ⊠ the **Navigation Pane**.

The *5B Potential Customers* table in this database contains similar fields to the *5B Customers* table in the 5B_Customer_Orders database.

3 Create a new query in **Query Design**. From the **Show Table** dialog box, add the **5B Potential Customers** table to the Query design workspace, and then **Close** the **Show Table** dialog box. Resize the field list.

4 In the **5B Potential Customers** field list, click **Customer#**, hold down Shift, and then click **Phone** to select all of the fields. Drag the selection down into the first column of the design grid.

Although you could click the asterisk (*) in the field list to add all of the fields to the design grid, it is easier to detect which fields have no match in the destination table when the field names are listed individually in the design grid.

5 On the **QUERY TOOLS DESIGN tab**, in the **Query Type group**, click the **Append** button. In the **Append** dialog box, click the **Another Database** option button, and then click the **Browse** button. Navigate to your **Access Chapter 5** folder, and then double-click **5B Customer Orders**.

The 5B Customer Orders database contains the destination table.

6 In the **Append** dialog box, click the **Table Name arrow**, click **5B Customers**, and then compare your screen with Figure 5.35.

Once you select the name of another database, the tables contained in that database display.

FIGURE 5.35

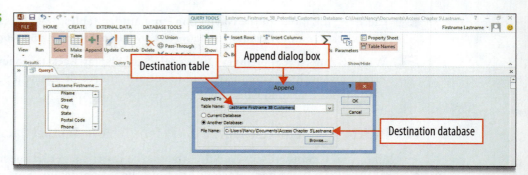

7 Click **OK**. In the design grid, notice that in the **Append To row**, Access found field name matches for all fields, except **LName** and **FName**.

8 In the design grid, click in the **Append To row** under **LName**, click the **arrow**, and then compare your screen with Figure 5.36.

A list displays the field names contained in the *5B Customers* table. If the field names are not exactly the same in the source and destination tables, Access will not designate them as matched fields. A **source table** is the table from which records are being extracted.

FIGURE 5.36

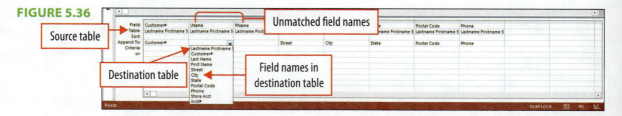

9 From the displayed list, click **Last Name**. Click in the **Append To** row under **FName**, and then click the **arrow**. In the displayed list, click **First Name**.

10 Save 💾 the query as **Lastname Firstname 5B Append to 5B Customers** and then **Run** the query, clicking **Yes** to append 9 rows. **Close** ✕ the query, and then **Open** » the **Navigation Pane**. **Close** the database, and then **Exit** ❎ this instance of Access.

ALERT! **To Trust or Not to Trust? That Is the Question!**

When you allow someone else to run an action query that will modify a table in your database, be sure that you can trust that individual. One mistake in the action query could destroy your table. A better way of running an action query that is dependent upon someone else's table is to obtain a copy of the table, place it in a database that you have created, and examine the table for malicious code. Once you are satisfied that the table is safe, you can create the action query to modify the data in your tables. Be sure to make a backup copy of the destination database before running action queries.

---

11 If necessary, on the taskbar, click the button for your 5B_Customer_Orders database. If you mistakenly closed the 5B_Customer_Orders database, reopen it. In the **Navigation Pane**, under **Tables**, double-click **5B Customers** to open the table in **Datasheet** view. **Close** « the **Navigation Pane**. Scroll down until **Customer# 9908** is displayed, and then compare your screen with Figure 5.37.

The last nine records—Customer#s 9900 through 9908—have been appended to the *5B Customers* table. The last two fields—Store Acct and Acct#—are blank because there were no corresponding fields in the *5B Potential Customers* table.

FIGURE 5.37

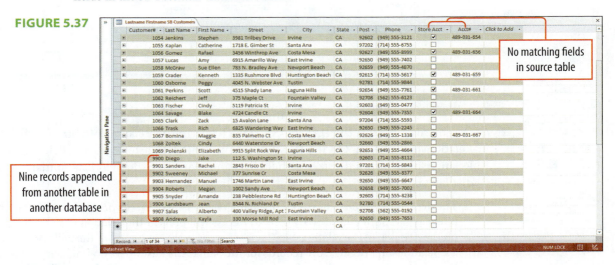

More Knowledge **Running the Same Append Query a Second Time**

If you run the same append query a second time with the same records in the source table and no primary key field is involved in the appending of records, you will have duplicate records in the destination table. If a primary key field is part of the records being duplicated, a message will display stating that Access cannot append all of the records due to one of several rule violations. If new records were added to the source table that were not originally appended to the destination table, clicking Yes in the message dialog box will enable those records to be added without adding duplicate records.

Objective 8 Create a Delete Query

Video A5-8

A **delete query** is an action query that removes records from an existing table in the same database. When information becomes outdated or is no longer needed, the records should be deleted from your database. Recall that one method you can use to find unnecessary records is to create a find unmatched query. Assuming outdated records have common criteria, you can create a select query, convert it to a delete query, and then delete all of the records at one time rather than deleting the records one by one. Use delete queries only when you need to remove many records quickly. Before running a delete query, you should back up the database because you cannot undo the deletion.

Activity 5.15 | Creating a Delete Query

A competing store has opened in Santa Ana, and the former customers living in that city have decided to do business with that store. In this activity, you will create a select query and then convert it to a delete query to remove records for clients living in Santa Ana.

1 With the **5B Customers** table open in **Datasheet** view, under **City**, click in any row. On the **HOME tab**, in the **Sort & Filter group**, click the **Descending** button to arrange the cities in descending alphabetical order.

2 At the top of the datasheet, in the record for **Customer# 1060**, click the **plus (+) sign** to display the subdatasheet. Notice that this customer has placed one order that has been shipped.

3 Display the subdatasheets for the four customers residing in Santa Ana, and then compare your screen with Figure 5.38.

The four customers residing in Santa Ana have not placed orders.

FIGURE 5.38

4 Collapse all of the subdatasheets by clicking each **minus (–) sign**.

5 On the ribbon, click the **DATABASE TOOLS tab**. In the **Relationships group**, click the **Relationships** button. On the **DESIGN tab**, in the **Relationships group**, click the **All Relationships** button. Resize the field lists and rearrange the field lists to match the layout displayed in Figure 5.39.

The *5B Customers* table has a one-to-many relationship with the *5B Orders* table, and referential integrity has been enforced. By default, Access will prevent the deletion of records from the table on the *one* side of the relationship if related records are contained in the table on the *many* side of the relationship. Because the records for the Santa Ana customers do not have related records in the related table, you will be able to delete the records from the *5B Customers* table, which is on the *one* side of the relationship.

To delete records from the table on the *one* side of the relationship that have related records in the table on the *many* side of the relationship, you must either delete the relationship or enable Cascade Delete Related Records. If you need to delete records on the *many* side of the relationship, you can do so without changing or deleting the relationship.

FIGURE 5.39

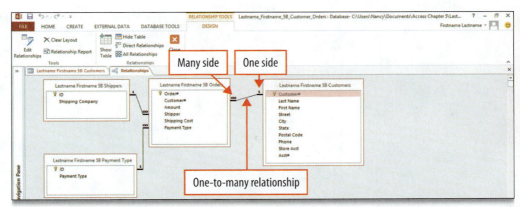

Many side

One side

One-to-many relationship

6 On the **tab row**, right-click any tab, and then click **Close All**, saving changes to the table and to the layout of the **Relationships** window.

7 Create a new query in **Query Design**. Add the **5B Customers** table to the Query design workspace, and then **Close** the **Show Table** dialog box. Resize the field list. From the field list, add **Customer#** and **City**, in the order specified, to the first and second columns in the design grid.

> Since you are deleting existing records based on criteria, you need to add only the field that has criteria attached to it—the City field. However, it is easier to analyze the results if you include another field in the design grid.

8 In the design grid, click in the **Criteria** row under **City**, type **Santa Ana** and then press ⬇.

> Access inserts the criteria in quotation marks because this is a Text field.

9 **Run** the query, and then compare your screen with Figure 5.40.

> Four records for customers in Santa Ana are displayed. If your query results display an empty record, switch to Design view and be sure that you typed the criteria correctly.

FIGURE 5.40

Customers living in Santa Ana

10 Switch to **Design** view. In the Query design workspace, to the right of the field list, right-click in the empty space. From the displayed shortcut menu, point to **Query Type**, and click **Delete Query**. Compare your screen with Figure 5.41. Alternatively, on the QUERY TOOLS DESIGN tab, in the Query Type group, click the Delete button.

> In the design grid, a Delete row is inserted above the Criteria row with the word *Where* in both columns. Access will delete all records *Where* the City is Santa Ana. If you include all of the fields in the query using the asterisk (*), Access inserts the word *From* in the Delete row, and all of the records will be deleted.

FIGURE 5.41

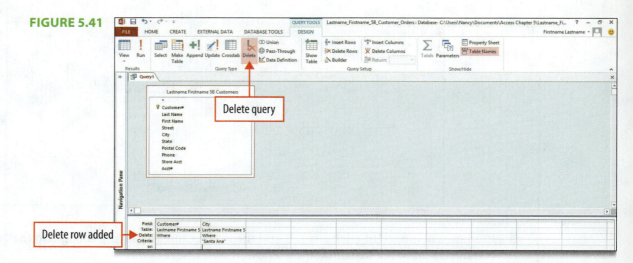

Delete query

Delete row added

11 Save the query as **Lastname Firstname 5B Delete Santa Ana Customers** and then **Run** the query. In the message box stating that *You are about to delete 4 row(s) from the specified table*, click **Yes**.

12 **Close** ✕ the query, and then **Open** » the **Navigation Pane**. Under **Queries**, notice the icon that is associated with a delete query—**5B Delete Santa Ana Customers**. Under **Tables**, open the **5B Customers** table in **Datasheet** view. Notice that the records are still in descending order by the **City** field, and notice that the four records for customers living in **Santa Ana** have been deleted from the table.

13 **Close** « the **Navigation Pane**, leaving the table open for the next activity. On the **HOME tab**, in the **Sort & Filter group**, click the **Remove Sort** button to clear all sorts from the **City** field.

Objective 9 | Create an Update Query

An *update query* is an action query that is used to add, change, or delete data in fields of one or more existing records. Combined with criteria, an update query is an efficient way to change data for a large number of records at one time, and you can change records in more than one table at a time. If you need to change data in a few records, you can use the Find and Replace dialog box. You are unable to use update queries to add or delete records in a table; use an append query or delete query as needed. Because you are changing data with an update query, you should back up your database before running one.

Video A5-9

Activity 5.16 | Creating an Update Query

The postal codes are changing for all of the customers living in Irvine or East Irvine to a consolidated postal code. In this activity, you will create a select query to extract the records from the *5B Customers* table for customers living in these cities and then convert the query to an update query so that you change the postal codes for all of the records at one time.

1 With the **5B Customers** table open in **Datasheet** view, click in the **City** field in any row. Sort the **City** field in **Ascending** order. Notice that there are five customers living in East Irvine with postal codes of 92650 and five customers living in Irvine with postal codes of 92602, 92603, and 92604.

2 **Close** ✕ the table, saving changes. Create a new query in **Query Design**. Add the **5B Customers** table to the Query design workspace, and then close the **Show Table** dialog box. Resize the field list.

3 In the **5B Customers** field list, double-click **City** to add the field to the first column of the design grid. Then add the **Postal Code** field to the second column of the design grid. In the design grid, click in the **Criteria row** under **City**, and then type **Irvine or East Irvine** Alternatively, type **Irvine** in the Criteria row, and then type **East Irvine** in the Or row. **Run** the query.

> Ten records display for the cities of Irvine or East Irvine. If your screen does not display ten records, switch to Design view and be sure you typed the criteria correctly. Then run the query again.

4 Switch to **Design** view, and then notice how Access changed the criteria under the **City** field, placing quotation marks around the text and capitalizing *or*. On the **QUERY TOOLS DESIGN tab**, in the **Query Type group**, click the **Update** button.

> In the design grid, an Update To row is inserted above the Criteria row.

5 In the design grid, click in the **Update To** row under **Postal Code**, type **92601** and then compare your screen with Figure 5.42.

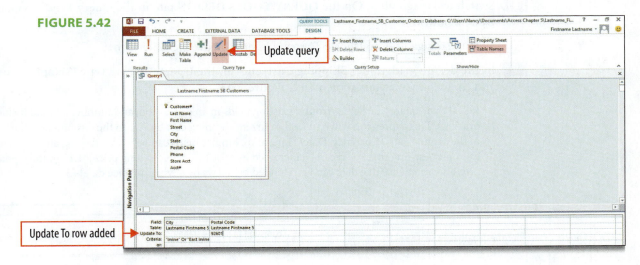

FIGURE 5.42

6 Save the query as **Lastname Firstname 5B Update Postal Codes** and then **Run** the query. In the message box stating that *You are about to update 10 row(s)*, click **Yes**.

7 Close the query, and then **Open** the **Navigation Pane**. Under **Queries**, notice the icon that is associated with an update query—**5B Update Postal Codes**. Under **Tables**, open the **5B Customers** table in **Datasheet** view. Notice that the 10 records for customers living in **East Irvine** and **Irvine** have **Postal** codes of **92601**.

8 View the table in **Print Preview**. Change the orientation to **Landscape**, and, if necessary, change the margins to ensure that the table prints on one page. If you are instructed to submit this result, create a paper or electronic printout, and then **Close** the **Print Preview** window. **Close** the table.

Activity 5.17 | Creating an Update Query with an Expression

There was a computer problem, and customers were overcharged for items shipped by FedEx. In this activity, you will create an update query to correct the field to reflect an accurate shipping cost. Any item shipped by FedEx will be discounted 7 percent.

1 Open the **5B Orders** table in **Datasheet** view, and **Close** « the **Navigation Pane**. Click the right side of the **Shipper** field to see the lookup list. Notice an entry of **1** means the order was shipped using FedEx. Press Esc to return to the field box. Sort the **Shipper** field from **Smallest to Largest**. Notice that there are five orders that were shipped using FedEx. Make note of the shipping cost for each of those items.

2 **Close** ✕ the table, saving changes. Create a new query in **Query Design**. From the **Show Table** dialog box, add the **5B Shippers** table and the **5B Orders** table to the Query design workspace, and then **Close** the **Show Table** dialog box. Resize the field lists.

3 From the **5B Shippers** field list, add **Shipping Company** to the design grid. From the **5B Orders** field list, add **Shipping Cost** to the design grid. In the **Criteria row** under **Shipping Company**, type **FedEx Run** the query.

> Five records display for FedEx. If your screen does not display five records, switch to Design view and be sure you typed the criteria correctly. Then run the query again.

4 Switch to **Design** view. On the **QUERY TOOLS DESIGN tab**, in the **Query Type group**, click the **Update** button.

> In the design grid, an Update To row is inserted above the Criteria row.

5 In the design grid, under **Shipping Cost**, click in the **Update To row**, type **[Shipping Cost]*.93** and then compare your screen with Figure 5.43.

> Recall that square brackets surround existing fields in an expression, and numbers do not include any brackets. This expression will reduce the current shipping cost by 7%, so the customers will pay 93% of the original cost. Currency, Date/Time, and Number fields can be updated using an expression. For example, a selling price field can be increased by 15% by keying [selling price]*1.15 in the Update To box, and an invoice due date can be extended by 3 days by keying [invoice date]+3 in the Update To box.

FIGURE 5.43

Criteria for records to be updated

Expression to update shipping cost

6 Save 💾 the query as **Lastname Firstname 5B Update FedEx Shipping Costs** and then **Run** the query. In the message box stating that *You are about to update 5 row(s)*, click **Yes**.

> The update query runs every time the query is opened, unless it is opened directly in Design view. To review or modify the query, right-click the query name, and then click Design view.

7 **Close** ✕ the query, and then **Open** » the **Navigation Pane**. Under **Tables**, open the **5B Orders** table in **Datasheet** view. Notice that the five records for orders shipped FedEx have lower shipping costs than they did prior to running the query, 93 percent of the original cost.

8 View the table in **Print Preview**. If you are instructed to submit this result, create a paper or electronic printout and then **Close** the **Print Preview** window. **Close** ✕ the **5B Orders** table.

More Knowledge **Restrictions for Update Queries**

It is not possible to run an update query with these types of table fields:

- Calculated fields, created in a table or in a query
- Fields that use total queries or crosstab queries as their source
- AutoNumber fields, which can change only when you add a record to a table
- Fields in union queries
- Fields in unique-values or unique-records queries
- Primary key fields that are common fields in table relationships, unless you set Cascade Update Related Fields

You cannot cascade updates for tables that use a data type of AutoNumber to generate the primary key field.

Objective 10 Modify the Join Type

Video A5-10

When multiple tables are included in a query, a *join* helps you extract the correct records from the related tables. The relationship between the tables, based upon common fields, is represented in a query by a join, which is displayed as the join line between the related tables. When you add tables to the Query design workspace, Access creates the joins based on the defined relationships. If you add queries to the Query design workspace or tables where the relationship has not been defined, you can manually create joins between the objects by dragging a common field from one object to the common field in the second. Joins establish rules about records to be included in the query results and combine the data from multiple sources on one record row in the query results.

Activity 5.18 | Viewing the Results of a Query Using an Inner Join

The default join type is the *inner join*, which is the most common type of join. When a query with an inner join is run, only the records where the common field exists in both related tables are displayed in the query results. All of the queries you have previously run have used an inner join. In this activity, you will view the results of a query that uses an inner join.

1 **Close** « the **Navigation Pane**. On the Ribbon, click the **DATABASE TOOLS tab**, and then in the **Relationships group** click the **Relationships** button. Notice the relationship between the **5B Customers** table and the **5B Orders** table.

> Because referential integrity has been enforced, it is easy to determine that the *5B Customers* table is on the *one* side of the relationship, and the *5B Orders* table is on the *many* side of the relationship. *One* customer can have *many* orders. The common field is Customer#.

2 In the **Relationships** window, double-click the **join line** between the **5B Customers** table and the **5B Orders** table. Alternatively, right-click the join line, and then click Edit Relationship, or click the line, and then in the Tools group, click the Edit Relationships button. Compare your screen with Figure 5.44.

> The Edit Relationships dialog box displays, indicating that referential integrity has been enforced and that the relationship type is *One-to-Many*. Because the relationship has been established for the tables, you can view relationship properties in the Relationships window.

> **A L E R T !** **Is Your Edit Relationships Dialog Box Empty?**
>
> If your Edit Relationships dialog box does not display as shown in Figure 5.44, you may have double-clicked near the join line and not on the join line. In the Edit Relationships dialog box, click Cancel, and then try again.

FIGURE 5.44

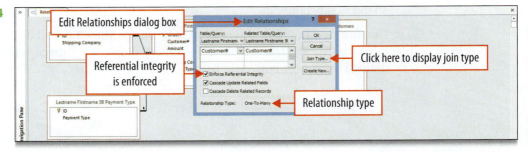

3 In the **Edit Relationships** dialog box, click **Join Type**, and then compare your screen with Figure 5.45. In the displayed **Join Properties** dialog box, notice that option **1** is selected—*Only include rows where the joined fields from both tables are equal.*

Option 1 is the default join type, which is an inner join. Options 2 and 3 are outer join types.

FIGURE 5.45

4 In the **Join Properties** dialog box, click **Cancel**. In the **Edit Relationships** dialog box, click **Cancel**. **Close** the **Relationships** window.

Because the relationships have been established and saved in the database, you should not change the join properties in the Relationships window. You should only change join properties in the Query design workspace.

5 Open ⟫ the **Navigation Pane**. In the **Navigation Pane**, open the **5B Orders** table and the **5B Customers** table, in the order specified, and then **Close** ⟪ the **Navigation Pane**.

 BY TOUCH   If tables are not displayed in the order specified, slide to rearrange—similar to dragging with a mouse.

6 With the **5B Customers** table active, on the **HOME tab**, in the **Sort & Filter group**, click the **Remove Sort** button to remove the ascending sort from the **City** field. Notice that the records are now sorted by the **Customer#** field—the primary key field.

7 In the third record, click the **plus (+) sign** to expand the subdatasheet—the related record in the *5B Orders* table—and then notice that Willie Smith has no related records—he has not placed any orders. Click the **minus (–) sign** to collapse the subdatasheets.

8 Expand the subdatasheet for **Customer# 1045**, and then notice that Joe Crocker has one related record in the *5B Orders* table—he has placed one order. Collapse the subdatasheet.

9 Expand the subdatasheet for **Customer# 1047**, and then notice that Robert Bland has two related records in the *5B Orders* table—he has placed *many* orders. Collapse the subdatasheet.

10 On the **tab row**, click the **5B Orders tab** to make the datasheet active, and then notice that **15** orders have been placed. On the **tab row**, right-click any tab, and then click **Close All**, saving changes, if prompted.

11 Create a new query in **Query Design**. From the **Show Table** dialog box, add the **5B Customers** table and the **5B Orders** table to the Query design workspace, and then close the **Show Table** dialog box. Resize both field lists.

12 From the **5B Customers** field list, add **Customer#**, **Last Name**, and **First Name**, in the order specified, to the design grid. In the design grid, under **Customer#**, click in the **Sort row**, click the **arrow**, and then click **Ascending**. **Run** the query, and then compare your screen with Figure 5.46. There is no record for **Willie Smith**, there is one record for **Customer# 1045**—Joe Crocker—and there are two records for **Customer# 1047**—Robert Bland.

Because the default join type is an inner join, the query results display records only where there is a matching Customer#—the common field—in both related tables, even though you did not add any fields from the *5B Orders* table to the design grid. All of the records display for the table on the *many* side of the relationship—*5B Orders*. For the table on the *one* side of the relationship—*5B Customers*—only those records that have matching records in the related table display. Recall that there were 30 records in the *5B Customers* table and 15 records in the *5B Orders* table.

FIGURE 5.46

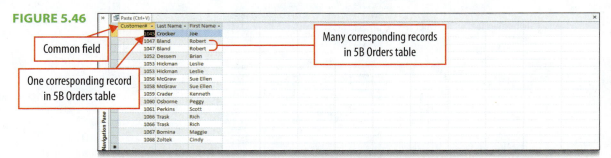

13 Switch to **Design** view. From the **5B Orders** field list, add **Order#** to the fourth column of the design grid, and then add **Amount** to the fifth column of the design grid. **Run** the query to display the results.

The same 15 records display but with two additional fields.

Activity 5.19 | Changing the Join Type to an Outer Join

An *outer join* is typically used to display records from both tables, regardless of whether there are matching records. In this activity, you will modify the join type to display all of the records from the *5B Customers* table, regardless of whether the customer has placed an order.

1 Switch to **Design** view. In the Query design workspace, double-click the **join line** to display the **Join Properties** dialog box. Alternatively, right-click the join line, and then click Join Properties. Compare your screen with Figure 5.47.

The Join Properties dialog box displays the tables used in the join and the common fields from both tables. Option 1—inner join type—is selected by default. Options 2 and 3 are two different types of outer joins.

Option 2 is a *left outer join*. Select a left outer join when you want to display all of the records on the *one* side of the relationship, whether or not there are matching records in the table on the *many* side of the relationship. Option 3 is a *right outer join*. Selecting a right outer join will display all of the records on the *many* side of the relationship, whether or not there are matching records in the table on the *one* side of the relationship. This should not occur if referential integrity has been enforced because all orders should have a related customer.

FIGURE 5.47

2 In the **Join Properties** dialog box, click the option button next to **2**, and then click **OK**. **Run** the query, and then compare your screen with Figure 5.48.

Thirty-four records display. There are thirty records in the *5B Customers* table; however, four customers have two orders, so there are two separate records for each of these customers. If a customer does not have a matching record in the *5B Orders* table, the Order# and Amount fields are left empty in the query results.

FIGURE 5.48

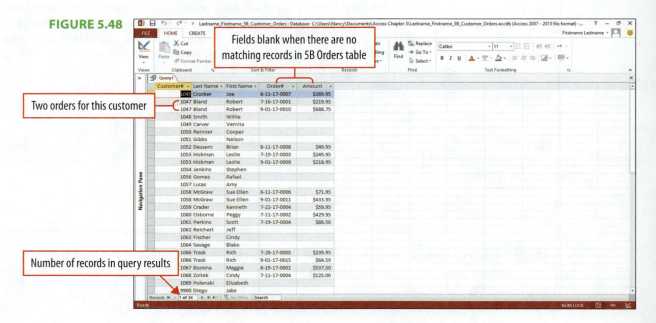

3 **Save** 💾 the query as **Lastname Firstname 5B Outer Join** View the query in **Print Preview**, ensuring that the table prints on one page. If you are instructed to submit this result, create a paper or electronic printout. **Close** the **Print Preview** window.

4 **Close** ✖ the query, and then **Open** 》 the **Navigation Pane**. **Close** the database, and then **Exit** Access.

5 As directed by your instructor, submit your database and the paper or electronic printouts of the four objects—three tables and a query—that are the result of this project. Specifically, in this project, using your own name you created the following database and printouts or electronic printouts:

1. Lastname_Firstname_5B_Customer_Orders	Database file
2. Lastname Firstname 5B August & September Orders	Table (printed or electronic printout)
3. Lastname Firstname 5B Customers	Table (printed or electronic printout)
4. Lastname Firstname 5B Orders	Table (printed or electronic printout)
5. Lastname Firstname 5B Outer Join	Query (printed or electronic printout)

More Knowledge Other Types of Joins

There are two other types of joins: cross joins and unequal joins. A ***cross join*** is not explicitly set in Access 2013. In a cross join, each row from one table is combined with each row in a related table. Cross joins are usually created unintentionally when you do not create a join line between related tables. In fact, the results of the query will probably not make much sense. In the previous query, you would create a cross join by deleting the join line between the 5B Customers table and the 5B Orders table. A cross join produces many records; depending on the number of records in both tables, the cross join can take a long time to run. A cross join using the aforementioned tables would result in 348 displayed records when the query is run (29 customers × 12 orders = 348 records).

An ***unequal join*** is used to combine rows from two data sources based on field values that are not equal. The join can be based on any comparison operator, such as greater than (>), less than (<), or not equal to (<>). The results in an unequal join using the not equal to comparison operator are difficult to interpret and can display as many records as those displayed in a cross join. Unequal joins cannot be created in Design view; they can be created only in SQL view.

END | You have completed Project 5B

END OF CHAPTER

SUMMARY

Queries are powerful database objects created to do more than extract data from tables and other queries; results can provide tools for analyzing, updating, and maintaining the integrity of the data.

Special-purpose queries are created to calculate fields, use aggregate functions, display data for easier analysis, find duplicate and unmatched records to avoid problems, and create prompts to use.

Action queries are used to create new tables, append and delete records, and update data in tables. Query results can be modified by changing from the default inner join to an outer join between tables.

GO! LEARN IT ONLINE

Review the concepts and key terms in this chapter by completing these online challenges, which you can find at **www.pearsonhighered.com/go.**

Matching and Multiple Choice:
Answer matching and multiple choice questions to test what you learned in this chapter. MyITLab®

Crossword Puzzle:
Spell out the words that match the numbered clues, and put them in the puzzle squares.

Flipboard:
Flip through the definitions of the key terms in this chapter and match them with the correct term.

END OF CHAPTER

REVIEW AND ASSESSMENT GUIDE FOR ACCESS CHAPTER 5

Your instructor may assign one or more of these projects to help you review the chapter and assess your mastery and understanding of the chapter.

Project	Apply Skills from These Chapter Objectives	Project Type	Project Location
		Review and Assessment Guide for Access Chapter 5	
5C	Objectives 1–5 from Project 5A	**5C Skills Review** A guided review of the skills from Project 5A.	On the following pages
5D	Objectives 6–10 from Project 5B	**5D Skills Review** A guided review of the skills from Project 5B.	On the following pages
5E	Objectives 1–5 from Project 5A	**5E Mastery (Grader Project)** A demonstration of your mastery of the skills in Project 5A with extensive decision making.	In MyITLab and on the following pages
5F	Objectives 6–10 from Project 5B	**5F Mastery (Grader Project)** A demonstration of your mastery of the skills in Project 5B with extensive decision making.	In MyITLab and on the following pages
5G	Objectives 1–3, 9 from Projects 5A and 5B	**5G Mastery (Grader Project)** A demonstration of your mastery of the skills in Projects 5A and 5B with extensive decision making.	In MyITLab and on the following pages
5H	Combination of Objectives from Projects 5A and 5B	**5H GO! Fix It** A demonstration of your mastery of the skills in Projects 5A and 5B by creating a correct result from a document that contains errors you must find.	Online
5I	Combination of Objectives from Projects 5A and 5B	**5I GO! Make It** A demonstration of your mastery of the skills in Projects 5A and 5B by creating a result from a supplied picture.	Online
5J	Combination of Objectives from Projects 5A and 5B	**5J GO! Solve It** A demonstration of your mastery of the skills in Projects 5A and 5B, your decision-making skills, and your critical thinking skills. A task-specific rubric helps you self-assess your result.	Online
5K	Combination of Objectives from Projects 5A and 5B	**5K GO! Solve It** A demonstration of your mastery of the skills in Projects 5A and 5B, your decision-making skills, and your critical thinking skills. A task-specific rubric helps you self-assess your result.	On the following pages
5L	Combination of Objectives from Projects 5A and 5B	**5L GO! Think** A demonstration of your understanding of the chapter concepts applied in a manner that you would use outside of college. An analytic rubric helps you and your instructor grade the quality of your work by comparing it to the work an expert in the discipline would create.	On the following pages
5M	Combination of Objectives from Projects 5A and 5B	**5M GO! Think** A demonstration of your understanding of the chapter concepts applied in a manner that you would use outside of college. An analytic rubric helps you and your instructor grade the quality of your work by comparing it to the work an expert in the discipline would create.	Online
5N	Combination of Objectives from Projects 5A and 5B	**5N You and GO!** A demonstration of your understanding of the chapter concepts applied in a manner that you would use in a personal situation. An analytic rubric helps you and your instructor grade the quality of your work.	Online

GLOSSARY

Action query A query that creates a new table or changes data in an existing table.

Aggregate function Performs a calculation on a column of data and returns a single value.

Append query An action query that adds new records to an existing table by adding data from another Access database or from a table in the same database.

Arithmetic operators Mathematical symbols used in building expressions.

Calculated field A field that obtains its data by using a formula to perform a calculation or computation.

Cross join A join that displays when each row from one table is combined with each row in a related table, usually created unintentionally when you do not create a join line between related tables.

Crosstab query A query that uses an aggregate function for data that is grouped by two types of information and displays the data in a compact, spreadsheet-like format. A crosstab query always has at least one row heading, one column heading, and one summary field.

Delete query An action query that removes records from an existing table in the same database.

Destination table The table to which you are appending records, attempting to match the fields.

Expression The formula that will perform a calculation.

Find Duplicates Query A query used to locate duplicate records in a table.

Find Unmatched Query A query used to locate unmatched records so they can be deleted from the table.

Inner join A join that allows only the records where the common field exists in both related tables to be displayed in query results.

Join A relationship that helps a query return only the records from each table you want to see, based on how those tables are related to other tables in the query.

Left outer join A join used when you want to display all of the records on the *one* side of a one-to-many relationship, whether or not there are matching records in the table on the *many* side of the relationship.

Make table query An action query that creates a new table by extracting data from one or more tables.

Multivalued fields Fields that hold multiple values.

Outer join A join that is typically used to display records from both tables, regardless of whether there are matching records.

Parameter A value that can be changed.

Parameter query A query that prompts you for criteria before running.

Right outer join A join used when you want to display all of the records on the *many* side of a one-to-many relationship, whether or not there are matching records in the table on the *one* side of the relationship.

Source table The table from which records are being extracted.

Static data Data that does not change.

Totals query A query that calculates subtotals across groups of records.

Unequal join A join used to combine rows from two data sources based on field values that are not equal; can be created only in SQL view.

Unmatched records Records in one table that have no matching records in a related table.

Update query An action query used to add, change, or delete data in fields of one or more existing records.

CHAPTER REVIEW

Apply 5A skills from these Objectives:

1 Create Calculated Fields in a Query

2 Use Aggregate Functions in a Query

3 Create a Crosstab Query

4 Find Duplicate and Unmatched Records

5 Create a Parameter Query

Derek Finkel, human resource specialist at S-Boards, Inc. Surf and Snowboard Shop, has a database containing employee data and payroll data. In the following Skills Review, you will create special-purpose queries to calculate data, summarize and group data, display data in a spreadsheet-like format, and find duplicate and unmatched records. You will also create a query that prompts an individual to enter the criteria. Your completed queries will look similar to Figure 5.49.

PROJECT FILES

For Project 5C, you will need the following file:

a05C_Employee_Payroll

You will save your database as:

Lastname_Firstname_5C_Employee_Payroll

PROJECT RESULTS

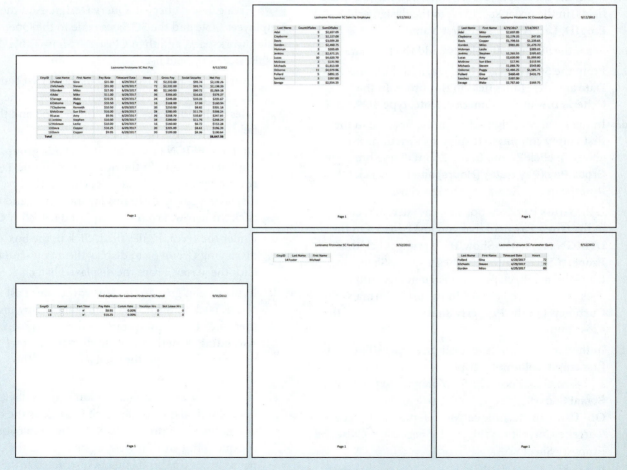

FIGURE 5.49

(Project 5C Employee Payroll continues on the next page)

CHAPTER REVIEW

1 **Start** Access. Locate and open the **a05C_ Employee_Payroll** file. Display **Backstage** view. **Save** the database in your **Access Chapter 5** folder as **Lastname_Firstname_5C_Employee_Payroll**

a. If necessary, enable the content or add the Access Chapter 5 folder to the Trust Center.

b. Rename the tables by adding your **Lastname Firstname** to the beginning of each table name. **Close** the **Navigation Pane**.

2 On the Ribbon, click the **CREATE tab**. In the **Queries group**, click the **Query Design** button. In the **Show Table** dialog box, select the following three tables— **5C Employees**, **5C Payroll**, and **5C Timecard**. **Add** the tables to the Query design workspace, and then click **Close**. Resize the field lists.

a. From the **5C Employees** field list, add the following fields, in the order specified, to the design grid: **EmpID**, **Last Name**, and **First Name**.

b. From the **5C Payroll** field list, add the **Pay Rate** field.

c. From the **5C Timecard** field list, add the **Timecard Date** and the **Hours** field in this order. In the **Criteria row** under **Timecard Date**, type **6/29/2017**

d. In the **Field row**, right-click in the first cell in the first empty column to display a shortcut menu, and then click **Zoom**. In the **Zoom** dialog box, type **Gross Pay:[Pay Rate]*[Hours]** and then click **OK**. Run the query. Return to **Design** view.

e. If the **Gross Pay** does not show as currency, click in the **Gross Pay** field that you just added. On the **DESIGN tab**, in the **Show/Hide group**, click the **Property Sheet** button. In the **Property Sheet**, on the **General tab**, click in the **Format** box, and then click the displayed **arrow**. In the list of formats, click **Currency**. On the **Property Sheet** title bar, click the **Close** button.

f. In the **Field row**, right-click in the first cell in the first empty column to display a shortcut menu, and then click **Zoom**. In the **Zoom** dialog box, type **Social Security:[Gross Pay]*0.042** and then click **OK**. Using the technique you just practiced, set a Currency format for this field if necessary. **Close** the Property Sheet.

g. In the **Field row**, right-click in the first cell in the first empty column to display a shortcut menu, and then click **Zoom**. In the **Zoom** dialog box,

type **Net Pay:[Gross Pay]-[Social Security]** and then click **OK**. **Run** the query to display the payroll calculations. Adjust column widths to display all field names and all data under each field.

h. In the **Records group**, click the **Totals** button. In the **Total row** under **Net Pay**, click in the empty box, and then click the **arrow** at the left edge. From the displayed list, click **Sum**.

i. On the **tab row**, right-click the **Query1 tab**, and then click **Save**. In the **Save As** dialog box, under **Query Name**, type **Lastname Firstname 5C Net Pay** and then click **OK**. View the query in **Print Preview**. Change the orientation to **Landscape** to ensure the table prints on one page. If you are instructed to submit this result, create a paper or electronic printout. **Close** the query.

3 Create a new query in **Query Design**. Add the **5C Employees** table and the **5C Sales** table to the Query design workspace, and then **Close** the **Show Table** dialog box. Resize both field lists.

a. From the **5C Employees** field list, add **Last Name** to the first field box in the design grid. From the **5C Sales** table, add **Sales** to both the second and third field boxes.

b. On the **DESIGN tab**, in the **Show/Hide group**, click the **Totals** button. In the design grid, in the **Total row** under the first **Sales** field, click in the box displaying *Group By* to display the arrow, and then click the **arrow**. From the displayed list, click **Count**.

c. Under the second **Sales** field, click in the box displaying *Group By* to display the arrow, and then click the **arrow**. From the displayed list, click **Sum**.

d. In the design grid, in the **Sort row** under **Last Name**, click in the box to display the arrow, and then click the **arrow**. From the displayed list, click **Ascending**. **Run** the query to display the total number of sales and the total amount of the sales for each associate.

e. If necessary, adjust column widths to display all field names and all data under each field. **Save** the query as **Lastname Firstname 5C Sales by Employee** View the query in **Print Preview**, ensuring that the query prints on one page. If you are instructed to submit this result, create a paper or electronic printout. **Close** the query.

(Project 5C Employee Payroll continues on the next page)

4 ▶ **Create** a new query in **Query Design**. Add the following tables to the Query design workspace: **5C Employees** and **5C Sales**. In the **Show Table** dialog box, click **Close**. Resize the field lists.

a. From the **5C Employees** table, add the **Last Name** and **First Name** fields. From the **5C Sales** table, add the **Timecard Date** and **Sales** fields. **Run** the query to display the sales by date. **Save** the query as **Lastname Firstname 5C Sales by Date** and then **Close** the query.

b. On the Ribbon, click the **CREATE tab**. In the **Queries group**, click the **Query Wizard** button. In the **New Query** dialog box, click **Crosstab Query Wizard**, and then click **OK**. In the middle of the dialog box, under **View**, click the **Queries** option button. In the list of queries, click **Query: 5C Sales by Date**, and then click **Next**.

c. Under **Available Fields**, double-click **Last Name** and **First Name**, and then click **Next**. In the displayed list of fields, double-click **Timecard Date**. Select an interval of **Date**. Click **Next**. Under **Functions**, click **Sum**. On the left side of the **Crosstab Query Wizard** dialog box, above the **Sample** area, clear the **Yes, include row sums** check box, and then click **Next**.

d. Under **What do you want to name your query?**, select the existing text, type **Lastname Firstname 5C Crosstab Query** and then click **Finish**. Adjust all of the column widths to display the entire field name and the data in each field. The result is a spreadsheet view of total sales by employee by payroll date. View the query in **Print Preview**, ensuring that the query prints on one page. If you are instructed to submit this result, create a paper or electronic printout. **Close** the query, saving changes.

5 ▶ On the **CREATE tab**, in the **Queries group**, click the **Query Wizard** button. In the **New Query** dialog box, click **Find Duplicates Query Wizard**, and then click **OK**.

a. In the first **Find Duplicates Query Wizard** dialog box, in the list of tables, click **Table: 5C Payroll**, and then click **Next**. Under **Available fields**, double-click **EmpID** to move it under **Duplicate-value fields**, and then click **Next**.

b. Under **Available fields**, add all of the fields to the **Additional query fields** box. Click **Next**. Click

Finish to accept the suggested query name—*Find duplicates for Lastname Firstname 5C Payroll*. Adjust all column widths. View the query in **Print Preview**, ensuring that the query prints on one page. If you are instructed to submit this result, create a paper or electronic printout. **Close** the query, saving changes.

6 ▶ On the **CREATE tab**, in the **Queries group**, click the **Query Wizard** button. In the **New Query** dialog box, click **Find Unmatched Query Wizard**, and then click **OK**.

a. In the first **Find Unmatched Query Wizard** dialog box, in the list of tables, click Table: 5C Employees, if necessary, and then click **Next**. In the list of tables, click **Table: 5C Payroll**, and then click **Next**. Under **Fields in '5C Employees'**, if necessary, click EmpID. Under **Fields in 5C Payroll**, if necessary, click EmpID. Click the **<=>** button. Click **Next**.

b. Under **Available fields**, double-click **EmpID**, **Last Name**, and **First Name** to move the field names under **Selected fields**. Click **Next**. In the last dialog box, under **What would you like to name your query?**, type **Lastname Firstname 5C Find Unmatched** and then click **Finish**.

c. Adjust all column widths. View the query in **Print Preview**, ensuring that the query prints on one page. If you are instructed to submit this result, create a paper or electronic printout. **Close** the query, saving changes if necessary.

7 ▶ **Create** a new query in **Query Design**. Add the **5C Employees** table and the **5C Timecard** table to the Query design workspace, and then **Close** the **Show Table** dialog box. Resize the field lists.

a. From the **5C Employees** field list, add **Last Name** and **First Name** to the first and second columns in the design grid. From the **5C Timecard** field list, add **Timecard Date** and **Hours** to the third and fourth columns in the design grid.

b. In the **Criteria row** under **Timecard Date** field, type **[Enter Date]**

c. In the **Criteria row**, right-click in the **Hours** field, and then click **Zoom**. In the **Zoom** dialog box, type **Between [Enter the minimum Hours] And [Enter the maximum Hours]** and then click **OK**.

(Project 5C Employee Payroll continues on the next page)

CHAPTER REVIEW

d. **Run** the query. In the **Enter Parameter Value** dialog box, type **6/29/17** and then click **OK**. Type **60** and then click **OK**. Type **80** and then click **OK**. Three employees have worked between 60 and 80 hours during the pay period for 6/29/17. They have earned vacation hours.

e. Adjust all column widths, and **Save** the query as **Lastname Firstname 5C Parameter Query** View the query in **Print Preview**, ensuring that the query prints on one page. If you are instructed to submit this result, create a paper or electronic printout. **Close** the query.

8 ▸ Open the **Navigation Pane**, **Close** the database, and then **Exit** Access.

9 ▸ As directed by your instructor, submit your database and the paper or electronic printouts of the six queries that are the result of this project. Specifically,

in this project, using your own name you created the following database and printouts or electronic printouts:

1. Lastname_Firstname_5C_Employee_Payroll	Database file
2. Lastname Firstname 5C Net Pay	Query (printed or electronic printout)
3. Lastname Firstname 5C Sales by Employee	Query (printed or electronic printout)
4. Lastname Firstname 5C Crosstab Query	Query (printed or electronic printout)
5. Find duplicates for Lastname Firstname 5C Payroll	Query (printed or electronic printout)
6. Lastname Firstname 5C Find Unmatched	Query (printed or electronic printout)
7. Lastname Firstname 5C Parameter Query	Query (printed or electronic printout)

END | You have completed Project 5C

CHAPTER REVIEW

Skills Review Project 5D Clearance Sale

Apply 5B skills from these Objectives:

6 Create a Make Table Query

7 Create an Append Query

8 Create a Delete Query

9 Create an Update Query

10 Modify the Join Type

Miles Gorden, purchasing manager for S-Boards, Inc. Surf and Snowboard Shop, must keep the tables in the database up to date and ensure that the queries display pertinent information. Two of the suppliers, Super Wave Boards and Boot City, will no longer provide merchandise for S-Boards, Inc. Surf and Snowboard Shop. This merchandise must be moved to a new discontinued items table. In the following Skills Review, you will create action queries that will create a new table, update records in a table, append records to a table, and delete records from a table. You will also modify the join type of relationships to display different subsets of the data when the query is run. Your completed queries will look similar to Figure 5.50.

PROJECT FILES

For Project 5D, you will need the following files:

a05D_Store_Items

a05D_Warehouse_Items

You will save your databases as:

Lastname_Firstname_5D_Store_Items

Lastname_Firstname_5D_Warehouse_Items

PROJECT RESULTS

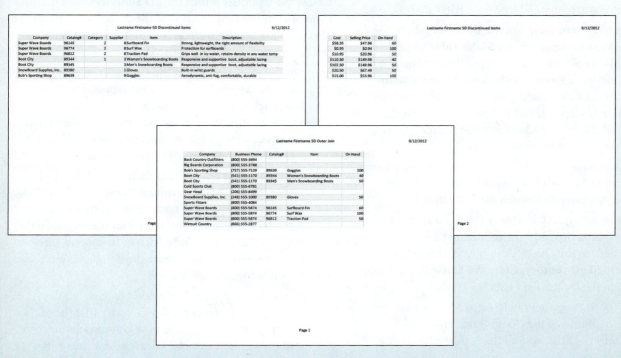

FIGURE 5.50

(Project 5D Clearance Sale continues on the next page)

CHAPTER REVIEW

1 **Start** Access. Locate and open the **a05D_Store_Items** file. Display **Backstage** view. **Save** the database in your **Access Chapter 5** folder as **Lastname_Firstname_5D_Store_Items**

a. If necessary, enable the content or add the Access Chapter 5 folder to the Trust Center.

b. Rename the tables by adding your **Lastname Firstname** to the beginning of each table name. **Close** the **Navigation Pane**.

2 Create a new query in **Query Design**. From the **Show Table** dialog box, add the following tables to the Query design workspace: **5D Suppliers** and **5D Inventory**. **Close** the **Show Table** dialog box, and then Resize the field lists.

a. From the **5D Suppliers** field list, add **Company** to the first column of the design grid. From the **5D Inventory** field list, double-click each field to add them all to the design grid.

b. In the design grid, click in the **Criteria row** under **Supplier**, type **8** and then **Run** the query. Notice that three items are supplied by *Super Wave Boards*.

c. Switch to **Design** view. On the **DESIGN tab**, in the **Query Type group**, click the **Make Table** button. In the **Make Table** dialog box, in the **Table Name** box, type **Lastname Firstname 5D Discontinued Items** In the **Make Table** dialog box, be sure that **Current Database** is selected, and then click **OK**. **Run** the query. In the displayed message box, click **Yes** to paste the rows to the new table.

d. **Close** the query, click **Yes** in the message box asking if you want to save changes, and then name the query **Lastname Firstname 5D SWB Items**

3 Create a new query in **Query Design**. From the **Show Table** dialog box, add the following tables, in the order specified, to the Query design workspace: **5D Suppliers** and **5D Inventory**. **Close** the **Show Table** dialog box, and then Resize the field lists.

a. From the **5D Suppliers** field list, add **Company** to the first column of the design grid. From the **5D Inventory** field list, add all fields in the field list to the design grid.

b. In the design grid, click in the **Criteria row** under **Supplier**, type **3** and then **Run** the query. Notice that one item is supplied by *Boot City*.

c. Switch to **Design** view. On the **DESIGN tab**, in the **Query Type group**, click the **Append** button. In the **Append** dialog box, click the **Table Name arrow**, and from the displayed list, click **5D Discontinued Items**, and then click **OK**.

d. **Run** the query. In the displayed message box, click **Yes** to append one row. **Close** the query, and then save it as **Lastname Firstname 5D Append Items**

4 On the Access window title bar, click the **Minimize** button. **Start** a second instance of Access. Navigate to the location where the student data files for this textbook are saved. Locate and open the **a05D_Warehouse_Items** file. Save the database in your **Access Chapter 5** folder as **Lastname_Firstname_5D_Warehouse_Items** If necessary, enable the content or add the Access Chapter 5 folder to the Trust Center.

5 Create a new query in **Query Design**. From the **Show Table** dialog box, add the **5D Suppliers** table and the **5D Discontinued Items** table to the Query design workspace, and then close the **Show Table** dialog box. Resize the field lists. From the **5D Suppliers** field list, add **Company** to the first column of the design grid. From the **5D Discontinued Items** field list, add all of the fields to the design grid in the order listed.

a. On the **DESIGN tab**, in the **Query Type group**, click the **Append** button. In the **Append** dialog box, click the **Another Database** option button, and then click the **Browse** button. Navigate to your **Access Chapter 5** folder, and then double-click **Lastname_Firstname_5D_Store_Items**.

b. In the **Append** dialog box, click the **Table Name arrow**, click **5D Discontinued Items**, and then click **OK**. **Save** the query as **Lastname Firstname 5D Append Warehouse** and then **Run** the query. In the displayed message box, click **Yes** to append three rows. **Close** the query. **Close** the database, and then **Exit** this instance of Access.

c. If necessary, from the Windows taskbar, click the 5D_Store_Items database. Verify that the **5D Discontinued Items** table now contains seven rows, and then close the table. Create a new query in **Query Design**. Add the **5D Inventory** table to the Query design workspace, and then **Close** the **Show Table** dialog box.

(Project 5D Clearance Sale continues on the next page)

CHAPTER REVIEW

d. Resize the field list. From the field list, add **Catalog#** and **On Hand**, in this order, to the first and second columns in the design grid. In the design grid, click in the **Criteria row** under **On Hand**, type **0** and then **Run** the query to display one record.

e. Switch to **Design** view. In the Query design workspace, right-click in the empty space. From the displayed shortcut menu, point to **Query Type**, and then click **Delete Query**.

f. Save the query as **Lastname Firstname 5D Delete Zero Inventory** and then **Run** the query. In the message box stating that *You are about to delete 1 row(s) from the specified table*, click **Yes**. **Close** the query. You have removed this item from the inventory.

6 Create a new query in **Query Design**. Add the **5D Discontinued Items** table to the Query design workspace, and then **Close** the **Show Table** dialog box. Resize the field list.

a. In the **5D Discontinued Items** field list, double-click **Catalog#** to add the field to the first column of the design grid. Then add the **Selling Price** field to the second column of the design grid.

b. On the **DESIGN tab**, in the **Query Type group**, click the **Update** button. In the design grid, click in the **Update To row** under **Selling Price**, and then type **[Selling Price]*0.75**

c. Save the query as **Lastname Firstname 5D Discounted Selling Prices** and then **Run** the query. In the message box stating that *You are about to update 7 row(s)*, click **Yes**. **Close** the query.

d. Open the **Navigation Pane**, and then double-click the **5D Discontinued Items** table to open it in **Datasheet** view. Close the **Navigation Pane**. Adjust all column widths. View the table in **Print Preview**. If you are instructed to submit this result, create a paper or electronic printout to fit on one page in **Landscape** orientation. **Close** the table, saving changes.

7 Create a new query in **Query Design**. From the **Show Table** dialog box, add the **5D Suppliers** table and the **5D Discontinued Items** table to the Query design workspace, and then **Close** the **Show Table** dialog box.

a. Resize both field lists. From the **5D Suppliers** table, drag the **ID** field to the **5D Discontinued Items** table **Supplier** field to create a join between the tables.

b. From the **5D Suppliers** field list, add **Company** and **Business Phone** to the first and second columns in the design grid. From the **5D Discontinued Items** field list, add **Catalog#**, **Item**, and **On Hand**, in this order, to the design grid. In the design grid, click in the **Sort row** under **Company**, click the **arrow**, and then click **Ascending**. **Run** the query.

c. Switch to **Design** view. Verify that the **5D Suppliers** table appears on the left, and the **5D Discontinued Items** table is on the right. Correct as necessary. In the Query design workspace, double-click the **join line** to display the **Join Properties** dialog box. Click the option button next to **2**, and then click **OK**. **Run** the query. Adjust all column widths. This query displays all of the supplier companies used by the shop, not just those with discontinued items.

d. Save the query as **Lastname Firstname 5D Outer Join** View the query in **Print Preview** in **Landscape** orientation. If you are instructed to submit this result, create a paper or electronic printout. **Close** the query.

8 Open the **Navigation Pane**, **Close** the database, and then **Exit** Access.

9 As directed by your instructor, submit your databases and the paper or electronic printouts of the two objects—one table and one query—that are the result of this project. Specifically, in this project, using your own name you created the following databases and printouts or electronic printouts:

1. Lastname_Firstname_5D_ Store_Items	Database file
2. Lastname_Firstname_5D_ Warehouse_Items	Database file
3. Lastname Firstname 5D Discontinued Items	Table (printed or electronic printout)
4. Lastname Firstname 5D Outer Join	Query (printed or electronic printout)

END | You have completed Project 5D

CONTENT-BASED ASSESSMENTS

Mastering Access   Project 5E Surfing Lessons

Gina Pollard, one of the owners of S-Boards, Inc. Surf and Snowboard Shop, has a database containing student, instructor, and surfing lesson data. In the following Mastering Access project, you will create special-purpose queries to calculate data, summarize and group data, display data in a spreadsheet-like format, and find duplicate and unmatched records. You will also create a query that prompts an individual to enter the criteria. Your completed queries will look similar to Figure 5.51.

Apply 5A skills from these Objectives:

1 Create Calculated Fields in a Query

2 Use Aggregate Functions in a Query

3 Create a Crosstab Query

4 Find Duplicate and Unmatched Records

5 Create a Parameter Query

PROJECT FILES

For Project 5E, you will need the following file:

a05E_Surfing_Lessons

You will save your database as:

Lastname_Firstname_5E_Surfing_Lessons

PROJECT RESULTS

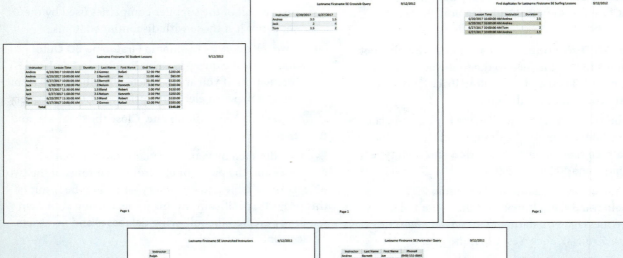

FIGURE 5.51

(Project 5E Surfing Lessons continues on the next page)

CONTENT-BASED ASSESSMENTS

1 **Start** Access. Locate and open the **a05E_Surfing_Lessons** file. Display **Backstage** view. Save the database in your **Access Chapter 5** folder as **Lastname_Firstname_5E_Surfing_Lessons** If necessary, enable the content or add the Access Chapter 5 folder to the Trust Center. Rename the tables by adding your **Lastname Firstname** to the beginning of each table name.

2 **Create** a query in **Query Design** using the **5E Surfing Lessons** table and the **5E Students** table. From the **5E Surfing Lessons** table, add the **Instructor** field, the **Lesson Time** field, and the **Duration** field to the first, second, and third columns of the design grid. From the **5E Students** table, add the **Last Name** and **First Name** fields to the fourth and fifth columns.

3 In the sixth column of the design grid, add a calculated field. In the **field name row**, type **End Time:[Duration]/24+[Lesson Time]** Display the field properties sheet, and then format this field as **Medium Time**. This field will display the time the lesson ends.

4 In the first blank column, in the **field name row**, add the calculated field **Fee:[Duration]*80** from the field properties sheet, and then format this field as **Currency**. Surfing lessons cost $80.00 an hour.

5 In the **Instructor** field, in the **Sort row**, click **Ascending**. In the **Lesson Time** field, in the **Sort row**, click **Ascending**. **Run** the query.

6 On the **HOME tab**, in the **Records group**, click the **Totals** button. In the **Fee** column, in the **Total row**, click the **down arrow**, and then click **Average**. Adjust field widths as necessary.

7 **Save** the query as **Lastname Firstname 5E Student Lessons** View the query in **Print Preview**, ensuring that the query prints on one page in **Landscape** orientation. If you are instructed to submit this result, create a paper or electronic printout. **Close** the query.

8 **Create** a new query using the **Crosstab Query Wizard**. Select the **Query: 5E Student Lessons**. Click **Next**. From the **Available Fields**, add **Instructor** to the **Selected Fields** column. Click **Next**. Double-click **Lesson Time**, and then click **Date**. Click **Next**. From the **Fields column**, select **Duration**, and then from **Functions**, select **Sum**. Clear the **Yes, include row sums** check box.

9 Click **Next**. Name the query **Lastname Firstname 5E Crosstab Query** Select **View the query**, and then click **Finish**. This query displays the instructor and the number of hours he or she taught by date. Adjust field widths as necessary.

10 View the query in **Print Preview**, ensuring that the query prints on one page. If you are instructed to submit this result, create a paper or electronic printout. **Close** the query, saving changes.

11 Click the **Query Wizard** button. In the **New Query** dialog box, click **Find Duplicates Query Wizard**. Search the **Table: 5E Surfing Lessons**, and select the **Lesson Time** field for duplicate information. Click **Next**. From **Available fields**, add the **Instructor** and **Duration** fields to the **Additional query fields** column. Accept the default name for the query. Click **Finish**. The query results show that there are duplicate lesson times. Adjust field widths as necessary.

12 View the query in **Print Preview**, ensuring that the query prints on one page. If you are instructed to submit this result, create a paper or electronic printout. **Close** and **Save** the query.

13 Click the **Query Wizard** button. In the **New Query** dialog box, click **Find Unmatched Query Wizard**. Select **Table: 5E Surfing Instructors**. From the **Which table or query contains the related records?** dialog box, click **Table: 5E Surfing Lessons**. Click **Instructor** as the **Matching** field. Display the one field **Instructor** in the query results. Name the query **Lastname Firstname 5E Unmatched Instructors** and then click **Finish**. Ralph is the only instructor who has no students.

14 View the query in **Print Preview**. If you are instructed to submit this result, create a paper or electronic printout. **Close** the query.

15 **Create** a query in **Design** view using the **5E Surfing Lessons** table and the **5E Students** table. From the **5E Surfing Lessons** table, add the **Instructor** field. From the **5E Students** table, add the **Last Name**, **First Name**, and **Phone#** fields in that order to the design grid. In the **Criteria row** under **Instructor**, type **[Enter Instructor's First Name]**

16 **Run** the query. In the **Enter Parameter Value** dialog box, type **Andrea** and then press Enter. The query displays Andrea's students and their phone numbers.

17 **Save** the query as **Lastname Firstname 5E Parameter Query** Adjust field widths as necessary.

(Project 5E Surfing Lessons continues on the next page)

CONTENT-BASED ASSESSMENTS

18 View the query in **Print Preview**, ensuring that the query prints on one page. If you are instructed to submit this result, create a paper or electronic printout. **Close** the query.

19 Open the **Navigation Pane**, **Close** the database, and then **Exit** Access.

20 As directed by your instructor, submit your database and the paper or electronic printouts of the five queries that are the result of this project. Specifically, in this project, using your own name you created the following database and printouts or electronic printouts:

1. Lastname_Firstname_5E_Surfing_Lessons	Database file
2. Lastname Firstname 5E Student Lessons	Query (printed or electronic printout)
3. Lastname Firstname 5E Crosstab Query	Query (printed or electronic printout)
4. Lastname Firstname Find duplicates…	Query (printed or electronic printout)
5. Lastname Firstname 5E Unmatched Instructors	Query (printed or electronic printout)
6. Lastname Firstname 5E Parameter Query	Query (printed or electronic printout)

END | You have completed Project 5E

CONTENT-BASED ASSESSMENTS

Mastering Access Project 5F Gift Cards

Karen Walker, sales manager for S-Boards, Inc. Surf and Snowboard Shop, has decided to offer gift cards for purchase at the shop. She has a database of the employees and the details of the cards they have sold. In the following Mastering Access project, you will create action queries that will create a new table, update records in a table, append records to a table, and delete records from a table. You will also modify the join type of the relationship to display a different subset of the data when the query is run. Your completed queries will look similar to Figure 5.52.

Apply 5B skills from these Objectives:

- **6** Create a Make Table Query
- **7** Create an Append Query
- **8** Create a Delete Query
- **9** Create an Update Query
- **10** Modify the Join Type

PROJECT FILES

For Project 5F, you will need the following file:

a05F_Gift_Cards

You will save your database as:

Lastname_Firstname_5F_Gift_Cards

PROJECT RESULTS

FIGURE 5.52

(Project 5F Gift Cards continues on the next page)

CONTENT-BASED ASSESSMENTS

1 **Start** Access. Locate and open the **a05F_Gift_Cards** file. Display **Backstage** view. Save the database in your **Access Chapter 5** folder as **Lastname_Firstname_5F_Gift_ Cards** If necessary, enable the content or add the Access Chapter 5 folder to the Trust Center. Rename the tables by adding your **Lastname Firstname** to the beginning of each table name.

2 Create a new query in **Query Design**. To the Query design workspace, add the **5F Employees**, **5F Sales**, and the **5F Inventory** tables. From the **5F Employees** table, add the **First Name** and **Last Name** fields to the first and second columns of the design grid. From the **5F Sales** table, add the following fields to the design grid in the order specified: **Sales Date** and **Quantity**. From the **5F Inventory** table, add the **Item** and **Cost** fields.

3 In the **Criteria row** under **Item**, type **Gift Cards** In the **Criteria row** under **Cost**, type **25 Or 50 Sort** the **Last Name** field in **Ascending** order.

4 On the **DESIGN tab**, click the **Make Table** button. Name the table **Lastname Firstname 5F $25 or $50 Gift Cards** Select **Current Database**, click **OK**, and then **Run** the query. **Close** the query, saving it as **Lastname Firstname 5F Make Table Query** Open the **5F $25 or $50 Gift Cards** table to display the two gift card purchases. **Close** the table.

5 Create a new query in **Query Design**. To the Query design workspace, add the **5F Employees**, **5F Sales**, and the **5F Inventory** tables. From the **5F Employees** table, add the **First Name** and **Last Name** fields to the first and second columns of the design grid. From the **5F Sales** table, add the following fields to the design grid in the following order: **Sales Date** and **Quantity**. From the **5F Inventory** table, add the **Item** and **Cost** fields.

6 In the **Criteria row** under **Item**, type **Gift Cards** In the **Criteria row** under **Cost**, type **100 Or 250 Sort** the **Last Name** field in **Ascending** order.

7 Click the **Append** button, and then append the records to the **5F $25 or $50 Gift Cards** table. Click **OK**. **Run** the query. Click **Yes** to append three rows. **Close** the query, saving it as **Lastname Firstname 5F Append Query** Open the **5F $25 or $50 Gift Cards** table to display all gift card purchases. **Close** the table, and then rename it **Lastname Firstname 5F Gift Cards**

8 View the table in **Print Preview**, ensuring that the table prints on one page. If you are instructed to submit this result, create a paper or electronic printout. **Close** the table.

9 Create a new query in **Query Design**. Add the **5F Inventory** table to the Query design workspace. From the **5F Inventory** table, add the **Catalog#** and **Item** fields to the first and second columns of the design grid. In the design grid, click in the **Criteria row** under **Item**, and type **Gift Cards**

10 **Run** the query to view the results. Switch to **Design** view, click the **Query Type: Delete** button, and then **Run** the query. Click **Yes** to delete five gift cards from the **5F Inventory** table. The gift cards are not to be counted as inventory items. **Close** and **Save** the query, naming it **Lastname Firstname 5F Delete Query**

11 Open the **5F Inventory** table. If you are instructed to submit this result, create a paper or electronic printout in **Landscape** orientation. **Close** the table.

12 Create a new query in **Query Design**. Add the **5F Employees** table to the Query design workspace. From the **5F Employees** table, add **Postal Code** to the first column of the design grid. In the design grid, click in the **Criteria row** under **Postal Code**, and then type **972*** **Run** the query to view the results. Switch to **Design** view. Click the **Query Type: Update** button.

13 In the design grid, click in the **Update To row** under **Postal Code**, and then type **92710**

14 **Run** the query. Click **Yes** to update two rows. **Close** the query, saving it as **Lastname Firstname 5F Update Postal Code** Open the **5F Employees** table. View the table in **Print Preview**, ensuring that the table prints on one page. If you are instructed to submit this result, create a paper or electronic printout. **Close** the table.

15 Create a new query in **Query Design**. Add the **5F Employees** and **5F Gift Cards** tables to the Query design workspace. From the **5F Employees** field list, click **Last Name**, and then drag to the **5F Gift Cards Last Name** field. Double-click the **join line**, and then select option **2**.

16 From the **5F Employees** field list, add **First Name** and **Last Name** to the first two columns of the design grid. From the **5F Gift Cards** field list, add **Cost** and **Quantity** field, in this order, to the design grid. **Run** the query to

(Project 5F Gift Cards continues on the next page)

CONTENT-BASED ASSESSMENTS

display the results, which include all 14 employees and not just gift card sellers. **Save** the query as **Lastname Firstname 5F Modified Join**

17 View the table in **Print Preview**, ensuring that the table prints on one page. If you are instructed to submit this result, create a paper or electronic printout. **Close** the query.

18 **Close** the database, and then **Exit** Access.

19 As directed by your instructor, submit your database and the paper or electronic printouts of the four objects—three tables and one query—that are the result of this project. Specifically, in this project, using your own name you created the following database and printouts or electronic printouts:

1. Lastname_Firstname_5F_Gift_Cards	Database file
2. Lastname Firstname 5F Gift Cards	Table (printed or electronic printout)
3. Lastname Firstname 5F Inventory	Table (printed or electronic printout)
4. Lastname Firstname 5F Employees	Table (printed or electronic printout)
5. Lastname Firstname 5F Modified Join	Query (printed or electronic printout)

END | You have completed Project 5F

CONTENT-BASED ASSESSMENTS

Mastering Access	Project 5G Advertising Options

Apply 5A and 5B skills from these Objectives:

1 Create Calculated Fields in a Query
2 Use Aggregate Functions in a Query
3 Create a Crosstab Query
9 Create an Update Query

Steven Michaels, one of the owners of S-Boards, Inc., is responsible for all of the advertising for the business. In the following Mastering Access project, you will create special-purpose queries to calculate data, and then summarize and group data for advertising cost analysis. You will also create a query that prompts an individual to enter the criteria for a specific type of advertisement media. Your completed queries will look similar to Figure 5.53.

PROJECT FILES

For Project 5G, you will need the following file:

a05G_Advertising_Options

You will save your database as:

Lastname_Firstname_5G_Advertising_Options

PROJECT RESULTS

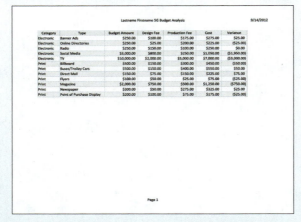

FIGURE 5.53

(Project 5G Advertising Options continues on the next page)

CONTENT-BASED ASSESSMENTS

1 **Start** Access. Locate and open the **a05G_Advertising_Options** file. Display **Backstage** view. Save the database in your Access Chapter 5 folder as **Lastname_Firstname_5G_Advertising_Options** If necessary, enable the content or add the Access Chapter 5 folder to the Trust Center. Rename the table by adding your **Lastname Firstname** to the beginning of the table names. Close the **Navigation Pane.**

2 Create a new query in **Query Design**. From the **5G Categories** table, add the **Category** field to the design grid. From the **5G Advertisements** table, add the **Type, Budget Amount, Design Fee,** and **Production Fee** fields to the design grid in this order.

3 In the first blank field column, add a calculated field. Type **Cost:[Design Fee]+[Production Fee]** In the next blank field column, add a second calculated field: **Variance:[Cost]-[Budget Amount]**

4 **Run** the query. Save it as **Lastname Firstname 5G Budget Analysis.** View the results in **Print Preview**, ensuring that it fits on one page in **Landscape** orientation. If you are instructed to submit this result, create a paper or electronic printout. **Close** the query.

5 Create a new query in **Query Design**. From the **5G Categories** table, add the **Category** field to the design grid. From the **5G Advertisements** table, add the **Objective** and **Budget Amount** fields to the design grid. On the **DESIGN tab**, in the **Show/Hide group**, click the **Totals** button. In the design grid, in the **Total row** under **Budget Amount**, click **Sum.**

6 **Run** the query. Save it as **Lastname Firstname 5G Budget by Category and Objective** View the results in **Print Preview**, ensuring that it fits on one page. If you are instructed to submit this result, create a paper or electronic printout. **Close** the query.

7 Create a new crosstab query using the **Query Wizard**. Select the **Query: 5G Budget Analysis.** For row headings, use **Type**, and for column headings, use **Category**. Select **Cost** for the calculated field, using the **Sum** function. Do not summarize each row. Save it as **Lastname Firstname 5G Crosstab Query**

8 Click **Finish** to view the cost in relation to the response rate for each type of advertisement.

9 View the query in **Print Preview**, ensuring that the query prints on one page. If you are instructed to submit this result, create a paper or electronic printout. **Close** the query.

10 Create a new query in **Query Design**. From the **5G Categories** table, add the **Category** field to the design grid. From the **5G Advertisements** table, add the **Budget Amount** field to the design grid. In the design grid, click in the **Criteria row** under **Category**, and type **Electronic**

11 Click the **Query Type: Update** button. In the design grid, click in the **Update To row** under **Budget Amount**, and type **[Budget Amount]*1.15**

12 **Run** the query. Click **Yes** to update five rows. **Close** the query, saving it as **Lastname Firstname 5G Update Electronics Budget** Open the **Navigation Pane.** Open the **5G Advertisements** table. View the table in **Print Preview**, ensuring that the table prints on one page. If you are instructed to submit this result, create a paper or electronic printout. **Close** the table.

13 **Close** the database, and then **Exit** Access.

14 As directed by your instructor, submit your database and the paper or electronic printouts of the four objects—three queries and one table—that are the result of this project. Specifically, in this project, using your own name you created the following database and printouts or electronic printouts:

1. Lastname_Firstname_5G_ Advertising_Options	Database file
2. Lastname Firstname 5G Budget Analysis	Query (printed or electronic printout)
3. Lastname Firstname 5G Budget by Category and Objective	Query (printed or electronic printout)
4. Lastname Firstname 5G Crosstab Query	Query (printed or electronic printout)
5. Lastname Firstname 5G Advertisements	Table (printed or electronic printout)

END | You have completed Project 5G

CONTENT-BASED ASSESSMENTS

GO! Fix It	Project 5H Contests	Online

GO! Make It	Project 5I Ski Trips	Online

GO! Solve It	Project 5J Applications	Online

Apply a combination of the 5A and 5B skills.

GO! Solve It	Project 5K Ski Apparel

PROJECT FILES

For Project 5K, you will need the following file:

a05K_Ski_Apparel

You will save your database as:

Lastname_Firstname_5K_Ski_Apparel

Miles Gorden is the purchasing manager for S-Boards, Inc. It is his responsibility to keep the clothing inventory current and fashionable. You have been asked to help him with this task. From the student files that accompany this textbook, open the **a05K_Ski_Apparel** database file, and then save the database in your **Access Chapter 5** folder as **Lastname_Firstname_5K_Ski_Apparel**

The database consists of a table of ski apparel for youth, women, and men. Create a query to identify the inventory by status of the items (promotional, in stock, and discontinued clothing), and the number of items that are in each category. Update the selling price of the discontinued items to 80 percent of the current selling price. Use a make table query to place the promotional items into their own table and use a delete query to remove those items from the *5K Ski Apparel* table. Save your queries using your last and first names followed by the query type. View the queries in Print Preview, ensuring that each query prints on one page. If you are instructed to submit this result, create a paper or electronic printout. Close the queries, and then close the database.

Performance Level

		Exemplary	Proficient	Developing
Performance Criteria	**Create 5K Totals Query**	Query created to display inventory by status	Query created with no more than two missing elements	Query created with more than two missing elements
	Create 5K Update Query	Query created to update clearance sale prices	Query created with no more than two missing elements	Query created with more than two missing elements
	Create 5K Make Table Query	Query created to make a table for promotional items	Query created with no more than two missing elements	Query created with more than two missing elements
	Create 5K Delete Query	Query created to delete promotional items from the Ski Apparel table	Query created with no more than two missing elements	Query created with more than two missing elements

END | You have completed Project 5K

OUTCOMES-BASED ASSESSMENTS

RUBRIC

The following outcomes-based assessments are open-ended assessments. That is, there is no specific correct result; your result will depend on your approach to the information provided. Make Professional Quality your goal. Use the following scoring rubric to guide you in how to approach the problem and then to evaluate how well your approach solves the problem.

The *criteria*—Software Mastery, Content, Format and Layout, and Process—represent the knowledge and skills you have gained that you can apply to solving the problem. The *levels of performance*—Professional Quality, Approaching Professional Quality, or Needs Quality Improvements—help you and your instructor evaluate your result.

	Your completed project is of Professional Quality if you:	Your completed project is Approaching Professional Quality if you:	Your completed project Needs Quality Improvements if you:
1-Software Mastery	Choose and apply the most appropriate skills, tools, and features and identify efficient methods to solve the problem.	Choose and apply some appropriate skills, tools, and features, but not in the most efficient manner.	Choose inappropriate skills, tools, or features, or are inefficient in solving the problem.
2-Content	Construct a solution that is clear and well organized, contains content that is accurate, appropriate to the audience and purpose, and is complete. Provide a solution that contains no errors in spelling, grammar, or style.	Construct a solution in which some components are unclear, poorly organized, inconsistent, or incomplete. Misjudge the needs of the audience. Have some errors in spelling, grammar, or style, but the errors do not detract from comprehension.	Construct a solution that is unclear, incomplete, or poorly organized; contains some inaccurate or inappropriate content; and contains many errors in spelling, grammar, or style. Do not solve the problem.
3-Format & Layout	Format and arrange all elements to communicate information and ideas, clarify function, illustrate relationships, and indicate relative importance.	Apply appropriate format and layout features to some elements, but not others. Overuse features, causing minor distraction.	Apply format and layout that does not communicate information or ideas clearly. Do not use format and layout features to clarify function, illustrate relationships, or indicate relative importance. Use available features excessively, causing distraction.
4-Process	Use an organized approach that integrates planning, development, self-assessment, revision, and reflection.	Demonstrate an organized approach in some areas, but not others; or, use an insufficient process of organization throughout.	Do not use an organized approach to solve the problem.

OUTCOMES-BASED ASSESSMENTS

PROJECT FILES

For Project 5L, you will need the following file:

a05L_Surfboards

You will save your document as:

Lastname_Firstname_5L_Surfboards

Miles Gorden, Purchasing Manager for S-Boards, Inc., is stocking the shop with a variety of surfboards and accessories for the upcoming season. In this project, you will open the **a05L_Surfboards** database and create queries to perform special functions. Save the database as **Lastname_Firstname_5L_Surfboards** Create a query to display the item, cost, selling price, on hand, and two calculated fields: Item Profit by subtracting the cost from the selling price, and Inventory Profit by multiplying Item Profit by the number on hand for each item. Be sure both fields display as Currency. Include a sum for the Inventory Profit column at the bottom of the query results. Check the supplier against the inventory using a find unmatched records query; display all fields in the supplier table. Create a query to show the organization that supplies each item, its email address, and then the item and on hand fields for each item in the inventory. Before running the query, create an outer join query using the *5L Suppliers* table and the *5L Inventory* table. Save your queries using your last and first names followed by the query type. View the queries in Print Preview, ensuring that the queries print on one page. If you are instructed to submit this result, create a paper or electronic printout. Close the queries.

END | You have completed Project 5L

GO! Think   Project 5M Shop Promotions   Online

You and GO!   Project 5N Club Directory   Online

Customizing Forms and Reports

GO! to Work
Video A6

6 ACCESS 2013

PROJECT 6A

OUTCOMES
Customize forms.

OBJECTIVES

1. Create a Form in Design View
2. Change and Add Controls
3. Format a Form
4. Make a Form User Friendly

PROJECT 6B

OUTCOMES
Customize reports.

OBJECTIVES

5. Create a Report Based on a Query Using a Wizard
6. Create a Report in Design View
7. Add Controls to a Report
8. Group, Sort, and Total Records in Design View

Jacek Chabraszewsk

In This Chapter

Forms provide a way to enter, edit, and display data from underlying tables. You have created forms using the Form button and wizard. Forms can also be created in Design view. Access provides tools to enhance the appearance of forms, like adding color, backgrounds, borders, or instructions to the person using the form. Forms can also be created from multiple tables if a relationship exists between the tables.

Reports display data in a professional-looking format. Like forms, reports can be created using a wizard or in Design view, and they can all be enhanced using Access tools. Reports can be based on tables or queries.

Rosebud Cafe is a "quick, casual" franchise restaurant chain with headquarters in Florida and locations throughout the United States. The founders wanted to create a restaurant where fresh flavors would be available at reasonable prices in a bright, comfortable atmosphere. The menu features quality ingredients in offerings like grilled meat and vegetable skewers, wraps, salads, frozen yogurt, smoothies, coffee drinks, and seasonal favorites. All 81 outlets offer wireless Internet connections and meeting space, making Rosebud Cafe the perfect place for groups and people who want some quiet time or to work with others.

PROJECT
6A Locations

PROJECT ACTIVITIES

In Activities 6.01 through 6.10, you will help Linda Kay, president, and James Winchell, vice president of franchising, create robust forms to match the needs of Rosebud Cafe. For example, the forms can include color and different types of controls and can manipulate data from several tables. You will customize your forms to make them easier to use and more attractive. Your completed form will look similar to Figure 6.1.

PROJECT FILES

For Project 6A, you will need the following files:

a06A_Locations
a06A_Logo
a06A_Background

You will save your database as:

Lastname_Firstname_6A_Locations

PROJECT RESULTS

FIGURE 6.1 Project 6A Locations

Video A6-1

Forms are usually created using the Form tool or the Form Wizard and then modified in Design view to suit your needs. Use Design view to create a form when these tools do not meet your needs, or if you want more control in the creation of a form. Creating or modifying a form in Design view is a common technique when additional controls, such as combo boxes or images, need to be added to the form.

Activity 6.01 | Creating a Form in Design View

In this activity, you will create a form in Design view that will enable employees to enter the daily sales data for each franchise of Rosebud Cafe.

1 ▶ **Start** Access. Navigate to the location where the student data files for this textbook are saved. Locate and open the **a06A_Locations** file. Display **Backstage** view. Click **Save As**, and then, under *File Types*, double-click **Save Database As**. In the **Save As** dialog box, navigate to the drive on which you will be saving your folders and projects for this chapter. Create a new folder named **Access Chapter 6** and then save the database as **Lastname_Firstname_6A_ Locations** in the folder.

2 ▶ Enable the content or add the **Access Chapter 6** folder to the Trust Center.

3 ▶ In the **Navigation Pane**, double-click **6A Sales** to open the table in **Datasheet** view. Take a moment to examine the fields in the table. In any record, click in the **Franchise#** field, and then click the **arrow**. This field is a Lookup field—the values are looked up in the *6A Franchises* table. The **Menu Item** field is also a Lookup field—the values are looked up in the *6A Menu Items* table.

4 ▶ **Close** ☒ the table, and then **Close** « the **Navigation Pane**. On the **CREATE tab**, in the **Forms group**, click the **Form Design** button.

The design grid for the Detail section displays.

5 ▶ On the **FORM DESIGN TOOLS DESIGN tab**, in the **Tools group**, click the **Property Sheet** button. Compare your screen with Figure 6.2. Notice that the *Selection type* box displays *Form*—this is the Property Sheet for the entire form.

Every object on a form, including the form itself, has an associated ***Property Sheet*** that can be used to further enhance the object. ***Properties*** are characteristics that determine the appearance, structure, and behavior of an object. This Property Sheet displays the properties that affect the appearance and behavior of the form. The left column displays the property name, and the right column displays the property setting. Some of the text in the property setting boxes may be truncated.

FIGURE 6.2

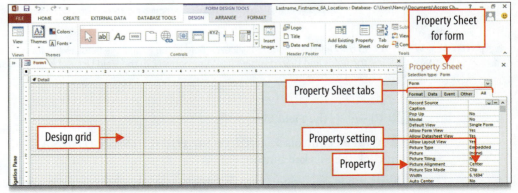

6 On the **Property Sheet**, click the **Format tab**, and then scroll down, if necessary, to display the **Split Form Orientation** property box. Point to the left edge of the **Property Sheet** until the ↔ pointer displays, and then drag to the left until the setting in the **Split Form Orientation** property box—**Datasheet on Top**—displays entirely.

7 On the **Property Sheet**, click the **Data tab**. Click the **Record Source property setting box arrow**, and then click **6A Sales**.

The *Record Source property* enables you to specify the source of the data for a form or a report. The property setting can be a table name, a query name, or an SQL statement.

8 **Close** ✕ the **Property Sheet**. On the **FORM DESIGN TOOLS DESIGN tab**, in the **Tools group**, click the **Add Existing Fields** button, and then compare your screen with Figure 6.3.

The Field List for the record source—6A Sales—displays.

FIGURE 6.3

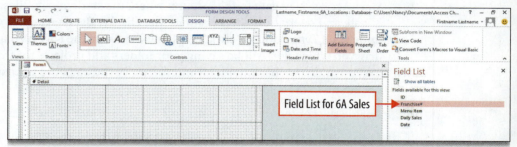

Field List for 6A Sales

9 In the **Field List**, click **Franchise#**. To select multiple fields, hold down Shift, and then click **Date**. Drag the selected fields onto the design grid until the top of the arrow of the pointer is **three dots** below the bottom edge of the **Detail section bar** and aligned with the **1.5-inch mark on the horizontal ruler**, as shown in Figure 6.4, and then release the mouse button.

Drag the fields to where the text box controls should display. If you drag to where the label controls should display, the label controls and text box controls will overlap. If you move the controls to an incorrect position, click the Undo button before moving them again.

FIGURE 6.4

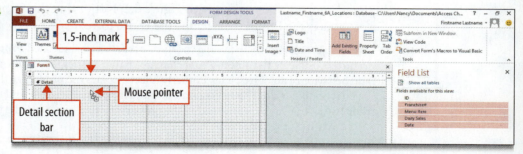

1.5-inch mark

Mouse pointer

Detail section bar

 **ANOTHER WAY**   In the Field List, double-click each field name to add the fields to the form. It is not possible to select all the fields and then double-click. Alternatively, in the Field List, right-click a field name, and then click Add Field to View.

---

10 **Close** ✕ the **Field List**.

11 With all controls selected, on the **FORM DESIGN TOOLS ARRANGE tab**, in the **Table group**, click the **Stacked** button.

When you create a form in Design view, the controls are not automatically grouped in a stacked or tabular layout. Grouping the controls makes it easier to format the controls and keeps the controls aligned.

12 ► Save ⊞ the form as **Lastname Firstname 6A Sales Form**

Activity 6.02 | Adding Sections to a Form

The only section that is automatically added to a form when it is created in Design view is the Detail section. In this activity, you will add a Form Header section and a Form Footer section.

1 ► Switch to **Form** view, and notice that the form displays only the data. There is no header section with a logo or name of the form.

2 ► Switch to **Design** view. On the **FORM DESIGN TOOLS DESIGN tab**, in the **Header/Footer group**, click the **Logo** button. Navigate to the location where the student data files for this textbook are saved. Locate and double-click **a06A_Logo** to insert the logo in the **Form Header** section.

Two sections—the Form Header and the Form Footer—are added to the form along with the logo. Sections can be added only in Design view.

3 ► On the selected logo, point to the right middle sizing handle until the ↔ pointer displays. Drag to the right until the right edge of the logo is aligned with the **1.5-inch mark on the horizontal ruler**.

4 ► In the **Header/Footer group**, click the **Title** button to insert the title in the **Form Header** section. Compare your screen with Figure 6.5.

The name of the form is inserted as a title into the Form Header section, and the label control is the same height as the logo.

FIGURE 6.5

5 ► Scroll down until the **Form Footer** section bar displays. Point to the top of the **Form Footer** section bar until the ⊞ pointer displays. Drag upward until the top of the **Form Footer** section bar aligns with the **2-inch mark on the vertical ruler**.

The height of the Detail section is decreased. Extra space at the bottom of the Detail section will cause blank space to display between records if the form is printed.

6 ► On the **FORM DESIGN TOOLS DESIGN tab**, in the **Controls group**, click the **Label** button [Aa]. Point to the **Form Footer** section until the plus sign (+) of the pointer aligns with the bottom of the **Form Footer** section bar and with the left edge of the **Date label control** in the **Detail** section. Drag downward to the bottom of the **Form Footer** section and to the right to **3 inches on the horizontal ruler**. Using your own first name and last name, type **Designed by Firstname Lastname** Press [Enter], and then compare your screen with Figure 6.6.

FIGURE 6.6

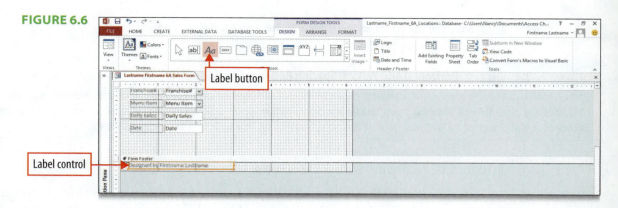

Label button

Label control

7 With the **label control** in the **Form Footer** section selected, hold down Shift, and then click each of the label controls in the **Detail** section. On the **FORM DESIGN TOOLS ARRANGE tab**, in the **Sizing & Ordering group**, click the **Align** button, and then select **Left**. **Save** 🖫 the form, and then switch to **Form** view.

The Form Header section displays the logo and the title of the form. The Form Footer section displays the label control that is aligned with the label controls in the Detail section. Both the Form Header and Form Footer sections display on every form page.

Objective 2   Change and Add Controls

Video A6-2

A *control* is an object, such as a label or text box, in a form or report that enables you to view or manipulate information stored in tables or queries. You have worked with label controls, text box controls, and, earlier in the chapter, logo controls, but there are more controls that can be added to a form. More controls are available in Design view than in Layout view. By default, when you create a form, Access uses the same field definitions as those in the underlying table or query.

Activity 6.03 | Changing Controls on a Form

In this activity, you will change a combo box control to a list box control.

1 Click the **Menu Item field arrow**.

Because the underlying table—*6A Sales*—designated this field as a lookup field, Access inserted a combo box control for this field instead of a text box control. The Franchise# field is also a combo box control. A *combo box* enables individuals to select from a list or to type a value.

2 Switch to **Design** view. In the **Detail** section, click the **Menu Item label control**, hold down Shift, and then click the **Menu Item combo box control**. On the **FORM DESIGN TOOLS ARRANGE tab**, in the **Table group**, click the **Remove Layout** button.

The Remove Layout button is used to remove a field from a stacked or tabular layout—it does not delete the field or remove it from the form. If fields are in the middle of a stacked layout column and are removed from the layout, the remaining fields in the column will display over the removed field. To avoid the clutter, first move the fields that you want to remove from the layout to the bottom of the column.

3 Click the **Undo** button 🔄. Point to the **Menu Item label control** until the 🏌 pointer displays. Drag downward until a thin orange line displays on the bottom edges of the **Date** controls.

> **ALERT!**   **Did the Control Stay in the Same Location?**
>
> In Design view, the orange line that indicates the location where controls will be moved is much thinner than—and not as noticeable as—the line in Layout view. If you drag downward too far, Access will not move the selected fields.

4 In the **Table group**, click the **Remove Layout** button to remove the **Menu Item** field from the stacked layout. Point to the selected controls, and then drag to the right and upward until the **Menu Item label control** is aligned with the **Franchise#** controls and with the **3.25-inch mark on the horizontal ruler**. Compare your screen with Figure 6.7.

FIGURE 6.7

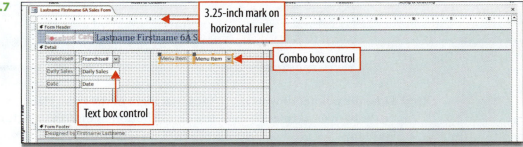

5 With the **Menu Item controls** selected, in the **Table group**, click the **Stacked** button. Click anywhere in the **Detail** section to deselect the second column.

> The Menu Item controls display in the second column and are grouped in a stacked layout. Recall that a stacked layout keeps the controls aligned and makes it easier to edit and move the controls.

6 Right-click the **Menu Item combo box control**. From the shortcut menu, point to **Change To**, and then click **List Box**.

> A *list box* enables individuals to select from a list but does not enable individuals to type anything that is not in the list. Based on the data in the underlying table or query, Access displays the control types to which you can change a field. The control type can be changed in Design view only.

7 Save 🖫 the form, and then switch to **Form** view. Notice the **Menu Item list box control** is not wide enough to display both columns and that there are horizontal and vertical scroll bars to indicate there is more data. Press Esc.

8 Click the **Menu Item list box control**. Scroll down until Menu Item *7839* displays. Switch to **Layout** view. Point to the right edge of the control until the ↔ pointer displays. Drag to the right until all of the Menu Item *7839* displays. Release the mouse button to display the resized list box.

9 Save 🖫 the form, and switch to **Design** view.

More Knowledge   **Validate or Restrict Data in Forms**

When you design tables, set field properties to ensure the entry of valid data by using input masks, validation rules, and default values. Any field in a form created with a table having these properties inherits the validation properties from the underlying table. Setting these properties in the table is the preferred method; however, you can also set the properties on controls in the form. If conflicting settings occur, the setting on the bound control in the form will override the field property setting in the table.

Activity 6.04 | Adding Controls to a Form

In this activity, you will add an image control and button controls to the form. An *image control* enables individuals to insert an image into any section of a form or report. A *button control* enables individuals to add a command button to a form or report that will perform an action when the button is clicked.

1 On the **FORM DESIGN TOOLS DESIGN tab**, in the **Controls group**, click the **Insert Image** button, and then click **Browse**. In the displayed **Insert Picture** dialog box, navigate to the location where the student data files for this textbook are saved and double-click **a06A_Logo**. Align the plus sign (+) of the pointer with the bottom of the **Form Header** section bar at **5.5-inches on the horizontal ruler**, as shown in Figure 6.8.

FIGURE 6.8

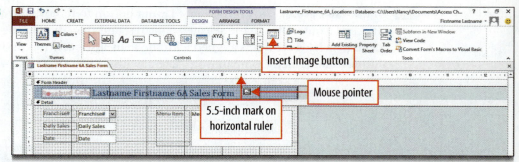

2 Drag the pointer downward to the lower right of the **Form Header** section to **6.75 inches on the horizontal ruler**. Release the mouse button to insert the picture in the **Form Header** section.

> Using the logo control inserts a picture in a predetermined location—the left side—of the Form Header section. The image control is used to insert a picture anywhere in the form. There is a second image control in the Controls gallery on the FORM DESIGN TOOLS DESIGN tab.

3 Click the **title's label control**. Point to the right edge of the **label control** until the pointer displays. Drag to the left until there is **one dot** between the right edge of the **label control** and the left edge of the **image control**. On the **FORM DESIGN TOOLS FORMAT tab**, in the **Font group**, click the **Center** button. Switch to **Form** view, and then compare your screen with Figure 6.9.

> The title is centered between the logo on the left and the image on the right, but the logo and the image are not the same size.

FIGURE 6.9

4 Switch to **Design** view, and then click the **image control**—the Rosebud Cafe image on the right side in the **Form Header** section. On the **FORM DESIGN TOOLS DESIGN tab**, in the **Tools group**, click the **Property Sheet** button. If necessary, on the Property Sheet, click the Format tab, and then compare your screen with Figure 6.10. Notice the **Width** and **Height** property settings.

> Your Width property setting and Height property setting may differ.

FIGURE 6.10

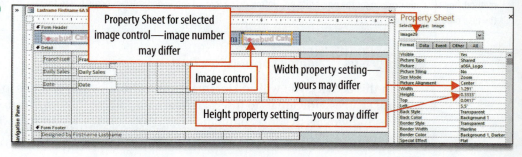

5 If necessary, change the Width property setting to 1.25 and then change the Height property setting to 0.5 In the **Form Header** section, on the left side, click the **logo control**, and then notice that the Property Sheet for the logo control displays. On the **Property Sheet**, change the **Width** property setting to **1.25** and then change the **Height** property setting to **0.5 Close** ✕ the **Property Sheet**.

> The width and height of the two controls are now the same.

6 With the logo control selected, hold down Shift, and then click the **image control**. On the **FORM DESIGN TOOLS ARRANGE tab**, in the **Sizing & Ordering group**, click the **Align** button, and then click **Bottom**. Click the **title's label control**. In the **Table group**, click **Remove Layout**, and then point to the left middle sizing handle until the ↔ pointer displays. Drag to the right until there is **one dot** between the right edge of the **logo control** and the left edge of the **title's label control**.

> The logo control and the image control are aligned at the bottom, and the title's label control is resized.

7 On the **FORM DESIGN TOOLS DESIGN tab**, at the right edge of the **Controls gallery**, click the **More** button ⬇, and verify that the **Use Control Wizards** option is active. Click the **Button** button ▭. Move the mouse pointer down into the **Detail** section. Align the plus sign (+) of the pointer at **1.5 inches on the vertical ruler** and **1.5 inches on the horizontal ruler**, and then click. Compare your screen with Figure 6.11.

> The Command Button Wizard dialog box displays. The first dialog box enables you to select an action for the button based on the selected category.

FIGURE 6.11

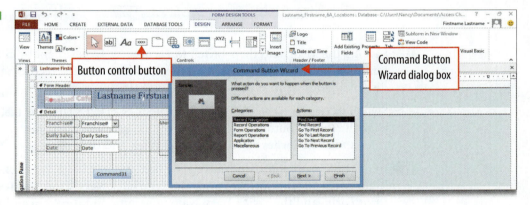

8 Take a moment to click the different categories to display the actions associated with each category. When you are finished, under **Categories**, click **Record Navigation**. Under **Actions**, click **Go to Previous Record**, and then click **Next**.

> The second Command Button Wizard dialog box displays, which enables you to select what will display on the button—either text or a picture. If you select picture, you can then click Browse to navigate to a location on your computer where pictures are saved, and then select any picture. If you select text, accept the default text or type new text. A preview of the button displays on the left side of the dialog box.

9 Next to **Picture**, verify **Go to Previous** is selected, and then click **Next**.

> The third Command Button Wizard dialog box displays, which enables you to name the button. If you need to refer to the button later—usually in creating macros—a meaningful name is helpful. The buttons created with the Command Button Wizard are linked to macros or programs.

10 In the text box, type **btnPrevRecord** and then click **Finish**.

> When creating controls that can later be used in programming, it is a good idea to start the name of the control with an abbreviation of the type of control—btn—and then a descriptive abbreviation of the purpose of the control.

11 Using the techniques you have just practiced, add a **button control** about **1 inch** to the right of the **Previous Record button control**. Under **Categories**, click **Record Navigation**, if necessary. Under **Actions**, click **Go to Next Record**. For **Picture**, click **Go to Next**, and then name the button **btnNxtRecord** and then click **Finish**. Do not be concerned if the button controls are not exactly aligned.

12 With the **Next Record button control** selected, hold down Shift, and then click the **Previous Record button control**. On the **FORM DESIGN TOOLS ARRANGE tab**, in the **Sizing & Ordering group**, click the **Align** button, and then click **Top**. Click the **Size/Space** button, and then click either **Increase Horizontal Spacing** button or **Decrease Horizontal Spacing** until there is approximately **1 inch** of space between the two controls. Compare your screen with Figure 6.12.

FIGURE 6.12

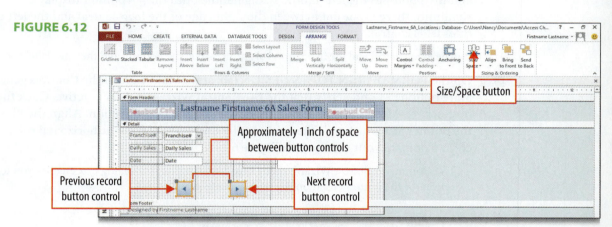

13 Save the form, and then switch to **Form** view. Experiment by clicking the **Next Record** button and the **Previous Record** button, and notice in the record navigator that you are displaying different records.

14 Switch to **Design** view. On the **FORM DESIGN TOOLS DESIGN tab**, in the **Controls group**, click the **Button** button [xxxx]. Align the plus sign (+) of the pointer at **1.5 inches on the vertical ruler** and at **5.5 inches on the horizontal ruler**, and then click.

15 In the **Command Button Wizard** dialog box, under **Categories**, click **Form Operations**. Under **Actions**, click **Print Current Form**, and then click **Next**. Click the **Text** option button to accept *Print Form*, and then click **Next**. Name the button **btnPrtForm** and then click **Finish**.

You will use this button to print one form when you are finished formatting the form.

16 Save the form.

More **Knowledge**   **Remove Form Controls**

To remove any control from a form, click the control to select it, and then press Del. To select more than one control at a time before deleting, select the controls by pressing Ctrl when you click each item.

Objective 3   Format a Form

Video A6-3

There are several methods you can use to modify the appearance of a form. Each section and control on a form has properties. Some properties can be modified by using buttons in the groups on a tab or by changing the property setting on the Property Sheet.

Activity 6.05 | Adding a Background Color

1 With **6A Sales Form** open in **Design** view, click the **Form Header** section bar.

The darkened bar indicates that the entire Form Header section of the form is selected.

2 On the **FORM DESIGN TOOLS FORMAT tab**, in the **Control Formatting group**, click the **Shape Fill** button. Under **Theme Colors**, in the second row, click the sixth color—**Red, Accent 2, Lighter 80%**.

The background color for the Form Header section changes to a light shade of red.

3 Double-click the **Form Footer** section bar to display the **Property Sheet** for the **Form Footer** section. On the **Property Sheet**, click the **Format tab**, if necessary, and then click in the **Back Color** property setting box—it displays Background 1. Click the **Build** button [...].

The color palette displays. Background 1 is a code used by Access to represent the color white. You can select an Access Theme Color, a Standard Color, a Recent Color, or click More Colors to select shades of colors.

4 Click **More Colors**. In the displayed **Colors** dialog box, click the **Custom tab**.

All colors use varying shades of Red, Green, and Blue.

5 In the **Colors** dialog box, click **Cancel**. On the **Property Sheet**, click the **Back Color property setting arrow**.

A list of color schemes display. These colors also display on the color palette under Access Theme Colors.

6 From the displayed list, experiment by clicking on different color schemes and viewing the effects of the background color change. You will have to click the **property setting arrow** each time to select another color scheme. When you are finished, click the **Build** button [...]. Under **Theme Colors**, in the second row, click the sixth color—**Red, Accent 2, Lighter 80%**. **Close** [×] the **Property Sheet**.

You can change the background color either by using the Background Color button in the Font group or by changing the Back Color property setting on the Property Sheet.

> **ANOTHER WAY**   Open the form in Layout view. To select a section, click in an empty area of the section. On the HOME tab, in the Text Formatting group, click the Background Color button.

7 Using one of the techniques you have just practiced, change the background color of the **Detail** section to **Red, Accent 2, Lighter 80%**. Switch to **Form** view, and then compare your screen with Figure 6.13.

FIGURE 6.13

8 **Save** [💾] the form, and then switch to **Design** view.

Activity 6.06 | Adding a Background Picture to a Form

In this activity, you will add a picture to the background of *6A Sales Form*.

1 With **6A Sales Form** open in **Design** view, locate the **Form selector**, as shown in Figure 6.14.

The *Form selector* is the box where the rulers meet, in the upper left corner of a form in Design view. Use the Form selector to select the entire form.

FIGURE 6.14

2 Double-click the **Form selector** to open the **Property Sheet** for the form.

3 On the **Property Sheet**, on the **Format tab**, click in the **Picture** property setting box. Click the **Build** button. Navigate to the location where the student data files for this textbook are saved. Locate and double-click **a06A_Background** to insert the picture in the form, and then compare your screen with Figure 6.15.

FIGURE 6.15

4 Click in the **Picture Alignment** property setting box, click the **arrow**, and then click **Form Center**.

The *Picture Alignment property* determines where the background picture for a form displays on the form. Center places the picture in the center of the page when the form is printed. Form Center places the picture in the center of the form data when the form is printed.

5 Click in the **Picture Size Mode** property setting box, and then click the **arrow** to display the options. From the displayed list, click **Stretch**.

The *Picture Size Mode property* determines the size of the picture in the form. The Clip setting retains the original size of the image. The Stretch setting stretches the image both vertically and horizontally to match the size of the form—the image may be distorted. The Zoom setting adjusts the image to be as large as possible without distorting the image. Both Stretch Horizontal and Stretch Vertical can distort the image. If you have a background color and set the Picture Type property setting to Stretch, the background color will not display.

6 **Close** the **Property Sheet**, **Save** the form, and then switch to **Layout** view. Compare your screen with Figure 6.16.

FIGURE 6.16

Background picture

Activity 6.07 | Modifying the Borders of Controls

In this activity, you will modify the borders of some of the controls on *6A Sales Form*. There are related property settings on the Property Sheet.

1 With **6A Sales Form** open in **Layout** view, click the **Franchise#** combo box control. Holding down ⇧Shift, click the **Daily Sales** text box control, and then click the **Date text box control**. On the **FORM LAYOUT TOOLS FORMAT tab**, in the **Control Formatting group**, click the **Shape Outline** button. Notice the options that are used to modify borders—Colors, Line Thickness, and Line Type. Compare your screen with Figure 6.17.

FIGURE 6.17

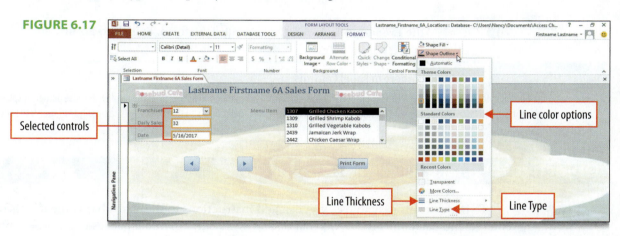

Selected controls

Line color options

Line Thickness

Line Type

2 Point to **Line Type** and point to each line type to display the **ScreenTip**. The second line type—**Solid**—is the default line type. Click the fifth line type—**Dots**—and then switch to **Form** view to display the results. Notice that the borders of the three controls display a line type of Dots. Switch to **Layout** view.

You can review the results in Layout view, but you would have to deselect the three controls.

3 With the three controls still selected, on the **FORM LAYOUT TOOLS FORMAT tab**, in the **Control Formatting group**, click the **Shape Outline** button. Point to **Line Thickness** and point to each line thickness to display the **ScreenTip**. The first line thickness—**Hairline**—is the default line thickness. Click the second line type—**1 pt**.

4 In the **Control Formatting group**, **click** the **Shape Outline** button. Under **Theme Colors**, point to each color to display the **ScreenTip**, and then in the first row, click the sixth color—**Red, Accent 2**. Switch to **Form** view to display the results.

The borders of the three controls display a line thickness of 1 point, and the color of the borders is a darker shade. A *point* is 1/72 of an inch.

5 Switch to **Layout** view. With the three controls still selected, on the **FORM LAYOUT TOOLS DESIGN tab**, in the **Tools group**, click the **Property Sheet** button, and then compare your screen with Figure 6.18. Notice the properties that are associated with the buttons on the ribbon with which you changed the borders of the selected controls.

Because multiple items on the form are selected, the Property Sheet displays Selection type: *Multiple selection*. You changed the property settings of the controls by using buttons, and the Property Sheet displays the results of those changes. You can also select multiple controls, open the Property Sheet, and make the changes to the properties. The Property Sheet displays more settings than those available through the use of buttons.

FIGURE 6.18

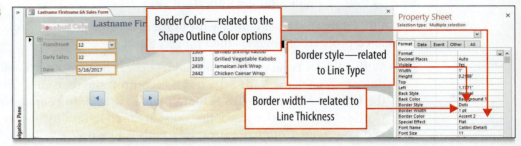

6 **Close** ☒ the **Property Sheet**, and then **Save** 💾 the form. Switch to **Form** view.

More Knowledge | Adding Borders to Label Controls

By default, the border style—line style—of a Label control is transparent, effectively hiding the border from the display. Because borders display around bound controls that contain data, it is recommended that you do not add borders to label controls so that individuals can easily distinguish the control that holds data.

Objective 4 | Make a Form User Friendly

Video A6-4

To make forms easy to use, you can add instructions to the status bar while data is being entered and custom ***ControlTips*** that display when an individual pauses the mouse pointer over a control on a form. Additionally, you can change the tab order of the fields on a form. ***Tab order*** refers to the order in which the fields are selected when the Tab key is pressed. By default, the tab order is created based on the order in which the fields are added to the form.

Activity 6.08 | Adding a Message to the Status Bar

When you created tables, you may have added a description to the field, and the description displayed in the status bar of the Access window. If a description is included for a field in the underlying table of a form, the text of the description will also display in the status bar when an individual clicks in the field on the form. In this activity, you will add a description to the Daily Sales field in the *6A Sales* table, and then ***propagate***—disseminate or apply—the changes to *6A Sales Form*. You will also add status bar text to a field on a form using the Property Sheet of the control.

1 With **6A Sales Form** open in **Form** view, click in the **Daily Sales** field. On the left side of the status bar, *Form View* displays—there is no text that helps an individual enter data.

2 ▸ **Close** × the form, and then **Open** « the **Navigation Pane**. Under **Tables**, right-click **6A Sales**, and then from the shortcut menu, click **Design View**. In the **Daily Sales** field, click in the **Description** box. Type **How many items were sold?** and then press Enter. Compare your screen with Figure 6.19.

A *Property Update Options button* displays in the Description box for the Date field. When you make changes to the design of a table, Access displays this button, which enables individuals to update the Property Sheet for this field in all objects that use this table as the record source.

FIGURE 6.19

3 ▸ Click the **Property Update Options** button 🖉, and then click **Update Status Bar Text everywhere Daily Sales is used**. In the displayed **Update Properties** dialog box, under **Update the following objects?**, notice that only one object—*Form: 6A Sales Form*—displays, and it is selected. In the **Update Properties** dialog box, click **Yes**. **Close** × the table, saving changes.

The changes in the Description field in the table will be propagated to *6A Sales Form*. If multiple objects use the *6A Sales* table as the underlying object, you can propagate the change to all of the objects.

4 ▸ In the **Navigation Pane**, under **Forms**, double-click **6A Sales Form** to open it in **Form** view. **Close** « the **Navigation Pane**. Click in the **Daily Sales** field, and then notice that on the left side of the status bar, *How many items were sold?* displays.

Access propagated the change made in the underlying table to the form.

5 ▸ Switch to **Design** view. Click the **Daily Sales text box control**. On the **FORM DESIGN TOOLS DESIGN tab**, in the **Tools group**, click the **Property Sheet** button.

6 ▸ On the **Property Sheet**, click the **Other tab**. Locate the **Status Bar Text** property, and notice the setting *How many items were sold?*

When Access propagated the change to the form, it populated the Status Bar Text property setting. The *Status Bar Text property* enables individuals to add descriptive text that will display in the status bar for a selected control.

7 ▸ In the **Detail** section, click the **Date text box control**, and then notice that the **Property Sheet** changes to display the properties for the **Date text box control**. Click in the **Status Bar Text** property setting box, type **Enter the date of sales report** and then Press Enter.

Entering a Status Bar Text on the Text Box Property Sheet does not display a Property Update Options button to propagate changes to the underlying table or add the information to the Description box for the field in the table.

8 ▸ **Save** 🖫 the form, and then switch to **Form** view. Click in the **Date** field, and then compare your screen with Figure 6.20.

The status bar displays the text you entered in the Status Bar Text property setting box.

FIGURE 6.20

Insertion point in Date textbox

Entered in Status Bar Text property setting box

9 ▶ Switch to **Design** view.

More Knowledge | **Conflicting Field Description and Status Bar Text Property Setting**

When you create a form, the fields inherit the property settings from the underlying table. You can change the Status Bar Text property setting for the form, and it will override the setting that is inherited from the table. If you later change field properties in Table Design view, the Property Update Options button displays—you must manually propagate those changes to the table's related objects; propagation is not automatic. An exception to this is entering Validation Rules—changes are automatically propagated.

Activity 6.09 | Creating Custom ControlTips

Another way to make a form easier to use is to add custom ControlTips to objects on the form. A ControlTip is similar to a ScreenTip, and temporarily displays descriptive text while the mouse pointer is paused over the control. This method is somewhat limited because most individuals press Tab or Enter to move from field to field and thus do not see the ControlTip. However, a ControlTip is a useful tool in a training situation when an individual is learning how to use the data entry form. In this activity, you will add a ControlTip to the Print Form button control.

1 ▶ With **6A Sales Form** open in **Design** view and the **Property Sheet** displayed, click the **Print Form** button. If necessary, click the Other tab to make it active. Notice the **Property Sheet** displays *Selection type: Command Button* and the **Selection type** box displays *btnPrtForm*, the name you gave to the button when you added it to the form.

2 ▶ Click in the **ControlTip Text** property setting box, type **Prints the selected record** and then press Enter. Compare your screen with Figure 6.21.

FIGURE 6.21

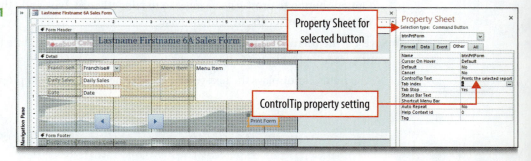

Property Sheet for selected button

ControlTip property setting

3 ▶ **Close** ☒ the **Property Sheet**, **Save** 🖫 the form, and then switch to **Form** view. Point to the **Print Form** button, and then compare your screen with Figure 6.22.

A ControlTip displays the message you typed for the ControlTip Text property setting.

FIGURE 6.22

Activity 6.10 | Changing the Tab Order

You can customize the order in which you enter data on a form by changing the tab order. Recall that tab order refers to the order in which the fields are selected each time Tab is pressed. As you press Tab, the focus of the form changes from one control to another control. *Focus* refers to the object that is selected and currently being acted upon.

1 With **6A Sales Form** open in **Form** view, in the record navigator, click the **New (blank) record** button. If necessary, click in the Franchise# combo box. Press Tab three times, and then notice that the insertion point moves from field to field, ending with the **Date** text box. Press Tab three more times, and then notice the **Print Form** button is the focus. The button displays with a darker border. Press Enter.

Because the focus is on the Print Form button, the Print dialog box displays.

2 In the **Print** dialog box, click **Cancel**. Switch to **Design** view.

3 On the **FORM DESIGN TOOLS DESIGN tab**, in the **Tools group**, click the **Tab Order** button, and then compare your screen with Figure 6.23.

The Tab Order dialog box displays. Under Section, Detail is selected. Under Custom Order, the fields and controls display in the order they were added to the form. To the left of each field name or button name is a row selector button.

As you rearrange fields on a form, the tab order does not change from the original tab order. This can make data entry chaotic because the focus is changed in what appears to be an illogical order. The Auto Order button will change the tab order based on the position of the controls in the form from left to right and top to bottom.

FIGURE 6.23

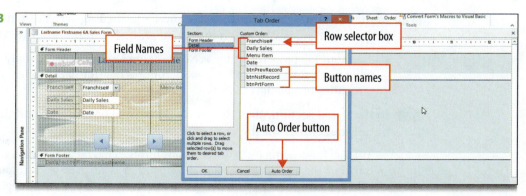

4 To the left of **Menu Item**, click the **row selector** box. Point to the **row selector** box, and then drag downward until a dark horizontal line displays between **Date** and **btnPrevRecord**.

The Menu Item field will now receive the focus after the Date field.

> **ALERT!** **Did the Field Stay in the Same Location?**
> You must point to the row selector box before dragging the field. If you point to the field name, the field will not be moved.

5 ▶ In the **Tab Order** dialog box, click **OK**. Save 🖫 the form, and then switch to **Form** view. In the record navigator, click the **Last Record** button. When the **Menu Item** field has the focus, it is easier to see it on a blank record. In the record navigator, click the **New (blank) record** button.

The insertion point displays in the Franchise# field.

6 ▶ Press Tab three times. Even though it is difficult to see, the focus changes to the **Menu Item** list box. Press Tab again, and then notice that the focus changes to the **btnPrevRecord** button.

Before allowing individuals to enter data into a form, you should always test the tab order to ensure that the data will be easy to enter.

7 ▶ Switch to **Design** view. In the **Detail** section, right-click the **Date text box control**, click **Properties**. If necessary, click the Other tab, and then compare your screen with Figure 6.24.

Text box controls have three properties relating to tab order: Tab Index, Tab Stop, and Auto Tab. Combo box controls and list box controls do not have an Auto Tab property.

FIGURE 6.24

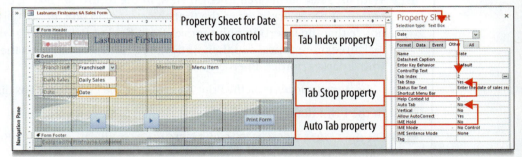

8 ▶ On the **Property Sheet**, click in the **Tab Index property setting box**, which displays *2*. Click the **Build** button ⸱⸱⸱ .

Tab Index settings begin with 0. Franchise# has a Tab Index setting of 0, which indicates that this field has the focus when the form is opened. Daily Sales has a Tab Index setting of 1—it will receive the focus when Tab is pressed one time. Date has a Tab Index setting of 2—it will receive the focus when Tab is pressed a second time. Menu Item has a Tab Index setting of 3—it will receive the focus when Tab is pressed a third time.

9 ▶ In the **Tab Order** dialog box, click **Cancel**. On the **Property Sheet**, notice that the **Tab Stop** property setting is **Yes**, which means individuals can press Tab to move to this field.

The Auto Tab property setting is No. It should be changed to Yes only when a text field has an input mask. Recall that an input mask controls how the data is entered into a field; for example, the formatting of a phone number.

10 ▶ In the **Detail** section, click the **Franchise# combo box control**, and then on the **Property Sheet**, notice the settings for the **Tab Index** and **Tab Stop** properties.

The Tab Index setting is 0, which means this field has the focus when the form page is displayed—it is first on the tab order list. The Tab Stop setting is Yes. Because an input mask cannot be applied to a combo box, there is no Auto Tab property. The Auto Tab property applies only to a text box control.

11 ▶ In the **Detail** section, click the **Previous Record button control**. On the **Property Sheet**, click in the **Tab Stop** property setting box, click the **arrow**, and then click **No**.

Changing the Tab Stop property setting to No means that the focus will not be changed to the button by pressing Tab.

12 Save 🖫 the form, and then switch to **Form** view. In the record navigator, click the **Last record** button. Press Tab two times, watching the focus change from the **Franchise#** field to the **Date** field. Press Tab two more times, and then compare your screen with Figure 6.25.

> Because the Tab Stop property setting for the Previous Record button control was changed to No, the button does not receive the focus by pressing the Tab key.

FIGURE 6.25

13 In the **Detail** section, click the **Previous Record** button.

> The previous record displays—you can still use the button by clicking on it.

14 Switch to **Design** view. Using the techniques you have just practiced, for the **Next Record** button and the **Print Form** button, change the **Tab Stop** property setting to **No**.

15 Close ✕ the **Property Sheet**. Save 🖫 the form, and then switch to **Form** view. Test the tab order by pressing Tab, making sure that the focus does not change to the **Next Record** button or the **Print Form** button.

> When the focus is on the Date field, pressing the Tab key moves the focus to the Franchise# field in the next record.

16 Navigate to **Record 5**—Franchise# 44. Unless you are required to submit your database electronically, in the **Detail** section, click the **Print Form** button. In the **Print** dialog box, under **Print Range**, click **Selected Record(s)**, and then click **OK**. If you are instructed to submit this result as an electronic printout, select the record using the selector bar, and then from **Backstage** view, click **Save As**. Click the **Save Object As** button, and double-click **PDF or XPS**. Navigate to the folder where you store your electronic printouts. Click the **Options** button, click **Selected records**, and then click **OK**. Click **Publish**.

17 Close ✕ the form, and then Close « the **Navigation Pane**. **Close** the database, and then **Exit** ⊠ Access.

18 As directed by your instructor, submit your database and the paper or electronic printout of the form that is the result of this project. Specifically, in this project, using your own name you created the following database and printout or electronic printout:

1. Lastname_Firstname_6A_Locations	Database file
2. Lastname_Firstname_6A_Sales_Form	Form (printed or electronic printout)

END | You have completed Project 6A

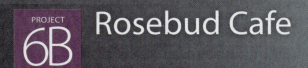

PROJECT ACTIVITIES

In Activities 6.11 through 6.18, you will create customized reports. The corporate office of Rosebud Cafe (RBC) maintains a database about the franchises, including daily sales of menu items per franchise, the franchise owners, and franchise fees and payments. Reports are often run to summarize data in the tables or queries. Creating customized reports will help the owners and officers of the company view the information in the database in a meaningful way. Your completed reports will look similar to Figure 6.26.

PROJECT FILES

For Project 6B, you will need the following files:

a06B_RBC
a06B_Logo

You will save your database as:

Lastname_Firstname_6B_RBC

PROJECT RESULTS

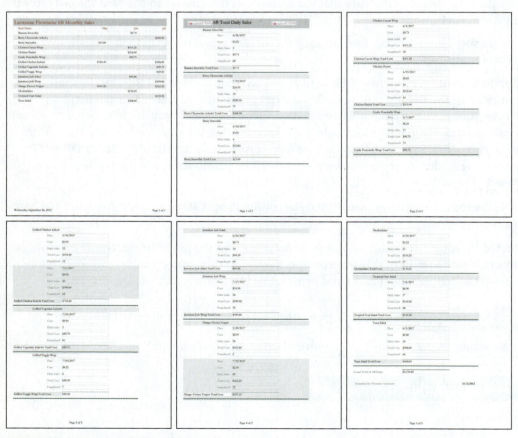

FIGURE 6.26 Project 6B Rosebud Cafe

Video A6-5

A report wizard is a more efficient way to start a report, although Design view does offer you more control as you create your report. Once the report has been created, its appearance can be modified in Design or Layout view.

Activity 6.11 | Creating a Report Using a Wizard

In this activity, you will use a wizard to create a report for Rosebud Cafe that displays the data from the 6B Total Daily Sales Crosstab Query.

1 **Start** Access. Navigate to the location where the student data files for this textbook are saved. Locate and open the **a06B_RBC** file. Save the database in your **Access Chapter 6** folder as **Lastname_Firstname_6B_RBC**

2 If you did not add the **Access Chapter 6** folder to the Trust Center, enable the content. In the **Navigation Pane**, under **Queries**, double-click **6B Total Daily Sales Crosstab Query**. Take a moment to study the data in the query, as shown in Figure 6.27.

> The data is grouped by Item Name and Month. The sum function calculates the total daily sales for each item per month.

FIGURE 6.27

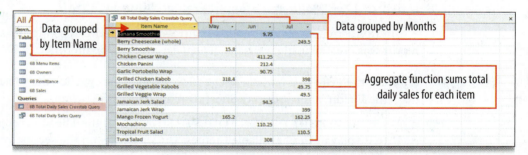

3 **Close** ☒ the query. With **6B Total Daily Sales Crosstab Query** still selected, **Close** « the **Navigation Pane**.

4 On the **CREATE tab**, in the **Reports group**, click the **Report Wizard** button.

5 Because the crosstab query was selected in the **Navigation Pane**, in the **Report Wizard** dialog box, in the **Tables/Queries** box, **Query: 6B Total Daily Sales Crosstab Query** displays. If it does not display, click the Tables/Queries arrow, and then click Query: 6B Total Daily Sales Crosstab Query.

6 Under **Available Fields**, notice there are more months than those that were displayed in **6B Total Daily Sales Crosstab Query**.

> Because there was data for the months of May, June, and July only, the other months were hidden from the display in the query. To hide a column in Datasheet view, right-click the column header, and then from the shortcut menu, click Hide Fields.

7 Under **Available Fields**, double-click each field name, in the order specified, to add the field names to the **Selected Fields** box: **Item Name**, **May**, **Jun**, and **Jul**.

8 In the **Report Wizard** dialog box, click **Next**. Because no grouping levels will be used, click **Next**.

9 To sort the records within the report by Item Name, click the **arrow** next to the **1** box. From the displayed list, click **Item Name**. Leave the sort order as **Ascending**, and then click **Next**.

10 Under **Layout**, verify the **Tabular** option button is selected. Under **Orientation**, verify the **Portrait** option button is selected, and then click **Next**.

11 In the **What title do you want for your report?** box, type **Lastname Firstname 6B Monthly Sales** and then click **Finish**. Compare your screen with Figure 6.28.

The report displays in Print Preview. Because this report uses a crosstab query as the record source, it displays calculated data grouped by two different types of information.

FIGURE 6.28

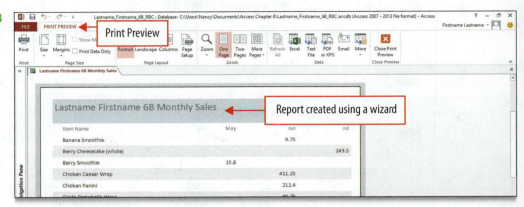

Activity 6.12 | Modifying a Report Created Using a Wizard

In this activity, you will modify controls in the report to change its appearance. Although the report was created using a wizard, its appearance can be modified in Design view and Layout view.

1 On the **Print Preview tab**, in the **Close Preview group**, click the **Close Print Preview** button. If the Field List or Property Sheet displays, close it.

2 On the **REPORT DESIGN TOOLS DESIGN tab**, in the **Themes group**, click the **Themes** button to display a list of available themes. Under **Office**, on the second row, click the second theme—**Organic**.

Themes simplify the process of creating professional-looking objects within one program or across multiple programs. A theme includes theme colors and theme fonts that will be applied consistently throughout the objects in the database. It is a simple way to provide professional, consistent formatting in a database.

3 If necessary, click anywhere in an empty area of the report to deselect the Item Name column. Click the **Report title text box control**. On the **REPORT DESIGN TOOLS FORMAT tab**, in the **Font group**, click the **Font Color button arrow** [A ▾]. Under **Theme Colors**, in the first row, click the eighth color—**Red, Accent 4**. If necessary, resize the title text box so the entire title is visible.

4 Select all of the controls in the **Page Header** section by pointing to the top left of the **Page Header** section, holding down your mouse button, dragging the mouse across the **Page Header controls** and to the bottom of the **Page Header** section, and then releasing the mouse button. Use the techniques you have practiced to change the font color to **Red, Accent 4**.

Any group of controls can be selected using this lasso method. It can be more efficient than holding down [Shift] while clicking each control.

 BY TOUCH   Use your finger to draw the circle and to highlight text.

---

5 **Save** [💾] the report, and then switch to **Layout** view.

6 > In the **Item Name** column, select any **text box control**. Hold down ⇧Shift and click the **Item Name label control** to select the entire column. Point to the right edge of the control until the ↔ pointer displays. Drag to the left until the box is approximately **2.5 inches** wide; be sure none of the data in the column is cut off.

7 > To select all of the text box controls, in the **May** column, click **15.8**. Holding down ⇧Shift, in the **Jun** and **Jul** columns, click a **text box control**. Compare your screen with Figure 6.29.

FIGURE 6.29

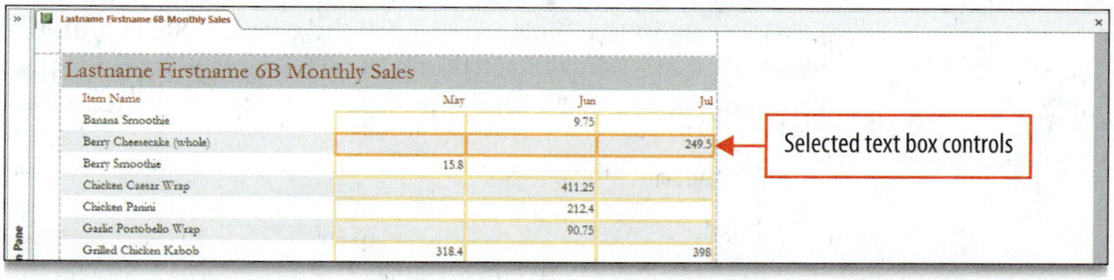

Item Name	May	Jun	Jul
Banana Smoothie		9.75	
Berry Cheesecake (whole)			249.5
Berry Smoothie	15.8		
Chicken Caesar Wrap		411.25	
Chicken Panini		212.4	
Garlic Portobello Wrap		90.75	
Grilled Chicken Kabob	318.4		398

Lastname Firstname 6B Monthly Sales

Selected text box controls

8 > On the **REPORT LAYOUT TOOLS DESIGN tab**, in the **Tools group**, click the **Property Sheet** button. Notice that the selection type is *Multiple selection*.

9 > On the **Property Sheet**, click the **Format tab**. Click the **Format property setting arrow**. From the displayed list, select **Currency**. Click the **Border Style property setting arrow**, and click **Short Dashes**. **Close** × the **Property Sheet**.

10 > **Save** 🖫 the report, and then switch to **Print Preview** view. If you are instructed to submit this result, create a paper or electronic printout. On the **Print Preview tab**, in the **Close Preview group**, click the **Close Print Preview** button.

11 > **Close** × the report, and then **Open** » the **Navigation Pane**.

Objective 6 | Create a Report in Design View

Video A6-6

You usually create a report using the Report tool or the Report Wizard, and then modify the report in Design view to suit your needs. Use Design view to create a report when these tools do not meet your needs or if you want more control in the creation of a report. Creating or modifying a report in Design view is a common technique when additional controls, such as calculated controls, need to be added to the report or properties need to be changed.

Activity 6.13 | Creating a Report in Design View

Creating a report with the Report tool or the Report Wizard is the easiest way to start the creation of a customized report, but you can also create a report from scratch in Design view. Once you understand the sections of a report and how to manipulate the controls within the sections, it is easier to modify a report that has been created using the report tools.

1 > In the **Navigation Pane**, open **6B Total Daily Sales Query** in **Design** view, and then notice the underlying tables that were used in the creation of the query. Notice the calculated field—*Total Cost*.

> Recall that a calculated field contains the field name, followed by a colon, and then an expression. In the expression, the existing field names must be enclosed in square brackets. The Total Cost was calculated by multiplying the value in the Cost field by the value in the Daily Sales field.

2 When you are finished, **Close** ✕ the query, and **Close** ≪ the **Navigation Pane**. On the **CREATE tab**, in the **Reports group**, click the **Report Design** button. When the design grid displays, scroll down to display all of the report sections.

Three sections are included in the blank design grid: the Page Header section, the Detail section, and the Page Footer section. A page header displays at the top of every printed page, and a page footer displays at the bottom of every printed page.

3 Select the report using the report selector, if necessary. On the **REPORT DESIGN TOOLS DESIGN tab**, in the **Tools group**, click the **Property Sheet** button, if necessary. On the **Property Sheet**, click the **Data tab**. Click the **Record Source property setting box arrow**, and then compare your screen with Figure 6.30. If necessary, increase the width of the Property Sheet.

FIGURE 6.30

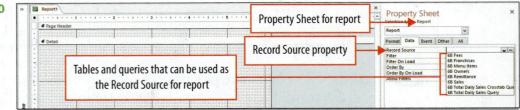

4 From the displayed list of tables and queries, click **6B Total Daily Sales Query**, and then **Close** ✕ the **Property Sheet**.

6B Total Daily Sales Query is the record source—underlying query—for this report.

5 On the **REPORT DESIGN TOOLS DESIGN tab**, in the **Tools group**, click the **Add Existing Fields** button to display the fields in **6B Total Daily Sales Query**.

6 In the **Field List**, click **Date**. Hold down Shift, and then click **Franchise#** to select all of the fields.

7 Drag the selected fields into the **Detail** section of the design grid until the top of the arrow of the pointer is **one dot** below the bottom edge of the **Detail** section bar and aligned with the **3-inch mark on the horizontal ruler**. **Close** ✕ the **Field List**, and then compare your screen with Figure 6.31.

FIGURE 6.31

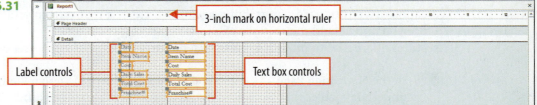

8 With the label controls and text box controls for the fields selected, click the **REPORT DESIGN TOOLS ARRANGE tab**. In the **Table group**, click the **Stacked** button to group the fields together for easier formatting.

9 On the **REPORT DESIGN TOOLS DESIGN tab**, in the **Themes group**, click the **Themes** button. Under **In This Database**, notice the theme used in this database—**Organic**. Press Esc to close the gallery.

10 Save 🖫 the report as **Lastname Firstname 6B Total Daily Sales**.

Activity 6.14 | Modifying the Sections of a Report

By default, a report created in Design view includes a Page Header section and a Page Footer section. Reports can also include a Report Header section and a Report Footer section. In this activity, you will add the Report Header and Report Footer sections and hide the Page Header section. Recall that a Report Header displays at the top of the first printed page of a report, and the Report Footer displays at the bottom of the last printed page of a report.

1 Right-click in the **Detail** section of the report, and click **Report Header/Footer**. Notice that the **Report Header** section displays at the top of the design grid. Scroll down to display the **Report Footer** section.

2 Scroll up to display the **Report Header** section. On the **REPORT DESIGN TOOLS DESIGN tab**, in the **Header/Footer group**, click the **Logo** button. Locate and double-click **a06B_Logo** to insert the logo in the **Report Header** section. On the selected logo, point to the right middle sizing handle until the ↔ pointer displays. Drag to the right until the right edge of the logo is aligned with the **1.5-inch mark on the horizontal ruler**.

3 On the **REPORT DESIGN TOOLS DESIGN tab**, in the **Header/Footer group**, click the **Title** button. In the **title's label control**, click to the left of your **Lastname**, delete your **Lastname Firstname** and the space, and then press Enter. On the **title's label control**, point to the right middle sizing handle until the ↔ pointer displays, and then double-click to adjust the size of the **label control** to fit the text. Alternatively, drag the right middle sizing handle to the left.

4 Scroll down until the **Page Footer** section bar displays. Point to the top edge of the **Page Footer** section bar until the ✛ pointer displays. Drag upward until the top of the **Page Footer** section bar aligns with the **2.25-inch mark on the vertical ruler**.

This prevents extra blank space from printing between the records.

5 Scroll up until the **Report Header** section displays. Point to the top edge of the **Detail** section bar until the ✛ pointer displays. Drag upward until the top edge of the **Detail** section bar aligns with the bottom edge of the **Page Header** section bar, and then compare your screen with Figure 6.32.

The Page Header and Page Footer sections are paired together. Likewise, the Report Header and Report Footer sections are paired together. You cannot remove only one section of the pair. If you wish to remove one section of a paired header/footer, decrease the height of the section. Alternatively, set the Height property for the section to 0. Because there is no space in the Page Header section, nothing will print at the top of every page. To remove both of the paired header/footer sections, right-click in the Detail section, and click the Page Header/Footer to deselect it.

FIGURE 6.32

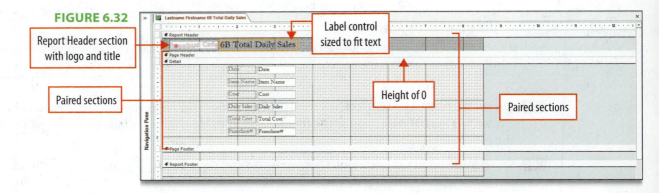

Report Header section with logo and title

Label control sized to fit text

Paired sections

Height of 0

Paired sections

6 Drag the right edge of the design grid to the left until it aligns with the **6.5-inch mark on the horizontal ruler**. **Save** the report.

The width of the report page is decreased, which will enable the report to fit within the margins of paper in portrait orientation.

Objective 7   Add Controls to a Report

Video A6-7

Reports are not used to manipulate data in the underlying table or query, so they contain fewer types of controls. You can add label controls, text box controls, images, hyperlinks, or calculated controls to a report.

Activity 6.15 | Adding Label and Text Box Controls to a Report

In this activity, you will add controls to the report that will contain the page number, the date, and your first name and last name.

1 On the **REPORT DESIGN TOOLS DESIGN tab**, in the **Header/Footer group**, click the **Page Numbers** button. In the displayed **Page Numbers** dialog box, under **Format**, click **Page N of M**. Under **Position**, click **Bottom of Page [Footer]**. Alignment should remain **Center**; click **OK**.

A text box control displays in the center of the Page Footer section. The control displays an expression that will display the page number. Every expression begins with an equal sign (=). "Page" is enclosed in quotation marks. Access interprets anything enclosed in quotation marks as text and will display it exactly as it is typed within the quotation marks, including the space. The & symbol is used for *concatenation*—linking or joining—of strings. A *string* is a series of characters. The word *Page* followed by a space will be concatenated—joined—to the string that follows the & symbol. [Page] is a reserved name that retrieves the current page number. This is followed by another & symbol that concatenates the page number to the next string—"of ". The & symbol continues concatenation of [Pages], a reserved name that retrieves the total number of pages in the report.

2 **Save** the report. On the **REPORT DESIGN TOOLS DESIGN tab**, in the **Views group**, click the **View button arrow**, and then click **Print Preview**. On the **Print Preview tab**, in the **Zoom group**, click the **Two Pages** button. Notice at the bottom of each page the format of the page number.

3 In the **Close Preview group**, click the **Close Print Preview** button.

4 On the **REPORT DESIGN TOOLS DESIGN tab**, in the **Controls group**, click the **Label** button **Aa**. Point to the **Report Footer** section until the plus sign (+) of the pointer aligns with the bottom edge of the **Report Footer** section bar and with the left edge of the **Report Footer** section. Drag downward to the bottom of the **Report Footer** section and to the right to the **2.5-inch mark on the horizontal ruler**. Using your own first name and last name, type **Submitted by Firstname Lastname** and then compare your screen with Figure 6.33.

FIGURE 6.33

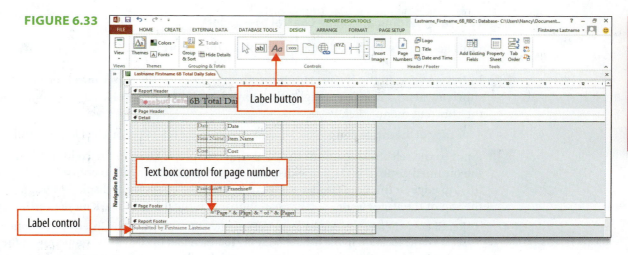

5 Click away from the **label box**, and then **Save** 💾 the report. On the **REPORT DESIGN TOOLS DESIGN tab**, in the **Header/Footer group**, click the **Date and Time** button. In the **Date and Time** dialog box, under **Include Date**, click the third option button, which displays the date as mm/dd/yyyy. Clear the **Include Time** check box, and then click **OK**.

A text box control with an expression for the current date displays in the Report Header section. It may display over the Report title.

6 In the **Report Header**, click the **Date text box control** to select it. On the **REPORT DESIGN TOOLS ARRANGE tab**, in the **Table group**, click the **Remove Layout** button so the **Date text box control** can be moved. Right-click the selected control, and click **Cut**. Point to the **Report Footer** section bar, right-click, and then click **Paste**. Drag the text box control until the right edge of the text box control aligns with the **6.25-inch mark on the horizontal ruler**. Click the **Title label control** to select it, point to the right middle sizing handle until the ↔ pointer displays, and then drag to the right until the right edge of the text box control aligns with the **4.5-inch mark on the horizontal ruler**.

7 **Save** 💾 the report, and then switch to **Layout** view. Notice that, for the first record, the data for the **Item Name** field does not fully display. Click the **Item Name text box control**, which partially displays *Banana Smoothie*. Point to the right edge of the **Item Name text box control** until the ↔ pointer displays. Drag to the right approximately **1.5 inches**. Because no ruler displays in Layout view, you will have to estimate the distance to drag.

Because the controls are in a stacked layout, the widths of all of the text box controls are increased.

8 Scroll down, observing the data in the **Item Name** field. Ensure that all of the data displays. If the data is not all visible in a record, use the technique you just practiced to increase the width of the text box control until all of the data displays.

9 Switch to **Design** view. Point to the right edge of the design grid until the ✛ pointer displays. If necessary, drag to the left until the right edge of the design grid aligns with the 6.5-inch mark on the horizontal ruler. Save 💾 the report.

The width of the report page will change with the addition of more text boxes, making it necessary to readjust the width so the report will fit within the margins of paper in portrait orientation.

More Knowledge **Adding a Hyperlink to a Report**

Add a hyperlink to a report in Design view by clicking the Insert Hyperlink button in the Controls group and then specifying the complete URL. To test the hyperlink, in Design view, right-click the hyperlink, click Hyperlink, and then click Open Hyperlink. The hyperlink is active—jumps to the target—in Design view, Report view, and Layout view. The hyperlink is not active in Print Preview view. If the report is exported to another Office application, the hyperlink is active when it is opened in that application. An application that can export data can create a file in a format that another application understands, enabling the two programs to share the same data.

Activity 6.16 | Adding an Image Control to a Report

In this activity, you will add image controls to the report header.

1 In **Design view**, in the **Report Header** section, right-click the **logo control**. From the displayed shortcut menu, click **Copy**. Right-click anywhere in the **Report Header** section, and then from the shortcut menu, click **Paste**.

A copy of the image displays on top and slightly to the left of the original logo control.

2 Point to the selected logo until the pointer displays. Drag to the right until the left edge of the outlined control is the same distance from the title as the logo control on the left. Point to the top edge of the **Page Header** section bar until the pointer displays. Drag upward until the top of the **Page Header** section bar aligns with the **0.5-inch mark on the vertical ruler**.

Recall that when you created a form in Design view, you clicked the Insert Image button and selected the location in the header section. You then had to change the properties of the image to match the size of the image in the logo control. Because you copied the original image from the logo, the images are the same size.

3 With the image control on the right selected, hold down Ctrl, and then click the **logo control**. On the **REPORT DESIGN TOOLS ARRANGE tab**, in the **Sizing & Ordering group**, click the **Align button**, and select **Bottom**. Compare your screen with Figure 6.34.

Both the logo control and the image control are aligned along the bottom edges.

FIGURE 6.34

Logo control

Image control

4 On the **REPORT DESIGN TOOLS DESIGN tab**, in the **Controls group**, click the **More** button, and then click the **Line** button. Point to the **Detail** section until the middle of the plus sign (+) of the pointer aligns at **2 inches on the vertical ruler** and **0 inches on the horizontal ruler**, as shown in Figure 6.35.

A *line control* enables an individual to insert a line in a form or report.

FIGURE 6.35

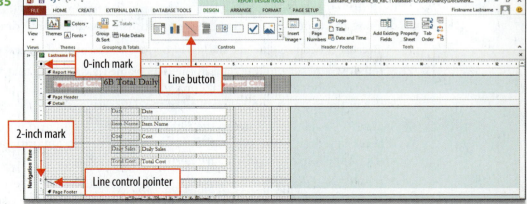

0-inch mark

Line button

2-inch mark

Line control pointer

5 Hold down Shift, click and then drag to the right to **6.5 inches on the horizontal ruler**, and then release the mouse button.

An orange line control displays. Holding down the Shift key ensures that the line will be straight.

On the **REPORT DESIGN TOOLS FORMAT tab**, in the **Control Formatting group**, click the **Shape Outline** button. Point to **Line Thickness** and then click the third line—**2 pt**. In the **Control Formatting group**, click the **Shape Outline** button. Under **Theme Colors**, on the fifth row, click the sixth color—**Teal, Accent 2, Darker 25%**.

7 ▶ **Save** 🖫 the report, and then switch to **Report** view. Compare your screen with Figure 6.36. Notice the horizontal line that displays between the records.

FIGURE 6.36

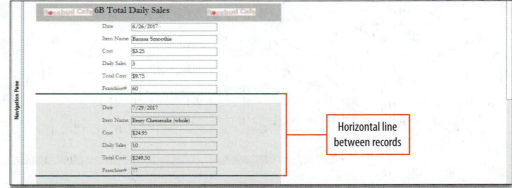

Horizontal line between records

8 ▶ Switch to **Design** view.

Objective 8 | Group, Sort, and Total Records in Design View

Video A6-8

Although it is much easier to create a report that is grouped and sorted using the Report Wizard, the same tasks can be completed in Design view. If a report has been created that was not grouped, you can modify the report in Design view to include grouping and summary data. Calculated controls are often added to reports to display summary information in reports with grouped records.

Activity 6.17 | Adding a Grouping and Sort Level to a Report

In this activity, you will add a grouping and sort order to the report, and then move a control from the Detail section to the Header section.

1 ▶ On the **REPORT DESIGN TOOLS DESIGN tab**, in the **Grouping & Totals group**, click the **Group & Sort** button, and then compare your screen with Figure 6.37.

The Group, Sort, and Total pane displays at the bottom of the screen. Because no grouping or sorting has been applied to the report, two buttons relating to these functions display in the Group, Sort, and Total pane.

FIGURE 6.37

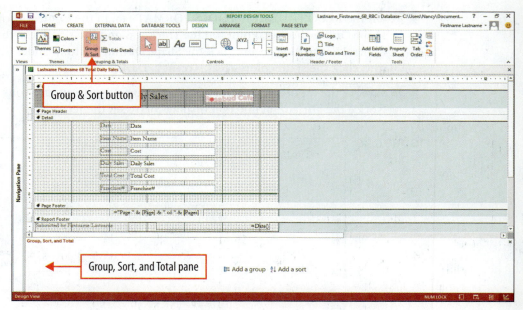

Group & Sort button

Group, Sort, and Total pane

2 In the **Group, Sort, and Total pane**, click the **Add a group** button. A list of fields that are used in the report displays, as shown in Figure 6.38.

FIGURE 6.38

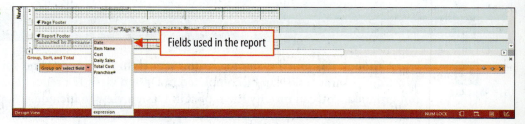

Fields used in the report

3 From the displayed list, click **Item Name**.

An empty Item Name Header section is inserted above the Detail section. The report will be grouped by the Item Name, and the Item Names will be sorted in ascending order.

4 In the **Detail** section, click the **Item Name text box control**. Point to the selected text box control until the ⁣ pointer displays. Drag downward until a thin orange line displays below the **Franchise#** controls.

The text box control for this field will be moved to the Item Name Header section in the report. Recall that moving the controls to the bottom of the stacked layout makes it easier to remove the controls from the stacked layout.

5 On the **REPORT DESIGN TOOLS ARRANGE tab**, in the **Table group**, click the **Remove Layout** button.

The label control and the text box control for the Item Name field are removed from the stacked layout.

6 Right-click the selected **Item Name text box control** to display the shortcut menu, and click **Cut**. Click the **Item Name Header** section bar to select it, right-click to display the shortcut menu, and click **Paste**.

The controls for the Item Name are moved from the Detail section to the Item Name Header section. Because the report is being grouped by this field, the controls should be moved out of the Detail section.

7 In the **Item Name Header** section, click the **Item Name label control**, and then press Delete. Click the **Item Name text box control** to select it, and then drag it to the right until the left edge of the control aligns with the **1-inch mark on the horizontal ruler**. Compare your screen with Figure 6.39.

Because the records are grouped by the data in the Item Name field, the name of the field is unnecessary.

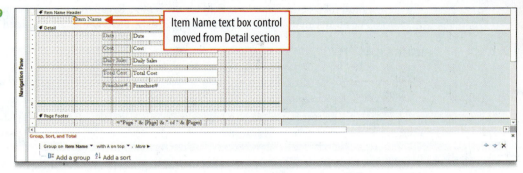

FIGURE 6.39

8 **Save** the report, and then switch to **Report** view. Scroll down, noticing the grouping of records, until the grouping for **Grilled Chicken Kabob** displays. Notice that there are two records, one for Franchise# 62 and another for Franchise# 12. For these two records, notice the dates.

9 Switch back to **Design** view. In the **Group, Sort, and Total pane**, click the **Add a sort** button, and then click **Date**. Notice that the date will be sorted from oldest to newest.

10 **Save** the report, and then switch to **Report** view. Scroll down until the **Grilled Chicken Kabob** grouping displays. Within the grouping, the two records are arranged in order by the date with the oldest date listed first.

11 Switch to **Design** view, and then **Close** the **Group, Sort, and Total pane**. Be sure to click the **Close** button located in the title bar and not the **Delete** button that is inside the pane.

Activity 6.18 | Adding Calculated Controls to a Report

In this activity, you will add an aggregate function and appropriate section to the report.

1 In the **Detail** section, click the **Total Cost text box control**. On the **REPORT DESIGN TOOLS DESIGN tab**, in the **Grouping & Totals group**, click the **Totals** button, and then compare your screen with Figure 6.40.

A list of **aggregate functions**—functions that group and perform calculations on multiple fields—displays. Before selecting the Totals button, the field that will be used in the aggregate function must be selected. If you wish to perform aggregate functions on multiple fields, you must select each field individually, and then select the aggregate function to apply to the field.

FIGURE 6.40

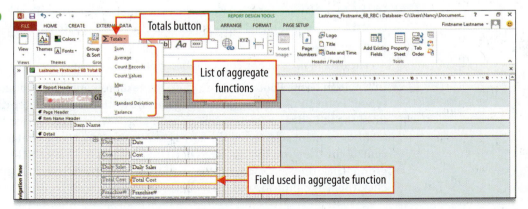

2 In the displayed list of aggregate functions, click **Sum**, and then compare your screen with Figure 6.41.

The Item Name Footer section is added to the report. A calculated control is added to the section that contains the expression that will display the sum of the Total Cost field for each grouping. A calculated control is also added to the Report Footer section that contains the expression that will display the grand total of the Total Cost field for the report. Recall that an expression begins with an equal sign (=). The Sum function adds or totals numeric data. Field names are included in square brackets.

FIGURE 6.41

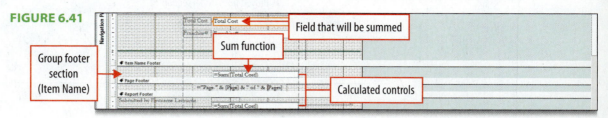

3 **Save** 💾 the report, and then switch to **Report** view. Notice that for the first grouping—**Banana Smoothie**—which only contains one record, the sum of the grouping displays below the horizontal line. Scroll down to the **Grilled Chicken Kabob** grouping, and then notice that the total for the grouping—**$716.40**—displays below the horizontal line for the second record in the grouping.

The placement of the horizontal line is distracting in the report, and there is no label attached to the grouping total.

4 Switch to **Design** view. On the **REPORT DESIGN TOOLS DESIGN tab**, in the **Controls group**, click the **Text Box** button 〔abl〕. Point to the **Item Name Footer** section until the plus sign (+) of the pointer aligns with the lower edge of the **Item Name Footer** section bar and with the **0.25-inch mark on the horizontal ruler**. Drag downward to the lower right of the **Item Name Footer** section and to the **2.5-inch mark on the horizontal ruler**.

5 Click inside the text box, and type **=[Item Name] & " Total Cost:"** ensuring that you include a space between the quotation mark and *Total* and that *Item Name* is enclosed in square brackets. Compare your screen with Figure 6.42.

Because a field name is included in the description of the total, a text box control must be used. This binds the control to the Item Name field in the underlying query, which makes this control a bound control. If you wish to insert only string characters as a description—for example, Total Cost—add a label control, which is an unbound control.

FIGURE 6.42

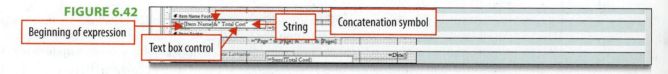

6 In the **Item Name Footer** section, click the **label control** that displays to the left of the text box control where you typed the expression. Press 〔Delete〕 to delete the text box control's associated **label control**.

The data in the text box control is descriptive and does not require an additional label control.

7 In the **Item Name Footer** section, click the **text box control** that contains the expression you typed. Point to the left middle sizing handle until the ↔ pointer displays. Drag to the left until the left edge of the text box control aligns with the left edge of the design grid. With the text box control selected, hold down 〔Shift〕. In the **Item Name Footer** section, click the **calculated control** for the sum. On the **REPORT DESIGN TOOLS ARRANGE tab**, in the **Sizing & Ordering group**, click the **Size/Space** button, and then click **To Tallest**. In the **Sizing & Ordering group**, click the **Align** button, and then click **Top** to align both controls at the top.

The two controls are now the same height and aligned at the top edges of the controls.

8 Point to the top of the **Page Footer** section bar until the ⊕ pointer displays. Drag downward to the top of the **Report Footer** section bar to increase the height of the **Item Name Footer** section so **four dots** display below the **Total Cost** controls.

9 In the **Detail** section, click the **line control**. Point to the **line control** until the pointer displays. Drag downward into the **Item Name Footer** section under the controls until there are approximately **two dots** between the **text box controls** and the **line control**, and then release the mouse button.

> The line control is moved from the Detail section to the Item Name Footer section.

10 Point to the top of the **Item Name Footer** section bar until the ⊕ pointer displays. Drag upward until approximately **two dots** display between the **Franchise#** controls and the top edge of the **Item Name Footer** section bar. Compare your screen with Figure 6.43.

> The height of the Detail section is changed.

FIGURE 6.43

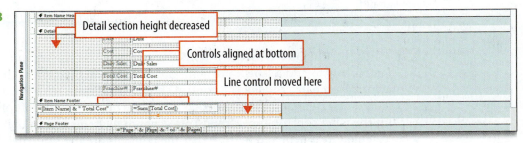

11 Save 🖫 the report, and then switch to **Report** view. Scroll down until the **Grilled Chicken Kabob** grouping displays, and then compare your screen with Figure 6.44.

> The report is easier to read with the horizontal line moved to the grouping footer section and with an explanation of the total for the grouping.

FIGURE 6.44

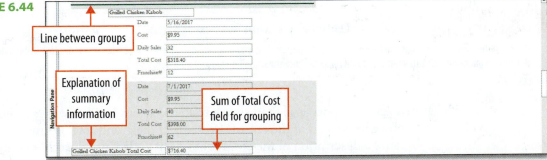

12 Hold down Ctrl, and then press End to move to the end of the report. Notice the sum of **$3,154.80**.

> By default, when you insert an aggregate function into a report, a calculated control for the grand total is inserted in the Report Footer section. The control is aligned with the text box control that is being used in the aggregate function. If the Report Footer section is not tall enough and multiple aggregate functions are used, the controls will display on top of one another.

13 Switch to **Design** view. In the **Report Footer** section, the calculated control displays *=Sum([Total Cost])*. Point to the bottom of the **Report Footer** section—not the section bar—until the ⊕ pointer displays. Drag downward until the height of the **Report Footer** section is approximately **1 inch**.

14 Click the label control that displays **Submitted by Firstname Lastname**. Hold down Shift, and then click the text box control that displays the **Date** expression. On the **REPORT DESIGN TOOLS ARRANGE tab**, in the **Sizing & Ordering group**, click the **Size/Space** button, and then click **To Tallest**. In the **Sizing & Ordering group**, click the **Align** button, and then click **Bottom**.

The two controls are the same height and aligned at the bottom edges of the controls.

15 Point to either of the selected controls until the pointer displays. Drag downward until the bottom edges of the controls align with the bottom edge of the Report Footer section, and then compare your screen with Figure 6.45.

The controls are moved to the bottom of the Report Footer section to increase readability and to make space to insert a label control for the grand total.

FIGURE 6.45

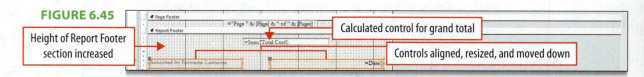

Height of Report Footer section increased

Calculated control for grand total

Controls aligned, resized, and moved down

16 Click the **REPORT DESIGN TOOLS DESIGN tab**. Use the techniques you have practiced previously to add a **label control** in the **Report Footer section** to the left of the calculated control—the left edge of the control should be aligned with the **0-inch mark on the horizontal ruler** and the right edge should be **one dot** to the left of the calculated control. In the label control, type **Grand Total Cost of All Items:** Align the label control with the calculated control and be sure that the controls are the same height. Compare your screen with Figure 6.46.

FIGURE 6.46

Label control

Controls aligned and same height

17 **Save** the report, and then switch to **Report** view. Hold down Ctrl, and then press End to move to the end of the report. Notice that the grand total is now easier to distinguish because a description of the control has been added and the other controls are moved down.

18 Switch to **Print Preview** view. If necessary, on the PRINT PREVIEW tab, in the Zoom group, click the Two Pages button. Look at the bottom of Page 1 and the top of Page 2, and notice that the grouping breaks across two pages. In the navigation area, click the **Next Page** button to display pages 3 and 4. Groupings are split between these pages. Compare your screen with Figure 6.47.

For a more professional-looking report, avoid splitting groupings between pages.

FIGURE 6.47

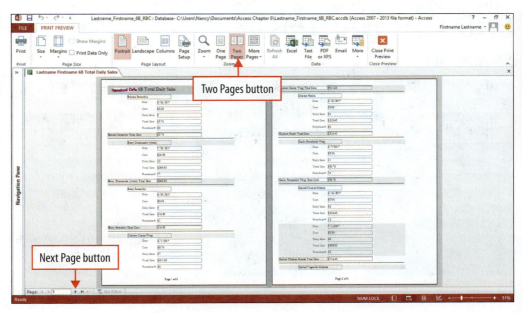

19 ▶ In the **Close Preview group**, click the **Close Print Preview** button. Switch to **Design** view. On the **DESIGN tab**, in the **Grouping & Totals group**, click the **Group & Sort** button.

20 ▶ In the displayed **Group, Sort, and Total pane**, on the **Group on Item Name** bar, click **More**. Click the **do not keep group together on one page arrow**, and then click **keep whole group together on one page**. **Close** ☒ the **Group, Sort, and Total pane**—do not click the **Delete** button.

21 ▶ **Save** 🖫 the report, and then switch to **Print Preview** view. In the navigation area, click the buttons to display pages in the report, and then notice that groupings are no longer split between pages. Also notice that more blank space displays at the bottom of some pages.

22 ▶ If you are instructed to submit this result, create a paper or electronic printout. On the **Print Preview tab**, in the **Close Preview group**, click the **Close Print Preview** button. **Close** ☒ the report. **Close** the database, and **Exit** ☒ Access.

More Knowledge | **Formatting a Report**

You can add a background picture to a report or change the background color of a report using the same techniques you used for forms.

---

23 ▶ As directed by your instructor, submit your database and the paper or electronic printouts of the two reports that are the result of this project. Specifically, in this project, using your own name you created the following database and printouts or electronic printouts:

1. Lastname_Firstname_6B_RBC	Database file
2. Lastname Firstname 6B Monthly Sales	Report (printed or electronic printout)
3. Lastname Firstname 6B Total Daily Sales	Report (printed or electronic printout)

END | You have completed Project 6B

END OF CHAPTER

SUMMARY

Forms are database objects used to interact with the data in tables. A form can be created in Design view. Sections and controls can be added, formatted, and modified to make the form user friendly.

Reports are database objects used to present data from tables or queries in a professional format. Grouping and sorting levels are added for organization, and then aggregate functions can summarize the data.

Controls added to forms and reports include label controls, image controls, command button controls, and line controls. Text box controls with expressions and concatenated strings are used to clarify data.

GO! LEARN IT ONLINE

Review the concepts and key terms in this chapter by completing these online challenges, which you can find at **www.pearsonhighered.com/go**.

Matching and Multiple Choice:
Answer matching and multiple choice questions to test what you learned in this chapter. **MyITLab®**

Crossword Puzzle:
Spell out the words that match the numbered clues, and put them in the puzzle squares.

Flipboard:
Flip through the definitions of the key terms in this chapter and match them with the correct term.

END OF CHAPTER

REVIEW AND ASSESSMENT GUIDE FOR ACCESS CHAPTER 6

Your instructor may assign one or more of these projects to help you review the chapter and assess your mastery and understanding of the chapter.

Project	Apply Skills from These Chapter Objectives	Project Type	Project Location
	Review and Assessment Guide for Access Chapter 6		
6C	Objectives 1–4 from Project 6A	**6C Skills Review** A guided review of the skills from Project 6A.	On the following pages
6D	Objectives 5–8 from Project 6B	**6D Skills Review** A guided review of the skills from Project 6B.	On the following pages
6E	Objectives 1–4 from Project 6A	**6E Mastery (Grader Project)** A demonstration of your mastery of the skills in Project 6A with extensive decision making.	In MyITLab and on the following pages
6F	Objectives 5–8 from Project 6B	**6F Mastery (Grader Project)** A demonstration of your mastery of the skills in Project 6B with extensive decision making.	In MyITLab and on the following pages
6G	Objectives 1–8 from Projects 6A and 6B	**6G Mastery (Grader Project)** A demonstration of your mastery of the skills in Projects 6A and 6B with extensive decision making.	In MyITLab and on the following pages
6H	Combination of Objectives from Projects 6A and 6B	**6H GO! Fix It** A demonstration of your mastery of the skills in Projects 6A and 6B by creating a correct result from a document that contains errors you must find.	Online
6I	Combination of Objectives from Projects 6A and 6B	**6I GO! Make It** A demonstration of your mastery of the skills in Projects 6A and 6B by creating a result from a supplied picture.	Online
6J	Combination of Objectives from Projects 6A and 6B	**6J GO! Solve It** A demonstration of your mastery of the skills in Projects 6A and 6B, your decision-making skills, and your critical thinking skills. A task-specific rubric helps you self-assess your result.	Online
6K	Combination of Objectives from Projects 6A and 6B	**6K GO! Solve It** A demonstration of your mastery of the skills in Projects 6A and 6B, your decision-making skills, and your critical thinking skills. A task-specific rubric helps you self-assess your result.	On the following pages
6L	Combination of Objectives from Projects 6A and 6B	**6L GO! Think** A demonstration of your understanding of the chapter concepts applied in a manner that you would use outside of college. An analytic rubric helps you and your instructor grade the quality of your work by comparing it to the work an expert in the discipline would create.	On the following pages
6M	Combination of Objectives from Projects 6A and 6B	**6M GO! Think** A demonstration of your understanding of the chapter concepts applied in a manner that you would use outside of college. An analytic rubric helps you and your instructor grade the quality of your work by comparing it to the work an expert in the discipline would create.	Online
6N	Combination of Objectives from Projects 6A and 6B	**6N You and GO!** A demonstration of your understanding of the chapter concepts applied in a manner that you would use in a personal situation. An analytic rubric helps you and your instructor grade the quality of your work.	Online

GLOSSARY

GLOSSARY OF CHAPTER KEY TERMS

Aggregate function A function that groups and performs calculations on multiple fields.

Button control A control that enables individuals to add a command button to a form or report that will perform an action when the button is clicked.

Combo box A control that enables individuals to select from a list or to type a value.

Concatenation Linking or joining strings.

Control An object, such as a label or text box, in a form or report that enables individuals to view or manipulate information stored in tables or queries.

ControlTip Displays descriptive text when the mouse pointer is paused over the control.

Focus An object that is selected and currently being acted upon.

Form selector The box in the upper left corner of a form in Design view where the rulers meet; used to select the entire form.

Image control A control that enables individuals to insert an image into any section of a form or report.

Line control A control that enables an individual to insert a line into a form or report.

List box A control that enables individuals to select from a list but does not enable individuals to type anything that is not in the list.

Picture Alignment property A property that determines where the background picture for a form displays on the form.

Picture Size Mode property A property that determines the proportion of a picture in a form.

Point A measurement that is 1/72 of an inch.

Propagate To disseminate or apply changes to an object.

Properties The characteristics that determine the appearance, structure, and behavior of an object.

Property Sheet A sheet that is available for every object on a form, including the form itself, to further enhance the object.

Property Update Options button An option button that displays when you make changes to the design of a table; it enables individuals to update the Property Sheet for a field in all objects that use a table as the record source.

Record Source property A property that enables you to specify the source of the data for a form or a report. The property setting can be a table name, a query name, or an SQL statement.

Status Bar Text property A form property that enables individuals to enter text that will display in the status bar for a selected control.

String A series of characters.

Tab order A setting that refers to the order in which the fields are selected when the Tab key is pressed.

Theme A design tool that simplifies the process of creating professional-looking objects within one program or across multiple programs; includes theme colors and theme fonts that will be applied consistently throughout the objects in a database.

CHAPTER REVIEW

Apply 6A skills from these Objectives:

1 Create a Form in Design View
2 Change and Add Controls
3 Format a Form
4 Make a Form User Friendly

Skills Review   Project 6C Party Orders

Marty Kress, vice president of marketing for the Rosebud Cafe franchise restaurant chain, wants to expand the chain's offerings to include party trays for advance order and delivery. In the following project, you will create a form to use for the data entry of these party order items. Your completed form, if printed, will look similar to Figure 6.48. An electronic version of the form will look slightly different.

PROJECT FILES

For Project 6C, you will need the following files:

a06C_Party_Orders
a06C_Logo
a06C_Rose

You will save your database as:

Lastname_Firstname_6C_Party_Orders

PROJECT RESULTS

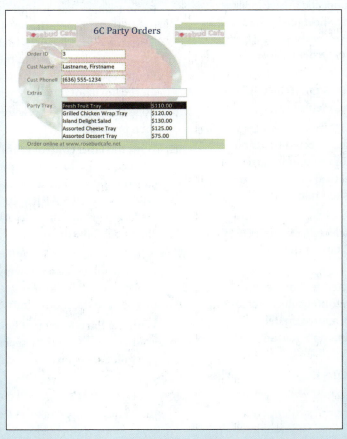

FIGURE 6.48

(Project 6C Party Orders continues on the next page)

CHAPTER REVIEW

1 **Start** Access. Locate and open the **a06C_Party_Orders** file. Save the database in your **Access Chapter 6** folder as **Lastname_Firstname_6C_Party_Orders** If necessary, click Enable Content.

2 Double-click **6C Party Orders** to open the table in **Datasheet** view. Take a moment to examine the fields in the table.

a. In any record, click in the **Party Tray** field, and then click the **arrow**. This field is a Lookup field in the *6C Trays* table. In any record, click in the **Extras** field, and then click the **arrow**. This field is a Lookup field in the *6C Menu Items* table.

b. **Close** the table, and then **Close** the **Navigation Pane**.

3 On the **CREATE tab**, in the **Forms group**, click the **Form Design** button.

a. If necessary, on the FORM DESIGN TOOLS DESIGN tab, in the Tools group, click the Property Sheet button. On the **Property Sheet**, click the **Data tab**. Click the **Record Source property setting box arrow**, and then click **6C Party Orders**. Close the **Property Sheet**.

4 On the **FORM DESIGN TOOLS DESIGN tab**, in the **Tools group**, click the **Add Existing Fields** button.

a. In the **Field List**, click **Order ID**, hold down Shift, and then click **Extras**. Drag the selected fields onto the design grid until the top of the pointer arrow is aligned at **0.25 inch on the vertical ruler** and **2 inches on the horizontal ruler**, and then release the mouse button. **Close** the **Field List**.

b. With all of the controls still selected, on the **FORM DESIGN TOOLS ARRANGE tab**, in the **Table group**, click the **Stacked** button.

c. Drag the left edge of the selected text box controls to the **0.5-inch mark on the horizontal ruler**. Increase the width of the text boxes by approximately **0.5 inches**. Save the form as **Lastname Firstname 6C Party Orders Form**

5 On the **FORM DESIGN TOOLS DESIGN tab**, in the **Header/Footer group**, click the **Logo** button.

a. Navigate to the location where the student data files for this textbook are saved. Locate and double-click **a06C_Logo** to insert the logo in the **Form Header**.

b. On the selected logo, point to the right middle sizing handle until the pointer displays. Drag to the right until the right edge of the logo is aligned with the **1.5-inch mark on the horizontal ruler**.

6 In the **Header/Footer group**, click the **Title** button.

a. In the **label control** for the title, replace the text with **6C Party Orders** and then press Enter.

b. Drag the right edge of the title to align it with the **4-inch mark on the horizontal ruler**.

c. With the title selected, on the **FORMAT tab**, in the **Font group**, click the **Center** button.

7 Scroll down until the **Form Footer** section bar displays. Point to the top of the **Form Footer** section bar until the pointer displays. Drag upward until the top of the **Form Footer** section bar aligns with the **2.5-inch mark on the vertical ruler**.

a. On the **FORM DESIGN TOOLS DESIGN tab**, in the **Controls group**, click the **Label** button. Point to the **Form Footer** section until the plus sign (+) of the pointer aligns with the bottom of the **Form Footer** section bar and the **0.25-inch mark on the horizontal ruler**. Drag downward to the bottom of the **Form Footer** section and to the right to the **3.25-inch mark on the horizontal ruler**.

b. Type **Order online at www.rosebudcafe.net** and then press Enter.

c. With the **label control** in the **Form Footer** section selected, hold down Shift, and then click the **Logo control** and the **Extras label control**. On the **FORM DESIGN TOOLS ARRANGE tab**, in the **Sizing & Ordering group**, click the **Align** button, and then click **Left**. **Save** the form.

8 Click and hold the **Party Tray text box control** until the pointer displays. Drag downward until a thin orange line displays on the bottom edges of the **Extras** controls and then release the mouse button.

a. With the **Party Tray text box control** selected, hold down Shift, and then click the **Party Tray label control**, **Extras text box control**, and **Extras label control**.

b. On the **FORM DESIGN TOOLS ARRANGE tab**, in the **Table group**, click the **Remove Layout** button to remove the *Extras* field and the *Party Tray* field from the stacked layout.

c. Click in the **Detail** section to deselect the controls. Right-click the **Party Tray combo box control**. From

(Project 6C Party Orders continues on the next page)

the shortcut menu, point to **Change To**, and then click **List Box**.

d. **Save** the form, and then switch to **Form** view. Notice that the **Party Tray list box control** is not wide enough to display all columns and that there are horizontal and vertical scroll bars to indicate there is more data. Click the **Extras combo box arrow** to see if any menu item names or prices are cut off. Press Esc.

e. Switch to **Design** view, and click the **Party Tray list box control**, if necessary. Point to the right edge of the control until the pointer displays. Drag to the right until the right edge of the control aligns with the **4.25-inch mark on the horizontal ruler**.

f. Switch to **Layout** view. Resize the **Extras combo box control** to be the same size as the **Party Tray list box control**. **Save** the form and switch to **Design** view. Click the **Form Header section bar**.

9 On the **FORM DESIGN TOOLS DESIGN tab**, in the **Controls group**, click the **Insert Image** button, and then click **Browse**. In the displayed **Insert Picture** dialog box, navigate to the location where the student data files for this textbook are saved.

a. Locate and double-click **a06C_Logo**.

b. Align the plus sign (+) with the bottom of the **Form Header** section bar and with the **4-inch mark on the horizontal ruler**. Drag downward to the top of the **Detail** section bar and to the right to the **5.25-inch mark on the horizontal ruler**.

c. Click the **image control**—the Rosebud Cafe image on the right side in the **Form Header** section—if necessary. On the **DESIGN tab**, in the **Tools group**, click the **Property Sheet** button. If necessary, on the Format tab, change the Width property setting to 1.25 and then change the Height property setting to 0.5.

d. In the **Form Header** section, click the **logo control**. On the **Property Sheet**, change the **Width** property setting to **1.25** and change the **Height** property setting to **0.5**. **Close** the **Property Sheet**.

e. With the logo control selected, hold down Shift, and then click the **image control**. On the **ARRANGE tab**, in the **Sizing & Ordering group**, click the **Align** button, and then click **Top**.

10 On the **FORM DESIGN TOOLS DESIGN tab**, in the **Controls group**, click the **Button** button.

a. Move the mouse pointer down into the **Detail** section. Align the plus sign (+) of the pointer at **0.25 inches on the vertical ruler** and **3.25 inches on the horizontal ruler**, and then click.

b. Under **Categories**, verify **Record Navigation** is selected. Under **Actions**, click **Find Record**, and then click **Next** two times. In the text box, type **btnFindRcrd** and then click **Finish**.

c. Using the technique you just practiced, add a **button control** right next to the **Find Record button**. Under **Categories**, click **Form Operations**. Under **Actions**, click **Print Current Form**, and then click **Next** two times. Name the button **btnPrtForm** Click **Finish**.

d. With the **Print Current Form button control** selected, hold down Shift, and then click the **Find Record button control**. On the **ARRANGE tab**, in the **Sizing & Ordering group**, click the **Align** button, and then click **Top**.

11 Switch to **Layout** view. Click in the **Form Footer** section to the right of the **label control**.

a. On the **FORMAT tab**, in the **Control Formatting group**, click the **Shape Fill** button. Under **Theme Colors**, in the third row, click the seventh color— **Olive Green, Accent 3, Lighter 60%**.

b. Using the technique you just practiced, change the color of the **Form Header** section to match the **Form Footer** section.

12 Switch to **Design** view, and then double-click the **Form selector** to open the **Property Sheet** for the form.

a. On the **Property Sheet**, on the **Format tab**, click in the **Picture** property setting box, and then click the **Build** button. Navigate to where the student data files for this textbook are saved. Locate and double-click **a06C_Rose** to insert the picture in the form.

b. Click in the **Picture Alignment** property setting box, click the **arrow**, and then click **Form Center**. **Close** the **Property Sheet**, and then **save** the form.

13 Switch to **Layout** view, click the **Order ID text box control**, hold down Shift, and then click the **Cust Name text box control** and the **Cust Phone# text box control**.

(Project 6C Party Orders continues on the next page)

CHAPTER REVIEW

a. On the **FORM LAYOUT TOOLS FORMAT tab**, in the **Control Formatting group**, click the **Shape Outline** button. Point to **Line Type**, and click the fifth line type—**Dots**.

b. On the **FORM LAYOUT TOOLS FORMAT tab**, in the **Control Formatting group**, click the **Shape Outline** button. Point to **Line Thickness**, and then click the second line type—**1 pt**.

c. In the **Control Formatting group**, click the **Shape Outline** button. Under **Theme Colors**, in the fifth row, click the seventh color—**Olive Green, Accent 3, Darker 25%**.

14 ▸ Switch to **Form** view, and then click in the **Cust Phone# text box control**. On the left side of the status bar, *Form View* displays—there is no text that helps an individual enter data. **Close** the form, **Save** your changes, and open the **Navigation Pane**.

a. Under **Tables**, right-click **6C Party Orders**; from the shortcut menu, click **Design View**. In the **Cust Phone#** field, click in the **Description** box. Type **Include area code for 10-digit dialing** and then press Enter.

b. Click the **Property Update Options** button, and then click **Update Status Bar Text everywhere Cust Phone# is used**. In the displayed **Update Properties** dialog box, click **Yes**. **Close** the table, saving changes.

15 ▸ Open **6C Party Order Form** in **Design** view. **Close** the **Navigation Pane**. On the **DESIGN tab**, in the **Tools** group, click the **Property Sheet** button.

a. In the **Detail** section, click the **Print Form** button. Notice that the **Property Sheet** is displayed for the button you selected.

b. On the **Other tab**, click in the **ControlTip Text property setting box**, type **Prints the Current Form** to replace the existing **Print Form** text, and then press Enter.

c. **Close** the **Property Sheet**, **Save** the form, and then switch to **Form** view. Point to the **Print Form** button to display the **ControlTip**.

16 ▸ Switch to **Design** view. In the **Detail** section, click the **Order ID text box control**, hold down Shift, and then click the **Find Record button control** and the **Print Current Form button control**.

a. On the **FORM DESIGN TOOLS DESIGN tab**, in the **Tools group**, click the **Property Sheet** button. If necessary, on the Property Sheet, click the Other tab. On the **Property Sheet**, click in the **Tab Stop** property setting box, click the **arrow**, and then click **No**.

b. Click the **Cust Name text box control**. Click in the **Tab Index** property setting box, and then type **0** **Close** the **Property Sheet**.

17 ▸ Switch to **Form** view. With the **Cust Name** control selected, click the **Find Record** button.

a. In the **Find and Replace** dialog box, in the **Find What** box, type **Gonzalez, Ricardo** Click **Find Next**. **Close** the **Find and Replace** dialog box.

b. In the **Cust Name text box**, type your **Lastname, Firstname** replacing Ricardo's name. Press Tab. In the **Cust Phone#** field, enter your phone number, and then press Enter. **Save** the form.

18 ▸ If you are instructed to submit this result, click the **Print Current Form** button to create a paper or electronic printout. If you are to submit your work electronically, follow your instructor's directions.

19 ▸ **Close** the form, **Close** the **Navigation Pane**, **Close** the database, and then **Exit** Access.

20 ▸ As directed by your instructor, submit your database and the paper or electronic printout of the one form that is the result of this project. Specifically, in this project, using your own name you created the following database and printout or electronic printout:

| 1. Lastname_Firstname_6C_Party_Orders | Database file |
| 2. Lastname Firstname 6C Party Orders | Form (printed or electronic printout) |

END | You have completed Project 6C

CHAPTER REVIEW

Skills Review Project 6D Catering

Apply 6B skills from these Objectives:

5 Create a Report Based on a Query Using a Wizard
6 Create a Report in Design View
7 Add Controls to a Report
8 Group, Sort, and Total Records in Design View

Each Rosebud Cafe location maintains a database about the orders that are placed for the catering entity of the business. Reports are run to summarize data in the tables or queries. Creating customized reports will help the managers of each location view the information in the database in a meaningful way. In this project, you will create customized reports. Your completed reports will look similar to Figure 6.49.

PROJECT FILES

For Project 6D, you will need the following files:

a06D_Catering
a06D_Logo

You will save your database as:

Lastname_Firstname_6D_Catering

PROJECT RESULTS

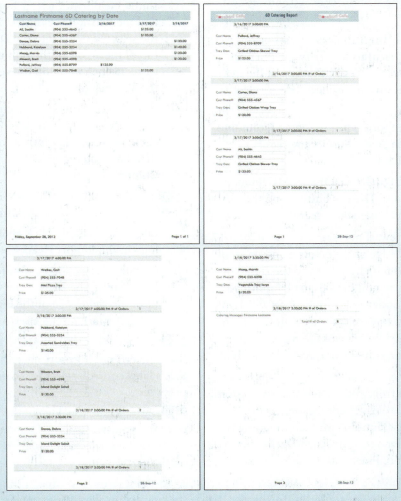

FIGURE 6.49

(Project 6D Catering continues on the next page)

CHAPTER REVIEW

1 **Start** Access. Locate and open the **a06D_Catering** file. Save the database in your **Access Chapter 6** folder as **Lastname_Firstname_6D_Catering** If necessary, click Enable Content.

2 In the Navigation Pane, under **Queries**, double-click **6D Catering Crosstab Query**. Take a moment to study the data in the query. **Close** the query, and then **Close** the **Navigation Pane**.

3 On the **CREATE tab**, in the **Reports group**, click the **Report Wizard** button.

a. Under **Tables/Queries**, verify **Query: 6D Catering Crosstab Query** is displayed. Under **Available Fields**, add all of the field names to the **Selected Fields** box. Click **Next** twice.

b. Click the **arrow** next to the **1** box, and then click **Cust Name**. Leave the sort order as **Ascending**, and then click **Next**.

c. Under **Layout**, verify the **Tabular** option button is selected. Under **Orientation**, verify the **Portrait** option button is selected. Verify the **Adjust the field width so all fields fit on a page** check box is selected. Click **Next**.

d. For the title of the report, type **Lastname Firstname 6D Catering by Date** Select **Modify the report's design**, and then click **Finish**.

4 On the **REPORT DESIGN TOOLS DESIGN tab**, in the **Themes group**, click the **Themes** button, and then in the first row click the third theme—**Integral**.

5 Switch to **Layout** view. If necessary, in the 3/16/2017 column, point to the left edge of the column and drag to the right approximately 0.5 inches. Point to the right edge of the **Cust Phone#** column and drag to the left until all of the data in the **Cust Phone#** column displays. Click in a blank area of the report to deselect the column. Switch to **Design** view. Drag the right edge of the report to the **7.75-inch mark on the horizontal ruler**, resizing the right column as necessary.

6 Select all of the controls in the **Page Header** section by pointing to the top left of the **Page Header** section, holding down your mouse button, and then dragging the mouse across the **Page Header controls** and to the bottom of the **Page Header** section. Release the mouse button.

a. On the **REPORT DESIGN TOOLS FORMAT tab**, in the **Font group**, click the **Font color button arrow**.

Under **Theme Colors**, on the first row, click the fourth color—**Dark Teal, Text 2**. In the **Font group**, click the **Bold button**.

7 **Save** the report, and then switch to **Print Preview**. If you are instructed to submit this result, create a paper or electronic printout. **Close Print Preview**. **Close** the report.

8 On the **CREATE tab**, in the **Reports group**, click the **Report Design** button.

a. On the **REPORT DESIGN TOOLS DESIGN tab**, in the **Tools group**, click the **Property Sheet** button. On the **Property Sheet**, click the **Data tab**. Click the **Record Source arrow**, click **6D Catering**, and then **Close** the **Property Sheet**.

b. On the **REPORT DESIGN TOOLS DESIGN tab**, in the **Tools group**, click the **Add Existing Fields** button.

c. In the **Field List**, click **Pickup Time**. Hold down Shift, and then click **Price** to select all of the fields. Drag the selected fields into the **Detail** section until the top of the arrow of the pointer is aligned with the **0.25-inch mark on the vertical ruler** and with the **1.5-inch mark on the horizontal ruler**.

d. With the controls still selected, on the **REPORT DESIGN TOOLS ARRANGE tab**, in the **Table group**, click the **Stacked** button. **Close** the **Field List**, and then **Save** the report as **Lastname Firstname 6D Catering Report**

9 On the **REPORT DESIGN TOOLS DESIGN tab**, in the **Header/Footer group**, click the **Logo** button.

a. Locate and double-click **a06D_Logo** to insert the logo in the **Report Header** section.

b. On the selected logo, point to the right middle sizing handle until the pointer displays. Drag to the right until the right edge of the logo is aligned with the **1.5-inch mark on the horizontal ruler**.

10 On the **REPORT DESIGN TOOLS DESIGN tab**, in the **Header/Footer group**, click the **Title** button. In the **title's label control**, select **Lastname Firstname**, and then press Delete.

11 Point to the top edge of the **Page Footer** section bar until the pointer displays. Drag upward until the top of the **Page Footer** section bar aligns with the **2-inch mark on the vertical ruler**.

12 Point to the top edge of the **Detail** section bar until the pointer displays. Drag upward until the top edge of

(Project 6D Catering continues on the next page)

CHAPTER REVIEW

the **Detail** section bar aligns with the bottom edge of the **Page Header** section bar. **Save** the report.

13 On the **REPORT DESIGN TOOLS DESIGN tab**, in the **Header/Footer group**, click the **Page Numbers** button.

  a. In the displayed **Page Numbers** dialog box, under **Format**, click **Page N**, if necessary. Under **Position**, click **Bottom of Page [Footer]**, and then click **OK**.

  b. Resize and move the **Page Number control box** until it fits between the **2-inch and 4-inch marks on the horizontal ruler**.

14 On the **REPORT DESIGN TOOLS DESIGN tab**, in the **Controls group**, click the **Label** button.

  a. Drag the plus sign (+) from the bottom edge of the **Report Footer** section bar at the **0.25-inch mark on the horizontal ruler** to the bottom of the **Report Footer** section at the **3-inch mark on the horizontal ruler**.

  b. Using your own first and last names, type **Catering Manager: Firstname Lastname** Press [Enter].

15 On the **REPORT DESIGN TOOLS DESIGN tab**, in the **Header/Footer group**, click the **Date & Time** button. In the **Date and Time** dialog box, under **Include Date**, click the second option button. Under **Include Time**, remove the check mark, and then click **OK**. **Save** the report.

  a. Click the **Date text box control**. On the **ARRANGE tab**, in the **Table group**, click the **Remove Layout** button.

  b. Right-click the selected control, and click **Cut**. Right-click the **Page Footer** section, and click **Paste**.

  c. Move the **Date text box control** and resize it until the right edge of the **text box control** aligns with the **6.25-inch mark on the horizontal ruler**.

  d. Click the **Title text box control** to select it, point to the right middle sizing handle until the pointer displays, and then drag to the left until the right edge of the text box control aligns with the **4.75-inch mark on the horizontal ruler**.

16 Drag the right edge of the design grid to the left until it aligns with the **6.5-inch mark on the horizontal ruler**. **Save** the report.

  a. Switch to **Layout** view. In the first record, click the **Tray Desc text box control**, and then point to the right edge of the control until the pointer displays. Drag to the right until all of the text displays in

the **Tray Desc text box control**—*Grilled Chicken Skewer Tray*.

17 Switch to **Design** view. In the **Report Header** section, right-click the **logo control**. From the displayed shortcut menu, click **Copy**. Right-click anywhere in the **Report Header** section, and then from the shortcut menu, click **Paste**.

  a. Point to the selected logo, and then drag to the right until the left edge of the outlined control aligns with the **4.75-inch mark on the horizontal ruler**.

  b. With the image control on the right selected, hold down [Ctrl], and then click the **logo control**. On the **ARRANGE tab**, in the **Sizing & Ordering group**, click the **Align** button, and then click **Bottom**.

  c. Resize the **Title text box control** so the right edge is **one dot** away from the image on its right. **Center** the title in the control. Drag the **Page Header section bar** up to the **0.5-inch mark on the vertical ruler**.

18 On the **REPORT DESIGN TOOLS DESIGN tab**, in the **Grouping & Totals group**, click the **Group & Sort** button.

  a. In the **Group, Sort, and Total Pane**, click the **Add a group** button. From the displayed list, click **Pickup Time**.

  b. Click the **by quarter arrow** that displays after **from oldest to newest**, and then click **by entire value**. Click in a blank area of the **Group, Sort, and Total Pane**. Click the **More arrow**, click the **do not keep group together on one page arrow**, and then click **keep whole group together on one page**.

  c. In the **Group, Sort, and Total Pane**, click the **Add a sort** button, and then click **Cust Name**. **Close** the **Group, Sort, and Total Pane**.

19 In the **Detail** section, click the **Pickup Time text box control**. Drag downward until a thin orange line displays at the bottom of the **Price** controls, and then release the mouse button.

  a. On the **ARRANGE tab**, in the **Table group**, click the **Remove Layout** button.

  b. Move the **Pickup Time text box control** into the **Pickup Time Header** section so the left edge of the **text box control** aligns with the **1-inch mark on the horizontal ruler**.

  c. In the **Pickup Time Header** section, click the **Pickup Time label control**, and then press [Delete].

(Project 6D Catering continues on the next page)

CHAPTER REVIEW

20 In the **Detail** section, click the **Tray Desc text box control**. On the **DESIGN tab**, in the **Grouping & Totals group**, click the **Totals** button. In the displayed list of aggregate functions, click **Count Records**.

21 In the **Pickup Time Footer** section, select the **Count text box control**, and then holding down Shift, in the **Report Footer** select the **Count text box control**.

a. On the **REPORT DESIGN TOOLS ARRANGE tab**, in the **Table group**, click the **Remove Layout** button.

b. Align and resize the control so the left edge of each control is even with the **5.5-inch marker on the horizontal ruler** and the right edge of each control is even with the **6-inch marker on the horizontal ruler**.

c. On the **REPORT DESIGN TOOLS DESIGN tab**, in the **Controls group**, click the **Text Box** button. Drag the plus sign (+) from the bottom edge of the **Pickup Time Footer** section bar at the **2.75-inch mark on the horizontal ruler** to the bottom of the **Pickup Time Footer** section and to the right to the **5.5-inch mark on the horizontal ruler**.

d. In the Unbound text box, type **=[Pickup Time] & " # of Orders:"** In the **Pickup Time Footer** section, click the **label control** that displays to the left of the **text box control**, and then press Delete.

e. In the **Pickup Time Footer** section, click the **text box control** that contains the expression you typed. Hold down Shift and click the **count calculated control** in the **Pickup Time Footer**. On the **ARRANGE tab**, in the **Sizing & Ordering group**, click **Size/Space**, and then click **To Tallest**. In the **Sizing & Ordering group**, click the **Align** button, and then click **Top**.

22 Drag the right edge of the design grid to the left until it aligns with the **6.5-inch mark on the horizontal ruler**. Switch to **Report** view. Hold down Ctrl, and then press End to move to the end of the report.

23 Switch to **Design** view. Point to the bottom of the **Report Footer** section, and then drag downward until it reaches the **0.5-inch mark on the vertical ruler**.

a. In the **Report Footer** section, click the **Count text box control**, and then drag downward until the bottom edge of the control aligns with the bottom edge of the **Report Footer** section.

b. Use the techniques you have practiced to add a label control in the **Report Footer** section to the left of the calculated control—the left edge of the control should be aligned with the **4-inch mark on the horizontal ruler**. In the **label control**, type **Total # of Orders:**

c. Align the label control with the calculated control and then be sure that the controls are the same height.

24 On the **REPORT DESIGN TOOLS DESIGN tab**, in the **Controls group**, click the **Line** button. Point to the bottom of the **Pickup Time Footer** section until the middle of the plus sign (+) of the pointer aligns with the top of the **Page Footer** section bar and the **0-inch mark on the horizontal ruler**. Hold down Shift, drag to the right to the **6.5-inch mark on the horizontal ruler**, and then release the mouse button and Shift.

25 On the **FORMAT tab**, in the **Control Formatting group**, click the **Shape Outline** button. Click **Line Thickness**, and then click the third line—**2 pt**. In the **Control Formatting group**, click the **Shape Outline** button. Under **Theme Colors**, in the first row, click the eighth color—**Green, Accent 4**. **Save** the report.

26 Switch to **Print Preview**. Adjust the margins or report width as needed. If you are instructed to submit this result, create a paper or electronic printout. **Close Print Preview**.

27 **Close** the report, and then **Close** the **Navigation Pane**. **Close** the database, and then **Exit** Access.

28 As directed by your instructor, submit your database and the paper or electronic printouts of the two reports that are the result of this project. Specifically, in this project, using your own name you created the following database and printouts or electronic printouts:

1. Lastname_Firstname_6D_Catering	Database file
2. Lastname Firstname 6D Catering by Date	Report (printed or electronic printout)
3. Lastname Firstname 6D Catering Report	Report (printed or electronic printout)

END | You have completed Project 6D

In the following project, you will create a form that will be used to enter the data for the monthly promotions that are offered to guests at the Rosebud Cafe restaurant franchise. Your task includes designing a form that will be attractive and provide easy data entry for the staff. Your completed form will look similar to Figure 6.50.

Apply 6A skills from these Objectives:

1 Create a Form in Design View

2 Change and Add Controls

3 Format a Form

4 Make a Form User Friendly

PROJECT FILES

For Project 6E, you will need the following files:

a06E_Monthly_Promotions
a06E_Logo
a06E_Dollar

You will save your database as:

Lastname_Firstname_6E_Monthly_Promotions

PROJECT RESULTS

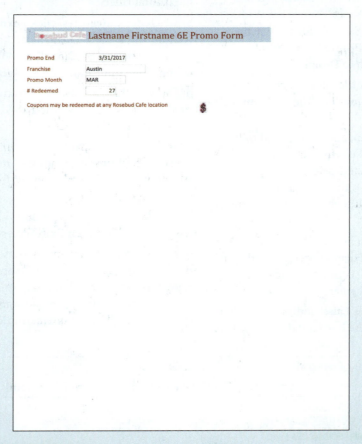

FIGURE 6.50

(Project 6E Monthly Promotions continues on the next page)

CONTENT-BASED ASSESSMENTS

1 **Start** Access. Locate and open the **a06E_Monthly_Promotions** file. Save the database in your **Access Chapter 6** folder as **Lastname_Firstname_6E_Monthly_Promotions** If necessary, click Enable Content.

2 Create a form in **Form Design**. For the **Record Source**, use the **6E Monthly Results** table. Select all of the fields, and then drag them onto the design grid until the top of the arrow is aligned with the **1-inch mark on the horizontal ruler** and the **0.25-inch mark on the vertical ruler. Save** the form as **Lastname Firstname 6E Promo Form**

3 With all of the text box controls selected, display the **Property Sheet**, and then click the **Format tab**. In the **Left** property box, type **1.5** and press Enter. Click anywhere in the **Detail** section to deselect the controls. Select the **Franchise text box control**, and then drag the right edge to the **3-inch mark on the horizontal ruler**. Select the **# Redeemed text box control**, and in the **Property Sheet**, change the **Width** to **0.75 Close** the Property Sheet. **Save** the form. Switch to **Form** view, and then click the **Promo Month text box control** to view the entries. Switch to **Design** view.

4 In the **Form Header**, insert the **a06E_Logo**. Widen the selected logo to the **1.5-inch mark on the horizontal ruler**.

5 In the **Header/Footer group**, add a **Title**, and then, if necessary, resize the **Title label control** so the entire title is visible. With the title selected, select all of the label controls. On the **FORMAT tab**, in the **Font group**, under **Theme Colors**, in the fifth row click the sixth color—**Red, Accent 2, Darker 25%**.

6 Scroll down until the **Form Footer** section bar displays. Point to the top of the **Form Footer**, and drag up until the top of the **Form Footer** section bar aligns with the **1.5-inch mark on the vertical ruler**.

7 In the **Form Footer**, insert a **Label** control so the left aligns with the **0-inch mark on the horizontal ruler** and

the right aligns with the **4-inch mark on the horizontal ruler**. Type **Coupons may be redeemed at any Rosebud Cafe location** Press Enter. Change the font color to **Red, Accent 2, Darker 25%**.

8 In the **Form Footer**, insert the **a06E_Dollar** image at the top of the **Form Footer** section and at the **4.25-inch mark on the horizontal ruler**.

9 Display the **Property Sheet**, and change the **Width** and **Height** to **0.35** Point to the bottom of the **Form Footer**; drag up until the bottom of the **Form Footer** section bar aligns with the **0.5-inch mark on the vertical ruler. Close** the **Property Sheet**.

10 In the **Detail** section, insert a **Button** control aligning the plus sign (+) of the pointer with the **0.5-inch mark on the vertical ruler** and the **3.5-inch mark on the horizontal ruler**.

11 Under **Categories**, click **Form Operations**. Under **Actions**, click **Close Form**. Select the **Text** option button. Name the button **btnCloseFrm** With the button selected, change the **Font Color** to **Red, Accent 2, Darker 25%**.

12 With the **Close Form** button selected, open the **Property Sheet**. Change the **Tab Stop** property to **No. Close** the **Property Sheet**.

13 If you are instructed to submit this result, create a paper or electronic printout of **record 8**. If you are to submit your work electronically, follow your instructor's directions.

14 Click the **Close Form** button, saving changes. **Close** the database, and then **Exit** Access.

15 As directed by your instructor, submit your database and the paper or electronic printout of the report that is the result of this project. Specifically, in this project, using your own name you created the following database and printout or electronic printout:

| 1. Lastname_Firstname_6E_Monthly_Promotions | Database file |
| 2. Lastname Firstname 6E Promo Form | Report (printed or electronic printout) |

END | You have completed Project 6E

CONTENT-BASED ASSESSMENTS

In the following project, you will create a report that will display the promotions that are offered to guests of the Rosebud Cafe restaurant franchise. You will also create a crosstab report that will summarize the results of the promotions. Creating customized reports will help the managers of each location view the information in the database in a meaningful way. Your completed reports will look similar to Figure 6.51.

Apply 6B skills from these Objectives:

5 Create a Report Based on a Query Using a Wizard

6 Create a Report in Design View

7 Add Controls to a Report

8 Group, Sort, and Total Records in Design View

PROJECT FILES

For Project 6F, you will need the following files:

a06F_Promotional_Results
a06F_Logo

You will save your database as:

Lastname_Firstname_6F_Promotional_Results

PROJECT RESULTS

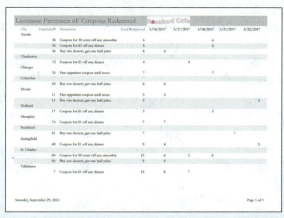

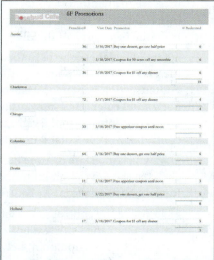

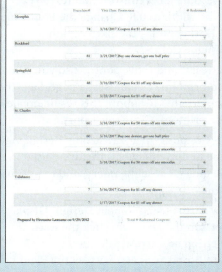

FIGURE 6.51

(Project 6F Promotional Results continues on the next page)

CONTENT-BASED ASSESSMENTS

1 **Start** Access. Locate and open the **a06F_ Promotional Results** file. Save the database in your **Access Chapter 6** folder as **Lastname_Firstname_6F_ Promotional_Results** If necessary, click Enable Content.

2 Under **Queries**, open the **6F Coupons Crosstab Query**. Take a moment to study the data in the query. **Close** the query, and then **Close** the **Navigation Pane**.

3 **Create** a report using the **Report Wizard**. From the **Query: 6F Coupons Crosstab Query**, select all of the fields. Under **Do you want to add any grouping levels?**, select **City**. **Sort** the records within the report by **Franchise#** in **Ascending** order. Under **Layout**, be sure the **Stepped** option button is selected. Under **Orientation**, click the **Landscape** option button. Be sure the **Adjust the field width so all fields fit on a page** check box is selected. For the title of the report, type **Lastname Firstname 6F Coupons Redeemed** Select **Modify the report's design**, and then click **Finish**.

4 Switch to **Layout** view. On the **DESIGN tab**, click the **Themes** button, and then apply the **Organic** theme. If any data is cut off, select the label control, and drag to the right to widen the column to display all data. Reduce the width of any columns that display a lot of blank space to allow for the widened columns.

5 Switch to **Design** view. Insert the **a06F_Logo** image so it appears from the **5.25-inch mark on the horizontal ruler** to the **7-inch mark**, and is the height of the **Report Header** section.

6 Select the five **Date label controls and textbox controls**. Change the width to **0.8**. Change the **Font Color** to **Teal, Accent 2, Darker 50%**—the sixth option in the sixth row under **Theme Colors**.

7 If necessary, resize and move controls so you can resize the report to print on one landscape page. **Save** the report. If you are instructed to submit this result, create a paper or electronic printout. **Close** the report.

8 Open the **6F Coupons** query. Switch to **Design** view, and then notice the underlying tables that were used in the creation of the query. **Close** the query, and then **Close** the **Navigation Pane**.

9 Create a new report using **Report Design**. Display the **Property Sheet**. On the **Data tab**, click the **Record Source** property setting box arrow, and then click **6F Coupons**. **Close** the **Property Sheet**. Display the **Field List**.

10 From the **Field List**, select all fields included in the query. Drag the selected fields into the **Detail** section of the design grid until the top of the pointer is aligned with the **0.25-inch mark on the vertical ruler** and the **1-inch mark on the horizontal ruler**. With the controls selected, on the **REPORT DESIGN TOOLS ARRANGE tab**, in the **Table group**, click the **Tabular** button. **Close** the **Field List**. Drag the **Page Footer section bar** up to the **0.5-inch mark on the vertical ruler**.

11 **Save** the report as **Lastname Firstname 6F Promotions** Switch to **Layout** view to be sure all data is visible in the report. If necessary, adjust the width of any columns where data is cut off. Switch to **Design** view.

12 On the **REPORT DESIGN TOOLS DESIGN tab**, click the **Group & Sort** button. Click the **Add a group** button, and then from the displayed list, click **City**. Apply **Keep whole group together on one page**. Click the **Add a sort** button, and then click **Visit Date**. **Close** the **Group, Sort, and Total Pane**.

13 In the **Page Header** section, click the **City** label control, and then press [Delete]. In the **Detail** section, delete the **City text box control**. Click the **City Header** section bar to select it, right-click to display the shortcut menu, and click **Paste**.

14 In the **Detail** section, click the **# Redeemed text box control**. On the **DESIGN tab**, click the **Totals** button, and then click **Sum**.

15 Insert the **a06F_Logo**. On the **Property Sheet**, increase the width to **1.75 inches** and the height to **0.5 inches**. Insert a **Title**. Delete your Lastname Firstname from the beginning of the title.

16 Add a **label control** to the **Report Footer**. Position the plus sign of the pointer at the bottom of the **Report Footer** section bar and the **4.5-inch mark on the horizontal ruler**. Drag upward to the top of the **Report Footer** section and to the right to the left edge of the Sum control box. Type **Total # Redeemed Coupons**

17 Click the **Date & Time** button. Under **Include Date**, click the second option button. Do not **Include Time**. Remove the **Date text box control** from the Layout.

18 Move the control to the left edge of the **Report Footer**. Click the **Date text box control** two times. Position the insertion point between the equal sign and the *D*. Type **"Prepared by Firstname Lastname on "&** and

(Project 6F Promotional Results continues on the next page)

then Press Enter. Click the **Title label control**, and resize it so the right edge aligns with the **4-inch mark on the horizontal ruler**. **Center** the text in the control. Resize the report to **7.75 inches wide**.

19 Select all of the controls in the **Report Footer**. Be sure they are all the same height and aligned at the bottom.

20 Switch to **Layout** view, and then adjust all controls to fit the data without extending beyond the right margin.

Save the report. If you are instructed to submit this result, create a paper or electronic printout. **Close** the report.

21 **Close** the database, and then **Exit** Access.

22 As directed by your instructor, submit your database and the paper or electronic printouts of the two reports that are the result of this project. Specifically, in this project, using your own name you created the following database and printouts or electronic printouts:

1. Lastname_Firstname_6F_Promotional Results	Database file
2. Lastname Firstname 6F Coupons Redeemed	Report (printed or electronic printout)
2. Lastname Firstname 6F Promotions	Report (printed or electronic printout)

END | You have completed Project 6F

CONTENT-BASED ASSESSMENTS

Project 6G Wireless Usage

Apply 6A and 6B skills from these Objectives:

1 Create a Form in Design View
2 Add and Change Controls
3 Format a Form
4 Make a Form User Friendly
5 Create a Report Based on a Query Using a Wizard

Marty Kress, vice president of marketing for Rosebud Cafe franchises, keeps a database on the wireless usage per franchise on a monthly basis. The individual restaurants report the number of customers using the wireless connections and the average length of usage per customer. In this project, you will design a form for the data entry of this data and design a report that can be used by Mr. Kress to plan next year's marketing strategies. Your completed work will look similar to Figure 6.52.

PROJECT FILES

For Project 6G, you will need the following files:

a06G_Wireless_Usage
a06G_Logo

You will save your database as:

Lastname_Firstname_6G_Wireless_Usage

PROJECT RESULTS

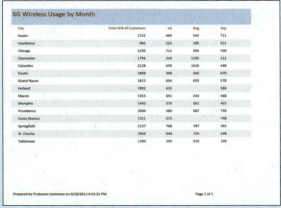

FIGURE 6.52

(Project 6G Wireless Usage continues on the next page)

CONTENT-BASED ASSESSMENTS

1 **Start** Access. Locate and open the **a06G_ Wireless_ Usage** file. Save the database in your **Access Chapter 6** folder as **Lastname_Firstname_6G_Wireless_Usage** If necessary, Enable Content.

2 Create a form in **Form Design**. For the **Record Source**, use the **6G Wireless Usage** table. Select all of the fields, and then drag them onto the design grid until the top of the arrow is aligned with the **1-inch mark on the horizontal ruler** and the **0.25-inch mark on the vertical ruler**. **Save** the form as **Lastname Firstname 6G Wireless Usage**

3 Apply a **Stacked** layout. Add a **Red, Accent 2** dashed outline to the **text box controls** in the **Detail** section.

4 Insert **a06G_Logo**. Widen the selected logo to the **1.5-inch mark on the horizontal ruler**.

5 Insert a **Title**. Delete Lastname Firstname and the following space, and then press [Enter]. Adjust the right edge of the title label control to just fit the text.

6 Add a **Button** in the **Detail** section at the **0.5-inch mark on the vertical ruler** and the **2.5-inch mark on the horizontal ruler**. Click **Record Operations**, and then **Add New Record**. Apply the **Go To New Picture**, and then name the button **btnNewRcrd** Add a button to print the record below the **Add New Record** button. Place a picture on it, and name it **btnPrtRcrd**

7 With the **New Record** and **Print Record** buttons selected, change the **Tab Stop** property to **No**. If necessary, Align the buttons at the Right.

8 Drag the top of the **Form Footer** section bar until it aligns with the **0.5-inch mark on the vertical ruler**. In the **Form Footer** section, insert a label aligned with the bottom of the **Form Footer** section bar and the left edge of the form. Type **Created by Firstname Lastname** and then press [Enter].

9 Switch to **Form** view. Click the **New Record** button. From the list of **Franchises**, select **Holland MI**. In the **Wireless Month text box control**, select **June 1** of the current year. In the **# of Customers text box control**, type **757** In the **Avg Minutes text box control**, type **25**

10 If you are instructed to submit this result, create a paper or electronic printout of the new, selected record only. **Close** the form and **Save** changes.

11 **Create** a report using the **Report Wizard**. From the **Query: 6G Wireless Crosstab Query**, select the **City, Total Of # of Customers, Jul, Aug,** and **Sep** fields. Do not add any grouping levels. **Sort** records within the report by **City**, in **Ascending** order. Use a **Tabular** layout and a **Landscape** orientation. Title your report as **6G Wireless Usage by Month**

12 Switch to **Design** view. Select the **Title** label control and all of the label controls in the **Page Header** section. Change the font color to **Orange, Accent 6, Darker 50%**. Reduce the width of the **Page # control** so the right edge aligns with the **8-inch mark on the horizontal ruler**.

13 Resize the **Jul, Aug,** and **Sep textbox controls** and **label controls** to **1 inch**. Move the controls so there is one dot between the monthly columns. Resize the report to **9.5 inches** wide.

14 Modify the **Page Footer** by adding **Prepared by Firstname Lastname on** before **Now()**. Widen the control to the **5-inch mark on the horizontal ruler**. Switch to **Print Preview**.

15 If you are instructed to submit this result, create a paper or electronic printout. **Close** the report and **Save** changes.

16 Close the **Navigation Pane**, **Close** the database, and then **Exit** Access.

17 As directed by your instructor, submit your database and the paper or electronic printouts of the two objects—one form and one report—that are the result of this project. Specifically, in this project, using your own name you created the following database and printouts or electronic printouts:

1. Lastname_Firstname_6G_Wireless_Usage	Database file
2. Lastname Firstname 6G Wireless Usage	Form (printed or electronic printout)
3. Lastname Firstname 6G Wireless Usage by Month	Report (printed or electronic printout)

END | You have completed Project 6G

CONTENT-BASED ASSESSMENTS

GO! Fix It	Project 6H Advertising Contracts	Online
GO! Make It	Project 6I Supply Orders	Online
GO! Solve It	Project 6J Menu Items	Online
GO! Solve It	Project 6K Birthday Coupons	

Apply a combination of the **6A** and **6B** skills.

PROJECT FILES

For Project 6K, you will need the following files:

a06K_Birthday_Coupons
a06K_Rose
a06K_Birthday
a06K_Cupcake

You will save your database as:

Lastname_Firstname_6K_Birthday_Coupons

The Vice President of Marketing, Marty Kress, encourages each location of the Rosebud Cafe franchise to offer birthday coupons to its customers as a promotional venture. Open the a06K_Birthday_Coupons database, and then save it as **Lastname_Firstname_6K_Birthday_Coupons** Use the 6K Birthdates table to create a form to enter the names, birthday months, and email addresses of the customers visiting one of the restaurants. Save the form as **Lastname Firstname 6K Birthday Form** Add a button control to print the current form. Include the Rose image as the logo and title the form **6K Happy Birthday** Remove the background from the Form Header. Resize the Detail area to 1 inch. Be sure all data is visible on the form. Add a new record using the form and your own information.

Create a report to display the customer name and email address grouped by birthday month using the months as a section header and sorted by customer name. Add the **a06K_Birthday** image as the logo, resized to 1 inch tall and wide. Add a title. Draw a line above the Birthday Month header control to separate the months; apply a Line Color and Line Type. Save the report as **Lastname Firstname 6K Birthdate Report**

Create a report based on the 6K First Quarter Birthdays query. Include both of the fields arranged in a tabular format. Save the report as **Lastname Firstname 6K First Quarter Birthdays** Add a title to the report, **Lastname Firstname 6K First Quarter Birthdays** Add the current date and time to the Report Header section. Delete the Page Footer controls, and resize the Page Footer section to 0. Apply a dotted outline to the label controls in the Page Header section; choose a Line Color and Line Thickness. Add a count of how many first quarter birthdays there are to the Report Footer. Include a descriptive label to the right of the count. Be sure the controls are sized the same and aligned. Adjust the width of the report to 7.5 inches, making necessary adjustments to textbox controls. Add the **a06K_Cupcake** image and place it in the lower right of the Report Footer. Resize it to 1 inch tall and wide. Save the changes. If you are instructed to submit the results, create a paper or electronic printout of the objects created.

(Project 6K Birthday Coupons continues on the next page)

CONTENT-BASED ASSESSMENTS

GO! Solve It **Project 6K Birthday Coupons** (continued)

	Performance Level		
Performance Criteria	**Exemplary**	**Proficient**	**Developing**
Create 6K Birthday Form	Form created with the correct fields and formatted as directed.	Form created with no more than two missing elements.	Form created with more than two missing elements.
Create 6K Birthdate Report	Report created with the correct fields and formatted as directed.	Report created with no more than two missing elements.	Report created with more than two missing elements.
Create 6K First Quarter Birthdays Report	Report created with the correct fields and formatted as directed.	Report created with no more than two missing elements.	Report created with more than two missing elements.

END | You have completed Project 6K

OUTCOMES-BASED ASSESSMENTS

RUBRIC

The following outcomes-based assessments are open-ended assessments. That is, there is no specific correct result; your result will depend on your approach to the information provided. Make Professional Quality your goal. Use the following scoring rubric to guide you in how to approach the problem and then to evaluate how well your approach solves the problem.

The *criteria*—Software Mastery, Content, Format and Layout, and Process—represent the knowledge and skills you have gained that you can apply to solving the problem. The *levels of performance*—Professional Quality, Approaching Professional Quality, or Needs Quality Improvements—help you and your instructor evaluate your result.

	Your completed project is of Professional Quality if you:	Your completed project is Approaching Professional Quality if you:	Your completed project Needs Quality Improvements if you:
1-Software Mastery	Choose and apply the most appropriate skills, tools, and features and identify efficient methods to solve the problem.	Choose and apply some appropriate skills, tools, and features, but not in the most efficient manner.	Choose inappropriate skills, tools, or features, or are inefficient in solving the problem.
2-Content	Construct a solution that is clear and well organized, contains content that is accurate, appropriate to the audience and purpose, and is complete. Provide a solution that contains no errors in spelling, grammar, or style.	Construct a solution in which some components are unclear, poorly organized, inconsistent, or incomplete. Misjudge the needs of the audience. Have some errors in spelling, grammar, or style, but the errors do not detract from comprehension.	Construct a solution that is unclear, incomplete, or poorly organized; contains some inaccurate or inappropriate content; and contains many errors in spelling, grammar, or style. Do not solve the problem.
3-Format & Layout	Format and arrange all elements to communicate information and ideas, clarify function, illustrate relationships, and indicate relative importance.	Apply appropriate format and layout features to some elements, but not others. Overuse features, causing minor distraction.	Apply format and layout that does not communicate information or ideas clearly. Do not use format and layout features to clarify function, illustrate relationships, or indicate relative importance. Use available features excessively, causing distraction.
4-Process	Use an organized approach that integrates planning, development, self-assessment, revision, and reflection.	Demonstrate an organized approach in some areas, but not others; or, use an insufficient process of organization throughout.	Do not use an organized approach to solve the problem.

OUTCOMES-BASED ASSESSMENTS

GO! Think   Project 6L Vacation Days

PROJECT FILES

For Project 6L, you will need the following files:

a06L_Vacation_Days
a06L_Logo

You will save your database as:

Lastname_Firstname_6L_Vacation_Days

In this project, you will create a report to display the information for the Rosebud Cafe employees and their vacation days. Open the **a06L_Vacation_Days** database and save it as **Lastname_Firstname_6L_Vacation_Days** From the *6L Vacation Days* table, add the following fields to the report: Employee Name, Days Allotted, and Days Taken. Add a calculated text box control to display the number of vacation days each employee has remaining (Days Allotted-Days Taken) with a label control to describe the field, and format the result as a General Number. Change the Theme to Ion. In the Report Header section, add the Rosebud Cafe logo and a descriptive title. Add a label control to the Report Footer section that reads **Report Designed by Firstname Lastname** Align the left edge with the label controls in the Detail section. Change the background color used in the Report Header and Report Footer sections, and change the font color so they are easy to read. Sort the report on Employee Name. Adjust all label and text controls to display all field names and data. Adjust the width of the report so it is 6 inches wide. Add a dotted line between employees to make it easier to read. Center page numbers in the page footer. Resize the Detail section to reduce the blank space. Close the space for the Page Header. Save the report as **Lastname Firstname 6L Vacation Information** If you are instructed to submit this result, create a paper or electronic printout.

END | You have completed Project 6L

OUTCOMES-BASED ASSESSMENTS

| GO! Think | Project 6M Seasonal Items | Online |
| You and GO! | Project 6N Club Directory | Online |

Creating Templates and Reviewing, Publishing, Comparing, Combining, and Protecting Presentations

GO! to Work
Video P4

PROJECT 4A

OUTCOMES
Create and Apply a Custom Template.

OBJECTIVES
1. Create a Custom Template by Modifying Slide Masters
2. Apply a Custom Template to a Presentation

PROJECT 4B

OUTCOMES
Review, Publish, Compare, Combine, and Protect Presentations.

OBJECTIVES
3. Create and Edit Comments
4. Compare and Combine Presentations
5. Prepare a Presentation for Distribution
6. Protect a Presentation

Luis Louro/Fotolia

In This Chapter

PowerPoint provides built-in templates to use when creating a new presentation. You can create your own customized templates and reuse them. You can review and comment on the content of a presentation by inserting and editing comments in the file. You can compare two versions of a presentation to view the differences between the presentations. PowerPoint also provides several ways to share presentations with others: converting to PDF or XPS format or printing handouts. You can check a presentation for compatibility with other versions, protect the presentation from further editing by marking it as Final, and password protect it.

Attorneys at **Thompson Henderson Law Partners** counsel their clients on a wide variety of issues, including contracts, licensing, intellectual property, and taxation, with emphasis on the unique needs of the entertainment and sports industries. Entertainment clients include production companies, publishers, talent agencies, actors, writers, artists—anyone involved in creating or doing business in the entertainment industry. Sports clients include colleges and universities, professional sports teams, and athletes. Increasingly, sports coaches and organizations with concerns about liability are also seeking the firm's counsel.

PROJECT ACTIVITIES

In Activities 4.01 through 4.10, you will design a template for the Thompson Henderson Law Partners to use to create presentations for meetings with the partners and clients. The template will contain formatting for the slide masters and shapes and images to add interest. Then you will use the template to create a presentation. You will also edit slide masters in an existing presentation in order to maintain uniformity in the slide designs. Your completed presentation will look similar to Figure 4.1.

PROJECT FILES

For Project 4A, you will need the following files:

New blank PowerPoint presentation
p04A_Law1.jpg

You will save your presentations as:

Firstname_Lastname_4A_Meeting_Template.potx
Firstname_Lastname_4A_Filing_Procedures.pptx

PROJECT RESULTS

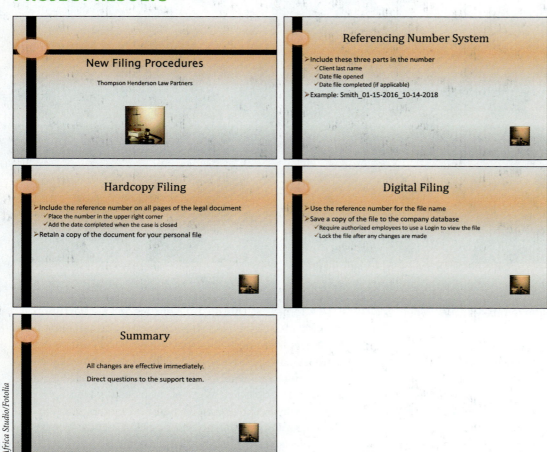

FIGURE 4.1 Project 4A Instructional Presentation

Video P4-1

A PowerPoint *template* is a predefined layout for a group of slides and is saved as a .potx file. You use a template to standardize the design of the slides in a presentation. A *slide master* is part of a template that stores information about the formatting and text that displays on every slide in a presentation. The stored information includes such items as the placement and size of text and object placeholders.

For example, if your company or organization has a logo that should be displayed on all slides of a presentation, the logo can be inserted one time on the slide master. That logo will then display in the same location on all slides of the presentation.

Activity 4.01 | Displaying and Editing Slide Masters

In this activity, you will change the Office Theme Slide Master background and the Title Slide Layout font and font size. You will start with a blank PowerPoint presentation file.

1 Start PowerPoint and then click **Blank Presentation**. On the Ribbon, click the **VIEW tab**. In the **Master Views group**, point to, but do not click, **Slide Master**. Read the **ScreenTip**: *Master slides control the look of your entire presentation, including colors, fonts, backgrounds, effects, and just about everything else. You can insert a shape or a logo on a slide master, for example, and it will show up on all your slides automatically.* Compare your screen with Figure 4.2.

In the Master Views group, notice the three views available—Slide Master, Handout Master, and Notes Master.

FIGURE 4.2

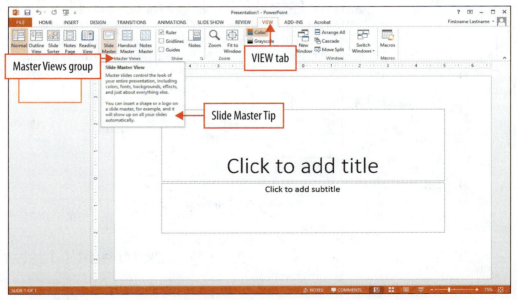

2 Click **Slide Master**. Take a moment to study the options associated with the **SLIDE MASTER tab**, as described in the table shown in Figure 4.3.

You are already familiar with editing themes, fonts, and colors by using the Edit Theme group, customizing a background by using the Background group, and modifying page setup and orientation by using the Size group. From the SLIDE MASTER tab, you can apply these changes to certain layouts or to the entire theme.

FIGURE 4.3

OPTIONS ON THE SLIDE MASTER TAB	
SCREEN ELEMENT	DESCRIPTION
Edit Master group	**Enables you to:**
Insert Slide Master	Add a new Slide Master to the presentation.
Insert Layout	Add a custom layout to the master slide set.
Delete	Remove this slide from your presentation.
Rename	Rename your custom layout so you can find it easily in the layout gallery.
Preserve	Preserve the selected master so that it remains with the presentation even if it is not used.
Master Layout group	**Enables you to:**
Master Layout	Choose the elements to include in the slide master.
Insert Placeholder	Add a placeholder to the slide layout to hold content, such as a picture, table, media, or text.
Title	Show or hide the title placeholder on this slide.
Footers	Show or hide the footer placeholders.

3 ▶ If necessary, scroll up, and then point to the first thumbnail to display the ScreenTip—**Office Theme Slide Master: used by slide(s) 1**. Compare your screen with Figure 4.4. Locate the **Title Slide Layout: used by slide(s) 1**, **Title and Content Layout: used by no slides**, and **Two Content Layout: used by no slide(s)** thumbnails.

In the Slide Master view, in the thumbnail pane, the larger slide image represents the slide master, and the associated layouts are smaller, positioned beneath it. The slide master is referred to as the Office Theme Slide Master. The *Office Theme Slide Master* is a specific slide master that contains the design, such as the background that displays on all slide layouts in the presentation. Changes made to it affect all slides in the presentation. Other common slide layouts include the Title Slide Layout, the Title and Content Layout, and the Two Content Layout.

FIGURE 4.4

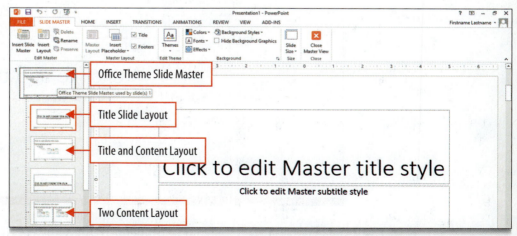

4 ▶ Click the first thumbnail—**Office Theme Slide Master**. In the **Background group**, click **Background Styles**. In the **Background Styles gallery**, locate **Style 10**, and then click it.

Notice that all slide layouts display with the same background style.

More Knowledge   **Slide Master - Add New Layouts**

You can create a custom layout in Slide Master view. In the Edit Master group, click Insert Layout. From there, you can make custom choices about four placeholders—Title, Date, Footer and Slide Number. In the Edit Master group, click the Rename button to assign a new name to your custom layout. Your custom layout is now available for use in a presentation and will display in the New Slide gallery.

5 Click the second thumbnail—**Title Slide Layout**. On the slide, click anywhere on the dashed border on the Master title style placeholder to display the border as a solid line. Click the **HOME tab**. In the **Font group**, change the font to **Lucida Sans Unicode**. Change the font size to **40**. Compare your screen with Figure 4.5.

The font and font size change affects only the Title Slide.

🔄 **BY TOUCH** Tap to select second thumbnail—Title Slide Layout. On the slide, tap anywhere on the dashed border on the Master title style placeholder to display the border as a solid line. Tap the HOME tab. In the Font group, slide the arrow to select the font to Lucida Sans Unicode. Tap and slide the arrow to change the font size to 40.

🔄 **ANOTHER WAY** You can also triple-click the text in the Master title style placeholder to select the text.

FIGURE 4.5

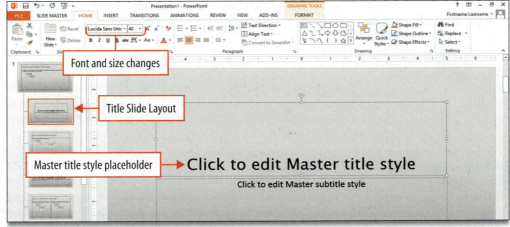

Activity 4.02 | Saving a Presentation as a Template

In this activity, you will save your design as a template.

1 Press F12 to display the **Save As** dialog box. At the right side of the **Save as type** box, click the **arrow** to display the file types. Point to, but do not click, **PowerPoint Template (*.potx)**. Compare your screen with Figure 4.6. Your display may differ slightly.

FIGURE 4.6

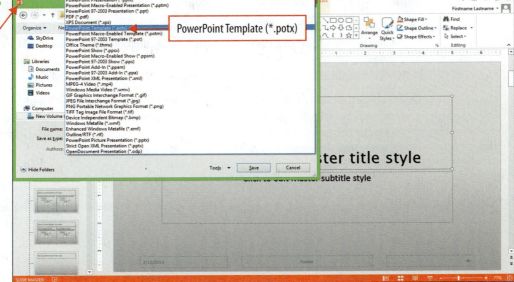

2 From the list of file types, click **PowerPoint Template (*.potx)**.

3 Navigate to the location where you are saving your work and create a new folder named **PowerPoint Chapter 4**

Your PowerPoint Chapter 4 folder is created. You will use this folder to store your templates.

More Knowledge | **Microsoft Office Templates Folder**

When Microsoft Office is installed, a Custom Office Templates folder is created in the Documents Library. You can save your templates to the Custom Office Templates folder to make them easier to find. However, for the projects in this chapter, you will save your files to your PowerPoint Chapter 4 folder.

4 Type the file name **Lastname_Firstname_4A_Meeting_Template** and then click **Save**.

The file extension .potx is automatically added to your file name. When working with templates, it is best to have the extension displayed so you can tell the difference between a template and a presentation file. The PowerPoint template will display in file documents library with gold at the top of the file icon.

More Knowledge | **Modifying a Template**

To make changes to a PowerPoint template, start PowerPoint, click FILE, click Open, navigate to the folder where the template is saved, click the file name, and then click Open. You can also open it from File Explorer. Navigate to the file, right-click, and then click Open. Do not double-click on the file name in File Explorer because that action will display a copy of the template, not the template itself.

Activity 4.03 | Formatting a Slide Master with a Gradient Fill

In this activity, you will modify a gradient fill to the slide master background. A *gradient fill* is a gradual progression of several colors blending into each other or shades of the same color blending into each other. A *gradient stop* allows you to apply different color combinations to selected areas of the background.

1 On the left, click the **Office Theme Slide Master** thumbnail—the first thumbnail.

2 On the **SLIDE MASTER tab, in** the **Background group**, click **Background Styles** to display the **Background Styles gallery**, and then click **Format Background**. At the right, in the **Format Background** pane, under **Fill**, click **Gradient fill**, if necessary. Click the **Type arrow** to display the list, and then click **Linear**, if necessary.

3 Under **Gradient stops**, at the right side, click **Add gradient stop** 🔲 one time. On the slider, drag the selected **gradient stop** to the left and then to the right and observe how the background changes on the slide and the percentage of gradation changes in the **Position** box. Position the stop at **75%**.

ANOTHER WAY | Instead of clicking Add gradient stop, you can click anywhere on the slider to add a gradient stop.

4 ▶ Click **Add gradient stop**  again to add another **gradient stop**, and then position it at **25%**. Click the **Color arrow**, and then, under **Theme Colors**, in the sixth column, fourth row, click **Orange, Accent 2, Lighter 40%**. Compare your screen with Figure 4.7.

Applying a gradient stop to the background makes the color vary smoothly from a darker to a lighter shade. The additional stop with a different color provides more interest.

🔄 ANOTHER WAY   You can position the gradient stop by typing the value or using the spin arrows in the Position spin box.

FIGURE 4.7

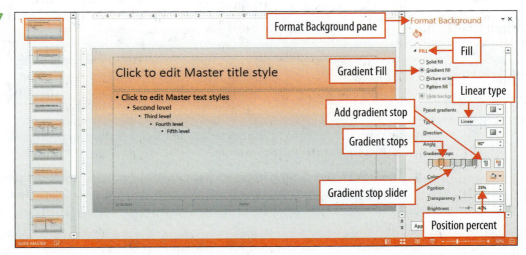

5 ▶ At the bottom of the **Format Background** pane, click **Apply to All**. At the top of the pane, click **Close** [✕].

All slide layout thumbnails are displayed with the gradient fill.

6 ▶ **Save** 🖫 the template.

Activity 4.04 | Formatting Slide Masters by Adding Pictures and Shapes

In this activity, you will add and format a shape, and then insert a picture into the shape. Then you will duplicate the shape, move the copied shape to a different slide layout, resize and recolor it.

1 ▶ Click the **Title Slide Layout** thumbnail—the second thumbnail—to make the **Title Slide Layout Master** the active slide layout.

2 ▶ On the **VIEW tab**, in the **Show group**, select the **Ruler** check box to display the horizontal and vertical rulers, if necessary. Click the **INSERT tab**. In the **Illustrations group**, click **Shapes**. From the list, under **Rectangles**, click the **Rectangle** shape—the first shape. Position the pointer at **2 inches on the right side of the horizontal ruler** and **3 inches on the upper half of the vertical ruler**, and then click to insert the shape. It looks like a square.

When you insert a shape, a DRAWING TOOLS tab is displayed above the ribbon tabs. A context-sensitive FORMAT tab is displayed under the DRAWING TOOLS tab. When you deselect the shape, the DRAWING TOOLS and FORMAT tabs disappear.

3 ▶ With the shape still selected, on the ribbon, on the **DRAWING TOOLS FORMAT tab**, in the **Shapes Styles group**, click **Shape Effects**. From the list, click **Bevel**. Point to some of the effects and note the changes made to the rectangle. In the first row, under **Bevel**, click the first effect—**Circle**. In the **Shapes Styles group**, click **Shape Outline**, and then click **No Outline**.

Removing the border softens the appearance of the shape.

4 With the rectangle still selected, in the **Size group**, change the **Shape Height** to **2"** and the **Shape Width** to **2"**. Compare your screen with Figure 4.8. If the placement of your rectangle

FIGURE 4.8

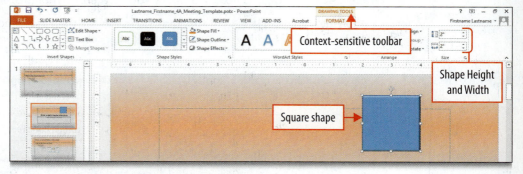

does not match, click on the shape, and then move it to match the position shown in Figure 4.8.

5 With the **FORMAT tab** selected, in the **Shape Styles group**, click **Shape Fill**, and then point to **Picture** to read the **ScreenTip**.

6 Click **Picture**. In the **Insert Pictures** dialog box, to the right of **From a file**, click **Browse**, navigate to the location where your data files are stored, and then click **p04A_Law1.jpg** Click **Insert**.

> The picture fills only the shape. When you add a picture inside the shape, a PICTURE TOOLS tab displays above the ribbon tabs with a FORMAT tab beneath it. One FORMAT tab is for the DRAWING TOOLS for the shape. The other FORMAT tab is for the PICTURE TOOLS for the picture you inserted. When you deselect the shape, both the DRAWING TOOLS and PICTURE TOOLS tabs disappear.

7 With the shape still selected, in the **Arrange group**, click **Align** to see the alignment options. Click **Align Center**. Click **Align** again, and then click **Align Bottom**.

> The shape with the picture aligns in the horizontal center at the bottom of the slide.

8 With the shape still selected, on the **HOME tab**, in the **Clipboard group**, click **Copy**. Click the **Title and Content Layout** thumbnail, which is the third thumbnail. In the **Clipboard group**, click **Paste**.

> The copied shape maintains the same format and position.

9 From the Ribbon, on the **DRAWING TOOLS FORMAT tab**, in the **Size group**, change the **Shape Height** to **1"** and the **Shape Width** to **1"**.

> The copied shape is resized.

10 With the shape still selected, hold down the [Shift] key, and then click on the dashed border of the content placeholder. In the **Arrange group**, click **Align**, and then click **Align Right**. Click **Align** again, and then click **Align Bottom**.

11 On the ribbon, on the **PICTURE TOOLS FORMAT tab**, in the **Adjust group**, click **Color**. Under **Recolor**, in the second row, click the third color—**Orange, Accent color 2 Dark**. Compare your screen with Figure 4.9.

> The logo now appears on the first slide of your presentation and then displays in a smaller format on slides using the title and content layout. If you wanted to have the logo on other slide layouts, you could copy the small logo to those layouts as well.

FIGURE 4.9

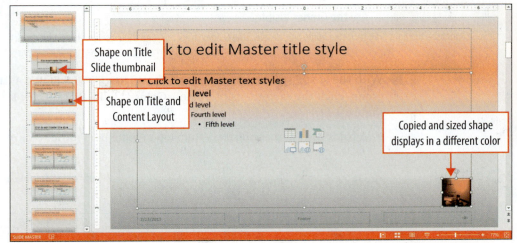

12 ▸ **Save** 🖫 the template. At the top of the **Format Shape** pane, click **Close** ✖, if necessary.

Activity 4.05 │ Formatting Slide Masters by Adding Shapes and Shape Effects

In this activity, you will add and format shapes, and then add a glow effect to shapes.

1 ▸ Click the **Office Theme Slide Master** thumbnail—the first thumbnail. On the **VIEW tab**, in the **Show group**, select the **Guides** check box to display the horizontal and vertical guides, if not already checked.

Light orange dotted guide lines display on the slide on both the horizontal and vertical rulers at zero.

2 ▸ At the top of the slide, move your mouse pointer over the orange dotted line until the mouse pointer changes into a double arrow 🔃. Drag the light orange dotted **vertical guide line** 🔃 to the left to **5.5 inches on the left side of the horizontal ruler**. Click the light orange dotted **horizontal guide line** 🔃 and drag it up to **2 inches on upper half of the vertical ruler**.

3 ▸ Click the **Title Slide Layout** thumbnail—the second thumbnail. Click the **INSERT tab**. In the **Illustrations group**, click **Shapes**. From the list, under **Rectangles**, click the **Rectangle** shape—the first shape. To insert the rectangle, position the pointer at **6 inches on the left side of the horizontal ruler**, aligning it with the top edge of the slide. Click and **drag across the top edge of the slide 0.5 inch to 5.5 inches on the horizontal ruler** to the edge of the vertical guide line, continue holding, and then **drag down along the vertical guide line** to the bottom edge of the slide, aligning it with the bottom edge of the slide, and then release. Compare your screen with Figure 4.10.

FIGURE 4.10

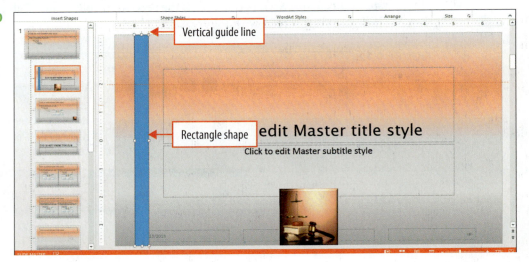

4 ▶ With the shape still selected, on the **DRAWING TOOLS FORMAT tab**, in the **Shapes Styles group**, click the second visible style—**Colored Fill – Black, Dark 1**. Compare your screen with Figure 4.11.

A black vertical shape displays from top to bottom on the left side of the slide.

🔄 **BY TOUCH**   Tap the FORMAT tab. In the Shapes Styles group, tap to select the second visible style—Colored Fill – Black, Dark 1.

FIGURE 4.11

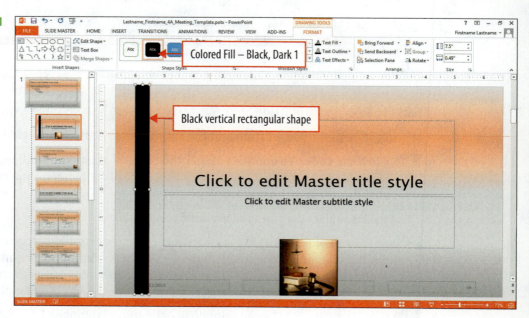

5 ▶ Click the **INSERT tab**. In the **Illustrations group**, click **Shapes**. From the list, under **Rectangles**, click the **Rectangle** shape. Position the pointer at **1.75 inches on the upper half of the vertical ruler**, aligning it with the left edge of the slide. **Drag up the edge of the slide .25 inches to 2.0 inches on the vertical ruler** to the edge of the horizontal guide line, continue holding, and then **drag to the right along the horizontal guide line**, aligning it with the right edge of the slide, and then release. With the shape still selected, on the ribbon, on the **DRAWING TOOLS FORMAT tab**, in the **Shapes Styles group**, click the second visible style—**Colored Fill – Black, Dark 1**. Compare your screen with Figure 4.12.

FIGURE 4.12

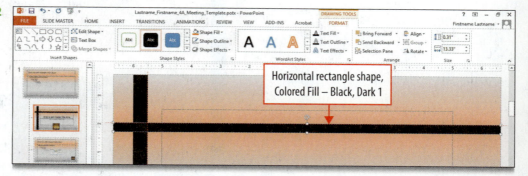

6 ▶ Click the **INSERT tab**. In the **Illustrations group**, click **Shapes**. From the list, under **Basic Shapes**, click the **Oval** shape—the second shape. Point to the intersection of the two black lines and click one time to insert the shape. With the oval still selected, in the **Size group**, change the **Shape Height** to **1"** and the **Shape Width** to **1.5"**. In the **Size group**, click the **dialog launcher** ▣. Click **Position** to expand. In the **Horizontal position** box, type **0.2** and then press Enter. In the **Vertical position** box, type **1.2** and then press Enter.

The oval shape is positioned over the intersection of the two black lines.

7 ▶ With the shape still selected, on the ribbon, in the **Shapes Styles group**, click the **More arrow** ▼. From the list, in the fourth row, click the third item—**Subtle Effect – Orange, Accent 2**. With the shape still selected, click the **Shape Effects arrow**. From the list, click **Glow**, and then under **Glow Variations**, in the second column, click the last item—**Orange, 18 pt glow, Accent color 2**. Compare your screen with Figure 4.13.

A black horizontal and vertical shape line with a soft glowing oval shape display on the upper portion of the slide.

FIGURE 4.13

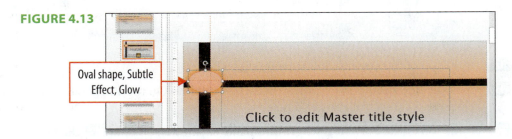

Oval shape, Subtle Effect, Glow

Click to edit Master title style

8 ▶ Click the **Office Theme Slide Master** thumbnail—the first thumbnail. Click the light orange dotted **vertical guide line** and drag to the left to **5.75 inches on the left side of the horizontal ruler**.

9 ▶ Click the **Title and Content Layout** thumbnail—the third thumbnail. Click the **INSERT tab**. In the **Illustrations group**, click **Shapes**. From the list, under **Rectangles**, click the **Rectangle** shape—the first shape. Position the pointer at **6.25 inches on the left side of the horizontal ruler**, aligning it with the top edge of the slide. Click and **drag across the top edge of the slide 0.5 inch to 5.75 inches on the horizontal ruler** to the edge of the vertical guide line, continue holding, and then **drag down along the vertical guide line** to the bottom edge of the slide, aligning it with the bottom edge of the slide, and then release. With the shape still selected, on the **DRAWING TOOLS FORMAT tab**, in the **Shapes Styles group**, click the second visible style—**Colored Fill – Black, Dark 1**. Compare your screen with Figure 4.14.

FIGURE 4.14

Vertical black rectangle shape

Click to edit Master text styles
• Second level

10 ▶ Click the **INSERT tab**. In the **Illustrations group**, click **Shapes**. From the list, under **Basic Shapes**, click the **Oval** shape. Click to insert the oval shape near the intersecting guide lines. With the oval shape selected, in the **Size group**, change the **Shape Height** to **0.7"** and the **Shape Width** to **1"**. In the **Size group**, click the **dialog launcher** ▣. In the **Format Shape** pane, under **Position**, in the **Horizontal position** box, type **0.2** and then press Enter. In the **Vertical position** box, type **0.8** and then press Enter. Compare your screen with Figure 4.15.

FIGURE 4.15

11 With the shape still selected, on the **DRAWING TOOLS FORMAT tab**, in the **Shapes Styles group**, click the **More arrow** ⬇. From the list, in the fourth row, click the third column—**Subtle Effect – Orange, Accent 2**. With the shape still selected, on the **DRAWING TOOLS FORMAT tab**, in the **Shapes Styles group**, click **Shape Effects**. From the list, click **Glow**, and then under **Glow Variations**, in the second column, click the last item—**Orange, 18 pt glow, Accent color 2**. Compare your screen with Figure 4.16.

FIGURE 4.16

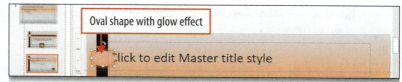

12 At the top of the **Format Shape** pane, click **Close** ✕.

13 Click the first thumbnail—**Office Theme Slide Master**. On the **VIEW tab**, in the **Show group**, select the **Guides** check box to deselect.

14 At the top of the **Format Background** pane, click **Close** ✕. **Save** 🖫 the template.

Activity 4.06 | Customizing Placeholders on a Slide Master

In this activity, you will change the size and position of the placeholders on the Title Slide master, format the footer placeholder, and then change the bullet types on the Title and Content Slide master.

1 Click the **Title Slide Layout** thumbnail to make it the active slide. Click anywhere on the dashed border for the **title placeholder**, hold down the Shift key, and then drag the entire placeholder so the top border is at **3.5 inches on the upper half of the vertical ruler**. Release the Shift key. Click anywhere on the dashed border for the **subtitle placeholder**, hold down the Shift key, and then drag the entire placeholder so the top border is at **0.5 inch on the upper half of the vertical ruler**. Release the Shift key.

Moving a placeholder does not change the size of it. Using the Shift key while dragging the placeholder constrains the placeholder to either perfect vertical movement or perfect horizontal movement.

2 With the **subtitle placeholder** still selected, drag the **bottom middle sizing handle** to **0.5 inches on the lower half of the vertical ruler** to decrease the size of the placeholder. Compare your screen with Figure 4.17.

Using the sizing handle changes the size of the placeholder.

FIGURE 4.17

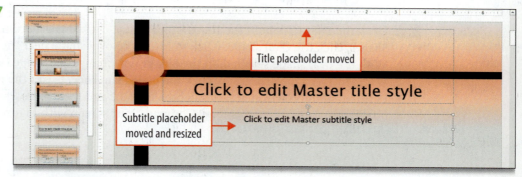

Title placeholder moved

Click to edit Master title style

Subtitle placeholder moved and resized

Click to edit Master subtitle style

3 ▶ Click the **Office Theme Slide Master** thumbnail to make it the active slide. Click anywhere in the first bulleted line. On the **HOME tab**, in the **Paragraph group**, click the **Bullets button arrow**, and then click **Bullets and Numbering**. In the **Bullets and Numbering** dialog box, click the **Bulleted tab** if necessary. Click **Arrow Bullets**. At the bottom left, click the **Color button arrow**. Under **Theme Colors**, in the sixth column, click the last color—**Orange, Accent 2, Darker 50%**. Compare your screen with Figure 4.18. Click **OK**.

FIGURE 4.18

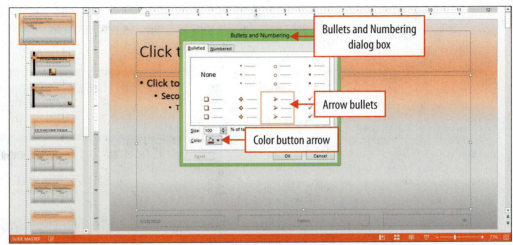

4 ▶ Click anywhere in the second bulleted line. Using the procedure that you used for the first bulleted line, display the **Bullets and Numbering** dialog box. Click the **Filled Square Bullets**. Click the **Color button arrow**, and then in the sixth row, last column, click **Orange, Accent 2, Darker 50%**. Click **OK**. Compare your screen with Figure 4.19.

All slides in the presentation will automatically display these custom bullets for the first two levels of the outline. If you intend to have more levels in your outline, you can continue customizing them.

FIGURE 4.19

More Knowledge   **Customizing Bullets on Different Slide Masters**

When you customize the bullets on the Office Theme Slide Master, the customized bullets are available on all slides. If you want different bullets on some of the slide masters, customize the slide masters, separately. For example, you could change the bullets on the Title and Content Layout and then change the bullets on the Two Content Layout.

---

5 ▶ With the first thumbnail, the **Office Theme Slide Master,** selected, click anywhere on the dashed border of the date placeholder, at the bottom left of the slide, to select the date. On the **HOME tab**, change the **font size** to **10**.

 **ANOTHER WAY**   Highlight the date to select the date placeholder.

6 Click the **Title Slide Layout** thumbnail. Select and drag the rectangle picture shape so the top of the rectangle aligns at **1.0 inches on the lower half of the vertical ruler**. On the **DRAWING TOOLS FORMAT tab**, in the **Arrange group**, click **Align**, and then select **Align Center**. Click outside to deselect the shape. Compare your screen with Figure 4.20.

ANOTHER WAY   Select the shape, and then hold down the Shift key and drag the shape to the desired location.

When you drag a shape, you might change the alignment by accident, so set the alignment again. The shape now clears the area reserved for the footer.

FIGURE 4.20

Title Slide Layout

Click to edit Master title style

Click to edit Master subtitle style

Date placeholder

Rectangular picture shape aligned center

7 With the **SLIDE MASTER tab** selected, in the **Close group**, click **Close Master View**.

ANOTHER WAY   On the status bar, click Normal to close the Master View.

8 **Save**  the template.

Activity 4.07 | Displaying and Editing the Handout Master

In this activity, you will edit the Handout Master for the meeting template you are building for the Thompson Henderson Law Partners. You can print your presentation in the form of handouts that your audience can use to follow along as you give your presentation, or keep for future reference. The *Handout Master* specifies the design of presentation handouts for an audience. You will learn how to change from landscape to portrait orientations, set the number of slides on a page, and specify whether you want to include the header, footer, date, and page number placeholders. Because you are working in a template file rather than a presentation file, the changes to the master affect presentations created from this template. You may change the settings in each presentation if you wish.

1 With the **Lastname_Firstname_4A_Meeting_Template** open, click the **VIEW tab**, and then in the **Master Views group**, click **Handout Master**. In the **Page Setup group**, click **Handout Orientation**, and then notice that the default orientation is **Portrait**. Click **Slide Size**, and then notice that the default orientation is **Widescreen**. Leave the settings as they are. Compare your screen with Figure 4.21.

The Portrait handout orientation means that the slides will print on paper that is 8.5" wide by 11" long. The Landscape handout orientation means that the slides will print on paper that is 11" wide by 8.5" long.

FIGURE 4.21

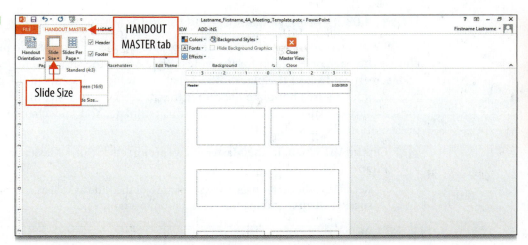

2 ▸ In the **Page Setup group**, click **Slides Per Page**. Click **3 Slides**. Compare your screen with Figure 4.22.

You can print the handouts with 1, 2, 3, 4, 6, or 9 slides per page.

FIGURE 4.22

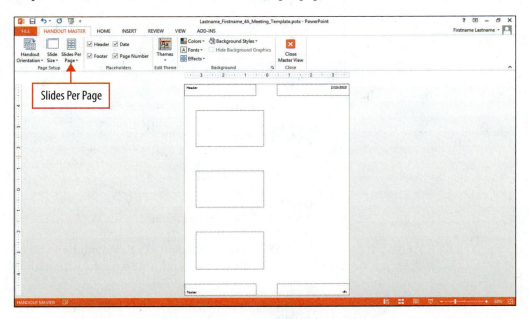

3 ▸ In the **Placeholders group**, click **Header** to clear the check mark. Compare your screen with Figure 4.23.

Notice that the Header placeholder disappears. The placeholders for the notes master include Header, Footer, Date, and Page Number.

FIGURE 4.23

4 ▸ In the **Close group**, click **Close Master View**.

5 ▸ **Save** 🖫 the template.

Activity 4.08 | Displaying and Editing the Notes Master

The *Notes Master* specifies how the speaker's notes display on the printed page. You can choose the page orientation for the notes page, switch the slide orientation between standard and widescreen, and select the placeholders that you want to display on the printed page. Because you are working in a template file rather than a presentation file, the changes to the master affect presentations created in the future from this template. You may change the settings in each presentation if you wish.

1 On the **VIEW tab**, in the **Master Views group**, click **Notes Master**. Compare your screen with Figure 4.24.

Recall that the Notes page shows a picture of the slide as well as appropriate notes to assist the speaker when delivering the presentation to a group.

FIGURE 4.24

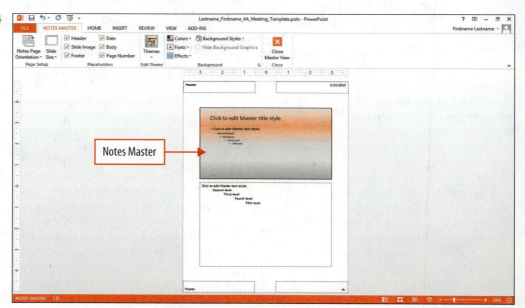

2 On the **NOTES MASTER tab**, click **Notes Page Orientation** and observe that the orientation is set for **Portrait**. Click the **Slide Size** and note that the orientation is set for **Widescreen**. Leave the settings as they are.

The orientation that you use to print the notes page is a matter of personal preference and what works best for the content of the presentation.

3 In the **Placeholders group**, click **Header** to clear the check mark. Compare your screen with Figure 4.25.

Notice that the Header placeholder disappears. The placeholders for the notes master include Header, Slide Image, Footer, Date, Body, and Page Number.

FIGURE 4.25

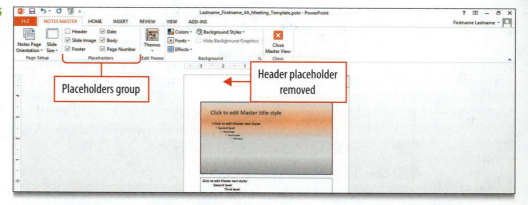

4 ▸ In the **Close group**, click **Close Master View**.

5 ▸ On the **INSERT tab**, in the **Text group** click **Header & Footer** to display the Header and Footer dialog box. click the **Notes and Handouts tab**. Under **Include on page**, select the **Date and time** check box, and then select **Fixed**. If necessary, clear the **Header** check box, and then select the **Page number** and **Footer** check boxes. In the footer box, using your own name, type **Lastname_Firstame_4A_Meeting_Template** and then click **Apply to All**.

6 ▸ Click the **FILE tab**, and then in the lower right portion of the screen, click **Show All Properties**. In the **Tags** box, type **template, meeting** and in the **Subject** box type, your course name and section number. In the **Author** box, right-click the existing author name, click **Edit Property**, replace the existing text with your first and last name, click outside the text box to deselect, and then click **OK**.

7 ▸ Save the template, and then close the template file but leave PowerPoint open.

Objective 2   Apply a Custom Template to a Presentation

Activity 4.09 | Applying a Template to a Presentation

Video P4-2

In this activity, you will use the meeting template to create a slide presentation that explains the new filing procedures to the law partners. Recall that you are saving your template in your PowerPoint Chapter 4 folder.

1 ▸ Click **FILE**, and then click **New**. Compare your screen with Figure 4.26. For complete descriptions of the templates and themes, see Figure 4.27.

> Several template options display—search online template and themes, categories for suggested searches, a blank presentation, and other pre-built themes. Recall that a PowerPoint template is a file that contains layouts, theme colors, theme fonts, theme effects, background styles, and content. It contains the complete blueprint for slides pertaining to a specific kind of presentation. A theme includes coordinated colors and matched backgrounds, fonts, and effects.

FIGURE 4.26

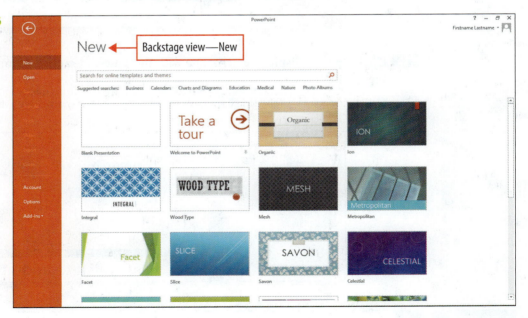

FIGURE 4.27

AVAILABLE TEMPLATES AND THEMES	
AVAILABLE TEMPLATES AND THEMES	**DESCRIPTION**
Search box	Search online templates and themes.
Suggested searches	Templates designed for specific uses, such as a Business, Calendars, Charts and Diagrams, Education, Medical, Nature, and Photo Albums.
Blank presentation	Default template that contains no content.
Themes	Templates with themes already added.

2 ▶ Click **Open**, and then navigate to the location where you are saving your files. Locate **Lastname_Firstname_4A_Meeting_Template.potx** Click the file name one time, and then compare your screen with Figure 4.28.

The extension for a PowerPoint template is *.potx* and the extension for a PowerPoint presentation is *.pptx*.

FIGURE 4.28

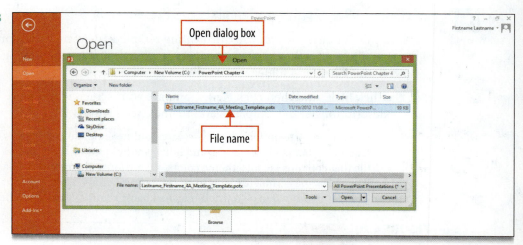

3 ▶ Click **Open** to display the template with the Title slide active. Compare your screen with Figure 4.29.

The file name on the title bar displays as Lastname_Firstname_4A_Meeting_Template.potx

FIGURE 4.29

More **Knowledge**   **Opening a Template**

If you need to edit a template, start PowerPoint. Click FILE, click Open, navigate to your storage location, and then open the file. You can also open a template by navigating to it in File Explorer, right-clicking the file name, and then clicking Open. Make sure that you see the .potx at the end of the file name in the title bar. To open a template saved in the Template folder on your computer, you have to know the path to the template.

4 ▸ Press F12 to display the **Save As** dialog box. Navigate to the location where you are saving your files, if necessary, and then at the right side of the **Save as type** box, click the arrow to display the file types. Click **PowerPoint Presentation (*.pptx),** and then save the file as **Lastname_Firstname_4A_Filing_Procedures**

> The file name on the title bar displays as Lastname_Firstname_4A_Filing_Procedures.pptx.

5 ▸ Click the title placeholder, and then type **New Filing Procedures** Click the subtitle placeholder, and then type **Thompson Henderson Law Partners**

🔄 **ANOTHER WAY**   Press the keyboard shortcut Ctrl + Enter to move to the subtitle placeholder.

6 ▸ On the **HOME tab,** in the **Slides group,** click the **New Slide button arrow.** The gallery shows the formatting you created for the slide layouts. Compare your screen with Figure 4.30.

FIGURE 4.30

7 ▸ Click **Title and Content** to add the slide and make it the active slide. In the title placeholder, press Ctrl + E to center the text. Type **Referencing Number System** Press Ctrl + Enter to move to the content placeholder. In the content placeholder, type **Include these three parts in the number** and then press Enter. In the **Paragraph group,** click **Increase List Level** [⬆] to increase the outline level. Type **Client last name** Press Enter, and then type **Date file opened** Press Enter, type **Date file completed (if applicable)** and then press Enter.

> When you increase an outline level, the text moves to the right. When you press Enter, the same outline level continues. When you press Ctrl + E, the text centers. When you press Ctrl + Enter, the cursor moves to the next placeholder.

🔄 **ANOTHER WAY**   Use the Tab key to increase the outline level. Use the Shift + Tab key combination to decrease the outline level.

8 ▸ In the **Paragraph group,** click **Decrease List Level** [⬅] to decrease the outline level. Type **Example: Smith_01-15-2016_10-14-2018**

> To move the text to the left, you need to decrease the outline level.

9 ▸ In the **Slides group,** click the **New Slide button arrow,** and then click **Title and Content** to add a third slide. Click in the title placeholder, press Ctrl + E, type **Hardcopy Filing** and then press Ctrl + Enter. Following the procedure explained for the previous slide, type the following bulleted items for the Hardcopy Filing slide in the content placeholder.

Include the reference number on all pages of the legal document

> **Place the number in the upper right corner**

> **Add the date completed when the case is closed**

Retain a copy of the document for your personal file

 **ANOTHER WAY**   To add a slide with the same layout as the previous slide, you can click New Slide without displaying the gallery.

10 At the bottom of the PowerPoint window, on the **status bar**, click **NOTES** to activate the notes pane, if necessary. In the **NOTES pane**, click in the placeholder and type **The ending date is the actual date that the case is closed. Until then, leave the ending date blank.** Compare your screen with Figure 4.31.

FIGURE 4.31

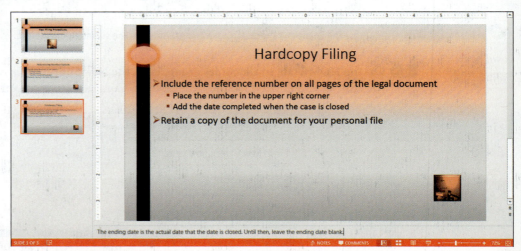

11 In the **Slides group,** click the **New Slide button arrow,** and then click **Title and Content** to add another slide. In the title placeholder, press Ctrl + E, type **Digital Filing** and then press Ctrl + Enter. In the content placeholder, type the following bulleted items, and then compare your screen with Figure 4.32:

Use the reference number for the file name

Save a copy of the file to the company database

    Require authorized employees to use a Login to view the file

    Lock the file after any changes are made

FIGURE 4.32

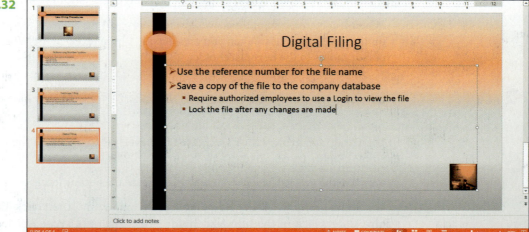

12 In the **Slides group,** click the **New Slide button arrow,** and then click **Title and Content** to add another slide. In the title placeholder, press Ctrl + E, type **Summary** In the content placeholder, type **All changes are effective immediately. Direct questions to the support team.** On the **HOME tab,** in the **Paragraph group,** click **Bullets** to remove the bullet. In the **Paragraph group,** click **Center.**

13 With the content placeholder selected, on the left side of the content placeholder, click the **middle sizing handle**, and then drag the sizing handle to **3.5 inches on the left side of the horizontal ruler**. On the right side of the content placeholder, drag the **middle sizing handle** to **3.5 inches on the right side of the horizontal ruler**. With the content placeholder still selected, at the bottom of the content placeholder, drag the **middle sizing handle** to **0.5 inches on the lower half of the vertical ruler** to reduce the size of the placeholder. Hold down the Shift key, and then click the top border of the content placeholder. Drag the entire placeholder down so the top is aligned at **1.5 inches on the upper half of the vertical ruler**. Release the Shift key. In the **Paragraph group**, click **Line Spacing**, and then click **1.5**. Compare your screen with Figure 4.33.

FIGURE 4.33

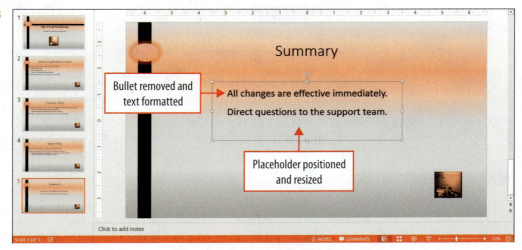

14 On the **INSERT tab**, in the **Text group**, click **Header & Footer** to display the **Header and Footer** dialog box. Click the **Notes and Handouts tab**. Under **Include on page**, select the **Date and time** check box, and then select **Fixed** and type today's date. If necessary, clear the **Header** check box, and then select the **Page number** and **Footer** check boxes. In the **Footer** box, using your own name, type **Lastname_Firstname_4A_Filing_Procedures** and then click **Apply to All**.

15 Click the **FILE tab**, and then in the lower right portion of the screen, click **Show All Properties**. In the **Tags** box, type **filing, number, system** and in the **Subject** box type your course name and section number. In the **Author** box, right-click the existing author name, click **Edit Property**, replace the existing text with your first and last name, click outside text box to deselect, and then click **OK**.

16 Save 💾 the presentation.

Activity 4.10 | Editing Slide Masters in an Existing Presentation

Occasionally, you might want to change the master design for a presentation created from your custom template. In this activity, you will change the bullet style on the Title and Content Layout slide master.

1 With **Lastname_Firstname_4A_Filing_Procedures** open, on the **VIEW tab**, in the **Master Views group**, click **Slide Master**.

2 Scroll up as necessary, and click the first thumbnail—**Office Theme Slide Master**. On the **SLIDE MASTER tab**, in **Background group**, click **Fonts**, and then click **Office 2007-2010**.

3 In the content placeholder, click the second bulleted line. On the **HOME tab**, in the **Paragraph group**, click the **Bullets button arrow**. Click **Checkmark Bullets**. Compare your screen with Figure 4.34.

FIGURE 4.34

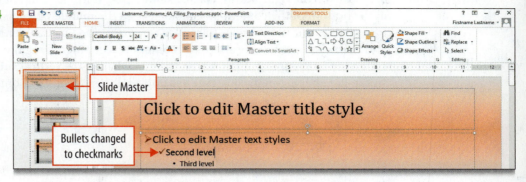

The title font is changed to Cambria (Heading). The second-level bullets are now displayed as checkmarks. Recall that changes made to the first thumbnail affect all slides.

4 On the **SLIDE MASTER tab**, in the **Close group**, click **Close Master View**. On the **SLIDE SHOW tab**, in the **Start Slide Show group**, click **From Beginning**. View the entire slide presentation.

ANOTHER WAY   Press F5 to start a slide show from the beginning.

Because you changed the second-level bullet to checkmarks on the slide master, all slides have checkmarks instead of square bullets. Changing the bullet style on the master slide saved you the time it would take to change the bullets on each slide.

5 Save your presentation. Print **Handouts 3 Slides**, or submit your presentation electronically as directed by your instructor.

The change that you made to the bullets affects only this presentation. The original meeting template still uses the square bullets. If you want the change to be permanent on the template, you should open the template and make the change in that file.

6 Click **Close** to close the presentation and **Exit** PowerPoint.

7 Submit **Lastname_Firstname_4A_Meeting_Template** and **Lastname_Firstname_4A_Filing_Procedures** as directed by your instructor.

END | You have completed Project 4A

Commented Presentation

PROJECT ACTIVITIES

In Activities 4.11 through 4.20, you will use reviewing comments to provide feedback to a presentation created by a colleague at the Thompson Henderson Law Partners firm. You will use editing tools, such as the thesaurus. You will compare two versions of a presentation to view the differences between the presentations. Then you will publish your presentation in both PDF and XPS formats. These formats preserve the document formatting and enable file sharing. You will save the presentation as Word handouts for the audience. Finally, you will check your presentation for compatibility with previous versions of PowerPoint and mark the presentation as final. You will password protect your presentation. Your completed presentation will look similar to Figure 4.35.

PROJECT FILES

For Project 4B, you will need the following files:

p04B_Entertainment_Basics.pptx
p04B_Entertainment_Basics2.pptx

You will save your presentations as:

Lastname_Firstname_4B_Entertainment_Basics.pptx
Lastname_Firstname_4B_Entertainment_Basics.pdf
Lastname_Firstname_4B_Entertainment_Basics.xps
Lastname_Firstname_4B_Entertainment_Basics.docx

PROJECT RESULTS

DGA/Fotolia; Scanrail/Fotolia; zentilia/Fotolia; Mitar/Fotolia

Figure 4.35 Project 4B Commented Presentation

Video P4-3

A *comment* is a note that you can attach to a letter or word on a slide or to an entire slide. People use comments to provide feedback on a presentation. A *reviewer* is someone who adds comments to the presentation to provide feedback.

Activity 4.11 | Adding Comments

In this activity, you will add comments to your meeting presentation. Comments may be added by the person who created the presentation, or other persons who are invited to provide suggestions.

1 ▸ Start PowerPoint. Locate and open the file **p04B_Entertainment_Basics.pptx** Navigate to the location where you are storing your folders and projects for this chapter, and then **Save** the file as **Lastname_Firstname_4B_Entertainment_Basics**

2 ▸ Make **Slide 2** the active slide. Click the **REVIEW tab**. In the **Comments group**, point to each of the buttons, and read the **ScreenTips**. Compare your screen with Figure 4.36. For a complete explanation of each of these buttons, see Figure 4.37.

FIGURE 4.36

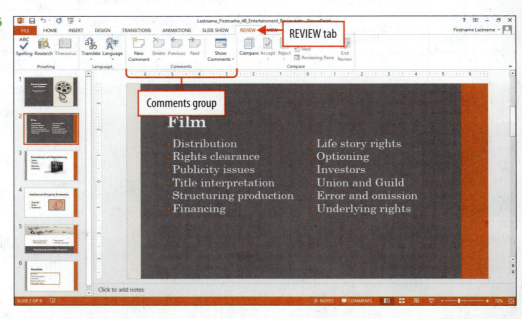

FIGURE 4.37

REVIEWING ELEMENTS	
SCREEN ELEMENT	**DESCRIPTION**
Comments group	
New Comment	Add a note about this part of the document.
Delete	Delete the selected comment.
Previous	Jump to the previous comment.
Next	Jump to the next comment.
Show Comments – Comments Pane	Show the Comments pane to view, add, and delete comments. Comments are not displayed during a slide show.
Show Comments – Show Markup	Show comments and other annotations.

3 In the **Comments group**, click **New Comment**. In the space provided in the Comments pane, type **Comprehensive List!** In the Comments group, all buttons become active. Compare your screen with Figure 4.38.

FIGURE 4.38

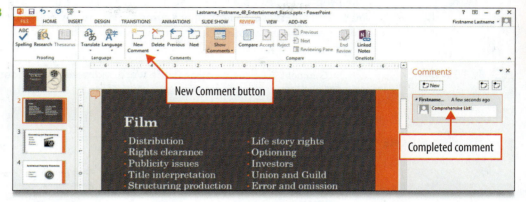

When there are no comments in the file, two buttons in the Comments group are active—New Comment and Show Comments which provides access to the Comments Pane. When a comment is added, the relevant buttons become active. When no placeholder or text is selected before adding a comment, by default the comment icon displays at the upper left corner of the slide. The comment displays in the Comments pane. The name of the person that entered the comment displays in the upper left corner of the comment box and the date or time displays in the upper right corner.

More Knowledge   **Comments**

The Comments pane allows you to view and track comments next to the text being discussed, see who replied to who and when, similar to a threaded style conversation. Additional participants can reply and join the conversation.

---

4 Make **Slide 3** the active slide. Click at the end of the third bulleted item, after *Directors*. In the **Comments** pane, click **New**. Type **What kind of directors?** Click outside the comment to deselect it. Compare your screen with Figure 4.39.

Placing the insertion point within a specific area of the slide will position the comment box at that place.

FIGURE 4.39

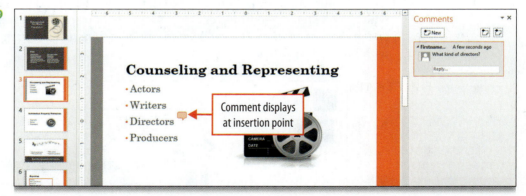

5 Make **Slide 4** the active slide. Select the word *Copyright*. Use the procedure explained in the previous steps to add this comment: **Add short definitions.** Click outside the comment to deselect it.

When you add a comment to selected text, the comment is displayed near the selected text.

6 Select **Slide 5**, and then enter this comment: **Is the word "agreements" necessary?** Click outside the comment. Drag the comment so it is positioned under the words *Production agreements.* Compare your screen with Figure 4.40.

When you add a new comment, the default location is the upper left corner of the slide unless you specify otherwise. You can drag a comment box to any position on the slide. Note that bold, underline, and italic are not available in the comment box.

FIGURE 4.40

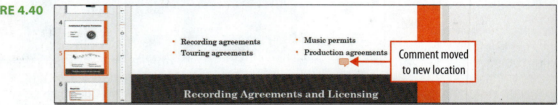

7 Save 💾 the presentation.

Activity 4.12 | Reading Comments

In this activity, you will learn how to navigate among the comments entered in a presentation.

1 On **Slide 2**, with the **REVIEW tab** selected, in the **Comments group**, click the **Show Comments arrow**, and then click **Show Markup**. Notice that the comment disappears and the **Comments** pane closes. Click the **Show Comments arrow**, and then click **Show Markup** again to redisplay the comment on the slide. Click the **Show Comments arrow**, and then click **Comments Pane** to redisplay the **Comments** Pane.

The Show Comments button Comments Pane and Show Markup options display a check mark when activated.

2 Make **Slide 1** the active slide. In the **Comments group**, click **Next**. The first comment displays in the **Comments** pane so you can read it. Click **Next** again to read the second comment, which is on **Slide 3**. Continue clicking **Next** until you see the message *PowerPoint reached the end of the presentation. Do you want to continue from the beginning?* Compare your screen with Figure 4.41. Click **Cancel**.

FIGURE 4.41

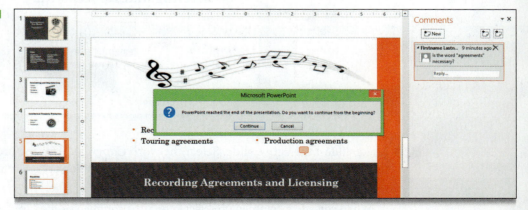

3 In the **Comments group**, click **Previous** to read the previous comment. Continue clicking **Previous** until you receive this message: *PowerPoint reached the beginning of the presentation. Do you want to continue from the end?* Click **Cancel**.

Use the Next and Previous buttons to read the comments in your presentation.

Activity 4.13 | Editing Comments

In this activity, you will learn how to edit a comment and how to delete a comment.

1 On **Slide 2**, in the **Comments** pane, under the first comment, click in the **Reply** box, and then type **Allow time to cover these**. Click outside the comment to close it. Compare your screen with Figure 4.42.

An additional comment by the same author is added in the Comments pane. The author's identifying information displays with the date and time of the comment. Two comment icons display in the upper left portion of the slide.

FIGURE 4.42

2 Click **Next** until you reach the comment on **Slide 4**. In the **Comments group**, click the **Delete button arrow**, and then read the three options: *Delete, Delete All Comments and Ink on This Slide,* and *Delete All Comments and Ink in This Presentation*. Compare your screen with Figure 4.43.

FIGURE 4.43

3 Click **Delete** to remove this comment.

The comment is deleted.

ANOTHER WAY    To delete a comment, you can also right-click the comment and then click Delete Comment.

4 On the **REVIEW tab**, in the **Comments group**, click the **Show Comments arrow**, and then click **Comments Pane**.

The Comments pane closes.

ANOTHER WAY   On the upper right corner of the Comments pane, click Close.

5 Save ⊟ the presentation.

Activity 4.14 | Using the Thesaurus

You can use the Thesaurus to replace a word in a presentation with a *synonym*—a word having the same or nearly the same meaning as another.

1 ▶ Display **Slide 5**. In the content placeholder on the right, in the second column, locate the word *permits*.

2 ▶ Right-click **permits**, and then on the shortcut menu, point to **Synonyms**. Compare your screen with Figure 4.44.

A list of words with the same meaning as *permits* displays.

FIGURE 4.44

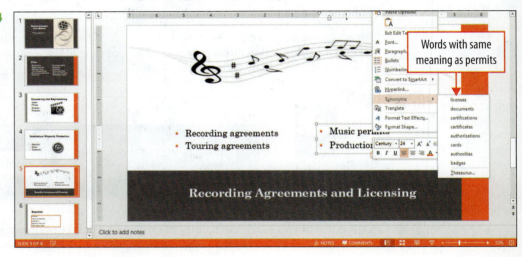

3 ▶ Click **licenses** to change the word *permits* to *licenses*.

4 ▶ Save 💾 your presentation.

More Knowledge | **The Thesaurus**

When a word is selected, you can display the Thesaurus pane by clicking on Thesaurus on the REVIEW tab, in the Proofing group, by pressing [Shift] + [F7], or by clicking Thesaurus on the Synonyms submenu on the shortcut menu. The Thesaurus pane displays a complete Thesaurus of synonyms and *antonyms*—words with an opposite meaning.

Objective 4 | Compare and Combine Presentations

Video P4-4

PowerPoint offers a way to compare and combine presentations by merging them into a single presentation, highlighting and listing the differences. You can then manually review the changes and choose the edits for the final presentation. This feature is useful if you work with others on presentations, or if you just want to see what differences exist between two versions of a presentation.

Activity 4.15 | Comparing and Combining Presentations

In this activity, you will view two versions of a presentation to compare their differences.

1 ▶ Click **Slide 1** to make it active. On the **REVIEW tab**, in the **Compare group**, click **Compare**. In the **Choose File to Merge with Current Presentation** dialog box, navigate to your student data files for this chapter, and then click **p04B_Entertainment_Basics2**, and then click **Merge**.

The Revisions pane opens on the right side of the slide. The Revisions pane is used to locate all instances in which the two presentations differ.

2 In the **Revisions** pane, verify that the **DETAILS tab** displays in orange, and if necessary, make it the active tab. Compare your screen with Figure 4.45.

The Revisions pane DETAILS tab is divided into two sections—Slide Changes and Presentation Changes. The Slide Changes section indicates differences between the two presentations for the active slide. The Presentation Changes section lists entire slides that were added or removed when the two presentations were merged.

FIGURE 4.45

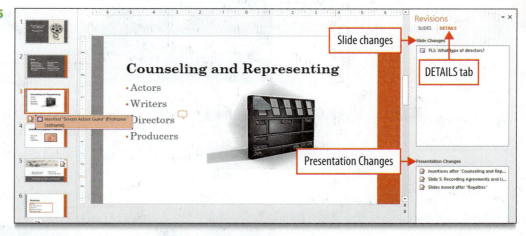

3 In the **Revisions** pane, under **Presentation Changes**, click **Insertions after "Counseling and Rep...** to display a **Revisions** check box in the **Slides and Outline** pane on the left. Compare your screen with Figure 4.46.

You can use the Revisions check box to accept or reject the addition of the slide. Your Lastname_Firstname_p04B_Entertainment_Basics presentation does not include this suggested revision; the slide is in the p04B_Entertainment_Basics2 presentation.

FIGURE 4.46

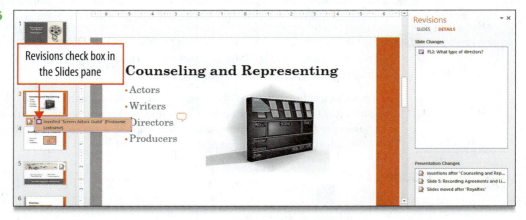

4 Select the **Revisions** check box that says *Inserted "Screen Actors Guild"*. Compare your screen with Figure 4.47.

The slide is inserted in your presentation. If the Revisions check box is left blank, the slide is not inserted.

FIGURE 4.47

> 5 ▶ Display **Slide 2** and notice that a **Revisions button** 📝 displays on the slide. Click the **Revisions** button to display the **Revisions** check box. Compare your screen with Figure 4.48.

This revision indicates that the word Capital has been inserted from the p04B_Entertainment_Basics2 presentation.

FIGURE 4.48

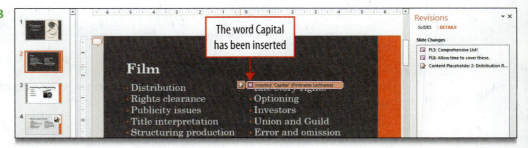

> 6 ▶ Select the **Revisions** check box that indicates *Inserted "Capital"* to accept the change and insert the word *Capital* in the last bullet of column 1.

> 7 ▶ Display **Slide 6**. In the **Revisions** pane, under **Presentation Changes**, click **Slide 6: Recording Agreements and Li…** to display a **Revisions** check box in the **Slides and Outline** pane on the left. Compare your screen with Figure 4.49.

You can use the Revisions check box to accept or reject the move of the "Recording Agreements and Licensing" slide after Slide 7: "Royalties". Your Lastname_Firstname_p04B_Entertainment_Basics presentation does not include this suggested revision; the slide moved is in the p04B_Entertainment_Basics2 presentation.

FIGURE 4.49

8 Do *not* select the **Revisions** check box on the **Slide 6** thumbnail.

9 In the **Revisions** pane, under **Presentation Changes**, click **Slides moved after "Royalties"** to display a **Revisions** check box under **Slide 7** in the **Slides and Outline** pane on the left. Do *not* select the **Revisions** check box under the **Slide 7** thumbnail.

> The revisions to Slides 6 and 7 are not accepted.

10 On the **REVIEW tab,** in the **Compare group**, click **End Review**, and then in the **Microsoft PowerPoint** dialog box, click **Yes**. **Save** 💾 your presentation.

> The presentation is now merged with the selected changes, the revisions to Slides 6 and 7 are not included, and the Revisions pane closes. The unapplied changes were discarded.

> **More Knowledge** | **View Multiple Presentations**
>
> You can view two presentations side by side to see the differences between them. On the VIEW tab, in the Window group, click Arrange All. The presentations display side by side on the screen.

Objective 5 | Prepare a Presentation for Distribution

Video P4-5

PowerPoint offers several ways to share, or distribute, a presentation. A common way is to create a PDF document that people who have Adobe Reader installed on their computers can read. You can also create an XPS document that people who have an XPS viewer can read. Another way to share a presentation is to create handouts in Microsoft Word.

Activity 4.16 | Publishing a Presentation in PDF and XPS Format

In this activity, you will save a presentation in PDF and XPS file formats. Adobe's *Portable Document Format (PDF)* preserves document formatting and enables file sharing. The PDF format is also useful if you intend to use commercial printing methods. *XML Paper Specification (XPS)* is Microsoft's electronic paper format, an alternative to the PDF format that also preserves document formatting and enables file sharing. When an XPS or PDF file is viewed online or printed, it retains the format that you intended, and the data in the file cannot be easily changed.

1 Open **Lastname_Firstname_4B_Entertainment_Basics**, if necessary. On the **INSERT tab**, in the **Text group**, click **Header & Footer** to display the **Header and Footer** dialog box. Click the **Notes and Handouts tab**. Under **Include on page**, select the **Date and time** check box, and then select **Fixed** and type today's date, if necessary. Clear the **Header** check box, if necessary, and then select the **Page number** and **Footer** check boxes. In the **Footer** box, using your own name, type **Lastname_Firstname_4B_Entertainment_Basics** and then click **Apply to All**.

2 Make **Slide 1** active. Click **FILE**, and then click **Export**. Under **Export**, **Create PDF/XPS Document** is selected. On the right side of your screen, read the explanation of a PDF/XPS document. Compare your screen with Figure 4.50.

> Presentations saved as PDF/XPS documents are saved in a fixed format. The document looks the same on most computers. Fonts, formatting, and images are preserved. Because content cannot be easily changed, your document is more secure. To view a PDF or XPS file, you must have a viewer installed on your computer. Free viewers are available on the web to view PDF and XPS documents.

FIGURE 4.50

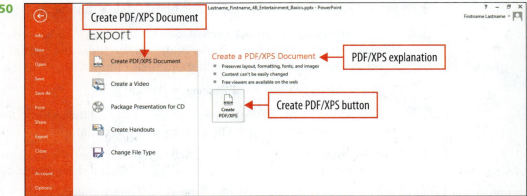

3 ▶ Click **Create PDF/XPS**. In the **Publish as PDF or XPS** dialog box, click the **Save as type arrow** to see the two file formats—PDF (*.pdf) and XPS Document (*.xps). Click **PDF (*.pdf)**. If necessary, click the option button for **Standard (publishing online and printing)** to select the print quality. If necessary, clear the **Open file after publishing** check box. Compare your screen with Figure 4.51.

Choose Standard (publishing online and printing) if the presentation requires high print quality. If the file size is more important than the print quality, click Minimum size (publishing online).

FIGURE 4.51

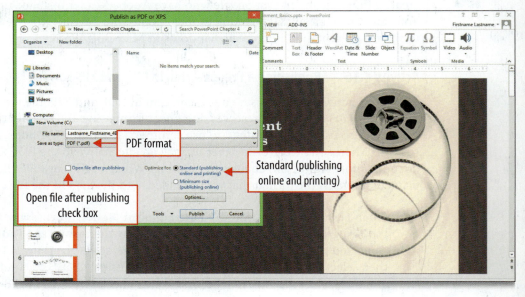

4 ▶ In the **Publish as PDF or XPS** dialog box, click **Options** located in the lower right area of the dialog box.

5 ▶ In the **Options** dialog box under **Publish options**, click the **Publish what arrow** to see the choices—Slides, Handouts, Notes pages, and Outline view. Click **Handouts**, and then on the right side of the dialog box, click the **Slides per page arrow**. Click **3**, and then view the preview showing how the printed page will look. Select the **Include comments and ink markup** check box. Compare your screen with Figure 4.52.

The options to publish a presentation as a PDF file are the same as the options to print the file.

FIGURE 4.52

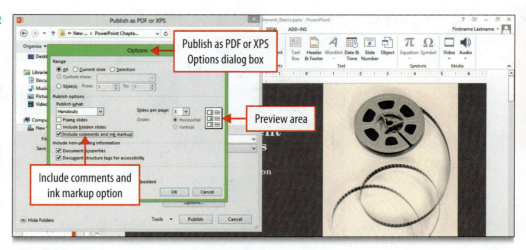

ANOTHER WAY   Enter the page number in the text box to change pages in the PDF.

6 ▶ Click **OK**. Click **Publish**. The document is published (saved) in PDF format in the location where you are saving your work.

Lastname_Firstname_4B_Entertainment_Basics.pdf is located in the same folder as your original PowerPoint presentation file.

N O T E   **Reading PDF Files**

A common application used to open PDF files is Adobe Reader. If you don't have Adobe Reader on your computer, you can download it free from www.adobe.com.

---

7 ▶ Click **FILE**, and then click **Export**. Under **Export**, **Create PDF/XPS Document** is selected. Click **Create PDF/XPS**. In the **Publish as PDF or XPS** dialog box, change the file type to **XPS Document (*.xps)**. Click **Options**. Click the **Publish what arrow**, and then click **Handouts**. Click **Include comments and ink markup**. Click **OK**. Select the **Open file after publishing** check box. Click **Publish**. The presentation is saved as an XPS document and opens in the XPS Viewer. Maximize your window and press Ctrl + N to view all 6 slides on one page. The menu bar on the XPS Viewer provides options to set permissions and digitally sign a document. Compare your screen with Figure 4.53.

The handouts are displayed with 6 slides per page. The comment numbers are displayed on the slides. Your file is saved on your storage media as Lastname_Firstname_4B_Entertainment_Basics. xps in the same folder as your original PowerPoint presentation file. You can only view XPS documents with an XPS Viewer, such as the one provided in Microsoft Windows. You can also download a free copy of the XPS Viewer at www.microsoft.com. Only presentations formatted in PowerPoint 2000 or later versions can be saved and viewed in the XPS Viewer.

FIGURE 4.53

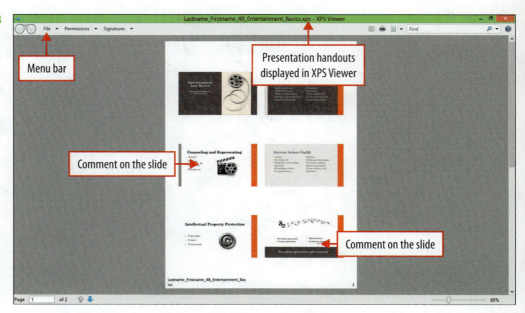

8 Click **File**, and then click **Exit** to close the file and XPS Viewer.

 **ANOTHER WAY**   To close the file and the viewer, press ⎡Alt⎤ + ⎡F4⎤.

Activity 4.17 | Creating Handouts in Microsoft Word

In this activity, you will create handouts that open in Microsoft Word.

1 In **PowerPoint**, click **FILE**, click **Export**, and then under **Export**, click **Create Handouts**. At the right, under **Create Handouts in Microsoft Word**, read the explanation. Compare your screen with Figure 4.54.

> The handout is a document that contains the slides and notes from the presentation. You can use Word to change the layout and format and even add additional content to the handout. If you link the handout file to your presentation, changes in your presentation will automatically update the handout content.

FIGURE 4.54

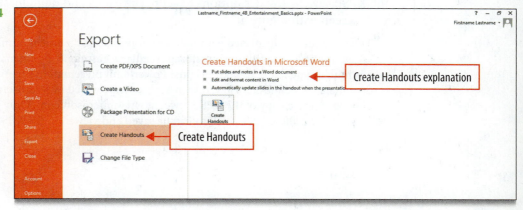

2 ▶ Click **Create Handouts** to display the **Send to Microsoft Word** dialog box. Under **Add slides to Microsoft Word document**, click **Paste link**. Compare your screen with Figure 4.55.

> To ensure that any changes you make to the PowerPoint presentation are reflected in the Word document, use Paste link. Each time you open the Word document, you will be prompted to accept or reject the changes. The link for the Word file and the PowerPoint file will be broken if either of the files are moved from their folder location.

FIGURE 4.55

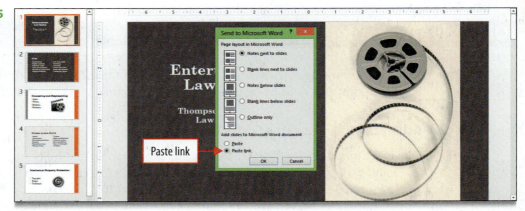

3 ▶ Click **OK**. Click **Word** on the taskbar to see the presentation slides displayed in a new Word document. Compare your screen with Figure 4.56.

FIGURE 4.56

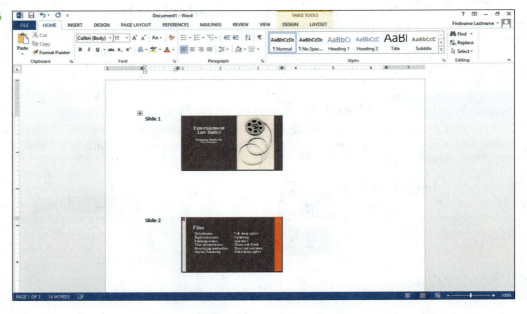

4 ▶ In the Word document, click the **INSERT tab**. In the **Header & Footer group**, click **Footer**, and then click **Edit Footer**. At the left, type **Lastname_Firstname_4B_Entertainment_Basics** Press the Tab key two times, and then type the current date. On the **DESIGN tab**, in the **Close group**, click **Close Header and Footer**.

5 ▶ Press F12 to display the **Save As** dialog box. Navigate to the location where you are saving your work, and then save the Word file as **Lastname_Firstname_4B_Entertainment_Basics** **Close** the Word document and return to the presentation file.

6 ▶ Click the **FILE tab** to display **Backstage** view. On the right, at the bottom of the **Properties** list, click **Show All Properties**.

7 On the list of **Properties**, click to the right of **Tags** to display an empty box, and then type **mission, agreements, licensing, film, royalties**

8 Click to the right of **Subject** to display an empty box, and then type your course name and section number. In the **Author** box, right-click the existing author name, click **Edit Property**, replace the existing text with your first and last name, click outside text box to deselect, and then click **OK**.

9 Save ▤ the presentation.

Objective 6   Protect a Presentation

Video P4-6

In the following activities, you will check the compatibility of your file with previous versions of PowerPoint as well as mark your presentation as final and then save it as read-only.

Activity 4.18 | Using the Compatibility Checker

The **Compatibility Checker** locates any potential compatibility issues between PowerPoint 2013 and earlier versions of PowerPoint. It will prepare a report to help you resolve any issues. PowerPoint 2013 files are compatible with 2007 and 2010 files because they use the same file format (.pptx). However, PowerPoint 2013 does not support saving files to PowerPoint 95 or earlier. If necessary, you can save the presentation in **compatibility mode**, which means to save it as a PowerPoint 97-2003 Presentation.

1 Click **FILE**. To the left of **Inspect Presentation**, click **Check for Issues**, and then click **Check Compatibility**. Read the report displayed in the **Microsoft PowerPoint Compatibility Checker** dialog box. Compare your screen with Figure 4.57.

The Compatibility Checker summary identifies parts of the presentation that cannot be edited in earlier versions because those features are not available.

> ### More Knowledge | Saving Presentations in Other File Formats
>
> If you exchange PowerPoint presentations with other people, you may save the presentation in other formats. Click FILE, click Export, click Change File Type, and then you may change the file type to PowerPoint 97-2003 Presentation. Other options include PowerPoint Show and PowerPoint Picture Presentation.

FIGURE 4.57

2 Click **OK**.

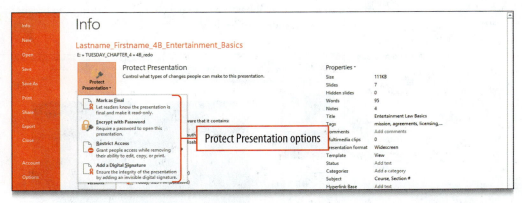

More Knowledge | **Check Accessibility**

You can check the presentation for content that people with disabilities might find difficult to read. To access this, on the Info tab, click the Check for Issues arrow, and then click Check Accessibility. An Accessibility Checker pane displays Inspection Results. You can then select and fix each issue listed in the pane to make the document accessible for people with disabilities. For example, you can add alternative text to describe a picture on the slide.

Activity 4.19 | Marking a Presentation as Final

In this activity, you will use the **_Mark as Final_** command to make your presentation document read-only in order to prevent changes to the document. Additionally, the Status property of the document is set to Final and the Mark as Final icon displays in the status bar.

1 ▶ Click **FILE**. Notice that Protect Presentation allows you to: _Control what types of changes people can make to this presentation._ Under **Info**, click the **Protect Presentation arrow**, and then examine the Protect Presentation options. Compare your screen with Figure 4.58.

The options to protect a presentation are Mark as Final, Encrypt with Password, Restrict Access, and Add a Digital Signature.

FIGURE 4.58

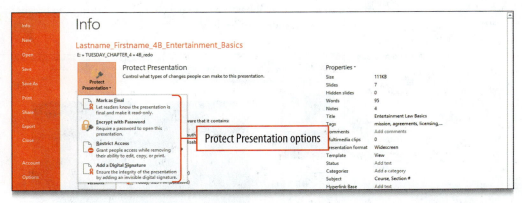

2 ▶ Click **Mark as Final**. Notice in the **Microsoft PowerPoint** dialog box that the presentation will be marked as final and then saved. Compare your screen with Figure 4.59.

The Mark as Final command helps prevent reviewers or readers from accidentally making changes to the document. Because the Mark as Final command is not a security feature, anyone who receives an electronic copy of a document that has been marked as final can edit that document by removing Mark as Final status from the document.

FIGURE 4.59

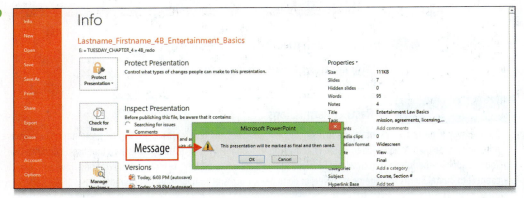

3 Click **OK**. A **Microsoft PowerPoint** dialog box displays that reminds you that the document will be saved as final. The message also tells you that a **Mark as Final** icon will display in the status bar. Compare your screen with Figure 4.60.

FIGURE 4.60

Marked as Final message

4 Click **OK**. Note the information bar at the top and the **Marked as Final** icon at the bottom left on the status bar. Compare your screen with Figure 4.61.

The information bar provides the option to edit the file even though you marked it as final, so be aware that others will be able to make changes. Marking the presentation as final tells others that you encourage them not to do this.

FIGURE 4.61

Information bar

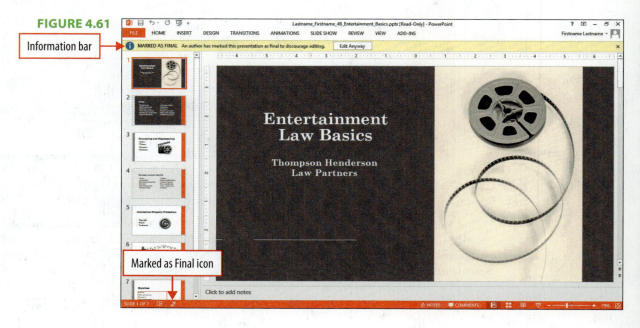

Marked as Final icon

5 On the information bar, click **Edit Anyway**.

You are free to make changes to the document.

More Knowledge | **Restrict Permissions**

Another way to protect a presentation is to restrict permissions. You can give others access to your presentation but remove their capability to edit, copy, or print. In order to do this, you need to install Windows Rights Management to restrict permissions that use a Windows Live ID or a Microsoft Windows account. You can apply for permissions from within PowerPoint—on the Info tab, click the Protect Presentation arrow, and then click Restrict Access. You can then connect to Digital Rights Management Servers or go to www.microsoft.com for more information.

Activity 4.20 | Changing the Presentation Password

In this activity, you will password protect the presentation.

1 Click **FILE**. Under **Info**, click the **Protect Presentation arrow**, and then click **Encrypt with Password**.

2 In the **Encrypt Document** dialog box, in the **Password** box, type **Go** and then click **OK**. Compare your screen with Figure 4.62.

FIGURE 4.62

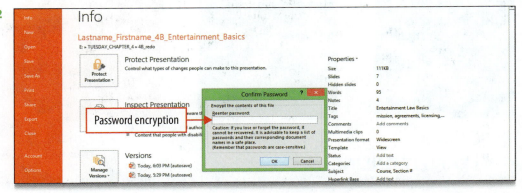

3 In the **Confirm Password** dialog box, type **Go** and then click **OK**. **Save** 🖫 the file. **Close** ☒ the file.

4 **Open** your **Lastname_Firstname_4B_Entertainment_Basics** file.

The Password dialog box displays and you are prompted to enter the password.

5 In the Password dialog box, type **Go** and then click **OK** to open the presentation.

More Knowledge | **Remove a Password**

To remove a password from an encrypted PowerPoint presentation, display the Encrypt Document dialog box, highlight the contents of the Password box, and then press Delete or Backspace. Click OK to accept the change.

---

6 Click **FILE**, click **Print**, and then under **Settings**, click the **Full Page Slides button arrow** to display the **Print Layout** gallery. Click **Handouts 3 Slides**. Display the **Print Layout** gallery again, and then check **Print Comments and Ink Markup** if necessary. Print the slides. If requested, submit your presentation electronically as directed by your instructor instead of printing.

7 Click **Close** ☒ to close the presentation, and then **Exit** PowerPoint.

END | You have completed Project 4B

END OF CHAPTER

SUMMARY

You designed a PowerPoint template containing formats, shapes, and images on the master pages; you then created a presentation based on this template; and you entered text for a meeting on the presentation.

You added comments into the presentation and practiced navigating through the presentation to read, edit, and delete comments in the presentation. You used the Thesaurus tool to edit your presentation.

You edited Handout and Notes Masters. You compared two versions of a presentation to view the differences between the presentations. You then merged the two presentations into a single presentation.

You prepared a presentation for distribution by publishing it in PDF and XPS formats. You checked the compatibility of the file, marked the presentation as Final, and password protected the presentation.

GO! LEARN IT ONLINE

Review the concepts and key terms in this chapter by completing these online challenges, which you can find at **www.pearsonhighered.com/go**.

Matching and Multiple Choice:
Answer matching and multiple choice questions to test what you learned in this chapter. MyITLab®

Crossword Puzzle:
Spell out the words that match the numbered clues, and put them in the puzzle squares.

Flipboard:
Flip through the definitions of the key terms in this chapter and match them with the correct term.

END OF CHAPTER
REVIEW AND ASSESSMENT GUIDE FOR POWERPOINT CHAPTER 4

Your instructor may assign one or more of these projects to help you review the chapter and assess your mastery and understanding of the chapter.

Review and Assessment Guide for PowerPoint Chapter 4			
Project	**Apply Skills from These Chapter Objectives**	**Project Type**	**Project Location**
4C	Objectives 1–2 from Project 4A	**4C Chapter Review** A guided review of the skills from Project 4A.	On the following pages
4D	Objectives 3–6 from Project 4B	**4D Chapter Review** A guided review of the skills from Project 4B.	On the following pages
4E	Objectives 1–2 from Project 4A	**4E Mastery (Grader Project)** A demonstration of your mastery of the skills in Project 4A with extensive decision making.	In MyITLab and on the following pages
4F	Objectives 3–6 from Project 4B	**4F Mastery (Grader Project)** A demonstration of your mastery of the skills in Project 4B with extensive decision making.	In MyITLab and on the following pages
4G	Objectives 1–6 from Projects 4A and 4B	**4G Mastery (Grader Project)** A demonstration of your mastery of the skills in Projects 4A and 4B with extensive decision making.	In MyITLab and on the following pages
4H	Combination of Objectives from Projects 4A and 4B	**4H GO! Fix It** A demonstration of your mastery of the skills in Projects 4A and 4B by creating a correct result from a document that contains errors you must find.	Online
4I	Combination of Objectives from Projects 4A and 4B	**4I GO! Make It** A demonstration of your mastery of the skills in Projects 4A and 4B by creating a result from a supplied picture.	Online
4J	Combination of Objectives from Projects 4A and 4B	**4J GO! Solve It** A demonstration of your mastery of the skills in Projects 4A and 4B, your decision-making skills, and your critical thinking skills. A task-specific rubric helps you self-assess your result.	Online
4K	Combination of Objectives from Projects 4A and 4B	**4K GO! Solve It** A demonstration of your mastery of the skills in Projects 4A and 4B, your decision-making skills, and your critical thinking skills. A task-specific rubric helps you self-assess your result.	On the following pages
4L	Combination of Objectives from Projects 4A and 4B	**4L GO! Think** A demonstration of your understanding of the chapter concepts applied in a manner that you would outside of college. An analytic rubric helps you and your instructor grade the quality of your work by comparing it to the work an expert in the discipline would create.	On the following pages
4M	Combination of Objectives from Projects 4A and 4B	**4M GO! Think** A demonstration of your understanding of the chapter concepts applied in a manner that you would outside of college. An analytic rubric helps you and your instructor grade the quality of your work by comparing it to the work an expert in the discipline would create.	Online
4N	Combination of Objectives from Projects 4A and 4B	**4N You and GO!** A demonstration of your understanding of the chapter concepts applied in a manner that you would in a personal situation. An analytic rubric helps you and your instructor grade the quality of your work.	Online

GLOSSARY

GLOSSARY OF CHAPTER KEY TERMS

Antonyms Words with an opposite meaning.

Comment A note that you can attach to a letter or word on a slide or to an entire slide. People use comments to provide feedback on a presentation.

Compatibility Checker A feature that locates potential compatibility issues between PowerPoint 2013 and earlier versions of PowerPoint.

Compatibility mode Saves a presentation as PowerPoint 97-2003 presentation. It also ensures that no new or enhanced features in PowerPoint 2013 are available while you work with a document, so that people who are using previous versions of PowerPoint will have full editing capabilities.

Gradient fill A gradual progression of several colors blending into each other or shades of the same color blending into each other.

Gradient stop Allows you to apply different color combinations to selected areas of the background.

Handout Master Includes the specifications for the design of presentation handouts for an audience.

Mark as Final Makes a presentation file read-only in order to prevent changes to the document. Adds a Marked as Final icon to the status bar.

Notes Master Includes the specifications for the design of the speaker's notes.

Office Theme Slide Master A specific slide master that contains the design, such as the background, that displays on all slide layouts in the presentation.

.potx The file extension for a PowerPoint template.

.pptx The file extension for a PowerPoint presentation.

Portable Document Format (PDF) A file format that creates an image that preserves the look of your file, but that cannot be easily changed; a popular format for sending documents electronically, because the document will display on most computers.

Reviewer A person who inserts comments into a presentation to provide feedback.

Slide Master Part of a template that stores information about the formatting and text that displays on every slide in a presentation. There are various slide master layouts.

Synonym A word having the same or nearly the same meaning as another.

Template A predefined layout for a group of slides saved as a .potx file.

XML Paper Specification (XPS) Microsoft's file format that preserves document formatting and enables file sharing. Files can be opened and viewed on any operating system or computer that is equipped with Microsoft XPS Viewer. Files cannot be easily edited.

CHAPTER REVIEW

| Skills Review | Project 4C Contract |

Apply 4A skills from these Objectives:

1 Create a Custom Template by Modifying Slide Masters

2 Apply a Custom Template to a Presentation

In the following Skills Review, you will create a template that Thompson Henderson Law Partners will use to prepare presentations for the initial meeting with a client. You will use the template to create a presentation for the musical group Billy and the Night Owls. Your completed presentation will look similar to Figure 4.63.

PROJECT FILES

Build from Scratch

For Project 4C, you will need the following files:

New blank Powerpoint presentation
p04C_Contract.jpg

You will save your files as:

Lastname_Firstname_4C_Contract_Template.potx
Lastname_Firstname_4C_Night_Owls.pptx

PROJECT RESULTS

Africa Studio/Fotolia

FIGURE 4.63

(Project 4C Contract continues on the next page)

CHAPTER REVIEW

1 ▶ Start PowerPoint, and then click **Blank Presentation**. Press F12 to display the **Save As** dialog box. Navigate to the location where you are saving your work, click the **Save as type box arrow**, and then click **PowerPoint Template (*.potx)**. **Save** your file as **Lastname_Firstname_4C_Contract_Template**

2 ▶ Click the **VIEW tab**. In the **Master Views group**, click **Slide Master**.

a. Scroll up, and then click the first thumbnail—**Office Theme Slide Master**. From the **SLIDE MASTER tab**, in the **Background group**, click **Background Styles**. In the **Background Styles gallery**, select **Style 9**.

b. Click the second thumbnail—**Title Slide Layout**. Click the dashed border on the Master title style placeholder, and then on the **HOME tab**, change the font size to **48 point**.

3 ▶ Click the **Office Theme Slide Master** thumbnail.

a. On the **SLIDE MASTER tab**, in the **Background group**, click **Background Styles**, and then click **Format Background**. Under **Fill**, click **Gradient fill**, if necessary. Click the **Type arrow**, and then click **Radial**.

b. Click **Add gradient stop** once, and then position the stop at **80%**.

c. Click the **Color arrow**, and then in the eighth column in the second row, click **Gold, Accent 4, Lighter 80%**.

d. Click **Apply to All**. **Close** the **Format Background** pane.

4 ▶ Click the **Title Slide Layout** thumbnail.

a. Click the **VIEW tab**. In the **Show group**, click the **Ruler** checkbox to display the horizontal and vertical rulers, if necessary.

b. Click the **INSERT tab**. In the **Illustrations group**, click **Shapes**. Under **Basic Shapes**, click the **Diamond** shape. At **2 inches on the right side of the horizontal ruler** and **3 inches on the upper half of the vertical ruler**, click to insert the shape.

c. On the ribbon, on the **DRAWING TOOLS FORMAT tab**, in the **Shapes Styles group**, click **Shape Effects**, point to **Preset**, and then click **Preset 2**. In the **Shapes Styles group**, click the **Shape Outline button arrow**, and then click **No Outline**.

d. With the diamond still selected, in the **Size group**, change the **Shape Height** to **1.5"** and the **Shape Width** to **1.5"**.

e. In the **Shape Styles group**, click **Shape Fill**, and then click **Picture**. **From a file** click **Browse**, navigate to the location where your data files are stored and then select **p04C_Contract.jpg** Click **Insert**.

f. With the shape still selected, in the **Arrange group**, click **Align**. Click **Align Center**. Click **Align** again, and then click **Align Bottom**.

g. On the ribbon, on the **PICTURE TOOLS FORMAT tab**, in the **Adjust group**, click **Color**. Under **Recolor**, click the second row, sixth color—**Blue, Accent color 5 Dark**.

h. With the shape still selected, on the **HOME tab**, in the **Clipboard group**, click **Copy**. Click the **Title and Content Layout** thumbnail. In the **Clipboard group**, click **Paste**.

i. Under the **DRAWING TOOLS FORMAT tab**, in the **Size group**, change the **Shape Height** to **1"** and the **Shape Width** to **1"**.

j. With the shape still selected, press the Shift key, and then click the content placeholder. In the **Arrange group**, click **Align**, and then select **Align Right**. Click **Align**, and then select **Align Top**.

5 ▶ Click the **Title Slide Layout** thumbnail.

a. Press the Shift key, and then drag the Master title placeholder up so the top aligns at **3 inches on the upper half of the vertical ruler**. Release the Shift key, and then click outside the placeholder. Press the Shift key, and then drag the Master subtitle placeholder up so the top aligns with **0 inch mark on the upper half of the vertical ruler**. Release the Shift key.

b. With the subtitle placeholder still selected, drag the **bottom middle sizing handle** to **1 inch on the lower half of the vertical ruler**.

c. Click the shape, and then drag the entire shape so the top aligns with **1.5 inches on the lower half of the vertical ruler**. On the **DRAWING TOOLS FORMAT tab**, in the **Arrange group**, click **Align**, and then click **Align Center**.

6 ▶ With the **Title Slide Layout** selected, on the **VIEW tab**, in the **Show group**, select the **Guides** check box to

(Project 4C Contract continues on the next page)

display the horizontal and vertical guides, if necessary. At the top of the slide, move your mouse pointer over the orange dotted line until the mouse pointer changes into a double arrow ⊹. Click the light orange dotted **vertical guide line** and drag to the left to **5.50 inches on the left side of the horizontal ruler**.

a. Click the **INSERT tab**. In the **Illustrations group**, click **Shapes**. Under **Rectangles**, click the **Rectangle** shape. Position the pointer at **6 inches on the left side of the horizontal ruler**, aligning it with the top edge of the slide. Click and **drag across the top edge of the slide .5 inch to 5.5 inches on the horizontal ruler** to the edge of the vertical guide line, continue holding, and then **drag down along the vertical guide line** to the bottom edge of the slide, and then release. With the shape still selected, on the **DRAWING TOOLS FORMAT tab**, in the **Shapes Styles group**, click **Colored Fill – Black, Dark 1**.

b. Click the **INSERT tab**. In the **Illustrations group**, click **Shapes**. Under **Basic Shapes**, click the **Diamond** shape. Click on the black line shape to insert the diamond shape. If necessary, with the diamond still selected, in the **Size group**, change the **Shape Height to 1"** and the **Shape Width to 1"**. With the shape still selected, in the **Size group**, click the **dialog launcher**. Click **Position** to expand. In the **Horizontal position box**, type 0.41 and then press Enter. In the **Vertical position box**, type 0.74 and then press Enter.

c. With the shape still selected, on the **DRAWING TOOLS FORMAT tab**, in the **Shapes Styles group**, click **More**. In the fourth row, click the sixth item— **Subtle Effect – Blue, Accent 5**. With the shape still selected, on the **DRAWING TOOLS FORMAT tab**, in the **Shapes Styles group**, click **Shape Effects**. Click **Glow**, and then under **Glow Variations**, in the fifth column, click the last item—**Blue, 18 pt glow, Accent color 5**. On the **VIEW tab**, in the **Show group**, select the **Guides** check box to deselect the box.

7 Click the **Title and Content Layout** thumbnail.

a. Click anywhere in the first bulleted line. Click the **HOME tab**. In the **Paragraph group**, click the **Bullets button arrow**, and then click **Bullets and Numbering**. In the **Bullets and Numbering** dialog box, click the

Bulleted tab if necessary. Click **Star Bullets**. Then click the **Color button arrow**. Under **Standard Colors**, click **Purple**. Click **OK**.

b. Click anywhere in the second bulleted line. Display the **Bullets and Numbering** dialog box. Click the **Filled Square Bullets**. Click the **Color button arrow**. Under **Standard Colors**, click **Purple**. Click **OK**.

8 Click the first thumbnail, the **Office Theme Slide Master**.

a. At the bottom left on the slide, click anywhere on the dashed border of the date placeholder.

b. With the **HOME tab** selected, change the **font size** to **10** and **Center** the date.

c. Click the **SLIDE MASTER tab**. In the **Close group**, click **Close Master View**.

9 On the **INSERT tab**, in the **Text group**, click **Header & Footer** to display the **Header and Footer** dialog box. Click the **Notes and Handouts tab**. Under **Include on page**, select the **Date and time** check box, and then select **Fixed** and type today's date. If necessary, clear the **Header** check box, and then select the **Page number** and **Footer** check boxes. In the **Footer** box, using your own name, type **Lastname_Firstname_4C_Contract_Template** and then click **Apply to All**.

10 Click the **FILE tab**, and then in the lower right portion of the screen, click **Show All Properties**. In the **Tags** box, type **template** and in the **Subject** box type your course name and section number. In the **Author** box, right-click the existing author name, click **Edit Property**, replace the existing text with your first and last name, click outside textbox to deselect, and then click **OK**.

11 Print **Handouts 4 Slides Horizontal**, or submit your presentation electronically as directed by your instructor.

12 Save the template.

13 Press F12 to display the **Save As** dialog box. If necessary, navigate to the location where you are saving your files, and then click the **Save as type box arrow**. Click **PowerPoint Presentation (*.pptx)**, and then **Save** the file as **Lastname_Firstname_4C_Night_Owls** in your storage location.

(Project 4C Contract continues on the next page)

CHAPTER REVIEW

14 Click **Slide 1**. In the title placeholder, type **Billy and the Night Owls** In the subtitle placeholder, type **Thompson Henderson Law Partners**

a. On the **HOME tab**, in the **Slides group**, click the **New Slide button arrow**, and then click **Title** and **Content**.

b. In the title placeholder, type **Performance Contract Basics**

c. In the content placeholder, type the following bulleted items, using the **Increase** and **Decrease List Level** buttons as needed to increase the second and third bulleted lines only:

A contract includes:

    Performance agreement outline

    Document of agreement

The contractee is the party for whom the performance service is provided

The contractor is the party that performs the service

15 In the **Slides group**, click the **New Slide button arrow**, and then click **Title and Content** to add a third slide.

a. In the title placeholder, type **Cross Licensing** and then press Ctrl + Enter.

b. Type the following bulleted items in the content placeholder:

Cross licensing is a legal agreement

Two or more parties may share rights to a performance

A royalty fee exchange may be included

Performance recording rights may be included

16 **Save** your presentation.

17 Click the **VIEW tab**. In the **Master Views group**, click **Handout Master**. In the **Page Setup group**, click **Slides Per Page**. Click **3 Slides**.

18 Click the **VIEW tab**. In the **Master Views group**, click **Notes Master**. In the **Placeholders group**, remove the **Body**.

19 In the **Close group**, click **Close Master View**.

20 On the **INSERT tab**, in the **Text group**, click **Header & Footer** to display the **Header and Footer** dialog box. Click the **Notes and Handouts tab**. In the **Footer** box, change the name to: **Lastname_Firstname_4C_Night_Owls** and then click **Apply to All**.

21 Click the **FILE tab**, and then in the lower right portion of the screen, click **Show All Properties**. In the **Tags** box, select any existing text, and then type **royalty, rights** If necessary, in the **Subject** box type your course name and section number. In the **Author** box, right-click the existing author name, click **Edit Property**, replace the existing text with your first and last name, click outside textbox to deselect, and then click **OK**.

22 Print **Handouts 4 Slides Horizontal**, or submit your presentation electronically as directed by your instructor.

23 **Save** the presentation. **Exit** PowerPoint.

END | You have completed Project 4C

CHAPTER REVIEW

Apply 4B skills from these Objectives:

3 Create and Edit Comments

4 Compare and Combine Presentations

5 Prepare a Presentation for Distribution

6 Protect a Presentation

Skills Review | Project 4D Athlete Taxes

In the following Skills Review, you will modify a presentation created by Thompson Henderson Law Partners as a brief overview of taxation issues to present to Finley Nagursky, who is a professional football player. You will add comments to the presentation, compare and combine presentations, prepare the document for distribution, and then password protect it. Your completed presentation will look similar to Figure 4.64.

PROJECT FILES

For Project 4D, you will need the following files:

p04D_Athlete_Taxes.pptx
p04D_Athlete_Taxes2.pptx

You will save your files as:

Lastname_Firstname_4D_Athlete_Taxes.pptx
Lastname_Firstname_4D_Athlete_Taxes.pdf
Lastname_Firstname_4D_Athlete_Taxes.xps

PROJECT RESULTS

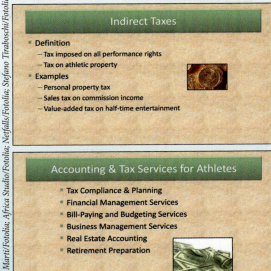
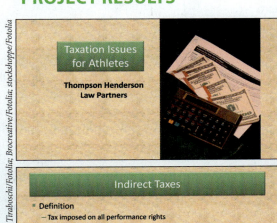

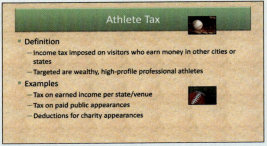

Pix by Marti/Fotolia; Africa Studio/Fotolia; Netfalls/Fotolia; Stefano Tiraboschi/Fotolia; Brocreative/Fotolia; stockshoppe/Fotolia

FIGURE 4.64

(Project 4D Athlete Taxes continues on the next page)

CHAPTER REVIEW

1 Start PowerPoint. Locate and open the file **p04D_Athlete_Taxes.pptx** Navigate to the location where you are storing your folders and projects for this chapter, and then **Save** the file as **Lastname_Firstname_4D_Athlete_Taxes**

2 Make **Slide 2** the active slide. Click the **REVIEW tab**. In the **Comments group**, click **New Comment**. In the space provided, on the **Comments** pane, type **It would be a good idea to add a couple more examples.**

3 Make **Slide 3** the active slide. Click at the end of the bulleted item that ends with *commission income*. In the **Comments group**, click **New Comment**. Type **I am glad you added this one.** Click outside the comment to close it.

4 Make **Slide 4** the active slide. In the last bulleted item, select the word *Deductions*. Use the procedure explained in the previous steps to add this comment: **Is this clear enough for the client to understand?**

5 Make **Slide 2** the active slide. In the **Comments** pane, click in the **Reply** box, and then type **Ask sports agents for more examples.**

6 Click **Next** until you reach the comment on **Slide 3**. In the **Comments group**, click **Delete** to remove this comment. **Close** the **Comments** pane.

7 On the **REVIEW tab**, in the **Compare group**, click **Compare**. In the **Choose File to Merge with Current Presentation** dialog box, navigate to your student data files for this chapter, and then click **p04D_Athlete_Taxes2**, and then click **Merge**.

   a.   In the **Revisions** pane, under **Presentations Changes**, click **Slide 2: Direct Taxes** to display a **Revisions** check box in the **Slides and Outline pane** on the left. Do *not* select the **Revisions** check box on **Slide 2**.

   b.   In the **Revisions** pane, under **Presentations Changes**, click **Slides moved after "Indirect Taxes"** to display a **Revisions** check box in the **Slides and Outline** pane on the left. Do *not* select the **Revisions** check box on **Slide 3**.

   c.   On **Slide 3** notice that a **Revisions** icon displays on the slide. Click the **Revisions** icon to display the **Revisions** check box. Select the **Revisions** check box that indicates *Inserted "all"* to accept the change and insert the word *all*.

   d.   In the **Revisions** pane, under **Presentations Changes**, click **Insertions after "Athlete Tax"** to display a

Revisions check box in the **Slides and Outline** pane on the left. Select the **Revisions** check box that indicates *Inserted "Accounting & Tax Services for Athletes"* to accept the change and insert the slide into the presentation.

   e.   On the **REVIEW tab**, in the **Compare group**, click **End Review**, and then click **Yes**.

8 Make **Slide 2** the active slide. Locate the word *sportspersons*. Right-click *sportspersons*, and then on the shortcut menu, point to **Synonyms**. Click **athletes** to change the word *sportspersons* to *athletes*.

9 On the **INSERT tab**, in the **Text group**, click **Header & Footer** to display the **Header and Footer** dialog box. Click the **Notes and Handouts tab**. If necessary, under **Include on page**, select the **Date and time** check box, and then select **Fixed**. If necessary, clear the **Header** check box, and then select the **Page number** and **Footer** check boxes. In the **Footer** box, select the existing text, and then using your own name, type **Lastname_Firstname_4D_Athlete_Taxes** and then click **Apply to All**.

10 Click the **FILE tab**, and then in the lower right portion of the screen, click **Show All Properties**. In the **Tags** box, type **direct taxes, athlete tax, indirect taxes** and in the **Subject** box type your course name and section number. In the **Author** box, right-click the existing author name, click **Edit Property**, replace the existing text with your first and last name, click outside textbox to deselect, and then click **OK**. **Save** the presentation.

11 Print **Handouts 4 Slides Horizontal**, or submit your presentation electronically as directed by your instructor.

12 Click **FILE**, and then click **Export**. Under **Export**, **Create PDF/XPS Document** is selected.

   a.   Click **Create PDF/XPS**. Click the **Save as type**, and then click **PDF(*.pdf)**. If necessary, select the option button **Standard (publishing online and printing)**. Clear **Open file after publishing** check box.

   b.   Click **Options**. Click the **Publish what arrow**, and then select **Handouts**. Click the **Slides per page arrow**, and then select **4**. Select the check box for **Include comments and ink markup**. Click **OK**.

   c.   Click **Publish**.

13 Click **FILE**, Click **Export**, **Create PDF/XPS Document** is selected.

(Project 4D Athlete Taxes continues on the next page)

CHAPTER REVIEW

a. Click **Create PDF/XPS**. Change the file type to **XPS Document (*.xps)**.

b. Click **Options**. Click the **Publish what arrow**, and then select **Handouts**. Click the **Slides per page arrow**, and then select **4**. Select the check box for **Include comments and ink markup**. Click **OK**. Select the **Open file after publishing** check box.

c. Click **Publish**.

d. **Close** the XPS file and viewer.

14 ▶ Click **FILE**, with **Info** selected, and then click **Protect Presentation arrow**, and then select **Mark as Final**. Click **OK**. Click **OK**.

15 ▶ Click **Edit Anyway**, click **FILE**, and then click **Protect Presentation arrow**. Click **Encrypt with Password**.

a. In the **Encrypt Document** dialog box, in the **Password** box, type **Go** and then click **OK**.

b. In the **Confirm password** dialog box, type **Go** and then click **OK**. **Save** the file. **Close** the file.

c. **Open** your **Lastname_Firstname_4D_Athlete_Taxes** file. The **Password** dialog box displays in which you are prompted to enter the password.

d. Type **Go** and then click **OK** to open the presentation.

16 ▶ **Close** the file. **Exit** PowerPoint. Submit your presentations electronically as directed by your instructor for:

> Lastname_Firstname_Athlete_Taxes.pptx
>
> Lastname_Firstname_Athlete_Taxes.pdf
>
> Lastname_Firstname_Athlete_Taxes.xps

END | You have completed Project 4D

CONTENT-BASED ASSESSMENTS

Mastering PowerPoint   Project 4E Sports Law

Apply 4A from these Objectives:

1 Create a Custom Template by Modifying Slide Masters

2 Apply a Custom Template to a Presentation

In the following Mastering PowerPoint project, you will edit a presentation you already prepared to explain the aspects of Title IX in Collegiate Sports Law and then save it as a template. You will use the template to personalize it for a presentation to Hugh Appleton, who is a College Athletic Director. Your completed presentation will look similar to Figure 4.65.

PROJECT FILES

For Project 4E, you will need the following files:

p04E_Sports_Law.pptx
p04E_Sports1.jpg

You will save your files as:

Lastname_Firstname_4E_Sports_Template.potx
Lastname_Firstname_4E_Sports_Law.pptx

PROJECT RESULTS

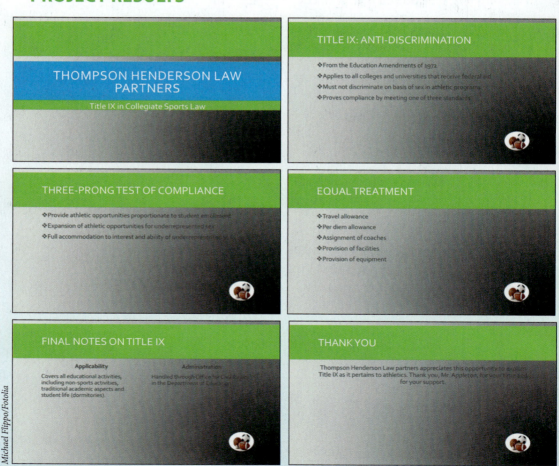

Michael Flippo/Fotolia

FIGURE 4.65

(Project 4E Sports Law continues on the next page)

CONTENT-BASED ASSESSMENTS

Mastering PowerPoint Project 4E Sports Law (continued)

1 Start PowerPoint. Locate and open the file **p04E_Sports_Law.pptx** Save the file as a **PowerPoint Template** in your **PowerPoint Chapter 4** folder, using the file name **Lastname_Firstname_4E_Sports_Template**

2 Click the **VIEW tab**, and then click **Slide Master**. Scroll up and click the **Banded Slide Master** thumbnail. Apply Background **Style 10**. Format the background with a **Radial Gradient fill**, and then apply it to all slides. On the first bulleted item, change the font size to **24**.

3 On the **Title Slide Layout** thumbnail, change the Master title style placeholder **font size** to **48 pts**. Change the Master subtitle style placeholder **font size** to **32 pts**.

4 On the **Title and Content Layout** thumbnail, insert an **Oval** shape and set the **Height** to **1.0"** and the **Width** to **1.25"**. Fill the shape with **p04E_Sports1.jpg** located in the student data files. Remove the **Shape Outline**, and then position the shape at the bottom right corner of the content placeholder.

5 Copy the shape to the **Two Content Layout** thumbnail.

6 Remove the Header from the **Handout Master**, and then **Close Master View**.

7 On the **INSERT tab**, in the **Text group**, click **Header & Footer** to display the **Header and Footer** dialog box. Click the **Notes and Handouts tab**. Under **Include on page**, select the **Date and time** check box, and then select **Fixed**. If necessary, clear the **Header** check box, and then select the **Page number** and **Footer** check boxes. In the **Footer** box, using your own name, type **Lastname_Firstname_4E_Sports_Template** and then click **Apply to All**.

8 Revise the document properties. In the **Author** box, right-click the existing author name, click **Edit Property**, replace the existing text with your first and last name,

click outside textbox to deselect, and then click **OK**. In the **Subject** box, type your course name and section number, and then in the **Tags** box, type **template**

9 **Save** the template. Print **Handouts 6 Slides Horizontal**, or submit your presentation electronically as directed by your instructor.

10 **Close** the template.

11 Create a **new presentation** using your template. **Save** the file as **Lastname_Firstname_4E_Sports_Law** in your storage location.

12 On **Slide 5**, in the left column, remove the bullet, center *Applicability*, and then add bold. Repeat the formatting for *Administration* in the second column.

13 Add a **Title and Content** slide. In the title placeholder, type **Thank You** In the content placeholder, type **Thompson Henderson Law Partners appreciates this opportunity to explain Title IX as it pertains to athletics. Thank you, Mr. Appleton, for your time and for your support.** Remove the bullet and center the text.

14 On the **Slide Master**, change the first-level bullets to **Star Bullets**. **Close** the Master View.

15 Change the footer on the handouts to include **Lastname_Firstname_4E_Sports_Law** and then click **Apply to All**.

16 Edit the document properties. In the **Author** box, add your Firstname Lastname. In the **Subject** box, type your course name and section number, and then in the **Tags** box, type **Title IX, discrimination**

17 **Save** the presentation. Print **Handouts 6 Slides Horizontal**, or submit your presentation electronically as directed by your instructor.

18 **Close** the presentation.

END | You have completed Project 4E

CONTENT-BASED ASSESSMENTS

In the following Mastering PowerPoint project, you will complete a presentation that covers various aspects of contracts in the entertainment industry, including royalties, minors, and advances. You will review the presentation and add comments, compare and combine presentations before preparing it for distribution. Your completed presentation will look similar to Figure 4.66.

Apply 4B skills from these Objectives:

3 Create and Edit Comments

4 Compare and Combine Presentations

5 Prepare a Presentation for Distribution

6 Protect a Presentation

PROJECT FILES

For Project 4F, you will need the following files:

p04F_Contract_Aspects.pptx
p04F_Contract_Aspects2.pptx

You will save your files as:

Lastname_Firstname_4F_Contract_Aspects.pptx
Lastname_Firstname_4F_Contract_Aspects.pdf
Lastname_Firstname_4F_Contract_Aspects.xps

PROJECT RESULTS

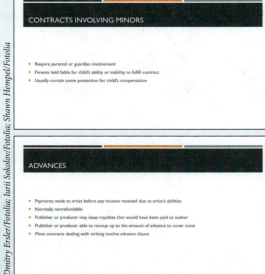
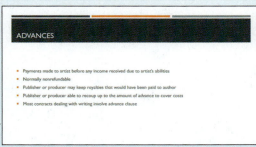

Dmitry Ersler/Fotolia; Iurii Sokolov/Fotolia; Shawn Hempel/Fotolia

FIGURE 4.66

(Project 4F Contract Aspects continues on the next page)

CONTENT-BASED ASSESSMENTS

1 Start PowerPoint. Locate and open the file **p04F_Contract_Aspects**. **Save** the file as **Lastname_Firstname_4F_Contract_Aspects**

2 Make **Slide 3** the active slide. At the end of the first bulleted item, add a comment, and then type **Are there any other points that should be added?**

3 On **Slide 4**, select *Intermediaries*, and then add this comment: **I think this term needs to be defined.**

4 On **Slide 5**, add this comment: **Excellent content!** Drag the comment so it is positioned right after *Advances*.

5 Edit the comment on **Slide 3**. Click in the *Reply* box, and then type **Should minor be defined?**

6 Delete the comment on **Slide 4**.

7 **Compare** and **Merge** the presentation with **p04F_Contract_Aspects2** from your student data files for this chapter. Accept the inserted slide **"Hold the Key to Your Future"**. **End Review**.

8 Change the word *payment* to *compensation* on **Slide 3**.

9 Insert a **Footer** on Notes and Handouts that includes the fixed date and time, page number, and file name.

10 Revise the document properties. In the **Author** box, replace the existing text with your first and last name. In the **Subject** box, type your course name and section number, and then in the **Tags** box, type **entertainment, royalties, minors, advances**

11 **Save** the presentation.

12 **Publish** the presentation as a **PDF** file. Set options to **Include comments and ink markup**, **Handouts**, **6 slides per page**, and **Horizontal**.

13 **Print** the PDF file, or submit your presentation electronically as directed by your instructor.

14 **Publish** the presentation as an **XPS** file using the same options as the PDF file. **Print** the XPS file, or submit your presentation electronically as directed by your instructor.

15 **Save** the file in your PowerPoint Chapter 4 folder. Mark your presentation as **Final**.

16 **Close** the presentation, and then **Exit** PowerPoint.

END | You have completed Project 4F

CONTENT-BASED ASSESSMENTS

Mastering PowerPoint Project 4G Film Production

Apply 4A and 4B skills from these Objectives:

1 Create a Custom Template by Modifying Slide Masters
2 Apply a Custom Template to a Presentation
3 Create and Edit Comments
4 Compare and Combine Presentations
5 Prepare a Presentation for Distribution
6 Protect a Presentation

In the following Mastering PowerPoint project, you will open a presentation explaining the legal aspects of film production and modify the slide masters. Frequently, Thompson Henderson Law Partners presents this information to college classes, so you will save the presentation as a template. Then you will create a presentation from the template and personalize it for the Film Production course at the local university. You will add some comments for other partners to see, edit it, save the presentation as an XPS file for the participants, and then password protect the presentation. Your completed presentation will look similar to Figure 4.67.

PROJECT FILES

For Project 4G, you will need the following files:

p04G_Film_Production.pptx
p04G_Film.jpg

You will save your files as:

Lastname_Firstname_4G_Film_Template.potx
Lastname_Firstname_4G_Film_Production.pptx
Lastname_Firstname_4G_Film_Production.xps

PROJECT RESULTS

FIGURE 4.67

(Project 4G Film Production continues on the next page)

CONTENT-BASED ASSESSMENTS

1 Start PowerPoint. Locate and open the file **p04G_Film_Production.pptx**, and then save it as a template with the name **Lastname_Firstname_4G_Film_Template**

2 In **Slide Master View**, on the Office Theme Slide Master, change the background to **Style 2**. Format the background with a **Gradient fill**, **Linear type**. Set gradient **stop 2** to **25%** and gradient **stop 3** to **75%**. Set the **stop 3** color to **Blue, Accent 1, Lighter 80%**, and then apply to all slides. Change the color of the first bullet to **Blue, Accent 5**.

3 Click the **Title Slide Layout** thumbnail. On the **VIEW tab**, in the **Show group**, click the **Guides** box. At the top of the slide, move your mouse pointer over the orange dotted line until the mouse pointer changes into a double arrow ⟦⊹⟧. Click the light orange dotted **vertical guide line** and drag to the left to **5.75 inches on the left side of the horizontal ruler**. On the **INSERT tab**, click **Shapes**, under **Rectangles**, click the **Rectangle** shape. Position the pointer at the **6.25 inches on the left side of the horizontal ruler**, aligning it with the top edge of the slide. Click and **drag across the top edge of the slide .5 inch to 5.75 inches on the horizontal ruler** to the edge of the vertical guide line, continue holding, and then **drag down along the vertical guide line** to the bottom edge of the slide, and then release. Apply the shape style **Colored Fill – Black, Dark 1**. Deselect the **Guides** check box.

4 Click the **Title and Content Layout** thumbnail. Insert a **Text Box** in the lower left corner of the content placeholder. Inside the shape, type **Thompson Henderson Law Partners** Change the font to **Palatino Linotype**, **12 pt**, **Bold**, and then **Center** the text. **Select** the text, and then change the **Height** to **0.5"** and the **Width** to **6.0"**. Use a **Shape Fill** to add **Gradient** with a **Light Variations** of **Linear Down**. **Align** the text box at the **center** and **bottom** of the slide.

5 Remove the Header on the **Handout Master**, and then **Close Master View**.

6 Insert the **Header & Footer**. On the **Notes and Handouts tab**, include a **Fixed** date and the **Page number** and **Footer**. In the **Footer** box, using your own name, type **Lastname_Firstname_4G_Film_Template** and then click **Apply to All**.

7 Revise the document properties. In the **Author** box, replace the existing text with your first and last name. In the **Subject** box, type your course name and section number, and then in the **Tags** box, type **template**

8 Print **Handouts 6 Slides Horizontal**, or submit your presentation electronically as directed by your instructor.

9 **Save** the template file, and then **Close** the template.

10 Create a new document from existing template **Lastname_Firstname_4G_Film_Template.potx**, and then save it as **Lastname_Firstname_4G_Film_Production.pptx**

11 On **Slide 1**, after *Presented to,* press ⟦Enter⟧, and then type **University Film Production Class**

12 In **Slide Master View**, on the **Title and Content Layout** slide, select all of the text in the first bulleted item, change the line spacing to **1.5**, and then **Close Master View**.

13 On **Slide 4**, after the third bulleted item, add this comment: **Maybe clarify that you mean the formation of an LLC.**

14 On **Slide 5**, select *Life rights*, and then add this comment: **Explain how life rights is considered intellectual property.**

15 On **Slide 4**, delete the comment.

16 On**Slide 2**, use the Thesaurus, to change *compensation* to *payment*.

17 On **Slide 3**, insert the picture file, **p04G_Film.jpg**, Crop to Shape using the Round Diagonal Corner Rectangle under Rectangles. Change the shape Height to 2.53", and position it to the right of the three bullet points. **Recolor** the picture to **Grayscale**.

18 Update the filename in the **Notes and Handouts Footer** to **Lastname_Firstname_4G_Film_Production** and then update the **Properties** with your name as the Author, and then in the **Tags** box, select the existing text, and then type **film production, LLC, intellectual property**

19 Print **Handouts 6 Slides Horizontal**, or submit your presentation electronically as directed by your instructor.

20 **Save** the presentation.

21 **Publish** the presentation as an **XPS file**, including the comments and ink markup and specifying handouts 6 slides per page. **Close** the **XPS Viewer**. **Print** the XPS file, or submit the file electronically as directed by your instructor.

22 Mark the presentation as **Final**, and then **Close** the file. **Exit** PowerPoint.

END | You have completed Project 4G

CONTENT-BASED ASSESSMENTS

Apply a combination of the **4A** and **4B** skills.

GO! Fix It Project 4H Labor Issues **Online**

GO! Make It Project 4I Consignment Contracts **Online**

GO! Solve It Project 4J Legal Guide **Online**

GO! Solve It Project 4K Actor Advice

PROJECT FILES

For Project 4K, you will need the following files:

p04K_Actor_Advice.pptx
p04K_Cinema.jpg

You will save your files as:

Lastname_Firstname_4K_Actor_Template.potx
Lastname_Firstname_4K_Actor_Advice.pptx
Lastname_Firstname_4K_Actor_Advice.pdf

Open **p04K_Actor_Advice** and save it as a template **Lastname_Firstname_4K_Actor_Template** Examine the slide content, and then modify the appropriate slide master with a background style or a theme. Adjust colors and fonts as needed. Insert a shape on the appropriate slide master so the shape displays only on Slide 1, and then insert **p04K_Cinema.jpg** in the shape, recolor it, and place it where it is visually pleasing on the slide. Add additional shape(s) for attractive style and color to the title slide to add interest. Change the bullet style for levels of bullets that are used. On the Notes and Handouts, insert the fixed date and time, page number, and a footer with the file name. Add your name, your course name and section number, and the tag **template** to the Properties.

Create a new presentation based on the template. Personalize the presentation for Julia Simpson. Save the presentation as **Lastname_Firstname_4K_Actor_Advice.pptx** On Slide 2, insert a comment. Update the Notes and Handouts footer with the correct file name, add the tags **contracts, paparazzi, media** and then change the author in the Properties. Save the presentation in a PDF file as handouts, including the comments. Mark the presentation as Final and save it. Print or submit electronically as directed by your instructor.

(Project 4K Actor Advice continues on the next page)

CONTENT-BASED ASSESSMENTS

GO! Solve It   Project 4K Actor Advice (continued)

Performance Level

Performance Criteria		Exemplary	Proficient	Developing
	Customized Office Theme Slide Master with a background or theme and bullet styles	Slide master was customized correctly with a background or theme and with bullet styles. Maintained good contrast.	Slide master was not customized with a background or theme and with bullet styles. Customization done on other slide masters.	No slide master customization was completed.
	Inserted a shape with the picture on the Title Slide Layout master and recolored it	Shape was inserted on the slide master and was sized, recolored and placed in an appropriate position.	The shape was not inserted or recolored on the appropriate slide master.	The shape was not inserted or recolored.
	Created and personalized a presentation. Saved presentation as PDF with comments and marked as Final	Presentation file was created, personalized, and included comments. Saved as PDF handouts with comments and marked as Final.	Presentation file was created, but was not personalized. May or may not have been saved as PDF and marked as Final.	A presentation file was not created from the template.

END | You have completed Project 4K

OUTCOMES-BASED ASSESSMENTS

RUBRIC

The following outcomes-based assessments are *open-ended assessments*. That is, there is no specific correct result; your result will depend on your approach to the information provided. Make *Professional Quality* your goal. Use the following scoring rubric to guide you in *how* to approach the problem and then to evaluate *how well* your approach solves the problem.

The *criteria*—Software Mastery, Content, Format and Layout, and Process—represent the knowledge and skills you have gained that you can apply to solving the problem. The *levels of performance*—Professional Quality, Approaching Professional Quality, or Needs Quality Improvements—help you and your instructor evaluate your result.

	Your completed project is of Professional Quality if you:	Your completed project is Approaching Professional Quality if you:	Your completed project Needs Quality Improvements if you:
1-Software Mastery	Choose and apply the most appropriate skills, tools, and features and identify efficient methods to solve the problem.	Choose and apply some appropriate skills, tools, and features, but not in the most efficient manner.	Choose inappropriate skills, tools, or features, or are inefficient in solving the problem.
2-Content	Construct a solution that is clear and well organized, contains content that is accurate, appropriate to the audience and purpose, and is complete. Provide a solution that contains no errors in spelling, grammar, or style.	Construct a solution in which some components are unclear, poorly organized, inconsistent, or incomplete. Misjudge the needs of the audience. Have some errors in spelling, grammar, or style, but the errors do not detract from comprehension.	Construct a solution that is unclear, incomplete, or poorly organized; contains some inaccurate or inappropriate content; and contains many errors in spelling, grammar, or style. Do not solve the problem.
3-Format & Layout	Format and arrange all elements to communicate information and ideas, clarify function, illustrate relationships, and indicate relative importance.	Apply appropriate format and layout features to some elements, but not others. Overuse features, causing minor distraction.	Apply format and layout that does not communicate information or ideas clearly. Do not use format and layout features to clarify function, illustrate relationships, or indicate relative importance. Use available features excessively, causing distraction.
4-Process	Use an organized approach that integrates planning, development, self-assessment, revision, and reflection.	Demonstrate an organized approach in some areas, but not others; or, use an insufficient process of organization throughout.	Do not use an organized approach to solve the problem.

OUTCOMES-BASED ASSESSMENTS

GO! Think   Project 4L Workshops

PROJECT FILES

For Project 4L, you will need the following file:

New blank PowerPoint presentation

You will save your files as:

Lastname_Firstname_4L_Venue_Template.potx
Lastname_Firstname_4L_Venue_Risks.pptx
Lastname_Firstname_4L_Venue_Risks.pdf

In this project, you will create a PowerPoint template for Thompson Henderson Law Partners to educate colleges, universities, and other sports venues about safety and security.

Create a template named **Lastname_Firstname_4L_Venue_Template.potx** Customize the slide masters, applying formatting as needed. In the Notes and Handouts, include the fixed date and time, page number, and file name in the footer. Add your name, course name and section number, and the tag **template** to the Properties.

Create a new presentation based on the template that addresses safety and security concerns. Save the presentation as **Lastname_Firstname_4L_Venue_Risks.pptx** Add three slides, each using a different layout. **Add** two comments. Update the Notes and Handouts footer with the new file name. Update your name, course name and section number, and the tags **venue, sports, risk** to the Properties. Export the presentation as Handouts 6 slides per page in a PDF file, including the comments. Mark the PowerPoint presentation as Final. Print or submit electronically as directed by your instructor.

END | You have completed Project 4L

OUTCOMES-BASED ASSESSMENTS

Build from
Scratch

GO! Think! Project 4M Intellectual Property **Online**

Build from
Scratch

You and GO! Project 4N Copyright **Online**

Build from
Scratch

GO! Cumulative Group Project Project 4O Bell Orchid Hotels
Online

Applying Advanced Graphic Techniques and Inserting Audio and Video

GO! to Work
Video P5

PROJECT 5A

OUTCOMES
Edit and format pictures and add sound to a presentation.

PROJECT 5B

OUTCOMES
Create and edit a photo album and crop pictures.

OBJECTIVES

1. Use Picture Corrections
2. Add a Border to a Picture
3. Change the Shape of a Picture
4. Add a Picture to a WordArt Object and Merge Shapes
5. Enhance a Presentation with Audio and Video

OBJECTIVES

6. Create a Photo Album
7. Edit a Photo Album and Add a Caption
8. Crop a Picture

vizafoto/Fotolia

In This Chapter

PowerPoint provides a variety of methods for formatting and enhancing graphic elements. PowerPoint provides sophisticated tools for changing the brightness, contrast, and shape of a picture; adding a border; and cropping a picture to remove unwanted areas. PowerPoint allows you to include audio and video effects in presentations, although the resulting files are quite large. You might want to introduce a slide with an audio effect or music, or have an audio effect or music play when the slide or a component on the slide, such as text or a graphic, is clicked. The inclusion of audio and video can enhance a presentation.

Cross Oceans Music produces and distributes recordings of innovative musicians from every continent in genres that include Celtic, jazz, New Age, reggae, flamenco, calypso, and unique blends of all styles. Company scouts travel the world attending world music festivals, concerts, performances, shows, and small local venues to find their talented roster of musicians and performers. These artists create new and exciting music using traditional and modern instruments and technologies. Cross Oceans' customers are knowledgeable about music and demand the highest quality digital recordings provided in state-of-the-art formats.

Enhance a Presentation with Graphics and Media

PROJECT ACTIVITIES

In Activities 5.01 through 5.11, you will change the sharpness or softness and the brightness and contrast of pictures. You will also add borders and change the outline shape of pictures. You will change the shape of a picture, add a WordArt object, and embed a picture and merge shapes. You will insert linked video files and add a trigger to the audio and video. Your completed presentation will look similar to Figure 5.1.

PROJECT FILES

For Project 5A, you will need the following files:

p05A_Cross_Oceans.pptx
p05A_Building.jpg
p05A_Island.jpg
p05A_mp3.jpg
p05A_Smooth_Jazz.wav
p05A_New_Age.wav
p05_Music_Video.avi

You will save your presentation as:

Lastname_Firstname_5A_Cross_Oceans.pptx

PROJECT RESULTS

Iapas77/Fotolia; qingwa/Fotolia; Giulio Meinardi/Fotolia; VanHart/Fotolia; RLG/Fotolia; Tsiumpa/Fotolia; Warren Goldswain/Fotolia; Pakhnyushchyy/Fotolia

FIGURE 5.1 Project 5A Cross Oceans Music

Objective 1 | Use Picture Corrections

Video P5-1

Pictures can be corrected to improve the brightness, contrast, or sharpness. For example, you can use Sharpen/Soften to enhance picture details or make a picture more appealing by removing unwanted blemishes. When you *sharpen* an image, the clarity of an image increases. When you *soften* an image, the picture becomes fuzzier. You can use *Presets* to choose common, built-in sharpness and softness adjustments from a gallery. You can also use a slider to adjust the amount of blurriness, or you can enter a number in the box next to the slider.

Another way to correct pictures is to use Brightness and Contrast. *Brightness* is the perceived radiance or luminosity of an image, and *contrast* is the difference between the darkest and lightest area of a picture. You can use *Presets* to choose common, built-in brightness and contrast combinations from a gallery, or you can use a slider to adjust the amount of brightness and contrast separately.

When you change the overall lightening and darkening of the image, you change the individual pixels in an image. *Pixel* is short for *picture element* and represents a single point in a graphic image. To increase brightness, more light or white is added to the picture by selecting positive percentages. To decrease brightness, more darkness or black is added to the image by selecting negative percentages.

Changing the contrast of a picture changes the amount of gray in the image. Positive percentages increase the intensity of a picture by removing gray; negative percentages decrease intensity by adding more gray.

When you *recolor* a picture, you change all colors in the image into shades of one color. This effect is often used to stylize a picture or make the colors match a background.

Activity 5.01 | Using Sharpen/Soften on a Picture

In this activity, you will change the sharpness of a picture so the text on the slide will have greater emphasis. You will also use the Presets, which allows you to apply one of five standard settings.

1 Start PowerPoint. Locate and open the file **p05A_Cross_Oceans** Press F12 to display the **Save As** dialog box, and then navigate to the location where you are storing your projects for this chapter. Create a new folder named **PowerPoint Chapter 5** and then in the **File name** box and using your own name, save the file as **Lastname_Firstname_5A_Cross_Oceans** Click **Save** or press Enter.

2 Make **Slide 1** the active slide, if necessary, and then click to select the picture.

3 On the **PICTURE TOOLS FORMAT tab**, in the **Arrange group**, click the **Send Backward button arrow**, and then click **Send to Back**.

 **ANOTHER WAY**   To move a picture behind all components on the slide, right-click the picture, point to Send to Back, and then click Send to Back.

The slide title words are now displayed in front of the picture so you can read the words. When you click Send Backward, there are two options. Send Backward moves the picture behind the subtitle text. Send to Back moves the picture behind both the title and subtitle text.

ALERT!   **Is the Text Visible?**

If you cannot read the text in front of a picture that has been sent to the back, move the picture or change the text color.

4 Compare your screen with Figure 5.2, and then take a moment to study the descriptions of the picture adjustment settings, as shown in the table in Figure 5.3.

FIGURE 5.2

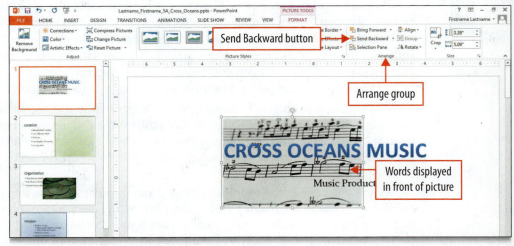

FIGURE 5.3

PICTURE ADJUSTMENT OPTIONS	
SCREEN ELEMENT	**DESCRIPTION**
Remove Background	Automatically remove unwanted portions of the picture. If needed, use marks to indicate areas to keep or remove from the picture.
Corrections	Improve the brightness, contrast, or sharpness of the picture.
Color	Change the color of the picture to improve quality or match document content.
Artistic Effects	Adds an artistic effect to a picture to make it look like a sketch or painting. You can access the Artistic Effects Options from this menu.
Compress Pictures	Compress pictures in the document to reduce its size. Reduces the image resolution and picture quality to make the file size smaller. There are two compression options: 　Apply only to this picture. The default is to compress the selected picture, but you can uncheck this option to compress all pictures in the document. 　Delete cropped areas of pictures. If you have cropped a picture, you can delete the cropped area to reduce the file size. However, if you want to undo the cropping, you have to insert the picture again. Provides four target output methods: 　Print (220 ppi): excellent quality on most printers and screens 　Screen (150 ppi): good for webpages and projectors 　E-mail (96 ppi): minimizes document size sharing 　Use document resolution (selected by default)
Change Picture	Change to a different picture, preserving the formatting and size of the current picture.
Reset Picture	Discards all formatting changes made to the picture.

5 On the **PICTURE TOOLS FORMAT tab**, in the **Adjust group**, click **Corrections**, and then click **Picture Corrections Options** to display the **Format Picture** pane. Under **Picture Corrections**, under **Sharpen/Soften**, drag the **Sharpness** slider to the left to -100% and observe the fuzzy effect on the picture. Drag the **Sharpness** slider to the right to **100%** and notice the sharpness of the picture.

6 Under **Sharpen/Soften**, click the **Presets arrow**. Compare your screen with Figure 5.4.

Five presets of variable sharp or soft picture corrections display.

FIGURE 5.4

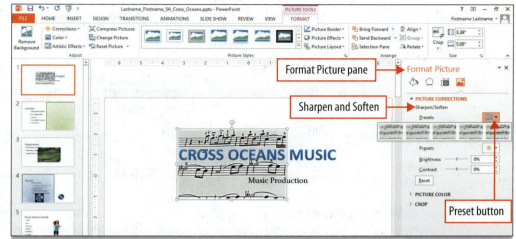

7 Click the fifth option—**Sharpen: 50%**.

The slider is now set at +50%, meaning that the picture is now sharper than the original picture.

More Knowledge	Using Picture Presets

The default for Sharpen/Soften is 0%. The Presets range from Soften: 50% to Sharpen: 50%. The slider settings range from -100% to +100%. Soften: 50% in Presets is the same as -50% on the slider.

8 Save 💾 the presentation.

Activity 5.02 | Changing the Brightness and Contrast of a Picture

In this activity, you will change the brightness and the contrast of a picture. You will also use the Presets, which allows you to select a combination of brightness and contrast settings.

1 With the image selected, on the **Format Picture** pane, under **Brightness/Contrast**, drag the **Brightness** slider to the left and then to the right. Watch how the picture brightness changes. In the **Brightness** box, select the text, type **20** and then press Enter.

2 Under **Brightness/Contrast**, drag the **Contrast** slider to the left and then to the right. Watch how the picture contrast changes. In the **Contrast** box, select the text, type **20** and then press Enter. Compare your screen with Figure 5.5.

The picture is enhanced so the slide title displays with more prominence.

FIGURE 5.5

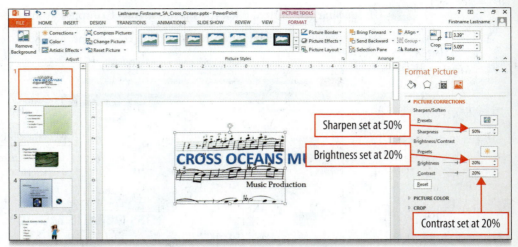

3 In the **Format Picture** pane, under **Brightness/Contrast**, click the **Presets arrow**. In the gallery, in the fourth row, fourth column, point to **Brightness: +20% Contrast: +20%** which is a combination of brightness and contrast you set. Compare your screen with Figure 5.6.

If you prefer, you may change brightness and contrast with one of the presets. The gallery displays the results on your picture to help you make a decision.

FIGURE 5.6

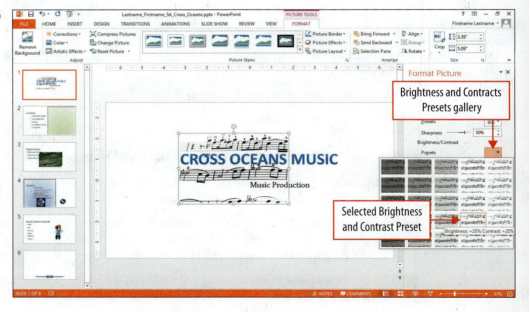

4 Click outside the **Brightness and Contrast** gallery to collapse it. **Close** the **Format Picture** pane, and then **Save** 💾 your changes.

Activity 5.03 | Recoloring a Picture

In this activity, you will recolor and reposition a picture.

1 Make **Slide 2** the active slide and click the **green shape**. On the **DRAWING TOOLS FORMAT tab**, in the **Shape Styles group**, click the **Shape Fill arrow**, and then click **Picture**. Navigate to the location where your student files are stored, and then insert the picture **p05A_Building.jpg**. Compare your screen with Figure 5.7.

The picture is aligned within the green shape and all of the text on the slide is visible.

FIGURE 5.7

2 ▶ On the **PICTURE TOOLS FORMAT tab**, in the **Adjust group**, click the **Color arrow**. Under **Recolor**, in the third row, second column, locate **Blue, Accent color 1 Light**, and then click to select it. Compare your screen with Figure 5.8.

🔁 **ANOTHER WAY**   On the Ribbon, click the PICTURE TOOLS FORMAT tab, in the Adjust group, click Color, and then click Picture Color Options to display the Format Picture pane.

FIGURE 5.8

3 ▶ With the picture on **Slide 3** selected, click the **VIEW tab**. In the **Show group**, select the **Gridlines** check box. Compare your screen with Figure 5.9.

The gridlines help you align objects at specific locations on the ruler.

FIGURE 5.9

4 On **Slide 3**, click to select the picture. On the **PICTURE TOOLS FORMAT tab**, in the **Arrange group**, click the **Send Backward button arrow**, and then click **Send to Back**.

5 With the picture selected, on the **PICTURE TOOLS FORMAT tab**, in the **Adjust group**, click the **Corrections arrow**, and then click **Picture Corrections Options**. On the **Format Picture** pane, under **PICTURE CORRECTIONS**, in the **Contrast** spin box, select the text, type **80** and then press [Enter].

This amount of contrast adds glare to the picture and makes the bulleted items difficult to read.

6 With the picture selected and the **Format Picture** pane displaying, use the method you prefer to change the **Brightness** to +40% and the **Contrast** to 20%. Change the **Sharpness** to 50%.

7 At the top of the **Format Picture** pane, click **Size & Properties** 🔲. Click **POSITION** to expand, if necessary. In the **Horizontal position** spin box, select the text, type **4.7** and then press [Enter]. In the **Vertical position** spin box, select the text, type **1.75** and then press [Enter]. Click outside the picture to deselect it. **Close** the **Format Picture** pane. Compare your screen with Figure 5.10.

Reducing the contrast and softness of the picture makes the picture fade into the background, allowing the content of the bulleted items to appear more prominently. Repositioning the picture makes the words easier to read.

FIGURE 5.10

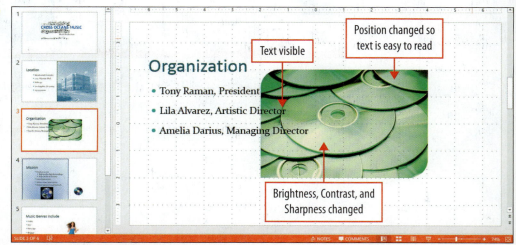

8 Select the picture. On the **PICTURE TOOLS FORMAT tab**, in the **Arrange group**, click **Selection Pane** to display the **Selection** pane. Compare your screen with Figure 5.11. Click **Content Placeholder 2** to select the content placeholder including the three names. Click **Title 1** to select the title placeholder—*Organization*. Click **Picture** 3 to select the picture on the slide.

> The Selection pane displays the shapes on the slide, making it easy to select the desired shape.

FIGURE 5.11

9 On the **PICTURE TOOLS FORMAT tab**, in the **Arrange group**, click the **Selection Pane** to close it.

 **ANOTHER WAY**   On the Selection pane, click Close ⊠ to close the Selection Pane.

10 Save 💾 your changes.

Objective 2   Add a Border to a Picture

Video P5-2

After you insert a picture into a slide, you can add a **border**, which is actually a frame, around the picture. It is possible to edit the color of the border and the line weight. The **line weight** is the thickness of the line measured in points (abbreviated as pt), similar to font sizes. It is sometimes also called line width.

You can also select the **line style**, which is how the line displays, such as a solid line, dots, or dashes. You can also change Line Width, Compound type, Dash type, Cap type, and Join type. Compound type is a line style composed of double or triple lines. Dash type is a style composed of various combinations of dashes. Cap type is the style you apply to the end of a line, and Join type is the style you specify to be used when two lines intersect at the corner.

Activity 5.04 | Adding a Border to a Picture

In this activity, you will add borders to pictures and then customize those borders by changing the color, line weight, and line style.

1 ▶ Make **Slide 4** the active slide. Right-click on the picture of the **CD**, and then click **Size and Position**. On the **Format Picture** pane, click **POSITION** to expand, if necessary. In the **Horizontal position** spin box, select the text, type **9.7** and then press ⏎. In the **Vertical position** spin box, select text, type **5.5** and then press ⏎.

The picture location changes and moves to the right side of the slide. Because the picture was selected, the title of the pane is Format Picture. The pane title is context sensitive depending on what type of object is selected. For example, if a shape has been selected, the pane title would display as Format Shape.

> **More Knowledge** | **Changing the Position of a Picture Using the Mouse**
>
> You can change the position of a picture by using the mouse to drag it to a new location on the slide. Hold down the ⇧ key before dragging a picture to move it in a straight line directly to the new location. You can also use the arrow keys and the gridlines to help position the picture.

2 ▶ With the picture still selected, on the **PICTURE TOOLS FORMAT tab**, in the **Picture Styles group**, click **Picture Border**, and then in the fifth column, click the first item—**Blue, Accent 1**. Click **Picture Border**, click **Weight**, and then click **2 1/4 pt**. Click **Picture Border**, click **Dashes**, and then click **Round Dot**. Deselect the picture, and then compare your screen with Figure 5.12.

The picture displays with a border. The color, style, and weight have all been set.

> **More Knowledge** | **Removing a Picture Border**
>
> To remove the border on a picture, click to select the picture. On the PICTURE TOOLS FORMAT tab, in the Picture Styles group, click Picture Border, and then click No Outline.

FIGURE 5.12

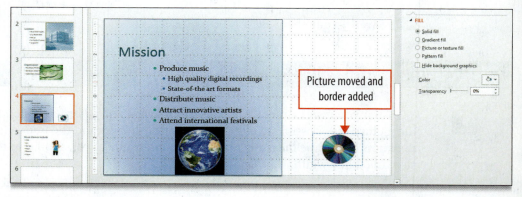

3 ▶ Click to select the picture of the globe. On the **Format Picture** pane, at the top, click **Size & Properties**; in the **Horizontal position** spin box, select the text, type **9.7** and then press ⏎. In the **Vertical position** spin box, select the text, type **3** and then press ⏎.

4 ▶ With the globe picture selected, on the **FORMAT tab**, in the **Picture Styles group**, click **Picture Border**, and then under **Standard Colors**, click **Yellow**. Click **Picture Border**, point to **Weight**, and then click **4 ½ pt**.

>  **ANOTHER WAY**
>
> To change the picture border color, on the Format Picture pane, at the top, click Fill & Line [icon], and then under Line, select the Solid line option, and then click the Color arrow. To change the border weight, click the Width spin box.

5 Click the **INSERT tab**. In the **Images group**, click **Pictures**. Navigate to the location where your student files are stored, and then insert the picture **p05A_mp3.jpg**. On the **Format Picture** pane, under **Size**, in the **Height** spin box, select the text, type **1.6** and then press Enter.

> The picture is sized proportionately.

 ANOTHER WAY   To size a picture proportionately, select the picture, and then drag a corner diagonally to the desired height or width.

6 Under **POSITION**, in the **Horizontal position** spin box, select the text, type **9.7** and then press Enter. In the **Vertical position** spin box, select the text, type **0.5** and then press Enter.

7 With the picture selected, on the **FORMAT tab**, in the **Picture Styles group**, click **Picture Border**, and then in the fifth column, click the last item—**Blue, Accent 1, Darker 50%**. Click **Picture Border**, point to **Weight**, and then click **More Lines** to display the **Format Picture** pane with the **Fill** and **Line** options displayed.

> Recall that the Format Picture pane displays the picture formatting types. The Line Style option is selected because you displayed the Picture Border first and then clicked More Lines.

8 Under **LINE**, in the **Width** spin box, select the text, type **9** and then press Enter. Scroll down as necessary, and then, click the **Join type arrow**, and then click **Miter**. Compare your screen with Figure 5.13.

> A *mitered* border is a border with corners that are square. The default is rounded corners. The Format Picture pane allows you to enter borders wider than the maximum 6 pt listed when you click Picture Border and select Weight.

FIGURE 5.13

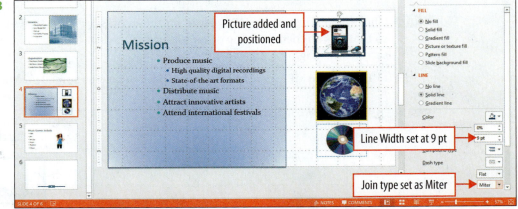

9 With the bordered picture of the MP3 player selected, on the **FORMAT tab**, in the **Picture Styles group**, click **Picture Effects**, point to **Reflection**, and then under **Reflection Variations**, click the first variation—**Tight Reflection, touching**. Deselect the picture, and then compare your screen with Figure 5.14.

 BY TOUCH   Tap the FORMAT tab. In the Picture Styles group, tap Picture Effects, point to Reflection, and then under Reflection Variations, tap the first variation—Tight Reflection, touching.

> The corners of the border are mitered borders, and a reflection is displayed below the picture.

FIGURE 5.14

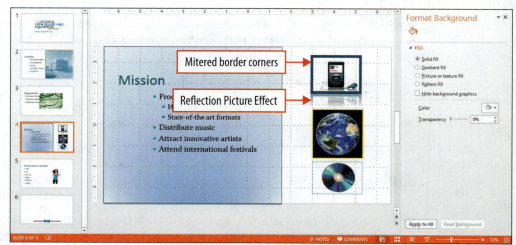

Mitered border corners

Reflection Picture Effect

10 Click the **CD picture** and then hold down Shift, and then click the other two pictures. Release the Shift key. All three pictures should be selected. On the **FORMAT tab**, in the **Arrange group**, click **Align**, and then click **Align Right**. Click anywhere off the slide to deselect the pictures.

The border of the mp3 player extends farther to the right than the other two pictures.

> **N O T E**   **Aligning Pictures**
>
> Use the alignment options on the FORMAT tab in the Arrange group to align pictures evenly. When you select Align Right, the selected pictures will align at the right side of the picture that is farthest to the right. Make sure that all pictures are selected before applying the alignment. The border size is not included in the alignment.

11 Click the picture of the **MP3 player**, and then press ← four times to nudge the picture border so that it is aligned with the other pictures. Deselect the picture, and then compare your screen with Figure 5.15.

Because the MP3 player picture has a wide border, it is now aligned better with the other pictures.

FIGURE 5.15

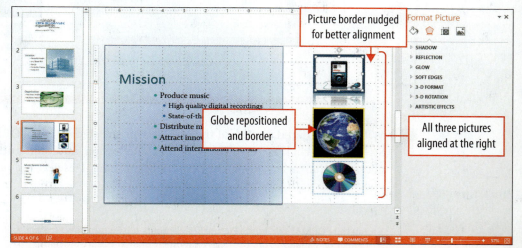

Picture border nudged for better alignment

Globe repositioned and border

All three pictures aligned at the right

12 On **Slide 5**, click to select the picture of the dancer. On the **FORMAT tab**, In the **Picture Styles group**, click **Picture Effects**, point to **Glow**, and then under **Glow Variations**, in the fourth row, click the first column—**Blue, 18 pt glow, Accent color 1**. Compare your screen with Figure 5.16.

The Picture Effect added a different kind of border.

FIGURE 5.16

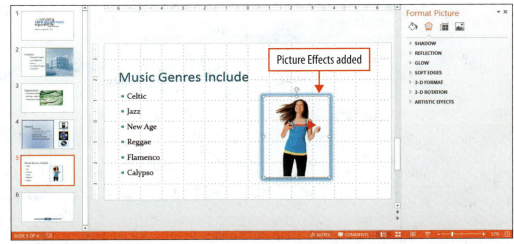

13 ▸ **Save** 💾 your changes.

Objective 3   Change the Shape of a Picture

Video P5-3

After you have inserted a picture, you can change the outline shape of the image. This is possible with or without the addition of a border. A large selection of shapes is available in PowerPoint. We apply several formatting techniques in this project so you can experiment with different options. Keep in mind, however, that applying too many formatting techniques can distract from the content of the presentation.

Activity 5.05 │ Changing the Shape of a Picture

In this activity, you will change a picture on your slide to a shape and then add a border.

1 ▸ With **Slide 5** as the active slide, on the **Format Picture** pane, at the top, click **Size & Properties** 📊. In the **Horizontal position** spin box, select the text, type **7.7** and then press Enter. In the **Vertical position** spin box, select the text, type **1.8** and then press Enter.

2 ▸ On the **PICTURE TOOLS FORMAT tab**, in the **Size group**, click the **Crop button arrow**, and then point to **Crop to Shape**. Under **Basic Shapes**, in the second row, point to the ninth symbol—**Plaque**, and then compare your screen with Figure 5.17.

FIGURE 5.17

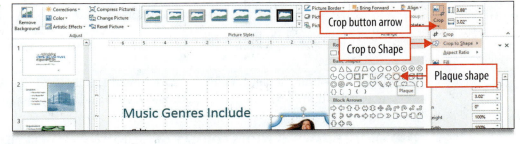

3 ▸ Click the **Plaque** shape. On the **PICTURE TOOLS FORMAT tab**, in the **Picture Styles group**, click **Picture Border**, and then in the fifth column, click the fifth row—**Blue, Accent 1, Darker 25%**. Click **Picture Border**, point to **Weight**, and then click **3 pt. Close** the **Format Picture** pane. Click to deselect the picture, and then compare your screen with Figure 5.18.

Without the border, applying the shape is confusing. Adding the border emphasized the shape.

FIGURE 5.18

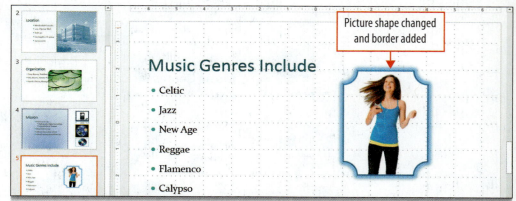

Picture shape changed
and border added

4 ▶ Click the **VIEW tab**. In the **Show group**, click to deselect the **Gridlines** check box.

5 ▶ Save 💾 your changes.

Objective 4 | Add a Picture to a WordArt Object and Merge Shapes

Video P5-4

A WordArt object may have a picture fill to add interest to a presentation. After adding the WordArt text, insert a picture fill that complements the WordArt message.

Activity 5.06 | Adding a WordArt Object and Embedding a Picture

In this activity, you will add a WordArt object containing text. Then you will insert a picture as a fill for the object. You will also recolor the picture.

1 ▶ Click **Slide 6**. On the **INSERT tab**, in the **Text group**, click **WordArt**. In the third row, point to the third item—**Fill – Blue, Accent 1, Outline – Background 1, Hard Shadow – Accent 1**, and then compare your screen with Figure 5.19.

FIGURE 5.19

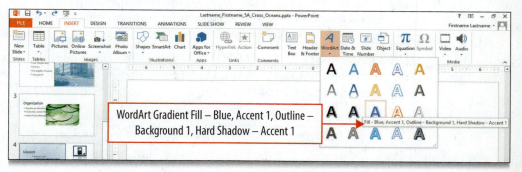

WordArt Gradient Fill – Blue, Accent 1, Outline –
Background 1, Hard Shadow – Accent 1

2 ▶ Click **Fill – Blue, Accent 1, Outline – Background 1, Hard Shadow – Accent 1**. In the **WordArt** object, with the text selected, type **Cross Oceans** and then press [Enter]. Type **Music** on the second line.

3 ▶ On the **DRAWING TOOLS FORMAT tab**, in the **Arrange group**, click **Align** 📇, and then select **Align Middle**. Deselect the **WordArt**, and then compare your screen with Figure 5.20.

FIGURE 5.20

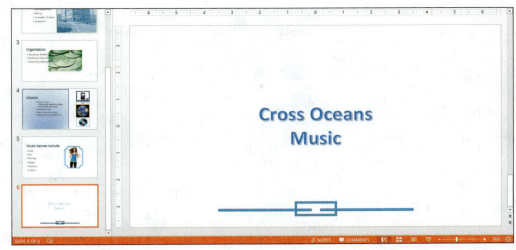

4 ▶ Click to select the WordArt object. On the **DRAWING TOOLS FORMAT tab**, in the **Shape Styles group**, click **Shape Fill**, and then click **Picture**. Navigate to the location where you are storing your files, click **p05A_Island.jpg**, and then click **Insert**. Compare your screen with Figure 5.21.

🔄 **ANOTHER WAY**   Double-click the file name to insert a picture.

FIGURE 5.21

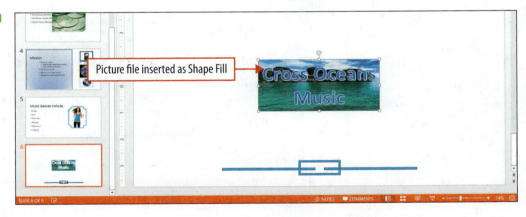

Picture file inserted as Shape Fill

5 ▶ With the WordArt object selected, on the **PICTURE TOOLS FORMAT tab**, in the **Adjust group**, click **Color**. Under **Recolor**, in the first row, in the fourth column, click **Washout**.

6 ▶ Right-click on the WordArt, and then click **Format Picture**. At the top, click **Size & Properties** 🖻. Under **SIZE**, under **Scale Width**, select the **Lock aspect ratio** check box. Under **SIZE**, in the **Height** spin box, select the text, type **2.5** and then press Enter. Compare your screen with Figure 5.22.

When *Lock aspect ratio* is selected, you can change one dimension (height or width) of an object, such as a picture, and the other dimension will automatically be changed to maintain the proportion.

FIGURE 5.22

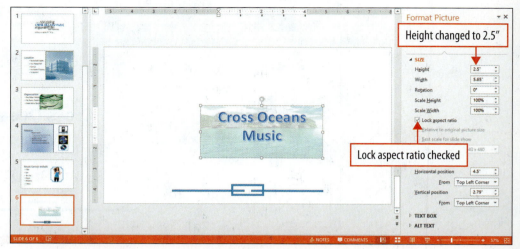

7 On the **PICTURE TOOLS FORMAT tab**, in the **Arrange group**, click **Align** [icon], and then select **Align Center**. Deselect the **WordArt**, and then compare your screen with Figure 5.23.

FIGURE 5.23

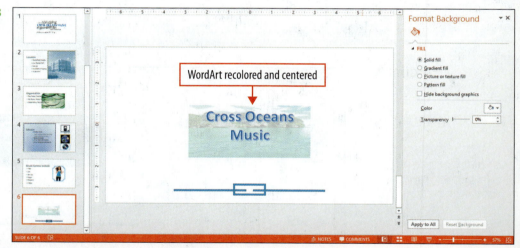

8 **Save** [icon] your changes.

Activity 5.07 | Merging Shapes

On occasion, the shape you want or need isn't listed in the Illustrations group. You can draw your own shapes and merge them together to create a new shape. In this activity, you will merge three separate shapes into one contiguous shape, move it to a new location, and then center the merged shape.

1 With **Slide 6** selected, at the bottom of the slide, hold down the [Ctrl] key and click to select the three blue shapes—a line, a frame box, and a line. Compare your screen with Figure 5.24.

FIGURE 5.24

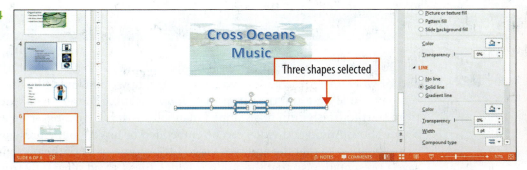

2 On the **DRAWING TOOLS FORMAT tab**, in the **Insert Shapes group**, click **Merge Shapes**, and then click **Union**. Compare your screen with Figure 5.25.

> The three shapes merge into one shape.

FIGURE 5.25

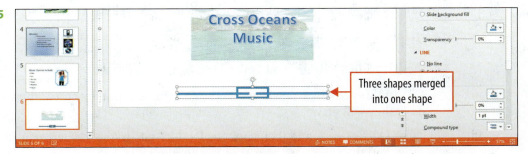

3 On the **Format Shape** pane, at the top, click **Size & Properties** . Under **POSITION**, in the **Horizontal position** spin box, select the text, type **3** and then press Enter. In the **Vertical position** spin box, select the text, type **6** and then press Enter. **Close** the **Format Shape** pane. Compare your screen with Figure 5.26.

> The merged shape is repositioned.

FIGURE 5.26

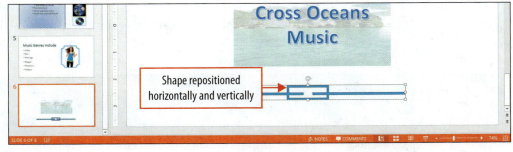

4 **Save** your changes.

Video P5-5

To further enhance a presentation, you can add audio and video. After you have applied audio and/or video to a presentation, you can control how you would like the files to play. A file can be set to play one time and then stop, or to *loop*, meaning the audio or video file will play repeatedly from start to finish until it is stopped manually. A *track*, or song, from a CD can also play during a slide show. Audio and video can be embedded or linked to the presentation. To *embed* is to save a presentation so that the audio or video file becomes part of the presentation file. To *link* is to save a presentation so that the audio or video file is saved separately from the presentation. Be sure to obtain permission to link or embed audio and video to a presentation to avoid violating the copyright.

> **ALERT!**   **Do You Have Permission to Use Audio in the Classroom?**
>
> If you are not allowed to play audio in your classroom or lab, use a headset for these activities. If you do not have a headset, ask your instructor how to proceed.

Activity 5.08 | Adding an Embedded Audio to a Presentation

In this activity, you will add audio to a presentation by embedding audio files and customizing how they will play.

1 Click **Slide 5**, and then click the **INSERT tab**. In the **Media group**, click the **Audio button arrow**, and then compare your screen with Figure 5.27.

FIGURE 5.27

2 Take a moment to study the options available for inserting audio into a presentation, as shown in the table in Figure 5.28.

FIGURE 5.28

SOUND OPTIONS	
SCREEN ELEMENT	**DESCRIPTION**
Online Audio	Displays the **Office.com** Clip Art pane so that you can search for royalty-free sound clip audio files in the Microsoft Office collection, both locally and online.
Audio on My PC	Enables you to insert audio clips such as music, narration, or audio bites from your computer or other computers that you are connected to. Compatible audio file formats include .mid or .midi, .mp3, and .wav.
Record Audio	Enables you to insert audio by recording the audio through a microphone and then naming and inserting the recorded audio.

3 From the displayed menu, click **Audio on My PC** to display the **Insert Audio** dialog box.

4 ▶ Above **Cancel**, click the **Audio Flies down arrow** to display the audio files supported by PowerPoint 2013, and then compare your screen with Figure 5.29. Take a moment to study the description of the Audio File Formats Supported in PowerPoint 2013, as shown in the table in Figure 5.30.

FIGURE 5.29

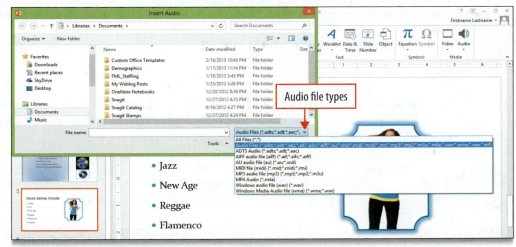

Audio file types

AUDIO FILE FORMATS SUPPORTED IN POWERPOINT 2013 SUPPORTED AUDIO FORMATS	
FILE FORMAT	**EXTENSION**
AIFF audio file	.aiff
AU audio file	.au
MIDI file	.mid or .midi
MP3 audio file	.mp3
MP4 audio	.m4a
Windows audio file	.wav
Windows Media Audio file	.wma

FIGURE 5.30

More Knowledge   **For the Best Audio and Video Playback Experience**

PowerPoint 2013 allows you to play back in several different video and audio file formats. For the best video playback experience, it is recommended that you use .mp4 videos encoded with H.264 video (a.k.a. MPEG-4 AVC) and AAC audio. For the best audio playback, it is recommended that you use .m4a files encoded with AAC audio. These formats are recommended for use with PowerPoint 2013 and for use with PowerPoint 2013 Web App.

---

5 ▶ Navigate to the location where your student files are stored, and click to select **p05A_Smooth_Jazz.wav**. At the bottom right of the **Insert Audio** dialog box, click the **Insert button arrow**, and then click **Insert**.

The AUDIO TOOLS tab displays on the Ribbon with the FORMAT and PLAYBACK tabs located under it. The PLAYBACK tab contains the Preview, Bookmarks, Editing, Audio Options, and Audio Styles groups. A speaker icon displays on the screen with Playback controls—Play/Pause, Move Back, Move Forward, Time, Mute/Unmute.

The audio files used in this activity are *.wav* files. These files are embedded in the PowerPoint presentation, meaning that the object, or audio file, is inserted into the presentation and becomes part of the saved presentation file. Because the audio is stored within the presentation file, this guarantees that the audio will play from any audio-enabled computer that you use to show the presentation.

The other method of inserting audio into a presentation is to link the audio file. When you link the audio file, it is stored outside the presentation. If your presentation includes linked files, you must copy both the presentation file and the linked files to the same folder if you want to show the presentation on another computer.

You can use the Optimized Media Compatibility feature, on the FILE Info tab, to make it easier to share your PowerPoint 2013 presentation that contains an audio file with others or to show this presentation on another computer.

6 ▶ On the **AUDIO TOOLS PLAYBACK** tab, in the **Audio Options group**, select the **Hide During Show** check box. Click the **Volume button arrow**, and then click **Medium**. In the **Start** box, select **Automatically**. Compare your screen with Figure 5.31.

🔄 **ANOTHER WAY** To adjust the audio volume, on the Windows taskbar, on the right side, click the Speakers icon, and then adjust the volume.

FIGURE 5.31

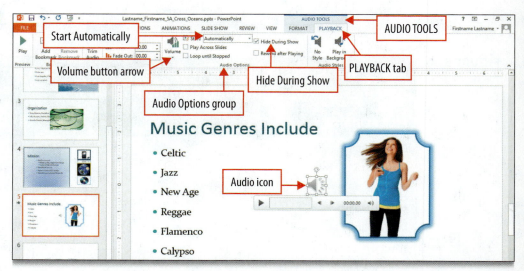

7 ▶ With **Slide 5** as the active slide, click the **SLIDE SHOW tab**. In the **Start Slide Show group**, click **From Current Slide**.

During a slide show presentation, the audio starts automatically when the slide displays. The audio plays one time and then stops. Because the audio icon is hidden, it does not display on the slide during the presentation of a slide show.

You can stop the audio by clicking the slide, by pressing Enter to advance to the next slide, or by pressing Esc.

You can play a song for the duration of your PowerPoint presentation slide show by selecting Play Across Slides in Audio options on the AUDIO TOOLS PLAYBACK tab. Often, this sets the mood while your audience views your slide show. Music downloaded from the Internet should be saved to your computer's hard drive first, and then inserted into your PowerPoint presentation. Adding audio will increase your file size. If file size is an issue, you can compress the audio file, keeping in mind that this will affect audio quality. On the FILE tab, under Info, click Compress Media, and then select the audio quality.

8 ⟩ Press Esc to end the slide show and return to **Normal** view.

It is possible to play sounds in Normal view. In the Slides and Outline pane, a small star-shaped icon displays to the left of the slide thumbnail. This is the *Play Animations button*. Click this small button to play the sound. Click the Play Animations button again to stop the sound or press Esc.

9 ⟩ Make **Slide 1** the active slide. Click the **INSERT tab**, and then in the **Media group**, click the **Audio arrow**. Click **Audio on My PC**. Navigate to the location where your student files are stored, click **p05A_New_Age.wav**, and then click **Insert**. Right-click the **Audio icon** 🔊 and then click **Size and Position**. Click **POSITION** to expand, if necessary. In the **Horizontal position** spin box, select the text, type **9** and then press Enter. In the **Vertical position** spin box, select the text, type **6** and then press Enter.

N O T E **Moving a Sound Icon**

You can move the audio icon away from the main content of the slide so that the icon is easier for the presenter to locate. Avoid placing the icon where it interferes with the text the audience is viewing.

---

10 ⟩ **Close** the Format Picture pane.

11 ⟩ On the **AUDIO TOOLS PLAYBACK tab**, to the right of **Start**, select **On Click**, if necessary. On the slide, on the **Sound Control Panel**, click **Play** ▶ to listen to the audio clip, and then click **Pause** ⏸ to stop the audio clip.

A L E R T ! **Is the Audio Not Audible? Is the Sound Control Panel Missing?**

Your PC may not have audio capability. If you know for a fact that your PC has audio capability, on the lower right side of the Windows taskbar, in the Notification area, click Speakers. To adjust speaker volume, drag the slider up to increase the volume. Make sure that the audio has not been muted. If the audio is muted, there will be a red stop symbol beside the speaker icon. Click the speaker icon and unmute the audio. Finally, make sure that you have your speakers turned on. If you cannot see the Sound Control Panel, click the speaker icon.

---

12 ⟩ On the **AUDIO TOOLS PLAYBACK tab**, in the **Audio Options group**, select the **Hide During Show** check box, and then compare your screen with Figure 5.32.

FIGURE 5.32

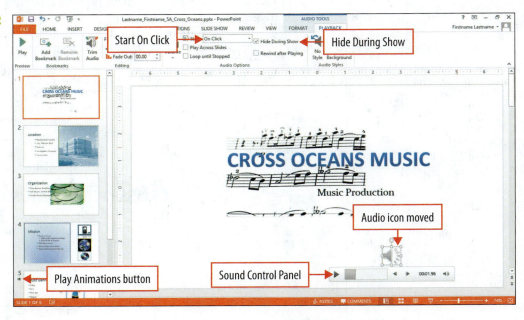

13 ⟩ Click the **SLIDE SHOW tab**. In the **Start Slide Show group**, click **From Beginning**. Click the slide, and notice that no audio plays. Instead, it takes you to the next slide.

14 Press Esc to end the slide show and return to **Normal** view.

15 Click **Slide 1**. Click to select the audio icon. Under **AUDIO TOOLS**, click the **PLAYBACK tab**.

16 In the **Audio Options group**, deselect the **Hide During Show** check box. Click the **SLIDE SHOW tab**. In the **Start Slide Show group**, click the **From Current Slide** button. Point to the **Audio** icon. On the control panel, click **Play**. Alternatively, you can click the top part of the audio icon to hear the sound.

After the slide show is started, there may be a delay before the mouse pointer becomes active.

17 Press Esc.

18 Save 💾 your changes.

Activity 5.09 | Setting a Trigger for an Embedded Audio in a Presentation

In this activity, you will set a trigger for an embedded audio. A **trigger** is a portion of text, a graphic, or a picture that, when clicked, causes the audio or video to play. You will display the Animation Pane to help you locate the trigger. The **Animation Pane** is an area used for adding and removing effects.

1 With **Slide 1** as the active slide, click to select the audio icon, if necessary.

2 Click the **ANIMATIONS tab**. In the **Advanced Animation group**, click **Animation Pane** to display the **Animation Pane** on the right side of the window. In the **Animation Pane**, the audio file name is displayed in the list.

3 In the **Advanced Animation group**, click the **Trigger button arrow**, and then point to **On Click of**. Compare your screen with Figure 5.33.

Notice the options to select for the trigger—Picture 8, Title 1, Subtitle 2 or the file name. The number after the trigger option may vary.

FIGURE 5.33

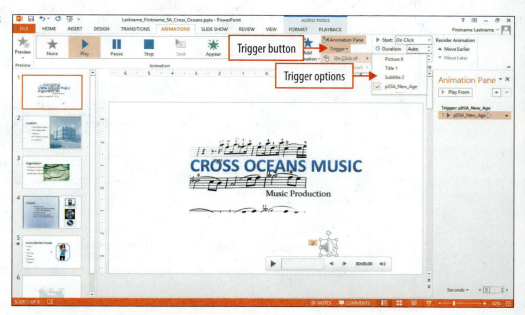

4 Click **Title 1**. Compare your screen with Figure 5.34.

At the right, in the Animation Pane, *Trigger: Title 1: Cross Oceans …* is displayed at the top of the list. Notice that it is identified as the trigger.

FIGURE 5.34

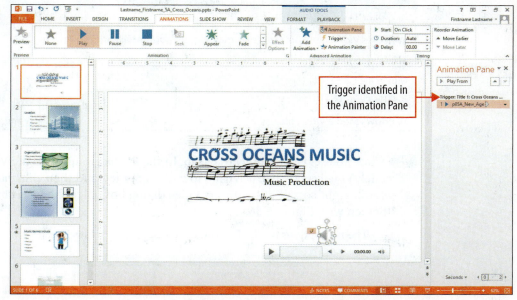

5 Close ☒ the **Animation Pane**. With the **Audio icon** 🔊 selected, on the **AUDIO TOOLS PLAYBACK tab**, in the **Audio Options group**, select the check box for **Hide During Show**.

6 Click the **SLIDE SHOW tab**. In the **Start Slide Show group**, click **From Current Slide**. Click the title *Cross Oceans Music* to start the audio. Press Esc.

The mouse pointer changes from an arrow to a hand and then back to an arrow when you move off the title.

7 Save 💾 your changes.

Activity 5.10 | Adding a Linked Video to a Presentation

In this activity, you will link a video to your presentation. A presentation with a linked video is smaller in file size than a presentation with an embedded video. To prevent possible problems with broken links, it is a good idea to copy the video into the same folder as your presentation and then link to it from there. Both the video file and the presentation file must be available when presenting your slide show.

1 In the location where your data files are stored, locate **p05_Music_Video.avi**, and then copy it into your **PowerPoint Chapter 5** folder. Take a moment to study the description of the Video File Formats Supported in PowerPoint 2013, as shown in the table in Figure 5.35.

> **N O T E**   **Copying a File**
>
> To copy a file on your storage device, display File Explorer and locate the file you want, right-click the file name, and then click Copy. Next, open the folder where you are saving your completed files, right-click, and then click Paste.

FIGURE 5.35

VIDEO FILE FORMATS SUPPORTED IN POWERPOINT 2013 SUPPORTED VIDEO FORMATS	
FILE FORMAT	**EXTENSION**
Windows Media file	.asf
Windows Video file (Some .avi files may require additional codecs)	.avi
MP4 Video file	.mp4, .m4v, .mov
Movie file	.mpg or .mpeg
Adobe Flash Media	.swf
Windows Media Video file	.wmv

2 Click **Slide 6**. Click the **INSERT tab**. In the **Media group**, click the **Video button arrow**, and then click **Video on My PC**. Navigate to your data files, and then click **p05_Music_Video.avi**. In the lower right corner of the **Insert Video** dialog box, click the **Insert button arrow**. Compare your screen with Figure 5.36.

The two options on the Insert list are Insert and Link to File.

FIGURE 5.36

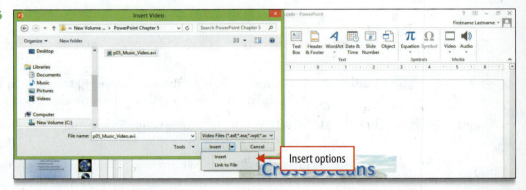

3 Click **Link to File**. With the video selected, on the **VIDEO TOOLS FORMAT tab**, in the **Size group**, change the **Video Height** to **1.5"**. Right-click the video, and then click **Size and Position** to display the **Format Video** pane. Click **POSITION** to expand, if necessary. In the **Horizontal position** spin box, select the text, type **5.5** and then press Enter. In the **Vertical position** spin box, select the text, type **0.5** and then press Enter. Compare your screen with Figure 5.37.

Moving and resizing the video allows you to see the content of the slide better.

FIGURE 5.37

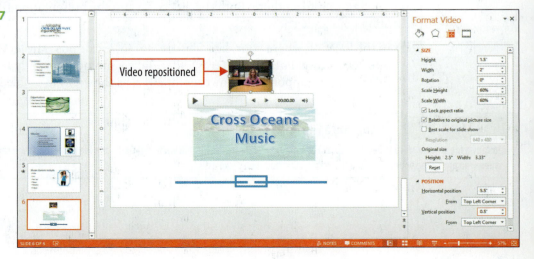

4 **Close** the **Format Video** pane. **Save** 💾 your changes.

Activity 5.11 | Changing the Trigger for a Linked Video in a Presentation

In this activity, you will use the Animation Pane to change the trigger that will play the video file from the video image to the WordArt shape. You will also set the video so it plays in full screen.

1 With **Slide 6** as the active slide, click to select the video, if necessary.

2 Click the **ANIMATIONS tab**. In the **Advanced Animation group**, click **Animation Pane** to display the **Animation Pane** on the right side of the window.

In the Animation Pane, the video file name is displayed in the list.

3 Click the **Trigger button arrow**, and then point to **On Click of**. Compare your screen with Figure 5.38.

Notice the options to select for the trigger—Freeform 6, Rectangle 1, and p05_Music_Video.avi. Rectangle represents the WordArt shape. The numbers after Freeform and Rectangle may vary.

FIGURE 5.38

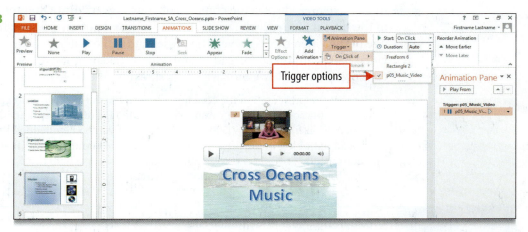

4 Click **Rectangle 1** (the number after Rectangle may vary). Compare your screen with Figure 5.39.

Rectangle refers to the WordArt.

FIGURE 5.39

5 On the **ANIMATIONS tab**, in the **Advanced Animation group**, click **Animation Pane** to close the **Animation Pane**. On the **VIDEO TOOLS PLAYBACK tab**, in the **Video Options group**, select the check box for **Hide While Not Playing**. Select the check box for **Play Full Screen**. Compare your screen with Figure 5.40.

FIGURE 5.40

6 ▶ Click the **SLIDE SHOW tab**. In the **Start Slide Show group**, click **From Current Slide**. Click the *Cross Oceans Music* WordArt to start the video. After the video plays, press Esc.

> The video plays in full screen. Allow the video to play completely. If you stop the video, the video will display on the slide. For that reason, you might want to resize the video to a smaller size.

7 ▶ In the **Start Slide Show group**, click **From Beginning** to view the entire presentation. Click the trigger on **Slide 1** to hear the audio. Click the trigger on **Slide 6** to view the video. Press Esc.

8 ▶ In **File Explorer**, display the contents of your **PowerPoint Chapter 5** folder. On the **View tab**, in the **Layout group**, click **Details**. Observe the size of the presentation file is larger than the size of the video file, however, the presentation file size would be substantially larger if the video had been linked instead of embedded. Take a moment to study the description of the Compression Quality Comparison, as shown in the table in Figure 5.41.

> Because the presentation file contains a link to the video file, the actual video file is not a part of the presentation file size. For example, the video for this presentation is about 3,100 KB and the presentation file is about 7,500 KB. Therefore, if you had embedded the video in the presentation instead of linking it, the presentation file would be about 10,500 KB. If you send this presentation electronically or transfer it to another location such as a USB drive, be sure to place both files in the same folder before sending or moving them.

More Knowledge   **Compressing Your Presentation Files**

If you are concerned about the size of your files or need to transmit them electronically, you may wish to consider using one of the compression methods. To display your options, on the FILE tab, under Info, click Compress Media. Refer to Figure 5.41 for an explanation of compression qualities. Under Media Size and Performance, the total file size of the media files in the presentation displays. These options will not display on the FILE Info tab unless you have a media file embedded in the presentation.

FIGURE 5.41

| COMPRESSION QUALITY COMPARISON ||
COMPRESSION METHOD	DESCRIPTION
No Compression	The original size of the presentation.
Presentation Quality	Save space while maintaining overall audio and video quality.
Internet Quality	Quality will be comparable to media which is streamed over the Internet.
Low Quality	Use when space is limited, such as when sending presentations via email.

A L E R T !   **Did You Change the Name of the Video File after Linking It to a Presentation?**

If you change the name of a video file after you link it to a presentation, the video will not play. You will have to link the file again.

9 Return to the PowerPoint presentation. On the **INSERT tab**, in the **Text group**, click **Header & Footer** to display the **Header and Footer** dialog box. Click the **Notes and Handouts tab**. Under **Include on page**, select the **Date and time** check box, and then select **Fixed**. If necessary, clear the **Header** check box, and then select the **Page number** and **Footer** check boxes. In the **Footer** box, using your own name, type **Lastname_Firstname_5A_Cross_Oceans** and then click **Apply to All**.

10 Click the **FILE tab**, and then in the lower right portion of the screen, click **Show All Properties**. In the **Tags** box, type **mission, genres** and in the **Subject** box type your course name and section number. In the **Author** box, right-click the existing author name, click **Edit Property**, replace the existing text with your first and last name, click outside text box to deselect, and then click **OK**.

11 Save 🖫 your changes. Print **Handouts 4 Slides Horizontal**, or submit your presentation electronically as directed by your instructor.

12 **Close** the presentation, and then **Exit** PowerPoint.

END | You have completed Project 5A

Create a Photo Album

PROJECT ACTIVITIES

In Activities 5.12 through 5.14, you will create a PowerPoint photo album to display business photos of jazz musicians promoted and recorded by Cross Oceans Music. You will insert photos, add an attention-getting theme, and select a layout. You will also add frames to the photos and provide captions. You will reorder pictures in a photo album, adjust the rotation of a photo album image, and change a photo album layout. You will experiment with tools that allow you to enter and format text in a text box and crop a photo to emphasize a key area of the photo. Your completed presentation will look similar to Figure 5.42.

PROJECT FILES

Build from Scratch

For Project 5B, you will need the following files:

You will save your presentation as:

New blank PowerPoint presentation
p05B_Jazz1.jpg
p05B_Jazz2.jpg
p05B_Jazz3.jpg
p05B_Jazz4.jpg
p05B_Jazz5.jpg
p05B_Jazz6.jpg
p05B_Jazz7.jpg

Lastname_Firstname_5B_Jazz_Album.pptx

PROJECT RESULTS

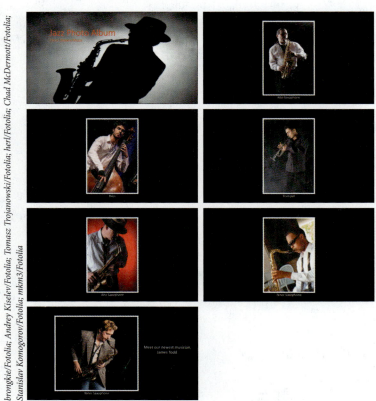

FIGURE 5.42 Project 5B Jazz Album

Video P5-6

In the following activity, you will create a PowerPoint photo album. In PowerPoint, a *photo album* is a stylized presentation format to display pictures; you can display 1, 2, or 4 photos on a slide. The format may include a title or caption for the photo(s). A placeholder is inserted with each photo when the photo is added to the album. PowerPoint provides an easy and powerful tool to aid you in creating an exciting photo album.

Activity 5.12 │ Creating a Photo Album

In this activity, you will create a photo album by inserting and customizing photos and selecting a theme. Each picture will be placed on its own slide.

1 Start PowerPoint. Click **Blank Presentation**. Click the **INSERT tab**. In the **Images group**, click the **Photo Album button arrow**, and then click **New Photo Album**. Compare your screen with Figure 5.43.

The Photo Album dialog box provides an easy and convenient way to insert and remove pictures; rearrange and rotate pictures; apply brightness and contrast; insert captions; and select a layout, theme, and frame shape.

FIGURE 5.43

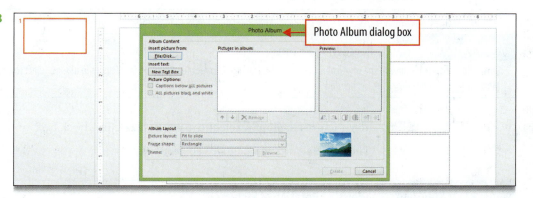

2 Under **Insert picture from**, click **File/Disk** to display the **Insert New Pictures** dialog box. Navigate to the location where your student files are stored, click **p05B_Jazz1.jpg**, and then click **Insert**. Compare your screen with Figure 5.44.

The file name displays as the first picture in the album, under Pictures in album, with a preview of the photograph.

ANOTHER WAY   When inserting pictures in the Photo Album dialog box, you can double-click the picture file name to insert it.

FIGURE 5.44

3 Using the technique you practiced, insert **p05B_Jazz2.jpg**, **p05B_Jazz3.jpg**, **p05B_Jazz4.jpg**, **p05B_Jazz5.jpg**, **p05B_Jazz6.jpg**, and **p05B_Jazz7.jpg**. Compare your screen with Figure 5.45.

FIGURE 5.45

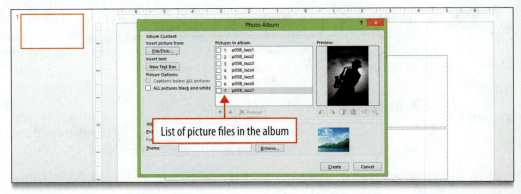

NOTE | **Inserting a Picture in the Photo Album Task Pane**

If the pictures you want to insert into your photo album are listed in a sequence on your storage location, you can click on the first file name in the list, hold down the Shift key and click on the last picture in the list, and then click Insert. If the pictures are not in a sequence, you can hold down the Ctrl key while clicking the pictures individually, and then click Insert.

More Knowledge | **Reordering Pictures**

PowerPoint inserts pictures in the photo album in alphabetical order. To reorder them, under Pictures in album, select the picture check box, and then click the Move up ↑ or Move down ↓ as needed.

---

4 Under **Pictures in album**, select the **p05B_Jazz7.jpg** check box, and then click **Remove**.

The photo album now contains six pictures.

More Knowledge | **Adjusting Rotation of Pictures**

Pictures display in either horizontal or vertical orientation in the Preview pane. If you wish to change the orientation, click the rotate left icon or rotate right icon to rotate the image in 90-degree increments located below the Preview pane.

---

5 Under **Album layout**, click the **Picture layout arrow** to display the options.

You can choose to insert 1, 2, or 4 pictures on a slide, with or without a title, or you can choose Fit to Slide.

6 Click **Fit to Slide**, if necessary.

In the Album Content area, the Captions below ALL pictures check box is dimmed and therefore unavailable. Also, in the Album Layout area, the Frame shape box is unavailable. In a photo album, the border around a picture is known as a *frame*, and a limited number of styles are available. When you select *Fit to Slide*, the picture occupies all available space on the slide with no room for a frame or a caption.

7 To the right of the **Theme** box, click **Browse** to display the **Choose Theme** dialog box. Scroll to view the available themes. Click **Cancel**. In the **Photo Album** dialog box, click **Create**.

Because you did not select a theme, the default theme is applied to the Photo Album. PowerPoint does not apply the theme to the photo album until you click Create. Notice that PowerPoint creates a title slide for the photo album. The name inserted in the subtitle, on the title slide, is the name associated with the owner or license holder of the software. It can be changed on the slide.

8 With **Slide 1** active, select the text in the subtitle placeholder, and then press Delete. Click the top edge of the subtitle placeholder to select it, and the press Delete.

9 In the title placeholder, click placing the insertion point to the left of the word *Photo*. Type **Jazz** and then press Spacebar. Click placing the insertion point to the right of the word *Album*. Press Enter. Type **Cross Oceans Music**

10 Select the text *Cross Oceans Music*. On the mini toolbar, change the font size to **24**. Select the text *Jazz Photo Album*. On the mini toolbar, change the font size to **54**. Select all the text in the title placeholder. On the mini toolbar, click **Bold**, and then click the **Font Color button arrow** [A]. Under **Standard** colors, click the first color—**Dark Red**. On the mini toolbar, click **Align Left**. On the **HOME tab**, in the **Paragraph group**, click the **Align Text arrow**, and then click **Top**. Click outside the placeholder to deselect. Compare your screen with Figure 5.46.

The title and subtitle font color, font size, and alignment are changed.

FIGURE 5.46

11 Press F12 to display the **Save As** dialog box, and then navigate to the location where you are storing your projects for this chapter. Using your own name, save the file as **Lastname_Firstname_5B_Jazz_Album**

Because PowerPoint creates the photo album in a new presentation, you should wait until you click Create before saving the photo album.

Objective 7 | Edit a Photo Album and Add a Caption

Video P5-7

After you create a PowerPoint photo album, it is possible to format the background of the title slide by adding and customizing a caption for each photo. A *caption* is text that helps to identify or explain a picture or graphic.

Activity 5.13 | Editing a Photo Album and Adding a Caption

In this activity, you will edit a photo album, change the picture layout, and add captions.

1 With **Slide 1** as the active slide, right-click the first thumbnail in the pane on the left to display the shortcut menu, and then click **Format Background**. In the **Format Background** pane, under **Fill**, select **Picture or texture fill**.

2 Under **Insert picture from**, click **File**. Navigate to the location where your student files are stored, click **p05B_Jazz7.jpg**, and then click **Insert**. Compare your screen with Figure 5.47.

This applies the background picture to the title slide only. Notice that the top of the picture is off the slide.

FIGURE 5.47

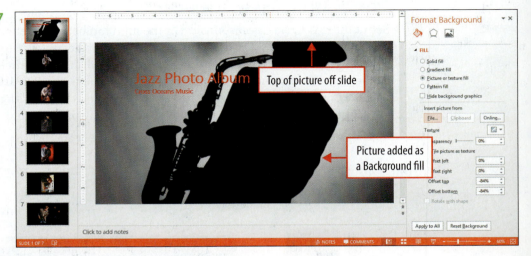

3 In the **Format Background** pane, in the **Offset top** spin box, select the text, type **-40**, and then press [Enter]. In the **Offset bottom** spin box, select the text, type **-60**, and then press [Enter]. **Close** the **Format Background** pane. Compare your screen with Figure 5.48.

This lowers the background silhouette to make the top visible on the slide. Because only the top and bottom offset were changed, the picture is a little distorted.

> **ALERT!** **Did Format Background Appear on the Context-Sensitive Menu?**
>
> If you did not see Format Background as a choice when you right-clicked the slide, you probably clicked on the Title or Subtitle placeholder. Right-click in another place on the slide, and you should see the appropriate options.

FIGURE 5.48

4 Click the **SLIDE SHOW tab**. In the **Start Slide Show group**, click **From Beginning**. Click through all the slides. Press [Esc] to return to **Normal** view.

The pictures fit to the slide and do not allow room for a caption.

5 Click the **INSERT tab**. In the **Images group**, click the **Photo Album button arrow**, and then click **Edit Photo Album** to display the **Edit Photo Album** dialog box. Under **Album Layout**, click the **Picture layout arrow** to display the options, and then click **1 picture**. Click the **Frame shape arrow**, to display the options, and then click **Simple Frame, White**.

6 In the **Album Content** area, under **Picture Options**, select the **Captions below ALL pictures** check box, and then compare your screen with Figure 5.49.

FIGURE 5.49

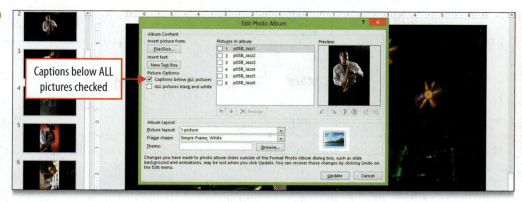

7 ▶ Click **Update**, and then make **Slide 2** the active slide. Compare your screen with Figure 5.50.

Notice that, by default, the file name displays as the caption.

FIGURE 5.50

8 ▶ With **Slide 2** as the active slide, click to select the picture caption placeholder. Double-click to select the caption, and then type **Alto Saxophone** Compare your screen with Figure 5.51.

FIGURE 5.51

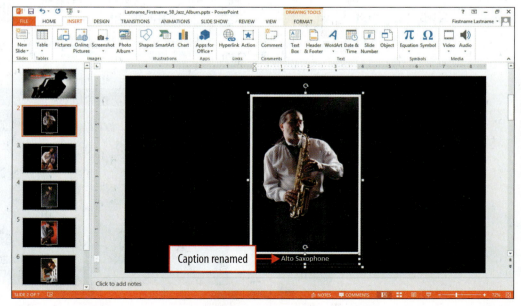

9 ▶ Using the technique you practiced, add the following captions to **Slides 3**, **4**, **5**, **6**, and **7**:

Slide 3	Bass
Slide 4	Trumpet
Slide 5	Alto Saxophone
Slide 6	Tenor Saxophone
Slide 7	Tenor Saxophone

10 ▶ On the **SLIDE SHOW tab**, in the **Start Slide Show group**, click **From beginning** to view the slides in the presentation.

11 ▶ Save 🖫 your changes.

Objective 8   Crop a Picture

Video P5-8

In the following activity, you will edit the PowerPoint photo album you created by cropping the picture. When you *crop* a picture, you remove unwanted or unnecessary areas of a picture. Images are often cropped to create more emphasis on the primary subject of the image. Recall that the Compress Picture pane provides the option to delete the cropped area of a picture. Deleting the cropped area reduces file size and also prevents people from being able to view the parts of the picture that you have removed. The *crop handles* are used like sizing handles to crop a picture, and the *Crop tool* is the mouse pointer used when removing areas of a picture.

Activity 5.14 | Cropping a Picture and Inserting a Textbox

1 ▶ Make **Slide 7** the active slide, if necessary. Click the picture one time to select the placeholder, and then click again to select the picture.

> Because the placeholder is inserted at the time the picture is inserted, you must click the picture two times in order to gain access to the crop feature.

2 ▶ On the **PICTURE TOOLS FORMAT tab**, in the **Size group**, click the **Crop arrow**, and then point to **Crop**. Compare your screen with Figure 5.52.

> **A L E R T !**   **Is the Crop Inactive?**
>
> If you cannot display the Crop tool and crop lines, click the picture two times.

FIGURE 5.52

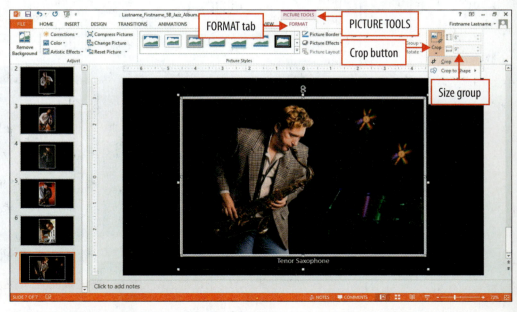

3 ▶ Click **Crop**. Position the **Crop pointer** 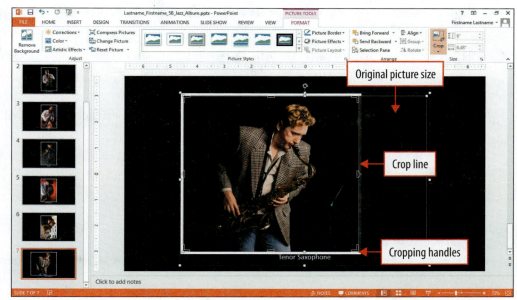 just inside the middle cropping handle on the right edge of the picture.

The mouse pointer assumes the shape of the crop line, in this case a straight vertical line with a short horizontal line attached.

4 ▶ Drag the pointer to the left until the right edge of the picture aligns with approximately the **2-inch mark to the right of 0** on the **horizontal ruler**, and then release the mouse button. Compare your screen with Figure 5.53.

The dark area to the right represents the area that will be removed. The caption is no longer centered under the picture.

FIGURE 5.53

> **Original picture size**
>
> **Crop line**
>
> **Cropping handles**

<table>
<tr><td>**N O T E**</td><td>**Does the Ruler Display?**</td></tr>
</table>

If the ruler does not display, on the VIEW tab, in the Show group, select the Ruler check box.

---

5 ▶ Click outside the picture to turn off cropping.

🔄 **ANOTHER WAY**   You can also turn off the cropping button by pressing Esc or by clicking Crop.

---

6 ▶ Under the picture, select the caption. On **the DRAWING TOOLS FORMAT tab**, in the **Size group**, in the **Width** spin box, select the text, type **6.5** and then press Enter.

The caption is now centered under the cropped picture.

7 ▶ Click the **INSERT tab**. In the **Text group**, click **Text Box**, and then click one time to the right of the picture. Compare your screen with Figure 5.54.

FIGURE 5.54

8 ▸ In the text box, type **Meet our newest musician,** press Enter, and then type **James Todd.**

🔄 **BY TOUCH**   Tap the INSERT tab. In the Text group, tap to select Text Box. Tap one time to the right of the picture. In the text box, type **Meet our newest musician, James Todd.**

9 ▸ Select both lines of text in the text box, and then increase the font size to **24. Center** ☰ the text.

🔄 **BY TOUCH**   Tap the HOME tab. In the Font group, slide the arrow to select the font size to 24. In the Paragraph group, tap Center to center the text.

> **N O T E**   **Selecting Text in Placeholders**
>
> Recall that you can click the border of a placeholder to select text. When the border is displayed as a solid border, you know the text is selected.

10 ▸ On the **DRAWING TOOLS FORMAT tab**, in the **Size group**, click the **Size and Position** dialog launcher 🔲 to display the **Format Shape** pane. Click **POSITION** to expand, if necessary. In the **Horizontal position** spin box, select the text, type **9** and then press Enter. In the **Vertical position** spin box, select the text, type **3** and then press Enter. Compare your screen with Figure 5.55.

FIGURE 5.55

11 ▸ **Close** the Format Shape pane. Click the **SLIDE SHOW tab**. In the **Start Slide Show group**, click **From Beginning**, and then view the presentation. Press Esc to return to **Normal** view.

🔄 **ANOTHER WAY**   To start the slide show from the beginning, make Slide 1 the active slide, and then press the F5 key or the Slide Show icon on the status bar.

650   **PowerPoint** | Chapter 5: APPLYING ADVANCED GRAPHIC TECHNIQUES AND INSERTING AUDIO AND VIDEO

12 On the **INSERT tab**, in the **Text group**, click **Header & Footer** to display the **Header and Footer** dialog box. Click the **Notes and Handouts tab**. Under **Include on page**, select the **Date and time** check box, and then select **Fixed**. If necessary, clear the **Header** check box, and then select the **Page number** and **Footer** check boxes. In the **Footer** box, using your own name, type **Lastname_Firstname_5B_Jazz_Album** and then click **Apply to All**.

13 Click the **FILE tab**, and then in the lower right portion of the screen, click **Show All Properties**. In the **Tags** box, type **jazz, photo, album** and in the **Subject** box type your course name and section number. In the **Author** box, right-click the existing author name, click **Edit Property**, replace the existing text with your first and last name, click outside text box to deselect, and then click **OK**.

14 Save 🖫 your changes. Print **Handouts 4 Slides Horizontal**, or submit your presentation electronically as directed by your instructor.

15 **Close** the presentation, and then **Exit** PowerPoint.

END | You have completed Project 5B

END OF CHAPTER

SUMMARY

In this chapter, you practiced completing a PowerPoint presentation by inserting and modifying pictures and images, and by changing the sharpness and softness as well as the brightness and contrast.

Next, you added borders to images. You added a mitered border, a colored border, and a weighted border. You recolored pictures, merged three shapes into one, and added audio and video to a slide show.

You added a WordArt object to the presentation and embedded a picture. You changed the method by which audio and video play in a slide show and created triggers for starting them. You added a video link.

You created and edited a photo album using the fit to slide layout option. You practiced cropping a picture using the crop tool to remove areas of a picture. You added captions to photos to add clarity.

GO! LEARN IT ONLINE

Review the concepts and key terms in this chapter by completing these online challenges, which you can find at **www.pearsonhighered.com/go.**

Matching and Multiple Choice: Answer matching and multiple choice questions to test what you learned in this chapter. MyITLab®

Crossword Puzzle: Spell out the words that match the numbered clues, and put them in the puzzle squares.

Flipboard: Flip through the definitions of the key terms in this chapter and match them with the correct term.

END OF CHAPTER

REVIEW AND ASSESSMENT GUIDE FOR POWERPOINT CHAPTER 5

Your instructor may assign one or more of these projects to help you review the chapter and assess your mastery and understanding of the chapter.

	Review and Assessment Guide for PowerPoint Chapter 5		
Project	**Apply Skills from These Chapter Objectives**	**Project Type**	**Project Location**
5C	Objectives 1–5 from Project 5A	**5C Skills Review** A guided review of the skills from Project 5A.	On the following pages
5D	Objectives 6–8 from Project 5B	**5D Skills Review** A guided review of the skills from Project 5B.	On the following pages
5E	Objectives 1–5 from Project 5A	**5E Mastering PowerPoint (Grader Project)** A demonstration of your mastery of the skills in Project 5A with extensive decision making.	In MyITLab and on the following pages
5F	Objectives 6–8 from Project 5B	**5F Mastering PowerPoint (Grader Project)** A demonstration of your mastery of the skills in Project 5B with extensive decision making.	In MyITLab and on the following pages
5G	Objectives 1–8 from Projects 5A and 5B	**5G Mastering PowerPoint (Grader Project)** A demonstration of your mastery of the skills in Projects 5A and 5B with extensive decision making.	In MyITLab and on the following pages
5H	Combination of Objectives from Projects 5A and 5B	**5H GO! Fix It** A demonstration of your mastery of the skills in Projects 5A and 5B by creating a correct result from a document that contains errors you must find.	Online
5I	Combination of Objectives from Projects 5A and 5B	**5I GO! Make It** A demonstration of your mastery of the skills in Projects 5A and 5B by creating a result from a supplied picture.	Online
5J	Combination of Objectives from Projects 5A and 5B	**5J GO! Solve It** A demonstration of your mastery of the skills in Projects 5A and 5B, your decision-making skills, and your critical thinking skills. A task-specific rubric helps you self-assess your result.	Online
5K	Combination of Objectives from Projects 5A and 5B	**5K GO! Solve It** A demonstration of your mastery of the skills in Projects 5A and 5B, your decision-making skills, and your critical thinking skills. A task-specific rubric helps you self-assess your result.	On the following pages
5L	Combination of Objectives from Projects 5A and 5B	**5L GO! Think** A demonstration of your understanding of the chapter concepts applied in a manner that you would outside of college. An analytic rubric helps you and your instructor grade the quality of your work by comparing it to the work an expert in the discipline would create.	On the following pages
5M	Combination of Objectives from Projects 5A and 5B	**5M GO! Think** A demonstration of your understanding of the chapter concepts applied in a manner that you would outside of college. An analytic rubric helps you and your instructor grade the quality of your work by comparing it to the work an expert in the discipline would create.	Online
5N	Combination of Objectives from Projects 5A and 5B	**5N You and GO!** A demonstration of your understanding of the chapter concepts applied in a manner that you would in a personal situation. An analytic rubric helps you and your instructor grade the quality of your work.	Online

GLOSSARY

GLOSSARY OF CHAPTER KEY TERMS

.wav (waveform audio data) A sound file that may be embedded in a presentation.

Animation Pane The area used for adding and removing effects.

Border A frame around a picture.

Brightness The perceived radiance or luminosity of an image.

Caption Text that helps to identify or explain a picture or a graphic.

Contrast The difference between the darkest and lightest area of a picture.

Crop Remove unwanted or unnecessary areas of a picture.

Crop handles Used like sizing handles to crop a picture.

Crop tool The mouse pointer used when removing areas of a picture.

Embed Save a file so that the audio or video file becomes part of the presentation file.

Fit to Slide The photo album option that allows the picture to occupy all available space on a slide with no room for a frame or caption.

Frame The border around a picture in a photo album.

Line style How the line displays, such as a solid line, dots, or dashes.

Line weight The thickness of a line measured in points.

Link Save a presentation so that the audio or video file is saved separately from the presentation.

Lock aspect ratio When this option is selected, you can change one dimension (height or width) of an object, such as a picture, and the other dimension will automatically be changed to maintain the proportion.

Loop The audio or video file plays repeatedly from start to finish until it is stopped manually.

Mitered A border with corners that are square.

Photo album A stylized presentation format to display pictures.

Pixel The term, short for picture element, represents a single point in a graphic image.

Play Animations button A small star-shaped icon that displays to the left of the slide thumbnail.

Presets Built-in sharpness and softness adjustments from a gallery.

Recolor The term used to change all the colors in the image to shades of one color.

Sharpen Increase the clarity of an image.

Soften Decrease the clarity of an image or make it fuzzy.

Track A song from a CD.

Trigger A portion of text, a graphic, or a picture that, when clicked, causes the audio or video to play.

CHAPTER REVIEW

Apply 5A skills from these Objectives:

1 Use Picture Corrections
2 Add a Border to a Picture
3 Change the Shape of a Picture
4 Add a Picture to a WordArt Object and Merge Shapes
5 Enhance a Presentation with Audio and Video

Skills Review | Project 5C Celtic Instruments

In the following Skills Review, you will modify pictures in a presentation about the instruments used in the Celtic music genre for the Cross Oceans Music company. You will change the brightness, contrast, and shapes of pictures and add borders to some pictures for emphasis. You will add WordArt and merge a shape. You will also add audio files that demonstrate the various instruments used in this type of music and a video file. Your completed presentation will look similar to Figure 5.56.

PROJECT FILES

For Project 5C, you will need the following files:

p05C_Celtic_Instruments.pptx
p05C_Flute.wav
p05_Music_Video.avi
p05C_Sheet_Music.jpg

You will save your presentation as:

Lastname_Firstname_5C_Celtic_Instruments.pptx

PROJECT RESULTS

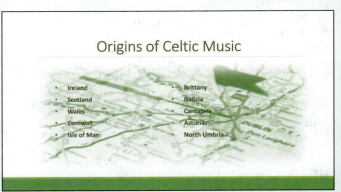

Klaus Eppele/Fotolia; miketea88/Fotolia

FIGURE 5.56

(Project 5C Celtic Instruments continues on the next page)

CHAPTER REVIEW

1 ▶ Start PowerPoint. Locate and open the file **p05C_Celtic_Instruments**. Using your own first and last name, save the file as **Lastname_Firstname_5C_Celtic_Instruments** in your **PowerPoint Chapter 5** folder.

2 ▶ Click **Slide 1**, if necessary, and then click to select the picture.

   a. On the **PICTURE TOOLS FORMAT tab**, in the **Size group**, click the **Crop button arrow**, and then click **Crop to Shape**. Under **Flowchart**, locate and click **Flowchart: Punched Tape**, which is in the second row, fourth from the left.

   b. In the **Adjust group**, click the **Corrections arrow**, and then click **Picture Corrections Options** to display the **Format Picture** pane. Under **Sharpen/Soften**, in the **Sharpness** spin box, select the text, type **-100** and then press Enter. Under **Brightness/Contrast**, click the **Presets arrow**, and then in the last row, third column, click **Brightness: 0% (Normal) Contrast: +40%**.

   c. In the **Arrange group**, click the **Send Backward button arrow**, and then click **Send to Back**.

   d. On **Format Picture** pane, at the top, click **Size & Properties**, and then click **POSITION** to expand, if necessary. To the right of **Horizontal position**, in the spin box, select the text, type **1** and then press Enter. To the right of **Vertical position**, in the spin box, select the text, type **2** and then press Enter. **Close** the Format Picture pane.

3 ▶ Make **Slide 2** the active slide, and then select the **picture**.

   a. On the **PICTURE TOOLS FORMAT tab**, in the **Arrange group**, click **Selection Pane**, and then in the **Selection** pane, click **Picture 6** (your picture number may vary), if necessary. In the **Adjust group**, click the **Corrections arrow**. Under **Brightness/Contrast**, locate and click **Brightness: 0% (Normal) Contrast: +20%**, which is in the fourth row, third column.

   b. In the **Arrange group**, click the **Send Backward button arrow**, and then click **Send to Back**.

   c. **Close** the **Selection** pane.

4 ▶ Make **Slide 3** the active slide.

   a. Click the **picture on the left**—the **flute**. On the **FORMAT tab**, in the **Size group**, click the **Crop button arrow**, and then click **Crop to Shape**. Under **Rectangles**, click the second rectangle—**Rounded Rectangle**.

   b. In the **Picture Styles group**, click **Picture Border**, and under **Theme** colors, click the first column, last row—**White, Background 1, Darker 50%**. In the **Pictures Styles group**, click **Picture Border**, click **Weight**, and then click **2 ¼ pt**.

   c. Click the **picture in the center**—the **accordion**. On the **FORMAT tab**, in the **Picture Styles group**, click the **More arrow**. Locate and click **Perspective Shadow, White**, which is in the third row, fourth column.

   d. Click the **picture on the right**—the **harp**. On the **FORMAT tab**, in the **Picture Styles group**, click the **More arrow**. Locate and click **Simple Frame, Black**, which is in the second row, second column.

5 ▶ Make **Slide 3** the active slide, if necessary.

   a. Click the **INSERT tab**. In the **Media group**, click the **Audio button arrow**, and then click **Audio on My PC**.

   b. Navigate to the location where your student files are stored. Locate and insert **p05C_Flute.wav**.

   c. On the **AUDIO TOOLS PLAYBACK tab**, click the **Start button arrow**, and then click **Automatically**. Click the **Hide During Show** check box.

   d. Move the speaker icon so it is on the left side of the picture of the accordion.

6 ▶ Make **Slide 4** the active slide.

   a. On the **INSERT tab**, in the **Text group**, click the **WordArt arrow**. In the second row, fifth column, click **Fill – Green, Accent 4, Sharp Bevel**.

   b. Type **Celtic Instruments** Press Enter, and then type **Presented by** Press Enter, and then type **Cross Oceans Music**

   c. Select the lines of text. On the **HOME tab**, in the **Font group**, click the **Font Color button arrow**. In the sixth column, fifth row, click **Green, Accent 2, Darker 25%**.

   d. On the **DRAWING TOOLS FORMAT tab**, in the **Size group**, click the **Size and Position** dialog launcher. In the **Format Shape** pane, to the right of **Horizontal position**, select the text, type **3.5** in the spin box, and then press Enter. In the **Format Shape** pane, to the right of **Vertical position**, select the text, type **1.0** in the spin box, and then press Enter.

(Project 5C Celtic Instruments continues on the next page)

e. On the **FORMAT tab**, in the **Shape Styles group**, click **Shape Fill**, and then click **Picture**. Navigate to the location where your student files are stored. Locate and click **p05C_Sheet_Music.jpg**, and then click **Insert**.

f. On the **PICTURE TOOLS FORMAT tab**, in the **Adjust group**, click **Color**. Under **Recolor**, locate and click **Green, Accent color 2 Light**. On the **PICTURE TOOLS FORMAT tab**, in the **Picture Styles group**, click the **Picture Effects arrow**, point to **Soft Edges**, and then click **10 Point**. Click to deselect the picture.

g. With **Slide 4** still selected, at the bottom of the slide, hold down the Ctrl key and click to select the **four green shapes** of the shamrock. On the **DRAWING TOOLS FORMAT tab**, in the **Insert Shapes group**, click **Merge Shapes**, and then click **Union**. Right-click the merged shape, and then click **Size and Position** to display the **Format Shape** pane. In the **Vertical position** spin box, select the text, type **5** and then press Enter. In the **Arrange group**, click the **Align button arrow**, and then click **Align Center**. **Close** the **Format Shape** pane.

7 In the location where your data files are stored, locate **p05_Music_Video.avi**, and then copy it into your **PowerPoint Chapter 5** folder.

8 Click **Slide 4**, and then click the **INSERT tab**. In the **Media group**, click the **Video button arrow**, and then click **Video on My PC**.

a. Navigate to the location where your student files are stored, click **p05_Music_Video.avi**, and then click the **Insert button arrow**. Click **Link to File**.

b. On the **VIDEO TOOLS FORMAT tab**, in the **Size group**, change the **Video Height** to **1.5"**.

c. On the **VIDEO TOOLS PLAYBACK tab**, select the check boxes for **Play Full Screen** and **Hide While Not Playing**.

d. Click the **ANIMATIONS tab**. In the **Advanced Animation group**, click the **Trigger** button, point to **On Click of**, and then click **Rectangle 5** (your Rectangle number may vary).

e. On the **Format Video** pane, at the top, click **Size & Properties**, click POSITION, to expand, if necessary. In the **Horizontal position** spin box, select the text, type **1** and then press Enter. In the **Vertical position** spin box, select the text, type **4.5** and then press Enter.

9 Click the **SLIDE SHOW tab**. In the **Start Slide Show group**, click **From Beginning**. Listen for the audio file, and then click the **WordArt** on **Slide 4** to view the video. Click **Esc** to exit the slide show.

10 On the **INSERT tab**, in the **Text group**, click **Header & Footer** to display the **Header and Footer** dialog box. Click the **Notes and Handouts tab**. Under **Include on page**, select the **Date and time** check box, and then select **Fixed**. If necessary, clear the **Header** check box, and then select the **Page number** and **Footer** check boxes. In the **Footer** box, using your own name, type **Lastname_Firstname_5C_Celtic_Instruments** and then click **Apply to All**.

11 Click the **FILE tab**, and then in the lower right portion of the screen, click **Show All Properties**. In the **Tags** box, type **Celtic, instruments, Ireland, Scotland** and in the **Subject** box type your course name and section number. In the **Author** box, right-click the existing author name, click **Edit Property**, replace the existing text with your first and last name, click outside the text box to deselect, and then click **OK**.

12 **Save** the presentation. Print **Handouts 4 Slides Horizontal**, or submit your presentation electronically as directed by your instructor. **Exit** PowerPoint.

END | You have completed Project 5C

CHAPTER REVIEW

Apply 5B skills from these Objectives:

6 Create a Photo Album

7 Edit a Photo Album and Add a Caption

8 Crop a Picture

In the following Skills Review, you will create a photo album for the Cross Oceans Music company. You will insert photos of musicians who record Celtic music and are represented by Cross Oceans. You will add captions and crop unwanted areas of photos. Your completed presentation will look similar to Figure 5.57.

Build from Scratch

PROJECT FILES

For Project 5D, you will need the following files:

New blank PowerPoint presentation
p05D_Mandolinist.jpg
p05D_Flautist.jpg
p05D_Harpist.jpg
p05D_Violinist.jpg
p05D_Bagpiper.jpg

You will save your presentation as:

Lastname_Firstname_5D_Celtic_Album.pptx

PROJECT RESULTS

FIGURE 5.57

(Project 5D Celtic Album continues on the next page)

CHAPTER REVIEW

1 Start PowerPoint, and then click **Blank Presentation**. Click the **INSERT tab**. In the **Images group**, click the **Photo Album button arrow**, and then click **New Photo Album**.

2 In the **Photo Album** dialog box, in the **Album Content** area, under **Insert picture from**, click **File/Disk** to display the **Insert New Pictures** dialog box. Navigate to the location where your student files are stored, click **p05D_Violinist.jpg**, and then click **Insert**.

3 Using the technique you practiced, insert the following pictures into the photo album in this order: **p05D_Flautist.jpg**, **p05D_Harpist.jpg**, **p05D_Mandolinst. jpg**, and **p05D_Bagpiper.jpg**.

4 Under **Album Layout**, click the **Picture layout arrow** to display the selections. Click **1 picture**.

5 Click the **Frame shape arrow** to display the frame shape selections, and then click **Rounded Rectangle**.

6 To the right of the **Theme** box, click the **Browse** button to display the **Choose Theme** pane. Click **Wisp**, and then click **Select**. In the **Photo Album** dialog box, click **Create**.

7 Press **F12** to display the **Save As** dialog box, and then navigate to the location where you are storing your projects for this chapter and save the file as **Lastname_Firstname_5D_Celtic_Album**

8 Click **Slide 1** in the Slides and Outline pane, if necessary. Right-click to display the shortcut menu.

  a. Click **Format Background** to display the Format Background pane.

  b. Select the **Gradient Fill** option, if necessary, and then click the **Type arrow** and select **Rectangular**.

  c. Click **Color**. In the ninth column, first row, click **Olive Green, Accent 5**.

  d. Click the **Direction** button. Locate and click **From Bottom Left Corner**.

  e. Under Gradient stops, click **Stop 2**. In the **Position** spin box, type **75** and then press **Enter**. Click **Apply to All**, and then **Close** the pane.

9 Position the insertion point to the left of *Photo Album*.

  a. Type **Celtic Music** and then press **Enter**.

  b. Select both lines of the title—*Celtic Music Photo Album*. Click the **FORMAT tab**. In the **WordArt Styles group**, click the **Text Fill arrow**, and then click the ninth column, last item—**Olive Green, Accent 5, Darker 50%**.

  c. Click **Text Effects**, point to **Shadow**, and then under **Perspective**, click **Perspective Diagonal Upper Left**.

  d. Increase the size of the title to **72 pts**.

10 Delete the subtitle text and replace it with **Cross Oceans Music**

11 Click the **INSERT tab**. In the **Images group**, click the **Photo Album button arrow**, and then click **Edit Photo Album**. In the **Edit Photo Album** dialog box, in the **Album Content** area, under **Picture Options**, select the **Captions below ALL pictures** check box, and then click **Update**.

12 Make **Slide 2** the active slide, and then click to select the caption. Select the text *p05D_* and then press **Delete**. The caption should now read *Violinist*

13 Using the technique you practiced, edit the captions for **Slides 3**, **4**, **5**, and **6** as follows:

  Flautist

  Harpist

  Mandolinist

  Bagpiper

14 On **Slide 6**, click two times to select the **picture of the Bagpiper**. On the **PICTURE TOOLS FORMAT tab**, in the **Size group**, click **Crop**.

  a. Drag the right middle cropping handle left to the **1.5-inch mark to the right of 0** on the **horizontal ruler**.

  b. Repeat the procedure to crop the left side to the **1.5-inch mark to the left of 0** on the **horizontal ruler**.

  c. Click **Crop** to turn off cropping.

15 Click the **SLIDE SHOW tab**. In the **Start Slide Show group**, click **From Beginning**. View the slide show, and then press **Esc** to exit.

(Project 5D Celtic Album continues on the next page)

CHAPTER REVIEW

16 On the **INSERT tab**, in the **Text group**, click the **Header & Footer** button to display the **Header and Footer** pane. Click the **Notes and Handouts tab**. Under **Include on page**, select the **Date and time** check box, and then select **Fixed**. If necessary, clear the **Header** check box, and then select the **Page number** and **Footer** check boxes. In the **Footer** box, using your own name, type **Lastname_ Firstname_5D_Celtic_Album** and then click **Apply to All**.

17 Click the **FILE tab**, and then in the lower right portion of the screen, click **Show All Properties**. In the **Tags** box, type **Celtic, music, album** and in the **Subject** box type your course name and section number. In the **Author** box, right-click the existing author name, click **Edit Property**, replace the existing text with your first and last name, click outside the text box to deselect, and then click **OK**.

18 **Save** the presentation. Print **Handouts 4 Slides Horizontal**, or submit your presentation electronically as directed by your instructor. Then **Close** your presentation, **Close** the **Blank Presentation**, and then **Exit** PowerPoint.

END | You have completed Project 5D

CONTENT-BASED ASSESSMENTS

Mastering PowerPoint　Project 5E Reggae Music

In the following Mastering PowerPoint project, you will modify pictures in a presentation used in educational seminars hosted by Cross Oceans Music. The presentation highlights Reggae music and its roots in jazz and rhythm and blues. You will add WordArt and a merged shape to the presentation. You will also add an audio file that represents this genre of music and format it to play across the slides in the slide show. You will also add a video file. Your completed presentation will look similar Figure 5.58.

Apply 5A skills from these Objectives:

1 Use Picture Corrections
2 Add a Border to a Picture
3 Change the Shape of a Picture
4 Add a Picture to a WordArt Object and Merge Shapes
5 Enhance a Presentation with Audio and Video

PROJECT FILES

For Project 5E, you will need the following files:

p05E_Reggae_Music.pptx
p05E_Reggae.wav
p05E_Music.jpg
p05_Music_Video.avi

You will save your presentation as:

Lastname_Firstname_5E_Reggae_Music.pptx

PROJECT RESULTS

luisapuccini/Fotolia; Alex White/Fotolia; satori/Fotolia; Lisa F. Young/Fotolia; megastocker/Fotolia; Pookeyman/Fotolia; miketea88/Fotolia

FIGURE 5.58

(Project 5E Reggae Music continues on the next page)

CONTENT-BASED ASSESSMENTS

1 Start PowerPoint. Locate and open the file **p05E_Reggae_Music**. Save the file in your chapter folder, using the file name **Lastname_Firstname_5E_Reggae_Music**

2 On the **title slide,** click to select the picture, click the **FORMAT tab,** and then set the **Sharpness** to **25%.** Set **Brightness** to **+20%** and **Contrast** to **-20%.**

3 Make **Slide 2** the active slide, and then click to select the **picture of the Jamaican flag.** On the **FORMAT tab,** click the **Crop button arrow,** and then crop the picture to the **Wave** shape, which is under Stars and Banners, in the second row, seventh shape.

4 Make **Slide 3** the active slide. Click the **picture,** and then send the picture to the back. In the **Adjust group,** click **Color,** and then under **Recolor,** in the first row, fourth column, click **Washout.**

5 Make **Slide 4** the active slide, and then click the picture. Set the **Brightness** to **+20%** and the **Contrast** to **+20%.** Change the picture border to **Turquoise, Accent 3, Darker 50%.** Crop the picture to an **Oval** shape.

6 Make **Slide 5** the active slide, and then click to select the **picture of the flag of Trinidad.** Use **Crop to Shape,** and then under **Stars and Banners,** change the picture shape to **Double Wave,** which is in the second row, the last shape.

7 Make **Slide 6** the active slide, and then click to select the picture. Set the **Brightness** to **25%,** and then **Send to Back.**

8 Make the **title slide** the active slide. Display the **Insert Audio** dialog box. From your student files, insert the audio file **p05E_Reggae.wav.** On the **PLAYBACK tab,** set the audio to **Hide During Show** and to start **Automatically.**

9 Make **Slide 7** the active slide. Insert **WordArt** with **Fill - Aqua, Accent 2, Outline - Accent 2.** Type **Reggae Music** on one line, type **Presented by** on the next line, and then type **Cross Oceans Music** on the third line. Change the **Font Color** to **Turquoise, Accent 3, Darker 25%.** With the **WordArt** selected, on the **DRAWING TOOLS FORMAT tab,** in the **Size group,** click the **Size and Position** dialog launcher. Click **POSITION** to expand, if necessary. Change the **Horizontal position** to **3** and the **Vertical position** to **1 Close** the Format Shape pane.

10 With **Slide 7** as the active slide, with **WordArt** selected, use **Shape Fill** to insert from your data files the picture **p05E_Music.jpg.** On the **PICTURE TOOLS FORMAT tab,** recolor the picture to **Aqua, Accent color 2 Light.** Set the **Sharpness** at **-100%.**

11 In the location where your data files are stored, locate **p05_Music_Video.avi,** and then copy it into your **PowerPoint Chapter 5** folder.

12 With **Slide 7** as the active slide, from your data files, insert **p05_Music_Video.avi** as a linked video. On the **PLAYBACK tab,** select the check boxes for **Play Full Screen** and **Hide While Not Playing.** On the **ANIMATIONS tab,** set a trigger for the video to play **On Click of Rectangle 3,** which is the WordArt shape. If necessary, use the **Selection** pane to identify the WordArt rectangle for the trigger. Right-click, and then click **Size and Position** to display the **Format Video** pane. Change the **Horizontal position** to **.05** and **Vertical position** to **4** Deselect the video. **Close** the Format Video pane.

13 With **Slide 7** selected, at the bottom of the slide, hold down the Ctrl key and click to select the **three turquoise shapes of the drum and each drum stick. Merge** the shapes using the **Union** option. Display the **Format Shape** pane. Click **POSITION** to expand, if necessary. Change the **Horizontal position** to **5.5** and the **Vertical position** to **4.5 Close** the **Format Shape** pane. Click to deselect the shape.

14 Start the slide show from the beginning. Listen for the audio file, and then click the **WordArt** on **Slide 7** to view the video.

15 Insert a footer on the notes and handouts, which includes a fixed date and time, the page number, and the file name.

16 Click the **FILE tab,** and then in the lower right portion of the screen, click **Show All Properties.** In the **Tags** box, type **Reggae, music** and in the **Subject** box type your course name and section number. In the **Author** box, right-click the existing author name, click **Edit Property,** replace the existing text with your first and last name, click outside the text box to deselect, and then click **OK.**

17 **Save** the presentation. Print **Handouts 4 Slides Horizontal,** or submit your presentation electronically as directed by your instructor. **Close** your presentation and **Exit** PowerPoint.

END | You have completed Project 5E

CONTENT-BASED ASSESSMENTS

Mastering PowerPoint   Project 5F CD Cover

In the following Mastering PowerPoint project, you will create a photo album of pictures of island settings for a CD entitled *Reggae Revisited*. One of these cover designs will be chosen by Cross Oceans Music to be the cover of the soon-to-be-released CD of Reggae and Jamaican music. Your completed presentation will look similar to Figure 5.59.

Apply 5B skills from these Objectives:

6 Create a Photo Album

7 Edit a Photo Album and Add a Caption

8 Crop a Picture

PROJECT FILES

For Project 5F, you will need the following files:

Build from Scratch

New blank PowerPoint presentation
p05F_Island1.jpg
p05F_Island2.jpg
p05F_Island3.jpg
p05F_Island4.jpg
p05F_Island5.jpg

You will save your presentation as:

Lastname_Firstname_5F_CD_Cover.pptx

PROJECT RESULTS

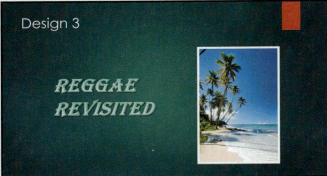

pavel Chernobrivets/Fotolia; PHB.cz/Fotolia; efired/Fotolia

FIGURE 5.59

(Project 5F CD Cover continues on the next page)

CONTENT-BASED ASSESSMENTS

1 Start a new **Blank Presentation** in PowerPoint. Click the **INSERT tab**. In the **Images group**, click the **Photo Album button arrow**, and then click **New Photo Album**.

2 From the student data files, insert the following pictures into the photo album: **p05F_Island1.jpg**, **p05F_Island2.jpg, p05F_Island3.jpg, p05F_Island4.jpg**, and **p05F_Island5.jpg**. In the **Picture layout** list, select **1 picture**. Select the **Ion** theme. **Create** a new **Photo Album**.

3 **Edit** the **Photo Album**, and remove the last two pictures, **p05F_Island4** and **p05F_Island5**, from the album. Change the **Picture layout** to **1 picture with title** and the **Frame shape** to **Simple Frame, White**.

4 Save the file in your chapter folder, using the file name **Lastname_Firstname_5F_CD_Cover**

5 Make the **title slide** the active slide. Change the subtitle text to **Cross Oceans Music** Apply **Bold**, and then change the font size to **24**.

6 Select the title text, *Photo Album*, and then change the font size to **48**. Delete the title text, *Photo Album*, and type **Design Entries for CD Cover** Press [Enter], and then type **Reggae & Jamaican Music** With both lines selected, on the **FORMAT tab**, in the **WordArt Styles group**, click the **More** button. In the second row, click the third style—**Gradient Fill – Green, Accent 4, Outline – Accent 4**.

7 Make **Slide 2** active. Change the title to **Design 1** Right-click the picture, and then click **Size and Position**. On the **Format Picture** pane, change the **Horizontal position** to **2** and the **Vertical position** to **2**.

8 Insert a text box in the blank area to the right of the picture. In the text box, type **Reggae** press [Enter], and then type **Revisited** Change the font to **Bauhaus 93** and the font size to **72**. On the **Format Shape** pane, change the **Horizontal position** to **7** and the **Vertical position** to **3**.

9 Make **Slide 3** active. Change the title to **Design 2** Select the picture, and then on the **Format Picture** pane, change the **Horizontal position** to **8** and the **Vertical position** to **2**.

10 Insert a text box in the blank area to the left of the picture. In the text box, type **Reggae** press [Enter], and then

type **Revisited** Change the font to **Brush Script MT** and the font size to **88**. Apply **Bold** and **Text Shadow**. On the **Format Shape** pane, change the **Horizontal position** to **2** and the **Vertical position** to **2.5**.

11 Make **Slide 4** active, and then change the title to **Design 3** Select the picture, and on the **Format Picture** pane, change the **Horizontal position** to **8** and the **Vertical position** to **2**.

12 Insert a text box in the middle of the slide, to the left of the picture. In the text box, type **Reggae** press [Enter], and then type **Revisited** Change the font to **Algerian** and the font size to **60**. Apply **Bold**, **Italic**, and **Text Shadow**. With the text box selected, on the **FORMAT tab**, in the **WordArt Styles group**, click **More**, and then in the second row, click the third column—**Gradient Fill - Green, Accent 4, Outline - Accent 4**. Select the **text box**, and then on the **Format Shape** pane, change the **Horizontal position** to **2** and the **Vertical position** to **3**.

13 Make **Slide 2** the active slide. Select the picture. On the **FORMAT tab**, click the **Crop** button, and then drag the left middle cropping handle to the **4-inch mark to the left of 0** on the **horizontal ruler**. Click outside the picture to deselect.

14 Review your presentation from the beginning.

15 Insert a footer on the notes and handouts, which includes a fixed date and time, the page number, and the file name.

16 Click the **FILE tab**, and then in the lower right portion of the screen, click **Show All Properties**. In the **Tags** box, type **design, CD, entries** and in the **Subject** box type your course name and section number. In the **Author** box, right-click the existing author name, click **Edit Property**, replace the existing text with your first and last name, click outside the text box to deselect, and then click **OK**.

17 **Save** the presentation. Print **Handouts 4 Slides Horizontal**, or submit your presentation electronically as directed by your instructor. **Close** your presentation, **Close** the **Blank Presentation**, and then **Exit** PowerPoint.

END | You have completed Project 5F

CONTENT-BASED ASSESSMENTS

Mastering PowerPoint Project 5G Jazz Origins and Percussion Album

Build from Scratch

In the following Mastering PowerPoint project, you will edit a short presentation about the origins and elements of jazz by changing the brightness, contrast, and shape of pictures and adding a border and merging a shape. You will also format the presentation to play a short jazz video across slides during the slide show. Finally, you will create a photo album showing some of the percussion instruments used in Cross Oceans Music jazz recordings. The album will contain an audio clip of music. Your completed presentations will look similar to Figure 5.60.

PROJECT FILES

For Project 5G, you will need the following files:

Presentation:
p05G_Jazz_Origins.pptx
p05_Music_Video.avi

Photo Album:
New blank PowerPoint presentation
p05G_Drums1.jpg
p05G_Drums2.jpg
p05G_Drums3.jpg
p05G_Drums4.jpg
p05G_Drums.wav

You will save your presentations as:

Lastname_Firstname_5G_Jazz_Origins.pptx
Lastname_Firstname_5G_Percussion_Album.pptx

PROJECT RESULTS

FIGURE 5.60

(Project 5G Jazz Origins and Percussion Album continues on the next page)

CONTENT-BASED ASSESSMENTS

1 Start PowerPoint. Locate and open the file **p05G_Jazz_Origins**, and then save the file as **Lastname_Firstname_5G_Jazz_Origins**

2 On **Slide 1**, insert the audio **p05G_Jazz.wav**. Move the audio file icon below the subtitle on the slide. Change to **Start Automatically** and **Hide During Show**. View the slide show **From Beginning** and test the sound.

3 On **Slide 2**, change the picture color to **Blue, Accent color 1 Light**, found under **Recolor** in the third row. **Crop** the picture to a **Rounded Rectangle** shape, found under **Rectangles**. Apply a **Picture Border—Blue, Accent 1**, found in the first row, fifth column. Set the border weight (also known as width) to **4 ½ pt**.

4 On **Slide 3**, on the picture, change the **Picture Effects** to **Soft Edges, 25 Point**.

5 Display **Slide 4**. On the **picture**, apply **+20% Brightness**. Change the picture shape to **Flowchart: Alternate Process**, found under **Flowchart**, in the first row. Add a picture border that is **Dark Blue, Background 2, Darker 50%**, found in the third column, last row of the gallery. Set the border weight (also known as width) to **2¼ pt**.

6 On **Slide 5**, at the bottom of the slide, hold down the [Ctrl] key, and then click to select the four blue shapes of the banner and stars. **Merge Shapes** using **Union** style. Right-click and then click **Size and Position** to display the **Format Shape** pane. Change the **Horizontal position** to **5.25** and the **Vertical position** to **6.0**.

7 With **Slide 5** selected, insert as a linked video **p05_Music_Video.avi**. Set it to play **Automatically, Hide While Not Playing**, and **Play Full Screen**. View your presentation from the beginning.

8 Insert a footer on the notes and handouts, which includes a fixed date and time, the page number, and the file name.

9 Click the **FILE tab**, and then in the lower right portion of the screen, click **Show All Properties**. In the **Tags** box, type **jazz, origins** and in the **Subject** box type your course name and section number. In the **Author** box, right-click the existing author name, click **Edit Property**, replace the existing text with your first and last name, click outside the text box to deselect, and then click **OK**.

10 **Save** the presentation. Print **Handouts 6 Slides Horizontal**, or submit your presentation electronically as directed by your instructor. **Close** your presentation.

11 Start PowerPoint, if necessary. Start a new **Blank Presentation**, and insert a **New Photo Album**. From the student data files, insert the following pictures into the photo album: **p05G_Drums1.jpg, p05G_Drums2.jpg, p05G_Drums3.jpg**, and **p05G_Drums4.jpg**.

12 Set the **Picture layout** to **Fit to Slide**. Do not add a theme so the default theme will be applied. Click to select the box **ALL pictures black and white**, and then create the photo album. In the location where you are storing your projects, save the file as **Lastname_Firstname_5G_Percussion_Album**

13 Make **Slide 1** the active slide. Replace the title—*Photo Album*—with **Jazz Percussion Instruments** Select the title, and then apply **Bold** and **Italics**.

14 Click to select the subtitle. Delete the subtitle text and replace it with **Cross Oceans Music**

15 On **Slide 1**, insert the audio file **p05G_Drums.wav**. Move the audio file icon below the subtitle on the slide. Change to **Start Automatically, Play Across Slides** and **Hide During Show**. View the slide show **From Beginning** and test the sound.

16 Insert a footer on the notes and handouts, which includes a fixed date and time, the page number, and the file name.

17 Click the **FILE tab**, and then in the lower right portion of the screen, click **Show All Properties**. In the **Tags** box, type **jazz, percussion** and in the **Subject** box type your course name and section number In the **Author** box, replace the existing text with your first and last name, if necessary.

18 **Save** the presentation. Print **Handouts 6 Slides Horizontal**, or submit your presentation electronically as directed by your instructor.

19 **Close** the presentation, and then **Exit** PowerPoint. Submit your work as directed for both **Lastname_Firstname_5G_Jazz_Origins** and **Lastname_Firstname_5G_Percussion_Album**.

END | You have completed Project 5G

CONTENT-BASED ASSESSMENTS

Apply a combination of the 5A and 5B skills.

GO! Fix It　Project 5H Caribbean Music and Strings Album　**Online**

Build from
Scratch

GO! Make It　Project 5I Salsa Music and Latin Album　**Online**

Build from
Scratch

GO! Solve It　Project 5J Flamenco Music and Brass Album　**Online**

Build from
Scratch

GO! Solve It　Project 5K New Age Music and Asian Album

PROJECT FILES

For Project 5K, you will need the following files:

Presentation:
p05K_NewAge_Music.pptx
p05K_Piano.wav
p05_Music_Video.avi

Photo Album:
New blank PowerPoint presentation
p05K_Cymbals.jpg
p05K_Flute.jpg
p05K_Hand_Drum.jpg
p05K_Lute.jpg

You will save your presentations as:

Lastname_Firstname_5K_NewAge_Music.pptx
Lastname_Firstname_5K_Asian_Album.pptx

In this presentation project, you will modify a short presentation that describes the elements of New Age music and create a photo album on Asian music. You will demonstrate your knowledge of the skills you have covered in this chapter.

Open **p05K_NewAge_Music**, and then save it as **Lastname_Firstname_5K_NewAge_Music** Improve the presentation by modifying the photos in the slides. Add the provided audio and video files and set the playback options.

Using the graphic files provided, create a photo album to highlight Asian musical instruments, and add captions or titles, if necessary. Save the album as **Lastname_Firstname_5K_Asian_Album**

For both presentations, insert a header and footer on the Notes and Handouts that includes the fixed date and time, the page number, and a footer with the file name. Add your name, course name and section number, and appropriate tags to the Properties. Print Handouts 6 slides per page or submit electronically as directed by your instructor.

(Project 5K New Age Music and Asian Album continues on the next page)

CONTENT-BASED ASSESSMENTS

GO! Solve It   Project 5K New Age Music and Asian Album (continued)

Performance Level

Performance Criteria		Exemplary	Proficient	Developing
	Modified photos in NewAge_Music.	Used a variety of picture corrections, shapes, and borders that enhanced the presentation.	Used some picture corrections, shapes, and borders to enhance the presentation.	Used few or no picture corrections, shapes, and borders to enhance the presentation.
	Added audio and video files and applied playback options.	Inserted audio and video files in appropriate places and applied playback options. Both played correctly. May have used a trigger.	Inserted the audio, but either the playback options were not set or the audio did not play back correctly. May have used a trigger.	Inserted the audio, but the playback options were not set and the audio did not play back correctly.
	Created a photo album—Asian Album, inserted pictures, added appropriate captions or titles.	The photo album had a theme, and the pictures were inserted. Used captions and titles as necessary and completed title slide.	The pictures were inserted, but there was no theme. Presentation and captions lacked consistency.	The photo album was not created.

END | You have completed Project 5K

OUTCOMES-BASED ASSESSMENTS

RUBRIC

The following outcomes-based assessments are *open-ended assessments*. That is, there is no specific correct result; your result will depend on your approach to the information provided. Make *Professional Quality* your goal. Use the following scoring rubric to guide you in *how* to approach the problem and then to evaluate *how well* your approach solves the problem.

The *criteria*—Software Mastery, Content, Format and Layout, and Process—represent the knowledge and skills you have gained that you can apply to solving the problem. The *levels of performance*—Professional Quality, Approaching Professional Quality, or Needs Quality Improvements—help you and your instructor evaluate your result.

	Your completed project is of Professional Quality if you:	Your completed project is Approaching Professional Quality if you:	Your completed project Needs Quality Improvements if you:
1-Software Mastery	Choose and apply the most appropriate skills, tools, and features and identify efficient methods to solve the problem.	Choose and apply some appropriate skills, tools, and features, but not in the most efficient manner.	Choose inappropriate skills, tools, or features, or are inefficient in solving the problem.
2-Content	Construct a solution that is clear and well organized, contains content that is accurate, appropriate to the audience and purpose, and is complete. Provide a solution that contains no errors in spelling, grammar, or style.	Construct a solution in which some components are unclear, poorly organized, inconsistent, or incomplete. Misjudge the needs of the audience. Have some errors in spelling, grammar, or style, but the errors do not detract from comprehension.	Construct a solution that is unclear, incomplete, or poorly organized; contains some inaccurate or inappropriate content; and contains many errors in spelling, grammar, or style. Do not solve the problem.
3-Format & Layout	Format and arrange all elements to communicate information and ideas, clarify function, illustrate relationships, and indicate relative importance.	Apply appropriate format and layout features to some elements, but not others. Overuse features, causing minor distraction.	Apply format and layout that does not communicate information or ideas clearly. Do not use format and layout features to clarify function, illustrate relationships, or indicate relative importance. Use available features excessively, causing distraction.
4-Process	Use an organized approach that integrates planning, development, self-assessment, revision, and reflection.	Demonstrate an organized approach in some areas, but not others; or, use an insufficient process of organization throughout.	Do not use an organized approach to solve the problem.

OUTCOMES-BASED ASSESSMENTS

Apply a combination of the **5A** and **5B** skills.

Build from
Scratch

GO! Think   Project 5L Ragtime and Woodwinds Music

PROJECT FILES

For Project 5L, you will need the following files:

Presentation:
p05L_Ragtime_Music.pptx
p05_Music_Video.avi
p05L_Entertainer.wav

Photo Album:
New blank PowerPoint presentation
p05L_Bass_Clarinet.jpg
p05L_Bassoon.jpg
p05L_Clarinet.jpg
p05L_Flute.jpg
p05L_Oboe.jpg
p05L_Saxophone.jpg

You will save your presentations as:

Lastname_Firstname_5L_Ragtime_Music.pptx
Lastname_Firstname_5L_Woodwinds_Album.pptx

In this project, you will edit a presentation about the history and structure of Ragtime music. Open **p05L_Ragtime_Music** and save it as **Lastname_Firstname_5L_Ragtime_Music** Modify the images on the slides. Add audio and video to the presentation. Set the audio file to start automatically and play across slides. Set the video to trigger On Click of Title.

Create a photo album using the provided pictures. Rotate, crop, and resize images as needed. Save it as **Lastname_Firstname_5L_Woodwinds_Album** Insert appropriate headers and footers, and then update the Properties on both files. Submit your files as directed.

END | You have completed Project 5L

Build from
Scratch

GO! Think   Project 5M Classical Music and Renaissance Album   Online

Build from
Scratch

You and GO!   Project 5N Swing Origins   Online

Delivering a Presentation

GO! to Work
Video P6

6

POWERPOINT 2013

PROJECT 6A

OUTCOMES
Apply slide transitions and custom animation effects.

OBJECTIVES
1. Apply and Modify Slide Transitions
2. Apply Custom Animation Effects
3. Modify Animation Effects

PROJECT 6B

OUTCOMES
Insert hyperlinks, create custom slide shows, and view presentations.

OBJECTIVES
4. Insert Hyperlinks
5. Create Custom Slide Shows
6. Present and View a Slide Presentation

Kzenon/Fotolia

In This Chapter

Microsoft PowerPoint provides a wide range of tools that can turn a lackluster presentation into one that captivates the attention of the audience. Animation can be applied to individual slides, a slide master, or a custom slide layout. Transitions and other animation effects can be applied to all slides or to selected slides. In addition, you can insert hyperlinks into a presentation to quickly link to a webpage, another slide, or a document. You may also want to create a custom show composed of selected slides. PowerPoint includes an annotation tool that enables you to write or draw on slides during a presentation.

Penn Liberty Motors has one of eastern Pennsylvania's largest inventories of popular new car brands, sport utility vehicles, hybrid cars, and motorcycles. Its sales, service, and finance staff are all highly trained and knowledgeable about Penn Liberty's products, and the company takes pride in its consistently high customer satisfaction ratings. Penn Liberty also offers extensive customization options for all types of vehicles through its accessories division. Custom wheels, bike and ski racks, car covers, and chrome accessories are just a few of the ways Penn Liberty customers make personal statements with their cars.

PROJECT
6A Penn Liberty Motors

PROJECT ACTIVITIES

In Activities 6.01 through 6.08, you will add slide transitions and animation effects to a presentation that outlines the organizational structure and location of Penn Liberty Motors. Your completed presentation will look similar to Figure 6.1.

PROJECT FILES

For Project 6A, you will need the following files:

p06A_Penn_Liberty.pptx
p06A_Tada.wav

You will save your presentation as:

Lastname_Firstname_6A_Penn_Liberty.pptx

PROJECT RESULTS

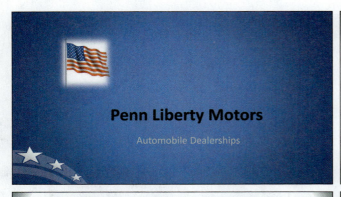

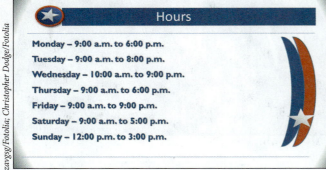
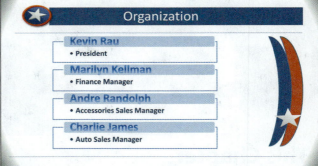

Sarunyu_foto/Fotolia; adisa/Fotolia; muro/Fotolia; zavgsg/Fotolia; Christopher Dodge/Fotolia

FIGURE 6.1 Project 6A Penn Liberty

Video P6-1

Transitions are motion effects that occur when a presentation moves from slide to slide in Slide Show view and affect how the content is revealed. When referring to transitions, ***animation*** is any type of motion or movement that occurs as the presentation moves from slide to slide. Different transitions can be applied to selected slides, or the same transition can be applied to all slides. *Animation* is also used in a second context in this chapter, meaning a special visual effect or sound effect that is added to text or an object.

You can modify the transitions by changing the ***transition speed***, which is the timing of the transition between all slides or between the previous slide and the current slide. It is also possible to apply a ***transition sound*** that will play as slides change from one to the next. Transition sounds are prerecorded sounds that can be applied and will play as the transition occurs.

Setting up a slide show also includes determining how you will advance the slide show from one slide to the next. You can set up the presentation to display each slide in response to the viewer clicking the mouse button or pressing the Enter key. You can also design the slide show so that the slides advance automatically after a set amount of time.

NOTE   Applying Transitions

In this project, you will learn how to apply and modify several kinds of transitions so that you are aware of how they work. When creating a presentation for an audience, however, you do not want to use too many transitions because they can be distracting and may destroy the professional appearance of your slide show. Remember, apply transitions in moderation.

Activity 6.01 | Applying and Modifying Slide Transitions

Slide transitions can be applied to all slides or to specific slides, and different transitions can be applied in one slide show. In this activity, you will modify slide transitions. In this case, modifications include changing the transition speed and sounds to be played during transitions.

1   Start PowerPoint. Locate and open the file **p06A_Penn_Liberty**. In the location where you are saving your work, create a new folder named **PowerPoint Chapter 6** and then **Save** the file as **Lastname_Firstname_6A_Penn_Liberty**

2   Make the **title slide** the active slide. Click the **TRANSITIONS tab**. In the **Transition to This Slide group**, click **More** ⬇ to display the **Transitions** gallery, and then compare your screen with Figure 6.2.

> The Transitions gallery includes the following types of slide transitions: Subtle, Exciting, and Dynamic Content.

FIGURE 6.2

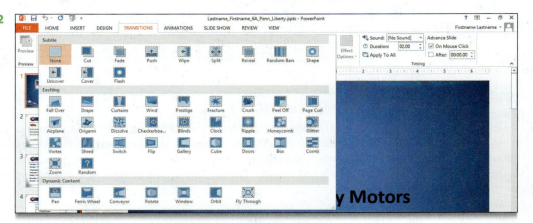

3 Under **Subtle**, click the fifth selection—**Wipe**.

The preview of the Wipe transition plays on Slide 1.

4 In the **Timing group**, click **Apply To All**. On the **TRANSITIONS tab**, in the **Preview group**, click **Preview**. Compare your screen with Figure 6.3.

 **ANOTHER WAY**   To preview a slide transition, in the Slide pane, click the Play Animations icon that displays to the left of the slide thumbnail.

The Wipe transition plays on Slide 1. In the Slides/Outline pane, a Play Animations icon displays next to every slide.

FIGURE 6.3

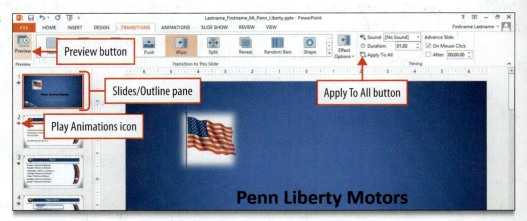

5 Click the **SLIDE SHOW tab**. In the **Start Slide Show group**, click **From Beginning**. Press Enter five times to view the entire slide show, and then press Enter or Esc to return to **Normal** view.

Because you selected Apply To All, the transition occurred between each slide.

6 Make **Slide 2** the active slide. Click the **TRANSITIONS tab**. In the **Transition to This Slide group**, click **More** ⬇.

7 In the **Transitions** gallery, under **Exciting**, in the second row, click **Clock**.

By not clicking Apply To All, the Clock transition will apply to Slide 2 only.

8 Using the technique you practiced, view the slide show **From Beginning**. When you are finished viewing the slide show, press Enter or Esc to return to **Normal** view.

The Clock transition occurs between Slide 1 and Slide 2. The transition between all the other slides remains set to Wipe.

 BY TOUCH   Tap to select the SLIDE SHOW tab. In the Start Slide Show group, tap From Beginning.

More Knowledge   **Animated GIFs and JPGs**

Many images are **GIF** (Graphics Interchange Format) or **JPG** (Joint Photographic Experts Group, also JPEG) files. GIFs are usually drawings, and JPGs are typically photos. GIF files are smaller in size and display faster than JPGs. Because of this, GIFs are frequently used on webpages. The image of the waving flag on the title slide is known as an **animated GIF**. An animated GIF is a file format made up of a series of frames within a single file. Animated GIFs create the illusion of movement by displaying the frames one after the other in quick succession. They can loop endlessly or present one or more sequences of animation and then stop.

9 If necessary, make **Slide 2** the active slide. Click the **TRANSITIONS tab**. In the **Timing group**, click in the **Duration** box, type **3** press Enter, and then compare your screen with Figure 6.4.

The number of seconds it takes to reveal the slide content is now three seconds, which is longer than the default value of one second.

FIGURE 6.4

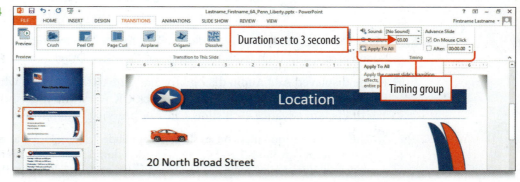

10 In the **Preview group**, click **Preview**.

The transition is displayed one time with the new speed setting. Slide 1 is displayed first and then three seconds later, Slide 2 appears.

11 Make **Slide 5** the active slide. Click the **Duration spin box up arrow** to display **05.00**. On the **SLIDE SHOW tab**, in the **Start Slide Show group**, click **From Beginning**. Click or press Enter to view the slides. Click or press Esc when finished.

Notice that when you clicked Slide 4 to advance to Slide 5, the transition duration was five seconds. Choose a speed that best displays the content.

12 If necessary, make **Slide 5** the active slide. On the **TRANSITIONS tab**, in the **Timing group**, click the **Sound button arrow**, and then compare your screen with Figure 6.5.

From the displayed list, you can choose from various prerecorded sound effects, choose your own sound effect by clicking Other Sound, or choose [No Sound] to remove a sound effect that was applied.

FIGURE 6.5

13 Click to select **Drum Roll**. In the **Preview group**, click **Preview**.

The Drum Roll plays on Slide 4 before Slide 5 is displayed. The overuse of any animation effects or sound effects can distract the audience from the content of the presentation. Keep your audience and your intent in mind. Whereas animations may enhance a light-hearted presentation, they can also trivialize a serious business presentation or cause viewer discomfort.

14 Make the **title slide** the active slide. On the **TRANSITIONS tab**, in the **Timing group**, click the **Sound arrow**, and then from the displayed list, click **Other Sound**.

15 In the displayed **Add Audio** dialog box, navigate to the location where your student files are stored, click **p06A_Tada.wav**, and then click **OK**. View the slide show **From Beginning**. Press Enter or click to advance each slide. Click or press Esc when finished.

The Wipe transition plays on all slides except Slide 2. The Clock transition plays on Slide 2. Sound occurs on Slides 1 and 5. The transition duration on Slide 2 is three seconds, and the transition duration on Slide 5 is five seconds. Transitions affect how the slide reveals on the screen.

16 Save 🖫 your changes.

Activity 6.02 | Advancing Slides Automatically

In this activity, you will customize a slide show by changing the Advance Slide method to advance slides automatically after a specified number of seconds.

1 Make **Slide 2** the active slide. Click the **TRANSITIONS tab**. In the **Timing group**, under **Advance Slide**, clear the **On Mouse Click** check box.

By clearing the On Mouse Click check box, viewers will no longer need to press Enter or click to advance the slide show. The slide show will advance automatically.

2 In the **Timing group**, under **Advance Slide**, click the **After spin box up arrow** to display **00:10.00**. Compare your screen with Figure 6.6.

🔁 **ANOTHER WAY**   To enter the time in the After box, click once in the box to select the current time, type 10, and then press Enter.

The time is entered in number of seconds. This automatic switching of slides is only effective if no one is providing an oral presentation along with the slides.

FIGURE 6.6

3 View the slide show **From Beginning**—press Enter one time to advance the slide show to **Slide 2**. Wait 10 seconds for the third slide to display. When **Slide 3** displays, press Esc.

NOTE   **Previewing Slides**

Previewing a slide will not advance to the next slide. Play the slide show From Beginning or From Current Slide in order to verify the time it takes to display the next slide.

4 ▸ Make **Slide 2** the active slide. On the **TRANSITIONS tab**, in the **Timing group**, change number in the **After** box to **5**. Compare your screen with Figure 6.7.

> If no person is speaking, set the number of seconds to allow people sufficient time to read the content. However, you may need to consider adding time to allow a speaker to make key points.

FIGURE 6.7

After timing changed to 5 seconds

5 ▸ **Save** 💾 your changes.

Objective 2 Apply Custom Animation Effects

Video P6-2

Like other effects that you can customize in PowerPoint, you can customize animation effects. In this context, *animation* refers to a special visual effect or sound effect added to text or an object. You can add animation to bulleted items, text, or other objects such as charts, graphics, or SmartArt graphics.

Animation can be applied as an ***Entrance effect***, which occurs as the text or object is introduced into the slide during a slide show, or as an ***Exit effect***, which occurs as the text or object leaves the slide or disappears during a slide show. For example, bulleted items can fly into, or move into, a slide and then fade away.

Animation can take the form of a ***Motion Paths effect***, which determines how and in what direction text or objects will move on a slide. Examples of an ***Emphasis effect*** include making an object shrink or grow in size, change color, or spin on its center.

The ***Animation Pane*** is the area that contains a list of the animation effects added to your presentation. From this pane, you can add or modify effects.

Activity 6.03 │ Adding Entrance Effects

In this activity, you will add entrance effects to text and objects by making them move in a specific manner as the text or graphic enters the slide.

1 ▸ Make **Slide 3** the active slide, and then click to select the content placeholder. Click the **ANIMATIONS tab**. In the **Advanced Animation group**, click **Add Animation**, and then compare your screen with Figure 6.8. Scroll the list to see all of the animation effects. Refer to Figure 6.9 for more information.

> There are four animation groups—Entrance, Emphasis, Exit, and Motion Paths. You have to scroll the list to see the Motion Paths animations.

FIGURE 6.8

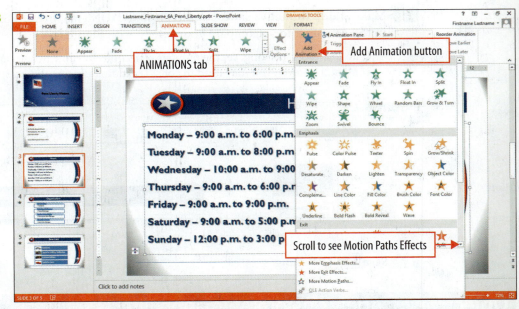

FIGURE 6.9

ANIMATION EFFECTS	
ANIMATION EFFECTS	**EXAMPLES**
Entrance	Fade gradually into focus, fly onto the slide from an edge, or bounce into view
Emphasis	Shrink or grow in size, change color, or spin on its center
Exit	Fly off the slide, disappear from view, or spiral off the slide
Motion Paths	Move up or down, left or right, or in a star or circular pattern

2 ▶ Under **Entrance**, click **Fade**.

Clicking Fade sets the text on the slide to display the various bulleted items one after the other, in order from top to bottom. Choose an animation that enhances the content of the slide.

3 ▶ In the **Advanced Animation group**, click **Animation Pane**, and then compare your screen with Figure 6.10.

The Animation Pane displays with the results of the animation you applied on Slide 3. In this case, the Animation Pane displays with the effect applied to the content placeholder selected. Each item on the slide content placeholder displays with a number next to it to indicate the order in which the items will display.

FIGURE 6.10

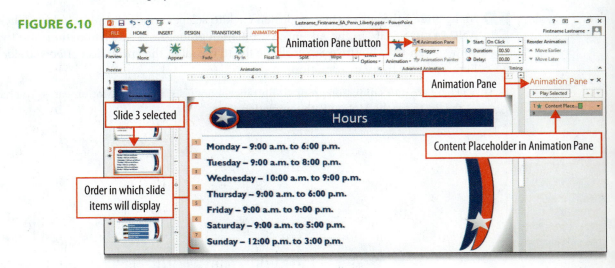

ALERT! **Do You Have Extra Items Displayed in the Animation Pane?**

If you clicked on an effect instead of pointing at it, you will have an extra item in the Animation Pane. Click the unwanted item in the Animation Pane, and then click the arrow and select Remove. If the item arrow does not display, click the correct placeholder on the slide or the item in the Animation Pane to make the item active.

ANOTHER WAY   To remove an effect in the Animation Pane, right-click the effect to display the options, and then select Remove. You can also just click on the effect and press the Delete key.

4 In the **Animation Pane**, below *Content Placeholder*, point to the **expand chevron** to display the ScreenTip *Click to expand contents*. Compare your screen with Figure 6.11.

The *chevron* is a V-shaped pattern that indicates that more information or options are available.

FIGURE 6.11

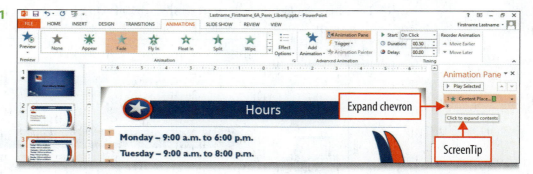

5 Click the **chevron** one time to expand the contents, and then compare your screen with Figure 6.12.

The numbers to the left of the items on the slide correspond with the item numbers in the Animation Pane.

FIGURE 6.12

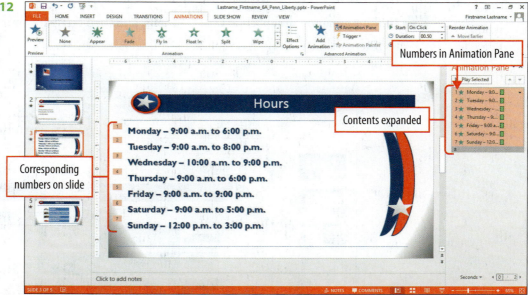

6 ▶ Right-click the **first entrance effect** for the content placeholder, and then, if necessary, click **Show Advanced Timeline.** In the **Animation Pane**, click **Play From** to test the animation.

At the bottom of the Animation Pane, a *timeline* displays the number of seconds the animation takes to complete.

<table>
<tr>
<td>A L E R T !</td>
<td>Did the Timeline Display?</td>
</tr>
</table>

If you cannot see the timeline at the bottom of the Animation Pane, right-click the entrance effect for the content placeholder, and then click Show Advanced Timeline. If the timeline is visible, the option is displayed as Hide Advanced Timeline.

7 ▶ Click the **hide chevron** to hide the contents. Click on **Slide 3**, and then under **Play All**, point to *Content Place…*, read the ScreenTip, *On Click Fade: Content Placeholder 2: Monday – 9:00 a.m. to 6:00…*, and then compare your screen with Figure 6.13.

The ScreenTip identifies the start setting, which is On Click, and the Effect, which is Fade.

FIGURE 6.13

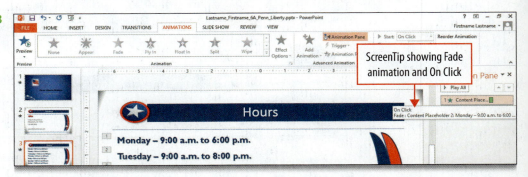

8 ▶ Make **Slide 5** the active slide. Click the **SmartArt graphic** containing the cars. On the **ANIMATIONS tab**, in the **Advanced Animation group**, click **Add Animation**. Under **Entrance**, click **Float In.**

The ANIMATIONS tab is inactive until a slide element is selected.

9 ▶ In the **Animation group**, click **Effect Options**, and then compare your screen with Figure 6.14.

After an animation effect is applied, the Effect Options becomes active. The sequence options are As One Object, All at Once, or One by One.

FIGURE 6.14

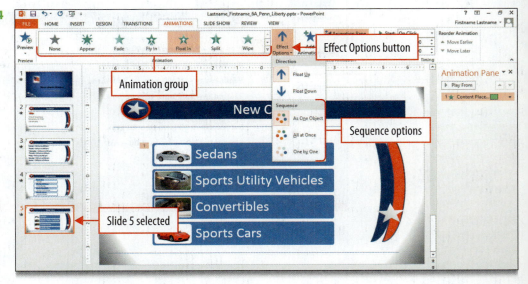

10 Under **Sequence**, click **One by One**.

Clicking One by One sets the shapes in the SmartArt graphic on Slide 5 as individual objects that display one at a time.

11 Make the **title slide** the active slide, and then click to select the title placeholder—*Penn Liberty Motors*. In the **Advanced Animation group**, click **Add Animation**, and then click **More Entrance Effects**. In the **Add Entrance Effect** dialog box, under **Moderate**, scroll if necessary, click **Rise Up**, and then compare your screen with Figure 6.15.

A preview of the Rise Up effect displays on the slide. The Add Entrance Effect dialog box provides additional effects.

FIGURE 6.15

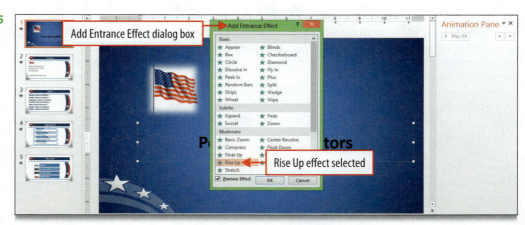

| N O T E | Automatic Preview |

To see the automatic preview of the effect more easily, you may want to move the dialog box to the side of the slide.

12 Click **OK**.

13 Click the **subtitle** placeholder. In the **Advanced Animation group**, click **Add Animation**, and then click **More Entrance Effects**. In the **Add Entrance Effect** dialog box, under **Moderate**, scroll if necessary, and then click **Rise Up**. Click **OK**. Compare your screen with Figure 6.16. In the **Animation Pane**, click **1 Title 1: Penn L…**, and then click **Play From** to test the animation.

The entrance effect for Slide 1 displays in the Animation Pane. The number 1 corresponds with the title placeholder. The number 2 corresponds with the subtitle placeholder. The numbers that appear on the slide in Normal view do not appear when you play the presentation.

FIGURE 6.16

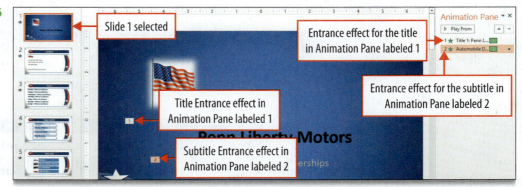

14 Save 💾 your changes.

Activity 6.04 | Adding Emphasis Effects

In this activity, you will add emphasis effects to text and graphics. These effects make the text or graphics move or change in a specified manner when you click the mouse or press Enter while the text or graphic is displayed on the slide. You will also reorder the effects.

1 With the **title slide** as the active slide, click to select the title placeholder—*Penn Liberty Motors*. On the **ANIMATIONS tab**, in the **Advanced Animation group**, click **Add Animation**, and then click **More Emphasis Effects** to display the **Add Emphasis Effect** dialog box.

The Add Emphasis Effect dialog box includes more emphasis effects than the Add Animations gallery and organizes them into groups—Basic, Subtle, Moderate, and Exciting effects. Use this dialog box if you do not find the effect you want in the gallery.

2 In the **Add Emphasis Effect** dialog box, under **Subtle**, click **Pulse**, and then click **OK**. In the **Animation Pane**, click **Play From** to see the **Pulse** effect on the title. Compare your screen with Figure 6.17.

A third item is displayed in the Animation Pane. The first one is for the entrance effect for the title placeholder, Penn Liberty Motors. The second one is for the entrance effect for the subtitle placeholder, Automobile Dealerships. The third one is for the emphasis effect for the title. The Pulse effect for the title is set to occur when the presenter clicks the mouse button. To make an item in the Animation Pane active, click the item or click on the placeholder on the slide. Notice that the numbers to the left of the title and subtitle on the slide correspond with the numbers for the effects in the Animation Pane.

FIGURE 6.17

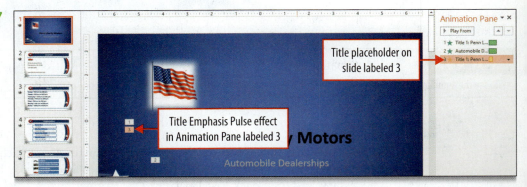

3 On the **SLIDE SHOW tab**, in the **Start Slide Show group**, click **From Current Slide**. Click to see the **title entrance** effect, click to see the **subtitle entrance** effect, and then click to see the **title emphasis** effect. Press Esc.

The sound effect played, the title moved up, the subtitle moved up, and then the title displayed the Pulse emphasis.

4 In the **Animation Pane**, click the third effect, the **emphasis** effect for the title—*3 Title1: Penn L....* At the top of the **Animation Pane**, on the right side, click the **Reorder move up arrow**. Compare your screen with Figure 6.18.

FIGURE 6.18

5 In the **Animation Pane**, click the first effect for the title—*1 Title1: Penn L...*, click **Play From**.

The order that the effects play is changed. The title moved up and displayed with the Pulse emphasis, and then the subtitle displayed.

6 Make **Slide 4** the active slide, and then click to select the title placeholder—*Organization*. Using the technique you practiced, display the **Add Emphasis Effect** dialog box. Under **Subtle**, click **Bold Flash**, and then click **OK**. In the **Animation Pane**, point to the animation to display the ScreenTip *On Click Bold Flash: Title 1: Organization*. Compare your screen with Figure 6.19.

FIGURE 6.19

7 On **Slide 4**, click to select the **SmartArt graphic**. On the **ANIMATIONS tab**, in the **Advanced Animation group**, click **Add Animation**, under **Entrance**, click **Zoom**. In the **Animation group**, click **Effect Options**. Click **Level at Once**. On the **Animation Pane**, click **Play Selected**.

The SmartArt levels display the names and then the organization titles.

8 In the **Animation Pane**, right-click on **Content Place...** and then click **Effect Options**. In the **Zoom** dialog box, click the **SmartArt Animation tab**, select the **Reverse order** check box, and then click **OK**. On the **Animation Pane**, click **Play Selected**.

Because the Reverse check box is selected, the SmartArt levels display the organization titles and then the names.

9 On the **SLIDE SHOW tab**, in the **Start Slide Show group**, click **From Current Slide**. Click to test the title emphasis effect. Click two times to test the **SmartArt Zoom** entrance effect. Click again to display **Slide 5.** When it appears, press Esc.

The title is displayed immediately. After the mouse click, the title blinks once and then returns to normal. The SmartArt levels displayed the organization titles first and then the names.

BY TOUCH Tap the SLIDE SHOW tab. In the Start Slide Show group, tap From Current Slide. Tap to test the title emphasis effect. Tap again to display Slide 5. When it appears, press Esc.

ALERT! **Did the Title Blink More Than Once?**

If the title blinked again on the second mouse click instead of advancing to Slide 5, you have applied the blink emphasis effect more than once. In the Animation Pane, right-click the extra effect, and then select Remove. Test the animation again.

10 Save your changes.

Activity 6.05 | Adding Exit Effects

In this activity, you will add exit effects to text and graphics. These effects make the text or graphics move or change in a specified manner when you click the mouse or press Enter while the text or graphic is displayed on the slide.

1 With the **title slide** as the active slide, click to select the **subtitle** placeholder. On the **ANIMATIONS tab**, in the **Advanced Animation group**, click **Add Animation**. From the displayed list, under **Exit**, scroll, if necessary to see the entire list. In the first row, click the third effect—**Fly Out**.

2 On the **SLIDE SHOW tab**, view the slide show **From Current Slide**. Click to display the title **Rise Up** entrance effect. Continue clicking to see the title **Pulse** emphasis effect, the subtitle **Rise Up** entrance effect, and then the subtitle **Fly Out** exit effect. Press Esc. In the **Animation Pane**, point to the fourth effect to see the ScreenTip *On Click Fly Out: Automobile Dealerships*. Compare your screen with Figure 6.20.

The order in which the effects play is determined by the sequence shown in the Animation Pane.

FIGURE 6.20

Fly Out exit effect added to the subtitle

3 In the **Animation Pane**, right-click the fourth animations effect, which is the subtitle **Fly Out** exit effect. From the options list, select **Remove** to remove the effect.

4 Select the **subtitle** placeholder on the **Slide 1** again. On the **ANIMATIONS tab**, in the **Advanced Animation group**, click **Add Animation**. Click **More Exit Effects**. Under **Moderate**, scroll if necessary, and then click **Sink Down** to see the **Sink Down** exit effect. Notice that the **Preview Effect** check box is selected. Click **OK**. In the **Animation Pane**, point to the fourth effect to see the ScreenTip *On Click Sink Down: Automobile Dealerships*. Compare your screen with Figure 6.21.

In the Animation Pane, the entrance effect for the title is marked with a green star, the emphasis effect for the title is marked with a gold star, the entrance effect for the subtitle is marked with a green star, and the exit effect for the subtitle is marked with a red star. The stars are displayed with different actions to help define the pattern selected. The ScreenTip clarifies what specific effect was applied.

FIGURE 6.21

Title entrance effect
Title emphasis effect
Subtitle entrance effect
Subtitle exit effect

5 View the slide show **From Current Slide**. Click four times to activate the title entrance, the title emphasis, the subtitle entrance, and the subtitle exit effects, and then press Esc.

Slide 1 is displayed with the sound effect. With each click, the title enters in an upward direction, the title blinks, the subtitle enters, and finally the subtitle exits.

6 With **Slide 5** as the active slide, click the **content placeholder** to select the **SmartArt** graphic. On the **ANIMATIONS tab**, click **Add Animation**, and then click **More Exit Effects**. Under **Basic**, click **Wipe**, and then click **OK**. Compare your screen with Figure 6.22.

The first effect in the Animation Pane identifies the entrance effect for the SmartArt. Because there are four items in the SmartArt, the items are numbered 1 through 4 on the slide. The second effect in the Animation Pane identifies the exit effect for the SmartArt. The corresponding numbers on the slide are 5 through 8.

FIGURE 6.22

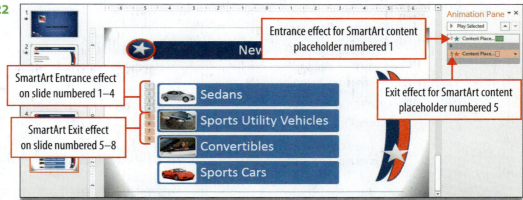

Entrance effect for SmartArt content placeholder numbered 1

SmartArt Entrance effect on slide numbered 1–4

SmartArt Exit effect on slide numbered 5–8

Exit effect for SmartArt content placeholder numbered 5

7 In the **Animation Pane**, click **1 Content Place….** Click **Play Selected** to see the entrance effects. Click **5 Content Place…** and then click **Play Selected** to the exit effects.

Each item in the SmartArt graphic entered separately with the Float In entrance, and then the items exited separately with the Wipe exit.

8 View the slide show **From Current Slide**. After the sound effect and Wipe transition are complete, click **four times** to see the cars enter, and then click **four more times** to see them exit. Click **two more times** to return to **Normal** view.

Because you are viewing the slide as it would be displayed in a slide show, you need to click or press
Enter in order to see the results.

9 Save 💾 your changes.

N O T E | **Selecting Effects**

Entrance, Emphasis, Exit, and Motion Paths effects may be selected from the Add Animation gallery or from the Add Effect dialog boxes. The Add Effect dialog box specific to each type of effect contains additional effects, which are categorized as Basic, Subtle, Moderate, and Exciting.

Activity 6.06 | Adding Motion Paths

Motion paths can also be applied to graphics. Built-in motion paths enable you to make text or a graphic move in a particular pattern, or you can design your own pattern of movement.

1 Make **Slide 2** the active slide. Click to select the **title** placeholder—*Location*. On the **ANIMATIONS tab**, in the **Advanced Animation group**, click **Add Animation**, and then click **More Motion Paths**. In the **Add Motion Path** dialog box, scroll down, and then under **Lines_Curves**, click **Left**, and click **OK**. Compare your screen with Figure 6.23.

The motion path graphic displays on the slide with a green dot at the beginning of the motion path, with a red dot at the end of the motion path, and with a dotted line in between.

FIGURE 6.23

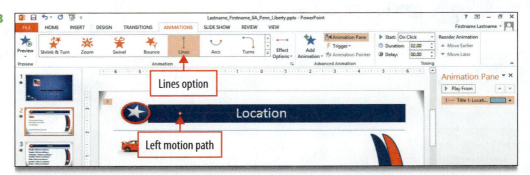

Lines option

Left motion path

2 View the slide show **From Current Slide**. Wait for the title to move to the left. When **Slide 3** displays, press [Esc].

> The transition on Slide 2 displayed first, and then the title moved to the left. Use motion paths very sparingly. They can be distracting, and the audience may watch the path of the text or graphic instead of listening to the presenter.

3 With **Slide 2** selected, in the **Animation Pane**, point to the **Motion Path** effect to display the **ScreenTip**. Compare your screen with Figure 6.24.

> The ScreenTip displays *On Click Left: Title 1: Location*. On the slide, the title placeholder displays a motion path graphic showing the direction of the movement.

FIGURE 6.24

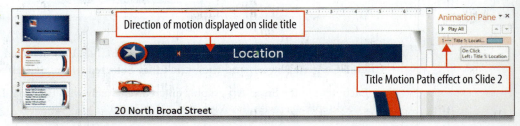

4 Click to select the **red car** picture. On the **ANIMATIONS tab**, in the **Advanced Animation group**, click **Add Animation**, and then click **More Motion Paths**. In the **Add Motion Path** dialog box, scroll down, and then under **Lines_Curves**, click **Right**. Click **OK**. Compare your screen with Figure 6.25.

> A motion path displays. The original car picture stays in place and a "ghost" image displays at the endpoint of the motion path. A green dot displays on the original image, a dotted line displays along the motion path, and a red dot displays on the "ghost" image at the endpoint of the motion path.

FIGURE 6.25

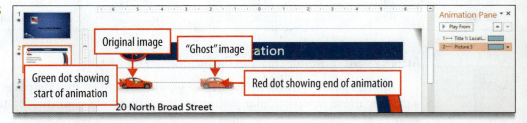

More Knowledge | **Relocating the Endpoint of a Motion Path**

You can change the location of the endpoints of the motion path by selecting and dragging an endpoint to a new location. Hold the [Shift] key to ensure that that the motion path remains in a straight line.

---

5 Save [icon] your changes.

Video P6-3

Entrance, Emphasis, and Exit effects as well as Motion Paths can be modified or customized by changing how they start, the speed at which they occur, and their direction. Effect settings such as timing delays and the number of times an effect is repeated can also be added. Effects can be set to start after a previous effect or simultaneously.

On Click allows you to start the animation effect when you click the slide or a trigger on the slide. On Click also allows you to display animation such as a motion path because the animation is triggered by the mouse click or, in some instances, by pressing Enter. Changing an animation start method to *After Previous* allows the animation effect to start immediately after the previous effect in the list finishes playing. Changing the start method to *With Previous* starts the animation effect at the same time as the previous effect in the list.

Activity 6.07 | Modifying Animation Effects

In this activity, you will modify the start method of some of the animation effects you added. You will also modify their speed and timing.

1 Click the **SLIDE SHOW tab**. In the **Start Slide Show group**, click **From Beginning**. Return to **Normal** view when finished.

On the title slide, you had to click for the title to enter, click for the title to blink, click for the subtitle to enter, and then click for the subtitle to exit. After clicking Slide 1, Slide 2 displayed after three seconds. The title moved to the left and the car picture moved to the right with each click. Slide 3 advanced automatically after five seconds. On Slide 3, the hours of each day of the week displayed one by one as you clicked the mouse or pressed Enter. On Slide 4, the title effect occurred when you clicked the mouse. On Slide 4, the SmartArt levels display the names and then the organization titles with two separate clicks.

On Slide 5, each type of vehicle displayed with separate mouse clicks, and each one exited with separate mouse clicks.

2 Make the **title slide** the active slide, and then click to select the **subtitle** placeholder.

ANOTHER WAY　If animation has been applied to a placeholder or to an object such as a picture or graphic, you can select the object or placeholder by clicking the small number that displays on the slide. This number corresponds with the list of objects in the Animation Pane.

The title slide subtitle is displayed with two numbers. Number 3 represents the entrance effect, and number 4 represents the exit effect. Numbers 1 and 2 are for the title placeholder.

3 In the **Animation Pane**, click on the fourth item in the list to select it, and then right-click the **subtitle Exit** effect, the fourth effect in the list. Compare your screen with Figure 6.26. The Start Options are defined in the table in Figure 6.27.

FIGURE 6.26

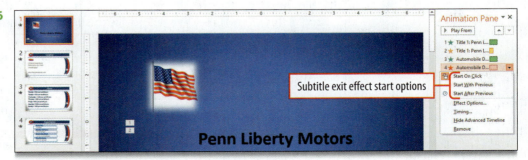

FIGURE 6.27

START OPTIONS	
SCREEN ELEMENT	**DESCRIPTION**
Start On Click	Animation begins when the slide is clicked. Displays with a mouse icon in the option list.
Start With Previous	Animation begins at the same time as the previous effect. One click executes all animation effects applied to the object. Displays with no icon in the option list.
Start After Previous	Animation begins after the previous effect in the list finishes. No additional click is needed. One click executes all animation effects applied to the object. Displays with a clock icon in the option list.

4 ▶ Click **Start After Previous**. View the slide show **From Current Slide**. Click three times to display the title entrance, the title emphasis, and then the subtitle entrance and exit effects. Press ⌨Esc.

🔁 **ANOTHER WAY**   To select a start method, on the ANIMATIONS tab, in the Timing group, click the Start arrow, and then select the method.

By changing On Click to After Previous, it was not necessary to click the mouse to initiate the subtitle exit effects. On the ANIMATIONS tab, in the Timing group, the Start box now displays After Previous. The exit effects applied to the subtitle displayed automatically. Notice that number 4 disappeared from the exit effect in the Animation Pane.

5 ▶ Make **Slide 3** the active slide. In the **Animation Pane**, right-click the **entrance effect** for the content placeholder, and then click **Effect Options**. In the **Fade** dialog box, click the **Timing tab**, and then click the **Start arrow**. Click **After Previous**.

6 ▶ Click the **Duration arrow**, and then select **1 seconds (Fast)**. Compare your screen with Figure 6.28.

The Fade dialog box is a context-sensitive dialog box for the entrance effect applied to the title. The name of the dialog box reflects which effect you are modifying. In this dialog box, you can modify more than one setting.

FIGURE 6.28

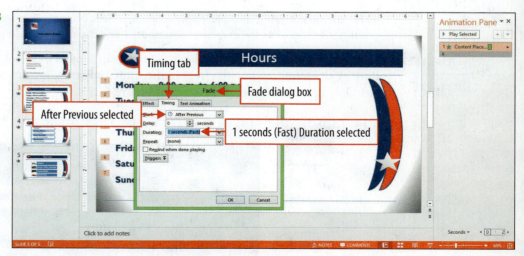

7 Click **OK**, and then view the slide show **From Current Slide**. After the last day displays, press Esc.

Each day displayed automatically without any mouse clicks.

8 Make **Slide 2** the active slide, and then click to select the content placeholder. On the **ANIMATIONS tab**, in the **Advanced Animation group**, click **Add Animation**, and then click **More Entrance Effects**. Under **Basic**, click **Fly In**, and then click **OK**. View the slide show **From Current Slide**, and then press Esc to return to **Normal** view.

The title is displayed and then moved to the left. The red car picture moved to the right. The items in the content placeholder fly in from the bottom one after the other. No mouse clicks were required.

9 Make **Slide 5** the active slide. In the **Animation Pane**, click **Play All**, and then view the slide show **From Current Slide**. After Wipe transition completes, click the mouse eight times. Press Esc.

The Play button displays all animations associated with the slide, in Normal view, regardless of how the animation is set to start. However, From Beginning or From Current Slide plays all animations applied to the slide in Slide Show view, and it displays them the way they will display in a slide show. If you are testing the effects with the Slide Show button and the animation is set to start On Click, you must click the mouse or press Enter to begin the animation.

10 In the **Animation Pane**, right-click the entrance effect for the SmartArt—the first effect. Click **Effect Options** to display the **Float Up** dialog box. On the **Timing tab**, click the **Start arrow**, and then select **After Previous**. Change the **Duration** to **0.5 seconds (Very Fast)**. Click **OK**. View the slide show **From Current Slide**. Press Esc to return to **Normal** view.

The SmartArt items enter without mouse clicks. To view the exit effect, you have to click the mouse for each one. The Duration speed was 0.5 seconds, which may be a little fast for a presentation, but appropriate for you to see the effect. Always choose a time suitable for your audience.

11 In the **Animation Pane**, right-click the exit effect for the SmartArt—the second effect. Click **Effect Options** to display the **Wipe** dialog box. On the **Timing tab**, click the **Start arrow**, and then select **After Previous**. If necessary, change the **Duration** to **0.5 seconds (Very Fast)**. Click **OK**. View the slide show **From Current Slide**. Press Esc.

The SmartArt items entered and exited without mouse clicks. Notice that the pictures entered and exited separately from the descriptions. The Duration speed was 0.5 seconds, which may be a little fast for a presentation, but appropriate for you to see the effect. Always choose a time suitable for your audience.

12 Save 💾 your changes.

Activity 6.08 | Setting Effect Options

In this activity, you will set effect options that include having an animation disappear from the slide after the animation effect, setting a time delay, and animating text.

1 With **Slide 2** as the active slide, in the **Animation Pane**, right-click the third effect, the **entrance effect** for the content placeholder, and then click **Effect Options** to display the **Fly In** dialog box.

The Fly In dialog box has three tabs—Effect, Timing, and Text Animation. On the Effect tab, you can change the Settings and the Enhancements. You can change the direction of the Fly In, add sound, and change the way text is animated.

2 On the **Effect tab**, under **Settings**, click the **Direction arrow**, and then click **From Left**.

3 Under **Enhancements**, click the **After animation arrow**. Compare your screen with Figure 6.29.

You can apply a color change to the animated text or object. You can also automatically hide the animated object after the animation takes place or hide the animated object on the next mouse click. Don't Dim is selected by default.

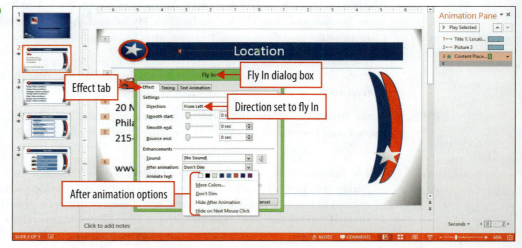

FIGURE 6.29

4 In the row of colors, click the fifth color—**Light Blue**. Click **OK**. View the slide show **From Current Slide**. When **Slide 3** displays, press ⌈Esc⌉.

The animation changes display automatically one at a time.

5 With **Slide 2** selected, in the **Animation Pane**, right-click the effect for the content placeholder, and then click **Effect Options**. In the **Fly In** dialog box, click the **Timing tab**. Click the **Duration arrow**, and then click **2 seconds (Medium)**. Compare your screen with Figure 6.30.

By using the Timing tab, you can change how the animation will start. You can also set a delay, in seconds, from when the slide displays until the text displays. You can select the speed and how many times you would like the animation to repeat. Selecting the *Rewind when done playing* check box will cause the animated text or object to disappear from the slide after the animation is completed, as opposed to remaining on the slide. From this tab you can also set a ***trigger***, which is a portion of text, a graphic, or a picture that, when clicked, produces a result. Recall that in Chapter 5 you practiced inserting sounds into slides and selecting a placeholder or object that would start the sound when clicked. Triggers are created for animation purposes using the same technique.

FIGURE 6.30

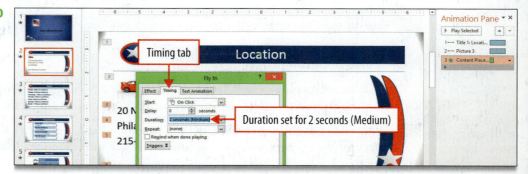

> **NOTE**   **Repeating an Animated List of Items**
>
> In the Fly In dialog box, on the Timing tab, if you elect to repeat a list of items that have animation applied to them, typing a number in the Repeat box will cause each line of text or each bulleted item to repeat before the next item displays. Repeating a list of two or three bulleted items might be used in a presentation as a special effect to emphasize the points but may produce unexpected and unwanted results, so be very cautious about using this option.

6 In the **Fly In** dialog box, click the **Text Animation tab**. Click the **Group text arrow**.

You can treat a list as one object and animate all paragraphs of text simultaneously. If your bulleted list has several levels of bulleted items, you can select how you want to animate the items. Use the Text Animation tab to set a delay in seconds, animate an attached shape, or reverse the order of the items.

7 If necessary, click **By 1st Level Paragraphs**, and then click **OK**.

8 On the **ANIMATIONS tab**, in the **Animation group**, click **Effect Options**, and then compare your screen with Figure 6.31.

🔁 **ANOTHER WAY**   To set the direction and sequence of bullet points, use the Effect Options button in the Animation group.

FIGURE 6.31

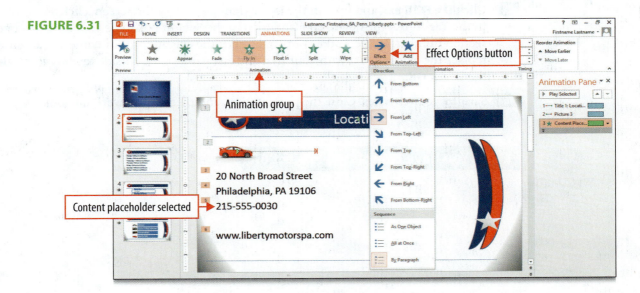

9 Click **From Bottom**. In the **Animation Pane**, click **Play Selected**.

The lines of text on the slide display from the bottom. On the ANIMATIONS tab, in the Animation group, the Effect Options button now points up, which means the items are coming from the bottom and moving upward.

10 With **Slide 2** active, click the **title** placeholder—*Location*. At the top of the **Animation Pane**, on the right side, click the **Reorder down-pointing arrow** two times. Click the **top item** in the list—**1 Picture 3**, and then click **Play From**. Compare your screen with Figure 6.32.

The order of the effects is changed. The car, address, and website are displayed first. The motion effect on the title is displayed last because the order of the effects was changed in the Animation Pane. You can easily reorder the list of animation sequences by selecting a placeholder and then clicking the reorder arrows at the top of the Animation Pane.

🔁 **ANOTHER WAY**   To reorder effects in the Animation Pane, you can click on the effect, and then drag it to the new position.

FIGURE 6.32

11 ▸ Click **2 Content Place…**. Under the **Content Placeholder**, click the **chevron** [icon], and then click **Play Selected** and watch the timeline. Click the **chevron** [icon] to hide the contents.

12 ▸ View the slide show **From Beginning**. Click when necessary to advance the slides.

13 ▸ On the **ANIMATIONS tab**, in the **Advanced Animation group**, click the **Animation Pane** to close the pane.

14 ▸ On the **INSERT tab**, in the **Text group**, click **Header & Footer** to display the **Header and Footer** dialog box. Click the **Notes and Handouts tab**. Under **Include on page**, select the **Date and time** check box, and then select **Fixed**. If necessary, clear the **Header** check box, and then select the **Page number** and **Footer** check boxes. In the **Footer** box, using your own name, type **Lastname_Firstname_6A_Penn_Liberty** and then click **Apply To All**.

15 ▸ Click **the FILE tab**, and then in the lower right portion of the screen, click **Show All Properties**. In the **Tags** box, type **hours, cars** and then in the **Subject** box, type your course name and section number. In the **Author** box, right-click the existing author name, click **Edit Property**, replace the existing text with your first and last name, click outside textbox to deselect, and then click **OK**.

16 ▸ **Save** [icon] your changes. **Close** the presentation, and then **Exit** PowerPoint. Submit your work as directed.

END | You have completed Project 6A

Penn Liberty Motors Advertisement

MyITLab®
Project 6B Training

PROJECT ACTIVITIES

In Activities 6.09 through 6.20, you will insert various types of hyperlinks into a presentation created by Penn Liberty Motors as an advertisement for the company. The focus of the ad is the location of Penn Liberty Motors in Philadelphia. You will create two custom slide shows from a single presentation to appeal to two different audiences. You will also annotate the presentation. Finally, you will organize your slides into sections and print selections from a presentation. Your completed presentation will look similar to Figure 6.33.

PROJECT FILES

For Project 6B, you will need the following files:

p06B_Advertisement.pptx
p06B_Blue_Car.jpg

You will save your files as:

Lastname_Firstname_6B_Advertisement.pptx
Lastname_Firstname_6B_History.docx

PROJECT RESULTS

kamonrat/Fotolia; Africa Studio/Fotolia; Sergey Drozdov/Fotolia; Storm/Fotolia; fergregory/Fotolia

FIGURE 6.33 Project 6B Advertisement

Video P6-4

In the following activities, you will insert hyperlinks into a PowerPoint presentation. Recall that *hyperlinks* are text or objects such as clip art, graphics, WordArt, or pictures that, when clicked, will move you to a webpage, an email address, another document or file, or another area of the same document. In a PowerPoint presentation, hyperlinks can also be used to link to a slide in the presentation, to a slide in a different presentation, or to a custom slide show.

Activity 6.09 │ Inserting a Hyperlink to Webpage

In this activity, you will insert a hyperlink into a slide that will connect to the Penn Liberty Motors webpage.

1 Start PowerPoint. Locate and open the file **p06B_Advertisement**. Navigate to the **PowerPoint Chapter 6** folder you created, and then **Save** the file as **Lastname_Firstname_6B_Advertisement**

2 Make the **Slide 5** the active slide. Click to select the textbox containing the webpage address *www.philadelphiazoo.org* and select the web address text.

3 Click the **INSERT tab**. In the **Links group**, click **Hyperlink** to display the **Insert Hyperlink** dialog box. If necessary, under **Link to**, click **Existing File or Web Page**. Compare your screen with Figure 6.34.

> The Insert Hyperlink dialog box provides an easy and convenient way to insert hyperlinks. You can link to an Existing File or Web Page (the default setting), a Place in This Document, Create New Document, or an E-mail Address. You can also browse the web, browse for a file, or change the text that displays in the ScreenTip.

FIGURE 6.34

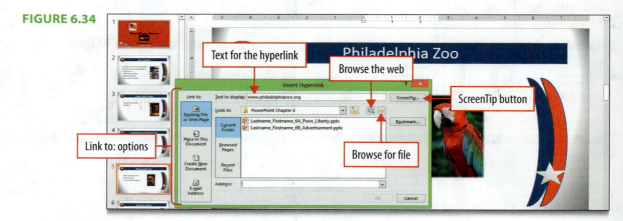

4 Click **ScreenTip**. In the **Set Hyperlink ScreenTip** dialog box, type **Philadelphia Zoo** Compare your screen with Figure 6.35.

FIGURE 6.35

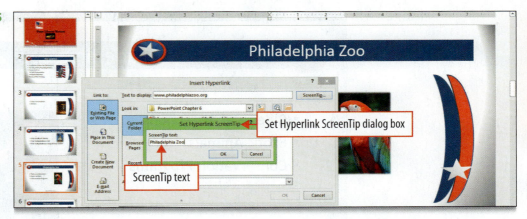

5 ▶ Click **OK**. In the **Address** box, delete the existing text, if any, and then type **http://www. philadelphiazoo.org** Compare your screen with Figure 6.36.

> The text you typed is a *URL*, or *Uniform Resource Locator*. A URL defines the address of documents and resources on the web.

FIGURE 6.36

Understanding Uniform Resource Locators

A Uniform Resource Locator, or URL, generally consists of the protocol and the IP address or domain name. The first part of the address is the ***protocol***. A protocol is a set of rules. ***HyperText Transfer Protocol (HTTP)*** is the protocol used on the World Wide Web to define how messages are formatted and transmitted. It also instructs the ***Web browser*** software how to display webpages. Web browsers, such as Internet Explorer, format webpages so that they display properly. The protocol is followed by a colon (:) and two forward slashes (/). The *www* stands for *World Wide Web*. The World Wide Web is a collection of websites. This is followed by the *domain name*. The domain name is a user friendly name that represents an *IP address*. An IP address, or Internet Protocol address, is a unique set of numbers, composed of a network ID and a machine ID, that identifies the web server where the webpage resides. The *suffix* part of the domain name, the portion after the dot (.), is the *high level domain name (HLDN)* or top level domain name, such as *.com*, *.org*, or *.gov*. This is the upper level domain to which the lower level domain belongs.

6 ▶ Click **OK**.

> The webpage address now displays with an underline and takes on the appearance of a hyperlink.

7 ▶ Start the slide show **From Current Slide**. On **Slide 5**, without clicking, point to the address *www.philadelphiazoo.org*, and then compare your screen with Figure 6.37.

> The Link Select pointer 🖑 displays. A ScreenTip displays with the text you typed.

FIGURE 6.37

BY TOUCH Tap the SLIDE SHOW tab. In the Start Slide Show group, tap From Current Slide. On slide 5, without clicking, point to the address *www.philadelphiazoo.org*.

8 With the **Link Select** pointer [image], click the **hyperlink**.

The webpage is displayed if you are connected to the Internet.

ALERT! **Did the www.philadelphiazoo.org Website Not Appear?**

As of this writing, the www.philadelphiazoo.org website was active. You might receive an error message stating that the Internet server could not be located.

9 Close the webpage, return to PowerPoint, and then press Esc.

10 Right-click anywhere on the URL **www.philadelphiazoo.org**, and then from the displayed shortcut menu, click **Remove Hyperlink**.

11 Click **Slide 9**. Select the text in the photo caption—*Philadelphia Museum of Art*. Click the **INSERT tab**. In the **Links group**, click **Hyperlink**.

12 To the right of the **Look in** box, click **Browse the Web** [image].

If you are connected to the Internet, your selected home page will display. From there, you can browse for a particular page.

13 In your browser address bar, type **www.philamuseum.org** and then press Enter.

14 On the status bar at the bottom of your screen, click **PowerPoint**.

ANOTHER WAY Press Alt + Tab to return to PowerPoint.

The website address is automatically displayed in the Insert Hyperlink dialog box Address box.

15 Click **OK**.

The caption now displays with an underline and takes on the appearance of a hyperlink.

16 Start the slide show **From Current Slide**. Point to the caption—*Philadelphia Museum of Art*, and then compare your screen with Figure 6.38.

It is not necessary to format the webpage hyperlink text in URL format as long as it is linked correctly to the webpage address. Any text or object can serve as a hyperlink.

FIGURE 6.38

17 Click to test your hyperlink. When you are finished, **Close** the webpage and return to PowerPoint. Press [Esc] to return to your presentation screen.

A L E R T !　　**Did the www.philamuseum.org Website Not Appear?**

As of this writing, the **www.philamuseum.org** website was active. You might receive an error message stating that the Internet server could not be located.

---

18 Save 🖫 your changes.

Activity 6.10 | Inserting a Hyperlink to a Slide in Another Presentation

In this activity, you will insert a hyperlink into a presentation that will link to the New Cars slide in a previously created presentation.

1 In **Normal** view, make **Slide 12** the active slide. Select the text in the picture caption—*Penn Liberty Motors New Car Selections*. Click the **INSERT tab**. In the **Links group**, click **Hyperlink** to display the **Insert Hyperlink** dialog box.

2 If necessary, under **Link to**, click to select **Existing File or Web Page**, and then navigate to the **PowerPoint Chapter 6** folder, if necessary, and click **Lastname_Firstname_6A_Penn_Liberty**. Compare your screen with Figure 6.39.

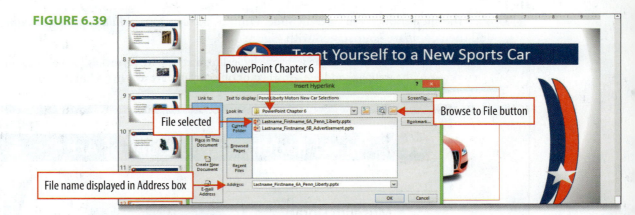

FIGURE 6.39

> PowerPoint Chapter 6
>
> File selected
>
> File name displayed in Address box
>
> Browse to File button

3 ▶ In the **Insert Hyperlink** dialog box, click **Bookmark** to display the **Select Place in Document** dialog box. Compare your screen with Figure 6.40.

> Notice that the slides from Lastname_Firstname_6A_Penn_Liberty are listed.

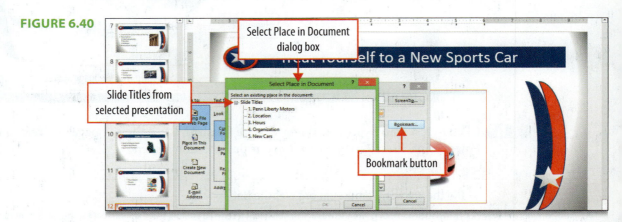

FIGURE 6.40

> Slide Titles from selected presentation
>
> Select Place in Document dialog box
>
> Bookmark button

4 ▶ In the **Select Place in Document** dialog box, click the fifth slide—*New Cars*—and then click **OK**. Compare your screen with Figure 6.41.

> The Address box contains the name of the presentation and the number and title of the slide.

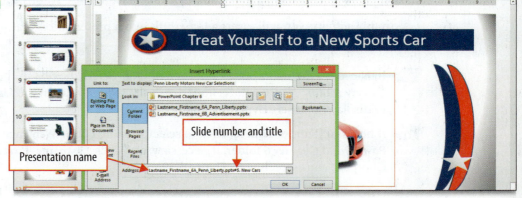

FIGURE 6.41

> Presentation name
>
> Slide number and title

5 ▶ Click **OK**. Click the **SLIDE SHOW tab**, and then in the **Set Up group**, click **Set Up Slide Show**. If necessary, in the **Set Up Show** dialog box, under **Show type**, select the **Presented by a speaker (full screen)** option button. If necessary, under **Advance slides**, click the **Manually** option button. Click **OK**.

6 Start the slide show **From Current Slide**, and then click the hyperlink. The hyperlink will move you to **Slide 5** of the other presentation. When the animations finish playing, press Esc to return to **Slide 12** of the current slide show. Press Esc to return to **Normal** view.

Because you selected Presented by a speaker (full screen), you were able to view Slide 5 from the Penn Liberty presentation.

7 Save 🖫 your changes.

Activity 6.11 | Inserting a Hyperlink to an Email Address

In this activity, you will insert a hyperlink that will open an email client and insert the recipient's email address and subject.

1 Make **Slide 6** the active slide. Select the text *Contact Us*. Click the **INSERT tab**. In the **Links group**, click **Hyperlink**.

2 In the **Insert Hyperlink** dialog box, under **Link to**, click to select **E-mail Address**.

3 In the **E-mail address** box, type **kevin@libertymotors.com**

4 In the **Subject** box, type **Discount Tickets** and then compare your screen with Figure 6.42.

The word *mailto:* displays before the email address. This is an *HTML* attribute instructing the Web browser software that this is an email address. HTML stands for **HyperText Markup Language** and is the language used to code webpages. The recently used email addresses with the associated subject also display for easy selection. You may not have any in your list.

FIGURE 6.42

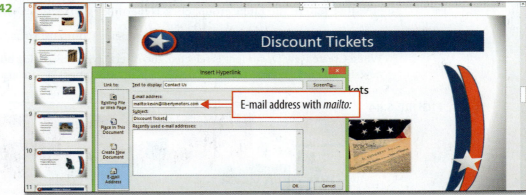

E-mail address with *mailto:*

5 Click **OK**.

6 Start the slide show **From Current Slide**, and when the slide show displays, click the hyperlink. Compare your screen with Figure 6.43.

An email program opens with the email address you typed in the To box. In this case, **Microsoft Outlook** opens. Microsoft Outlook is the program, or **email client**, that facilitates the sending and receiving of electronic messages. This enables you to type an email message and click Send from within the PowerPoint presentation. An email client is a software program that enables you to compose and send an email message.

FIGURE 6.43

7 **Close** the email program without saving changes to the email message, and then press Esc.

8 **Save** 🖫 your changes.

Activity 6.12 │ Inserting a Hyperlink to a New File

In this activity, you will insert a hyperlink that will allow you to create a new file.

1 In **Normal** view, make the **title slide** the active slide. Click to select the image of the flag. Click the **INSERT tab**. In the **Links group**, click **Hyperlink**.

2 Under **Link to**, click to select **Create New Document**. Compare your screen with Figure 6.44.

When Create New Document is selected, the Insert Hyperlink dialog box allows you to create a new document from PowerPoint. The file can be a document, a spreadsheet, or a presentation.

FIGURE 6.44

3 In the **Name of new document** box, substitute your own first name and last name, and then type **Lastname_Firstname_6B_History.docx** Make sure that you type the file extension—.docx

4 If necessary, click **Change**, and then navigate to your **PowerPoint Chapter 6** folder and click **OK**.

In this case, you are creating a Microsoft Word document. The *file extension* or file type identifies the format of the file or the application that was used to create it. If the *full path* listed is incorrect, click Change, and then navigate to the PowerPoint Chapter 6 folder you created. The full path includes the location of the drive, the folder, and any subfolders in which the file is contained.

> **NOTE** **File Name and File Extension**
>
> Typing the file extension with the file name in the Name of new document box is the only way that Windows recognizes which application to start. If you do not type a file extension in the Name of new document box, Windows will assume you are creating a presentation and will start a new PowerPoint presentation because you are currently using PowerPoint.

5 Under **When to edit**, make sure the **Edit the new document now** option button is selected, and then compare your screen with Figure 6.45.

FIGURE 6.45

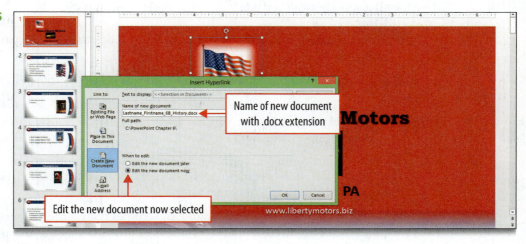

6 Click **OK** to open a new Microsoft Word file named **Lastname_Firstname_6B_History.docx**.

> **ALERT!** **Did You Have Trouble Displaying the Word Document?**
>
> If you made an error in the process of creating the hyperlink to create a new document and tried to do it again, you may find that the Word document does not display. If that happens, look in your chapter folder. If a file named Lastname_Firstname_6B_History.docx displays, delete the file. Return to PowerPoint, and then enter the hyperlink again.

7 Type **Penn Liberty Motors was founded in 1903 by Martin Rau.** Press Enter two times, and then type **Lastname_Firstname_6B_History.docx** Compare your screen with Figure 6.46.

FIGURE 6.46

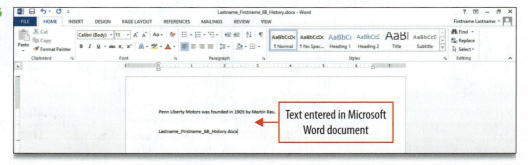

8 Save 🖫 the document, and then **Exit** ⊠ Microsoft Word.

9 Start the slide show **From Current Slide**, and when the slide show displays, click the flag image to display the Word document.

The flag image contains the hyperlink to the Word document.

10 **Exit** Word ⊠. Press ⌈Esc⌉ to return to **Normal** view.

11 Save 🖫 your changes.

Activity 6.13 | Creating an Action Button

An *action button* is a built-in button shape that you can add to your presentation and then assign an action to occur upon the click of a mouse or with a mouse over. It is a type of hyperlink, created by inserting an action button from the list of shapes. Action buttons have built-in actions or links associated with them, or you can change the action that occurs when the action button is clicked. Action buttons are generally used in self-running slide shows.

1 In **Normal** view, make **Slide 5** the active slide. Click the **INSERT tab**. In the **Illustration group**, click **Shapes**.

2 At the bottom of the list, under **Action Buttons**, click the fourth button—**Action Button: End**.

3 Position the ⊞ pointer at the lower right corner—at the **3-inch mark to the right of 0** on the **horizontal ruler** and at the **3-inch mark below 0** on the **vertical ruler**. Click once to display the **Action Settings** dialog box.

The Action Settings dialog box displays. Because the action associated with the End button is to link to the last slide in the presentation, *Last Slide* displays in the Hyperlink to box. The action button on the slide is too large, but you will resize it later.

4 Click the **Hyperlink to: arrow**, and then scroll to review the list of options, which includes other slides in the presentation, a custom show, a URL, other files, and other PowerPoint presentations. Click **Last Slide** to close the list, and then compare your screen with Figure 6.47.

There are two tabs in the Action Settings dialog box. You can set the action to occur on a Mouse Click or *Mouse Over*. Mouse Over means that the action will occur when the presenter points to (hovers over) the action button. It is not necessary to click.

FIGURE 6.47

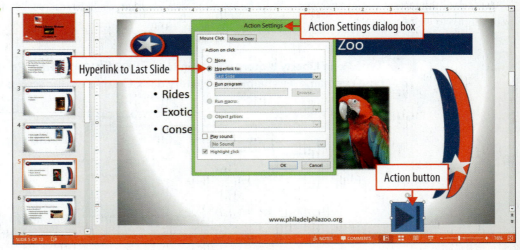

5 ▸ Click the **Mouse Over tab**. Click the **Hyperlink to:** option, click the **Hyperlink to: arrow**, and then select **Last Slide**. Select the **Play sound** check box, click the **Play sound check box arrow**, scroll down, and then click **Chime**. Click **OK**.

6 ▸ With the action button still selected, on the **DRAWING TOOLS FORMAT tab**, in the **Size group**, change the **Shape Height** 🔼 to **0.5"**. Change the **Shape Width** 🔽 to **0.5"**. Compare your screen with Figure 6.48.

The action button is displayed at the bottom right of the slide.

FIGURE 6.48

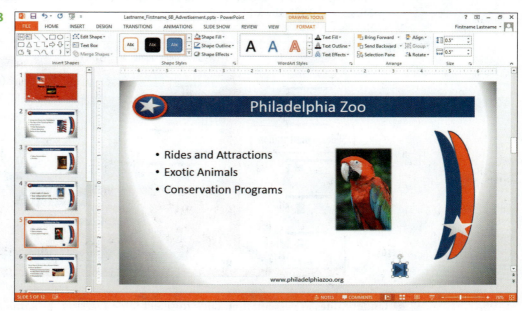

7 ▸ Start the slide show **From Current Slide**, and then move the mouse over the action button.

The chime effect is played when the mouse was over the action button, and then the last slide in the presentation is displayed.

8 ▸ Press [Esc], and then **Save** 💾 your changes.

Objective 5 Create Custom Slide Shows

Video P6-5

A ***custom slide show*** displays only the slides you want to display to an audience in the order you select. You still have the option of running the entire presentation in its sequential order. Custom shows provide you with the tools to create different slide shows to appeal to different audiences from the original presentation.

There are two types of custom shows—basic and hyperlinked. A ***basic custom slide show*** is a separate presentation saved with its own title containing some of the slides from the original presentation. A ***hyperlinked custom slide show*** is a quick way to navigate to a separate slide show from within the original presentation. For example, if your audience wants to know more about a topic, you could have hyperlinks to slides that you could quickly access when necessary.

Activity 6.14 │ Creating a Basic Custom Slide Show

In this activity, you will create basic custom slide shows from an existing presentation. You will then save them as separate custom shows that can be run from the SLIDE SHOW tab.

1 Make the **title slide** the active slide. On the **SLIDE SHOW tab**, in the **Start Slide Show group**, click **Custom Slide Show button arrow**, and then click **Custom Shows** to display the **Custom Shows** dialog box.

2 Click **New** to display the **Define Custom Show** dialog box, In the **Slide show name** box, delete the text, and then type **Historic** Compare your screen with Figure 6.49.

> From the Define Custom Show dialog box, you can name a custom slide show and select the slides that will be included in the slide show. All the slides in the current presentation are displayed in the Slides in presentation box. The slides you want to include in the custom show will display in the Slides in custom show box.

FIGURE 6.49

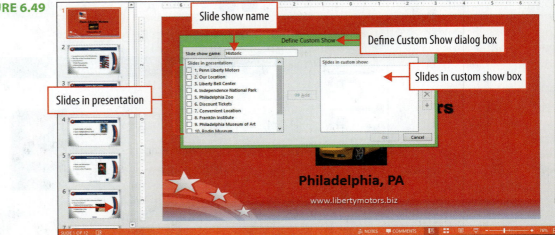

3 Under **Slides in presentation**, click to select **Slide 1**. Using the same technique, click to select **Slides 2, 3, 4, 5**, and **6**. Compare your screen with Figure 6.50.

FIGURE 6.50

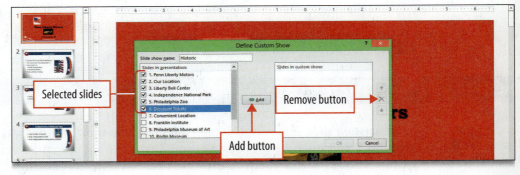

4 Click **Add**. Under **Slides in presentation**, click to select **Slide 12** and add it to the custom show. Compare your screen with Figure 6.51.

> Slide 12 is renumbered as Slide 7 in the custom show.

FIGURE 6.51

Slide 12 added and renumbered in custom show

5 Click **OK**. Compare your screen with Figure 6.52.

FIGURE 6.52

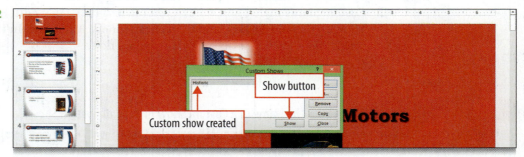

Show button

Custom show created

6 In the **Custom Shows** dialog box, click **Show** to preview your custom show. Click through the slides. When you are finished viewing the slide show, press `Esc`.

The Historic custom slide show included only seven slides.

ALERT!   **Did the Presentation Not Display?**

If the first slide of the presentation did not display automatically, press `Esc`. On the SLIDE SHOW tab, in the Set Up group, click the Set Up Slide Show. In the Set Up Show dialog box, select the *Presented by a speaker (full screen)* option button, and then click OK.

7 On the **SLIDE SHOW tab**, in the **Start Slide Show group**, click **Custom Slide Show arrow**.

The custom show—Historic—displays, and you can start the show from this list also.

8 Click **Historic** to view the slide show again. When you are finished viewing the slide show, press `Enter` or `Esc`.

9 Click **Custom Slide Show arrow** again. Click **Custom Shows** to display the **Custom Shows** dialog box, and then click **New**. In the **Slide show name** box, delete the text, and type **Cultural**

10 Under **Slides in presentation**, click to select **Slides 6, 7, 8, 9, 10, 11,** and **12**. Click **Add**. Under **Slides in presentation**, click to select **Slide 1,** and then add it to the custom slide show.

Slide 1 is now Slide 8 in the Cultural custom show.

11 Under **Slides in custom show**, click **Slide 8**. Click the **Up arrow** seven times to move **Slide 8** so it is in the **Slide 1** position in the custom show, and then compare your screen with Figure 6.53.

FIGURE 6.53

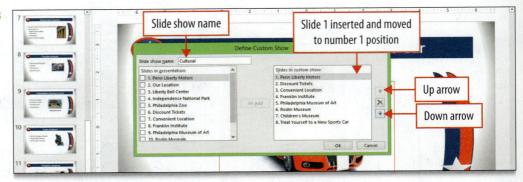

12 ▸ Click **OK**. In the **Custom Shows** dialog box, click **Show** to preview your custom show. When you are finished viewing the slide show, press Enter or Esc.

Eight slides displayed.

13 ▸ In the **Start Slide Show group**, click **Custom Slide Show arrow**. Click **Custom Shows** to display the **Custom Shows** dialog box. Click **Cultural**, and then click **Edit**. In the **Slides in custom show** list, click **2. Discount Tickets**, and then click **Remove**. Click **OK**. In the **Custom Shows** dialog box, click **Show**. Press Enter or Esc when you are done.

Seven slides displayed.

ALERT!   **Did You Click the Name of a Custom Show Instead of Custom Shows?**

To edit a specific custom show, when you click Custom Slide Show, make sure you click Custom Shows to allow you to select the show and edit it. If you clicked a custom show by accident, press Esc and try again.

14 ▸ Click **Custom Slide Show arrow**, and then click **Custom Shows** to display the **Custom Shows** dialog box. Click **New**. In the **Slide show name** box, delete the text, and then type **Location**

15 ▸ In the **Slides in presentation** box, click to select **Slides 2, 3, 4, 5,** and **6**. Click **Add**. Click **OK**.

16 ▸ In the **Custom Shows** dialog box, click **Show** to preview your custom show. When you are finished viewing the slide show, press Enter, or Esc.

17 ▸ In the **Start Slide Show group**, click **Custom Slide Show arrow**. Compare your screen with Figure 6.54.

Three custom shows are displayed in the list—Historic, Cultural, and Location.

FIGURE 6.54

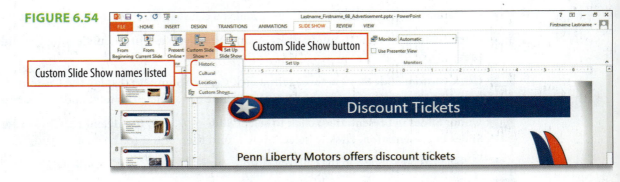

18 ▸ **Save** 🔖 your changes.

Activity 6.15 | Creating a Hyperlinked Custom Slide Show

In this activity, you will create a hyperlinked custom slide show from an existing presentation by selecting the slides that will be shown in the custom show. These slides can be hyperlinked to the original presentation.

1 In **Normal** view, make the **title slide** the active slide. Click to select the picture of the car.

2 On the **INSERT tab**, in the **Links group**, click **Hyperlink**. In the **Insert Hyperlink** dialog box, under **Link to:**, click **Place in This Document**. In the **Insert Hyperlink** dialog box, under **Select a place in this document:**, scroll down to display the **Custom Shows**.

3 Under **Select a place in this document**, below **Custom Shows**, click **Location**, and then select the **Show and return** check box. Compare your screen with Figure 6.55.

FIGURE 6.55

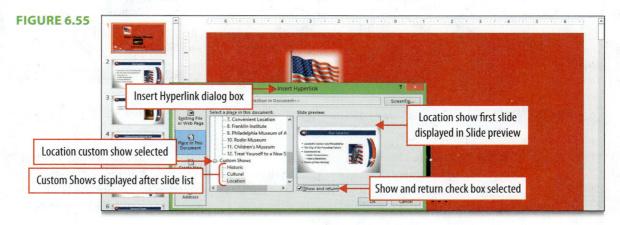

4 Click **OK**. Start the slide show **From Beginning**, and then click the picture of the **car** on the title slide. When the presentation returns to the title slide, press Esc.

The slides in the custom show—Location—will display, and after the last slide, the presentation will return to the title slide.

5 Save 💾 your changes.

Objective 6   Present and View a Slide Presentation

Video P6-6

In the following activities, you will use the navigation tools included with PowerPoint to view slide shows. You can start a slide show from the beginning or from any slide you choose. The *navigation tools* include buttons that display on the slides during a slide show that enable you to perform actions such as move to the next slide, the previous slide, the last viewed slide, or the end of the slide show. Additionally, you can add an *annotation*, which is a note or a highlight that can be saved or discarded.

Activity 6.16 | Duplicating and Hiding a Slide

In this activity, you will duplicate one slide at the end of the presentation. You will hide two slides so that they do not display during the slide show and unhide one slide.

1 Make **Slide 12** the active slide. On the **HOME tab**, in the **Slides group**, click the **New Slide arrow**, and then from the displayed list, click **Duplicate Selected Slides**. Compare your screen with Figure 6.56.

FIGURE 6.56

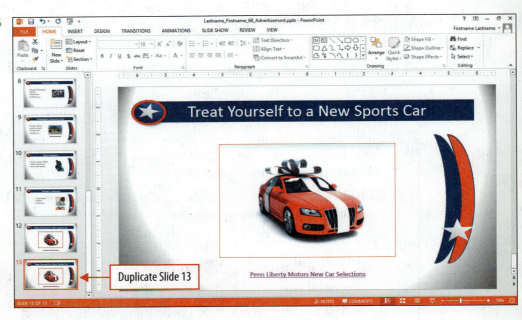

Duplicate Slide 13

↻ **ANOTHER WAY**   Right-click Slide 13, and then click Duplicate Slide.

2 With **Slide 13** selected, right-click the picture of the car, and then click **Change Picture**. In the **Insert Pictures** dialog box, on the right of **From a file**, click **Browse**. Navigate to the location where you are storing your student data files, and then insert the file **p06B_Blue_Car.jpg**. In the slide title placeholder, select the words *New Sports Car* and then type **Sedan** Compare your screen with Figure 6.57.

The slide is duplicated and the picture and the slide title are changed.

FIGURE 6.57

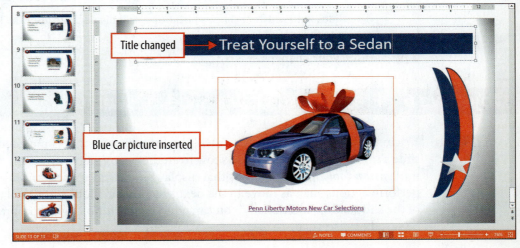

Title changed

Blue Car picture inserted

3 Make **Slide 6** the active slide. On the **SLIDE SHOW tab**, in the **Set Up group**, click **Hide Slide**. Compare your screen with Figure 6.58.

In the Slides/Outline pane, the number displayed to the left of the slide thumbnail has a diagonal line through it.

FIGURE 6.58

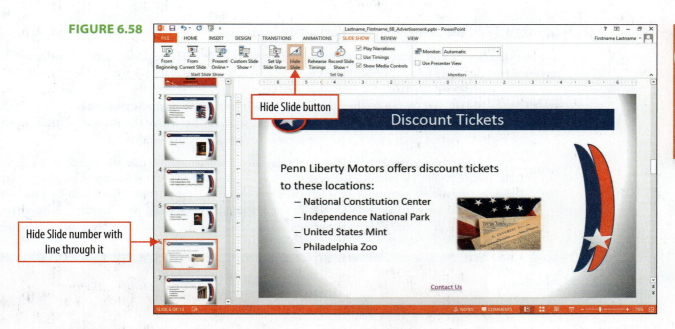

Hide Slide button

Hide Slide number with line through it

Discount Tickets

Penn Liberty Motors offers discount tickets to these locations:
— National Constitution Center
— Independence National Park
— United States Mint
— Philadelphia Zoo

Contact Us

4 ▶ Make **Slide 12** the active slide. Right-click the thumbnail for **Slide 12** to display the shortcut menu, and then compare your screen with Figure 6.59.

You can hide a slide from the shortcut menu. Make sure you right-click the thumbnail.

FIGURE 6.59

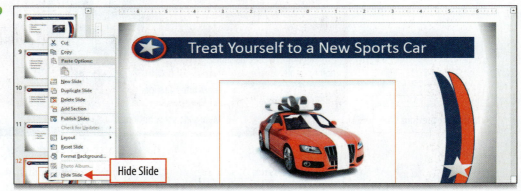

Hide Slide

Treat Yourself to a New Sports Car

5 ▶ Click **Hide Slide**.

6 ▶ Right-click the **Slide 6** thumbnail to display the shortcut menu again, and then click **Hide Slide** to unhide **Slide 6**.

Slide 6 is displayed. Only one slide is hidden—Slide 12.

N O T E **Hiding and Displaying a Slide**

On the SLIDE SHOW tab, in the Setup group, the Hide Slide button is a toggle button. Recall that a toggle button performs an action when clicked and then reverses the previous action when clicked again. In the shortcut menu, Hide Slide is also a toggle command.

---

7 ▶ **Save** 🖫 your changes.

Activity 6.17 | Using the Onscreen Navigation Tools

In this activity, you will use the onscreen navigation tools and the slide shortcut menu to navigate to a desired slide in the slide show.

1 On the **SLIDE SHOW tab** in the **Start Slide Show group**, click **From Beginning**. Move the mouse to the bottom left corner of the screen to reveal six buttons. Move the mouse pointer to the right to reveal each one. Compare your screen with Figure 6.60.

Notice that six semitransparent buttons display for a few seconds and then disappear. If you move the mouse pointer, they display again for a few seconds. The buttons display as long as you are moving the mouse pointer or when you point to them. The buttons are Return to the previous slide, Advance to the next slide, Pen and laser pointer tools, See all slides, Zoom into the slide, and More slide show options. As you move the mouse over them, they can be seen.

FIGURE 6.60

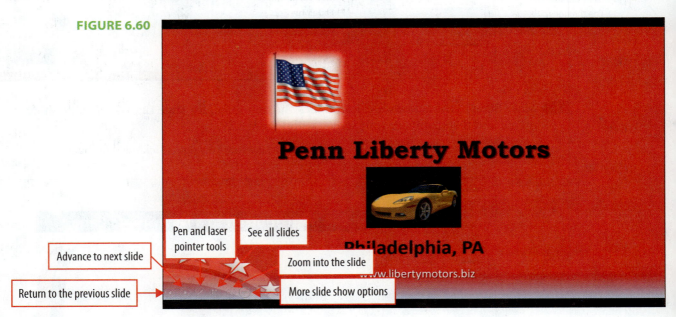

2 At the lower left corner of the screen, click **Advance to the next slide**, and then click **Return to the previous slide**.

The slide advances from Slide 1 to Slide 2; then the slide returns from Slide 2 to Slide 1.

3 Click the fourth button—**See all slides**. Compare your screen with Figure 6.61.

All slides display on the screen. Slide 12, the hidden slide, is dimmed and the number 12 has a line through it.

More Knowledge | **Zoom Slider**

The Zoom Slider in the bottom right corner of the screen allows you to change the zoom level so you can change the number of slides that are visible on the screen at one time.

FIGURE 6.61

Slide 12, the hidden slide is dimmed and a line is through the number 12

4 ▶ Click **Slide 7** to display it. Right-click anywhere on the slide, click **Custom Show**, and then click **Historic**. Click to view each of the slides in the custom show. When the slide show is finished, press Esc.

You right-clicked Slide 7 to display the shortcut menu, and then you viewed the Historic custom show.

5 ▶ On the **SLIDE SHOW tab**, in the **Start Slide Show group**, click **From Beginning**. At the lower left corner of the screen, click **More slide show options** ⊙, and then click **Show Presenter View**. Compare your screen with Figure 6.62.

Slide Show view changes to Presenter View.

More Knowledge | **Arrow Options**

Arrow Options display on the More slide show options menu. When the Arrow Options is set for Visible, the mouse pointer displays on the Slide show. When the Arrow Options is set for Hidden, the mouse pointer does not display. The default setting is Automatic.

FIGURE 6.62

6 In Presenter View, below the large slide, click **Black or unblack slide show** 🖵. Compare your screen with Figure 6.63.

> The large slide changes to black in Presenter View. This is useful when you do not want your presentation to display; for example, before your presentation begins.

FIGURE 6.63

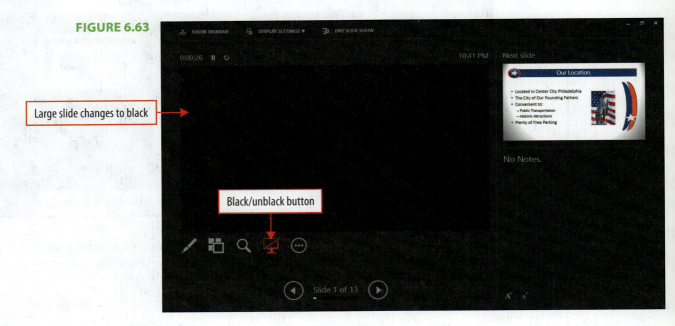

Large slide changes to black

Black/unblack button

7 Click **Black or unblack slide show** 🖵 to make the large slide visible again.

🔁 **ANOTHER WAY**   Click the slide to make the large slide visible again.

More Knowledge   **AutoExtend Feature in Presenter View**

The AutoExtend feature in Presenter View allows you to project to a second screen. The Swap Presentation View and Slide Show is located in the DISPLAY SETTINGS which allows you to swap the screens that the presentation displays on. The Duplicate Slide Show display setting allows you to display a slide show on more than one monitor.

---

8 Below the large slide, click **More slide show options** ⊙, and then click **Hide Presenter View** to return to the slide show.

Activity 6.18 | Using the Annotation Tool

In this activity, you will use the Pen and laser tools to highlight and annotate information on a slide.

1 At the lower left corner of the screen, click the third button—**Pen and laser tools**. Compare your screen with Figure 6.64. Take a moment to review the Pen and Laser Pointer Tool options, as described in the table shown in Figure 6.65.

FIGURE 6.64

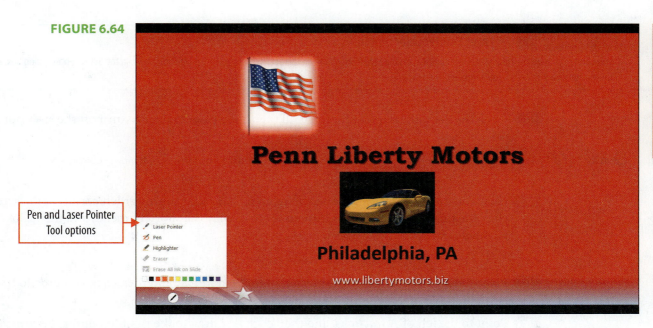

Pen and Laser Pointer
Tool options

FIGURE 6.65

PEN AND LASER POINTER TOOLS	
SCREEN ELEMENT	**DESCRIPTION**
Laser Pointer	Changes your mouse pointer into a laser pointer.
Pen	Allows you to write or circle items on the slide.
Highlighter	Allows you to emphasize parts of the slide.
Eraser	Removes areas of an annotation.
Erase All Ink on Slide	Removes all annotations on a slide.
Ink Color	Displays a selection of colors for highlighting or writing with the pen.

 2 Click **Laser Pointer** and move the mouse around the screen. Compare your screen with Figure 6.66.

The mouse pointer displays as a large red dot.

FIGURE 6.66

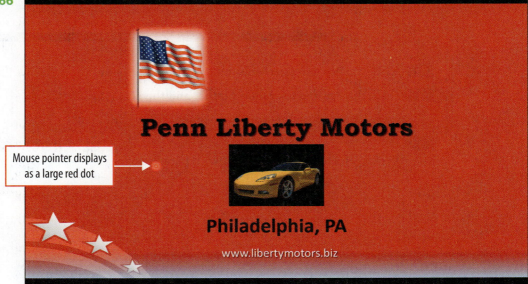

Mouse pointer displays
as a large red dot

3   Click the **Pen and laser tool** button, and then click **Laser Pointer** to turn off the laser pointer.

🔄 **ANOTHER WAY**   You can also press Esc to turn off the laser pointer and return to the default mouse pointer.

4   Click the **Advance to next slide** button to go to **Slide 2**. At the lower left corner of the screen, click the third button—**Pen and laser tools** to display the shortcut menu, and then click **Highlighter**.

     The mouse pointer displays as a yellow rectangle.

5   Place the highlighter pointer to the left of the *P* in *Public*, and then click and drag to the right to highlight *Public Transportation*.

6   Point to the left of *Attractions*, and then click and drag to the right to highlight *Attractions*. Compare your screen with Figure 6.67.

FIGURE 6.67

7   Click the **Pen and laser tools** button. At the bottom of the list, click the color—**Red**.

8   Click the **Pen and laser tools** button, and then click **Pen**.

     The Pen and laser tool displays as a small red circle or dot.

9   Point above the word *Parking*, and then click and drag to draw a circle around the word *Parking*. Compare your screen with Figure 6.68.

FIGURE 6.68

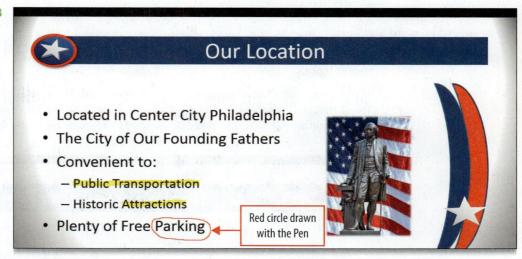

> Red circle drawn with the Pen

10 Click the **Pen and laser tools** button, and then click **Eraser**. Click one time on the circle to remove the circle. It is not necessary to drag the eraser.

11 Click the **Pen and laser tools** button, and then click **Pen**. Using the technique you practiced, draw a circle around the word *Free*.

12 Press [Esc] two times. In the displayed dialog box, which prompts you to keep your annotations, click **Keep**.

13 **Save** 🖫 your changes.

Activity 6.19 | Creating a Self-Running Presentation

In this activity, you will set up a presentation to run without an individual present to run the slide show. Normally, self-running presentations run on a *kiosk*. A kiosk is a booth that includes a computer and a monitor that may have a touchscreen. Usually, kiosks are located in an area such as a mall, a trade show, or a convention—places that are frequented by many people.

1 With the **title slide** as the active slide, click the **SLIDE SHOW tab**, if necessary. In the **Set Up group**, click **Rehearse Timings**. Compare your screen with Figure 6.69.

The presentation slide show begins, the Recording toolbar displays, and the Slide Time box begins timing the presentation.

FIGURE 6.69

Recording toolbar

Next slide

Repeat

Total presentation time

Slide Time box

Pause recording

2 Wait until the **Slide Time** box ⌗0:00:09⌗ displays **10** (**seconds**), and then click **Next** ➡.

ALERT! | **Did Your Time Get Past 10 Seconds?**

If you spent longer on the slide than 10 seconds, you can revise your timing. On the Rehearsal toolbar, click the Repeat button ↺, and then click Resume Recording to restart recording the time for the current slide.

---

3 Repeat this step for every slide.

4 After you set the time for the last slide, a dialog box displays with the total time for the slide show and prompts you to save the slide timings or discard them. Compare your screen with Figure 6.70.

If you are not satisfied with the slide times for your slide show, you can rehearse the times again. On the SLIDE SHOW tab, in the Set Up group, click the Rehearse Timings button, and time the slides. When you finish, you will be asked if you want to keep the new slide timings. Answer Yes if you do.

FIGURE 6.70

5 Click **Yes**.

6 On the PowerPoint **status bar**, click **Slide Sorter**. With the slides displayed, drag the **Zoom slider** to **70%**. Compare your screen with Figure 6.71.

Slide Sorter view displays with the time of each slide in the presentation. Your slide times may not be timed at exactly 10 seconds. There is a delay between the click and the actual time, but that is not critical.

FIGURE 6.71

7 > On the **SLIDE SHOW tab**, in the **Set Up group**, click **Set Up Slide Show**. Compare your screen with Figure 6.72.

The Set Up Show dialog box displays. The options in the Set Up Show dialog box are described in the table shown in Figure 6.73.

FIGURE 6.72

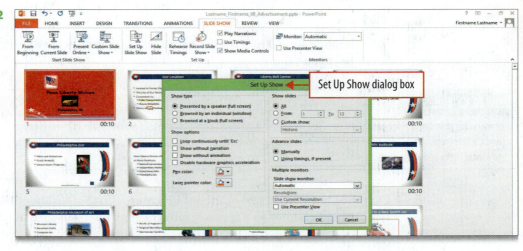

FIGURE 6.73

SET UP SHOW OPTIONS	
SCREEN ELEMENT	**DESCRIPTION**
Show type	Presented by a speaker (full screen) is used to present to a live audience.
	Browsed by an individual (window) enables your audience to view the presentation from a hard drive, CD, or the Internet.
	Browsed at kiosk (full screen) delivers a self-running show that can run without a presenter in an unattended booth or kiosk. You can also send someone a self-running presentation on a CD.
Show options	Loop continuously until the ⌷Esc⌷ key is pressed is used when the show is unattended.
	Show without narration suppresses any recorded audio in the presentation.
	Show without animation suppresses the animation in the presentation.
	Disable hardware graphics acceleration.
	Pen color allows you to select a pen color for the slide show.
	Laser pointer color allows you to select a laser pointer color for the slide show.
Show slides	All: Shows all of the slides.
	From: Selects a range of slides to view.
	Custom show: Shows a custom show.
Advance slides	Manually lets you advance the slides yourself.
	Using timings, if present, activates the timings you set for each slide.
Multiple monitors	If your computer supports using multiple monitors, a PowerPoint presentation can be delivered on two monitors. Slide show monitor gives you the option to select the monitor that the slide show will display, or you can let PowerPoint select the monitor automatically.
	Resolution allows you to use the current resolution or select another resolution that your monitor supports.
	Use Presenter View allows you to run the PowerPoint presentation from one monitor while the audience views it on a second monitor. This enables you to run other programs that will not be visible to your audience.

8 Under **Advance slides**, click to select **Using timings, if present**. Under **Show type**, select **Browsed at a kiosk (full screen)**.

Under Show options, the Loop continuously until "Esc" check box is selected by default. This option refers to playing a sound file or animation continuously. Advance slides options are disabled.

9 Click **OK**.

10 Start the slide show **From Beginning**. Wait 10 seconds per slide, and then view a few slides. Press [Esc] to end the show.

NOTE | **To Change the Slide Show Timings**

If you want new timings for your slides, you can rehearse the timings again. On the SLIDE SHOW tab, in the Set Up group, click the Rehearse Timings button, and then set new timings for each slide in the presentation. When all slides have been timed, you will be asked whether you want to keep the new timings or to cancel them and keep the old timings.

---

11 On the **SLIDE SHOW tab**, in the **Set Up group**, click **Set Up Slide Show** button. Under **Show type**, select **Presented by a speaker (full screen)**. Under **Advance slides**, click **Manually**. Click **OK**.

The timings are saved with the presentation. When you want to use them for a kiosk, click the Set Up Slide Show button, select Using timings, if present and then Browsed at a kiosk (full screen).

12 On the **VIEW tab**, in the **Presentation Views group**, click **Normal**.

Activity 6.20 | Printing Selections from a Presentation

In this activity, you will print selections from a presentation. You will select three slides to print.

1 Hold down [Ctrl] and click to select **Slides 1, 2**, and **6** thumbnails.

2 On the **FILE tab**, click **Print**. Under **Settings**, click the **Print All Slides arrow**, and then point to **Print Selection**. Compare your screen with Figure 6.74.

The Print All Slides list displays. Print Selection—Only print the selected slides is highlighted.

FIGURE 6.74

ANOTHER WAY   To print selected files, on the FILE tab, click Print, and then under Setting, in the Slides box, type the numbers of the slides that you want to print. Enter slide numbers and/or slide ranges. For example, 1, 3, 5–12.

3 ▸ Press ⌈Esc⌉ to return to **Normal** view.

4 ▸ On the **INSERT tab**, in the **Text group**, click **Header & Footer** to display the **Header and Footer** dialog box. Click the **Notes and Handouts tab**. Under **Include on page**, select the **Date and time** check box, and then select **Fixed**. If necessary, clear the **Header** check box, and then select the **Page number** and **Footer** check boxes. In the **Footer** box, using your own name, type **Lastname_Firstname_6B_Advertisement** and then click **Apply To All**.

5 ▸ Click **the FILE tab**, and then in the lower right portion of the screen, click **Show All Properties**. In the **Tags** box, type **discount, tourist, attractions** In the **Subject** box, type your course name and section number. In the **Author** box, right-click the existing author name, click **Edit Property**, replace the existing text with your first and last name, click outside textbox to deselect, and then click **OK**.

6 ▸ **Save** 🖫 your changes. **Close** your presentation, and then **Exit** PowerPoint. Submit your work as directed by your instructor.

END | You have completed Project 6B

END OF CHAPTER

SUMMARY

You used techniques related to viewing and presenting a slide show by adding and modifying slide transitions and various animation effects, including entrance, exit, emphasis effects, and motion paths.

Within a slide show, you also inserted hyperlinks to quickly link to a webpage, an email address, another document or file, another area of the same document, and other slides within a slide show.

You practiced hiding slides and creating a basic custom slide show and a hyperlinked custom slide show. You created action buttons, assigned an action to the buttons, and used the onscreen navigation tools.

You practiced using annotation tools such as the pen and laser pointer tools that enabled you to write or draw on slides during a presentation. You also created a self-running slide show that runs in a loop.

GO! LEARN IT ONLINE

Review the concepts and key terms in this chapter by completing these online challenges, which you can find at **www.pearsonhighered.com/go.**

Matching and Multiple Choice:
Answer matching and multiple choice questions to test what you learned in this chapter. MyITLab®

Crossword Puzzle:
Spell out the words that match the numbered clues, and put them in the puzzle squares.

Flipboard:
Flip through the definitions of the key terms in this chapter and match them with the correct term.

END OF CHAPTER

REVIEW AND ASSESSMENT GUIDE FOR POWERPOINT CHAPTER 6

Your instructor may assign one or more of these projects to help you review the chapter and assess your mastery and understanding of the chapter.

6

POWERPOINT

Review and Assessment Guide for PowerPoint Chapter 6			
Project	**Apply Skills from These Chapter Objectives**	**Project Type**	**Project Location**
6C	Objectives 1–3 from Project 6A	**6C Skills Review** A guided review of the skills from Project 6A.	On the following pages
6D	Objectives 4–6 from Project 6B	**6D Skills Review** A guided review of the skills from Project 6B.	On the following pages
6E	Objectives 1–3 from Project 6A	**6E Mastery (Grader Project)** A demonstration of your mastery of the skills in Project 6A with extensive decision making.	In MyITLab and on the following pages
6F	Objectives 4–6 from Project 6B	**6F Mastery (Grader Project)** A demonstration of your mastery of the skills in Project 6B with extensive decision making.	In MyITLab and on the following pages
6G	Objectives 1–6 from Projects 6A and 6B	**6G Mastery (Grader Project)** A demonstration of your mastery of the skills in Projects 6A and 6B with extensive decision making.	In MyITLab and on the following pages
6H	Combination of Objectives from Projects 6A and 6B	**6H GO! Fix It** A demonstration of your mastery of the skills in Projects 6A and 6B by creating a correct result from a document that contains errors you must find.	Online
6I	Combination of Objectives from Projects 6A and 6B	**6I GO! Make It** A demonstration of your mastery of the skills in Projects 6A and 6B by creating a result from a supplied picture.	Online
6J	Combination of Objectives from Projects 6A and 6B	**6J GO! Solve It** A demonstration of your mastery of the skills in Projects 6A and 6B, your decision-making skills, and your critical thinking skills. A task-specific rubric helps you self-assess your result.	Online
6K	Combination of Objectives from Projects 6A and 6B	**6K GO! Solve It** A demonstration of your mastery of the skills in Projects 6A and 6B, your decision-making skills, and your critical thinking skills. A task-specific rubric helps you self-assess your result.	On the following pages
6L	Combination of Objectives from Projects 6A and 6B	**6L GO! Think** A demonstration of your understanding of the chapter concepts applied in a manner that you would outside of college. An analytic rubric helps you and your instructor grade the quality of your work by comparing it to the work an expert in the discipline would create.	On the following pages
6M	Combination of Objectives from Projects 6A and 6B	**6M GO! Think** A demonstration of your understanding of the chapter concepts applied in a manner that you would outside of college. An analytic rubric helps you and your instructor grade the quality of your work by comparing it to the work an expert in the discipline would create.	Online
6N	Combination of Objectives from Projects 6A and 6B	**6N You and GO!** A demonstration of your understanding of the chapter concepts applied in a manner that you would in a personal situation. An analytic rubric helps you and your instructor grade the quality of your work.	Online

GLOSSARY

GLOSSARY OF CHAPTER KEY TERMS

Action button A built-in button shape that you can add to your presentation and then assign an action to occur upon the click of a mouse or with a mouse over.

After Previous A custom animation that starts the animation effect immediately after the previous effect in the list finishes playing.

Animated GIF A file format made up of a series of frames within a single file that creates the illusion of animation by displaying the frames one after the other in quick succession.

Animation 1. Any type of motion or movement that occurs as the presentation moves from slide to slide. 2. A special visual effect or sound effect added to text or an object.

Animation Pane The area that contains a list of the animation effects added to your presentation. From this pane, you can add or modify effects.

Annotation A note or a highlight that can be saved or discarded.

Basic custom slide show A separate presentation saved with its own title containing some of the slides from the original presentation.

Chevron A V-shaped symbol that indicates more information or options are available.

Custom slide show Displays only the slides you want to display to an audience in the order you select.

Email client A software program that enables you to compose and send an email message.

Emphasis effect An animation effect that, for example, makes an object shrink or grow in size, change color, or spin on its center.

Entrance effect An animation effect that occurs when the text or object is introduced into the slide during a slide show.

Exit effect An animation effect that occurs when the text or object leaves the slide or disappears during a slide show.

File extension Also called the file type, it identifies the format of the file or the application used to create it.

Full path Includes the drive, the folder, and any subfolders in which a file is contained.

GIF Stands for Graphics Interchange Format. It is a file format used for graphic images, such as drawings.

Hyperlinked custom slide show A quick way to navigate to a separate slide show from within the original presentation.

Hyperlinks Navigation elements that, when clicked, will take you to another location, such as a webpage, an email address, another document, or a place within the same document. In a PowerPoint presentation, hyperlinks can also be used to link to a slide in the presentation, to a slide in a different presentation, or to a custom slide show.

HyperText Markup Language (HTML) The language used to code webpages.

HyperText Transfer Protocol (HTTP) The protocol used on the World Wide Web to define how messages are formatted and transmitted.

JPG (JPEG) Stands for Joint Photographic Experts Group. It is a file format used for photos.

Kiosk A booth that includes a computer and a monitor that may have a touchscreen.

Microsoft Outlook An example of an email client.

Motion path effect An animation effect that determines how and in what direction text or objects will move on a slide.

Mouse Over Refers to an action that will occur when the mouse pointer is placed on (over) an action button. No mouse click is required.

Navigation tools Buttons that display on the slides during a slide show that allow you to perform actions such as move to the next slide, the previous slide, the last viewed slide, or the end of the slide show.

On Click Starts the animation effect when you click the slide or a trigger on the slide.

Protocol A set of rules.

Timeline A graphical representation that displays the number of seconds the animation takes to complete.

Transition sound A prerecorded sound that can be applied and will play as slides change from one to the next.

Transition speed The timing of the transition between all slides or between the previous slide and the current slide.

Transitions Motion effects that occur when a presentation moves from slide to slide in Slide Show view and affect how content is revealed.

Trigger A portion of text, a graphic, or a picture that, when clicked, causes the audio or video to play.

Uniform Resource Locator (URL) Defines the address of documents and resources on the web.

Web browser A software application used for retrieving, presenting, and searching information resources on the World Wide Web. It formats webpages so that they display properly.

With Previous A custom animation that starts the animation effect at the same time as the previous effect in the list.

CHAPTER REVIEW

Apply 6A skills from these Objectives:

1 Apply and Modify Slide Transitions

2 Apply Custom Animation Effects

3 Modify Animation Effects

Skills Review | Project 6C Vintage Car

In the following Skills Review, you will modify a PowerPoint presentation advertising the annual Vintage Car Event hosted by Penn Liberty Motors. You will apply slide transitions and custom animation effects to the slide show to generate interest in the event. Your completed presentation will look similar to Figure 6.75.

PROJECT FILES

For Project 6C, you will need the following file:

p06C_Vintage_Cars.pptx

You will save your presentation as:

Lastname_Firstname_6C_Vintage_Cars.pptx

PROJECT RESULTS

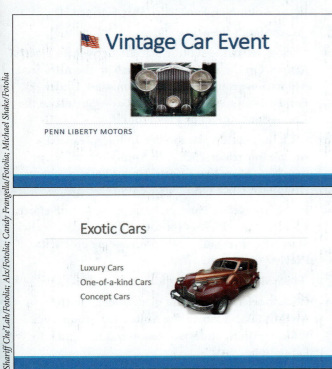

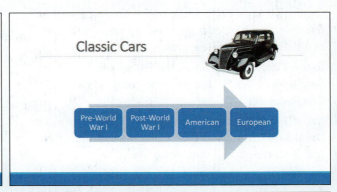

Shariff Che'Lah/Fotolia; Alx/Fotolia; Candy Frangella/Fotolia; Michael Shake/Fotolia

FIGURE 6.75

(Project 6C Vintage Car continues on the next page)

CHAPTER REVIEW

1 Start PowerPoint. Locate and open the file **p06C_Vintage_Cars**. Using your own first and last name, **Save** the file as **Lastname_Firstname_6C_Vintage_Cars** in your **PowerPoint Chapter 6** folder.

2 Make the **title slide** the active slide.

a. Click the **TRANSITIONS tab**. In the **Transition to This Slide group**, click **More**. In the **Transitions** gallery, under **Subtle**, in the first row, click **Shape**.

b. In the **Timing group**, click **Apply To All**.

3 Make **Slide 2** the active slide.

a. In the **Transition to This Slide group**, click **More**. In the **Transitions** gallery, under **Subtle**, in the first row, click the fourth transition—**Push**.

b. On the **TRANSITIONS tab**, in the **Timing group**, in the **Duration** box, click **spin box up arrow to 02.00**, and then in the **Preview group**, click **Preview**.

c. In the **Timing group**, click the **Sound arrow**, and then select **Click**. In the **Preview group**, click **Preview**.

d. In the **Timing group**, under **Advance Slide**, clear the **On Mouse Click** check box. Click once in the **After** spin box, type **3** and then press ⏎.

4 Make **Slide 2** the active slide.

a. Select the **SmartArt** graphic. On the **ANIMATIONS tab**, in the **Advanced Animation group**, click **Add Animations**, and then under **Entrance**, click **Zoom**.

b. On the **ANIMATIONS tab**, in the **Animation group**, click **Effect Options**, and then click **One by One**.

c. In the **Advanced Animation group**, click **Animation Pane**. In the **Animation Pane**, click **Play Selected**.

d. In the **Animation Pane**, right-click **Content Place…** and then click **Effect Options**. In the **Zoom** dialog box, click the **SmartArt Animation tab**, select the **Reverse order** check box, and then click **OK**.

5 Make **Slide 3** the active slide.

a. Apply the same Step 3 transition sound, and duration slide settings and advance slide mouse settings that you applied to **Slide 2**.

b. Click the **SLIDE SHOW tab**, and then view the slide show **From Beginning**. Wait for **Slides 2** and **3** to advance after three seconds.

c. On Slide 3, click the **content placeholder**. On the **ANIMATIONS tab**, in the **Advanced Animation group**, click **Add Animation**, and then under **Entrance**, click on **Fly In**.

d. In the **Animation Pane**, below *Content Placeholder*, click the **chevron** to expand the contents. In the **Animation Pane**, click **Play Selected**.

6 Make **Slide 4** the active slide.

a. Select the content placeholder. On the **ANIMATIONS tab**, in the **Advanced Animation group**, click **Add Animation**. Under **Entrance**, click **Wipe**.

b. In the **Animation group**, click **Effect Options**, under **Sequence**, select **All at Once**.

c. In the **Animation Pane**, click **Play Selected**.

7 Make **Slide 1** the active slide.

a. Click to select the subtitle placeholder—*Penn Liberty Motors*. On the **ANIMATIONS tab**, in the **Advanced Animation group**, click **Add Animation**. Under **Emphasis**, in the first row, click **Grow/Shrink**. In the **Animation Pane**, click **Play From**.

b. Click the **subtitle** placeholder. In the **Advanced Animation group**, click **Add Animation**, and then click **More Exit Effects**. Under **Basic**, select **Disappear**. Click **OK**.

c. In the **Animation Pane**, right-click the second effect, which is the exit effect for the subtitle, and then click **Start After Previous**. In the **Preview group**, click **Preview** to view the effect.

8 Make **Slide 4** the active slide.

a. Click to select the content placeholder. On the **ANIMATIONS tab**, in the **Animation group**, click **Effect Options**, under **Sequence**, and then click **By Paragraph**.

b. In the **Animation Pane**, click the **chevron** to expand all effects, if necessary. With all three animations selected, right-click the first effect—**Model A Cars**, and then click **Effect Options** to display the **Wipe** dialog box. On the **Timing tab**, click the **Start arrow**, and then select **After Previous**. Change the **Duration** to **1 seconds (Fast)**. Click **OK**.

c. Click to select the **title** placeholder. In **the Advanced Animation group**, click **Add Animation**. Under **Motion Paths**, scroll if necessary, click **Shapes**.

(Project 6C Vintage Car continues on the next page)

CHAPTER REVIEW

d. Click the **car picture**. On the **ANIMATIONS tab**, in the **Advanced Animation group**, click **Add Animation**, and then click **More Motion Paths**. In the **Add Motion Path** dialog box, scroll down, and then under **Lines_Curves**, click **Left**. Click **OK**.

9 Make **Slide 3** the active slide.

a. Click to select the content placeholder. In the **Animation Pane**, right-click the first entrance effect—*Luxury Cars,* and then select **Effect Options** to display the **Fly In** dialog box. On the **Effect tab**, under the **Settings**, click the **Direction arrow**, and then click **From Bottom-Left**.

b. Under **Enhancements**, click the **After animation arrow**. In the row of colors, click the fifth color—**Teal**. Click the **Animate text arrow**, if necessary, and then click **All at Once**.

c. On the **Timing tab**, click the **Duration arrow**, and then click **1 seconds (Fast)**.

d. On the **Text Animation tab**, click the **Group text arrow**, select **All Paragraphs at Once**, and then click **OK**.

e. Click to select the **title** placeholder. On the **ANIMATIONS tab**, in the **Advanced Animation group**, click **Add Animation**. Under **Emphasis**, select **Pulse**. In the **Animation Pane**, click **Play From**.

f. At the top of the **Animation Pane**, click the **Reorder up arrow** to move the title—*Title 1: Exotic*

Cars—to the top of the list. Click **Play From** in the **Animation Pane**.

g. Click on **SLIDE SHOW tab**, and then view the slide show **From Beginning**.

10 **Close** the **Animation Pane**.

11 On the **INSERT tab**, in the **Text group**:

a. Click **Header & Footer** to display the **Header and Footer** dialog box.

b. Click the **Notes and Handouts tab**. Under **Include on page**, select the **Date and time** check box, and then select **Fixed**. If necessary, clear the **Header** check box, and then select the **Page number and Footer** check boxes. In the **Footer** box, using your own name, type **Lastname_Firstname_6C_Vintage_Cars** and then click **Apply To All**.

12 Click the **FILE tab**, and then in the lower right portion of the screen, click **Show All Properties**.

a. In the **Tags** box, type **vintage cars, Penn Liberty** In the **Subject** box, type your course name and section number.

b. In the **Author** box, right-click the existing author name, click **Edit Property**, replace the existing text with your first and last name, click outside text box to deselect, and then click **OK**.

13 Print **Handouts 4 Slides Horizontal**, or submit your presentation electronically as directed by your instructor.

14 **Save** the presentation. **Exit** PowerPoint.

END | You have completed Project 6C

CHAPTER REVIEW

Apply 6B skills from these Objectives:

4 Insert Hyperlinks

5 Create Custom Slide Shows

6 Present and View a Slide Presentation

In the following Skills Review, you will modify a PowerPoint presentation that showcases safety features of the cars sold by Penn Liberty Motors. You will insert hyperlinks to a webpage and the email address of the company's safety director. You will also create custom slide shows of standard safety features available on all vehicles and custom safety features available on select vehicles. You will annotate the slide show and then create a self-running version of the presentation for use in a kiosk. Your completed presentation will look similar to Figure 6.76.

PROJECT FILES

For Project 6D, you will need the following files:

p06D_Safety.pptx
p06D_ESC.docx
p06D_Customer_Service.jpg

You will save your files as:

Lastname_Firstname_6D_Safety.pptx
Lastname_Firstname_6D_ESC_Benefits.docx

PROJECT RESULTS

Tstumpa/Fotolia; Sarunyu_foto/Fotolia; Tomasz Zajda/Fotolia; Toniflap/Fotolia; Eduard Stelmakh/

FIGURE 6.76

(Project 6D Safety continues on the next page)

CHAPTER REVIEW

1 ▶ Start PowerPoint. Locate and open the file **p06D_Safety**. **Save** the file as **Lastname_Firstname_6D_Safety** in your **PowerPoint Chapter 6** folder.

2 ▶ Make the **title slide** the active slide.

a. Click to select the picture of the car.

b. Click the **INSERT tab**. In the **Links group**, click **Hyperlink**. In the **Insert Hyperlink** dialog box, under **Link to**, click **Existing File or Web Page**.

c. In the **Address** box, type **www.nhtsa.dot.gov** This is the website for the National Highway Traffic Safety Administration.

d. Click **ScreenTip**. In the **Set Hyperlink ScreenTip** dialog box, type **National Highway Traffic Safety Administration** Click **OK**. Click **OK** again.

3 ▶ Confirm that the **title slide** is the active slide.

a. In the subtitle, click and drag to select *Safety Features*.

b. On the **INSERT tab**, in the **Links group**, click **Hyperlink**.

c. Under **Link to**, click **Place in This Document**. Scroll down, click **13. Penn Liberty Motors Safety Team**, and then click **OK**.

4 ▶ Make **Slide 13** the active slide.

a. Click and drag to select *Email Your Concerns*. On the **INSERT tab**, in the **Links group**, click **Hyperlink**. Under **Link to**, click **E-mail Address**. In the **Email address** box, type **safetyteam@libertymotors.com** In the **Subject** box, type **Safety First** Click **OK**.

b. Click and drag to select the second bulleted item—*Available to Customers*. Click the **INSERT tab**. In the **Links group**, click **Hyperlink** to display the **Insert Hyperlink** dialog box. Click **Existing File or Web Page**.

c. Navigate to the **PowerPoint Chapter 6** folder and select **Lastname_Firstname_6B_Advertisement**. In the **Insert Hyperlink** dialog box, click **Bookmark** to display the **Select Place in Document** dialog box. Click the last slide—*Treat Yourself to a New Sedan*—and then click **OK**. Click **OK** to close the **Insert Hyperlink** dialog box.

d. Click the **SLIDE SHOW tab**, and then in the **Set Up group**, click **Set Up Slide Show**. In the **Set Up Show** dialog box, under **Show type**, select the **Presented by a speaker (full screen)** option button, if necessary. Under **Advance slides**, click **Manually**, and then click **OK**.

e. View slide show **From Current Slide**. Click the hyperlinks to test them.

5 ▶ Make **Slide 10** the active slide.

a. Click to select the picture of the dashboard. Click the **INSERT tab**. In the **Links group**, click **Hyperlink**. In the **Insert Hyperlink** dialog box, under **Link to**, click **Existing File or Web Page**.

b. Click the **Browse for File**, navigate to the location where your student files are stored, and then double-click **p06D_ESC.docx**. Click **OK**.

6 ▶ **Slide 10** should be the active slide.

a. In the title, select (*ESC*). On the **INSERT tab**, in the **Links group**, click **Hyperlink**. In the **Insert Hyperlink** dialog box, click **ScreenTip**. Type **Benefits** Click **OK**.

b. Under **Link to**, click **Create New Document**. In the **Name of new document** box, substitute your own first name and last name and type **Lastname_Firstname_6D_ESC_Benefits.docx** Make sure the **Edit the new document now** option button is selected, and then click **OK**.

c. When Microsoft Word displays, type **Benefits of ESC** and then press Enter. Type **Save between 6,000 and 11,000 lives annually.** Press Enter. Type **Prevent up to 275,000 injuries each year.** Press Enter two times, and then type **Lastname_Firstname_6D_ESC_Benefits.docx**

d. **Save** your document in the **PowerPoint Chapter 6** folder, and then **Exit** Microsoft Word.

e. View the slide show **From Current Slide**. Click to test the hyperlink. **Close** Word, and then press Esc to return to **Normal** view.

7 ▶ Make **Slide 7** the active slide.

a. Click the **INSERT tab**. In the **Illustrations group**, click **Shapes**.

b. At the bottom of the list, under **Action Buttons**, click the third button—**Action Button: Beginning**.

c. Position the ✛ pointer at the **4.5-inch mark left of 0** on the **horizontal ruler** and at the **3-inch mark below 0** on the **vertical ruler**, and then click once to insert the shape and display the **Action Settings** dialog box.

(Project 6D Safety continues on the next page)

CHAPTER REVIEW

d. In the **Action Settings** dialog box, click the **Mouse Over tab**. Click the **Hyperlink to** option button, click the **Hyperlink to arrow**, and select **First Slide**. Click the **Play sound** check box, click the **Play sound check box arrow**, and then select **Chime**. Click **OK**.

e. On the **FORMAT tab**, in the **Size group**, change the **Height** to **0.5"** and the **Width** to **0.5"**.

f. View the slide show **From Current Slide**, click or mouse over the **action button** to test it. Press Esc.

8 If necessary, make the **title slide** the active slide.

a. Click the **SLIDE SHOW tab**. In the **Start Slide Show group**, click **Custom Slide Show arrow**, and then click **Custom Shows**. In the **Custom Shows** dialog box, click **New**. In the **Slide show name** box, remove existing text, and type **Standard Safety Features**

b. In the **Slides in presentation** box, click to select **Slides 1, 2, 3, 4**, and **5**. Click **Add**. Scroll to and then click **Slide 13**, and then click **Add** to add it to the slides in the custom show. Click **OK**.

c. Click **Edit**. Under **Slides in presentation**, click **Slide 6** and add it to the custom show. Under **Slides in custom show**, click **Slide 7**, and then click the **up arrow** so the new slide is before the *Penn Liberty Motors Safety Team* slide. Click **OK**.

d. In the **Custom Shows** dialog box, click **New**. In the **Slide show name** box, remove existing text and type **Optional Safety Features**

e. In the **Slides in presentation** box, click to select **Slides 7, 8, 9, 10, 11, 12, and 13**. Click **Add**. Click **OK**, and then **Close** the **Custom Shows** dialog box.

f. In the **Start Slide Show group**, click **Custom Slide Show arrow**. Click **Standard Safety Features**, and then view the slides. Repeat the procedure to view **Optional Safety Features**.

9 Make the **title slide** the active slide, if necessary.

a. Click to select the picture of the flag. On the **INSERT tab**, in the **Links group**, click **Hyperlink**. In the **Insert Hyperlink** dialog box, under **Link to**, click **Place in This Document**.

b. In the **Insert Hyperlink** dialog box, under **Select a place in this document**, scroll down to display the **Custom Shows**. Select **Optional Safety Features**, and then click the **Show and return** check box. Click **OK**.

c. View the slide show **From Beginning**, and then click the flag to view the custom show. When the **title slide** displays, press Esc.

10 Make **Slide 13** the active slide.

a. On the **HOME tab**, in the **Slides group**, click the **New Slide arrow**, and then from the displayed list, click **Duplicate Selected Slides**.

b. On **Slide 14**, right-click the picture, and then click **Change Picture**. In the **Insert Pictures** dialog box, on the right of **From a file**, click **Browse**. Navigate to the location where you are storing your student data files, and then insert the file **p06D_Customer_Service.jpg**. On the slide title, select the words **Safety Team**, and then type **Customer Service** Place the insertion point before *Customer* and then press Enter.

c. Make **Slide 6** the active slide. Click the **SLIDE SHOW tab**. In the **Set Up group**, click **Hide Slide**.

d. Make **Slide 13** the active slide. Right-click the thumbnail for **Slide 13** to display the shortcut menu. Click **Hide Slide**.

e. Right-click the **Slide 6** thumbnail to display the shortcut menu again, and then click **Hide Slide** to unhide **Slide 6**.

11 On the **SLIDE SHOW tab**, in the **Start Slide Show group**, click **From Beginning**. Move the mouse to the bottom left corner of the screen to reveal the six navigation buttons. Move the mouse pointer to the right to reveal each button.

a. At the lower left corner of the screen, click the **Advance next** button. Click the **Advance previous** button. Click the fourth button—**See all slides**.

b. Click **Slide 7** to display it. Right-click anywhere on the slide, click **Custom Show**, and then click **Standard Safety Features**. Click to view each of the slides in the custom show. When the slide show is finished, press Esc.

c. On the **SLIDE SHOW tab**, in the **Start Slide Show group**, click **From Beginning**. At the lower left corner of the screen, click the **More slide show options** button, and then click **Show Presenter View**.

d. In **Presenter View**, below the large slide, click the **Black or unblack slide show** button.

(Project 6D Safety continues on the next page)

CHAPTER REVIEW

e. Click the **Black or unblack slide show** button to make the large slide visible again.

f. Below the large slide, click **See all slides**, and then click **Slide 8**. Click **More slide show options**, and then click **Hide Presenter View**.

12 At the lower left corner of the screen, click the third button—**Pen and laser pointer tools.** Click **Laser Pointer** and move the mouse around the screen. Click the **Pen and laser pointer tools** button, and then click **Laser Pointer** to turn it off.

a. At the lower left corner of the screen, click the third button—**Pen and laser pointer tools,** and then click **Highlighter**.

b. Place the highlighter pointer to the left of the *S* in *Seat-Belt*, and then click and drag to the right to highlight *Seat-Belt Use.*

c. Click the **Pen and laser pointer tools** button, and then click **Pen**. Circle the first bulleted item— *Built-in Sensors Detect.*

d. Click the **Pen and laser pointer tools** button, and then click the second ink color—**Black**. Circle the last bullet—*Includes On-Off Switch.*

e. Click **Pen and laser pointer tools** button, click **Eraser**, and then click to delete the black annotation on the last bulleted item.

f. Press Esc two times. In the displayed dialog box, which prompts you to keep your annotations, click **Keep**.

13 Make the **title slide** the active slide.

a. On the **SLIDE SHOW tab**, in the **Set Up group**, click **Rehearse Timings**.

b. In the **Slide Time** display, wait for four seconds, and then click **Next Slide arrow**. Repeat for all slides. When prompted, click **Yes** to save the timings.

c. On the **PowerPoint task bar**, click the **Slide Sorter icon**, and then after the slides display, drag the **Zoom slider** to **70%**.

d. In the **Set Up group**, click **Set Up Slide Show**. In the **Set Up Show** dialog box, under **Advance slides**, select

Using timings, if present. Under **Show type**, select the **Browsed at a kiosk (full screen)** option button. Click **OK**.

e. View the slide show **From Beginning** and view all slides. When **Slide 1** appears again, press Esc.

f. On the **SLIDE SHOW tab**, in the **Set Up group**, click **Set Up Slide Show**. Under **Show type**, select **Presented by a speaker (full screen)**. Under **Advance slides**, select **Manually**. Click **OK**.

g. On the **VIEW tab**, in the **Presentation Views**, click **Normal** to return to **Normal** view.

14 Hold down Ctrl and click thumbnails to select **Slides 1, 2, 3, 4, 5, 6, 7, 8, 9, 10, 11, 12,** and **14.**

a. On the **FILE tab**, click **Print**. Under **Settings**, click the **Print All Slides arrow**, and then point to **Print Selection**. Press Esc to return to **Normal** view.

15 On the **INSERT tab**, in the **Text group**:

a. Click **Header & Footer** to display the **Header and Footer** dialog box.

b. Click the **Notes and Handouts tab**. Under **Include on page**, select the **Date and time** check box, and then select **Fixed**. If necessary, clear the **Header** check box, and then select the **Page number and Footer** check boxes. In the **Footer** box, using your own name, type **Lastname_Firstname_6D_Safety** and then click **Apply To All**.

16 Click the **FILE tab**, and then in the lower right portion of the screen, click **Show All Properties**.

a. In the **Tags** box, type **safety, seat belts** If necessary, in the **Subject** box type your course name and section number.

b. In the **Author** box, right-click the existing author name, click **Edit Property**, replace the existing text with your first and last name, click outside textbox to deselect, and then click **OK**.

17 Print **Handouts 9 Slides Horizontal**, or submit your presentation electronically as directed by your instructor.

18 **Save** the presentation. **Exit** PowerPoint.

END | You have completed Project 6D

CONTENT-BASED ASSESSMENTS

Mastering PowerPoint | Project 6E Race Car

In the following Mastering PowerPoint project, you will modify a PowerPoint presentation advertising the Annual Race Car Rally hosted by Penn Liberty Motors. You will apply slide transitions and custom animation effects to the slide show to make the slide show more dynamic. The purpose is to appeal to race car enthusiasts. Your completed presentation will look similar to Figure 6.77.

PROJECT FILES

For Project 6E, you will need the following files:

p06E_Race_Car.pptx   p06E_Tires1.wav
p06E_Fast_Car.wav   p06E_Drag_Race.wav
p06E_Car_Horn.wav

You will save your presentation as:

Lastname_Firstname_6E_Race_Car.pptx

PROJECT RESULTS

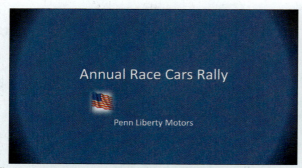

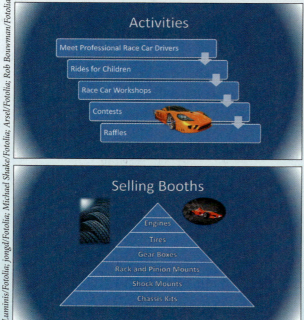

Luminis/Fotolia; jongd1/Fotolia; Michael Shake/Fotolia; Arsel/Fotolia; Rob Bouwman/Fotolia

FIGURE 6.77

(Project 6E Race Car continues on the next page)

CONTENT-BASED ASSESSMENTS

1 Start PowerPoint. Locate and open the file **p06E_ Race_Car**. **Save** the file in your **PowerPoint Chapter 6** folder using the file name **Lastname_Firstname_6E_Race_Car**

2 Make the **title slide** the active slide. Display the **Transitions** gallery, and then under **Subtle**, in the first row, click the third transition—**Fade**. Set the **Duration** to **1.50**, and then click **Apply To All**.

3 Make **Slide 2** the active slide. Click the **content placeholder** to select the **SmartArt** graphic. In the **Add Animation** gallery, under **Entrance**, click **Fly In**. Click **Effect Options**. Under **Sequence**, choose **Level at Once**.

4 Open the **Animation Pane**, right-click the entrance effect for content placeholder, and then click **Effect Options**. Change the **Direction** to **From Left**. On the **Timing tab**, set the **Duration** to **1 seconds (Fast)**.

5 On **Slide 2**, click to select the **car** graphic, and then apply the **Fly In** entrance effect. Change **Direction** to **From Top-Left**, set the **Duration** to **2 seconds (Medium)**, and then set the **Start** to **After Previous**.

6 On the **TRANSITIONS tab**, in the **Timing group**, insert the sound file **p06E_Fast_Car.wav** from the student data files.

7 Make **Slide 3** the active slide. Select the **SmartArt** graphic, and then apply the **Fly In** entrance animation effect. Click **Effect Options**, under **Sequence**, and then select **One by One**. Click **Effect Options** again, and then select **From Top**. Change the **Duration** to **1 seconds (Fast)**.

8 On **Slide 3**, click to select the **car** picture, and then add the **Fly In** entrance effect. In the **Animation Pane**, right-click the entrance effect for the picture, select **Effect Options**, and then change the **Direction** to **From Top-Right**. Under **Enhancements**, add the sound file **p06E_Car_Horn.wav** from your student data files. Change the **Start** to **After Previous** and the **Duration** to **2 seconds (Medium)**.

9 View the slide show **From Current Slide** to test the transition and animation entrance effects on **Slide 3**.

10 Make **Slide 4** the active slide. Click to select the **SmartArt** graphic. Click **Add Animation**, and then click the **Wipe** entrance effect. With the **SmartArt** selected, click **Effect Options**, and then under **Sequence**, click **One by One**. In the **Animation Pane**, right-click **Content Place…** and then click **Effect Options**. In **Wipe** dialog

box, on the **Timing tab**, click the **Start arrow**, and then click **After Previous**. Click the **SmartArt Animation tab**, select the **Reverse order** check box, and then click **OK**.

11 On **Slide 4**, click to select the **car picture**. Click **Add Animation**, and then click **More Exit Effects**. Under **Moderate**, click **Basic Zoom**. In the **Animation Pane**, right-click **Picture 4**, and then click **Effect Options**. Under **Enhancements**, click the **Sound arrow**, and add the sound file **p06E_Tires1.wav** from your student data files.

12 View the slide show **From Current Slide** to test the transition and animation entrance effects on **Slide 4**.

13 Make **Slide 5** the active slide. Select the **title** placeholder. Click **Add Animation**. Select **More Motion Paths**, and then under **Lines_Curves**, select **Arc Up**.

14 On **Slide 5**, select the **car picture**. Click **Add Animation**, under **More Motion Paths**, click **Diagonal Down Right**.

15 On **Slide 5**, select the **SmartArt** graphic. Display the **Animations** gallery. Under **Exit**, click **Fade**. Click **Effect Options,** and then select **One by One**. Click to select the **car picture**, and then apply the **Grow/Shrink** emphasis effect. Click **Effect Options**, and then under **Amount**, select **Smaller**. Select the car graphic if necessary, and then insert the sound file **p06E_Drag_Race.wav** from your student data files.

16 View the slide show **From Current Slide** to test the transition and animation entrance effects on **Slide 5**.

17 Make the **title slide** the active slide. Click to select the **title** placeholder. Display the **Add Animation** gallery, and then click **More Entrance Effects**. Under **Basic**, select **Blinds**. In the **Animation Pane**, right-click the entrance effect for the title, and then click **Effect Options**. Set the **Start** to **With Previous** and the **Duration** to **1 seconds (Fast)**. On the **TRANSITIONS tab**, in the **Timing group**, apply the **Whoosh** sound.

18 Start the slide show **From Beginning**, and then view the animation effects. When you are finished, return to **Normal** view.

19 Insert a footer on the notes and handouts that includes a fixed date and time, the page number, and the file name.

20 Click the **FILE tab**, and then in the lower right portion of the screen, click **Show All Properties**. In the **Tags** box, type **race, exhibition, event** In the **Subject**

(Project 6E Race Car continues on the next page)

CONTENT-BASED ASSESSMENTS

box, type your course name and section number. In the **Author** box, right-click the existing author name, click **Edit Property**, replace the existing text with your first and last name, click outside textbox to deselect, and then click **OK**.

21 Print **Handouts 6 Slides Horizontal**, or submit your presentation electronically as directed by your instructor.

22 **Save** the presentation. **Exit** PowerPoint.

END | You have completed Project 6E

CONTENT-BASED ASSESSMENTS

Mastering PowerPoint | Project 6F Custom Detail Aspects

In the following Mastering PowerPoint project, you will modify a PowerPoint presentation listing many of the customization services available at Penn Liberty Motors to give a vehicle a unique appearance. You will insert hyperlinks and create custom slide shows of interior and exterior detailing. You will annotate the slide show and create a self-running version of the presentation for use in the automobile dealership. Your completed presentation will look similar to Figure 6.78.

Apply 6B skills from these Objectives:

4 Insert Hyperlinks

5 Create Custom Slide Shows

6 Present and View a Slide Presentation

PROJECT FILES

For Project 6F, you will need the following file:

p06F_Custom_Detail.pptx

You will save your files as:

Lastname_Firstname_6F_Custom_Detail.pptx
Lastname_Firstname_Dashboard.docx

PROJECT RESULTS

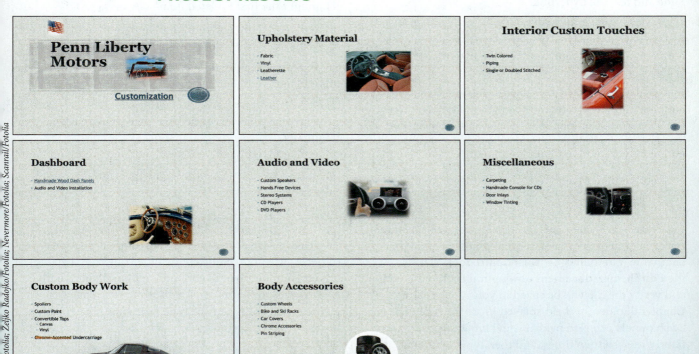

FIGURE 6.78

shock/Fotolia; Zeljko Radojko/Fotolia; Nevermore/Fotolia; Scanrail/Fotolia

(Project 6F Custom Detail Aspects continues on the next page)

CONTENT-BASED ASSESSMENTS

1 Start PowerPoint. Locate and open the file **p06F_Custom_Detail**. **Save** the file in your **PowerPoint Chapter 6** folder using the file name **Lastname_Firstname_6F_Custom_Detail**

2 Make the **title slide** the active slide, if necessary. Click to select the picture of the **car**. Display the **Insert Hyperlink** dialog box, and then type the address **www.dmv.state.pa.us** Include the **ScreenTip Pennsylvania Driver and Vehicle Services** View **From Current Slide** and test the hyperlink. Note: As of this writing, the *www.dmv.state.pa.us* website was active. You might receive an error message stating that the Internet server could not be located.

3 Make **Slide 7** the active slide. At the bottom right corner of the slide, insert an **Action Button: Forward or Next**, which is found in the last row of the **Shapes** gallery. Size the button **0.5"** wide and high. View **From Current Slide** and test the hyperlink.

4 Make **Slide 2** the active slide. Select *Leather*. Insert a hyperlink to **Place in This Document**, and then click **3. Interior Custom Touches**. Test the hyperlink.

5 Make **Slide 8** the active slide. Select *Contact Us*, and then add a **Hyperlink** to an **Email Address**. For the email address, type **customteam@libertymotors.com** Include the **ScreenTip**, **Contact us for all your customization needs.** Test the link, and then **Close** the email program. Notice that if you are using a campus computer, the actual email program may not work as it would at home.

6 Make **Slide 4** the active slide. Select the first bulleted item—*Handmade Wood Dash Panels*. Set up a **Hyperlink** to **Create New Document**. In the **Name of new document** box, substitute your own last and first name and type **Lastname_Firstname_6F_Dashboard.docx** Make sure the **Edit the new document now** option button is selected and verify the file will be saved in your **PowerPoint Chapter 6** folder. In the displayed Word document, type **Dash panels are also available in aluminum and carbon fiber.** Press Enter two times, and then type **Lastname_Firstname_6F_Dashboard.docx** Save the document **PowerPoint Chapter 6**, and then **Exit** Word.

7 Create a new custom slide show named **Interior Customization** Add **Slide 1** through **Slide 6**. Create

another custom slide show named **Body Customization** Add **Slide 1**, **Slide 7**, and **Slide 8**. Move the *Body Accessories* slide so it is number 2 in the list. Remove **Slide 1**.

8 Make the **title slide** the active slide. Double-click to select the subtitle *Customization*. Insert a hyperlink to **Place in This Document**. Scroll down to custom shows, and then click **Body Customization**. Select the **Show and return** check box, and then click **OK**. View **From Current Slide** and test the link to view the 2 slides, and then return to the title slide.

9 Hide **Slide 5**.

10 View the slideshow and use the onscreen navigation tools to go to **Slide 7**. Click the **Pen and laser tools** button, and then click **Highlighter**. Change the **Ink Color** to **Red**. In the last bulleted item, highlight *Chrome-Accented*. Highlight the first bulleted item—*Spoilers*.

11 Remove the highlighting on *Spoilers*.

12 **Keep** your ink annotations. Return to **Normal** view.

13 Make the **title slide** the active slide. Set each slide to display for four seconds.

14 Set the presentation to be **Presented by a speaker (full screen)** and then under Advance slides, click **Manually**.

15 Insert a footer on the notes and handouts that includes a fixed date and time, the page number, and the file name.

16 Click the **FILE tab**, and then in the lower right portion of the screen, click **Show All Properties**. In the **Tags** box, type **dashboard, custom, accessories** If necessary, in the **Subject** box type your course name and section number. In the **Author** box, right-click the existing author name, click **Edit Property**, replace the existing text with your first and last name, click outside textbox to deselect, and then click **OK**.

17 Print **Handouts 9 Slides Horizontal**, or submit your presentation electronically as directed by your instructor.

18 **Save** the presentation. **Exit** PowerPoint.

END | You have completed Project 6F

CONTENT-BASED ASSESSMENTS

Mastering PowerPoint   Project 6G Repairs

In the following Mastering PowerPoint project, you will modify a PowerPoint presentation that advertises Penn Liberty Motors' Repair Department and lists the types of repairs performed and the goodwill customer services available. You will apply slide transitions and custom animation effects, insert hyperlinks, and create custom slide shows. You will annotate the slide show and create a self-running version of the presentation. Your completed presentation will look similar to Figure 6.79.

Apply 6A and 6B skills from these Objectives:

1 Apply and Modify Slide Transitions
2 Apply Custom Animation Effects
3 Modify Animation Effects
4 Insert Hyperlinks
5 Create Custom Slide Shows
6 Present and View a Slide Presentation

PROJECT FILES

For Project 6G, you will need the following files:

p06G_Repairs.pptx
p06G_Emergency.docx

You will save your presentation as:

Lastname_Firstname_6G_Repairs.pptx

PROJECT RESULTS

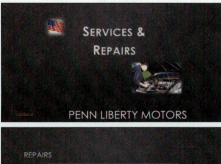

FIGURE 6.79

Uwe Annas/Fotolia; Anton Gvozdikov/Fotolia

(Project 6G Repairs continues on the next page)

CONTENT-BASED ASSESSMENTS

1 Start PowerPoint. Locate and open the file **p06G_Repairs**, and then **Save** the file as **Lastname_Firstname_6G_Repairs**

2 Make the **title slide** the active slide. Apply a **Wipe** transition to all slides.

3 Make **Slide 2** the active slide. Select the **SmartArt** graphic. Add the **Fly In** entrance effect, set the **Effect Options** to **One by One**, and then set the **Start** to **After Previous**. In the **Animation Pane**, select **Effect Options**. Set the **Direction** to **From Left**, and then change the **Duration** to **2 seconds (Medium)**.

4 Make **Slide 3** the active slide. Select the **SmartArt** graphic. Apply the **Fly In** entrance effect, set the **Effect Options** to **As One Object**, and then change the **Direction** to **From Left** and the **Duration** to **2 seconds (Medium)**.

5 Make **Slide 4** the active slide. Select the **SmartArt** graphic, and then add the **Fade** entrance animation effect. Change the **Effect Options** to **One by One**. Change the **Start** to **After Previous**.

6 Make **Slide 5** the active slide. Using the same techniques, apply the same animation entrance effects to the **SmartArt** graphic as you applied to **Slide 4**.

7 Make **Slide 6** the active slide. Select the **SmartArt** graphic. Apply the **Wipe** entrance animation effect. Set the **Effect Options** to **One by One**, the **Start** to **After Previous**, the **Direction** to **From Left**, and the **Duration** to **1 seconds (Fast)**.

8 Make **Slide 7** the active slide. Using the same techniques, apply the same animation effects to the **SmartArt** graphic as you applied to **Slide 6**.

9 Make **Slide 7** the active slide. At the bottom right corner of the slide, insert an **Action Button: Home**, which is found in the last row of the **Shapes** gallery. Size the button about **0.5"** wide and high. Test the hyperlink.

10 Make the **title slide** the active slide. Select the picture of the **car mechanic**, and then set up a **Hyperlink** to **Link to** an **Existing File or Web Page**. Navigate to the location where your student files are stored, and then

click **p06G_Emergency.docx**. For the **ScreenTip**, type **24-Hour Phone Number** Test the hyperlink.

11 Make **Slide 6** the active slide. Select the picture, and then set up a **Hyperlink** to **Place in This Document**. Select **7. Customer Service**. Test the hyperlink.

12 Make **Slide 1** the active slide. Select *Contact Us*, and then set up a **Hyperlink** to an **E-mail Address**. For the **Address**, type **repairs@libertymotors.com** Test the hyperlink.

13 Set up a new custom slide show named **Warranty and Maintenance** Add **Slides 1**, **3**, **4**, and **5** to the custom slide show. Set up a second custom slide show named **Insurance Claims** Add **Slide 6** and **Slide 7** to the custom slide show.

14 Make **Slide 2** the active slide. Select the picture. Set up a **Hyperlink** to a **Place in This document**. Scroll down to the custom shows, and then click **Insurance Claims**. Click the **Show and return** check box. Test the hyperlink.

15 View the slide show **From Beginning**. Use the **Navigation tools** to go to **Slide 4**. Click the **Pen and laser pointer tools**, and then click **Pen**. In the gray area before each of the five text line items, draw a check mark. **Keep the ink annotations**.

16 Insert a footer on the notes and handouts that includes a fixed date and time, the page number, and the file name.

17 Click the **FILE tab**, and then in the lower right portion of the screen, click **Show All Properties**. In the **Tags** box, type **insurance, maintenance, warranty** If necessary, in the **Subject** box type your course name and section number. In the **Author** box, right-click the existing author name, click **Edit Property**, replace the existing text with your first and last name, click outside textbox to deselect, and then click **OK**.

18 Print **Handouts 9 Slides Horizontal**, or submit your presentation electronically as directed by your instructor.

19 **Save** the presentation. **Exit** PowerPoint.

END | You have completed Project 6G

CONTENT-BASED ASSESSMENTS

Apply a combination of the **6A** and **6B** skills.

GO! Fix It	Project 6H Staff	Online

GO! Make It	Project 6I Auto Show	Online

GO! Solve It	Project 6J Leasing	Online

GO! Solve It	Project 6K Special Orders	

PROJECT FILES

For Project 6K, you will need the following file:

p06K_Special_Orders.pptx

You will save your presentation as:

Lastname_Firstname_6K_Special_Orders.pptx

In this project, you will customize a slide show showcasing special-order vehicles, such as limousines, motorcycles, and race cars, available at Penn Liberty Motors. You will apply transitions and customized entrance and exit animation effects.

Open **p06K_Special_Orders**, and then save it as **Lastname_Firstname_6K_Special_Orders** Apply transitions and add entrance and exit animation effects. Insert a hyperlink to the Specialized Inventory text for the email address: **custom@libertymotors.com** Use hyperlinks to link the picture of a vehicle to its features. Create at least two basic custom shows to appeal to two different vehicle enthusiasts, and then insert a hyperlink to one of the custom shows. Create an action button.

Insert a Header & Footer on the Notes and Handouts that includes a footer with the text **Lastname_Firstname_6K_Special_Orders** In the Properties, add your name, course name and section number for the subject, and the tags **classic, limousines** Save your presentation. Print Handouts 4 slides per page, or submit electronically as directed by your instructor.

(Project 6K Special Orders continues on the next page)

CONTENT-BASED ASSESSMENTS

Performance Level

Performance Element	Exemplary	Proficient	Developing
Formatted slide show with a variety of transitions and effects.	Slide show included relevant transitions and effects.	Slide show included a variety of transitions and effects, but they were not appropriate for the presentation.	Slide show contained no transitions and effects.
Inserted hyperlinks to website, to email address, and to place in the slide show.	All hyperlinks worked correctly.	One of the hyperlinks did not work correctly.	Hyperlinks were not created, or they did not work correctly.
Created two custom slide shows and linked one of them.	Created two custom shows and one was linked correctly.	Created one custom show and did not link.	No custom slide shows were created.
Created an action button.	The action button produced the intended result.	Action button was created but did not work properly.	No action button was created.

Performance Criteria

END | You have completed Project 6K

OUTCOMES-BASED ASSESSMENTS

RUBRIC

The following outcomes-based assessments are *open-ended assessments*. That is, there is no specific correct result; your result will depend on your approach to the information provided. Make *Professional Quality* your goal. Use the following scoring rubric to guide you in *how* to approach the problem and then to evaluate *how well* your approach solves the problem.

The *criteria*—Software Mastery, Content, Format and Layout, and Process—represent the knowledge and skills you have gained that you can apply to solving the problem. The *levels of performance*—Professional Quality, Approaching Professional Quality, or Needs Quality Improvements—help you and your instructor evaluate your result.

	Your completed project is of Professional Quality if you:	Your completed project is Approaching Professional Quality if you:	Your completed project Needs Quality Improvements if you:
1-Software Mastery	Choose and apply the most appropriate skills, tools, and features and identify efficient methods to solve the problem.	Choose and apply some appropriate skills, tools, and features, but not in the most efficient manner.	Choose inappropriate skills, tools, or features, or are inefficient in solving the problem.
2-Content	Construct a solution that is clear and well organized, contains content that is accurate, appropriate to the audience and purpose, and is complete. Provide a solution that contains no errors in spelling, grammar, or style.	Construct a solution in which some components are unclear, poorly organized, inconsistent, or incomplete. Misjudge the needs of the audience. Have some errors in spelling, grammar, or style, but the errors do not detract from comprehension.	Construct a solution that is unclear, incomplete, or poorly organized; contains some inaccurate or inappropriate content; and contains many errors in spelling, grammar, or style. Do not solve the problem.
3-Format & Layout	Format and arrange all elements to communicate information and ideas, clarify function, illustrate relationships, and indicate relative importance.	Apply appropriate format and layout features to some elements, but not others. Overuse features, causing minor distraction.	Apply format and layout that does not communicate information or ideas clearly. Do not use format and layout features to clarify function, illustrate relationships, or indicate relative importance. Use available features excessively, causing distraction.
4-Process	Use an organized approach that integrates planning, development, self-assessment, revision, and reflection.	Demonstrate an organized approach in some areas, but not others; or, use an insufficient process of organization throughout.	Do not use an organized approach to solve the problem.

OUTCOMES-BASED ASSESSMENTS

Apply a combination of the **6A** and **6B** skills.

Build from
Scratch

GO! Think   Project 6L Car Purchase

PROJECT FILES

For Project 6L, you will need the following files:

New blank PowerPoint presentation
p06L_Off_Lease.docx

You will save your presentation as:

Lastname_Firstname_6L_Car_Purchase.pptx

Penn Liberty Motors has launched a new sales initiative to sell used cars. In this project, you will create a presentation with a minimum of six slides comparing the benefits of buying a new car versus buying a used car. In addition, certified lease cars should be part of the presentation. Insert a hyperlink on one slide to hyperlink to the **p06L_Off_Lease.docx** file provided in the student files. Include transitions and custom animation effects in the presentation. Create a self-running slide show.

Insert a Header & Footer on the Notes and Handouts that includes the date and time fixed, the page number, and a footer with the text **Lastname_Firstname_6L_Car Purchase** In Properties, add your name and course information and the tags **certification, lease** Save your presentation. Print Handouts 6 slides per page, or submit electronically as directed by your instructor.

END | You have completed Project 6L

Build from
Scratch

GO! Think   Project 6M Security   Online

Build from
Scratch

You and GO!   Project 6N Digital Sound   Online

Glossary

Action button A built-in button shape that you can add to your presentation and then assign an action to occur upon the click of a mouse or with a mouse over.

Action query A query that creates a new table or changes data in an existing table.

Additive The term that describes the behavior of a filter when each additional filter that you apply is based on the current filter, and that further reduces the number of records displayed.

Address bar (Internet Explorer) The area at the top of the Internet Explorer window that displays, and where you can type, a URL—Uniform Resource Locator—which is an address that uniquely identifies a location on the Internet.

Address bar (Windows) The bar at the top of a folder window with which you can navigate to a different folder or library, or go back to a previous one.

Advanced Filter A filter that can specify three or more criteria for a particular column, apply complex criteria to two or more columns, or specify computed criteria.

After Previous A custom animation that starts the animation effect immediately after the previous effect in the list finishes playing.

Aggregate function Performs a calculation on a column of data and returns a single value.

Alignment The placement of text or objects relative to the left and right margins.

Alignment guides Green lines that display when you move an object to assist in alignment.

All Markup A Track Changes view that displays the document with all revisions and comments visible.

And comparison operator The comparison operator that requires each and every one of the comparison criteria to be true.

Animated GIF A file format made up of a series of frames within a single file that creates the illusion of animation by displaying the frames one after the other in quick succession.

Animation 1. Any type of motion or movement that occurs as the presentation moves from slide to slide. 2. A special visual effect or sound effect added to text or an object.

Animation Pane The area that contains a list of the animation effects added to your presentation. From this pane, you can add or modify effects.

Annotation A note or a highlight that can be saved or discarded.

Antonyms Words with an opposite meaning.

App The term that commonly refers to computer programs that run from the device software on a smartphone or a tablet computer—for example, iOS, Android, or Windows Phone—or computer programs that run from the browser software on a desktop PC or laptop PC—for example Internet Explorer, Safari, Firefox, or Chrome.

App for Office A webpage that works within one of the Office applications, such as Excel, and that you download from the Office Store.

Append A feature that allows you to add data to an existing table.

Append query An action query that adds new records to an existing table by adding data from another Access database or from a table in the same database.

Apps for Office 2013 and SharePoint 2013 A collection of downloadable apps that enable you to create and view information within your familiar Office programs.

Area chart A chart type that shows trends over time.

Arguments The values that an Excel function uses to perform calculations or operations.

Arithmetic operators Mathematical symbols used in building expressions.

Arrange All The command that tiles all open program windows on the screen.

Ascending The term that refers to the arrangement of text that is sorted alphabetically from A to Z, numbers sorted from lowest to highest, or dates and times sorted from earliest to latest.

Auditing The process of examining a worksheet for errors in formulas.

Author The owner, or creator, of the original document.

AutoFilter menu A drop-down menu from which you can filter a column by a list of values, by a format, or by criteria.

AutoFit A table feature that automatically adjusts column widths or the width of the entire table.

AutoFit Contents A table feature that resizes the column widths to accommodate the maximum field size.

Axis A line that serves as a frame of reference for measurement and that borders the chart plot area.

Back up A feature that creates a copy of the original database to protect against lost data.

Backstage tabs The area along the left side of Backstage view with tabs to display screens with related groups of commands.

Backstage view A centralized space for file management tasks; for example, opening, saving, printing, publishing, or sharing a file. A navigation pane displays along the left side with tabs that group file-related tasks together.

Balloon The outline shape in which a comment or formatting change displays.

Bar chart A chart type that shows a comparison among related data.

Basic custom slide show A separate presentation saved with its own title containing some of the slides from the original presentation.

Border A frame around a picture.

Border Painter A table feature that applies selected formatting to specific borders of a table.

Brightness The perceived radiance or luminosity of an image.

Building blocks Reusable pieces of content or other document parts—for example, headers, footers, and page number formats—that are stored in galleries.

Building Blocks Organizer A feature that enables you to view—in a single location—all of the available building blocks from all the different galleries.

Button control A control that enables individuals to add a command button to a form or report that will perform an action when the button is clicked.

Calculated field A field that obtains its data by using a formula to perform a calculation or computation.

Caption A title that is added to a Word object and numbered sequentially; or, text that helps to identify or explain a picture or graphic.

Category labels The labels that display along the bottom of a chart to identify the categories of data.

Cell The intersection of a column and row.

Cell margins The amount of space between a cell's content and the left, right, top, and bottom borders of the cell.

Cell spacing The distance between the individual cells in a table.

Cell style A defined set of formatting characteristics, such as font, font size, font color, cell borders, and cell shading.

Center alignment The alignment of text or objects that is centered horizontally between the left and right margins.

Change Case A formatting command that allows you to quickly change the capitalization of selected text.

Character style A style, indicated by the symbol **a**, that contains formatting characteristics that you apply to text, such as font name, font size, font color, bold emphasis, and so on.

Chart A visual representation of numerical data.

Chart area The entire chart and all of its elements.

Chart data range The group of cells with red, purple, and blue shading that is used to create a chart.

Chart Elements A Word feature that displays commands to add, remove, or change chart elements, such as the legend, gridlines, and data labels.

Chart elements Objects that make up a chart.

Chart Filters A Word feature that displays commands to define what data points and names display on a chart.

Chart sheet A workbook sheet that contains only a chart.

Chart style The overall visual look of a chart in terms of its graphic effects, colors, and backgrounds.

Chart Styles A Word feature that displays commands to apply a style and color scheme to a chart.

Chevron A V-shaped symbol that indicates more information or options are available.

Circular reference An Excel error that occurs when a formula directly or indirectly refers to itself.

Click The action of pressing and releasing the left button on a mouse pointing device one time.

Click and type pointer The text select—I-beam—pointer with various attached shapes that indicate which formatting—left-aligned, centered, or right-aligned—will be applied when you double-click in a blank area of a document.

Clip art Downloadable predefined graphics available online from Office.com and other sites.

Clipboard A temporary storage area that holds text or graphics that you select and then cut or copy.

Cloud computing Refers to applications and services that are accessed over the Internet, rather than to applications that are installed on your local computer.

Cloud storage Online storage of data so that you can access your data from different places and devices.

Collaborate To work with others as a team in an intellectual endeavor to complete a shared task or to achieve a shared goal.

Column chart A chart in which the data is arranged in columns and that is useful for showing data changes over a period of time or for illustrating comparisons among items.

Combine A Track Changes feature that allows you to review two different documents containing revisions, both based on an original document.

Combo box A control that enables individuals to select from a list or to type a value.

Comma delimited file A file type that saves the contents of the cells by placing commas between them and an end-of-paragraph mark at the end of each row; also referred to as a CSV (comma separated values) file.

Commands An instruction to a computer program that causes an action to be carried out.

Comment A note that you can attach to a letter or word on a slide or to an entire slide. People use comments to provide feedback on a presentation.

Common dialog boxes The set of dialog boxes that includes Open, Save, and Save As, which are provided by the Windows programming interface, and which display and operate in all of the Office programs in the same manner.

Compare A Track Changes feature that enables you to review differences between an original document and the latest version of the document.

Comparison operators Symbols that evaluate each value to determine if it is the same (=), greater than (>), less than (<), or in between a range of values as specified by the criteria.

Compatibility Checker A feature that locates potential compatibility issues between PowerPoint 2013 and earlier versions of PowerPoint.

Compatibility mode Saves a presentation as PowerPoint 97-2003 presentation. It also ensures that no new or enhanced features in PowerPoint 2013 are available while you work with a document, so that people who are using previous versions of PowerPoint will have full editing capabilities.

Compound criteria The use of two or more criteria on the same row—all conditions must be met for the records to be included in the results.

Compound filter A filter that uses more than one condition—and one that uses comparison operators.

Compressed file A file that has been reduced in size and thus takes up less storage space and can be transferred to other computers quickly.

Compressed folder A folder that has been reduced in size and thus takes up less storage space and can be transferred to other computers quickly; also called a *zipped* folder.

Concatenation Linking or joining strings.

Context menus Menus that display commands and options relevant to the selected text or object; also called *shortcut menus*.

Context-sensitive commands Commands that display on a shortcut menu that relate to the object or text that you right-clicked.

Contextual tabs Tabs that are added to the ribbon automatically when a specific object, such as a picture, is selected, and that contain commands relevant to the selected object.

Contiguous Items that are adjacent to one another.

Contrast The difference between the darkest and lightest area of a picture.

Control An object, such as a label or text box, in a form or report that enables individuals to view or manipulate information stored in tables or queries.

ControlTip Displays descriptive text when the mouse pointer is paused over the control.

Copy A command that duplicates a selection and places it on the Clipboard.

Criteria Conditions that you specify in a logical function or filter.

Criteria range An area on your worksheet where you define the criteria for the filter, and that indicates how the displayed records are filtered.

Crop Remove unwanted or unnecessary areas of a picture.

Crop handles Used like sizing handles to crop a picture.

Crop tool The mouse pointer used when removing areas of a picture.

Cross join A join that displays when each row from one table is combined with each row in a related table, usually created unintentionally when you do not create a join line between related tables.

Crosstab query A query that uses an aggregate function for data that is grouped by two types of information and displays the data in a compact, spreadsheet-like format. A crosstab query always has at least one row heading, one column heading, and one summary field.

CSV (comma separated values) file A file type in which the cells in each row are separated by commas and an end-of-paragraph mark at the end of each row; also referred to as a *comma delimited file*.

Custom Filter A filter with which you can apply complex criteria to a single column.

Custom list A sort order that you can define.

Custom slide show Displays only the slides you want to display to an audience in the order you select.

Cut A command that removes a selection and places it on the Clipboard.

Cycle A category of SmartArt graphics that illustrates a continual process.

Data labels Labels that display the value, percentage, and/or category of each particular data point and can contain one or more of the choices listed—Series name, Category name, Value, or Percentage.

Data marker A column, bar, area, dot, pie slice, or other symbol in a chart that represents a single data point; related data points form a data series.

Data point A value that originates in a worksheet cell and that is represented in a chart by a data marker; or, the cells that contain numerical data used in a chart.

Data range border The blue line that surrounds the cells containing numerical data that display in the chart.

Data series Related data points represented by data markers; each data series has a unique color or pattern represented in the chart legend.

Data table A range of cells that shows how changing certain values in your formulas affect the results of those formulas and that makes it easy to calculate multiple versions in one operation.

Data validation A technique by which you can control the type of data or the values that are entered into a cell by limiting the acceptable values to a defined list.

Database An organized collection of facts related to a specific topic.

Default The term that refers to the current selection or setting that is automatically used by a computer program unless you specify otherwise.

Default value A value displayed for new records.

Defined name A word or string of characters in Excel that represents a cell, a range of cells, a formula, or a constant value; also referred to as simply a *name*.

Delete query An action query that removes records from an existing table in the same database.

Dependent cells Cells that contain formulas that refer to other cells.

Descending The term that refers to the arrangement of text that is sorted alphabetically from Z to A, numbers sorted from highest to lowest, or dates and times sorted from latest to earliest.

Deselect The action of canceling the selection of an object or block of text by clicking outside of the selection.

Desktop In Windows, the screen that simulates your work area.

Desktop app The term that commonly refers to a computer program that is installed on your computer and requires a computer operating system like Microsoft Windows or Apple OS to run.

Destination table The table to which you are appending records, attempting to match the fields.

Detail data The subtotaled rows that are totaled and summarized; typically adjacent to and either above or to the left of the summary data.

Dialog box A small window that contains options for completing a task.

Dialog Box Launcher A small icon that displays to the right of some group names on the ribbon, and which opens a related dialog box or pane providing additional options and commands related to that group.

Direct formatting The process of applying each format separately, for example bold, then font size, then font color, and so on.

Distribute Columns A command that adjusts the width of the selected columns so that they are equal.

Distribute Rows A command that causes the height of the selected rows to be equal.

Document properties Details about a file that describe or identify it, including the title, author name, subject, and keywords that identify the document's topic or contents; also known as *metadata*.

Drag The action of holding down the left mouse button while moving your mouse.

Dynamic An attribute applied to data in a database that changes.

Edit The process of making changes to text or graphics in an Office file.

Ellipsis A set of three dots indicating incompleteness; an ellipsis following a command name indicates that a dialog box will display if you click the command.

Email client A software program that enables you to compose and send an email message.

Embed Save a file so that the audio or video file becomes part of the presentation file.

Embedded chart A chart that is inserted into the same worksheet that contains the data used to create the chart.

Embedding The process of inserting an object, such as a chart, into a Word document so that it becomes part of the document.

Emphasis effect An animation effect that, for example, makes an object shrink or grow in size, change color, or spin on its center.

Enhanced ScreenTip A ScreenTip that displays more descriptive text than a normal ScreenTip.

Entrance effect An animation effect that occurs when the text or object is introduced into the slide during a slide show.

Error Checking command A command that checks for common errors that occur in formulas.

Error value The result of a formula that Excel cannot evaluate correctly.

Exit effect An animation effect that occurs when the text or object leaves the slide or disappears during a slide show.

Expression A combination of functions, field values, constants, and operators that produces a result; or, a formula that will perform a calculation.

Expression Builder A feature used to create formulas (expressions) in calculated fields, query criteria, form and report properties, and table validation rules.

Extract To decompress, or pull out, files from a compressed form.

Extract area The location to which you copy records when extracting filtered rows.

Field A specific type of data such as name, employee number, or social security number that is stored in columns.

Field property An attribute or a characteristic of a field that controls the display and input of data.

File A collection of information stored on a computer under a single name, for example, a Word document or a PowerPoint presentation.

File Explorer The program that displays the files and folders on your computer, and which is at work anytime you are viewing the contents of files and folders in a window.

File extension Also called the file type, it identifies the format of the file or the application used to create it.

Fill The inside color of an object.

Filtering A process in which only the rows that meet the criteria display; rows that do not meet the criteria are hidden.

Financial functions Pre-built formulas that perform common business calculations such as calculating a loan payment on a vehicle or calculating how much to save each month to buy something; financial functions commonly involve a period of time such as months or years.

Find A command that finds and selects specific text or formatting.

Find Duplicates Query A query used to locate duplicate records in a table.

Find Unmatched Query A query used to locate unmatched records so that they can be deleted from the table.

Fit to Slide The photo album option that allows the picture to occupy all available space on a slide with no room for a frame or caption.

Flagged A highlighted word that Spell Check does not recognize from the Office dictionary.

Focus An object that is selected and currently being acted upon.

Folder A container in which you store files.

Folder window In Windows, a window that displays the contents of the current folder, library, or device, and contains helpful parts so that you can navigate the Windows file structure.

Font A set of characters with the same design and shape.

Font styles Formatting emphasis such as bold, italic, and underline.

Footer A reserved area for text or graphics that displays at the bottom of each page in a document.

Form selector The box in the upper left corner of a form in Design view where the rulers meet; used to select the entire form.

Formatting The process of establishing the overall appearance of text, graphics, and pages in an Office file—for example, in a Word document.

Formatting marks Characters that display on the screen, but do not print, indicating where the Enter key, the Spacebar, and the Tab key were pressed; also called *nonprinting characters*.

Formula A mathematical expression that contains functions, operators, constants, and properties, and returns a value to a cell.

Formula Auditing Tools and commands accessible from the Formulas tab that help you check your worksheet for errors.

Frame The border around a picture in a photo album.

Freeze Panes A command that enables you to select one or more rows or columns and freeze (lock) them into place so that they remain on the screen while you scroll; the locked rows and columns become separate panes.

Full path Includes the drive, the folder, and any subfolders in which a file is contained.

Function A predefined formula that performs calculations by using specific values in a particular order.

Future value (Fv) The value at the end of the time periods in an Excel function; the cash balance you want to attain after the last payment is made—usually zero for loans.

Gallery An Office feature that displays a list of potential results instead of just the command name.

GIF Stands for Graphics Interchange Format. It is a file format used for graphic images, such as drawings.

Go To A command that moves to a specific cell or range of cells that you specify.

Go To Special A command that moves to cells that have special characteristics, for example, to cells that are blank or to cells that contain constants, as opposed to formulas.

Goal Seek One of Excel's What-If Analysis tools that provides a method to find a specific value for a cell by adjusting the value of one other cell—find the right input when you know the result you want.

Gradient fill A gradual progression of several colors blending into each other or shades of the same color blending into each other.

Gradient stop Allows you to apply different color combinations to selected areas of the background.

Gridlines Nonprinting lines that indicate cell borders; or, lines in the plot area that aid the eyes in determining the plotted values.

Groups On the Office ribbon, the sets of related commands that you might need for a specific type of task.

Handout Master Includes the specifications for the design of presentation handouts for an audience.

Header A reserved area for text or graphics that displays at the top of each page in a document.

Header row The first row of a table containing column titles.

Hierarchy A category of SmartArt graphics used to create an organization chart or show a decision tree.

HLOOKUP An Excel function that looks up values that are displayed horizontally in a row.

Horizontal axis (*X*-axis) The axis that displays along the lower edge of a chart.

Horizontal Category axis (x-axis) The area along the bottom of a chart that identifies the categories of data; also referred to as the *x-axis*.

HTML (Hypertext Markup Language) A language web browsers can interpret.

Hyperlink Navigation elements that, when clicked, will take you to another location, such as a webpage, an email address, another document, or a place within the same document. In a PowerPoint presentation, hyperlinks can also be used to link to a slide in the presentation, to a slide in a different presentation, or to a custom slide show.

Hyperlinked custom slide show A quick way to navigate to a separate slide show from within the original presentation.

HyperText Markup Language (HTML) The language used to code webpages.

HyperText Transfer Protocol (HTTP) The protocol used on the World Wide Web to define how messages are formatted and transmitted.

Hyphenation A tool in Word that controls how words are split between two lines.

Image control A control that enables individuals to insert an image into any section of a form or report.

Index A special list created in Access to speed up searches and sorting.

Info tab The tab in Backstage view that displays information about the current file.

Ink Revision marks made directly on a document by using a stylus on a Tablet PC.

Inner join A join that allows only the records where the common field exists in both related tables to be displayed in query results.

Input mask A field property that determines how the data displays and is stored.

Insertion point A blinking vertical line that indicates where text or graphics will be inserted.

Instance Each simultaneously running Access session.

Interest The amount charged for the use of borrowed money.

Iterative calculation When Excel recalculates a formula over and over because of a circular reference.

Join A relationship that helps query return only the records from each table you want to see, based on how those tables are related to other tables in the query.

JPG (JPEG) Stands for Joint Photographic Experts Group. It is a file format used for photos.

Keep lines together A formatting feature that prevents a single line from displaying by itself at the bottom of a page or at the top of a page.

Keep with next A formatting feature that keeps a heading with its first paragraph of text on the same page.

Keyboard shortcut A combination of two or more keyboard keys, used to perform a task that would otherwise require a mouse.

KeyTip The letter that displays on a command in the ribbon and that indicates the key you can press to activate the command when keyboard control of the ribbon is activated.

Keywords Custom file properties in the form of words that you associate with a document to give an indication of the document's content; used to help find and organize files. Also called *tags*.

Kiosk A booth that includes a computer and a monitor that may have a touchscreen.

Labels Column and row headings that describe the values and help the reader understand the chart.

Landscape orientation A page orientation in which the paper is wider than it is tall.

Layout Options A button that displays when an object is selected and that has commands to choose how the object interacts with surrounding text.

Left outer join A join used when you want to display all of the records on the *one* side of a one-to-many relationship, whether or not there are matching records in the table on the *many* side of the relationship.

Legend A chart element that identifies the patterns or colors that are assigned to the categories in the chart.

Line charts A chart type that is useful to display trends over time; time displays along the bottom axis and the data point values are connected with a line.

Line control A control that enables an individual to insert a line into a form or report.

Line style How the line displays, such as a solid line, dots, or dashes.

Line weight The thickness of a line measured in points.

Link Save a presentation so that the audio or video file is saved separately from the presentation.

Linked style A style, indicated by the symbol ¶a, that behaves as either a character style or a paragraph style, depending on what you select.

List A series of rows that contains related data that you can group adding subtotals; or, a category or SmartArt graphics used to show nonsequential information.

List box A control that enables individuals to select from a list but does not enable individuals to type anything that is not in the list.

List style A style that applies a format to a list.

Live Preview A technology that shows the result of applying an editing or formatting change as you point to possible results—*before* you actually apply it.

Location Any disk drive, folder, or other place in which you can store files and folders.

Lock aspect ratio When this option is selected, you can change one dimension (height or width) of an object, such as a picture, and the other dimension will automatically be changed to maintain the proportion.

Lock Tracking A feature that prevents reviewers from turning off Track Changes and making changes that are not visible in markup.

Locked [cells] In a protected worksheet, data cannot be inserted, modified, deleted, or formatted in these cells.

LOOKUP An Excel function that looks up values in either a one-row or one-column range.

Lookup field A way to restrict data entered in a field.

Lookup functions A group of Excel functions that look up a value in a defined range of cells located in another part of the workbook to find a corresponding value.

Loop The audio or video file plays repeatedly from start to finish until it is stopped manually.

Major sort A term sometimes used to refer to the first sort level in the Sort dialog box.

Major unit value A number that determines the spacing between tick marks and between the gridlines in the plot area.

Make table query An action query that creates a new table by extracting data from one or more tables.

Mark as Final Makes a presentation file read-only in order to prevent changes to the document. Adds a Marked as Final icon to the status bar.

Markup The formatting Word uses to denote a document's revisions visually.

Markup area The space to the right or left of a document where comments and formatting changes display in balloons.

Matrix A category of SmartArt graphics used to show how parts relate to a whole.

Memorandum (Memo) A written message sent to someone working in the same organization.

Merge A table feature that combines two or more adjacent cells into one cell so that the text spans across multiple columns or rows.

Metadata Details about a file that describe or identify it, including the title, author name, subject, and keywords that identify the document's topic or contents; also known as *document properties*.

Microsoft Outlook An example of an email client.

Mini toolbar A small toolbar containing frequently used formatting commands that displays as a result of selecting text or objects.

Mitered A border with corners that are square.

Motion Path effect An animation effect that determines how and in what direction text or objects will move on a slide.

Mouse Over Refers to an action that will occur when the mouse pointer is placed on (over) an action button. No mouse click is required.

MRU Acronym for *most recently used*, which refers to the state of some commands that retain the characteristic most recently applied; for example, the Font Color button retains the most recently used color until a new color is chosen.

Multilevel list A list in which the items display in a visual hierarchical structure.

Multivalued fields Fields that hold multiple values.

Name A word or string of characters in Excel that represents a cell, a range of cells, a formula, or a constant value; also referred to as *a defined name*.

Navigate The process of exploring within the organizing structure of Windows.

Navigation pane In a folder window, the area on the left in which you can navigate to, open, and display favorites, libraries, folders, saved searches, and an expandable list of drives.

Navigation tools Buttons that display on the slides during a slide show that allow you to perform actions such as move to the next slide, the previous slide, the last viewed slide, or the end of the slide show.

Nested table A table inserted in a cell of an existing table.

No Markup A Track Changes view that displays the document in its final form—with all proposed changes included and comments hidden.

Noncontiguous Items that are not adjacent to one another.

Nonprinting characters Characters that display on the screen, but do not print, indicating where the Enter key, the Spacebar, and the Tab key were pressed; also called *formatting marks*.

Normal The default style in Word for new documents and which includes default styles and customizations that determine the basic look of a document; for example, it includes the Calibri font, 11 point font size, line spacing at 1.08, and 8 pt spacing after a paragraph.

Notes Master Includes the specifications for the design of the speaker's notes.

Notification bar An area at the bottom of an Internet Explorer window that displays information about pending downloads, security issues, add-ons, and other issues related to the operation of your computer.

Nper The abbreviation for *number of time periods* in various Excel functions.

Numerical data Numbers that represent facts.

Object A text box, picture, table, or shape that you can select and then move and resize.

Office Theme Slide Master A specific slide master that contains the design, such as the background, that displays on all slide layouts in the presentation.

Office Web Apps The free online companions to Microsoft Word, Excel, PowerPoint, Access, and OneNote.

On Click Starts the animation effect when you click the slide or a trigger on the slide.

One-variable data table A data table that changes the value in only one cell.

Open dialog box A dialog box from which you can navigate to, and then open on your screen, an existing file that was created in that same program.

Option button In a dialog box, a round button that enables you to make one choice among two or more options.

Options dialog box A dialog box within each Office application where you can select program settings and other options and preferences.

Or comparison operator The comparison operator that requires only one of the two comparison criteria that you specify to be true.

Organization chart A type of graphic that is useful to depict reporting relationships within an organization.

Organizer A dialog box where you can modify a document by using styles stored in another document or template.

Original A Track Changes view that displays the original, unchanged document with all revisions and comments hidden.

Outer join A join that is typically used to display records from both tables, regardless of whether there are matching records.

Pane A portion of a worksheet window bounded by and separated from other portions by vertical and horizontal bars.

Paragraph style A style, indicated by ¶, that includes everything that a character style contains, plus all aspects of a paragraph's appearance; for example text alignment, tab stops, line spacing, and borders.

Paragraph symbol The symbol ¶ that represents the end of a paragraph.

Parameter A value that can be changed.

Parameter query A query that prompts you for criteria before running.

Password An optional element of a template added to prevent someone from disabling a worksheet's protection.

Paste The action of placing text or objects that have been copied or cut from one location to another location.

Paste Options gallery A gallery of buttons that provides a Live Preview of all the Paste options available in the current context.

Path The location of a folder or file on your computer or storage device.

PDF (Portable Document Format) A file format developed by Adobe Systems that creates a representation of electronic paper that displays your data on the screen as it would look when printed, but that cannot be easily changed.

Person Card A feature that allows you to communicate with a reviewer—using email messsage, instant messaging, phone, or video—directly from a comment.

Photo album A stylized presentation format to display pictures.

Picture A category of SmartArt graphics that is used to display pictures in a diagram.

Picture Alignment property A property that determines where the background picture for a form displays on the form.

Picture Size Mode property A property that determines the proportion of a picture in a form.

Pie chart A chart type that shows the proportion of parts to a whole.

Pixel The term, short for picture element, represents a single point in a graphic image.

Play Animations button A small star-shaped icon that displays to the left of the slide thumbnail.

Plot area The area bounded by the axes of a chart, including all the data series.

PMT function An Excel function that calculates the payment for a loan based on constant payments and a constant interest rate.

Point The action of moving your mouse pointer over something on your screen.

Pointer Any symbol that displays on your screen in response to moving your mouse.

Points A measurement of the size of a font; there are 72 points in an inch.

Portable Document Format (PDF) A file format that creates an image that preserves the look of your file, but that cannot be easily changed; a popular format for sending documents electronically, because the document will display on most computers.

Portrait orientation A page orientation in which the paper is taller than it is wide.

.potx The file extension for a PowerPoint template.

.pptx The file extension for a PowerPoint presentation.

Precedent cells Cells that are referred to by a formula in another cell.

Present value (Pv) The total amount that a series of future payments is worth now; also known as the *principal*.

Presets Built-in sharpness and softness adjustments from a gallery.

Principal The total amount that a series of future payments is worth now; also known as the *Present value (Pv)*.

Print Preview A view of a document as it will appear when you print it.

Process A category of SmartArt graphics that is used to show steps in a process or timeline.

Progress bar In a dialog box or taskbar button, a bar that indicates visually the progress of a task such as a download or file transfer.

Propagate To disseminate or apply changes to an object.

Properties The characteristics that determine the appearance, structure, and behavior of an object.

Property Sheet A sheet that is available for every object on a form, including the form itself, to further enhance the object.

Property Update Options button An option button that displays when you make changes to the design of a table; it enables individuals to update the Property Sheet for a field in all objects that use a table as the record source.

Protected View A security feature in Office 2013 that protects your computer from malicious files by opening them in a restricted environment until you enable them; you might encounter this feature if you open a file from an email message or download files from the Internet.

Protection This prevents anyone from altering the formulas or changing other template components.

Protocol A set of rules.

pt The abbreviation for *point*; for example, when referring to a font size.

Pyramid A category of SmartArt graphics that uses a series of pictures to show relationships.

Query A process of restricting records through the use of criteria conditions that will display records that will answer a question about the data.

Quick Access Toolbar In an Office program window, the small row of buttons in the upper left corner of the screen from which you can perform frequently used commands.

Quick Parts All of the reusable pieces of content that are available to insert into a document, including building blocks, document properties, and fields.

Quick Tables Tables that are stored as building blocks.

Rate In the Excel PMT function, the term used to indicate the interest rate for a loan.

Read-only A property assigned to a file that prevents the file from being modified or deleted; it indicates that you cannot save any changes to the displayed document unless you first save it with a new name.

Recolor The term used to change all the colors in the image to shades of one color.

Recommended Charts An Excel feature that helps you choose a chart type by previewing suggested charts based upon the patterns in your data.

Record All the categories of data pertaining to one person, place, thing, event, or idea.

Record Source property A property that enables you to specify the source of the data for a form or a report. The property setting can be a table name, a query name, or an SQL statement.

Relationship A category of SmartArt graphics that is used to illustrate connections.

Required A field property that ensures a field cannot be left empty.

Reveal Formatting A pane that displays the formatted selection and includes a complete description of formats applied.

Reviewer An individual who reviews and marks changes on a document or presentation.

Reviewing Pane A separate scrollable window that shows all of the changes and comments that currently display in a document.

Revisions Changes made to a document.

Ribbon A user interface in both Office 2013 and File Explorer that groups the commands for performing related tasks on tabs across the upper portion of the program window.

Right outer join A join used when you want to display all of the records on the *many* side of a one-to-many relationship, whether or not there are matching records in the table on the *one* side of the relationship.

Right-click The action of clicking the right mouse button one time.

Rotation handle A circle that displays on the top side of a selected object used to rotate the object up to 360 degrees.

Sans serif font A font design with no lines or extensions on the ends of characters.

Scale The range of numbers in the data series that controls the minimum, maximum, and incremental values on the value axis.

Scaling The group of commands by which you can reduce the horizontal and vertical size of the printed data by a percentage or by the number of pages that you specify.

Scope The location within which a defined name is recognized without qualification—usually either to a specific worksheet or to the entire workbook.

ScreenTip A small box that displays useful information when you perform various mouse actions such as pointing to screen elements or dragging.

Scroll bar A vertical or horizontal bar in a window or a pane to assist in bringing an area into view, and which contains a scroll box and scroll arrows.

Scroll box The box in the vertical and horizontal scroll bars that can be dragged to reposition the contents of a window or pane on the screen.

Selecting Highlighting, by dragging with your mouse, areas of text or data or graphics, so that the selection can be edited, formatted, copied, or moved.

Serif font A font design that includes small line extensions on the ends of the letters to guide the eye in reading from left to right.

SharePoint Collaboration software with which people in an organization can set up team sites to share information, manage documents, and publish reports for others to see.

Sharpen Increase the clarity of an image.

Shortcut menu A menu that displays commands and options relevant to the selected text or object; also called a *context menu*.

Show Preview A formatting feature that displays a visual representation of each style in the Styles window.

Simple Markup The default Track Changes view that indicates revisions by vertical red lines in the left margin and indicates comments by icons in the right margin.

Sizing handles Small squares that indicate a picture or object is selected.

SkyDrive Microsoft's free cloud storage for anyone with a free Microsoft account.

Slide Master Part of a template that stores information about the formatting and text that displays on every slide in a presentation. There are various slide master layouts.

SmartArt graphic A visual representation of information and ideas.

Soften Decrease the clarity of an image or make it fuzzy.

Sort The process of arranging data in a specific order.

Sort dialog box A dialog box in which you can sort data based on several criteria at once, and that enables a sort by more than one column or row.

Source table The table from which records are being extracted.

Sparklines Tiny charts that fit within a cell and give a visual trend summary alongside data.

Split The command that enables you to view separate parts of the same worksheet on your screen; splits the window into multiple resizable panes to view distant parts of the worksheet at one time.

Split button A button divided into two parts and in which clicking the main part of the button performs a command and clicking the arrow opens a menu with choices.

Split Table A table feature that divides an existing table into two tables in which the selected row—where the insertion point is located—becomes the first row of the second table.

Standardization All forms created within the organization will have a uniform appearance; the data will always be organized in the same manner.

Start search The search feature in Windows 8 in which, from the Start screen, you can begin to type and by default, Windows 8 searches for apps; you can adjust the search to search for files or settings.

Static data Data that does not change.

Status bar The area along the lower edge of an Office program window that displays file information on the left and buttons to control how the window looks on the right.

Status Bar Text property A form property that enables individuals to enter text that will display in the status bar for a selected control.

String A series of characters.

Style A group of formatting commands, such as font, font size, font color, paragraph alignment, and line spacing that can be applied to a paragraph with one command.

Style Inspector A pane that displays the name of the selected style with formats applied and contains paragraph- and text-level formatting options.

Style set A group of styles that are designed to work together.

Styles pane A window that displays a list of styles and contains tools to manage styles.

Subfolder A folder within a folder.

Subtotal command The command that totals several rows of related data together by automatically inserting subtotals and totals for the selected cells.

Synchronization The process of updating computer files that are in two or more locations according to specific rules—also called *syncing*.

Synchronous scrolling The setting that causes two documents to scroll simultaneously.

Syncing The process of updating computer files that are in two or more locations according to specific rules—also called *synchronization*.

Synonym A word having the same or nearly the same meaning as another.

System tables Tables used to keep track of multiple entries in an attachment field that you cannot view or work with.

Tab delimited text file A file type in which cells are separated by tabs; this type of file can be readily exchanged with various database programs.

Tab order A setting that refers to the order in which the fields are selected when the Tab key is pressed.

Table array A defined range of cells, arranged in a column or a row, used in a VLOOKUP or HLOOKUP function.

Table style A style that includes formatting for the entire table and specific table elements, such as rows and columns.

Tabs (ribbon) On the Office ribbon, the name of each activity area.

Tags Custom file properties in the form of words that you associate with a document to give an indication of the document's content; used to help find and organize files. Also called *keywords*.

Taskbar The area along the lower edge of the desktop that displays buttons representing programs.

Template (Excel) A special workbook which may include formatting, formulas, and other elements, that is used as a pattern for creating other workbooks.

Template (PowerPoint) A predefined layout for a group of slides saved as a .potx file.

Template (Word) A preformatted document that you can use as a starting point and then change to suit your needs.

Text box A movable, resizable container for text or graphics.

Text Pane The pane that displays to the left of the graphic, is populated with placeholder text, and is used to build a graphic by entering and editing text.

Theme A design tool that simplifies the process of creating professional-looking objects within one program or across multiple programs; includes theme colors and theme fonts that will be applied consistently throughout the objects in a database.

Theme template A stored, user-defined set of colors, fonts, and effects that can be shared with other Office programs.

Tick mark labels Identifying information for a tick mark generated from the cells on the worksheet used to create the chart.

Tick marks The short lines that display on an axis at regular intervals.

Timeline A graphical representation that displays the number of seconds the animation takes to complete.

Title bar The bar at the top edge of the program window that indicates the name of the current file and the program name.

Toggle button A button that can be turned on by clicking it once, and then turned off by clicking it again.

Toolbar In a folder window, a row of buttons with which you can perform common tasks, such as changing the view of your files and folders or burning files to a CD.

Totals query A query that calculates subtotals across groups of records.

Trace Dependents command A command that displays arrows that indicate what cells are affected by the value of the currently selected cell.

Trace Error command A tool that helps locate and resolve an error by tracing the selected error value.

Trace Precedents command A command that displays arrows to indicate what cells affect the value of the cell that is selected.

Tracer arrow An indicator that shows the relationship between the active cell and its related cell.

Track A song from a CD.

Track Changes A feature that makes a record of the changes made to a document.

Transition sound A prerecorded sound that can be applied and will play as slides change from one to the next.

Transition speed The timing of the transition between all slides or between the previous slide and the current slide.

Transitions Motion effects that occur when a presentation moves from slide to slide in Slide Show view and affect how content is revealed.

Trendline A graphic representation of trends in a data series, such as a line sloping upward to represent increased sales over a period of months.

Trigger A portion of text, a graphic, or a picture that, when clicked, causes the audio or video to play.

Triple-click The action of clicking the left mouse button three times in rapid succession.

Trust Center A security feature that checks documents for macros and digital signatures.

Trusted Documents A security feature in Office that remembers which files you have already enabled; you might encounter this feature if you open a file from an email message or download files from the Internet.

Trusted source A person or organization that you know will not send you databases with malicious content.

Two-variable data table A data table that changes the values in two cells.

Type argument An optional argument in the PMT function that assumes that the payment will be made at the end of each time period.

Unequal join A join used to combine rows from two data sources based on field values that are not equal; can be created only in SQL view.

Uniform Resource Locator (URL) Defines the address of documents and resources on the web.

Unlocked [cells] Cells in a protected worksheet that may be filled in.

Unmatched records Records in one table that have no matching records in a related table.

Update query An action query used to add, change, or delete data in fields of one or more existing records.

URL The acronym for *Uniform Resource Locator*, which is an address that uniquely identifies a location on the Internet.

USB flash drive A small data storage device that plugs into a computer USB port.

Validation list A list of values that are acceptable for a group of cells; only values in the list are valid and any value *not* in the list is considered invalid.

Validation rule An expression that precisely defines the range of data that will be accepted in a field.

Validation text The error message that displays when an individual enters a value prohibited by the validation rule.

Vertical axis (*Y*-axis) The axis that displays along the left side of a chart.

Vertical change bar A line that displays in the left margin next to each line of text that contains a revision.

Vertical Value axis (y-axis) A numerical scale on the left side of a chart that shows the range of numbers for the data points; also referred to as the *y-axis*.

View Side by Side A view that displays two open documents in separate windows, next to each other on the screen.

VLOOOKUP An Excel function that looks up values that are displayed vertically in a column.

Walls and floor The areas surrounding a 3-D chart that give dimension and boundaries to the chart.

Watch Window A window that displays the results of specified cells.

.wav (waveform audio data) A sound file that may be embedded in a presentation.

Web browser A software application used for retrieving, presenting, and searching information resources on the World Wide Web. It formats webpages so that they display properly.

What-If Analysis The process of changing the values in cells to see how those changes affect the outcome of formulas in a worksheet.

Wildcard A character, for example the asterisk or question mark, used to search a field when you are uncertain of the exact value or when you want to widen the search to include more records.

Window A rectangular area on a computer screen in which programs and content appear, and which can be moved, resized, minimized, or closed.

With Previous A custom animation that starts the animation effect at the same time as the previous effect in the list.

Word Options A collection of settings that you can change to customize Word.

WordArt A feature with which you can insert decorative text in your document.

.xlsx file name extension The default file format used by Excel 2013 to save an Excel workbook.

XML Paper Specification (XPS) Microsoft's file format that preserves document formatting and enables file sharing. Files can be opened and viewed on any operating system or computer that is equipped with Microsoft XPS Viewer. Files cannot be easily edited.

XPS (XML Paper Specification) A file type, developed by Microsoft, which creates a representation of electronic paper that displays your data on the screen as it would look when printed.

Zero-length string An entry created by typing two quotation marks with no spaces between them ("") to indicate that no value exists for a required text or memo field.

Zipped folder A folder that has been reduced in size and thus takes up less storage space and can be transferred to other computers quickly; also called a *compressed* folder.

Zoom The action of increasing or decreasing the size of the viewing area on the screen.

Index

creating
- append queries, 462–465
- calculated fields
  - *based on one field and number, 442–443*
  - *based on two fields, 439–442*
- ControlTips, 512–513
- crosstab queries, 448–451
- custom
  - *building blocks, 149–151*
  - *field formats, 109–111*
  - *styles, 54–56*
  - *table style, 99–104*
  - *table style from Table Styles gallery, 102*
  - *theme colors, 155–156*
  - *theme template, 156–157*
- custom slide shows, 703–707
- custom table styles, 269–271
- data tables, 208–209
- defined names using row and column titles, 217
- delete queries, 465–468
- document by using building blocks, 157–162
- folders, 14–17
- forms, Design view, 499–502
- handouts, in Word, 588–590
- input masks, 402–406
- line charts, 332–333
- lookup fields, 399–401
- make table queries, 459–461
- Microsoft accounts, 42–43
- multilevel charts, 49–96
- multilevel lists, 60–64
- multilevel lists with bullets, 60–61
- new styles, 54–56
- organization charts in SmartArt graphics, 338–339
- parameter queries
  - *with multiple criteria, 455–457*
  - *with one criterion, 454–455*
- Photo Album, 643–645
- reports
  - *Design view, 519–522*
  - *Report Wizard, 517–518*
- select query
  - *for crosstab query, 448–449*
  - *for make table query, 459–460*
- SmartArt graphics, 336–337
- sparklines, 323–324
- table style, 101–102
- tables
  - *Design view, 395–398*
  - *with Design view, 395–398*
- theme fonts, 155–156
- theme template, 155–157
- totals query, 446–448
- update queries, 468–470
- validation lists, 225–227
- validation rules, 410–412
- validation text, 410–412
- worksheets based on templates, 351–353

criteria
- compound, 294
- custom, 290–291
- definition, 288
- parameter queries
  - *with multiple criteria, 455–457*
  - *with one criterion, 454–455*
- **criteria range, definition, 292**
- **crop handles, definition, 648, 654**
- **Crop tool, 648, 654**
- **cropping, 638–641**
- **cross joins, 475, 478**
- **crosstab queries, creating, 448–451**
- **Crosstab Query Wizard dialog box, 449–450**
- **CSV (comma separated values) file, 277, 279–280**
- **Currency data type, 396**
- **current date, as default value, 408**
- **custom building blocks**
  - creating, 149–151
  - deleting, 161–162
  - saving as Quick Table, 152–153
- **custom criteria, 290–291**
- **custom field formats, creating, 109–111**
- **custom filters, 288, 290–291**
- **custom lists, 286–287**
- **Custom Office Templates folder, 560**
- **Custom Shows dialog box, 704–707**
- **custom slide shows**
  - basic, 703–707, 722
  - definition, 703, 722
  - hyperlinked, 703, 707, 722
- **custom styles, creating, 54–56**
- **custom table style, applying, 99–104**
- **custom themes, newsletter with, 148–162**
- **custom theme templates, creating, 156–157**
- **customer handouts, 50–64**
- **Customize Input Mask Wizard dialog box, 403**
- **customizing**
  - building blocks, 160–161
  - placeholders, on slide master, 566–568
  - settings for existing styles, 56–58
- **Cut command, 35**
- **cutting, definition, 35**
- **Cycle, SmartArt graphic, 336**

D

- **dark exclamation point, 460**
- **Dash type, 623**
- **data**
  - circling invalid, 236–237
  - column charts, 328–331
  - detail, 298
  - dynamic, 385, 418
  - editing, 74

inserting
- *charts, 70–74*
- *into named ranges, 216*
- numerical, 70
- recovering from backups, 377
- restricting in forms, 503
- saving
  - *in CSV (comma separated values) file format, 279–280*
  - *in other file formats, 277–281*
  - *as PDFs or XPS files, 280–281*
- static, 459, 478
- subtotaling, outlining, and grouping a list of, 297–299
- validating, 225–228, 503
- **data labels, 75**
  - definition, 327
- **data markers, definition, 327**
- **data points, definition, 327**
- **data series**
  - definition, 327
  - formatting in a line chart, 334–335
- **data tables**
  - calculating options with, 209–212
  - creating, 208–209
  - definition, 208
  - one-variable, 208
  - two-variable, 208–209
- **data types**
  - aggregate functions with, 445
  - changing, 391–392
  - list of, 396
- **data validation, 225, 227, 503**
  - definition, 402, 418
  - validation rules
    - *creating, 410–412*
    - *definition, 409, 418*
  - validation text
    - *creating, 410–412*
    - *definition, 409, 418*
- **databases.** *See also* **Trusted Locations**
  - backing up, 377
  - definition, 283
- **Datasheet view (Access), adding and moving fields, 388–390**
- **date text box controls, 509, 511, 513–514, 523**
- **date placeholder, 567–568**
- **dates**
  - current date as default value, 408
  - date and time separators (input mask characters), 404
  - Date/Time data type, 396
  - display formats, 406
- **decimal separator (.), 404**
- **default settings, restoring, 180–181**
- **default values**
  - definition, 408, 418
  - setting, 408
- **defaults, definition, 8**
- **Define Custom Show dialog box, 704**
- **defined names**
  - changing, 216

X

x-axis, definition, 327
.xlsx file name extension, definition, 277
XPS (XML Paper Specification)
Create PDF/XPS, 19
definition, 19, 280, 585, 596
presentations as, 585–588
Publish as PDF or XPS dialog box, 19–20, 586–587
saving Excel data as, 280–281
XPS Viewer, 281, 585, 587–588, 596

Y

y-axis, definition, 327
Yes/No data type, 396

Z

zero-length string (" "), 407, 418
zipped folders, definition, 4
Zoom dialog box, 456
Zoom Slider, 710
zooming, 30
definition, 19